Co

BEST

Mandarin
Chinese
Dictionary
英汉·汉英词典

HarperCollins Publishers
Westerhill Road
Bishopbriggs
Glasgow
G64 2QT
Great Britain

First Edition 2007
First published in this format 2011

Reprint 10 9 8 7 6 5 4 3 2 1 0

ISBN 978-0-00-742824-3

Collins Gem® and Bank of English®
are registered trademarks of
HarperCollins Publishers Limited

www.collinslanguage.com

A catalogue record for this book is
available from the British Library

HarperCollins Publishers,
10 East 53rd Street,
New York, NY 10022

COLLINS CHINESE GEM DICTIONARY.
First US Edition 2007

ISBN 978-0-06-114190-4

www.harpercollins.com

Typeset by Thomas Callan

Printed in Italy by
LEGO Spa, Lavis (Trento), ITALY.

Acknowledgements
We would like to thank those
authors and publishers who kindly
gave permission for copyright
material to be used in the Collins
Word Web. We would also like to
thank Times Newspapers Ltd for
providing valuable data.

EDITORIAL COORDINATION
Gaëlle Amiot-Cadey
Marianne Noble

CONTRIBUTORS
顾越施
谢曦
孙有玲
李跃
Eugene Benoit
Daphne Day

目录　　　　　　　　　　CONTENTS

商标说明
认为是商标的词语都相应
地注有商标符号。
无论加注或漏注商标符号都
不应被认作影响任何商标
的法律地位。

NOTE ON TRADEMARKS
Words which we have reason to
believe constitute trademarks
have been designated as such.
However, neither the presence nor
the absence of such designation
should be regarded as affecting
the legal status of any trademark.

William Collins' dream of knowledge for all began with the publication of his first book in 1819. A self-educated mill worker, he not only enriched millions of lives, but also founded a flourishing publishing house. Today, staying true to this spirit, Collins books are packed with inspiration, innovation, and practical expertise. They place you at the centre of a world of possibility and give you exactly what you need to explore it.

Language is the key to this exploration, and at the heart of Collins Dictionaries is language as it is really used. New words, phrases, and meanings spring up every day, and all of them are captured and analysed by the Collins Word Web. Constantly updated, and with over 2.5 billion entries, this living language resource is unique to our dictionaries.

Words are tools for life. And a Collins Dictionary makes them work for you.

Collins. Do more.

INTRODUCTION

Learning Chinese is definitely a challenge. However, in some ways Chinese is not particularly complicated. Words do not change with gender, number or even tense, and there are not many complicated grammatical traps for the unwary. However, other things about it make it hard for native English speakers to learn.

CHINESE PRONUNCIATION

THE FOUR TONES

Chinese is a tonal language – the pitch of any syllable affects its meaning.

There are four tones: first tone (high, even pitch); second (rising pitch); third tone (falling and then rising) and fourth tone (falling pitch). There is also a fifth (or neutral) tone, which is pronounced so quietly and quickly that there is no discernible tone at all.

Tones are a very important part of the pronunciation – and wrong tones can cause real confusion.

EXAMPLES OF DIFFERENCES IN TONES:

First tone	Second tone	Third tone	Fourth tone	Neutral tone
mā	má	mǎ	mà	ma
妈	麻	马	骂	吗
mother	hemp	horse	curse; swear	[question particle]

It may seem unnatural to native speakers of English to have pitch so rigidly attached to words, but the tone is as fundamental a part of any syllable as are its vowels and consonants.

PINYIN

Pinyin, the Chinese phonetic alphabet, was first introduced to help children learn to write characters, and foreigners and speakers of non-Mandarin dialects to pronounce Standard Chinese correctly. It is also very useful for dictionaries, as it provides an alphabetical order by which characters can be sorted. However, *pinyin* is not used much in China. Although signs in China are sometimes written in *pinyin*, do not expect people to understand *pinyin* as they would characters – in short, it should not be regarded as a substitute for learning Chinese characters. It is, however, a good, accurate guide to pronunciation.

CHINESE CHARACTERS

The Chinese script has a history that goes back at least three thousand years.

Although there are tens of thousands of known characters, a lot of these are archaic (some so old that even their meanings are unknown). An educated Chinese person will know roughly 4-6000 characters, and 2-3000 is considered sufficient for basic literacy (newspapers and the like).

Each character has to be learned individually – with the shape of the character, the sound of it and the meaning learned together as a unit.

There is no way of predicting the sound and meaning of an unknown Chinese character with any degree of accuracy. This does not mean, however, that there is no system behind the characters at all. All characters contain at least one of the component parts known as "radicals", and almost all radicals have an element of meaning; if you are familiar with these, not only will using a dictionary be much easier, it will also help you identify more of the building blocks of the characters you are trying to learn.

SIMPLIFIED AND COMPLEX CHARACTERS

In the 1950s and 60s the government of the People's Republic of China simplified the Chinese script, in an effort to improve the literacy rate by making characters easier to write. It is these simplified characters which are used in this dictionary.

CHINESE GRAMMAR

Compared to many languages, Chinese grammar is not particularly complicated.

Words do not change according to gender, number or case the way they do in many European languages. Sentence structure is generally straightforward, and there are not many exceptions to the grammatical rules (unlike English).

TALKING ABOUT TIME

It is sometimes said that Chinese has no tenses. This is not quite true, but speakers of Chinese talk about time in a way that is quite different from ours.

The English tense system is based on the idea of before and after the point of view of the narrator. Things that happened before the time in which we are talking take the past tense, those that are in the process of going on, the present, and things that have yet to take place, the future. This is shown by a change in the verbs. Chinese verbs, on the other hand, do not change with tense, but an aspect marker is placed before or after the verb. Some of the most common are 了 le (for completed actions – usually *but not always* in the past), 过 guò (for events that have already taken place), 要 yào (for things that are going to happen) and 在 zài (for things that are in the process of happening). These are no more than generalizations, however, and it is important not to use them indiscriminately as substitutes for English tenses, as that is not what they are for.

Adverbs of time are often used to show what time relation events have to each other, such as 已经 yǐjing (already), 曾经 céngjìng (once), or specific times or dates.

明年我去中国。 Míngnián wǒ qù Zhōngguó.
(literally: Next year I go China.) I'm going to China next year.

MEASURE WORDS

These are not unique to Chinese – you occasionally see something similar in English.

> a *gaggle* of geese
> a *piece* of fruit
> six *pints* of milk etc.

They do not occur very often in English. In Chinese, however, measure words are mandatory when giving a number of nouns. It is important to remember to put them in – and also to get them right, as there are a lot of measure words in Chinese.

一只青蛙	yī zhī qīngwā	one frog
三部电影	sān bù diànyǐng	three films
五封信	wǔ fēng xìn	five letters

Different measure words are used for different types of objects. 张 zhāng is used for flat things, such as tickets, sheets and tables. 条 tiáo is used to talk about long, thin things such as ribbons, or fish. The most common measure word is 个 gè, and it is a useful "default setting" for when you cannot remember the exact term you need.

WORD ORDER

Because of the less specific nature of the Chinese view of time, the tendency to avoid redundancy and the lack of cases to show a word's function in the sentence, word order is important in Chinese. It generally follows a subject-verb-object pattern, although there are certain particles or rhetorical constructions that change the order slightly. If the word order is wrong, it can be very hard to unscramble the sense of a phrase or sentence.

All this may seem a little intimidating to a beginner. However, the challenge of learning Chinese is in direct proportion to the pleasure of being able to use it. Not only is it an absorbing and intriguing language, which can express both brutal frankness and extreme delicacy, it also brings with it great opportunities to learn about a new and very different country and culture. And there could be no better time to begin that exploration than now, when China is taking a greater role in the world.

Esther Tyldesley, University of Edinburgh

HOW TO USE THE DICTIONARY

On the following pages you will find an outline of how information is presented in your Collins Chinese Dictionary. We hope that this will help you to get the most out of your dictionary, not simply from its comprehensive wordlist, but also from the information provided in each entry.

CHINESE-ENGLISH SIDE

HEAD ENTRIES

On the Chinese side, head entries are ordered traditionally, that is by single-character entries with multiple-character entries beginning with the same character nested below them.

标	biāo
标本	biāoběn
标点	biāodiǎn
标记	biāojì
标题	biāotí
标志	biāozhì
标准	biāozhǔn

表	biǎo
表达	biǎodá

Single character entries are ordered by pinyin, that is alphabetically and then by tone. In Chinese, there are four tones, each represented by a different mark above the relevant vowel:

¯	first tone	(flat tone)	mā
´	second tone	(rising tone)	má
ˇ	third tone	(falling rising tone)	mǎ
`	fourth tone	(falling tone)	mà
	light or no tone		ma

Where characters have the same pinyin and tone, they are ordered by the number of strokes in the character, with the smallest number of strokes first.

八	bā
巴	bā
芭	bā
疤	bā

Where characters have the same pinyin, tone, and number of strokes, they are ordered by the first stroke in the character, as follows:

一 丨 丿 丶

The multiple-character entries nested below single-character entries are similarly ordered by the pinyin (including tone), and then by the number of strokes.

蒸	zhēng
蒸气	zhēngqì
蒸汽	zhēngqì

Polyphones, that is characters with more than one pronunciation, are crossed-referred to the alternative pinyin.

斗 dǒu [名] 1 (指容器) cup 2 (斗状物) ▶ 烟斗 yāndǒu pipe ▶ 漏斗 lòudǒu funnel
→ *see also*/另见 dòu

斗 dòu [动] 1 (打斗) fight ▶ 斗鸡 dòujī cock fighting 2 (战胜) beat
→ *see also*/另见 dǒu

RADICAL AND CHARACTER INDEX

If you do not know the pronunciation for the Chinese character that you are looking for, you can use the index before the start of the Chinese-English side. For further information on how to use the radical index, see the introduction to that section.

THE STRUCTURE OF ENTRIES

On the Chinese side there are two levels of entry (single-character entries and multiple-character entries), both of which have essentially the same entry structure. Pinyin romanization is given for both types of entry.

Parts of speech are given in square brackets after the pinyin. Where a word has more than one part of speech, Roman numerals are used. For a full list of all parts of speech used, see page xxii.

Where an entry has more than one meaning, it is divided into categories, which are shown by an Arabic numeral.

When expressing yourself in another language, it is important to be aware of when you can use certain words and expressions and with whom – you would communicate very differently with a business colleague than with a friend. To help you, we have labelled words and expressions appropriately throughout the dictionary.

A full list of field and register labels used in the dictionary is shown on page xxiii.

EXAMPLES

Word examples are preceded by a shaded arrow ▶. Fuller examples are preceded by an empty arrow ▷.

TRANSLATIONS

Translations are shown in normal roman type after the part of speech or indicator. In general, we have only given one translation per meaning, since we believe this is the most accurate and helpful approach.

In a few cases, there is no equivalent at all, and an explanation rather than a translation has to be given. In such cases it is shown in italics:

压岁钱 yāsuìqián [名] *traditional
gifts of money given to children
during the Spring Festival*

British and American English variants are shown where appropriate,
and alternative parts of translations are preceded by 或 ('or'):

大学 dàxué [名] university (英)
或 college (美)

HEADWORDS
The words you look up in the dictionary – 'headwords' – are listed
alphabetically. Homonyms (words which are written in the same way
but have different pronunciations) are shown as separate headwords
and differentiated by the use of superscript numbers. For example:

bow¹ [bəu] N [c] **1** (*knot*) 蝴蝶结
húdiéjié [个 gè] **2** (*weapon*) 弓
gōng [把 bǎ]
bow² [bau] I vi (*with head, body*) 鞠
躬 jūgōng II vt [+ *head*] 低头 dītóu

American spellings of words are always shown, at the headword
which is spelled in the British way:

axe, (*US*) **ax** [æks] N [c] 斧 fǔ
[把 bǎ]

Irregular past tenses and plural forms are also shown as headwords
in their alphabetical position and cross-referred to the base form. For
example:

children ['tʃɪldrən] N PL *of* **child**

went [wɛnt] PT *of* **go**

THE STRUCTURE OF ENTRIES

Parts of speech are given in upper case after the phonetic spelling of the headword. We have used the notations C, U and S and PL in square brackets after each word to show whether nouns are countable, uncountable, singular or plural. C means that the noun is countable, and has a plural form (eg *I'm reading a book; she's bought several books*). U means that the noun is not normally counted, and is not used in the plural (eg *Lesley refused to give me more information*). S (for singular noun) means the noun is always singular, and is usually preceded by *a*, *an* or *the* (eg *We need to persuade people to repect the environment*). PL means the noun is always plural, and is used with plural verbs or pronouns (eg *These clothes are ready to wear*). For a full list of all parts of speech used, see page xxii.

hairdryer ['heədraɪə'] N [c] 吹风
机 chuīfēngjī [个 gè]

hair gel N [U] 发胶 fàjiāo

kick-off ['kɪkɔf] N [s] 开场时间
kāichǎng shíjiān

Where an entry has more than one meaning, it is divided into categories, which are shown by an Arabic numeral. You will often find information in round brackets and *italics* after the meaning category number. This information functions as a 'signpost' to help the user select the right translation when there is more than one to choose from. This 'signpost' or indicator may give a synonym of the headword, typical contexts in which the word might appear or a label indicating the subject field in which the word is used.

A full list of field and register labels used in the dictionary is shown on page xxiii.

link [lɪŋk] I N [c] 1 联系 liánxì [种
zhǒng] 2 (*Comput*) (*also:* **hyperlink**)
超链接 chāoliànjiē [个 gè] II vт
1 [+ *places, objects*] 连接 liánjiē
2 [+ *people, situations*] 联系 liánxì

PHRASES

All phrases are given in bold and preceded by a shaded arrow ▶. For example:

half-time [ˈhɑːfˈtaɪm] (*Sport*) N [U]
半场 bànchǎng ▶ **at half-time** 半
场时 bànchǎng shí

TRANSLATIONS

Translations are shown in normal roman type after the part of speech or indicator. In general, we have only given one translation per meaning, since we believe this is the most accurate and helpful approach. In a few cases, there is no equivalent at all, and an explanation rather than a translation has to be given.

au pair [ˈəʊˈpɛəʳ] N [C] 为学习语言
而住在当地人家里并提供家政服务
的外国年轻人

PINYIN

Pinyin romanization is given for all translations, except where, as above, there is no real equivalent in Chinese and an explanation rather than a translation has been given.

MEASURE WORDS

Measure words are given after translations of nouns which are countable and take a measure word. They are given in square brackets, with their pinyin. For more information on measure words, see the introduction on page vii.

banknote [ˈbæŋknəʊt] N [C] 纸
币 zhǐbì [张 zhāng]

KEYWORDS

Certain commonly used words, such as have and do, have been treated in special depth because they constitute basic elements of English and have very many uses and meaning. We have given them a special design to make it easier to find the meaning of construction you are looking for.

KEYWORD

have [hæv] (*pt, pp* had) I vt 1 有
yǒu ▸ he has *or* he has got blue
eyes/dark hair 他长着蓝眼睛/黑
头发 tā zhǎngzhe lán yǎnjīng/hēi
tóufa ▸ do you have *or* have you
got a car/phone? 你有车/电话
吗? nǐ yǒu chē/diànhuà ma? ▸ to
...

LANGUAGE NOTES

Language notes have been given at certain entries on the Chinese side, for example, 盏 zhǎn and 捆 bā. These are intended to give learners more information about certain important aspects of the Chinese language.

CULTURAL NOTES

A number of entries include cultural notes, giving an insight into Chinese life and culture. These notes cover many subject areas including political institutions and systems, national festivals and Chinese traditions and customs.

如何使用本辞典

接下来的几页概要地叙述本词典内容的组织方式。希望此说明能让使用者不但能通过广泛的选词而且还能通过每个词条中的信息最有效地使用本词典。

汉英部分

顺序

在汉语部分，词目按传统顺序排列，即单字词条下嵌入以相同汉字开头的多字词条。

标	biāo
标本	biāoběn
标点	biāodiǎn
标记	biāojì
标题	biāotí
标志	biāozhì
标准	biāozhǔn

表	biǎo
表达	biǎodá

单字词条按拼音字母顺序排列，再按声调顺序排列。注意，轻声排在四声之后。同音字按笔画的多寡排列，笔画少的在前，笔画多的在后。

八	bā
巴	bā
芭	bā
疤	bā

笔画相同的同音字按起笔笔画排列，顺序为：一丨丿、乛

单字词条下的多字词条也先按照拼音（包括声调），再按照笔画数进行排序。

xvi

蒸	zhēng
蒸气	zhēngqì
蒸汽	zhēngqì

多音字，即有一个以上发音的汉字，会标明"另见"，后接
另一个发音。

斗 dǒu [名] **1**(指容器) cup **2**(斗状
物) ▶ 烟斗 yāndǒu pipe ▶ 漏斗
lòudǒu funnel
→ *see also* 另见 dòu

斗 dòu [动] **1**(打斗) fight ▶ 斗鸡
dòujī cock fighting **2**(战胜) beat
→ *see also* 另见 dǒu

部首与汉字索引
如果使用者不知道所使用汉字的发音，部首目录和检字表位于
汉英部分之前。有关如何使用部首索引，参见部首和汉字索
引的第一部分。

词目构成
汉语部分的词条有两个层次，单字词条和多字词条，但它们的
构成方式基本相同。所有词条都标注汉语拼音。

词性在方括号中用中文标注，紧随拼音之后。如果有一个以上
的词性，用罗马数字标识。词性列表参见第xxii页。

如果一个词条有一个以上的词义，则归入不同的意类，用阿拉
伯数字标出。当一个词条有多种含义时，读者可以根据阿拉伯
数字后圆括号中的信息找到利用的语境，进而查到正确的翻
译。圆括号中的信息起到"路标"的功能，此"路标"标示了
主词条的同义词或近义词，以及使用主词条的典型语境。

专业学科领域及修辞色彩缩略语列表见xxiii页。

例子

以词的形式出现的例子，前面用实心灰色箭头▶标出。更完整的例子，前面用空心箭头▷标出。

翻译

一般情况下，作为最精确、有效的办法，每个意义只提供一个翻译。 在某些情况下，如果根本没有相应的翻译对等语，则提供该词的解释，而不是翻译，用斜体表示。

> 压岁钱 yāsuìqián [名] *traditional gifts of money given to children during the Spring Festival*

以-s结尾的名词，若用作复数，则标注为pl，若用作单数，则标注为sg

> 奥林匹克运动会 Àolínpǐkè Yùndònghuì [名] Olympic Games (PL)

> 算术 suànshù [名] maths (SG) (英), math (美)

必要时，同时给出英式英语和美式英语两种翻译，可供选择的部分前标有 "或"：

> 大学 dàxué [名] university (英) 或 college (美)

英汉部分

同音异义词

书写相同但发音完全不同的单词作为单独的词条出现，并且用数字上标加以区分：

bow[1] [bəʊ] N [c] **1** (*knot*) 蝴蝶结
húdiéjié [个 gè] **2** (*weapon*) 弓
gōng [把 bǎ]
bow[2] [baʊ] I vi (*with head, body*) 鞠
躬 jūgōng II vt [+ *head*] 低头 dītóu

如上所示，数字上标明确表明该单词的发音完全不同。

单词的拼写变化也作为单独的词条录入，并参见首先出现的拼写形式，单词的美式拼写总是在括号中给出：

pajamas [pəˈdʒɑːməz] (*US*) N PL
= **pyjamas**

axe, (*US*) **ax** [æks] N [c] 斧 fǔ
[把 bǎ]

不规则动词的时态变化和不规则名词的复数形式作为单独的词条出现，并且指示参照原形：

children [ˈtʃɪldrən] N PL *of* **child**

went [wɛnt] PT *of* **go**

如果一个单词有一个以上的词义，则归入不同的意类，用阿拉伯数字区别出。进一步的词义区分在括号中用斜体表示。当一个词条有多种含义时，读者可以根据阿拉伯数字括号中的信息找到相关的语境，进而查到正确的翻译。圆括号中的信息起到"路标"的功能，在此"路标"标示了主词条的同义词或近义词，以及使用主词条的典型语境。

专业学科领域及修辞色彩缩略语列表见 xxiii 页。

link [lɪŋk] I N [c] **1** 联系 liánxì [种
zhǒng] **2** (Comput) (*also*: **hyperlink**)
超链接 chāoliànjiē [个 gè] II vt
1 [+ *places, objects*] 连接 liánjiē
2 [+ *people, situations*] 联系 liánxì

短语

短语用黑体表示，并跟在实心灰色箭头标志▶后。短语包括不同种类的固定结构，感叹语和其他语法结构：

to have a baby
in the background
to pack one's bags

例子

例句用斜体表示，并跟在空心箭头标志▷后。英语中最常用单词，都给出了大量的例子及在相应语境中的翻译，有助于读者在具体的语境中正确使用单词。

翻译

一般情况下，作为最精确、有效的办法，每个意义只提供一个翻译。 在某些情况下，如果根本没有相应的翻译对等语，则提供该词的解释，而不是翻译。

au pair ['əu,peə] N [c] 为学习语言
而住在当地人家里并提供家政服务
的外国年轻人

拼音

词条及动词词组翻译都标注有拼音。如果该词条没有相应的翻译，则给出相关的解释以帮助读者理解，并省略拼音。

量词

量词在可数名词的翻译之后，和拼音一起括在方括号中。关于量词的详细信息请见序言中的XXX页。

banknote ['bæŋknaut] N [c] 纸
币 zhǐbì [张 zhāng]

关键词

对于一些极其常用的词，例如have 和 do，我们给予了长篇的注释。这类词是构成英语的基本要素，语意众多，用法复杂。本词典对该类词作了特别的外观设计，便于读者查阅。

○ **KEYWORD**

have [hæv] (pt, pp **had**) I VT 1 有
yǒu ▸ he has or he has got blue
eyes/dark hair 他长着蓝眼睛/黑
头发 tā zhǎngzhe lán yǎnjīng/hēi
tóufa ▸ do you have or have you
got a car/phone? 你有车/电话
吗? nǐ yǒu chē/diànhuà ma? ▸ to

语言注释
为了帮助读者更加准确、熟练地掌握并运用英语，我们对一些
易混淆词进行了详细的比较说明。

文化注释
对于英语国家中特有的文化现象，我们都加注了说明和解释。

略语表/REFERENCE LIST

PARTS OF SPEECH   词性

abbreviation	*ABBR*	简
adjective	*ADJ*	形
adverb	*ADV*	副
auxiliary verb	*AUXVB*	助动
conjunction	*CONJ*	连
compound	*CPD*	复合词
definite article	*DEFART*	定冠词
indefinite article	*INDEFART*	不定冠词
interjection	*INT*	叹
noun	*N*	名
noun abbreviation	*N ABBR*	名词缩写
singular noun	*N SING*	单数名词
noun (plural)	*N(PL)*	名词
noun plural	*NPL*	复数名词
numeral	*NUM*	数
plural	*PL*	复数
plural adjective	*PLADJ*	复数形容词
plural pronoun	*PL PRON*	复数代词
past participle	*PP*	过去分词
prefix	*PREFIX*	前缀
preposition	*PREP*	介
pres part	*PRES PART*	现在分词
pronoun	*PRON*	代
past tense	*PT*	过去时
suffix	*SUFFIX*	后缀
verb	*VB*	动
intransitive verb	*VI*	不及物动词
transitive verb	*VT*	及物动词
indicates that particle cannot	*VT FUS*	及物动词
be separated from the main verb		

SUBJECT FIELD LABELS

专业学科领域

Administration	*Admin*	行政
Agriculture	*Agr*	农
Anatomy	*Anat*	解剖
Architecture	*Archit*	建筑
Art		艺术
Astrology	*Astrol*	占星术
Astronomy	*Astron*	天文
Motoring	*Aut*	汽车
Aviation	*Aviat*	航空
Badminton		羽毛球
Baseball		棒球
Biology	*Bio*	生物
Bookkeeping		簿记
Botany	*Bot*	植物
Bowls		滚木球
Boxing		拳击
Cards		纸牌
Chemistry	*Chem*	化
Chess		国际象棋
Cinema	*Cine*	电影
Climbing		登山
Clothing		服饰
Commerce	*Comm*	商
Computing	*Comput*	计算机
Cricket		板球
Cooking	*Culin*	烹饪
Drawing		绘画
Drugs		药品
Economics	*Econ*	经济
Electricity	*Elec*	电子
Fencing		击剑
Finance	*Fin*	金融
Fishing		钓鱼
Football		足球

SUBJECT FIELD LABELS

专业学科领域

Geography	*Geo*	地理
Geology	*Geol*	地质
Geometry	*Geom*	几何
Golf		高尔夫
Grammar	*Gram*	语法
History	*Hist*	历史
Industry	*Ind*	工业
Insurance		保险
Law		法
Linguistics	*Ling*	语言
Literature	*Liter*	文学
Mathematics	*Math*	数
Medicine	*Med*	医
Meteorology	*Met*	气象
Military	*Mil*	军
Mining	*Min*	矿
Music	*Mus*	音乐
Mythology	*Myth*	神
Nautical	*Naut*	航海
Parliament	*Parl*	议会
Philosophy	*Phil*	哲
Photography	*Phot*	摄影
Physics	*Phys*	物
Physiology	*Physiol*	生理
Politics	*Pol*	政治
Police		警察
Post office	*Post*	邮政
Psychology	*Psych*	心理
Publishing		出版
Radio	*Rad*	广播
Railways	*Rail*	铁路
Religion	*Rel*	宗
Rugby		橄榄球
Science	*Sci*	科学

SUBJECT FIELD LABELS 专业学科领域

School	Scol	教育
	Sewing	缝纫
Sociology	Sociol	社会
Space		宇航
Sport		体育
Technical usage	Tech	术语
Telecommunications	Tel	电信
Tennis		网球
Texting		手机短信
Theatre	Theat	戏剧
Television	TV	电视
University	Univ	大学
Zoology	Zool	动

REGISTER LABELS 修辞色彩缩略语

dialect		方
euphemism		婉
formal	frm	正式
formerly		旧
humorous		诙谐
informal	inf	非正式
literary	liter	文
offensive		侮辱
old-fashioned	o.f.	过时
offensive	infl	疑讳/讳
pejorative	pej	贬
humble		谦
respectful		敬
slang		俚
spoken language		口
written		书
polite		客套
literal	lit	字
figurative	fig	喻

英语发音指导/GUIDE TO ENGLISH PHONETICS

CONSONANTS/辅音

[b]	baby
[t]	tent
[d]	daddy
[k]	cork kiss chord
[g]	gag guess
[s]	so rice kiss
[z]	cousin buzz
[ʃ]	sheep sugar
[ʒ]	pleasure beige
[tʃ]	church
[dʒ]	judge general
[f]	farm raffle
[v]	very rev
[θ]	thin maths
[ð]	that other
[l]	little ball
[r]	rat rare
[m]	mummy comb
[n]	no ran
[ŋ]	singing bank
[h]	hat reheat
[x]	loch

SEMIVOWELS/半元音

[j]	yet
[w]	wet

VOWELS/元音

[iː]	heel
[ɪ]	hit pity
[ɛ]	set tent
[æ]	bat apple
[ɑː]	after car calm
[ʌ]	fun cousin
[ə]	over above
[əː]	urn fern work
[ɔ]	wash pot
[ɔː]	born cork
[u]	full soot
[uː]	pool lewd

DIPHTHONGS/双元音

[ɪə]	beer tier
[ɛə]	tear fair there
[eɪ]	date plaice day
[aɪ]	life buy cry
[au]	owl foul now
[əu]	low no
[ɔɪ]	boil boy oily
[uə]	poor tour

不规则动词/ENGLISH IRREGULAR VERBS

PRESENT	PT	PP
arise	arose	arisen
awake	awoke	awoken
be (am, is, are; being)	was, were	been
bear	bore	born(e)
beat	beat	beaten
begin	began	begun
bend	bent	bent
bet	bet, betted	bet, betted
bid (at auction)	bid	bid
bind	bound	bound
bite	bit	bitten
bleed	bled	bled
blow	blew	blown
break	broke	broken
breed	bred	bred
bring	brought	brought
build	built	built
burn	burnt, burned	burnt, burned
burst	burst	burst
buy	bought	bought
can	could	(been able)
cast	cast	cast
catch	caught	caught
choose	chose	chosen
cling	clung	clung
come	came	come
cost	cost	cost
creep	crept	crept
cut	cut	cut
deal	dealt	dealt
dig	dug	dug
do (does)	did	done
draw	drew	drawn
dream	dreamed, dreamt	dreamed, dreamt
drink	drank	drunk
drive	drove	driven
eat	ate	eaten
fall	fell	fallen
feed	fed	fed
feel	felt	felt
fight	fought	fought
find	found	found
fling	flung	flung
fly	flew	flown
forbid	forbad(e)	forbidden
forecast	forecast	forecast
forget	forgot	forgotten
forgive	forgave	forgiven
freeze	froze	frozen
get	got	got, (US) goten
give	gave	given
go (goes)	went	gone
grind	ground	ground
grow	grew	grown
hang	hung	hung
hang (execute)	hanged	hanged
have	had	had
hear	heard	heard
hide	hid	hidden
hit	hit	hit
hold	held	held
hurt	hurt	hurt
keep	kept	kept
kneel	knelt, kneeled	knelt, kneeled
know	knew	known
lay	laid	laid
lead	led	led
lean	leant, leaned	leant, leaned
leap	leapt, leaped	leapt, leaped
learn	learnt, learned	learnt, learned
leave	left	left
lend	lent	lent
let	let	let
lie (lying)	lay	lain
light	lit, lighted	lit, lighted
lose	lost	lost
make	made	made
may	might	–
mean	meant	meant

PRESENT	PT	PP	PRESENT	PT	PP
meet	met	met	spell	spelt,	spelt,
mistake	mistook	mistaken		spelled	spelled
mow	mowed	mown,	spend	spent	spent
		mowed	spill	spilt,	spilt,
must	(had to)	(had to)		spilled	spilled
pay	paid	paid	spin	spun	spun
put	put	put	spit	spat	spat
quit	quit,	quit,	spoil	spoiled,	spoiled,
	quitted	quitted		spoilt	spoilt
read	read	read	spread	spread	spread
rid	rid	rid	spring	sprang	sprung
ride	rode	ridden	stand	stood	stood
ring	rang	rung	steal	stole	stolen
rise	rose	risen	stick	stuck	stuck
run	ran	run	sting	stung	stung
saw	sawed	sawed,	stink	stank	stunk
		sawn	stride	strode	stridden
say	said	said	strike	struck	struck
see	saw	seen	swear	swore	sworn
sell	sold	sold	sweep	swept	swept
send	sent	sent	swell	swelled	swollen,
set	set	set			swelled
sew	sewed	sewn	swim	swam	swum
shake	shook	shaken	swing	swung	swung
shear	sheared	shorn,	take	took	taken
		sheared	teach	taught	taught
shed	shed	shed	tear	tore	torn
shine	shone	shone	tell	told	told
shoot	shot	shot	think	thought	thought
show	showed	shown	throw	threw	thrown
shrink	shrank	shrunk	thrust	thrust	thrust
shut	shut	shut	tread	trod	trodden
sing	sang	sung	wake	woke,	woken,
sink	sank	sunk		waked	waked
sit	sat	sat			
sleep	slept	slept	wear	wore	worn
slide	slid	slid	weave	wove	woven
sling	slung	slung	weep	wept	wept
slit	slit	slit	win	won	won
smell	smelt,	smelt,	wind	wound	wound
	smelled	smelled	wring	wrung	wrung
sow	sowed	sown,	write	wrote	written
		sowed			
speak	spoke	spoken			
speed	sped,	sped,			
	speeded	speeded			

数字/NUMBERS

CARDINAL NUMBERS/基数

nought (英), naught (美), zero	0	零 (líng)
one	1	一 (yī)
two	2	二 (èr)
three	3	三 (sān)
four	4	四 (sì)
five	5	五 (wǔ)
six	6	六 (liù)
seven	7	七 (qī)
eight	8	八 (bā)
nine	9	九 (jiǔ)
ten	10	十 (shí)
eleven	11	十一 (shíyī)
twelve	12	十二 (shí'èr)
thirteen	13	十三 (shísān)
fourteen	14	十四 (shísì)
fifteen	15	十五 (shíwǔ)
sixteen	16	十六 (shíliù)
seventeen	17	十七 (shíqī)
eighteen	18	十八 (shíbā)
nineteen	19	十九 (shíjiǔ)
twenty	20	二十 (èrshí)
twenty-one	21	二十一 (èrshíyī)
twenty-two	22	二十二 (èrshí'èr)
twenty-three	23	二十三 (èrshísān)
thirty	30	三十 (sānshí)
forty	40	四十 (sìshí)
fifty	50	五十 (wǔshí)
sixty	60	六十 (liùshí)
seventy	70	七十 (qīshí)
eighty	80	八十 (bāshí)
ninety	90	九十 (jiǔshí)
one hundred	100	一百 (yìbǎi)

a hundred and one	101	一百零一 (yìbǎi líng yī)
two hundred and twelve	212	二百一十二 (èrbǎi yīshí'èr)
one thousand	1,000	一千 (yìqiān)
one thousand and one	1,001	一千零一 (yìqiān líng yī)
two thousand five hundred	2,500	二千五百 (èrqiān wǔbǎi)
a hundred thousand	100,000	十万 (shíwàn)
one million	1,000,000	一百万 (yìbǎi wàn)
one billion	1,000,000,000	十亿 (shíyì)

ORDINAL NUMBERS/序数

first	1st	第一 (dì-yī)
second	2nd	第二 (dì-èr)
third	3rd	第三 (dì-sān)
fourth	4th	第四 (dì-sì)
fifth	5th	第五 (dì-wǔ)
sixth	6th	第六 (dì-liù)
seventh	7th	第七 (dì-qī)
eighth	8th	第八 (dì-bā)
ninth	9th	第九 (dì-jiǔ)
tenth	10th	第十 (dì-shí)
hundredth	100th	第一百 (dì-yībǎi)
hundred and first	101st	第一百零一 (dì-yībǎi líng yī)
thousandth	1,000th	第一千 (dì-yīqiān)

FRACTIONS AND PERCENTAGES/ 分数、小数和百分数

a half	½	二分之一 (èr fēn zhī yī)
a third	⅓	三分之一 (sān fēn zhī yī)
a quarter	¼	四分之一 (sì fēn zhī yī)
two-thirds	⅔	三分之二 (sān fēn zhī èr)
nought (英) or naught (美) point five	0.5	零点五 (líng diǎn wǔ)
six point eight nine	6.89	六点八九 (liù diǎn bājiǔ)
ten per cent	10%	百分之十 (bǎi fēn zhī shí)
one hundred per cent	100%	百分之百 (bǎi fēn zhī bǎi)

部 首 检 字 表
RADICAL INDEX

检字方法说明:

(1) 根据字的部首在部首目录中查到该部首所在检字表中的号码;

(2) 按此号码在检字表中找到该部首,并根据字的笔画(字的笔画数不含其部首)查到该字的汉语拼音。

How to use this index:

(1) Use pages 2 – 4 to identify the radical. Note the number preceding it.

(2) In the index on pages 5 – 45, use this number to find all the characters appearing in this dictionary which contain the radical. Characters are ordered according to the number of strokes. The pinyin given will lead you to the correct entry.

部 首 目 录

检 字 表

(1)		开	kāi	**5 strokes**		面 miàn
一部		夫	fū	亚	yà	**9 strokes**
		天	tiān	再	zài	哥 gē
一	yī	无	wú	百	bǎi	**15 strokes**
1 stroke		专	zhuān	而	ér	整 zhěng
七	qī	五	wǔ	夹	jiā	
2 strokes		不	bù	**6 strokes**		**(2)**
三	sān	互	hù	严	yán	**丨部**
干	gān; gàn	牙	yá	更	gēng; gèng	
于	yú	丑	chǒu	束	shù	**3 strokes**
下	xià	**4 strokes**		两	liǎng	中 zhōng
丈	zhàng	末	mò	来	lái	内 nèi
与	yǔ	未	wèi	求	qiú	**4 strokes**
才	cái	正	zhēng;	**7 strokes**		北 běi
万	wàn		zhèng	表	biǎo	旧 jiù
上	shàng	世	shì	事	shì	申 shēn
3 strokes		可	kě	**8 strokes**		电 diàn
丰	fēng	平	píng	甚	shèn	由 yóu
井	jǐng	东	dōng	巷	xiàng	史 shǐ
		册	cè	歪	wāi	出 chū
		丝	sī			

5 strokes		升	shēng	乖	guāi	丸	wán
师	shī	长	cháng	质	zhì	之	zhī
曲	qǔ		zhǎng	周	zhōu	**3 strokes**	
肉	ròu	币	bì	**8 strokes**		为	wéi；wèi
6 strokes		反	fǎn	拜	bài	**4 strokes**	
串	chuàn	乌	wū	重	chóng	主	zhǔ
7 strokes		**4 strokes**			zhòng	半	bàn
非	fēi	生	shēng	复	fù	头	tóu
畅	chàng	失	shī	**9 strokes**		**5 strokes**	
8 strokes		甩	shuǎi	乘	chéng	兴	xīng；xìng
临	lín	乐	lè；yuè	**11 strokes**		农	nóng
		5 strokes		甥	shēng	**6 strokes**	
(3)		年	nián	**13 strokes**		良	liáng
丿 部		丢	diū	舞	wǔ	**7 strokes**	
		乒	pīng	疑	yí	学	xué
1 stroke		向	xiàng	**14 strokes**		**8 strokes**	
九	jiǔ	后	hòu	靠	kào	举	jǔ
2 strokes		**6 strokes**					
千	qiān	我	wǒ	**(4)**		**(5)**	
川	chuān	每	měi	、 部		乙（乚 一	
及	jí	龟	guī			丁）部	
久	jiǔ	系	xì	**2 strokes**			
3 strokes		**7 strokes**					
午	wǔ	垂	chuí	义	yì		

1 stroke		亟 qì	**4 strokes**	**2 strokes**
了 le; liǎo			考 kǎo	厅 tīng
		(6)	协 xié	历 lì
2 strokes		**二 部**	毕 bì	
乞 qǐ			华 huá	**3 strokes**
也 yě		二 èr		厉 lì
飞 fēi		**1 stroke**	**5 strokes**	
习 xí		亏 kuī	克 kè	**4 strokes**
乡 xiāng				压 yā
		2 strokes	**6 strokes**	厌 yàn
3 strokes		元 yuán	直 zhí	
尺 chǐ		云 yún	丧 sāng; sàng	**6 strokes**
巴 bā			卖 mài	厕 cè
孔 kǒng		**6 strokes**		
书 shū		些 xiē	**7 strokes**	**7 strokes**
			南 nán	厘 lí
4 strokes				厚 hòu
司 sī		(7)	**8 strokes**	
民 mín		**十 部**	真 zhēn	**8 strokes**
				原 yuán
5 strokes		十 shí	**10 strokes**	
尽 jǐn; jìn			博 bó	**10 strokes**
买 mǎi		**2 strokes**		厨 chú
		支 zhī		厦 xià
6 strokes			(8)	雁 yàn
乱 luàn		**3 strokes**	**厂 部**	
		古 gǔ		(9)
7 strokes			厂 chǎng	**匚 部**
承 chéng				

2 strokes

区	qū
匹	pǐ
巨	jù

4 strokes

5 strokes

| 医 | yī |

(10)

刂 部

3 strokes

| 刊 | kān |

4 strokes

刑	xíng
列	liè
划	huá; huà
刚	gāng
创	chuāng
	chuàng

5 strokes

| 别 | bié |
| 利 | lì |

| 删 | shān |
| 判 | pàn |

6 strokes

刺	cì
到	dào
制	zhì
刮	guā
刹	shā
剁	duò
刻	kè
刷	shuā

7 strokes

削	xiāo
前	qián
剃	tì

8 strokes

剔	tī
剥	bāo
剧	jù

9 strokes

| 副 | fù |

10 strokes

| 剩 | shèng |
| 割 | gē |

(11)

卜 部

| 卜 | bo |

3 strokes

卡	kǎ; qiǎ
占	zhàn
外	wài

6 strokes

| 卧 | wò |

8 strokes

| 桌 | zhuō |

(12)

冂 部

4 strokes

| 同 | tóng |
| 网 | wǎng |

(13)

亻 部

1 stroke

| 亿 | yì |

2 strokes

什	shén
仇	chóu
化	huà
仍	réng
仅	jǐn

3 strokes

仨	sā
代	dài
付	fù
仙	xiān
们	men
仪	yí
他	tā
仔	zǐ

4 strokes

伟	wěi
传	chuán
休	xiū
伍	wǔ
优	yōu
件	jiàn

任	rèn	佛	fó	倾	qīng	**14 strokes**	
伤	shāng			倒	dǎo; dào	儒	rú
价	jià	**6 strokes**		俱	jù		
伦	lún	供	gōng	倡	chāng	**(14)**	
份	fèn	使	shǐ	倍	bèi	**八 部**	
仰	yǎng	佰	bǎi	健	jiàn		
仿	fǎng	例	lì	**9 strokes**		八	bā
伙	huǒ	侄	zhí	做	zuò	**2 strokes**	
伪	wěi	侧	cè	偿	cháng	分	fēn; fèn
似	sì	佩	pèi	偶	ǒu	公	gōng
5 strokes		依	yī	偷	tōu	**3 strokes**	
估	gū	**7 strokes**		停	tíng	只	zhī; zhǐ
体	tǐ	便	biàn; pián	偏	piān	**4 strokes**	
何	hé	俩	liǎ	假	jiǎ; jià	共	gòng
但	dàn	修	xiū	**10 strokes**		并	bìng
伸	shēn	保	bǎo	傲	ào	关	guān
作	zuò	促	cù	傍	bàng	**5 strokes**	
伯	bó	俄	é	储	chǔ	兵	bīng
佣	yōng; yòng	侮	wǔ	**11 strokes**		兑	duì
低	dī	俭	jiǎn	催	cuī	弟	dì
你	nǐ	俗	sú	傻	shǎ	**6 strokes**	
住	zhù	信	xìn	像	xiàng	其	qí
位	wèi	侵	qīn	**12 strokes**		具	jù
伴	bàn	**8 strokes**					
伺	cì	借	jiè	僧	sēng		
		值	zhí				

典	diǎn	**2 strokes**		**10 strokes**		**2 strokes**
卷	juǎn	介	jiè	舒	shū	**4 strokes**
单	dān	从	cóng			朵	duǒ
7 strokes		今	jīn	**(16)**		**5 strokes**
养	yǎng	仓	cāng	**勹 部**		壳	ké
首	shǒu	以	yǐ			秃	tū
8 strokes		**3 strokes**		**1 stroke**		**6 strokes**
益	yì	令	lìng	勺	sháo	凭	píng
9 strokes		**4 strokes**		**2 strokes**		**12 strokes**
黄	huáng	全	quán	勿	wù	凳	dèng
兽	shòu	会	huì；kuài	匀	yún		
10 strokes		合	hé	**3 strokes**		**(18)**
普	pǔ	企	qǐ	句	jù	**儿 部**
曾	céng	伞	sǎn	匆	cōng		
12 strokes		**5 strokes**		包	bāo	儿	ér
舆	yú	余	yú	**9 strokes**		**2 strokes**
		含	hán	够	gòu	允	yǔn
(15)		**6 strokes**				**3 strokes**
人(入)部		舍	shè	**(17)**		兄	xiōng
		命	mìng	**几 部**		**4 strokes**
人	rén	**8 strokes**				光	guāng
入	rù	拿	ná	几	jī；jǐ	先	xiān
1 stroke		**9 strokes**		**1 stroke**			
个	gè	盒	hé	凡	fán		

8 strokes	**7 strokes**	**(20)**	**10 strokes**
党　dǎng	哀　āi		寒　hán
9 strokes	亭　tíng	冫部	
兜　dōu	亮　liàng		**(21)**
	帝　dì	**2 strokes**	冖部
(19)	**8 strokes**	斗　dǒu; dòu	
亠部	衰　shuāi	**4 strokes**	**3 strokes**
	高　gāo	冲　chōng	写　xiě
1 stroke	离　lí	chòng	**4 strokes**
亡　wáng	旁　páng	次　cì	军　jūn
2 strokes	**9 strokes**	决　jué	**7 strokes**
六　liù	毫　háo	冰　bīng	冠　guàn
3 strokes	商　shāng	**5 strokes**	**8 strokes**
市　shì	率　shuài	冻　dòng	冤　yuān
4 strokes	**10 strokes**	况　kuàng	**10 strokes**
交　jiāo	就　jiù	冷　lěng	幂　mì
产　chǎn	**11 strokes**	**8 strokes**	
充　chōng	禀　bǐng	准　zhǔn	**(22)**
6 strokes	**12 strokes**	凋　diāo	讠(言)部
变　biàn	裹　guǒ	凉　liáng; liàng	
京　jīng	豪　háo	**9 strokes**	**2 strokes**
享　xiǎng	**15 strokes**	凑　còu	计　jì
夜　yè	赢　yíng	减　jiǎn	订　dìng

认	rèn	诘	jí	**10 strokes**		**2 strokes**		
讥	jī	诚	chéng	谢	xiè	队	duì	
3 strokes		话	huà	谣	yáo	**4 strokes**		
讨	tǎo	诞	dàn	谦	qiān	阵	zhèn	
让	ràng	询	xún			阳	yáng	
训	xùn	该	gāi	**(23)**		阶	jiē	
议	yì	详	xiáng	**卩 部**		阴	yīn	
记	jì	**7 strokes**				防	fáng	
4 strokes		语	yǔ; yù	**1 stroke**		**5 strokes**		
讲	jiǎng	误	wù	卫	wèi	陆	liù; lù	
许	xǔ	诱	yòu	**3 strokes**		阿	ā	
论	lùn	说	shuō	印	yìn	陈	chén	
讽	fěng	**8 strokes**		**4 strokes**		阻	zǔ	
设	shè	请	qǐng	危	wēi	附	fù	
访	fǎng	读	dú	**5 strokes**		**6 strokes**		
5 strokes		课	kè	却	què	陌	mò	
证	zhèng	调	diào; tiáo	即	jí	降	jiàng	
评	píng	谈	tán	**7 strokes**		限	xiàn	
诉	sù	谊	yì	卸	xiè	**7 strokes**		
词	cí	**9 strokes**				陡	dǒu	
译	yì	谋	móu	**(24)**		除	chú	
6 strokes		谎	huǎng	**阝(在左)部**		险	xiǎn	
试	shì	谚	yàn			院	yuàn	
诗	shī	谜	mí					

8 strokes		6 strokes		2 strokes		3 strokes	
陶	táo	耶	yē	切	qiē	功	gōng
陷	xiàn	郁	yù	**3 strokes**		务	wù
陪	péi	郊	jiāo	召	zhào	加	jiā
9 strokes		郑	zhèng	**4 strokes**		**4 strokes**	
随	suí	**8 strokes**		负	fù	动	dòng
隐	yǐn	都	dōu;dū	争	zhēng	劣	liè
10 strokes		部	bù	色	sè;shǎi	**5 strokes**	
隔	gé			**5 strokes**		劳	láo
11 strokes		**(26)**		免	miǎn	助	zhù
障	zhàng	**凵 部**		初	chū	男	nán
12 strokes				**6 strokes**		努	nǔ
隧	suì	**2 strokes**		兔	tù	劲	jìn
		凶	xiōng	**9 strokes**		**6 strokes**	
(25)		**6 strokes**		象	xiàng	势	shì
阝(在右)部		画	huà	剪	jiǎn	**7 strokes**	
		7 strokes				勉	miǎn
4 strokes		幽	yōu	**(28)**		勇	yǒng
邪	xié			**力 部**		**11 strokes**	
那	nà	**(27)**				勤	qín
5 strokes		**刀 部**		力	lì		
邮	yóu			**2 strokes**		**(29)**	
邻	lín	刀	dāo	办	bàn	**厶 部**	

3 strokes		双	shuāng	(31)	差	chā
去	qù	**3 strokes**		**叾 部**		chà
台	tái	发	fā；fà			chāi
4 strokes		圣	shèng	**4 strokes**	(33)
牟	mù	对	duì	延	yán	**土 部**
5 strokes		**4 strokes**		**6 strokes**		
县	xiàn	戏	xì	建	jiàn	土	tǔ
6 strokes		观	guān			**3 strokes**
叁	sān	欢	huān	(32)	寺	sì
参	cān	**5 strokes**		**工 部**	地	de；dì
	shēn	鸡	jī		场	chǎng
8 strokes		**6 strokes**		工	gōng	在	zài
能	néng	取	qǔ	**2 strokes**	至	zhì
		叔	shū	巧	qiǎo	尘	chén
(30)		受	shòu	左	zuǒ	**4 strokes**
又 部		艰	jiān	**3 strokes**	坛	tán
		7 strokes		式	shì	坏	huài
又	yòu	叙	xù	巩	gǒng	坟	fén
1 stroke		**8 strokes**		**4 strokes**	块	kuài
叉	chā	难	nán	贡	gòng	坚	jiān
2 strokes		桑	sāng	攻	gōng	坐	zuò
友	yǒu	**11 strokes**		**6 strokes**	社	shè
劝	quàn	叠	dié	项	xiàng		

5 strokes		10 strokes		10 strokes		扰	rǎo
坦	tǎn	填	tián	鼓	gǔ	拒	jù
垃	lā	塌	tā			找	zhǎo
幸	xìng	墓	mù	(35)		批	pī
坡	pō	塑	sù	扌部		扯	chě
						抄	chāo
6 strokes		11 strokes				折	shé
型	xíng	墙	qiáng	1 stroke			zhé
垮	kuǎ			扎	zhā	抓	zhuā
城	chéng	12 strokes				抢	qiǎng
垫	diàn	增	zēng	2 strokes		抑	yì
		墨	mò	打	dá; dǎ	抛	pāo
7 strokes				扑	pū	投	tóu
埋	mái	17 strokes		扔	rēng	抗	kàng
		(34)				抖	dǒu
8 strokes		士部		3 strokes		护	hù
堵	dǔ			扛	káng	扭	niǔ
域	yù			扣	kòu	把	bǎ
堆	duī	4 strokes		托	tuō	报	bào
培	péi	声	shēng	执	zhí		
基	jī			扩	kuò	5 strokes	
堂	táng	7 strokes		扪	mén	抹	mā; mǒ
堕	duò	壶	hú	扫	sǎo; sào	拓	tuò
						拔	bá
9 strokes		9 strokes		4 strokes		拣	jiǎn
塔	da; tǎ	喜	xǐ	扶	fú	担	dān; dàn
堤	dī	壹	yī	技	jì		

押	yā	挺	tǐng	捣	dǎo	搜	sōu
抽	chōu	括	kuò	挨	āi;ái	援	yuán
拐	guǎi	拾	shí	**8 strokes**		搀	chān
拖	tuō	挑	tiāo;tiǎo	捧	pěng	搁	gē
拍	pāi	指	zhǐ	措	cuò	搓	cuō
拆	chāi	挣	zhèng	描	miáo	搂	lǒu
拎	līn	挤	jǐ	捷	jié	搅	jiǎo
拥	yōng	拼	pīn	排	pái	握	wò
抵	dǐ	挖	wā	掉	diào	揉	róu
抱	bào	按	àn	捶	chuí	**10 strokes**	
拉	lā	挥	huī	推	tuī	摄	shè
拦	lán	挪	nuó	掀	xiān	摸	mō
拌	bàn	**7 strokes**		掏	tāo	摆	bǎi
拧	níng;nǐng	捞	lāo	掂	diān	携	xié
招	zhāo	捕	bǔ	掖	yè	搬	bān
披	pī	捂	wǔ	接	jiē	摇	yáo
拨	bō	振	zhèn	掸	dǎn	搞	gǎo
抬	tái	捉	zhuō	控	kòng	摊	tān
拇	mǔ	捆	kǔn	探	tàn	**11 strokes**	
6 strokes		损	sǔn	据	jū;jù	摘	zhāi
		捌	bā	掺	chān	摔	shuāi
挂	guà	捡	jiǎn	**9 strokes**		**12 strokes**	
持	chí	挫	cuò	搭	dā	撕	sī
拮	jié	换	huàn	提	dī;tí	撒	sā;sǎ
拷	kǎo	挽	wǎn	插	chā	撑	chēng
挡	dǎng						

撮	cuō	花	huā	获	huò	**11 strokes**	
播	bō	苍	cāng	**8 strokes**		蔫	niān
撞	zhuàng	芭	bā	著	zhù	**12 strokes**	
撤	chè	苏	sū	萝	luó	蔬	shū
13 strokes		**5 strokes**		菜	cài	**13 strokes**	
操	cāo	茉	mò	菠	bō	薯	shǔ
擅	shàn	苦	kǔ	萤	yíng	薪	xīn
14 strokes		茂	mào	营	yíng	薄	báo; bò
擦	cā	苹	píng	**9 strokes**		**14 strokes**	
16 strokes		苗	miáo	募	mù	藏	cáng
攒	zǎn	英	yīng	董	dǒng	**15 strokes**	
		范	fàn	葡	pú	藕	ǒu
(36)		茄	qié	葱	cōng	藤	téng
艹 部		**6 strokes**		落	là; luò	**16 strokes**	
		荏	chá	葵	kuí	蘑	mó
1 stroke		草	cǎo	**10 strokes**			
艺	yì	茶	chá	蒜	suàn	(37)	
2 strokes		荒	huāng	蓝	lán	**寸 部**	
艾	ài	荣	róng	幕	mù		
节	jié	荤	hūn	蒙	mēng	寸	cùn
		荫	yīn		méng	**3 strokes**	
3 strokes		荔	lì		Měng		
芝	zhī	药	yào		zhēng	寻	xún
4 strokes		**7 strokes**		蒸	zhēng	导	dǎo
芽	yá	莲	lián				

4 strokes		**(40)**		**9 strokes**		尝 cháng
寿 shòu		**大部**		奥 ào		**8 strokes**
6 strokes						常 cháng
封 fēng		大 dà; dài		**(41)**		**9 strokes**
耐 nài		**1 stroke**		**尢部**		辉 huī
7 strokes		太 tài				赏 shǎng
射 shè		**3 strokes**				掌 zhǎng
9 strokes		夸 kuā		**1 stroke**		**17 strokes**
尊 zūn		夺 duó		尤 yóu		耀 yào
		尖 jiān		**2 strokes**		
(38)		**5 strokes**		龙 lóng		**(43)**
弋部		奉 fèng				**口部**
		奇 qí		**(42)**		
6 strokes		奋 fèn		**小部**		口 kǒu
贰 èr		态 tài				**2 strokes**
		6 strokes		小 xiǎo		右 yòu
(39)		牵 qiān		**1 stroke**		叶 yè
廾(在下)部		美 měi		少 shǎo		叮 dīng
		奖 jiǎng		少 shào		号 hào
		7 strokes		**3 strokes**		叼 diāo
3 strokes		套 tào		当 dāng		叫 jiào
异 yì		**8 strokes**		当 dàng		另 lìng
		奢 shē		**6 strokes**		叨 dāo
				省 shěng		叹 tàn

3 strokes	吧 ba	**7 strokes**	**10 strokes**
吐 tǔ;tù	**5 strokes**	唇 chún	嗷 áo
吓 xià	味 wèi	哲 zhé	嗜 shì
吊 diào	哎 āi	哮 xiào	嗝 gé
吃 chī	呼 hū	哨 shào	嗓 sǎng
吸 xī	呢 ne;ní	哭 kū	**11 strokes**
吗 ma	咖 gā;kā	哦 ó;ò	嘛 ma
各 gè	知 zhī	唤 huàn	**12 strokes**
名 míng	和 hé	啊 ā;á	噎 yē
4 strokes	**6 strokes**	**8 strokes**	嘲 cháo
吞 tūn	咸 xián	啦 lā;la	**13 strokes**
否 fǒu	哄 hòng	唱 chàng	嘴 zuǐ
呆 dāi	哑 yǎ	唾 tuò	器 qì
呕 ǒu	虽 suī	啤 pí	噪 zào
吨 dūn	品 pǐn	售 shòu	**17 strokes**
呀 yā	咽 yān;yàn	**9 strokes**	嚷 rǎng
吵 chǎo	咱 zán	喷 pēn	
员 yuán	响 xiǎng	喇 lǎ	(44)
听 tīng	哈 hā	喊 hǎn	口 部
吩 fēn	哆 duō	喂 wèi	
吻 wěn	咬 yǎo	喉 hóu	**2 strokes**
吹 chuī	咳 ké	喧 xuān	四 sì
告 gào	哪 nǎ	善 shàn	
吝 lìn	哟 yō		
启 qǐ	咨 zī		

3 strokes	4 strokes	岳	yuè	7 strokes
因 yīn	帐 zhàng	6 strokes		徒 tú
团 tuán	希 xī	炭 tàn		8 strokes
回 huí	5 strokes	峡 xiá		得 dé; de; děi
4 strokes	帖 tiě	8 strokes		9 strokes
园 yuán	帘 lián	崖 yá		街 jiē
围 wéi	6 strokes	崭 zhǎn		循 xún
困 kùn	帮 bāng	崇 chóng		10 strokes
5 strokes	带 dài			微 wēi
国 guó	9 strokes	(47)		12 strokes
固 gù	幅 fú	彳 部		德 dé
图 tú	帽 mào			
7 strokes		3 strokes		(48)
圆 yuán	(46)	行 háng; xíng		彡 部
8 strokes	山 部	4 strokes		
圈 quān		彻 chè		4 strokes
	山 shān	5 strokes		形 xíng
(45)	3 strokes	征 zhēng		6 strokes
巾 部	岁 suì	往 wǎng		须 xū
	4 strokes	6 strokes		8 strokes
2 strokes	岛 dǎo	待 dāi; dài		彩 cǎi
布 bù	5 strokes	律 lǜ		
帅 shuài	岸 àn	很 hěn		

12 strokes	猎 liè	**2 strokes**	**6 strokes**
影 yǐng	猫 māo	处 chǔ·chù	饺 jiǎo
	猕 mí	冬 dōng	饼 bǐng
(49)	猛 měng		**7 strokes**
犭 部	**9 strokes**	**4 strokes**	饿 è
	猩 xīng	麦 mài	**8 strokes**
2 strokes	猴 hóu	条 tiáo	馄 hún
犯 fàn	**10 strokes**	**5 strokes**	馅 xiàn
4 strokes	猿 yuán	备 bèi	**9 strokes**
狂 kuáng	**13 strokes**	**7 strokes**	馋 chán
犹 yóu	獭 tǎ	夏 xià	**11 strokes**
5 strokes			馒 mán
狐 hú	**(50)**	**(52)**	
狗 gǒu	**夕 部**	**饣 部**	**(53)**
6 strokes			**丬 部**
狭 xiá	夕 xī	**2 strokes**	
狮 shī	**3 strokes**	饥 jī	**4 strokes**
独 dú	多 duō	**4 strokes**	状 zhuàng
狱 yù	**8 strokes**	饭 fàn	**6 strokes**
7 strokes	梦 mèng	饮 yǐn	将 jiāng
狼 láng		**5 strokes**	
8 strokes	**(51)**	饰 shì	**(54)**
猜 cāi	**夂 部**	饱 bǎo	**广 部**
猪 zhū		饲 sì	

广 guǎng	**11 strokes**	恨 hèn	懊 ào
3 strokes	腐 fǔ	**7 strokes**	**13 strokes**
庄 zhuāng	**15 strokes**	恭 gōng	懒 lǎn
庆 qìng	鹰 yīng	悄 qiāo	
4 strokes		**8 strokes**	(56)
床 chuáng	(55)	情 qíng	**门 部**
应 yīng;yìng	**忄 部**	惭 cán	
5 strokes		悼 dào	门 mén
店 diàn	**1 stroke**	惟 wéi	**2 strokes**
庙 miào	忆 yì	惊 jīng	闪 shǎn
底 de;dǐ	**3 strokes**	惦 diàn	**3 strokes**
废 fèi	忙 máng	惨 cǎn	问 wèn
6 strokes	**4 strokes**	惯 guàn	闯 chuǎng
度 dù	怀 huái	**9 strokes**	**4 strokes**
庭 tíng	忧 yōu	愤 fèn	闲 xián
7 strokes	快 kuài	慌 huāng	间 jiān
席 xí	**5 strokes**	愉 yú	闷 mēn;mèn
座 zuò	性 xìng	**10 strokes**	**5 strokes**
8 strokes	怕 pà	慎 shèn	闹 nào
廊 láng	怪 guài	**11 strokes**	**6 strokes**
庸 yōng	**6 strokes**	慢 màn	闻 wén
康 kāng	恢 huī	慷 kāng	**7 strokes**
鹿 lù	恰 qià	**12 strokes**	阅 yuè
		懂 dǒng	

9 strokes

阔 kuò

(57)
氵 部

2 strokes

汇 huì
汉 hàn

3 strokes

汗 hán;hàn
污 wū
江 jiāng
池 chí
汤 tāng

4 strokes

沙 shā
汽 qì
沟 gōu
没 méi;mò
沉 chén

5 strokes

沫 mò

浅 qiǎn
法 fǎ
泄 xiè
河 hé
泪 lèi
油 yóu
沿 yán
泡 pào
注 zhù
泳 yǒng
泥 ní
波 bō
治 zhì

6 strokes

洪 hóng
洒 sǎ
洞 dòng
测 cè
洗 xǐ
活 huó
派 pài
洋 yáng
浑 hún
浓 nóng

7 strokes

酒 jiǔ
涉 shè
消 xiāo
海 hǎi
涂 tú
浴 yù
浮 fú
流 liú
浪 làng
涨 zhǎng
涩 sè

8 strokes

清 qīng
添 tiān
淋 lín
淹 yān
渠 qú
渐 jiàn
混 hùn
渊 yuān
渔 yú
淘 táo
液 yè
淡 dàn

深 shēn
渗 shèn

9 strokes

港 gǎng
湖 hú
湿 shī
温 wēn
渴 kě
滑 huá
湾 wān
渡 dù
游 yóu

10 strokes

满 mǎn
源 yuán
溪 xī
溜 liū
滚 gǔn

11 strokes

漱 shù
漂 piāo
　　 piào
漫 màn
滴 dī
演 yǎn

漏	lòu	**5 strokes**		密	mì	**4 strokes**
12 strokes		宝	bǎo	**9 strokes**		进	jìn
潮	cháo	宗	zōng	富	fù	远	yuǎn
澳	ào	定	dìng	寓	yù	违	wéi
13 strokes		宠	chǒng	**10 strokes**		运	yùn
激	jī	审	shěn	塞	sāi	还	hái; huán
17 strokes		官	guān	**11 strokes**		连	lián
灌	guàn	实	shí	赛	sài	近	jìn
		6 strokes		察	chá	返	fǎn
———		宣	xuān	蜜	mì	迎	yíng
(58)		室	shì			这	zhè
宀 部		宫	gōng	(59)		迟	chí
		宪	xiàn	辶 部		**5 strokes**	
2 strokes		客	kè			述	shù
宁	nìng	**7 strokes**		**2 strokes**		迪	dí
它	tā	害	hài	边	biān	迫	pò
3 strokes		宽	kuān	**3 strokes**		**6 strokes**	
宇	yǔ	家	jiā	达	dá	选	xuǎn
守	shǒu	宵	xiāo	迈	mài	适	shì
安	ān	宴	yàn	过	guò	追	zhuī
字	zì	宾	bīn	迅	xùn	逃	táo
4 strokes		**8 strokes**		巡	xún	送	sòng
完	wán	寄	jì			迷	mí
灾	zāi	宿	sù			退	tuì
						逊	xùn

7 strokes		遛	liù	**4 strokes**		己	jǐ
速	sù	**11 strokes**		层	céng	已	yǐ
逗	dòu	遭	zāo	屁	pì		
逐	zhú	**12 strokes**		尾	wěi	**(63)**
逝	shì	遵	zūn	局	jú	**弓 部**
逞	chěng	**13 strokes**		尿	niào	
造	zào	邀	yāo			**1 stroke**
透	tòu	避	bì	**5 strokes**		引	yǐn
途	tú			居	jū	**4 strokes**
逛	guàng	**(60)**		届	jiè	张	zhāng
逢	féng	**彐 (彑) 部**		**6 strokes**		**5 strokes**
递	dì			屋	wū	弥	mí
通	tōng	**2 strokes**		屎	shǐ	弦	xián
8 strokes		归	guī	**7 strokes**		**6 strokes**
逻	luó	**4 strokes**		展	zhǎn	弯	wān
逮	dǎi; dài	灵	líng	**8 strokes**		**7 strokes**
9 strokes		**5 strokes**		屠	tú	弱	ruò
逼	bī	录	lù	**9 strokes**		**8 strokes**
遇	yù			犀	xī	弹	dàn; tán
遗	yí	**(61)**		属	shǔ	**9 strokes**
道	dào	**尸 部**				强	qiáng
遂	suí			**(62)**			qiǎng
遍	biàn	**尸**	shī	**己 (巳) 部**		
10 strokes						
遥	yáo					

(64)		3 strokes		姜	jiāng	3 strokes	
子 部		如	rú	姿	zī	红	hóng
		妇	fù	娃	wá	纤	xiān
子	zǐ	她	tā	姥	lǎo	级	jí
2 strokes		好	hǎo; hào	姨	yí	约	yuē
孕	yùn	妈	mā	7 strokes		纪	jǐ; jì
3 strokes		4 strokes		娱	yú	4 strokes	
存	cún	妥	tuǒ	8 strokes		纬	wěi
孙	sūn	妩	wǔ	娶	qǔ	纯	chún
4 strokes		妙	miào	婴	yīng	纱	shā
孝	xiào	妖	yāo	婚	hūn	纷	fēn
5 strokes		妨	fáng	婶	shěn	纸	zhǐ
孤	gū	5 strokes		9 strokes		纺	fǎng
6 strokes		妻	qī	媒	méi	纽	niǔ
孩	hái	委	wěi	嫂	sǎo	5 strokes	
(65)		妹	mèi	婿	xù	线	xiàn
女 部		姑	gū	10 strokes		练	liàn
		姐	jiě	媳	xí	组	zǔ
女	nǚ	姓	xìng	嫌	xián	绅	shēn
		始	shǐ			细	xì
2 strokes		6 strokes		(66)		织	zhī
奶	nǎi	要	yāo; yào	**纟 部**		终	zhōng
		威	wēi	2 strokes		绊	bàn
		耍	shuǎ	纠	jiū	经	jīng

6 strokes		缠 chán	**8 strokes**		**1 stroke**	
绑	bǎng	**11 strokes**	骑	qí	玉	yù
结	jiē;jié	缩 suō	**9 strokes**		**3 strokes**	
绕	rào		骗	piàn	玖	jiǔ
给	gěi	**(67)**	骚	sāo	**4 strokes**	
绝	jué	**马 部**			玩	wán
统	tǒng		**(68)**		环	huán
7 strokes		马 mǎ	**幺 部**		现	xiàn
绣	xiù	**3 strokes**			玫	méi
继	jì	驮 tuó	**1 stroke**		**5 strokes**	
8 strokes		驯 xùn	幻	huàn	珐	fà
绳	shéng	**4 strokes**	**2 strokes**		珊	shān
维	wéi	驴 lú	幼	yòu	玻	bō
绸	chóu	**5 strokes**			皇	huáng
综	zōng	驾 jià	**(69)**		**6 strokes**	
绿	lǜ	驼 tuó	**巛 部**		班	bān
9 strokes		**6 strokes**			**7 strokes**	
缅	miǎn	骂 mà	**8 strokes**		球	qiú
缆	lǎn	骄 jiāo	巢	cháo	理	lǐ
缎	duàn	骆 luò			望	wàng
缓	huǎn	**7 strokes**	**(70)**		**8 strokes**	
编	biān	验 yàn	**王 部**		琴	qín
缘	yuán					
10 strokes		王 wáng				
缝 féng;fèng						

(71)		杏	xìng	树	shù
韦 部		极	jí	亲	qīn
		权	chā	柒	qī
8 strokes		**4 strokes**		染	rǎn
韩	hán	林	lín	架	jià
		枝	zhī	柔	róu
(72)		杯	bēi	**6 strokes**	
木 部		柜	guì	栽	zāi
		板	bǎn	框	kuàng
木	mù	松	sōng	栖	xī
1 stroke		枪	qiāng	档	dàng
本	běn	构	gòu	桥	qiáo
术	shù	枕	zhěn	桃	táo
		果	guǒ	格	gé
2 strokes		采	cǎi	校	xiào
朴	pǔ	**5 strokes**		核	hé
机	jī	某	mǒu	样	yàng
权	quán	标	biāo	根	gēn
杀	shā	查	chá	栗	lì
杂	zá	相	xiāng; xiàng	柴	chái
3 strokes		柳	liǔ	案	àn
杆	gān	柿	shì	**7 strokes**	
材	cái	栏	lán	检	jiǎn
村	cūn	柠	níng	梳	shū
				梯	tī

桶	tǒng	
梭	suō	
梨	lí	
8 strokes		
棒	bàng	
棋	qí	
椰	yē	
植	zhí	
森	sēn	
椅	yǐ	
棵	kē	
棍	gùn	
棉	mián	
椭	tuǒ	
集	jí	
9 strokes		
楼	lóu	
概	gài	
10 strokes		
模	mó; mú	
榜	bǎng	
11 strokes		
横	héng	
	hèng	

樱	yīng	车	chē; jū	**2 strokes**	**6 strokes**

(81) 日 部	6 strokes	15 strokes	(84) 贝 部
日　　　rì	晒　shài	曝　bào	
	晓　xiǎo		
2 strokes	晃　huàng	(82)	3 strokes
早　zǎo	晕　yūn; yùn	曰 部	财　cái
3 strokes	7 strokes		4 strokes
旱　hàn	匙　chí	5 strokes	责　zé
时　shí	晨　chén	冒　mào	败　bài
旷　kuàng	晚　wǎn	7 strokes	账　zhàng
4 strokes	8 strokes	冕　miǎn	贬　biǎn
旺　wàng	暂　zàn	8 strokes	购　gòu
昆　kūn	晴　qíng	替　tì	货　huò
明　míng	暑　shǔ	最　zuì	贪　tān
易　yì	量　liǎng		贫　pín
昏　hūn	liàng	(83)	贯　guàn
5 strokes	景　jǐng	水 部	5 strokes
春　chūn	晾　liàng		贵　guì
是　shì	智　zhì	水　shuǐ	贴　tiē
显　xiǎn	9 strokes	1 stroke	贷　dài
星　xīng	暖　nuǎn	永　yǒng	贸　mào
昨　zuó	暗　àn	5 strokes	费　fèi
香　xiāng	11 strokes	泉　quán	贺　hè
	暴　bào		

6 strokes	牛 niú	毛 máo	效 xiào
贿 huì	**4 strokes**	**8 strokes**	**7 strokes**
资 zī	牧 mù	毯 tǎn	教 jiāo; jiào
8 strokes	物 wù		救 jiù
赌 dǔ	**5 strokes**	(89)	敏 mǐn
赔 péi	牲 shēng	**气 部**	敢 gǎn
10 strokes	**6 strokes**		**8 strokes**
赚 zhuàn	特 tè	气 qì	散 sǎn; sàn
12 strokes	牺 xī	**6 strokes**	敬 jìng
赠 zèng		氧 yǎng	敞 chǎng
赞 zàn	(87)		**9 strokes**
	手 部	(90)	数 shǔ; shù
(85)		**攵 部**	
见 部	手 shǒu		(91)
	6 strokes	**2 strokes**	**片 部**
见 jiàn	拳 quán	收 shōu	
4 strokes	**11 strokes**	**3 strokes**	片 piàn
规 guī	摩 mó	改 gǎi	**8 strokes**
5 strokes	**15 strokes**	**5 strokes**	牌 pái
觉 jué	攀 pān	政 zhèng	
		故 gù	(92)
(86)	(88)	**6 strokes**	**斤 部**
牛(牜) 部	**毛 部**	敌 dí	

斤	jīn	**4 strokes**		育	yù	脱	tuō
4 strokes		爸	bà	**5 strokes**		**8 strokes**	
欣	xīn			胡	hú	期	jī;qī
7 strokes		(95)		背	bēi;bèi	朝	cháo
断	duàn	**月 部**		胃	wèi	脾	pí
9 strokes				胆	dǎn	腋	yè
新	xīn	月	yuè	胜	shèng	腕	wàn
		2 strokes		胖	pàng	**9 strokes**	
(93)		有	yǒu	脉	mài	腻	nì
爪(爫) 部		肌	jī	胎	tāi	腰	yāo
		肋	lèi	**6 strokes**		腥	xīng
4 strokes		**3 strokes**		胯	kuà	腮	sāi
爬	pá	肝	gān	脆	cuì	腺	xiàn
6 strokes		肚	dǔ	胸	xiōng	腿	tuǐ
舀	yǎo	肠	cháng	胳	gē	**10 strokes**	
爱	ài	**4 strokes**		脏	zāng	膜	mó
		肾	shèn	胶	jiāo	**11 strokes**	
(94)		肺	fèi	脑	nǎo	膝	xī
父 部		肿	zhǒng	脊	jǐ	**13 strokes**	
		服	fú;fù	朗	lǎng	臀	tún
父	fù	朋	péng	**7 strokes**		(96)	
2 strokes		股	gǔ	脚	jiǎo	**欠 部**	
爷	yé	肛	āng	脖	bó		
		肥	féi	脯	pú		
				脸	liǎn		

欠	qiàn	**5 strokes**		**5 strokes**		**4 strokes**	
4 strokes		段	duàn	施	shī	炖	dùn
欧	ōu	**9 strokes**		**6 strokes**		炒	chǎo
7 strokes		毁	huǐ	旅	lǚ	炊	chuī
欲	yù	殿	diàn	**7 strokes**		炎	yán
8 strokes		**11 strokes**		旋	xuán; xuàn	炉	lú
款	kuǎn	毅	yì	**10 strokes**		**5 strokes**	
欺	qī	(99)		旗	qí	炸	zhá; zhà
9 strokes		**文 部**		(101)		炮	pào
歇	xiē			**火 部**		烂	làn
10 strokes		文	wén			**6 strokes**	
歌	gē	**2 strokes**		火	huǒ	烤	kǎo
(97)		齐	qí	**1 stroke**		烦	fán
风 部				灭	miè	烧	shāo
		(100)		**2 strokes**		烟	yān
风	fēng	**方 部**		灰	huī	烫	tàng
11 strokes				灯	dēng	**8 strokes**	
飘	piāo	方	fāng	**3 strokes**		焰	yàn
(98)		**4 strokes**		灿	càn	**9 strokes**	
殳 部		放	fàng			煤	méi
		房	fáng			**10 strokes**	
						熄	xī

11 strokes	8 strokes	6 strokes	(106)
熨 yùn	煮 zhǔ	扇 shān	心部
12 strokes	焦 jiāo	shàn	
燃 rán	然 rán	8 strokes	心 xīn
15 strokes	9 strokes	雇 gù	1 stroke
爆 bào	照 zhào		必 bì
	10 strokes	(105)	3 strokes
(102)	熬 āo	礻部	忘 wàng
斗部	熊 xióng		忍 rěn
	11 strokes	1 stroke	4 strokes
6 strokes	熟 shú	礼 lǐ	念 niàn
料 liào	12 strokes	4 strokes	忽 hū
7 strokes	燕 yàn	视 shì	5 strokes
斜 xié		5 strokes	思 sī
	(104)	祖 zǔ	怎 zěn
(103)	户部	神 shén	急 jí
灬部		祝 zhù	总 zǒng
	户 hù	7 strokes	怒 nù
5 strokes	4 strokes	祸 huò	6 strokes
点 diǎn	所 suǒ	9 strokes	恐 kǒng
6 strokes	肩 jiān	福 fú	恶 ě;è
烈 liè	5 strokes		恋 liàn
热 rè	扁 biǎn		

7 strokes

悬	xuán
患	huàn
悠	yōu
您	nín

8 strokes

惹	rě
悲	bēi
惩	chéng

9 strokes

想	xiǎng
感	gǎn
愚	yú
愁	chóu
意	yì
慈	cí

10 strokes

愿	yuàn

(107)

聿(聿)部

9 strokes

肆	sì

(108)

毋(毋母)部

1 stroke

母	mǔ

5 strokes

毒	dú

(109)

示 部

示	shì

6 strokes

票	piào

8 strokes

禁	jìn

(110)

石 部

石	shí

3 strokes

矿	kuàng
码	mǎ

4 strokes

研	yán
砖	zhuān
砚	yàn
砍	kǎn

5 strokes

砸	zá
破	pò

6 strokes

硕	shuò

7 strokes

硬	yìng
确	què

8 strokes

碑	bēi
碎	suì
碰	pèng
碗	wǎn
碌	liù

9 strokes

碟	dié
碳	tàn
磁	cí

10 strokes

磕	kē
磅	bàng

11 strokes

磨	mó;mò

(111)

龙 部

6 strokes

聋	lóng
袭	xí

(112)

业 部

业	yè

(113)

目 部

目	mù	**10 strokes**		(115)		shèng
2 strokes		瞒	mán	**罒部**	盘	pán
盯	dīng	瞎	xiā		盖	gài
3 strokes		**11 strokes**		**4 strokes**	盗	dào
盲	máng	瞥	piē	罚	fá	(117)
4 strokes		**12 strokes**		**8 strokes**	**钅部**	
盼	pàn	瞧	qiáo	罪	zuì	
看	kān;kàn	瞪	dèng			**2 strokes**
盾	dùn			(116)	针	zhēn
眉	méi	(114)		**皿部**	钉	dīng
5 strokes		**田部**				**3 strokes**
眠	mián			**3 strokes**	钓	diào
6 strokes	田	tián	盂	yú	金	jīn
眶	kuàng	**4 strokes**		**4 strokes**		**4 strokes**
睁	zhēng	界	jiè	盆	pén	钙	gài
眼	yǎn	**5 strokes**		**5 strokes**	钝	dùn
8 strokes	留	liú	盏	zhǎn	钞	chāo
睦	mù	畜	chù;xù	盐	yán	钢	gāng
瞄	miáo	**6 strokes**		监	jiān	钥	yào
睡	shuì	略	lüè	盎	àng	钩	gōu
9 strokes	累	lěi;lèi	**6 strokes**			**5 strokes**
瞅	chǒu	**7 strokes**		盔	kuī	钱	qián
		番	fān	盛	chéng	钻	zuān

铁	zuàn	**10 strokes**	**4 strokes**	**9 strokes**
铁	tiě	锷 niè	秒 miǎo	稳 wěn
铃	líng	镇 zhèn	种 zhǒng	**11 strokes**
铅	qiān	镑 bàng	zhòng	穆 mù
6 strokes		**11 strokes**	秋 qiū	**12 strokes**
铝	lǚ	镜 jìng	科 kē	黏 nián
铜	tóng		**5 strokes**	
铲	chǎn	(118)	秤 chèng	(120)
银	yín	**矢 部**	租 zū	**白 部**
7 strokes			积 jī	
铺	pū		秩 zhì	白 bái
销	xiāo	**7 strokes**	称 chèn	**3 strokes**
锁	suǒ	短 duǎn	chēng	的 de; dí; dì
锅	guō	**8 strokes**	秘 mì	
锈	xiù	矮 ǎi	**6 strokes**	(121)
锋	fēng		移 yí	**瓜 部**
8 strokes		(119)	**7 strokes**	
错	cuò	**禾 部**	稍 shāo	瓜 guā
锚	máo		shào	**14 strokes**
锤	chuí		程 chéng	瓣 bàn
键	jiàn	**2 strokes**	稀 xī	
锯	jù	秀 xiù	税 shuì	(122)
9 strokes		私 sī	**8 strokes**	**用 部**
锻	duàn	**3 strokes**	稠 chóu	
		季 jì		

用　　yòng

(123)
鸟 部

鸟　　niǎo

4 strokes

鸦　　yā

5 strokes

鸭　　yā
鸵　　tuó
鸳　　yuān

6 strokes

鸽　　gē

7 strokes

鹅　　é

8 strokes

鹌　　ān

11 strokes

鹦　　yīng

(124)
广 部

4 strokes

疮　　chuāng
疯　　fēng
疫　　yì
疤　　bā

5 strokes

症　　zhèng
病　　bìng
疼　　téng
疲　　pí

6 strokes

痒　　yǎng

7 strokes

痤　　cuó
痛　　tòng

8 strokes

痴　　chī
痰　　tán

9 strokes

瘦　　shòu
瘊　　hóu

10 strokes

瘤　　liú

瘫　　tān

11 strokes

瘾　　yǐn
瘸　　qué

12 strokes

癌　　ái

16 strokes

癫　　diān

(125)
立 部

立　　lì

4 strokes

竖　　shù

5 strokes

站　　zhàn
竞　　jìng

6 strokes

章　　zhāng

7 strokes

童　　tóng

9 strokes

端　　duān

(126)
穴 部

穴　　xué

2 strokes

究　　jiū
穷　　qióng

3 strokes

空　　kōng
　　　kòng

4 strokes

突　　tū
穿　　chuān
窃　　qiè

5 strokes

窄　　zhǎi
容　　róng

7 strokes

窝　　wō
窗　　chuāng

(127) 衤部	(128) 疋部	(132) 老(耂)部	(135) 页部
2 strokes	6 strokes	老　lǎo	页　yè
补　bǔ	蛋　dàn		2 strokes
3 strokes	(129) 皮部	(133) 耳部	顶　dǐng
衬　chèn	皮　pí	耳　ěr	3 strokes
4 strokes			顺　shùn
袄　ǎo	7 strokes	4 strokes	4 strokes
5 strokes	(130) 矛部	耽　dān	顽　wán
袜　wà		5 strokes	顾　gù
袖　xiù	矛　máo	职　zhí	顿　dùn
被　bèi		聊　liáo	预　yù
7 strokes	(131) 耒部	6 strokes	5 strokes
裤　kù		联　lián	领　lǐng
裙　qún	4 strokes	9 strokes	7 strokes
8 strokes	耕　gēng	聪　cōng	频　pín
褂　guà		(134) 西(覀)部	8 strokes
裸　luǒ		西　xī	颗　kē
9 strokes			9 strokes
褪　tuì			题　tí
			颜　yán

额 é	蚂 mǎ;mà	**10 strokes**	舌 shé
10 strokes	**4 strokes**	蟒 mǎng	**5 strokes**
颠 diān	蚕 cán	**11 strokes**	甜 tián
13 strokes	蚊 wén	螺 luó	**7 strokes**
颤 chàn	**5 strokes**	**13 strokes**	辞 cí
	蛇 shé	蟹 xiè	**8 strokes**
(136)	**6 strokes**	**15 strokes**	舔 tiǎn
虍 部	蛙 wā	蠢 chǔn	
	7 strokes		(140)
2 strokes	蜗 wō	(138)	**⺮(竹) 部**
虎 hǔ	蛾 é	**缶 部**	
5 strokes	蜂 fēng		竹 zhú
虚 xū	**8 strokes**	**3 strokes**	**3 strokes**
	蜚 fēi	缸 gāng	竿 gān
(137)	蜡 là	**4 strokes**	**4 strokes**
虫 部	蝇 yíng	缺 quē	笔 bǐ
	蜘 zhī	**17 strokes**	笑 xiào
虫 chóng	蝉 chán	罐 guàn	笋 sǔn
2 strokes	**9 strokes**		**5 strokes**
虱 shī	蝶 dié	(139)	笨 bèn
3 strokes	蝴 hú	**舌 部**	笼 lóng
虾 xiā	蝎 xiē		笛 dí
蚁 yǐ	蝙 biān		符 fú

第　　dì

6 strokes

等　　děng
策　　cè
筒　　tǒng
答　　dā; dá

7 strokes

签　　qiān
筷　　kuài
简　　jiǎn

8 strokes

算　　suàn
管　　guǎn

9 strokes

箱　　xiāng
箭　　jiàn
篇　　piān

10 strokes

篮　　lán

(141)
臼 部

---

7 strokes

舅　　jiù

(142)
自 部

自　　zì

(143)
血 部

血　　xiě; xuè

(144)
舟 部

4 strokes

舱　　cāng
航　　háng

5 strokes

船　　chuán

6 strokes

艇　　tǐng

---

(145)
衣 部

衣　　yī

5 strokes

袋　　dài

6 strokes

裂　　liè
装　　zhuāng

(146)
羊 部

羊　　yáng

4 strokes

羞　　xiū

5 strokes

着　　zháo

6 strokes

美　　xiàn

7 strokes

群　　qún

---

(147)
米 部

米　　mǐ

3 strokes

类　　lèi

4 strokes

粉　　fěn

5 strokes

粘　　zhān
粗　　cū
粒　　lì

7 strokes

粮　　liáng

8 strokes

精　　jīng
粽　　zòng

9 strokes

糊　　hú

10 strokes

糙　　cāo
糖　　táng
糕　　gāo

11 strokes

糟 zāo

紧 jǐn

6 strokes

紫 zǐ

11 strokes

繁 fán

---

(158) 足部

足　　zú

4 strokes

距　　jù
跃　　yuè

5 strokes

跌　　diē
跑　　pǎo

6 strokes

跨　　kuà
跳　　tiào
踩　　duò
跪　　guì
路　　lù
跟　　gēn

8 strokes

踢　　tī
踩　　cǎi
踏　　tà

9 strokes

踹　　chuài
蹄　　tí

11 strokes

蹦　　bèng

12 strokes

蹲　　dūn
蹭　　cèng
蹿　　cuān
蹬　　dēng

(159) 身部

身　　shēn

6 strokes

躲　　duǒ

8 strokes

躺　　tǎng

(160) 采部

5 strokes

释　　shì

(162) 豸部

3 strokes

豺　　chái
豹　　bào

7 strokes

貌　　mào

(163) 角部

角　　jiǎo

6 strokes

触　　chù
解　　jiě

(164) 言(訁见讠)部

言　　yán

7 strokes

誓　　shì

12 strokes

警　　jǐng

13 strokes

譬　　pì

(165) 辛部

辛　　xīn

7 strokes

辣　　là

9 strokes

辨　　biàn
辩　　biàn

10 strokes

(166) 青部

青　　qīng

6 strokes

静　　jìng

(167) 雨部	(168) 齿部	4 strokes	8 strokes
雨　　yǔ	齿　　chǐ	鱿　　yóu	9 strokes
3 strokes	6 strokes	6 strokes	鞭　　biān
雪　　xuě	龈　　yín	鲜　　xiān	
5 strokes		7 strokes	(173) 骨部
雷　　léi	(169) 隹部	鲨　　shā	
零　　líng		9 strokes	骨　　gǔ
雾　　wù	4 strokes	鳄　　è	
雹　　báo	雄　　xióng	12 strokes	(174) 鬼部
6 strokes	6 strokes	鳝　　shàn	
需　　xū	雌　　cí	鳞　　lín	鬼　　guǐ
7 strokes	8 strokes		4 strokes
霉　　méi	雕　　diāo	(172) 革部	魂　　hún
9 strokes			魁　　kuí
霜　　shuāng	(171) 鱼部	革　　gé	5 strokes
11 strokes		4 strokes	魅　　mèi
霭　　ǎi	鱼　　yú	靴　　xuē	11 strokes
13 strokes		6 strokes	魔　　mó
露　　lòu;lù		鞋　　xié	
		鞍　　ān	

(175) 食 部	(177) 彡 部	(180) 黑 部	鼠 shǔ
			(182) 鼻 部

a

hard going!

哀 āi [形] (悲痛) sad

哀悼 āidào [动] mourn

挨 āi [动] 1 (靠近) be next to ▷两个孩子挨着门坐。Liǎng gè háizi āi zhe mén zuò. The two children sat by the door. 2 (逐个) ▷挨个儿 āigèr one by one
→ see also/另见 ái

挨 ái [动] 1 (遭受) suffer ▷挨饿 ái'è suffer from hunger ▷挨骂 áimà get told off 2 (艰难度过) endure
挨打 áidǎ [动] be beaten up

癌 ái [名] cancer ▷癌症 áizhèng cancer

矮 ǎi [形] 1 (指人) short 2 (指物) low

艾 ài [名] (植) mugwort
艾滋病 àizībìng [名] AIDS

阿 ā [前缀] (方) 阿爸 ābà dad
阿拉伯 Ālābó [名] Arabia
阿拉伯数字 Ālābó shùzì [名] Arabic numerals (PL)
阿姨 āyí [名] (指年长妇女) auntie

啊 ā [叹] oh ▷啊！着火了！Ā! Zháohuǒ le! Oh! It's caught fire!

哎 āi [叹] 1 (表示惊讶或不满) oh ▷哎！这么贵！Āi! Zhème guì! Oh! It's so expensive! 2 (表示提醒) hey ▷哎！别踩了那朵花。Āi! Bié cǎi le nà duǒ huā. Hey! Careful not to tread on that flower.

哎呀 āiyā [叹] oh ▷哎呀，这条路真难走！Āiyā, zhè tiáo lù zhēn nán zǒu! Oh, this road is

爱 ài [动] 1 (恋) love ▷爱人 àirén husband or wife, partner ▷我爱你。Wǒ ài nǐ. I love you. 2 (喜欢) enjoy ▷爱上网 ài shàngwǎng enjoy surfing the net 3 (容易) ▷她爱晕车。Tā ài yùnchē. She tends to get car sick.
爱好 àihào [动] be keen on ▷她有广泛的爱好。Tā yǒu guǎngfàn de àihào. She has many hobbies.
爱护 àihù [动] take care of
爱情 àiqíng [名] love

安 ān I [形] 1 (安定) quiet ▷不安

bù'ān anxious **2** (平安) safe ▸治安 zhì'ān public order **II** [动] **1** (使安静) calm ▸安心 ānxīn calm the nerves **2** (安装) fit ▸门上加锁门 mén shàng ān bǎ suǒ fit a lock on the door

安定 āndìng **I** [形] stable **II** [动] stabilize ▸安定局面 āndìng júmiàn stabilize the situation

安家 ānjiā [动] **1** (also: 安置家庭) settle in **2** (结婚) get married

安检 ānjiǎn [名] security check

安静 ānjìng [形] **1** (无声) quiet **2** (平静) peaceful

安乐死 ānlèsǐ [名] euthanasia

安排 ānpái [动] arrange

安全 ānquán [形] safe ▸注意安全。 Zhùyì ānquán. Be sure to take care. ▸人身安全 rénshēn ānquán personal safety

安全套 ānquántào [名] condom

安慰 ānwèi **I** [动] comfort **II** [形] reassured

安心 ānxīn [动] (形容心情) stop worrying

安装 ānzhuāng [动] install

鹌 ān see below/见下文

鹌鹑 ānchún [名] quail

鞍 ān [名] saddle ▸马鞍 mǎ'ān saddle

岸 àn [名] edge ▸河岸 hé'àn river bank ▸海岸 hǎi'àn seashore

按 àn **I** [动] **1** (用手压) press ▸按电钮 àn diànniǔ press a button ▸按

门铃 àn ménlíng push a doorbell **2** (人) push ▸按...下去 **3** (抑制) restrain ▸按不住心头怒火 àn bùzhù xīntóu nùhuǒ be unable to restrain one's fury **II** [介] (按照) according to ▸按制度办事 àn zhìdù bànshì do things by the book

按揭 ànjiē [名] mortgage

按摩 ànmó [动] massage

按照 ànzhào [介] according to ▸按照课本 ànzhào kèběn according to the text book

案 àn [名] (案件) case ▸案子 ànzi case

案件 ànjiàn [名] case

暗 àn **I** [形] (昏暗) dim ▸今晚月光很暗。 Jīnwǎn yuèguāng hěn àn. Tonight the moon is dim. **II** [副] secretly

暗号 ànhào [名] secret signal

暗杀 ànshā [动] assassinate

暗示 ànshì [动] hint

暗自 ànzì [副] secretly

肮 āng see below/见下文

肮脏 āngzāng [形] **1** (不干净) filthy **2** (喻) (不道德) vile

盎 àng [形] (书) abundant

盎司 àngsī [量] ounce

熬 áo [动] **1** (煮) stew ▸熬粥 áozhōu make porridge **2** (忍受) endure

熬夜 áoyè [动] stay up late

袄 ǎo [名] coat ▶ 棉袄 mián'ǎo padded jacket

傲 ào [形] proud
傲慢 àomàn [形] arrogant
傲气 àoqì [名] arrogance

奥 ào [形] profound
奥林匹克运动会 Àolínpǐkè Yùndònghuì [名] Olympic Games (PL)

澳 ào [名] bay
澳大利亚 Àodàlìyà [名] Australia

懊 ào [形] 1 (后悔) regretful 2 (恼怒) annoyed
懊悔 àohuǐ [动] regret

八 bā [数] eight ▶ 八月 bāyuè August

巴 bā [名] ▶ 下巴 xiàbā chin ▶ 尾巴 wěibā tail ▶ 嘴巴 zuǐbā mouth
巴士 bāshì [名] bus
巴掌 bāzhang [名] (手掌) palm

芭 bā [名] banana
芭蕾舞 bālěiwǔ [名] ballet

疤 bā [名] scar

捌 bā [数] eight

This is the complex character for eight, which is mainly used in banks, on receipts, etc.

拔 bá [动] 1 (抽出) pull ... up ▶ 拔草 bá...cǎo weed 2 (取下) pull ... out

▷拔牙 báyá pull out a tooth **3**(挑选) choose ▷选拔人才 xuǎnbá réncái select talented people **4**(超出) exceed ▶海拔 hǎibá height above sea level

把 bǎ I [动] **1**(握住) hold **2**(看守) guard II [名](把手) handle III [量] **1** ▷一把刀 yī bǎ dāo a knife ▷一把剪子 yī bǎ jiǎnzi a pair of scissors

measure word, used for objects with a handle

2 handful ▷一把米 yī bǎ mǐ a handful of rice

measure word, used for the quantity of something that can be held in a hand

3 ▷两把花 liǎng bǎ huā two bunches of flowers

measure word, used for something that can be bundled together

IV [介] ▷把门关好 bǎ mén guān hǎo shut the door ▷把作业做完 bǎ zuòyè zuò wán finish doing one's homework ▷她把书放在桌子上了。Tā bǎ shū fàngzài zhuōzi shàng le. She put the book on the table.

把 bǎ is used to alter the word order of a sentence, especially when the verb is a complex one. The normal word order of Subject + Verb + Object, becomes Subject + 把 + Object + Verb. It is very commonly used when the verb implies a change of place, or when the verb is followed by certain complements. For instance, a word-for-word translation of the sentence, 我把书放在那儿。 Wǒ bǎ shū fàngzài nàr. (I put the book there) is 'I 把 book put there'.

把手 bǎshou [名] handle

把握 bǎwò I [动] grasp ▷把握时机 bǎwò shíjī seize the opportunity II [名] certainty ▷没把握 méi bǎwò there is no certainty

爸 bà [名] father

爸爸 bàba [名] dad

吧 ba [助] **1**(在句尾表示建议) ▷我们回家吧。 Wǒmen huíjiā ba. Let's go home. ▷吃吧！ Chī ba! Eat! ▷再想想吧。 Zài xiǎngxiǎng ba. Think about it again. **2**(在句尾表示推测的肯定) ▷你听说了吧？ Nǐ tīngshuō le ba? You may have heard about this. ▷他明天走吧？ Tā míngtiān zǒu ba? He is leaving tomorrow?

Adding 吧 ba at the end of a sentence forms a suggestion, e.g. 我们走吧。Wǒmen zǒu ba. (Let's go). But adding 吗 ma at the end of a sentence forms a question, e.g. 我们走吗？ Wǒmen zǒu ma? (Shall we go?).

白 bái I [形] **1**(白色) white ▶白

糖 báitáng white sugar ►白领 báilǐng white-collar **2** (明亮) bright ►白天 báitiān daytime **3** (平淡) plain ►白开水 bái kāishuǐ boiled water ►白米饭 bái mǐfàn boiled rice **II** [副] (无结果) in vain ►白费 báifèi waste ►白等 báiděng wait in vain

白菜 báicài [名] Chinese cabbage

白酒 báijiǔ [名] clear spirit

白人 báirén [名] white people (PL)

百 bǎi [数] hundred

百分之百 bǎi fēn zhī bǎi absolutely

百万 bǎiwàn [数] million

百 bǎi [数] hundred

This is the character for hundred which is used in banks, on receipts, cheques etc.

摆 bǎi [动] **1** (放置) arrange ►摆放 bǎifàng place **2** (摇动) sway ►摆动 bǎidòng sway ►她向我摆手。 Tā xiàng wǒ bǎi shǒu. She waved her hand at me.

摆设 bǎishè [动] furnish and decorate

败 bài [动] (打败) defeat

败坏 bàihuài [动] (打败) corrupt **II** [形] corrupt

拜 bài [动] (会见) pay a visit ►拜访 bàifǎng visit

拜年 bàinián [动] pay a New Year call

拜托 bàituō [动] ►拜托您给看会儿我女儿。 Bàituō nín gěi kān huìr wǒ nǚr. Would you be kind enough to look after my daughter for a while?

班 bān **I** [名] **1** (班级) class ►班长 bānzhǎng class monitor **2** (交通) scheduled trip ►班机 bānjī scheduled flight ►末班车 mòbānchē the last bus **3** (轮班) shift ►上班 shàngbān go to work ►下班 xiàbān finish work ►晚班 wǎnbān night shift **4** (军) squad **II** [量] ►下一班船 xià yī bān chuán the next boat **5** ►错过一班飞机 cuòguò yī bān fēijī miss a flight

measure word, used for scheduled transportations

班级 bānjí [名] classes (PL)

搬 bān [动] **1** (移动) take ... away ►把这些东西搬走。 Bǎ zhèxiē dōngxi bān zǒu. Take these things away. **2** (迁移) move ►搬家 bānjiā move house

板 bǎn **I** [名] (片状硬物) board **II** [动] put on a stern expression ►板着脸 bǎn zhe liǎn pull a long face

办 bàn [动] **1** (处理) handle ►办事 bànshì handle affairs ►我们该怎么办? Wǒmen gāi zěnme bàn? What should we do? **2** (创设) set ... up ►办工厂 bàn gōngchǎng set up a factory **3** (经营) run ►办学 bànxué run a school **4** (展览)

stage ▷办画展 bàn huàzhǎn stage an art exhibition

办法 bànfǎ [名] way ▷想办法 xiǎng bànfǎ find a way ▷联系办法 liánxì bànfǎ means of contact

办公 bàngōng [动] work

办理 bànlǐ [动] handle

半 bàn I [数] 1 (二分之一) half ▷半价 bàn jià half price ▷半年 bàn nián half a year 2 (在中间) middle ▷半夜 bànyè midnight II [副] partially ▷半新半旧 bàn xīn almost new

半导体 bàndǎotǐ [名] 1 (指物质) semiconductor 2 (收音机) transistor radio

半岛 bàndǎo [名] peninsula

半径 bànjìng [名] radius

半球 bànqiú [名] hemisphere

半天 bàntiān [名] for quite a while ▷他等了半天。Tā děng le bàntiān. He waited for quite a while.

伴 bàn [名] company ▷做伴 zuòbàn keep company

拌 bàn [动] (搅和) mix

绊 bàn [动] (使跌倒) trip

瓣 bàn I [名] (指花儿) petal II [量] ▷几瓣蒜 jǐ bàn suàn a few cloves of garlic ▷一瓣橘子 yī bàn júzi a segment of orange

measure word, used to describe flower petals and segments of fruits

帮 bāng [动] (帮助) help ▷我帮他买票。Wǒ bāng tā mǎi piào. I helped him get the tickets.

帮忙 bāngmáng [动] help ▷请您帮我个忙。Qǐng nín bāng wǒ ge máng. Please can you help me out?

帮助 bāngzhù [动] help ▷谢谢您的帮助。Xièxie nín de bāngzhù. Thank you for your help.

绑 bǎng [动] tie up

榜 bǎng [名] list of names

榜样 bǎngyàng [名] model

棒 bàng I [名] (棍子) cudgel ▷棒子 bàngzi club II [形] (口) great ▷他英语说得很棒。Tā Yīngyǔ shuō de hěn bàng. He speaks great English.

傍 bàng [动] be close to

傍晚 bàngwǎn [名] dusk

磅 bàng [量] pound

镑 bàng [名] pound

包 bāo I [动] 1 (包裹) wrap 2 (包含) include 3 (担保) guarantee 4 (约定专用) hire ▷包车 bāo chē hire a car ▷包飞机 bāo fēijī charter a plane II [名] 1 (包裹) parcel 2 (口袋) bag ▷背包 bēibāo backpack ▷钱包 qiánbāo wallet 3 (疙瘩) lump III [量] packet ▷一包烟 yī bāo yān a packet of cigarettes ▷一包衣服 yī bāo yīfu a bag of clothes measure word, used to describe things that are wrapped up

包含 bāohán [动] contain

包括 bāokuò [动] include

包子 bāozi [名] *steamed stuffed bun*

包子 bāozi

包子 bāozi are bigger than 饺子 jiǎozi. Shaped like buns, they are usually stuffed with meat or vegetable fillings, and are steamed rather than boiled.

剥 bāo [动] peel

雹 báo [名] hail ▷电子 báozi hailstone

薄 báo [形] 1 (不厚) thin 2 (冷淡) cold ▷我对她不薄。Wǒ duì tā bù báo. I treat her very well.

宝 bǎo I [名] treasure II [形] precious

宝贵 bǎoguì [形] valuable

饱 bǎo [形] full ▷我吃饱了。Wǒ chī bǎo le. I am full.

保 bǎo [动] 1 (保护) protect 2 (保持) keep ▷保密 bǎomì keep ... secret ▷保鲜膜 bǎoxiān mó Clingfilm® (英), Saran wrap® (美) 3 (保证) ensure

保安 bǎo'ān [名] security guard

保持 bǎochí [动] maintain ▷保持警惕 bǎochí jǐngtì stay vigilant

保存 bǎocún [动] preserve

保护 bǎohù [动] protect ▷保护环

境 bǎohù huánjìng protect the environment

保龄球 bǎolíngqiú [名] (体育运动) bowling

保留 bǎoliú [动] 1 (保存不变) preserve 2 (意见) hold back ▷你可以保留自己的意见。Nǐ kěyǐ bǎoliú zìjǐ de yìjiàn. You can keep your opinions to yourself.

保姆 bǎomǔ [名] 1 (做家务的女工) domestic help 2 (保育员) nanny

保守 bǎoshǒu [形] conservative

保卫 bǎowèi [动] defend

保险 bǎoxiǎn I [名] insurance II [形] safe

保证 bǎozhèng [动] guarantee

保重 bǎozhòng [动] take care of oneself

报 bào I [动] (告诉) report II [名] 1 (报纸) newspaper ▷日报 rìbào daily ▷报社 bàoshè newspaper office 2 (刊物) periodical ▷画报 huàbào glossy magazine

报仇 bàochóu take revenge

报酬 bàochóu [名] pay

报到 bàodào [动] register

报道 bàodào [动] report ▷电视台报道了这条新闻。Diànshì tái bàodào le zhè tiáo xīnwén. The television station reported this item of news. II [名] report ▷一篇关于克隆人的报道 yī piān guānyú kèlóng rén de bàodào a report about human cloning

报复 bàofù [动] retaliate

报告 bàogào I [动] report ▷向主管部门报告 xiàng zhǔguǎn bùmén bàogào report to the department in charge II [名] report ▷在大会上作报告 zài dàhuì shàng zuò bàogào give a talk at the conference

报关 bàoguān [动] declare

报刊 bàokān [名] newspapers and periodicals (PL)

报名 bàomíng [动] sign up

报失 bàoshī [动] report a loss

报销 bàoxiāo [动] (费用) claim for

报纸 bàozhǐ [名] newspaper

抱 bào [动] 1 (手臂围住) carry in one's arms 2 (领养) adopt 3 (心里存有) cherish ▷对某事抱幻想 duì mǒushì bào huànxiǎng have illusions about sth

抱歉 bàoqiàn I [形] sorry II [动] apologize

抱怨 bàoyuàn [动] complain

豹 bào [名] leopard

暴 bào [形] (猛烈) violent ▷暴雨 bàoyǔ rainstorm

爆 bào [动] 1 (猛烈破裂) explode ▷爆炸 bàozhà explode 2 (突然发生) break out ▷爆发 bàofā break out

杯 bēi I [名] 1 (杯子) cup ▷玻璃杯 bōli bēi glass ▷酒杯 jiǔbēi wineglass ▷杯子 bēizi cup 2 (奖杯) cup ▷世界杯 Shìjièbēi World Cup II [量] cup, glass ▷一杯咖啡 yī bēi kāfēi a cup of coffee ▷两杯水 liǎng bēi shuǐ two glasses of water

背 bēi [动] 1 (驮) carry ... on one's back 2 (担负) take ... on ▷背起重任 bēi qǐ zhòngrèn take on great responsibility
→ see also / 另见 bèi

悲 bēi [形] (悲伤) sad

悲惨 bēicǎn [形] miserable

悲观 bēiguān [形] pessimistic

悲伤 bēishāng [形] sad

碑 bēi [名] tablet ▷纪念碑 jìniànbēi monument

北 běi [名] north ▷北方 běifāng the North ▷北京 Běijīng Beijing ▷北部 běibù the north

北极 běijí [名] the North Pole

备 bèi [动] 1 (具备) have 2 (准备) prepare

备份 bèifèn [动] (计算机) keep a backup copy

备用 bèiyòng [动] backup ▷备用光盘 bèiyòng guāngpán backup CD

备注 bèizhù [名] (注解说明) notes (PL)

背 bèi I [名] 1 (指身体) back ▷背疼 bèiténg backache 2 (指反面) back ▷背面 bèimiàn reverse side 3 (指后面) behind ▷背后 bèihòu behind II [动] (背诵) recite
→ see also / 另见 bēi

背景 bèijǐng [名] (指景物，情况) background

背诵 bèisòng [动] recite

被 bèi I [名] quilt ▸ 被子 bèizi quilt II [介] ▸ 他被哥哥打了一顿。Tā bèi gēge dǎ le yī dùn. He was beaten up by his elder brother. III [助] ▸ 他被跟踪了。Tā bèi gēnzōng le. He was followed.

倍 bèi [名] times (PL) ▸ 这本书比那本书厚三倍。Zhè běn shū bǐ nà běn shū hòu sānbèi. This book is three times thicker than that one. ▸ 物价涨了两倍。Wùjià zhǎng le liǎngbèi. Prices have doubled.

本 běn I [名] 1 (本子) book ▸ 笔记本 bǐjìběn notebook 2 (版本) edition ▸ 手抄本 shǒuchāo běn hand-written copy II [形] 1 (自己的) one's own ▸ 本人 běnrén oneself 2 (现今) this ▸ 本月 běnyuè this month III [副] originally ▸ 我本想亲自去一趟。Wǒ běn xiǎng qīnzì qù yītàng. I originally wanted to go myself. IV [量] ▸ 几本书 jǐ běn shū a few books

measure word, used for counting books, magazines, dictionaries, etc.

本地 běndì [名] locality ▸ 她是本地人。Tā shì běndì rén. She is a native of this place.

本科 běnkē [名] undergraduate course ▸ 本科生 běnkē shēng undergraduate

本来 běnlái I [形] original ▸ 本来的打算 běnlái de dǎsuàn the original plan II [副] (原先) at first ▸ 我本来以为你已经走了。Wǒ běnlái yǐwéi nǐ yǐjīng zǒu le. At first, I thought you had left.

本领 běnlǐng [名] skill

本身 běnshēn [名] itself

本事 běnshi [名] ability

本质 běnzhì [名] essence

笨 bèn [形] 1 (不聪明) stupid 2 (不灵巧) clumsy ▸ 他嘴很笨。Tā zuǐ hěn bèn. He's quite inarticulate.

蹦 bèng [动] leap

逼 bī [动] 1 (强迫) force 2 (强取) press for ▸ 逼债 bīzhài press for repayment of a debt 3 (逼近) close in on

逼近 bījìn [动] close in on

逼迫 bīpò [动] force

鼻 bí [名] (鼻子) nose

鼻涕 bítì [名] mucus

鼻子 bízi [名] nose

比 bǐ I [动] 1 (比较) compare ▸ 比比过去，现在的生活好多了。Bǐbǐ guòqù, xiànzài de shēnghuó hǎo duō le. Life now is much better compared to then. 2 (较量) compete ▸ 他们要比比谁游得快。Tāmen yào bǐbǐ shuí yóu de kuài. They are competing to see who swims the fastest. II [介] 1 (指得分) ▸ 零比零 líng bǐ líng nil-nil (英), no score (美) 2 (相对) ▷今年冬天比去年冷。 Jīnnián dōngtiān bǐ qùnián lěng. It is colder this winter than last winter.

比 bǐ is used to express comparisons: to say that X is taller than Y, simply say X 比 Y 高. e.g. 上海比南京大。(Shànghǎi bǐ Nánjīng dà. (Shanghai is bigger than Nanjing.)

比方 bǐfāng [名] analogy ▷比方说 bǐfāng shuō for example

比分 bǐfēn [名] score

比基尼 bǐjīní [名] bikini

比较 bǐjiào I [动] compare II [副] relatively ▷这里的水果比较新鲜。Zhèlǐ de shuǐguǒ bǐjiào xīnxiān. The fruit here is relatively fresh.

比例 bǐlì [名] proportion

比率 bǐlǜ [名] ratio

比如 bǐrú [连] for instance

比赛 bǐsài [名] match

彼 bǐ [代] 1 (那个) that 2 (对方) the other side

彼此 bǐcǐ [代] (双方) both sides

笔 bǐ I [名] 1 (工具) pen ▷圆珠笔 yuánzhūbǐ ball-point pen 2 (笔画) brush stroke II [量] (款项) ▷一笔钱 yī bǐ qián a sum of money measure word, used for money

笔记 bǐjì [名] (记录) note ▷记笔记 jì bǐjì take notes

笔记本电脑 bǐjìběn diànnǎo [名] laptop

币 bì [名] coin ▷货币 huòbì currency ▷外币 wàibì foreign currency

必 bì [副] 1 (必然) certainly 2 (必须) ▷必修课 bìxiūkè compulsory course

必然 bìrán I [形] inevitable II [名] necessity

必须 bìxū [副] ▷你们必须准时来上班。Nǐmen bìxū zhǔnshí lái shàngbān. You must start work on time.

必要 bìyào [形] essential

毕 bì [动] finish

毕业 bìyè [动] graduate

避 bì [动] 1 (躲开) avoid ▷避风 bìfēng shelter from the wind 2 (防止) prevent

避免 bìmiǎn [动] avoid

避难 bìnàn [动] take refuge

避孕 bìyùn [动] use contraceptives ▷避孕药 bìyùn yào the pill

边 biān [名] 1 (边线) side ▷街边 jiē biān liǎngbiān both sides of the street 2 (边缘) edge ▷路边 lù biān roadside 3 (边界) border 4 (旁边) side ▷在床边 zài chuáng biān by the bed

边…边… biān… biān… ▷边吃边谈 biān chī biān tán talk while eating

边疆 biānjiāng [名] border area

边界 biānjiè [名] border

边境 biānjìng [名] border

边缘 biānyuán [名] edge

编 biān *see below*/ 见下文 biān gēcí 作)
biānchéng program **2** (创作)
write ▷编歌词 biān gēcí write
lyrics **3** (捏造) fabricate ▷编谎话
biān huǎnghuà fabricate a lie
编辑 biānjí I [动] edit II [名] editor

蝙 biān *see below*/ 见下文
蝙蝠 biānfú [名] bat

鞭 biān I [名] **1** (鞭子) whip **2** (爆竹)
firecracker

鞭炮 biānpào [名] firecracker

鞭炮 biānpào

> Firecrackers are believed
> by the Chinese to scare
> off evil spirits and attract
> the god of good fortune
> to people's doorsteps,
> especially in the
> celebration of the Spring
> Festival and at weddings.

贬 biǎn [动] (降低) reduce ▷贬值
biǎnzhí depreciate

贬义词 biǎnyì cí [名] derogatory
expression

扁 biǎn [形] flat ▷自行车胎扁了。
Zìxíngchē tāi biǎn le. The bicycle
tyre is flat.

变 biàn [动] **1** (改变) change ▷小
城的面貌变了。Xiǎochéng de
miànmào biàn le. The

appearance of the town has
changed. **2** (变成) become ▷他
变成熟了。Tā biàn chéngshú le.
He's become quite grown up.

变化 biànhuà I [动] change II [名]
change

便 biàn I [形] **1** (方便) convenient
▷轻便 qīngbiàn portable **2** (简
单) simple ▷便饭 biànfàn
simple meal II [动] excrete ▷小
便 xiǎobiàn urinate ▷大便
dàbiàn defecate III [副] ▷稍等
片刻演出便开始。Shāoděng
piànkè yǎnchū biàn kāishǐ. The
performance is about to start in
a moment.
→ *see also*/ 另见 pián

便利 biànlì I [形] convenient
II [动] facilitate

便士 biànshì [量] pence

便条 biàntiáo [名] note

便携式 biànxiéshì [形] portable

便于 biànyú be easy to ▷便
于联系 biànyú liánxì be easy
to contact

遍 biàn I [副] all over ▷找了个遍
zhǎo le ge biàn search high
and low II [量] ▷我说了两遍。
Wǒ shuō le liǎng biàn. I said it
twice.

> measure word, used for
> the number of times the
> same action takes place

辨 biàn [动] distinguish ▷辨别
biànbié distinguish

辨认 biànrèn [动] identify

辩 biàn [动] debate ▶辩论 biànlùn argue

标 biāo [名] 1 (记号) mark 2 (标准) standard II [动] mark

标本 biāoběn [名] (样品) specimen

标点 biāodiǎn [名] punctuation

标记 biāojì [名] mark

标题 biāotí [名] 1 (指文章, 书) title 2 (指新闻) headline

标志 biāozhì [名] sign

标准 biāozhǔn [名] I standard ▶道德标准 dàodé biāozhǔn moral standard II [形] standard ▶标准时间 biāozhǔn shíjiān standard time

表 biǎo [名] 1 (计时器) watch ▶手表 shǒubiǎo wristwatch 2 (计量器) meter ▶电表 diànbiǎo electricity meter 3 (表格) form ▶火车时间表 huǒchē shíjiān biǎo train timetable ▶填申请表 tián shēnqǐng biǎo fill in the application form 4 (指亲戚) cousin ▶表哥 biǎogē cousin

表达 biǎodá [动] express

表格 biǎogé [名] form

表面 biǎomiàn [名] surface

表明 biǎomíng [动] show

表示 biǎoshì I [动] (表达) express II [名] 1 (言行或表情) gesture 2 (意见) attitude

表现 biǎoxiàn I [动] (显出) show II [名] (指行为, 作风) performance

表演 biǎoyǎn I [动] (演出) perform II [名] performance

表扬 biǎoyáng [动] praise

别 bié I [形] (其他) other II [副] (不要) ▷别忘了关灯。 Bié wàng le guāndēng. Don't forget to turn off the light.

别人 biérén [名] other people

别墅 biéshù [名] villa

别针 biézhēn [名] safety pin

宾 bīn [名] guest

宾馆 bīnguǎn [名] hotel

冰 bīng I [名] ice II [动] 1 (使感觉寒冷) be freezing ▷这水冰手。 Zhè shuǐ bīng shǒu. This water is freezing. 2 (冰镇) cool ▶冰镇 bīngzhèn iced

冰淇淋 bīngqílín [名] ice cream

冰箱 bīngxiāng [名] fridge

兵 bīng [名] 1 (军队) the army ▶当兵 dāng bīng join the army 2 (士兵) soldier

饼 bǐng [名] (面食) cake ▶月饼 yuèbǐng moon cake

饼干 bǐnggān [名] biscuit (英), cookie (美)

并 bìng I [动] 1 (合并) merge 2 (并拢) bring ... together ▷把脚并起来 bǎ jiǎo bìng qǐlái bring your feet together II [副] (表示强调) really ▷他今晚并不想出去。 Tā jīnwǎn bìng bù xiǎng chūqù. He really doesn't want to go out this evening. III [连] and ▶他会

说法语,并在学习西班牙语。
Tā huì shuō Fǎyǔ, bìng zài xuéxí Xībānyá yǔ He can speak French, and he is studying Spanish at the moment.

并且 bìngqiě [连] **1**(和) and ▷她聪明并且用功。Tā cōngmíng bìngqiě yònggōng. She is clever and diligent. **2**(此外) also

丙 bǐng [名] (疾病) disease ▷心脏病 xīnzàng bìng heart disease ▷生病 shēngbìng become ill ▷他去看病了。Tā qù kànbìng le. He went to see a doctor. **II** [动] be ill ▷他病得不轻。Tā bìng de bùqīng. He was seriously ill.

病毒 bìngdú [名] virus

病房 bìngfáng [名] ward

病菌 bìngjūn [名] bacteria

病人 bìngrén [名] **1**(指医院里) patient **2**(指家里) invalid

波 bō [名] (指水,声音,电) wave

发 bō [动] **1**(号码) dial ▷拨电话号码 bō diànhuà hàomǎ dial the phone number **2**(频道) change over to

玻 bō see below/见下文

玻璃 bōli [名] glass

菠 bō see below/见下文

菠菜 bōcài [名] spinach

菠萝 bōluó [名] pineapple

播 bō [动] (电视,收音机) broadcast ▷播放 bōfàng broadcast

伯 bó [名] (伯父) uncle

伯伯 bóbo [名] **1**(伯父) uncle **2**(用于称呼) uncle

脖 bó [名] neck ▷脖子 bózi neck

博 bó [形] abundant

博物馆 bówùguǎn [名] museum

补 bǔ [动] **1**(衣服, 鞋, 车胎, 袜子) mend **2**(牙) fill **3**(增加) add

补充 bǔchōng **I** [动] add **II** [形] supplementary ▷补充说明 bǔchōng shuōmíng additional explanation

补考 bǔkǎo [动] resit

补习 bǔxí [动] take extra lessons

补助 bǔzhù [名] subsidy

捕 bǔ [动] catch

捕捉 bǔzhuō [动] **1**(抓住) seize **2**(捕拿) hunt down

不 bù [副] **1**(用于否定句) not ▷不诚实 bù chéngshí dishonest ▷他不抽烟。Tā bù chōuyān. He doesn't smoke. **2**(用于否定回答) no ▷"你累了吧?" "不,不累。" "Nǐ lèi le ba?" "Bù, bùlèi." "Are you tired?" — "No, I'm not." **3**(客套) ▷不客气。Bù kèqì. Please don't mention it. ▷不谢。Bù xiè. You're welcome. Negating sentences in Chinese is very straightforward: just use 不 bù before the verb. E.g. 我不喝酒。Wǒ bù hējiǔ (I don't drink alcohol). The only exception is the verb 有 yǒu, to have, for which you must use 没 méi. E.g. 我没有钱。Wǒ méiyǒu qián. (I don't have any money). 不 bù is fourth tone unless it is followed by another fourth tone syllable, in which case it is usually pronounced as a second tone, eg. 不要 búyào. For more information on tones, please see the introduction.

不必 bùbì [副] ▷明天你们不必来了。Míngtiān nǐmen bùbì lái le. You don't have to come tomorrow.

不但 bùdàn [连] not only ▷这辆车的设计不但美观，而且实用。Zhè liàng chē de shèjì bùdàn měiguān, érqiě shíyòng. The design of this car is not only beautiful, but it's also practical.

不得了 bùdéliǎo [形] (表示程度) extreme ▷这孩子淘气得不得了。Zhè háizi táoqì de bùdéliǎo. This child is terribly naughty.

不断 bùduàn [副] continually ▷沙漠不断扩大。Shāmò bùduàn kuòdà. The desert is expanding all the time.

不敢 bùgǎn [动] not dare

不管 bùguǎn [连] no matter ▷不管出什么事，我们都要保持镇定。Bùguǎn chū shénme shì, wǒmen dōuyào bǎochí zhèndìng. Whatever happens, we must remain calm.

不过 bùguò I [副] 1 (仅仅) only ▷不过是点小伤。Bùguò shì diǎn xiǎoshāng. It's only a slight injury. 2 (非常) can't be better ▷这是最简单不过的方法。Zhè shì zuì jiǎndān bùguò de fāngfǎ. This is by far the easiest method. II [连] but ▷他很喜欢新学校，不过离家太远了。Tā hěn xǐhuān xīn xuéxiào, bùguò lí jiā tài yuǎn le. He really likes his new school, but it's a very long way from home.

不仅 bùjǐn 1 (不止) not just ▷这不仅是学校的问题。Zhè bùjǐn shì xuéxiào de wèntí. This is not just the school's problem 2 (不但) not only ▷这地毯不仅质量好，而且价格便宜。Zhè dìtǎn bùjǐn zhìliàng hǎo, érqiě jiàgé piányí. Not only is the carpet good quality, it's also cheap.

不久 bùjiǔ [名] ▷他们不久就要结婚了。Tāmen bùjiǔ jiùyào jiéhūn le. They are getting married soon.

不论 bùlùn [连] no matter ▷不论是谁，都必须遵守法规。Bùlùn shì shuí, dōu bìxū zūnshǒu fǎguī. No matter who you are, you have to abide by the regulations.

不满 bùmǎn [形] dissatisfied

不免 bùmiǎn [副] inevitably

不然 bùrán [连] otherwise ▷多

谢你提醒我，不然我就忘了。
Duōxiè nǐ tíxǐng wǒ, bùrán wǒ jiù wàng le. Thanks very much for reminding me, or I would have forgotten about it.

不如 bùrú [动] not be as good as ▷城里太吵，不如住在郊区。Chénglǐ tài chǎo, bùrú zhùzài jiāoqū. The city is too noisy - it's better living in the suburbs.

不少 bùshǎo [形] a lot of ▷她有不少好朋友。Tā yǒu bùshǎo hǎo péngyou. She has a lot of good friends.

不同 bùtóng [形] different

不幸 bùxìng I [形] 1 (不幸运) unhappy 2 (出人意料) unfortunate II [名] disaster

不要紧 bùyàojǐn [形] 1 (不严重) not serious ▷他的病不要紧。Tā de bìng bùyàojǐn. His illness is not serious. 2 (没关系) it doesn't matter

不一定 bùyídìng [副] may not ▷她未必会回电话。Tā wèibì huì huí diànhuà. She may not return your call.

不止 bùzhǐ [副] 1 (不停地) incessantly ▷大笑不止 dàxiào bùzhǐ laugh incessantly 2 (多于) more than ▷不止一次 bùzhǐ yīcì on more than one occasion

布 bù [名] cloth

布置 bùzhì [动] 1 (房间等) decorate 2 (任务, 作业) assign

步 bù [名] 1 (脚步) step ▷步伐

bùfá pace 2 (阶段) stage ▷步骤 bùzhòu step 3 (地步) situation

步行 bùxíng [动] go on foot

部 bù I [名] 1 (部分) part ▷东部 dōng bù the eastern part 2 (部门) department ▷总部 zǒngbù headquarters (PL) ▷部长 bùzhǎng department head ▷教育部 jiàoyù bù education department II [量] 1 一部电话 yī bù diànhuà a telephone ▷三部电影 sān bù diànyǐng three films measure word, used for films, phones, etc.

部队 bùduì [名] armed forces (PL)

部分 bùfen [名] part

部门 bùmén [名] department

部位 bùwèi [名] place

C

擦 cā [动] 1(抹) wipe ... clean 2(指用水) wash 3(皮鞋) polish 4(摩擦) rub 5(涂) apply 6(火柴) strike 7(破) scrape ▶ 擦伤 cāshāng scrape 8(挨着) brush 9(瓜果) shred

猜 cāi [动] 1(猜测) guess 2(猜疑) suspect

猜测 cāicè I [动] speculate II [名] speculation

猜想 cāixiǎng [动] suppose

猜疑 cāiyí [动] have unfounded suspicions about

才 cái I [名] 1(才能) ability ▶ 多才多艺 duōcái duōyì multi-talented 2(人才) talent ▶ 奇才 qícái extraordinary talent II [副] 1(刚) just ▷ 我才到家, 电话就响了。 Wǒ cái dào jiā, diànhuà jiù xiǎng le. Just as I arrived home, the phone rang. 2(表示晚) not...until ▷ 我10点才到单位。 Wǒ shídiǎn cái dào dānwèi I didn't arrive at work until ten o'clock. 3(表示条件) only...if ▷ 学生只有用功, 才能取得好成绩。 Xuéshēng zhǐyǒu yònggōng, cái néng qǔdé hǎo chéngjì. Students will only be able to do well if they study hard. 4(表示情况改变) only after ▷ 他解释后, 我才明白了他为什么那么难过。 Tā jiěshì hòu, wǒ cái míngbai tā wèishénme nàme nánguò. It was only after he explained that I understood why he was so sad. 5(程度低) only ▷ 他才学会上网。 Tā cái xuéhuì shàngwǎng. He has only just learned how to use the Internet.

才华 cáihuá [名] talent

才能 cáinéng [名] ability

才子 cáizǐ [名] talented man

材 cái [名] (指物) material ▶ 教材 jiàocái teaching material

材料 cáiliào [名] 1(原料) material 2(资料) material 3(人才) talent

财 cái [名] wealth

财富 cáifù [名] wealth

财政 cáizhèng [名] finance

裁 cái [动] 1(衣服, 纸) cut 2(减) cut ▶ 裁员 cáiyuán cut staff 3(判断) decide

裁缝 cáifeng [名] **1**(指男装)tailor **2**(指女装)dressmaker

裁判 cáipàn **I**[名]judgment **II**[动]make a decision

采 cǎi [动] **1**(摘)pick **2**(选)choose **3**(开采)extract **4**(采集)gather

采访 cǎifǎng [动]interview

采购 cǎigòu **I**[动]purchase **II**[名]buyer

采取 cǎiqǔ [动]adopt

采用 cǎiyòng [动]adopt

彩 cǎi [名](颜色)colour(英), color(美)

彩电 cǎidiàn [名]colour(英)或color(美)TV

彩色 cǎisè [名](指胶片)colour(英)或color(美)film

彩排 cǎipái [动]rehearse

彩票 cǎipiào [名]lottery ticket

彩色 cǎisè [名]colour(英), color(美)

踩 cǎi [动](脚)step on

菜 cài [名] **1**(植物)vegetable **2**(饭食)dish

菜单 càidān [名]menu

菜谱 càipǔ [名] **1**(菜单)menu **2**(指书)cookbook

参 cān [动](加入)join ▷ 参军 cānjūn enlist
→ see also/另见 shēn

参观 cānguān [动]tour

参加 cānjiā [动]take part in ▷ 参加新年晚会 cānjiā

xīnnián wǎnhuì attend a New Year's party ▷ 参加民主党 cānjiā Mínzhǔ Dǎng join the Democratic Party

参考 cānkǎo **I**[动]consult **II**[名]reference ▷ 参考书 cānkǎo shū reference book

参谋 cānmóu **I**[名] **1**(顾问)advisor **2**(指军职)staff officer **II**[动]give advice

参与 cānyù [动]participate in

餐 cān **I**[名]meal **II**[量]meal

餐车 cānchē [名] **1**(指推车)food trolley **2**(指车厢)buffet(英)或dining(美)car

餐巾 cānjīn [名]napkin

餐具 cānjù [名]eating utensils (PL)

餐厅 cāntīng [名]canteen

残 cán [形] **1**(指器物)defective **2**(指人或动物)disabled **3**(剩余)remaining

残废 cánfèi [动]be disabled

残疾 cánjí [名]disability ▷ 残疾人 cánjí rén people with disabilities

残酷 cánkù [形]brutal

残忍 cánrěn [形]cruel

蚕 cán [名]silkworm

惭 cán see below/见下文

惭愧 cánkuì [形]ashamed

惨 cǎn [形](悲惨)tragic

灿 càn see below/见下文

灿烂 cànlàn [形]glorious

仓 cāng [名] store

仓库 cāngkù [名] storehouse

苍 cāng [形] (指鬓发) grey (英), gray (美)

苍白 cāngbái [形] 1 (脸色) pale 2 (文章,表演等) bland

苍蝇 cāngying [名] fly

舱 cāng [名] 1 (用于载人) cabin ▸头等舱 tóuděngcāng first-class cabin 2 (用于装物) hold ▸货舱 huòcāng cargo hold

藏 cáng [动] 1 (隐藏) hide 2 (储存) store 3 (收集) collect ▸藏书 cángshū collect books
→ see also / 另见 zàng

操 cāo [名] (体育活动) exercise

操场 cāochǎng [名] sports ground

操心 cāoxīn [动] concern

操作 cāozuò [动] operate

糙 cāo [形] poor

草 cǎo [名] 1 (植物) grass ▸草地 cǎodì lawn, meadow 2 (用作材料) straw

草稿 cǎogǎo [名] rough draft

草帽 cǎomào [名] straw hat

草莓 cǎoméi [名] strawberry

草率 cǎoshuài [形] rash

草原 cǎoyuán [名] grasslands (PL)

册 cè I [名] book ▸手册 shǒucè handbook ▸相册 xiàngcè photo album II [量] 1 (指同一本书) copy 2 (指不同本书) volume

厕 cè [名] toilet ▸公厕 gōngcè public toilet

厕所 cèsuǒ [名] toilet

侧 cè I [名] side ▸两侧 liǎngcè both sides II [动] turn ... away ▸我侧过脸去。 Wǒ cè guò liǎn qù. I turned my face away.

侧面 cèmiàn I [形] 1 (非official) unofficial 2 (指方位) side II [名] side

测 cè [动] 1 (测量) measure 2 (推测) predict

测量 cèliáng I [动] measure II [名] survey

测试 cèshì [动] test II [名] test

测验 cèyàn [动] test II [名] test

策 cè [名] suggestion

策划 cèhuà I [动] design II [名] planning

策略 cèlüè I [名] strategy II [形] strategic

层 céng I [量] 1 (指建筑物) floor 2 (指覆盖物) layer 3 (步) step 4 (指含义) layer II [名] (指物,状态) layer

曾 céng [副] once

曾经 céngjīng [副] once

蹭 cèng [动] 1 (摩擦) rub 2 (沾上) smear 3 (指速度) creep along

叉 chā [名] 1 (器具) fork 2 (餐具) fork 3 (符号) cross

叉子 chāzi [名] 1 (符号) cross 2 (餐具) fork

差 chā [名] difference
→ *see also*/另见 chà, chāi

差别 chābié [名] difference

差错 chācuò [名] **1** (错误) mistake **2** (意外) accident

差距 chājù [名] difference

差异 chāyì [名] difference

插 chā [动] insert ▷ 我能不能插一句? Wǒ néng bùnéng chā yījù? Can I interrupt just a second?

插曲 chāqǔ [名] **1** (音乐) incidental music **2** (事件) interlude

插入 chārù [动] insert

插图 chātú [名] illustration

插销 chāxiāo [名] **1** (闩) bolt **2** (插头) electrical plug

插嘴 chāzuǐ [动] interrupt

插座 chāzuò [名] socket (英), outlet (美)

茶 chá [名] tea ▷ 红茶 hóngchá black tea ▷ 茶杯 chábēi teacup ▷ 茶壶 cháhú teapot ▷ 茶馆 cháguǎn teahouse ▷ 泡茶 pào chá make tea

茶具 chájù [名] tea set

茶叶 cháyè [名] tea leaves (PL)

查 chá [动] **1** (检查) inspect **2** (调查) investigate **3** (字典, 词典) look ... up

查号台 cháhàotái [名] directory inquiries (SG) (英) 或 assistance (美)

查阅 cháyuè [动] look ... up

查找 cházhǎo [动] look for

察 chá [动] check ▷ 观察 guānchá observe

察觉 chájué [动] detect

杈 chà [名] branch

差 chà I [动] **1** (不相同) be different from ▷ 你比他差得远了。Nǐ bǐ tā chà de yuǎn le. You are not nearly as good as him. **2** (缺欠) be short of ▷ 差3个人 chà sān gè rén be three people short II [形] **1** (错误) mistaken **2** (不好) poor ▷ 质量差 zhìliàng chà poor quality
→ *see also*/另见 chā, chāi

差不多 chà bu duō I [形] very similar II [副] almost

拆 chāi [动] **1** (打开) tear ... open **2** (拆毁) dismantle

差 chāi [动] send ▷ 出差 chūchāi go on a business trip
→ *see also*/另见 chā, chà

差事 chāishi [名] **1** (任务) assignment **2** (差使) position

柴 chái [名] firewood

柴油 cháiyóu [名] diesel

豺 chái [名] jackal

掺 chān [动] mix

搀 chān [动] **1** (搀扶) support ... by the arm **2** (混合) mix

馋 chán [形] greedy

缠 chán [动] **1** (缠绕) twine **2** (纠

缠) pester

蝉 chán [名] cicada

产 chǎn [动] 1(生育) give birth to 2(出产) produce

产量 chǎnliàng [名] yield

产品 chǎnpǐn [名] product

产权 chǎnquán [名] property rights (PL) ▷知识产权 zhīshì chǎnquán intellectual property

产生 chǎnshēng [动] produce

产业 chǎnyè [名] 1(财产) property 2(工业生产) industry

铲 chǎn I [名] shovel II [动] shovel

颤 chàn [动] tremble

颤抖 chàndǒu [动] shiver

长 cháng I [形] long II [名] (长度) length
→ see also/ 另见 zhǎng

长城 Chángchéng [名] the Great Wall

长城 Chángchéng

As one of the longest man-made mega structures in world, the Great Wall of China is nearly 4,000 miles in length, reaching from the border of Xinjiang province in the west to the eastern coast just north of Beijing. It is probably the most famous of China's landmarks, and was made a UNESCO World Heritage site in 1987. It was used

records of fortifications being built along the route which date from the 3rd century BC, although most of what remains today was built during the Ming dynasty (1368-1644). Built as a defence mechanism, its primary function was to withstand invasions by the northern tribes.

长处 chángchu [名] strong point

长度 chángdù [名] length

长江 Cháng Jiāng [名] the Yangtze

长久 chángjiǔ [形] long-term

长跑 chángpǎo [动] go long-distance running

长寿 chángshòu [形] long-lived ▷祝您长寿！ Zhù nín chángshòu! Here's to a long life!

长寿面 chángshòumiàn [名] long-life noodles (PL)

长寿面 chángshòumiàn

In the Chinese tradition, long-life noodles are eaten on a birthday. They are very long, thin noodles symbolizing longevity.

长途 chángtú [形] long-distance ▷长途电话 chángtú diànhuà long-distance phone call ▷长途旅行 chángtú lǚxíng long journey

肠 cháng [名] intestines (PL)

肠子 chángzi [名] intestines (PL)

尝 cháng [动] taste ▸品尝 pǐncháng taste

尝试 chángshì [动] try

常 cháng I [形] 1 (平常) common 2 (经常) frequent ▸常客 chángkè regular guest II [副] often

常常 chángcháng [副] often

常识 chángshí [名] 1 (非专业知识) general knowledge 2 (生活经验) common sense

偿 cháng [动] 1 (归还) repay 2 (满足) fulfil ▸如愿以偿 rúyuànyícháng fulfil one's dreams

偿还 chánghuán [动] repay

厂 chǎng [名] (工厂) factory

场 chǎng I [名] 1 (地方) ground ▸排球场 páiqiúchǎng volleyball court ▸市场 shìchǎng market 2 (舞台) stage ▸上场 shàngchǎng go on stage 3 (戏剧片段) scene 4 (物) field II [量] 1 (比赛, 演出) ▸一场足球赛 yī chǎng zúqiú sài a football match ▸两场音乐会 liǎng chǎng yīnyuèhuì two concerts measure word, used for games and shows 2 (病) ▸一场重病 yī chǎng zhòngbìng a serious illness measure word, used for illnesses 3 (灾害, 战争, 事故) ▸一场火灾 yī chǎng huǒzāi a fire ▸一场战争 yī chǎng zhànzhēng a war ▸几场事故 jǐ chǎng shìgù

several accidents measure word, used for afflictions, wars, accidents, etc.

场地 chǎngdì [名] space ▸运动场地 yùndòng chǎngdì sports area

场合 chǎnghé [名] occasion

场所 chǎngsuǒ [名] place ▸公共场所 gōnggòng chǎngsuǒ public place

敞 chǎng I [形] spacious ▸宽敞 kuānchǎng spacious II [动] be open ▸大门敞着 Dàmén chǎng zhe. The main door is open.

畅 chàng I [形] 1 (无阻碍) smooth ▸畅通 chàngtōng unimpeded 2 (舒畅) untroubled ▸他心情不畅。Tā xīnqíng bùchàng. He's troubled by something. II [副] uninhibitedly ▸畅饮 chàngyǐn drink one's fill

畅快 chàngkuài [形] carefree

畅所欲言 chàng suǒ yù yán speak freely

畅通 chàngtōng [动] be open

畅销 chàngxiāo [动] have a ready market

倡 chàng [动] initiate

倡议 chàngyì [动] propose

唱 chàng [动] (发出乐音) sing ▸独唱 dúchàng solo ▸合唱 héchàng chorus

唱歌 chànggē [动] sing

唱戏 chàngxì [动] perform opera

抄 chāo [动] 1 (誊写) copy 2 (抄袭) plagiarize

抄袭 chāoxí [动] (剽窃) plagiarize

钞 chāo [名] banknote

钞票 chāopiào [名] banknote

超 chāo I [动] 1 (超过) exceed 2 (不受限制) transcend ▶超现实 chāoxiànshí surreal II [形] super ▷超低温 chāodīwēn ultra-low temperature

超级 chāojí [形] super ▶超级大国 chāojí dàguó superpower ▶超级市场 chāojí shìchǎng supermarket

超人 chāorén [名] superman

超市 chāoshì [名] supermarket

超重 chāozhòng [动] 1 (超过载重量) overload 2 (超过标准重量) be overweight

巢 cháo [名] nest

朝 cháo I [名] (朝代) dynasty II [动] face III [介] towards ▷他朝着我走过来。Tā cháo zhe wǒ zǒu guòlai. He was walking towards me.

朝鲜 Cháoxiǎn [名] North Korea

嘲 cháo [动] ridicule

嘲笑 cháoxiào [动] laugh at

潮 cháo I [名] 1 (潮汐) tide 2 (社会运动) movement ▶工潮 gōngcháo labour (英) 或 labor (美) movement ▶思潮 sīcháo Zeitgeist II [形] damp

潮流 cháoliú [名] 1 (水流) tide 2 (发展趋势) trend

潮湿 cháoshī [形] damp

潮水 cháoshuǐ [名] tidal waters (PL)

吵 chǎo I [动] 1 (发出噪音) make a racket 2 (争吵) squabble II [形] noisy

吵架 chǎojià [动] quarrel

吵闹 chǎonào [动] 1 (争吵) bicker 2 (打扰) disturb

吵嘴 chǎozuǐ [动] bicker

炒 chǎo [动] 1 (烹调) stir-fry 2 (地皮、外汇等) speculate ▷炒股 chǎogǔ speculate in stocks and shares 3 (方) (解雇) sack ▷炒鱿鱼 chǎo yóuyú be fired

车 chē [名] 1 (运输工具) vehicle ▶小汽车 xiǎoqìchē car ▶公共汽车 gōnggòngqìchē bus 2 (带轮的装置) wheel ▶风车 fēngchē windmill

车费 chēfèi [名] fare

车祸 chēhuò [名] traffic accident

车间 chējiān [名] workshop

车库 chēkù [名] garage

车辆 chēliàng [名] vehicle

车轮 chēlún [名] wheel

车胎 chētāi [名] tyre (英), tire (美)

车厢 chēxiāng [名] coach

车站 chēzhàn [名] 1 (火车的) railway station 2 (汽车的) bus stop

扯 chě [动] (拉) pull

彻 chè [动] penetrate ▸彻夜 chèyè all night

彻底 chèdǐ [形] thorough

撤 chè [动] 1 (除去) take ... away ▸撤职 chèzhí dismiss from one's job 2 (退) move away

撤退 chètuì [动] withdraw

撤销 chèxiāo [动] 1 (职务) dismiss 2 (计划) cancel 3 (法令) rescind

尘 chén [名] 1 (尘土) dirt ▸灰尘 huīchén dust 2 (尘世) the material world ▸尘世 chénshì worldly affairs (PL)

尘土 chéntǔ [名] dust

沉 chén I [动] 1 (向下落) sink 2 (指情绪) become grave II [形] 1 (指程度深) deep ▸昨晚我睡得很沉。 Zuówǎn wǒ shuì de hěn chén. Last night I slept very deeply. 2 (重) heavy 3 (不舒服) heavy ▸我两条腿发沉。 Wǒ liǎng tiáo tuǐ fāchén. My legs feel heavy.

沉静 chénjìng [形] 1 (肃静) quiet 2 (指性格) placid

沉闷 chénmèn [形] 1 (天气, 气氛) depressing 2 (心情) depressed 3 (指性格) introverted

沉没 chénmò [动] sink

沉默 chénmò I [形] taciturn II [动] be silent

沉痛 chéntòng [形] 1 (心情) grieving 2 (教训) bitter

沉稳 chénwěn [形] 1 (稳重) steady 2 (安稳) peaceful

沉重 chénzhòng [形] heavy

沉着 chénzhuó [形] calm

陈 chén [动] 1 (陈列) set ... out 2 (陈述) state

陈旧 chénjiù [形] out-of-date

陈列 chénliè [动] display

陈述 chénshù [动] state

晨 chén [名] morning ▸早晨 zǎochén early morning

衬 chèn [名] lining ▸衬衫 chènshān shirt

衬托 chèntuō [动] set ... off

称 chèn [动] match ▸相称 xiāngchèn match ▸对称 duìchèn be symmetrical
→ see also/另见 chēng

称心 chènxīn [动] be satisfactory

趁 chèn [介] ▸趁这个机会我讲几句话。 Chèn zhè ge jīhuì wǒ jiǎng jǐ jù huà. I would like to take this opportunity to say a few words.

称 chēng I [动] 1 (叫) call 2 (说) say 3 (测量) weigh II [名] name ▸简称 jiǎnchēng short form
→ see also/另见 chèn

称呼 chēnghu I [动] call II [名] form of address

称赞 chēngzàn [动] praise

撑 chēng [动] 1 (抵住) prop ... up 2 (船) punt 3 (坚持住) keep ... up 4 (张开) open 5 (容不下) fill to bursting ▸少吃点吧, 别撑着! Shǎo chī diǎn ba, bié chēng zhe!

Don't eat so much, you'll burst!

成 chéng I [动] 1 (成功) accomplish ▷ 那件事成了。Nà jiàn shì chéng le. The job is done. 2 (成为) become II [形] (可以) OK ▷ 成！就这么定了。Chéng! Jiù zhème dìng le. OK – that's agreed.

成本 chéngběn [名] cost

成分 chéngfèn [名] 1 (组成部分) composition 2 (社会阶层) status

成功 chénggōng [动] succeed

成果 chéngguǒ [名] achievement

成绩 chéngjì [名] success

成就 chéngjiù I [名] achievement II [动] achieve

成立 chénglì [动] 1 (建立) found 2 (有根据) be tenable

成年 chéngnián [动] 1 (指动植物) mature 2 (指人) grow up

成人 chéngrén I [名] adult II [动] grow up

成熟 chéngshú [形] 1 (指果实) ripe 2 (指思想) mature 3 (指机会) ripe

成为 chéngwéi [动] become

成问题 chéng wèntí [动] be a problem

成语 chéngyǔ [名] idiom

成员 chéngyuán [名] member

成长 chéngzhǎng [动] grow up

诚 chéng [形] honest ▷忠诚 zhōngchéng loyal ▷诚心 chéngxīn sincere

诚恳 chéngkěn [形] sincere

诚实 chéngshí [形] honest

承 chéng [动] 1 (承受) bear 2 (承担) undertake

承担 chéngdān [动] 1 (责任) bear 2 (工作) undertake 3 (费用) bear

承诺 chéngnuò I [动] undertake II [名] commitment

承认 chéngrèn [动] 1 (认可) acknowledge 2 (政权) recognize

承受 chéngshòu [动] 1 (禁受) bear 2 (经受) experience

城 chéng [名] 1 (城墙) city wall ▷城外 chéngwài outside the city 2 (城市) city ▷进城 jìnchéng go to town 3 (城镇) town

城堡 chéngbǎo [名] castle

城市 chéngshì [名] city

乘 chéng [动] 1 (搭坐) travel by ▷乘火车 chéng huǒchē travel by train 2 (利用) take advantage of 3 (几倍于) multiply ▷8乘5等于40。Bǎ chéng wǔ děngyú sìshí. Eight times five is forty.

乘法 chéngfǎ [名] multiplication

乘方 chéngfāng [名] (数) power

乘客 chéngkè [名] passenger

乘务员 chéngwùyuán [名] conductor

盛 chéng [动] 1 (装) ladle ... out 2 (容纳) contain → see also/另见 shèng

程 chéng [名] 1 (规矩) rule ▷章程 zhāngchéng constitution 2 (程序) procedure ▷议程

yìchéng agenda ▶课程 kèchéng curriculum **3**(距离) distance ▶路程 lùchéng journey **4**(道路) journey

程度 chéngdù [名] **1**(水平) level **2**(限度) extent

程式 chéngshì [名] form

程序 chéngxù [名] **1**(次序) procedure **2**(计算机) program

惩 chéng [动] punish

惩罚 chéngfá [动] punish

橙 chéng *see below/见下文*

橙子 chéngzi [名] orange

逞 chěng [动] (夸耀) flaunt

逞能 chěngnéng [动] show off

秤 chèng [名] scales (PL)

吃 chī [动] **1**(咀嚼吞咽) eat ▶吃药 chīyào take medicine **2**(就餐) eat in **3**(依靠) live off ▶吃劳保 láobǎo live off welfare **4**(消灭) wipe ... out **5**(耗费) withstand ▶吃力 chīlì strenuous **6**(吸收) absorb

吃醋 chīcù [动] be jealous

吃惊 chījīng [动] surprise

吃苦 chīkǔ [动] put up with hardship

吃亏 chīkuī [动] **1**(受损失) lose out **2**(条件不利) be at a disadvantage

吃香 chīxiāng [形] (口) popular

痴 chī I [形] idiotic II [名] obsession

痴呆 chīdāi [形] idiotic

痴迷 chīmí [形] infatuated

池 chí [名] (池塘) pond ▶泳池 yǒngchí swimming pool

池塘 chítáng [名] pond

迟 chí [形] **1**(慢) slow **2**(晚) late

迟到 chídào [动] be late

迟钝 chídùn [形] (贬) slow

迟早 chízǎo [副] sooner or later

持 chí [动] **1**(拿着) hold **2**(支持) support ▶坚持 jiānchí maintain

持久 chíjiǔ [形] protracted

持续 chíxù [动] go on

匙 chí [名] spoon

尺 chǐ I [量] *unit of length, equal to a third of a metre* II [名] ruler ▶尺子 chǐzi ruler

尺寸 chǐcun [名] **1**(长度) size **2**(分寸) sense of propriety

尺码 chǐmǎ [名] (尺寸) size

齿 chǐ [名] (器官) tooth ▶牙齿 yáchǐ tooth

耻 chǐ [名] **1**(羞愧) shame **2**(耻辱) disgrace

耻辱 chǐrǔ [名] disgrace

赤 chì [形] (红色) red

赤道 chìdào [名] the equator

赤裸裸 chìluǒluǒ [形] **1**(光身子) stark naked **2**(喻) (毫不掩饰) undisguised

翅 chì [名] **1**(翅膀) wing **2**(鳍) fin

翅膀 chìbǎng [名] wing

冲 chōng [动] 1 (向前闯) rush forward 2 (猛撞) clash ▶冲撞 chōngzhuàng collide 3 (浇) pour boiling water on 4 (冲洗) rinse 5 (指胶片) develop
→ see also/另见 chòng

冲刺 chōngcì [动] (字) sprint

冲动 chōngdòng [动] be impulsive

冲浪 chōnglàng [动] surf

冲突 chōngtū [动] 1 (激烈争斗) conflict 2 (相抵触) clash II [名] (矛盾) conflict

冲洗 chōngxǐ [动] 1 (洗涤) wash 2 (指胶片) develop

充 chōng [动] 1 (满) fill ▶充电 chōngdiàn charge a battery 2 (担任) act as 3 (假装) pass ... off as

充当 chōngdāng [动] act as

充分 chōngfèn I [形] ample II [副] fully

充满 chōngmǎn [动] 1 (填满) fill 2 (有) brim with

充其量 chōngqíliàng [副] at best

充实 chōngshí I [形] rich II [动] enrich

充足 chōngzú [形] sufficient

虫 chóng [名] insect ▶虫子 chóngzi insect

重 chóng [动] 1 (重复) repeat 2 (重叠) overlap II [副] again
→ see also/另见 zhòng

重叠 chóngdié [动] overlapping

重逢 chóngféng [动] reunite

重复 chóngfù [动] repeat

重新 chóngxīn [副] again

崇 chóng [形] high

崇拜 chóngbài [动] worship

崇高 chónggāo [形] lofty

宠 chǒng [动] spoil

宠爱 chǒng'ài [动] dote on

宠物 chǒngwù [名] pet

冲 chòng I [形] (指气味刺鼻) pungent 2 (劲儿足) vigorous II [介] 1 (对着) at 2 (凭) because of 3 [动] (口) (正对) face
→ see also/另见 chōng

抽 chōu [动] 1 (取出) take ... out 2 (取出部分) take ▶抽时间 chōu shíjiān find time 3 (吸) inhale ▶抽烟 chōuyān smoke 3 (抽血) chōuxiě take blood 4 (抽缩) shrink 5 (打) whip

抽搐 chōuchù [动] twitch

抽风 chōufēng [动] 1 (指疾病) have convulsions 2 (喻) (不合常理) lose the plot

抽奖 chōujiǎng [动] draw prizes

抽筋 chōujīn [动] (口) (肌肉痉挛) have cramp

抽空 chōukòng [动] find the time

抽签 chōuqiān [动] draw lots

抽水 chōushuǐ [动] 1 (吸水) pump water 2 (缩水) shrink

抽屉 chōuti [名] drawer

抽象 chōuxiàng [形] abstract

仇 chóu [名] 1 (仇敌) enemy 2 (仇恨) hatred ▶报仇 bàochóu avenge

仇恨 chóuhèn [动] hate

绸 chóu [名] silk ▸丝绸 sīchóu silk

酬 chóu [动] (报答) reward

酬金 chóujīn [名] remuneration

酬劳 chóuláo I [动] repay II [名] repayment

酬谢 chóuxiè [动] repay

稠 chóu [形] 1 (浓度大) thick 2 (稠密) dense

稠密 chóumì [形] dense

愁 chóu [动] be anxious ▸忧愁 yōuchóu be worried

丑 chǒu [形] 1 (丑陋) ugly 2 (令人厌恶) disgraceful

丑陋 chǒulòu [形] ugly

丑闻 chǒuwén [名] scandal

瞅 chǒu [动] (方) look at

臭 chòu [形] 1 (指气味) smelly 2 (惹人厌恶) disgusting 3 (拙劣) lousy

出 chū [动] 1 (与入相对) go out ▸出国 chūguó go abroad ▸出游 chūyóu go sightseeing 2 (到来) appear ▸出庭 chūtíng appear in court 3 (超出) exceed ▸出轨 chūguǐ derail 4 (给) give out 5 (产生) produce 6 (发生) occur ▸出事 chūshì have an accident 7 (显现) come out ▸出血 chūxiě bleed ▸出汗 chūhàn sweat 8 (显露) ▸出名 chūmíng become famous

出版 chūbǎn [动] publish

出差 chūchāi [动] go away on business

出发 chūfā [动] 1 (离开) set out 2 (表示着眼点) take ... as a starting point

出口 chūkǒu I [动] (指贸易) export II [名] exit

出路 chūlù [名] 1 (指道路) way out 2 (前途) prospects (PL) 3 (销路) market

出名 chūmíng [动] become famous

出勤 chūqín [动] (按时到) show up on time ▸出勤率 chūqínlǜ ratio of attendance

出色 chūsè [形] outstanding

出身 chūshēn I [动] come from II [名] background

出生 chūshēng [动] be born

出售 chūshòu [动] sell

出席 chūxí [动] attend

出现 chūxiàn [动] appear

出院 chūyuàn [动] leave hospital

出租 chūzū [动] let ▸有房出租 yǒu fáng chūzū room to let

出租汽车 chūzū qìchē [名] taxi

初 chū I [名] original II [形] 1 (第一) first ▸初恋 chūliàn first love 2 (最低) primary ▸初级 chūjí primary 3 (开始) early ▸初冬 chūdōng early winter

初步 chūbù [形] fundamental

初期 chūqī [名] initial stage

除 chú I [动] 1 (去掉) get rid of ▸开除 kāichú dismiss ▸去除 qùchú

remove **2** (指算术) divide ▸除法 chúfǎ division ▸16除8等于2. Shíliù chú bā děngyú èr. Sixteen divided by eight is two. **II** [介] (除了不包括) except ▸除彼得外大家都来了。 Chú Bǐdé wài dàjiā dōu lái le. Everyone came except Peter. **2** (除此以外) apart from

除非 chúfēi **I** [连] unless ▸除非他要我去,否则我不去。 Chúfēi tā yào wǒ qù, fǒuzé wǒ bù qù. I won't go unless he wants me to. **II** [介] other than

除了 chúle [介] **1** (表示不包括) except ▸除了你其他人都参加了会议。 Chúle nǐ qítā rén dōu cānjiā le huìyì. Everyone else attended the meeting except you. **2** (除此以外) apart from ▸他除了学习英语,还学习日语。 Tā chúle xuéxí Yīngyǔ, hái xuéxí Rìyǔ. Apart from studying English, he also studies Japanese. **3** (表示非此即彼) apart from ... the only ... ▸他除了工作就是睡觉。 Tā chúle gōngzuò jiùshì shuìjiào. The only thing he does apart from work is sleep.

除夕 chúxī [名] New Year's Eve

厨 chú [名] **1** (厨房) kitchen ▸厨房 chúfáng kitchen **2** (厨师) cook

厨师 chúshī [名] cook

橱 chú [名] cabinet

橱窗 chúchuāng [名] **1** (指商店的展示窗) shop (英) 或 store (美)

window **2** (用于展览图片等) display case

处 chǔ [动] **1** (交往) get on with **2** (在) be in **3** (办理) deal with **4** (处罚) penalize → see also/另见 chù

处罚 chǔfá [动] punish

处方 chǔfāng [名] prescription

处分 chǔfèn **I** [动] punish **II** [名] punishment

处境 chǔjìng [名] situation

处理 chǔlǐ [动] **1** (解决) deal with **2** (减价) sell ... at a reduced price ▸处理品 chǔlǐ pǐn goods sold at a discount **3** (加工) treat

处于 chǔyú [动] be in a position ▸处于困境 chǔyú kùnjìng be in a difficult position

储 chǔ [动] store

储备 chǔbèi **I** [动] store ... up **II** [名] reserve

储藏 chǔcáng [动] **1** (保藏) store **2** (蕴藏) contain

储存 chǔcún [动] stockpile

储蓄 chǔxù **I** [动] save **II** [名] savings (PL)

处 chù [名] **1** (地方) place ▸益处 yìchù profit **2** (部门) department ▸人事处 rénshì chù human resources department → see also/另见 chǔ

畜 chù → see also/另见 xù

畜生 chùsheng [名] beast

触 chù [动] 1 (接触) touch 2 (触动) move

触犯 chùfàn [动] violate

触及 chùjí [动] touch

触摸 chùmō [动] touch

踹 chuài [动] (踢) kick

川 chuān [名] (河流) river

穿 chuān [动] 1 (弄破纸等) pierce 2 (谎言, 事实) expose 3 (通过) pass through ▷ 穿过人群 chuān guò rénqún pass through the crowd 4 (穿针) chuān zhēn thread a needle 4 (串) piece ... together ▷ 穿珍珠 chuān zhūzhū string pearls together 5 (衣服, 鞋帽, 首饰等) wear 6 (表示透彻) penetrate

穿着 chuānzhuó [名] outfit

传 chuán [动] 1 (交给) hand ... down 2 (传授) pass ... on 3 (传播) spread 4 (传导) conduct 5 (表达) express ▷ 传真情 chuán zhēnqíng express one's feelings 6 (命令) summon 7 (传染) infect
→ see also/另见 zhuàn

传播 chuánbō [动] disseminate

传达 chuándá I [动] pass ... on II [名] receptionist ▷ 传达室 chuándá shì reception room

传单 chuándān [名] leaflet

传媒 chuánméi [名] (传播媒介) media (PL)

传票 chuánpiào [名] (指法院) summons (SG)

传奇 chuánqí [形] legendary

传染 chuánrǎn [动] infect

传说 chuánshuō [名] legend

传统 chuántǒng I [名] tradition II [形] 1 (世代相传) traditional 2 (保守) conservative

传真 chuánzhēn [动] (指通讯方式) fax ▷ 给我发个传真吧。 Gěi wǒ fā ge chuánzhēn ba. Please send me a fax.

船 chuán [名] boat, ship

串 chuàn I [动] 1 (连贯) string ... together 2 (勾结) conspire 3 (指信号) get mixed up 4 (走动) drop by II [量] bunch ▷ 两串钥匙 liǎng chuàn yàoshi two bunches of keys ▷ 一串珍珠 yī chuàn zhēnzhū a string of pearls

创 chuāng [名] wound ▷ 创可贴 chuāngkětiē plaster (英), Band-Aid® (美)
→ see also/另见 chuàng

创伤 chuāngshāng [名] 1 (指肉体) wound 2 (指精神) trauma

疮 chuāng [名] (指疾病) ulcer ▷ 口疮 kǒuchuāng mouth ulcer ▷ 冻疮 dòngchuāng chilblain

窗 chuāng [名] window ▷ 窗子 chuāngzi window

窗户 chuānghu [名] window

窗口 chuāngkǒu [名] 1 (字) window 2 (喻) (渠道) vehicle 3 (喻) (反映处) window

床 chuáng [名] bed ▷ 单人床 dānrénchuáng single bed ▷ 床

单 chuángdān bed sheet ▶床
上床 shàngchuáng go to bed

闯 chuǎng [动] 1(冲) rush 2(磨炼)
steel oneself 3(惹) stir ... up ▶闯
祸 chuǎnghuò cause trouble

创 chuàng [动] create ▶独创
dúchuàng make an original
creation
→ see also/另见 chuāng

创建 chuàngjiàn [动] establish

创立 chuànglì [动] establish

创业 chuàngyè [动] carve out
a career

创意 chuàngyì [名] creativity

创造 chuàngzào [动] create

创作 chuàngzuò I [动] create
II [名] work

吹 chuī [动] 1(出气) blow ▶吹蜡烛
chuī làzhú blow out a candle 2(演
奏) play ▶吹口琴 chuī kǒuqín
play the harmonica 3(夸口)
boast 4(口)(破裂) fall through
▶我和女友吹了。 Wǒ hé nǚyǒu
chuī le. I've broken up with my
girlfriend.

吹风 chuīfēng [动] (吹干)
blow-dry

吹牛 chuīniú [动] brag

吹捧 chuīpěng [动] flatter

吹嘘 chuīxū [动] boast

炊 chuī [动] cook ▶炊具 chuījù
cooking utensil

垂 chuí [动] (一头向下) hang down

垂直 chuízhí [形] vertical

捶 chuí [动] pound

锤 chuí I [名] hammer II [动]
hammer

春 chūn [名] (春季) spring

春节 Chūn Jié [名] Chinese New
Year

春节 Chūn Jié

Chinese New Year, or
Spring Festival, is the
most important festival
of the year and falls on
the first day of the lunar
calendar. Traditionally
families gather together,
children receive money in
red envelopes, and in some
parts of China everyone
helps make and eat a
festival feast. On greeting
people over this festival it
is traditional to wish them
wealth and happiness, by
saying 恭喜发财 gōngxǐ
fācái.

春卷 chūnjuǎn [名] spring roll

春天 chūntiān [名] spring

纯 chún [形] 1(纯净) pure 2(纯熟)
skilful (英), skillful (美)

纯粹 chúncuì I [形] pure II [副]
purely

纯洁 chúnjié I [形] pure II [动]
purify

纯净 chúnjìng [形] pure

唇 chún [名] lip

蠢 chǔn [形] **1**(愚蠢) stupid **2**(笨拙) clumsy

戳 chuō **I**[动](穿过) poke **II**[名] seal

戳子 chuōzi [名] seal

辍 chuò [动] stop

辍学 chuòxué [动] give up one's studies

词 cí [名] **1**(语句) words (PL) ▸台词 táicí lines ▸闭幕词 bìmùcí closing speech **2**(语言单位) word

词典 cídiǎn [名] dictionary

词汇 cíhuì [名] vocabulary

词语 cíyǔ [名] word

词组 cízǔ [名] phrase

瓷 cí [名] (物) porcelain

辞 cí [动] **1**(辞职) resign **2**(辞退) dismiss

辞职 cízhí [动] resign

慈 cí [形] kind

慈爱 cí'ài [形] affectionate

慈善 císhàn [形] charitable

慈祥 cíxiáng [形] kind

磁 cí [名] (物) magnetism

磁场 cíchǎng [名] magnetic field

磁盘 cípán [名] disk

雌 cí [形] female ▸雌性 cíxìng female

此 cǐ [代] (这) this ▸此时此刻 cǐshí cǐkè right now

此外 cǐwài [连] apart from this

次 cì **I**[名] ranking ▸档次 dàngcì grade **2**[名] mìngcì position **II**[形] **1**(第二) second ▸次日 cìrì next day **2**(差) inferior ▸次品 cìpǐn inferior product **III**[量] time ▸初次 chūcì first time ▸屡次 lǚcì repeatedly

次序 cìxù [名] order

次要 cìyào [形] secondary

刺 cì [动] sting

刺耳 cì'ěr [形] **1**(指声音) ear-piercing **2**(响) (指言语) jarring

刺激 cìjī [动] **1**(指生物现象) stimulate **2**(推动) stimulate **3**(打击) provoke

刺猬 cìwei [名] hedgehog

匆 cōng [副] hastily

匆忙 cōngmáng [形] hurried

葱 cōng [名] spring onion

聪 cōng **I**[名] hearing **II**[形] **1**(指听力) acute **2**(聪明) clever

聪明 cōngmíng [形] clever

从 cóng **I**[动] **1**(跟随) follow **2**(顺从) comply with ▸服从 fúcóng obey **3**(从事) participate in **II**[名] follower **III**[形] (从属) subordinate ▸从犯 cóngfàn accessory **IV**[介] **1**(起于) from ▸从明天起 cóng míngtiān qǐ from tomorrow onwards **2**(经过) ▸飞机从我们头顶飞过。Fēijī cóng wǒmen tóudǐng fēiguò. The plane passed over our heads.

从此 cóngcǐ [副] after that

从此 cóng'cǐ [连] thus

从来 cónglái [副] ▷ 她从来说过。Tā cónglái wèi shuōguò. She never said it.

从前 cóngqián [名] 1 (过去) past ▷ 希望你比从前快乐。Xīwàng nǐ bǐ cóngqián kuàilè. I hope you are happier than you were before. 2 (很久以前) once upon a time

从事 cóngshì [动] 1 (投身) undertake 2 (处理) deal with

凑 còu [动] 1 (聚集) gather ... together 2 (碰) encounter 3 (接近) approach

凑合 còuhe [动] 1 (聚集) gather ... together 2 (排凑) improvise 3 (将就) get by

凑巧 còuqiǎo [形] lucky

粗 cū [形] 1 (横剖面大) thick 2 (颗粒大) coarse 3 (声音粗) gruff 4 (糙) crude

粗暴 cūbào [形] rough

粗糙 cūcāo [形] 1 (不光滑) rough 2 (不细致) crude

粗话 cūhuà [名] obscene language

粗鲁 cūlǔ [形] crude

粗心 cūxīn [形] careless

粗野 cūyě [形] rough

促 cù I [形] urgent II [动] 1 (催) press 2 (靠近) be near

促进 cùjìn [动] promote

促使 cùshǐ [动] press for

醋 cù [名] (指调味品) vinegar

催 cuī [动] 1 (敦促) hurry ▶催促 cuīcù hurry 2 (加快) speed ... up ▶催眠 cuīmián hypnotize

脆 cuì [形] 1 (易碎) brittle 2 (指食物) crispy

脆弱 cuìruò [形] fragile

村 cūn [名] village ▶村子 cūnzi village

存 cún [动] 1 (存在) exist 2 (储存) store 3 (储蓄) save ▶存款 cúnkuǎn savings (PL) 4 (寄存) check ... in ▶存行李 cún xíngli check in one's bags 5 (保留) retain 6 (心里怀着) harbour (英), harbor (美)

存档 cúndàng [动] file

存放 cúnfàng [动] deposit

存心 cúnxīn [副] deliberately

存在 cúnzài [动] exist

存折 cúnzhé [名] passbook

寸 cùn [量] unit of length, approximately 3 cm

搓 cuō [动] rub

撮 cuō [动] (聚集) scoop ... up

痤 cuó see below/见下文

痤疮 cuóchuāng [名] acne

挫 cuò [动] (挫折) defeat ▶挫折 cuòzhé setback

措 cuò [动] 1 (安排) handle 2 (筹划) make plans

措施 cuòshī [名] measure

错 cuò I [形] (不正确) incorrect
II [动] (避开) miss III [名] fault
▷这是我的错。Zhè shì wǒ de
cuò. This is my fault.

错过 cuòguò [动] miss ▷错过
机会 cuòguò jīhuì miss an
opportunity

错误 cuòwù I [形] wrong II [名]
mistake

d

搭 dā [动] 1 (建造) put ... up ▷搭帐
篷 dā zhàngpeng put up a tent
2 (挂) hang ▷我把大衣搭在胳
膊上。Wǒ bǎ dàyī dā zài gēbo
shàng. I hung my overcoat over
my arm. 3 (坐) take ▷他每个月
搭飞机去上海。Tā měi ge yuè
dā fēijī qù Shànghǎi. He takes the
plane to Shanghai every month.
▷搭便车 dā biànchē get a lift
4 (连接) join ▷搭伙 dāhuǒ join
forces ▷两家公司终于搭上了关
系。Liǎng jiā gōngsī zhōngyú
dā shàng le guānxi. The two
companies finally joined forces.
5 (抬) carry

搭档 dādàng I [名] partner II [动]
team up

搭配 dāpèi [动] 1 (安排) combine 2 (配合) pair up 3 (指语言) collocate

答 dā [动] answer
→ see also/另见 dá

答理 dālǐ [动] (理睬) bother 2 (打招呼) acknowledge

答应 dāying [动] 1 (回答) answer 2 (同意) agree 3 (承诺) promise

打 dá [量] dozen
→ see also/另见 dǎ

达 dá [动] 1 (数量,目标) reach 2 (指时间) last 3 (通) ▷ 直达 zhídá non-stop journey 4 (表示) express ▷ 转达 chuándá convey

达到 dádào [动] 1 (要求,水平,目的) achieve ▷ 达到目的 dádào mùdì achieve an aim ▷ 达到要求 dádào yāoqiú satisfy requirements 2 (指过程) reach

答 dá [动] 1 (回答) answer 2 (还报) repay ▷ 报答 bàodá repay
→ see also/另见 dā

答案 dá'àn [名] answer

答复 dáfù [动] respond

答卷 dájuàn I [名] answer sheet II [动] answer exam questions

打 dǎ I [动] 1 (指暴力) hit ▷ 殴打 ōudǎ beat up ▷ 打人 dǎrén beat sb up 2 (敲) beat ▷ 打鼓 dǎ gǔ beat a drum 3 (破) break ▷ 我把暖瓶给打了。Wǒ bǎ nuǎnpíng gěi dǎ le. I broke the Thermos®. 4 (发出) send ▷ 打电话 dǎ diànhuà make a phone call ▷ 打手电 dǎ shǒudiàn shine a torch 5 (做游戏) play ▷ 打篮球 dǎ lánqiú play basketball 6 (表示动作) ▷ 打喷嚏 dǎ pēntì sneeze ▷ 打滚 dǎgǔn roll about 7 (建造) build ▷ 打基础 dǎ jīchǔ build the foundation 8 (涂抹) polish ▷ 打蜡 dǎ là wax 9 (交涉) deal with ▷ 打交道 dǎ jiāodao socialize ▷ 打官司 dǎ guānsi file a lawsuit 10 (制造) make ▷ 打家具 dǎ jiājù make furniture 11 (搅拌) beat ▷ 打两个鸡蛋 dǎ liǎng ge jīdàn beat two eggs 12 (编织) knit ▷ 打毛衣 dǎ máoyī knit a sweater 13 (捕捉) catch ▷ 打猎 dǎliè go hunting 14 (画) draw ▷ 打草稿 dǎ cǎogǎo draw up a draft 15 (举) hold ▷ 打伞 dǎ sǎn hold an umbrella 16 (揭开) open ▷ 打开 dǎkāi open 17 (穿凿) dig ▷ 打耳洞 dǎ ěrdòng pierce one's ears 18 (收集) gather ▷ 打柴火 dǎ cháihuǒ gather firewood 19 (从事) do ▷ 打杂儿 dǎzár do odd jobs 20 (用) make ▷ 打比喻 dǎ bǐyù make a comparison 21 (捆) pack ▷ 打行李 dǎ xíngli pack one's bags 22 (拨动) flick ▷ 打字 dǎzì type ▷ 打字机 dǎzìjī typewriter II [介] from ▷ 打今儿起 dǎ jīnr qǐ from today
→ see also/另见 dá

打败 dǎbài [动] defeat

打扮 dǎban [动] make oneself up

打倒 dǎdǎo [动] 1 (击倒在地) knock down 2 (指口号) down with 3 (推翻) overthrow

打的 dǎ dī [动] take a taxi

打动 dǎdòng [动] move

打赌 dǎdǔ [动] bet

打发 dǎfa [动] 1 (时间) while away 2 (哄走) get rid of 3 (派) send

打工 dǎgōng [动] temp

打火机 dǎhuǒjī [名] lighter

打击 dǎjī I [动] crack down on II [名] (指精神上) blow

打架 dǎjià [动] have a fight

打开 dǎkāi [动] 1 (开启) open 2 (扩展) expand 3 (开) turn ... on

打气 dǎqì [动] (球，轮胎) inflate

打扫 dǎsǎo [动] clean

打算 dǎsuàn I [动] plan II [名] plan

打听 dǎtīng [动] ask about

打印机 dǎyìnjī [名] printer

打仗 dǎzhàng [动] fight a war

打招呼 dǎ zhāohu [动] (问好) greet

打折 dǎzhé [动] discount

大 dà [形] 1 (数量，体积，面积) big ▷大街 dàjiē street ▷一大批 yīdàpī a large amount of 2 (指力气) great ▷他劲儿真大！Tā jìn'r zhēn dà! He's so strong! 3 (重要) important 4 (强) strong ▷大风 dà fēng strong wind 5 (指声音) loud ▷大声 dàshēng loudly 6 (雨，雪) heavy 7 (指年龄) old ▷你多大了？Nǐ duōdà le? How old are you? ▷他比我大。Tā bǐ wǒ dà. He's older than me. 8 (指程度) ▷大笑 dàxiào roar with

laughter 9 (老大) eldest ▷大姐 dà jiě eldest sister

→ see also/另见 dài

大胆 dàdǎn [形] bold

大地 dàdì [名] the land

大方 dàfang [形] 1 (慷慨) generous 2 (不拘束) natural 3 (不俗气) tasteful

大概 dàgài I [名] general idea II [形] approximate III [副] probably

大伙儿 dàhuǒr [代] everybody

大家 dàjiā [代] everybody

大款 dàkuǎn [名] (贬) moneybags (sc)

大量 dàliàng [形] (数量多) large amount of ▷大量资金 dàliàng zījīn a large investment ▷大量 裁员 dàliàng cáiyuán lay off a large number of people

大陆 dàlù [名] 1 (指各大洲) continent 2 (指中国) the mainland ▷中国大陆 Zhōngguó dàlù mainland China

大米 dàmǐ [名] rice

大人 dàrén [名] adult

大使 dàshǐ [名] ambassador

大使馆 dàshǐguǎn [名] embassy

大事 dàshì [名] important event

大提琴 dàtíqín [名] cello

大小 dàxiǎo [名] (尺寸) size

大写 dàxiě [名] (指字母) capital letter

大型 dàxíng [形] large-scale

大选 dàxuǎn [名] general election

大学 dàxué [名] university (英) 或 college (美)

大学生 dàxuéshēng [名] university (英) 或 college (美) student

大雪 dàxuě [名] heavy snow

大衣 dàyī [名] overcoat

大雨 dàyǔ [名] downpour

大约 dàyuē [副] 1 (指数量) approximately 2 (可能) probably

大众 dàzhòng [名] the people (PL)

大自然 dàzìrán [名] nature

呆 dāi I [形] 1 (傻) slow-witted 2 (发愣) blank ▷发呆 fādāi stare blankly II [动] stay ▷我在北京呆了个一星期了。 Wǒ zài Běijīng dāi le yī ge xīngqī. I stayed in Beijing for a week.

待 dāi [动] stay ▷你再多待一会儿。 Nǐ zài duō dāi yīhuǐr. Do stay a little longer.
→ see also/另见 dài

逮 dǎi [动] catch
→ see also/另见 dài

大 dài see below/见下文

大夫 dàifu [名] doctor
→ see also/另见 dàifu

代 dài I [动] 1 (替) do ... on behalf of 2 (指问候) send regards to ▷你见到他时，代我问好。 Nǐ jiàndào tā shí, dài wǒ wènhǎo. When you see him, say hello from me. 3 (代理) act as ▷校长代 xiàozhǎng acting headmaster II [名] 1 (时代) times 2 (古

代) gǔdài ancient times 2 (辈分) generation 3 (朝代) dynasty ▷清代 Qīng dài Qing Dynasty

代表 dàibiǎo I [名] representative II [动] 1 (代表) stand in for 2 (委托) represent 3 (指意义，概念) be representative of III [形] archetypal

代价 dàijià [名] cost

代理 dàilǐ [动] 1 (暂时替代) act on behalf of 2 (委托) represent

代理人 dàilǐrén [名] agent

代码 dàimǎ [名] code

代数 dàishù [名] algebra

代替 dàitì [动] substitute for

带 dài I [名] 1 (长条物) strap ▷皮带 pídài leather belt ▷磁带 cídài cassette ▷录像带 lùxiàngdài videotape 2 (轮胎) tyre (英) 或 tire (美) ▷车带 chēdài car tyre (英) 或 tire (美) 3 (区域) zone ▷热带 rèdài the tropics (PL) II [动] 1 (携带) take ▷别忘了带钱包！ Bié wàng le dài qiánbāo! Don't forget to take your wallet! 2 (捎带) ▷你出去时带点牛奶回来，好吗？ Nǐ chūqù shí dài diǎn niúnǎi huílai, hǎo ma? Can you buy some milk when you're out? 3 (呈现) wear ▷面带笑容 miàn dài xiàoróng wear a smile on one's face 4 (含有) have 5 (连带) come with 6 (指导) direct 7 (领) lead 8 (养) bring up ... up

带动 dàidòng [动] (指进步) drive

带领 dàilǐng [动] 1 (领着) guide

2 (指挥) lead

带头 dàitóu [动] take the initiative

待 dài [动] **1** (对待) treat **2** (招待) entertain **3** (等待) wait for → see also/另见 dāi

待业 dàiyè [动] be unemployed

待遇 dàiyù [名] pay

贷 dài [动] **1** (指银行) lend **2** (指借钱方) take out a loan **II** [名] loan

贷款 dàikuǎn [动] lend **II** [名] loan

袋 dài [名] bag **II** [量] bag

袋鼠 dàishǔ [名] kangaroo

逮 dài [动] capture → see also/另见 dǎi

逮捕 dàibǔ [动] arrest

戴 dài [动] (眼镜, 帽子, 小装饰品等) wear

单 dān **I** [形] **1** (一个) single ▶单身 dānshēn single **2** (奇数) odd **3** (仅供) solitary **4** (独) simple **5** (薄弱) weak **6** (衣, 裤) thin **II** [副] only ▶成功不能单凭运气。 Chénggōng bùnéng dān píng yùnqì. To be successful you can't rely only on luck. **III** [名] **1** (单子) sheet ▶床单 chuángdān bed sheet **2** (列表) list ▶菜单 càidān menu

单程 dānchéng [名] single trip

单纯 dānchún **I** [形] simple **II** [副]

单词 dāncí [名] word

单单 dāndān [副] only

单调 dāndiào [形] monotonous

单独 dāndú [形] **1** (独自) alone **2** (独立) unaided

单位 dānwèi [名] **1** (指标准量) unit **2**

单元 dānyuán [名] unit ▶单元房 dānyuán fáng self-contained flat (英) 或 apartment (美)

单子 dānzi [名] **1** (指床上用品) sheet **2** (列表) list

担 dān [动] **1** (挑) carry ... on one's shoulder **2** (负) take ... on → see also/另见 dàn

担保 dānbǎo [动] guarantee

担当 dāndāng [动] take ... on

担架 dānjià [名] stretcher

担任 dānrèn [动] hold the post of

担心 dānxīn [动] worry

耽 dān see below/见下文

耽误 dānwu [动] delay

胆 dǎn [名] (胆量) courage

胆固醇 dǎngùchún [名] cholesterol

胆量 dǎnliàng [名] guts (PL)

胆子 dǎnzi [名] guts (PL)

掸 dǎn [动] brush

掸子 dǎnzi [名] duster

但 dàn **I** [连] but **II** [副] only ▶但愿 dànyuàn wish

但是 dànshì [连] but ▶虽然下雨, 但是不冷。 Suīrán xiàyǔ, dànshì bù lěng. Even though it's raining, it's not cold.

担 dàn [名] load
→ see also/另见 dān

担子 dànzi [名] (责任)
responsibility

诞 dàn [动] be born

诞生 dànshēng [动] be born

淡 dàn [形] 1(指味道淡淡) weak
2(指减淡) bland 3(颜色浅)
light 4(稀薄)light 5(不热情)
indifferent 6(不红火)slack

淡季 dànjì [名] low season

蛋 dàn [名] (卵) egg ▸鸡蛋 jīdàn
egg

蛋白质 dànbáizhì [名] protein

蛋糕 dàngāo [名] cake

弹 dàn [名] (子弹) bullet ▸子弹
zǐdànbullet ▸原子弹 yuánzǐdàn
atomic bomb
→ see also/另见 tán

当 dāng I [介] 1(向) in front of ▸当
众 dāngzhòng in public 2(正当全
班 dāng zhe quánbānin front of
the whole class 2(正在) ▸当我
们当时, 电影已开始了。 Dāng
wǒmen dào shí, diànyǐng yǐ
kāishǐ le.When we arrived the
film had already started. ▸当他
在美国时, 他爷爷去世了。 Dāng
tā zài Měiguó shí, tā yéye qùshì
le.His grandfather passed away
while he was in America. II [动]
1(担任) act as ▸当经理 dāng
jīnglǐact as manager 2(掌管)
be in charge ▸当家 dāngjiārule

the roost
→ see also/另见 dàng

当场 dāngchǎng [副] there and
then

当初 dāngchū [名] those days

当代 dāngdài [名] the present
▸当代文学 dāngdài wénxué
contemporary literature

当地 dāngdì [名] locality ▸当地风
俗 dāngdì fēngsúlocal customs

当今 dāngjīn [名] the present

当面 dāngmiàn [动] do ... face
to face

当年 dāngnián [名] those days

当前 dāngqián I [动] be faced
with II [名] present ▸当前的
目标 dāngqián de mùbiāo the
present aim

当然 dāngrán I [副] of course
II [形] natural

当时 dāngshí [名] ▸我当时高兴
极了。 Wǒ dāngshí gāoxìng jí
le.I was ecstatic at the time.

当心 dāngxīn [动] be careful

挡 dǎng [动] (拦) keep off ▸别挡
路! Bié dǎnglù! Keep off the
road!

党 dǎng [名] (政党) party ▸党员
dǎngyuánparty member

当 dàng I [形] appropriate ▸不当
bùdànginappropriate II [动]
1(作为) treat ... as 2(认为) assume
▸我当你明白了。 Wǒ dàng
nǐ míngbai le. I assumed you'd
understood. 3(抵押) pawn 4(指当

时间和地点) ▶当天 dàngtiān that day ▶当场 dàngchǎng on the spot

→ see also/另见 dāng

当年 dàngnián [名] that same year

当铺 dàngpù [名] pawnshop

当作 dàngzuò [动] regard ... as

档 dàng [名] 1(档案) file 2(等级) grade

档案 dàng'àn [名] files (PL)

档次 dàngcì [名] grade

刀 dāo [名] (指工具) knife ▶刀子 dāozi knife

叨 dāo see below/见下文

叨唠 dāolao [动] prattle on

导 dǎo [动] 1(引导) guide 2(传导) conduct 3(开导) give guidance 4(导演) direct

导弹 dǎodàn [名] missile

导火线 dǎohuǒxiàn [名] 1(字) fuse 2(喻) trigger

导师 dǎoshī [名] 1(字) tutor 2(喻) mentor

导演 dǎoyǎn I [动] direct II [名] director

导游 dǎoyóu I [动] guide II [名] tour guide

导致 dǎozhì [动] lead to ▶粗心导致她没考上。Cūxīn dǎozhì tā méi kǎo shàng. Because of her carelessness she failed the exam.

岛 dǎo [名] island ▶岛国 dǎoguó

island nation ▶半岛 bàndǎo peninsula

倒 dǎo [动] 1(横躺) fall ▶摔倒 shuāidǎo fall down ▶卧倒 wòdǎo lie down 2(失败) fail ▶倒闭 dǎobì go bankrupt 3(食欲) spoil ▶倒胃口 dǎo wèikǒu lose one's appetite 4(换) change ▶倒班 dǎobān change shifts

→ see also/另见 dào

倒霉 dǎoméi [形] unlucky

倒塌 dǎotā [动] collapse

捣 dǎo [动] 1(捶打) crush 2(搅乱) make trouble

捣乱 dǎoluàn [动] 1(扰乱) disturb 2(制造麻烦) make trouble

到 dào [动] 1(达到) arrive ▶火车到了。 Huǒchē dào le. The train has arrived. ▶到点了!Dào diǎn le! Time is up! 2(去) go ▶我到厦门旅游。 Wǒ dào Xiàmén lǚyóu. I'm going to Xiamen on a tour. 3(用作动词的补语) ▶听到这个消息我很吃惊。 Tīngdào zhè ge xiāoxi wǒ hěn chījīng. When I heard the news I was very surprised. ▶你的要求我办不到。 Nǐ de yāoqiú wǒ bàn bù dào. I can't handle your demands.

到处 dàochù [名] all places (PL)

到达 dàodá [动] arrive

到底 dàodǐ I [动] 1(坚持到底) jiānchí dàodǐ keep going until the end II [副] 1(究竟) ▶你到底在干什么? Nǐ dàodǐ zài gàn shénme? What on earth are you up to? 2 (毕竟) after all 3 (终于) at last

倒 dào I [动] 1 (颠倒) ▷他把地图挂倒了。Tā bǎ dìtú guà dào le. He hung the map up upside down. ▷姓和名写倒了。Xìng hé míng xiě dào le. The first name and surname were written the wrong way round. 2 (后退) reverse ▷倒车 dàochē reverse a car 3 (倾倒) empty out ▷倒垃圾 dào lājī empty the rubbish out ▷倒杯茶 dào bēi chá pour a cup of tea II [副] 1 (表示意料之外) unexpectedly 2 (反而) instead 3 (表示让步) ▷这房子地段虽好，就是太小。Zhè fángzi dìduàn suī hǎo, jiùshì tài xiǎo. Although the location of the house is good, it's still too small. 4 (表示转折) but 5 (表示不耐烦) ▷你倒是说呀！Nǐ dào shì shuō ya! Can you get on with it please! 6 (表示责怪) ▷他说得倒漂亮。Tā shuō de dào piàoliang. He's all talk.

→ see also/ 另见 dǎo

倒立 dàolì [动] 1 (物) be upside down 2 (人) do a handstand

倒计时 dàojìshí [动] count down

倒退 dàotuì [动] go back

倒影 dàoyǐng [名] reflection

悼 dào [动] mourn

悼念 dàoniàn [动] mourn

盗 dào I [动] 1 (偷窃) rob ▷盗窃 dàoqiè steal II [名] 1 (盗贼) robber ▷海盗 hǎidào

pirate

盗版 dàobǎn I [动] pirate ▷盗版软件 dàobǎn ruǎnjiàn pirated software II [名] pirate copy

盗贼 dàozéi [名] thieves (PL)

道 dào I [名] 1 (路) road ▷近道 jìndào shortcut 2 (方法) way ▷生财之道 shēngcái zhī dào the road to riches 3 (技艺) art ▷茶道 chádào tea ceremony 4 (道教) the Tao ▷ (线) line ▷道儿 héngdàor horizontal line 6 (水流途径) channel ▷下水道 xiàshuǐdào sewer II [量] 1 ▷一道阳光 yī dào yángguāng a beam of sunlight ▷两道泪痕 liǎng dào lèihén two tear streaks

  measure word, used for things in the shape of a long strip

2 ▷第二道门 dì'èr dào mén the second door ▷一道墙 yī dào qiáng a wall

  measure word, used for doors, walls, etc.

3 ▷三道题 sān dào tí three questions ▷两道命令 liǎng dào mìnglìng two orders

  measure word, used for orders, questions, procedures, etc.

4 (次) ▷我还要办一道手续。Wǒ háiyào bàn yī dào shǒuxù I still need to complete one formality. ▷刷了两道漆 shuā le liǎng dào qī paint two coats ▷五道菜 wǔ dào cài five dishes

measure word, used for dishes or courses of a meal

道德 dàodé [名] morals (PL)

道教 Dàojiào [名] Taoism

道理 dàolǐ [名] 1 (规律) principle ▷ 他 讲 了 流畅。 Tā dé le liúgǎn. He caught flu. 3 (计算) equal ▷ 四 减 二 等 于 二。 Sì jiǎn èr dé èr. Four minus two equals two. 4 (完成) be ready ▷ 晚饭得了。 Wǎnfàn dé le. Dinner is ready. 5 (适合) be suitable ▷ 得体 détǐ appropriate II [叹] 1 (表示同意，禁止) OK ▷ 得，就 这么 决定 了。 Dé, jiù zhème juédìng le. OK, that's settled then. 2 (表示无可奈何) Oh no! ▷ 得，我 又 没 考 及格！ Dé, wǒ yòu méi kǎo jígé! Oh no, I failed again! III [动词] 版权 所有，不得 转载。 Bǎnquán suǒyǒu, bù dé zhuǎnzǎi. All rights reserved, copying not allowed.
→ see also/另见 de, děi

道路 dàolù [名] path

道歉 dàoqiàn [动] apologize

得 dé I [动] 1 (得到) get ▷ 得 奖 déjiǎng win a prize 2 (病) catch (情理) sense

道路 dàolù [名] path

道歉 dàoqiàn [动] apologize

得 dédào [动] get ▷ 得到 帮助 dédào bāngzhù get help

得意 déyì [形] pleased with oneself

得罪 dézuì [动] offend

德 dé [名] 1 (品行) morality ▷ 品德 pǐndé moral character 2 (恩惠) kindness ▷ 恩德 ēndé kindness

3 (德国) Germany ▷ 德国 Déguó Germany ▷ 德语 Déyǔ German

地 de [助] ▷ 刻苦 地 学习 kèkǔ de xuéxí study hard ▷ 努力 地 工作 nǔlì de gōngzuò work hard
→ see also/另见 dì

Use 地 after adjectives to form adverbs.

的 de [助] 1 (用于定语后) ▷ 昂贵 的 价格 ángguì de jiàgé high price ▷ 他 的 哥哥 tā de gēge his elder brother ▷ 经理 的 秘书 jīnglǐ de mìshū the manager's secretary 2 (名词化) ▷ 画画 的 huàhuà de painter 3 (用于是…的 强调结构) ▷ 我 的 嗓子 是 喊哑 的。 Wǒ de sǎngzi shì hǎnyǎ de. My voice became hoarse from shouting.
→ see also/另见 dí, dì

Use 的 to link descriptive words, phrases and clauses to the noun they describe, e.g. 她 是 一 个 很漂亮 的 女人。 Tā shì yīgè hěn piàoliang de nǚrén. (She is a very beautiful woman.); 这 是 他 昨天 给 我 的 书。 Zhè shì tā zuótiān gěi wǒ de shū. (This is the book which he gave me yesterday.)

的话 dehuà [助] ▷ 见到 她 的 话，替 我 问好。 Jiàndào tā de huà, tì wǒ wènhǎo. Please give her my regards if you see her.

得 de [助] 1 (用于动词后面) ▷ 这种 野菜 能 吃 Zhè zhǒng yěcài chī

de. This wild herb is edible. **2**(动词或补语中间) ▷她拿得动。 Tā ná de dòng. She can carry it. ▷我写得完。 Wǒ xiě de wán. I am able to finish writing it. **3**(动词和形容词后面) ▷他英语学得很快。 Tā Yīngyǔ xué de hěn kuài. He's learning English very quickly. ▷风大得很。 Fēng dà de hěn. The wind's very strong.

→ *see also* / 另见 dé, děi

> Most adverbial phrases follow the verb and are joined to it by 得 de. Such statements are often evaluations or judgements, and contain the idea of *to the extent of* or *to the degree that*, e.g. 她说得很流利。 Tā shuō de hěn liúlì. (She speaks very fluently.).

得 děi **I**[动](口)(需要) need ▷买房得多少钱? Mǎifáng děi duōshao qián? How much money do you need to buy a house? **II**[助动](口)**1**(必要) must ▷我们得6点出发。 Wǒmen děi liùdiǎn chūfā. We have to leave at six. **2**(表示推测) will ▷快走, 电影得开始了。 Kuài zǒu, diànyǐng děi kāishǐ le. Get a move on, the film's just about to start.

→ *see also* / 另见 dé, de

灯 dēng [名] light ▷台灯 táidēng desk lamp ▷红绿灯 hónglǜdēng traffic lights [PL]

灯塔 dēngtǎ [名] lighthouse

登 dēng [动] **1**(由低到高) go up **2**(刊登) publish **3**(踩踏板) pedal **4**(踩) get up onto

登记 dēngjì [动] register

登录 dēnglù [动] log in ▷登录网站 dēnglù wǎngzhàn log in to a website

蹬 dēng [动] pedal

等 děng **I**[名] **1**(等级) grade ▷中等 zhōngděng medium ▷二等奖 èr děng jiǎng second prize **2**(类) kind **II**[动] **1**(相同) equal ▷等于 děngyú be equal to **2**(等待) wait ▷等车 děngchē wait for a bus **III**[连] (到时) when ▷他来了, 我们再讨论。 Děng tā lái le, wǒmen zài tǎolùn. We'll talk about it when he comes. **IV**[助] **1**(列举未尽的) etc. **2**(煞尾的) namely

等待 děngdài [动] wait

等到 děngdào [连] when

等等 děngděng [助] and so on

等号 děnghào [名](数) equals sign

等候 děnghòu [动] expect

等级 děngjí [名] grade

等于 děngyú [动] **1**(相等于) equal **2**(等同) be equivalent to

凳 dèng [名] stool ▷板凳 bǎndèng wooden stool ▷凳子 dèngzi stool

瞪 dèng [动] **1**(表示生气) glare at **2**(睁大) open one's eyes wide

低 dī I [形] 1 (指高度，程度) low ▷他喜欢低声说话。Tā xǐhuan dī shēng shuōhuà. He likes to speak quietly. 2 (指等级) junior ▷我比她低两届。Wǒ bǐ tā dī liǎngjiè. I am two years below her. II [动] (头) bend

低潮 dīcháo [名] low ebb

低调 dīdiào [名] low-key

低级 dījí [形] 1 (不高级) inferior 2 (庸俗) vulgar

堤 dī [名] dyke

提 dī [动] carry
→ see also / 另见 tí

提防 dīfang [动] guard against

滴 dī I [动] 1 (指液体) drip ▷水滴 shuǐdī drop of water III [量] drop ▷几滴墨水 jǐ dī mòshuǐ a few drops of ink

的 dí see below / 见下文
→ see also / 另见 de, dì

的确 díquè [副] really

迪 dí [动] (书) enlighten

迪斯科 dísīkē [名] disco

敌 dí I [名] enemy II [动] oppose III [形] equal

敌人 dírén [名] enemy

笛 dí [名] 1 (音) flute 2 (警笛) siren

笛子 dízi [名] bamboo flute

底 dǐ I [名] 1 (最下部分) bottom ▷鞋底 xiédǐ sole ▷底下 dǐxia under 2 (末尾) end ▷年底 niándǐ the end of the year

底层 dǐcéng [名] 1 (指建筑) ground floor 2 (最下部) bottom

抵 dǐ [动] 1 (支撑) support 2 (抵抗) resist 3 (补偿) compensate for 4 (抵押) mortgage 5 (抵消) offset 6 (代替) be equal to

抵达 dǐdá [动] reach

抵抗 dǐkàng [动] resist

抵押 dǐyā [动] mortgage

地 dì [名] 1 (地球) the Earth ▷地球 dìqiú the Earth 2 (陆地) land 3 (土地) fields (PL) 4 (地点) location ▷目的地 mùdìdì destination
→ see also / 另见 de

地步 dìbù [名] 1 (处境) state, situation 2 (程度) extent

地带 dìdài [名] zone

地道 dìdào [名] tunnel

地道 dìdao [形] 1 (真正) genuine 2 (纯正) pure 3 (指质量) well done

地点 dìdiǎn [名] location

地方 dìfāng [名] locality ▷地方政府 dìfāng zhèngfǔ local government

地方 dìfang [名] 1 (区域) place ▷你是哪个地方的人？Nǐ shì nǎ ge dìfang de rén? Where do you come from? 2 (空间) room 3 (身体部位) ▷我这个地方痛。Wǒ zhè ge dìfang tòng. I ache here. 4 (部分) part ▷有不明白的地方吗？Yǒu bù míngbai de dìfang ma? Are there any parts that are not clear?

地理 dìlǐ [名] geography

地面 dìmiàn [名] 1 (地表) the Earth's surface 2 (指房屋) floor

地球仪 dìqiúyí [名] globe

地区 dìqū [名] area

地摊 dìtān [名] stall

地毯 dìtǎn [名] carpet

地铁 dìtiě [名] 1 (also: 地下铁道) underground (英) 或 subway (美) 2 (列车) underground (英) 或 subway (美) train ▷坐地铁 zuò dìtiě take the underground (英) 或 subway (美)

地图 dìtú [名] map

地位 dìwèi [名] position ▷平等的地位 píngděng de dìwèi equal status ▷历史地位 lìshǐ dìwèi place in history

地下 dìxià [名] underground

地下室 dìxiàshì [名] basement

地震 dìzhèn [名] earthquake

地址 dìzhǐ [名] address ▷通信地址 tōngxìn dìzhǐ postal address

地址簿 dìzhǐbù [名] address book

地主 dìzhǔ [名] landlord

弟 dì [名] younger brother ▶表弟 biǎodì cousin ▶弟弟 dìdi younger brother

弟兄 dìxiong [名] brothers (PL)

弟子 dìzǐ [名] disciple

的 dì [名] target ▶目的 mùdì goal
 ▷ see also/另见 de, dí

帝 dì [名] 1 (君主) emperor

帝国 dìguó [名] empire

递 dì [动] (传送) pass

第 dì ▶第三产业 dìsān chǎnyè tertiary industry ▶第三世界 dì sān shìjiè the Third World ▶第一次世界大战 dì yī cì shìjiè dàzhàn the First World War

第六感觉 dìliù gǎnjué [名] sixth sense

第一手 dìyīshǒu [形] first-hand

掂 diān [动] weigh in one's hand

颠 diān [动] 1 (颠簸) jolt 2 (跌落) fall

颠倒 diāndǎo [动] ▷这张照片上下颠倒了。 Zhè zhāng zhàopiàn shàngxià diāndǎo le. The photo is upside down.

典 diǎn [名] 1 (标准) standard 2 (书籍) standard work ▶词典 cídiǎn dictionary 3 (典故) allusion 4 (仪礼) ceremony

典礼 diǎnlǐ [名] ceremony ▷毕业典礼 bìyè diǎnlǐ graduation ceremony

典型 diǎnxíng [形] (代表性) representative

点 diǎn I [名] 1 (时间单位) o'clock ▷早上8点 zǎoshang bā diǎn eight o'clock in the morning 2 (钟点) ▷到点了。 Dào diǎn le. It's time. 3 (小滴液体) drop ▷雨点 yǔdiǎn raindrops (PL) 4 (痕迹) stain 5 (指字、画) dot 6 (指几何) point 7 (小数点) decimal point ▷五点六 wǔ diǎn liù five point six ▷ (标志) 终点 zhōngdiǎn end point **9**(方面) point ▶优点 yōudiǎn strong point ▶重点 zhòngdiǎn focal point **II** [量] **1**(画点) make a dot **2**(头) nod ▶点头 diǎntóu nod one's head **3**(药水等) apply ▶点眼药 diǎn yǎnyào apply eye drops **4**(查对) check ▶点名 diǎnmíng call the register **5**(指定) select ▶点菜 diǎncài order food **6**(灯, 火, 烟等) light ▶点烟 diǎn yān light a cigarette **7**(点缀) decorate **III** [量] **1**(少量) a little ▶有一点问题。 Yǒu yì diǎn wèntí. There is a bit of a problem. ▶她会说一点日语。 Tā huì shuō yì diǎn Rìyǔ. She can speak a little Japanese. **2**(事项) item ▶议事日程上有6点。 Yìshì rìchéng shàng yǒu liù diǎn. There are six items on the agenda. ▶我们有4点建议。 Wǒmen yǒu sì diǎn jiànyì. We have four recommendations.

点击 diǎnjī [动] click

点头 diǎntóu [动] nod

点心 diǎnxin [名] snack

点子 diǎnzi [名] **1**(关键部分) key point **2**(主意) idea

电 diàn **I** [名] **1**(能源) electricity ▶电能 diànnéng electric power ▶发电站 fādiànzhàn electric power station ▶停电了。 Tíng diàn le. There's been a power cut. **2**(电报) telegram **II** [动] **1**(触电) get an electric shock **2**(发电报) send a telegram ▶电贺 diànhè congratulate by telegram

电报 diànbào [名] telegram

电池 diànchí [名] battery

电动 diàndòng [形] electric

电话 diànhuà [名] **1**(电话机) telephone ▶办公室的电话占线。 Bàngōngshì de diànhuà zhànxiàn. The office phone is engaged (英) 或 busy (美). ▶别挂电话! Bié guà diànhuà! Don't hang up! (打, 接, 回) call ▶接电话 jiē diànhuà answer the phone

电话号码 diànhuà hàomǎ [名] phone number

电脑 diànnǎo [名] computer ▶手提电脑 shǒutí diànnǎo laptop

电器 diànqì [名] electrical appliance

电视 diànshì [名] television, TV ▶彩色电视 cǎisè diànshì colour (英) 或 color (美) television ▶看电视 kàn diànshì watch television

电台 diàntái [名] station

电影 diànyǐng [名] film (英) 或 movie (美)

电影院 diànyǐngyuàn [名] cinema

电子 diànzǐ [名] electron ▶电子表 diànzǐ biǎo digital watch ▶电子游戏 diànzǐ yóuxì electronic game ▶电子商务 diànzǐ shāngwù e-commerce ▶电子图书 diànzǐ túshū e-book ▶电子邮件 diànzǐ yóujiàn e-mail

店 diàn [名] **1**(商店) shop (英) 或 store (美) **2**(旅店) hotel

垫 diàn I [名] cushion ▶鞋垫 xiédiàn insole II [动] 1 (铺) insert 2 (付钱) pay

惦 diàn see below/见下文

惦记 diànjì [动] think about

殿 diàn [名] palace ▶宫殿 gōngdiàn palace

叼 diāo [动] have ... in one's mouth

凋 diāo [动] wither

凋谢 diāoxiè [动] wither

雕 diāo I [动] carve II [名] 1 (指艺术) sculpture ▶石雕 shídiāo stone sculpture 2 (鸟) vulture

雕刻 diāokè I [动] carve II [名] carving

雕塑 diāosù [名] sculpture

吊 diào [动] (悬挂) hang

钓 diào [动] fish ▶钓鱼 diàoyú go fishing

调 diào I [动] transfer II [名] 1 (口音) accent 2 (曲调) melody ▶走调 zǒudiào be out of tune 3 (音) key
→ see also/另见 tiáo

调查 diàochá [动] investigate

掉 diào [动] 1 (落下) fall 2 (落后) fall behind 3 (遗失) lose 4 (减少) reduce 5 (转回) turn ... round ▶把车头掉过来 bǎ chētóu diào guòlái turn the car round 6 (互换) swap ▶掉换 diàohuàn swap

跌 diē [动] fall down

叠 dié [动] 1 (又加义) pile ... up 2 (信, 纸, 衣, 被) fold

碟 dié see below/见下文

碟子 diézi [名] saucer

蝶 dié [名] butterfly ▶蝴蝶 húdié butterfly

叮 dīng [动] (蚊虫) bite

叮嘱 dīngzhǔ [动] warn

盯 dīng [动] stare at

钉 dīng [名] nail

顶 dǐng I [名] top ▶头顶 tóudǐng top of one's head ▶山顶 shāndǐng mountain top II [动] 1 (指用头) carry ... on one's head 2 (拱起) lift ... up 3 (支撑) prop ... up 4 (撞) butt 5 (迎着) face 6 (顶撞) be rude to 7 (承担) undertake 8 (相当) ▷他干活一个人能顶两个。Tā gànhuó yī ge rén néng dǐng liǎng ge. He can do as much work as two people. 9 (顶替) take the place of III [量] ▷一项帽子 yī dǐng màozi a hat ▷一项蚊帐 yī dǐng wénzhàng a mosquito net

measure word, used for things with a pointy tip, such as caps and hats

IV [副] extremely ▶顶棒 dǐng bàng extremely good

顶点 dǐngdiǎn [名] (最高点) top

顶峰 dǐngfēng [名] summit

顶替 dǐngtì [动] 1 (代替) take the place of 2 (冒名) assume

顶嘴 dǐngzuǐ [动] answer back

订 dìng [动] 1(确立) draw ... up 2(预订) order ▸订报 dìngbào subscribe to a newspaper 3(校正) revise 4(装订) fasten ... together

订单 dìngdān [名] order form

订购 dìnggòu [动] order

订婚 dìnghūn [动] get engaged

订货 dìnghuò [动] order goods

订金 dìngjīn [名] deposit

定 dìng I [形] 1(平静) calm 2(不变的) settled ▸定论 dìnglùn final conclusion 3(规定的) fixed ▸定义 dìngyì definition II [动] 1(决定) decide ▸定计划 dìng jìhuà decide on a plan 2(固定) settle 3(预定) order III [副] definitely

定居 dìngjū [动] settle

定期 dìngqī I [动] set a date II [形] fixed III [副] regularly

丢 diū [动] 1(遗失) lose 2(扔掉) throw away 3(投) toss

丢脸 diūliǎn [动] lose face

丢人 diūrén [动] lose face

东 dōng [名] 1(方向) east ▸东南亚 Dōngnányà Southeast Asia 2(主人) owner ▸股东 gǔdōng shareholder 3(东道主) host

东西 dōngxi [名] 1(物品) thing ▸他今天买了不少东西。Jīntiān tā mǎi le bùshǎo dōngxi. He did quite a bit of shopping today.

冬 dōng [名] winter

冬眠 dōngmián [动] hibernate

冬天 dōngtiān [名] winter

董 dǒng [名] director

董事 dǒngshì [名] director

董事会 dǒngshìhuì [名] (指企业) board of directors

懂 dǒng [动] understand ▸懂得 dǒngdé understand

懂行 dǒngháng [动] (方) know the ropes

动 dòng [动] 1(指改变位置) move ▸不许动! Bùxǔ dòng! Freeze! 2(行动) act 3(用作补) ▸她太累了, 走不动。 Tā tài lèi le, zǒu bù dòng. She's too tired – she can't go on. 4(使用) use ▸我们得动脑筋。 Wǒmen děi dòng nǎojīn. We must use our brains. 5(触动) affect 6(感动) move ▸动人 dòngrén moving

动机 dòngjī [名] motive

动静 dòngjìng [名] 1(声音) sound 2(情况) movement

动力 dònglì [名] 1(指机械) power 2(力量) strength

动脉 dòngmài [名] artery

动身 dòngshēn [动] begin

动手 dòngshǒu [动] 1(开始做) get to work 2(用手摸) touch ▸只许看, 不许动手。 Zhǐxǔ kàn, bùxǔ dòngshǒu. You can look, but don't touch. 3(打人) strike a blow

动物 dòngwù [名] animal

动物园 dòngwùyuán [名] zoo

动员 dòngyuán [动] mobilize

动作 dòngzuò I [名] movement II [动] make a move

冻 dòng [动] freeze ▶冻死 dòngsǐ freeze to death

洞 dòng [名] 1 (孔) hole 2 (穴) cave

洞穴 dòngxué [名] cave

都 dōu [副] 1 (全部) all ▶全体成员 quántǐ chéngyuán all the members 2 (表示理由) all ▶都是他的错。Dōu shì tā de cuò. It's all his fault. 3 (甚至) even ▶老师待他比亲生父母都好。Lǎoshī dài tā bǐ qīnshēng fùmǔ dōu hǎo. The teacher treated him even better than his parents. 4 (已经) already ▶都到冬天了！Dōu dào dōngtiān le! It's winter already! → see also/另见 dū

兜 dōu [名] 1 (衣袋) pocket ▶裤兜 kùdōu trouser pocket 2 (拎兜) bag ▶网兜 wǎngdōu string bag

兜风 dōufēng [动] (游逛) go for a spin

兜圈子 dōuquānzi [动] (喻) (拐弯抹角) beat about the bush

斗 dǒu [名] 1 (指容器) cup 2 (斗状物) ▶烟斗 yāndǒu pipe ▶漏斗 lòudǒu funnel → see also/另见 dòu

抖 dǒu [动] 1 (颤抖) shiver 2 (甩动) shake

陡 dǒu [形] steep

斗 dòu [动] 1 (打斗) fight ▶斗鸡 dòujī cock fighting 2 (战胜) beat → see also/另见 dǒu

斗争 dòuzhēng [动] 1 (努力奋斗) struggle 2 (打击) combat 3 (奋斗) fight for

豆 dòu [名] bean

豆子 dòuzi [名] (豆类作物) bean

逗 dòu [动] (引逗) tease

逗号 dòuhào [名] comma

逗留 dòuliú [动] stay

都 dū [名] (首都) capital → see also/另见 dōu

都市 dūshì [名] metropolis

毒 dú I [名] poison II [形] (有毒) poisonous

毒品 dúpǐn [名] drug

独 dú I [形] only ▶独生子 dúshēngzǐ only son ▶独生女 dúshēngnǚ only daughter II [副] 1 (独自) alone (惟independently) only

独裁 dúcái [动] dictate

独立 dúlì [动] 1 (指国家) declare independence ▶独立宣言 dúlì xuānyán declaration of independence 2 (指个人) be independent

独身 dúshēn [动] be single

独特 dútè [形] distinctive

独自 dúzì [副] alone

读 dú [动] 1 (朗读) read aloud 2 (阅读) read 3 (上学) go to school

读书 dúshū [动] 1 (阅读) read 2 (学习) study 3 (上学) go to school

读者 dúzhě [名] reader

堵 dǔ I [动] 1 (堵塞) block ▷ 堵车 dǔchē traffic jam 2 (发闷) suffocate II [量] ▷ 一堵墙 yī dǔ qiáng a wall

measure word, used for walls

堵塞 dǔsè [动] block up

赌 dǔ [动] 1 (赌博) gamble 2 (打赌) bet

赌博 dǔbó [动] gamble

赌注 dǔzhù [名] bet

肚 dù [名] belly

肚子 dùzi [名] (腹部) stomach

度 dù I [名] 1 (限度) limit 2 (气量) tolerance ▷ 大度 dàdù magnanimous 3 (考虑) consideration 4 (程度) degree ▷ 厚度 hòudù thickness II [量] 1 (指经度或纬度) degree ▷ 北纬42度 běiwěi sìshí'èr dù latitude 42 degrees north 2 (指电量) kilowatt-hour 3 (指温度) degree ▷ 零下十度 língxià shí dù minus ten degrees 4 (指弧度或角度) degree 5 (次) time III [动] spend

渡 dù [动] 1 (越过) cross 2 (指用船) ferry 3 (喻) (通过) survive ▷ 渡关 dù nánguān go through a difficult time

端 duān I [名] 1 (头) end 2 (开头) beginning ▷ 开端 kāiduān beginning II [动] carry

端午节 Duānwǔjié [名] Dragon Boat Festival

端午节 Duānwǔjié

Dragon Boat Festival is celebrated on the fifth day of the fifth month of the Chinese lunar calendar. The two main activities which take place at this time are dragon boat racing and eating 粽子 zòngzi.

端正 duānzhèng [形] 1 (不歪斜) upright 2 (正派) proper

短 duǎn I [形] short ▷ 短期 duǎnqī short-term II [动] owe III [名] weakness

短处 duǎnchu [名] weakness

短裤 duǎnkù [名] 1 (指女式内裤) pants (PL) 2 (指男式内裤) briefs (PL) 3 (指夏装) shorts (PL)

短缺 duǎnquē [名] lack

短信 duǎnxìn [名] text message

短暂 duǎnzàn [形] brief

段 duàn [量] 1 (用于长条物) ▷ 一段铁轨 yī duàn tiěguǐ a section of railway ▷ 一段木头 yī duàn mùtou a chunk of wood

measure word, used for a part of something that is thin and long

2 (指时期) period ▷ 一段时间

yī duàn shíjiān a period of time **3**(指路程) stretch **4**(部分) piece

断 duàn [动] **1**(分成段) break **2**(断绝) break ... off **3**(判断) decide

断定 duàndìng [动] determine

断言 duànyán [动] assert

缎 duàn [名] satin

锻 duàn [动] forge

锻炼 duànliàn [动] **1**(身身体) work out **2**(磨炼) toughen

堆 duī [动] **1**(堆积) pile ▷别把垃圾堆在这里。Bié bǎ lājī duī zài zhèlǐ. Don't pile the rubbish in here. **II** [名] pile **III** [量] pile ▷一堆石头 yī duī shítou a pile of stones

队 duì [名] **1**(行列) line **2**(集体) team ▷队长 duìzhǎng team leader ▷队员 duìyuán team member

队伍 duìwu [名] **1**(军队) troops (PL) **2**(集体) contingent

对 duì **I** [动] **1**(回答) answer **2**(对待) treat **3**(朝着) face **4**(接触) come into contact with **5**(适合) suit ▷对脾气 duì píqìxué one's temperament ▷今天的菜很对他的胃口。Jīntiān de cài hěn duì tā de wèikǒu. Today's meal was definitely to his liking. **6**(调整) adjust **7**(核对) check ▷对表 duì biǎo set one's watch **8**(加law) add **II** [形] **1**(对面) opposite **2**(正确) correct **III** [介] **1**(朝) at **2**(对于) ▷吸烟对健康有害。Xīyān

duì jiànkāng yǒuhài. Smoking is harmful to your health. **IV** [量] pair ▷一对夫妻 yī duì fūqī married couple

对比 duìbǐ [动] contrast ▷鲜明的对比 xiānmíng de duìbǐ marked contrast

对不起 duìbuqǐ [动] (愧疚) be sorry ▷对不起，借过。Duìbuqǐ, jièguò. Excuse me- may I just get through?

对称 duìchèn [形] symmetrical

对待 duìdài [动] treat

对方 duìfāng [名] other side

对付 duìfu [动] **1**(应对) deal with **2**(将就) make do

对话 duìhuà **I** [名] dialogue **II** [动] hold talks

对立 duìlì [动] counter

对面 duìmiàn [名] **1**(对过) the opposite ▷正前方 the front

对手 duìshǒu [名] **1**(指比赛) opponent **2**(指能力) match

对象 duìxiàng [名] **1**(目标) object **2**(指男女朋友) partner

对应 duìyìng [动] correspond

对于 duìyú [介] ▷对于这篇文章，大家理解不一。Duìyú zhè piān wénzhāng, dàjiā lǐjiě bù yī. Not everyone understands this article in the same way.

兑 duì [动] **1**(互换) exchange **2**(汇兑) cash

兑换 duìhuàn [动] convert

吨 dūn [量] ton

蹲 dūn [动] (弯腿) squat

炖 dùn [动] stew

钝 dùn [形] 1 (不锋利) blunt 2 (不灵活) dim

顿 dùn I [动] (停顿) pause II [量] ▷一顿饭 yī dùn fàn a meal ▷挨了一顿打 āi le yī dùn dǎ take a beating measure word, used for meals

顿时 dùnshí [副] immediately

多 duō I [形] 1 (数量大) a lot of ▷很多书 hěn duō shū a lot of books 2 (相差大) more ▷我比你大多了。Wǒ bǐ nǐ dà duō le. I'm much older than you are. 3 (过出) too many ▷她喝多了。Tā hē duō le. She drank too much. 4 (过分) excessive ▷多疑 duōyí over-suspicious II [数] ▷2年多前 liǎngnián duō qiánover two years ago III [数] be more than ▷多个人就多份力量。Duō ge rén jiù duō fèn lìliàng. The more people we have, the stronger we will be. IV [副] 1 (用在疑问句中) how ▷从北京到上海有多远? Cóng Běijīng dào Shànghǎi yǒu duō yuǎn? How far is it from Beijing to Shanghai? ▷你儿子多大了? Nǐ érzi duō dà le? How old is your son? 2 (表示感叹) how ▷多美的城市! Duō měi de chéngshì! How beautiful this town is! 3 (表示任何一种程度) however ▷给我一把尺,多长都

行。Gěi wǒ yī bǎ chǐ, duō cháng dōu xíng. Give me a ruler – any length will do.

多媒体 duōméitǐ [名] multimedia

多么 duōme [副] 1 (用于询问程度) how ▷他到底有多么聪明? Tā dàodǐ yǒu duōme cōngming? How clever is he really? 2 (用在感叹句) ▷多么蓝的天啊! Duōme lán de tiān ya! What a clear day! 3 (表示程度深) no matter how

多少 duōshǎo I [副] 1 (或多或少) somewhat ▷这笔买卖多少能赚点钱。Zhè bǐ mǎimai duōshǎo néng zhuàn diǎn qián. We're bound to earn some money from this deal. 2 (稍微) slightly

多少 duōshao I [代] (用于询问数量) ▷这台电视机多少钱? Zhè tái diànshìjī duōshao qián? How much is this television? ▷今天有多少人到会? Jīntiān yǒu duōshao rén dàohuì? How many people attended the meeting today? II [数] ▷你们有多少我们要多少。Nǐmen yǒu duōshao wǒmen yào duōshao. We want everything you've got.

多数 duōshù [名] the majority

多余 duōyú [形] 1 (超出需要量的) surplus 2 (不必要的) redundant

哆 duō see below/ 见下文

哆嗦 duōsuo [动] tremble

夺 duó [动] 1 (抢) seize 2 (争取) compete for 3 (剥夺) deprive 4 (决定) resolve

夺取 duóqǔ [动] 1 (武力强取) capture 2 (努力争取) strive for

朵 duǒ [量] ▷朵朵白云 duǒ duǒ báiyún white clouds ▷几朵玫瑰 jǐ duǒ méiguì some roses measure word, used for clouds and flowers

躲 duǒ [动] 1 (隐藏) hide 2 (避让) avoid

躲避 duǒbì [动] 1 (回避) run away from 2 (躲藏) hide

躲藏 duǒcáng [动] hide

剁 duò [动] chop

堕 duò [动] fall

堕落 duòluò [动] go to the bad

堕胎 duòtāi [动] have an abortion

跺 duò [动] stamp

e

俄 é [名] (also: 俄罗斯 Éluósī) Russia ▷俄国 Éguó Russia

俄语 Éyǔ [名] Russian language

鹅 é [名] goose

蛾 é [名] moth ▷蛾子 ézi moth

额 é [名] forehead ▷额头 étóu forehead

恶 ě see below/见下文
→ see also/另见 è, wù

恶心 ěxin I [动] feel nauseous II [形] nauseating

恶 è I [名] evil II [形] 1 (凶恶) ferocious 2 (恶劣) evil
→ see also/另见 ě, wù

恶劣 èliè [形] bad

恶梦 èmèng [名] nightmare

饿 è I [形] hungry ▷ 我很饿。 Wǒ hěn è. I'm very hungry. II [动] starve

鳄 è [名] crocodile, alligator ▷ 鳄鱼 èyú crocodile, alligator

儿 ér [名] 1 (小孩子) child 2 (儿子) son ▷ 儿子 érzi son

儿女 érnǚ [名] children (PL)

儿童 értóng [名] child

而 ér [连] 1 (并且) and ▷ 美丽而聪明 měilì ér cōngmíng beautiful and clever 2 (但是) but ▷ 浓而不烈 nóng ér bù liè strong but not overpowering ▷ 她不是学生，而是老师。 Tā bù shì xuéshēng,ér shì lǎoshī. She isn't a student, but a teacher.

而且 érqiě [连] and what's more ▷ 他会讲英语，而且讲得好。 Tā huì jiǎng Yīngyǔ,érqiě jiǎng de hǎo. He can speak English, and what's more he speaks it very well.

耳 ěr [名] (耳朵) ear ▷ 耳朵 ěrduo ear

二 èr [数] two ▷ 二月 èryuè February ▷ 第二次 dì èr cì the second time

二十 èrshí [数] twenty

贰 èr [数] two
This is the complex character for two, which is mainly used in banks, on receipts, etc.

f

发 fā [动] 1 (送出) send ▷ 发工资 fā gōngzī pay wages 2 (发射) emit ▷ 发光 fāguāng shine 3 (产生) produce ▷ 发电 fādiàn generate electricity ▷ 发芽 fāyá sprout 4 (表达) express ▷ 发言 fāyán speak 5 (扩大) develop ▷ 发扬 fāyáng carry on 6 (兴旺) prosper ▷ 发家 fājiā make a family fortune 7 (使膨胀) ▷ 发面 fāmiàn leaven, dough 8 (散开) spread ▷ 发散 fāsàn diverge 9 (揭开) uncover ▷ 发掘 fājué unearth ▷ 揭发 jiēfā expose 10 (变得) become ▷ 发霉 fāméi go mouldy (英) 或 moldy (美) 11 (流露) ▷ 发愁 fāchóu worry ▷ 发脾气 fā píqi lose one's temper 12 (感到) feel 13 (起程) leave ▷ 出发 chūfā

set out
→ see also/另见 fà

发表 fābiǎo [动] 1(宣布) announce 2(刊登) publish

发财 fācái [动] make a fortune

发出 fāchū [动] 1(发送) send out 2(散发) give out

发达 fādá I [形] developed II [动] promote

发动 fādòng [动] 1(启动) start 2(发起) launch 3(鼓动) mobilize

发动机 fādòngjī [名] engine

发抖 fādǒu [动] 1(因恐惧等) tremble 2(因寒冷等) shiver

发挥 fāhuī [动] 1(充分利用) bring ... into play 2(详尽论述) elaborate

发火 fāhuǒ [动] 1(着火) catch fire 2(爆炸) detonate 3(发脾气) lose one's temper

发霉 fāméi [动] go mouldy (英) 或 moldy (美)

发明 fāmíng [动] invent

发票 fāpiào [名] 1(收据) receipt 2(发货清单) invoice

发烧 fāshāo [动] have a temperature

发生 fāshēng [动] happen

发现 fāxiàn [动] discover

发言 fāyán [动] make a speech

发扬 fāyáng [动] carry on

发音 fāyīn [动] pronounce

发展 fāzhǎn [动] 1(变化) develop 2(扩大) expand

罚 fá [动] punish ▷ 罚款 fákuǎn fine

罚款 fákuǎn I [动] fine II [名] fine

法 fǎ [名] 1(法律) law 2(方法) method ▷ 用法 yòngfǎ use 3(标准) model 4(佛理) Buddhism 5(法术) magic ▷ 戏法 xìfǎ conjuring tricks

法国 Fǎguó [名] France

法律 fǎlù [名] law

法庭 fǎtíng [名] court

法语 Fǎyǔ [名] French

法院 fǎyuàn [名] court

发 fà [名] hair
→ see also/另见 fā

番 fān [量] ▷ 三番五次 sānfān-wǔcì time and time again ▷ 经过几番挫折他明白了许多道理。Jīngguò jǐfān cuòzé tā míngbai le xǔduō dàoli. After a few false starts he picked up quite a lot. measure word, used for actions

番茄 fānqié [名] tomato

翻 fān [动] 1(换位置) turn over 2(寻找) rummage 3(推翻) reverse 4(越过) get across 5(增加) multiply 6(翻译) translate 7(翻脸) fall out

翻译 fānyì I [动] translate II [名] translator

凡 fán I [名] 1(人世间) mortal world 2(大概) approximation II [形] 1(平凡) ordinary II [副] (总共)

烦 fán I [名] trouble II [动] (谦) trouble III [形] (厌烦) fed up

烦恼 fánnǎo [形] worried

繁 fán I [形] numerous II [动] propagate

繁华 fánhuá [形] bustling

繁忙 fánmáng [形] busy

繁荣 fánróng [形] flourishing

繁体字 fántǐzì [名] complex characters (PL)

繁体字 fántǐzì
Complex characters, also known as traditional Chinese characters, had been used as the Chinese script for centuries in all parts of China until 1956 when the government of the People's Republic of China carried out a programme of simplifying these characters in an effort to improve the literacy rate by making characters easier to write. Since then, 简体字 jiǎntǐzì 'simplified characters', have become the dominant form of the Chinese script. However, for various cultural and political reasons, many Chinese-speaking regions and communities did not accept these changes, and

continue to use the old system. Hong Kong and Taiwan are among these regions.

繁殖 fánzhí [动] breed

反 fǎn I [名] 1 (相反) opposite 2 (造反) rebellion II [动] 1 (转换) turn 2 (回) return 3 (反对) oppose 4 (背叛) rebel III [形] opposite IV [副] 1 (相反地) on the contrary 2 (从反面) again ▶反思 fǎnsī review

反动 fǎndòng I [形] reactionary II [名] reaction

反对 fǎnduì [动] oppose

反复 fǎnfù [副] 1 (重复) repeatedly 2 (多变) capriciously

反抗 fǎnkàng [动] resist

反面 fǎnmiàn I [名] other side II [形] negative

反应 fǎnyìng [名] 1 (反响) response 2 (指机体) reaction 3 (指物理, 化学) reaction

反映 fǎnyìng [动] 1 (反照) reflect 2 (汇报) report

反正 fǎnzhèng [副] anyway

返 fǎn [动] return

返回 fǎnhuí [动] come back

犯 fàn [动] 1 (违犯) violate 2 (侵犯) attack 3 (错误, 罪行等) commit II [名] criminal

犯法 fànfǎ [动] break the law

犯规 fànguī [动] break the rules

犯人 fànrén [名] prisoner

犯罪 fànzuì [动] commit a crime

饭 fàn [名] 1 (餐) meal ▷ 晚饭 wǎnfàn supper 2 (米饭) rice

饭店 fàndiàn [名] 1 (住宿) hotel 2 (吃饭) restaurant

饭馆 fànguǎn [名] restaurant

饭厅 fàntīng [名] dining room

范 fàn [名] 1 (模范) model ▷ 典范 diǎnfàn model 2 (范围) limit ▷ 规范 guīfàn standard 3 (模子) pattern

范围 fànwéi [名] limit

方 fāng I [名] 1 (方向) direction ▷ 南方 nánfāng the South 2 (方形) square ▷ 长方形 chángfāngxíng rectangle 3 (方面) side 4 (方法) method 5 (地方) place 6 (方) prescription 7 (数) (乘方) power II [形] 1 (方形) square 2 (正直) honest

方案 fāng'àn [名] plan

方便 fāngbiàn [形] 1 (便利) convenient 2 (适宜) appropriate

方法 fāngfǎ [名] method

方面 fāngmiàn [名] 1 (指人) side 2 (指物) aspect

方式 fāngshì [名] way

方向 fāngxiàng [名] direction

方言 fāngyán [名] dialect

方针 fāngzhēn [名] policy

防 fáng [动] 1 (防备) prevent 2 (防守) defend II [名] (堤) dyke

防止 fángzhǐ [动] prevent

妨 fáng [动] obstruct

妨碍 fáng'ài [动] obstruct

房 fáng [名] 1 (房子) house 2 (房间) room ▷ 书房 shūfáng study 3 (家族) ▷ 远房亲戚 yuǎnfáng qīnqi a distant relative

房东 fángdōng [名] landlord

房屋 fángwū [名] building

仿 fǎng [动] 1 (仿效) copy 2 (类似) be like

仿佛 fǎngfú I [连] as if II [形] similar

访 fǎng [动] 1 (访问) call on ▷ 访谈 fǎngtán call in for a chat 2 (调查) investigate

访问 fǎngwèn [动] visit

纺 fǎng I [动] spin II [名] silk

纺织 fǎngzhī [动] ▷ 纺织品 fǎngzhīpǐn textiles (PL)

放 fàng [动] 1 (使自由) release ▷ 解放 jiěfàng free 2 (暂时停止) ▷ 放学了。School is now over. 3 (放纵) let oneself go 4 (赶牲畜吃草) graze 5 (驱逐) expel ▷ 流放 liúfàng banish 6 (发出) send out ▷ 放炮 fàngpào fire a gun 7 (点燃) set ... off 8 (借出收息) loan 9 (扩展) ▷ 把照片放大 bǎ zhàopiàn fàngdà enlarge a photo 10 (花开) bloom 11 (搁置) put ... to one side 12 (弄倒) cut down 13 (使处于) put 14 (加进) add 15 (控制自己) ▷ 放严肃点 fàng yánsù diǎn become more serious 16 (放映) project 17 (保存) leave

放大 fàngdà [动] enlarge

放假 fàngjià [动] go on holiday (英) 或 vacation (美)

放弃 fàngqì [动] give ... up

放松 fàngsōng [动] relax

放心 fàngxīn [动] set one's mind at rest

放学 fàngxué [动] finish school

飞 fēi I [动] 1 (鸟、虫、飞机) fly 2 (空中游动) flutter 3 (挥发) evaporate II [副] swiftly

飞机 fēijī [名] aeroplane (英), airplane (美)

飞行 fēixíng [动] fly

非 fēi I [名] 1 (错误) wrong ▶是非 shìfēi right and wrong 2 (also: 非洲 Fēizhōu) Africa II [动] 1 (非议) blame 2 (不合于) run counter to ▶非法 fēifǎ illegal 3 (不是) not be 4 (强硬) insist on III [副] (必须) ▶我不让他去，他非去不可。 wǒ bù ràng tā qù, tā fēi qù bù kě. I've tried to stop him, but he simply has to go.

非常 fēicháng I [形] exceptional II [副] very

非典 fēidiǎn [名] (非典型性肺炎) SARS

非法 fēifǎ [形] illegal

非洲 Fēizhōu [名] Africa

肥 féi I [名] fertilizer II [动] 1 (使肥沃) fertilize 2 (暴富) get rich III [形] 1 (脂肪多) fat 2 (肥沃) fertile 3 (肥大) loose

肥胖 féipàng [形] fat

肥皂 féizào [名] soap

肺 fèi [名] lung

废 fèi I [动] abandon II [形] 1 (不用的) waste 2 (没用的) useless 3 (残废的) disabled

费 fèi I [名] fee ▶车费 chēfèi bus fare II [形] expensive III [动] spend

费用 fèiyòng [名] expense

分 fēn I [动] 1 (分开) divide ▶分离 fēnlí separate ▶分裂 fēnliè split 2 (分配) assign 3 (辨别) distinguish II [名] 1 (分支) branch 2 (分数) fraction ▶分母 fēnmǔ denominator 3 (数字) 1 (分数) fraction ▶四分之三 sì fēn zhī sān three quarters 2 (十分之一) unit of Chinese currency, equal to a hundredth of a yuan 4 (指时间) minute ▶5点过5分 wǔ diǎn guò wǔ fēn 5 minutes past 5 5 (指弧度或角度) minute ▶36度20分 sānshíliù dù èrshí fēn jiǎo 36 degrees 20 minutes 6 (百分之一) per cent ▶月利1分 yuèlì yī fēn monthly interest of 1 per cent → see also/另见 fèn

分别 fēnbié I [动] 1 (离别) split up 2 (辨别) distinguish II [名] difference

分开 fēnkāi [动] separate

分配 fēnpèi [动] assign

分手 fēnshǒu [动] 1 (告别) say goodbye 2 (指男女关系) break up

分数 fēnshù [名] mark

分析 fēnxī [动] analyse(英), analyze(美)

吩 fēn *see below*/见下文

吩咐 fēnfù [动] instruct

纷 fēn [形] 1(多) numerous ▸纷繁 fēnfán numerous 2(乱) confused ▸纷扰 fēnrǎo confusion

纷纷 fēnfēn I [形] diverse II [副] one after another

坟 fén [名] grave

坟墓 fénmù [名] grave

粉 fěn I [名] 1(粉末) powder 2(粉丝) vermicelli II [动] 1(成碎末) crumble ▸粉碎 fěnsuì crush 2(变成粉状) pulverize III [形] 1(白色) white 2(粉红色) pink

粉笔 fěnbǐ [名] chalk

粉红 fěnhóng [形] pink

粉末 fěnmò [名] powder

分 fèn [名] 1(成分) component 2(限度) limit ▸过分 guòfèn excessive ▸see also/另见 fēn

分量 fènliàng [名] weight

份 fèn I [名] 1(一部分) part ▸股份 gǔfèn share 2(指划分单位) ▸年份 niánfèn year II [量] 1(指食物) portion 2(指报刊) copy

奋 fèn [动] 1(振作) exert oneself ▸勤奋 qínfèn diligent 2(举起) raise

奋斗 fèndòu [动] fight

愤 fèn [形] indignant ▸气愤 qìfèn indignant

愤怒 fènnù [形] angry

丰 fēng [形] 1(丰富) abundant 2(大) great

丰富 fēngfù I [形] abundant II [动] enrich

丰收 fēngshōu [动] have a good harvest

风 fēng I [名] 1(指空气流动) wind 2(风气) trend 3(景象) scene ▸风光 fēngguāng scenery 4(态度) manner ▸风度 fēngdù bearing 5(消息) information II [形] 1(传闻的) rumoured(英), rumored(美) 2(风干) air ▸风干 fēnggān air-dry

风格 fēnggé [名] 1(气度) manner 2(特点) style

风景 fēngjǐng [名] scenery

风水 fēngshuǐ [名] feng shui

风俗 fēngsú [名] custom

风险 fēngxiǎn [名] risk

封 fēng I [动] (封闭) seal II [名] envelope III [量] ▸一封信 yī fēng xìn a letter

封建 fēngjiàn I [名] feudalism II [形] feudal

疯 fēng I [形] mad II [副] madly

疯子 fēngzi [名] lunatic

锋 fēng [名] 1(尖端) point 2(带头的) vanguard 3(锋面) front

锋利 fēnglì [形] 1(工具) sharp 2(言论) cutting

蜂 fēng I [名] 1 (黄蜂) wasp 2 (蜜蜂) bee II [副] in swarms

蜂蜜 fēngmì [名] honey

逢 féng [动] come across

缝 féng [动] sew
→ see also/另见 fèng

讽 fěng [动] mock ▶讥讽 jīfěng satirize

讽刺 fěngcì [动] ridicule

奉 fèng [动] 1 (献给) present 2 (接受) receive 3 (尊重) respect 4 (信仰) believe in 5 (伺候) attend to

奉献 fèngxiàn [动] dedicate

缝 fèng [名] 1 (接合处) seam 2 (缝隙) crack
→ see also/另见 féng

缝隙 fèngxì [名] crack

佛 fó [名] 1 (佛教) Buddhism 2 (佛像) Buddha

佛教 fójiào [名] Buddhism

否 fǒu I [动] deny II [副] 1 (书) (不) no 2 (是,能,可) or not ▶他明天是否来参加聚会? tā míngtiān shìfǒu lái cānjiā jùhuì? Is he coming to the party tomorrow or not?

否定 fǒudìng I [动] negate II [形] negative

否认 fǒurèn [动] deny

否则 fǒuzé [连] otherwise

夫 fū [名] 1 (丈夫) husband 2 (男子) man 3 (劳动者) manual worker

夫妇 fūfù [名] husband and wife

夫妻 fūqī [名] husband and wife

夫人 fūren [名] Mrs

扶 fú [动] 1 (稳住) steady 2 (搀起) help up 3 (扶助) help

服 fú I [名] clothes (PL) II [动] 1 (吃) take ▶服药 fúyào take medicine 2 (担任) serve ▶服役 fúyì serve in the army 3 (服从) comply with 4 (使信服) convince 5 (适应) adapt
→ see also/另见 fù

服从 fúcóng [动] obey

服务 fúwù [动] serve

服务员 fúwùyuán [名] 1 (指商店里) attendant 2 (指饭馆里) waiter, waitress 3 (指宾馆里) room attendant

服装 fúzhuāng [名] clothing

浮 fú I [动] float II [形] 1 (表面上) superficial 2 (可移动) movable 3 (暂时) temporary 4 (轻浮) slapdash 5 (空虚) empty ▶浮夸 fúkuā exaggerated 6 (多余) surplus

浮肿 fúzhǒng [动] puff up

符 fú I [名] 1 (标记) mark 2 (图形) Daoist motif II [动] be in keeping with

符号 fúhào [名] mark

符合 fúhé [动] match

幅 fú I [名] 1 (指布) width 2 (泛指大小) size ▶幅度 fúdùrange II [量] ▶一幅画 yī fú huà a painting ▶三幅书法 sān fú shūfǎ calligraphies measure word, used for paintings, portraits and Chinese calligraphies

福 fú [名] good fortune

辅 fú [动] complement
辅导 fǔdǎo [动] coach

腐 fú I [形] rotten II [名] bean curd
腐败 fǔbài [动] rot II [形] corrupt

父 fù [名] 1 (父亲) father 2 (指男性长辈) senior male relative ▶ 祖父 zǔfù grandfather
父母 fùmǔ [名] parents
父亲 fùqīn [名] father

付 fù [动] 1 (事物) hand over ▶ 托付 tuōfù entrust 2 (钱) pay ▶ 偿付 chángfù pay back
付账 fùzhàng [动] pay the bill

负 fù I [动] 1 (书) (背) carry on one's back ▶ 负重 fùzhòng carry a heavy load 2 (担负) bear 3 (遭受) suffer 4 (享有) enjoy 5 (拖欠) be in arrears 6 (背弃) turn one's back on 7 (失败) lose II [形] negative ▶ 负数 fùshù negative number
负担 fùdān I [动] bear II [名] burden
负责 fùzé [动] be responsible II [形] conscientious

妇 fù [名] 1 (妇女) woman ▶ 妇科 fùkē gynaecology (英), gynecology (美) 2 (已婚女人) married woman 3 (妻) wife
妇女 fùnǚ [名] woman

附 fù [动] 1 (附带) attach 2 (靠近) get close to 3 (依从) depend on
附近 fùjìn I [形] nearby II [名] vicinity

服 fù [量] dose
→ see also/另见 fú

复 fù I [形] 1 (重复) duplicated ▶ 复制 fùzhì reproduce 2 (繁复) complex II [动] 1 (转) turn 2 (回答) reply 3 (恢复) recover 4 (报复) take revenge III [副] again ▶ 复查 fùchá re-examine
复活节 Fùhuó Jié [名] (宗) Easter
复习 fùxí [动] revise
复印 fùyìn [动] photocopy
复杂 fùzá [形] complex

副 fù I [形] 1 (辅助) deputy 2 (附属) subsidiary ▶ 副业 fùyè subsidiary business II [名] assistant ▶ 大副 dàfù first mate III [动] correspond to IV [量] (套) pair ▶ 一副手套 yī fù shǒutào a pair of gloves ▶ 一副冷面孔 yī fù lěng miànkǒng a cold expression ▶ 一副笑脸 yī fù xiàoliǎn a smiling face

measure word, used for expressions

副作用 fùzuòyòng [名] side effect

富 fù I [形] 1 (有钱) rich 2 (丰富) abundant II [名] wealth III [动] enrich
富有 fùyǒu I [形] wealthy II [动] be full of

g

咖 gā *see below*/见下文
→ *see also*/另见 kā

咖喱 gālí [名] curry

---

could be here.

改 gǎi [动] 1(改变) change 2(修改) alter 3(改正) correct

改变 gǎibiàn [动] change ▷我改变了主意。 Wǒ gǎibiàn le zhǔyi. I changed my mind.

改革 gǎigé [动] reform ▷改革开放 gǎigé kāifàng reform and opening up

改善 gǎishàn [动] improve

改正 gǎizhèng [动] correct ▷改正缺点 gǎizhèng quēdiǎn mend one's ways

钙 gài [名] (化) calcium

盖 gài I [名] (指器皿) cover ▷盖子 gàizi lid II [动] 1(蒙上) cover 2(遮掩) cover ... up 3(打上) stamp 4(压过) block ... out 5(建造) build

概 gài [名] (大略) outline

概括 gàikuò I [动] summarize II [形] brief

概念 gàiniàn [名] concept

该 gāi I [动] 1(应当) ought to 2(轮到) be the turn of 3(活该) serve ... right ▷活该 huógāi serve ... right II [助动] 1(应当) should ▷工作明天就完成了。 Gōngzuò míngtiān gāi wánchéng le. The work should be finished by tomorrow. 2(表示推测) ▷再不吃的话，菜都该凉了。 Zài bù chī dehuà, cài dōu gāi liáng le. If we keep waiting the food is only going to get colder. 3(用于加强语气) ▷要是他能在这儿这么好啊! Yàoshi tā néng zài zhèr zhè duō hǎo a! It would be great if he

干 gān I [动] have to do with ▷不干我事。 Zhè bù gān wǒ shì. This has nothing to do with me. II [形] 1(无水) dry 2(不用水) dry ▷干洗 gānxǐ dry-clean 3(干涸) dried-up III [名] 豆腐干 dòufugān dried tofu ▷葡萄干 pútaogān raisin IV [副] (白白) in vain
→ *see also*/另见 gàn

干杯 gānbēi [动] drink a toast ▷"干杯!" "Gānbēi!" "Cheers!"

干脆 gāncuì [形] direct

干旱 gānhàn [形] arid

干净 gānjìng [形] **1** (无尘) clean **2** (一点不剩) complete ▷请把汤喝干净。Qǐng bǎ tāng hē gānjìng. Please finish your soup.

干扰 gānrǎo [动] disturb

干预 gānyù [动] interfere

干燥 gānzào [形] dry

杆 gān [名] post

肝 gān [名] liver

竿 gān [名] pole ▷竿子 gānzi pole

赶 gǎn [动] **1** (追) catch ▷赶公共汽车 gǎn gōnggòng qìchē catch a bus **2** (加快) rush ▷赶着回家 gǎn zhe huíjiā rush home **3** (驱赶) drive **4** (驱逐) drive ... out

赶紧 gǎnjǐn [副] quickly

赶快 gǎnkuài [副] at once ▷我们得赶快走了！Wǒmen děi gǎnkuài zǒu le! We must be at once!

赶上 gǎnshàng [动] catch up with

赶忙 gǎnmáng [副] hurriedly

敢 gǎn [动] **1** (有胆量) dare ▷敢于 gǎnyú dare to **2** (有把握) be sure

感 gǎn **I** [动] **1** (觉得) feel **2** (感动) move ▷感人 gǎnrén moving **II** [名] sense ▷成就感 chéngjiùgǎn a sense of achievement ▷方向感 fāngxiànggǎn a sense of direction

感到 gǎndào [动] feel ▷我感到幸运。Wǒ gǎndào xìngyùn. I

feel lucky.

感动 gǎndòng [动] move ▷他容易被感动。Tā róngyì bèi gǎndòng. He's very easily moved.

感恩节 Gǎn'ēn Jié [名] Thanksgiving

感激 gǎnjī [动] appreciate

感觉 gǎnjué **I** [名] feeling **II** [动] **1** (感到) feel **2** (认为) sense

感冒 gǎnmào [动] catch a cold

感情 gǎnqíng [名] **1** (心理反应) emotion **2** (喜爱) feelings (PL)

感染 gǎnrǎn [动] (传染) infect

感想 gǎnxiǎng [名] thoughts (PL)

感谢 gǎnxiè [动] thank ▷感谢您的指导。Gǎnxiè nín de zhǐdǎo. Thank you for your guidance.

感兴趣 gǎn xìngqù [动] be interested in ▷他对绘画感兴趣。Tā duì huìhuà gǎn xìngqù. He's interested in painting.

干 gàn [动] **1** (做) do ▷干活 gànhuó work **2** (担任) act as ▷他干过队长。Tā gànguò duìzhǎng. He acted as team leader.
→ see also/另见 gān

干部 gànbù [名] cadre

刚 gāng [形] strong **II** [副] **1** (恰好) just ▷水温刚好。Shuǐwēn gāng hǎo. The temperature of the water was just right. **2** (仅仅) just ▷这儿刚够放一把椅子。Zhèr gāng gòu fàng yī bǎ yǐzi. There is just enough room for a chair. **3** (不久以前) only just ▷小

宝宝刚会走路。Xiǎo bǎobao gāng huì zǒulù. The baby has only just started walking.

刚才 gāngcái [名] just now

刚刚 gānggāng [副] just

刚好 gānghǎo I [形] just right II [副] luckily

钢 gāng [名] steel ▷钢铁 gāngtiě steel

钢笔 gāngbǐ [名] fountain pen

钢琴 gāngqín [名] piano

缸 gāng [名] (器物) vat ▷鱼缸 yúgāng fish bowl

港 gǎng [名] 1 (港湾) harbour (英), harbor (美) 2 (香港) Hong Kong ▷香港 Xiānggǎng Hong Kong ▷港币 gǎngbì Hong Kong dollar

港口 gǎngkǒu [名] port

高 gāo [形] 1 (指高度) tall ▷高楼 gāolóu tall building 2 (指标准或程度) high ▷高标准 gāo biāozhǔn high standard 3 (指等级) senior ▷高中 gāozhōng senior school 4 (指声音) high-pitched 5 (指年龄) old 6 (指价格) high

高大 gāodà [形] (字) huge

高档 gāodàng [形] top quality

高等 gāoděng [形] higher ▷高等教育 gāoděng jiàoyù higher education

高级 gāojí [形] 1 (指级别) senior ▷高级法院 gāojí fǎyuàn high court 2 (超过一般) high-quality ▷高级英语 gāojí Yīngyǔ advanced English ▷高级宾馆 gāojí bīnguǎn luxury hotel

高考 gāokǎo [名] college entrance examination

高科技 gāokējì [形] hi-tech

高速 gāosù [形] rapid

高速公路 gāosù gōnglù [名] motorway (英), freeway (美)

高兴 gāoxìng I [形] happy II [动] enjoy

高原 gāoyuán [名] plateau

高中 gāozhōng [名] (also: 高级中学) senior school (英), high school (美)

糕 gāo [名] cake ▷蛋糕 dàngāo cake

搞 gǎo [动] 1 (干) do 2 (弄) get

告 gào [动] 1 (陈述) tell 2 (控诉) sue

告别 gàobié [动] say goodbye

告诉 gàosu [动] tell

告状 gàozhuàng [动] (抱怨) complain

哥 gē [名] 1 (哥哥) elder brother 2 (亲热称呼) brother

哥哥 gēge [名] elder brother

哥儿们 gērmen [名] (朋友) mate (英), buddy (美)

胳 gē see below/见下文

胳膊 gēbo [名] arm

鸽 gē [名] dove ▷鸽子 gēzi dove

搁 gē [动] 1 (放) put 2 (搁置) put aside

割 gē [动] cut

歌 gē I [名] song II [动] sing

歌剧 gējù [名] opera

歌曲 gēqǔ [名] song

歌手 gēshǒu [名] singer

革 gé I [名] leather II [动] (改变) change

革命 gémìng [动] revolutionize ▷工业革命 gōngyè gémìng industrial revolution

格 gé [名] (格子) check

格式 géshì [名] format

格外 géwài [副] 1 (特别) especially 2 (额外) additionally

隔 gé [动] 1 (阻隔) separate 2 (间隔) be apart

隔壁 gébì [名] next door ▷隔壁邻居 gébì línjū next-door neighbour (英) 或 neighbor (美)

嗝 gé [名] 1 (饱嗝) burp ▷打饱嗝 dǎ bǎogé burp 2 (冷嗝) hiccup ▷打冷嗝 dǎ lěnggé hiccup

个 gè I [名] (指身材或大小) size ▷个头儿 gètóur build II [量] (表示个数) ▷6个桃子 liù gè táozi six peaches ▷两个月 liǎng gè yuè two months

This is the most useful and common measure word, and can be used as the default measure word when you are unsure. It can be used for people, objects, fruits, countries, cities, companies, dates, weeks, months, ideas etc. (表示动量) ▷开个会 kāi gè huì have a meeting ▷冲个澡 chōng gè zǎo have a shower the most useful measure word, used for actions

个别 gèbié [形] 1 (单个) individual 2 (少数) a couple

个人 gèrén I [名] individual II [代] oneself ▷就他个人而言 jiù tā gèrén éryán as far as he's concerned ▷在我个人看来，这是个好主意。Zài wǒ gèrén kànlái, zhè shì gè hǎo zhǔyi. As far as I'm concerned this is a good idea.

个体 gètǐ [名] 1 (指生物) individual 2 (指经济形态) ▷个体经营 gètǐ jīngyíng private enterprise

个性 gèxìng [名] personality ▷他个性很强。Tā gèxìng hěn qiáng. He has a very strong personality.

个子 gèzi [名] stature ▷高个子女人 gāo gèzi nǚrén a tall woman

各 gè I [代] each II [副] individually

各个 gègè I [代] each II [副] one by one

各种 gèzhǒng [代] all kinds

各自 gèzì [代]

给 gěi I [动] 1 (给予) give 2 (让) let II [介] 1 (为) for ▷我给妻子做早餐。Wǒ gěi qīzi zuò zǎocān.

I made breakfast for my wife.
2(向)to ▷留给他 liú gěi tā leave
it to him ▷递给我 dì gěi wǒ pass
it to me

根 gēn [名] (指植物) root ▷祸根
huògēn the root of the problem
II [量] ▷一根绳子 yì gēn shéngzi
a rope ▷一根头发 yì gēn tóufa
a hair

measure word, used for
long thin objects, body
parts and plants

根本 gēnběn **I** [名] root **II** [形]
fundamental **III** [副] **1**(完全)
at all **2**(彻底) thoroughly ▷根
本转变态度 gēnběn zhuǎnbiàn
tàidù completely change one's
attitude

根据 gēnjù **I** [介] according to
II [名] basis

根源 gēnyuán [名] cause

跟 gēn **I** [名] heel **II** [动] **1**(跟随)
follow **2**(嫁) marry **III** [介] **1**(同)
with ▷我跟朋友去公园了。 Wǒ
gēn péngyou qù gōngyuán le. I
went to the park with friends.
2(向) ▷跟我说这件事。 Gēn
wǒ shuōshuo zhè jiàn shì. Tell me
what happened. **3**(表示比较) as
▷他的教育背景跟我相似。 Tā
de jiàoyù bèijǐng gēn wǒ xiāngsì.
His educational background is
similar to mine. **IV** [连] and

跟随 gēnsuí [动] follow

跟头 gēntou [名] fall ▷翻跟头 fān
gēntou do a somersault

跟踪 gēnzōng [动] tail

更 gēng [动] (改变) change ▷更正
gēngzhèng correct
→ see also/另见 gèng

更改 gēnggǎi [动] alter

更换 gēnghuàn [动] change

更替 gēngtì [动] replace

更新 gēngxīn [动] **1**(事物) replace
▷更新网站内容 gēngxīn
wǎngzhàn nèiróng update web
content **2**(森林) renew

更衣室 gēngyīshì [名] fitting
room

耕 gēng [动] plough

耕地 gēngdì **I** [动] plough **II** [名]
cultivated land

更 gèng [形] (更加) even more ▷天
更黑了。 Tiān gèng hēi le. It's
getting even darker.
→ see also/另见 gēng

更加 gèngjiā [副] even more

工 gōng [名] **1**(指人) worker ▷童
工 tónggōng child labour **2**(指阶
级) the working class **3**(工作或
劳动) work **4**(工程) project **5**(工
业) industry

工厂 gōngchǎng [名] factory

工程 gōngchéng [名] engineering
project

工程师 gōngchéngshī [名]
engineer

工夫 gōngfu [名] **1**(时间) time
2(空闲) spare time

工具 gōngjù [名] **1**(器具) tool
2(喻) instrument

工人 gōngrén [名] worker

工业 gōngyè [名] industry

工艺品 gōngyìpǐn [名] handicraft item

工资 gōngzī [名] pay

工作 gōngzuò [名] 1(劳动) work 2(职业) job 3(业务) work

公 gōng I [形] 1(非私有) public ▸公共 gōnggòng public 2(共识) general 3(公正) fair 4(雄性) male II [名] 1(公务) official business 2(敬) (老先生) ▸王公 Wáng gōng Mr Wang 3(丈夫的父亲) father-in-law ▸公公 gōnggong father-in-law

公安 gōng'ān [名] public security

公布 gōngbù [动] announce

公厕 gōngcè [名] public toilet

公尺 gōngchǐ [名] metre (英), meter (美)

公费 gōngfèi [名] public expense

公分 gōngfēn [名] centimetre (英), centimeter (美)

公共 gōnggòng [形] public

公共汽车 gōnggòng qìchē [名] bus

公共汽车站 gōnggòng qìchēzhàn [名] 1(指总站) bus station 2(指路边站) bus stop

公斤 gōngjīn [名] kilogram

公开 gōngkāi I [形] public II [动] make public

公里 gōnglǐ [名] kilometre (英), kilometer (美)

公路 gōnglù [名] motorway

公民 gōngmín [名] citizen

公平 gōngpíng [形] fair

公社 gōngshè [名] commune

公司 gōngsī [名] company

公用 gōngyòng [形] public

公寓 gōngyù [名] 1(旅馆) boarding house 2(楼房) flat (英), apartment (美)

公元 gōngyuán [名] A.D.

公园 gōngyuán [名] park

公正 gōngzhèng [形] impartial

公众 gōngzhòng [名] public

公主 gōngzhǔ [名] princess

功 gōng [名] 1(功劳) contribution 2(成效) achievement

功夫 gōngfu [名] martial arts

功课 gōngkè [名] homework

功劳 gōngláo [名] contribution

功能 gōngnéng [名] function ▸多功能电话 duōgōngnéng diànhuà multi-functional telephone

攻 gōng [动] (攻打) attack

攻击 gōngjī [动] (进攻) attack

供 gōng [动] 1(供应) supply 2(提供) provide

供给 gōngjǐ [动] supply

供求 gōngqiú [名] supply and demand

供应 gōngyìng [动] supply

宫 gōng [名] (皇宫) palace ▸宫殿 gōngdiàn palace

恭 gōng [形] respectful

恭维 gōngwéi [动] flatter

恭喜 gōngxǐ [动] congratulate

巩 gǒng *see below*/见下文

巩固 gǒnggù I [形] solid II [动] strengthen

共 gòng I [形] common II [动] share III [副] 1 (一齐) together 2 (总共) altogether IV [名] (also: 共产党) the communist party

共产党 gòngchǎndǎng [名] the communist party

共产主义 gòngchǎnzhǔyì [名] communism

共和国 gònghéguó [名] republic

共同 gòngtóng I [形] common II [副] together

贡 gòng [名] tribute

贡献 gòngxiàn I [动] devote II [名] contribution

沟 gōu [名] ditch

沟通 gōutōng [动] communicate

钩 gōu [名] 1 (钩子) hook 2 (符号) tick [动] 3 (用钩子挂) hook 4 (编织、缝) crochet

狗 gǒu [名] dog

构 gòu I [动] 1 (组成) compose 2 (结成) form 3 (建造) construct II [名] (结构) structure

构成 gòuchéng [动] 1 (造成) constitute 2 (组成) compose

构造 gòuzào [名] structure

购 gòu [动] buy

购买 gòumǎi [动] buy

购物 gòuwù [动] go shopping ▷她爱购物。Tā ài gòuwù. She likes shopping.

够 gòu I [形] enough ▷5个就够了。Wǔ gè jiù gòu le. Five is enough. II [动] reach

估 gū [动] guess

估计 gūjì [动] reckon

姑 gū [名] 1 (姑母) aunt 2 (丈夫的姐妹) sister-in-law

姑娘 gūniang [名] girl

姑姑 gūgu [名] aunt

孤 gū [形] (孤单) alone

孤单 gūdān [形] (寂寞) lonely

孤独 gūdú [形] solitary

孤儿 gū'ér [名] orphan

古 gǔ I [名] ancient times (PL) II [形] ancient

古代 gǔdài [名] antiquity

古典 gǔdiǎn I [名] classics (PL) II [形] classical

古董 gǔdǒng [名] (古代器物) antique

古迹 gǔjì [名] historic site

古老 gǔlǎo [形] ancient

股 gǔ I [名] 1 (指绳或线) strand 2 (股份) share II [量] (气体、气味) whiff

股票 gǔpiào [名] share

股市 gǔshì [名] stock market

骨 gǔ [名] bone

骨头 gǔtou [名] (字) bone

鼓 gǔ I [名] drum II [动] 1 ▸ 鼓掌 gǔzhǎng applaud 2 (凸起, 胀大) bulge ▸他鼓着嘴。Tā gǔ zhe zuǐ. He puffed his cheeks out. III [形] bulging ▸她的书包鼓鼓的。Tā de shūbāo gǔgǔ de. Her schoolbag was full to bursting.

鼓励 gǔlì [动] encourage

鼓舞 gǔwǔ I [动] inspire II [形] inspiring

固 gù I [形] strong ▸坚固 jiāngù solid ▸牢固 láogù firm II [副] (坚定) firmly

固定 gùdìng I [形] fixed II [动] fix

固体 gùtǐ [名] solid

固执 gùzhí [形] stubborn

故 gù [名] 1 (变故) incident 2 (原因) reason

故宫 gùgōng [名] the Forbidden City

故宫 gùgōng

As the largest collection of ancient wooden structures in the world, 故宫 gùgōng formed the imperial palaces of the Ming (1368–1644) and Qing (1644–1911) dynasties. It is located at what was once the exact centre of the old city of Beijing, just to the north of Tiananmen Square. It is now a major tourist attraction, both for the architecture of its 800-plus wooden buildings, and for the many artistic and cultural treasures which are housed within them. In 1987 it was declared a World Heritage Site by UNESCO.

故事 gùshì [名] story

故乡 gùxiāng [名] birthplace

故意 gùyì [副] deliberately

故障 gùzhàng [名] fault ▸这台机器出了故障。Zhè tái jīqì chū le gùzhàng. This machine is faulty.

顾 gù [动] 1 (看) look ▸回顾 huígù look back ▸环顾 huángù look around 2 (注意, 照管) attend to ▸照顾 zhàogù attend to

顾客 gùkè [名] customer

顾问 gùwèn [名] consultant

雇 gù [动] 1 (雇佣) employ 2 (租赁) hire

雇员 gùyuán [名] employee

雇主 gùzhǔ [名] employer

瓜 guā [名] (植) melon

刮 guā [动] 1 (指用刀) shave 2 (涂抹) smear 3 (风) blow

挂 guà [动] 1 (悬, 吊) hang 2 (中断电话) hang up

挂号 guàhào I [动] register II [形] registered ▸挂号信 guàhàoxìn registered mail

挂历 guàlì [名] calendar

褂 guà [名] gown ▸褂子 guàzi

gown

乖 guāi[形](听话) well-behaved

拐 guǎiI[名]1(拐杖) walking stick 2(拐角处) turn II[动]1(转变方向) turn ▷向左/右拐 xiàng zuǒ/yòu guǎi turn left 2(拐骗) swindle

拐卖 guǎimài[动] abduct and sell

怪 guàiI[形] strange II[动]1(觉得奇怪) be surprised 2(责怪) blame III[副](口) really IV[名] monster

怪不得 guàibude[连] no wonder

关 guānI[动]1(合拢) close 2(圈起来) imprison 3(停业) close down 4(中断,终止) turn ... off ▷关灯 guān dēng turn off the light 5(牵连) concern ▷这不关他的事。Zhè bù guān tā de shì.This matter does not concern him. II[名]1(守卫处所) pass 2(出入境收税处) customs (PL) ▷海关 hǎiguān customs (PL) 3(转折点) critical point 4(关联部分) ▷关节 guānjié joint ▷关键 guānjiàn key

关闭 guānbì[动]1(合拢) close 2(歇业或停办) close down

关怀 guānhuái[动] be concerned about

关税 guānshuì[名] customs duty

关系 guānxìI[名](联系) relation II[动] impact on

关心 guānxīn[动] be concerned about

关于 guānyú[介] on

关照 guānzhào[动](关心照顾) look after

关注 guānzhù[动] pay close attention to

观 guānI[动] look ▷围观 wéiguān gather round to watch ▷旁观 pángguān look on II[名] view

观察 guānchá[动] observe

观点 guāndiǎn[名] point of view

观看 guānkàn[动] watch

观念 guānniàn[名] concept

观众 guānzhòng[名] spectator

官 guān[名]1(公职人员) official 2(器官) organ

官司 guānsi[名] lawsuit

官员 guānyuán[名] official

管 guǎnI[名]1(管子) pipe ▷水管 shuǐguǎn water pipe ▷管子 guǎnzi tube 2(乐器) wind instrument ▷双簧管 shuānghuángguǎn oboe 3(管状物) tube II[动]1(负责) be in charge of 2(管辖) have jurisdiction over 3(管教) discipline 4(过问) interfere ▷这事不用你管。 Zhè shì bù yòng nǐ guǎn. It's no use you interfering in this. 5(保证) guarantee ▷管保 guǎnbǎo guarantee 6(提供) provide

管道 guǎndào[名] pipeline

管理 guǎnlǐ[动]1(负责) be in charge 2(保管) take care of 3(看管) keep guard over ▷企业管理 qǐyè guǎnlǐ business management

管用 guǎnyòng [形] effective

贯 guàn I [动] 1 (贯穿) pass through 2 (连贯) keep following II [名] ancestral home ▷籍贯 jíguàn place of origin

贯彻 guànchè [动] implement

贯穿 guànchuān [动] run through

冠 guàn I [动] crown II [名] crown

冠军 guànjūn [名] champion

惯 guàn [动] 1 (习惯) be used to ▷我吃西餐已经惯了。Wǒ chī xīcān yǐjīng guàn le. I'm already used to Western food. 2 (纵容) spoil ▷惯孩子 guàn háizi spoil the children

灌 guàn [动] 1 (灌溉) irrigate 2 (注入) pour ... into

罐 guàn I [名] 1 (盛茶叶, 糖等) jar 2 (易拉罐) can 3 (煤气) cylinder ▷煤气罐 méiqìguàn gas cylinder II [量] can ▷两罐啤酒 liǎng guàn píjiǔ two cans of beer ▷五罐苏打水 wǔ guàn sūdǎshuǐ five cans of soda water

罐头 guàntou [名] tin ▷金枪鱼罐头 jīnqiāngyú guàntou tinned tuna fish

光 guāng I [名] 1 (指物质) light ▷月光 yuèguāng moonlight ▷阳光 yángguāng sunlight 2 (景物) scenery ▷风光 fēngguāng scenery 3 (荣誉) glory ▷增光 zēngguāng bring glory II [动] 1 (光大) glorify (露出) bare III [形] 1 (光滑) smooth ▷光滑 guānghuá smooth 2 (露出) bare ▷光脚 guāngjiǎo barefooted 3 (穷尽) used up ▷钱都用光了。Qián dōu yòng guāng le. All the money's used up. IV [副] just ▷他光说不做。Tā guāng shuō bù zuò. He's all talk.

光临 guānglín [动] be present

光明 guāngmíng I [名] light II [形] bright

光盘 guāngpán [名] CD

光荣 guāngróng [形] glorious

光线 guāngxiàn [名] light

广 guǎng [形] 1 (宽阔) broad 2 (多) numerous

广播 guǎngbō [动] broadcast

广场 guǎngchǎng [名] square

广大 guǎngdà [形] 1 (宽广) vast 2 (众多) numerous

广泛 guǎngfàn [形] wide-ranging ▷广泛开展活动 guǎngfàn kāizhǎn huódòng initiate a wide range of activities

广告 guǎnggào [名] advertisement

广阔 guǎngkuò [形] broad

逛 guàng [动] stroll

归 guī [动] 1 (返回, 还给) return 2 (合并) group ... together ▷归类 guīlèi categorise 3 (属于) be under the charge of ▷这本书归他所有。Zhè běn shū guī tā suǒyǒu. This book belongs to him.

归功于 guīgōngyú [动] give credit to

归还 guīhuán [动] return

龟 guī [名] tortoise ▶乌龟 wūguī tortoise

规 guī [名] 1 (工具) compasses (PL) 2 (规则) rule

规定 guīdìng I [动] stipulate II [名] regulation

规范 guīfàn [名] standard ▶一定要规范市场秩序。yídìng yào guīfàn shìchǎng zhìxù We must standardize the market economy.

规矩 guīju I [名] norm II [形] well-behaved ▶他办事总是规矩。Tā bànshì zǒngshì guīju. He always plays by the rules.

规律 guīlǜ [名] law

规模 guīmó [名] scale

规则 guīzé I [名] regulation II [形] orderly

规章 guīzhāng [名] regulations (PL)

轨 guǐ [名] (轨道) rail ▶轨道 guǐdào track

鬼 guǐ [名] 1 (灵魂) ghost 2 (勾当) dirty trick 3 (不良行为者) ▶酒鬼 jiǔguǐ drunkard

鬼混 guǐhùn [动] hang around

鬼脸 guǐliǎn [名] grimace ▶做鬼脸 zuò guǐliǎn make a funny face

柜 guì [名] (柜子) cupboard ▶衣柜 yīguì wardrobe ▶保险柜 bǎoxiǎnguì safe

柜台 guìtái [名] counter

贵 guì [形] 1 (指价格) expensive 2 (值得珍视) valuable ▶贵宾 guìbīn VIP

贵重 guìzhòng [形] valuable

贵族 guìzú [名] aristocrat

跪 guì [动] kneel ▶跪下 guìxià kneel down

滚 gǔn I [动] 1 (滚动) roll ▶滚动 gǔndòng roll 2 (走开) get lost ▶滚烫 gǔntàng boiling hot II [形] 1 (滚动的) rolling 2 (沸腾的) boiling

棍 gùn [名] (棍子) stick ▶棍子 gùnzi stick

锅 guō [名] (指炊具) pot ▶炒菜锅 chǎocàiguō wok ▶火锅 huǒguō hotpot

国 guó I [名] country II [形] (国家) national ▶国徽 guóhuī national emblem ▶国歌 guógē national anthem ▶国旗 guóqí national flag

国产 guóchǎn [形] domestic

国画 guóhuà [名] traditional Chinese painting

国会 guóhuì [名] parliament

国籍 guójí [名] nationality

国际 guójì [形] international

国家 guójiā [名] state

国力 guólì [名] national strength

国民 guómín [名] citizen

国内 guónèi [形] domestic

国庆节 guóqìngjié [名] National Day

国庆节 guóqìngjié
(National Day) falls on 1 October, and commemorates the anniversary of the founding of the People's Republic of China in 1949. The PRC was declared by Chairman Mao Zedong, in Tiananmen Square in Beijing.

国王 guówáng [名] king

国务院 guówùyuàn [名] the State Council

国务院 guówùyuàn, the State Council, is the highest executive and administrative organ of the PRC government, headed by the Premier, and overseeing all the various ministries.

国营 guóyíng [形] state-run

果 guǒ [名] 1 (果子) fruit ▷果子 guǒzi fruit 2 (结局) outcome ▷效果 xiàoguǒ result ▷成果 chéngguǒ achievement

果断 guǒduàn [形] resolute

果然 guǒrán [副] really

果实 guǒshí [名] 1 (果子) fruit

2 (成果) fruits (PL)

果真 guǒzhēn [副] really

裹 guǒ [动] (缠绕) wrap

过 guò I [动] 1 (经过) pass through 2 (度过) spend ▷你假期怎么过的? Nǐ jiàqī zěnme guò de? How did you spend your holiday? 3 (过去) pass 4 (超过) be more than ▷年过半百 nián guò bàn bǎi over fifty years old 5 (生活) live ▷我们过得很好。Wǒmen guò de hěn hǎo. We live well. 6 (庆祝) celebrate ▷过生日 guò shēngrì celebrate a birthday II [名] fault III [介] past ▷现在是9点8分。Xiànzài shì jiǔ diǎn guò bā fēn. It is now eight minutes past nine.

When 过 guò is used as a verb suffix to indicate a past action, it often corresponds to the present perfect tense (e.g. 'I have done') in English, stressing that the subject has experienced something, e.g. 我去过中国三次 Wǒ qùguo Zhōngguó sān cì (I have been to China three times).

过程 guòchéng [名] process

过道 guòdào [名] corridor

过分 guòfèn [形] excessive

过后 guòhòu [副] later

过奖 guòjiǎng [动] flatter ▷您过奖了。Nín guòjiǎng le. I'm flattered.

过来 guòlái [动] come over

过滤 guòlǜ [动] filter

过敏 guòmǐn [名] (医) allergy

过期 guòqī [动] expire

过年 guònián [动] celebrate the new year

过去 guòqù [名] the past

过去 guòqu [动] pass by

过日子 guò rìzi [动] live

过时 guòshí [形] outdated

过世 guòshì [动] pass away

过头 guòtóu [形] excessive

过瘾 guòyǐn [动] do to one's heart's content

过于 guòyú [副] too

h

哈 hā I [叹] aha II [拟] ha ha ▷哈哈大笑 hā hā dàxiào roar with laughter

还 hái [副] 1 (仍旧) still, yet ▷那家老饭店还很兴旺。Nà jiā lǎo fàndiàn hái hěn xīngwàng. The old restaurant is still thriving. ▷她还没回来。Tā hái méi huílái. She hasn't come back yet. 2 (更加) even more
→ see also/另见 huán

还是 háishì I [副] 1 (仍然) still 2 (最好) had better ▷你还是先完成作业吧。Nǐ háishì xiān wánchéng zuòyè ba. You'd better finish your homework first. II [连] or ▷你是去巴黎还是去伦敦？Nǐ shì qù Bālí háishì qù Lúndūn? Are you going to Paris or London?

孩 hái [名] child

孩子 háizi [名] child

海 hǎi [名] (海洋) ocean ▸地中海 Dìzhōnghǎi the Mediterranean Sea

海边 hǎibiān [名] coast

海拔 hǎibá [名] elevation

海报 hǎibào [名] poster

海滨 hǎibīn [名] seaside

海关 hǎiguān [名] customs (PL)

海军 hǎijūn [名] the navy

海绵 hǎimián [名] sponge

海滩 hǎitān [名] beach

海峡 hǎixiá [名] strait

海鲜 hǎixiān [名] seafood

海洋 hǎiyáng [名] ocean

害 hài [动] 1 (损害) harm 2 (杀害) kill II [名] harm ▸害处 hàichu harm III [形] harmful ▸害虫 hàichóng pest

害怕 hàipà [动] be afraid

害羞 hàixiū [动] be shy

含 hán [动] 1 (用嘴) keep ... in the mouth 2 (包含) contain

含量 hánliàng [名] content

含义 hányì [名] meaning

寒 hán [形] (冷) cold ▸寒风 hánfēng chilly wind

寒假 hánjià [名] winter holiday

寒冷 hánlěng [形] cold

韩 hán [名] see below/见下文

韩国 Hánguó [名] South Korea

喊 hǎn [动] 1 (大声叫) shout ▸喊叫 hǎnjiào cry out 2 (叫) call

汉 hàn [名] (汉族) the Han (PL) ▸汉人 Hànrén the Han people (PL)

汉语 Hànyǔ [名] Chinese

汉字 Hànzì [名] Chinese characters (PL)

汉族 Hànzú [名] the Han (PL)

汗 hàn [名] sweat ▸汗水 hànshuǐ sweat

旱 hàn [形] dry ▸旱灾 hànzāi drought

行 háng I [名] 1 (行列) row ▸第一行 dìyī háng first row 2 (行业) profession ▸同行 tóngháng people in the same profession II [量] line ▸一行字 yī háng zì a line of words
→ see also/另见 xíng

行业 hángyè [名] industry

航 háng [动] 1 (指船) sail 2 (指飞机) fly

航班 hángbān [名] (指客机) scheduled flight

航空 hángkōng [动] fly ▸航空信 hángkōngxìn airmail ▸航空公司 hángkōng gōngsī airline

毫 háo [名] (千分之一) ▸毫米 háomǐ millimetre (英), millimeter (美) ▸毫升 háoshēng millilitre (英), milliliter (美)

毫不 háobù [副] not at all

毫无 háowú [副] without the slightest

豪 háo [形] grand ▶豪华 háohuá luxurious

好 hǎo I [形] 1 (令人满意) good ▷他脾气好。Tā píqi hǎo. He's good-natured. 2 (容易) easy ▷这事不好办。Zhè shì bù hǎo bàn. This won't be easy to manage. 3 (健康) well ▷你身体好吗？Nǐ shēntǐ hǎo ma? Are you keeping well? 4 (亲密) good ▷我们是好朋友。Wǒmen shì hǎo péngyou. We're good friends. 5 (表示问候) ▷你好！Nǐ hǎo! Hello! ▷大家好。Dàjiā hǎo. Hello everyone. 6 (表示完成) ▷工作找好了。Gōngzuò zhǎo hǎo le. I've found work. ▷衣服洗好了。Yīfu xǐ hǎo le. The clothes have been washed. ▷表示答应，结束等) ▷好，我们现在就去！Hǎo, wǒmen xiànzài jiù qù! OK, let's go then! II [副] 1 (强调多或久) ▷我等了好久她才来。Wǒ děng le hǎo jiǔ tā cái lái. I'd waited for a long time before she arrived. 2 (表示程度深) ▷他话说得好快。Tā huà shuō de hǎo kuài. He speaks so quickly. III [名] (问候) regards (PL) ▷请代我向你太太问好。Qǐng dài wǒ xiàng nǐ tàitai wènhǎo. Please send my regards to your wife.
→ see also/另见 hào

好吃 hǎochī [形] delicious

好处 hǎochu [名] 1 (益处) benefit 2 (利益) profit

好久 hǎojiǔ [副] for a long time

好看 hǎokàn [形] 1 (漂亮) nice-looking 2 (精彩) good ▷这本书很好看。Zhè běn shū hěn hǎokàn. This book is very good.

好受 hǎoshòu [形] comfortable

好容易 hǎoróngyì [副] with great effort

好听 hǎotīng [形] 1 (指声音，音乐) lovely 2 (指言语) nice

好玩儿 hǎowánr [形] fun

好像 hǎoxiàng [副] apparently

好笑 hǎoxiào [形] funny

好些 hǎoxiē [形] quite a great deal of

号 hào I [名] 1 (名称) name ▶外号 wàihào nickname 2 (商店) firm ▶商号 shānghào firm 3 (标记) sign ▶逗号 dòuhào comma 4 (次序) number 5 (日期) date ▷6月1号 liùyuè yī hào the first of June 6 (大小) size 7 (乐器) brass instrument ▶小号 xiǎohào trumpet II [动] (脉) take ▶号脉 hàomài take a pulse

号码 hàomǎ [名] number

号召 hàozhào [动] appeal

好 hào [动] 1 (喜爱) like 2 (容易) be easy
→ see also/另见 hǎo

好奇 hàoqí [形] curious

喝 hē [动] drink

合 hé [动] **1**(闭) close **2**(合在一起)join ▶合资 hézī joint venture **3**(折合) be equal to **4**(符合) tally with

合并 hébìng [动] merge

合唱 héchàng [名] chorus

合法 héfǎ [形] legal

合格 hégé [形] qualified

合理 hélǐ [形] rational

合身 héshēn [形] fitted

合适 héshì [形] appropriate

合算 hésuàn [动] be worthwhile

合同 hétong [名] contract

合作 hézuò [动] cooperate

何 hé [代](什么) ▶何时 héshí when ▶何人 hérén who ▶何地 hédì where

和 hé I [连] and II [介] with ▷这事和你没关系。 Zhè shì hé nǐ méi guānxì. This has nothing to do with you. III [名](总数) total IV [动] draw ▷这场比赛和了。 Zhè chǎng bǐsài hé le. The match was a draw.

和蔼 hé'ǎi [形] affable

和好 héhǎo [动] reconcile

和睦 hémù [形] harmonious

和平 hépíng [名](指战争) peace

和气 héqì I [形] polite II [名] peace

和数 héshù [名] sum

河 hé [名](河) river

核 hé [名](指水果) stone

盒 hé [名] box

盒子 hézi [名] box

贺 hè [动] congratulate

贺卡 hèkǎ [名] greetings card

黑 hēi [形] **1**(指颜色) black ▶黑板 hēibǎn blackboard **2**(暗) dark **3**(秘密) secret ▶黑市 hēishì black market **4**(反动) ▶黑社会 hēishèhuì gangland ▶黑手党 hēishǒudǎng the Mafia

黑暗 hēi'àn [形] **1**(指光线) dark **2**(腐败) corrupt

黑人 hēirén [名] black person

很 hěn [副] very

恨 hèn [动] **1**(憎恶) hate **2**(后悔) regret

哼 hēng [动](唱) hum

横 héng I [名] horizontal II [形] **1**(竖,线,行) horizontal **2**(左右向) sideways ▶横躺 héngtǎng lie sideways **3**(指横截) across ▶人行横道 rénxíng héngdào zebra crossing III [动] turn ... lengthways

红 hóng I [形] **1**(指颜色) red ▶红旗 hóngqí red flag ▶红十字会 Hóngshízìhuì the Red Cross **2**(形容受欢迎) popular ▶走红 zǒuhóng be popular ▶红人 hóngrén rising star **3**(形容成功) successful ▶红运 hóngyùn lucky **II** [名](红利) bonus ▶分红 fēnhóng get a bonus

红茶 hóngchá [名] black tea

红绿灯 hónglùdēng [名] traffic lights (PL)

红色 hóngsè [形] red

洪 hóng [名] (指洪水) flood ▷洪水 hóngshuǐ flood

喉 hóu [名] throat

喉咙 hóulong [名] throat

猴 hóu [名] monkey

猴子 hóuzi [名] monkey

后 hòu [名] 1 (背面) the back ▷房后有个车库。Fánghòu yǒu gè chēkù. At the back of the house is a garage. 2 (指时间) ▷后天 hòutiān the day after tomorrow 3 (指次序) the last ▷后排 hòupái the last row

后边 hòubian [名] back

后代 hòudài [名] 1 (指时代) later generations (PL) 2 (子孙) offspring

后果 hòuguǒ [名] consequence

后悔 hòuhuǐ [动] regret

后来 hòulái [副] afterwards ▷我后来再也没有见过他。Wǒ hòulái zài yě méi jiànguo tā. I didn't see him again after that.

后门 hòumén [名] back door

后面 hòumiàn I [名] back II [副] later

后年 hòunián [名] the year after next

后退 hòutuì [动] retreat

厚 hòu [形] 1 (书,衣服,脸皮) thick 2 (雪,土) deep 3 (指感情) profound

厚道 hòudao [形] kind

呼 hū [动] 1 (排气) exhale 2 (喊) shout ▷呼喊 hūhǎn shout 3 (叫) call ▷呼叫 hūjiào call ▷呼救 hūjiù call for help

呼机 hūjī [名] pager

呼噜 hūlu [名] (口) snore

呼吸 hūxī [动] breathe

忽 hū [副] suddenly

忽然 hūrán [副] suddenly

忽视 hūshì [动] ignore

狐 hú see below/见下文

狐狸 húli [名] fox

胡 hú I [名] 1 (髭) moustache (英), mustache (美) 2 (长在下颚, 两腮) beard II [副] recklessly

胡乱 húluàn [副] 1 (随便) casually 2 (任意) wilfully

胡闹 húnào [动] play around

胡说 húshuō [动] talk nonsense

胡同 hútòng [名] lane

胡子 húzi [名] 1 (髭) moustache (英), mustache (美) 2 (指长在下颚, 两腮) beard

壶 hú [名] pot

湖 hú [名] lake

蝴 hú see below/见下文

蝴蝶 húdié [名] butterfly

糊 hú [动] paste

糊里糊涂 húlǐhútú confused

糊涂 hútu [形] 1 (不明白)

confused **2** (混乱) chaotic

虎 hǔ [名] tiger

互 hù [副] mutually

互联网 hùliánwǎng [名] the Internet

互相 hùxiāng [副] mutually

户 hù [名] **1** (门) door **2** (住户) family **2** (户头) bank account ▸ 账户 zhànghù account

户口 hùkǒu [名] (户籍) registered permanent residence

护 hù [动] (保护) protect

护士 hùlì [动] nurse

护士 hùshi [名] nurse

护照 hùzhào [名] passport

花 huā I [名] **1** (指植物) flower **2** (烟火) fireworks (PL) II [形] **1** (多彩) multi-coloured (英), multi-colored (美) **2** (有花的) floral ▸ 花篮 huālán flower basket **3** (模糊) blurred ▸ 头昏眼花 tóuyūn yǎnhuā muddle-headed and bleary-eyed **4** (虚假) superficial ▸ 花招 huāzhāo trick III [动] spend ▸ 花钱 huā qián spend money ▸ 花工夫 huā gōngfu put in effort

花费 huāfèi [动] spend ▸ 留学的花费很大。 liúxué de huāfèi hěn dà. It's very expensive to study abroad.

花生 huāshēng [名] peanut

花纹 huāwén [名] decorative design

花园 huāyuán [名] garden

花招 huāzhāo [名] trick

划 huá [动] **1** (拨水) row **2** (合算) be worthwhile ▸ 划不来 huábulái not worth it **3** (擦) scratch → see also/另见 huà

华 huá [名] China ▸ 华人 huárén Chinese person

华丽 huálì [形] resplendent

华侨 huáqiáo [名] overseas Chinese

华人 huárén [名] Chinese

滑 huá I [形] **1** (光滑) slippery **2** (油滑) crafty II [动] slip

滑冰 huábīng [动] ice skate

滑动 huádòng [动] slide

滑稽 huájī [形] comical

滑坡 huápō [动] **1** (字) slide **2** (喻) drop

滑雪 huáxuě [动] ski

化 huà I [名] chemistry ▸ 化肥 huàféi chemical fertilizer II [动] **1** (变化) change ▸ 化装 huàzhuāng disguise oneself **2** (消化) digest

化工 huàgōng [名] chemical industry

化石 huàshí [名] fossil

化学 huàxué [名] chemistry

化验 huàyàn [动] test

化妆 huàzhuāng [动] make oneself up

划 huà [动] **1** (划分) demarcate

▶划分 huàfēn divide 2 (划拨) transfer 3 (计划) plan
→ see also/另见 huá

画 huà I [动] 1 (用铅笔) draw 2 (用刷状) paint II [名] 1 (用铅笔) drawing 2 (用刷状, 笔画) painting ▶油画 yóuhuà oil painting 2 (笔画) stroke III [形] painted

画报 huàbào [名] pictorial

画家 huàjiā [名] painter

画像 huàxiàng [名] portrait

画展 huàzhǎn [名] art exhibition

话 huà I [名] words (PL) ▶说话 shuōhuà talk ▶对话 duìhuà conversation ▶谎话 huǎnghuà lie II [动] talk about ▶话旧 huàjiù reminisce

话剧 huàjù [名] stage play

话题 huàtí [名] subject

怀 huái I [名] 1 (胸前) bosom 2 (胸怀) mind II [动] 1 (思念) think of 2 (存有) keep ... in mind 3 (有孕) become pregnant

怀念 huáiniàn [动] yearn for

怀疑 huáiyí [动] 1 (认为是真) suspect 2 (认为不可能) doubt

怀孕 huáiyùn [动] be pregnant

坏 huài I [形] 1 (不好) bad 2 (程度深) extreme II [动] go off ▷空调坏了。Kōngtiáo huài le. The air-conditioning has broken down. III [名] dirty trick

坏处 huàichu [名] harm

坏蛋 huàidàn [名] (讳) bastard

坏话 huàihuà [名] (不利的话) bad words (PL)

欢 huān [形] 1 (快乐) happy 2 (活跃) vigorous

欢呼 huānhū [动] cheer

欢快 huānkuài [形] cheerful

欢乐 huānlè [形] joyful

欢心 huānxīn [名] favour (英), favor (美)

欢迎 huānyíng [动] welcome ▷欢迎来中国。Huānyíng lái Zhōngguó. Welcome to China.

还 huán [动] 1 (回) return 2 (归还) return ▶还债 huánzhài repay a debt 3 (回报) repay ▶还价 huánjià haggle ▶还击 huánjī fight back
→ see also/另见 hái

环 huán [名] 1 (圆圈) ring ▶耳环 ěrhuán earring 2 (环节) element ▶环节 huánjié element II [动] surround

环保 huánbǎo [名] (also: 环境保护 huánjìng bǎohù) environmental protection

环境 huánjìng [名] environment ▷生活环境 shēnghuó huánjìng living conditions (PL)

环绕 huánrào [动] surround

缓 huǎn I [形] 1 (慢) slow 2 (缓和) relaxed II [动] 1 (推迟) delay 2 (恢复) revive

缓慢 huǎnmàn [形] slow

幻 huàn [形] unreal

幻想 huànxiǎng I [动] dream II [名] fantasy

换 huàn [动] 1(交换) exchange 2(更换) replace

唤 huàn [名] summon

唤醒 huànxǐng [动] (叫醒) wake up

患 huàn I [动] 1(害) suffer from ▶患者 huànzhě sufferer 2(忧虑) worry II [名] trouble

荒 huāng [形] 1(荒芜) waste 2(荒凉) desolate 3(短缺) short 4(荒歉) famine

慌 huāng [形] nervous

慌忙 huāngmáng [形] hurried

慌张 huāngzhāng [形] nervous

皇 huáng [名] emperor ▶皇帝 huángdì emperor ▶皇后 huánghòu empress

皇宫 huánggōng [名] palace

黄 huáng I [形] 1(指颜色) yellow 2(色情) pornographic II [名] 1(蛋黄) yolk 2(黄金) gold

黄瓜 huángguā [名] cucumber

黄河 Huánghé [名] Yellow River

黄昏 huánghūn [名] dusk

黄金 huángjīn [名] gold

黄色 huángsè [名] 1(指颜色) yellow 2(色情) pornographic

黄油 huángyóu [名] butter

谎 huǎng [名] lie

谎言 huǎngyán [名] lie

晃 huàng [动] shake

晃动 huàngdòng [动] rock

灰 huī I [名] 1(灰烬) ash 2(尘土) dust 3(石灰) lime II [动] (消沉) be disheartened ▶灰暗 huī'àn gloomy

灰尘 huīchén [名] dust

灰色 huīsè [名] (指颜色) grey(英), gray(美)

灰心 huīxīn [动] lose heart

恢 huī [形] vast

恢复 huīfù [动] recover

挥 huī [动] 1(挥舞) wave 2(抹掉) wipe ... away 3(指挥) command 4(散出) scatter ▶挥发 huīfā evaporate

回 huí I [动] 1(旋转) circle 2(还) return 3(掉转) turn around ▶回头 huítóu turn one's head 4(答复) reply ▶回信 huíxìn reply to a letter II [量] 1(次数) time ▶我去过两回。Wǒ qùguo liǎng huí. I have been there twice. 2(章) chapter

回报 huíbào [动] (报答) repay

回避 huíbì [动] avoid

回答 huídá [动] answer

回复 huífù [动] (答复) reply

回顾 huígù [动] look back

回合 huíhé [名] round

回话 huíhuà [动] reply

回扣 huíkòu [名] commission

回教 Huíjiào [名] Islam

回来 huílái [动] come back

回去 huíqù [动] go back

回声 huíshēng [名] echo

回收 huíshōu [动] 1 (再利用) recycle 2 (收回) retrieve

回信 huíxìn [动] write in reply

回忆 huíyì [动] recall

毁 huǐ [动] 1 (破坏) destroy 2 (诽谤) defame

毁坏 huǐhuài [动] destroy

汇 huì I [动] 1 (汇合) converge 2 (聚集) gather 3 (划拨) transfer II [名] 1 (外汇) foreign exchange 2 (聚集物) collection ▶词汇 cíhuì vocabulary

汇报 huìbào [动] report

汇集 huìjí [动] collect

汇率 huìlǜ [名] exchange rate

会 huì I [动] 1 (聚合) assemble 2 (见面) meet ▶会客 huìkè receive a guest 3 (理解) understand ▶领会 lǐnghuì understand 4 (通晓) be able to ▶会武术 huì wǔshù be able to do martial arts II [助动] 1 (能做) can ▶我不会下象棋。Wǒ bùhuì xià xiàngqí. I can't play chess. 2 (擅长) ▶会过日子 huì guò rìzi know how to economize 3 (可能) might ▶明天会更热。Míngtiān huì gèng rè. Tomorrow might be hotter. III [名] 1 (集会) gathering 2 (团体) association ▶学生会 xuéshēnghuì student union 3 (城市) city ▶大都

会 dàdūhuì metropolis 4 (时机) opportunity ▶机会 jīhuì opportunity

→ see also/另见 kuài

Both 会 huì and 要 yào can be used to express the future tense. 会 huì is usually used to express a possible or probable outcome, e.g. 明天会下雨 míngtiān huì xiàyǔ (it might rain tomorrow); 要 yào refers to something definite, e.g. 我明天要上班 wǒ míngtiān yào shàngbān (I am going to work tomorrow). 会 huì, 能 néng, and 可以 kěyǐ can all be used to express ability and are sometimes used interchangeably. Strictly, 会 huì should express a learned ability, e.g. 我会说法语 wǒ huì shuō Fǎyǔ (I can speak French), while 能 néng should be used to express physical ability, e.g. 我能跑得很快 wǒ néng pǎo de hěn kuài (I can run very fast).

会话 huìhuà [动] converse

会见 huìjiàn [动] meet

会谈 huìtán [动] hold talks

会议 huìyì [名] 1 (集会) meeting 2 (机构) council

会员 huìyuán [名] member

贿 huì [名] bribe ▶贿赂 huìlù bribe

昏 hūn I [名] dusk II [形] 1 (黑暗) dark ▷昏暗 hūn'àn dim 2 (迷糊) muddled III [动] faint

昏迷 hūnmí [动] be unconscious

荤 hūn [名] meat

婚 hūn I [名] marriage II [动] marry

婚礼 hūnlǐ [名] wedding ceremony

婚姻 hūnyīn [名] marriage

浑 hún [形] 1 (浑浊) muddy 2 (糊涂) muddled

浑蛋 húndàn [名] (讳) bastard

浑身 húnshēn [副] from head to toe

浑浊 húnzhuó [形] murky

馄 hún see below/见下文

馄饨 húntún [名] wonton

馄饨 húntún

In Chinese cooking, 馄饨 húntún is a kind of dumpling filled with spiced minced meat and other ingredients such as chopped mushrooms, shrimps etc. It is usually served in the soup in which it is cooked. The English name for 馄饨 comes from the Cantonese pronunciation, wantan.

魂 hún [名] (灵魂) soul

混 hùn I [动] 1 (搀杂) mix 2 (蒙混) pass off ... as 3 (苟且生活) drift ▷混日子 hùn rìzi drift through the days II [副] aimlessly

混合 hùnhé [动] mix

混乱 hùnluàn [形] 1 (无秩序) chaotic 2 (无条理) disordered

混淆 hùnxiáo [动] confuse

活 huó I [动] 1 (生存) live 2 (使生存) keep ... alive II [形] 1 (有生命) alive 2 (不固定) flexible 3 (不死板) lively 4 (逼真) lifelike III [副] completely IV [名] 1 (工作) work 2 (产品) product

活动 huódòng I [动] 1 (运动) take exercise 2 (行动) operate 3 (动用关系) use connections II [名] activity III [形] movable

活该 huógāi [动] (口) serve ... right

活力 huólì [名] vitality

活泼 huópō [形] lively

活期 huóqī [形] current ▷活期账号 huóqī zhànghào current account

活跃 huóyuè [动] 1 (使有生气) invigorate 2 (积极从事) be active

火 huǒ I [名] 1 (火焰) fire 2 (枪支弹药) ammunition 3 (医) (指内火) internal heat 4 (喻) (愤怒) rage II [动] be in a rage III [形] 1 (红色) flaming red ▷火红 huǒhóng flaming red 2 (兴旺) prosperous

火柴 huǒchái [名] match

火车 huǒchē [名] train

火鸡 huǒjī [名] turkey

火警 huǒjǐng [名] fire alarm

火山 huǒshān [名] volcano

火腿 huǒtuǐ [名] ham

火焰 huǒyàn [名] flame

火药 huǒyào [名] gunpowder

伙 huǒ I [名] 1 (同伴) companion 2 (指集体) partnership 3 (伙食) meals (PL) II [量] group

伙伴 huǒbàn [名] companion

伙食 huǒshí [名] meals (PL)

或 huò [连] or

或许 huòxǔ [副] perhaps

或者 huòzhě I [副] maybe II [连] or

货 huò [名] 1 (货币) currency 2 (货物) goods (PL) 3 (人) person ▸ 蠢货 chǔnhuò idiot

货币 huòbì [名] currency

货物 huòwù [名] goods (PL)

祸 huò [名] I [名] misfortune II [动] harm

几 jī [名] small table ▸ 茶几 chájī tea table

→ see also/另见 jǐ

几乎 jīhū [副] almost

讥 jī [动] mock

讥笑 jīxiào [动] jeer

饥 jī [形] hungry [名] famine

饥饿 jī'è [形] starving

机 jī I [名] 1 (机器) machine ▸ 发动机 fādòngjī engine 2 (飞机) aeroplane (英), airplane (美) ▸ 客机 kèjī airliner 3 (枢纽) pivot ▸ 转机 zhuǎnjī turning point 4 (机会) opportunity 5 (机能) 有机体 yǒujītǐ organism II [形] quick-witted ▸ 机智 jīzhì ingenious

机场 jīchǎng [名] airport

机关 jīguān [名] **1**(部门) department **2**(机械) mechanism

机会 jīhuì [名] opportunity

机灵 jīling [形] clever

机器 jīqì [名] machine

机械 jīxiè I [名] machinery II [形] rigid

机遇 jīyù [名] opportunity

肌 jī [名] muscle

肌肉 jīròu [名] muscle

鸡 jī [名] chicken ▸公鸡 gōngjī cock ▸母鸡 mǔjīhen

鸡蛋 jīdàn [名] egg

积 jī I [动] accumulate II [形] long-standing III [名] (数) product

积极 jījí [形] **1**(肯定的) positive **2**(热心的) active

积极性 jījíxìng [名] positive attitude

积累 jīlěi [动] accumulate

积蓄 jīxù I [动] save II [名] savings (PL)

基 jī I [名] base II [形] primary ▸基层 jīcéng grass roots

基本 jīběn [形] **1**(根本) basic **2**(主要) essential **3**(基础) elementary II [副] basically

基础 jīchǔ I [名] foundation II [形] basic

基督教 jīdūjiào [名] Christianity

基金 jījīn [名] fund

激 jī I [动] **1**(涌起) surge **2**(刺激)

catch a chill **3**(唤起) excite **4**(冰) chill II [形] violent

激动 jīdòng [动] excite ▸激动的孩子 jīdòng de háizi excited child ▸令人激动的电影 lìng rén jīdòng de diànyǐng exciting film

激光 jīguāng [名] laser

激烈 jīliè [形] intense

及 jí I [动] **1**(到达) reach **2**(比得上) be as good as **3**(赶上) be in time for II [连] and

及格 jígé [动] pass

及时 jíshí I [形] timely II [副] without delay

级 jí I [名] **1**(等级) level **2**(年级) year (英), grade (美) **3**(台阶) step II [量] step ▸100多级台阶 yìbǎi duō jí táijiē a staircase of more than 100 steps

极 jí I [名] **1**(顶点) extreme **2**(指地球或磁极) pole ▸南极 nánjí the South Pole II [动] go to an extreme III [形] extreme ▸极限 jíxiàn limit IV [副] very

极其 jíqí [副] extremely

即 jí I [动] **1**(书) (就是) mean **2**(靠近) approach **3**(到) ▸即位 jíwèi ascend the throne **4**(就着) ▸即兴演唱 jíxìng yǎnchàng ad-lib II [形] present ▸即日 jírì this very day III [副] immediately

即将 jíjiāng [副] soon

即使 jíshǐ [连] even if

急 jí I [形] **1**(着急) anxious **2**(急躁) impatient **3**(猛烈) ▸水流急

shuǐliú hěn jí.There's a strong current. **4**(紧急) urgent **II**[名] priority **III**[动] worry

急救 jíjiù [动] give first-aid

急忙 jímáng [副] hurriedly

急诊 jízhěn [名] emergency treatment

集 jí **I**[动] gather **II**[名] **1**(集市) market ▶赶集 gǎnjí go to market **2**(集子) anthology ▶诗集 shījí an anthology of poems **3**(册) part

集合 jíhé [动] assemble

集体 jítǐ [名] collective

集团 jítuán [名] group

集中 jízhōng [动] concentrate

几 jǐ [数] **1**(用于疑问句) ▶昨天来了几位客人? Zuótiān lái le jǐ wèi kèrén? How many customers came yesterday? **2**(用于陈述句) ▶几本书 jǐ běn shū several books ▶十几本书 shíjǐ běn shū more than ten books ▶几十本书 jǐshí běn shū several tens of books ▷ see also/另见 jī

己 jǐ [名] self ▶自己 zìjǐ oneself

挤 jǐ [动] **1**(拥挤) crowd **2**(事情, 会议, 约会) be close **3**(推人) elbow one's way **4**(贬)(指社交) push one's way **5**(牙膏, 颜料) squeeze ... out 挤奶 jǐnǎi milk **6**(时间) make **7**(排斥) rob ... of

计 jì **I**[动] **1**(核算) calculate ▶共计 gòngjì total **2**(计谋) plan **3**(考虑) bother **II**[名] **1**(计谋) strategy

2(测量仪器) gauge ▶温度计 wēndùjì thermometer

计划 jìhuà **I**[名] plan **II**[动] plan

计算 jìsuàn [动] **1**(数) calculate **2**(筹划) plan **3**(暗算) scheme

计算机 jìsuànjī [名] computer

计算器 jìsuànqì [名] calculator

记 jì **I**[动] **1**(指往事) remember **2**(写) record **II**[名] **1**(指事或文章) record ▶游记 yóujì travel journal ▶日记 rìjì diary **2**(标志) mark **3**(指皮肤) birthmark

记得 jìde [动] remember

记号 jìhao [名] mark

记录 jìlù **I**[动] (写下) write ... down **II**[名] **1**(材料) record **2**(指人) secretary **3**(成绩) record

记忆 jìyì **I**[动] remember **II**[名] memory

记者 jìzhě [名] journalist

纪 jì **I**[名] **1**age ▶中世纪 zhōngshìjì the Middle Ages (PL) **2**(指地质) period ▶侏罗纪 zhūluójì the Jurassic period **3**(纪律) discipline ▶军纪 jūnjì record

纪律 jìlǜ [名] discipline

纪念 jìniàn **I**[动] commemorate **II**[名] memento

技 jì [名] **1**(技艺) skill ▶技能 jìnéng skill ▶技巧 jìqiǎo technique **2**(本领) ability ▶绝技 juéjì unique ability

技巧 jìqiǎo [名] technique

技术 jìshù [名] technology

技术员 jìshùyuán [名] technician

季 jì [名] season ▶春季 chūnjì spring ▶旺季 wàngjì busy season

季节 jìjié [名] season

既 jì I [副] already ▶既定 jìdìng fixed II [连] (表示兼而有之) ▶他既高又壮。Tā jì gāo yòu zhuàng. He's tall and strong. 2 (既然) since

既然 jìrán [连] since

继 jì I [副] 1 (接续) continuously ▶继任 jìrèn succeed to a post 2 (接连) successively ▶相继 xiāngjì one after another II [动] continue

继承 jìchéng [动] 1 (遗产, 文化等) inherit 2 (遗志, 未竟事业) take ... on

继续 jìxù I [动] continue II [名] continuation

寄 jì [动] 1 (邮递) post (英), mail (美) 2 (付托) place 3 (依附) depend on

加 jiā [动] 1 (相加) ▶2加2等于4。Èr jiā èr děngyú sì. Two plus two is four. 2 (增加) increase 3 (添加) add

加工 jiāgōng [动] 1 (制作) process 2 (完善) polish

加拿大 Jiānádà [名] Canada

加强 jiāqiáng [动] strengthen

加油 jiāyóu [动] 1 (加燃料) refuel 2 (加劲儿) make more effort ▶快, 加油! Kuài, jiāyóu! Come on, come on!

夹 jiā I [动] 1 (钳) get hold of 2 (携带) carry 3 (夹在腋下) ... under one's arm 4 (限制) ▶两边高楼夹着一条狭窄的街道。Liǎngbiān gāolóu jiāzhe yī tiáo xiázhǎi de jiēdào. A narrow street hemmed in by tall buildings on either side. 4 (带) mix ... with II [名] folder

家 jiā I [名] 1 (家庭) family 2 (住所) home 3 (学派) school of thought 4 (指人) ▶船家 chuánjiā boatman ▶农家 nóngjiā peasant ▶专家 zhuānjiā expert II [形] 1 (饲养的) domestic ▶家畜 jiāchù domestic animal 2 (嫡亲的) ▶家兄 jiāxiōng elder brother III [量] ▶一家公司 yī jiā gōngsī a company ▷两家人 liǎng jiā rén two families measure word, used for families, companies, banks, factories, restaurants, hotels etc.

家伙 jiāhuo [名] 1 (工具) tool 2 (武器) weapon 3 (人) guy

家具 jiājù [名] furniture

家庭 jiātíng [名] family

家务 jiāwù [名] housework

家乡 jiāxiāng [名] hometown

家长 jiāzhǎng [名] 1 (一家之长) head of the family 2 (父母) parent

假 jiǎ I [形] 1 (虚伪) false 2 (不真) artificial ▶假发 jiǎfà wig 3 (借) ▶假话 jiǎhuà lie II [连] if ▶假如 jiǎrú if

→ see also/另见 jià

假如 jiǎrú [连] if

假设 jiǎshè I [动] suppose II [名] hypothesis

假装 jiǎzhuāng [动] pretend

介 jià [名] 1 (价格) price ▸ 物价 wùjiàjià price 2 (价值) value

价格 jiàgé [名] price

价钱 jiàqin [名] price

价值 jiàzhí [名] value

驾 jià I [动] 1 (驾驭) harness 2 (驾驶) drive II [代] (敬) ▸ 劳驾 láojià excuse me

驾驶 jiàshǐ [动] steer

驾照 jiàzhào [名] driving licence (英), driver's license (美)

架 jià I [名] 1 (架子) frame ▸ 书架 shūjià bookshelf ▸ 脚手架 jiǎoshǒujià scaffolding 2 (指行为) ▸ 吵架 chǎojià quarrel ▸ 打架 dǎjià fight II [动] 1 (撑起) support 2 (招架) ward ... off 3 (绑架) kidnap 4 (挽扶) support ... under the arm III [量] 1 ▸ 5架飞机 wǔ jià fēijī five planes ▸ 一架钢琴 yī jià gāngqín a piano

measure word, used for pianos, aircrafts, machines etc.

驾 jià [名] holiday ▸ 暑假 shǔjià summer holiday ▸ 病假 bìngjià sick leave

→ see also/另见 jiǎ

假条 jiàtiáo [名] note

尖 jiān I [形] 1 (锐利) pointed 2 (指声音) shrill 3 (敏锐) sensitive 4 (吝啬) stingy 5 (尖刻) biting II [名] 1 (尖端) tip ▸ 笔尖 bǐjiān pen tip 2 (精华) the best

尖锐 jiānruì [形] 1 (锋利) sharp 2 (敏锐) penetrating 3 (刺耳) shrill

坚 jiān I [形] hard II [名] stronghold III [副] firmly ▸ 坚信 jiānxìn firmly believe

坚持 jiānchí [动] go on

坚定 jiāndìng [形] steadfast

坚决 jiānjué [副] resolutely

坚强 jiānqiáng [形] strong

坚硬 jiānyìng [形] hard

间 jiān I [介] between ▸ 课间 kèjiān between lessons II [名] 1 (范围) ▸ 晚间 wǎnjiān in the evening ▸ 田间 tiánjiān field 2 (屋子) room ▸ 房间 fángjiān room ▸ 卫生间 wèishēngjiān toilet III [量] ▸ 两间客厅 liǎng jiān kètīng two living rooms ▸ 一间病房 yī jiān bìngfáng one ward

measure word, used for rooms, lounges, hospital wards etc.

肩 jiān see below/见下文

肩膀 jiānbǎng [名] shoulder

艰 jiān [形] difficult ▸ 艰辛 jiānxīn hardship

艰巨 jiānjù [形] formidable

艰苦 jiānkǔ [形] harsh

艰难 jiānnán [形] hard

监 jiān **I** [动] supervise ▸监视 jiānshì keep watch **II** [名] **1**(监狱) prison ▸探监 tànjiān visit a prison **2**(负责人) inspector ▸总监 zǒngjiān chief-inspector

监督 jiāndū [动] supervise

监狱 jiānyù [名] prison

拣 jiǎn [动] choose

俭 jiǎn [形] frugal

俭朴 jiǎnpǔ [形] economical

捡 jiǎn [动] pick ... up

检 jiǎn [动] **1**(检查) examine ▸体检 tǐjiǎn medical examination **2**(检点) show restraint

检查 jiǎnchá **I** [动] examine **II** [名] self-criticism

减 jiǎn [动] **1**(减去) subtract **2**(减少) reduce **3**(降低) decrease ▸减退 jiǎntuì fail

减肥 jiǎnféi [动] slim

减轻 jiǎnqīng [动] reduce

减少 jiǎnshǎo [动] reduce

剪 jiǎn **I** [名] scissors (PL) **II** [动] **1**(铰) cut **2**(除去) eliminate

剪刀 jiǎndāo [名] scissors (PL)

简 jiǎn **I** [形] simple **II** [动] simplify ▸简化 jiǎnhuà simplify

简单 jiǎndān [形] **1**(不复杂) simple **2**(草率) casual **3**(平凡) ▸这孩子能说两门外语，真不简单。 Zhè háizi néng shuō liǎng mén wàiyǔ, zhēn bù jiǎndān. It is quite extraordinary that this child can speak two foreign languages.

简体字 jiǎntǐzì [名] simplified characters (PL)

简体字 jiǎntǐzì
简体字 jiǎntǐzì (simplified characters) are the type of Chinese characters used today throughout Mainland China, and mostly derive from the PRC government's efforts during the 1950s and 60s to make the script more accessible and improve literacy. The alternative and older form of the script, known as complex or traditional characters, 繁体字 fántǐzì, is used predominantly in Taiwan, Hong Kong and many overseas Chinese communities. The two systems are closely related and if you have learnt one then, with a little effort, the other form should not pose too many problems!

见 jiàn **I** [动] **1**(看到) see ▸罕见 hǎnjiàn rare **2**(接触) come into contact with ▸汽油见火就着。 Qìyóu jiàn huǒ jiù zháo. Petrol ignites on contact with a flame. **3**(看得出) be visible ▸见效 jiànxiào take effect **4**(参照) see ▸见上图 jiàn shàngtú see the above diagram (会见)

meet ▶接见 jiējiàn receive **II** [名] opinion ▶偏见 piānjiàn prejudice **III** [助动] (书) 请见谅。 Qǐng jiànliàng. Please excuse me.

见面 jiànmiàn [动] meet

件 jiàn **I** [量] item ▶一件衣服 yī jiàn yīfu an item of clothing ▶两件事 liǎng jiàn shì two things **II** [名] correspondence ▶急件 jíjiàn urgent letter

建 jiàn [动] **1**(建造) build **2**(建立) found **3**(提出) propose ▶建议 jiànyì propose

建立 jiànlì [动] establish

建设 jiànshè [动] build

建议 jiànyì [动] propose

建筑 jiànzhù **I** [动] build **II** [名] building

建筑师 jiànzhùshī [名] architect

健 jiàn **I** [形] ▶强健 qiángjiàn strong and healthy ▶健全 jiànquán sound **II** [动] **1**(使强健) strengthen ▶健身 jiànshēn keep fit **2**(善于) be good at ▶健谈 jiàntán be good at small-talk

健康 jiànkāng [形] healthy

健忘 jiànwàng [形] forgetful

渐 jiàn [副] gradually

渐渐 jiànjiàn [副] gradually

键 jiàn [名] key

键盘 jiànpán [名] keyboard

箭 jiàn [名] arrow

江 jiāng [名] **1**(大河) river **2**(长江) Yangtze

将 jiāng **I** [副] ▷他将成为一名医生。 Tā jiāng chéngwéi yī míng yīshēng. He is going to become a doctor. **II** [动] **1**(下棋用语) check **2**(激) egg … on **III** [介] with ▷请将车停在路边。 Qǐng jiāng chē tíng zài lùbiān. Please stop the car by the side of the road.

将军 jiāngjūn [名] general

将来 jiānglái [名] future

将要 jiāngyào [副] ▷她将要做妈妈了。 Tā jiāngyào zuò māma le. She is going to be a mother.

姜 jiāng [名] ginger

讲 jiǎng [动] **1**(说) speak **2**(解释) explain **3**(谈) discuss **4**(讲求) emphasize ▶讲卫生 jiǎng wèishēng pay attention to hygiene

讲话 jiǎnghuà [动] **1**(说话) speak **2**(发言) address

讲台 jiǎngtái [名] dais

讲座 jiǎngzuò [名] course of lectures

奖 jiǎng **I** [动] encourage ▶夸奖 kuājiǎng praise **II** [名] award

奖金 jiǎngjīn [名] bonus

奖励 jiǎnglì [动] encourage and reward

奖品 jiǎngpǐn [名] trophy

奖学金 jiǎngxuéjīn [名] scholarship

降 jiàng [动] **1**(落下) drop **2**(降低)

reduce ▶降价 jiàngjià reduce prices

降低 jiàngdī [动] reduce

降落 jiàngluò [动] land

酱 jiàng I [名] 1 (调味品) soya bean (英) 或 soybean (美) paste 2 (糊状食品) paste ▶果酱 guǒjiàng jam II [形] 酱肘子 jiàngzhǒuzi knuckle of pork in soy sauce

酱油 jiàngyóu [名] soy sauce

交 jiāo I [动] 1 (交出) hand ... in 2 (给付) pay 3 (托付) entrust 4 (结交) associate with ▶交友 jiāoyǒu make friends ▶交情 (交情) friendship ▶深交 shēnjiāo deep friendship

交叉 jiāochā I [动] 1 (相交) intersect 2 (穿插) alternate II [形] overlapping

交换 jiāohuàn [动] exchange

交际 jiāojì [动] socialize

交警 jiāojǐng [名] traffic police

交流 jiāoliú [动] exchange

交谈 jiāotán [动] talk

交通 jiāotōng [名] traffic

交往 jiāowǎng [动] have contact

交易 jiāoyì I [动] trade II [名] transaction

郊 jiāo [名] suburbs (PL) ▶郊外 jiāowài outskirts (PL)

郊区 jiāoqū [名] suburbs (PL)

骄 jiāo [形] 1 (骄傲) arrogant ▶骄气 jiāoqì arrogance 2 (书) (猛烈) fierce

骄傲 jiāo'ào I [形] 1 (傲慢) arrogant 2 (自豪) proud II [名] pride

胶 jiāo I [名] 1 (黏性物品) glue ▶万能胶 wànnénggjiāo all-purpose glue 2 (橡胶) rubber ▶胶鞋 jiāoxié rubber boots (PL) II [动] glue

胶卷 jiāojuǎn [名] film

胶囊 jiāonáng [名] capsule

教 jiāo [动] teach
→ see also/另见 jiào

焦 jiāo [形] 1 (成黄黑色) burnt 2 (着急) agitated ▶心焦 xīnjiāo feel agitated

焦急 jiāojí [形] anxious

角 jiǎo [名] 1 (指动物) horn 2 (军号) bugle 3 (数) angle ▶直角 zhíjiǎo right angle 4 (角落) corner ▶墙角 qiángjiǎo corner of a wall

角度 jiǎodù [名] 1 (数) angle 2 (视角) point of view

角落 jiǎoluò [名] corner

饺 jiǎo [名] Chinese dumpling ▶水饺 shuǐjiǎo Chinese dumpling

饺子 jiǎozi [名] dumpling

饺子 jiǎozi

Chinese dumplings, wrapped with a thin doughy skin, are usually filled with minced meat and mixed vegetables. They are normally steame or boiled, and served with vinegar, soy sauce and other spices.

脚 jiǎo [名] 1 (指人, 动物) foot ▸脚印 jiǎoyìn footprint 2 (指物体的) base ▸山脚 shānjiǎo foot of a mountain

觉 jiǎo [动] 1 (搅拌) stir 2 (混杂) mix 3 (搅扰) disturb

搅拌 jiǎobàn [动] stir

叫 jiào [动] 1 (喊叫) shout 2 (招呼) call 3 (菜, 车) order 4 (称为) be called 5 (吩咐) order

叫喊 jiàohǎn [动] yell

叫做 jiàozuò [动] be called

较 jiào [动] 1 (比较) compare ▸较量 jiàoliàng test one's strength 2 (书) (计较) dispute

教 jiào I [动] teach ▸教导 jiàodǎo instruct II [名] religion
→ see also/另见 jiāo

教材 jiàocái [名] teaching materials (PL)

教科书 jiàokēshū [名] textbook

教练 jiàoliàn [名] coach

教师 jiàoshī [名] teacher

教室 jiàoshì [名] classroom

教授 jiàoshòu I [名] professor II [动] lecture in

教学 jiàoxué [名] 1 (知识传授) teaching 2 (教与学) teaching and study

教训 jiàoxun I [名] lesson II [动] teach ... a lesson

教育 jiàoyù I [名] education II [动] educate

教员 jiàoyuán [名] teacher

阶 jiē [名] 1 (台阶) step 2 (官阶) rank

阶段 jiēduàn [名] stage

阶级 jiējí [名] class

结 jiē [动] 1 bear ▸结果 jiéguǒ bear fruit
→ see also/另见 jié

结实 jiēshi [形] 1 (坚固耐用) sturdy 2 (健壮) strong

接 jiē [动] 1 (靠近) draw near 2 (连接) connect 3 (托付) catch 4 (接收) receive ▸接电话 jiē diànhuà answer the phone 5 (迎接) meet 6 (接替) take over

接触 jiēchù [动] (交往) come into contact with

接待 jiēdài [动] receive

接到 jiēdào [动] receive

接见 jiējiàn [动] have an interview with

接近 jiējìn I [动] approach II [形] approachable

接受 jiēshòu [动] accept

接着 jiēzhe [动] 1 (用手接) catch 2 (紧跟着) follow

街 jiē [名] 1 (街道) street 2 (方) (集市) market

街道 jiēdào [名] 1 (马路) street 2 (社区) neighbourhood (英), neighborhood (美)

节 jié I [名] 1 (连接处) joint 2 (段

落) paragraph **3** (节日) festival ► 圣诞节 Shèngdàn Jié Christmas **4** (事项) item ► 细节 xìjié details (PL) **5** (节操) moral fibre (英) 或 fiber (美) ► 气节 qìjié integrity **II** [动] **1** (节约) save **2** (删节) abridge **III** [量] (指部分) section ► 一节管子 yī jié guǎnzi a length of pipe **2** ► 三节课 sān jié kè three classes ► 四节车厢 sì jié chēxiāng four carriages ► 两节电池 liǎng jié diànchí two batteries measure word, used for school classes, carriages, batteries etc.

节目 jiémù [名] programme (英), program (美)

节拍 jiépāi [名] beat

节日 jiérì [名] festival

节省 jiéshěng [动] conserve

节约 jiéyuē [动] save

结 jié **I** [动] **1** (编织) tie ► 结网 jiéwǎng weave a net **2** (结合) unite **3** (凝聚) freeze ► 结冰 jiébīng ice up **4** (了结) settle up ► 结账 jiézhàng settle up **II** [名] (绳扣) knot ► 活结 huójié slip-knot **2** (字据) written undertaking **3** (生理) node → see also/另见 jiē

结构 jiégòu [名] composition

结果 jiéguǒ **I** [名] result **II** [副] in the end

结合 jiéhé [动] **1** (联系) combine **2** (成夫妇) become husband and wife

结婚 jiéhūn [动] get married

结论 jiélùn [名] conclusion

结束 jiéshù [动] end

捷 jié **I** [形] (快) quick ► 敏捷 mǐnjié nimble **II** [名] victory

捷径 jiéjìng [名] short cut

姐 jiě [名] elder sister

姐姐 jiějie [名] elder sister

姐妹 jiěmèi [名] sisters (PL)

解 jiě [动] **1** (分开) divide ► 解剖 jiěpōu dissect **2** (解开) untie **3** (解除) relieve **4** (解答) answer ► 解题 jiětí solve a problem **5** (理解) understand

解答 jiědá [动] answer

解放 jiěfàng [动] liberate

解雇 jiěgù [动] fire

解决 jiějué [动] **1** (处理) resolve **2** (消灭) annihilate

解释 jiěshì [动] explain

介 jiè [动] be situated between

介绍 jièshào [动] **1** (使相识) introduce **2** (推荐) sponsor **3** (了解) give an introduction to

届 jiè **I** [动] (到) fall due ► 届期 jièqī at the appointed time **II** [量] **1** (指要上学的学年) year ► 82届毕业生 bā èr jiè bìyèshēng the class of '82 **2** (指大会, 首脑) ► 第10届奥运会 dì shí jiè Àoyùnhuì the tenth Olympic Games ► 第26届总统 dì èrshíliù jiè zǒngtǒng the twenty-sixth president measure word, used for conferences, sports events, trade fairs, terms of office etc.

界 jiè [名] 1 (界限) boundary (PL) 2 (阶层) circles (PL) 3 (范围) range 4 (类别) category

借 jiè [动] 1 (借入) borrow 2 (借出) lend 3 (假托) use ... as a means of 4 (凭借) make use of

借口 jièkǒu I [动] use ... as an excuse II [名] excuse

借助 jièzhù [动] enlist the help of

斤 jīn [量] unit of weight, equal to 500 grams

今 jīn I [形] 1 (现在的) present 2 (当前的) current II [名] today

今后 jīnhòu [副] from now on

今年 jīnnián [名] this year

今天 jīntiān [名] today

金 jīn I [名] 1 (化) gold 2 (金属) metal ▸五金 wǔjīn hardware 3 (钱) money II [形] golden ▸金发 jīnfà blonde hair

金融 jīnróng [名] finance

金属 jīnshǔ [名] metal

金子 jīnzi [名] gold

仅 jǐn [副] only

仅仅 jǐnjǐn [副] just

尽 jǐn I [副] 1 (尽量) as far as possible ▸尽快 jǐnkuài as early as possible 2 (最) most 3 (表示继续) constantly II [介] 1 (不超过)

take no more than 2 (考虑在先) give priority to
→ see also / 另见 jìn

尽管 jǐnguǎn I [副] without reserve ▸ 有话尽管说。 Yǒu huà jǐnguǎn shuō. If there's something you'd like to say please don't hold back. II [连] even though

尽量 jǐnliàng [副] to the best of one's ability

尽早 jǐnzǎo [副] as soon as possible

紧 jǐn I [形] 1 (不松) tight 2 (牢固) secure 3 (接近) close 4 (急迫) pressing 5 (严格) strict 6 (拮据) short of money II [动] tighten

紧急 jǐnjí [形] urgent

紧张 jǐnzhāng [形] 1 (激烈) intense 2 (不安) nervous 3 (不足) in short supply

尽 jìn I [动] 1 (完) exhaust 2 (达到极限) go to extremes 3 (充分发挥) go to ... the full 4 (努力完成) strive to accomplish II [形] complete
→ see also / 另见 jǐn

尽力 jìnlì [动] try one's hardest

尽量 jìnliàng [动] do all one can

进 jìn [动] 1 (前进) advance 2 (进入) enter 3 (接纳) bring ... in ▸进货 jìnhuò stock up 4 (吃食) eat 5 (呈上) submit 6 (改进) enter ▸进球 jìnqiú score a goal

进步 jìnbù [动] improve II [形] advanced

进攻 jìngōng [动] attack

进化 jìnhuà [动] evolve

进口 jìnkǒu [动] import

近来 jìnlái [动] come in

进去 jìnqù [动] enter

进入 jìnrù [动] **1**(走进) enter **2**(到了) reach **3**(到位) get inside

进行 jìnxíng [动] carry ... out

进修 jìnxiū [动] take a refresher course

近 jìn [形] **1**(不远) near ▸近日 jìnrì recently **2**(接近) close **3**(亲近) close to

近来 jìnlái [副] recently

近视 jìnshì [形] short-sighted (英), near-sighted (美)

劲 jìn [名] **1**(力气) strength **2**(情绪) spirit **3**(态度) manner **4**(趣味) fun

禁 jìn I [动] **1**(禁止) forbid **2**(监禁) imprison ▸禁闭 jìnbì lock ... up II [名] taboo
→ see also/另见 jīn

禁止 jìnzhǐ [动] forbid

京 jīng [名] **1**(首都) capital **2**(北京) Beijing

京剧 jīngjù [名] Beijing opera

京剧 jīngjù
京剧 jīngjù is a form of Chinese traditional opera which enjoys a history of over two hundred years, and is regarded as one of the most important Chinese cultural heritages. The performances combine singing, acting, music, dialogue, dancing and acrobatics. Different roles follow different patterns of acting, which are all rather symbolic, suggestive and exaggerated.

经 jīng I [名] **1**(经线) warp **2**(中医) channels (PL) **3**(经度) longitude **4**(经典) scripture ▸佛经 fójīng Buddhist sutra II [动] **1**(经营) run **2**(经商) be in business **3**(经受) endure **3**(经过) ▸途经西安 tújīng Xī'ān go via Xī'an III [形] regular

经常 jīngcháng I [形] day-to-day II [副] often

经过 jīngguò I [动] **1**(通过) pass **2**(延续) ▸经过3年的恋爱，他们终于结婚了。 Jīngguò sān nián de liàn'ài, tāmen zhōngyú jiéhūn le. Having been together for three years, they finally got married. **3**(经历) ▸企业经过裁员缩减了经费开支。 Qǐyè jīngguò cáiyuán suōjiǎn le jīngfèi kāizhī. Business expenditure was reduced through staff cutbacks. II [名] course

经济 jīngjì I [名] **1**(社会生产关系) economy **2**(个人财政状况) financial situation II [形] **1**(有关国民经济) economic **2**(实惠) economical ▸经济舱 jīngjìcāng

经济舱 economy-class cabin

经理 jīnglǐ [名] manager

经历 jīnglì [动] experience

经验 jīngyàn [名] experience

惊 jīng [动] 1 (紧张) start 2 (惊动) startle

惊奇 jīngqí [形] surprised

惊人 jīngrén [形] amazing

惊喜 jīngxǐ [动] be pleasantly surprised

惊讶 jīngyà [形] astonished

精 jīng I [形] 1 (经挑选的) refined ▸ 精兵 jīngbīng crack troops 2 (完美) excellent 3 (细密) precise 4 (心细) sharp 5 (精通) skilled II [名] 1 (精华) essence ▸ 酒精 jiǔjīng alcohol 2 (精力) energy III [副] (方) extremely

精彩 jīngcǎi [形] wonderful

精力 jīnglì [名] energy

精确 jīngquè [形] precise

精神 jīngshén [名] 1 (主观世界) mind 2 (宗旨) gist

精神 jīngshen [名] energy II [形] energetic

精通 jīngtōng [动] be proficient in

井 jǐng I [名] 1 (用于取水) well 2 (井状物) ▸ 天井 tiānjǐng skylight ▸ 矿井 kuàngjǐng mine shaft II [形] neat

景 jǐng [名] 1 (风景) scenery 2 (情形) situation ▸ 背景 bèijǐng background 3 (布景) scene ▸ 外景 wàijǐng outdoor scene II [动] admire

景点 jǐngdiǎn [名] scenic spot

景色 jǐngsè [名] scenery

警 jǐng I [形] alert ▸ 警惕 jǐngtì on the alert II [动] 1 (使警觉) warn 2 (戒备) be on the alert III [名] 1 (危急) alarm ▸ 报警 bàojǐng raise the alarm 2 (警察) police ▸ 巡警 xúnjǐng an officer on the beat

警报 jǐngbào [名] alarm

警察 jǐngchá [名] police

警告 jǐnggào [动] warn

竞 jìng [动] compete

竞赛 jìngsài [名] competition

竞争 jìngzhēng [动] compete

敬 jìng I [动] 1 (尊重) respect 2 (恭敬地给) offer II [形] respectful

敬度 jìngdù [动] revere

敬礼 jìnglǐ [动] salute

静 jìng [形] 1 (不动) still 2 (无声) quiet

镜 jìng [名] 1 (镜子) mirror 2 (指光学器具) lens ▸ 眼镜 yǎnjìng glasses

镜子 jìngzi [名] mirror

纠 jiū [动] 1 (缠绕) entangle 2 (集合) assemble 3 (督察) supervise 4 (改正) correct

纠正 jiūzhèng [动] correct

究 jiū [动] investigate II [副] actually

究竟 jiūjìng I [名] outcome II [副] actually

九 jiǔ [数] nine

九月 jiǔyuè [名] September

久 jiǔ [形] 1 (时间长) long 2 (时间长短) long

玖 jiǔ [数] nine

This is the complex character for 'nine', which is mainly used in banks, on receipts etc. to prevent mistakes and forgery.

酒 jiǔ [名] alcohol ▷ 葡萄酒 pútaojiǔ wine ▷ 敬酒 jìngjiǔ propose a toast

旧 jiù I [形] 1 (过时) old 2 (陈旧) used II [名] old friend

救 jiù [动] save

救护车 jiùhùchē [名] ambulance ▷ 救命啊！Jiùmìng a! Help!

救命 jiùmìng [动] save a life

就 jiù I [动] 1 (靠近) move close to 2 (开始) take ... up 3 (完成) accomplish 4 (趁) take the opportunity 5 (搭配着吃) eat ... with II [副] 1 (强调时间短) shortly 2 (早已) already 3 (表示紧接着) as soon as 4 (表示条件关系) then 5 (强调数量多) as much as 6 (仅仅) only 7 (原本) already 8 (表示坚决) simply 9 (强调事实) exactly 10 (表示容忍) even though III [连] even if IV [介] on

就是 jiùshì I [副] 1 (表示坚决) still 3 (表示强调) really 4 (确定范围) only II [助] ▷ 你干就是了，没人说你。 Nǐ gàn jiùshì le, méi rén shuō nǐ. Just go ahead and do it – no one will blame you! III [连] even if

就算 jiùsuàn [连] even if

舅 jiù [名] 1 (母父) uncle 2 (妻子的弟弟) brother-in-law

舅舅 jiùjiu [名] uncle

居 jū I [动] 1 (住) live 2 (在) be II [名] house

居住 jūzhù [动] live

局 jú [名] 1 (棋盘) chessboard 2 (次) game ▷ 平局 píngjú draw 3 (形势) situation ▷ 时局 shíjú current political situation 4 (聚会) gathering ▷ 饭局 fànjú dinner party 5 (圈套) ruse ▷ 骗局 piànjú fraud 6 (部分) part 7 (机关部门) department 8 (业务机构) office II [量] set ▷ 我赢了这局棋。 Wǒ yíng le zhè jú qí. I won the chess game.

局长 júzhǎng [名] director

橘 jú [名] tangerine

橘子 júzi [名] orange ▷ 橘子汁 júzi zhī orange juice

举 jǔ I [动] 1 (往上托) raise ▷ 举重 jǔzhòng weightlifting 2 (兴起) mobilize ▷ 举兵 jǔbīng dispatch troops 3 (选举) elect 4 (提出) cite ▷ 举例 jǔlì cite an example II [动] act III [形] all

举办 jǔbàn [动] hold

举行 jǔxíng [动] hold

巨 jù [形] huge

巨大 jùdà [形] huge

巨人 jùrén [名] giant

句 jù I [名] sentence II [量] ▷说几句话 shuō jǐ jù huà say a few words ▷写两句诗 xiě liǎng jù shī write two lines of verse measure word, used for sentences, and lines in a speech, song or poem

句子 jùzi [名] sentence

拒 jù [动] 1 (抵抗) resist 2 (拒绝) refuse

拒绝 jùjué [动] refuse

具 jù I [动] have II [名] utensil ▷玩具 wánjù toy

具备 jùbèi [动] have

具体 jùtǐ [形] 1 (明确) detailed 2 (特定) particular

具有 jùyǒu [动] have

俱 jù [副] ▷面面俱到 miàn miàn jù dào attend to each and every aspect

俱乐部 jùlèbù [名] club

剧 jù I [名] drama ▷喜剧 xǐjù comedy II [形] severe ▷剧变 jùbiàn dramatic change

剧场 jùchǎng [名] theatre (英), theater (美)

剧烈 jùliè [形] severe

剧院 jùyuàn [名] 1 (剧场) theatre

(英), theater (美) 2 (剧团) company

据 jù I [动] 1 (占据) occupy ▷盘据 pánjù forcibly occupy 2 (凭借) rely on ▷据点 jùdiǎn stronghold II [介] according to III [名] evidence ▷收据 shōujù receipt

据说 jùshuō [动] be said

距 jù [名] distance

距离 jùlí [动] be at a distance from

锯 jù I [名] saw II [动] saw

卷 juǎn I [动] 1 (裹成筒形) roll ... up 2 (撮起) sweep ... up 3 (喻) (牵涉) be swept up in II [动] roll III [量] roll ▷一卷卫生纸 yī juǎn wèishēngzhǐ a roll of toilet paper

决 jué I [动] 1 (决定) decide 2 (执行死刑) execute 3 (决口) burst 4 (定胜负) decide on a result ▷决战 juézhàn decisive battle II [副] under any circumstances III [形] decisive ▷果决 guǒjué resolute

决定 juédìng [动] 1 (打定主意) decide 2 (表示条件关系) determine

决心 juéxīn [名] determination

觉 jué I [动] 1 (感觉) feel 2 (觉悟) become aware of II [名] sense ▷知觉 zhījué consciousness

觉得 juéde [动] 1 (感到) feel 2 (认为) think

觉悟 juéwù [名] awareness

绝 jué I [动] 1 (断绝) cut ... off ▷隔绝 géjué isolate 2 (穷尽) exhaust

3 (无后代) have no descendants **4** (死) die **II** [形] **1** (不通) hopeless ▶绝路 juélù blind alley **2** (高超) superb **III** [副] **1** (最) extremely ▶绝密 juémì top secret **2** (绝对) absolutely

绝对 juéduì **I** [形] absolute **II** [副] absolutely

绝望 juéwàng [动] feel desperate

军 jūn **I** [名] **1** (军队) army ▶参军 cānjūn enlist **2** (指军队编制单位) regiment **3** (指集体) forces (PL) **II** [形] military ▶军费 jūnfèi military expenditure

军队 jūnduì [名] troops (PL)

军官 jūnguān [名] officer

军人 jūnrén [名] soldier

军事 jūnshì [名] military affairs (PL)

K

咖 kā *see below*/见下文
→ *see also*/另见 gā

咖啡 kāfēi [名] coffee ▶速溶咖啡 sùróng kāfēi instant coffee

卡 kǎ **I** [量] (卡路里) calorie **II** [名] (卡片) card

卡车 kǎchē [名] lorry (英), truck (美)

卡拉OK kǎlā'ōukèi [名] karaoke

卡通 kǎtōng [名] cartoon

开 kāi [动] **1** (打开) open ▶开门 kāimén open the door **2** (银行, 商店) be open **3** (绽放) bloom **4** (松开) come undone **5** (驾驶) drive ▶开汽车 kāi qìchē drive a car **6** (办) open ... up ▶开公司 kāi gōngsī start up a business

7 (开始) start ▶开课 kāikè give a course ▶开学 kāixué start school ▶开演 kāiyǎn start the show **8** (举行) hold ▶开会 kāihuì have a meeting **9** (写出) write ... out **10** (灯, 电器, 煤气) turn on ▶开灯 kāi dēng turn on the light **11** (沸腾) boil ▶水刚开。Shuǐ gāng kāi. The water was just boiled. **12** (饭) serve ▶开饭了。Kāi fàn le. Dinner is ready.

开刀 kāidāo [动] operate on

开放 kāifàng [动] **1** (解禁) open ▷对外开放政策 duìwài kāifàng zhèngcè the opening-up policy **2** (开朗) be open-minded

开关 kāiguān [名] switch

开户 kāihù [动] open an account

开会 kāihuì [动] have a meeting

开课 kāikè [动] **1** (开学) start **2** (授课) teach a course

开朗 kāilǎng [形] (指性格) cheerful

开明 kāimíng [形] enlightened

开幕 kāimù [动] **1** (指演出) start **2** (指会) open

开辟 kāipì [动] **1** (开通) open ... up **2** (开发) develop

开始 kāishǐ I [动] start, begin II [名] beginning

开水 kāishuǐ [名] boiling water

开头 kāitóu I [动] begin II [名] beginning

开玩笑 kāi wánxiào [动] joke ▷别拿我开玩笑。 Bié ná wǒ kāi wánxiào. Don't make fun of me.

开心 kāixīn [形] happy

开展 kāizhǎn [动] launch

开支 kāizhī [动] spend

刊 kān I [动] (出版) publish II [名] periodical ▶报刊 bàokān the press

刊登 kāndēng [动] publish

刊物 kānwù [名] periodical

看 kān [动] **1** (照料) look after ▶看家 kānjiā look after the house **2** (看管) watch over
→ see also/另见 kàn

砍 kǎn [动] **1** (劈) chop **2** (减) cut

看 kàn [动] **1** (观看) look at ▶看到 kàndào see ▶看电视 kàn diànshì watch TV **2** (阅读) read **3** (认为) think ▶看成 kànchéng consider **4** (拜访) visit ▶看望 kànwàng visit **5** (照料) look after **6** (对待) treat **7** (诊治) treat ▶看病 kànbìng see a doctor **8** (取决于) depend on
→ see also/另见 kān

看不起 kàn bu qǐ [动] look down on

看待 kàndài [动] regard ▷当朋友看待 péngyou kàndài regard as a friend

看法 kànfǎ [名] opinion

看好 kànhǎo [动] look good

看见 kànjiàn [动] see

看来 kànlái [动] seem

康 kāng [形] (健康) healthy ▶康复 kāngfù recover

慷 kāng *see below*/见下文

慷慨 kāngkǎi [形] (大方) generous

扛 káng [动] shoulder

抗 kàng [动] 1 (抵抗) resist 2 (抗拒) refuse

抗议 kàngyì [动] protest

考 kǎo [动] 1 (测试) have an exam ▶考上 kǎoshang pass the entrance exam 2 (查看) check ▶考察 kǎochá investigate

考虑 kǎolù [动] consider

考试 kǎoshì [动] sit an exam

考验 kǎoyàn [动] test

拷 kǎo [动] (拷贝) copy

烤 kǎo [动] 1 (指东西) roast ▶烤鸭 kǎoyā 2 (指人体) warm oneself ▶烤火 kǎohuǒ warm oneself by a fire

靠 kào [动] 1 (倚) lean 2 (近) keep to 3 (依赖) rely on 4 (信赖) trust

科 kē [名] 1 (指学科) discipline ▶文科 wénkē humanities (PL) 2 (指部门) department

科技 kējì [名] science and technology

科目 kēmù [名] subject

科学 kēxué I [名] science II [形] scientific

科学家 kēxuéjiā [名] scientist

科学研究 kēxué yánjiū scientific research

棵 kē [量] ▷一棵水仙 yī kē shuǐxiān a narcissus ▷三百棵树 sānbǎi kē shù three hundred trees

measure word, used for plants, trees and vegetables

颗 kē [量] ▷一颗种子 yī kē zhǒngzi seed ▷一颗汗珠 yī kē hànzhū a bead of sweat

measure word, used for small, round objects

磕 kē [动] bump

壳 ké [名] shell

咳 ké [动] cough

咳嗽 késou [动] cough

可 kě I [动] (同意) approve II [助动] 1 (可以) can 2 (值得) III [连] but

可爱 kě'ài [形] adorable

可悲 kěbēi [形] lamentable

可靠 kěkào [形] reliable

可乐 kělè [名] Coke®

可怜 kělián I [形] pitiful II [动] pity

可能 kěnéng I [形] possible II [副] maybe III [名] possibility ▶可能性 kěnéngxìng possibility

可怕 kěpà [形] frightening

可是 kěshì [连] but ▷这个小镇不大,可是很热闹。Zhè ge xiǎozhèn bù dà, kěshì hěn rènào. This is a small town, but it's very lively.

可惜 kěxī I [形] regrettable II [副] regrettably

可笑 kěxiào [形] 1 (令人耻笑)

ridiculous 2 (引人发笑) funny

可以 kěyǐ I [助动] 1 (能够) can 2 (有权) may II [形] (不坏) not bad

> 可以 kěyǐ, 能 néng, and 会 huì can all be used to express ability and are sometimes used interchangeably. Both 可以 kěyǐ and 能 néng can express being able to do something because you have been granted permission, e.g. 你可以/能借我的照相机 nǐ kěyǐ/néng jiè wǒ de zhàoxiàngjī (you may/can borrow my camera). Strictly, 能 néng should be used to express physical ability, e.g. 我能跑得很快 wǒ néng pǎo de hěn kuài (I can run very fast), while 会 huì should express a learned ability, e.g. 我会说法语 wǒ huì shuō Fǎyǔ (I can speak French).

渴 kě I [形] thirsty ▸渴望 kěwàng long for II [副] eagerly

克 kè I [动] 1 (克制) restrain 2 (战胜) overcome II [量] gram

克服 kèfú [动] (战胜) overcome

克隆 kèlóng [动] clone

刻 kè [动] 1 (雕刻) engrave II [名] 1 (雕刻物品) engraving 2 (指十五分钟) quarter

刻苦 kèkǔ [形] hardworking

客 kè [名] 1 (客人) visitor ▸客厅 kètīng living room 2 (旅客) traveller (英), traveler (美) ▸客车 kèchē passenger train 3 (顾客) customer ▸客户 kèhù customer

客观 kèguān [形] objective

客气 kèqi I [形] polite II [动] be polite

客人 kèrén [名] guest

课 kè [名] 1 (学科) subject 2 (学时) class 3 (单元) lesson

课本 kèběn [名] textbook

课程 kèchéng [名] course ▸课程表 kèchéngbiǎo school timetable

课堂 kètáng [名] classroom

课题 kètí [名] (论题) topic

课文 kèwén [名] text

肯 kěn [助动] be willing

肯定 kěndìng I [动] confirm II [形] 1 (确定的) affirmative 2 (明确的) clear III [副] certainly

空 kōng I [形] empty ▸空虚 kōngxū empty II [名] sky ▸空中小姐 kōngzhōng xiǎojiě stewardess

→ see also/另见 kòng

空间 kōngjiān [名] space

空军 kōngjūn [名] air force

空调 kōngtiáo [名] air conditioner

空气 kōngqì [名] (大气) air

空前 kōngqián [形] unprecedented

孔 kǒng [名] hole

孔子 Kǒngzǐ [名] Confucius

孔子 Kǒngzǐ

孔子 Kǒngzǐ, Confucius, (trad. 551-479 BC) was a hugely influential thinker. A posthumous compilation of his sayings, 《论语》 Lúnyǔ, The Analects, is China's most important philosophical work, and was the key text on which much of the traditional Chinese education system was based.

恐 kǒng fear

恐怖 kǒngbù I [形] terrifying II [名] terror ▶恐怖主义 kǒngbù zhǔyì terrorism

恐龙 kǒnglóng [名] dinosaur

恐怕 kǒngpà [副] 1 (担心) fearfully 2 (大概) probably

空 kòng I [动] leave ... empty II [形] vacant ▶空白 kòngbái blank ▶空缺 kòngquē vacancy III [名] 1 (空间) space 2 (时间) free time ▶空儿 kòngr spare time ▶有空 yǒu kòng have free time
→ see also / 另见 kōng

控 kòng [动] 1 (控制) control 2 (控告) charge

控制 kòngzhì [动] control

口 kǒu [名] 1 (嘴) mouth ▶口才 kǒucái eloquence ▶口吃 kǒuchī stammering ▶口红 kǒuhóng lipstick 2 (丁) 家口 jiākǒu family member ▶口味 kǒuwèi taste 3 (指容器) rim ▶瓶口 píngkǒu the mouth of a bottle 4 (指端口) 出口 chūkǒu exit ▶入口 rùkǒu entrance ▶窗口 chuāngkǒu window 5 (缝) split II [量] ▷我家有五口人。 Wǒ jiā yǒu wǔ kǒu rén. There are five people in my family.

measure word, used for the number of people in a family

口袋 kǒudài [名] bag

口号 kǒuhào [名] slogan

口气 kǒuqì [名] (语气) tone

口头 kǒutóu [名] 1 (嘴) word 2 (口语) ▷口头作文 kǒutóu zuòwén oral composition

口信 kǒuxìn [名] message

口音 kǒuyīn [名] (方言) accent

口语 kǒuyǔ [名] spoken language

扣 kòu I [动] 1 (拉紧) fasten 2 (朝下) put ... upside down 3 (抓) arrest ▶扣留 kòuliú arrest 4 (减) deduct ▶扣除 kòuchú II [名] button ▶扣子 kòuzi button

哭 kū [动] cry

苦 kǔ I [形] 1 (苦涩) bitter 2 (艰苦) hard II [动] (苦害) be hard on III [副] painstakingly ▶苦练 kǔ liàn train hard IV [名] suffering ▶吃苦 chīkǔ bear hardships

苦难 kǔnàn I [名] hardship II [形] hard

苦恼 kǔnǎo [形] distressed

库存 kùcún [名] stock

裤 kù [名] trousers (PL)(英), pants (PL)(美) ▶裤子 kùzi trousers (PL) (英), pants (PL)(美)

夸 kuā [动] 1(夸大) exaggerate 2(夸奖) praise

夸奖 kuājiǎng [动] praise

夸张 kuāzhāng I [形] exaggerated II [名] hyperbole

垮 kuǎ [动] 1(坍塌) collapse ▶垮台 kuǎtái collapse 2(伤身) wear down

胯 kuà [名] hip

跨 kuà [动] 1(迈步) step 2(骑) mount 3(超越) surpass ▶跨国 kuàguó transnational

会 kuài [名] accounting ▶财会 cáikuài finance and accounting → 另见 huì

会计 kuàijì [名] 1(指工作) accounting 2(指人员) accountant

块 kuài I [名] lump II [量] piece ▷ 一块蛋糕 yí kuài dàngāo a piece of cake ▷ 一块方糖 yí kuài fāngtáng a lump of sugar

快 kuài I [形] 1(快速) 2(赶快) 3(灵敏) quick ▷他脑子快。 Tā nǎozi kuài. He's quick-witted. 4(锋利) sharp 5(直爽) straightforward ▷爽快 shuǎngkuài frank II [副] soon ▶快要 kuàiyào soon

快餐 kuàicān [名] fast food

快活 kuàihuo [形] delighted

快乐 kuàilè [形] happy

筷 kuài [名] chopsticks (PL) ▶筷子 kuàizi chopsticks (PL)

宽 kuān I [形] 1(距离大) wide 2(范围广) broad ▶宽敞 kuānchang spacious 3(宽大) lenient ▶宽容 kuānróng tolerant II [名] width

宽带 kuāndài [名] broadband

款 kuǎn [名] 1(项目) section 2(钱) sum of money ▶现款 xiànkuǎn cash 3(样式) style ▶款式 kuǎnshì style

狂 kuáng I [形] 1(疯狂) crazy ▶发狂 fākuáng go crazy 2(猛烈) violent ▶狂风 kuángfēng gale 3(狂妄) arrogant 4(狂热) wild II [副] wildly

旷 kuàng [形] (空阔) spacious ▶旷野 kuàngyě wilderness II [动] neglect ▶旷课 kuàngkè play truant

况 kuàng [名] situation ▶状况 zhuàngkuàng condition

况且 kuàngqiě [连] besides

矿 kuàng [名] 1(矿场) mine 2(矿石) ore

框 kuàng I [名] 1(框架) frame 2(方框) box II [动] 1(画圈) box 2(口)(限制) limit

框架 kuàngjià [名] 1(指建筑) frame 2(指文书) framework

眶 kuàng [名] socket ▶眼眶

yǎnkuàng eye socket

亏 kuī I [动] 1 (亏损) lose 2 (欠缺) lack 3 (亏负) allow ... to suffer losses II [副] luckily ▷ 亏你把我叫醒, 要不我就出到了。 Kuī nǐ bǎ wǒ jiào xǐng, yào bù wǒ jiù chídào le. It's lucky you woke me up or I would have been late.

盔 kuī [名] helmet

葵 kuí see below/ 见下文
葵花 kuíhuā [名] sunflower

魁 kuí I [名] 1 (首) ▷ 夺魁 duókuí win first place II [形] well-built ▷ 魁梧 kuíwú tall and sturdy

昆 kūn see below/ 见下文
昆虫 kūnchóng [名] insect

捆 kǔn I [动] tie ... up II [量] bundle ▷ 一捆书 yī kǔn shū a bundle of books

困 kùn I [动] 1 (困扰) be stricken 2 (限制) trap II [形] 1 (瞌睡) sleepy 2 (困难) difficult
困难 kùnnan [形] 1 (指事情) difficult ▷ 克服困难 kèfú kùnnan overcome difficulties 2 (指经济) poor

扩 kuò [动] expand
扩大 kuòdà [动] expand

括 kuò [动] 1 (包括) include 2 (加括号) bracket
括弧 kuòhú [名] bracket

阔 kuò [形] 1 (宽广) wide 2 (阔气) wealthy

拉 lā see below/ 见下文
垃圾 lājī [名] rubbish (英), garbage (美) ▷ 垃圾食品 lājī shípǐn junk food

拉 lā [动] 1 (用力移动) pull 2 (载运) transport ▷ 出租车司机拉我到了机场。 Chūzūchē sījī lā wǒ dào le jīchǎng. The taxi driver took me to the airport. 3 (演奏) play ▷ 拉小提琴 lā xiǎotíqín play the violin

喇 lǎ see below/ 见下文
喇叭 lǎba [名] 1 (管乐器) trumpet 2 (扩音器) loudspeaker

落 là [动] 1 (遗漏) be missing 2 (忘记) leave
→ see also/ 另见 luò

辣 là [形] (指味道) hot ▸ 辣酱 làjiàng chilli sauce ▸ 辣椒 làjiāo chillies

蜡 là [名] candle ▸ 蜡烛 làzhú candle

啦 la [助] ▸ 你回来啦! Nǐ huílai la! Hey – you're back!

来 lái I [动] 1 (到来) come ▸ 家里来了几个客人。Jiā lǐ lái le jǐ gè kèrén. Some guests came to the house. 2 (发生) happen ▸ 刚到家, 麻烦来了。Gāng dào jiā, máfan lái le. As soon as I got home, the trouble started. 3 (泛指做事) ▸ 请来碗面条。Qǐng lái wǎn miàntiáo. A bowl of noodles, please. ▸ 你累了, 让我来。Nǐ lèi le, ràng wǒ lái. You're tired – let me do it. 4 (表示要做) ▸ 请你来帮个忙。Can you help me with this? 5 (表示目的) ▸ 我要想个法子来对付他。Wǒ yào xiǎng gè fǎzi lái duìfu tā. I must think of a way to deal with him. 6 (表示朝向) ▸ 服务员很快就把饭菜端了上来。Fúwùyuán hěnkuài jiù bǎ fàncài duān le shànglai. Soon the waiter had brought the food to the table. II [形] coming ▸ 来年 láinián the coming year III [助] 1 (表示持续) ▸ 几年来 jǐ nián lái in the last few years 2 (表示概数) about ▸ 10来公斤重 10 lái gōngjīn zhòng about 10 kilos

来不及 láibùjí [动] lack sufficient time for

来得及 láidejí [动] have enough time for

来回 láihuí I [动] 1 (去了再来) make a round trip ▸ 从住宅小区到市中心来回有多远? Cóng zhùzhái xiǎoqū dào shìzhōngxīn láihuí yǒu duō yuǎn? How far is it from the residential area to town and back? 2 (来来去去) move back and forth II [名] round trip ▸ 我从学校到家一天跑两个来回。Wǒ cóng xuéxiào dào jiā yì tiān pǎo liǎng gè láihuí. I make the round trip from school to home twice a day.

来往 láiwǎng [动] have dealings with

来自 láizì [动] come from

拦 lán [动] stop

栏 lán [名] 1 (栏杆) fence ▸ 栏杆 lángān railing 2 (部分版面) column ▸ 栏目 lánmù column

蓝 lán [形] blue ▸ 蓝色 lánsè blue ▸ 蓝天 lántiān sky

篮 lán [名] (篮子) basket ▸ 篮子 lánzi basket

篮球 lánqiú [名] basketball

缆 lán [名] (似缆之物) cable

缆车 lǎnchē [名] cable car

懒 lǎn [形] 1 (懒惰) lazy 2 (疲倦) lethargic

懒得 lǎnde [动] not feel like ▸ 天

太热，我懒得出门。 Tiān tài rè, wǒ lǎn de chūmén. I don't feel like going out, it's too hot.

懒惰 lǎnduò [形] lazy

烂 làn I [形] 1 (破烂) worn-out 2 (头绪乱) messy ▷烂摊子 làn tānzi a shambles II [动] be rotten ▷西瓜烂了。 Xīguā làn le. The watermelon has gone off.

狼 láng [名] wolf

廊 láng [名] corridor ▷走廊 zǒuláng corridor

朗 lǎng [形] 1 (明亮) bright 2 (响亮) clear

朗读 lǎngdú [动] read ... aloud
朗诵 lǎngsòng [动] recite

浪 làng I [名] wave ▷浪潮 làngcháo tide II [形] wasteful ▷浪费 làngfèi squander

浪费 làngfèi [动] waste
浪漫 làngmàn [形] romantic

捞 lāo [动] (取) take ▷捕捞 bǔlāo fish for

劳 láo [动] 1 (劳动) work 2 (烦劳) trouble ▷劳您帮我看下行李。 Láo nín bāng wǒ kàn xià xíngli. Would you mind keeping an eye on my luggage?

劳动 láodòng [名] labour (英), labor (美) ▷脑力劳动 nǎolì láodòng brain work
劳动力 láodònglì [名] 1 (劳动能力) labour (英), labor (美) 2 (人力) workforce

劳驾 láojià [动] (客套) excuse me

老 lǎo I [形] 1 (年岁大的) old 2 (有经验的) experienced ▷老手 lǎoshǒu veteran 3 (旧的) old ▷老同学 lǎo tóngxué old school friend 4 (火候大的) over-done II [名] (老人) old people III [副] 1 (经常) always 2 (长久) for a long time 3 (非常) very ▷老远 lǎoyuǎn very far

老百姓 lǎobǎixìng [名] ordinary people
老板 lǎobǎn [名] boss
老虎 lǎohǔ [名] tiger
老家 lǎojiā [名] home ▷我老家在上海。 Wǒ lǎojiā zài Shànghǎi. Shanghai is my hometown.
老练 lǎoliàn [形] experienced
老年 lǎonián [名] old age
老婆 lǎopo [名] (妻子) wife
老师 lǎoshī [名] teacher
老实 lǎoshi [形] 1 (诚实规矩) honest 2 (不聪明) naive
老鼠 lǎoshǔ [名] mouse
老外 lǎowài [名] foreigner

姥 lǎo see below/见下文
姥姥 lǎolao [名] (口) (母方的) granny
姥爷 lǎoye [名] (口) (母方的) grandpa

乐 lè I [形] happy II [动] 1 (乐于) take pleasure in 2 (笑) laugh
→ see also/另见 yuè
乐观 lèguān [形] optimistic

乐趣 lèqù [名] delight

乐意 lèyì [动] be willing to ▷他不乐意帮我们。Tā bù lèyì bāng wǒmen. He's unwilling to help us.

了 le [助] 1 (表示动作或变化已完成) ▷他买了这本书。Tā mǎi le zhè běn shū. He's bought this book. 2 (表示对未来的假设已完成) ▷下个月我考完了试回家。Xià gè yuè wǒ kǎo wán le shì huíjiā. I'll go home next month once my exams are over. 3 (在句尾，表示出现变化) ▷下雨了。Xiàyǔ le. It's raining. 4 (在句尾，表示提醒，劝告或催促) ▷该回家了。Gāi huíjiā le. It's time to go home. ▷别喊了！Bié hǎn le! Stop shouting!

→ see also/另见 liǎo

The usage of 了 le is one of the most complex parts of Chinese grammar, partly because it has two completely different functions. It can indicate completion of an action, e.g. 他喝了三杯啤酒 tā hē le sān bēi píjiǔ (he drank three glasses of beer). Sometimes, when placed at the end of a clause or a sentence, it usually indicates a change of some kind, e.g. 天黑了 tiān hēi le (it's gone dark).

雷 léi [名] (雷电) thunder ▷雷电 léidiàn thunder and lightning

累 léi [动] (积累) accumulate ▷累积 léijī accumulate
→ see also/另见 lèi

累计 lèijì [动] add up

肋 lèi [名] rib ▷肋骨 lèigǔ rib

泪 lèi [名] tear ▷眼泪 yǎnlèi tears (PL) ▷流泪 liúlèi shed tears

类 lèi I [名] kind ▷分类 fēnlèi classify ▷类型 lèixíng type II [动] be similar to ▷类似 lèisì similar to

类别 lèibié [名] category

类似 lèisì [形] similar

累 lèi I [形] tired II [动] (使劳累) tire ▷别累着自己。Bié lèizhe zìjǐ. Don't tire yourself out.
→ see also/另见 léi

冷 lěng [形] 1 (温度低) cold 2 (不热情) frosty ▷冷淡 lěngdàn give the cold shoulder to

冷藏 lěngcáng [动] refrigerate

冷冻 lěngdòng [动] freeze ▷冷冻食品 lěngdòng shípǐn frozen food

冷静 lěngjìng [形] (沉着) cool-headed

冷饮 lěngyǐn [名] cold drink

厘 lí see below/见下文

厘米 límǐ [量] centimetre (英), centimeter (美)

离 lí [动] 1 (分离) leave 2 (距离) be far away from ▷我家离办公室不

太远。Wǒ jiā lí bàngōngshì bù tài yuǎn. My home is quite near to the office.

离 lí is used to express separation of two things, or distance of one thing from another: to say that X is far away from Y, say "X 离 Y 远", e.g. 我家离火车站不远 wǒ jiā lí huǒchēzhàn bù yuǎn (my home is not far from the train station).

离婚 líhūn [动] divorce

离开 líkāi [动] depart

梨 lí [名] pear

礼 lǐ [名] 1 (仪式) ceremony 2 (表示尊敬) courtesy 3 (礼物) present

礼拜 lǐbài [名] (星期) week

礼貌 lǐmào [名] manners (PL)

礼堂 lǐtáng [名] hall

礼物 lǐwù [名] present

里 lǐ [名] 1 (反面) inside 2 (里边) inner ▷里屋 lǐwū inner room II [介] in ▷屋子里 wūzi lǐ in the room III [副] 1 (这里) here ▷这里 zhèlǐ here ▷那里 nàlǐ there IV [量] lǐ, a Chinese unit of length, equal to 1/3 of a mile ▷英里 yīnglǐ mile

理 lǐ [名] 1 (道理) reason ▷合理 hélǐ reasonable 2 (自然科学) natural science ▷理科 lǐkē science II [动] 1 (管理) manage ▷理财 lǐcái manage the finances 2 (整理) tidy ▷理发 lǐfà get a hair cut 3 (表示态度) acknowledge ▷理睬 lǐcǎi pay attention

理解 lǐjiě [动] understand

理论 lǐlùn [名] theory

理想 lǐxiǎng I [名] ideal II [形] ideal

理由 lǐyóu [名] reason

力 lì [名] 1 (物) force 2 (功能) strength 3 (体力) physical strength

力量 lìliang [名] 1 (力气) strength ▷这一拳力量很大。Zhè yī quán lìliang hěndà. That was a very powerful punch. 2 (能力) power 3 (作用) strength ▷这种药的力量大。Zhèzhǒng yào de lìliang dà. This medicine is very strong.

力气 lìqi [名] strength

历 lì [名] (经历) experience

历史 lìshǐ [名] history

严 lì [形] 1 (严格) strict 2 (严肃) stern

厉害 lìhai [形] terrible ▷他口渴得厉害。Tā kǒukě de lìhai. He was terribly thirsty.

立 lì [动] 1 (站) stand 2 (竖立) stand ... up 3 (建立) ▷立功 lìgōng make contributions 4 (制定) set ... up ▷立法 lìfǎ legislate II [形] upright ▷立柜 lìguì wardrobe

立方 lìfāng I [名] cube II [量] cubic ▷立方米 lìfāngmǐ cubic metre (英) or meter (美)

立即 lìjí [副] immediately

立刻 lìkè [副] immediately

利 lì I [形] (锋利) sharp II [名] 1 (利

益) interest ▸利弊 lìbì pros and
cons (PL) 2 (利润) profit and
interest ▸暴利 bàolì staggering
profits (PL) III [动] benefit

利害 lìhai [形] terrible ▸天冷得
利害。Tiān lěng de lìhai. It's
terribly cold today.

利率 lìlǜ [名] interest rate

利润 lìrùn [名] profit

利息 lìxī [名] interest

利益 lìyì [名] benefit

利用 lìyòng [动] 1 (物) use 2 (人)
exploit

例 lì [名] (例子) example ▸举例 jǔlì
give an example

例如 lìrú [动] give an example ▸大
商场货物齐全，例如服装，食
电，食品等。Dà shāngchǎng
huòwù qíquán, lìrú fúzhuāng,
jiādiàn, shípǐn děng. The big
shopping centre sells all kinds
of goods, for example, clothes,
household appliances and food.

例外 lìwài [动] be an exception

例子 lìzi [名] example

荔 lì see below/ 见下文

荔枝 lìzhī [名] lychee

栗 lì [名] chestnut ▸栗子 lìzi
chestnut

粒 lì [量] ▸一粒珍珠 yílì zhēnzhū
a pearl ▸三粒种子 sānlì zhǒngzi
three seeds

measure word, used for
small round objects, such
as sand, grains, pills etc.

俩 liǎ [数] (口) (两个) two ▸我俩
wǒ liǎ the two of us

连 lián I [动] (连接) ▸连接 liánjiē
link II [副] in succession ▸连看
了几眼 lián kàn le jǐ yǎn glance
at several times III [介] 1 (包括)
including ▸连他4人 lián tā sì rén
four people, including him 2 (甚
至) even

连接 liánjiē [动] connect

连忙 liánmáng [副] at once

连续 liánxù [动] go on without
stopping ▸他连续干了3天，
觉都没睡。Tā liánxù gàn le
sān tiān, jiào dōu méi shuì. He
worked for three days in a row
without sleeping.

帘 lián [名] curtain (英)，drape (美)
▸窗帘 chuānglián curtain (英)，
drape (美)

莲 lián [名] lotus ▸莲花 liánhuā
lotus flower

联 lián [动] unite ▸联赛 liánsài
league match

联合 liánhé I [动] (人) unite II [形]
joint

联合国 Liánhéguó [名] United
Nations, UN

联络 liánluò [动] contact ▸联络
方式 liánluò fāngshì ways to
maintain contact

联系 liánxì [动] connect ▸理论
联系实际 lǐlùn liánxì shíjì apply
theory to practice ▸促进经济贸
易联系 cùjìn jīngjì màoyì liánxì

encourage economic and trade relations

脸 liǎn [名] 1(面部) face 2(前部) front ▸门脸 ménliǎn shop front (英), storefront (美) 3(情面) face ▸脸面 liǎnmiàn face

脸色 liǎnsè [名] (气色) complexion

练 liàn I [动] practise (英), practice (美) ▸练武 liànwǔ practise martial arts II [形] experienced ▸熟练 shúliàn skilful (英), skillful (美)

练习 liànxí [动] practise (英), practice (美) II [名] exercise

恋 liàn [动] 1(恋爱) love ▸相恋 xiāngliàn fall in love with each other 2(想念) miss ▸恋家 liànjiā be homesick

恋爱 liàn'ài [动] love ▸谈恋爱 tán liàn'ài be in love

恋人 liànrén [名] lover

良 liáng [形] good

良好 liánghǎo [形] good

良心 liángxīn [名] conscience

凉 liáng [形] (冷) cool
→ see also/另见 liàng

凉快 liángkuai [形] cool

量 liáng [动] (衡量) measure
→ see also/另见 liàng

粮 liáng [名] grain

粮食 liángshi [名] food

两 liǎng I [数] 1(表示具体数目)

two ▸两个小时 liǎng gè xiǎoshí two hours 2(表示不定数目) a few ▸说两句 shuō liǎng jù say a few words II [量] liang, a Chinese unit of weight, equal to 50 grams

When citing numbers, including cardinal numbers, ordinal numbers, telephone numbers and serial numbers etc., 二 èr is used for the number two. However, when you want to talk about two things, you must use 两 liǎng and a measure word, e.g. 两个人 liǎng gè rén (2 people), 两杯茶 liǎng bēi chá (2 cups of tea) etc.

亮 liàng I [形] (光线) bright II [动] (发光) shine ▸灯还亮着。 Dēng hái liàng zhe. The lights are still lit.

凉 liàng [动] let ... cool
→ see also/另见 liáng

辆 liàng [量] ▸一辆汽车 yī liàng qìchē a car ▸两辆自行车 liǎng liàng zìxíngchē two bicycles measure word, used for vehicles and bicycles

量 liàng [名] 1(限度) capacity 2(数量) quantity
→ see also/另见 liáng

晾 liàng [动] 1(弄干) dry 2(晒干) air

聊 liáo [动] (口) chat ▸聊天室 liáotiānshì chat room

聊天儿 liáotiānr [动] (口) chat

了 liǎo [动] 1 (完毕) finish 2 (放在动词之后表示可能) ▷办不了 bàn bù liǎo not be able to handle ▷受得了 shòu de liǎo be able to bear ▶ see also/另见 le

了不起 liǎobuqǐ [形] amazing

了解 liǎojiě [动] 1 (知道) understand 2 (打听) find ... out

料 liào [名] (材料) material ▶木料 mùliào timber

列 liè I [动] 1 (排列) set ... out 2 (安排) list ▶列举 lièjǔ list II [名] (行列) rank 2 (类别) category

列车 lièchē [名] train

劣 liè [形] bad ▶恶劣 èliè bad

劣质 lièzhì [形] poor-quality

烈 liè [形] (强烈) strong ▶激烈 jīliè fierce ▶烈性酒 lièxìngjiǔ strong liquor

猎 liè [动] hunt ▶打猎 dǎliè go hunting

裂 liè [动] split ▶分裂 fēnliè split ▶破裂 pòliè break

裂口 lièkǒu [名] split

拎 līn [动] carry

邻 lín [名] neighbour (英), neighbor (美) ▶邻居 línjū

邻近 línjìn [动] be close to

邻居 línjū [名] neighbour (英), neighbor (美)

林 lín [名] 1 (树林) wood 2 (林业) forestry ▶林业 línyè forestry

临 lín I [动] 1 (靠近) face ▶临危 línwēi face danger 2 (到达) reach ▶光临 guānglín presence 3 (将要) be about to ▶临产 línchǎn be in labour (英) 或 labor (美)

临近 línjìn [动] be close to ▷考试临近了。Kǎoshì línjìn le. The exams are approaching.

临时 línshí [副] temporarily

淋 lín [动] drench ▶淋浴 línyù [动] take a shower

鳞 lín [名] scale

吝 lín [形] stingy ▶吝啬 lìnsè stingy

灵 líng I [形] 1 (灵活) nimble ▶灵敏 língmǐn agile 2 (灵验) effective II [名] 1 (灵魂) soul 2 (神灵) deity ▶精灵 jīnglíng spirit

灵活 línghuó [形] 1 (敏捷的) agile 2 (机动的) flexible

铃 líng [名] 1 (响器) bell ▶铃铛 língdang small bell 2 (铃状物) ▶哑铃 yǎlíng dumb-bell

零 líng I [名] 1 (零数) zero 2 (零头) odd ▷她年纪七十有零。Tā niánjì qīshí yǒu líng. She's seventy-odd years old. II [形] 1 (零碎的) odd ▶零活 línghuó odd jobs (PL) ▶零钱 língqián small change 2 (部分的) spare ▶零件 língjiàn spare parts (PL) III [动] [连] ▷两年零三个月 liǎng nián líng sān gè yuè two years and three months ▷ 五元零二分 wǔ yuán líng èr fēn two fen

零钱 língqián [名] small change

零食 língshí [名] snack

零售 língshòu [动] retail

零用钱 língyòngqián [名] pocket money (英), allowance (美)

领 lǐng I [名] 1 (衣领) collar 2 (脖颈) neck II [动] 1 (带领) lead 2 (占有) possess ▷ 占领 zhànlǐng occupy

领带 lǐngdài [名] tie

领导 lǐngdǎo I [动] lead ▷ 他领导有方。Tā lǐngdǎo yǒufāng. He's an effective leader. II [名] leader

领土 lǐngtǔ [名] territory

领先 lǐngxiān [动] lead ▷ 他在比赛中遥遥领先。Tā zài bǐsài zhōng yáoyáo lǐngxiān. He took a runaway lead in the competition.

领袖 lǐngxiù [名] leader

领养 lǐngyǎng [动] adopt

另 lìng I [代] another II [副] separately

另外 lìngwài I [代] other ▷ 我不喜欢这些衣服，我喜欢另外那些。Wǒ bù xǐhuan zhèxiē yīfu, wǒ xǐhuan lìngwài nàxiē. I don't like these clothes – I like the others. II [副] in addition

令 lìng I [名] (命令) order II [动] 1 (令) order 2 (使) make

溜 liū [动] (走开) sneak off

溜达 liūda [动] go for a stroll

留 liú [动] 1 (不走) stay 2 (使) keep ... back ▷ 挽留 wǎnliú persuade ... to stay 3 (注意) be careful ▷ 留神 liúshén be careful 4 (保留) keep 5 (积攒) grow ▷ 留胡子 liú húzi grow a beard 6 (接受) accept 7 (遗留) leave ... behind 8 (留学) study abroad ▷ 留英 liú Yīng study in Britain

留步 liúbù [动] stop here

留念 liúniàn [动] keep as a souvenir

留神 liúshén [动] be on the alert

留心 liúxīn [动] take note

留学 liúxué [动] study abroad

留言 liúyán [动] leave a message

留意 liúyì [动] look ... out

流 liú I [动] (流动) flow ▷ 漂流 piāoliú drift II [名] 1 (水流) current ▷ 洪流 hóngliú torrent 2 (等级) grade ▷ 一流 yīliú first-class

流传 liúchuán [动] spread

流动 liúdòng [动] (移动) flow

流感 liúgǎn [名] the flu

流利 liúlì [形] fluent

流氓 liúmáng [名] 1 (下流) perversion 2 (歹徒) hooligan

流水 liúshuǐ [名] (流动水) running water

流行 liúxíng [动] be fashionable

瘤 liú [名] tumour (英), tumor

(美)▶瘤子 liúzi tumour (英),
tumor (美)

柳 liǔ [名] willow ▶柳树 liǔshù
willow

六 liù [数] six

六月 liùyuè [名] June

陆 liù [数] six
→ see also/另见 lù

This is the complex
character for "six", which
is mainly used in banks,
on receipts etc. to prevent
mistakes and forgery.

遛 liù [动] 1 (指人) take a stroll 2 (指
动物) walk ▶遛狗 liùgǒu walk
the dog

龙 lóng [名] dragon

龙卷风 lóngjuǎnfēng [名] tornado

龙头 lóngtóu [名] tap (英), faucet
(美)

聋 lóng [形] deaf

聋子 lóngzi [名] ▷他是个聋子。
Tā shì gè lóngzi. He's deaf.

笼 lóng [名] (笼子) cage ▶笼子
lóngzi cage

楼 lóu [名] 1 (楼房) tall building
▷教学楼 jiàoxué lóu teaching
block 2 (楼层) floor

楼房 lóufáng [名] multi-storey
building

楼梯 lóutī [名] stairs (PL)

搂 lǒu [动] embrace

漏 lòu [动] 1 (雨, 水) leak 2 (消
息, 风声) divulge 3 (词, 句) leave
... out

漏斗 lòudǒu [名] funnel

露 lòu [动] reveal
→ see also/另见 lù

露马脚 lòumǎjiǎo [动] give
oneself away

炉 lú [名] stove

炉灶 lúzào [名] kitchen range

卤 lǔ I [名] 1 (盐卤) bittern 2 (卤
汁) thick gravy II [动] stew ... in
soy sauce

陆 lù [名] land
→ see also/另见 liù

陆地 lùdì [名] land

录 lù I [名] record II [动] 1 (记载)
record ▶记录 jìlù take notes 2 (录
音) tape-record

录取 lùqǔ [动] admit ▷她被剑桥
大学录取了。Tā bèi Jiànqiáo
Dàxué lùqǔ le. She was given
a place at the University of
Cambridge.

录像 lùxiàng [动] video (英),
videotape (美)

录音 lùyīn [动] record

鹿 lù [名] deer

路 lù [名] 1 (道路) road ▶路标
lùbiāo signpost 2 (路程) journey
▷一路平安 yī lù píng'ān have a
safe journey 3 (门路) means ▶财
路 cáilù a means of getting rich
4 (条理) sequence ▶思路 sīlù

train of thought 5(路线) route
▸8路公车 bālù chē No. 8 bus

路程 lùchéng [名] journey

路过 lùguò [动] pass through

路口 lùkǒu [名] crossing (英),
intersection (美)

路线 lùxiàn [名] 1(指交通) route
2(指思想) line

露 lù I [名] (水珠) dew II [动] reveal
▸暴露 bàolù expose
▸ see also/另见 lòu

露天 lùtiān [名] the open air ▸露
天剧场 lùtiān jùchǎng open-air
theatre $ 或 theater $

露营 lùyíng [动] camp out

驴 lǘ [名] donkey

旅 lǚ [动] travel ▸差旅费 chāilǚfèi
travel expenses (PL)

旅馆 lǚguǎn [名] hotel

旅客 lǚkè [名] passenger

旅途 lǚtú [名] journey

旅行 lǚxíng [动] travel

旅游 lǚyóu [名] tour ▸旅游业
lǚyóu yè tourism ▸去国外旅游
qù guówài lǚyóu travel abroad

铝 lǚ [名] aluminium (英),
aluminum (美)

律 lǜ [名] law ▸纪律 jìlǜ discipline

律师 lǜshī [名] lawyer

绿 lǜ [形] green ▸绿灯 lǜdēng
green light

绿化 lǜhuà [动] make ... green
▸绿化荒山 lǜhuà huāngshān

plant trees on the mountains

绿卡 lǜkǎ [名] green card

绿洲 lǜzhōu [名] oasis

乱 luàn I [形] 1(没有秩序的)
disorderly ▸杂乱 záluàn messy
2(心绪不宁的) disturbed II [名]
(指冲突) chaos ▸战乱 zhànluàn
war chaos

乱哄哄 luànhōnghōng [形]
chaotic

乱七八糟 luànqībāzāo in a mess

略 lüè I [名] 1(简述) summary 2(计
谋) plan ▸策略 cèlüè tactic
II [动] 1(夺取) capture ▸侵略
qīnlüè invade 2(简化) simplify
▸省略 shěnglüè omit

伦 lún [名] (人伦) human
relationships (PL)

伦敦 Lúndūn [名] London

伦理 lúnlǐ [名] ethics (SG)

轮 lún I [名] 1(轮子) wheel 2(轮船)
steamship II [动] take turns ▸侵略
qīnlüè invade 2(简化) simplify
▸省略 shěnglüè omit

轮船 lúnchuán [名] steamship

轮换 lúnhuàn [动] take turns

轮廓 lúnkuò [名] outline

轮流 lúnliú [副] in turns

轮椅 lúnyǐ [名] wheelchair

论 lùn I [名] 1(文章) essay 2(学
说) theory ▸相对论 xiāngduì
lùn theory of relativity II [动]
(分析) discuss ▸评论 pínglùn
comment on

论文 lùnwén [名] dissertation

萝 luó [名] trailing plant
萝卜 luóbo [名] turnip ▸ 胡萝卜 húluóbo carrot

逻 luó [动] patrol
逻辑 luóji [名] logic

螺 luó [名] (指动物) snail
螺钉 luódīng [名] screw

裸 luǒ [动] expose
裸体 luǒtǐ [形] naked

骆 luò see below/见下文
骆驼 luòtuo [名] camel

落 luò [动] 1 (掉下) fall 2 (下降) go
down ▸ 降落 jiàngluò descend
3 (降下) lower 4 (衰败) decline
▸ 衰落 shuāiluò wane 5 (落后) fall
behind 6 (归属) fall to
→ see also/另见 là

落后 luòhòu I [动] fall behind
II [形] backward

妈 mā [名] (口) (母亲) mum (英),
mom (美)
妈妈 māma [名] (口) mum (英),
mom (美)

抹 mā [动] (擦) wipe
→ see also/另见 mǒ
抹布 mābù [名] cloth

麻 má I [名] (指植物) hemp II [形]
(麻木) numb
麻烦 máfan I [形] problematic
II [名] trouble III [动] trouble
▸ 不好意思, 麻烦您了。 Bùhǎo
yìsi, máfan nín le. Sorry to
trouble you.

麻将 májiàng [名] mahjong

麻将 májiàng
The game of mahjong
is usually played by four

people. 144 tiles appearing like dominoes and bearing various designs are drawn and discarded until one player has an entire hand of winning combinations. The game requires strategy as well as luck. In China, mahjong is also a popular gambling game.

麻醉 mázuì [动] (医) anaesthetize (英), anesthetize (美)

马 mǎ [名] horse

马达 mǎdá [名] motor

马虎 mǎhu [形] careless

马拉松 mǎlāsōng [名] marathon

马路 mǎlù [名] road

马上 mǎshàng [副] right away ▷他马上就到。Tā mǎshàng jiù dào. He'll be right here right away.

马戏 mǎxì [名] circus

码 mǎ [名] numeral ▷页码 yèmǎ page number

码头 mǎtou [名] pier

蚂 mǎ see below/见下文

蚂蚁 mǎyǐ [名] ant

骂 mà [动] 1(侮辱) insult 2(斥责) tell ... off

吗 ma [助] (表示疑问) ▷你去银行吗? Nǐ qù yínháng ma? Are you going to the bank?

吗 ma is added to the end of any statement to turn it into a simple yes/no question, e.g. 你忙吗? Nǐ máng ma? (Are you busy?), whereas 呢 ne is added to the end of a statement to form a tentative question, or to indicate that a response is expected, e.g. 你好吗? 我很好, 你呢? Nǐ hǎo ma? Wǒ hěn hǎo, nǐ ne? (How are you? Fine, and you?)

嘛 ma [助] 1(表示显而易见) ▷事实就是这样嘛! Shìshí jiùshì zhèyàng ma! That's the way things are! 2(表示期望) ▷别不高兴嘛! Bié bù gāoxìng ma! Please don't be unhappy.

埋 mái [动] 1(盖住) bury 2(隐藏) hide
→ see also/另见 mán

埋葬 máizàng [动] bury

买 mǎi [动] 1(购买) buy ▷不是每个人都买得起房。Bùshì měigè rén dōu mǎideqǐ fáng. Not everyone can afford to buy a flat. ▷我去市场买东西。Wǒ qù shìchǎng mǎi dōngxi. I'm going shopping in the market. 2(换取) win ... over ▷买通 mǎitōng buy ... off

买单 mǎidān [动] (方) pay a bill ▷买单! Mǎidān! The bill, please!

买卖 mǎimai [名] 1(生意) business 2(商店) shop (英), store (美)

迈 mài [动] step ▸迈步 màibù stride

麦 mài [名] (麦类粮食) wheat ▸燕麦 yànmài oats (PL)

麦克风 màikèfēng [名] microphone, mike (口)

卖 mài [动] (出售) sell ▸书都卖完了。Shū dōu mài wán le. The books are all sold out.

卖弄 màinong [动] show off

脉 mài [名] (脉搏) pulse ▸号脉 hàomài feel a pulse

脉搏 màibó [名] pulse

埋 mán see below/见下文
→ see also/另见 mái

埋怨 mányuàn [动] 1 (指责) blame 2 (抱怨) complain

馒 mán see below/见下文

馒头 mántou [名] steamed bun

瞒 mán [动] hide the truth from ▸别瞒着我们！Bié mán zhe wǒmen! Don't keep us in the dark!

满 mǎn I [形] 1 (充实) full 2 (全) complete II [动] 1 (使充满) fill 2 (到) reach ▸孩子刚满六岁。Háizi gāng mǎn liùsuì. The child has just turned six years old. III [副] fully

满意 mǎnyì [动] be satisfied

满足 mǎnzú [动] 1 (感到满意) be satisfied 2 (使满足) satisfy

漫 màn [动] overflow

漫长 màncháng [形] endless

漫画 mànhuà [名] comic strip

漫延 mànyán [动] spread

慢 màn I [形] (缓慢) slow II [动] slow ▸慢点儿！Màn diǎn! Slow down! ▸钟慢了十分钟。Zhōng màn le shí fēnzhōng. The clock is ten minutes slow.

忙 máng I [形] busy II [动] be busy with ▸你这一段忙什么呢？Nǐ zhè yīduàn máng shénme ne? What's been keeping you busy recently?

盲 máng [形] blind ▸文盲 wénmáng illiterate

盲目 mángmù [形] blind

盲文 mángwén [名] braille

蟒 mǎng [名] (动物) python

猫 māo [名] cat

猫儿眼 māoryǎn [名] spyhole

毛 máo I [名] 1 (毛发) hair ▸羽毛 yǔmáo feather 2 (指食物上) mould (英), mold (美) ▸面包上长毛了。Miànbāo shàng zhǎng máo le. The bread is mouldy (英) or moldy (美). 3 (指动物) fur ▸毛皮 máopí fur 4 (羊毛) wool ▸毛衣 máoyī sweater 5 (中国货币单位) mao unit of Chinese currency, 1/10 yuan II [形] (不纯) gross ▸毛重 máozhòng gross weight

毛笔 máobǐ [名] brush pen

毛病 máobìng [名] 1 (缺点) shortcoming

3(疾病) illness

毛巾 máojīn [名] towel

毛孔 máokǒng [名] pore

矛 máo [名] spear

矛盾 máodùn **I** [名] **1**(相抵之处) conflict **2**(哲) contradiction **II** [形] uncertain

锚 máo [名] anchor

茂 mào [形] **1**(茂盛) luxuriant **2**(丰富) abundant

茂盛 màoshèng [形] flourishing

冒 mào [动] **1**(往外) give ... off ▷锅冒烟了。 Guō mào yān le. The wok is giving off smoke. **2**(不顾) risk ▷冒生命危险 mào zhe shēngmìng wēixiǎn putting one's life at risk **3**(假充) pretend to be ▷冒牌 màopáibogus

冒充 màochōng [动] pass ... off as

冒牌 màopái [动] pirate ▷冒牌商品 màopái shāngpǐnpirated goods

冒险 màoxiǎn [动] take a risk

贸 mào [动] trade ▷外贸 wàimào foreign trade

贸易 màoyì [名] trade

帽 mào [名] (帽子) hat

帽子 màozi [名] (字) hat

貌 mào [名] (相貌, 外表) appearance

没 méi **I** [动] not have ▷没关系 méiguānxì it doesn't matter ▷屋子里没人。 Wūzi lǐ méi rén.

There's no one in the room. **II** [副] not ▷他没看过大海。 Tā méi kànguò dàhǎi. He's never seen the sea before.

→ see also/另见 mò

Constructing negating sentences in Chinese is very straightforward: just use 不 bùbefore the verb, e.g. 我不喝酒。 Wǒ bù hējiǔ. (I don't drink alcohol). The only exception is the verb 有 yǒu, for which you must use 没 méi, e.g. 我没有钱。 Wǒ méiyǒu qián. (I don't have any money).

没错儿 méicuòr [句] that's right

没劲 méijìn **I** [动] have no energy **II** [形] uninteresting

没门儿 méiménr [动] (不可能) be impossible

没事 méishì **1**(有空) be free ▷我今晚没事。 Wǒ jīnwǎn méishì. I'm free tonight. **2**(不要紧) ▷没事。 Méishì. It doesn't matter.

没有 méiyǒu **I** [动] **1**(不具有) not have **2**(不存在) there is not **3**(全都) ▷没有一个答案是正确的。 Méiyǒu yígè dá'àn shì zhèngquè de. None of the answers are correct. **4**(不如) be not as ... as ... ▷他没有你努力。 Tā méiyǒu nǐ nǔlì. He's not as hard-working as you. **5**(不到) be less than ▷他们干了这两个小时就休息了。 Tāmen gàn le méiyǒu liǎngge xiǎoshí jiù xiūxi le. They had been working for less than two hours when they took a rest. II [副] 1(尚未) not yet ▷她还没有到。Tā hái méiyǒu dào. She hasn't arrived yet. 2(未曾) never before ▷我没有吃过西餐。Wǒ méiyǒu chīguò xīcān. I have never eaten Western food before.

没辙 méizhé [动] (方) not be able to do anything about

攻 méi see below/见下文

玫瑰 méigui [名] rose

眉 méi [名] (眉毛) eyebrow ▷眉毛 méimao eyebrow

媒 méi [名] 1(媒人) matchmaker ▷做媒 zuòméi be a matchmaker 2(媒介) intermediary

媒体 méitǐ [名] media

煤 méi [名] coal

煤气 méiqì [名] 1(指燃料) gas 2(指有毒气体) carbon monoxide ▷煤气中毒 méiqì zhòngdú carbon monoxide poisoning

霉 méi [动] 1(指食物) mould (英), mold (美) 2(指衣服) mildew

每 měi I [形] every, each ▷每次 měicì every time ▷每个晚上 měi gè wǎnshang every evening II [副] every time ▷每走一步，他的脚都很疼。Měi zǒu yī bù, tā de jiǎo dōu hěn téng. His feet ache with every step he takes.

美 měi I [形] 1(美丽) beautiful 2(好) good ▷我们的明天会更美。Wǒmen de míngtiān huì gèng měi. Our future will be even better. II [名] 1(美丽) beauty 2(美洲) North and South America ▷南美 Nánměi South America ▷北美 Běiměi North America 3(美国) the USA

美国 Měiguó [名] the US, the USA ▷美国人 Měiguórén American

美好 měihǎo [形] wonderful

美丽 měilì [形] beautiful

美满 měimǎn [形] perfectly satisfactory

美容 měiróng [动] make oneself more beautiful ▷美容店 měiróng diàn beauty salon ▷美容手术 měiróng shǒushù cosmetic surgery

美食 měishí [名] delicacy

美术 měishù [名] 1(造型艺术) fine arts (PL) 2(绘画) painting

美元 měiyuán [名] US dollar

妹 mèi [名] 1(指同胞) younger sister 2(指亲戚) ▷表妹 biǎomèi cousin

妹妹 mèimei (指同胞) younger sister

魅 mèi [名] demon

魅力 mèilì [名] charm

闷 mēn I [形] stuffy II [动] 1(盖) cover ... tightly 2(不出声) keep silent 3(使自己处于) shut oneself in
→ see also/另见 mèn

闷热 mēnrè [形] muggy

门 mén I [名] 1 (指出入口) door ▶门口 ménkǒu entrance 2 (指开关装置) switch ▶电门 diànmén switch II [量] 5门课 wǔ mén kè five courses ▶一门新技术 yī mén xīn jìshù a new technology measure word, used for academic subjects, courses and technology

门类 ménlèi [名] category

门卫 ménwèi [名] guard

门诊 ménzhěn [名] outpatient department

闷 mèn [形] 1 (烦) low 2 (无聊) bored
→ see also/另见 mēn

们 men [后缀] ▶我们 wǒmen we, us ▶你们 nǐmen you ▶他们 tāmen they, them

蒙 mēng [动] 1 (欺骗) deceive 2 (乱猜) make a wild guess
→ see also/另见 méng, Měng

蒙骗 mēngpiàn [动] deceive

蒙 méng I [动] 1 (遮盖) cover 2 (受到) receive II [形] ignorant ▶启蒙 qǐméng enlighten
→ see also/另见 mēng, Měng

蒙混 ménghùn [动] deceive ▶蒙混过关 ménghùn guòguān muddle through

猛 měng [形] 1 (凶猛) fierce [副] 2 (猛烈) fiercely 3 (忽然) suddenly

猛烈 měngliè [形] fierce

蒙 Měng [名] Mongolia ▶蒙古 Měnggǔ Mongolia ▶蒙古人 Měnggǔrén Mongolian ▶内蒙古 Nèiměnggǔ Inner Mongolia
→ see also/另见 mēng, méng

梦 mèng I [名] 1 (睡梦) dream ▶白日梦 báirìmèng daydream 2 (幻想) illusion ▶做梦 zuòmèng have a dream 2 (幻想) illusion ▶做梦 zuòmèng have a dream 2 (幻想) illusion ▶梦 dream

梦话 mènghuà [名] 1 (字) ▶说梦话 shuō mènghuà talk in one's sleep 2 (喻) nonsense

梦想 mèngxiǎng [动] dream

弥 mí [动] fill

弥补 míbǔ [动] make ... up

迷 mí I [动] 1 (迷失) be lost ▶迷路 mílù lose one's way 2 (迷恋) become obsessed with 3 (迷惑) be deluded II [名] fan ▶球迷 qiúmí sports fan ▶足球迷 zúqiú mí football fan

迷你 mínǐ [形] mini ▶迷你裙 mínǐ qún mini-skirt

迷信 míxìn [动] 1 (鬼神) be superstitious about 2 (人或事) have blind faith in

猕 mí see below/见下文

猕猴桃 míhóutáo [名] kiwi fruit

谜 mí [名] 1 (谜语) riddle 2 (神秘) mystery

谜语 míyǔ [名] riddle

米 mǐ I [名] 1 (稻米) rice ▶米饭 mǐfàn cooked rice II [量] meter, metre (英)

秘 mì I [形] secret II [动] keep ... secret III [名] secretary

秘密 mìmì [名] secret ▷一定要保守秘密！ Yīdìng yào bǎoshǒu mìmì! You must keep this a secret!

秘书 mìshū [名] secretary

密 mì I [形] 1 (空隙小) dense 2 (关系近) close ▷亲密 qīnmì intimate 3 (精致) meticulous ▷精密 jīngmì precise 4 (秘密) secret ▷保密 bǎomì keep sth a secret

密度 mìdù [名] density

密封 mìfēng [动] seal ... tightly

密码 mìmǎ [名] 1 (口令) password 2 (符号系统) code

密切 mìqiè [形] close

幂 mì [名] (数) power

蜜 mì I [名] honey II [形] sweet

蜜蜂 mìfēng [名] bee

蜜月 mìyuè [名] honeymoon

眠 mián [动] (睡) sleep ▷失眠 shīmián suffer from insomnia 2 (冬眠) hibernate

棉 mián [名] cotton

棉花 miánhua [名] (指植物) cotton

棉衣 miányī [名] cotton-padded clothing

免 miǎn [动] 1 (除去) exempt ▷免试 miǎnshì be exempt from an exam 2 (避免) avoid ▷免不了 miǎnbùliǎo be unavoidable 3 (不要) not be allowed ▷闲人免进 xiánrén miǎnjìn staff only

免费 miǎnfèi [动] be free of charge ▷注册一个免费电子邮箱 zhùcè yīgè miǎnfèi diànzǐ yóuxiāng register for free e-mail

免疫 miǎnyì [名] immunity

勉 miǎn [动] 1 (努力) strive 2 (勉励) encourage 3 (勉强) force ... to carry on

勉强 miǎnqiǎng I [动] 1 (尽力) push oneself hard ▷做事不要太勉强。 Zuòshì bùyào tài miǎnqiǎng. Don't push yourself too hard. 2 (强迫) force ▷不要勉强孩子学钢琴。 Bùyào miǎnqiǎng háizi xué gāngqín. Don't force the child to study the piano. II [形] 1 (不情愿) reluctant ▷我让他帮忙，他勉强答应了。 Wǒ ràng tā bāngmáng, tā miǎnqiǎng dāyìng le. I asked him to help, and he reluctantly agreed. 2 (凑合) barely enough ▷他挣的钱勉强够自己花。 Tā zhèng de qián miǎnqiǎng gòu zìjǐ huā. The money he earned was barely enough to support himself. 3 (牵强) far-fetched ▷这个理论有点勉强。 Zhège lǐlùn yǒudiǎn miǎnqiǎng. This theory is a bit far-fetched.

冕 miǎn [名] 1 (皇冠) crown ▷加冕 jiāmiǎn be crowned 2 (冠军头衔) title ▷卫冕 wèimiǎn defend one's title

缅 miǎn [形] (书) remote

缅甸 Miǎndiàn [名] Myanmar

面 miàn I [名] 1 (脸) face 2 (表面) surface 3 (方位) aspect ▶前面 qiánmiàn front 4 (情面) self-respect 5 (粉末) powder ▶辣椒面 làjiāomiàn chilli powder 6 (磨成粉的粮食) flour ▶面粉 miànfěn flour 7 (面条) noodles (PL) II [动] (朝) face III [量] (用于扁平物)
▷一面墙 yī miàn qiáng a wall ▷两面镜子 liǎng miàn jìngzi two mirrors

measure word, used for objects with a flat surface, such as walls, mirrors, drums etc.

2 (指见面的次数) ▷我只见过她一面。 Wǒ zhǐ jiànguò tā yī miàn. I've only met her once before. ▷我们见过几面。 Wǒmen jiànguò jǐ miàn. We've met a few times.

measure word, used for encounters between two people

面包 miànbāo [名] bread ▶面包房 miànbāofáng bakery

面对 miànduì [动] face

面积 miànjī [名] area

面临 miànlín [动] face

面貌 miànmào [名] 1 (面容) features (PL) 2 (喻) appearance

面前 miànqián [名] ▷在困难面前 zài kùnnan miànqián in the face of difficulties

面试 miànshì [动] have an interview

面条 miàntiáo [名] noodles (PL) ▷意大利面条 Yìdàlì miàntiáo spaghetti

面子 miànzi [名] 1 (体面) face ▷丢面子 diū miànzi lose face 2 (情面) feelings (PL) ▷给我点面子，你就答应吧！ Gěi wǒ diǎn miànzi, nǐ jiù dāying ba! Show some respect for my feelings and say yes!

苗 miáo [名] (指植物) seedling ▶树苗 shùmiáo sapling

苗条 miáotiao [形] slim

描 miáo [动] 1 (画) trace 2 (涂抹) touch ... up

描述 miáoshù [动] describe

描写 miáoxiě [动] describe

瞄 miáo [动] fix one's eyes on

瞄准 miáozhǔn [动] (对准) take aim

秒 miǎo [量] (指时间) second ▷5秒 wǔ miǎo five seconds

妙 miào [形] 1 (好) wonderful 2 (巧妙) ingenious

庙 miào [名] temple

灭 miè [动] 1 (熄灭) go out 2 (使熄灭) extinguish ▶灭火器 mièhuǒqì fire extinguisher 3 (淹没) submerge 4 (消亡) perish 5 (消灭) kill

灭绝 mièjué [动] (消亡) become extinct

民 mín [名] 1 (人民) the people (PL) 2 (人) person ▸网民 wǎngmín Internet user 3 (民间) folk 4 (非军方) civilian

民歌 míngē [名] folk song

民间 mínjiān [名] 1 (百姓中间) folk ▸民间传说 mínjiān zhuànshuō folklore 2 (非官方) ▸民间组织 mínjiān zǔzhī non-governmental organization

民警 mínjǐng [名] civil police

民主 mínzhǔ I [名] democracy II [形] democratic

民族 mínzú [名] nationality ▸少数民族 shǎoshù mínzú ethnic minority

敏 mǐn [形] 1 (快) quick ▸敏感 mǐngǎn sensitive 2 (聪明) clever ▸机敏 jīmǐn quick-witted

敏捷 mǐnjié [形] quick

名 míng I [名] 1 (名字) name ▸书名 shū míng book title 2 (名声) reputation II [形] famous ▸名著 míngzhù classics (PL) III [量] 1 (指人) ▸5名工人 wǔ míng gōngrén five workers ▸10名教师 shí míng jiàoshī ten teachers

measure word, used for people of any profession

2 (指名次) ▸期末考试她得了第一名。Qīmò kǎoshì tā dé le dìyī míng. She came first in the end-of-term exams.

measure word, used for rankings in competitions and exams

名称 míngchēng [名] name

名次 míngcì [名] ranking

名单 míngdān [名] list of names

名额 míng'é [名] quota

名牌 míngpái [名] famous name ▸名牌服装 míngpái fúzhuāng designer clothing

名片 míngpiàn [名] business card

名气 míngqì [名] fame

名人 míngrén [名] famous person

名声 míngshēng [名] reputation

名胜 míngshèng [名] tourist site

名字 míngzi [名] name ▸你叫什么名字? Nǐ jiào shénme míngzi? What's your name?

明 míng I [形] 1 (亮) bright 2 (清楚) clear 3 (公开) open II [名] 1 (视力) sight ▸失明 shīmíng lose one's eyesight 2 (光明) light III [动] 1 (懂) understand ▸明理 mínglǐ be understanding 2 (显示) show ▸表明 biǎomíng indicate

明白 míngbai I [形] 1 (清楚) clear 2 (聪明) sensible 3 (公开) explicit II [动] understand

明亮 míngliàng [形] 1 (亮堂) bright 2 (发亮) shining 3 (明白) clear

明确 míngquè I [形] clear-cut II [动] clarify

明显 míngxiǎn [形] obvious

明星 míngxīng [名] star

明智 míngzhì [形] sensible

命 mìng [名] 1 (性命) life 2 (命

运) fate **3**(寿命) lifespan **4**(命令) order

命令 mìnglìng [动] order

命名 mìngmíng [动] name

命运 mìngyùn [名] fate

摸 mō [动] **1**(触摸) stroke **2**(摸黑行动) feel one's way ▸摸索 mōsuǒ grope

模 mó **I**[名] model ▸模型 móxíng model **II**[动] imitate
→ see also/另见 mú

模范 mófàn [名] model

模仿 mófǎng [动] imitate

模糊 móhu [形] blurred

模拟 mónǐ [动] imitate ▸模拟考试 mónǐ kǎoshì mock exam

模式 móshì [名] pattern

模特儿 mótèr [名] model

模型 móxíng [名] **1**(样品) model **2**(模具) mould (英), mold (美)

膜 mó [名] (膜状物) film ▸保鲜膜 bǎoxiānmó clingfilm (英), plastic wrap (美)

摩 mó [动] (摩擦) rub ... together

摩擦 mócā **I**[动] rub **II**[名] **1**(阻力) friction **2**(冲突) conflict

摩托车 mótuōchē [名] motorbike

磨 mó **I**[动] **1**(摩擦) rub **2**(指用磨料) grind ▸磨刀 módāo sharpen a knife **3**(折磨) wear ... down **4**(纠缠) pester **5**(拖延) dawdle
→ see also/另见 mò

磨擦 mócā [动] rub

磨蹭 móceng [形] sluggish

磨合 móhé [动] (适应) adapt to each other

磨炼 móliàn [动] steel

磨损 mósǔn [动] wear ... out

蘑 mó [名] mushroom

蘑菇 mógu [名] mushroom

魔 mó **I**[名] **1**(魔鬼) demon **2**(魔法) magic **II**[形] magic

魔法 mófǎ [名] magic

魔鬼 móguǐ [名] devil

魔术 móshù [名] magic

魔术师 móshùshī [名] magician

抹 mǒ [动] **1**(涂抹) apply **2**(擦) wipe **3**(去除) erase
→ see also/另见 mā

末 mò [名] (尾) end ▸世纪末 shìjì mò the end of the century

末尾 mòwěi [名] end

没 mò [动] **1**(沉没) sink **2**(漫过) overflow **3**(隐没) disappear ▸出没 chūmò appear and disappear
→ see also/另见 méi

没收 mòshōu [动] confiscate

沫 mò [名] foam ▸泡沫 pàomò bubble

茉 mò see below/见下文

茉莉 mòlì [名] jasmine

陌 mò [名] (书) footpath

陌生 mòshēng [形] unfamiliar

陌生人 mòshēngrén [名] stranger

墨 mò **I**[名] (墨汁) ink ▸墨汁

mòzhǐ ink II [形] dark ▶墨镜 mòjìng sunglasses

默 mò [动] 1 (不出声) do ... silently ▶默哀 mò'āi pay ... silent tribute 2 (默写) write ... from memory

磨 mó I [名] mill ▶磨坊 mòfáng mill II [动] grind
→ see also/另见 mó

谋 móu [名] plan ▶阴谋 yīnmóu plot

谋杀 móushā [动] murder

谋生 móushēng [动] make a living

某 mǒu [代] (指不确定的人或事) ▶某人 mǒurén somebody

模 mú [名] mould (英), mold (美)
→ see also/另见 mó

模样 múyàng [名] (相貌) looks (PL)

母 mǔ I [名] 1 (母亲) mother 2 (指长辈女子) ▶祖母 zǔmǔ grandmother 3 (喻) (基础) origin II [形] (雌性) female ▶母牛 mǔniú cow

母亲 mǔqīn [名] mother

拇 mǔ [名] see below/见下文

拇指 mǔzhǐ [名] 1 (指手) thumb 2 (指脚) big toe

木 mù I [名] 1 (树) tree 2 (木材) wood II [形] (僵) numb

木材 mùcái [名] timber

木匠 mùjiang [名] carpenter

木偶 mù'ǒu [名] puppet

木头 mùtou [名] wood

目 mù [名] 1 (眼睛) eye 2 (条目) item

目标 mùbiāo [名] 1 (对象) target 2 (目的) goal

目的 mùdì [名] 1 (指地点) destination 2 (结果) aim 3 (企图) intention

目光 mùguāng [名] 1 (视线) gaze 2 (神情) look

目录 mùlù [名] 1 (指事物) catalogue (英), catalog (美) 2 (指书刊) table of contents

目前 mùqián [名] present ▶到目前为止 dào mùqián wéizhǐ to date ▶我们目前的任务 wǒmen mùqián de rènwù our current tasks

牧 mù [动] herd

牧民 mùmín [名] herdsman

牧师 mùshi [名] priest

牧业 mùyè [名] animal husbandry

募 mù [动] (钱款) raise

募捐 mùjuān [动] collect donations

墓 mù [名] grave

墓碑 mùbēi [名] gravestone

墓地 mùdì [名] graveyard

幕 mù [名] (帷幔) curtain ▶银幕 yínmù the silver screen

睦 mù [动] get on ▶和睦 hémù harmonious

穆 mù [形] solemn

穆斯林 mùsīlín [名] Muslim

n

No, no, it was nothing.

哪些 nǎxiē [代] which

那 nà **I** [代] that ▷ 那些人 nàxiē rén those people **II** [连] then ▷ 你想买，那就买吧。 nǐ xiǎng mǎi, nà jiù mǎi ba. If you want to buy it, then buy it.

那边 nàbiān [名] that side

那个 nàge [代] (指代人, 事或物) that

那里 nàlǐ [代] ▷ 我去过那里。 wǒ qùguo nàlǐ. I've been there. ▷ 我也要去那里吗？ wǒ yě yào qù nàlǐ ma? Shall I go over there as well?

那么 nàme [代] **1**(表示程度) ▷ 你不该那么相信他。 nǐ bù gāi nàme xiāngxìn tā. You shouldn't trust him so much. **2**(表示方式) ▷ 你别那么想。 nǐ bié nàme xiǎng. Don't think in that way.

那些 nàxiē [代] those

那样 nàyàng [副] ▷ 我没有说过那样的话。 wǒ méiyǒu shuōguo nàyàng de huà. I never said anything like that.

奶 nǎi [名] milk ▷ 酸奶 suānnǎi yoghurt

奶酪 nǎilào [名] cheese

奶奶 nǎinai [名] (父方的) granny

耐 nài [动] **1**(指人) endure ▷ 耐性 nàixìng patience **2**(指材料) be resistant ▷ 耐用 nàiyòng enduring

耐力 nàilì [名] stamina

拿 ná [动] **1**(握) hold **2**(得) get

哪 nǎ [代] **1**(什么) which ▷ 你喜欢哪种音乐？ nǐ xǐhuan nǎ zhǒng yīnyuè? What kind of music do you like? ▷ 哪个人是李先生？ nǎ gè rén shì Lǐ Xiānsheng? Which one is Mr Li? **2**(任何一个) any ▷ 你哪天来都行。 nǐ nǎ tiān lái dōu xíng. You can come any day.

哪个 nǎge [代] which

哪里 nǎlǐ [代] **1**(用于问处所) ▷ 你住在哪里？ nǐ zhù zài nǎlǐ? Where do you live? **2**(指某一地方) ▷ 我们应该在哪里见过。 wǒmen yīnggāi zài nǎlǐ jiànguo. I'm sure we've met somewhere before. **3**(谦) ▷ 哪里, 哪里, 你过奖了。 nǎlǐ, nǎlǐ, nǐ guòjiǎng le.

耐心 nàixīn [形] patient

男 nán [名] (男性) male

男孩子 nánháizi [名] boy

男朋友 nánpéngyou [名] boyfriend

男人 nánrén [名] man

南 nán [名] south ▸东南 dōngnán south-east ▸西南 xīnán south-west

南边 nánbiān [名] the south

南部 nánbù [名] southern part

南方 nánfāng [名] the South

南极 nánjí [名] South Pole

难 nán [形] 1 (困难) hard 2 (不好) bad, baffle

难道 nándào [副] ▸你难道还不明白吗？ nǐ nándào hái bù míngbai ma? How can you not understand? ▸难道你就不累？ nándào nǐ jiù bù lèi? Aren't you tired?

难过 nánguò I [动] have a hard time II [形] upset

难看 nánkàn [形] 1 (丑) ugly 2 (不体面) ashamed

难免 nánmiǎn [动] be unavoidable

难受 nánshòu [动] 1 (指身体) not feel well 2 (指心情) feel down

脑 nǎo [名] 1 (生理) brain 2 (脑筋) head 3 (头部) head 4 (头领) leader ▸首脑 shǒunǎo head

脑袋 nǎodai [名] head

脑子 nǎozi [名] brain

闹 nào I [形] noisy II [动] 1 (吵闹) have a row ▸闹别扭 nào bièniu fall out 2 (病、灾难) suffer from ▸闹肚子 nào dùzi have diarrhoea (英) 或 diarrhea (美)

闹钟 nàozhōng [名] alarm clock

呢 ne [助] 1 (表示疑问) ▸你们都走，我呢？ nǐmen dōu zǒu, wǒ ne? If you all go, what about me? ▸我到底错在哪儿呢？ wǒ dàodǐ cuò zài nǎr ne? What did I actually do wrong? 2 (表示陈述) ▸离北京还远着呢。lí Běijīng hái yuǎnzhe ne. Beijing is still quite far. 3 (表示持续) ▸老师还在办公室呢。lǎoshī hái zài bàngōngshì ne. The teacher is still in the office.

→ see also / 另见 ní

呢 ne is added to the end of a statement to form a tentative question, or to indicate that a response is expected, e.g. 你好吗？我很好，你呢？Nǐ hǎo ma? Wǒ hěn hǎo, nǐ ne? (How are you? Fine, and you?). It may also be used to stress continuity, e.g. 我还在吃饭呢 Wǒ hái zài chīfàn ne (I am still eating dinner), whereas 吗 ma is added to the end of any statement to turn it into a simple yes/no question, e.g. 你忙吗？Nǐ máng ma? (Are you busy?)

内 nèi [名] (里头) inside ▸室内 shìnèi indoor ▸内地 nèidì inland ▸他在一个月内完成了任务。 tā zài yī gè yuè nèi wánchéng le rènwu. He finished the task within a month.

内部 nèibù [形] internal

内服 nèifú [动] take orally

内行 nèiháng [名] expert

内科 nèikē [名] internal medicine

内容 nèiróng [名] content

内向 nèixiàng [形] introverted

能 néng I [名] 1 (能力) ability 2 (物) (能量) energy 能量 néngliàng energy II [形] capable III [助动] can

能，会huì，and可以kěyǐ can all be used to express ability and are sometimes used interchangeably. Strictly, 能néng should be used to express physical ability, e.g. 我能跑得很快wǒ néng pǎo de hěn kuài (I can run very fast), while 会huì should express a learned ability, e.g. 我会说法语wǒ huì shuō fǎyǔ (I can speak French). Both 能néng and 可以kěyǐ can express being able to do something because you have been granted permission, e.g. 你能/可以借我的照相机 nǐ

néng/kěyǐ jiè wǒ de zhàoxiàngjī (You can/may borrow my camera).

能干 nénggàn [形] capable

能够 nénggòu [动] be able to

能力 nénglì [名] ability

能源 néngyuán [名] energy

呢 ní [名] woollen cloth
→ see also / 另见 ne

呢子 nízi [名] woollen cloth

泥 ní [名] (土) mud

你 nǐ [代] 1 (称对方) you 2 (你的) your ▸你家有几口人？ nǐ jiā yǒu jǐ kǒu rén? How many people are there in your family?

你们 nǐmen [代] you (PL)

腻 nì [形] (太油) oily

蔫 niān [形] (枯萎) withered

年 nián I [名] 1 (时间单位) year 2 (元旦或春节) New Year 3 (岁数) age II [形] annual

年代 niándài [名] (时代) period

年级 niánjí [名] year (英), grade (美)

年纪 niánjì [名] age

年龄 niánlíng [名] age

年轻 niánqīng [形] young

黏 nián [形] sticky

念 niàn [动] 1 (读) read 2 (上学) study

念叨 niàndao [动] (唠叨) nag

念书 niànshū [动] study

念头 niàntou [名] idea

鸟 niǎo [名] bird

尿 niào I [名] urine ▷撒尿 sāniào urinate II [动] urinate

镊 niè [名] tweezers (PL) ▶镊子 nièzi tweezers (PL)

您 nín [代] you ▷您慢走! nín màn zǒu! Mind how you go!

宁 níng [形] peaceful
→ see also/另见 nìng

拧 níng [动] 1 (毛巾, 衣服) wring 2 (皮肤) pinch

柠 níng see below/见下文

柠檬 níngméng [名] lemon

宁 nìng [副] ▶宁愿 nìngyuàn would rather
→ see also/另见 níng

牛 niú [名] 1 (指动物) cow ▷公牛 gōngniú bull 2 (指肉) beef ▶牛肉 niúròu beef

牛奶 niúnǎi [名] milk

牛仔裤 niúzǎikù [名] jeans (PL)

扭 niǔ [动] 1 (掉转) turn around 2 (拧) twist 3 (崴) sprain

纽 niǔ [名] (扣子) button ▶纽扣 niǔkòu button

纽约 Niǔyuē [名] New York

农 nóng [名] 1 (农业) agriculture (农民) farmer

农场 nóngchǎng [名] farm

农村 nóngcūn [名] the countryside

农历 nónglì [名] lunar calendar

农民 nóngmín [名] farmer

农业 nóngyè [名] agriculture

浓 nóng [形] 1 (指气味, 味道) strong 2 (指浓雾) thick 3 (指兴趣) great ▷他对语言有很浓的兴趣。tā duì yǔyán yǒu hěn nóng de xìngqù. He has a great interest in languages.

浓缩 nóngsuō I [动] condense II [形] condensed

弄 nòng [动] 1 (搞) make 2 (设法取得) get

努 nǔ [动] (劲力) make an effort ▷我们再努把力。wǒmen zài nǔ bǎ lì. Let's make one last effort.

努力 nǔlì [动] try hard ▷我会尽最大努力。wǒ huì jìn zuìdà nǔlì. I'll try my very best.

怒 nù I [形] (生气) angry ▶恼怒 nǎonù furious II [名] anger ▶发怒 fānù lose one's temper

女 nǚ [名] 1 (女子) woman ▷女演员 nǚyǎnyuán actress 2 (女儿) daughter ▶子女 zǐnǚ children

女儿 nǚ'ér [名] daughter

女孩子 nǚháizi [名] girl

女朋友 nǚpéngyou [名] girlfriend

女人 nǚrén [名] woman

女士 nǚshì [名] 1 (指称呼) Ms. 2 (对妇女的尊称) lady

女婿 nǚxu [名] son-in-law

暖 nuǎn I [形] warm II [动] warm

暖和 nuǎnhuo I [形] warm II [动] warm up

暖气 nuǎnqì [名] heating

暖水瓶 nuǎnshuǐpíng [名] Thermos® flask

挪 nuó [动] move ▶挪动 nuódong move

哦 ó [叹] oh ▶哦，他也来了。Ó, tā yě láile. Oh, he's come too.
→ see also/另见 ò

哦 ò [叹] oh ▶哦，我明白了。Ò, wǒ míngbai le. Oh, now I understand.
→ see also/另见 ó

欧 ōu [名] (欧洲) Europe ▶欧洲 Ōuzhōu Europe

欧元 ōuyuán [名] euro

呕 ǒu [动] vomit

呕吐 ǒutù [动] vomit

偶 ǒu [名] 1 (人像) image ▶木偶 mù'ǒu puppet 2 (双数) even number ▶偶数 ǒushù even number

偶尔 ǒu'ěr[副] occasionally

偶然 ǒurán[形] chance

藕 ǒu[名] lotus root

P

爬 pá[动] 1(前移) crawl 2(上移) climb ►爬山 páshānclimb a mountain 3(起床) get up 4(升迁) be promoted

怕 pà[动] 1(惧怕) fear 2(担心) be afraid 3(估计) may be

拍 pāi I[动] 1(击打) beat 2(拍摄) shoot 3(发) send 4(拍马屁) flatter II[名] 1(用具) bat (英), paddle (美) 2(节奏) beat

拍照 pāizhào[动] take a photograph

拍子 pāizi[名] 1(用具) bat (英), paddle (美) ►网球拍子 wǎngqiú pāizitennis racket 2(节奏) beat

排 pái I[动] 1(摆放) put ... in

order **2** (排演) rehearse **3** (除去) drain **II** [名] **1** (行列) row **2** (指 军队) platoon **3** (指水运) raft **III** [量] row

排队 páiduì [动] queue (英), stand in line (美)

排球 páiqiú [名] volleyball

牌 pái [名] **1** (标志板) board ▸ 门 牌 ménpái house number ▸ 招牌 zhāopái shop sign **2** (商标) brand

派 pài **I** [名] **1** (学派) ▸ 学派 xuépài school of thought **2** (风度) manner **II** [动] **1** (分配) set **2** (委 派) send **3** (安排) assign

派对 pàiduì [名] party

攀 pān [动] **1** (向上爬) climb **2** (指 关系) seek friends in high places ▸ 高攀 gāopān be a social climber **3** (拉扯) chat

攀登 pāndēng [动] scale

盘 pán **I** [名] **1** (盘子) tray **2** (盘状 物) ▸ 棋盘 qípán chessboard **3** (行情) quotation **II** [动] **1** (绕) wind ▸ 盘旋 pánxuán wind **2** (核 查) examine ▸ 盘问 pánwèn interrogate **3** (清点) make an inventory ▸ 盘货 pánhuò stocktake **4** (转让) transfer **III** [量] **1** (指物量) ▸ 三盘录像 带 sān pán lùxiàngdài three videotapes **2** (指动量) game

measure word, used for videotapes, cassettes and board games

盘子 pánzi [名] plate

判 pàn **I** [动] **1** (分辨) distinguish ▸ 判明 pànmíng ascertain **2** (评 定) judge **3** (裁决) sentence ▸ 审 判 shěnpàn try **II** [副] clearly

判断 pànduàn [动] judge

盼 pàn [动] **1** (盼望) long **2** (看) look ▸ 左顾右盼 zuǒgù-yòupàn look around

盼望 pànwàng [动] long

旁 páng **I** [名] side **II** [形] (口) other

旁边 pángbiān [名] side **II** [副] beside

胖 pàng [形] fat

抛 pāo [动] **1** (投掷) throw **2** (丢下) leave ... behind **3** (暴露) bare ▸ 抛 头露面 pāotóu-lùmiàn appear in public **4** (脱手) dispose of

抛弃 pāoqì [动] desert

跑 pǎo [动] **1** (奔) run **2** (逃) escape **3** (奔波) run around **4** (漏) leak

跑步 pǎobù [动] run

泡 pào **I** [名] **1** (指气体) bubble **2** (泡状物) ▸ 灯泡 dēngpào light bulb **II** [动] **1** (浸) soak **2** (消磨) dawdle **3** (沏) infuse ▸ 泡茶 pào chá make tea

泡沫 pàomò [名] foam

炮 pào [名] **1** (武器) cannon **2** (爆 竹) firecracker

陪 péi [动] **1** (相伴) go with ▸ 我 要陪母亲去医院。wǒ yào péi mǔqīn qù yīyuàn I have to go to the hospital with my mother.

2(协助)assist

陪同 péitóng I[动] accompany II[名] guide

培 péi[动] foster

培训 péixùn[动] train

培养 péiyǎng[动] cultivate

培育 péiyù[动] 1(培植养育) cultivate 2(培养教育) nurture

赔 péi[动] 1(赔偿) make good 2(亏本) make a loss

赔偿 péicháng[动] compensate

佩 pèi[动] 1(佩带) wear 2(佩服) admire ▶钦佩 qīnpèi esteem

佩服 pèifú[动] admire

配 pèi I[动] 1(指两性) marry 2(指动物) mate 3(调和) mix ▶配药 pèiyào make up a prescription 4(分配) allocate ▶配售 pèishòu ration 5(衬托) match 6(符合) fit II[名] spouse

配合 pèihé I[动] cooperate II[形] complementary

喷 pēn[动] gush

喷泉 pēnquán[名] fountain

喷嚏 pēntì[名] sneeze

盆 pén[名] 1(盛具) basin ▶脸盆 liǎnpén washbasin 2(盆状物) ▶骨盆 gǔpén pelvis

朋 péng[名] friend

朋友 péngyou[名] 1(指友谊) friend 2(女友) girlfriend 3(男友) boyfriend

捧 pěng I[动] 1(托) hold ... in both hands 2(奉承) flatter II[量] handful

碰 pèng[动] 1(撞击) hit 2(遇见) bump into 3(试探) take a chance

碰见 pèngjiàn[动] encounter

碰巧 pèngqiǎo[副] by chance

批 pī I[动] 1(指示) comment ▶批示 pīshì comment 2(批评) criticize II[名] wholesale III[量] 1(指人) group 2(指物) batch

批判 pīpàn[动] 1(驳斥) repudiate 2(批评) criticize

批评 pīpíng[动] criticize

批准 pīzhǔn[动] approve

披 pī[动] 1(搭) drape ... over one's shoulders 2(开裂) split

皮 pí I[名] 1(表皮) skin 2(皮革) leather ▶漆皮 qīpí patent leather 3(外皮) covering 4(表面) surface 5(薄片) sheet ▶奶皮 nǎipí skin on the milk 6(指橡胶) rubber II[形] 1(韧) thick-skinned 2(变韧的) rubbery 3(顽皮) naughty

皮包 píbāo[名] leather handbag

皮肤 pífū[名] skin

疲 pí[形] 1(疲劳) tired 2(厌倦) tired of

疲倦 píjuàn[形] tired

疲劳 píláo[形] 1(劳累) weary 2(衰退) weakened

啤 pí see below/见下文

啤酒 píjiǔ[名] beer

脾 pí [名] spleen

脾气 píqi [名] 1 (怒气) temper 2 (性情) temperament

匹 pǐ I [动] match II [量] 1 (指动物) ▷ 三匹马 sān pǐ mǎ three horses 2 (指布料) bolt

measure word, used for horses, mules, donkeys and bolts of silk

屁 pì I [名] wind ▷ 放屁 fàngpì fart II [形] meaningless

屁股 pìgu [名] 1 (指人) bottom 2 (指后部) rear

譬 pì [名] analogy ▷ 譬如 pìrú for example ▷ 譬喻 pìyù metaphor

譬如 pìrú [动] take ... for example

偏 piān [形] 1 (倾斜的) slanting 2 (不公的) biased

偏见 piānjiàn [名] prejudice

偏偏 piānpiān [副] 1 (表示主观) persistently 2 (表示客观) contrary to expectation 3 (表示范围) only

篇 piān I [名] 1 (文章) writing ▷ 篇章 piānzhāng sections (PL) 2 (单张纸) sheet ▷ 歌篇儿 gēpiānr song sheet II [量] ▷ 三篇文章 sān piān wénzhāng three articles

measure word, used for articles, essays etc.

便 pián see below/见下文 → see also/另见 biàn

便便 piánpián [形] fat

便宜 piányi I [形] cheap II [名]

small gains (PL) III [动] let ... off lightly

片 piàn I [名] 1 (指薄度) piece ▷ 纸片 zhǐpiàn scraps of paper 2 (指地区) area II [动] slice III [形] (不全) incomplete ▷ 片面 piànmiàn one-sided 2 (简短) brief IV [量] 1 (指片状物) ▷ 两片药 liǎng piàn yào two tablets ▷ 几片树叶 jǐ piàn shùyè some leaves ▷ 一片面包 yī piàn miànbāo a slice of bread 2 (指水陆) stretch

measure word, used for thin flat objects

片面 piànmiàn I [名] one side II [形] one-sided

骗 piàn [动] 1 (欺骗) deceive 2 (骗得) swindle ▷ 骗钱 piànqián swindle

骗子 piànzi [名] swindler

漂 piāo [动] 1 (浮) float 2 (流动) drift → see also/另见 piào

飘 piāo [动] 1 (飞扬) flutter 2 (指腿、脚) wobble

飘扬 piāoyáng [动] flutter

票 piào [名] 1 (作凭证) ticket 2 (指钞票) note (英), bill (美) 3 (指戏曲) amateur performance

漂 piào see below/见下文 → see also/另见 piāo

漂亮 piàoliang [形] 1 (好看) good-looking 2 (精彩) wonderful

拼 pīn [动] 1 (合) join together

2(竭尽全力) go all out ▶拼命 pīnmìng with all one's might **3**(字，词) spell ▷你能拼一下这个词吗? nǐ néng pīn yíxià zhège cí ma? Can you spell this word?

拼命 pīnmìng [动] **1**(不要命) risk one's life **2**(努力) go all out

拼音 pīnyīn [名] Pinyin

贫 pín **I** [形] **1**(穷) poor ▶贫民 pínmín the poor **2**(少) deficient ▶贫血 pínxuè anaemia (英), anemia (美) **II** [动] (方) be a chatterbox

贫苦 pínkǔ [形] poverty-stricken

贫穷 pínqióng [形] poor

频 pín [副] frequently

频繁 pínfán [形] frequent

频率 pínlǜ [名] **1**(物) frequency **2**(指心脏) rate

品 pǐn **I** [名] **1**(物品) article ▶商品 shāngpǐn merchandise **2**(等级) grade ▶精品 jīngpǐn special product **3**(种类) type ▶品种 pǐnzhǒng variety **4**(品质) character ▶品德 pǐndé moral character **II** [动] taste

品尝 pǐncháng [动] savour (英), savor (美)

品德 pǐndé [名] moral character

品格 pǐngé [名] character

品质 pǐnzhì [名] **1**(品德) character **2**(质量) quality

品种 pǐnzhǒng [名] **1**(动) breed **2**(植) species **3**(指产品) kind

乒 pīng **I** [拟] bang **II** [名] (also: 乒乓球) table tennis

乒乓球 pīngpāngqiú [名] table tennis

平 píng **I** [形] **1**(平坦) flat ▶平原 píngyuán plain **2**(安定) calm **3**(普通) ordinary **4**(平均) even ▶平分 píngfēn fifty-fifty **5**(指比分) 平局 píngjú a draw **II** [动] **1**(夷平) level **2**(指成绩) equal **3**(镇压) suppress

平安 píng'ān [形] safe and sound

平常 píngcháng **I** [形] common **II** [副] usually

平等 píngděng [形] equal

平凡 píngfán [形] uneventful

平方 píngfāng [名] **1**(数) square **2**(平方米) square metre (英) 或 meter (美)

平衡 pínghéng [名] balance ▶平衡收支 pínghéng shōuzhī balance revenue and expenditure

平静 píngjìng [形] calm

平均 píngjūn [形] average

平时 píngshí [副] usually

平原 píngyuán [名] plain

评 píng [动] **1**(评论) criticize ▶批评 pīpíng criticize ▶书评 shūpíng book review **2**(评判) judge ▶评分 píngfēn mark **3**(选) select

评估 pínggū [动] evaluate

评论 pínglùn [动] review

苹 píng see below / 见下文

苹果 píngguǒ [名] apple

凭 píng I [动] rely on II [名] evidence ▶凭据 píngjù credentials (PL) III [连] no matter

瓶 píng [名] bottle

瓶子 píngzi [名] bottle

坡 pō [名] slope ▶山坡 shānpō slope

迫 pò I [动] 1 (逼迫) force 2 (接近) approach II [形] urgent

迫切 pòqiè [形] pressing

破 pò I [形] 1 (受损) broken 2 (烂) lousy II [动] 1 (受损) cut 2 (破除) break 3 (例外) pòlì make an exception 4 (钱, 工夫) spend 4 (揭穿) expose ▶破案 pò'àn solve a case 5 (打败) defeat

破坏 pòhuài [动] 1 (建筑, 环境, 文物, 公物) destroy 2 (团结, 社会秩序) undermine 3 (协定, 法规, 规章) violate 4 (计划) bring ... down 5 (名誉) damage

破裂 pòliè [动] 1 (谈判) break down 2 (感情) break up 3 (外交关系) break off

扑 pū [动] 1 (冲向) rush at 2 (专注于) devote 3 (扑打) swat 4 (翅膀) beat

扑克 pūkè [名] poker

铺 pū [动] 1 (摊开) spread 2 (铺) lay
→ see also/ 另见 pù

葡 pú see below/ 见下文

葡萄 pútao [名] grape

朴 pǔ see below/ 见下文

朴实 pǔshí [形] 1 (简朴) simple 2 (诚实) honest

朴素 pǔsù [形] 1 (衣着) plain 2 (生活) simple 3 (语言) plain

普 pǔ [形] general

普遍 pǔbiàn I [形] common II [副] commonly

普通 pǔtōng [形] common

普通话 pǔtōnghuà [名] Mandarin

铺 pù [名] 1 (商店) shop ▶杂货铺 záhuòpù general store 2 (床) plank bed ▶卧铺 wòpù berth
→ see also/ 另见 pū

q

七 qī [数] seven

七月 qīyuè [名] July

妻 qī [名] wife ▶ 未婚妻 wèihūnqī fiancée

妻子 qīzǐ [名] wife

柒 qī [数] seven

This is the complex character for "seven", which is mainly used in banks, on receipts, etc. to prevent mistakes and forgery.

期 qī I [名] 1 (预定时间) time limit ▶ 到期 dàoqī expire 2 (一段时间) period of time ▶ 假期 jiàqī holiday II [量] 1 (指训练班) class 2 (指杂志, 报纸) edition III [动]

expect

期待 qīdài [动] await

期间 qījiān [名] period of time

期望 qīwàng I [名] expectations (PL) II [动] expect

欺 qī [动] 1 (欺骗) deceive 2 (欺负) bully

欺负 qīfu [动] bully

欺骗 qīpiàn [动] deceive

齐 qí I [形] 1 (整齐) neat 2 (一致) joint 3 (完备) ready II [动] 1 (达到) reach 2 (取齐) level III [副] at the same time

其 qí [代] (书) 1 (他的) his 2 (她的) her 3 (它的) its 4 (他们的, 她们的, 它们的) their 5 (他) him 6 (她) her 7 (它) it 8 (他们, 她们, 它们) them 9 (那个) that

其次 qícì [代] 1 (下一个) next ▷ 我 其次要做的事是什么？ Qícì yào zuò de shì shì shénme? What are we going to do next? 2 (次要的) the second

其实 qíshí [副] actually

其他 qítā [代] other ▷ 我不知道，你问其他人吧。Wǒ bù zhīdào, nǐ wèn qítā rén ba. I don't know, ask someone else. ▷ 还有其他事情没有？ Háiyǒu qítā shìqíng méiyǒu? Is there anything else?

其余 qíyú [代] the rest

其中 qízhōng [名] among which ▷ 我有六套西服，其中两套是黑色的。 Tā yǒu liù tào xīfú, qízhōng liǎng tào shì hēisè de. He has six suits, of which two are black.

奇 qí I [形] 1 (非常少见的) strange ▶奇闻 qíwén fantastic story ▶奇事 qíshì miracle 2 (出人意料的) unexpected ▶奇袭 qíxí surprise attack ▶奇遇 qíyù lucky encounter II [动] (惊奇) jīngqí surprise III [副] unusually

奇怪 qíguài [形] strange

奇迹 qíjì [名] miracle

骑 qí I [动] ride II [名] cavalry

棋 qí [名] chess ▶围棋 wéiqí go (board game)

旗 qí [名] flag ▶锦旗 jǐnqí silk banner

旗袍 qípáo [名] cheongsam (board game)

旗子 qízi [名] flag

乞 qǐ [动] beg ▶行乞 xíngqǐ begging

乞丐 qǐgài [名] beggar

乞求 qǐqiú [动] beg

企 qǐ [动] look forward to

企图 qǐtú I [动] plan II [名] (贬) plan

企业 qǐyè [名] enterprise

启 qǐ [动] 1 (打开) open ▶开启 kāiqǐ open 2 (开导) enlighten 3 (开始) start

启发 qǐfā I [动] inspire II [名] inspiration

起 qǐ I [动] 1 (起来) rise ▶起立 qǐlì stand up 2 (取出) remove 3 (长出) form ▶脚上起泡 jiǎoshang qǐ pào form a blister on one's foot 4 (产生) become 5 (拟订) sketch out ▶起草 qǐcǎo draft 6 (建立) establish II [量] ▶一起交通事故 yī qǐ jiāotōng shìgù a traffic accident ▶一起火灾 yī qǐ huǒzāi a fire

measure word, used for accidents

起床 qǐchuáng [动] get up

起点 qǐdiǎn [名] starting point

起飞 qǐfēi [动] take off ▶飞机准时起飞。 Fēijī zhǔnshí qǐfēi. The plane took off on time.

起来 qǐlái [动] 1 (站起或坐起) get up 2 (起床) get up

气 qì I [名] 1 (气体) gas ▶毒气 dúqì poison gas 2 (空气) air ▶这球没气了。 Zhè qiú méi qì le. This ball is deflated. 3 (气息) breath 4 (精神) mood 5 (气味) smell ▶臭气 chòuqì stink 6 (习气) manner ▶孩子气 háiziqì childishness 7 (怒气) anger 8 (怒) qì II [动] 1 (生气) be angry 2 (使生气) provoke

气氛 qìfēn [名] atmosphere

气功 qìgōng [名] qigong

气候 qìhòu [名] climate

气温 qìwēn [名] temperature

气象 qìxiàng [名] 1 (大气现象) weather 2 (气象学) meteorology 3 (情景)

atmosphere

汽 qì[名] 1(气体) vapour (英), vapor (美) 2(蒸气) steam

汽车 qìchē[名] car ▶公共汽车 gōnggòng qìchē bus

汽水 qìshuǐ[名] fizzy drink

汽油 qìyóu[名] petrol (英), gasoline (美)

器 qì[名] 1(器具) utensil ▶乐器 yuèqì musical instrument ▶瓷器 cíqì china 2(器官) organ

器官 qìguān[名] organ

恰 qià[副] 1(适当) appropriately 2(刚好) exactly

恰当 qiàdàng[形] appropriate

恰好 qiàhǎo[副] luckily

千 qiān I [数] thousand II [形] many

千万 qiānwàn I [数] ten million II [副] ▷你千万别做傻事。Nǐ qiānwàn bié zuò shǎshì. You absolutely mustn't do anything stupid.

牵 qiān[动] 1(拉住) pull 2(牵涉) involve

铅 qiān[名] (化) lead

铅笔 qiānbǐ[名] pencil

谦 qiān[形] modest

谦虚 qiānxū I [形] modest II [动] speak modestly

签 qiān I [动] 1(名字) sign 2(意见) endorse 3(指占卜, 赌博, 比赛) lot 2(标志) label ▶书

签 shūqiān bookmark 3(细棍子) stick ▶牙签 yáqiān toothpick

签名 qiānmíng[动] sign

签证 qiānzhèng[名] visa

签字 qiānzì[动] sign one's name

前 qián I [形] 1(正面的) front 2(指次序) first 3(从前的) former ▶前夫 qiánfū ex-husband 4(未来的) future II [动] advance

前进 qiánjìn[动] 1(向前走) advance 2(发展) make progress

前面 qiánmiàn[副] in front

前年 qiánnián[名] the year before last

前天 qiántiān[名] the day before yesterday

前途 qiántú[名] future

前夕 qiánxī[名] eve

钱 qián[名] money

钱包 qiánbāo[名] 1(女用) purse 2(男用) wallet

浅 qiǎn[形] 1(指深度) shallow 2(指难度) easy 3(指学识) lacking in knowledge 4(指颜色) light ▶浅蓝色 qiǎnlánsè light blue ▶浅绿色 qiǎnlǜsè pale green 5(指时间) short

欠 qiàn[动] 1(钱, 情) owe 2(缺乏) lack 3(移动) raise ... slightly

枪 qiāng[名] 1(旧式兵器) spear 2(兵器) gun ▶手枪 shǒuqiāng pistol

强 qiáng I [形] 1(力量大) strong 2(程度高) able 3(好) better 4(略多于) extra ▶三分之一强

fēn zhī yī qiáng a third extra
II [动] force
→ see also/另见 qiǎng

强大 qiángdà [形] powerful

强盗 qiángdào [名] robber

强调 qiángdiào [动] stress

强度 qiángdù [名] intensity

强奸 qiángjiān [动] rape

强烈 qiángliè [形] intense

墙 qiáng [名] wall

抢 qiǎng [动] 1 (抢夺) rob 2 (抢夺) grab 3 (抢先) forestall 4 (赶紧) rush

抢劫 qiǎngjié [动] rob

强 qiǎng [动] 1 (勉强) make an effort 2 (迫使) force
→ see also/另见 qiáng

强迫 qiǎngpò [动] force

悄 qiāo see below/见下文

悄悄 qiāoqiāo [副] 1 (悄然无声) quietly 2 (不让知道) stealthily

敲 qiāo [动] 1 (击) knock 2 (敲诈) blackmail

敲诈 qiāozhà [动] extort

桥 qiáo [名] bridge

桥梁 qiáoliáng [名] bridge

瞧 qiáo [动] look

巧 qiǎo [形] 1 (手、口) nimble 2 (有技能的) skilful (英), skillful (美) 3 (恰好) coincidental 4 (虚浮的) false

巧克力 qiǎokèlì [名] chocolate

巧妙 qiǎomiào [形] clever

切 qiē [动] cut

茄 qié [名] aubergine (英), eggplant (美)

茄子 qiézi [名] aubergine (英), eggplant (美)

窃 qiè I [动] steal II [副] surreptitiously

窃听 qiètīng [动] eavesdrop

窃贼 qièzéi [名] thief

侵 qīn [动] invade

侵略 qīnlüè [动] invade

亲 qīn I [名] 1 (父母) parent 2 (亲戚) relative 3 (婚姻) marriage ▶定亲 dìngqīn engagement 4 (新娘) bride II [形] 1 (指血缘近) blood 2 (指感情好) intimate III [副] personally IV [动] 1 (亲吻) kiss 2 (亲近) be close to

亲爱 qīn'ài [形] dear

亲近 qīnjìn [形] close

亲密 qīnmì [形] close ▶亲密朋友 qīnmì péngyǒu close friend ▶亲密无间 qīnmì wújiàn be as thick as thieves

亲戚 qīnqi [名] relative

亲切 qīnqiè [形] warm

亲热 qīnrè [形] affectionate

亲自 qīnzì [副] personally

琴 qín [名] ▶钢琴 gāngqín piano ▶小提琴 xiǎotíqín violin

勤 qín I [形] hard-working II [副] regularly III [副] 1 (勤务) duty

▶值勤 zhíqín be on duty **2**(到场) attendance ▶考勤 kǎoqín check attendance

勤奋 qínfèn [形] diligent

勤劳 qínláo [形] hard-working

青 qīng I [形] **1**(指颜色) green **2**(指伤害) black **3**(指年纪) young ▶青年 qīngnián youth II [名] **1**(指青草) grass **2**(指庄稼) unripe crops (PL)

青年 qīngnián [名] youth

青少年 qīngshàonián [名] teenager

轻 qīng I [形] **1**(指重量) light **2**(指数量或程度) ▶他们年纪很轻。Tāmen niánjì hěnqīng. They are quite young. **3**(指无足轻重) not important **4**(指轻松愉快) relaxed ▶轻音乐 qīngyīnyuè light music II [副] **1**(指少用力) gently **2**(轻率) rashly III [动] disparage

轻松 qīngsōng [形] relaxing

轻易 qīngyì [副] **1**(容易) easily **2**(随便) rashly

倾 qīng I [动] **1**(斜) lean **2**(塌) collapse **3**(倒出) empty out **4**(用尽) exhaust II [名] tendency

倾向 qīngxiàng I [动] incline to II [名] tendency

清 qīng I [形] **1**(纯净) clear **2**(寂静) quiet **3**(清楚) distinct ▶分清 fēnqīng distinguish **4**(完全) settled **5**(纯洁) pure II [动] **1**(清除) get rid of **2**(结清) settle **3**(清

点) check **4**(清理) put in order

清楚 qīngchu I [形] clear II [动] understand

清洁 qīngjié [形] clean

清静 qīngjìng [形] quiet

清明节 Qīngmíng Jié [名] Tomb Sweeping Festival

清明节 Qīngmíng Jié, **Clear and Bright Festival** sometimes translated literally as **Tomb Sweeping Festival**, is celebrated on the 4th, 5th, or 6th of April. It is traditionally the time when Chinese families visit graves to honour their dead ancestors.

情 qíng [名] **1**(感情) feeling ▶热情 rèqíng warmth **2**(情面) kindness **3**(爱情) love **4**(情况) condition ▶实情 shíqíng true state of affairs

情节 qíngjié [名] **1**(内容) plot **2**(事实) circumstances (PL)

情景 qíngjǐng [名] sight

情况 qíngkuàng [名] **1**(状况) situation **2**(变化) military development

情侣 qínglǚ [名] lovers (PL)

情人节 Qíngrén Jié [名] Valentine's Day

情形 qíngxíng [名] situation

情绪 qíngxù [名] **1**(心理状态)

mood **2** (不很开心) moodiness

晴 qíng [形] fine

晴朗 qínglǎng [形] sunny

请 qǐng [动] **1** (请求) ask ▷请他进来。 Qǐng tā jìnlái. Ask him to come in. **2** (邀请) invite ▷ (敬) ▷请这边走。 Qǐng zhèbiān zǒu. This way, please. ▷请大家安静一下。 Qǐng dàjiā ānjìng yīxià. Everyone quiet, please.

请假 qǐngjià [动] ask for leave

请教 qǐngjiào [动] consult

请客 qǐngkè [动] treat

请求 qǐngqiú [动] ask

请问 qǐngwèn [动] ▷请问怎么出去？ Qǐngwèn zěnme chūqù? Could you show me the way out, please?

请勿 qǐngwù [动] ▷请勿吸烟。 Qǐngwù xīyān. No smoking.

庆 qìng I [动] celebrate II [名] festival ▷国庆 guóqìng National Day

庆贺 qìnghè [动] celebrate

庆祝 qìngzhù [动] celebrate

穷 qióng I [形] poor II [名] limit III [副] **1** (彻底) thoroughly **2** (极端) extremely

秋 qiū [名] **1** (指季节) autumn (英), fall (美) **2** (指庄稼) harvest time **3** (指一年) year **4** (指厄运期) period

秋天 qiūtiān [名] autumn (英), fall (美)

求 qiú I [动] **1** (请求) request **2** (追求) strive for II [名] demand

球 qiú [名] **1** (数) (球体) sphere **2** (指球状) ball ▷雪球 xuěqiú snowball **3** (指体育) ball ▷篮球 lánqiú basketball ▷足球 zúqiú football **4** (指比赛) ball game **5** (地球) the Earth ▷全球 quánqiú the whole world

球场 qiúchǎng [名] court

球迷 qiúmí [名] fan

区 qū I [动] distinguish II [名] **1** (地区) area **2** (指行政单位) region ▷自治区 zìzhìqū autonomous region

区别 qūbié [动] distinguish

区分 qūfēn [动] differentiate

区域 qūyù [名] area

趋 qū [动] **1** (走) hasten **2** (趋向) tend to become

趋势 qūshì [名] trend

趋向 qūxiàng I [动] tend to II [名] trend

渠 qú [名] ditch

渠道 qúdào [名] **1** (水道) irrigation ditch **2** (途径) channel

曲 qǔ [名] **1** (指歌曲) song **2** (指乐曲) music

曲子 qǔzi [名] tune

取 qǔ [动] **1** (拿到) take **2** (得到) obtain **3** (采取) adopt **4** (选取) choose

取得 qǔdé [动] get

取消 qǔxiāo [动] cancel

娶 qǔ [动] marry

去 qù I [动] 1 (到) go 2 (除) get rid of 3 (距) be apart 4 (发) send II [形] past

去年 qùnián [名] last year

去世 qùshì [动] pass away

趣 qù I [名] interest ▶志趣 zhìqù interest II [形] interesting

趣味 qùwèi [名] taste

圈 quān I [名] 1 (环形物) circle ▶北极圈 Běijíquān Arctic Circle 2 (界) group II [动] circle

圈套 quāntào [名] trap

权 quán I [名] 1 (权力) power ▶当权 dāngquán be in power 2 (权利) right 3 (形势) ▶主动权 zhǔdòngquán initiative ▶控制权 kòngzhìquán control 4 (权宜) expediency II [副] for the time being

权力 quánlì [名] power

全 quán I [形] 1 (齐全) complete 2 (整个) whole II [副] entirely III [动] keep ... intact

全部 quánbù [形] whole

全面 quánmiàn [形] comprehensive

全体 quántǐ [名] everyone

泉 quán [名] spring ▶温泉 wēnquán hot spring

拳 quán [名] fist

拳头 quántóu [名] fist

拳击 quánjī [名] boxing

鬈 quán [形] curly

劝 quàn [动] 1 (说服) advise 2 (勉励) encourage

劝告 quàngào [动] advise

缺 quē I [动] 1 (缺乏) lack 2 (残破) be incomplete 3 (缺席) be absent II [名] vacancy ▶补缺 bǔquē fill a vacancy

缺点 quēdiǎn [名] shortcoming

缺乏 quēfá [动] lack

缺口 quēkǒu [名] 1 (口子) gap 2 (缺额) shortfall

缺少 quēshǎo [动] lack

缺席 quēxí [动] be absent

缺陷 quēxiàn [名] defect

瘸 qué [动] be lame

却 què I [动] 1 (后退) step back 2 (使退却) back ... back 3 (拒绝) decline ▶推却 tuīquè decline 4 (表示完成) ▶冷却 lěngquè cool off ▶忘却 wàngquè forget II [副] however

确 què I [副] 1 (确实地) really 2 (坚定地) firmly ▶确信 quèxìn firmly believe

确定 quèdìng I [动] determine II [形] definite

确实 quèshí I [形] true II [副] really

裙 qún [名] skirt

裙子 qúnzi [名] skirt

群 qún I [名] crowd II [量] 1 (指动物) herd, flock ▶一群羊 yī qún

miányáng a flock of sheep ▷一群
蜜蜂 yī qún mìfēng a swarm of
bees ▷一群奶牛 yī qún nǎiniú a
herd of cows 2(指人) group ▷一
群学生 yī qún xuésheng a group
of students

群众 qúnzhòng [名] the masses
(PL)

r

然 rán [代] so

然而 rán'ér [连] however

然后 ránhòu [连] afterwards

燃 rán [动] 1(燃烧) burn 2(点
燃) light

燃料 ránliào [名] fuel

燃烧 ránshāo [动] burn

染 rǎn [动] 1(着色) dye 2(感染)
contract 3(沾染) catch

嚷 rǎng [动] 1(喊叫) howl 2(吵闹)
make a racket

让 ràng I [动] 1(退让) make
allowances 2(允许) let 3(转让)
transfer II [介] by

扰 rǎo [动] (搅扰) disturb ▷打扰

dǎrǎo disturb

绕 rào [动] 1 (缠绕) wind 2 (围绕) go round 3 (迂回) make a detour

惹 rě [动] 1 (引起) stir up 2 (触动) provoke 3 (招) make

热 rè I [名] 1 (物) heat 2 (高烧) fever ▶发烧 fāshāo have a fever II [形] 1 (温度高) hot 2 (走俏) popular III [动] heat

热爱 rè'ài [动] love

热狗 règǒu [名] hot dog

热烈 rèliè [形] heated

热闹 rènao [形] lively

热情 rèqíng I [名] passion II [形] enthusiastic

热线 rèxiàn [名] 1 (指电话或电报) hotline 2 (指交通) busy route

热心 rèxīn [形] warm-hearted

人 rén [名] 1 (人类) human being 2 (人权) rénquán human rights (PL) 2 (指某种人) person ▶军人 jūnrén soldier ▶中国人 Zhōngguórén a Chinese person/Chinese people 3 (人手) manpower

人才 réncái [名] (指能力) talent

人工 réngōng [形] man-made

人口 rénkǒu [名] 1 (地区人数) population 2 (家庭人数) people

人类 rénlèi [名] mankind, humankind

人们 rénmen [名] people

人民 rénmín [名] the people

人民币 rénmínbì [名] Renminbi, RMB

人生 rénshēng [名] life

人体 réntǐ [名] the human body

人物 rénwù [名] 1 (能人) figure 2 (艺术形象) character

忍 rěn [动] (忍受) endure

忍耐 rěnnài [动] show restraint

忍受 rěnshòu [动] bear

认 rèn [动] 1 (识) know 2 (承认) admit

认得 rènde [be] acquainted with

认识 rènshi I [动] know II [名] understanding

认为 rènwéi [动] think

认真 rènzhēn I [形] serious II [动] take ... seriously

任 rèn I [动] 1 (聘) appoint ▶委任 wěirèn appoint 2 (听凭) let II [名] (职责) responsibility

任何 rènhé [形] any ▷任何人都不能迟到。Rènhé rén dōu bù néng chídào. No one can be late.

任务 rènwu [名] task

扔 rēng [动] 1 (掷) throw 2 (丢) throw ... away

仍 réng [副] still

仍然 réngrán [副] (表示继续) still

日 rì I [名] 1 (太阳) sun ▶日出 rìchū sunrise ▶日落 rìluò sunset 2 (白天) daytime 3 (天) day ▶明

日 míngrì tomorrow **4** (每天) every day ▷ 城市面貌日见改善。 Chéngshì miànmào rìjiàn gǎishàn. The city looks better and better every day. **5** (指某一天) day ▷ 生日 shēngrì birthday **6** (also: 日本) Japan

日报 rìbào [名] daily paper

日本 Rìběn [名] Japan

日常 rìcháng [形] everyday

日记 rìjì [名] diary

日历 rìlì [名] calendar

日期 rìqī [名] date

日用品 rìyòngpǐn [名] daily necessities

日语 Rìyǔ [名] Japanese

日元 Rìyuán [名] Japanese yen

日子 rìzi [名] **1** (日期) date **2** (时间) day **3** (生活) life

荣 róng [形] (光荣) glorious

荣幸 róngxìng [形] honoured (英), honored (美) ▷ 认识您，我感到非常荣幸。 Rènshi nín wǒ gǎndào fēicháng róngxìng. I feel honoured to know you.

荣誉 róngyù [名] (指名声) honour (英), honor (美)

容 róng **I** [动] **1** (容纳) fit ▷ 容纳 róngnà hold ▷ 容量 róngliàng capacity ▷ 容器 róngqì container **2** (容忍) tolerate ▷ 容忍 róngrěn tolerate **3** (允许) allow **II** [名] (相貌) appearance ▷ 容貌 róngmào features (PL)

容易 róngyì [形] **1** (简便) easy **2** (较

可能) likely

柔 róu [形] **1** (软) soft **2** (柔和) gentle

柔软 róuruǎn [形] soft

揉 róu [动] (搓) rub

肉 ròu [名] **1** (指人) flesh **2** (指动物) meat ▷ 猪肉 zhūròu pork **3** (指瓜果) flesh

如 rú [动] **1** (好似) be like **2** (比得上) be as good as ▷ 不如 bùrú not as good as **3** (例如)

如此 rúcǐ [代] so ▷ 他的态度是如此恶劣。 Tā de tàidù jìng rúcǐ èliè. His attitude was so unpleasant.

如果 rúguǒ [连] if

如何 rúhé [代] how ▷ 此事如何解决？ Cǐ shì rúhé jiějué? How are we going to sort this out? ▷ 你今后如何打算？ Nǐ jīnhòu rúhé dǎsuàn? What are your plans for the future?

儒 rú (儒家) Confucianism ▷ 儒家 Rújiā Confucianism

入 rù [动] **1** (进入) enter ▷ 入场 rùchǎng enter **2** (参加) join ▷ 入学 rùxué enrol ▷ 入境 rùjìng [动] enter a country

入口 rùkǒu [名] (门) entrance

软 ruǎn [形] **1** (柔) soft ▷ 软年 ruǎnhuò soft **2** (温和) gentle **3** (软弱) weak ▷ 软弱 ruǎnruò weak

软件 ruǎnjiàn [名] (计算机) software

软卧 ruǎnwò [名] light sleeper

软饮料 ruǎnyǐnliào [名] soft drink

弱 ruò [形] 1(弱小) weak 2(年幼) young 3(软弱) weak

弱点 ruòdiǎn [名] weakness

S

仨 sā [数] (口) three ▶哥仨 gēsā three brothers

撒 sā [动] 1(手, 网) let ... go 2(贬) (疯, 野) lose control of oneself ▶撒野 sāyě have a tantrum → see also/另见 sǎ

撒谎 sāhuǎng [动] (口) lie

撒娇 sājiāo [动] behave like a spoiled child

撒气 sāqì [动] 1(球, 车胎) get a puncture 2(发泄怒气) take one's anger out on ▶别拿我撒气！ Bié ná wǒ sāqì! Don't take your anger out on me!

撒手 sāshǒu [动] (松手) let go

洒 sǎ [动] 1(泼) sprinkle 2(指不小心) spill

洒脱 sǎtuo [形] carefree

撒 sǎ [动] 1 (散布) scatter 2 (散落) spill
→ see also/另见 sā

腮 sāi [名] cheek

腮帮子 sāibāngzi [名] (口) cheek

塞 sāi I [动] stuff ... into II [名] cork

塞子 sāizi [名] cork

赛 sài [名] match ▷演讲比赛 yǎnjiǎng bǐsài debating contest II [动] compete

赛车 sàichē I [动] race II [名] (指汽车) racing car

赛季 sàijì [名] season

赛跑 sàipǎo [动] race

三 sān [数] 1 (指数目) three ▷三月 sānyuè March 2 (表示序数) third 3 (表示多数) several ▷三思 sānsī think twice

三角 sānjiǎo [名] triangle ▷三角恋爱 sānjiǎo liàn'ài love triangle

三明治 sānmíngzhì [名] sandwich

三围 sānwéi [名] vital statistics (PL)

三心二意 sān xīn èr yì half-hearted ▷他工作三心二意的。Tā gōngzuò sān xīn èr yì de. He's half-hearted about his work.

叁 sān [数] three
This is the complex character for "three", which is mainly used in banks, on receipts, etc. to prevent mistakes and forgery.

伞 sǎn [名] umbrella

散 sǎn I [动] loosen II [形] loose
→ see also/另见 sàn

散漫 sǎnmàn [形] slack

散文 sǎnwén [名] prose

散 sàn [动] 1 (分离) break up ▷乌云散了。Wūyún sàn le. The dark clouds scattered. 2 (散布) give ... out 3 (排除) dispel
→ see also/另见 sǎn

散布 sànbù [动] 1 (传单) distribute 2 (谣言) spread

散步 sànbù [动] go for a stroll

丧 sāng [名] funeral
→ see also/另见 sàng

丧事 sāngshì [名] funeral arrangements (PL)

桑 sāng [名] mulberry

桑那浴 sāngnàyù [名] sauna

嗓 sǎng [名] 1 (嗓子) throat 2 (嗓音) voice

嗓门 sǎngmén [名] voice

嗓子 sǎngzi [名] 1 (喉咙) throat 2 (嗓音) voice

丧 sàng [动] lose
→ see also/另见 sāng

丧气 sàngqì [动] lose heart

丧失 sàngshī [动] lose

骚 sāo [动] disturb

骚扰 sāorǎo [动] harass ▷性骚扰 xìng sāorǎo sexual harassment

扫 sǎo [动] 1 (打扫) sweep 2 (除去)

扫黄 sǎohuáng anti-pornography campaign → see also/另见 sào

扫除 sǎochú [动] 1 (打扫) sweep ... up 2 (除掉) eliminate

扫盲 sǎománg [动] eliminate illiteracy

扫描 sǎomiáo [动] scan

扫描仪 sǎomiáoyí [名] scanner

扫兴 sǎoxìng [形] disappointed

嫂 sǎo [名] (哥哥之妻) sister-in-law

嫂子 sǎozi [名] (口) sister-in-law

扫 sào see below/见下文 → see also/另见 sǎo

扫帚 sàozhou [名] broom

色 sè [名] (颜色) colour (英), color (美) → see also/另见 shǎi

色彩 sècǎi [名] 1 (颜色) colour (英), color (美) 2 (指情调) tone

色盲 sèmáng [名] colour (英) 或 color (美) blindness

色情 sèqíng [形] pornographic

涩 sè [形] (味道) astringent

森 sēn [形] (形容树多) wooded

森林 sēnlín [名] forest

僧 sēng [名] Buddhist monk ▶僧人 sēngrén Buddhist monk

杀 shā [动] 1 (杀死) kill 2 (战斗) fight 3 (削弱) reduce

杀毒 shādú [动] get rid of a virus ▶杀毒软件 shādú ruǎnjiàn anti-virus software

杀害 shāhài [动] murder

杀价 shājià [动] bargain ▷我很会杀价。Wǒ hěn huì shājià. I'm a very good bargainer.

杀手 shāshǒu [名] killer

沙 shā [名] (石粒) sand

沙尘 shāchén [名] dust

沙尘暴 shāchénbào [名] sandstorm

沙发 shāfā [名] sofa

沙锅 shāguō [名] casserole

沙皇 shāhuáng [名] tsar

沙漠 shāmò [名] desert

沙滩 shātān [名] beach

沙哑 shāyǎ [形] hoarse

沙眼 shāyǎn [名] trachoma

沙子 shāzi [名] sand

纱 shā [名] (指织品) gauze

纱布 shābù [名] gauze

刹 shā [动] brake

刹车 shāchē I [动] 1 (停止机器) brake 2 (停止制止) put a stop to II [名] brake

鲨 shā [名] shark ▶鲨鱼 shāyú shark

傻 shǎ [形] 1 (蠢) stupid 2 (死心眼) inflexible

傻瓜 shǎguā [名] fool

傻子 shǎzi [名] fool

厦 shà [名] tall building ▷摩天大厦 mótiān dàshà skyscraper

色 shǎi [名] colour (英), color (美)
→ see also/另见 sè

色子 shǎizi [名] dice

晒 shài [动] 1 (阳光照射) shine upon ▶他被晒黑了。Tā bèi shài hēi le. He's tanned. 2 (吸收光热) lie in the sun ▶她在沙滩上晒太阳。Tā zài shātān shàng shài tàiyang. She was sunbathing on the beach.

山 shān [名] (地质) mountain ▶小山 xiǎoshān hill

山村 shāncūn [名] mountain village

山洞 shāndòng [名] cave

山峰 shānfēng [名] peak

山谷 shāngǔ [名] valley

山脚 shānjiǎo [名] foothills (PL)

山林 shānlín [名] wooded hill

山脉 shānmài [名] mountain range

山坡 shānpō [名] mountainside

山区 shānqū [名] mountainous area

山水 shānshuǐ [名] 1 (风景) scenery 2 (画) landscape painting

山珍海味 shān zhēn hǎi wèi [名] exotic delicacies (PL)

删 shān [动] delete

删除 shānchú [动] delete

珊 shān see below/见下文

珊瑚 shānhú [名] coral

扇 shān [动] 1 (扇子) fan 2 (耳光) slap
→ see also/另见 shàn

闪 shǎn I [动] 1 (闪避) dodge 2 (受伤) sprain 3 (突然出现) flash 4 (闪耀) shine II [名] lightning ▶打闪了。Dǎshǎn le. Lightning flashed.

闪电 shǎndiàn [名] lightning

闪动 shǎndòng [动] flash

闪烁 shǎnshuò [动] (忽明忽暗) twinkle

扇 shàn I [名] (扇子) fan II [量] ▶一扇窗 yī shàn chuāng a window ▶两扇门 liǎng shàn mén two doors
measure word, used for doors, windows, screens etc.
→ see also/另见 shān

善 shàn I [形] 1 (善良) kind 2 (良好) good ▶善事 shànshì good deeds 3 (友好) friendly II [动] 1 (擅长) be an expert at 2 (容易) be prone to ▶善忘 shànwàng forgetful

善良 shànliáng [形] kind-hearted

善于 shànyú [动] be good at

擅 shàn [动] be expert at

擅长 shàncháng [动] be skilled in

鳝 shàn [名] eel ▶鳝鱼 shànyú eel

伤 shāng I [动] 1 (身体部位) injure ▶扭伤 niǔshāng sprain 2 (感情) hurt II [名] injury

伤残 shāngcán [名] the disabled (PL)

伤风 shāngfēng [动] catch a cold

伤害 shānghài [动] 1 (感情) hurt 2 (身体) damage

伤痕 shānghén [名] scar

伤口 shāngkǒu [名] wound

伤心 shāngxīn [形] sad

商 shāng I [动] discuss ▶协商 xiéshāng negotiate II [名] 1 (商业) commerce ▶经商 jīngshāng trade 2 (商人) businessman, businesswoman 3 (数) quotient

商标 shāngbiāo [名] trademark

商场 shāngchǎng [名] shopping centre (英), mall (美)

商店 shāngdiàn [名] shop (英), store (美)

商量 shāngliáng [动] discuss

商品 shāngpǐn [名] commodity

商人 shāngrén [名] businessman, businesswoman

商谈 shāngtán [动] negotiate

商务 shāngwù [名] business ▶电子商务 diànzǐ shāngwù e-commerce

商业 shāngyè [名] commerce

赏 shǎng I [动] 1 (赏赐) award 2 (欣赏) admire 3 (赏识) appreciate II [名] reward

赏识 shǎngshí [动] think highly of

上 shàng I [名] 1 (指方位) upper part 2 (指等级，质量) ▶上级 shàngjí higher authorities (PL)

3 (指时间，次序) ▶上星期 shàng xīngqī last week ▶上半年 shàng bànnián the first half of the year II [动] 1 (向上) ▶上楼 shànglóu go upstairs 2 (按点前往) go ▶上学 shàngxué go to school ▶上班 shàngbān go to work 3 (去) go to ▶他上天津开会去了。 Tā shàng Tiānjīn kāihuì qù le. He went to Tianjin to attend a meeting. 4 (出场) make an entrance 5 (添补) fill ▶上货 shànghuò stock up 6 (饭，菜) serve ▶上菜 shàng cài serve food 7 (安装) fix ▶上螺丝 shàng luósī fix a screw 8 (涂) apply ▶上涂料 shàng túliào apply paint 9 (登载) appear ▶上杂志 shàng zázhì appear in a magazine 10 (拧紧) tighten ▶我的表已上弦了。 Wǒde biǎo yǐ shàngxián le. I've wound up my watch. 11 (车，船，飞机) board 12 (表示到目的) ▶当上老师 dāngshàng lǎoshī become a teacher III [介] 1 (在物体表面) on ▶椅子上 yǐzi shàng on the chair 2 (表示范围) in ▶报纸上 bàozhǐ shàng in the newspaper

上当 shàngdàng [动] be taken in

上等 shàngděng [形] first-class

上帝 Shàngdì [名] God

上吊 shàngdiào [动] hang oneself

上级 shàngjí [名] higher authorities (PL)

上来 shànglái [动] 1 (指动作趋向) ▶饭菜端上来了。 Fàncài

duān shànglái le. The meal was brought to the table. **2**(表示成功) ▷ 这个问题我答不上来。Zhège wèntí wǒ dá bù shànglái. I can't answer this question.

上面 shàngmian [名] **1**(指位置高) ▷ 他住在我上面。Tā zhùzài wǒ shàngmian. He lives above me. **2**(物体表面) ▷ 墙上面挂着相片。Qiáng shàngmian guà zhe zhāopiàn. Photographs were hanging on the walls. **3**(以上的部分) ▷ 上面我们分析了各种可能性。Shàngmian wǒmen fēnxī le gèzhǒng kěnéngxìng. As can be seen above, we have made an analysis of all possibilities.

上年纪 shàng niánjì [动] get old

上去 shàngqù [动] **1**(指由低到高) go up **2**(提高) improve

上身 shàngshēn [名] upper body

上升 shàngshēng [动] **1**(往高处移) ascend **2**(增加) increase

上市 shàngshì [动] appear on the market

上司 shàngsi [名] superior

上诉 shàngsù [动] appeal

上网 shàngwǎng [动] go online

上午 shàngwǔ [名] morning

上衣 shàngyī [名] top

上瘾 shàngyǐn [动] be addicted to

上涨 shàngzhǎng [动] rise

烧 shāo [动] **1**(着火) burn **2**(加热) heat ▷ 烧水 shāo shuǐ boil water **3**(烹) braise **4**(烤) roast ▷ 烧鸡 shāojī roast chicken **5**(发烧) have a temperature

烧烤 shāokǎo [动] barbecue

稍 shāo [副] slightly
→ see also/另见 shào

稍微 shāowēi [副] a little

勺 sháo [名] ladle

少 shǎo **I**[形] few ▷ 屋里家具太少。Wū lǐ jiājù tài shǎo. There is very little furniture in the room. **II**[动] **1**(缺) lack ▷ 汤里少了葱。Tāng lǐ shǎo le cōng. There is no onion in the soup. **2**(丢) be missing ▷ 她发现钱包里的钱少了一百块。Tā fāxiàn qiánbāo lǐ de qián shǎo le yìbǎi kuài. She discovered that one hundred kuai were missing from her purse.
→ see also/另见 shào

少量 shǎoliàng [名] a little

少数 shǎoshù [名] minority

少数民族 shǎoshù mínzú [名] ethnic minorities (PL)

少数民族 shǎoshù mínzú

少数民族 shǎoshù mínzú refers to China's ethnic minorities. There are 56 distinct ethnic groups in China, of which the Han is by far the largest, accounting for over 90% of the population. The other 55 minorities are mainly located in the southwestern and northwestern provinces. Five regions have been set up as ethnic minorities autonomous regions.

少 shào [形] young ▶少女 shàonǚ young girl
→ see also/另见 shǎo

少年 shàonián [名] youth

哨 shào [名] (哨子) whistle

哨子 shàozi [名] whistle

稍 shào see below/见下文
→ see also/另见 shāo

稍息 shàoxī [动] stand at ease

奢 shē [形] extravagant

奢侈 shēchǐ [形] luxurious

舌 shé [名] tongue

舌头 shétou [名] tongue

折 shé [动] (折断) snap ▶他的腿折了。Tāde tuǐ shé le. He broke his leg.
→ see also/另见 zhé

蛇 shé [名] snake

设 shè [动] 1 (摆设) set ... up 2 (想) plan 3 (假定) suppose ▶设想 shèxiǎng envisage

设备 shèbèi [名] equipment

设计 shèjì [动] design ▶服装设计 fúzhuāng shèjì fashion design

设施 shèshī [名] facilities (PL)

社 shè [名] organization ▶旅行社 lǚxíngshè travel agent

社会 shèhuì [名] society ▶社会福利 shèhuì fúlì social welfare

社交 shèjiāo [名] social contact

社区 shèqū [名] community

舍 shè [名] house ▶宿舍 sùshè dormitory

射 shè [动] 1 (发) shoot 2 (喷) spout 3 (放出) emit ▶照射 zhàoshè shine

射击 shèjī I [动] fire II [名] shooting

射门 shèmén [动] shoot

射线 shèxiàn [名] (电磁波) ray

涉 shè [动] (牵涉) involve ▶涉嫌 shèxián be a suspect

涉及 shèjí [动] involve

摄 shè [动] 1 (吸取) absorb 2 (摄影) take a photo

摄像 shèxiàng [动] make a video

摄影 shèyǐng [动] 1 (照相) take a photo 2 (拍电影) shoot a film (英) 或 movie (美)

谁 shéi [代] 1 (表示问人) who ▶谁在门外？Shéi zài mén wài? Who's at the door? 2 (指任何一个人) whoever ▶谁先到谁买票。Shéi xiān dào shéi mǎi piào. Whoever arrives first buys the tickets.

申 shēn [动] express

申请 shēnqǐng [动] apply ▶申请工作 shēnqǐng gōngzuò apply for a job

伸 shēn [动] stretch

伸手 shēnshǒu [动](伸出手) hold out one's hand

身 shēn [名] 1(身体) body 2(生命) life 3(自己) oneself

身材 shēncái [名] figure

身份 shēnfèn [名](地位) position

身份证 shēnfènzhèng [名] identity card

身体 shēntǐ [名] body

参 shēn [名] ginseng ▶人参 rénshēn ginseng → see also/另见 cān

绅 shēn [名] gentry

绅士 shēnshì [名] gentleman

深 shēn I [形] 1(指深度) deep 2(指距离) remote 3(深奥) difficult 4(深刻) deep ▶印象深 yìnxiàng shēn a deep impression 5(密切) close 6(浓重) dark ▶深蓝 shēnlán dark blue 7(指时间久) late ▶深夜 shēnyè late at night II [名] depth III [副] very ▶深信 shēnxìn firmly believe

深奥 shēn'ào [形] profound

深度 shēndù I [名] depth II [形] extreme

深化 shēnhuà [动] deepen

深刻 shēnkè [形] deep

深入 shēnrù I [动] penetrate II [形] thorough

深远 shēnyuǎn [形] far-reaching

深造 shēnzào [动] pursue advanced studies

什 shén see below/见下文

什么 shénme [代] 1(表示疑问) what ▷你要什么? Nǐ yào shénme? What do you want? 2(表示虚指) something ▷他们在商量着什么。Tāmen zài shāngliàng zhe shénme. They are discussing something. 3(表示任指) anything ▷我什么都不怕。Wǒ shénme dōu bùpà. I'm not afraid of anything. 4(表示惊讶,不满) what ▷什么! 他拒绝出席会议! Shénme! Tā jùjué chūxí huìyì! What! He refused to attend the meeting! 5(表示责难) ▷你在胡说什么! Nǐ zài húshuō shénme! What's that rubbish!

什么的 shénmede and so on [代] ▷餐桌上摆满了香蕉,李子,苹果什么的。Cānzhuō shàng bǎimǎn le xiāngjiāo, lǐzi, píngguǒ shénme de. The dining table was loaded with bananas, plums, apples and so on.

神 shén I [名] 1(宗) god 2(精神) spirit ▶走神 zǒushén be absent-minded II [形](高超) amazing ▶神奇 shénqí magical

神话 shénhuà [名] myth

神经 shénjīng [名] nerve

神秘 shénmì [形] mysterious

神气 shénqì I [名] manner II [形] 1(精神) impressive 2(得意) cocky

神圣 shénshèng [形] sacred

神态 shéntài [名] look

神仙 shénxiān [名] immortal

神学 shénxué [名] theology

审 shěn [动] 1(审查) go over 2(审讯) try ▶审案子 shěn ànzi try a case

审查 shěnchá [动] examine

审判 shěnpàn [动] try

审问 shěnwèn [动] interrogate

妯 shěn [名] aunt

肾 shèn [名] kidney

甚 shèn I [形] extreme II [副] very
甚至 shènzhì [副] even

渗 shèn [动] seep

慎 shèn [形] careful
慎重 shènzhòng [形] cautious

升 shēng I [动] 1(由低往高) rise 2(提升) promote ▶升职 shēngzhí be promoted II [量] litre (英), liter (美)

升级 shēngjí [动] 1(升高年级) go up 2(规模扩大) escalate 3(指电脑) upgrade

升值 shēngzhí [动] appreciate

生 shēng I [动] 1(生育) give birth to ▶生孩子 shēng háizi have a baby 2(长) grow 3(活) live ▶生死 shēngsǐ life and death 4(患) get ▶生病 shēngbìng get ill 5(点) light ▶生火 shēnghuǒ light a fire II [名] 1(生命) life 2(生平) life ▶今生 jīnshēng this life 3(学生) student ▶新生 xīnshēng new student III [形] 1(活的) living 2(未熟的) unripe 3(未煮的) raw

4(生疏) unfamiliar

生产 shēngchǎn [动] 1(制造) produce 2(生孩子) give birth to

生存 shēngcún [动] survive

生动 shēngdòng [形] lively

生活 shēnghuó I [名] life II [动] 1(居住) live 2(生存) survive

生计 shēngjì [名] livelihood

生理 shēnglǐ [名] physiology

生命 shēngmìng [名] life

生命力 shēngmìnglì [名] vitality

生气 shēngqì [动] get angry

生人 shēngrén [名] stranger

生日 shēngrì [名] birthday

生态 shēngtài [名] ecology

生物 shēngwù [名] living things (PL)

生物学 shēngwùxué [名] biology

生肖 shēngxiào [名] animal of the Chinese zodiac

生效 shēngxiào [动] come into effect

生意 shēngyi [名] business

生育 shēngyù [动] give birth to

生长 shēngzhǎng [动] 1(植物) grow 2(生物) grow up

声 shēng [名] 1(声音) sound 2(名声) reputation 3(声调) tone (of Chinese phonetics)

声波 shēngbō [名] sound wave

声调 shēngdiào [名] tone

声明 shēngmíng [动] state

声望 shēngwàng [名] prestige

声音 shēngyīn [名] **1**(指人) voice **2**(物音) sound

牲 shēng [名] (家畜) domestic animal

牲畜 shēngchù [名] livestock

甥 shēng [名] nephew ▷外甥 wàishēng nephew ▷外甥女 wàishēngnǚ niece

绳 shéng [名] rope

绳子 shéngzi [名] rope

省 shěng I [动] **1**(节约) save ▷省钱 shěng qián save money **2**(免掉) leave ... out II [名] province

省会 shěnghuì [名] provincial capital

省略 shěnglüè [动] leave ... out

省事 shěngshì [动] save trouble

省心 shěngxīn [动] save worry

圣 shèng I [形] holy ▷圣诞节 Shèngdàn Jié Christmas II [名] (圣人) sage

圣诞 Shèngdàn [名] Christmas

圣经 Shèngjīng [名] the Bible

胜 shèng [动] **1**(赢) win **2**(打败) defeat **3**(好于) be better than

胜利 shènglì [动] **1**(打败对方) be victorious **2**(获得成功) be successful

盛 shèng [形] **1**(兴盛) flourishing **2**(强烈) intense **3**(盛大) grand ▷盛宴 shèngyàn sumptuous dinner **4**(深厚) abundant ▷盛情 shèngqíng great kindness **5**(盛

行) popular ▷盛行 shèngxíng be in fashion

→ see also/另见 chéng

盛大 shèngdà [形] magnificent

剩 shèng [动] be left ▷剩下 shèngxià remain

尸 shī [名] corpse

尸体 shītǐ [名] corpse

失 shī I [动] **1**(丢失) lose **2**(未得到) fail **3**(背弃) break II [名] mistake ▷过失 guòshī error

失败 shībài [动] fail

失眠 shīmián [动] be unable to sleep

失眠症 shīmiánzhèng [名] insomnia

失明 shīmíng [动] go blind

失望 shīwàng I [形] disappointed II [动] lose hope

失误 shīwù [动] slip up

失效 shīxiào [动] **1**(不起作用) stop working **2**(没有法力) be no longer valid

失信 shīxìn [动] go back on one's word

失业 shīyè [动] be unemployed, be out of work

失踪 shīzōng [动] be missing

师 shī [名] (老师) teacher

师傅 shīfu [名] (口) master

诗 shī [名] poetry

诗歌 shīgē [名] poetry

诗人 shīrén [名] poet

虱 shī[名]louse

狮 shī *see below*/见下文
狮子 shīzi[名]lion

施 shī[动]1(实行)carry ... out ▶施工 shīgōng construct 2(给予)exert ▶施压 shīyā exert pressure 3(肥料)apply ▶施肥 shīféi spread fertilizer
施行 shīxíng[动](执行)implement

湿 shī[形]wet
湿润 shīrùn[形]moist

十 shí[名]ten ▶十月 shíyuè October ▶十一月 shíyīyuè November ▶十二月 shí'èryuè December
十分 shífēn[副]extremely
十字路口 shízì lùkǒu[名]crossroads(PL)

石 shí[名]stone
石油 shíyóu[名]oil

时 shí[名]1(指时间单位)hour 2(指规定时间)time ▶准时 zhǔnshí on time 3(时常)▶不时 shíbùshí from time to time 4(时尚)fashion ▶入时 rùshí fashionable ▶过时 guòshí out-of-date 5(时候)time ▶当时 dāngshí at that time 6(机会)opportunity 7(语法)tense ▶过时 guòqùshí past tense
时差 shíchā[名]time difference
时常 shícháng[副]often
时代 shídài[名]1(指时期)age

2(指人生)period
时候 shíhou[名]time ▶你什么时候上班? Nǐ shénme shíhou shàngbān? What time do you go to work?
时机 shíjī[名]opportunity
时间 shíjiān[名]time ▶时间到了。Shíjiān dào le. Time's up! ▶办公时间 bàngōng shíjiān working hours
时刻 shíkè I[名]moment II[副]constantly
时刻表 shíkèbiǎo[名]timetable (英),schedule(美)
时髦 shímáo[形]fashionable
时期 shíqī[名]period
时区 shíqū[名]time zone
时事 shíshì[名]current affairs (PL)
时装 shízhuāng[名]fashion

实 shí[形]1(实心)solid 2(真实)true ▶实话 shíhuà truth
实际 shíjì I[名]reality II[形]1(实有的)real 2(合乎事实的)practical
实践 shíjiàn I[动]practise(英),practice(美)II[名]practice
实力 shílì[名]strength
实情 shíqíng[名]actual state of affairs
实施 shíshī[动]implement
实习 shíxí[动]practise(英),practice(美)
实习生 shíxíshēng[名]trainee
实现 shíxiàn[动]realize

实行 shíxíng [动] put ... into practice

实验 shíyàn I [动] test II [名] experiment

实验室 shíyànshì [名] laboratory

实用 shíyòng [形] practical

实在 shízài I [形] honest II [副] really

拾 shí I [动] pick ... up II [数] ten
This is the complex character for "ten", which is mainly used in banks, on receipts, etc. to prevent mistakes and forgery.

食 shí I [动] eat II [名] 1 (食物) food ▸主食 zhǔshí staple ▸狗食 gǒushí dog food 2 (指天体) eclipse ▸日食 rìshí solar eclipse

食品 shípǐn [名] food

食谱 shípǔ [名] recipe

食堂 shítáng [名] canteen

食物 shíwù [名] food

食欲 shíyù [名] appetite

史 shǐ [名] history

史诗 shǐshī [名] epic

史实 shǐshí [名] historical fact

使 shǐ I [动] 1 (使用) use 2 (让) make II [名] envoy ▸大使 dàshǐ ambassador

使馆 shǐguǎn [名] embassy

使用 shǐyòng [动] use ▸使用说明 shǐyòng shuōmíng operating instructions (PL)

始 shǐ [动] start

始终 shǐzhōng [副] all along

屎 shǐ [名] 1 (粪便) excrement 2 (眼, 耳) wax ▸耳屎 ěrshǐ ear wax

示 shì [动] show

示范 shìfàn [动] demonstrate

示威 shìwēi [动] demonstrate

世 shì [名] 1 (生) life ▸来世 láishì afterlife 2 (代) generation ▸世仇 shìchóu family feud 3 (时期) age 4 (世界) world ▸世上 shìshàng in this world

世纪 shìjì [名] century

世界 shìjiè [名] world

市 shì [名] 1 (城市) city 2 (市场) market

市场 shìchǎng [名] market

市民 shìmín [名] city residents (PL)

式 shì [名] 1 (样式) style 2 (典礼) ceremony 3 (子) formula ▸公式 gōngshì formula

式样 shìyàng [名] style

事 shì [名] 1 (事情) thing ▸私事 sīshì private matter 2 (事故) accident ▸出事 chūshì have an accident 3 (事端) trouble ▸闹事 nàoshì make trouble 4 (责任) responsibility 5 (工作) job 6 (用于问答) problem ▸有事吗? 没事。Yǒushì ma? Méishì. Are you OK? — I'm fine.

事故 shìgù [名] accident

事件 shìjiàn [名] event

事情 shìqing [名] matter

事实 shìshí [名] fact ▷事实上 shìshí shàng in fact

事务 shìwù [名] work

事物 shìwù [名] thing

事业 shìyè [名] 1(用于个人) undertaking 2(用于社会) activity

势 shì [名] 1(势力) force 2(姿态) gesture 3(趋势) tendency

势力 shìli [名] power

势利 shìli [形] snobbish

势利眼 shìliyǎn [名] snob

势头 shìtóu [名] momentum

饰 shì I [动] 1(装饰) decorate 2(扮演) play II [名] ornament ▷首饰 shǒushì jewellery (英), jewelry (美)

饰物 shìwù [名] ornaments (PL)

饰演 shìyǎn [动] play

试 shì I [动] try ▷我可以试一下这双鞋吗？Wǒ kěyǐ shì yīxià zhè shuāng xié ma? Can I try on this pair of shoes? II [名] examination

试卷 shìjuàn [名] exam paper

试题 shìtí [名] exam question

试验 shìyàn [动] test

试用 shìyòng [动] try ... out

试用期 shìyòngqī [名] probation

视 shì I [动] 1(看到) look at 2(看待) look on

视觉 shìjué [名] vision

视力 shìlì [名] sight

柿 shì see below/见下文

柿子 shìzi [名] persimmon, sharon fruit

是 shì I [动] be ▷我是学生。Wǒ shì xuésheng. I am a student. II [名] right ▷是非 shìfēi right and wrong III [副] yes

是 shì is the verb 'to be'. It is omitted when used with adjectives, e.g. 我很忙 wǒ hěn máng (I am very busy).

适 shì [形] 1(适合) suitable 2(恰好) well 3(舒服) well

适当 shìdàng [形] appropriate

适合 shìhé [形] suitable

适应 shìyìng [动] adapt

室 shì [名] room ▷办公室 bàngōngshì office

室外 shìwài [名] outdoor

逝 shì [动] (人) die

逝世 shìshì [动] (书) pass away

释 shì [动] (解释) explain

释放 shìfàng [动] release

嗜 shì [动] be addicted to

嗜好 shìhào [名] hobby

誓 shì I [动] swear ▷发誓 fāshì vow II [名] vow

誓言 shìyán [名] oath

收 shōu [动] 1(归拢) put ... away 2(取回) take ... back 3(接纳) accept 4(结束) stop ▷收工 shōugōng stop work 5(获得) gain ▷收入 shōurù income

收获 shōuhuò [动] 1(指庄稼) harvest 2(指成果) gain

收集 shōují [动] collect

收据 shōujù [名] receipt

收拾 shōushi [动] 1(整顿) tidy 2(修理) repair 3(口)(惩罚) punish

收缩 shōusuō [动] 1(指物理现象) contract 2(紧缩) cut back

收听 shōutīng [动] listen to

收音机 shōuyīnjī [名] radio

手 shǒu [名] 1(指人体) hand 2(指人) expert ▷选手 xuǎnshǒu player

手表 shǒubiǎo [名] watch

手电筒 shǒudiàntǒng [名] torch (英), flashlight (美)

手段 shǒuduàn [名] 1(方法) method 2(贬)(花招) trick

手风琴 shǒufēngqín [名] accordion

手工 shǒugōng I [名] craft II [动] make ... by hand

手机 shǒujī [名] mobile phone (英), cell phone (美)

手绢 shǒujuàn [名] handkerchief

手铐 shǒukào [名] handcuffs (PL)

手枪 shǒuqiāng [名] pistol

手势 shǒushì [名] sign

手术 shǒushù I [名] operation II [动] operate

手套 shǒutào [名] glove ▷一副手套 yī fù shǒutào a pair of gloves

手腕 shǒuwàn [名] (指人体) wrist

手续 shǒuxù [名] procedure

手语 shǒuyǔ [名] sign language

手掌 shǒuzhǎng [名] palm

手纸 shǒuzhǐ [名] toilet paper

手指 shǒuzhǐ [名] finger

手镯 shǒuzhuó [名] bracelet

守 shǒu [动] 1(防卫) guard 2(遵循) observe ▷守法 shǒufǎ observe the law

守则 shǒuzé [名] regulation

首 shǒu I [名] 1(脑袋) head 2(头领) leader II [形] 1(第一) first ▷首富 shǒufù the richest person 2(最早) first III [量] ▷一首诗 yī shǒu shī one poem ▷两首歌 liǎng shǒu gē two songs

measure word, used for music, songs and poems

首都 shǒudū [名] capital

首领 shǒulǐng [名] chief

首脑 shǒunǎo [名] head of state

首饰 shǒushì [名] jewellery (英), jewelry (美)

首席 shǒuxí [形] chief

首先 shǒuxiān [副] 1(最早) first 2(第一) first

首相 shǒuxiàng [名] prime minister

首要 shǒuyào [形] primary

寿 shòu [名] (寿命) lifespan

寿命 shòumìng [名] life

受 shòu [动] 1(接受) receive 2(遭受) suffer 3(忍受) bear

受罪 shòuzuì [动] 1(指苦难) suffer 2(指不愉快的事) have a hard time

兽 shòu [名] beast

兽医 shòuyī [名] vet

售 shòu [动] sell

售货员 shòuhuòyuán [名] shop assistant

瘦 shòu [形] 1(指人) thin 2(指食用肉) lean 3(指衣服, 鞋袜) tight

书 shū I [动] write ▸ 书写 shūxiě write II [名] 1(册子) book ▸ 书包 shūbāo school bag ▸ 书架 shūjià bookcase ▸ 书桌 shūzhuō desk ▸ 精装书 jīngzhuāngshū hardback 2(书)(信) letter ▸ 情书 qíngshū love letter 3(文件) document ▸ 申请书 shēnqǐngshū application documents (PL)

书店 shūdiàn [名] bookshop

书法 shūfǎ [名] calligraphy

书籍 shūjí [名] books (PL)

书记 shūjì [名] secretary

书面语 shūmiànyǔ [名] written language

书信 shūxìn [名] letter

书展 shūzhǎn [名] book fair

叔 shū [名] (指父亲的弟弟) uncle

叔叔 shūshu [名] 1(指父亲的弟弟) uncle 2(指亲戚以外的辈男性) uncle

梳 shū I [名] comb ▸ 梳子 shūzi comb, brush II [动] comb

舒 shū [动] 1(指身体) stretch out

2(指心情) relax

舒服 shūfu [形] comfortable

舒适 shūshì [形] cosy (英), cozy (美)

输 shū [动] 1(运送) transport 2(失败) lose

输出 shūchū [动] (指从内到外) emit

输入 shūrù [动] (指从外到内) enter

输送 shūsòng [动] 1(物品) convey 2(人员) transfer

蔬 shū [名] vegetable

蔬菜 shūcài [名] vegetable

熟 shú [形] 1(指果实) ripe 2(指食物) cooked 3(熟悉) familiar ▸ 他对北京很熟。 Tā duì Běijīng hěn shú. He knows Beijing well. 4(熟练)

熟练 shúliàn [形] skilled

熟人 shúrén [名] old acquaintance

熟食 shúshí [名] cooked food

熟悉 shúxī I [动] know well II [形] familiar

属 shǔ I [动] 1(生物) genus 2(家属) family member II [动] 1(隶属) be under 2(指属相) ▸ 你属什么？ Nǐ shǔ shénme? What sign of the Chinese zodiac are you?

属相 shǔxiang [名] (口) sign of the Chinese zodiac

属于 shǔyú [动] belong to

暑 shǔ [名] 1(热) heat 2(盛夏)

midsummer

暑假 shǔjià [名] summer holidays (英) (PL), vacation (美)

鼠 shǔ [名] 1 (家鼠) mouse ▸老鼠 lǎoshǔ mouse 2 (比家鼠大, 尾巴长) rat

鼠标 shǔbiāo [名] mouse

数 shǔ [动] 1 (数目) count 2 (指名次) rank 3 (列举) list
→ see also/另见 shù

薯 shǔ [名] potato ▸红薯 hóngshǔ sweet potato

术 shù [名] 1 (技艺) skill 2 (策略) tactic

术语 shùyǔ [名] terminology

束 shù I [动] 1 (捆) tie 2 (约束) restrain II [量] 1 (指花) bunch ▸一束鲜花 yī shù xiānhuā a bunch of flowers 2 (指光) ray ▸一束阳光 yī shù yángguāng a ray of sunlight

束缚 shùfù [动] 1 (书) (捆绑) tie 2 (局限) restrain

述 shù [动] state

述说 shùshuō [动] give an account

树 shù I [名] tree II [动] (建立) establish

树立 shùlì [动] establish

树林 shùlín [名] wood

树木 shùmù [名] trees (PL)

树阴 shùyīn [名] shade

竖 shù I [形] vertical II [动] erect III [名] vertical stroke

数 shù [名] 1 (数目) number 2 (语法) ▸单数 dānshù singular ▸复数 fùshù plural
→ see also/另见 shǔ

数据 shùjù [名] data (PL)

数据库 shùjùkù [名] database

数量 shùliàng [名] quantity

数码 shùmǎ I [名] numeral II [形] digital

数码相机 shùmǎ xiàngjī [名] digital camera

数目 shùmù [名] amount

数学 shùxué [名] mathematics (SG)

数字 shùzì [名] 1 (指系统) numeral 2 (数据) figure

漱 shù [动] gargle

漱口 shùkǒu [动] rinse one's mouth out

刷 shuā I [名] brush ▸牙刷 yáshuā toothbrush II [动] (清除) scrub

刷卡 shuākǎ [动] swipe a card

刷牙 shuāyá [动] brush one's teeth

刷子 shuāzi [名] brush

耍 shuǎ [动] 1 (方) (玩) play 2 (戏弄) mess ... around 3 (贬) (施展) play ▸别再耍小聪明了。Bié zài shuǎ xiǎocōngmíng le. Don't play those petty tricks again.

耍花招 shuǎ huāzhāo [动] play tricks

衰 shuāi I [形] declining II [动] decline

衰老 shuāilǎo [形] ageing

衰弱 shuāiruò [形] weak

摔 shuāi [动] 1 (跌倒) fall 2 (下落) fall out ▷ 他从床上摔了下来。Tā cóng chuáng shàng shuāi le xiàlái. He fell out of bed. 3 (跌坏) break

摔跤 shuāijiāo I [动] (摔倒) fall over II [名] wrestling

甩 shuǎi [动] 1 (抡) swing 2 (扔) fling 3 (抛开) throw ... off

甩卖 shuǎimài [动] sell at a reduced price

帅 shuài I [名] commander-in-chief II [形] handsome

率 shuài [动] command

率领 shuàilǐng [动] lead

双 shuāng I [形] 1 (两个) two 2 (偶数) even ▷ 双数 shuāngshù even number 3 (加倍) double II [量] pair ▷ 一双鞋 yī shuāng xié a pair of shoes ▷ 一双袜子 yī shuāng wàzi a pair of socks

双胞胎 shuāngbāotāi [名] twins (PL)

双方 shuāngfāng [名] both sides (PL)

双休日 shuāngxiūrì [名] the weekend

霜 shuāng [名] frost

谁 shuí [代] → shéi

水 shuǐ [名] 1 (物质) water 2 (指江河湖海) waters (PL) 3 (汁) liquid

▶ 消毒水 xiāodúshuǐ disinfectant

▶ 墨水 mòshuǐ ink

水彩 shuǐcǎi [名] 1 (指颜料) watercolour (英), watercolor (美) 2 (指画) watercolour (英), watercolor (美)

水果 shuǐguǒ [名] fruit

水晶 shuǐjīng [名] crystal

水库 shuǐkù [名] reservoir

水泥 shuǐní [名] cement

水平 shuǐpíng I [名] standard II [形] horizontal

水手 shuǐshǒu [名] sailor

水银 shuǐyín [名] mercury

水灾 shuǐzāi [名] flood

税 shuì [名] tax

税收 shuìshōu [名] tax revenue

税务局 shuìwùjú [名] tax office

睡 shuì [动] sleep

睡觉 shuìjiào [动] sleep

睡眠 shuìmián [动] sleep

顺 shùn I [介] 1 (指方向) with 2 ▶ 顺时针 shùnshízhēn clockwise 2 (沿) along 3 (趁便) ▶ 顺便 shùnbiàn on the way II [动] 1 (朝同一方向) follow 2 (使有条理) put ... in order 3 (顺从) obey 4 (合意) be to one's liking ▶ 顺心 shùnxīn as one would wish III [形] successful ▷ 他找工作很顺。Tā zhǎo gōngzuò hěn shùn. His job hunt has been very successful.

顺便 shùnbiàn [副] 1 (指乘方便)

on the way 2 (说，问) by the way ▷顺便问一下，他给你回电话了吗？ Shùnbiàn wèn yīxià, tā gěi nǐ huí diànhuà le ma? By the way, did he call you back?

顺风 shùnfēng [动] (指祝福) ▷一路顺风！Yīlù shùnfēng! Bon voyage!

顺利 shùnlì [副] smoothly

顺序 shùnxù [名] order

说 shuō [动] 1 (用语言表达意思) say 2 (解释) explain 3 (责备) tell ... off

说服 shuōfú [动] persuade

说话 shuōhuà I [动] 1 (用语言表达意思) say 2 (闲谈) chat II [副] (马上) any minute

说明 shuōmíng I [动] 1 (解释明白) explain 2 (证明) prove II [名] explanation ▷产品使用说明 chǎnpǐn shǐyòng shuōmíng instruction manual

硕 shuò [形] large

硕士 shuòshì [名] master's degree

司 sī [动] take charge of

司机 sījī [名] driver

丝 sī [名] 1 (指蚕) silk 2 (指像丝的) thread ▷铁丝 tiěsī wire

丝绸 sīchóu [名] silk

私 sī [形] 1 (个人的) private ▷私事 sīshì private affairs 2 (自私的) selfish ▷无私 wúsī unselfish 3 (暗地里的) secret 4 (非法的) illegal

私人 sīrén [形] 1 (属于个人的) private 2 (人与人之间的) personal

私生活 sīshēnghuó [名] private life

私下 sīxià [副] privately

私营 sīyíng [动] run privately

私有 sīyǒu [形] private ▷私有化 sīyǒuhuà privatization

私自 sīzì [副] without permission

思 sī [名] thought ▷思路 sīlù train of thought

思考 sīkǎo [动] think

思念 sīniàn I [动] miss II [名] longing

思维 sīwéi [名] thinking

思想 sīxiǎng [名] 1 (指有体系) thought 2 (念头) idea

撕 sī [动] tear

死 sǐ I [动] die II [形] 1 (死亡的) dead 2 (不可调和的) implacable ▷死敌 sǐdí sworn enemy 3 (不能通过的) impassable ▷死胡同 sǐhútòng dead end 4 (确切的) fixed 5 (脑筋) slow-witted 6 (规定) rigid 7 (水) still III [副] 1 (拼到) to the death ▷死战 sǐzhàn fight to the death 2 (表示固执或坚决) stubbornly ▷死等 sǐ děng wait indefinitely 3 (表示到达极点) extremely ▷累死我了。Lèi sǐ wǒ le. I'm completely exhausted.

死机 sǐjī [动] crash

死尸 sǐshī [名] corpse

死亡 sǐwáng [动] die

死刑 sǐxíng [名] death penalty

死者 sǐzhě [名] the deceased

四 sì [数] four

四季 sìjì [名] the four seasons (PL)

四声 sìshēng [名] *the four tones of Standard Chinese pronunciation*

四月 sìyuè [名] April

四肢 sìzhī [名] limbs (PL)

四周 sìzhōu [名] all sides

寺 sì [名] 1 (指佛教) temple, Tibetan Buddhist temple 2 (指伊斯兰教) mosque ▷清真寺 qīngzhēnsì mosque

似 sì I [动] (像) be like ▷他的脸似一样白。 Tā de liǎn sì zhǐ yīyàng bái. His face was as white as a sheet of paper. II [副] apparently

似乎 sìhū [副] apparently

饲 sì [动] raise ▷饲养 sìyǎng raise

饲料 sìliào [名] fodder

肆 sì [名] four

> This is the complex character for "four", which is mainly used in banks, on receipts, etc. to prevent mistakes and forgery.

松 sōng I [名] (树) pine tree II [动] 1 (放开) relax 2 (鞋带, 腰带) loosen III [形] loose

松弛 sōngchí [形] 1 (放松) relaxed 2 (松散) lax

送 sòng [动] 1 (信, 邮包, 外卖) deliver 2 (礼物) give ▷你准备送他什么结婚礼物? Nǐ zhǔnbèi

sòng tā shénme jiéhūn lǐwù? What are you going to give him as a wedding present? 3 (送行) see ... off ▷他把女朋友送到家。 Tā bǎ nǚpéngyou sòng dào jiā. He saw his girlfriend home.

送行 sòngxíng [动] see ... off

搜 sōu [动] search

搜查 sōuchá [动] search

搜集 sōují [动] gather

搜索 sōusuǒ [动] search for

搜索引擎 sōusuǒ yǐnqíng [名] search engine

苏 sū [动] revive

苏打 sūdá [名] soda

苏格兰 Sūgélán [名] Scotland ▷苏格兰短裙 Sūgélán duǎnqún kilt

俗 sú I [名] (风俗) custom ▷民俗 mínsú folk custom ▷入乡随俗 rùxiāng suísú when in Rome, do as the Romans do II [形] 1 (大众的) popular 2 (庸俗) vulgar

俗气 súqì [形] vulgar

俗语 súyǔ [名] common saying

诉 sù [动] 1 (说给人) tell ▷诉说 sùshuō tell 2 (倾吐) pour ... out ▷诉苦 sùkǔ complain 3 (控告) accuse ▷上诉 shàngsù appeal to a higher court

素 sù I [形] plain II [名] 1 (蔬菜, 瓜果等食物) vegetable 2 (有根本性质的) element ▷维生素 wéishēngsù vitamin

素描 sùmiáo [名] sketch

素食 sùshí [名] vegetarian food

素食者 sùshízhě [名] vegetarian

素质 sùzhì [名] character

速 sù I [名] speed II [形] quick ▸速算 sùsuàn quick calculation

速成 sùchéng [动] take a crash course

速递 sùdì [动] send by express delivery

速度 sùdù [名] speed

速溶 sùróng [动] dissolve quickly ▸速溶咖啡 sùróng kāfēi instant coffee

宿 sù [动] stay

宿舍 sùshè [名] dormitory

塑 sù I [动] model II [名] mould (英), mold (美)

塑料 sùliào [名] plastic

塑像 sùxiàng [名] statue

酸 suān I [形] 1 (指味道) sour 2 (伤心) sad 3 (迂腐) pedantic 4 (疼) sore II [名] acid

酸奶 suānnǎi [名] yoghurt

蒜 suàn [名] garlic

算 suàn [动] 1 (计算) calculate 2 (计算进去) count 3 (谋划) plan ▸暗算 ànsuàn plot against 4 (当作) be considered as 5 (由某人负责) blame 6 (数说) count 7 (作罢) ▸算了吧！suàn le ba! Forget it! 8 (推测) suppose

算命 suànmìng [动] tell sb's fortune ▸算命先生 suànmìng xiānsheng fortune teller

算盘 suànpán [名] (计算用具) abacus

算术 suànshù [名] maths (sɡ) (英), math (美)

算账 suànzhàng [动] 1 (计算账目) work out accounts 2 (把事情扯平) get even with

虽 suī [连] although ▸他个子虽小, 力气却很大。Tā gèzi suī xiǎo, lìqi què hěn dà. Although he isn't big, he's very strong.

虽然 suīrán [连] although ▸虽然她很年轻, 可是却很成熟。Suīrán tā hěn niánqīng, kěshì què hěn chéngshú. Although she is very young, she is quite mature.

随 suí [动] 1 (跟随) follow 2 (顺从) go along with 3 (任凭) let ... do as they like ▸孩子大了, 随他去吧。Háizi dà le, suí tā qù ba. The child's grown up — let him do as he wishes.

随便 suíbiàn I [动] do as one wishes II [形] 1 (随意) casual 2 (欠考虑的) thoughtless III [副] ▸大家随便坐。Dàjiā suíbiàn zuò. Everyone can sit where they like.

随和 suíhe [形] easygoing

随身 suíshēn [副] ▸随身行李 suíshēn xíngli hand luggage

随身听 suíshēntīng [名] Walkman®

随时 suíshí [副] at any time

随手 suíshǒu [副] on one's way
▷请随手关门。 Qǐng suíshǒu guānmén. Please close the door on your way.

随着 suízhe [动] follow

岁 suì [名] year ▷他20岁了。 Tā èrshí suì le. He's 20 years old.

岁数 suìshu [名] age

碎 suì I [动] 1 (破碎) break 2 (使粉碎) smash ▷碎纸机 suìzhǐjī shredder II [形] (不完整) broken

隧 suì [名] tunnel

隧道 suìdào [名] tunnel

孙 sūn [名] grandchild

孙女 sūnnǚ [名] granddaughter

孙子 sūnzi [名] grandson

损 sǔn [动] 1 (减少) decrease 2 (损坏) harm 3 (损失) damage

损害 sǔnhài [动] 1 (健康) damage 2 (利益) harm 3 (名誉) ruin 4 (关系) damage

损坏 sǔnhuài [动] damage

损失 sǔnshī I [动] lose II [名] loss

笋 sǔn [名] bamboo shoot

缩 suō [动] 1 (收缩) contract 2 (收回去) withdraw

缩减 suōjiǎn [动] 1 (经费) cut 2 (人员) reduce

缩水 suōshuǐ [动] shrink

缩写 suōxiě I [名] abbreviation II [动] abridge

所 suǒ I [名] 1 (处所) place 2 (用于机构名称) office ▷派出所 pàichūsuǒ local police station ▷诊所 zěnsuǒ clinic I [量] ▷三所医院 sān suǒ yīyuàn three hospitals ▷一所大学 yī suǒ dàxué a university measure word, used for buildings, houses, hospitals, schools, universities, etc.

III [助] 1 (表示被动) ▷他被金钱所迷惑。 Tā bèi jīnqián suǒ míhuò. He's obsessed with money. 2 (表示强调) ▷这正是大家所不理解的。 Zhè zhèng shì dàjiā suǒ bù lǐjiě de. This is the bit that no-one understands.

所谓 suǒwèi [形] 1 (通常说的) what is known as ▷中医所谓"上火"不止是指嗓子疼一种症状。 Zhōngyī suǒwèi "shànghuǒ" bùzhǐ shì zhǐ sǎngzi téng yīzhǒng zhèngzhuàng. What is known in Chinese medicine as "excess internal heat" covers a lot more than sore throats and the like. 2 (形容不认可) so-called

所以 suǒyǐ [连] (表示结果) so ▷路上堵车，所以我迟到了。 Lù shàng dǔchē, suǒyǐ wǒ chídào le. There was a lot of traffic, so I am late.

所有 suǒyǒu I [动] own II [名] possession III [形] all

索 suǒ I [名] 1 (绳子) rope 2 (链子) chain II [动] 1 (找) search ▷探索 tànsuǒ explore 2 (要) request

索赔 suǒpéi [动] claim damages

索引 suǒyǐn [名] index

锁 suǒ I [名] lock II [动] (用锁锁住) lock

锁链 suǒliàn [名] chain

ㄊ

他 tā [代] (另一人) he ▷他的包 tā de bāo his bag ▷我还记得他。 Wǒ hái jìde tā. I still remember him.

他们 tāmen [代] they ▷他们的老师 tāmen de lǎoshī their teacher ▷我给他们写信。 Wǒ gěi tāmen xiěxìn. I wrote to them.

他人 tārén [名] others (PL)

它 tā [代] it

它们 tāmen [代] they

她 tā [代] she ▷她的帽子 tā de màozi her hat ▷我给她发了个短信。 Wǒ gěi tā fā le gè duǎnxìn. I sent her a text message.

塌 tā [动] (倒塌) collapse

塌实 tāshi [形] 1(不浮躁) steady 2(放心) at peace

塔 tǎ [名] 1(指佛教建筑物) pagoda 2(指塔形物) tower

塔楼 tǎlóu [名] tower block

獭 tǎ [名] 1(指佛教建筑) otter ▷水獭 shuǐtǎ otter

踏 tà [动] (踩) step onto

胎 tāi [名] 1(母体内的幼体) foetus(英), fetus(美) ▷怀胎 huáitāi be pregnant 2(轮胎) tyre(英), tire(美)

胎儿 tāi'ér [名] foetus(英), fetus(美)

台 tái I [名] 1(指建筑) tower ▷观测台 guāncètái observation tower 2(指讲话,表演) stage ▷舞台 wǔtái stage 3(指作座子用) stand ▷蜡台 làtái candlestick 4(台形物) ▷窗台 chuāngtái window sill ▷站台 zhàntái platform 5(桌子或类似物) table ▷梳妆台 shūzhuāngtái dressing table ▷写字台 xiězìtái desk 6(指电话服务) telephone service ▷查号台 cháhào tái directory inquiries (pl) 7(指广播电视) station ▷电视台 diànshìtái television station 8(also: 台湾) Taiwan II [量] 1(指机器) ▷一台电脑 yī tái diànnǎo a computer ▷一百台电视 yībǎi tái diànshì one hundred TVs 2(指戏剧,戏曲) ▷两台京剧 liǎng tái Jīngjù two Beijing Opera performances ▷一台舞剧 yī tái wǔjù a ballet

measure word, used for machines, equipment, stage performances, etc.

台风 táifēng [名] typhoon

台阶 táijiē [名] (指建筑物) step

台历 táilì [名] desk calendar

台球 táiqiú [名] 1(指美式) pool 2(指英式) billiards (sc)

抬 tái [动] 1(举) raise 2(搬) carry

抬头 táitóu [动] (昂头) raise one's head

太 tài I [形] 1(高或大) highest 2(辈分高) senior ▷太爷爷 tài yéye great-grandfather II [副] 1(程度过分) too ▷这部电影太长。 Zhè bù diànyǐng tài cháng. This film is too long. 2(指程度极高) so ▷我太高兴了。 Wǒ tài gāoxìng le. I am so happy.

太极拳 tàijíquán [名] Tai-chi

太空 tàikōng [名] space

太平洋 Tàipíngyáng [名] the Pacific Ocean

太太 tàitai [名] 1(妻子) wife 2(指对年老者) lady 3(对已婚妇女) Mrs

太阳 tàiyáng [名] sun

态 tài [名] 1(状态) state ▷常态 chángtài normality ▷体态 tǐtài posture 2(语言) voice

态度 tàidù [名] 1(举止神情) manner 2(看法) attitude

贪 tān [动] 1(贪污) be corrupt 2(不满足) crave 3(好处,便宜) covet II [形] greedy

贪吃 tānchī [动] be greedy

贪婪 tānlán [形] greedy

贪玩 tānwán [动] be too fond of a good time

贪污 tānwū [动] embezzle

贪心 tānxīn I [形] greedy II [名] greed

摊 tān I [动] 1 (摆开) spread ... out ▸摊开地图 tānkāi dìtú spread out a map 2 (指烹调) fry ▸他摊了个鸡蛋。Tā tān le ge jīdàn. He fried an egg. 3 (分担) share II [名] stall

摊贩 tānfàn [名] street trader

瘫 tān I [名] paralysis II [形] paralysed (英), paralyzed (美)

瘫痪 tānhuàn I [名] paralysis II [动] be paralysed (英) 或 paralyzed (美)

坛 tán [名] 1 (土台) raised plot ▸花坛 huātán raised flower bed 2 (台子) platform ▸论坛 lùntán forum

谈 tán I [动] talk ▸谈生意 tán shēngyi discuss business II [名] talk

谈话 tánhuà [动] chat

谈论 tánlùn [动] discuss

谈判 tánpàn [动] negotiate

谈心 tánxīn [动] have a heart-to-heart talk

弹 tán [动] 1 (指弹性) spring ▸球弹不起来了。Qiú tán bù qǐlái le. The ball doesn't bounce. 2 (棉花，羊毛) fluff ▸ up 3 (灰，球)

flick 4 (乐器) play ▸弹钢琴 tán gāngqín play the piano → see also/另见 dàn

弹簧 tánhuáng [名] spring

弹力 tánlì [名] elasticity

弹性 tánxìng [名] 1 (弹力) elasticity 2 (喻) flexibility ▸弹性工作制 tánxìng gōngzuò zhì flexible working system

痰 tán [名] phlegm

坦 tǎn [形] 1 (平整) flat ▸平坦 píngtǎn flat 2 (直率) candid 3 (心里安定) calm ▸坦然 tǎnrán composed

坦白 tǎnbái I [形] candid II [动] confess

坦率 tǎnshuài [形] frank

毯 tǎn [名] 1 (指地上) carpet ▸地毯 dìtǎn carpet 2 (指床上) blanket ▸毛毯 máotǎn wool blanket 3 (指墙上) tapestry ▸壁毯 bìtǎn tapestry

叹 tàn [动] (叹气) sigh

叹气 tànqì [动] sigh

炭 tàn [名] charcoal

探 tàn I [动] 1 (试图发现) explore ▸探险 tànxiǎn explore 2 (看望) visit ▸探亲 tànqīn visit one's relatives 3 (伸出去) stick ▸ out 4 (过问) inquire ▸打探 dǎtàn scout II [名] scout ▸侦探 zhēntàn detective

探测 tàncè [动] survey

探索 tànsuǒ [动] probe

探讨 tàntǎo [动] investigate

探望 tànwàng [动] (看望) visit

碳 tàn [名] carbon

汤 tāng [名] (指食物) soup

汤药 tāngyào [名] herbal medicine

堂 táng I [名] 1 (房屋) hall ▷礼堂 lǐtáng auditorium ▷课堂 kètáng classroom ▷教堂 jiàotáng church 2 (厅) hall II [量] ▷两堂课 liǎng táng kè two lessons measure word, used for school lessons

糖 táng [名] 1 (指做饭) sugar 2 (糖果) sweet

躺 tǎng [动] lie

烫 tàng I [形] very hot ▷这汤真烫。Zhè tāng zhēn tàng. This soup is boiling hot. II [动] 1 (人) scald ▷... up 3 (熨) iron 4 (头发) perm

烫手 tàngshǒu [形] scalding

趟 tàng [量] 1 (指旅程) ▷我已经去了好几趟。Wǒ yǐjīng qù le hǎo jǐ tàng. I've made several trips. 2 (指公车, 地铁等) ▷他错过了一趟车。Tā cuòguò le yī tàng chē. He missed the bus. measure word, used for journeys, visits, scheduled public transport, etc.

掏 tāo [动] 1 (拿出) take ... out 2 (挖) dig 3 (偷) steal

逃 táo [动] 1 (逃跑) run away 2 (逃避) flee

逃避 táobì [动] escape ▷逃避责任 táobì zérèn shirk responsibility ▷逃避关税 táobì guānshuì evade customs duties

逃跑 táopǎo [动] escape

桃 táo [名] peach ▶桃子 táozi peach

陶 táo [名] pottery

陶瓷 táocí [名] ceramics (PL)

陶器 táoqì [名] pottery

陶醉 táozuì [动] be intoxicated

淘 táo [动] 1 (米) wash 2 (金子) pan for ▷淘金 táojīn pan for gold II [形] naughty

淘气 táoqì [形] naughty

淘汰 táotài [动] eliminate

讨 tǎo [动] 1 (债) demand 2 (饭, 钱) beg 3 (讨论) discuss

讨论 tǎolùn [动] discuss

讨厌 tǎoyàn I [形] 1 (可恶) disgusting 2 (指难办) nasty II [动] dislike

套 tào I [名] (套子) cover ▶手套 shǒutào glove ▶避孕套 bìyùntào condom II [动] (罩在外面) slip ... on III [量] set ▷一套西装 yī tào xīzhuāng a suit ▷两套邮票 liǎng tào yóupiào two sets of stamps measure word, used for suits, collections of books, tools, etc.

套餐 tàocān [名] set meal

特 tè I [形] special II [副] 1 (特地)

especially **2**(非常) extremely

特别 tèbié I [形] peculiar II [副] **1**(格外) exceptionally **2**(特地) specially

特此 tècǐ [副] hereby

特地 tèdì [副] especially

特点 tèdiǎn [名] characteristic

特价 tèjià [名] bargain price ▷ 特价商品 tèjià shāngpǐn bargain

特例 tèlì [名] special case

特区 tèqū [名] special zone

特权 tèquán [名] privilege

特色 tèsè [名] characteristic

特殊 tèshū [形] special

特务 tèwu [名] special agent

特征 tèzhēng [名] characteristic

疼 téng I [形] sore ▷ 我牙疼。Wǒ yá téng. I have toothache. II [动] love

藤 téng [名] vine ▷ 藤椅 téngyǐ cane chair

剔 tī [动] (牙，指甲) pick

梯 tī [名] ladder ▷ 电梯 diàntī lift (英), elevator (美) ▷ 楼梯 lóutī stairs (PL)

踢 tī [动] kick ▷ 踢足球 tī zúqiú play football

提 tí [动] **1**(拿) carry **2**(升) raise ▷ 提拔 tíbá promote **3**(提前) bring forward **4**(提出) put ... forward ▷ 他提了个建议。Tā tí le ge jiànyì. He put forward a proposal. **5**(提取) collect **6**(谈

起) mention ▷ 别再提那件事了。Bié zài tí nà jiàn shì le. Don' mention that subject again.

提倡 tíchàng [动] promote

提出 tíchū [动] put ... forward

提纲 tígāng [名] synopsis

提高 tígāo [动] raise ▷ 提高效率 tígāo xiàolǜ increase efficiency

提供 tígōng [动] provide

提前 tíqián I [动] bring ... forward II [副] early

提问 tíwèn [动] ask a question

提醒 tíxǐng [动] remind

提议 tíyì I [动] propose II [名] proposal

题 tí I [名] subject ▷ 标题 biāotí title II [动] inscribe

题材 tícái [名] theme

题目 tímù [名] **1**(标题) title **2**(考题) question

蹄 tí [名] hoof

体 tǐ [名] **1**(身体) body ▷ 人体 réntǐ human body **2**(物体) substance ▷ 液体 yètǐliquid

体操 tǐcāo [名] gymnastics (SG)

体会 tǐhuì I [动] come to understand II [名] understanding

体积 tǐjī [名] volume

体检 tǐjiǎn [名] physical examination

体力 tǐlì [名] physical strength

体贴 tǐtiē [动] show consideratio for

体温 tǐwēn [名] temperature

体系 tǐxì [名] system

体现 tǐxiàn [动] embody

体型 tǐxíng [名] physique

体验 tǐyàn [动] learn from experience

体育 tǐyù [名] 1 (课程) P.E. 2 (运动) sport ▷体育比赛 tǐyù bǐsài sports event

体育场 tǐyùchǎng [名] stadium

体育馆 tǐyùguǎn [名] gym

体重 tǐzhòng [名] weight

剃 tì [动] shave

替 tì I [动] (代) replace II [介] for ▷别替他操心了。 Bié tì tā cāoxīn le. Don't worry about him.

天 tiān I [名] 1 (天空) sky 2 (一昼夜) day ▷昨天 zuótiān yesterday 3 (一段时间内) ▷ Tiān hái zǎo ne. It's still so early. 4 (季节) season ▷秋天 qiūtiān autumn (英), fall (美) 5 (天气) weather ▷阴天 yīntiān overcast weather ▷天很热。 Tiān hěn rè. It's a very hot day. 6 (自然界) nature 7 (造物主) God ▷天知道！ Tiān zhīdào! God knows! 8 (神的住所) Heaven II [形] (头顶的) overhead ▷天桥 tiānqiáo overhead walkway

天才 tiāncái [名] 1 (才能) talent 2 (人) genius

天鹅 tiān'é [名] swan

天空 tiānkōng [名] sky

天气 tiānqì [名] weather ▷天气预报 tiānqì yùbào weather forecast

天然 tiānrán [形] natural

天生 tiānshēng [形] inherent ▷这孩子天生聋哑。 Zhè háizi tiānshēng lóngyǎ. This child was born deaf-mute.

天使 tiānshǐ [名] angel

天堂 tiāntáng [名] Heaven

天下 tiānxià [名] the world

天线 tiānxiàn [名] aerial

天性 tiānxìng [名] nature

天真 tiānzhēn [形] innocent

添 tiān [动] (增加) add

田 tián [名] 1 (耕地) field 2 (开采地) field ▷油田 yóutián oilfield

田径 tiánjìng [名] track and field sports (PL)

田野 tiányě [名] open country

甜 tián [形] 1 (指味道) sweet 2 (指睡觉) sound

甜点 tiándiǎn [名] dessert

甜食 tiánshí [名] sweet

填 tián [动] 1 (塞满) fill 2 (填写) complete ▷填表格 tián biǎogé fill in a form

填充 tiánchōng [动] 1 (填上) stuff 2 (补足) fill ... in

填空 tiánkòng [动] (指考试) fill in the blanks

填写 tiánxiě [动] fill ... in

舔 tiǎn [动] lick

挑 tiāo [动] 1(肩扛) carry ... on a carrying pole 2(挑选) choose 3(挑剔) nitpick
→ see also/另见 tiǎo

挑食 tiāoshí [动] be a fussy eater

挑剔 tiāoti [动] nitpick

挑选 tiāoxuǎn [动] select

条 tiáo I [名] 1(细树枝) twig 2(长条) strip 3(层次) order 4(分项) item 5(律令) article 6(短书信) note II [量] 1(用于细长东西) ▷两条腿 liǎng tiáo tuǐ two legs ▷一条烟 yī tiáo yān a multipack of cigarettes 2(指分事项的) ▷一条新闻 yī tiáo xīnwén an item of news 3(指与人有关) ▷一条人命 yī tiáo rénmìng a life measure word, used for long thin things, news, human lives, etc.

条件 tiáojiàn [名] 1(客观因素) condition 2(要求) requirement 3(状况) circumstances (PL)

条理 tiáolǐ [名] order

条约 tiáoyuē [名] treaty

调 tiáo [动] 1(使和谐) harmonize ▷失调 shītiáo imbalance 2(使均匀) blend 3(给钢琴调音) gěi gāngqín tiáo yīn tune a piano 3(调解) mediate
→ see also/另见 diào

调节 tiáojié [动] adjust

调料 tiáoliào [名] seasoning

调皮 tiáopí [形] (顽皮) naughty

调整 tiáozhěng [动] adjust

挑 tiǎo [动] 1(扯起一头) raise 2(向上拨) prick
→ see also/另见 tiāo

挑战 tiǎozhàn [动] challenge ▷面临新挑战 miànlín xīn tiǎozhàn face a new challenge

跳 tiào [动] 1(跃) jump ▷跳高 tiàogāo high jump ▷跳水 tiàoshuǐ diving ▷跳远 tiàoyuǎn long jump 2(弹起) bounce 3(起伏地动) beat ▷心跳 xīntiào heartbeat 4(越过) jump over ▷跳过几页 tiàoguò jǐ yè jump a few pages

跳槽 tiàocáo [动] change jobs

跳舞 tiàowǔ [动] dance

跳跃 tiàoyuè [动] jump

贴 tiē I [动] 1(粘) stick 2(紧挨) be close to 3(贴补) subsidize II [名] allowance

帖 tiě [名] 1(请帖) invitation ▷请帖 qǐngtiě invitation 2(小卡片) card

铁 tiě [名] (金属) iron

铁道 tiědào [名] railway (英), railroad (美)

铁路 tiělù [名] railway (英), railroad (美)

厅 tīng [名] 1(大degree) hall ▷客厅 kètīng sitting room ▷餐厅 cāntīng canteen 2(机关) office

听 tīng I [动] 1(收听) listen to 2(听从) obey ▷听老师的话 tīng lǎoshī de huà as the teacher

says II [名] tàin III [量] can ▸一听
啤酒 yì tīng píjiǔ a can of beer

听话 tīnghuà I [动] obey II [形]
obedient

听见 tīngjiàn [动] hear

听讲 tīngjiǎng [动] attend a
lecture

听说 tīngshuō [动] hear

听众 tīngzhòng [名] audience

亭 tíng [名] 1 (亭子) pavilion 2 (小
房子) kiosk ▸电话亭 diànhuàtíng
phone box(英), phone booth
(美)

庭 tíng [名] 1 (书) (厅堂) hall 2 (院
子) courtyard 3 (法庭) law court

庭院 tíngyuàn [名] courtyard

停 tíng [动] 1 (止) stop 2 (停留)
stop off 3 (停放) park

停车场 tíngchēchǎng [名] car
park(英), car lot(美)

停顿 tíngdùn I [动] 1 (中止) halt
2 (指说话) pause II [名] pause

停止 tíngzhǐ [动] stop ▸停止营业
tíngzhǐ yíngyè cease trading

挺 tǐng [副] very

艇 tǐng [名] boat ▸游艇 yóutǐng
yacht ▸救生艇 jiùshēngtǐng
lifeboat

通 tōng I [动] 1 (连接) connect with
▸通商 tōngshāng have trade
relations with ▸通风 tōngfēng
ventilate 2 (使不堵) clear ... out
▸通下水道 tōng xiàshuǐdào clear
a drain 3 (传达) inform ▸通信
tōngxìn correspond by letter ▸通

电话 tōng diànhuà communicate
by telephone 4 (通晓)
understand ▸精通 jīngtōng be
expert in II [名] expert ▸外语通
wàiyǔ tōng an expert in foreign
languages III [形] 1 (没有障碍)
open ▸电话打通了。Diànhuà
dǎ tōng le. The call has been put
through. 2 (顺畅) workable 3 (通
顺) coherent 4 (普通) common
5 (整个) overall IV [副] 1 (全部)
completely 2 (一般) normally

通常 tōngcháng I [形] normal
II [名] normal circumstances
(PL)▸我通常7点起床。Wǒ
tōngcháng qīdiǎn qǐchuáng.
Under normal circumstances, I
get up at seven o'clock.

通道 tōngdào [名] (指出入)
passageway ▸地下通道 dìxià
tōngdào tunnel

通过 tōngguò I [动] 1 (经过)
pass ▸通过边境线 tōngguò
biānjìngxiàn cross the border
2 (同意) pass II [介] by means of

通俗 tōngsú [形] popular

通宵 tōngxiāo [名] all night

通信 tōngxìn [动] correspond

通讯 tōngxùn I [名] dispatch
II [动] communicate

通用 tōngyòng [动] be in common
use

同 tóng I [动] 1 (一样) be the same
▸不同 bùtóng be different 2 (共
同) do ... together ▸同居 tóngjū
cohabit II [介] 1 (跟) with 2 (指
比较) as

同伴 tóngbàn [名] companion

同等 tóngděng [形] of the same level

同类 tónglèi I [形] of the same kind II [名] the same kind

同盟 tóngméng [名] alliance

同情 tóngqíng [动] sympathize ▷表示同情 biǎoshì tóngqíng express sympathy

同时 tóngshí I [名] at the same time ▷同时发生 tóngshí fāshēng occur simultaneously II [连] besides

同事 tóngshì [名] colleague

同性恋 tóngxìngliàn [名] homosexuality

同学 tóngxué [名] 1 (指同校) fellow student 2 (指同班) classmate

同样 tóngyàng [形] 1 (一样) same 2 (情况类似) similar

同意 tóngyì [动] agree

同志 tóngzhì [名] comrade

铜 tóng [名] copper

铜牌 tóngpái [名] bronze medal

童 tóng [名] (小孩) child ▷神童 shéntóng child prodigy

童话 tónghuà [名] fairy tale

童年 tóngnián [名] childhood

统 tǒng I [名] ▷系统 xìtǒng system ▷血统 xuètǒng bloodline II [动] command III [副] all

统计 tǒngjì [名] statistics (PL) ▷人口统计 rénkǒu tǒngjì

census II [动] count

统统 tǒngtǒng [副] entirely

统一 tǒngyī I [动] 1 (使成一体) unite 2 (使一致) unify ▷统一 思想 tǒngyī sīxiǎng reach a common understanding II [形] unified

统治 tǒngzhì [动] rule

桶 tǒng I [名] bucket ▷汽油桶 qìyóu tǒng petrol (英) 或 gasoline (美) drum ▷啤酒桶 píjiǔ tǒng beer barrel II [量] barrel ▷一桶 柴油 yī tǒng cháiyóu a barrel of diesel oil ▷两桶牛奶 liǎng tǒng niúnǎi two churns of milk

筒 tǒng [名] 1 (竹管) bamboo tube 2 (粗管状物) ▷笔筒 bǐtǒng pen holder ▷邮筒 yóutǒng post box (英)、mailbox (美) 3 (指衣服) ▷长筒袜 chángtǒngwà stockings (PL)

痛 tòng I [动] 1 (疼) ache ▷头痛 tóutòng have a headache ▷胃痛 wèitòng have a stomach ache 2 (悲伤) grieve ▷哀痛 āitòng sorrow II [副] deeply ▷痛打 tòngdǎ give a sound beating to

痛苦 tòngkǔ [形] painful

痛快 tòngkuài [形] 1 (高兴) joyful 2 (尽兴) to one's heart's content ▷玩个痛快 wán gè tòngkuài play to one's heart's content 3 (爽快) straightforward

偷 tōu I [动] (窃) steal II [副] stealthily

偷空 tōukòng [动] take time off

偷懒 tōulǎn [动] be lazy

偷窃 tōuqiè [动] steal

偷偷 tōutōu [副] secretly

头 tóu I [名] 1 (脑袋) head ▷点头 diǎntóu nod one's head 2 (发型) hair ▷平头 píngtóu crew cut ▷梳头 shūtóu comb one's hair 3 (顶端) tip 4 (开始) beginning 5 (头目) head ▷谁是你们的头儿? Shéi shì nǐmen de tóur? Who's your boss? II [形] 1 (第一) first ▷头奖 tóujiǎng first prize ▷头等 tóuděng first class 2 (领头) leading 3 (以前) first ▷头几年 tóu jǐ nián first few years III [量] 1 (指动物) ▷3头母牛 sān tóu mǔniú three cows 2 (指蒜) ▷一头蒜 yī tóu suàn a bulb of garlic

    measure word, used for cows, bulls, and vegetable bulbs

头发 tóufa [名] hair

头领 tóulǐng [名] leader

头脑 tóunǎo [名] brains (PL)

头衔 tóuxián [名] title

投 tóu [动] 1 (扔) throw 2 (放进去) put ... in 3 (跳下去) throw oneself 4 (投射) cast 5 (寄) post

投入 tóurù I [形] 1 (指专注) engrossed 2 (指逼真) realistic II [动] 1 (放入) put ... in 2 (参加) throw oneself into

投诉 tóusù I [动] lodge a complaint II [名] appeal

投降 tóuxiáng [动] surrender

投资 tóuzī I [动] invest II [名] investment

透 tòu I [动] 1 (渗透) penetrate 2 (泄露) leak out 3 (显露) appear II [形] 1 (透彻) thorough 2 (程度深) complete ▷我浑身都湿透了。 Wǒ húnshēn dōu shī tòu le. I'm soaked to the skin.

透彻 tòuchè [形] incisive

透露 tòulù [动] disclose

透明 tòumíng [形] transparent

秃 tū [形] 1 (指毛发) bald 2 (指山) barren 3 (指树) bare

秃顶 tūdǐng [动] be bald

秃子 tūzi [名] (口) baldy

突 tū [副] suddenly

突出 tūchū I [动] give prominence to ▷他从不突出自己。 Tā cóng bù tūchū zìjǐ. He never pushes himself forward. II [形] (明显) noticeable ▷突出的特点 tūchū de tèdiǎn prominent feature

突击 tūjī I [动] 1 (突然袭击) assault 2 (加快完成) do a rush job II [名] from nowhere

突破 tūpò [动] 1 (防线, 界线) break through 2 (僵局, 难关) make a breakthrough 3 (限额) surpass 4 (记录) break

突然 tūrán I [形] sudden II [副] suddenly

图 tú I [名] 1 (图画) picture 2 (地图) map 3 (计划) plan II [动] 1 (贪图) seek ▷图一时痛快 tú yíshí tòngkuài seek momentary gratification 2 (谋划) scheme

图案 tú'àn [名] design

图画 túhuà [名] picture

图书 túshū [名] books (PL)

图书馆 túshūguǎn [名] library

图像 túxiàng [名] image

图章 túzhāng [名] seal

徒 tú [名] (徒弟) apprentice ▶徒弟 túdì apprentice

途 tú [名] way ▶旅途 lǚtú journey ▶前途 qiántú prospect

途径 tújìng [名] channel

涂 tú [动] 1 (抹) spread ... on ▷涂油漆 tú yóuqī apply paint 2 (乱写乱画) scribble 3 (改动) cross ... out

涂改 túgǎi [动] alter

涂料 túliào [名] paint

屠 tú I [动] 1 (动物) slaughter 2 (人) massacre II [名] butcher

屠夫 túfū [名] (字) butcher

屠杀 túshā [动] massacre

土 tǔ I [名] 1 (泥) soil 2 (土地) land ▶领土 lǐngtǔ territory II [形] 1 (地方) local 2 (民间) folk 3 (不时髦) unfashionable

土地 tǔdì [名] 1 (田地) land 2 (疆域) territory

土豆 tǔdòu [名] potato

土话 tǔhuà [名] local dialect

土壤 tǔrǎng [名] soil

土著 tǔzhù [名] indigenous peoples (PL)

吐 tǔ [动] (排出口外) spit
→ see also/另见 tù

吐 tù [动] vomit
→ see also/另见 tǔ

吐沫 tùmo [名] saliva

兔 tù [名] 1 (野兔) hare 2 (家兔) rabbit

团 tuán I [名] 1 (球形物) ball 2 (组织) group ▶剧团 jùtuán drama company 3 (军) regiment II [动] 1 (聚合) unite ▷团聚 tuánjù reunite 2 (揉成球状) roll into a ball III [形] round IV [量] ▷一团面 yī tuán miàn a lump of dough ▷一团毛线 yī tuán máoxiàn a ball of wool

▨ measure word, used for rolled up round things

团伙 tuánhuǒ [名] gang

团结 tuánjié [动] unite

团体 tuántǐ [名] organization

团圆 tuányuán [动] reunite

推 tuī [动] 1 (门、窗、车) push 2 (使用工具) scrape ▷他推了个光头。Tā tuī le ge guāngtóu. He's shaved his head. 3 (录) push forward 4 (推断) deduce 5 (辞让) decline 6 (推迟) shift 7 (推迟) postpone 8 (举荐) elect

推测 tuīcè [动] infer

推辞 tuīcí [动] decline

推出 tuīchū [动] put ... off

推出 tuīchū [动] bring ... out

推动 tuīdòng [动] promote

推广 tuīguǎng [动] popularize

推荐 tuījiàn [动] recommend

推销 tuīxiāo [动] promote

腿 tuǐ [名] 1 (下肢) leg ▶大腿 dàtuǐ thigh ▶小腿 xiǎotuǐ calf 2 (支撑物) leg

退 tuì [动] 1 (后移) retreat 2 (使后移) cause ... to withdraw 3 (退出) quit 4 (减退) recede 5 (减弱) fade 6 (退还) return 7 (撤销) cancel

退步 tuìbù I [动] 1 (落后) lag behind 2 (让步) give way II [名] leeway

退让 tuìràng [动] make a concession

退缩 tuìsuō [动] hold back

退休 tuìxiū [动] retire

褪 tuì [动] 1 (衣服) take ... off 2 (毛) shed 3 (颜色) fade

吞 tūn [动] 1 (整个咽下) swallow 2 (吞并) take over

吞并 tūnbìng [动] annex

吞没 tūnmò [动] 1 (据为己有) misappropriate 2 (淹没) engulf

臀 tún [名] buttock

托 tuō I [动] 1 (撑) support 2 (委托) entrust 3 (依赖) rely on II [名] tray

托儿所 tuō'érsuǒ [名] nursery

托福 tuōfú [名] TOEFL, Test of English as a Foreign Language

托付 tuōfù [动] entrust

托运 tuōyùn [动] ship

拖 tuō [动] 1 (拉) pull 2 (地板) mop 3 (下垂) trail 4 (拖延) delay

拖延 tuōyán [动] delay

脱 tuō [动] 1 (皮肤, 毛发) shed 2 (衣服, 鞋帽) take ... off 3 (摆脱) escape 4 (颜色) fade 5 (油脂) skim

脱臼 tuōjiù [动] dislocate

脱离 tuōlí [动] 1 (关系) break off 2 (危险) get away from

脱落 tuōluò [动] 1 (毛发, 牙齿) lose 2 (油漆, 墙皮) come off

脱水 tuōshuǐ [动] dehydrate

驮 tuó [动] carry on one's back

驼 tuó I [名] camel ▶骆驼 luòtuo camel II [形] hunchbacked ▶驼背 tuóbèi be hunchbacked

鸵 tuó see below/见下文

鸵鸟 tuóniǎo [名] ostrich

妥 tuǒ [形] 1 (适当) appropriate 2 (停当) ready

妥当 tuǒdang [形] appropriate

妥善 tuǒshàn [形] appropriate

妥协 tuǒxié [动] compromise

椭 tuǒ see below/见下文

椭圆 tuǒyuán [名] oval

拓 tuò [动] open ... up

拓展 tuòzhǎn [动] expand

唾 tuò I [名] saliva II [动] spit

唾沫 tuòmo [名] (口) saliva

W

挖 wā[动] 1(掘) dig ▸挖掘 wājué excavate 2(耳朵, 鼻子) pick

蛙 wā[名] frog
　蛙泳 wāyǒng[名] breaststroke

娃 wá[名](方) baby
　娃娃 wáwa[名] 1(小孩) baby 2(玩具) doll

瓦 wǎ[名] tile
　瓦斯 wǎsī[名] gas

袜 wà[名] sock ▸长筒袜 chángtǒngwà stocking
　袜子 wàzi[名] sock

歪 wāi[形](倾斜) slanting
　歪斜 wāixié[形] crooked

外 wài I[名] 1(范围以外) outside 2(外国) foreign country II[形] 1(外国的) foreign 2(其他的) other ▸外人 wàirén outsider III[副] besides
　▸外边 wàibian outside
　外表 wàibiǎo[名] exterior
　外地 wàidì[名] other parts of the country ▸外地人 wàidìrén person from another part of the country
　外公 wàigōng[名] maternal grandfather
　外国 wàiguó[名] foreign country
　外国人 wàiguórén[名] foreign person
　外号 wàihào[名] nickname
　外汇 wàihuì[名](外币) foreign currency
　外交 wàijiāo[名] foreign affairs ▸外交部 wàijiāobù Ministry of Foreign Affairs
　外交官 wàijiāoguān[名] diplomat
　外科 wàikē[名] surgery ▸外科医生 wàikē yīshēng surgeon
　外卖 wàimài[名] takeaway(英), takeout(美)
　外贸 wàimào[名] foreign trade
　外婆 wàipó[名] maternal grandmother
　外企 wàiqǐ[名] foreign enterprise
　外伤 wàishāng[名] injury
　外商 wàishāng[名] foreign businessman
　外甥 wàisheng[名] nephew
　外孙 wàisūn[名] grandson

外套 wàitào [名] overcoat

外文 wàiwén [名] foreign language

外向 wàixiàng [形] (指性格) extrovert

外语 wàiyǔ [名] foreign language

弯 wān I [形] curved II [动] bend III [名] bend

湾 wān [名] bay

豌 wān see below/见下文

豌豆 wāndòu [名] pea

丸 wán [名] (指药) pill ▷丸药 wányào pill II [量] ▷他要吃一丸药。Tā fú le yī wán yào. He took a pill.

完 wán I [形] whole II [动] 1 (完成) complete 2 (耗尽) run out 3 (了结) finish

完成 wánchéng [动] complete

完美 wánměi [形] perfect

完全 wánquán I [形] complete II [副] completely

完整 wánzhěng [形] complete

玩 wán [动] 1 (玩耍) play 2 (游玩) have a good time ▷我去泰国玩了一个星期。Wǒ qù Tàiguó wán le yī gè xīngqī. I went to Thailand for a week's holiday. 3 (做客) visit 4 (表示祝愿) enjoy ▷玩得好! Wán de hǎo! Enjoy yourself!

玩具 wánjù [名] toy

玩笑 wánxiào [名] joke ▷他喜欢跟人开玩笑。Tā xǐhuan gēn rén kāi wánxiào. He likes to play jokes on people.

玩意儿 wányìr [名] (口) 1 (东西) thing 2 (玩具) toy 3 (器械) gadget

顽 wán [形] 1 (难以摆脱的) stubborn ▷顽固 wángù stubborn 2 (淘气) naughty ▷顽皮 wánpí mischievous

挽 wán [动] 1 (拉) hold 2 (卷起) roll ... up

晚 wǎn I [形] late ▷晚秋 wǎnqiū late autumn ▷我起晚了。Wǒ qǐ wǎn le. I got up late. II [名] evening

晚安 wǎn'ān [形] good night

晚饭 wǎnfàn [名] dinner

晚会 wǎnhuì [名] party

晚年 wǎnnián [名] old age

晚上 wǎnshang [名] evening

碗 wǎn [名] bowl

万 wàn [数] ten thousand

万岁 wànsuì [动] long live

万一 wànyī [连] if by any chance

腕 wàn [名] 1 (指手) wrist 2 (指脚) ankle

腕子 wànzi [名] 1 (指手) wrist 2 (指脚) ankle

亡 wáng [动] die ▷死亡 sǐwáng die

王 wáng [名] king

王国 wángguó [名] kingdom

王子 wángzǐ [名] prince

网 wǎng [名] 1 (工具) net 2 (网状

物) web **3** (系统) network ▶互联网 Hùliánwǎng the Internet

网吧 wǎngbā [名] Internet café

网络 wǎngluò [名] network

网民 wǎngmín [名] Internet user

网球 wǎngqiú [名] tennis ▶网球场 wǎngqiúchǎng tennis court

网页 wǎngyè [名] web page

网站 wǎngzhàn [名] website

网址 wǎngzhǐ [名] web address

往 wǎng I [介] to II [形] past ▶往事 wǎngshì past events (PL)

往往 wǎngwǎng [副] often

忘 wàng [动] forget

忘记 wàngjì [动] forget

旺 wàng [形] **1** (火) roaring **2** (人, 生意) flourishing **3** (花) blooming

旺季 wàngjì [名] **1** (指生意) peak season **2** (指水果, 蔬菜) season

旺盛 wàngshèng [形] **1** (精力, 生命力) full of energy **2** (植物) thriving

望 wàng [动] **1** (向远处看) look into the distance **2** (察看) watch **3** (希望) hope

危 wēi I [形] dangerous II [动] endanger

危害 wēihài [动] harm

危机 wēijī [名] crisis

危险 wēixiǎn I [形] dangerous II [名] danger

威 wēi [名] power

威力 wēilì [名] power

威士忌 wēishìjì [名] whisky

威胁 wēixié [动] threaten

威信 wēixìn [名] prestige

威严 wēiyán I [形] dignified II [名] dignity

微 wēi I [形] tiny ▶微米 wēimǐ micron ▶微秒 wēimiǎo microsecond II [副] slightly

微波炉 wēibōlú [名] microwave oven

微风 wēifēng [名] gentle breeze

微量元素 wēiliàng yuánsù [名] trace element

微妙 wēimiào [形] delicate

微弱 wēiruò [形] faint

微生物 wēishēngwù [名] micro-organism

微小 wēixiǎo [形] tiny

微笑 wēixiào [动] smile

微型 wēixíng [形] mini

为 wéi I [动] **1** (是) be **2** (充当) act as II [介] by
→ see also/另见 wèi

为难 wéinán I [形] embarrassed II [动] make things difficult for

为期 wéiqī [动] be scheduled for

为首 wéishǒu [动] make a point of

为止 wéizhǐ ▷到上周末为止 dào shàngzhōu mò wéizhǐ by the end of last week

违 wéi [动] break ▶违章 wéizhāng break regulations

违背 wéibèi [动] go against

违法 wéifǎ I [动] break the law II [形] illegal

违反 wéifǎn [动] go against

违犯 wéifàn [动] violate

围 wéi I [动] surround II [名] 1 (四周) all sides 2 (周长) measurement ▶三围 sānwéi vital statistics ▶胸围 xiōngwéi chest measurement

围棋 wéiqí [名] go (board game)

围棋 wéiqí

围棋 wéiqí is a popular strategic board game in China, Japan and other East-Asian countries. It originated in ancient China. It is known as go in Japan. It is played by two players alternately placing black and white round stone pieces on the intersections of a square grid on a square game board. To win, the player must control a larger area on the game board than his/her opponent.

围绕 wéirào [动] 1 (物体) revolve around 2 (话题) centre (英) 或 center (美) on

惟 wéi I [副] 1 (单) only 2 (书) (只是) but only

惟一 wéiyī [形] only

维 wéi I [动] 1 (连接) hold ... together 2 (保持) maintain II [名] dimension

维持 wéichí [动] 1 (保持) maintain 2 (资助) support

维护 wéihù [动] safeguard

维生素 wéishēngsù [名] vitamin

维修 wéixiū [动] maintain

伟 wěi [形] great

伟大 wěidà [形] great

伟哥 wěigē [名] (医) Viagra®

伟人 wěirén [名] great man

伪 wěi [形] false

伪钞 wěichāo [名] counterfeit note (英) 或 bill (美)

伪君子 wěijūnzǐ [名] hypocrite

伪造 wěizào [动] forge

伪装 wěizhuāng I [动] disguise II [名] disguise

尾 wěi [名] 1 (尾巴) tail ▶尾巴 wěiba tail 2 (末端) end 3 (残余) remainder ▶扫尾 sǎowěi finish off

尾气 wěiqì [名] exhaust (英), tailpipe (美)

纬 wěi [名] (地理) latitude ▶纬线 wěixiàn latitude

纬度 wěidù [名] latitude

委 wěi I [动] entrust II [名] 1 (委员) committee member ▶委员 wěiyuán committee member 2 (委员会) committee ▶委员会 wěiyuán huì committee

委屈 wěiqu [名] unjust treatment

委托 wěituō [动] entrust

委婉 wěiwǎn [形] (指言词) tactful

卫 wèi [动] protect

卫生 wèishēng I [名] 1 (干净) hygiene 2 (扫除) clean-up II [形] hygienic

卫生间 wèishēngjiān [名] toilet (英), rest room (美)

卫生纸 wèishēngzhǐ [名] toilet paper (英) 或 tissue (美)

卫星 wèixīng [名] satellite

为 wèi [介] for ▷ 我真为你高兴！ Wǒ zhēn wèi nǐ gāoxìng! I am really happy for you!
→ see also/另见 wéi

为了 wèile [介] in order to

为什么 wèishénme [副] why

未 wèi [副] not

未必 wèibì [副] not necessarily

未成年人 wèichéngniánrén [名] minor

未婚夫 wèihūnfū [名] fiancé

未婚妻 wèihūnqī [名] fiancée

未来 wèilái [名] future

位 wèi I [名] 1 (位置) location 2 (地位) position 3 (数学) digit ▷ 两位数 liǎng wèi shù two-digit number II [量] ▷ 两位教授 liǎng wèi jiàoshòu two professors ▷ 一位父亲 yī wèi fùqin a father measure word, used for people

位于 wèiyú [动] be located

位置 wèizhi [名] 1 (地点) location 2 (地位) place 3 (职位) position

位子 wèizi [名] 1 (座位) seat 2 (职

位) position

味 wèi [名] 1 (滋味) taste 2 (气味) smell

味道 wèidao [名] (滋味) taste

味精 wèijīng [名] monosodium glutamate

胃 wèi [名] stomach

胃口 wèikǒu [名] 1 (食欲) appetite 2 (喜好) liking

喂 wèi I [动] feed ▷ 喂养 wèiyǎng raise II [叹] 1 (指打电话) hello 2 (指招呼) hey

温 wēn I [形] 1 (不冷不热) warm 2 (平和) mild II [动] (加热) warm ... up III [名] temperature

温度 wēndù [名] temperature

温和 wēnhé [形] 1 (指性情, 态度) mild 2 (指气候) temperate

温暖 wēnnuǎn [形] warm

温泉 wēnquán [名] hot spring

温柔 wēnróu [形] gentle

温室 wēnshì [名] greenhouse ▷ 温室效应 wēnshì xiàoyìng the greenhouse effect

文 wén [名] 1 (字) writing 2 (书面语) written language ▷ 中文 Zhōngwén the Chinese language 3 (文章) essay 4 (指社会产物) culture 5 (文科) humanities (PL)

文化 wénhuà [名] 1 (精神财富) culture 2 (知识) education

文件 wénjiàn [名] 1 (公文) document 2 (计算机) file

文具 wénjù [名] stationery

文科 wénkē [名] humanities (PL)

文盲 wénmáng [名] illiterate

文明 wénmíng I [名] civilization II [形] civilized

文凭 wénpíng [名] diploma

文物 wénwù [名] cultural relic

文学 wénxué [名] literature

文艺 wényì [名] 1 (文学艺术) art and literature 2 (文学) literature 3 (演艺) performing arts (PL)

文章 wénzhāng [名] (著作) essay

文字 wénzì [名] 1 (指符号) script 2 (指文章) writing

闻 wén I [动] (嗅) smell II [名] (消息) news (SG) ▶新闻 xīnwén news

蚊 wén [名] mosquito ▶蚊子 wénzi mosquito

吻 wěn I [名] kiss II [动] kiss

稳 wěn I [形] 1 (平稳) steady 2 (坚定) firm 3 (稳重) composed 4 (可靠) reliable 5 (肯定) sure II [动] keep calm

稳定 wěndìng I [形] steady II [动] settle

问 wèn [动] 1 (提问) ask 2 (问候) send regards to 3 (干预) ask about II [名] question ▶疑问 yíwèn doubt

问候 wènhòu [动] send regards to

问题 wèntí [名] 1 (疑问) question 2 (困难) problem 3 (故障) fault 4 (分项) issue

窝 wō [名] (栖息地) nest

蜗 wō see below/见下文

蜗牛 wōniú [名] snail

我 wǒ [代] 1 (自己, 作主语) I 2 (自己, 作宾语) me

我们 wǒmen [代] 1 (作主语) we 2 (作宾语) us

卧 wò I [动] 1 (躺) lie 2 (趴伏) sit II [名] berth

卧铺 wòpù [名] berth

卧室 wòshì [名] bedroom

握 wò [动] 1 (抓) grasp 2 (掌握) master

握手 wòshǒu [动] shake hands

乌 wū I [名] crow ▶乌鸦 wūyā crow II [形] black ▶乌云 wūyún black cloud

乌龟 wūguī [名] tortoise

乌黑 wūhēi [形] jet-black

污 wū [形] 1 (肮脏) dirty 2 (腐败) corrupt ▶贪污 tānwū be corrupt

污染 wūrǎn [动] pollute

污辱 wūrǔ [动] (侮辱) insult

屋 wū [名] 1 (房子) house 2 (房间) room

屋顶 wūdǐng [名] roof

屋子 wūzi [名] room

无 wú I [动] (没有) not have ▶无效 wúxiào invalid ▶无形 wúxíng invisible II [副] not ▶无论如何 wúlùn rúhé in any case

无耻 wúchǐ [形] shameless

无辜 wúgū I [动] be innocent II [名] the innocent

无关 wúguān [动] have nothing to do with

无赖 wúlài [名] rascal

无论 wúlùn [连] no matter what

无情 wúqíng [形] 1 (指感情) heartless 2 (不留情) ruthless

无数 wúshù I [形] countless II [动] be uncertain

无所谓 wúsuǒwèi [动] 1 (谈不上) never mind 2 (不在乎) be indifferent

无限 wúxiàn [形] boundless

无线电 wúxiàndiàn [名] radio

无须 wúxū [副] needlessly

无知 wúzhī [形] ignorant

五 wǔ [名] five ▶五月 wǔyuè May ▶五分之一 wǔ fēn zhī yī one fifth

五官 wǔguān [名] the five sense organs

午 wǔ [名] noon

午饭 wǔfàn [名] lunch

午夜 wǔyè [名] midnight

伍 wǔ [名] (五) five

This is the complex character for "five", which is mainly used in banks, on receipts, etc. to prevent mistakes and forgery.

武 wǔ [形] 1 (军事的) military 2 (勇猛) valiant ▶威武 wēiwǔ powerful

武力 wǔlì [名] 1 (军事力量)

military strength 2 (暴力) force

武器 wǔqì [名] weapon

武士 wǔshì [名] warrior

武术 wǔshù [名] martial arts circles (PL)

侮 wǔ [动] (侮辱) insult ▶侮辱 wǔrǔ insult

舞 wǔ I [名] dance II [动] (跳舞) dance

舞蹈 wǔdǎo [名] dance

舞台 wǔtái [名] stage

勿 wù [副] not ▶请勿吸烟 qǐng wù xīyān no smoking

务 wù I [名] business ▶任务 rènwù task II [副] without fail

务必 wùbì [副] without fail

物 wù [名] 1 (东西) thing ▶物体 wùtǐ body 2 (物产) produce ▶物产 wùchǎn produce 3 (动物) creature 4 (指哲学) matter

物价 wùjià [名] price

物理 wùlǐ [名] (指学科) physics (SG)

物业 wùyè [名] property

物质 wùzhì [名] 1 (哲) matter 2 (非精神) material things (PL)

物种 wùzhǒng [名] species (SG)

误 wù I [名] mistake II [形] 1 (不正确) erroneous ▶误会 wùhuì misunderstand 2 (非故意) accidental ▶误伤 wùshāng accidentally injure II [动] (耽误) miss ▶快点儿，别误了火车！

Kuàidiǎnr, bié wù le huǒchē!
Hurry up – we don't want to miss the train!

雾 wù [名] fog

夕 xī [名] 1 (傍晚) sunset ▷夕阳 xīyáng setting sun 2 (晚上) evening ▷除夕 chúxī New Year's Eve

西 xī [名] 1 (方向) west ▷西北 xīběi northwest ▷西南 xīnán southwest 2 (疆域) the West ▷西藏 Xīzàng Tibet

西班牙 Xībānyá [名] Spain ▷西班牙人 Xībānyárén Spaniard ▷西班牙语 Xībānyáyǔ the Spanish language

西餐 xīcān [名] Western food

西方 xīfāng [名] the West

西服 xīfú [名] Western clothes

西瓜 xīguā [名] watermelon

西红柿 xīhóngshì [名] tomato

西药 xīyào [名] Western medicine

西医 xīyī [名] (药品) Western medicine

吸 xī [动] 1 (气，水等) draw ... in ▶吸烟 xīyān smoke cigarettes 2 (吸收) absorb 3 (吸引) attract

吸尘器 xīchénqì [名] vacuum cleaner

吸收 xīshōu [动] 1 (摄取) absorb 2 (接纳) recruit

吸引 xīyǐn [动] attract

希 xī

希望 xīwàng I [动] hope II [名] hope

牺 xī see below/见下文

牺牲 xīshēng [动] 1 (献身) sacrifice oneself 2 (放弃) sacrifice

稀 xī [形] 1 (稀疏) rare 2 (稀疏) sparse 3 (水多的) watery ▶稀饭 xīfàn rice porridge

稀少 xīshǎo [形] sparse

稀有 xīyǒu [形] rare

犀 xī [名] rhinoceros ▶犀牛 xīniú rhinoceros

溪 xī [名] brook

熄 xī [动] put ... out ▶熄灯 xīdēng put out the light

熄灭 xīmiè [动] put ... out

膝 xī [名] knee ▶膝盖 xīgài knee

习 xī [动] 1 (学习) practise (英), practice (美) ▶习武 xíwǔ study

martial arts 2 (熟悉) be used to ▶习以为常 xí yǐ wéi cháng become used to II [名] custom ▶习俗 xísú custom ▶习气 xíqì bad habit

习惯 xíguàn I [动] be used to II [名] habit

习性 xíxìng [名] habits (PL)

席 xī [名] 1 (编织物) mat ▶竹席 zhúxí bamboo mat 2 (座位) seat ▶席位 xíwèi seat ▶出席 chūxí be present 3 (宴席) feast ▶酒席 jiǔxí banquet

袭 xī [动] 1 (攻击) make a surprise attack ▶空袭 kōngxí air raid 2 (仿做) follow the pattern of ▶抄袭 chāoxí plagiarize

袭击 xíjī [动] attack

媳 xī [名] daughter-in-law

媳妇 xífù [名] 1 (儿子的妻子) daughter-in-law 2 (晚辈的妻子) wife

洗 xī [动] 1 (衣，碗等) wash ▶洗衣店 xǐyīdiàn Launderette (英), Laundromat® (美) 2 (胶卷) develop 3 (录音，录像) wipe 4 (麻将，扑克) shuffle

洗衣机 xǐyījī [名] washing machine

洗澡 xǐzǎo [动] have a bath

喜 xī I [形] 1 (高兴) happy 2 (可贺的) celebratory II [动] 1 (爱好) like ▶喜爱 xǐ'ài like 2 (适宜) suit

喜爱 xǐ'ài [动] like

喜欢 xǐhuan [动] like

喜剧 xǐjù [名] comedy

戏 xì I [动] (嘲弄) joke ▸戏弄 xìnòng tease II [名] 1 (戏剧) show ▸京戏 jīngxì Beijing Opera ▸马戏 mǎxì circus

戏法 xìfǎ [名] magic

戏剧 xìjù [名] theatre (英), theater (美)

戏曲 xìqǔ [名] Chinese opera

戏院 xìyuàn [名] theatre (英), theater (美)

系 xì I [名] 1 (系统) system 2 (部门) department II [动] (拴) tie
→ see also/另见 jì

系列 xìliè [名] series (SG)

系统 xìtǒng [名] system

细 xì I [形] 1 (绳, 线等) thin 2 (沙, 粮等) fine 3 (声, 语等) gentle 4 (节, 则等) detailed ▸细节 xìjié details (PL) II [副] 1 (详细) minutely 2 (细致) xìxiāng consider carefully

细胞 xìbāo [名] cell

细菌 xìjūn [名] germ

细心 xìxīn [形] careful

细致 xìzhì [副] meticulously

虾 xiā [名] shrimp ▸龙虾 lóngxiā lobster ▸对虾 duìxiā prawn

瞎 xiā [形] (失明) blind

瞎话 xiāhuà [名] lie

峡 xiá [名] gorge ▸海峡 hǎixiá strait

峡谷 xiágǔ [名] canyon

狭 xiá [形] narrow ▸狭窄 xiázhǎi narrow

下 xià I [动] 1 (走下) go down ▸下山 xià shān go down the mountain ▸下楼 xià lóu go downstairs ▸下船 xià chuán disembark from a boat ▸下床 xià chuáng get out of bed 2 (落下) fall ▸下雨 xiàyǔ rain ▸下雪 xiàxuě snow 3 (传发) issue 4 (锅煮) put ... in 5 (给出) give 6 (开始) begin ▸下笔 xiàbǐ start to write 7 (结束) finish ▸下班 xiàbān finish work ▸下课 xiàkè finish class 8 (生下) ▸下蛋 xià dàn lay an egg 9 (用于动词后, 表示脱离物体) ▸拧下灯泡 nǐng xià dēngpào unscrew a light bulb 10 (用于动词后, 表示动作完成) ▸记录下会议内容 jìlù xià huìyì nèiróng take the minutes at a meeting II [名] 1 (低) ▸下层 xiàcéng lower level 2 (另) ▸下次 xiàcì next time ▸下个星期 xià gè xīngqī next week 3 (指方位或时间) ▸楼下 lóuxià downstairs ▸树下 shù xià under the tree 4 (指范围, 情况, 条件) ▸在朋友的帮助下 zài péngyou de bāngzhù xià with help from friends ▸在压力下 zài yālì xià under pressure III [量] time ▸拍了几下 pāi le jǐ xià tapped a few times ▸拧了两下 nǐng le liǎng xià turned a couple of times

下岗 xiàgǎng [动] 1 (完工) leave one's post 2 (失业) be laid off

下海 xiàhǎi [动] (指经商) go into

business

下级 xiàjí [名] subordinate

下来 xiàlái [动] 1 (指由高到低) come down ▷ 我上不去了，你下来吧。Wǒ bù shàngqu le, nǐ xiàlái ba. I won't come up - you come down. 2 (指作物成熟) be harvested 3 (用于动词后，指脱离物体) ▷ 他把眼镜摘了下来。Tā bǎ yǎnjìng zhāi le xiàlái. He took off his glasses. 4 (用于动词后，表示完成) ▷ 暴乱平息了下来了。Bàoluàn píngxī xiàlái le. The riot has calmed down. 5 (表示出现某种状态) ▷ 灯光暗了下来。Dēngguāng àn le xiàlái. The light started to fade.

下流 xiàliú [形] dirty

下面 xiàmiàn I [副] 1 (指位置) underneath 2 (指次序) next II [名] lower levels (PL)

下去 xiàqù [动] 1 (指由高到低) go down 2 (指时间的延续) continue 3 (用于动词后，指空间上) ▷ 从楼上跳了下去 cóng lóu shàng tiào xiàqù jump from a building 4 (时间上的持续) ▷ 唱下去 chàng xiàqù keep singing 5 (指数量下降) ▷ 高烧已经退下去了。Gāoshāo yǐjīng tuì xiàqù le. His temperature has already gone down. 6 (指程度深化) ▷ 天气有可能热下去。Tiānqì yǒu kěnéng rè xiàqù. The weather will probably go on getting hotter.

下网 xiàwǎng (计算机) go offline

下午 xiàwǔ [名] afternoon

下载 xiàzài [动] download

吓 xià [动] frighten ▶吓人 xiàrén scary

吓唬 xiàhu [动] frighten

夏 xià [名] summer

夏令营 xiàlìngyíng [名] summer camp

夏天 xiàtiān [名] summer

仙 xiān [名] immortal ▶仙人 xiānrén immortal

先 xiān [形] (指时间) earlier ▶事先 shìxiān beforehand

先后 xiānhòu [副] successively

先进 xiānjìn [形] advanced

先生 xiānsheng [名] 1 (指男士) Mr 2 (老师) teacher 3 (丈夫) husband

纤 xiān [形] fine

纤维 xiānwéi [名] fibre

掀 xiān [动] lift

掀起 xiānqǐ [动] 1 (揭起) lift 2 (涌起) surge

鲜 xiān I [形] 1 (新鲜) fresh 2 (鲜美) delicious II [名] 1 (鲜美) delicacy ▶海鲜 hǎixiān seafood

鲜艳 xiānyàn [形] brightly-coloured (英), brightly-colored (美)

闲 xián I [形] 1 (不忙) idle 2 (安静) quiet 3 (闲置) unused ▶闲房 xiánfáng empty house II [名] leisure

闲话 xiánhuà [名] 1(流言) gossip 2(废话) digression

闲事 xiánshì [名] other people's business

弦 xián [名] 1(指乐器) string 2(指钟表) spring

咸 xián [形] salted ▷咸菜 xiáncài pickled vegetables (PL)

嫌 xián [动] dislike ▷他嫌这儿吵，搬走了。 Tā xián zhèr chǎo, bānzǒu le. He found it too noisy here and moved away.

嫌弃 xiánqì [动] cold-shoulder

嫌疑 xiányí [名] suspicion

显 xiǎn [动] 1(表现) display 2(呈现) be apparent

显然 xiǎnrán [副] obviously

显示 xiǎnshì [动] demonstrate

显眼 xiǎnyǎn [形] conspicuous

显著 xiǎnzhù [形] striking

险 xiǎn [形] 1(险要) strategic 2(危险) dangerous

县 xiàn [名] county

现 xiàn [形] 1(现在) present ▷现状 xiànzhuàng present situation 2(现有) ready ▷现金 xiànjīn cash

现场 xiànchǎng [名] scene ▷现场报道 xiànchǎng bàodào live report

现成 xiànchéng [形] ready-made

现代 xiàndài [名] modern times (PL)

现代化 xiàndàihuà [名] modernization

现实 xiànshí [名] reality

现象 xiànxiàng [名] phenomenon

现在 xiànzài [名] now

现状 xiànzhuàng [名] the current situation

限 xiàn I [动] limit II [名] limit

限期 xiànqī I [动] set a deadline II [名] deadline

限制 xiànzhì [动] restrict

线 xiàn [名] 1(指细长物品) thread ▷电线 diànxiàn electric wire 2(交通干线) line

线索 xiànsuǒ [名] clue

宪 xiàn [名] constitution

宪法 xiànfǎ [名] constitution

陷 xiàn I [名] 1(书)(陷阱) trap 2(过失) fault ▷缺陷 quēxiàn defect II [动] 1(沉入) get bogged down 2(凹进) sink 3(卷入) get involved

陷害 xiànhài [动] frame

陷阱 xiànjǐng [名] trap

馅 xiàn [名] stuffing ▷饺子馅 jiǎozi xiàn jiaozi filling

羡 xiàn [动] admire

羡慕 xiànmù [动] envy

献 xiàn [动] 1(给) give ▷献血 xiànxiě donate blood 2(表演) show

腺 xiàn [名] gland

乡 xiāng [名] 1(乡村) countryside 2(家乡) home town

乡村 xiāngcūn [名] village

乡下 xiāngxia [名] countryside

相 xiāng [副] (互相) mutually ▸相差 xiāngchà differ
→ see also/另见 xiàng

相处 xiāngchǔ [动] get along

相当 xiāngdāng I [动] match II [形] appropriate III [副] quite

相对 xiāngduì I [动] be opposite II [形] 1 (非绝对的) relative 2 (比较的) comparative

相反 xiāngfǎn I [形] opposite II [连] on the contrary

相关 xiāngguān [动] be related

相互 xiānghù I [形] mutual II [副] ▸相互理解 xiānghù lǐjiě understand each other

相识 xiāngshí [动] be acquainted

相似 xiāngsì [形] similar

相同 xiāngtóng [形] identical

相像 xiāngxiàng [动] be alike

相信 xiāngxìn [动] believe

香 xiāng I [形] 1 (芳香) fragrant 2 (美味) delicious 3 (睡得熟的) sound II [名] 1 (香料) spice 2 (烧的香) incense

香波 xiāngbō [名] shampoo

香肠 xiāngcháng [名] sausage

香港 Xiānggǎng [名] Hong Kong

香蕉 xiāngjiāo [名] banana

香料 xiāngliào [名] spice

香水 xiāngshuǐ [名] perfume

香烟 xiāngyān [名] (卷烟) cigarette

香皂 xiāngzào [名] soap

箱 xiāng [名] 1 (箱子) box 2 (箱状物) ▸信箱 xìnxiāng postbox (英), mailbox (美)

箱子 xiāngzi [名] box

详 xiáng [形] detailed

详情 xiángqíng [名] details (PL)

详细 xiángxì [形] detailed

享 xiǎng [动] enjoy

享受 xiǎngshòu [动] enjoy

响 xiǎng I [名] 1 (回声) echo 2 (声音) sound II [动] sound ▸手机响了。Shǒujī xiǎng le. The mobile (英) or cell (美) phone was ringing. III [形] loud and clear

响亮 xiǎngliàng [形] loud and clear

响应 xiǎngyìng [动] respond

想 xiǎng [动] 1 (思考) think ▸想办法 xiǎng bànfǎ think of a way 2 (推测) reckon 3 (打算) want to 4 (想念) miss

In a positive sentence, both 想 xiǎng and 要 yào can be used to express "want to". To express "I don't want to", it is more common to use 不想 bù xiǎng, as the expression 不要 bù yào is stronger and indicates a definite decision, meaning "I shall not (under any circumstances)".

想法 xiǎngfǎ [名] opinion

想念 xiǎngniàn [动] miss

想像 xiǎngxiàng I [动] imagine II [名] imagination

向 xiàng I [名] direction II [动] 1(对着) face 2(偏袒) side with III [介] to ▷我向他表示了感谢。Wǒ xiàng tā biǎoshì le gǎnxiè. I expressed my thanks to him.

向导 xiàngdǎo [名] guide

向来 xiànglái [副] always

项 xiàng I [名] (项目) item ▷事项 shìxiàng item II [量] item ▷三项要求 sān xiàng yāoqiú three requirements ▷两项任务 liǎng xiàng rènwu two tasks

项链 xiàngliàn [名] necklace

项目 xiàngmù [名] 1(事项) item 2(指工程计划) project

巷 xiàng [名] lane

相 xiàng [名] 1(相貌) appearance 2(姿势) posture 3(官位) minister ▷外相 wàixiàng foreign minister 4(相片) photograph ▷照相 zhàoxiàng take a photograph → see also/另见 xiāng

相貌 xiàngmào [名] appearance

相片 xiàngpiàn [名] photograph

象 xiàng [名] 1(大象) elephant 2(样子) appearance

象棋 xiàngqí [名] Chinese chess

象棋 xiàngqí

象棋 xiàngqí is a very popular board game in China. It is a game of skill, played by two players on a board which imitates a battle field with a river in between two opposing sides. There are some similarities between the Chinese chess and international chess.

象牙 xiàngyá [名] ivory

象征 xiàngzhēng [动] symbolize

像 xiàng I [名] portrait ▷画像 huàxiàng paint portraits ▷雕像 diāoxiàng statue II [动] 1(相似) look like 2(比如) ▷像他这样的好孩子，谁不喜欢呢！Xiàng tā zhèyàng de hǎo háizi, shéi bù xǐhuan ne! Who doesn't like good children like this one! III [副] as if ▷像要下雪了。 Xiàng yào xiàxuě le. It looks as if it might snow.

橡 xiàng [名] 1(橡树) oak 2(橡树) rubber tree

橡胶 xiàngjiāo [名] rubber

橡皮 xiàngpí [名] rubber (英), eraser (美)

削 xiāo [动] peel

消 xiāo [动] 1(消失) disappear 2(使消失) remove

消除 xiāochú [动] eliminate

消防 xiāofáng [名] fire fighting

消费 xiāofèi [动] consume

消耗 xiāohào [动] consume

消化 xiāohuà [动] digest

消极 xiāojí [形] 1(反面) negative

2(消沉) demoralized

消灭 xiāomiè [动] **1**(消失) die out
2(除掉) eradicate

消失 xiāoshī [动] vanish

消息 xiāoxi [名] news (sG)

宵 xiāo [名] night ▷通宵 tōngxiāo
all night

销 xiāo [动] **1**(熔化) melt **2**(除
去) cancel **3**(销售) market **4**(消
费) spend

销路 xiāolù [名] market

销售 xiāoshòu [动] sell

小 xiǎo [形](不大) small ▷年龄小
niánlíng xiǎo young

小便 xiǎobiàn I [动] urinate II [名]
urine

小吃 xiǎochī [名] **1**(非正餐) snack
2(冷盘) cold dish

小丑 xiǎochǒu [名](滑稽演员)
clown

小儿科 xiǎo'érkē [名](医)
paediatrics (英) 或 pediatrics
(美) department

小费 xiǎofèi [名] tip

小伙子 xiǎohuǒzi [名] lad

小姐 xiǎojiě [名] **1**(称呼) Miss
2(女子) young lady

小看 xiǎokàn [动] underestimate

小麦 xiǎomài [名] wheat

小名 xiǎomíng [名] pet name

小气 xiǎoqi [形] **1**(气量小) petty
2(吝啬) stingy

小区 xiǎoqū [名] housing estate

小时 xiǎoshí [名] hour

小说 xiǎoshuō [名] novel

小提琴 xiǎotíqín [名] violin

小偷 xiǎotōu [名] thief

小心 xiǎoxīn I [动] be careful
II [形] careful

小学 xiǎoxué [名] primary school
(英), elementary school (美)

小学生 xiǎoxuéshēng [名]
primary school pupil (英),
elementary school student (美)

小组 xiǎozǔ [名] group

晓 xiǎo I [名] dawn II [动] **1**(知道)
know **2**(使人知道) tell

晓得 xiǎode [动] know

孝 xiào I [动] be dutiful ▷孝子
xiàozǐ filial son II [名] filial piety

孝顺 xiàoshùn I [动] show filial
obedience II [形] filial

校 xiào [名](学校) school

校长 xiàozhǎng [名] principal

哮 xiào I [名] wheezing II [动]
wheeze

哮喘 xiàochuǎn [名] asthma

笑 xiào [动] **1**(欢笑) laugh **2**(嘲
笑) laugh at

笑话 xiàohua I [名] joke II [动]
laugh at

效 xiào I [名] effect II [动] **1**(仿效)
imitate **2**(献出) devote ... to

效果 xiàoguǒ [名] **1**(结果) effect
2(戏剧) effects (PL)

效率 xiàolǜ [名] efficiency

效益 xiàoyì [名] returns (PL)

些 xiē [量] **1** (不定量) some **2** (略微) a little

歇 xiē [动] (休息) rest

歇息 xiēxi [动] **1** (休息) have a rest **2** (睡觉) go to sleep

蝎 xiē [名] scorpion ► 蝎子 xiēzi scorpion

协 xié **I** [动] assist **II** [副] jointly ► 协议 xiéyì agree on

协会 xiéhuì [名] association

协调 xiétiáo **I** [动] coordinate **II** [形] coordinated

协议 xiéyì [名] agreement

协助 xiézhù [动] help

协作 xiézuò [动] collaborate

邪 xié [形] (不正当) evil

邪恶 xié'è [形] evil

斜 xié **I** [形] (不正) slanting **II** [动] slant

斜坡 xiépō [名] slope

携 xié **1** (携带) carry **2** (拉着) hold

携带 xiédài [动] carry

鞋 xié [名] shoe

鞋匠 xiéjiàng [名] cobbler

写 xiě [动] **1** (书写) write **2** (写作) write **3** (描写) describe **4** (绘画) draw

写作 xiězuò [动] write

血 xiě [名] (口) blood → see also/另见 xuè

泄 xiè [动] (泄露) let ... out

泄露 xièlòu [动] let ... out

卸 xiè [动] **1** (搬下) unload ► 卸车 xièchē unload a vehicle **2** (除去) remove ► 卸妆 xièzhuāng remove one's makeup **3** (拆卸) strip **4** (解除) be relieved of ► 卸任 xièrèn step down

谢 xiè [动] **1** (感谢) thank ► 多谢 Duōxiè! Thanks a lot! **2** (认错) apologize **3** (拒绝) decline ► 谢绝 xièjué decline **4** (脱落) wither

谢谢 xièxie [动] thank you, thanks (口)

蟹 xiè [名] crab ► 螃蟹 pángxiè crab

心 xīn [名] **1** (心脏) heart **2** (思想) mind ► 用心 yòngxīn attentively ► 谈心 tánxīn heart-to-heart talk **3** (中心) centre (英), center (美)

心得 xīndé [名] what one has learned

心理 xīnlǐ [名] psychology

心灵 xīnlíng [名] mind

心情 xīnqíng [名] frame of mind

心愿 xīnyuàn [名] one's heart's desire

心脏 xīnzàng [名] heart

心脏病 xīnzàngbìng [名] heart disease

辛 xīn [形] **1** (辣) hot **2** (辛苦) laborious **3** (痛苦) bitter

辛苦 xīnkǔ **I** [形] laborious **II** [动] trouble ► 辛苦你了! Xīnkǔ nǐ le! Thanks for taking the trouble!

辛勤 xīnqín [形] hardworking

欣 xīn [形] glad

欣赏 xīnshǎng [动] 1(赏识) admire 2(享受) enjoy

新 xīn I [形] (跟旧相对) new II [副] newly

新潮 xīncháo I [形] fashionable II [名] new trend

新陈代谢 xīn chén dàixiè [名] metabolism

新郎 xīnláng [名] bridegroom

新年 xīnnián [名] 1(指一段时间) New Year 2(指元旦当天) New Year's Day

新娘 xīnniáng [名] bride

新闻 xīnwén [名] news (sG)

新鲜 xīnxiān [形] 1(指食物) fresh 2(指植物) tender 3(清爽) fresh 4(奇异) novel

新颖 xīnyǐng [形] original

薪 xīn [名] (薪水) salary

薪水 xīnshui [名] salary

信 xìn I [动] 1(相信) believe ▶轻信 qīngxìn readily believe 2(信奉) believe in ▶信教 xìnjiào be religious II [名] 1(书信) letter ▶信箱 xìnxiāng letterbox (英), mailbox (美) 2(信息) message 3(信用) trust ▶失信 shīxìn lose trust

信贷 xìndài [名] credit

信封 xìnfēng [名] envelope

信号 xìnhào [名] signal

信件 xìnjiàn [名] letter

信赖 xìnlài [动] trust

信任 xìnrèn [动] trust

信息 xìnxī [名] information

信心 xìnxīn [名] faith

信仰 xìnyǎng [动] believe in ▶他没有宗教信仰。 Tā méiyǒu zōngjiào xìnyǎng. He has no religious faith.

信用 xìnyòng [名] 1(指信任) word 2(指借贷) credit

信用卡 xìnyòngkǎ [名] credit card

信誉 xìnyù [名] reputation

兴 xīng [动] 1(旺盛) prosper 2(流行) be popular 3(使盛行) promote
→ see also/另见 xìng

兴奋 xīngfèn [动] be excited

兴盛 xīngshèng [形] prosperous

兴旺 xīngwàng [形] prosperous

星 xīng [名] 1(指天体) star ▶星星 xīngxing star 2(指名人) star ▶球星 qiúxīng football star

星期 xīngqī [名] 1(周) week 2(指某天) day ▶星期天 xīngqītiān Sunday ▶星期三 xīngqīsān Wednesday ▶明天星期几? Míngtiān xīngqī jǐ? What day is it tomorrow?

猩 xīng [名] orang-utan ▶黑猩猩 hēixīngxīng chimpanzee

腥 xīng [形] fishy

刑 xíng [名] (刑罚) punishment ▶死刑 sǐxíng the death penalty

行 xíng I [动] 1 (走) walk ▸步行 bùxíng go on foot 2 (流通) be current ▸发行 fāxíng issue 3 (做) do ▸行医 xíngyī practise (英) 或 practice (美) medicine II [形] 1 (可以) OK 2 (能干) capable III [名] 1 (旅行) travel 2 (行为) conduct ▸暴行 bàoxíng act of cruelty

→ see also/另见 háng

行动 xíngdòng [动] 1 (行走) move about 2 (活动) take action

行李 xínglǐ [名] luggage

行人 xíngrén [名] pedestrian

行驶 xíngshǐ [动] travel

行为 xíngwéi [名] behaviour (英), behavior (美)

行走 xíngzǒu [动] walk

形 xíng [名] 1 (形状) shape 2 (形体) body

形成 xíngchéng [动] form

形容 xíngróng [动] describe

形式 xíngshì [名] form

形象 xíngxiàng [名] image

形状 xíngzhuàng [名] shape

型 xíng [名] type ▸体型 tǐxíng build ▸血型 xuèxíng blood group

型号 xínghào [名] model

醒 xǐng [动] 1 (神志恢复) come to 2 (睡醒) wake up 3 (醒悟) become aware ▸提醒 tíxǐng remind

兴 xìng [名] excitement

→ see also/另见 xīng

兴趣 xìngqù [名] interest ▸他对

集邮有浓厚的兴趣。 Tā duì jíyóu yǒu nónghòu de xìngqù. He has a deep interest in stamp-collecting.

杏 xìng [名] apricot

幸 xìng I [形] lucky II [副] fortunately

幸福 xìngfú I [名] happiness II [形] happy

幸亏 xìngkuī [副] fortunately

幸运 xìngyùn I [名] good luck II [形] lucky

性 xìng [名] 1 (性格) character ▸任性 rènxìng stubborn 2 (性能) function ▸酸性 suānxìng acidity 3 (性别) gender ▸男性 nánxìng male 4 (情欲) sex 5 (性质) 可靠性 kěkàoxìng reliability ▸实用性 shíyòngxìng utility 6 (语法) gender ▸阳性 yángxìng masculine

性别 xìngbié [名] sex

性感 xìnggǎn [形] sexy

性格 xìnggé [名] personality

性质 xìngzhì [名] character

姓 xìng I [动] ▸我姓李。 Wǒ xìng Lǐ. My surname is Li. II [名] surname

姓名 xìngmíng [名] full name

凶 xiōng [形] 1 (不幸的) unlucky 2 (凶恶) ferocious ▸凶相 xiōngxiàng fierce look 3 (厉害) terrible

凶狠 xiōnghěn [形] vicious

凶手 xiōngshǒu [名] murderer

兄 xiōng [名] brother

兄弟 xiōngdi [名] brother

胸 xiōng [名] 1 (胸部) chest 2 (心胸) heart

胸脯 xiōngpú [名] chest

雄 xióng [形] 1 (公的) male ▶雄性 xióngxìng male 2 (有气魄的) imposing 3 (强有力的) strong

熊 xióng [名] bear

熊猫 xióngmāo [名] panda

休 xiū [动] 1 (停止) stop 2 (休息) rest

休息 xiūxi [动] rest

休闲 xiūxián [动] (悠闲) be at leisure ▶休闲服装 xiūxián fúzhuāng casual clothes

修 xiū [动] 1 (修理) mend 2 (兴建) build 3 (剪) trim

修改 xiūgǎi [动] alter

修建 xiūjiàn [动] build

修理 xiūlǐ [动] repair

修饰 xiūshì [动] 1 (修整装饰) decorate 2 (修改润饰) polish

修养 xiūyǎng [名] 1 (水平) accomplishments (PL) 2 (指态度) gentility

羞 xiū [形] shy ▶害羞 hàixiūbe shy

秀 xiù I [形] 1 (清秀) elegant 2 (优异) outstanding II [名] talent ▶新秀 xīnxiùnew talent

秀气 xiùqi [形] 1 (清秀) delicate

2 (文雅) refined

袖 xiù [名] sleeve ▶袖子 xiùzi sleeve

袖珍 xiùzhēn [形] pocket-sized ▶袖珍收音机 xiùzhēn shōuyīnjī pocket radio

绣 xiù I [动] embroider II [名] embroidery

锈 xiù [名] rust ▶生锈 shēngxiù go rusty

须 xū I [副] ▶必须 bìxūmust II [名] beard

须要 xūyào [动] need

须知 xūzhī [名] essentials (PL)

虚 xū [形] 1 (空着) empty 2 (胆怯) timid 3 (虚假) false 4 (虚心) modest 5 (弱) weak

虚构 xūgòu [动] fabricate

虚假 xūjiǎ [形] false

虚荣 xūróng [名] vanity

虚弱 xūruò [形] frail

虚伪 xūwěi [形] hypocritical

虚心 xūxīn [形] open-minded

需 xū I [动] need II [名] needs (PL) ▶军需 jūnxūmilitary requirements (PL)

需求 xūqiú [名] demand

需要 xūyào I [动] need II [名] needs (PL) ▶日常生活需要 rìcháng shēnghuó xūyào necessities of life

许 xǔ [动] 1 (称赞) praise 2 (答应) promise 3 (允许) allow

许多 xǔduō [形] many ▷他养了许多金鱼。Tā yǎng le xǔduō jīnyú. He keeps a lot of goldfish.

叙 xù [动] 1(谈) chat 2(记述) recount

叙事 xùshì [动] narrate

叙述 xùshù [动] recount

畜 xù [动] raise
→ see also/另见 chù

畜牧 xùmù [动] rear ▷畜牧业 xùmùyè animal husbandry

酗 xù see below/见下文

酗酒 xùjiǔ [动] get drunk

婿 xù [名] (女婿) son-in-law ▷女婿 nǚxù son-in-law

宣 xuān [动] 1(宣布) announce 2(疏导) lead ... off ▷宣泄 xuānxiè get ... off one's chest

宣布 xuānbù [动] announce

宣称 xuānchēng [动] announce

宣传 xuānchuán [动] disseminate ▷宣传工具 xuānchuán gōngjù means of dissemination

宣告 xuāngào [动] proclaim

宣誓 xuānshì [动] take an oath

宣言 xuānyán [名] declaration

宣扬 xuānyáng [动] advocate

宣战 xuānzhàn [动] declare war

喧 xuān [动] make a noise

喧哗 xuānhuá I [形] riotous II [动] create a disturbance

喧闹 xuānnào [形] rowdy

悬 xuán [动] 1(挂) hang 2(设想) imagine 3(挂念) be concerned about 4(未定) be unresolved

悬挂 xuánguà [动] hang

悬念 xuánniàn [名] suspense

悬崖 xuányá [名] precipice

旋 xuán I [动] 1(旋转) revolve 2(返回) return II [名] spiral
→ see also/另见 xuàn

旋律 xuánlǜ [名] melody

旋钮 xuánniǔ [名] knob

旋涡 xuánwō [名] whirlpool

旋转 xuánzhuǎn [动] revolve

选 xuǎn I [动] 1(挑选) choose 2(选举) vote II [名] 1(指人) selection ▷人选 rénxuǎn selection of people 2(作品集) collection ▷文选 wénxuǎn collected works (PL)

选拔 xuǎnbá [动] select

选举 xuǎnjǔ [动] elect

选民 xuǎnmín [名] electorate

选手 xuǎnshǒu [名] contestant

选修 xuǎnxiū [动] choose to study ▷选修课程 xuǎnxiū kèchéng optional course

选择 xuǎnzé [动] choose ▷别无选择 biéwú xuǎnzé have no choice

旋 xuàn [动] spin
→ see also/另见 xuán

旋风 xuànfēng [名] whirlwind

靴 xuē [名] boot

靴子 xuēzi [名] boot

穴 xué [名] 1(洞) den 2(穴位)

acupuncture point

穴位 xuéwèi [名] acupuncture point

学 xué I [动] 1 (学习) study ▷学英语 xué Yīngyǔ learn English 2 (模仿) imitate II [名] 1 (学问) learning ▷博学 bóxué erudition 2 (学科) science ▷生物学 shēngwùxué biology ▷化学 huàxué chemistry 3 (学校) school ▷大学 dàxué university ▷中学 zhōngxué senior school (英), high school (美) ▷小学 xiǎoxué primary school (英), elementary school (美)

学费 xuéfèi [名] tuition fee

学科 xuékē [名] subject

学历 xuélì [名] educational background

学生 xuésheng [名] student

学士 xuéshì [名] (指学位) bachelor's degree

学术 xuéshù [名] learning

学说 xuéshuō [名] theory

学位 xuéwèi [名] degree

学问 xuéwen [名] learning

学习 xuéxí [动] study

学校 xuéxiào [名] school

学业 xuéyè [名] studies (PL)

学者 xuézhě [名] scholar

雪 xuě [名] snow ▷下雪 xiàxuě to snow

雪花 xuěhuā [名] snowflake

血 xuè [名] (血液) blood

→ see also/另见 xiě

血统 xuètǒng [名] blood relation

血型 xuèxíng [名] blood type

血压 xuèyā [名] blood pressure

血液 xuèyè [名] 1 (血) blood 2 (主要力量) lifeblood

血缘 xuèyuán [名] blood relation

熏 xūn [动] 1 (烟气接触物体) blacken 2 (熏制) smoke ▷熏肉 xūnròu smoked meat

寻 xún [动] search

寻常 xúncháng [形] usual

寻求 xúnqiú [动] seek

寻找 xúnzhǎo [动] look for

巡 xún [动] patrol

巡逻 xúnluó [动] patrol

询 xún [动] inquire

询问 xúnwèn [动] ask

循 xún [动] abide by

循环 xúnhuán [动] circulate

训 xùn I [动] 1 (教导) teach 2 (训练) train II [名] rule

训练 xùnliàn [动] train

迅 xùn [形] swift

迅速 xùnsù [形] swift

驯 xùn I [形] tame II [动] tame

驯服 xùnfú I [形] tame II [动] tame

y

压 yā I [动] 1 (施力) press 2 (超越) outdo 3 (使稳定) control 4 (压制) suppress 5 (积压) put ... off II [名] pressure

压力 yālì [名] 1 (物) pressure 2 (指对人) pressure 3 (负担) burden

压迫 yāpò [动] 1 (压制) oppress 2 (挤压) put pressure on

压岁钱 yāsuìqián [名] traditional gifts of money given to children during the Spring Festival

压抑 yāyì [动] suppress

呀 yā [叹] (表示惊异) oh ▷ 呀! 已经12点了! Yā! Yǐjīng shí'èr diǎn le! Oh! It's 12 o'clock already!

押 yā [动] (抵押) leave ... as a security

押金 yājīn [名] deposit

鸦 yā [名] crow

鸦片 yāpiàn [名] opium

鸭 yā [名] duck

牙 yá [名] (牙齿) tooth

牙齿 yáchǐ [名] tooth

牙床 yáchuáng [名] gum

牙膏 yágāo [名] toothpaste

牙签 yáqiān [名] toothpick

牙刷 yáshuā [名] toothbrush

牙痛 yátòng [名] toothache

牙医 yáyī [名] dentist

芽 yá [名] (指植物) sprout

崖 yá [名] cliff

哑 yǎ [形] 1 (不能说话) mute 2 (不说话) speechless 3 (嘶哑) hoarse

哑巴 yǎba [名] mute

哑铃 yǎlíng [名] dumbbell

哑语 yǎyǔ [名] sign language

轧 yà [动] (碾) roll

亚 yà I [形] inferior ▶ 亚军 yàjūn runner-up II [名] Asia

亚洲 Yàzhōu [名] Asia ▷ 她是亚洲人。Tā shì Yàzhōurén. She's Asian.

咽 yān [名] pharynx
→ see also/另见 yàn

咽喉 yānhóu [名] (字) throat

烟 yān [名] 1 (指气体) smoke 2 (烟草) tobacco ▶ 香烟 xiāngyān cigarette

烟草 yāncǎo [名] **1**(指植物) tobacco plant **2**(烟草制品) tobacco

烟花 yānhuā [名] firework

烟灰缸 yānhuīgāng [名] ashtray

烟民 yānmín [名] smokers (PL)

淹 yān [动] (淹没) flood

淹没 yānmò [动] **1**(漫过) submerge **2**(喻) drown ... out

延 yán [动] **1**(延长) extend **2**(推迟) delay

延长 yáncháng [动] extend

延迟 yánchí [动] delay

严 yán [形] **1**(严密) tight **2**(严格) strict

严格 yángé [形] strict

严谨 yánjǐn [形] (严密谨慎) meticulous

严厉 yánlì [形] severe

严肃 yánsù [形] **1**(庄重) solemn **2**(严格认真) severe

严重 yánzhòng [形] serious

言 yán I [动] speak II [名] **1**(话) speech **2**(字) words (PL)

言论 yánlùn [名] speech ▷ 言论自由 yánlùn zìyóu freedom of speech

言情片 yánqíngpiān [名] romantic film (英) 或 movie (美)

言语 yányǔ [名] language

岩 yán [名] rock

炎 yán I [形] scorching II [名] (炎症) inflammation

炎黄子孙 Yán-Huáng zǐsūn [名] Chinese people

炎热 yánrè [形] scorching hot

炎症 yánzhèng [名] inflammation

沿 yán I [介] (along II [动] (依照) follow III [名] edge

沿岸 yán'àn [名] bank

沿海 yánhǎi [名] coast

研 yán [动] (研究) research ▶ 研究院 yánjiūyuàn research institute ▶ 研究生 yánjiūshēng postgraduate student

研究 yánjiū [动] **1**(探求) research **2**(商讨) discuss

盐 yán [名] salt

颜 yán [名] **1**(字) face **2**(颜色) colour (英), color (美)

颜料 yánliào [名] colouring (英), coloring (美)

颜色 yánsè [名] (色彩) colour (英), color (美)

眼 yǎn [名] **1**(眼睛) eye **2**(小洞) small hole

眼光 yǎnguāng [名] **1**(视线) gaze **2**(观察能力) vision **3**(观点) perspective

眼红 yǎnhóng [动] be jealous

眼界 yǎnjiè [名] horizons (PL)

眼睛 yǎnjing [名] eye

眼镜 yǎnjìng [名] glasses (PL)

眼泪 yǎnlèi [名] tear

眼力 yǎnlì [名] **1**(视力) eyesight **2**(鉴别能力) judgement

眼神 yǎnshén [名] **1**(指神态) expression **2**(方)(视力) eyesight

演 yǎn [动] (表演) perform

演出 yǎnchū [动] perform

演讲 yǎnjiǎng [动] make a speech

演示 yǎnshì [动] demonstrate

演说 yǎnshuō [动] make a speech

演员 yǎnyuán [名] performer

演奏 yǎnzòu [动] perform

厌 yàn [动] (厌恶) detest

厌烦 yànfán [动] be sick of

厌恶 yànwù [动] loathe

砚 yàn [名] ink stone ▶砚台 yàntai ink stone

咽 yàn [动] swallow
→ see also/另见 yān

宴 yàn [动] (脸向上) host a dinner ▶宴请 yànqǐng invite ... to dinner

宴会 yànhuì [名] banquet

验 yàn [动] (检查) test

验光 yànguāng have an eye test

验血 yànxiě [动] have a blood test

谚 yàn [名] saying ▶谚语 yànyǔ proverb

雁 yàn [名] wild goose

焰 yàn [名] flame

燕 yàn [名] swallow

燕麦 yànmài [名] oats (PL)

燕尾服 yànwěifú [名] tailcoat

羊 yáng [名] sheep ▶山羊

shānyáng goat

羊毛 yángmáo [名] wool

羊绒衫 yángróngshān [名] cashmere

阳 yáng [名] **1**(阴的对立面) Yang (from Yin and Yang) **2**(太阳) sun ▶阳光 yángguāng sunlight

阳台 yángtái [名] balcony

阳性 yángxìng [名] **1**(医) positive **2**(语言) masculine

洋 yáng I [名] (海洋) ocean II [形] (外国的) foreign

洋白菜 yángbáicài [名] cabbage

洋葱 yángcōng [名] onion

仰 yǎng [动] (脸向上) look up

仰望 yǎngwàng [动] look up

养 yǎng I [动] **1**(供给) provide for **2**(饲养) keep ▷我爱养花。 Wǒ ài yǎng huā. I like growing flowers. **3**(生育) give birth to **4**(培养) form ▷养成习惯 yǎng chéng xíguàn form a habit II [形] foster ▶养母 yǎngmǔ foster mother ▶养子 yǎngzǐ adopted son

养活 yǎnghuó [动] (口) **1**(提供生活费用) support **2**(饲养) raise **3**(生育抚养) give birth to

养料 yǎngliào [名] nourishment

养育 yǎngyù [动] bring up

养殖 yǎngzhí [动] breed

氧 yǎng [名] oxygen ▶氧气 yǎngqì oxygen

痒 yǎng [动] itch

样 yàng I [名] 1(模样) style 2(标准的) sample II [量] type ▷3样水果 sān yàng shuǐguǒ three types of fruit

样品 yàngpǐn [名] sample

样式 yàngshì [名] style

样子 yàngzi [名] 1(模样) appearance 2(神情) expression

妖 yāo [名] evil spirit

妖精 yāojing [名] (妖怪) demon

要 yāo [动] 1(求) ask 2(邀请) invite → see also/另见 yào

Both 要 yào and 会 huì can be used to express the future tense. 要 yào refers to something definite, e.g. 我明天要上班 wǒ míngtiān yào shàngbān (I am going to work tomorrow); 会 huì is usually used to express a possible, or probable outcome, e.g. 明天会下雨 míngtiān huì xiàyǔ (It might rain tomorrow).

要求 yāoqiú I [动] demand II [名] request

腰 yāo [名] 1(身体中部) waist 2(裤腰) waist

腰包 yāobāo [名] wallet

腰带 yāodài [名] belt

腰果 yāoguǒ [名] cashew nut

腰围 yāowéi [名] waistline

腰子 yāozi [名] kidney

邀 yāo [动] (邀请) invite

邀请 yāoqǐng [动] invite

谣 yáo [名] 1(歌谣) folk song ▶歌谣 gēyáo folk song 2(谣言) rumour (英), rumor (美) ▶谣言 yáoyán hearsay

谣传 yáochuán I [动] be rumoured (英) 或 rumored (美) II [名] rumour (英), rumor (美)

摇 yáo [动] shake

摇动 yáodòng [动] 1(摇东西) wave 2(晃) shake

摇滚乐 yáogǔnyuè [名] rock and roll

摇晃 yáohuàng [动] shake

摇篮 yáolán [名] cradle

遥 yáo [形] distant ▶遥控器 yáokòngqì remote control

遥控 yáokòng [动] operate by remote control

遥远 yáoyuǎn [形] 1(指距离) distant 2(指时间) far-off

咬 yǎo [动] 1(指用嘴) bite 2(夹住) grip

舀 yǎo [动] ladle

药 yào [名] 1(指治病) medicine 2(指化学物品) chemical

药材 yàocái [名] herbal medicine

药方 yàofāng [名] prescription

药物 yàowù [名] medicine

要 yào I [形] important II [动] 1(想得到) want ▶我女儿要一个新书包。Wǒ nǚ'ér yào yī gè xīn shūbāo. My daughter wants a new schoolbag. **2**(要求) ask ▷ 老师要我们安静。Lǎoshī yào wǒmen ānjìng. The teacher asked us to be quiet. **III** [助动] **1**(应该) should ▷ 饭前要洗手。Fàn qián yào xǐshǒu. You should wash your hands before you eat. **2**(需要) need ▷ 我要上厕所。Wǒ yào shàng cèsuǒ. I need the toilet. **3**(表示意志) want ▷ 我要学开车。Wǒ yào xué kāichē. I want to learn to drive. **4**(将要) be about to ▷ 我们要放暑假了。Wǒmen yào fàng shǔjià le. We're about to break for summer vacation. **IV** [连](如果) if ▷ 你要碰见他，替我问声好。Nǐ yào pèngjiàn tā, tì wǒ wèn shēng hǎo. If you meet him, say hello from me.

→ see also/另见 yāo

> In a positive sentence, both 要 yào and 想 xiǎng can be used to express "want to". To express "I don't want to", it is more common to use 不想 bù xiǎng, as the expression 不要 bù yào is stronger and indicates a definite decision, meaning "I shall not (under any circumstances)".

要不 yàobù [连] **1**(否则) otherwise ▷ 快点走，要不你要迟到了。Kuàidiǎn zǒu, yào bù nǐ yào chídào le. Go quickly, otherwise you'll be late. **2**(表示选择) either ... or ▷ 我们要不

去看电影，要不去喝咖啡厅，你说呢？Wǒmen yàobù qù kàn diànyǐng, yàobù qù kāfēitīng, nǐ yào ne? We can either go to see a film or go to a coffee shop – which would you prefer?

要紧 yàojǐn [形] **1**(重要) important **2**(严重) serious

要领 yàolǐng [名] **1**(要点) gist **2**(基本要求) main points (PL)

要么 yàome [连] either ... or ▷ 要么学文，要么学理。Yàome xué wén, yàome xué lǐ. You either study arts or science.

要是 yàoshi [连] if ▷ 要是你不满意，可以随时退货。Yàoshi bù mǎnyì, kěyǐ suíshí tuìhuò. If you're not satisfied, you can return the goods at any time.

钥 yào see below/见下文
钥匙 yàoshi [名] key

耀 yào [动] (照射) shine

耶 yē see below/见下文
耶稣 Yēsū [名] Jesus

椰 yē [名] coconut
椰子 yēzi [名] **1**(树) coconut tree **2**(果实) coconut

噎 yē [动] (堵塞) choke

爷 yé [名] (祖父) (paternal) grandfather
爷爷 yéye [名] (口) (祖父) (paternal) granddad

也 yě [副] **1**(同样) also ▷ 他也去过中国。Tā yě qùguò Zhōngguó.

He's been to China too. **2** (表示转折) still ▷即使他来了，也帮不上忙。Jíshǐ tā lái le, yě bāng bù shàng máng. Even if he comes, it still won't be of any use.

也许 yěxǔ [副] perhaps

野 yě I [名] **1** (野外) open country ▷野餐 yěcān picnic II [形] **1** (野生) wild ▷野菜 yěcài wild herbs (PL) **2** (蛮横) rude ▷粗野 cūyě rough **3** (无约束) unruly

野餐 yěcān [动] have a picnic

野蛮 yěmán [形] **1** (蒙昧) uncivilized **2** (残暴) brutal

野生 yěshēng [形] wild

野兽 yěshòu [名] wild animal

野外 yěwài [名] open country

野心 yěxīn [名] ambition

野营 yěyíng [名] camp

业 yè [名] **1** (行业) industry ▷饮食业 yǐnshí yè the food and drink industry **2** (职业) job ▷就业 jiùyè obtain employment ▷失业 shīyè be unemployed **3** (学业) studies (PL) ▷毕业 bìyè graduate **4** (产业) property ▷家业 jiāyè family property

业务 yèwù [名] profession

业余 yèyú I [名] spare time II [形] amateurish

业主 yèzhǔ [名] owner

叶 yè [名] (叶子) leaf

页 yè I [名] page II [量] page

页码 yèmǎ [名] page number

夜 yè [名] night

夜班 yèbān [名] night shift

夜猫子 yèmāozi [名] (方) **1** (猫头鹰) owl **2** (喻) (晚睡者) night owl

夜生活 yèshēnghuó [名] nightlife

夜市 yèshì [名] night market

夜总会 yèzǒnghuì [名] nightclub

夜宵 yèxiāo [名] late-night snack

液 yè [名] liquid

液体 yètǐ [名] liquid

腋 yè [名] (夹肢窝) armpit ▷腋毛 yèmáo underarm hair

一 yī [数] **1** (指数目) one ▷一辈子 yíbèizi a lifetime **2** (相同) ▷一类人 yí lèi rén the same sort of people **3** (全) ▷一屋子烟 yì wūzi yān full of smoke

—— yī is pronounced as 1st tone when it is used by itself to mean the number one, for example in telephone numbers etc. When it is followed by another syllable it changes its tone depending on the tone of the subsequent syllable. If the subsequent syllable is 1st, 2nd or 3rd tone then it is pronounced as 4th tone yì. If the subsequent syllable is a 4th tone, then it is pronounced as a 2nd tone yí. For consistency, changes of tone in pinyin are not shown in this book.

一般 yībān [形] 1(一样) same ▷ 他们俩一般大。 Tāmen liǎ yībān dà. The two of them are the same age. 2(普通) ordinary

一半 yībàn [名] half

一边 yībiān I [名] (一面) side II [副] at the same time

一道 yídào [副] together

一点儿 yìdiǎnr [量] 1(一些) some ▷ 你行李太多了，我帮你提一点儿吧。 Nǐ xíngli tàiduō, wǒ bāng nǐ tí yìdiǎnr ba. You've got so much luggage - let me help you with some of it. 2(很少) a little ▷ 这件事我一点儿都不知道。 Zhè jiàn shì wǒ yìdiǎnr dōu bù zhīdào. I know nothing about this.

一定 yídìng I [形] 1(规定的) definite 2(固定的) fixed 3(相当) certain 4(特定) given II [副] 1(必定) definitely ▷ 放心，我一定去机场接你。 Fàngxīn, wǒ yídìng qù jīchǎng jiē nǐ. Don't worry, I'll definitely pick you up at the airport.

一共 yígòng [副] altogether ▷ 这套书一共多少本？ Zhè tào shū yígòng duōshao běn? How many books are there in this set?

一⋯⋯就⋯⋯ yī⋯⋯jiù⋯⋯ [副] as soon as ▷ 我一到家就给你打电话。 Wǒ yī dào jiā jiù gěi nǐ dǎ diànhuà. I'll call you as soon as I get home.

一连 yìlián [副] on end ▷ 一连下了几个月的雨。 Yìlián xià le jǐ

gè yuè de yǔ. It's been raining for months on end.

一路 yílù [名] 1(行程) journey ▷ 一路顺利吗？ Yílù shùnlì ma? Did you have a good journey? 2(一起) the same way ▷ 咱俩是一路。 Zán liǎ shì yílù. We're going the same way.

一面 yímiàn I [名] (一面) aspect ▷ 积极的一面 jījí de yímiàn a positive aspect II [副] at the same time ▷ 她一面听音乐，一面看小说。 Tā yímiàn tīng yīnyuè, yímiàn kàn xiǎoshuō. She was listening to music and reading a novel at the same time.

一齐 yìqí [副] simultaneously

一起 yìqǐ I [名] the same place II [副] together

一切 yíqiè [代] 1(全部) all 2(全部事物) everything

一时 yìshí I [名] 1(一个时期) time 2(短暂时间) moment II [副] 1(临时) for the moment 2(时而) sometimes

一同 yìtóng [副] together

一下 yíxià I [量] ▷ 我去问一下。 Wǒ qù wèn yíxià. I'll just go and ask.

measure word, used after verbs to indicate one's attempts to do something II [副] at once ▷ 天一下就冷了。 Tiān yíxià jiù lěng le. All at once the weather turned cold.

一向 yíxiàng [副] always

一些 yìxiē [量] 1(部分) some 2(几

个) a few 3 (略微) a little ▷她感觉好一些了。Tā gǎnjué hǎo yīxiē le. She feels a little better.

一样 yīyàng [形] same ▷他俩爱好一样。Tā liǎ àihào yīyàng. They have the same hobbies.

一再 yīzài [副] repeatedly

一直 yīzhí [副] 1 (不变向) straight 2 (不间断) always ▷大风一直刮了两天两夜。Dàfēng yīzhí guā le liǎng tiān liǎng yè. The gale blew for two days and two nights. 3 (指一定范围) all the way ▷从南一直到北 cóng nán yīzhí dào běi from the south all the way to the north

一致 yīzhì I [形] unanimous II [副] unanimously

衣 yī [名] (衣服) clothing ▷衣裳 yīshang clothes (PL)

衣服 yīfu [名] clothes (PL)

医 yī I [名] 1 (医生) doctor 2 (医 medicine ▷中医 zhōngyī Chinese traditional medicine II [动] cure

医疗 yīliáo [动] treat ▷免费医疗制度 miǎnfèi yīliáo zhìdù system of free medical care

医生 yīshēng [名] doctor

医术 yīshù [名] medical skill

医务室 yīwùshì [名] clinic

医学 yīxué [名] medicine

医药 yīyào [名] medicine

医院 yīyuàn [名] hospital

医治 yīzhì [动] cure

依 yī [动] 1 (依靠) depend on 2 (依从) comply with

依旧 yījiù [副] still

依据 yījù I [动] go by II [名] basis

依靠 yīkào I [动] rely on II [名] support

依赖 yīlài [动] depend on

依然 yīrán [副] still

依照 yīzhào [介] according to

壹 yī [数] one
This is the complex character for "one", which is mainly used in banks, on receipts, etc. to prevent mistakes and forgery.

仪 yí [名] 1 (外表) appearance 2 (礼节) ceremony 3 (仪器) meter

仪器 yíqì [名] meter

仪式 yíshì [名] ceremony

姨 yí [名] 1 (母亲的姐妹) aunt 2 (妻子的姐妹) sister-in-law

移 yí [动] 1 (移动) move 2 (改变) change

移动 yídòng [动] move

移民 yímín I [动] emigrate II [名] immigrant

遗 yí [动] 1 (遗失) lose 2 (留下) leave ... behind

遗产 yíchǎn [名] legacy

遗传 yíchuán [动] inherit

遗憾 yíhàn I [名] regret II [动] be a pity

遗弃 yíqì [动] 1 (车,船等) abandon 2 (妻,子等) desert

遗书 yíshū [名] (书面遗言) last letter (of dying man)

遗体 yítǐ [名] remains (PL)

遗忘 yíwàng [动] forget

遗址 yízhǐ [名] ruins (PL)

遗嘱 yízhǔ [名] will

疑 yí [动] doubt

疑难 yínán [形] knotty

疑问 yíwèn [名] question

疑心 yíxīn I [名] suspicion II [动] suspect

已 yǐ [副] already

已经 yǐjīng [副] already

以 yǐ (书) I [动] use ▷以强凌弱 yǐ qiáng líng ruò use one's strength to humiliate the weak II [介] (依照) by 2 (因为) for 3 (表示界限) ▷以内 yǐnèi within ▷以南 yǐnán to the south III [连] ▷我们要改进技术，以提高生产效率。Wǒmen yào gǎijìn jìshù, yǐ tígāo shēngchǎn xiàolù. We should improve the technology so as to increase production.

以便 yǐbiàn [连] in order that

以后 yǐhòu [名] ▷两年以后 liǎng nián yǐhòu two years later ▷以后我们去看电影。Yǐhòu wǒmen qù kàn diànyǐng. Afterwards we're going to see a film.

以及 yǐjí [连] as well as

以来 yǐlái [名] ▷入冬以来 rù dōng yǐlái since the beginning of the winter

以免 yǐmiǎn [连] in case

以前 yǐqián [名] ▷10年以前 shí nián yǐqián ten years ago ▷他以前是老师。Tā yǐqián shì lǎoshī. She was a teacher before.

以为 yǐwéi [动] think

以下 yǐxià [名] (低于某点) ▷30岁以下 sānshí suì yǐxià under thirty

以致 yǐzhì [连] so that

蚁 yǐ [名] ant ▷蚂蚁 mǎyǐ ant

椅 yǐ [名] chair

椅子 yǐzi [名] chair

亿 yì [数] hundred million

义 yì I [名] 1 (正义) righteousness 2 (情谊) human relationship 3 (意义) meaning II [形] 1 (正义的) just 2 (拜认的) adopted ▷义父 yìfù adoptive father

义卖 yìmài [动] sell ... for charity

义气 yìqì I [名] loyalty II [形] loyal

义务 yìwù I [名] duty II [形] compulsory

艺 yì [名] 1 (技能) skill ▷手艺 shǒuyì craftsmanship 2 (艺术) art

艺人 yìrén [名] (演员) performer

艺术 yìshù I [名] 1 (文艺) art 2 (方法) skill ▷管理艺术 guǎnlǐ yìshù management skills II [形] artistic

艺术家 yìshùjiā [名] artist

忆 yì [动] remember ▷记忆 jìyì memory

议 yì[名] opinion ▸建议 jiànyì propose II[动] discuss ▸商议 shāngyì discuss

议程 yìchéng[名] agenda

议会 yìhuì[名] parliament

议论 yìlùn I[动] discuss II[名] talk

议题 yìtí[名] topic

议员 yìyuán[名] MP(英), congressman, congresswoman (美)

异 yì[形] 1(不同) different ▸差异 chāyì difference 2(奇异) strange 3(另外) other ▸异国 yìguó foreign country II[动] separate ▸离异 líyì separate

异常 yìcháng[形] unusual

异性 yìxìng[名] (指性别) the opposite sex

译 yì[动] translate

译文 yìwén[名] translation

译者 yìzhě[名] translator

译制 yìzhì[动] dub

抑 yì[动] repress

抑郁 yìyù[形] depressed

抑制 yìzhì[动] 1(生理) inhibit 2(控制) control

易 yì[形] (容易) easy ▸易传染 yì chuánrǎn easily transmissible

易拉罐 yìlāguàn[名] can

疫 yì[名] epidemic

疫苗 yìmiáo[名] inoculation

益 yì[名] benefit II[形]

beneficial III[动] increase IV[副] increasingly

益处 yìchù[名] benefit

谊 yì[名] friendship ▸友谊 yǒuyì friendship

意 yì[名] 1(意思) meaning 2(心愿) wish ▸好意 hǎoyì good intention

意见 yìjiàn[名] 1(看法) opinion 2(不满) objection

意识 yìshí I[名] consciousness II[动] realize

意思 yìsi[名] 1(意义) meaning 2(意见) idea 3(愿望) wish 4(趣味) interest ▸有意思 yǒu yìsi interesting ▸没意思 méi yìsi boring 5(心意) token

意图 yìtú[名] intention

意外 yìwài I[名] accident II[形] unexpected

意义 yìyì[名] 1(含义) meaning 2(作用) significance

毅 yì[形] resolute

毅力 yìlì[名] perseverance

因 yīn I[连] because II[介] because of ▸昨天他因病缺课。 Zuótiān tā yīn bìng quēkè. He missed a class yesterday because of illness. III[名] cause ▸病因 bìngyīn cause of the illness

因此 yīncǐ[连] so

因而 yīn'ér[连] therefore

因素 yīnsù[名] 1(成分) element 2(因) factor

因特网 Yīntèwǎng [名] the Internet

因为 yīnwei [连] because

阴 yīn I [形] 1(指天气) overcast 2(阴险的) insidious ▸阴谋 yīnmóuplot 3(物) negative ▸阴性 yīnxìngnegative II [名] 1(阳的对立面) Yin (*from Yin and Yang*) 2(指月亮) the moon ▸阴历 yīnlì lunar calendar 3(阴凉处) shade ▸树阴 shùyīnthe shade

阴暗 yīn'àn [形] gloomy

阴部 yīnbù [名] private parts (PL)

阴凉 yīnliáng [形] shady and cool

音 yīn [名] 1(声音) sound 2(消息) news (SG)

音量 yīnliàng [名] volume

音响 yīnxiǎng [名] 1(指声音) acoustics (PL) 2(指设备)

音像 yīnxiàng [名] audio and video

音乐 yīnyuè [名] music

音乐会 yīnyuèhuì [名] concert

银 yín I [名] 1(指)(金属) silver 2(指)(货币) money ▸收银台 shōuyíntáicashier's desk II [形] silver

银行 yínháng [名] bank

银河 yínhé [名] the Milky Way

银幕 yínmù [名] screen

银牌 yínpái [名] silver medal

龈 yín [名] gum ▸牙龈 yáyíngum

引 yǐn [动] 1(牵引) draw 2(引导) lead ▸引路 yǐnlùlead the way

3(引起) cause 4(引用) cite

引导 yǐndǎo [动] 1(带领) lead 2(启发诱导) guide

引进 yǐnjìn [动] 1(人) recommend 2(物) import

引力 yǐnlì [名] gravitation

引起 yǐnqǐ [动] cause

引擎 yǐnqíng [名] engine

引用 yǐnyòng [动] (引述) quote

引诱 yǐnyòu [动] 1(诱导) induce 2(诱惑) tempt

饮 yǐn I [动] drink II [名] drink

饮料 yǐnliào [名] drink

饮食 yǐnshí [名] food and drink

饮用水 yǐnyòngshuǐ [名] drinking water

隐 yǐn [动] conceal

隐藏 yǐncáng [动] conceal

隐瞒 yǐnmán [动] cover ... up

隐私 yǐnsī [名] private matters (PL)

瘾 yǐn [名] (嗜好) addiction ▸上瘾 shàngyǐnbe addicted to

印 yìn I [名] 1(图章) stamp 2(痕迹) print II [动] (留下痕迹) print

印刷 yìnshuā [动] print

印象 yìnxiàng [名] impression

印章 yìnzhāng [名] seal

荫 yìn [形] shady

荫凉 yìnliáng [形] shady and cool

应 yīng I [动] 1(答应) answer 2(应允) agree II [助动] should

→ see also/另见 yìng

应当 yìngdāng [助动] should

应该 yìnggāi [助动] should

应允 yìngyǔn [动] consent

英 yīng [名] 1 (才能出众者) hero ▷ 精英 jīngyīng elite 2 (英国) Britain

英镑 yīngbàng [名] pound sterling

英国 Yīngguó [名] Great Britain ▷ 英国的 Yīngguó de British

英国人 Yīngguórén [名] the British

英俊 yīngjùn [形] (漂亮的) handsome

英雄 yīngxióng I [名] hero II [形] heroic

英勇 yīngyǒng [形] brave

英语 yīngyǔ [名] English

婴 yīng [名] baby

婴儿 yīng'ér [名] baby

樱 yīng [名] 1 (樱桃) cherry ▷ 樱桃 yīngtáo cherry 2 (樱花) cherry blossom ▷ 樱花 yīnghuā cherry blossom

鹦 yīng see below/见下文

鹦鹉 yīngwǔ [名] parrot

鹰 yīng [名] eagle

迎 yíng [动] 1 (接待) welcome 2 (对着) meet

迎合 yínghé [动] cater to

迎接 yíngjiē [动] welcome

萤 yíng [名] firefly ▷ 萤火虫 yínghuǒchóng firefly

营 yíng I [动] (经营) operate II [名] 1 (军队驻地) barracks (PL) 2 (军队编制) battalion 3 (营地) camp ▷ 营地 yíngdì camp

营救 yíngjiù [动] rescue

营销 yíngxiāo [动] sell

营养 yíngyǎng [名] nourishment

营业 yíngyè [动] do business

蝇 yíng [名] fly ▷ 苍蝇 cāngyíng fly

赢 yíng [动] 1 (胜) win 2 (获利) gain

赢利 yínglì [名] gain

影 yǐng [名] 1 (影子) shadow 2 (照片) photograph 3 (电影) film (英), movie (美)

影片 yǐngpiàn [名] 1 (胶片) film 2 (电影) film (英), movie (美)

影响 yǐngxiǎng I [动] affect II [名] influence

影印 yǐngyìn [动] photocopy

应 yìng [动] 1 (回答) answer ▷ 回应 huíyìng answer 2 (满足) respond to 3 (顺应) comply with 4 (应付) handle ▷ 应急 yìngjí handle an emergency

→ see also/另见 yīng

应酬 yìngchou I [动] socialize with II [名] social engagement

应付 yìngfu [动] 1 (采取办法) handle 2 (敷衍) do half-heartedly 3 (将就) make do with

应聘 yìngpìn [动] accept an offer

应用 yìngyòng I [动] apply II [形]

applied

硬 yìng I [形] 1 (坚固) hard 2 (刚强) firm 3 (能干的) strong II [副] obstinately

硬币 yìngbì [名] coin

硬件 yìngjiàn [名] 1 (计算机) hardware 2 (设备) equipment

硬盘 yìngpán [名] hard disk

哟 yō [叹] (表示轻微的惊异或赞叹) oh

佣 yōng I [动] hire II [名] servant ▸佣人 yōngrén servant
→ see also/另见 yòng

拥 yōng [动] 1 (抱) embrace 2 (围着) gather round 3 (拥挤) swarm 4 (拥护) support

拥抱 yōngbào [动] embrace

拥护 yōnghù [动] support

拥挤 yōngjǐ I [形] crowded II [动] crowd

拥有 yōngyǒu [动] have

庸 yōng [形] (不高明) mediocre

庸俗 yōngsú [形] vulgar

永 yǒng I [形] (书) everlasting II [副] forever

永恒 yǒnghéng [形] everlasting

永久 yǒngjiǔ [形] eternal

永远 yǒngyuǎn [副] eternally

泳 yǒng [名] swim ▸蛙泳 wāyǒng breaststroke

泳道 yǒngdào [名] lane

勇 yǒng [形] brave

勇敢 yǒnggǎn [形] brave

勇气 yǒngqì [名] courage

用 yòng I [动] 1 (使用) use 2 (需要) need 3 (消费) consume ▸用餐 yòngcān have a meal II [名] 1 (费用) expense ▸家用 jiāyòng household expenses (PL) 2 (用处) use ▸没用 méiyòng useless

用处 yòngchu [名] use

用功 yònggōng I [形] hardworking II [动] work hard

用户 yònghù [名] user ▷网络用户 wǎngluò yònghù internet user

用具 yòngjù [名] tool

用力 yònglì [动] exert oneself

用品 yòngpǐn [名] goods (PL)

用途 yòngtú [名] use

佣 yòng see below/见下文
→ see also/另见 yōng

佣金 yòngjīn [名] commission

优 yōu [形] (优良) excellent

优点 yōudiǎn [名] strong point

优良 yōuliáng [形] fine

优美 yōuměi [形] elegant

优势 yōushì [名] advantage

优先 yōuxiān [动] have priority

优秀 yōuxiù [形] outstanding

优越 yōuyuè [形] superior

忧 yōu I [形] anxious II [动] worry III [名] anxiety

忧伤 yōushāng [形] sad

忧郁 yōuyù [形] depressed

幽 yōu [形] (暗) dim ▸幽暗 yōu'àn

gloomy

幽默 yōumò [形] humorous

悠 yōu [形] 1 (久远) remote 2 (闲适) leisurely

悠久 yōujiǔ [形] long-standing

悠闲 yōuxián [形] leisurely

尤 yóu [副] especially

尤其 yóuqí [副] especially

由 yóu I [动] 1 (听凭) give in to 2 (经过) go through II [介] 1 (归) by 2 (根据) ▷由此可见… yóu cǐ kě jiàn… from this we can see… 3 (从) from 4 (由于) due to III [名] cause ▷理由 lǐyóu reason

由于 yóuyú [介] as a result of

邮 yóu I [动] post (英), mail (美) II [名] 1 (邮寄) post (英), mail (美) 2 (邮票) stamp

邮递 yóudì [动] send … by post (英) or mail (美)

邮电 yóudiàn [名] post and telecommunications

邮寄 yóují [动] post (英), mail (美)

邮件 yóujiàn [名] post (英), mail (美)

邮局 yóujú [名] post office

邮票 yóupiào [名] stamp

邮政 yóuzhèng [名] postal service

邮资 yóuzī [名] postage

犹 yóu [副] still

犹豫 yóuyù [形] hesitant

油 yóu I [名] oil II [形] oily

油滑 yóuhuá [形] slippery

油腻 yóunì I [形] greasy II [名] greasy food

油漆 yóuqī I [名] varnish II [动] varnish

鱿 yóu [名] squid

鱿鱼 yóuyú [名] squid

游 yóu [动] 1 (游泳) swim 2 (游览) tour

游客 yóukè [名] tourist

游览 yóulǎn [动] tour

游牧 yóumù [动] live a nomadic life

游说 yóushuì [动] lobby

游戏 yóuxì I [名] game II [动] play

游行 yóuxíng [动] march

游泳 yóuyǒng I [动] swim II [名] swimming

游泳池 yóuyǒngchí [名] swimming pool

友 yǒu I [名] friend ▷男友 nányǒu boyfriend II [形] friendly ▷友好 yǒuhǎo friendly

友爱 yǒu'ài [形] affectionate

友情 yǒuqíng [名] friendship

友人 yǒurén [名] friend

友谊 yǒuyì [名] friendship

有 yǒu [动] 1 (具有) have 2 (存在) ▷院子里有一棵大树。Yuànzi li yǒu yī kē dàshù. There's a big tree in the courtyard. 3 (发生) occur ▷我的生活有了一些变化。Wǒ de shēnghuó yǒu le yīxiē biànhuà. A few changes have occurred in my life. 4 (表

示程度)have ▷他特别有学问。Tā tèbié yǒu xuéwèn. He's extremely knowledgeable. **5** (某)有时候 yǒushíhou sometimes ▷有一次,他得了冠军。Yǒu yì cì, tā dé le guànjūn. He won a prize once.

有的 yǒude [名] some ▷展出的作品,有的来自本土,有的来自海外。Zhǎnchū de zuòpǐn, yǒude láizì běntǔ, yǒude láizì hǎiwài. Of the articles on display, some are local, others are from overseas.

有关 yǒuguān [动] **1** (有关系) be relevant **2** (涉及到) be about

有利 yǒulì [形] favourable (英), favorable (美)

有趣 yǒuqù [形] interesting

有限 yǒuxiàn [形] limited

有限公司 yǒuxiàn gōngsī [名] limited company

有线电视 yǒuxiàn diànshì [名] cable TV

有幸 yǒuxìng [形] fortunate

有意思 yǒuyìsi I [形] **1** (有意义) significant **2** (有趣味) interesting II [动] be interested in

又 yòu [副] **1** (重复) again **2** (同时) ▷他是一个好教师,又是一个好妈妈。Tā shì yí gè hǎo jiàoshī, yòu shì yí gè hǎo māma. She's both a good teacher and a great mother. **3** (也) too **4** (另外) another **5** (再加上) and ▷一又三

分之二 yī yòu sān fēn zhī èr one and two thirds **6** (可是) but

右 yòu [名] **1** (右边) right ▷右边 yòubiān right side ▷请向右转。Qǐng xiàng yòu zhuǎn. Please turn right. **2** (右翼) the Right

幼 yòu I [形] young II [名] child ▷幼儿园 yòu'éryuán nursery school (英), kindergarten (美)

幼儿 yòu'ér [名] small child

幼年 yòunián [名] infancy

幼小 yòuxiǎo [形] young

幼稚 yòuzhì [形] **1** (书) (年龄很小) young **2** (头脑简单) naive

诱 yòu [动] **1** (诱导) guide **2** (引诱) entice

诱饵 yòu'ěr [名] bait

诱惑 yòuhuò [动] **1** (引诱) entice **2** (吸引) attract

于 yú [介] **1** (在) in **2** (向) from **3** (对) to **4** (从) from **5** (比) than ▷大于 dàyú bigger than

于是 yúshì [连] so

余 yú [名] **1** (零头) ▷500余人 wǔbǎi yú rén more than five hundred people **2** (指时间) ▷课余 kèyú extra-curricular

余地 yúdì [名] room

盂 yú [名] jar ▷痰盂 tányú spittoon (英), cuspidor (美)

鱼 yú [名] fish ▷鱼肉 yúròu fish

娱 yú I [动] amuse II [名] amusement

娱乐 yúlè I [动] have fun II [名] entertainment

渔 yú [动] (捕鱼) fish ▶渔业 yúyè fisheries

愉 yú [形] happy

愉快 yúkuài [形] happy ▶祝你旅行愉快! Zhù nǐ lǚxíng yúkuài! Have a pleasant journey!

愚 yú I [形] foolish ▶愚蠢 yúchǔn foolish II [动] fool

愚昧 yúmèi [形] ignorant

舆 yú [形] popular

舆论 yúlùn [名] public opinion

与 yú I [介] with II [连] and

宇 yú [名] 1 (房屋) house 2 (四方) the universe

宇航 yǔháng I [动] travel through space II [名] space travel

宇航员 yǔhángyuán [名] astronaut

宇宙 yǔzhòu [名] universe

羽 yǔ [名] 1 (羽毛) feather 2 (翅膀) wing

羽毛 yǔmáo [名] feather

羽毛球 yǔmáoqiú [名] 1 (指运动) badminton 2 (指球体) shuttlecock

雨 yǔ [名] rain ▶下雨 xiàyǔ to rain

雨衣 yǔyī [名] waterproofs (PL)

雨水 yǔshuǐ [名] (降水) rain

语 yǔ I [名] (语言) language ▶手语 shǒuyǔ sign language II [动] talk

语调 yǔdiào [名] tone

语法 yǔfǎ [名] grammar

语句 yǔjù [名] sentence

语气 yǔqì [名] 1 (口气) tone of voice 2 (语法) mood

语文 yǔwén [名] 1 (语言文字) language 2 (中文) Chinese 3 (语言与文学) language and literature

语言 yǔyán [名] language

语音 yǔyīn [名] pronunciation

语音信箱 yǔyīn xìnxiāng [名] voice mail

语种 yǔzhǒng [名] language

玉 yù [名] (玉石) jade

玉米 yùmǐ [名] (指植物) maize (英), corn (美)

郁 yù [形] (烦闷) gloomy

郁闷 yùmèn [形] melancholy

育 yù I [动] 1 (生育) give birth to 2 (养活) raise ▶养育 yǎngyù bring up II [名] education ▶教育 jiàoyù education

狱 yù [名] (监狱) prison ▶监狱 jiānyù prison

浴 yù [动] wash

浴盆 yùpén [名] bath

浴室 yùshì [名] bathroom

预 yù [副] in advance

预报 yùbào [动] predict ▶天气预报 tiānqì yùbào weather forecast

预备 yùbèi [动] prepare

预测 yùcè [动] predict

预防 yùfáng [动] prevent

预感 yùgǎn [动] have a premonition

预计 yùjì [动] estimate

预见 yùjiàn [动] foresee

预科 yùkē [名] foundation course

预料 yùliào [动] predict

预算 yùsuàn [名] budget

预习 yùxí [动] prepare for lessons

预言 yùyán [动] predict

域 yù [名] region ▶领域 lǐngyù realm

欲 yù [名] desire

欲望 yùwàng [名] desire

遇 yù I [动] meet ▶遇到 yùdào meet II [名] 1 (待遇) treatment 2 (机会) opportunity

寓 yù I [动] 1 (居住) live 2 (寄托) imply II [名] residence ▶公寓 gōngyù flat (英), apartment (美)

寓言 yùyán [名] fable

鸳 yuān [名] mandarin duck

鸳鸯 yuānyāng [名] (指鸟) mandarin duck

冤 yuān [名] 1 (冤枉) injustice ▶冤枉 yuānwang treat unfairly 2 (冤仇) enmity

元 yuán I [名] 1 (始) first 2 (首) chief ▶元首 yuánshǒu head of state 3 (主) fundamental ▶元素 yuánsù element 4 (整体) component ▶单元 dānyuán unit 5 (圆形货币) coin ▶金元 jīnyuán gold coin II [量] yuan ▶5元钱 wǔ yuán qián five yuan

元旦 Yuándàn [名] New Year's Day

元件 yuánjiàn [名] part

元帅 yuánshuài [名] commander-in-chief

元宵 yuánxiāo [名] sweet round dumplings made of glutinous rice, usually eaten with the broth in which they are cooked

元宵节 Yuánxiāo Jié [名] the Lantern Festival

元宵节 Yuánxiāo Jié
The Lantern Festival is celebrated on the 15th day of the Lunar Chinese New Year. The traditional food which is eaten at this festival is called 元宵 yuánxiāo or 汤圆 tāngyuán, a traditional sweet dumpling made of glutinous rice, with various sweet fillings.

园 yuán [名] 1 (指菜地或果林) garden 2 (指游乐场所) park

园丁 yuándīng [名] (园艺工人) gardener

园林 yuánlín [名] garden

园艺 yuányì [名] gardening

员 yuán [名] 1 (指工作或学习的人) ▶理发员 lǐfàyuán hairdresser 2 (成员) member

员工 yuángōng [名] staff (PL)

原 yuán [形] **1**(本来的) original **2**(未加工的) raw ▸原油 yuányóu crude oil

原来 yuánlái I [形] original II [副] **1**(起初) originally **2**(其实) all along

原理 yuánlǐ [名] principle

原谅 yuánliàng [动] forgive

原料 yuánliào [名] (指烹饪) ingredient

原始 yuánshǐ [形] **1**(古老) primitive **2**(最初) original

原先 yuánxiān I [形] original II [副] originally

原因 yuányīn [名] reason

原则 yuánzé [名] principle

原著 yuánzhù [名] the original

原子 yuánzǐ [名] atom

圆 yuán I [形] **1**(圆形的) round ▸圆圈 yuánquān circle **2**(球形的) spherical **3**(圆满的) satisfactory II [名] (数) (圆周) circle

圆规 yuánguī [名] compasses (PL)

圆满 yuánmǎn [形] satisfactory

圆舞曲 yuánwǔqǔ [名] waltz

援 yuán [动] (援助) help ▸支援 zhīyuán support

援救 yuánjiù [动] rescue

援助 yuánzhù [动] help

缘 yuán [名] **1**(缘故) cause **2**(缘分) fate **3**(边缘) edge

缘分 yuánfèn [名] fate

缘故 yuángù [名] cause

猿 yuán [名] ape

猿猴 yuánhóu [名] apes and monkeys (PL)

猿人 yuánrén [名] ape-man

源 yuán [名] source ▸水源 shuǐyuán source

远 yuǎn [形] (指距离) far ▸远程 yuǎnchéng long-distance **2**(指血统) distant **3**(指程度) far

远大 yuǎndà [形] far-reaching

远方 yuǎnfāng [名] afar

远见 yuǎnjiàn [名] foresight

远亲 yuǎnqīn [名] distant relative

远视 yuǎnshì [名] (医) long sightedness

远足 yuǎnzú [动] hike

院 yuàn [名] **1**(院落) courtyard ▸院子 yuànzi yard **2**(指机关和处所) ▸电影院 diànyǐngyuàn cinema (英), movie theater (美) **3**(学院) college **4**(医院) hospital

愿 yuàn [名] (愿望) wish II [助动] ▸我不愿说。Wǒ bù yuàn shuō. I don't want to say anything.

愿望 yuànwàng [名] wish

愿意 yuànyì [动] **1**(同意) be willing to **2**(希望) wish

约 yuē I [动] **1**(束缚) restrict **2**(商定) arrange **3**(邀请) invite II [形] brief ▸简约 jiǎnyuē brief III [副] about

约会 yuēhuì [名] **1**(指工作) appointment **2**(指恋人) date

约束 yuēshù [动] bind

月 yuè [名] 1(月球) the moon ▶满月 mǎnyuè full moon 2(月份) month ▶三月 sānyuè March 3(每月) monthly ▶月薪 yuèxīn monthly salary

月饼 yuèbing [名] mooncake

月饼 yuèbing

Mooncakes, the traditional festival food for 中秋节 Zhōngqiū Jié (the Mid-Autumn Festival), are round cakes made of a variety of sweet fillings including beanpaste, egg and peanut.

月份 yuèfèn [名] month

月光 yuèguāng [名] moonlight

月经 yuèjīng [名] (例假) period

月亮 yuèliang [名] the moon

月票 yuèpiào [名] monthly ticket

乐 yuè [名] music ▶器乐 qìyuè instrumental music ▶民乐 mínyuè folk music
→ see also/另见 lè

乐队 yuèduì [名] band

乐器 yuèqì [名] musical instrument

乐曲 yuèqǔ [名] music

乐团 yuètuán [名] philharmonic orchestra

岳 yuè [名] 1(高山) mountain 2(妻子的父母) parents-in-law (PL)

岳父 yuèfù [名] father-in-law

岳母 yuèmǔ [名] mother-in-law

阅 yuè [动] 1(看) read 2(检阅) inspect 3(经历) experience

阅读 yuèdú [动] read

阅览 yuèlǎn [动] read

阅历 yuèlì [动] experience

跃 yuè [动] leap ▶跳跃 tiàoyuè jump

越 yuè I [动] 1(跨过) jump over 2(超过) exceed II [副] ▶越发 yuèfā increasingly

越来越 yuèláiyuè [副] more and more ▷天气越来越暖和了。 Tiānqì yuèláiyuè nuǎnhuo le. The weather is getting warmer and warmer.

越野 yuèyě [动] go cross-country

越…越… yuè…yuè… [副] the more … the more … ▷越早越好 yuè zǎo yuè hǎo the earlier the better

晕 yūn [动] 1(晕眩) feel dizzy 2(昏迷) faint ▷她晕过去了。 Tā yūn guòqu le. She passed out.
→ see also/另见 yùn

云 yún [名] cloud

云彩 yúncai [名] cloud

匀 yún I [形] even II [动] 1(使均匀) even … out 2(分) apportion

匀称 yúnchèn [形] well-proportioned

允 yǔn [动] allow

允许 yǔnxǔ [动] allow

孕 yùn I [动] be pregnant ▶怀

孕 huáiyùn be pregnant **II** [名] pregnancy

运 yùn **I** [动] **1** (运动) move **2** (搬运) transport **3** (运用) use **II** [名] luck ▶好运 hǎoyùn good luck

运动 yùndòng **I** [动] (物) (运) move **II** [名] **1** (体育活动) sport **2** (大规模) movement

运动鞋 yùndòngxié [名] trainer

运动员 yùndòngyuán [名] athlete

运河 yùnhé [名] canal

运气 yùnqi [名] luck

运输 yùnshū [动] transport

运算 yùnsuàn [动] calculate

运行 yùnxíng [动] move

运用 yùnyòng [动] make use of

运转 yùnzhuǎn [动] (指机器) run

运作 yùnzuò [动] operate

晕 yùn [动] feel giddy ▶晕机 yùnjī be airsick ▶晕车 yùnchē be carsick ▶晕船 yùnchuán be seasick

→ see also/ 另见 yūn

熨 yùn [动] iron

熨斗 yùndǒu [名] iron

杂 zá **I** [形] miscellaneous ▶复杂 fùzá complicated **II** [动] mix

杂货 záhuò [名] groceries (PL)

杂技 zájì [名] acrobatics (PL)

杂志 zázhì [名] magazine

砸 zá [动] **1** (撞击) pound **2** (打破) break ▶杯子砸坏了。 Bēizi záhuài le. The cup was broken.

灾 zāi [名] **1** (灾害) disaster ▶水灾 shuǐzāi flood **2** (不幸) misfortune

灾害 zāihài [名] disaster

灾难 zāinàn [名] disaster

栽 zāi [动] **1** (种) plant ▶栽花 zāi huā grow flowers **2** (摔倒) tumble

再 zài [副] **1** (又) again ▶你再说一遍。 Nǐ zài shuō yī biàn. Say that again. **2**(更) more ▸请把音量放得再大些。 Qǐng bǎ yīnliàng fàngde zài dàxiē. Please turn the volume up a bit. **3**(继续)▸我不能再等了。 Wǒ bùnéng zài děng le. I can't wait any longer. **4**(接着) then ▸你做完功课再看小说。 Nǐ zuòwán gōngkè zài kàn xiǎoshuō. You can read your book when you've finished your homework. **5**(另外) besides ▸再说 zàishuō besides

再见 zàijiàn [动] say goodbye ▸再见! Zàijiàn! Goodbye!

再三 zàisān [副] again and again

在 zài I [动] **1**(存在) live **2**(处于) be ▸你的书在桌子上。 Nǐ de shū zài zhuōzi shang. Your book is on the table. ▸我父母在纽约。 Wǒ fùmǔ zài Niǔyuē. My parents are in New York. **3**(在于) rest with II [副] 情况在改变。 Qíngkuàng zài gǎibiàn. Things are changing. ▸他们在看电视。 Tāmen zài kàn diànshì. They're watching TV. III [介] at ▸在机场等候 zài jīchǎng děnghòu wait at the airport ▸在历史上 zài lìshǐ shang in history

在乎 zàihu [动] care

在于 zàiyú [动] **1**(存在) lie in **2**(取决于) depend on

咱 zán [代] **1**(咱们) we **2**(方) (我) I

咱们 zánmen [代] **1**(我们) we **2**(方) (我) I

攒 zǎn [动] save

暂 zàn I [形] brief II [副] temporarily

暂时 zànshí [名] ▸暂时的需要 zànshí de xūyào temporary need

赞 zàn [动] **1**(帮助) assist ▸赞助 zànzhù assistance **2**(称颂) commend ▸赞赏 zànshǎng admire

赞成 zànchéng [动] approve

赞美 zànměi [动] praise

赞同 zàntóng [动] approve of

赞扬 zànyáng [动] pay tribute to

脏 zāng [形] dirty ▸脏话 zānghuà dirty word

遭 zāo [动] meet with ▸遭殃 zāoyāng suffer

遭到 zāodào [动] encounter

遭受 zāoshòu [动] suffer

糟 zāo I [名] dregs (PL) II [动] **1**(浪费) waste ▸糟蹋 zāota spoil **2**(腌制) flavour (英) (美) with alcohol III [形] **1**(腐烂) rotten **2**(弄坏) messy

糟糕 zāogāo [形] terrible ▸真糟糕,我的钥匙丢了。 Zhēn zāogāo, wǒ de yàoshi diū le. Oh no, I've lost my key!

早 zǎo I [名] morning II [副] a long time ago III [形] early

早安 zǎo'ān [名] ▸早安! Zǎo'ān! Good morning!

早餐 zǎocān [名] breakfast

早晨 zǎochen [名] morning

早饭 zǎofàn [名] breakfast

早晚 zǎowǎn I [名] morning and evening II [副] 1 (迟早) sooner or later 2 (方) (将来) some day

早上 zǎoshang [名] morning

造 zào [动] 1 (制作) make 2 (瞎编) concoct ▶造谣 zàoyáo start a rumour (英) 或 rumor (美)

造成 zàochéng [动] cause

造反 zàofǎn [动] rebel

造型 zàoxíng [名] model

噪 zào [动] (嚷) clamour (英), clamor (美) ▶噪音 zàoyīn noise

责 zé I [名] responsibility ▶负责 fùzé be responsible for II [动] (备) blame ▶指责 zhǐzé censure

责备 zébèi [动] blame

责任 zérèn [名] responsibility

怎 zěn [代] (方) ▶你怎能相信他的话？ Nǐ zěn néng xiāngxìn tā de huà? How can you believe him?

怎么 zěnme I [代] ▶你看这事我该怎么办？ Nǐ kàn zhè shì wǒ gāi zěnme bàn? What do you think I should do about this? ▶你昨天怎么没来上课？ Nǐ zuótiān zěnme méi lái shàngkè? Why weren't you in class yesterday? II [副] (泛指方式) ▶我是怎么想就怎么说。 Wǒ shì zěnme xiǎng jiù zěnme shuō. I say whatever I think. ▶他最近怎么样？ Tā zuìjìn zěnme yàng? How has he been doing?

怎样 zěnyàng [副] how

增 zēng [动] increase

增加 zēngjiā [动] increase

增长 zēngzhǎng [动] increase

赠 zèng [动] present ▶捐赠 juānzèng donate

赠品 zèngpǐn [名] gift

扎 zhā [动] 1 (刺) prick 2 (住下) set up camp 3 (钻进) plunge into

扎实 zhāshi [形] 1 (结实) sturdy 2 (实在) solid

炸 zhá [动] fry
→ see also/另见 zhà

炸 zhà [动] 1 (爆破) blow ... up 2 (破裂) explode 3 (逃离) run scared
→ see also/另见 zhá

炸弹 zhàdàn [名] bomb

炸药 zhàyào [名] explosive

摘 zhāi [动] 1 (取) pick 2 (选) select 3 (借) borrow

窄 zhǎi [形] 1 (不宽敞) narrow 2 (气量小) narrow-minded 3 (不宽裕) hard up

粘 zhān [动] stick

盏 zhǎn I [名] small cup II [量] ▶一盏灯 yī zhǎn dēng a lamp measure word, used for lamps and lights

展 zhǎn [动] 1 (进行) develop 2 (施展) give free rein to 3 (暂缓) postpone II [名] exhibition

展出 zhǎnchū [动] exhibit

展开 zhǎnkāi [动] 1 (张开) spread 2 (进行) develop

展览 zhǎnlǎn [名] exhibition

展品 zhǎnpǐn [名] exhibit

崭 zhǎn *see below*/见下文

崭新 zhǎnxīn [形] brand-new

占 zhàn [动] (占用) occupy

战 zhàn I [名] war II [动] 1 (战斗) fight 2 (发抖) shiver

战斗 zhàndòu [动] fight

战胜 zhànshèng [动] overcome

战士 zhànshì [名] soldier

战争 zhànzhēng [名] war

站 zhàn I [动] 1 (站立) stand 2 (停下) stop II [名] 1 (停车地点) stop ▷公共汽车站 gōnggòng qìchēzhàn bus stop 2 (服务机构) centre (英), center (美)

张 zhāng I [动] 1 (打开) open 2 (展开) stretch 3 (夸大) exaggerate ▷夸张 kuāzhāng exaggerate 4 (看) look 5 (开业) open for business 6 (陈设) lay ... on II [量] (指平的物体) ▷一张海报 yī zhāng hǎibào a poster ▷一张书桌 yī zhāng shūzhuō a desk 2 (指嘴或脸) ▷一张大嘴 yī zhāng dà zuǐ a big mouth ▷一张脸 yī zhāng liǎn a face

measure word, used for flat objects such as newspaper, maps, paintings, cards, tickets, pancakes; furniture such as beds, desks, sofas; mouths and faces

章 zhāng [名] 1 (作品) article ▷文章 wénzhāng article 2 (章节) chapter 3 (条理) order 4 (章程) regulation ▷宪章 xiànzhāng charter 5 (图章) seal 6 (标志) badge (英), button (美)

长 zhǎng I [形] 1 (大) older ▷他年长我 3 岁。Tā niánzhǎng wǒ sān suì. He's three years older than me. 2 (排行第一) oldest ▷长兄 zhǎngxiōng oldest brother II [名] 1 (年长者) ▷兄长 xiōngzhǎng elder brother 2 (头领) head ▷校长 xiàozhǎng head teacher III [动] 1 (生) form 2 (发育) grow (增加) increase

→ *see also*/另见 cháng

涨 zhǎng [动] increase

掌 zhǎng I [名] 1 (手掌) palm 2 (人的脚底) sole 3 (动物的脚掌) foot 4 (掌形物) ▷仙人掌 xiānrénzhǎng cactus 5 (U型铁) horseshoe 6 (鞋掌) sole II [动] 1 (打) slap 2 (钉) sole 3 (主持) be in charge of

掌握 zhǎngwò [动] control

丈 zhàng [名] (长度单位) Chinese unit of length, equal to 3.3 metres

丈夫 zhàngfu [名] husband

帐 zhàng [名] (窗帘) curtain ▷蚊帐 wénzhàng mosquito net

帐篷 zhàngpeng [名] tent

账 zhàng [名] 1 (账目) accounts (PL) 2 (账簿) ledger 3 (债务) credit ▷赊账 shēzhàng buy on credit

账单 zhàngdān [名] bill

账号 zhànghào [名] account number

障 zhàng I [名] barrier II [动] hinder

障碍 zhàng'ài I [动] hinder II [名] obstacle

招 zhāo I [动] 1 (挥动) beckon 2 (招收) recruit 3 (引来) attract 4 (惹怒) provoke 5 (坦白) confess II [名] 1 (计策) trick 2 (下棋) move

招待 zhāodài [动] entertain ▶招待会 zhāodàihuì reception

招呼 zhāohu [动] 1 (呼唤) call 2 (问候) greet 3 (吩咐) tell

着 zháo [动] 1 (挨) touch 2 (受到) be affected by 3 (燃烧) be lit 4 (入睡) fall asleep

着急 zháojí [形] worried

找 zhǎo [动] 1 (寻找) look for 2 (退余额) give change ▶找钱 zhǎoqián give change 3 (求见) call on

召 zhào [动] summon

召开 zhàokāi [动] hold

照 zhào I [动] 1 (照射) light up 2 (映现) reflect 3 (拍摄) take a photograph 4 (照看) look after 5 (对照) contrast 6 (遵照) refer to ▶参照 cānzhào consult 7 (明白) understand II [名] 1 (照片) photograph 2 (执照) licence (英), license (美) III [介] 1 (按照) according to 2 (向着) in the direction of

照常 zhàocháng [副] as usual

照顾 zhàogu [动] 1 (照料) look after 2 (考虑) consider

照看 zhàokàn [动] look after

照料 zhàoliào [动] take care of

照片 zhàopiàn [名] photograph

照相 zhàoxiàng [动] take a picture

照相机 zhàoxiàngjī [名] camera

折 zhé I [动] 1 (断裂) break 2 (损失) lose 3 (弯曲) wind 4 (回转) turn back 5 (使信服) convince 6 (折合) convert … into 7 (折叠) fold II [名] 1 (折子) notebook ▶存折 cúnzhé bank book 2 (折扣) discount → see also/另见 shé

折叠 zhédié [动] fold

折扣 zhékòu [名] discount

折磨 zhémó [动] torment

哲 zhé I [形] wise II [名] sage

哲学 zhéxué [名] philosophy

这 zhè [代] (指人或事物) this

这边 zhèbiān [副] here

这个 zhège [代] this ▷这个可比那个好多了。 Zhège kě bǐ nàge hǎo duō le. This one is much better than that one.

这么 zhème [代] 1 (指程度) so ▷今天这么热。 Jīntiān zhème rè. It's so hot today. 2 (指方式) so ▷我看就应该这么做。 Wǒ kàn jiù yīnggāi zhème zuò. I think it should be done this way.

这儿 zhèr [副] here

这些 zhèxiē [代] these (PL)

这样 zhèyàng [代] **1**(指程度)so ▶乡村的风景这样美。Xiāngcūn de fēngjǐng zhèyàng měi. The scenery in the countryside is so beautiful. **2**(指状态)such ▶再这样下去可不行。Zài zhèyàng xiàqù kě bùxíng. It really won't do to carry on like this.

针 zhēn [名] **1**(工具)needle **2**(针状物)▶表针 biǎozhēn hand (on watch) **3**(针剂)injection **4**(缝合)stitch

针对 zhēnduì [动] **1**(对准)be aimed at **2**(按照)have ... in mind

真 zhēn I [形] true ▶真话 zhēnhuà truth ▶真品 zhēnpǐn genuine product II [副] really ▶他真勇敢。Tā zhēn yǒnggǎn. He is really brave.

真理 zhēnlǐ [名] truth

真实 zhēnshí [形] true

真正 zhēnzhèng [形] true

枕 zhěn I [名] pillow II [动] rest one's head on

枕头 zhěntou [名] pillow

阵 zhèn [名] **1**(军)(阵形)battle formation **2**(军)(阵地)position **3**(时间)a while

振 zhèn [动] **1**(振动)vibrate **2**(振作)boost

振动 zhèndòng [动] vibrate

镇 zhèn I [名] **1**(城镇)town **2**(重地)garrison II [动] **1**(抑制)suppress **2**(守卫)guard **3**(安定)calm **4**(冷却)cool III [形] calm ▶镇静 zhènjìng calm

镇定 zhèndìng [形] calm

正 zhēng see below/见下文 → see also/另见 zhèng

正月 zhēngyuè [名] first month of the lunar year

争 zhēng [动] **1**(争夺)contend **2**(争论)argue

争论 zhēnglùn [动] argue

争取 zhēngqǔ [动] strive for

征 zhēng I [动] **1**(征讨)mount a military expedition **2**(召集)draft ▶征兵 zhēngbīng conscript **3**(征收)levy ▶征税 zhēngshuì levy taxes **4**(征求)solicit ▶征订 zhēngdìng solicit subscriptions II [名] **1**(征程)journey ▶长征 chángzhēng the Long March **2**(迹象)sign ▶特征 tèzhēng feature

征服 zhēngfú [动] conquer

征求 zhēngqiú [动] solicit

征兆 zhēngzhào [名] sign

睁 zhēng [动] open

蒸 zhēng [动] **1**(指烹饪方法)steam **2**(蒸发)evaporate

蒸气 zhēngqì [名] vapour (英), vapor (美)

蒸汽 zhēngqì [名] steam

整 zhěng I [形] **1**(完整)whole **2**(整齐)tidy II [动] **1**(整理)sort ... out **2**(修理)repair **3**(习惯)punish

整个 zhěnggè [形] whole

整理 zhěnglǐ [动] sort ... out

整齐 zhěngqí [形] 1 (有序的) orderly 2 (均匀的) even

正 zhèng I [形] 1 (不偏不斜) straight ▷ 正前方 zhèng qiánfāng directly ahead ▷ 这片挂得不正。Zhè zhàopiàn guà de bù zhèng. This photograph is not hung straight. 2 (居中的) main 3 (正面) right 4 (正直) upright ▷ 公正 gōngzhèng just 5 (正当) right ▷ 正轨 zhèngguǐ the right track 6 (纯正) pure ▷ 这道菜的味儿不正。Zhè dào cài de wèir bù zhèng. This dish does not taste authentic. 7 (规范的) regular 8 (主要的) principal ▷ 正餐 zhèngcān main meal 9 (指图形) regular 10 (物) positive 11 (数) (大于零的) positive ▷ 正数 zhèngshù positive number II [动] 1 (使不歪) straighten ▷ 正 (改正) put ... right III [副] 1 (恰好) just 2 (正在) right now ▷ 天正刮着风。Tiān zhèng guā zhe fēng. It's windy right now.

→ see also/另见 zhēng

正常 zhèngcháng [形] normal

正当 zhèngdàng [形] legitimate

正确 zhèngquè [形] correct

正式 zhèngshì [形] official

正在 zhèngzài [副] right now

证 zhèng I [动] prove II [名] 1 (证据) evidence ▷ 物证 wùzhèng material evidence ▷ 身份

证 shēnfènzhèng identity card

证明 zhèngmíng I [动] prove II [名] certificate

政 zhèng [名] 1 (政治) politics (SG) 2 (事务) affairs (PL)

政策 zhèngcè [名] policy

政党 zhèngdǎng [名] political party

政府 zhèngfǔ [名] government

政权 zhèngquán [名] political power

政治 zhèngzhì [名] politics (SG)

挣 zhèng [动] 1 (赚钱) earn ▷ 挣钱 zhèngqián earn money 2 (摆脱) break free

之 zhī [助] (的) ▷ 父母之爱 fùmǔ zhī ài parental love

之后 zhīhòu [介] after

之间 zhījiān [介] 1 (指两者) between 2 (指三者或三者以上) among

之前 zhīqián [介] before

之上 zhīshàng [介] above

之下 zhīxià [介] below

之一 zhīyī [代] one of

之中 zhīzhōng [介] amid

支 zhī I [动] 1 (支撑) prop ... up 2 (伸出) raise 3 (支持) bear 4 (调度) send 5 (付出) pay ... out 6 (领取) get II [量] 1 (指乐曲) ▷ 一支钢琴曲 yī zhī gāngqín qǔ a piano tune 2 (指细长物) ▷ 一支钢笔 yī zhī gāngbǐ a pen 3 (指队伍) ▷ 一支军队 yī zhī bùduì an army unit measure word, used for songs, tunes, troops, and stick-like objects

支持 zhīchí [动] 1(鼓励) support 2(支撑) hold out

支出 zhīchū I [动] spend II [名] expenditure

支付 zhīfù [动] pay

支票 zhīpiào [名] cheque (英), check (美) ▷把支票兑换成现金 bǎ zhīpiào duìhuàn chéng xiànjīn cash a cheque

支援 zhīyuán [动] help

只 zhī [量] ▷一只拖鞋 yī zhī tuōxié a slipper ▷两只小船 liǎng zhī xiǎochuán two boats ▷三只小鸟 sān zhī xiǎo niǎo three birds → see also/另见 zhǐ

measure word, used for one of a pair such as gloves, eyes, feet; also used for animals, insects, birds and boats

芝 zhī see below/见下文

芝麻 zhīma [名] sesame

枝 zhī [名] branch

知 zhī I [动] 1(知道) know 2(使知道) inform II [名] knowledge

知道 zhīdào [动] know ▷这事我可不知道。Zhè shì wǒ kě bù zhīdào. I really know nothing about this.

知识 zhīshi [名] knowledge

织 zhī [动] knit

蜘 zhī see below/见下文

蜘蛛 zhīzhū [名] spider

执 zhí [动] 1(拿着) hold 2(执掌) take charge of 3(坚持) stick to 4(执行) carry out II [名] written acknowledgment ▷回执 huízhí receipt

执行 zhíxíng [动] carry out

执照 zhízhào [名] licence (英), license (美)

直 zhí I [形] 1(不弯曲) straight 2(竖的) vertical 3(公正) upstanding 4(直爽) candid II [动] straighten III [副] 1(直接) straight 2(不断地) continuously 3(简直) simply

直到 zhídào [介] until

直接 zhíjiē [形] direct

直升机 zhíshēngjī [名] helicopter

侄 zhí [名] nephew

侄女 zhínǚ [名] niece

侄子 zhízi [名] nephew

值 zhí I [名] 1(价值) value 2(数) value II [动] 1(值得) be worth 2(碰上) just happen to be 3(轮到) be on duty

值班 zhíbān [动] be on duty

值得 zhíde [动] be worth ▷这书值得买。Zhè shū zhíde mǎi. This book is worth buying.

职 zhí [名] 1(职位) post 2(职责) duty

职工 zhígōng [名] 1(员工) staff 2(工人) blue-collar worker

职业 zhíyè [名] occupation

职员 zhíyuán [名] member of staff

植 zhí [动] 1 (栽种) plant 2 (树立) establish

植物 zhíwù [名] plant ▸ 草本植物 cǎoběn zhíwù herbs

止 zhǐ I [动] 1 (停止) stop 2 (截止) end II [副] only

只 zhǐ [副] only ▸ 我只在周末有时间。Wǒ zhǐ zài zhōumò yǒu shíjiān. I only have time at the weekend.
→ see also/另见 zhī

只好 zhǐhǎo [副] have to

只是 zhǐshì I [副] merely II [连] but

只要 zhǐyào [连] so long as

只有 zhǐyǒu [副] only

纸 zhǐ [名] paper

纸币 zhǐbì [名] note (英), bill (美)

指 zhǐ I [名] finger ▸ 中指 zhōngzhǐ middle finger ▸ 无名指 wúmíngzhǐ ring finger II [动] 1 (对着) point to 2 (点明) point ... out 3 (针对) refer to 4 (依靠) rely on

指出 zhǐchū [动] point ... out

指导 zhǐdǎo [动] instruct

指挥 zhǐhuī I [动] command II [名] 1 (指挥官) commander 2 (乐队指挥) conductor

指南针 zhǐnánzhēn [名] compass

指示 zhǐshì [动] instruct

指责 zhǐzé [动] criticize

至 zhì I [动] arrive II [介] to ▸ 从东到西 cóng dōng zhì xī from east to west III [副] 1 (至于) to ▸ 至于 zhìyú as to 2 (最) extremely ▸ 至少 zhìshǎo at least

至今 zhìjīn [副] so far

至少 zhìshǎo [副] at least

至于 zhìyú [介] as to

制 zhì I [动] 1 (制造) make 2 (拟订) work ... out 3 (约束) restrict II [名] system

制订 zhìdìng [动] work ... out

制定 zhìdìng [动] draw ... up

制度 zhìdù [名] system

制造 zhìzào [动] 1 (物品) manufacture 2 (气氛, 局势) create

制作 zhìzuò [动] make ▸ 制作网页 zhìzuò wǎngyè create a web page ▸ 制作商 zhìzuòshāng manufacturer

质 zhì I [名] 1 (性质) nature ▸ 本质 běnzhì nature 2 (质量) quality 3 (物质) matter 4 (抵押品) pledge ▸ 人质 rénzhì hostage II [形] simple ▸ 质疑 zhìyí cast doubt on

质量 zhìliàng [名] 1 (物) mass 2 (优劣) quality

治 zhì [动] 1 (治理) control 2 (医治) cure 3 (消灭) exterminate 4 (惩办) punish 5 (研究) research

治安 zhì'ān [名] security ▸ 社会治安 shèhuì zhì'ān public order

治疗 zhìliáo [动] cure

秩 zhì[名] order

秩序 zhìxù[名] sequence

智 zhì I [形] wise II [名] wisdom

智慧 zhìhuì[名] intelligence

智力 zhìlì[名] intelligence

智商 zhìshāng[名] IQ

中 zhōng I [名] 1(中心) centre (英), center (美) 2(中国) China ▶中央 zhōngyāng central 2(中国) China ▶中餐 zhōngcān Chinese food 3(两端之间的) the middle ▶中层 zhōngcéng mid-level 4(不偏不倚) impartial ▶适中 shìzhōng moderate 5(在过程里的) course II [动] be suitable for

中国 Zhōngguó[名] China

中国人 Zhōngguórén[名] Chinese person

中华人民共和国 Zhōnghuá Rénmín Gònghéguó[名] People's Republic of China

中华人民共和国 Zhōnghuá Rénmín Gònghéguó

The People's Republic of China was declared in Tiananmen Square on October 1st 1949 by Chairman Mao Zedong.

中华 Zhōnghuá[名] China

中间 zhōngjiān[名] 1(中心) middle 2(之间) ▶我站在他俩中间。 Wǒ zhàn zài tā liǎ zhōngjiān. I was standing in between the both of them.

中介 zhōngjiè[名] agency ▶房产

中介 fángchǎn zhōngjiè estate agent

中年 zhōngnián[名] middle age

中秋节 Zhōngqiū Jié[名] Mid-Autumn Festival

中秋节 Zhōngqiū Jié

The Mid-Autumn Festival is celebrated on the 15th day of the 8th month of the Chinese lunar calendar. Traditionally families gather to observe the moon and eat 月饼 yuèbǐng, mooncakes. The roundness of both the full moon and the cakes symbolize the unity of the family.

中文 Zhōngwén[名] Chinese

中午 zhōngwǔ[名] noon

中心 zhōngxīn[名] centre (英), center (美)

中学 zhōngxué[名] high school (英), senior school (美)

中旬 zhōngxún[名] the middle ten days of a month

中央 zhōngyāng[名] 1(中心地) centre (英), center (美) 2(最高机构) central government

中药 zhōngyào[名] Chinese medicine

中医 zhōngyī[名] 1(医学) traditional Chinese medicine 2(医生) doctor of traditional Chinese medicine

终 zhōng I [动] die II [副] in the

end III [形] all ▶终身 zhōngshēn all one's life

终点 zhōngdiǎn [名] 1 (尽头) terminus 2 (体育) finish

终于 zhōngyú [副] finally

终止 zhōngzhǐ [动] stop

钟 zhōng [名] 1 (响器) bell 2 (记时器) clock 3 (指时间) ▶5点钟 wǔ diǎnzhōng five o'clock

钟表 zhōngbiǎo [名] clocks and watches

钟头 zhōngtóu [名] hour

肿 zhǒng [动] swell

种 zhǒng I [名] 1 (物种) species (SG) 2 (人种) race 3 (种子) seed 4 (胆量) courage II [量] kind, type ▶各种商品 gè zhǒng shāngpǐn all kinds of commodities ▶3种选择 sān zhǒng xuǎnzé three choices
→ see also/另见 zhòng

种子 zhǒngzi [名] seed

种族 zhǒngzú [名] race

种 zhòng [动] sow ▶种田 zhòngtián farm ▶种痘 zhòngdòu vaccinate
→ see also/另见 zhǒng

重 zhòng I [名] weight II [形] 1 (重量大) heavy 2 (程度深) strong 3 (重要) important ▶重任 zhòngrèn important task (不轻率) serious ▶稳重 wěnzhòng staid III [动] stress ▶注重 zhòngshì pay attention to
→ see also/另见 chóng

重大 zhòngdà [形] major

重点 zhòngdiǎn [名] key point

重量 zhòngliàng [名] weight

重视 zhòngshì [动] attach importance to

重要 zhòngyào [形] important

周 zhōu I [名] 1 (圈子) circle 2 (星期) week II [动] 1 (环绕) circle 2 (接济) give ... financial help III [形] 1 (普遍) widespread 2 (完备) thorough

周到 zhōudào [形] thorough

周末 zhōumò [名] weekend

周围 zhōuwéi [名] the vicinity

猪 zhū [名] pig

猪肉 zhūròu [名] pork

竹 zhú [名] bamboo

竹子 zhúzi [名] bamboo

逐 zhú [动] 1 (追赶) chase 2 (驱逐) drive ... away II [副] one after another

逐步 zhúbù [副] step by step

逐渐 zhújiàn [副] gradually

主 zhǔ I [名] 1 (接待者) host ▶东道主 dōngdàozhǔ host 2 (所有者) owner ▶房主 fángzhǔ home-owner 3 (当事人) person concerned 4 (主见) idea 5 (上帝) God II [形] main III [动] 1 (主持) take charge ▶主办 zhǔbàn take charge of 2 (主张) be in favour (英) 或 favor (美) of 3 (从自身出发) look at ... subjectively ▶主观 zhǔguān subjective

主动 zhǔdòng [形] voluntary

主观 zhǔguān [形] subjective

主人 zhǔrén [名] 1 (接待者) host 2 (雇佣者) master ▶ 女主人 nǚzhǔrén mistress 3 (所有者) owner

主任 zhǔrèn [名] director

主席 zhǔxí [名] chairman, chairwoman

主要 zhǔyào [形] major

主义 zhǔyì [名] doctrine ▶ 社会主义 shèhuì zhǔyì socialism ▶ 浪漫主义 làngmàn zhǔyì romanticism

主意 zhǔyi [名] 1 (办法) idea 2 (主见) opinion

主张 zhǔzhāng I [动] advocate II [名] standpoint

煮 zhǔ [动] boil

助 zhù [动] help

助手 zhùshǒu [名] assistant

住 zhù [动] 1 (居住) live. 2 (停止) stop. 3 (作动词补语)

住宿 zhùsù [动] stay

住院 zhùyuàn [动] be hospitalized

住宅 zhùzhái [名] house

住址 zhùzhǐ [名] address

注 zhù I [动] 1 (灌入) pour ▶ 注射 zhùshè inject 2 (集中) concentrate 3 (解释) explain II [名] 1 (记载) record ▶ 注册 zhùcè enrol (英), enroll (美) 2 (赌注) bet

注意 zhùyì [动] be careful

祝 zhù [动] wish

祝贺 zhùhè [动] congratulate

著 zhù I [形] marked II [动] 1 (显出) show 2 (写作) write III [名] work

著名 zhùmíng [形] famous

著作 zhùzuò [名] writings (PL)

抓 zhuā [动] 1 (拿住) grab 2 (划过) scratch 3 (提拿) catch 4 (掌握) take control of 5 (吸引) attract 6 (把握住) seize

抓紧 zhuājǐn [动] make the most of

专 zhuān [动] 1 (集中) concentrate 2 (独占) dominate ▶ 专卖 zhuānmài monopoly

专家 zhuānjiā [名] expert

专门 zhuānmén I [形] specialized II [副] especially

专心 zhuānxīn [形] single-minded

专业 zhuānyè [名] special field of study

砖 zhuān [名] brick

转 zhuǎn [动] 1 (改换) turn ▶ 转弯 zhuǎnwān turn a corner ▶ 转学 zhuǎnxué change schools 2 (传送) pass ... on ▶ 转送 zhuǎnsòng deliver
→ see also / 另见 zhuàn

转变 zhuǎnbiàn [动] transform

转告 zhuǎngào [动] pass on

转 zhuàn [动] turn
→ see also / 另见 zhuǎn

赚 zhuàn [动] 1 (获得利润) make a profit 2 (挣钱) earn

庄 zhuāng [名] 1 (指村庄) village

2(指土地) manor ▶庄园 zhuāngyuán manor **3**(指商店) ▶茶庄 cházhuāng teahouse ▶饭庄 fànzhuāng restaurant

庄稼 zhuāngjia [名] crops (PL)

庄严 zhuāngyán [形] solemn

装 zhuāng **I** [动] **1**(修饰) dress up ▶装饰 zhuāngshì decorate **2**(假装) pretend **3**(装载) load **4**(装配) install **II** [名](服装) clothing ▶套装 tàozhuāng matching outfit

状 zhuàng [名] **1**(形状) shape **2**(情况) state **3**(症状) ▶症状 zhèngzhuàng symptom **3**(诉状) complaint ▶告状 gàozhuàng bring a case **4**(证书) certificate ▶奖状 jiǎngzhuàng certificate

状况 zhuàngkuàng [名] condition

状态 zhuàngtài [名] condition

撞 zhuàng [动] **1**(碰撞) collide **2**(碰见) bump into **3**(试探) try **4**(闯) dash

撞车 zhuàngchē [动] **1**(车辆相撞) collide **2**(发生分歧) clash

追 zhuī [动] **1**(追赶) chase **2**(追究) investigate **3**(追求) seek **4**(回溯) reminisce

追捕 zhuībǔ [动] pursue and capture

追求 zhuīqiú [动] **1**(争取) seek **2**(求爱) chase after

准 zhǔn **I** [动] **1**(准许) allow **2**(批准) pīzhǔn ratify **3**(依据) be in accord with **II** [名] standard **III** [形] **1**(准确) accurate ▶准时 zhǔnshí

punctual **2**(类似) quasi

准备 zhǔnbèi [动] **1**(筹划) prepare **2**(打算) plan

准确 zhǔnquè [形] accurate

准时 zhǔnshí [形] punctual

捉 zhuō [动] **1**(握住) clutch **2**(捕捉) catch

桌 zhuō **I** [名] table ▶书桌 shūzhuō desk **II** [量] table ▷一桌菜 yī zhuō càia table covered in dishes

桌子 zhuōzi [名] table

咨 zī [动] consult

咨询 zīxún [动] seek advice from

姿 zī [名] **1**(容貌) looks (PL) **2**(姿势) posture

姿势 zīshì [名] posture

资 zī **I** [名] **1**(钱财) money ▶外资 wàizī foreign capital ▶邮资 yóuzī postage **2**(资质) ability ▶天资 tiānzī natural ability **3**(资格) qualifications (PL) **4**(资历) zīlì record of service **II** [动] **1**(资助) aid ... financially **2**(提供) provide

资本 zīběn [名] (本钱) capital

资格 zīgé [名] **1**(条件) qualifications (PL) **2**(身份) seniority

资金 zījīn [名] funds (PL)

资料 zīliào [名] **1**(必需品) means (PL) **2**(材料) material

资源 zīyuán [名] resources (PL)

子 zǐ **I** [名] **1**(儿子) son ▶母子 mǔzǐ mother and son **2**(人) person

▶男子 nánzǐ man **3**(种子) seed
▶瓜子 guāzǐ melon seed **4**(卵) egg ▶鱼子 yúzǐ fish roe **5**(粒状物) ▶棋子 qízǐ chess piece **6**(铜子) coin **II**[形]**1**(幼小) young **2**(附属) affiliated

子女 zǐnǚ[名]children

仔 zǐ[形]young

仔细 zǐxì[形]**1**(细心) thorough **2**(小心) careful

紫 zǐ[形]purple

自 zì **I**[代]oneself **II**[副]certainly **III**[介]from

自从 zìcóng[介]since

自动 zìdòng[形]**1**(主动的) voluntary **2**(机械的) automatic

自动取款机 zìdòng qǔkuǎnjī[名]cashpoint(英), ATM(美)

自费 zìfèi[形]self-funded

自己 zìjǐ **I**[代]oneself **II**[形]our

自觉 zìjué **I**[动]be aware of **II**[形]conscientious

自来水 zìláishuǐ[名]tap water

自然 zìrán **I**[名]nature **II**[形]natural **III**[副]naturally

自杀 zìshā[动]commit suicide

自私 zìsī[形]selfish

自我 zìwǒ[代]self

自信 zìxìn[形]self-confident

自行车 zìxíngchē[名]bicycle

自学 zìxué[动]teach oneself

自由 zìyóu **I**[名]freedom **II**[形]free

自愿 zìyuàn[动]volunteer

自助餐 zìzhùcān[名]self-service buffet

字 zì[名]**1**(文字) character **2**(字音) pronunciation **3**(书法作品) calligraphy ▶字画 zìhuà painting and calligraphy **4**(字体) script **5**(字据) written pledge

字典 zìdiǎn[名]dictionary

字母 zìmǔ[名]letter

宗 zōng[名]**1**(祖宗) ancestor **2**(家族) clan **3**(宗派) school ▶正宗 zhèngzōng orthodox school **4**(宗旨) purpose

宗教 zōngjiào[名]religion

综 zōng[动]summarize ▶综述 zōngshù sum … up

综合 zōnghé **I**[动]synthesize **II**[形]comprehensive

总 zǒng **I**[动]gather ▶总括 zǒngkuò sum … up **II**[形]**1**(全部的) total **2**(为首的) chief ▶总部 zǒngbù headquarters(PL)[名]**1**(一直) always **2**(毕竟) after all

总理 zǒnglǐ[名]premier

总是 zǒngshì[副]always

总算 zǒngsuàn[副]**1**(最终) finally **2**(大体上) all things considered

总统 zǒngtǒng[名]president

粽 zòng[名]see below/见下文

粽子 zòngzi[名]glutinous rice dumplings

粽子 zòngzi

The traditional festival food for the Dragon

Boat Festival are large pyramid-shaped glutinous rice dumplings wrapped in reed or bamboo leaves, often with sweet or meat fillings.

走 zǒu [动] 1 (行走) walk ▸走路 zǒulù walk ▸出去走走 chūqù zǒuzǒu go out for a walk 2 (跑动) run 3 (运行) move 4 (离开) leave ▸我先走。Wǒ xiān zǒu. I'll leave first. 5 (来往) visit 6 (通过) go through 7 (漏出) leak 8 (改变) depart from 9 (去世) die

走道 zǒudào [名] path

走动 zǒudòng [动] 1 (行走) walk about 2 (来往) visit each other

走后门 zǒu hòumén use one's connections

走廊 zǒuláng [名] corridor

租 zū I [动] 1 (租用) (房屋) rent (租用) (汽车，自行车，录像带) rent (英)，hire (美) 3 (出租) rent out II [名] rent ▸房租 fángzū rent

足 zú I [名] foot ▸足迹 zújì footprint II [形] ample 1 (充足) chōngzú adequate III [副] 1 (达到某种程度) as much as 2 (足以) enough

足够 zúgòu [动] be enough

足球 zúqiú [名] football

阻 zǔ [动] block

阻止 zǔzhǐ [动] stop

组 zǔ I [动] form II [名] group

组成 zǔchéng [动] form

组织 zǔzhī I [动] organize II [名] 1 (集体) organization 2 (指器官) tissue 3 (指纺织) weave

祖 zǔ [名] 1 (祖辈) grandparent 2 (祖宗) ancestor 3 (首创者) founder

祖父 zǔfù [名] grandfather

祖国 zǔguó [名] motherland

祖母 zǔmǔ [名] grandmother

祖先 zǔxiān [名] ancestors (PL)

钻 zuān [动] 1 (打洞) drill 2 (穿过) go through 3 (钻研) bury one's head in
→ see also/另见 zuàn

钻研 zuānyán [动] study ... intensively

钻 zuàn [名] 1 (工具) drill 2 (钻石) diamond
→ see also/另见 zuān

钻石 zuànshí [名] 1 (金刚石) diamond 2 (宝石) jewel

嘴 zuǐ [名] 1 (口) mouth 2 (嘴状物) ▸茶壶嘴 cháhú zuǐ spout of a teapot 3 (话) words (PL) ▸插嘴 chāzuǐ interrupt

最 zuì [副] most ▸最难忘的海外之旅 zuì nánwàng de hǎiwài zhī lǚ the most unforgettable trip abroad ▸这家饭店服务最好。Zhè jiā fàndiàn fúwù zuì hǎo. The service at this restaurant is the best.

最初 zuìchū I [形] initial II [副] at first

最好 zuìhǎo I [形] best II [副] had better

最后 zuìhòu I [形] final II [副] at last

最近 zuìjìn [形] recent

罪 zuì I [名] 1 (恶行) crime ▶犯罪 fànzuì commit a crime 2 (过失) blame 3 (苦难) hardship 4 (刑罚) punishment ▶死罪 sǐzuì death sentence II [动] blame

罪犯 zuìfàn [名] criminal

醉 zuì I [形] 1 (饮酒过量的) drunk ▶醉鬼 zuìguǐ drunk 2 (用酒泡制的) steeped in wine II [动] drink too much

尊 zūn I [形] senior II [动] respect

尊敬 zūnjìng [动] respect

尊重 zūnzhòng I [动] respect II [形] serious ▶放尊重些! Fàng zūnzhòng xiē! Behave yourself!

遵 zūn [动] follow

遵守 zūnshǒu [动] observe

昨 zuó [名] 1 (昨天) yesterday ▶昨日 zuórì yesterday 2 (过去) the past

昨天 zuótiān [名] yesterday

左 zuǒ I [名] 1 (左边) left ▶左边 zuǒbian the left II [形] 1 (相反的) conflicting 2 (进步的) leftist ▶左派 zuǒpài left-wing

左边 zuǒbian [名] the left side

左右 zuǒyòu I [名] 1 (左和右) left and right 2 (跟随者) attendants

(PL) 3 (上下) ▶他身高1点75米 左右。Tā shēngāo yī diǎn qī wǔ mǐ zuǒyòu. He is about 1.75 metres tall. II [动] control

作 zuò I [动] 1 (起) rise 2 (写) write ▶作家 zuòjiā writer 3 (作曲) zuòqǔ compose music 3 (装) pretend 4 (犯) do 5 (当) take ... as ▶废 zuòfèi become invalid 6 (发作) feel II [名] work ▶杰作 jiézuò masterpiece

作罢 zuòbà [动] drop

作家 zuòjiā [名] writer

作品 zuòpǐn [名] work

作为 zuòwéi I [名] 1 (行为) action 2 (成绩) accomplishment 3 (干头系) scope II [动] (当作) regard ... as

作文 zuòwén [名] write an essay

作业 zuòyè I [名] work II [动] do work

作用 zuòyòng I [动] affect II [名] 1 (影响) effect 2 (活动) action

作者 zuòzhě [名] author

坐 zuò [动] 1 (坐下) sit ▶坐在窗口 zuò zài chuāngkǒu sit by the window 2 (乘坐) travel by ▶坐飞机 zuò fēijī travel by plane

座 zuò I [名] 1 (坐位) seat ▶座号 zuòhào seat number 2 (垫子) stand 3 (星座) constellation ▶双子座 Shuāngzǐ Zuò Gemini II [量] ▶一座山 yī zuò shān a mountain ▶三座桥 sān zuò qiáo three bridges ▶五座办公楼 wǔ zuò bàngōnglóu five office buildings measure word, used for mountains, buildings, bridges, etc.

座谈 zuòtán [动] discuss

座位 zuòwèi [名] seat

做 zuò [动] 1 (制造) make 2 (写作) write 3 (从事) do ▷ 做生意 zuò shēngyi do business 4 (举行) hold ▷ 做寿 zuòshòu hold a birthday party 5 (充当) be ▷ 做大会主席 zuò dàhuì zhǔxí chair a meeting 6 (用作) be used as 7 (结成) become ▷ 做朋友 zuò péngyou be friends

做法 zuòfǎ [名] method

做客 zuòkè [动] be a guest

做梦 zuòmèng [动] dream

a

A & E (Brit) N ABBR (= accident and emergency) 急诊室 jízhěnshì

abbey ['æbɪ] N [c] 大修道院 dà xiūdàoyuàn [座 zuò]

abbreviation [əbriːvɪ'eɪʃən] N [c] 缩写 suōxiě [个 gè]

ability [ə'bɪlɪtɪ] N [s] ▸ **ability (to do sth)** (做某事的)能力 (zuò mǒushì de) nénglì

able ['eɪbl] ADJ ▸ **to be able to do sth** (have skill, ability) 能够做某事 nénggòu zuò mǒushì; (have opportunity) 可以做某事 kěyǐ zuò mǒushì

abolish [ə'bɒlɪʃ] VT [+ system, practice] 废止 fèizhǐ

abortion [ə'bɔːʃən] (Med) N [c/u] 流产 liúchǎn [次 cì] ▸ **to have an abortion** 流产 liúchǎn

KEYWORD

a [eɪ, ə] (before vowel or silent h: **an**)
INDEF ART **1** (article) 一个 yīgè ▸ **a man** 一个男人 yīgè nánrén ▸ **a girl** 一个女孩 yīgè nǚhái ▸ **an elephant** 一只大象 yīzhī dàxiàng ▸ **she's a doctor** 她是一名医生 tā shì yìmíng yīshēng ▸ **they haven't got a television** 他们没有电视 tāmen méiyǒu diànshì **2** (one) 一 yī ▸ **a year ago** 一年前 yīnián qián
3 (expressing ratios, prices etc) ▸ **five hours a day/week** 一天/一周5个小时 yìtiān/yìzhōu wǔge xiǎoshí ▸ **100 km an hour** 每小时100公里 měi xiǎoshí yībǎi gōnglǐ

KEYWORD

about [ə'baut] I PREP (relating to) 关于 guānyú ▸ **a book about London** 关于伦敦的一本书 guānyú Lúndūn de yìběn shū ▸ **what's it about?** 这是关于什么的? zhèshì guānyú shénme de? ▸ **we talked about it** 我们谈到了这事 wǒmen tándào le zhèshì ▸ **to be sorry/pleased/angry about sth** 对某事感到抱歉/开心/生气 duì mǒushì gǎndào bàoqiàn/kāixīn/shēngqì ▸ **what or how about eating out?** 出去吃怎么样? chūqù chī zěnmeyàng? II ADV **1** (approximately) 大约 dàyuē ▸ **about a hundred/thousand people** 大约

100/1000人 dàyuē yìbǎi/yìqiān rén
2 (place) 在 zài ▸**to leave things lying about** 把东西到处乱放 bǎ dōngxī dàochù luànfàng ▸**to be about to do sth** 正要做某事 zhèng yào zuò mǒushì

above [əˈbʌv] **I** PREP (higher than) 在⋯上面 zài⋯shàngmiàn **II** ADV (in position) 在上面 zài shàngmiàn **III** ADJ ▸**the above address** 上述 地址 shàngshù dìzhǐ ▸**above all** 首先 shǒuxiān

abroad [əˈbrɔːd] ADV **1** (be) 在国 外 zài guówài **2** (go) 到国外 dào guówài

absence [ˈæbsəns] N **1** [c/u] (of person) 缺席 quēxí [次 cì] **2** [s] (of thing) 缺乏 quēfá

absent [ˈæbsənt] ADJ 缺席 的 quēxí de ▸**to be absent** 不 在 bùzài

absolutely [æbsəˈluːtlɪ] ADV (utterly) 绝对地 juéduì de

absorbent cotton [əbˈzɔːbənt-] (US) N [u] 脱脂棉 tuōzhīmián

abuse [n əˈbjuːs, vb əˈbjuːz] **I** N **1** [u] (insults) 辱骂 rǔmà **2** [u] (ill-treatment: physical) 虐待 nüèdài; (sexual) 猥亵 wěixiè **3** [c/u] (misuse: of power, alcohol, drug) 滥用 lànyòng [种 zhǒng] **II** VT **1** (ill-treat: physically) 虐待 nüèdài **2** (sexually) [+ child] 猥亵 wěixiè

academic [ækəˈdemɪk] **I** ADJ 学 术的 xuéshù de **II** N 大学教师 dàxué jiàoshī

academy [əˈkædəmɪ] N [c] **1** 学会 xuéhuì [个 gè] **2** (school, college) 学

院 xuéyuàn [个 gè]

accelerate [ækˈseləreɪt] VI (Aut) 加速 jiāsù

accelerator [ækˈseləreɪtə^r] (Aut) N [c] 加速器 jiāsùqì [个 gè]

accent [ˈæksənt] N [c] 口音 kǒuyīn ▸**to speak with an (Irish/French) accent** 讲话带 (爱尔兰/法国) 口音 jiǎnghuà dài (Ài'ěrlán/Fǎguó) kǒuyīn

accept [əkˈsept] VT 接受 jiēshòu

access [ˈækses] **I** N [u] ▸**access (to sth)** (to building, room) 进入 (某 物) jìnrù (mǒuwù); (to information, papers) (某物的) 使用权 (mǒuwù de) shǐyòngquán **II** VT (Comput) 存取 cúnqǔ

accident [ˈæksɪdənt] N [c] **1** (involving vehicle) 事故 shìgù [个 gè] **2** (mishap) 意外 yìwài [个 gè] ▸**to have an accident** 出 事故 chū shìgù ▸**by accident** (unintentionally) 无意中 wúyì zhōng; (by chance) 偶然 ǒurán

accidental [æksɪˈdentl] ADJ 意外 的 yìwài de

accident and emergency (Brit) N [c] 急诊室 jízhěnshì [个 gè]

accommodation [əkɒməˈdeɪʃə n] **I** N [u] 住处 zhùchù **II** ACCOMMODATIONS (US) NPL = **accommodation**

accompany [əˈkʌmpənɪ] VT **1** (frm: escort) 陪伴 péibàn **2** (Mus) 为⋯伴奏 wèi⋯bànzòu

according [əˈkɔːdɪŋ] ▸**according to** PREP [+ person] 据⋯所说 jù⋯suǒshuō; [+ account, information] 根据 gēnjù

account [əˈkaʊnt] N [c] 1 (*with bank, at shop*) 账户 zhànghù [个 gè] 2 (*report*) 描述 miáoshù [番 fān] ▶to take sth into account, take account of sth 考虑到某事 kǎolǜ dào mǒushì

accountant [əˈkaʊntənt] N [c] 会计师 kuàijìshī [位 wèi]

accuracy [ˈækjʊrəsɪ] N [u] 1 (*of information, measurements*) 准确 zhǔnquè 2 (*of device*) 精确 jīngquè

accurate [ˈækjʊrɪt] ADJ [+ information, measurement, instrument] 精确的 jīngquè de; [+ description, account, person, aim] 准确的 zhǔnquè de

accuse [əˈkjuːz] VT 1 ▶to accuse sb of (doing) sth 指责某人 (做) 某事 zhǐzé mǒurén (zuò) mǒushì 2 ▶to be accused of sth (*of crime*) 被指控某事 bèi zhǐkòng mǒushì

ache [eɪk] I VI 痛 tòng II N [c] 疼痛 téngtòng [种 zhǒng] ▶I've got (a) stomach/toothache 我胃/牙痛 wǒ wèi/yá tòng

achieve [əˈtʃiːv] VT [+ victory, success, result] 取得 qǔdé

achievement [əˈtʃiːvmənt] N [c] 成就 chéngjiù [个 gè]

acid [ˈæsɪd] N [c/u] (*Chem*) 酸 suān [种 zhǒng]

across [əˈkrɒs] I PREP 1 (*moving from one side to the other of*) 穿过 chuānguò 2 (*situated on the other side of*) 在…对面 zài…duìmiàn 3 (*extending from one side to the other of*) 跨越 kuàyuè II ADV 1 (*from one side to the other*) 从一边到另一边

cóng yībiān dào lìngyībiān 2 ▶ **across from** (*opposite*) 在…对面 zài…duìmiàn 3 ▶ **across at/to** (*towards*) 朝向 cháoxiàng 4 (*in width*) 宽 kuān

act [ækt] VI 1 (*take action*) 行动 xíngdòng 2 (*behave*) 举止 jǔzhǐ ▷They were acting suspiciously. 他们举止可疑。tāmen jǔzhǐ kěyí. 3 (*in play, film*) 演戏 yǎnxì ▶ **acts of sabotage** 破坏行动 pòhuài xíngdòng

action [ˈækʃən] N 1 [u] (*steps, measures*) 行动 xíngdòng 2 [c] (*deed*) 行为 xíngwéi [种 zhǒng] ▶to take action 采取行动 cǎiqǔ xíngdòng

active [ˈæktɪv] ADJ 1 活跃的 huóyuè de 2 [+ volcano] 活的 huó de

activity [ækˈtɪvɪtɪ] I N [c] 活动 huódòng [项 xiàng] II **activities** NPL 活动 huódòng

actor [ˈæktər] N [c] 演员 yǎnyuán

actress [ˈæktrɪs] N [c] 女演员 nǚ yǎnyuán [个 gè]

actual [ˈæktjʊəl] ADJ 真实的 zhēnshí de

actually [ˈæktjʊəlɪ] ADV 1 实际地 shíjì de 2 (*in fact*) 事实上 shìshíshàng ▶ **actually, we have the same opinion** 实际上我们有同样的观点 shíjì shàng wǒmen yǒu tóngyàng de guāndiǎn

AD ADV ABBR (= **Anno Domini**) 公元 gōngyuán

ad [æd] (*inf*) N (*advertisement*) 广告 guǎnggào

adapt [ə'dæpt] I VT 使适合 shǐ shìhé II VI ▸ **to adapt (to)** 适应 shìyìng

adaptor [ə'dæptə*] (Elec) N [c] 转接器 zhuǎnjiēqì [个 gè]

add [æd] VT 1 (put in, put on) 加入 jiārù 2 ▸ **to add (together)** (calculate total of) 加(起来) jiā (qǐlái)

addict ['ædɪkt] N [c] ▸ **drug/heroin addict** 吸毒/海洛因成瘾的人 xīdú/hǎiluòyīn chéngyǐn de rén [个 gè]

addicted [ə'dɪktɪd] ADJ ▸ **to be addicted to sth** 对某事上瘾 duì mǒushì shàngyǐn

addition [ə'dɪʃən] N [u] (Math) 加法 jiāfǎ ▸ **in addition to** 除…之外 chú…zhīwài

address [ə'drɛs] N [c] 地址 dìzhǐ [个 gè]

adjective ['ædʒɛktɪv] N [c] 形容词 xíngróngcí [个 gè]

adjust [ə'dʒʌst] VT [+ device, position, setting] 校准 jiàozhǔn

adjustable [ə'dʒʌstəbl] ADJ 可调节的 kě tiáojié de

admire [əd'maɪə*] VT 钦佩 qīnpèi

admit [əd'mɪt] VT 1 (confess) 承认 chéngrèn 2 (accept) [+ defeat, responsibility] 接受 jiēshòu ▸ **he admits that…** 他承认… tā chéngrèn… ▸ **to be admitted to hospital** 住进医院 zhùjìn yīyuàn

adolescent [ædəu'lɛsnt] N [c] 青少年 qīngshàonián [个 gè]

adopt [ə'dɒpt] VT 1 [+ plan, approach, attitude] 采用 cǎiyòng 2 [+ child] 收养 shōuyǎng

adopted [ə'dɒptɪd] ADJ 被收养的 bèi shōuyǎng de

adoption [ə'dɒpʃən] N [c/u] [of child] 收养 shōuyǎng

adult ['ædʌlt] N [c] 成年人 chéngniánrén [个 gè] II ADJ (grown-up) 成年的 chéngnián de

advance [əd'vɑːns] ADJ [+ notice, warning] 预先的 yùxiān de ▸ **in advance** (book, prepare, plan) 提前 tíqián

advanced [əd'vɑːnst] ADJ 1 (highly developed) 先进的 xiānjìn de 2 (Scol) [+ student, pupil] 高年级的 gāoniánjí de; [+ course, work] 高等的 gāoděng de

advantage [əd'vɑːntɪdʒ] N [c] 1 (benefit) 好处 hǎochù [种 zhǒng] 2 (favourable factor) 有利因素 yǒulì yīnsù [个 gè] ▸ **to take advantage of** [+ person] 利用 lìyòng; [+ opportunity] 利用 lìyòng

adventure [əd'vɛntʃə*] N [c] 冒险活动 màoxiǎn huódòng [次 cì]

adverb ['ædvə:b] N [c] 副词 fùcí [个 gè]

advert ['ædvə:t] (Brit) N 广告 guǎnggào

advertise ['ædvətaɪz] I VI 做广告 zuò guǎnggào II VT 1 [+ product, event] 为…做广告 wèi…zuò guǎnggào 2 [+ job] 刊登 kāndēng

advertisement [əd'və:tɪsmənt] (Comm) N [c] 广告 guǎnggào [则 zé]

advice [əd'vaɪs] N [u] 忠告 zhōnggào ▸ **a piece of advice** 一条建议 yītiáo jiànyì

advise [əd'vaɪz] VT ▸ **to advise**

sb to do sth 劝某人做某事 quàn mǒurén zuò mǒushì

aerial [ˈɛərɪəl] (Brit) N [c] 天线 tiānxiàn [根 gēn]

aerobics [ɛəˈrəubɪks] N [u] 有氧健身操 yǒuyǎng jiànshēncāo

aeroplane [ˈɛərəpleɪn] (Brit) N [c] 飞机 fēijī [架 jià]

affair [əˈfɛəʳ] I N 1 [s] (matter, business) 事情 shìqíng 2 [c] (romance) 风流韵事 fēngliú yùnshì [桩 zhuāng] II **affairs** NPL 1 (matters) 事务 shìwù 2 (personal concerns) 私事 sīshì ▶**to have an affair (with sb)** (和某人)发生暧昧关系 (hé mǒurén) fāshēng àimèi guānxì

affect [əˈfɛkt] VT 影响 yǐngxiǎng

afford [əˈfɔːd] VT ▶**to be able to afford (to buy/pay) sth** 买/支付得起某物 mǎi/zhīfùdeqǐ mǒuwù

afraid [əˈfreɪd] ADJ (frightened) 害怕的 hàipà de ▶**to be afraid of sb/sth** 害怕某人/某物 hàipà mǒurén/mǒuwù ▶**to be afraid to do sth/of doing sth** 怕做某事 pà zuò mǒushì ▶**to be afraid that...** (worry, fear) 担心… dānxīn…; (expressing apology, disagreement) 恐怕… kǒngpà… ▶**I'm afraid so/not** 恐怕是/不是的 kǒngpà shì/bùshì de

Africa [ˈæfrɪkə] N 非洲 Fēizhōu

African [ˈæfrɪkən] I ADJ 非洲的 Fēizhōu de II N [c] (person) 非洲人 Fēizhōurén [个 gè]

after [ˈɑːftəʳ] I PREP 1 (in time) 在…以后 zài…yǐhòu 2 (in place, order) 在…后面 zài…hòumiàn

II ADV (afterwards) 以后 yǐhòu III CONJ (once) 在…以后 zài…yǐhòu ▶**the day after tomorrow** 后天 hòutiān ▶**it's ten after eight** (US) 现在是8点过10分 xiànzài shì bādiǎn guò shífēn ▶**after all** 毕竟 bìjìng ▶**after doing sth** 做完某事后 zuòwán mǒushì hòu

after, afterwards 和 **later** 用于表示某事发生在说话的时间，或者某个特定事件之后。**after** 可以和 **not long, shortly** 等连用。*After dinner she spoke to him...Shortly after, she called me.* 在无须指明某个特定时间或事件时，可以用 **afterwards**。*Afterwards we went to a night club...You'd better come and see me later.* **afterwards** 可以和 **soon, shortly** 连用。*Soon afterwards, he came to the clinic.* **later** 表示某事发生在说话之后，可以和 **a little, much** 或 **not much** 等连用。*A little later, the lights went out...I learned all this much later.* 可以用 **after, afterwards** 和 **later** 后跟表示时间段的词语，表示某事发生的时间。*...five years after his death...She wrote about it six years later/afterwards.*

afternoon [ˈɑːftəˈnuːn] N [c/u] 下午 xiàwǔ ▶**this afternoon** 今天下午 jīntiān xiàwǔ ▶**tomorrow/yesterday**

afternoon 明天/昨天下午
míngtiān/zuótiān xiàwǔ ▶(good)
afternoon! (hello) 下午好!
xiàwǔ hǎo!

after-shave (lotion) ['ɑːftə
ʃeɪv-] N [U] 须后(润肤)水 xūhòu
(rùnfū) shuǐ

afterwards ['ɑːftəwədz], (US)
afterward ['ɑːftəwəd] ADV 以
后 yǐhòu

again [ə'ɡɛn] ADV 又一次地 yòu
yīcì de ▶again and again/time
and again 一再 yīzài

against [ə'ɡɛnst] PREP 1 (leaning
on, touching) 紧靠在 jǐnkào zài
2 (opposed to) 反对 fǎnduì 3 (in
game or competition) 同…对抗
tóng...duìkàng 4 ▶ to protect
against sth 保护免受某种伤
害 bǎohù miǎnshòu mǒuzhǒng
shānghài ▶they'll be playing
against Australia 他们将在比赛
中同澳大利亚队对抗 tāmen jiāng
zài bǐsài zhōng tóng Àodàlìyà duì
duìkàng ▶against the law/rules
违反法律/规则 wéifǎn fǎlǜ/guīzé
▶against one's will 违背自己的
意愿 wéibèi zìjǐ de yìyuàn

age [eɪdʒ] N 1 [C/U] 年龄 niánlíng
2 [C] (period in history) 时代 shídài
[个 gè] ▶what age is he? 他多大
了? tā duōdà le? ▶at the age of
20 20岁时 èrshí suì shí ▶an age,
ages (inf) 很长时间 hěncháng
shíjiān ▶the Stone/Bronze/Iron
Age 石器/铜器/铁器时代 shíqì/
tóngqì/tiěqì shídài

aged¹ ['eɪdʒd] ADJ ▶aged 10 10岁
shí suì

aged² ['eɪdʒɪd] NPL ▶the aged 老
人 lǎorén

agent ['eɪdʒənt] N [C] 代理人
dàilǐrén [个 gè]

aggressive [ə'ɡrɛsɪv] ADJ 好斗的
hàodòu de

ago [ə'ɡəu] ADV ▶2 days ago 两
天前 liǎngtiān qián ▶long ago/a
long time ago 很久以前 hěnjiǔ
yǐqián ▶how long ago? 多久以
前? duōjiǔ yǐqián?

agony ['æɡənɪ] N [C/U] 痛苦
tòngkǔ [阵 zhèn]

agree [ə'ɡriː] VI 1 (have same
opinion) 同意 tóngyì 2 ▶ to agree
to sth/to do sth 同意某事/做某
事 tóngyì mǒushì/zuò mǒushì ▶to
agree with sb about sth 关于某
事赞同某人的看法 guānyú mǒushì
zànchéng mǒurén de kànfǎ ▶to
agree on sth [+ price, arrangement]
商定某事 shāngdìng mǒushì

agreement [ə'ɡriːmənt] N 1 [C]
▶an agreement (on sth) (decision,
arrangement) (关于某事的) 协议
(guānyú mǒushì de) xiéyì [个 gè]
2 [U] (consent) 同意 tóngyì

agricultural [æɡrɪ'kʌltʃərəl] ADJ
农业的 nóngyè de

agriculture ['æɡrɪkʌltʃər] N
农业 nóngyè

ahead [ə'hɛd] ADV 1 (in front)
在前地 zàiqián de 2 (in work,
achievements) 提前地 tíqián de
3 (in competition) 领先地 lǐngxiān
de 4 (in the future) 在未来 zài
wèilái ▶the days/months ahead
今后几天/几个月 jīnhòu jǐtiān/jǐgè
yuè ▶ahead of time/schedule

提前 tíqián ▸right or straight
ahead 笔直向前 bǐzhí xiàngqián
▸go ahead! (giving permission) 干
吧! gànba!

aid [eɪd] N [U] 援助 yuánzhù

AIDS [eɪdz] N ABBR (= acquired
immune deficiency syndrome)
艾滋病 àizībìng

aim [eɪm] I VT ▸to aim sth (at
sb/sth) [+ gun, camera] 将某物
瞄准(某人/某物) jiāng mǒuwù
miáozhǔn (mǒurén/mǒuwù) II VI
(with weapon) 瞄准 miáozhǔn III N
[c] (objective) 目标 mùbiāo [个 gè]
▸to aim at sth (with weapon) 瞄
准某物 miáozhǔn mǒuwù ▸to
aim to do sth 打算做某事 dǎsuàn
zuò mǒushì

air [eəʳ] I N [U] 空气 kōngqì II CPD
[+ travel] 乘飞机 chéng fēijī;
[+ fare] 飞机 fēijī ▸in/into/
through the air 在/进入/穿过天
空 zài/jìnrù/chuānguò tiānkōng
▸by air (flying) 乘飞机 chéng fēijī

air-conditioned [ˈeəkənˈdɪʃənd]
ADJ 装有空调的 zhuāngyǒu
kōngtiáo de

air conditioning [-kənˈdɪʃənɪŋ]
N [U] 空气调节 kōngqì tiáojié

air force N [c] 空军 kōngjūn
[支 zhī]

air hostess (Brit) N [c] 空中小姐
kōngzhōng xiǎojiě [位 wèi]

airline [ˈeəlaɪn] N [c] 航空公司
hángkōng gōngsī [家 jiā]

airmail [ˈeəmeɪl] N [U] ▸by
airmail 航空邮寄 hángkōng yóujì

airplane [ˈeəpleɪn] (US) N [c] 飞机
fēijī [架 jià]

airport [ˈeəpɔːt] N [c] 飞机场
fēijīchǎng [个 gè]

aisle [aɪl] N [c] 过道 guòdào [条
tiáo] ▸aisle seat (on plane) 靠过
道的位置 kào guòdào de zuòwèi

alarm [əˈlɑːm] N 1 [c] (warning
device) 警报 jǐngbào [个 gè] 2 [c]
(on clock) 闹钟 nàozhōng [个 gè]

alarm clock N [c] 闹钟 nàozhōng
[个 gè]

Albania [ælˈbeɪnɪə] N 阿尔巴尼
亚 Ā'ěrbāníyà

album [ˈælbəm] N [c] 1 册子 cèzi
[本 běn] 2 (LP) 唱片 chàngpiàn
[张 zhāng]

alcohol [ˈælkəhɒl] N [U] 酒 jiǔ

alcoholic [ˌælkəˈhɒlɪk] I N [c] 酒
鬼 jiǔguǐ [个 gè] II ADJ [+ drink] 含
酒精的 hán jiǔjīng de

alert [əˈlɜːt] N [c] (situation) ▸a
security alert 安全警戒 ānquán
jǐngjiè [个 gè]

A level (Brit) N [c/U] 中学中高
级考试

Algeria [ælˈdʒɪərɪə] N 阿尔及利
亚 Ā'ěrjílìyà

alike [əˈlaɪk] ADJ ▸to be/look
alike 是/看起来相似的 shì/
kànqǐlái xiāngsì de

alive [əˈlaɪv] ADJ (living) ▸to be
alive 活着 huózhe de ▸alive
and well 安然无恙的 ānrán
wúyàng de

KEYWORD

all [ɔːl] I ADJ 所有的 suǒyǒu de
▸all day/night 整日/夜 zhěngrì/
yè ▸all big cities 所有的大城市

suǒyǒu de dàchéngshì
II PRON **1** 全部 quánbù ▶all I
could do was apologize 我所能
做的全部就是道歉 wǒ suǒ néng
zuò de quánbù jiùshì dàoqiàn ▶I
ate it all, I ate all of it 我把它全都
吃了 wǒ bǎ tā quán dōu chīle ▶all
of us 我们的所有人 wǒmen
zhōng de suǒyǒu rén ▶we all sat
down 我们都坐下了 wǒmen dōu
zuòxià le ▶is that all? 那就是全部
吗? nà jiùshì quánbù ma?
2 (in expressions) ▶after all
(considering) 毕竟 bìjìng ▶in all
总共 zǒnggòng ▶best of all 最好
不过的是 zuìhǎo bùguò de shì
III ADV 1 (emphatic) 完全 wánquán
▶he was doing it all by himself
他完全是自己做的 tā wánquán shì
zìjǐ zuò de ▶all alone 孤零零的
gūlínglíng de
2 (in scores) ▶the score is 2 all 比
分2比2平 bǐfēn èr bǐ èr píng

allergic [ə'lɜːdʒɪk] ADJ [+ reaction,
response] 过敏的 guòmǐn de ▶to
be allergic to sth 对某物过敏 duì
mǒuwù guòmǐn

allergy ['ælədʒɪ] (Med) N [C/U] 过
敏症 guòmǐnzhèng [种 zhǒng]
▶to have an allergy to sth 对
某物有过敏症 duì mǒuwù yǒu
guòmǐnzhèng

allow [ə'lau] VT 1 (permit) 允许
yǔnxǔ 2 [+ sum, time, amount] 留
出 liúchū ▶to allow sb to do sth
允许某人做某事 yǔnxǔ mǒurén
zuò mǒushì

all right I ADJ ▶to be all right

(satisfactory) 还不错的 hái bùcuò
de; (well, safe) 安然无恙的 ānrán
wúyàng de **II** ADV 1 (satisfactorily) 顺利地 shùnlì
de 2 (without problem) 没问题地 méi wèntí de 3 (as
answer) 可以 kěyǐ

almond ['ɑːmənd] N [C/U] (nut)
杏仁 xìngrén [颗 kē]

almost ['ɔːlməust] ADV 差不多
chàbùduō

alone [ə'ləun] I ADJ 独自的
dúzì de II ADV (unaided) 独自地
dúzì de ▶to leave sb/sth alone
(undisturbed) 不要打扰某人/某物
bùyào dǎrǎo mǒurén/mǒuwù

along [ə'lɒŋ] I PREP 1 沿着
yánzhe 2 [+ road, corridor, river] 沿
着 yánzhe II ADV 沿着 yánzhe
▶along with (together with)
与……一起 yǔ……yìqǐ

alphabet ['ælfəbɛt] N ▶the
alphabet 字母表 zìmǔbiǎo

already [ɔːl'rɛdɪ] ADV ▶yǐjīng
▶I have already started making
dinner 我已经开始做晚餐了 wǒ
yǐjīng kāishǐ zuò wǎncān le ▶is it
five o'clock already? (expressing
surprise) 已经到5点了吗? yǐjīng
dào wǔdiǎn le ma?

also ['ɔːlsəu] ADV 1 (too) 也 yě
2 (moreover) 同样 tóngyàng

alternate [ɔl'tɜːnət] ADJ 1 交替的
jiāotì de 2 (US: alternative) 供替换
的 gōng tìhuàn de

alternative [ɔl'tɜːnətɪv] I ADJ
1 (Brit) 另外的 lìngwài de
2 (non-conventional) 非常规的
fēi chángguī de II N ▶(an)
alternative (to) ……的替代
……de tìdài [个 gè] ▶to have no

alternative (but to) (除…外)别无选择 (chú…wài) biéwú xuǎnzé

alternatively [ɔːl'tɜːnətɪvlɪ] ADV 或者 huòzhě

although [ɔːl'ðəʊ] CONJ **1** 尽管 jǐnguǎn **2** (but) 但是 dànshì

altogether [ɔːltə'ɡeðə'] ADV **1** (completely) 完全 wánquán **2** (in total) 总共 zǒnggòng ▸ how much is that altogether? 总共多少钱？zǒnggòng duōshǎo qián?

always ['ɔːlweɪz] ADV 总是 zǒngshì ▸ He's always late 他总是迟到 tā zǒngshì chídào

am [æm] VB see **be**

a.m. ADV ABBR (= ante meridiem) 上午 shàngwǔ

amateur ['æmətə'] N [c] 业余爱好者 yèyú àihàozhě [个 gè]

amaze [ə'meɪz] VT 使惊讶 shǐ jīngyà ▸ to be amazed (at/by/that...) (对/被…) 惊讶 (duì/bèi…) jīngyà

amazing [ə'meɪzɪŋ] ADJ 令人惊讶的 lìng rén jīngyà de

ambassador [æm'bæsədə'] N [c] 大使 dàshǐ [位 wèi]

ambition [æm'bɪʃən] N [c] ▸ an ambition to do sth (做某事的) 志向 (zuò mǒushì de) zhìxiàng [个 gè] ▸ to achieve one's ambition 实现自己的抱负 shíxiàn zìjǐ de bàofù

ambitious [æm'bɪʃəs] ADJ 雄心勃勃的 xióngxīn bóbó de

ambulance [æm'bjʊlǝns] N [c] 救护车 jiùhùchē [辆 liàng]

America [ə'mɛrɪkə] N 美洲 Měizhōu

American [ə'mɛrɪkən] **I** ADJ 美国的 Měiguó de **II** N [c] (person) 美国人 Měiguórén [个 gè]

among(st) [ə'mʌn(st)] PREP 在…当中 zài…dāngzhōng 如果指两个以上的人或物，用 **among** 或 **amongst**。如果指两个人或物，用 **between**。...an area between Mars and Jupiter...an opportunity to discuss these issues amongst the trees. **amongst** 是有些过时的表达方式。注意，如果你 **between** 某些东西或某些人，他们在你的两侧。如果你 **among** 或 **amongst** 某些东西或某些人，他们在你的周围。...the bag standing on the floor between us...the sound of a pigeon among the trees.

amount [ə'maʊnt] N [c/u] (quantity) 数量 shùliàng; [of money] 数额 shù'é [个 gè]; [of work] 总量 zǒngliàng [个 gè]

amp [æmp] N [c] 安培 ānpéi

amplifier ['æmplɪfaɪə'] N [c] 扬声器 yángshēngqì [个 gè]

amuse [ə'mjuːz] VT (distract, entertain) 给…消遣 gěi…xiāoqiǎn ▸ to be amused at/by sth 被某事逗乐 bèi mǒushì dòulè

amusement arcade N [c] 游乐场 yóulèchǎng [个 gè]

an [æn, ən] DEF ART see **a**

aluminium [æljʊ'mɪnɪəm], (US) **aluminum** [ə'luːmɪnəm] N [U] 铝 lǚ

anaesthetic, (US) **anesthetic** [ænɪsˈθetɪk] N [c/u] 麻醉剂 mázuìjì [种 zhǒng] ▶**local anaesthetic** 局部麻醉 júbù mázuì ▶**general anaesthetic** 全身麻醉 quánshēn mázuì

analyse, (US) **analyze** [ˈænəlaɪz] VT 分析 fēnxī

analysis [əˈnæləsɪs] (pl **analyses** [əˈnæləsiːz]) N [c/u] 分析 fēnxī [种 zhǒng]

analyze [ˈænəlaɪz] (US) VT = **analyse**

ancestor [ˈænsɪstəʳ] N [c] 祖先 zǔxiān [位 wèi]

ancient [ˈeɪnʃənt] ADJ 1 [+ Greece, Rome, monument] 古代的 gǔdài de 2 (very old) 古老的 gǔlǎo de

and [ænd] CONJ 和 hé ▶**men and women** 男人和女人 nánrén hé nǚrén ▶**better and better** 越来越好 yuè lái yuè hǎo ▶**to try and do sth** 试着做某事 shìzhe zuò mǒushì

anesthetic [ænɪsˈθetɪk] (US) = **anaesthetic**

anger [ˈæŋgəʳ] N [u] 生气 shēngqì

angry [ˈæŋgrɪ] ADJ 生气的 shēngqì de ▶**to be angry with sb/about sth** 对某人/某事生气 duì mǒurén/mǒushì shēngqì ▶**to make sb angry** 使某人生气 shǐ mǒurén shēngqì

animal [ˈænɪməl] N [c] 动物 dòngwù [只 zhī]

ankle [ˈæŋkl] (Anat) N [c] 踝 huái [个 gè]

anniversary [ænɪˈvəːsərɪ] N [c] 1 ▶**anniversary (of sth)** (某事的) 周年纪念 (mǒushì de) zhōunián jìniàn [个 gè] 2 (also: **wedding anniversary**) 结婚周年纪念 jiéhūn zhōunián jìniàn [个 gè]

announce [əˈnauns] VT 宣布 xuānbù ▶**the government has announced that...** 政府宣称... zhèngfǔ xuānchēng...

announcement [əˈnaunsmənt] N [c] 1 宣布 xuānbù 2 (at airport or station) 通告 tōnggào [个 gè] ▶**to make an announcement** 发表声明 fābiǎo shēngmíng

annoy [əˈnɔɪ] VT 使烦恼 shǐ fánnǎo

annoyed [əˈnɔɪd] ADJ 烦恼的 fánnǎo de ▶**to be annoyed at sth/with sb** 对某事/某人感到厌烦 duì mǒushì/mǒurén gǎndào yànfán

annoying [əˈnɔɪɪŋ] ADJ [+ noise, habit, person] 讨厌的 tǎoyàn de

annual [ˈænjuəl] ADJ 1 [+ meeting, report] 每年的 měinián de 2 [+ sales, income, rate] 年度的 niándù de

anorak [ˈænəræk] N [c] 连帽防风夹克 liánmào fángfēng jiákè [件 jiàn]

another [əˈnʌðəʳ] I ADJ 1 ▶**another book** (one more) 另一本书 lìng yī běn shū 2 (a different one) 另外的 lìngwài de 3 ▶**another 5 years/miles/kilos** 再有5年/英里/公斤 zài yǒu wǔ nián/yīnglǐ/gōngjīn II PRON 1 (one more) 再一个 zài yī gè 2 (a different one) 不同的一个 bùtóng de yīgè ▶**another**

answer ['ɑːnsəʳ] I N [c] 1 *(reply)* 回答 huídá [个 gè]; *(to letter)* 回信 huíxìn [封 fēng] 2 *(solution)* 答案 dá'àn [个 gè] II VI *(reply)* 回答 huídá; *(to telephone ringing, knock at door)* 应答 yìngdá III VT *(+ person)* 答复 dáfù; *(+ question)* 回答 huídá; *(+ letter)* 回复 huífù ▸**to answer the phone** 接听电话 jiētīng diànhuà

answering machine ['ɑːnsərɪŋ-] N [c] 电话答录机 diànhuà dálùjī [台 tái]

Antarctic [ænt'ɑːktɪk] N ▸**the Antarctic** 南极 Nánjí

anthem ['ænθəm] N [c] 赞美诗 zànměishī [首 shǒu]

antibiotic ['æntɪbaɪ'ɒtɪk] N [c] 抗生素 kàngshēngsù [种 zhǒng]

antique [æn'tiːk] N [c] 古董 gǔdǒng [件 jiàn]

antiseptic [æntɪ'sɛptɪk] N [c/u] 杀菌剂 shājùnjì [种 zhǒng]

anxious ['æŋkʃəs] ADJ 忧虑的 yōulǜ de

KEYWORD

any ['ɛnɪ] I ADJ 1 *(in negatives, in questions)* 一些的 yīxiē de ▸**I haven't any chocolate/sweets** 我没有巧克力/糖了 wǒ méiyǒu qiǎokèlì/táng le ▸**there was hardly any food** 几乎没有食物了 jīhū méiyǒu shíwù le ▸**have you got any chocolate/sweets?** 你有巧克力/糖吗? nǐ yǒu qiǎokèlì/táng ma? 2 *(in "if" clauses)* 任何的 rènhé de

▸**if there are any tickets left** 如果有票剩下的话 rúguǒ yǒu piào shèngxià de huà

3 *(no matter which)* 任意的 rènyì de ▸**take any card you like** 拿你喜欢的任意一张卡 ná nǐ xǐhuan de rènyì yì zhāng kǎ

4 *(in expressions)* ▸**any day now** 从现在起的任何一天 cóng xiànzài qǐ de rènhé yītiān ▸**(at) any moment** (在) 任何时候 (zài) rènhé shíhòu ▸**any time** *(whenever)* 不论何时 bùlùn héshí; *(also: at any time)* 在任何时候 zài rènhé shíhòu

II PRON 1 *(in negatives)* 一些 yīxiē ▸**I didn't eat any (of it)** 我 (这) 一点也没吃 wǒ (zhè) yīdiǎn yě méi chī ▸**I haven't any (of them)** 我一个也没有 wǒ yígè yě méiyǒu 2 *(in questions)* 一些 yīxiē ▸**have you got any?** 你有吗? nǐ yǒu ma? 3 *(in "if" clauses)* 任何 rènhé ▸**if any of you would like to take part,...** 如果你们中任何人想参加的话, ... rúguǒ nǐmen zhōng rènhé rén xiǎng cānjiā de huà, ... 4 *(no matter which ones)* 无论哪一个 wúlùn nǎ yīgè ▸**help yourself to any of the books** 无论哪本书你随便拿 wúlùn nǎběn shū nǐ suíbiàn ná

III ADV 1 *(with negative)* 丝毫 sīháo ▸**I don't play tennis any more** 我不再打网球了 wǒ bùzài dǎ wǎngqiú le ▸**don't wait any longer** 不再等了 bùzài děng le 2 *(in questions)* 一点...点儿

▶do you want any more soup/
sandwiches? 你还想要多喝点汤/三
明治吗？ nǐ hái xiǎng zài yào diǎn
tāng/sānmíngzhì ma?

anybody ['ɛnɪbɒdɪ] PRON =
anyone

anyhow ['ɛnɪhau] ADV = **anyway**

anyone ['ɛnɪwʌn] PRON 1 (in
negatives, "if" clauses) 任何人
rènhé rén 2 (in questions) 任何
一个人 rènhé yīgè rén ▶I can't
see anyone 我见不到任何人 wǒ
jiànbùdào rènhé rén ▶did anyone
see you? 有人看到你吗？ yǒurén
kàndào nǐ ma? ▶anyone could
do it 任何人都能做到 rènhé rén
dōunéng zuòdào

anything ['ɛnɪθɪŋ] PRON (in
negatives, questions, "if" clauses)
任何事 rènhé shì ▶I can't see
anything 我什么也看不见 wǒ
shénme yě kànbùjiàn ▶hardly
anything 几乎没有任何东西 jīhū
méiyǒu rènhé dōngxi ▶did you
find anything? 你找到些什么
吗？ nǐ zhǎodào xiē shénme ma?
▶if anything happens to me…
如果任何事情发生在我身上…
rúguǒ rènhé shìqíng fāshēng zài
wǒ shēnshàng… ▶you can say
anything you like 你可以畅所欲
言 nǐ kěyǐ chàng suǒ yù yán

anyway ['ɛnɪweɪ] ADV 1 (besides)
无论如何 wúlùn rúhé 2 (all the
same) 还是 háishì 3 (in short) 总
之 zǒngzhī ▶I shall go anyway 不
论如何我要走了 bùlùn rúhé wǒ
yào zǒu le

anywhere ['ɛnɪwɛəʳ] ADV (in
negatives, questions, "if" clauses) 任
何地方 rènhé dìfāng ▶I can't see
him anywhere 我哪里都见不到
他 wǒ nálǐ dōu jiànbùdào tā

apart [ə'pɑːt] ADV (couple, family)
分开 fēnkāi ▶to take sth apart
拆卸某物 chāixiè mǒuwù ▶apart
from (excepting) 除去 chúqú

apartment [ə'pɑːtmənt] N [c]
(US) 公寓 gōngyù [处 chù]

apologize [ə'pɒlədʒaɪz] VI 道歉
dàoqiàn ▶to apologize to sb (for
sth) 向某人（为某事）道歉 xiàng
mǒurén (wèi mǒushì) dàoqiàn

apology [ə'pɒlədʒɪ] N [c/U] 道歉
dàoqiàn [个 gè]

apostrophe [ə'pɒstrəfɪ] N [c] 撇
号 piěhào [个 gè]

apparently [ə'pærəntlɪ] ADV 表
面看来 biǎomiàn kànlái

appear [ə'pɪəʳ] VI 1 (seem) 看起来
kànqǐlái 2 (come into view, begin to
develop) 出现 chūxiàn ▶to appear
to be/have 看起来是/有 kànqǐlái
shì/yǒu

appendicitis [əpɛndɪ'saɪtɪs] N [U]
阑尾炎 lánwěiyán

appetite ['æpɪtaɪt] N [c/U] 食
欲 shíyù

applause [ə'plɔːz] N [U] 掌声
zhǎngshēng

apple ['æpl] N [c] 苹果 píngguǒ
[个 gè]

appliance [ə'plaɪəns] (frm) N [c] 器
具 qìjù [件 jiàn]

applicant ['æplɪkənt] N [c] 申请
人 shēnqǐngrén [个 gè]

application [æplɪ'keɪʃən] N

[c] 申请 shēnqǐng [份 fèn] **2** [c] (Comput: program) 应用程序 yìngyòng chéngxù [个 gè]

application form N [c] 申请表格 shēnqǐng biǎogé [份 fèn]

apply [ə'plaɪ] VI (make application) 提出申请 tíchū shēnqǐng ▸ **to apply for sth** [+ job, grant, membership] 申请某事 shēnqǐng mǒushì

appointment [ə'pɔɪntmənt] N [c] (arranged meeting) 约会 yuēhuì [个 gè]; (with hairdresser, dentist, doctor) 预约 yùyuē [个 gè] ▸ **to make an appointment (with sb)** (to see hairdresser, dentist, doctor) (和某人) 预约 (hé mǒurén) yùyuē

appreciate [ə'priːʃɪeɪt] VT (be grateful for) 感谢 gǎnxiè ▸ **I (really) appreciate your help** 我 (十分) 感谢你的帮助 wǒ (shífēn) gǎnxiè nǐde bāngzhù

approach [ə'prəʊtʃ] **I** VI [person, car] 走近 zǒu jìn; [event, time] 临近 línjìn **II** VT1 (draw near to) 向…靠近 xiàng…kàojìn **2** [+ situation, problem] 处理 chǔlǐ **III** N [c] (to a problem, situation) 方式 fāngshì [种 zhǒng]

approval [ə'pruːvəl] N [u] 批准 pīzhǔn

approve [ə'pruːv] VI 赞成 zànchéng

approximate [ə'prɒksɪmɪt] ADJ 近似的 jìnsì de

apricot ['eɪprɪkɒt] N [c/u] 杏子 xìngzi [个 gè]

April ['eɪprəl] N [c/u] 四月 sìyuè; see also **July**

apron ['eɪprən] N [c] 围裙 wéiqún [条 tiáo]

Aquarius [ə'kwɛərɪəs] N [u] (sign) 宝瓶座 Bǎopíng Zuò gè

Arab ['ærəb] **I** ADJ 阿拉伯的 Ālābó de **II** N [c] 阿拉伯人 Ālābórén [个 gè]

Arabic ['ærəbɪk] N [u] (language) 阿拉伯语 Ālābóyǔ

arch [ɑːtʃ] N [c] 拱 gǒng [个 gè]

archaeology [ɑːkɪ'ɒlədʒɪ] N [u] 考古学 kǎogǔxué

archeology [ɑːkɪ'ɒlədʒɪ] (US) = **archaeology**

architect ['ɑːkɪtekt] N [c] 建筑师 jiànzhùshī [位 wèi]

architecture ['ɑːkɪtektʃər] N [u] 建筑学 jiànzhùxué

Arctic ['ɑːktɪk] N ▸ **the Arctic** 北极 Běijí

are [ɑːr] VB see **be**

area ['ɛərɪə] N **1** [c] (region, zone) 地区 dìqū [个 gè] **2** [c] (of room, building etc) 区 qū [个 gè] **3** [c/u] (Math, Geom) 面积 miànjī [个 gè] **4** [c] (part) 部分 bùfen [个 gè] ▸ **in the London area** 在伦敦周边地区 zài Lúndūn zhōubiān dìqū

area code (esp US) N [c] 区号 qūhào [个 gè]

Argentina [ɑːdʒən'tiːnə] N 阿根廷 Āgēntíng

argue [ˈɑːgjuː] VI (quarrel) ▸ **to argue (with sb) (about sth)** (为某事) (和某人) 争吵 (wèi mǒushì) (hé mǒurén) zhēngchǎo

argument ['ɑːgjumənt] N [c/u] (quarrel) 争吵 zhēngchǎo [阵 zhèn] ▸ **an argument for/against sth**

赞成/反对某事的论据 zànchéng/fǎnduì mǒushì de lùnjù

Aries ['ɛərɪz] N [U] (sign) 白羊座 Báiyáng Zuò

arithmetic [ə'rɪθmətɪk] N [U] (Math) 算术 suànshù

arm [ɑːm] I N [c] 1 胳膊 gēbo [条 tiáo] 2 (of jacket, shirt etc) 袖子 xiùzi [只 zhī] II arms NPL (weapons) 武器 wǔqì

armchair ['ɑːmtʃɛəʳ] N [c] 扶手椅 fúshǒuyǐ [把 bǎ]

armed [ɑːmd] ADJ 武装的 wǔzhuāng de

army ['ɑːmɪ] ▸ **the army** 军队 jūnduì

around [ə'raʊnd] I ADV (about) 到处 dàochù II PREP 1 (encircling) 围绕 wéirào 2 (near) 在附近 zài fùjìn 3 大约 dàyuē

arrange [ə'reɪndʒ] I VT 1 (organize) 安排 ānpái 2 (put in order) 整理 zhěnglǐ II VI ▸ **to arrange to do sth** 安排做某事 ānpái zuò mǒushì

arrangement [ə'reɪndʒmənt] I N [c] 1 (agreement) 约定 yuēdìng [个 gè] 2 (grouping, layout) 布置 bùzhì [种 zhǒng] II arrangements NPL (plans, preparations) 安排 ānpái

arrest [ə'rɛst] VT 逮捕 dàibǔ ▸ **to be under arrest** 被逮捕 bèi dàibǔ

arrival [ə'raɪvl] N [c/U] 到达 dàodá

arrive [ə'raɪv] VI 1 到达 dào 2 (letter, meal) 来 lái

arrow ['ærəʊ] N [c] 1 (weapon) 箭 jiàn [支 zhī] 2 (sign) 箭头标志 jiàntóu biāozhì [个 gè]

art [ɑːt] I N [U] 1 艺术 yìshù 2 [U] (activity of drawing, painting etc) 美

术 měishù 3 [c] (skill) 技艺 jìyì [项 xiàng] II arts NPL ▸ **the arts** 艺术活动 yìshù huódòng III CPD ▸ **arts** [+ graduate, student, course] 文科 wénkē ▸ **work of art** 艺术品 yìshùpǐn

art gallery N [c] 美术馆 měishùguǎn [个 gè]

article ['ɑːtɪkl] N [c] 1 (item) 物品 wùpǐn [件 jiàn] 2 (in newspaper) 文章 wénzhāng [篇 piān] 3 (Ling) 冠词 guàncí [个 gè]

artificial [ɑːtɪ'fɪʃəl] ADJ 人造的 rénzào de

artist ['ɑːtɪst] N [c] 画家 huàjiā [位 wèi]

● **KEYWORD**

as [æz, əz] I CONJ 1 (referring to time) 当…时 dāng…shí ▸ **he came in as I was leaving** 我离开时他进来了 wǒ líkāi shí tā jìnlái le 2 (since, because) 因为 yīnwèi ▸ **you can't come, I'll go on my own** 既然你不能来，我就自己去 jìrán nǐ bùnéng lái, wǒ jiù zìjǐ qù 3 (referring to manner, way) 像…一样 xiàng…yíyàng ▸ **as you can see** 如你所见 rú nǐ suǒ jiàndào de ▸ **it's on the left as you go in** 在你进入时的左侧 zài nǐ jìnrù shí de zuǒcè

II PREP 1 (in the capacity of) 作为 zuòwéi ▸ **he works as a salesman** 他做推销员的工作 tā zuò tuīxiāoyuán de gōngzuò 2 (when) 在…时 zài…shí ▸ **he was very energetic as**

III ADV **1** (in comparisons) ▸ as big/good/easy etc as... 像……一样大/好/容易 [等] xiàng... yíyàng dà/hǎo/róngyì [děng] ▸ you're as tall as he is or as him 你和他一样高 nǐ hé tā yíyàng gāo ▸ as soon as 一……就…… yī...jiù... **2** (in expressions) ▸ as if or though 好像 hǎoxiàng

ash [æʃ] N [U] 灰末 huīmò

ashamed [əˈʃeɪmd] ADJ ▸ to be/feel ashamed 感到羞愧 gǎndào xiūkuì ▸ to be ashamed of sb/sth 对某人/某事感到羞愧 duì mǒurén/mǒushì gǎndào xiūkuì

ashtray [ˈæʃtreɪ] N [c] 烟灰缸 yānhuīgāng [个 gè]

Asia [ˈeɪʃə] N 亚洲 Yàzhōu

Asian [ˈeɪʃən] **I** ADJ 亚洲的 Yàzhōu de **II** N [c] (person) 亚洲人 Yàzhōurén [个 gè]

ask [ɑːsk] **I** VT **1** ▸ to ask (sb) a question 问 (某人) 一个问题 wèn (mǒurén) yīgè wèntí **2** (invite) 邀请 yāoqǐng **II** VI **1** 问 wèn ▸ to ask sb whether/why... 问 (某人) 是否/为什么…… wèn (mǒurén) shìfǒu/wèishénme... ▸ to ask sb to do sth 请求某人做事 qǐngqiú mǒurén zuò mǒushì ▸ to ask to do sth 要求做某事 yāoqiú zuò mǒushì ▸ to ask sb the time 向某人询问时间 xiàng mǒurén xúnwèn shíjiān ▸ to ask sb about sth 向某人打听某事 xiàng mǒurén dǎtīng mǒushì ▸ I asked

him his name 我问他叫什么 wǒ wèn tā jiào shénme ▸ ask for sth FUS **1** [+ thing] 要 yào **2** [+ person] 找 zhǎo

asleep [əˈsliːp] ADJ 睡着的 shuìzháo de ▸ to be asleep 睡着了 shuìzháo le ▸ to fall asleep 入睡 rùshuì

aspirin [ˈæsprɪn] N [c] (tablet) 阿司匹林药片 āsīpǐlín yàopiàn [片 piàn]

assemble [əˈsɛmbl] **I** VT [+ machinery, object] 装配 zhuāngpèi **II** VI (gather) 聚集 jùjí

assembly [əˈsɛmbli] N **1** [c] (meeting) 集会 jíhuì [个 gè] **2** [U] 装配 zhuāngpèi

assignment [əˈsaɪnmənt] N [c] 任务 rènwù [项 xiàng]; (for student) 作业 zuòyè [个 gè]

assistance [əˈsɪstəns] N [U] 帮助 bāngzhù

assistant [əˈsɪstənt] N [c] **1** (helper) 助手 zhùshǒu [个 gè] **2** (Brit: in shop) 营业员 yíngyèyuán [个 gè]

assortment [əˈsɔːtmənt] N [c] ▸ an assortment of sth 各种各样的某物 gèzhǒng gèyàng de mǒuwù [种 zhǒng]

assume [əˈsjuːm] VT (suppose) 假设 jiǎshè

assure [əˈʃuəʳ] VT 使确信 shǐ quèxìn

asterisk [ˈæstərɪsk] N [c] 星号 xīnghào [个 gè]

asthma [ˈæsmə] N [U] 哮喘 xiàochuǎn

astonishing [əˈstɒnɪʃɪŋ] ADJ 惊人的 jīngrén de

astronaut [ˈæstrənɔːt] N [c] 宇航员 yǔhángyuán [位 wèi]

astronomy [əˈstrɒnəmɪ] N [u] 天文学 tiānwénxué

KEYWORD

at [æt] PREP **1** (position, time, age) 在 zài ▸ **we had dinner at a restaurant** 我们在一家饭店吃了饭 wǒmen zài yījiā fàndiàn chī le fàn ▸ **at home** 在家 zàijiā ▸ **at work** 在工作 zài gōngzuò ▸ **to be sitting at a table/desk** 坐在桌边/书桌边 zuòzài zhuōbiān/shūzhuōbiān ▸ **there's someone at the door** 门口有人 ménkǒu yǒurén; (towards) ▸ **to throw sth at sb** 向某人扔某物 xiàng mǒurén rēng mǒuwù ▸ **at four o'clock** 在4点钟 zài sìdiǎn zhōng ▸ **at Christmas** 在圣诞节 zài Shèngdànjié

2 (referring to price, speed) 以 yǐ ▸ **apples at £2 a kilo** 苹果每公斤两镑 píngguǒ měi gōngjīn liǎngbàng ▸ **at 50 km/h** 以每小时50公里的速度 yǐ měi xiǎoshí wǔshí gōnglǐ de sùdù

3 (in expressions) ▸ **not at all** (in answer to question) 一点也不 yīdiǎn yě bù; (in answer to thanks) 别客气 bié kèqi

ate [eɪt] PT of **eat**

athlete [ˈæθliːt] N [c] 运动员 yùndòngyuán [名 míng]

athletics [æθˈlɛtɪks] N [u] 田径运动 tiánjìng yùndòng

Atlantic [ətˈlæntɪk] I ADJ 大西洋的 Dàxīyáng de ▸ **the Atlantic (Ocean)** 大西洋 Dàxīyáng

atlas [ˈætləs] N [c] 地图册 dìtúcè [本 běn]

atmosphere [ˈætməsfɪəʳ] N **1** [c] [of planet] 大气层 dàqìcéng [个 gè] **2** [s] 气氛 qìfēn

attach [əˈtætʃ] VT 附上 fùshàng

attachment [əˈtætʃmənt] N [c] [of tool, computer file] 附件 fùjiàn [个 gè]

attack [əˈtæk] I VT **1** [+ person] 袭击 xíjī [+ place, troops] 攻击 gōngjī **3** (criticise) 抨击 pēngjī II VI (Mil, Sport) 进攻 jìngōng III N **1** [c/u] [on person] 袭击 xíjī [次 cì] **2** [c/u] (military assault) 攻击 gōngjī [次 cì] **3** [c/u] [of illness] 发作 fāzuò [阵 zhèn] ▸ **an attack on sb** (assault) 袭击某人 xíjī mǒurén; (criticism) 抨击某人 pēngjī mǒurén

attempt [əˈtɛmpt] I N [c] (try) 尝试 chángshì [个 gè] II VI ▸ **to attempt to do sth** 试图做某事 shìtú zuò mǒushì ▸ **an attempt to do sth** 做某事的企图 zuò mǒushì de qǐtú

attend [əˈtɛnd] VT **1** [+ school, church, course] 上 shàng **2** [+ lecture, conference] 参加 cānjiā

attention [əˈtɛnʃən] N **1** (concentration) 注意 zhùyì **2** (care) 照料 zhàoliào ▸ **to pay attention (to sth/sb)** 关注 (某事/某人) guānzhù (mǒushì/mǒurén)

attitude [ˈætɪtjuːd] N [c/u] 看法 kànfǎ [个 gè]

attorney [əˈtəːnɪ] (US) N [c] (lawyer) 律师 lǜshī [位 wèi]

attract [əˈtrækt] VT 吸引 xīyǐn

attraction [əˈtrækʃən] I N [u] (charm, appeal) 吸引力 xīyǐnlì II attractions NPL (also: tourist attractions) (amusements) 游览胜地 yóulǎn shèngdì

attractive [əˈtræktɪv] ADJ [+ man, woman] 有魅力的 yǒu mèilì de; [+ thing, place] 吸引人的 xīyǐn rén de ▶ he was very attractive to women 他对女人很有吸引力 tā duì nǚrén hěn yǒu xīyǐnlì

auburn [ˈɔːbən] ADJ 赤褐色的 chìhèsè de

auction [ˈɔːkʃən] I N [c] 拍卖 pāimài [次 cì] II VT 拍卖 pāimài

audience [ˈɔːdɪəns] N [c] 1 (in theatre) 观众 guānzhòng [位 wèi] 2 (Rad, TV) 听众 tīngzhòng [位 wèi]

August [ˈɔːgəst] N [c/u] 八月 bāyuè; see also **July**

aunt [ɑːnt] N [c] (father's sister) 姑母 gūmǔ [位 wèi]; (father's older brother's wife) 伯母 bómǔ [位 wèi]; (father's younger brother's wife) 婶母 shěnmǔ [位 wèi]; (mother's sister) 姨母 yímǔ [位 wèi]; (mother's brother's wife) 舅母 jiùmǔ [位 wèi]

auntie, aunty [ˈɑːntɪ] (inf) N = aunt

au pair [ˈəuˈpɛəʳ] N [c] 为学习语言而住在当地人家里并提供家政服务的外国年轻人

Australia [ɔsˈtreɪlɪə] N 澳大利亚 Àodàlìyà

Australian [ɔsˈtreɪlɪən] I ADJ 澳大利亚的 Àodàlìyà de II N [c] (person) 澳大利亚人 Àodàlìyàrén [个 gè]

Austria [ˈɔstrɪə] N 奥地利 Àodìlì

author [ˈɔːθəʳ] N [c] (writer: of novel) 作家 zuòjiā [位 wèi]; [of text] 作者 zuòzhě [个 gè]

autobiography [ɔːtəbaɪˈɒgrəfɪ] N [c] 自传 zìzhuàn [部 bù]

automatic [ɔːtəˈmætɪk] I ADJ 自动的 zìdòng de II N (car) 自动挡 zìdòngdǎng [个 gè]

automatically [ɔːtəˈmætɪklɪ] ADV 1 (by itself) 自动地 zìdòng de 2 (without thinking) 无意识地 wúyìshí de 3 (as a matter of course) 自然而然地 zìrán'érrán de

automobile [ˈɔːtəməbiːl] (US) N [c] 汽车 qìchē [辆 liàng]

autumn [ˈɔːtəm] (Brit) N [c/u] 秋季 qiūjì [个 gè] ▶ in (the) autumn 在秋季 zài qiūjì

available [əˈveɪləbl] ADJ 1 可得 kě yòng de 2 [+ person] 有空的 yǒukòng de

avalanche [ˈævəlɑːnʃ] N [c] 雪崩 xuěbēng [次 cì]

average [ˈævərɪdʒ] I N [c] 1 (Math: mean) 平均数 píngjūnshù [个 gè] 2 ▶ the average (for sth/sb) (某物/某人的) 平均水平 (mǒuwù/mǒurén de) píngjūn shuǐpíng [个 gè] II ADJ (ordinary) 普通的 pǔtōng de ▶ on average 平均 píngjūn ▶ above/below the average 高于/低于平均水平 gāoyú/dīyú píngjūn shuǐpíng

avoid [əˈvɔɪd] VT 1 [+ person,

obstacle] 避免 bìmiǎn **2** [+ *trouble, danger*] 防止 fángzhǐ ▶ **to avoid doing sth** 避免做某事 bìmiǎn zuò mǒushì

awake [əˈweɪk] (*pt* **awoke**, *pp* **awoken** *or* **awakened**) ADJ ▶ **to be awake** 醒着的 xǐngzhe de

award [əˈwɔːd] I N [c] (*prize*) 奖 jiǎng [个 gè] II VT [+ *prize*] 授予 shòuyǔ

aware [əˈwεəʳ] ADJ ▶ **to be aware of sth** (*know about*) 意识到某事 yìshi dào mǒushì; (*be conscious of*) 觉察到某事 chájué dào mǒushì ▶ **to be aware that...** 知道… zhīdào…

away [əˈweɪ] I ADV **1** (*move, walk*) …开 …kāi **2** (*not present*) 不在 bùzài II ADJ [+ *match, game*] 客场 的 kèchǎng de ▶ **a week/month away** 还有一个星期/月 háiyǒu yígè xīngqī/yuè ▶ **two kilometres away** 离这里两公里远 lí zhèlǐ liǎng gōnglǐ yuǎn

awful [ˈɔːfəl] I ADJ **1** 糟糕的 zāogāo de **2** [+ *shock, crime*] 可怕 的 kěpà de **3** ▶ **to look/feel awful** (*ill*) 看起来/感觉很糟糕的 kàn qǐlái/gǎnjué hěn zāogāo de II ADV (*US: very*) 十分地 shífēn de ▶ **an awful lot (of)** (*amount*) 大量 的 dàliàng de; (*number*) 非常多的 fēichángduō de

awkward [ˈɔːkwəd] ADJ **1** [+ *movement*] 笨拙的 bènzhuō de **2** [+ *time, question*] 令人尴尬的 lìng rén gāngà de

axe, (*US*) **ax** [æks] N [c] 斧 fǔ [把 bǎ]

b

baby [ˈbeɪbɪ] N [c] 婴儿 yīng'ér [个 gè] ▶ **to have a baby** 生孩子 shēng háizi

baby carriage (*US*) N [c] 婴儿车 yīng'ér chē [辆 liàng]

babysit [ˈbeɪbɪsɪt] (*pt, pp* **babysat**) VI 代人照看孩子 dài rén zhàokàn háizi

babysitter [ˈbeɪbɪsɪtəʳ] N [c] 代 人照看孩子的人 dài rén zhàokàn háizi de rén [个 gè]

bachelor [ˈbætʃələʳ] N [c] **1** (*unmarried man*) 单身汉 dānshēnhàn [个 gè] **2** ▶ **Bachelor of Arts/Science** 文/理科学士学 位 wén/lǐkē xuéshì xuéwèi [个 gè]

back [bæk] I N [c] **1** 背部 bèibù [个 gè] **2** 背面 bèimiàn [个 gè]; [of house, door, book] 后面 hòumiàn

[个 gè]; [of car] 后部 hòubù [个 gè] II VT 1 (support) 支持 zhīchí; (financially) 资助 zīzhù 2 (reverse) 倒 dào III ADJ [+ garden, door, room, wheels] 后面的 hòumiàn de IV ADV 1 (not forward) 向后 xiàng hòu 2 (returned) 回 huí ▶ to be back 回来 huílai ▶ can I have it back? 我能要回它吗? wǒ néng yàohuí tā ma?

▶ back down VI 做出让步 zuòchū ràngbù

▶ back out VI (withdraw) 退出 tuìchū

▶ back up VT 1 [+ statement, theory] 证实 zhèngshí 2 (Comput) [+ disk] 备份 bèifèn

backache ['bækeɪk] N [c/u] 背痛 bèitòng [阵 zhèn]

background ['bækɡraʊnd] N [c] [of picture, scene, events] 背景 bèijǐng [个 gè] 2 [c/u] [of person: origins] 出身 chūshēn [种 zhǒng]; (experience) 经验 jīngyàn [种 zhǒng] ▶ in the background 在背后 zài bèihòu

backing ['bækɪŋ] N [u] (support) 支持 zhīchí; (financial) 资助 zīzhù

backpack ['bækpæk] N [c] 双肩背包 shuāngjiān bèibāo [个 gè]

backpacker ['bækpækə'] N [c] 背包旅行者 bèibāo lǚxíngzhě [名 míng]

■ BACKPACKER

backpacker 一词指预算紧张的青年旅行者。他们把全部的随身物品放在一个背包

里，尽可能地节省开支，为的是能延长旅行时间而多看一个地区，多看一些地方。

backstroke ['bækstrəʊk] N [u] (also: **the backstroke**) 仰泳 yǎngyǒng

backup ['bækʌp] I ADJ (Comput) [+ copy, file, disk] 备份的 bèifèn de II N [u] (support) 支持 zhīchí

backward ['bækwəd] ADV (esp US) = **backwards**

backwards ['bækwədz] ADV 向后地 xiànghòu de

backyard [bæk'jɑːd] N [c] 后院 hòuyuàn [个 gè]

bacon ['beɪkən] N [u] 腌猪肉 yān zhūròu

bad [bæd] ADJ 1 [+ weather, health, conditions, temper] 坏的 huài de; [+ actor, driver] 不胜任的 bù shèngrèn de; [+ behaviour, habit] 不良的 bùliáng de 2 (wicked) 恶 è de 3 (naughty) 不听话的 bù tīnghuà de 4 [+ mistake, accident, headache] 严重的 yánzhòng de 5 [+ back, arm] 有病的 yǒubìng de 6 (rotten) 腐烂的 fǔlàn de ▶ to be bad for sth/sb 对某事/某物有害 duì mǒushì/mǒuwù yǒuhài ▶ not bad 不错 bùcuò

badge [bædʒ] N [c] (Brit) 徽章 huīzhāng [个 gè]

badly ['bædlɪ] ADV 1 (poorly) 不令人满意地 bù lìng rén mǎnyì de 2 (damaged, injured) 严重地 yánzhòng de

badminton ['bædmɪntən] N [u] 羽毛球 yǔmáoqiú

bad-tempered ['bæd'tempəd]
ADJ 脾气坏的 píqì huài de

bag [bæg] N [c] **1** 袋 dài [个 gè]
2 (suitcase) 行李箱 xínglǐxiāng [个
gè] **3** (handbag) 手袋 shǒudài [个
gè] ▶ **to pack one's bags** 准备离
开 zhǔnbèi líkāi

baggage ['bægɪdʒ] N [U] 行
李 xínglǐ

baggage (re)claim N [U] 行李领
取 xínglǐ lǐngqǔ

bake [beɪk] VT 烤 kǎo

baker ['beɪkə'] N [c] (also:
baker's) 面包店 miànbāodiàn [个
家 jiā]

bakery ['beɪkərɪ] N [c] 面包房
miànbāofáng [个 gè]

balance ['bæləns] N **1** [U] 平衡
pínghéng **2** [c] (in bank account) 余
额 yú'é [笔 bǐ] **3** [s] (remainder to
be paid) 余欠之数 yúqiàn zhī shù
▶ **to keep/lose one's balance**
保持/失去平衡 bǎochí/shīqù
pínghéng

balcony ['bælkənɪ] N [c] 露
台 lùtái [个 gè]; (covered) 阳台
yángtái [个 gè]

bald [bɔ:ld] ADJ 秃的 tū de ▶ **to go
bald** 变秃 biàntū

ball [bɔ:l] N [c] 球 qiú [个 gè]

ballet ['bæleɪ, US bæˈleɪ] N [U] 芭
蕾舞 bāléiwǔ

ballet dancer N [c] 芭蕾舞演员
bāléiwǔ yǎnyuán [位 wèi]

balloon [bəˈlu:n] N [c] 气球 qìqiú
[只 zhī]

ballpoint (pen) ['bɔ:lpɔɪnt(-)] N
[c] 圆珠笔 yuánzhūbǐ [支 zhī]

ban [bæn] I N [c] 禁止 jìnzhǐ [种

zhǒng] II VT 禁止 jìnzhǐ

banana [bəˈnɑ:nə] N [c] 香蕉
xiāngjiāo [只 zhī]

band [bænd] N [c] **1** (group) 群 qún
2 (Mus) 乐队 yuèduì [个 gè]

bandage ['bændɪdʒ] N [c] 绷带
bēngdài [条 tiáo]

Band-Aid® ['bændeɪd] (US) N [c]
邦迪创可贴 Bāngdí chuàngkětiē
[贴 tiē]

bang [bæŋ] I N [c] **1** (noise) 砰的
一声 pēng de yīshēng; (of gun,
exhaust) 爆炸声 bàozhà shēng [阵
zhèn] **2** (blow) 撞击 zhuàngjī [下
xià] II VT ▶ **one's head, elbow** 撞
zhuàng III **bangs** NPL (US: fringe)
刘海 liúhǎi ▶ **to bang into sth/sb**
猛撞某物/某人 měngzhuàng
mǒuwù/mǒurén

Bangladesh [bæŋgləˈdɛʃ] N 孟加
拉国 Mèngjiālāguó

bank [bæŋk] N [c] **1** (Fin) 银行
yínháng [家 jiā] **2** (of river, lake) 岸
àn [个 gè]

bank account N [c] 银行账户
yínháng zhànghù [个 gè]

bank card N [c] **1** (Brit: for cash
machine) 银行卡 yínhángkǎ [张
zhāng] **2** (US: credit card) 信用
卡 yínháng xìnyòngkǎ [张 zhāng]

bank holiday (Brit) N [c] 法定假
期 fǎdìng jiàqī [个 gè]

banknote ['bæŋknəʊt] N [c] 纸
币 zhǐbì [张 zhāng]

bar [bɑ:'] N [c] **1** 酒吧 jiǔbā [个 gè]
2 (counter) 吧台 bātái [个 gè] **3** 条
tiáo **4** (tablet: of soap, chocolate)
块 kuài

barbecue ['bɑ:bɪkju:] N [c] 烧烤

聚会 shāokǎo jùhuì [次 cì]

barefoot(ed) ['beəfut(ɪd)] ADV 赤脚地 chìjiǎo de

barely ['beəlɪ] ADV 几乎不 jīhū bù

bargain ['ba:gɪn] N [c] 1 *(good buy)* 廉价品 liánjiàpǐn [件 jiàn] 2 *(deal, agreement)* 协议 xiéyì [个 gè]

barge [ba:dʒ] N [c] 驳船 bóchuán [艘 sōu]

bark [ba:k] VI *[dog]* 叫 jiào

barmaid ['ba:meɪd] *(esp Brit)* N [c] 酒吧女侍 jiǔbā nǚshì [个 gè]

barman ['ba:mən] *(pl* **barmen)** *(esp Brit)* N [c] 酒吧男侍 jiǔbā nánshì [个 gè]

barrel ['bærəl] N [c] 桶 tǒng [个 gè]

barrier ['bærɪər] N [c] 关口 guānkǒu [个 gè]

bartender ['ba:tendər] *(US)* N [c] 酒吧侍者 jiǔbā shìzhě [个 gè]

base [beɪs] N [c] 1 *(bottom)* 底部 dǐbù [个 gè] 2 *(basis)* 根基 gēnjī [个 gè] 3 基地 jīdì [个 gè]; *(for individual, organization)* 总部 zǒngbù [个 gè] ▶ **to be based on sth** 以某物为根据 yǐ mǒuwù wéi gēnjù ▶ **I'm based in London** 我长驻伦敦 wǒ chángzhù Lúndūn

baseball ['beɪsbɔ:l] N [U] 棒球 bàngqiú

basement ['beɪsmənt] N [c] 地下室 dìxiàshì [间 jiān]

basic ['beɪsɪk] ADJ 基本的 jīběn de; *see also* **basics**

basically ['beɪsɪklɪ] ADV 1 *(fundamentally)* 基本上 jīběnshang 2 *(in fact, put simply)* 简而言之 jiǎn ér yán zhī

basics ['beɪsɪks] NPL ▶ **the basics** 基本点 jīběndiǎn

basin ['beɪsn] N [c] 1 *(bowl)* 盆 pén [个 gè] 2 *(also:* **wash basin)** 洗脸盆 xǐliǎnpén [个 gè] 3 *[of river, lake]* 流域 liúyù [个 gè]

basket ['ba:skɪt] N [c] 筐 kuāng [个 gè]

basketball ['ba:skɪtbɔ:l] N [U] 篮球 lánqiú

bat [bæt] N [c] 1 *(animal)* 蝙蝠 biānfú [只 zhī] 2 *(for cricket, baseball)* 球板/棒 qiúbǎn/bàng [块 zhī] 3 *(Brit: for table tennis)* 球拍 qiúpāi [只 zhī]

bath [ba:θ] N [c] 1 *(Brit: bathtub)* 浴缸 yùgāng [个 gè] 2 *(act of bathing)* 洗澡 xǐzǎo [次 cì] ▶ **to have** *or* **take a bath** 洗澡 xǐzǎo

bathe [beɪð] VI 1 *(esp Brit)* 戏水 xìshuǐ 2 *(esp US: have a bath)* 洗澡 xǐzǎo

bathroom ['ba:θrum] N [c] 1 卫生间 wèishēngjiān [个 gè] 2 *(US: toilet)* 厕所 cèsuǒ [处 chù] ▶ **to go to the bathroom** *(US)* 去卫生间 qù wèishēngjiān

bathtub ['ba:θtʌb] *(US)* N [c] 浴缸 yùgāng [个 gè]

battery ['bætərɪ] N [c] 1 电池 diànchí [块 kuài] 2 *(in car)* 电瓶 diànpíng [个 gè]

battle ['bætl] N [c] 1 *(Mil)* 战役 zhànyì [场 chǎng] 2 *(fig: struggle)* 斗争 dòuzhēng [场 chǎng]

bay [beɪ] N [c] 湾 wān [个 gè]

BC ADV ABBR *(= before Christ)* 公

元前 gōngyuán qián

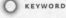

🔑 KEYWORD

be [biː] (pt **was, were**, pp **been**)

I VI **1** (with complement) 是 shì
▶I'm English/Chinese 我是英国人/中国人 wǒ shì Yīngguórén/Zhōngguórén ▶she's tall/pretty 她长得高/漂亮 tā zhǎngde gāo/piàoliang ▶this is my mother 这是我妈妈 zhèshì wǒ māma ▶who is it? 是谁啊? shì shuí a? ▶be careful/quiet! 当心/安静! dāngxīn/ānjìng!

2 (referring to time, date) 是 shì
▶it's 5 o'clock 现在是5点钟 xiànzài shì wǔdiǎnzhōng

3 (describing weather) 天热/冷 tiān rè/lěng ▶it's hot/cold 天热/冷 tiān rè/lěng

4 (talking about health) 怎么样 zěnmeyàng ▶how are you? 你身体怎么样? nǐ shēntǐ zěnmeyàng?

5 (talking about age) 有 yǒu ▶how old are you? 你多大了? nǐ duōdà le?

6 (talking about place) 在 zài
▶Madrid is in Spain 马德里在西班牙 Mǎdélǐ zài Xībānyá ▶the supermarket isn't far from here 超市离这儿不远 chāoshì lí zhè'er bùyuǎn ▶I won't be here tomorrow 我明天不在这儿 wǒ míngtiān bùzài zhè'er ▶have you been to Beijing? 你去过北京吗? nǐ qùguò Běijīng ma? ▶we've been here for ages 我们已经在这里好久了 wǒmen yǐjīng zài zhèlǐ hǎojiǔ le ▶the meeting will be in

the canteen 会议将在食堂举行 huìyì jiāng zài shítáng jǔxíng

7 (referring to distance) 有 yǒu ▶it's 10 km to the village 这儿离村庄有10公里 zhè'er lí cūnzhuāng yǒu shí gōnglǐ

8 (cost) 花 huā ▶how much was the meal? 这顿饭花了多少钱? zhèdùn fàn huāle duōshǎo qián? ▶that'll be £5 please 请付5英镑 qǐng fù wǔyīngbàng

9 (linking clauses) 是 shì ▶the problem is that ... 问题是… wèntí shì...

II AUX VB **1** (forming continuous tenses) ▶what are you doing? 你在干什么? nǐ zài gàn shénme?
▶they're coming tomorrow 他们明天来 tāmen míngtiān lái

2 (forming passives) ▶to be murdered 被谋杀 bèi móushā ▶he was killed in a car crash 他在一场车祸中丧生 tā zài yīchǎng chēhuò zhōng sàngshēng

3 (in tag questions) ▶it was fun, wasn't it? 有意思，是不是? yǒu yìsi, shì bù shì? ▶he's good-looking, isn't he? 他长得不错，是不是? tā zhǎngde bùcuò, shìbùshì?

beach [biːtʃ] N [c] 海滩 hǎitān [片 piàn]

beads [biːdz] NPL (necklace) 项链 xiàngliàn

beam [biːm] N [c] (of wood, metal) 梁 liáng [根 gēn]

bean [biːn] N [c] 豆 dòu [粒 lì] ▶coffee/cocoa beans

豆 kāfēi/kěkě dòu

bear [bɛəʳ] (pt **bore**, pp **borne**)
I N [c] 熊 xióng [头 tóu] II VT
1 (tolerate) 容忍 róngrěn 2 (endure)
忍受 rěnshòu

beard [bɪəd] N [c] 胡须 húxū
[根 gēn]

beat [bi:t] (pt **beat**, pp **beaten**) VT
[+ opponent, record] 击败 jībài

beaten ['bi:tn] PP of **beat**

beautiful ['bju:tɪful] ADJ 1 美丽的
měilì de 2 [+ shot, performance] 精
彩的 jīngcǎi de

beautifully ['bju:tɪflɪ] ADV 极好
地 jíhǎo de

beauty ['bju:tɪ] N 美 měi

became [bɪ'keɪm] PT of **become**

because [bɪ'kɒz] CONJ 因为
yīnwéi ▶ **because of** 因为 yīnwéi
我们在解释一件事发生
的原因时，可以使用
because, **as** 或 **since**。
because 最为常用，并且
是唯一可以回答ització **why**
提出的问题。'Why can't
you come?' – 'Because I'm
too busy.' 在引出含有原因
的从句时，尤其是在书面
语中，我们可以用 **as** 或
since 代替 **because**。
I was rather nervous, as I
hadn't seen her for a long
time…Since the juice is quite
strong, you should always
dilute it.

become [bɪ'kʌm] (pt **became**,
pp **become**) VI 1 (+ noun) 成为
chéngwéi 2 (+ adj) 变 biàn

bed [bɛd] N [c] 床 chuáng [张
zhāng] ▶ **to go to bed** 去睡觉 qù

shuìjiào

bed and breakfast N [U] 住宿加
早餐 zhùsù jiā zǎocān

bedding ['bɛdɪŋ] N [U] 床上用品
chuángshang yòngpǐn

bedroom ['bɛdrum] N [c] 卧室
wòshì [间 jiān]

bee [bi:] N [c] 蜜蜂 mìfēng [只 zhī]

beef [bi:f] N [U] 牛肉 niúròu
▶ **roast beef** 烤牛肉 kǎo niúròu

beefburger ['bi:fbə:gəʳ] (Brit) N
[c] 牛肉汉堡包 niúròu hànbāobāo
[个 gè]

been [bi:n] PP of **be**

beer [bɪəʳ] N [U] 啤酒 píjiǔ
▶ **would you like a beer?** 你想喝
一瓶啤酒吗? nǐ xiǎng hē yīpíng
píjiǔ ma?

beet [bi:t] N [c] (US: red vegetable)
甜菜根 tiáncàigēn [根 gēn]

beetle ['bi:tl] N [c] 甲虫 jiǎchóng
[只 zhī]

beetroot ['bi:tru:t] (Brit) N [c/U]
甜菜根 tiáncàigēn [根 gēn]

before [bɪ'fɔ:ʳ] I PREP 之
前 zhīqián II CONJ 在…之前
zài…zhīqián III ADV 以前 yǐqián
▶ **before doing sth** 在做某事之
前 zài zuò mǒushì zhīqián ▶ I've
never seen it before 我以前从没
见过 wǒ yǐqián cóngméi jiànguò

beg [bɛg] VI [beggar] 乞讨 qǐtǎo ▶ I
beg your pardon (apologizing) 对
不起 duìbùqǐ; (not hearing) 请再说
一遍 qǐng zàishuō yībiàn

began [bɪ'gæn] PT of **begin**

beggar ['bɛgəʳ] N [c] 乞丐 qǐgài
[个 gè]

begin [bɪ'gɪn] (pt **began**, pp

begun [bɪ'gʌn] I vt 开始 kāishǐ II vi 开始 kāishǐ ▸ **to begin doing** or **to do sth** 开始做某事 kāishǐ zuò mǒushì

beginner [bɪ'gɪnəʳ] N [c] 初学者 chūxuézhě [位 wèi]

beginning [bɪ'gɪnɪŋ] N [c] 开始 kāishǐ [个 gè] ▸ **at the beginning** 开始时 kāishǐ shí

begun [bɪ'gʌn] PP of **begin**

behave [bɪ'heɪv] vi 表现 biǎoxiàn

behaviour, (US) **behavior** [bɪ'heɪvjəʳ] N [u] 举止 jǔzhǐ

behind [bɪ'haɪnd] I PREP 在…后面 zài…hòumiàn II ADV (at/towards the back) 在/向后面 zài/xiàng hòumiàn ▸ **to be behind (schedule)** 落后于 (计划) luòhòu yú (jìhuà) ▸ **to leave sth behind** (forget) 忘记 wàngjì

beige [beɪʒ] ADJ 灰棕色的 huīzōngsè de

Beijing [beɪˈdʒɪŋ] N 北京 Běijīng

Belgian [ˈbɛldʒən] I ADJ 比利时的 Bǐlìshí de II N [c] (person) 比利时人 Bǐlìshírén [个 gè]

Belgium [ˈbɛldʒəm] N 比利时 Bǐlìshí

believe [bɪ'liːv] vt 相信 xiāngxìn ▸ **to believe that ...** 认为… rènwéi…

bell [bɛl] N [c] (on door) 门铃 ménlíng [个 gè]

belong [bɪ'lɔŋ] vi ▸ **to belong to** [+ person] 属于 shǔyú; [+ club, society] 是…的成员 shì…de chéngyuán

belongings [bɪ'lɔŋɪŋz] NPL 所有物 suǒyǒuwù

below [bɪ'ləu] I PREP 1 (beneath) 在…之下 zài…zhīxià 2 (less than) 低于 dīyú II ADV 1 (beneath) 下面 xiàmiàn 2 (less) 以下 yǐxià ▸ **below zero** 零度以下 língdù yǐxià ▸ **temperatures below normal** or **average** 低于正常 (或) 平均温度 dīyú zhèngcháng (huò) píngjūn wēndù

belt [bɛlt] N [c] 腰带 yāodài [条 tiáo]

bench [bɛntʃ] N [c] 长椅 chángyǐ [条 tiáo]

bend [bɛnd] (pt, pp **bent**) I vt 使弯曲 shǐ wānqū II vi 1 屈身 qūshēn 2 [road, river] 转弯 zhuǎnwān III N [c] (in road, river) 弯 wān [个 gè] ▸ **bend down** vi 弯腰 wānyāo

beneath [bɪ'niːθ] I PREP 在…之下 zài…zhīxià II ADV 在下面 zài xiàmiàn

benefit [ˈbɛnɪfɪt] I N [c/u] 好处 hǎochù [个 gè] II vi 受益 shòuyì ▸ **to benefit from sth** 从某事中获益 cóng mǒushì zhōng huòyì

bent [bɛnt] I PT, PP of **bend** II ADJ 弯曲的 wānqū de

berth [bɜːθ] N [c] 卧铺 wòpù [张 zhāng]

beside [bɪ'saɪd] PREP 在…旁边 zài…pángbiān; see also **besides**

besides [bɪ'saɪdz] I ADV (also: **beside**) (in addition) 另外 lìngwài II PREP (also: **beside**) (in addition to, as well as) 除了…之外 chú…zhīwài

> **besides** 引出的事物包括在我们所谈及的事情之内。She is very intelligent besides being very beautiful.

不过，当我们说 **the only person besides** 另外某人时，或 **the only thing besides** 另外某物时，我们指在某一特定场合或上下文中的惟一其他人或物。*There was only one person besides me who knew where the money was hidden.* 介词 **except** 后面通常跟我们的陈述中惟独不包括的那些物，人，事的名词或代词形式。*She spoke to everyone except me.* **except** 也可作连词，引导从句或副词短语。*There was nothing more to do now except wait.* **except for** 还可以引出连词 **that, when** 或 **if** 引导的从句。*The house stayed empty, except when we came for the holidays.* **except for** 是用在名词前的介词短语，用来引出某人或某物，说明要不是有某人或某物，所陈述的便为全部事实。*Everyone was late except for Richard.*

best [best] **I** ADJ 最好的 zuìhǎo de **II** ADV 最 zuì **III** N ▸ **the best** 最好的事物 zuìhǎo de shìwù ▸ **the best thing to do is** 最好是…… zuìhǎo shì… ▸ **to do** or **try one's best** 尽某人最大的努力 jìn mǒurén zuìdà de nǔlì

bet [bet] (*pt, pp* **bet** or **betted**) **I** N [c] 赌注 dǔzhù [个 gè] **II** VT 1 ▸ **to bet sb 100 pounds that…** 就……和某人赌100英镑 jiù…hé mǒurén

dǔ yìbǎi yīngbàng 2 (*expect, guess*) ▸ **to bet (that)** 断定 duàndìng **III** VI ▸ **to be on** [+ *horse, result*] 下赌注于 xià dǔzhù yú

better ['betər] **I** ADJ 1 (*comparative of good*) 更好的 gènghǎo de 2 (*after an illness or injury*) 好转的 hǎozhuǎn de **II** ADV (*comparative of well*) 更好地 gènghǎo de ▸ **to get better** (*improve*) 变得更好 biàndé gènghǎo; [*sick person*] 渐愈 jiànyù ▸ **to feel better** 感觉好一些 gǎnjué hǎo yìxiē ▸ **I'd better go** or **I had better go** 我得走了 wǒ děi zǒule

between [bɪ'twi:n] **I** PREP 1 (*in space*) 在……中间 zài…zhōngjiān 2 (*in time*) 介于……之间 jièyú…zhījiān 3 (*in amount, age*) 介于……之间 jièyú…zhījiān **II** ADV ▸ **in between** (*in space*) 在……中间 zài…zhōngjiān; (*in time*) 期间 qíjiān ▸ **to choose between** 从中选一个 cóngzhōng xuǎn yīgè ▸ **to be shared/divided between people** 由大家一起分享／分用 yóu dàjiā yīqǐ fēnxiǎng/fēnyòng

beyond [bɪ'jɔnd] **I** PREP 1 在……的另一边 zài…de lìng yībiān 2 [+ *time, date, age*] 迟于 chíyú **II** ADV 1 (*in space*) 在另一边 zài lìng yībiān 2 (*in time*) 在……之后 zài…zhīhòu

Bible ['baɪbl] (*Rel*) N [c] ▸ **the Bible** 圣经 Shèngjīng 部 bù]

bicycle ['baɪsɪkl] N [c] 自行车 zìxíngchē [辆 liàng] ▸ **to ride a bicycle** 骑自行车 qí zìxíngchē

big [bɪg] ADJ 1 大的 dà de

2 [+ *change, increase, problem*] 大
的 dà de

bike [baɪk] N [c] **1** (*bicycle*) 自行车
zìxíngchē [辆 liàng] **2** (*motorcycle*)
摩托车 mótuōchē [部 bù]

bikini [bɪ'ki:nɪ] N [c] 比基尼 bǐjīní
[套 tào]

bill [bɪl] N [c] **1** (*requesting payment*)
账单 zhàngdān [个 gè] **2** (*Brit: in
restaurant*) 账单 zhàngdān [个 gè]
3 (*US: banknote*) 钞票 chāopiào
[张 zhāng]

billfold ['bɪlfəʊld] (*US*) N [c] 钱夹
qiánjiā [个 gè]

billion ['bɪljən] N [c] 十亿 shíyì

bin [bɪn] N [c] (*Brit*) 垃圾箱
lājīxiāng [个 gè]

binoculars [bɪ'nɒkjʊləz] N PL
双筒望远镜 shuāngtǒng
wàngyuǎnjìng

biochemistry [baɪə'kemɪstrɪ] N
[u] 生物化学 shēngwù huàxué

biography [baɪ'ɒɡrəfɪ] N [c] 传记
zhuànjì [部 bù]

biology [baɪ'ɒlədʒɪ] N [u] 生物学
shēngwùxué

bird [bə:d] N [c] 鸟 niǎo [只 zhī]

Biro® ['baɪərəʊ] (*Brit*) N [c] 圆珠笔
yuánzhūbǐ [支 zhī]

birth [bə:θ] N [c/u] 出生 chūshēng

birth certificate N [c] 出生证明
chūshēng zhèngmíng [个 gè]

birth control N [u] 节育 jiéyù

birthday ['bə:θdeɪ] I N [c] 生日
shēngrì [个 gè] II CPD [+ *cake, card,
present*] 生日 shēngrì

biscuit ['bɪskɪt] N [c] **1** (*Brit*) 饼干
bǐnggān [片 piàn] **2** (*US*) 小圆饼
xiǎoyuánbǐng [张 zhāng]

bishop ['bɪʃəp] N [c] 主教 zhǔjiào
[位 wèi]

bit [bɪt] I PT OF **bite** II N [c] **1** (*esp
Brit: piece*) 少许 shǎoxǔ **2** (*esp
Brit: part*) 部分 bùfen [个 gè]
3 (*Comput*) 比特 bǐtè [个 gè] ▸ **a
bit mad/dangerous** 有点疯狂/危
险 yǒudiǎn fēngkuáng/wēixiǎn
▸ **for a bit** (*inf*) 一会儿 yíhuìr
▸ **quite a bit** 好多 hǎoduō

bite [baɪt] (*pt* **bit**, *pp* **bitten** ['bɪtn])
I VT 咬 yǎo II N [c] **1** (*mouthful*) 一
口 yìkǒu **2** (*from dog*) 咬伤 yǎoshāng
(*from snake, mosquito*) 咬
痕 yǎohén [处 chù] ▸ **to bite one's
nails** 咬指甲 yǎo zhǐjiǎ

bitter ['bɪtə'] ADJ [+ *taste*] 苦
的 kǔ de

black [blæk] I ADJ **1** 黑色的 hēisè
de **2** [+ *person*] 黑人的 hēirén de
3 [+ *tea, coffee*] 不加牛奶的 bù jiā
niúnǎi de II N [u] 黑色 hēisè ▸ **black
out** (*faint*) 暂时失去知
觉 zànshí shīqù zhìjué

blackboard ['blækbɔ:d] N [c] 黑
板 hēibǎn [个 gè]

blackmail ['blækmeɪl] I N [u] 敲
诈 qiāozhà II VT 敲诈 qiāozhà

blade [bleɪd] N [c] 刀片 dāopiàn

blame [bleɪm] I N [u] (*for mistake,
crime*) 责备 zébèi II VT ▸ **to blame
sb for sth** 为某事责备某人 wèi
mǒushì zébèi mǒurén ▸ **to be to
blame (for sth)** 该 (为某事) 负责
任 gāi (wèi zérèn) 为 zérèn ▸ **to
blame sth on sb** 把某事归罪于某
人 bǎ mǒushì guīzuì yú mǒurén

blank [blæŋk] ADJ 空白的
kòngbái de

blanket ['blæŋkɪt] N [C] 毛毯 máotǎn [床 chuáng]

blast [blɑːst] N [C] (explosion) 爆炸 bàozhà [次 cì]

blaze [bleɪz] I N [C] 大火 dàhuǒ [场 chǎng] II VI (fire) 熊熊燃烧 xióngxióng ránshāo

blazer ['bleɪzə'] N [C] 上装 shàngzhuāng [件 jiàn]

bleed [bliːd] (pt, pp **bled** [bled]) VI 流血 liúxuè ▸ **my nose is bleeding** 我流鼻血了 wǒ liú bíxuè le

blender ['blendə'] N [C] 搅拌器 jiǎobànqì [个 gè]

bless [bles] VT (Rel) 赐福 cìfú ▸ **bless you!** (after sneeze) 上帝保佑! shàngdì bǎoyòu!

blew [bluː] PT OF **blow**

blind [blaɪnd] I ADJ 失明的 shīmíng de II N (for window) 向上卷的帘子 xiàng shàng juǎn de liánzi III **the blind** NPL (blind people) 盲人 mángrén ▸ **to go blind** 失明 shīmíng

blink [blɪŋk] VI 眨眼睛 zhǎ yǎnjīng

blister ['blɪstə'] N [C] 水泡 shuǐpào [个 gè]

blizzard ['blɪzəd] N [C] 暴风雪 bàofēngxuě [场 chǎng]

block [blɔk] I N [C] 1 街区 jiēqū [个 gè] 2 (of stone, wood, ice) 块 kuài II VT [+ entrance, road] 堵塞 dǔsè ▸ **block of flats** or (US) **apartment block** 公寓楼 gōngyùlóu ▸ **3 blocks from here** 离这里有3个街区那么远 lí zhèlǐ yǒu sāngè jiēqū nàme yuǎn

blond(e) [blɔnd] ADJ 1 [+ hair] 金色的 jīnsè de 2 [+ person] 金发的人 jīnfà de rén

blood [blʌd] N [U] 血液 xuèyè

blood pressure N [U] 血压 xuèyā ▸ **to have high/low blood pressure** 有高/低血压 yǒu gāo/dī xuèyā ▸ **to take sb's blood pressure** 量某人的血压 liáng mǒurén de xuèyā

blood test N [C] 验血 yànxuè [次 cì] ▸ **to have a blood test** 验血 yànxuè

blouse [blauz, US blaus] N [C] 女士衬衫 nǚshì chènshān [件 jiàn]

blow [bləu] (pt **blew**, pp **blown**) I N [C] 1 (punch) 拳打 quándǎ [顿 dùn] 2 打击 dǎjī [个 gè] II VT 1 [wind, sand, dust etc] 吹 chuī 2 [person] 吹气 chuīqì III VT [wind] 吹 chuī ▸ **to blow one's nose** 擤鼻子 xǐng bízi

▸ **blow away** I VT 吹走 chuīzǒu II VI 刮跑 guāpǎo ▸ **blow down** VT [+ tree, house] 刮倒 guādǎo ▸ **blow out** VT [+ flame, candle] 吹灭 chuīmiè ▸ **blow up** I VI (explode) 爆炸 bàozhà II VT 1 (destroy) 使爆炸 shǐ bàozhà 2 (inflate) 冲气 chōngqì

blow-dry ['bləudraɪ] N [C] 吹风定型 chuīfēng dìngxíng

blown [bləun] PP OF **blow**

blue [bluː] I ADJ 蓝色的 lánsè de II N 蓝色 lánsè III **blues** NPL (Mus) ▸ **the blues** 蓝调 lándiào

blunt [blʌnt] ADJ 1 (not sharp) 钝的 dùn de 2 [+ person, remark] 直率的 zhíshuài de

blush [blʌʃ] VI 脸红 liǎnhóng

board [bɔːd] I N 1 [c] (piece of wood) 木板 mùbǎn [块 kuài] 2 [c] (also: **noticeboard**) 公告板 gōnggàobǎn [块 kuài] 3 (also: **blackboard**) 黑板 hēibǎn [个 gè] 4 [c] (for chess) 盘 pán 5 [U] (at hotel) 膳食 shànshí II VT [+ ship, train, plane] 上 shàng III VI (frm: on ship, train, plane) 登上 dēngshang ▶ **board and lodging** 食宿 shísù ▶ **on board** 在船/车/飞机上 zài chuán/chē/fēijī shàng

boarding card ['bɔːdɪŋ-] N [c] 登机卡 dēngjīkǎ [个 zhāng]

boarding school N [c/U] 寄宿学校 jìsù xuéxiào [个 gè]

boast [bəust] I VI ▶ **to boast (about or of)** 说(关于某事的)大话 shuō (guānyú mǒushì de dàhuà) II VT 自夸 zìkuā [种 zhǒng]

boat [bəut] N [c] 1 (small vessel) 船 chuán [艘 sōu] 2 (ship) 轮船 lúnchuán [艘 sōu] ▶ **to go by boat** 乘船去 chéngchuán qù

body [ˈbɒdɪ] N [c] 1 身体 shēntǐ [个 gè] 2 [c] (corpse) 尸体 shītǐ [具 jù]

bodybuilding [ˈbɒdɪˌbɪldɪŋ] N [U] 健身 jiànshēn

bodyguard [ˈbɒdɪgɑːd] N [c] 保镖 bǎobiāo [个 gè]

boil [bɔɪl] I VT 1 [+ water] 烧开 shāokāi 2 [+ eggs, potatoes] 煮 zhǔ II VI [liquid] 沸腾 fèiténg III N (Med) 疖子 jiēzi ▶ **to boil a kettle** 烧开水 shāo kāishuǐ

boiler [ˈbɔɪləʳ] N [c] (device) 锅炉 guōlú [个 gè]

boiling (hot) [ˈbɔɪlɪŋ-] (inf) ADJ ▶ **I'm boiling (hot)** 我太热了 wǒ tài rè le

bolt [bəult] N [c] 1 (to lock door) 插销 chāxiāo [个 gè] 2 (used with nut) 螺钉 luódīng [颗 kē]

bomb [bɒm] I N [c] 炸弹 zhàdàn [颗 kē] II VT 轰炸 hōngzhà

bomber [ˈbɒməʳ] N [c] 1 (Aviat) 轰炸机 hōngzhàjī [架 jià] 2 (terrorist) 投放炸弹的人 tóufàng zhàdàn de rén [个 gè]

bombing [ˈbɒmɪŋ] N [c/U] 轰炸 hōngzhà [阵 zhèn]

bone [bəun] N 1 [c/U] 骨头 gǔtou [根 gēn] 2 [c] (in fish) 刺 cì [根 gēn]

bonfire [ˈbɒnfaɪəʳ] N [c] 1 (as part of a celebration) 篝火 gōuhuǒ [堆 duī] 2 (to burn rubbish) 火堆 huǒduī [个 gè]

bonnet [ˈbɒnɪt] N [c] (Brit: of car) 引擎罩 yǐnqíngzhào [个 gè]

bonus [ˈbəunəs] N [c] 1 (extra payment) 红利 hónglì [份 fèn] 2 (additional benefit) 额外收获 éwài shōuhuò [份 fèn]

book [buk] I N [c] 1 (novel etc) 书 shū [本 běn] 2 [of stamps, tickets] 册 cè II VT [+ ticket, table, seat, room] 预订 yùdìng ▶ **fully booked** 预订一空 yùdìng yīkōng ▶ **book into** (Brit) VT FUS [+ hotel] 登记入住 dēngjì rùzhù

bookcase [ˈbukkeɪs] N [c] 书橱 shūchú [个 gè]

booklet [ˈbuklɪt] N [c] 小册子 xiǎocèzi [本 běn]

bookshelf [ˈbukʃelf] N [c] 书架 shūjià [个 gè]

bookshop ['bukʃɔp] (Brit) N [c] 书店 shūdiàn [家 jiā]

bookstore ['bukstɔːr] (esp US) N = **bookshop**

boot [buːt] N [c] 1 靴子 xuēzi [双 shuāng]; (for football, walking) 鞋鞋 xié [双 shuāng] 2 (Brit: of car) 车后行李箱 chē hòu xínglǐxiāng [个 gè] ▸ **boot up** (Comput) I VT 使运行 shǐ yùnxíng II VI 开始运行 kāishǐ yùnxíng

border ['bɔːdər] N [c] 边界 biānjiè [条 tiáo]

bore [bɔːr] I PT of **bear** II VT 1 [+ hole] 钻 zuān 2 [+ oil well, tunnel] 开凿 kāizáo 3 [+ person] 使厌烦 shǐ yànfán ▸ **to be bored (with sth)** (对某事) 不感兴趣 (duì mǒushì) bùgǎn xìngqù

boring ['bɔːrɪŋ] ADJ 乏味的 fáwèi de

born [bɔːn] ADJ ▸ **to be born** [baby] 出生 chūshēng

borrow ['bɔrəu] VT 借 jiè

boss [bɔs] N [c] 1 (employer) 老板 lǎobǎn 2 (inf: leader) 领导 lǐngdǎo [位 wèi]

both [bəuθ] I ADJ 两者都 liǎngzhě dōu II PRON 1 (things) 两个 liǎnggè 2 (people) 两个 liǎnggè III CONJ ▸ **both A and B** A和B两者都人和B liǎngzhě dōu rén hé B liǎngzhě dōu ▸ **both of us went** or **we both went** 我们两个都去了 wǒmen liǎnggè dōuqù le

bother ['bɔðər] I VT 1 (worry) 烦扰 fánrǎo 2 (disturb) 打扰 dǎrǎo II VI 在乎 zàihu III N [u] (trouble) 麻烦 máfan ▸ **don't bother** 不用 búyòng le

bottle ['bɔtl] N 1 [c] 瓶子 píngzi [个 gè] 2 [c] (amount contained) 一瓶 yīpíng 3 [c] (baby's) 奶瓶 nǎipíng [个 gè] ▸ **a bottle of wine/milk** 一瓶葡萄酒/牛奶 yīpíng pútáojiǔ/niúnǎi

bottle opener N [c] 开瓶器 kāipíngqì [个 gè]

bottom ['bɔtəm] I N 1 [c] [of container, sea] 底部 dìbù [个 gè] 2 [c] [of page, list] 下端 xiàduān [个 gè] 3 [u/s] [of class, league] 最后一名 zuìhòu yīmíng 4 [c] [of hill, tree, stairs] 最底部 zuìdǐbù [个 gè] 5 [c] (buttocks) 臀部 túnbù [个 gè] II ADJ (lowest) 最下面的 zuì xiàmian de ▸ **at the bottom of** 在…的底部 zài…de dǐbù

bought [bɔːt] PT, PP of **buy**

bound [baund] ADJ ▸ **to be bound to do sth** (certain) 一定做某事 yīdìng zuò mǒushì

boundary ['baundrɪ] N [c] 边界 biānjiè [个 gè]

bow¹ [bəu] N [c] 1 (knot) 蝴蝶结 húdiéjié [个 gè] 2 (weapon) 弓 gōng [把 bǎ]

bow² [bəu] I VI (with head, body) 鞠躬 jūgōng II VT [+ head] 低头 dītóu

bowl [bəul] N [c] 1 碗 wǎn [个 gè] 2 (contents) 一碗的量 yī wǎn de liàng 3 (for washing clothes/dishes) 盆 pén [个 gè]

bowling ['bəulɪŋ] N [u] 保龄球 bǎolíngqiú ▸ **to go bowling** 打保龄球 dǎ bǎolíngqiú

bow tie [bəu-] N [c] 蝶形领结 diéxíng lǐngjié [个 gè]

box [bɔks] I N [c] 1 盒

子 hézi [个 gè] 2 (contents) 盒
hé子 3 (also: cardboard box)
纸箱 zhǐxiāng [个 gè] 4 (crate) 箱 xiāng
II VI (Sport) 拳击 quánjī

boxer ['bɒksə'] N [c] 拳击运动员
quánjī yùndòngyuán [位 wèi]

boxer shorts, boxers NPL 平角
裤 píngjiǎokù

boxing ['bɒksɪŋ] (Sport) N [U] 拳
击 quánjī

Boxing Day (Brit) N [c/U] 圣诞节
后的第一天，是公共假日
shèngdàn jié hòu de dì-yī tiān, shì
gōnggòng jiàrì

boy [bɔɪ] N [c] 1 (male child) 男孩
nánhái [个 gè] 2 (young man) 男青
年 nán qīngnián [个 gè]

boyfriend ['bɔɪfrɛnd] N [c] 男朋
友 nánpéngyou [个 gè]

bra [brɑ:] N [c] 胸罩 xiōngzhào
[件 jiàn]

bracelet ['breɪslɪt] N [c] 手镯
shǒuzhuó [只 zhī]

braid [breɪd] N [c] (US: plait) 辫子
biànzi [条 tiáo]

brain [breɪn] N [c] 脑 nǎo [个 gè]

brainy ['breɪnɪ] ADJ (inf) 聪明的
cōngmíng de

brake [breɪk] **I** N [c] (Aut) 刹车
shāchē [个 gè] **II** VI (driver, vehicle)
刹车 shāchē

branch [brɑ:ntʃ] N [c] 1 (of tree) 树
枝 shùzhī [条 tiáo] 2 (of shop) 分店
fēndiàn [家 jiā]; (of bank, company)
分支机构 fēnzhī jīgòu [个 gè]

brand [brænd] N [c] 牌子 páizi
[块 kuài]

brand-new ['brænd'nju:] ADJ 全
新的 quánxīn de

brandy ['brændɪ] N [c/U] 白兰地
酒 báilándìjiǔ [瓶 píng]

brass [brɑ:s] N [U] 铜 tóng

brave [breɪv] ADJ 1 勇敢的
yǒnggǎn de 2 [+ attempt, smile,
action] 英勇的 yīngyǒng de

Brazil [brə'zɪl] N 巴西 Bāxī

bread [brɛd] N [U] 面包 miànbāo

break [breɪk] (pt broke, pp
broken) **I** VT 1 打碎 dǎsuì 2 [+ leg,
arm] 弄断 nòngduàn 3 [+ promise,
contract] 违背 wéibèi 4 [+ law,
rule] 违反 wéifǎn 5 [+ record] 打
破 dǎpò **II** VI 1 破碎 pòsuì **III** N 1
(rest) 休息 xiūxi [次 cì] 2 (pause,
interval) 间歇 jiànxiē [个 gè] 3 [+
(fracture) 骨折 gǔzhé [次 cì] 4
(holiday) 休假 xiūjià [次 cì] ▸ to
break the news to sb 委婉地向
某人透露消息 wěiwǎn de xiàng
mǒurén tòulù xiāoxi ▸ to **take a
break** (for a few minutes) 休息一下
xiūxi yīxià ▸ **without a break** 连
续不断 liánxù bùduàn

▸ **break down** VI 坏掉 huàidiào

▸ **break in** VI (burglar) 破门而入
pòmén ér rù

▸ **break into** VT FUS [+ house] 强
行进入 qiángxíng jìnrù

▸ **break off** VT 1 [+ branch, piece
of chocolate] 折断 zhéduàn 2 [+
engagement, relationship] 断
绝 duànjué

▸ **break out** VI 1 (begin) 爆发
bàofā 2 (escape) 逃脱 táotuō

▸ **break up** VI 1 [+ couple, marriage]
破裂 pòliè 2 [+ meeting, party] 纷
纷离去 fēnfēn líqù **II** VT 1 [+ meeting,
demonstration] 驱散 qūsàn ▸ to
break up with sb 与某人分手

tóng mǒurén fēnshǒu

breakdown ['breɪkdaʊn] N [c]
1 (Aut) 故障 gùzhàng [个 gè] **2** [of
system, talks] 中断 zhōngduàn
[次 cì] **3** [of marriage] 破裂 pòliè
[个 gè] **4** (Med) (also: **nervous
breakdown**) 精神崩溃 jīngshén
bēngkuì [阵 zhèn] ▶ **to have a
breakdown** 精神崩溃 jīngshén
bēngkuì

breakfast ['brekfəst] N [c/u] 早
餐 zǎocān [顿 dùn]

break-in ['breɪkɪn] N [c] 闯入
chuǎngrù

breast [brest] N **1** [c] [of woman]
乳房 rǔfáng [个 gè] **2** [c/u] 胸脯肉
xiōngpúròu [块 kuài]

breath [breθ] N **1** [c/u] (intake of
air) 呼吸 hūxī [下 xià] **2** [u] (air
from mouth) 口气 kǒuqì ▶ **out of
breath** 上气不接下气 shàngqì
bùjiē xiàqì ▶ **bad breath** 口臭
kǒuchòu ▶ **to get one's breath
back** (Brit) 恢复正常呼吸 huīfù
zhèngcháng hūxī ▶ **to hold one's
breath** 屏住呼吸 bǐngzhù hūxī

breathe [briːð] I VT [+ air] 呼吸
hūxī II VI 呼吸 hūxī
▶ **breathe in** VI 吸入 xīrù
▶ **breathe out** VI 呼出 hūchū

breed [briːd] (pt, pp **bred** [bred])
I VT [+ animals] 繁殖 fánzhí II N [c]
品种 pǐnzhǒng [个 gè]

breeze [briːz] N [c] 微风 wēifēng
[阵 zhèn]

brewery ['bruːərɪ] N [c] 啤酒厂
píjiǔchǎng [家 jiā]

bribe [braɪb] I N [c] 贿赂 huìlù [种
zhǒng] II VT 行贿 xínghuì ▶ **to**

bribe sb to do sth 贿赂某人去做
某事 huìlù mǒurén qù zuò mǒushì

brick [brɪk] N [c/u] 砖 zhuān
[块 kuài]

bride [braɪd] N [c] 新娘 xīnniáng
[个 gè]

bridegroom ['braɪdgruːm] N [c]
新郎 xīnláng [个 gè]

bridesmaid ['braɪdzmeɪd] N [c]
伴娘 bànniáng [个 gè]

bridge [brɪdʒ] N **1** [c] 桥 qiáo [座
zuò] **2** [u] (Cards) 桥牌 qiáopái

brief [briːf] I ADJ **1** 短暂的
duǎnzàn de **2** [+ description, speech]
简短的 jiǎnduǎn de II **briefs** NPL
1 (for men) 男式三角内裤 nánshì
sānjiǎo nèikù **2** (for women) 女式
三角内裤 nǚshì sānjiǎo nèikù

briefcase ['briːfkeɪs] N [c] 公事包
gōngshìbāo [个 gè]

briefly ['briːflɪ] ADV 简短地
jiǎnduǎn de

bright [braɪt] ADJ **1** [+ light] 亮
的 liàng de **2** [+ person] 聪明的
cōngming de; [+ idea] 巧妙的
qiǎomiào de **3** [+ colour] 鲜亮的
xiānliàng de

brilliant ['brɪljənt] ADJ **1** [+ person,
mind] 才华横溢的 cáihuá héngyì
de **2** [+ idea, performance] 出色的
chūsè de **3** (esp Brit: inf: wonderful)
棒极了的 bàngjíle de

bring [brɪŋ] (pt, pp **brought**) VT
(with you) 带来 dàilái; (to sb) 拿
来 nálái
▶ **bring along** VT 随身携带
suíshēn xiédài
▶ **bring back** VT (return) 带回来
dài huílái

▶ **bring forward** VT [+ *meeting*] 提前 tíqián

▶ **bring round** VT [+ *unconscious person*] 使苏醒 shǐ sūxǐng

▶ **bring up** VT **1** [+ *child*] 抚养 fǔyǎng **2** [+ *question, subject*] 提出 tíchū

Britain ['brɪtən] (*also*: **Great Britain**) 英国 Yīngguó ▶ **in Britain** 在英国 zài Yīngguó

> **BRITAIN**
>
> **Britain** 或 **Great Britain** 由英格兰, 威尔士, 苏格兰和北爱尔兰组成。如指整个不列颠, 应慎用 **England** 和 **English**, 以免引起英格兰以外地区, 如苏格兰和北爱尔兰人的不满。**United Kingdom** 作为王国的官方称谓, 常简略为 **the UK**, 覆盖大不列颠及北爱尔兰。**British Isles** 包括大不列颠, 北爱尔兰, 爱尔兰共和国 (不隶属 **the UK**) 和四周岛屿。

British ['brɪtɪʃ] I ADJ 英国的 Yīngguó de II NPL ▶ **the British** 英国人 Yīngguórén

broad [brɔːd] ADJ 宽的 kuān de ▶ **in broad daylight** 光天化日之下 guāng tiān huà rì zhīxià

broadband ['brɔːdbænd] N (*Comput*) 宽带 kuāndài

broadcast ['brɔːdkɑːst] (*pt, pp* **broadcast**) I N [c] 广播 guǎngbō [段 duàn] II VT 播送 bōsòng

broccoli ['brɒkəlɪ] N [U] 花椰菜 huāyēcài

brochure ['brəʊʃjʊəʳ, US brəʊʃʊr] N [c] 小册子 xiǎocèzi [本 běn]

broil [brɔɪl] (*US*) VT 烤 kǎo

broke [brəʊk] I PT *of* **break** II ADJ (*inf*: *penniless*) 身无分文的 shēn wú fēnwén de

broken ['brəʊkən] I PP *of* **break** II ADJ **1** 破碎的 pòsuì de **2** [+ *machine*] 坏损的 huàisǔn de ▶ **a broken leg** 折断的腿 zhéduàn de tuǐ

bronchitis [brɒŋ'kaɪtɪs] N [U] 支气管炎 zhīqìguǎnyán

bronze [brɒnz] N **1** [U] (*metal*) 青铜 qīngtóng **2** [c] (*Sport*) (*also*: **bronze medal**) 铜牌 tóngpái [块 kuài]

brooch [brəʊtʃ] N [c] 胸针 xiōngzhēn [枚 méi]

brother ['brʌðəʳ] N [c] 兄弟 xiōngdì [个 gè]; (*elder*) 哥哥 gēge [个 gè]; (*younger*) 弟弟 dìdi [个 gè]

brother-in-law ['brʌðərɪnlɔː] N [c] (*older sister's husband*) 姐夫 jiěfu [个 gè]; (*younger sister's husband*) 妹夫 mèifu [个 gè]; (*husband's older brother*) 大伯子 dàbǎizi [个 gè]; (*husband's younger brother*) 小叔子 xiǎoshūzi [个 gè]; (*wife's older brother*) 内兄 nèixiōng [个 gè]; (*wife's younger brother*) 内弟 nèidì [个 gè]

brought [brɔːt] PT, PP *of* **bring**

brown [braʊn] I ADJ **1** 褐色的 hèsè de; [+ *hair, eyes*] 棕色的 zōngsè de **2** (*tanned*) 晒黑的 shàihēi de II N [U] (*colour*) 褐色 hèsè

browse [brauz] VI (on the internet) 浏览 liúlǎn

bruise [bruːz] N [c] 青瘀 qīngyū [块 kuài]

brush [brʌʃ] I N [c] 1 刷子 shuāzi [把 bǎ]; (for hair) 发刷 fàshuā [把 bǎ]; (artist's) 画笔 huàbǐ [支 zhī] II VT 1 [+ carpet etc] 刷 shuā 2 [+ hair] 梳 shū ▸ **to brush one's teeth** 刷牙 shuā yá

Brussels sprout [ˈbrʌslz-] N [c] 芽甘蓝 yágānlán [个 gè]

bubble [bʌbl] N [c] 泡 pào [个 gè]

bubble gum N [U] 泡泡糖 pàopàotáng

bucket [ˈbʌkɪt] N [c] 1 (pail) 桶 tǒng [个 gè] 2 (contents) 一桶 yītǒng

buckle [bʌkl] I N [c] (on shoe, belt) 扣环 kòuhuán [个 gè] II VT [+ shoe, belt] 扣住 kòuzhù

Buddhism [ˈbudɪzəm] N [U] 佛教 Fójiào

Buddhist [ˈbudɪst] I ADJ 佛教的 Fójiào de II N [c] 佛教徒 Fójiàotú [个 gè]

buffet [ˈbufeɪ, US buˈfeɪ] N [c] 1 (in station) 餐厅 cāntīng [个 gè] 2 (food) 自助餐 zìzhùcān [顿 dùn]

bug [bʌg] N [c] 1 (esp US: insect) 虫子 chóngzi [只 zhī] 2 (Comput: in program) 故障 gùzhàng [种 zhǒng] 3 (inf: virus) 病菌 bìngjūn [种 zhǒng]

build [bɪld] (pt, pp built) I N [c/U] [of person] 体格 tǐgé [种 zhǒng] II VT [+ house, machine] 建造 jiànzào

▸ **build up** VI (accumulate) 积

聚 jījù

builder [ˈbɪldəʳ] N [c] (worker) 建筑工人 jiànzhù gōngrén [位 wèi]

building [ˈbɪldɪŋ] N [c] 建筑物 jiànzhùwù [座 zuò]

built [bɪlt] I PT, PP of **build** II ADJ ▸ **well-/heavily-built** [+ person] 体态优美/粗笨的 tǐtài yōuměi/cūbèn de

bulb [bʌlb] N [c] 1 (Elec) 电灯泡 diàndēngpào [个 gè] 2 (Bot) 球茎 qiújīng [个 gè]

Bulgaria [bʌlˈgɛərɪə] N 保加利亚 Bǎojiālìyà

bull [bul] N [c] 公牛 gōngniú [头 tóu]

bullet [ˈbulɪt] N [c] 子弹 zǐdàn [发 fā]

bulletin [ˈbulɪtɪn] N [c] 公告 gōnggào [个 gè]

bulletin board c 1 (Comput) 公共留言板 gōnggòng liúyánbǎn 2 (US: noticeboard) 布告栏 bùgàolán

bully [ˈbulɪ] I N [c] 恃强凌弱者 shìqiáng língruò zhě [个 gè] II VT 欺侮 qīwǔ

bum [bʌm] (inf) N [c] 1 (Brit: backside) 屁股 pìgu [个 gè] 2 (esp US: tramp) 流浪汉 liúlànghàn [个 gè]

bump [bʌmp] I N [c] 1 肿包 zhǒngbāo [个 gè] 2 (on road) 隆起物 lóngqǐwù [个 gè] II VT (strike) 碰 pèng

▸ **bump into** VT FUS 1 [+ obstacle, person] 撞到 zhuàngdào 2 (inf: meet) 碰见 pèngjiàn

bumpy [ˈbʌmpɪ] ADJ 崎岖不平的 qíqū bùpíng de

bunch [bʌntʃ] N [C] 1 (of flowers)
束 shù 2 (of keys, bananas, grapes)
串 chuàn

bungalow ['bʌŋɡələu] N [C] 平房
píngfáng [间 jiān]

bunk [bʌŋk] N [C] 铺位 pùwèi

burger ['bəːɡəʳ] N [C] 汉堡包
hànbǎobāo [个 gè]

burglar ['bəːɡləʳ] N [C] 窃贼 qièzéi
[个 gè]

burglary ['bəːɡlərɪ] N 1 [C] (act) 盗
窃 dàoqiè [次 cì] 2 [U] (crime) 盗窃
罪 dàoqièzuì

burn [bəːn] I vt 1 焚烧 fénshāo
2 [+ fuel] 燃烧 ránshāo II vi 1 (fire,
flame) 燃烧 ránshāo 2 (house,
car) 烧着 shāozháo III N [C] 烧
伤 shāoshāng [次 cì] ▸ **I've burnt
myself!** 我把自己烫伤了！wǒ bǎ
zìjǐ tàngshāng le
▸ **burn down** vi (house) 烧毁
shāohuǐ

burnt [bəːnt] PT, PP of **burn**

burst [bəːst] (pt, pp **burst**) vi (pipe,
tyre) 爆裂 bàoliè ▸ **to burst into
flames** 突然着火 túrán zháohuǒ
▸ **to burst into tears** 突然大哭
起来 túrán dàkū qǐlái ▸ **to burst
out laughing** 突然大笑起来 túrán
dàxiào qǐlái

bury ['bɛrɪ] vt 1 掩埋 yǎnmái
2 [+ dead person] 埋葬 máizàng

bus [bʌs] N [C] 公共汽车
gōnggòng qìchē [辆 liàng]

bus driver N [C] 公共汽车司机
gōnggòng qìchē sījī [位 wèi]

bush [buʃ] N [C] 灌木 guànmù

[棵 kē]

business ['bɪznɪs] N 1 [C] (firm) 公
司 gōngsī [家 jiā] 2 [U] (occupation)
商业 shāngyè 3 [U] (trade) 生意
shēngyì ▸ **to be away on business**
出差 chūchāi ▸ **to do business
with sb** 和某人做生意 hé mǒurén
zuò shēngyì

businessman ['bɪznɪsmən]
(pl **businessmen**) N [C] 商人
shāngrén [个 gè]

businesswoman ['bɪznɪswumən]
(pl **businesswomen**) N [C] 女商人
nǚ shāngrén [个 gè]

bus station N [C] 公共汽车
gōnggòng qìchē chēzhàn [个 gè]

bus stop N [C] 公共汽车站
gōnggòng qìchē zhàn [个 gè]

bust [bʌst] N [C] 胸部 xiōngbù

busy ['bɪzɪ] ADJ 1 忙的 máng de
2 [+ shop, street] 繁忙的 fánmáng
de 3 [+ schedule, time, day] 忙碌的
mánglù de 4 (esp US) (Tel) 占线的
zhànxiàn de ▸ **I'm busy** 我正忙着
呢 wǒ zhèng mángzhe ne

KEYWORD

but [bʌt] CONJ (yet, however) 但
是 dànshì ▸ **I'd love to come, but
I'm busy** 我想来，但是有事
xiǎnglái, dànshì yǒushì ▸ **not
only ... but also** 不但…而且
bùdàn…érqiě

butcher ['butʃəʳ] N [C] 1 肉商
ròushāng 2 (shop) (also:
butcher's) 肉铺 ròupù [个 gè]

butter ['bʌtəʳ] N [C] 黄油

huángyóu

butterfly ['bʌtəflaɪ] N [c] 蝴蝶 húdié [只 zhī]

button ['bʌtn] N [c] 1 (on clothes) 钮扣 niǔkòu [颗 kē] 2 (on machine) 按钮 ànniǔ [个 gè] 3 (US: badge) 徽章 huīzhāng [个 gè]

buy [baɪ] (pt, pp bought) I vт 买 mǎi II N [c] (purchase) 所买之物 suǒ mǎi zhī wù [件 jiàn] ▸ **to buy sb sth** 给某人买某物 gěi mǒurén mǎi mǒuwù ▸ **to buy sth off** or **from sb** 从某人处购买某物 cóng mǒurén chù gòumǎi mǒuwù

buzz [bʌz] vɪ (insect, machine) 发出嗡嗡声 fāchū wēngwēngshēng

○ **KEYWORD**

by [baɪ] I PREP 1 (referring to cause, agent) 被 bèi ▸ **a painting by Picasso** 毕加索的画 Bìjiāsuǒ de huà ▸ **surrounded by a fence** 由篱笆围着 yóu líba wéizhe

2 (referring to manner, means) ▸ **by bus/car/train** 乘公共汽车/汽车/火车 chéng gōnggòng qìchē/qìchē/huǒchē ▸ **to pay by cheque** 以支票支付 yǐ zhīpiào zhīfù ▸ **by moonlight/candlelight** 借助月光/烛光 jièzhù yuèguāng/zhúguāng

3 (via, through) 经由 jīngyóu ▸ **he came in by the back door** 他从后门进来 tā cóng hòumén jìnlai

4 (close to, beside) 靠近 kào jìn ▸ **he was standing by the door** 他正站在门边 tā zhèng zhànzài ménbiān ▸ **the house by the river** 河边的房子 hébiān de fángzi

5 (with times, dates, years) 以前 yǐqián ▸ **by 4 o'clock** 4点以前 sìdiǎn yǐqián ▸ **by April 7** 4月7号以前 sìà yuè qī hào yǐqián ▸ **by now/then** 到如今/那时 dào rújīn/nàshí

6 (during) ▸ **by day/night** 在白天/晚上 zài báitiān/wǎnshang

7 (specifying degree of change) 相差 xiāngchà ▸ **crime has increased by 10 per cent** 犯罪率上升了10% fànzuìlǜ shàngshēng le bǎi fēn zhī shí

8 (in measurements) ▸ **a room 3 metres by 4** 一间长3米宽4米的房间 yī jiān cháng sān mǐ kuān sì mǐ de fángjiān

9 (Math) ▸ **to divide/multiply by 3** 被3除/乘 bèi sān chú/chéng

10 ▸ **by myself/himself** etc (unaided) 我/他 {等} 自己 wǒ/tā {děng} zìjǐ; (alone) 我/他 {等} 单独 wǒ/tā {děng} dāndú

II ADV see **go by**, **pass by** etc

如果你说 I'll be home by ten o'clock，你的意思是你要在10点或10点以前到家，但绝不会晚于10点。如果你说 I'll be home before ten o'clock，你的意思是10点是你到家的最晚时间，你可能比点以前就到家了。如果你说 I'll be at home until ten o'clock，你的意思是10点以前你会在家里，但10点以后就不在了。当我们谈论某人或某事或剧本，导演了一部电影，或了一部乐曲或画了一幅画时，我们说一部作品是 **by** 那个人或是 **written by** 那个人。 *a collection of piano pieces by Mozart* 当我们谈到某人给你写信或留言时，我们说信或留言是 *from* 那个人。 *He received a letter from his brother.*

C

bye(-bye) ['baɪ('baɪ)] (*inf*) INT 再见 zàijiàn

cab [kæb] N [c] 出租车 chūzūchē [辆 liàng]

cabbage ['kæbɪdʒ] N [c/u] 卷心菜 juǎnxīncài [头 tóu]

cabin ['kæbɪn] N [c] **1** (*on ship*) 船舱 chuáncāng [个 gè] **2** (*on plane*) 机舱 jīcāng [个 gè]

cable ['keɪbl] N **1** [c/u] (*rope*) 缆绳 lǎnshéng [根 gēn] **2** [c/u] (*Elec*) 电缆 diànlǎn [根 gēn]

cable television N [u] 有线电视 yǒuxiàn diànshì

cactus ['kæktəs] (*pl* **cactuses** *or* **cacti** ['kæktaɪ]) N [c] 仙人掌 xiānrénzhǎng [棵 kē]

cafeteria [kæfɪ'tɪərɪə] N [c] 自助餐厅 zìzhù cāntīng [个 gè]

cage [keɪdʒ] N [c] 笼子 lóngzi [个 gè]

cagoule [kə'gu:l] N [c] 连帽防雨
长夹克衫 liánmào fángyǔ cháng
jiákèshān [件 jiàn]

cake [keɪk] N [c/u] 蛋糕 dàngāo
[块 kuài], (small) 糕点 gāodiǎn
[块 kuài]

calculate ['kælkjuleɪt] VT 计
算 jìsuàn

calculation [kælkju'leɪʃən] N
[c/u] (Math) 计算 jìsuàn

calculator ['kælkjuleɪtə'] N [c]
计算器 jìsuànqì [个 gè]

calendar ['kæləndə'] N [c] 日历
rìlì [本 běn]

calf [kɑ:f] (pl calves) N [c] 1 小
牛 xiǎoniú [头 tóu] 2 (Anat) 腿肚
tuǐdù [个 gè]

call [kɔ:l] I VT 1 (name) 为…取名
wèi…qǔmíng 2 (address as) 称
呼 chēnghu 3 (label as) 说成
shuōchéng shì 4 (shout) 喊
hǎn 5 (Tel) 打电话 dǎ diànhuà
6 (summon) 召唤 zhàohuàn II VI 1
(telephone) 打电话 dǎ diànhuà
III N 1 [c] (shout) 大喊 dà hǎn 2
[c] (Tel) 打电话 dǎ diànhuà 3 [c]
(visit) 探访 tànfǎng [次 cì] ▶to
be called sth [person] 被叫某
名 bèijiào mǒumíng; [object] 被
称为某物 bèi chēngwéi mǒuwù
▶who's calling? (Tel) 请问是谁?
qǐngwèn shìshuí? ▶to make a
phone call 打电话 dǎ diànhuà
▶to give sb a call 打电话给某人
dǎ diànhuà gěi mǒurén
▶call back I VI (Tel) 再打电话 zài
dǎ diànhuà II VT (Tel) 给…回电话
gěi…huí diànhuà
▶call off VT 取消 qǔxiāo

call centre, (US) **call center**
N [c] (Tel) 电话中心 diànhuà
zhōngxīn [个 gè]

calm [kɑ:m] ADJ 1 冷静的 lěngjìng
de 2 (+ sea) 平静的 píngjìng de
▶calm down I VT [+ person,
animal] 使平静 shǐ píngjìng II VI
[person] 平静下来 píngjìng xiàlái

calorie ['kælərɪ] N [c] 卡路里
kǎlùlǐ

calves [kɑ:vz] NPL of **calf**

Cambodia [kæm'bəudɪə] N 柬埔
寨 Jiǎnpǔzhài

camcorder ['kæmkɔ:də'] N [c]
摄像放像机 shèxiàng fàngxiàng
jī [部 bù]

came [keɪm] PT of **come**

camel ['kæməl] N [c] 骆驼 luòtuo
[头 tóu]

camera ['kæmərə] N [c] 1 (Phot)
照相机 zhàoxiàngjī [架 jià] 2 (Cine,
TV) 摄影机 shèyǐngjī [部 bù]

cameraman ['kæmərəmæn]
(pl **cameramen**) N [c] 摄影师
shèyǐngshī [位 wèi]

camp [kæmp] N 1 (for refugees,
prisoners, soldiers) 营 yíng II VI 扎
营 zhāyíng ▶to go camping 外出
露营 wàichū lùyíng

campaign [kæm'peɪn] N [c] 运动
yùndòng [场 chǎng]

camper ['kæmpə'] N [c] 1 (person)
野营者 yěyíngzhě [个 gè] 2 (also:
camper van) 野营车 yěyíngchē
[辆 liàng]

camping ['kæmpɪŋ] N [u] 野
营 yěyíng

campsite ['kæmpsaɪt] N [c] 营地
yíngdì [个 gè]

campus ['kæmpəs] N [C] 校园 xiàoyuán [个 gè]

can¹ [kæn] N [C] **1** (for food, drinks) 罐头 guàntou [个 gè]; (for petrol, oil) 罐 guàn [个 gè] **2** (contents) 一听所装的量 yītīng suǒ zhuāng de liàng [听 tīng] **3** (contents and container) 一罐 yíguàn

 KEYWORD

can² [kæn] (negative **cannot**, **can't**, conditional, pt **could**) AUX VB **1** (be able to) 能 néng ▶can I help you? (in shop) 您要买点儿什么？nín yào mǎidiǎnr shénme?; (in general) 我能帮你吗 wǒ néng bāngnǐ ma? ▶you can do it if you try 如果试验的话你会是能做的 rúguǒ shìshì de huà nǐ shì néng zuò de ▶I can't hear/see anything 我什么也听/看不见 wǒ shénme yě tīng/kàn bùjiàn **2** (know how to) 会 huì ▶I can swim/drive 我会游泳/开车 wǒ huì yóuyǒng/kāichē **3** (permission, requests) 可以 kěyǐ ▶can I use your phone? 我可以用你的电话吗？wǒ kěyǐ yòng nǐde diànhuà ma? ▶can you help me? 你可以帮我一下吗？nǐ kěyǐ bāng wǒ yíxià ma? **4** (possibility) 可能 kěnéng ▶he can be very unpleasant 他有时会非常不高兴 tā yǒushí huì fēicháng bù gāoxìng

can, **could** 和 **be able to** 都是用来表示某人有能力做某事，后接原形动词。

can 或 **be able to** 的现在式都可以指现在，但 **can** 更为常用。They can all read and write...The snake is able to catch small mammals. **could** 或 **be able to** 的过去式可用来指过去。**will** 或 **shall** 加 **be able to** 则用于表示将来。指在某一特定时间能够做某事，用 **be able to**。After treatment he was able to return to work. **can** 和 **could** 用于表示可能性。**could** 指的是某个特定情况下的可能性，而 **can** 则表示一般情况下的可能性。Many jobs could be lost...Too much salt can be harmful. 在谈论过去的时候，使用 **could have** 加过去分词形式。It could have been much worse. 在谈论规则或法律许可的时候，用 **can** 表示现在，用 **could** 表示过去。They can leave at any time. 注意，当表示请求时，**can** 和 **could** 两者都可。Can I have a drink?...Could we put the fire on? 但表示建议时只能使用 **could**。You could phone her and ask.

Canada ['kænədə] N 加拿大 Jiānádà

Canadian [kə'neɪdɪən] I ADJ 加拿大的 Jiānádà de II N [C] (person) 加拿大人 Jiānádàrén [个 gè]

canal [kə'næl] N 运河 yùnhé

[条 tiáo]

cancel ['kænsəl] VT 取消 qǔxiāo

cancer ['kænsə'] N 1 [c/u] (Med) 癌症 áizhèng [种 zhǒng] 2 (Astrol) ▶ Cancer [U] (sign) 巨蟹座 Jùxiè Zuò

candidate ['kændɪdeɪt] N [c] 1 (for job) 候选人 hòuxuǎnrén [位 wèi] 2 (in exam) 报考者 bàokǎozhě [个 gè]

candle ['kændl] N [c] 蜡烛 làzhú [根 gēn]

candy ['kændɪ] (US) N [c/u] 糖果 tángguǒ [块 kuài]

canned [kænd] ADJ 罐装的 guànzhuāng de

cannot ['kænɔt] = **can not**

canoe [kə'nu:] N [c] 独木船 dúmùchuán [艘 sōu]

canoeing [kə'nu:ɪŋ] N [U] 划独木船 huá dúmùchuán

can opener [-'əupnə'] N [c] 开罐器 kāi guànqì [个 gè]

can't [kɑ:nt] = **can not**

canteen [kæn'ti:n] N [c] 食堂 shítáng [个 gè]

canvas ['kænvəs] N [U] 帆布 fānbù

cap [kæp] N [c] 帽 mào [顶 dǐng]

capable ['keɪpəbl] ADJ 有能力的 yǒu nénglì de ▶ **to be capable of doing sth** 有做某事的能力 yǒu zuò mǒushì de nénglì

capacity [kə'pæsɪtɪ] N [s] (of container, ship) 容量 róngliàng; (of stadium, theatre) 可容纳人数 kě róngnà rénshù

capital ['kæpɪtl] N 1 [c] (city) 首都 shǒudū [个 gè] 2 [U] (money)

资本 zīběn 3 [c] (also: **capital letter**) 大写字母 dàxiě zìmǔ [个 gè] ▶ **capital R/L** etc 大写字母 R/L 〔等〕 dàxiě zìmǔ R/L (děng)

capitalism ['kæpɪtəlɪzəm] N [U] 资本主义 zīběn zhǔyì

Capricorn ['kæprɪkɔ:n] N [U] (sign) 摩羯座 Mójié Zuò

captain ['kæptɪn] N [c] 1 (of ship) 船长 chuánzhǎng [位 wèi] 2 (of plane) 机长 jīzhǎng [位 wèi] 3 (of team) 队长 duìzhǎng [个 gè]

capture ['kæptʃə'] VT (+ animal) 捕获 bǔhuò; (+ person) 俘虏 fúlǔ

car [kɑ:'] N [c] 1 (Aut) 汽车 qìchē [辆 liàng] 2 (US) (Rail) 车厢 chēxiāng [节 jié] ▶ **by car** 乘汽车 chéng qìchē

caravan ['kærəvæn] N [c] (Brit) 活动住房 huódòng zhùfáng [处 chù]

card [kɑ:d] N 1 [c] 卡片 kǎpiàn [张 zhāng] 2 [c] (playing card) 扑克牌 pūkèpái [张 zhāng] 3 [c] (greetings card) 贺卡 hèkǎ [张 zhāng] 4 [c] (also: **business card**) 名片 míngpiàn [张 zhāng] 5 [c] (bank card, credit card) 信用卡 xìnyòngkǎ [张 zhāng] ▶ **to play cards** 打牌 dǎpái

cardigan ['kɑ:dɪgən] N [c] 开襟毛衣 kāijīn máoyī [件 jiàn]

care [kɛə'] I N [U] 照顾 zhàogù II VI 关心 guānxīn ▶ **with care** 小心 xiǎoxīn ▶ **take care!** (saying goodbye) 慢走! mànzǒu! ▶ **to take care of sb** 照顾某人 zhàogù mǒurén ▶ **to take care of sth** (+ possession, clothes) 保管某

物 bǎoguǎn mǒuwù; [+ *problem, situation*]
处理某种情况 chǔlǐ mǒuwù
▶ I don't care 我不在乎 wǒ bù zàihu
▶ care about VT FUS [+ *person, thing, idea*] 关心 guānxīn
▶ care for VT FUS 照顾 zhàogù

career [kə'rɪər] N [c] 1 (*job, profession*) 事业 shìyè [项 xiàng] 2 (*working life*) 生涯 shēngyá [个 gè]

careful ['keəful] ADJ 1 小心的 xiǎoxīn de 2 [+ *work, thought, analysis*] 仔细的 zǐxì de ▶ (be) **careful!** 小心! xiǎoxīn! ▶ to be **careful with sth** [+ *money*] 谨慎地使用某物 jǐnshèn de shǐyòng mǒuwù; [+ *fragile object*] 小心对待某物 xiǎoxīn duìdài mǒuwù

carefully ['keəfəlɪ] ADV 1 (*cautiously*) 小心地 xiǎoxīn de 2 (*methodically*) 用心地 yòngxīn de

careless ['keəlɪs] ADJ [+ *person, worker*] 粗心的 cūxīn de; [+ *driving*] 疏忽的 shūhu de; [+ *mistake*] 疏忽造成的 shūhu zàochéng de ▶ **it was careless of him to let the dog out** 他真不当心，把狗放了出去 tā zhēn bù dāngxīn, bǎ gǒu fàng le chūqù

caretaker ['keəteɪkər] N [c] (*Brit*) 看门人 kānménrén [个 gè]

car ferry N [c] 汽车渡轮 qìchē dùlún [艘 sōu]

cargo ['kɑːgəu] (*pl* **cargoes**) N [c/u] 货物 huòwù [批 pī]

car hire (*Brit*) N [u] 汽车出租 qìchē chūzū

Caribbean [kærɪ'biːən] N ▶ **the Caribbean (Sea)** 加勒比海 Jiālèbǐhǎi

carnival ['kɑːnɪvl] N 1 [c/u] (*festival*) 狂欢节 kuánghuānjié [个 gè] 2 [c] (*US*) 游艺团 yóuyìtuán [个 gè]

car park (*Brit*) N [c] 停车场 tíngchēchǎng [处 chù]

carpenter ['kɑːpɪntər] N [c] 木匠 mùjiàng [个 gè]

carpet ['kɑːpɪt] N [c] (*fitted*) 地毯 dìtǎn [条 tiáo]; (*rug*) 小地毯 xiǎo dìtǎn [块 kuài]

car rental N [u] 汽车出租 qìchē chūzū

carriage ['kærɪdʒ] N [c] (*Brit*) (*Rail*) 车厢 chēxiāng [节 jié]

carrier bag (*Brit*) N [c] 购物袋 gòuwùdài [个 gè]

carrot ['kærət] N [c/u] 胡萝卜 húluóbo [根 gēn]

carry ['kærɪ] I VT [+ *person*] 提 bào; (*by hand with the arm down*) 提 tí; (*on one's back*) 背 bēi; (*by hand*) 拿 ná 2 (*transport*) [*ship, plane*] 运载 yùnzài
▶ **carry on** I VI 继续 jìxù II VT (*continue*) [+ *work, tradition*] 继续做 jìxù zuò ▶ to **carry on with sth** 继续做某事 jìxù zuò mǒushì ▶ to **carry on doing sth** 继续做某事 jìxù zuò mǒushì
▶ **carry out** VT [+ *order, instruction*] 执行 zhíxíng

cart [kɑːt] N [c] 1 大车 dàchē [辆 liàng] 2 (*US*) (*also*: **shopping cart**) 手推车 shǒutuīchē [辆 liàng]

carton [kɑː'tən] N (*esp US*:

cardboard box) 纸箱 zhǐxiāng [个 gè] 2 (of milk, juice, yoghurt) 容器 róngqì [个 gè]

cartoon [kɑːˈtuːn] N [c] 1 (drawing) 漫画 mànhuà [幅 fú] 2 (Brit: comic strip) 系列幽默picture xìliè yōumò huà [套 tào] 3 (animated) 卡通片 kǎtōngpiàn [部 bù]

cartridge [ˈkɑːtrɪdʒ] N [c] 1 (for gun) 弹壳 dànké [个 gè] 2 (for printer) 墨盒 mòhé [个 gè]

case [keɪs] N 1 [c] (instance) 情况 qíngkuàng [种 zhǒng] 2 [c] (container) 盒子 hézi [个 gè] 3 [c] (Brit) (also: suitcase) 行李箱 xínglíxiāng [个 gè] ▶ lower/upper case 小/大写 xiǎo/dàxiě ▶ in case he comes 以防万一他会来 yǐfáng wànyī tā huì lái ▶ in any case 无论如何 wúlùn rúhé ▶ just in case 以防万一 yǐfáng wànyī ▶ in that case 既然是那样 jìrán shì nàyàng

cash [kæʃ] I N [u] 1 (notes and coins) 现金 xiànjīn 2 (money) 现款 xiànkuǎn II VT 兑现 duìxiàn ▶ to pay (in) cash 付现金 fù xiànjīn

cashew [kæˈʃuː] N [c] (also: cashew nut) 腰果 yāoguǒ [颗 kē]

cashier [kæˈʃɪə] N [c] 出纳员 chūnàyuán [个 gè]

casino [kəˈsiːnəʊ] N [c] 赌场 dǔchǎng [个 gè]

cassette [kæˈsɛt] N [c] 磁带 cídài [盘 pán]

cast [kɑːst] (pt, pp cast) N [c] (Theat) 演员表 yǎnyuánbiǎo [份 fèn]

castle [ˈkɑːsl] N [c] 城堡

chéngbǎo [座 zuò]

casual [ˈkæʒjuːl] ADJ 1 (chance) 漫不经心的 màn bù jīngxīn de 2 (unconcerned) 随便的 suíbiàn de 3 (informal) 非正式的 fēizhèngshì de

casualty [ˈkæʒjultɪ] N [c] (of war, accident: injured) 伤病员 shāngbìngyuán [个 gè]; (dead) 伤亡人员 shāngwáng rényuán [批 pī] 2 (Brit: in hospital) 急诊室 jízhěnshì

cat [kæt] N [c] 猫 māo [只 zhī]

catalogue, (US) catalog [ˈkætəlɒg] N [c] 1 (for mail order) 目录 mùlù [个 gè] 2 (of exhibition) 目录 mùlù [个 gè] 3 (of library) 书目 shūmù [个 gè]

catastrophe [kəˈtæstrəfɪ] N [c] 大灾难 dàzāinàn [场 chǎng]

catch [kætʃ] (pt, pp caught) VT 1 (+ animal, fish) 捕获 bǔhuò; (+ thief, criminal) 抓获 zhuāhuò 2 (+ ball) 接 jiē 3 (+ bus, train, plane) 赶上 gǎnshang 4 (discover) (+ person) 发现 fāxiàn 5 (+ flu, illness) 染上 rǎnshàng ▶ to catch sb doing sth 撞见某人做某事 zhuàngjiàn mǒurén zuò mǒushì ▶ catch up VI 追上 zhuīshang

category [ˈkætɪgərɪ] N [c] 种类 zhǒnglèi [个 gè]

catering [ˈkeɪtərɪŋ] N [u] 饮食业 yǐnshíyè

cathedral [kəˈθiːdrəl] N [c] 大教堂 dàjiàotáng [个 gè]

Catholic [ˈkæθəlɪk] I ADJ 天主教的 Tiānzhǔjiào de II N [c] 天主教徒 Tiānzhǔjiào tú [个 gè]

cattle ['kætl] NPL 牛 niú

caught [kɔːt] PT, PP of **catch**

cauliflower ['kɔlɪflauə'] N [c/u] 菜花 càihuā [头 tóu]

cause [kɔːz] I N [c] 起因 qǐyīn [个 gè] II VT 导致 dǎozhì ▶**to cause sb to do sth** 促使某人做某事 cùshǐ mǒurén zuò mǒushì ▶**to cause sth to happen** 导致某事发生 dǎozhì mǒushì fāshēng

cautious ['kɔːʃəs] ADJ 谨慎的 jǐnshèn de

cave [keɪv] N [c] 山洞 shāndòng [个 gè]

CD N ABBR (= **compact disc**) 激光唱片 jīguāng chàngpiàn

CD player N [c] 激光唱机 jīguāng chàngjī [部 bù]

CD-ROM [siːdiːˈrɔm] N ABBR (= **compact disc read-only memory**) 光盘只读存储器 guāngpán zhǐdú cúnchǔ qì ▶ **on CD-ROM** 光盘版 guāngpán bǎn

ceiling ['siːlɪŋ] N [c] 天花板 tiānhuābǎn [块 kuài]

celebrate ['selɪbreɪt] VT 庆祝 qìngzhù

celebrity [sɪˈlebrɪtɪ] N [c] 名人 míngrén [位 wèi]

cell [sel] N [c] **1** (Bio) 细胞 xìbāo [个 gè] **2** (in prison) 牢房 láofáng [间 jiān]

cellar ['selə'] N [c] 地下室 dìxiàshì [间 jiān]; (for wine) 酒窖 jiǔjiào

cello ['tʃeləu] N [c] 大提琴 dàtíqín [把 bǎ]

cement [səˈment] N [u] (concrete) 水泥 shuǐní

cemetery ['semɪtrɪ] N [c] 墓地 mùdì [处 chù]

cent [sent] N [c] 分 fēn

center ['sentə'] (US) N = **centre**

centigrade ['sentɪgreɪd] ADJ 摄氏的 Shèshì de

centimetre, (US)**centimeter** ['sentɪmiːtə'] N [c] 厘米 límǐ

central ['sentrəl] ADJ 中心的 zhōngxīn de

central heating N [u] 中央供暖系统 zhōngyāng gōngnuǎn xìtǒng

centre, (US)**center** ['sentə'] N **1** [c] 中心 zhōngxīn [个 gè] **2** [c] (building) 中心 zhōngxīn [个 gè] ▶**to be at the centre of sth** 是某事的关键 shì mǒushì de guānjiàn ▶**to centre** or **be centred on** (focus on) 集中于 jízhōng yú

century ['sentjuri] N [c] 世纪 shìjì [个 gè] ▶**the 21st century** 21世纪 èrshíyī shìjì ▶**in the twenty-first century** 在21世纪 zài èrshíyī shìjì

cereal ['siːrɪəl] N **1** [c] (plant, crop) 谷类植物 gǔlèi zhíwù [种 zhǒng] **2** [c/u] (also: **breakfast cereal**) 谷类食品 gǔlèi shípǐn [种 zhǒng]

ceremony ['serɪmənɪ] N [c] 典礼 diǎnlǐ [个 gè]

certain ['səːtən] ADJ **1** (sure) 肯定的 kěndìng de **2** (some) 某些 mǒuxiē ▶**to be certain that...** 肯定… kěndìng… ▶**to make certain that...** 证实… zhèngshí… ▶**to be certain of** 肯定 kěndìng ▶**a certain amount of sth** 一定量的某物 yídìngliàng de mǒuwù ▶**to know sth for certain** 确定某事

quèdìng mǒushì

certainly ['sɜːtənlɪ] ADV
1 (undoubtedly) 无疑地 wúyí
de **2** (of course) 当然 dāngrán
▸**certainly not** 绝对不行 juéduì
bùxíng

certificate [sə'tɪfɪkɪt] N [c] **1** (of
birth, marriage) 证 zhèng [张
zhāng] **2** (diploma) 结业证书 jiéyè
zhèngshū [个 gè]

chain [tʃeɪn] N **1** [c/u] 链条
liàntiáo [根 gēn] **2** [c] (jewellery) 链
子 liànzi [条 tiáo]

chair [tʃeə'] N [c] 椅子 yǐzi [把 bǎ];
(armchair) 扶手椅 fúshǒuyǐ [把 bǎ]

chairman ['tʃeəmən] (pl
chairmen) N [c] 主席 zhǔxí
[位 wèi]

chalk [tʃɔːk] N [c/u] (for writing) 粉
笔 fěnbǐ [支 zhī]

challenge ['tʃælɪndʒ] I N [c/u]
1 (hard task) 挑战 tiǎozhàn [个
gè] **2** (to rival, competitor) 挑
战 tiǎozhàn [个 gè] II VT
[+ rival, competitor] 向…挑战
xiàng…tiǎozhàn ▸**to challenge
sb to a fight/game** 挑战某人
打架/比赛 tiǎozhàn mǒurén
dǎjià/bǐsài

champagne ['ʃæm'peɪn] N [u]
香槟酒 xiāngbīn jiǔ [瓶 píng]

champion ['tʃæmpɪən] N [c] 冠
军 guànjūn [位 wèi]

championship ['tʃæmpɪənʃɪp] N
[c] 锦标赛 jǐnbiāo sài [届 jiè]

chance [tʃɑːns] N **1** N [c/u]
(likelihood, possibility) 可能
性 kěnéngxìng [种 zhǒng] **2** [u]
(opportunity) 机会 jīhuì **3** [u]

(luck) 运气 yùnqì II ADJ [+ meeting,
discovery] 偶然的 ǒurán de ▸he
hasn't much chance of winning
他赢的机会不大 tā yíng de jīhuì
búdà ▸**the chance to do sth** 做某
事的机会 zuò mǒushì de jīhuì ▸**by
chance** 偶然 ǒurán

change [tʃeɪndʒ] I VT **1** 改变
gǎibiàn **2** [+ wheel, battery] 换
huàn **3** [+ trains, buses] 换乘
huàn **4** [+ clothes] 换 huàn **5** [+ job,
address] 更改 gēnggǎi **6** [+ nappy]
换 huàn **7** [+ money] 兑换 duìhuàn
II VI **1** 变化 biànhuà **2** (change
clothes) 换衣 huànyī **3** (on bus,
train) 换车 huànchē III N **1** [c/u]
(alteration) 转变 zhuǎnbiàn [种
zhǒng] **2** [s] (novelty) 变化 biànhuà
3 [u] (money returned) 找头 zhǎotou ▸**to
change one's mind** 改变主意
gǎibiàn zhǔyì ▸**for a change** 为了
改变一下 wèile gǎibiàn yíxià ▸**a
change of clothes/underwear**
一套换洗的衣服/内衣 yí tào
huànxǐ de yīfu/nèiyī ▸**small
change** 零钱 língqián ▸**to give
sb change for or of 10 pounds** 给
某人10英镑的零钱 gěi mǒurén
shí yīngbàng de língqián ▸**keep
the change!** 不用找了！bùyòng
zhǎole!

changing room (Brit) N [c] **1** (in
shop) 试衣室 shìyīshì [间 jiān]
2 (Sport) 更衣室 gēngyīshì [间
jiān]

channel ['tʃænl] N [c] **1** (TV) 频
道 píndào [个 gè] **2** (for water) 沟
渠 gōuqú [条 tiáo] ▸**the (English)**

Channel 英吉利海峡 Yīngjílì hǎixiá

chaos ['keɪɒs] N [U] 混乱 hùnluàn

chapel ['tʃæpl] N [c] (in hospital, prison, school) 附属教堂 fùshǔ jiàotáng [个 gè]

chapter ['tʃæptər] N [c] 章 zhāng

character ['kærɪktər] N 1 [c] 特性 tèxìng [种 zhǒng] 2 [c] (in novel, film) 角色 juésè [个 gè] 3 [c] (letter, symbol) 字母 zìmǔ [个 gè]

characteristic [kærɪktə'rɪstɪk] N [c] 特征 tèzhēng ▸ to be characteristic of sb/sth 反映某人/某物的特性 fǎnyìng mǒurén/mǒuwù de tèxìng

charge [tʃɑːdʒ] I N [c] 费用 fèiyòng [笔 bǐ] II VT 1 [+ sum of money] 要价 yàojià; [+ customer, client] 收费 shōufèi 2 (also: **charge up**) [+ battery] 使充电 shǐ chōngdiàn III PHRASES NPL 费 fèi ▸ free of charge 免费 miǎnfèi ▸ to be in charge (of sth/sb) (of person, machine) 主管 (某事/某人) zhǔguǎn (mǒushì/mǒurén) ▸ how much do you charge? 你收费多少? nǐ shōufèi duōshǎo? ▸ to charge sb £20 for sth 因某物收某人20英镑 yīn mǒuwù shōu mǒurén èrshí yīngbàng

charity ['tʃærɪtɪ] N [c] (organization) 慈善机构 císhàn jīgòu [个 gè] ▸ to give money to charity 把钱捐给慈善团体 bǎ qián juāngěi císhàn tuántǐ

charm [tʃɑːm] N [c/u] [of place, thing] 魅力 mèilì [种 zhǒng]; [of person] 迷人的特性 mírén de tèxìng [个 gè]

charming ['tʃɑːmɪŋ] ADJ [+ person] 迷人的 mírén de; [+ place, custom] 吸引人的 xīyǐn rén de

chart [tʃɑːt] N [c] 图表 túbiǎo [个 gè]

charter flight N [c] 包机 bāojī [架 jià]

chase [tʃeɪs] VT 追赶 zhuīgǎn

chat [tʃæt] I VI (also: **have a chat**) 聊天 liáotiān II N [c] (conversation) 聊天 liáotiān [次 cì]

chatroom (Comput) N [c] 聊天室 liáotiānshì [个 gè]

chat show (Brit) N [c] 访谈节目 fǎngtán jiémù [个 gè]

chauvinist ['ʃəʊvɪnɪst] N [c] (also: **male chauvinist**) 大男子主义者 dànánzǐzhǔyìzhě [个 gè]

cheap [tʃiːp] ADJ 1 便宜的 piányí de 2 [+ ticket] 降价的 jiàngjià de; [+ fare, rate] 廉价的 liánjià de

cheat [tʃiːt] I VI 作弊 zuòbì II VT 欺骗 qīpiàn III N [c] (in games, exams) 作弊者 zuòbìzhě [个 gè] ▸ cheat on (inf) VT FUS 不忠实于 bù zhōngshí yú

check [tʃek] I VT 1 核对 héduì; [+ passport, ticket] 检查 jiǎnchá 2 (also: **check in**) [+ luggage] 托运 tuōyùn II VI (investigate) 检查 jiǎnchá III N [c] 1 (inspection) 检查 jiǎnchá [次 cì] 2 (US: in restaurant) 账单 zhàngdān [张 zhāng] 3 (US) = **cheque** 4 (pattern: gen pl) 方格图案 fānggé tú'àn [个 gè] 5 (US: mark) 勾号 gōuhào [个 gè] IV ADJ (also: **checked**) 方格图案的 fānggé tú'àn de

check sth against sth 将某物与某物相比较 jiāng mǒuwù yǔ mǒuwù xiāng bǐjiào ▸ **to check with sb** 向某人证实 xiàng mǒurén zhèngshí ▸ **to keep a check on sb/sth** (watch) 监视某人/某物 jiānshì mǒurén/mǒuwù
▸ **check in** VI (at hotel, clinic) 登记 dēngjì; (at airport) 办理登机手续 bànlǐ dēngjī shǒuxù
▸ **check into** VT 登记入住 dēngjì rùzhù
▸ **check out** VI (of hotel) 结账离开 jiézhàng líkāi

checkbook ['tʃekbuk] (US) N = **cheque book**

checked [tʃekt] ADJ see **check**

checkers ['tʃekəz] (US) NPL 西洋跳棋 xīyáng tiàoqí

check-in ['tʃekɪn] (also: **check-in desk**) N [c] 旅客验票台 lǚkè yànpiào tái [个 gè]

checkout ['tʃekaut] N [c] 付款台 fùkuǎntái [个 gè]

check-up ['tʃekʌp] N [c] (by doctor) 体检 tǐjiǎn [次 cì]; (by dentist) 牙科检查 yákē jiǎnchá [次 cì]

cheek [tʃiːk] N 1 [c] 面颊 miànjiá [个 gè] 2 [U] 厚颜无耻 hòuyánwúchǐ ▸ **to have the cheek to do sth** 居然有脸做某事 jūrán yǒuliǎn zuò mǒushì

cheeky ['tʃiːki] (esp Brit) ADJ 恬不知耻的 tián bù zhī chǐ de

cheer [tʃɪə] I VI 欢呼 huānhū II N [c] 喝彩 hècǎi [阵 zhèn] ▸ **cheers!** (esp Brit: toast) 干杯! gānbēi!
▸ **cheer up** VI 振作起来 zhènzuò qǐlái

cheerful ['tʃɪəful] ADJ 兴高采烈的 xìnggāocǎiliè de

cheese [tʃiːz] N [c/u] 干酪 gānlào [块 kuài]

chef [ʃef] N [c] 厨师 chúshī [位 wèi]

chemical ['kemɪkl] N [c] 化学剂 huàxué jì [种 zhǒng]

chemist ['kemɪst] N [c] 1 (Brit) (also: **chemist's**) 药商 yàoshāng [个 gè] 2 (scientist) 化学家 huàxuéjiā [位 wèi]

chemistry ['kemɪstrɪ] N [U] 化学 huàxué

cheque, (US) **check** [tʃek] N [c] 支票 zhīpiào [张 zhāng] ▸ **to pay by cheque** 用支票付款 yòng zhīpiào fùkuǎn

cheque book, (US) **checkbook** ['tʃekbuk] N [c] 支票簿 zhīpiào bù [本 běn]

cherry ['tʃerɪ] N [c] 1 (fruit) 樱桃 yīngtáo [颗 kē] 2 (also: **cherry tree**) 樱桃树 yīngtáo shù [棵 kē]

chess [tʃes] N [U] 象棋 xiàngqí

chest [tʃest] N [c] 1 胸部 xiōngbù 2 (box) 箱子 xiāngzi [个 gè]

chestnut ['tʃesnʌt] N [c] 栗子 lìzi [颗 kē]

chew [tʃuː] VT 嚼 jiáo

chewing gum ['tʃuːɪŋ-] N [U] 口香糖 kǒuxiāngtáng

chick [tʃɪk] N [c] 小鸟 xiǎoniǎo [只 zhī]

chicken ['tʃɪkɪn] N [c] 1 鸡 jī [只 zhī] 2 [c/u] (meat) 鸡肉 jīròu [块 kuài]

chickenpox ['tʃɪkɪnpɒks] N [U] 水痘 shuǐdòu

chief [tʃiːf] I N [c] 首领 shǒulǐng
[个 gè] II ADJ 首要的 shǒuyào de

child [tʃaɪld] (pl **children**) N [c]
1 儿童 értóng [个 gè] 2 (son,
daughter) 孩子 háizi [个 gè]
▸ she's just had her second child
她刚生了第二个孩子 tā gāng
shēng le dì'èr gè háizi

child minder (Brit) N [c] 保姆
bǎomǔ [个 gè]

children [ˈtʃɪldrən] NPL of **child**

Chile [ˈtʃɪlɪ] N 智利 Zhìlì

chill [tʃɪl] VT [+ food, drinks] 使冷冻
shǐ lěngdòng ▸ to catch a chill 着
凉 zháoliáng

chilli, (US) **chili** [ˈtʃɪlɪ] N [c/u] 辣
椒 làjiāo [个 gè]

chilly [ˈtʃɪlɪ] ADJ 相当冷的
xiāngdāng lěng de

chimney [ˈtʃɪmnɪ] N [c] 烟囱
yāncōng [节 jié]

chin [tʃɪn] N [c] 下巴 xiàba [个 gè]

China [ˈtʃaɪnə] N 中国 Zhōngguó

china [ˈtʃaɪnə] N [u] (crockery) 瓷
器 cíqì

Chinese [tʃaɪˈniːz] (pl **Chinese**)
I ADJ 中国的 Zhōngguó de II N 1
[c] (person) 中国人 Zhōngguórén
[个 gè] 2 [u] (language) 汉语
Hànyǔ

chip [tʃɪp] N [c] 1 (Brit) 薯条
shǔtiáo [根 gēn] 2 (US: snack) 薯片
shǔpiàn [片 piàn] 3 (Comput) (also:
microchip) 集成电路芯片 jíchéng
diànlù piàn [块 kuài]

chiropodist [kɪˈrɒpədɪst] (Brit) N
[c] 足医 zúyī [位 wèi]

chocolate [ˈtʃɒklɪt] N 1 N [u] (drinking
chocolate) 巧克力 qiǎokèlì 2 [c/u]

chocolate) 巧克力饮料 qiǎokèlì
yǐnliào (糖 táng) 3 [c] (piece of
confectionery) 巧克力糖 qiǎokèlì
táng [块 kuài] II CPD [+ cake,
pudding, mousse] 巧克力味的
qiǎokèlìwèi de
▸ bar of chocolate 巧克力条
qiǎokèlì tiáo ▸ piece of chocolate
一块巧克力 yīkuài qiǎokèlì

choice [tʃɔɪs] N 1 [c/u] (between
items) 选择 xuǎnzé [个 gè] 2 [c]
(option) 选择 xuǎnzé [个 gè] ▸ a
wide choice 多种多样 duōzhǒng
duōyàng ▸ to have no/little
choice 没有/没有太多选择
méiyǒu/méiyǒu tàiduō xuǎnzé

choir [ˈkwaɪəʳ] N [c] 合唱团
héchàngtuán [个 gè]

choke [tʃəuk] VI (on food, drink) 噎
住 yēzhù; (with smoke, dust) 呛
qiàng ▸ to choke on sth 被某物噎
了 bèi mǒuwù yēle

choose [tʃuːz] (pt **chose**, pp
chosen) I VT 挑选 tiāoxuǎn II VI
▸ to choose between 在…之间作
出选择 zài…zhījiān zuòchū xuǎnzé
▸ to choose to do sth 选择做某事
xuǎnzé zuò mǒushì

chop [tʃɒp] I VT 1 [+ vegetables, fruit,
meat] 切碎 qiēsuì 2 (Culin) 排骨
páigǔ [根 gēn]
▸ chop down VT [+ tree] 砍倒
kǎndǎo
▸ chop up VT 切碎 qiēsuì

chopsticks [ˈtʃɒpstɪks] NPL 筷
子 kuàizi

chose [tʃəuz] PT of **choose**

chosen [ˈtʃəuzn] PP of **choose**

Christ [kraɪst] N 耶稣 Yēsū

christening [ˈkrɪsnɪŋ] N 洗

Christian ['krɪstɪən] I ADJ 基督教的 Jīdūjiào de II N [c] 基督徒 Jīdūtú [个 gè]

Christian name N [c] 教名 jiàomíng [个 gè]

Christmas ['krɪsməs] N [c/u] 1 圣诞节 Shèngdàn Jié [个 gè] 2 (period) 圣诞节期间 Shèngdàn Jié qījiān ▸ **Happy** or **Merry Christmas!** 圣诞快乐! Shèngdàn Kuàilè! ▸ **at Christmas** 在圣诞节 zài Shèngdànjié ▸ **for Christmas** 为了圣诞节 wèile Shèngdànjié

Christmas Eve N [c/u] 圣诞夜 Shèngdàn Yè [个 gè]

Christmas tree N [c] 圣诞树 Shèngdàn shù [棵 kē]

church [tʃɜːtʃ] N [c/u] 教堂 jiàotáng [座 zuò]

cider ['saɪdə'] N [c/u] 1 (Brit: alcoholic) 苹果酒 píngguǒ jiǔ [瓶 píng] 2 (US: non-alcoholic) 苹果汁 píngguǒ zhī [瓶 píng]

cigar [sɪ'gɑː'] N [c] 雪茄烟 xuějiā yān [支 zhī]

cigarette [sɪgə'rɛt] N [c] 香烟 xiāngyān [支 zhī]

cinema ['sɪnəmə] N [c] (Brit) 电影院 diànyǐng yuàn [个 gè]

circle ['sɜːkl] N [c] 圆圈 yuánquān [个 gè]

circular ['sɜːkjulə'] N [c] (letter) 供传阅的函件 gōng chuányuè de hánjiàn [封 fēng]

circumstances ['sɜːkəmstənsɪz] NPL 情况 qíngkuàng ▸ **in** or **under the circumstances** 在这种情况下 zài zhèzhǒng qíngkuàng xià

circus ['sɜːkəs] N [c] 马戏团 mǎxì tuán [个 gè]

citizen ['sɪtɪzn] N [c] 公民 gōngmín [个 gè]

citizenship ['sɪtɪznʃɪp] N [u] 公民身份 gōngmín shēnfèn

city ['sɪtɪ] N [c] 城市 chéngshì [座 zuò] ▸ **the City** (Brit) (Fin) 英国伦敦商业区 Yīngguó Lúndūn shāngyèqū

THE CITY

the City (伦敦商业区)是伦敦的一部分,位于市内的东部。很多重要的金融机构都将总部设在这里,譬如英格兰银行,伦敦证券交易所和其他几个主要银行。这些金融机构的所在地通常称为 **the City**。在历史上,这个地区是伦敦的心脏,有自己的市长和警力。

---

city centre (esp Brit) N [c] 市中心 shì zhōngxīn [个 gè]

civilization [sɪvɪlaɪ'zeɪʃən] N [c/u] 文明 wénmíng [种 zhǒng]

civilized ['sɪvɪlaɪzd] ADJ (+ society, people) 文明的 wénmíng de

civil war N [c/u] 内战 nèizhàn [场 chǎng]

claim [kleɪm] I VT 1 (+ expenses, rights, inheritance) 要求 yāoqiú 2 (+ compensation, damages, benefit) 索取 suǒqǔ II VI (for insurance) 提出索赔 tíchū suǒpéi

[c] 索赔 suǒpéi [项 xiàng] ▸to **claim** or **make a claim on one's insurance** 提出保险索赔的要求 tíchū bǎoxiǎn suǒpéi de yāoqiú ▸**insurance claim** 保险索赔要求 bǎoxiǎn suǒpéi de yāoqiú

clap [klæp] vi 鼓掌 gǔzhǎng

clarinet [klærɪ'net] (Mus) n [c] 单簧管 dānhuángguǎn [根 gēn]

class [klɑːs] I n 1 [c] (Scol: group of pupils) 班级 bānjí [个 gè]; (lesson) 课 kè [堂 táng] 2 [c/u] (social) 阶级 jiējí [个 gè] II vt (categorize) ▸to **class** sb/sth as 将某人/某物分类为 jiāng mǒurén/mǒuwù fēnlèi wéi

classic ['klæsɪk] n [c] 经典 jīngdiǎn [种 zhǒng]

classical ['klæsɪkl] ADJ 1 (traditional) 传统的 chuántǒng de 2 (Mus) 古典的 gǔdiǎn de

classmate ['klɑːsmeɪt] n [c] 同学 tóngxué [位 wèi]

classroom ['klɑːsrum] n [c] 教室 jiàoshì [间 jiān]

claw [klɔː] n [c] 爪子 zhuǎzi [只 zhī]

clay [kleɪ] n [u] 黏土 niántǔ

clean [kliːn] I ADJ 1 干净的 gānjìng de; (+water) 清洁的 qīngjié de II vt (+car, cooker) 弄干净 nòng gānjìng; (+room) 打扫 dǎsǎo ▸a **clean driving licence** or (US) **record** 未有违章记录的驾照 wèiyǒu wéizhāng jìlù de jiàzhào ▸to **clean one's teeth** (Brit) 刷牙 shuāyá

▸**clean up** [+room, place] 打扫干净 dǎsǎo gānjìng; [+mess] 整理 zhěnglǐ

cleaner ['kliːnəʳ] n [c] (person) 清洁工 qīngjié gōng [位 wèi]

clear [klɪəʳ] I ADJ 1 [+explanation, account] 明确的 míngquè de 2 (visible) 清晰的 qīngxī de 3 (audible) 清晰的 qīngxī de 4 (obvious) 无疑的 wúyí de 5 (transparent) 透明的 tòumíng de 6 (unobstructed) 畅通的 chàngtōng de II vt [+place, room] 清空 qīngkōng III vi [weather, sky] 变晴 biànqíng; [fog, smoke] 消散 xiāosàn ▸to be **clear about sth** 很明确某事 hěn míngquè mǒushì ▸to **make o.s. clear** 表达清楚 biǎodá qīngchǔ ▸to **clear the table** 收拾饭桌 shōushí fànzhuō

▸**clear away** 清除 qīngchú
▸**clear off** (inf) vi (leave) 走开 zǒukāi

▸**clear up** I vt 1 [+room, mess] 清理 qīnglǐ 2 [+mystery, problem] 澄清 chéngqīng II vi (tidy up) 清理 qīnglǐ

clearly ['klɪəlɪ] ADV 1 明确地 míngquè de; (think) 清醒地 qīngxǐng de; (see) 清楚地 qīngchu de; (speak, hear) 清晰地 qīngxī de 2 (visible, audible) 清楚地 qīngchu de 3 (obviously) 显然 xiǎnrán

clever ['klevəʳ] ADJ 1 聪明的 cōngmíng de 2 (sly, crafty) 耍小聪明的 shuǎ xiǎocōngmíng de 3 [+device, arrangement] 巧妙的 qiǎomiào de

click [klɪk] n [c] (Comput) ▸with **a click of one's mouse** 按一下鼠标 àn yīxià shǔbiāo [下 xià] ▸to **click on** (Comput) 点击某处

diǎnjī mǒuchù

client ['klaɪənt] N [c] *(of lawyer)* 委托人 wěituōrén [个 gè]; *(of company, restaurant, shop)* 顾客 gùkè [位 wèi]

cliff [klɪf] N [c] 悬崖 xuányá [个 gè]

climate ['klaɪmɪt] N [c/U] 气候 qìhòu [种 zhǒng]

climb [klaɪm] I VT *(also: climb up)* [+ tree] 爬 pá; [+ mountain, hill] 攀登 pāndēng; [+ ladder] 登 dēng; [+ stairs, steps] 上 shàng II VI *(person)* 攀爬 pānpá III N [c] 攀登 pāndēng [次 cì] ▸**to go climbing** 去爬山 qù páshān

climber ['klaɪməʳ] N [c] 登山者 dēngshānzhě [个 gè]

climbing ['klaɪmɪŋ] N [U] 攀登 pāndēng

clingfilm ['klɪŋfɪlm] *(Brit)* N [U] 保鲜纸 bǎoxiān zhǐ

clinic ['klɪnɪk] *(Med)* N [c] 诊所 zhěnsuǒ [家 jiā]

cloakroom ['kləʊkrʊm] N [c] 1 *(for coats)* 衣帽间 yīmàojiān [个 gè] 2 *(Brit: bathroom)* 厕所 cèsuǒ [处 chù]

clock [klɒk] N [c] 钟 zhōng [个 gè] ▸**around the clock** *(work, guard)* 日夜不停 rìyè bùtíng ▸**clock in** VI *(for work)* 打卡上班 dǎkǎ shàngbān ▸**clock off** VI *(from work)* 打卡下班 dǎkǎ xiàbān ▸**clock on** VI = **clock in** ▸**clock out** VI = **clock off**

close¹ [kləʊs] I ADJ 1 近的 jìn de 2 [+ relative] 直系的 zhíxì de

3 [+ contest] 势均力敌的 shìjūnlìdí de II ADV *(near)* 紧紧地 jǐnjǐn de ▸**close to** *(near)* 近 jìn ▸**a close friend** 一位密友 yīwèi mìyǒu ▸**close by, close at hand** 在近旁 zài jìnpáng

close² [kləʊz] I VT 1 关 guān 2 [+ shop, factory] 关闭 guānbì II VI 1 关 guān 2 *(shop, library)* 关门 guānmén ▸**close down** VI *(factory, business)* 关闭 guānbì

closed [kləʊzd] ADJ [+ door, window] 关着的 guānzhe de; [+ shop, library] 关着门的 guānzhe mén de; [+ road] 封锁着的 fēngsuǒzhe de

closely ['kləʊslɪ] ADV 1 *(examine, watch)* 仔细地 zǐxì de 2 *(connected)* 密切地 mìqiè de

closet ['klɒzɪt] N [c] *(US)* 壁橱 bìchú [个 gè]

cloth [klɒθ] N [c/U] 1 *(fabric)* 布料 bùliào [块 kuài] 2 [c] *(for cleaning, dusting)* 布 bù [块 kuài] 3 [c] *(tablecloth)* 桌布 zhuōbù [块 kuài]

clothes [kləʊðz] NPL 衣服 yīfu ▸**to take one's clothes off** 脱衣服 tuō yīfu

cloud [klaʊd] N 1 [c/U] 云 yún [片 piàn] 2 [c] *(of smoke, dust)* 雾 wù [团 tuán] ▸**cloud over** VI 阴云密布 yīnyún mìbù

cloudy ['klaʊdɪ] ADJ 多云的 duōyún de ▸**it's cloudy** 天阴 tiānyīn

clown [klaʊn] N [c] 小丑 xiǎochǒu [个 gè]

club [klʌb] N [c] **1** 俱乐部 jùlèbù
[个 gè] **2** (Sport) 俱乐部 jùlèbù [个
gè] **3** (nightclub) 夜总会 yèzǒnghuì
[家 jiā]

clue [kluː] N [c] **1** (in investigation)
线索 xiànsuǒ [条 tiáo] **2** (in
crossword, game) 提示 tíshì [个 gè]
▸ **I haven't a clue** (inf) 我一无所知
wǒ yī wú suǒ zhī

clumsy [ˈklʌmzɪ] ADJ 笨手笨脚的
bènshǒubènjiǎo de

clutch [klʌtʃ] N [c] (Aut) 离合器
líhéqì [个 gè]

coach [kəʊtʃ] I N [c] **1** (Brit) 长
途汽车 chángtú qìchē [辆 liàng]
2 (Sport) 教练 jiàoliàn [位 wèi]
II VT (Sport) 训练 xùnliàn

coal [kəʊl] N [u] 煤 méi

coast [kəʊst] N [c] 海岸 hǎi'àn
[个 gè]

coat [kəʊt] N [c] **1** (overcoat) 外套
wàitào [件 jiàn] **2** [of animal] 皮毛
pímáo [层 céng]

coat hanger N [c] 衣架 yījià
[个 gè]

cocaine [kəˈkeɪn] N [u] 可卡因
kěkǎyīn

cock [kɒk] N [c] (Brit) 公鸡 gōngjī
[只 zhī]

cocoa [ˈkəʊkəʊ] N [u] 可可 kěkě

coconut [ˈkəʊkənʌt] N [c] (nut)
椰子 yēzi [个 gè]

cod [kɒd] (pl cod or cods) N [c]
(fish) 鳕鱼 xuěyú [条 tiáo]

code [kəʊd] N [c] **1** (cipher) 密
码 mìmǎ [个 gè] **2** [Tel] 区号
qūhào [个 gè] **3** [c/u] (Comput, Sci)
编码 biānmǎ [个 gè]

coffee [ˈkɒfɪ] N **1** [c/u] 咖啡 kāfēi [杯

[c] (cup of coffee) 一杯咖啡 yībēi
kāfēi [杯 bēi] ▸ **black coffee** 黑咖
啡 hēi kāfēi ▸ **white coffee** 牛奶
咖啡 niúnǎi kāfēi

coffin [ˈkɒfɪn] N [c] 棺材 guāncai
[口 kǒu]

coin [kɔɪn] N [c] 硬币 yìngbì
[枚 méi]

coincidence [kəʊˈɪnsɪdəns] N
[c/u] 巧合 qiǎohé [种 zhǒng]

Coke® [kəʊk] N [u] (drink) 可可
乐 Kěkǒu Kělè

cold [kəʊld] I ADJ **1** [+ water, object]
凉的 liáng de; [+ weather, room,
meat] 冷的 lěng de II N **1** (weather) ▸ **the cold** 寒冷 hánlěng **2** (illness) 感冒
gǎnmào [次 cì] ▸ **it's cold** 天气寒
冷 tiānqì hánlěng ▸ **to be or feel
cold** [person] 感到冷 gǎndào lěng
▸ **to catch (a) cold** 患感冒 huàn
gǎnmào

collapse [kəˈlæps] VI **1** 倒坍
dǎotān; [person] 倒下 dǎoxià

collar [ˈkɒlə^r] N [c] 领子 lǐngzi
[个 gè]

collarbone [ˈkɒləbəʊn] N [c] 锁
骨 suǒgǔ [根 gēn]

colleague [ˈkɒliːg] N [c] 同事
tóngshì [个 gè]

collect [kəˈlɛkt] VT **1** 采集 cǎijí
2 (as hobby) 收集 shōují [个 gè]
3 (Brit: fetch) [+ person] 接 jiē; [+ object]
取 qǔ **4** [+ money, donations] 募捐
mùjuān ▸ **to call collect, make
a collect call** (US) [Tel] 打对方付
款的电话 dǎ duìfāng fùkuǎn de
diànhuà

collection [kəˈlɛkʃən] N [c] (of

art, stamps) 收藏品 shōucáng pǐn [件 jiàn] **2** [c] *(for charity, gift)* 募捐 mùjuān [次 cì]

collector [kəˈlɛktəʳ] N [c] 收藏家 shōucáng jiā [位 wèi]

college [ˈkɔlɪdʒ] N **1** [c/u] *(for further education)* 学院 xuéyuàn [个 gè] **2** [c] *(of university)* 学院 xuéyuàn [个 gè] ▸ **to go to college** 上大学 shàng dàxué

collide [kəˈlaɪd] VI 碰撞 pèngzhuàng ▸ **to collide with sth/sb** 与某物/某人碰撞 yǔ mǒuwù/mǒurén pèngzhuàng

collision [kəˈlɪʒən] N [c/u] *(of vehicles)* 碰撞 pèngzhuàng [下 xià]

colonel [ˈkəːnl] N [c] 上校 shàngxiào [位 wèi]

color *etc* [ˈkʌləʳ] (US) = **colour** *etc*

colour, (US) **color** [ˈkʌləʳ] I N **1** [c/u] 颜色 yánsè [种 zhǒng] **2** [c] *(skin colour)* 肤色 fūsè [种 zhǒng] II VT 给…着色 gěi…zhuósè III CPD [+ *film, photograph, television*] 彩色 cǎisè ▸ **in colour** [+ *film, illustrations*] 彩色 cǎisè

colourful, (US) **colorful** [ˈkʌləful] ADJ 色彩鲜艳的 sècǎi xiānyàn de

colour television, (US) **color television** [ˈtɛlɪvɪʒən] N [c] 彩色电视 cǎisè diànshì [台 tái]

column [ˈkɔləm] N [c] *(Archit)* 支柱 zhīzhù [个 gè]

comb [kəum] I N [c] 梳子 shūzi [把 bǎ] II VT 梳理 shūlǐ

combination [kɔmbɪˈneɪʃən] N [c] 混合 hùnhé [种 zhǒng]

combine [kəmˈbaɪn] I VT ▸ **to**

combine sth with sth 将某物与某物结合起来 jiāng mǒuwù yǔ mǒuwù jiéhé qǐlái II VI *(qualities, situations)* 结合 jiéhé; [*people, groups*] 组合 zǔhé ▸ **a combined effort** 协力 xiélì

○ KEYWORD

come [kʌm] *(pt* **came**, *pp* **come**) VI **1** 来 lái ▸ **come here!** 到这儿来! dào zhèr lái! ▸ **can I come too?** 我也能来吗? wǒ yěnéng láima? ▸ **come with me** 跟我来 gēn wǒ lái ▸ **a girl came into the room** 一个女孩进了房间 yīgè nǚhái jìnle fángjiān ▸ **why don't you come to lunch on Saturday?** 何不星期六过来吃午饭呢? hébù xīngqīliù guòlái chī wǔfàn ne? ▸ **he's come here to work** 他已经到了这儿工作 tā yǐjìng dàole zhèr gōngzuò **2** ▸ **to come to** *(reach)* 达到 dàdào; *(amount to)* 达到 dádào ▸ **to come to a decision** 做出决定 zuòchū juédìng ▸ **the bill came to £40** 账单共计40英镑 zhàngdān gòngjì sìshí yīngbàng **3** *(be, become)* ▸ **to come first/ second/last etc** *(in series)* 排在第一/第二/最后〔等〕 páizài dìyī/dì'èr/zuìhòu〔děng〕; *(in competition, race)* 位居第一/第二/最后〔等〕 wèijū dìyī/dì'èr/zuìhòu〔děng〕 ▸ **come across** VT FUS 偶然发现 ǒurán fāxiàn ▸ **come apart** VI 裂成碎片 lièchéng suìpiàn ▸ **come back** VI *(return)* 回来

huílái

▶ **come down** VI 1 (*price*) 降低 jiàngdī

2 (*plane*) 坠落 zhuìluò

3 (*descend*) 降下 jiàngxià

▶ **come forward** VI (*volunteer*) 自告奋勇 zìgàofènyǒng

▶ **come from** VT FUS 来自 láizì ▶I **come from London** 我来自伦敦 wǒ láizì Lúndūn ▶ **where do you come from?** 你是哪里人? nǐ shì nǎlǐ rén?

▶ **come in** VI 进来! jìnrù ▶ **come in!** 进来! jìnlái!

▶ **come off** VI (*button, handle*) 脱落 tuōluò

▶ **come on** VI (*progress*) 进展 jìnzhǎn ▶ **come on!** (*giving encouragement*) 来! lái!; (*hurry up*) 快一点! kuàiyìdiǎn!

▶ **come out** VI 1 (*person*) 出去 chūqù

2 (*sun*) 出现 chūxiàn

3 (*book*) 出版 chūbǎn; (*film*) 上映 shàngyìng

▶ **come through** VT FUS (*survive*) 经历…而幸存 jīnglì...ér xìngcún

▶ **come to** VI (*regain consciousness*) 苏醒 sūxǐng

▶ **come up** VI 1 (*approach*) 走近 zǒujìn

2 (*meet*) 突然出现 tūrán chūxiàn

▶ **come up to** VT FUS 1 (*approach*) 走近 zǒujìn

2 (*meet*) ▶ **the film didn't come up to our expectations** 电影没有我们预期的那么好 diànyǐng méiyǒu wǒmen yùqí de nàme hǎo

comedian [kə'miːdɪən] (*Theat, TV*) N [c] 喜剧演员 xǐjù yǎnyuán [个 gè]

comedy ['kɒmɪdɪ] N 1 [U] (*humour*) 幽默 yōumò 2 [c] (*play, film*) 喜剧 xǐjù [部 bù]

comfortable ['kʌmfətəbl] ADJ 1 (*person*) ▶ **to be comfortable** 舒服的 shūfu de 2 (*+ furniture, room, clothes*) 使人舒服的 shǐ rén shūfu de ▶ **to make o.s. comfortable** 自在点 zìzài diǎn

comma ['kɒmə] N [c] 逗号 dòuhào [个 gè]

command [kə'mɑːnd] N 1 [c] (*order*) 命令 mìnglìng [项 xiàng] 2 [c] (*Comput*) 指令 zhīlìng [个 gè]

comment ['kɒment] I N [c/u] 评论 pínglùn [种 zhǒng] II VI ▶ **to comment (on sth)** (对某事) 表述意见 (duì mǒushì) fābiǎo yìjiàn ▶ **"no comment"** "无可奉告" "wú kě fèng gào"

commentary ['kɒməntərɪ] N [c/u] 实况报道 shíkuàng bàodào [段 duàn]

commentator ['kɒmənteɪtə] N [c] 解说员 jiěshuōyuán [位 wèi]

commercial [kə'mɜːʃəl] I ADJ 1 (*+ success, failure*) 从盈利角度出发 cóng yínglì jiǎodù chūfā; (*+ television, radio*) 商业性的 shāngyè xìng de 2 (*advertisement*) 广告 guǎnggào [则 zé]

commit [kə'mɪt] VT 犯 fàn ▶ **to commit suicide** 自杀 zìshā

committee [kə'mɪtɪ] N [c] 委员会 wěiyuánhuì [个 gè]

的 chángjiàn de ▸to have sth in common (with sb) 有某些共同点 yǒu mǒuxiē gòngtóngdiǎn; (things) 有共同的某特征 yǒu gòngtóng de mǒutèzhēng ▸to have sth in common with sb/sth 与某人/某物有某共同点 yǔ mǒurén/mǒuwù yǒu mǒu gòngtóngdiǎn

common sense N [U] 常识 chángshí

communicate [kəˈmjuːnɪkeɪt] VI 联络 liánluò

communication [kəmjuːnɪˈkeɪʃən] I N [U] 交流 jiāoliú II **communications** NPL 通讯 tōngxùn

communism [ˈkɒmjʊnɪzəm] N [U] 共产主义 gòngchǎnzhǔyì

community [kəˈmjuːnɪti] N [c] 社区 shèqū [个 gè]

commute [kəˈmjuːt] VI 乘车上下班 chéngchē shàngxiàbān ▸to commute to/from London/Brighton 去/从伦敦/布赖顿乘车上下班 qù/cóng Lúndūn/Bùlàidùn chéngchē shàngxià bān

compact disc N [c] 激光唱片 jīguāng chàngpiàn [张 zhāng]

company [ˈkʌmpəni] N 1 [c] (firm) 公司 gōngsī [个 gè] 2 [U] (companionship) 交往 jiāowǎng ▸to keep sb company 陪伴某人 péibàn mǒurén

comparatively [kəmˈpærətɪvli] ADV [+ easy, safe, peaceful] 相对地 xiāngduì de

compare [kəmˈpɛə] I VT 比

较 bǐjiào II VI ▸to compare favourably/unfavourably (with sth/sb) 比得上/比不上(某物/某人)bǐdeshàng/bǐbùshang (mǒuwù/mǒurén) ▸to compare sb/sth to 把某人/某物比作 bǎ mǒurén/mǒuwù bǐzuò ▸compared with or to 与…相比 yǔ…xiāngbǐ ▸how does he compare with his predecessor? 和他前任比起来他怎么样？ hé tā qiánrèn bǐ qǐlái tā zěnmeyàng?

comparison [kəmˈpærɪsn] N [c/U] 比较 bǐjiào [种 zhǒng] ▸in or by comparison (with) (与…)比较起来 (yǔ…) bǐjiào qǐlái

compartment [kəmˈpɑːtmənt] N [c] (Rail) 隔间 géjiān [个 gè]

compass [ˈkʌmpəs] N [c] 指南针 zhǐnánzhēn [个 gè]

compatible [kəmˈpætɪbl] ADJ [+ people] 意气相投的 yìqì xiāngtóu de; (Comput) 兼容的 jiānróng de ▸to be compatible with sth (Comput) 与某物兼容 yǔ mǒuwù jiānróng

compensation [kɒmpənˈseɪʃən] N [U] 赔偿金 péicháng jīn ▸compensation for sth 因某事而获得的赔偿金 yīn mǒushì ér huòdé de péichángjīn

compete [kəmˈpiːt] VI [companies, rivals] 竞争 jìngzhēng; (in contest, game) 比赛 bǐsài ▸to compete for sth [companies, rivals] 争夺某物 zhēngduó mǒuwù; (in contest, game) 争夺某物 zhēngduó mǒuwù ▸to compete with sb/sth (for sth) [companies, rivals] 与某

人/某物竞争(以得到某物) yǔ mǒurén/mǒuwù jìngzhēng (yǐ dédào mǒuwù); (in contest, game) 与某人/某物竞争(以获得某奖项) yǔ mǒurén/mǒuwù jìngzhēng (yǐ huòdé jiǎngxiàng)

competent ['kɒmpɪtənt] ADJ 称职的 chènzhí de; [+ piece of work] 合格的 hégé de

competition [kɒmpɪ'tɪʃən] N 1 [U] (rivalry) 竞争 jìngzhēng 2 [c] (contest) 竞赛 jìngsài [项 xiàng] ▸ in competition with 与…竞争 yǔ…jìngzhēng

competitive [kəm'pɛtɪtɪv] ADJ 1 [+ industry, society] 竞争性的 jìngzhēngxìng de 2 [+ person] 求胜心切的 qiúshèngxīnqiè de

competitor [kəm'pɛtɪtər] N [c] 1 (in business) 竞争对手 jìngzhēng duìshǒu [个 gè] 2 (participant) 参赛者 cānsàizhě [个 gè]

complain [kəm'pleɪn] VI ▸ to complain (about sth) (就某事) 投诉 (jiù mǒushì) tóusù; (grumble) (就某事) 诉苦 (jiù mǒushì) sùkǔ ▸ to complain to sb (about sth) (就某事) 向某人投诉 (jiù mǒushì) xiàng mǒurén tóusù

complaint [kəm'pleɪnt] N 1 抱怨 bàoyuàn [个 gè] ▸ to make a complaint (to sb) (向某人) 投诉 (xiàng mǒurén) tóusù

complete [kəm'pli:t] I ADJ 1 完全的 wánquán de 2 (whole) 整个的 zhěnggè de 3 (finished) 完成的 wánchéng de II VT 1 完成 wánchéng 2 [+ form, coupon] 填写 tiánxiě ▸ complete with 附

带 fùdài

completely [kəm'pli:tlɪ] ADV (different, satisfied, untrue) 完全 wánquán; (forget, destroy) 彻底 chèdǐ

complexion [kəm'plɛkʃən] N [c] 面色 miànsè [种 zhǒng]

complicated ['kɒmplɪkeɪtɪd] ADJ 复杂的 fùzá de

compliment [n 'kɒmplɪmənt, vb 'kɒmplɪmɛnt] I N [c] 赞美 zànměi [种 zhǒng] II VT 赞美 zànměi ▸ to pay sb a compliment 赞美某人 zànměi mǒurén ▸ to compliment sb on sth 为某事赞美某人 wèi mǒushì zànměi mǒurén

composer [kəm'pəʊzər] N [c] 作曲家 zuòqǔjiā [位 wèi]

comprehension [kɒmprɪ'hɛnʃən] N 1 [U] (understanding) 理解 lǐjiě 2 [c/U] (Scol) 理解力练习 lǐjiělì liànxí [项 xiàng]

comprehensive [kɒmprɪ'hɛnsɪv] I ADJ 1 [+ review, list] 全面的 quánmiàn de 2 (of insurance) 综合的 zōnghé de II N [c] (Brit) (also: **comprehensive school**) 综合性中学 zōnghéxìng zhōngxué [所 suǒ]

compulsory [kəm'pʌlsərɪ] ADJ 必须的 bìxū de; [+ course] 必修的 bìxiū de

computer [kəm'pju:tər] I N [c] 计算机 jìsuànjī [台 tái] II CPD [+ language, program, system, technology etc] 电脑 diànnǎo

computer game N [c] 电脑游戏 diànnǎo yóuxì [局 jú]

computer programmer

computer science N [U] 计算机科学 jìsuànjī kēxué

computing [kəm'pjuːtɪŋ] I N [U] 计算机运用 jìsuànjī yùnyòng; (also: **computing studies**) 计算机学 jìsuànjīxué II CPD [+ course, skills] 电脑 diànnǎo

concentrate ['kɒnsəntreit] VI 集中精力 jízhōng jīnglì ▸ to **concentrate on sth** (keep attention on) 全神贯注于某事 quán shén guàn zhù yú mǒushì; (focus on) 集中注意力于某事 jízhōng zhùyìlì yú mǒushì

concentration [kɒnsən'treiʃən] N [U] 专心 zhuānxīn

concern [kən'səːn] I N [U] (anxiety) 担忧 dānyōu II VT (worry) 使担忧 shǐ dānyōu ▸ **concern for sb** 为某人担忧 wèi mǒurén dānyōu ▸ **as far as I'm concerned** 据我看来 jù wǒ kànlái ▸ **the people concerned** (in question) 有关人士 yǒuguān rénshì

concerned [kən'səːnd] ADJ (worried) 担心的 dānxīn de ▸ to **be concerned about sb/sth** 担心某人/某事 dānxīn mǒurén/mǒushì

concerning [kən'səːnɪŋ] PREP 关于 guānyú

concert ['kɒnsət] N [c] 音乐会 yīnyuèhuì [个 gè]

concert hall N [c] 音乐厅 yīnyuètīng [个 gè]

conclusion [kən'kluːʒən] N 1 [s] (end) 结尾 jiéwěi 2 [c] (deduction) 结论 jiélùn [个 gè] ▸ to **come to**

the **conclusion that...** 得出的结论是… déchū de jiélùn shì...

concrete ['kɒŋkriːt] I N [U] 混凝土 hùnníngtǔ II ADJ 1 [+ block, floor] 混凝土的 hùnníngtǔ de 2 [+ proposal, evidence] 确实的 quèshí de

condemn [kən'dɛm] VT (denounce) 谴责 qiǎnzé

condition [kən'dɪʃən] I N 1 [s] (state) 状态 zhuàngtài 2 [c] (stipulation) 条件 tiáojiàn [个 gè] II **conditions** NPL 环境 huánjìng ▸ **in good/poor condition** 状况良好/不好 zhuàngkuàng liánghǎo/bùhǎo ▸ **weather conditions** 天气形势 tiānqì xíngshì ▸ **on condition that...** 在…条件下 zài...tiáojiàn xià

conditional [kən'dɪʃənl] I ADJ 有条件的 yǒu tiáojiàn de II N (Ling) ▸ the **conditional** 条件从句 tiáojiàn cóngjù

conditioner [kən'dɪʃənə'] N [c/u] 护发素 hùfàsù [种 zhǒng]

condom ['kɒndəm] N [c] 安全套 ānquán tào [只 zhī]

conduct [kən'dʌkt] VT [+ orchestra, choir] 指挥 zhǐhuī

conductor [kən'dʌktə'] N [c] 1 [of orchestra] 指挥家 zhǐhuījiā [位 wèi] 2 (US: on train) 列车员 lièchēyuán [位 wèi] 3 (on bus) 售票员 shòupiàoyuán [位 wèi]

cone [kəun] N 1 (shape) 圆锥体 yuánzhuītǐ [个 gè] 2 (also: **ice cream cone**) 锥形蛋卷冰淇淋 zhuīxíng dànjuǎn bīngqílín [个 gè]

conference ['kɒnfərəns] N [c] 会议

议 huìyì [次 cì]

confess [kən'fɛs] VI 坦白 tǎnbái
▸ to confess to sth/to doing sth
承认某事/做了某事 chéngrèn
mǒushì/zuòle mǒushì

confession [kən'fɛʃən] N [c/u]
(admission) 坦白 tǎnbái [种 zhǒng]
▸ to make a confession 坦白
tǎnbái

confidence ['kɔnfɪdns] N 1
[u] (faith) 信赖 xìnlài 2 [u]
(self-assurance) 自信 zìxìn ▸ in
confidence 秘密地 mìmì de

confident ['kɔnfɪdənt] ADJ (self-
assured) 自信的 zìxìn de ▸ to be
confident that... 有信心… yǒu
xìnxìn…

confidential [kɔnfɪ'dɛnʃəl] ADJ
机密的 jīmì de

confirm [kən'fə:m] VT 肯定
kěndìng [+ appointment, date] 确
认 quèrèn

confiscate ['kɔnfɪskeɪt] VT 没
收 mòshōu ▸ to confiscate sth
from sb 没收某人的某物 mòshōu
mǒurén de mǒuwù

confuse [kən'fju:z] VT 1 (perplex)
把…弄糊涂 bǎ…nòng hútú 2 (mix
up) 混淆 hùnxiáo

confused [kən'fju:zd] ADJ 困惑
的 kùnhuò de

confusing [kən'fju:zɪŋ] ADJ 含混
不清的 hánhùn bùqīng de

confusion [kən'fju:ʒən] N 1 [c/u]
(uncertainty) 惶惑 huánghuò [种
zhǒng] 2 [u] (mix-up) 混淆 hùnxiáo

congratulate [kən'grætjuleɪt]
VT 祝贺 zhùhè ▸ to congratulate
sb on sth/on doing sth 祝贺某

人某事/做某事 zhùhè mǒurén
mǒushì/zuò mǒushì

congratulations
[kəngrætjuˈleɪʃənz] NPL 祝贺
zhùhè ▸ congratulations on your
engagement! 祝贺你订婚了！
zhùhè nǐ dìnghūn le!

Congress ['kɔngrɛs] N (US)
▸ Congress 国会 guóhuì

congressman ['kɔngrɛsmən] (pl
congressmen) (US) N [c] 国会议
员 guóhuì yìyuán [位 wèi]

congresswoman
['kɔngrɛswumən] (pl
congresswomen) (US) N [c] 女国
会议员 nǚ guóhuì yìyuán [位 wèi]

connection [kə'nɛkʃən] N 1
(link) 联系 liánxì [种 zhǒng] 2
(Elec) 接头 jiētóu [个 gè] 3
[c] (train, plane) 联运 liányùn [种
zhǒng] ▸ what is the connection
between them? 他们之间有什么
关系？ tāmen zhījiān yǒu shénme
guānxì?

conscience ['kɔnʃəns] N [c] 是非
感 shìfēi gǎn [种 zhǒng] ▸ to have
a guilty/clear conscience 感到
内疚/问心无愧 gǎndào nèijiù/wèn
xīn wú kuì

conscientious [kɔnʃɪ'ɛnʃəs] ADJ
认真的 rènzhēn de

conscious ['kɔnʃəs] ADJ 1 (awake)
清醒的 qīngxǐng de 2 [+ decision,
effort] 蓄意的 xùyì de ▸ to be
conscious of sth 意识到某事
yìshí dào mǒushì

consciousness ['kɔnʃəsnɪs] N
[u] (Med) 知觉 zhījué ▸ to lose
consciousness 失去知觉 shīqù

zhíjué

consequence ['kɒnsɪkwəns] N [c] 后果 hòuguǒ [种 zhǒng]

consequently ['kɒnsɪkwəntlɪ] ADV 所以 suǒyǐ

conservation [kɒnsə'veɪʃən] N [U] (of environment) 环保 huánbǎo; (of energy) 节约 jiéyuē

conservative [kən'sɜːvətɪv] I ADJ 1 (traditional) 保守的 bǎoshǒu de 2 (Brit) (Pol) 保守党 bǎoshǒudǎng II N [c] (Brit) (Pol) ▶ **Conservative** 保守党人士 bǎoshǒudǎng rénshì [名 míng]

conservatory [kən'sɜːvətrɪ] N [c] 暖房 nuǎnfáng [间 jiān]

consider [kən'sɪdə'] VT 1 (think about) 考虑 kǎolǜ 2 (take into account) 考虑到 kǎolǜ dào

considerate [kən'sɪdərɪt] ADJ 体贴的 tǐtiē de

considering [kən'sɪdərɪŋ] I PREP 考虑到 kǎolǜ dào II CONJ ▶ **considering (that)...** 考虑到... kǎolǜ dào...

consist [kən'sɪst] VI ▶ **to consist of** 由...组成 yóu...zǔchéng

consonant ['kɒnsənənt] N [c] 辅音 fǔyīn [个 gè]

constant ['kɒnstənt] ADJ 1 [+ threat, pressure, pain, reminder] 不断的 búduàn de 2 [+ interruptions, demands] 重复的 chóngfù de 3 [+ temperature, speed] 恒定的 héngdìng de

constantly ['kɒnstəntlɪ] ADV 1 (repeatedly) 不断地 búduàn de 2 (uninterruptedly) 持续地 chíxù de

constipated ['kɒnstɪpeɪtɪd] ADJ

便秘的 biànmì de

construct [kən'strʌkt] VT 建造 jiànzào

construction [kən'strʌkʃən] N 1 [U] (of building, road, machine) 建造 jiànzào 2 [c] (structure) 建筑 jiànzhù [座 zuò]

consult [kən'sʌlt] VT (+ doctor, lawyer, friend) 咨询 zīxún; (+ book, map) 查阅 cháyuè

consumer [kən'sjuːmə'] N [c] (of goods, services) 消费者 xiāofèizhě [个 gè]; (of resources) 使用者 shǐyòngzhě [个 gè]

contact ['kɒntækt] I N 1 [c/U] (communication) 联络 liánluò [种 zhǒng] 2 [c] (person) 熟人 shúrén [个 gè] II VT 联系 liánxì ▶ **to be in contact with sb** 与某人有联络 yǔ mǒurén yǒu liánluò

contact lenses NPL 隐形眼镜 yǐnxíng yǎnjìng

contain [kən'teɪn] VT (+ objects) 装有 zhuāngyǒu; (+ component, ingredient) 含有 hányǒu

container [kən'teɪnə'] N [c] 1 (box, jar etc) 容器 róngqì [个 gè] 2 (for transport) 集装箱 jízhuāngxiāng [个 gè]

content[1] ['kɒntent] I N [U] 内容 nèiróng II **contents** NPL (of bottle, packet) 所盛之物 suǒshèng zhī wù

content[2] [kən'tent] ADJ 满足的 mǎnzú de

contest ['kɒntest] N [c] 比赛 bǐsài [项 xiàng]

contestant [kən'testənt] N [c] 参赛者 cānsàizhě [位 wèi]

context ['kɒntekst] N [of

word, phrase] 上下文 shàngxiàwén
[个 gè]

continent ['kɒntɪnənt] N
[c] 大陆 dàlù [个 gè] ▶**on the
Continent** (Brit) 在欧洲大陆 zài
Ōuzhōu dàlù

continental breakfast N [c] 欧
洲大陆式早餐 Ōuzhōu dàlù shì
zǎocān [顿 dùn]

continue [kən'tɪnjuː] VI 1 继续
jìxù 2 [speaker] 继续说 jìxù shuō
▶**to continue to do sth** or **doing
sth** 持续做某事 chíxù zuò mǒushì
▶**to continue with sth** 继续某事
jìxù mǒushì

continuous [kən'tɪnjuəs] ADJ 连
续不停的 liánxù bù tíng de

contraception [kɒntrə'sɛpʃən] N
[U] 避孕 bìyùn

contraceptive [kɒntrə'sɛptɪv]
N [c] (drug) 避孕药 bìyùn yào [片
piàn]; (device) 避孕工具 bìyùn
gōngjù [种 zhǒng]

contract ['kɒntrækt] N [c] 合同
hétong [份 fèn]

contradict [kɒntrə'dɪkt] VT 驳
斥 bóchì

contradiction [kɒntrə'dɪkʃən] N
[c/U] 矛盾 máodùn [种 zhǒng]

contrary ['kɒntrərɪ] N [c/U]
▶**the contrary** 相反 xiāngfǎn
▶**on the contrary** 正相反 zhèng
xiāngfǎn

contrast [n 'kɒntrɑːst, vb
kən'trɑːst] I N [c/U] 明显的差异
míngxiǎn de chāyì [种 zhǒng]
2 ▶**to be a contrast to sth** 与
某物截然不同 yǔ mǒuwù jiérán
bùtóng [个 gè] II VI 1 ▶**to**

with sth 与某事形成对照 yǔ
mǒushì xíngchéng duìzhào ▶**to
contrast sth with sth** 将某物与
某物进行对比 jiāng mǒuwù yǔ
mǒuwù jìnxíng duìbǐ

contribute [kən'trɪbjuːt] I VI
▶**to contribute (to sth)** (with
money) (给某事) 捐助 (gěi
mǒushì) juānzhù II VT ▶**to
contribute 10 pounds (to sth)**
(给某事) 捐助10英镑 (gěi mǒushì)
juānxiàn shí yīngbàng

contribution [kɒntrɪ'bjuːʃən] N
[c] 捐献 juānxiàn [次 cì]

control [kən'trəul] I VT [+ country,
organization] 统治 tǒngzhì;
[+ person, emotion, disease, fire] 控
制 kòngzhì II N [U] [of country,
organization] 控制权 kòngzhì
quán III **controls** NPL [of vehicle,
machine, TV] 操纵装置 cāozòng
zhuāngzhì ▶**to control o.s.** 克制
自己 kèzhì zìjǐ ▶**to be in control
(of sth)** (of situation, car) 控制着
(某事) kòngzhì zhe (mǒushì) ▶**to
be under control** (fire, situation)
处于控制之下 chǔyú kòngzhì
zhīxià ▶**circumstances beyond
our control** 不在我们控制中的
中的情况 bùzài wǒmen kòngzhì
zhīzhōng de qíngkuàng

controversial [kɒntrə'vəːʃl]
ADJ 有争议的 yǒu zhēngyì de;
[+ book, film] 引起争论的 yǐnqǐ
zhēnglùn de

convenient [kən'viːnɪənt] ADJ
[+ method, system, time] 方便
的 fāngbiàn de; [+ place] 近便的
jìnbiàn de

conventional [kən'venʃənl] ADJ
符合习俗的 fúhé xísú de;
[+ method, product] 传统的
chuántǒng de

conversation [kɒnvə'seɪʃən]
N [c/u] 交谈 jiāotán [次 cì] ►to
have a conversation (about
sth/with sb) (和某人)谈(某事)
(hé mǒurén) tán (mǒushì)

convert [kən'vɜːt] VT (transform)
[+ substance] 使转化成 shǐ
zhuǎnhuà; [+ building] 改建
gǎijiàn ►to convert sth into sth
[+ substance] 将某物转化成某物
jiāng mǒuwù zhuǎnhuà chéng
mǒuwù; [+ building] 将某建筑改建
成某建筑 jiāng mǒujiànzhù gǎijiàn
chéng mǒujiànzhù

convince [kən'vɪns] VT 1 (cause to
believe) 使信服 shǐ xìnfú 2 (persuade)
说服 shuōfú ►to convince sb to do sth
说服某人去做某事 shuōfú mǒurén
qù zuò mǒushì

cook [kuk] I VT [+ food, meat,
vegetables] 烹调 pēngtiáo;
[+ meal] 做 zuò II VI 1 [person] 做
饭 zuòfàn 2 [food] 烧 shāo III N
[c] 厨师 chúshī [位 wèi] ►a good
cook 会做饭的人 huì zuòfàn
de rén

cooker ['kukə*] (Brit) N [c] 厨灶
chúzào [个 gè]

cookie ['kukɪ] N [c] 1 (US: for
eating) 小甜饼 xiǎotiánbǐng [块
kuài] 2 (Comput) 记忆块 jìyì kuài
[个 gè]

cooking ['kukɪŋ] N [u] 烹调
pēngtiáo

cool [kuːl] I ADJ 1 (凉的 liáng de

2 (calm, unemotional) 冷静的
lěngjìng de 3 (inf: good) 顶呱呱的
dǐngguāguā de; (fashionable) 酷
kù de II VT 使变凉 shǐ biànliáng
III VI 冷下来 lěngxiàlái IV N
►to keep/lose one's cool (inf)
保持冷静/失去自制而激动起来
bǎochí lěngjìng/shīqù zìzhì ér
jīdòng qǐlái ►to keep sth cool
保持某物的凉度 bǎochí mǒuwù
de liángdù

►**cool down** VI 变凉 biànliáng

co-operate [kəu'ɒpəreɪt] VI
1 (collaborate) 合作 hézuò 2 (be
helpful) 配合 pèihé

cope [kəup] VI 对付 duìfù

copper ['kɒpə*] N [u] 铜 tóng

copy ['kɒpɪ] I N 1 [c] 复制品
fùzhìpǐn [件 jiàn] 2 [c] 本/张/份
běn/zhāng/fèn II VT 模仿 mófǎng
►**to make a copy of sth** 复印某物
fùyìn mǒuwù

cork [kɔːk] N [c] 瓶塞 píngsāi
[个 gè]

corkscrew ['kɔːkskruː] N [c] 瓶塞
钻 píngsāizuàn [个 gè]

corn [kɔːn] N 1 [u] (Brit: cereal crop)
谷物 gǔwù 2 [u] (US: maize) 玉米
yùmǐ ►**corn on the cob** 玉米(棒
子) yùmǐ (bàngzi)

corner ['kɔːnə*] N [c] 1 角落
jiǎoluò [个 gè] 2 [of road] 街角
jiējiǎo [个 gè]

corpse [kɔːps] N [c] 死尸 sǐshī
[具 jù]

correct [kə'rekt] I ADJ 正确的
zhèngquè de; [+ decision, means,
procedure] 适当的 shìdàng de
II VT [+ mistake, fault, person] 纠

正 jiūzhèng

correction [kəˈrekʃən] N [c] 修改 xiūgǎi [次 cì]

corridor [ˈkɒrɪdɔːʳ] N [c] (in house, building) 走廊 zǒuláng [条 tiáo]; (on train) 车厢过道 chēxiāng guòdào [个 gè]

corruption [kəˈrʌpʃən] N [U] 贪赃舞弊 tānzāng wǔbì

cosmetics [kɒzˈmetɪks] NPL (beauty products) 化妆品 huàzhuāng pǐn

cost [kɒst] (pt, pp **cost**) I N [c] 价格 jiàgé [种 zhǒng] II VT 价格为 jiàgé wéi ▸ **how much does it cost?** 多少钱? zhè duōshǎo qián? ▸ **it costs 5 pounds/too much** 价格为5英镑/太高 jiàgé wéi wǔ yīngbàng/tàigāo ▸ **the cost of living** 生活费用 shēnghuó fèiyòng

costume [ˈkɒstjuːm] N [c/U] 戏装 xìzhuāng [套 tào]

cot [kɒt] N [c] 1 (Brit: child's) 幼儿床 yòu'ér chuáng [张 zhāng] 2 (US: bed) 帆布床 fānbù chuáng [张 zhāng]

cottage [ˈkɒtɪdʒ] N [c] 村舍 cūnshè [个 gè]

cotton [ˈkɒtn] I N [U] 1 (fabric) 棉布 miánbù 2 (thread) 棉线 miánxiàn II CPD [+ dress, sheets] 棉布 miánbù

cotton wool (Brit) N [U] 脱脂棉 tuōzhī mián

couch [kautʃ] N [c] 长沙发 cháng shāfā [个 gè]

cough [kɒf] I VI 咳嗽 késou II N [c] 咳嗽 késou [阵 zhèn] ▸ **to**

have a cough 咳嗽 késou

◯ **KEYWORD**

could [kud] AUX VB 1 (referring to past) ▸ **we couldn't go to the party** 我们没能去参加聚会 wǒmen méi néng qù cānjiā jùhuì ▸ **he couldn't read or write** 他不会读也不会写 tā bùhuì dú yě bùhuì xiě

2 (possibility) ▸ **he could be in the library** 他可能在图书馆 tā kěnéng zài túshūguǎn ▸ **you could have been killed!** 可能你连命都没了! kěnéng nǐ lián mìng dōu méile!

3 (in conditionals with "if") ▸ **if we had more time, I could finish this** 如果有更多时间,我能够完成的 rúguǒ yǒu gèngduō shíjiān, wǒ nénggòu wánchéng de ▸ **we'd have a holiday, if we could afford it** 如果能支付得起的话,我们就去度假了 rúguǒ néng zhīfù de qǐ de huà, wǒmen jiù qù dùjià le

4 (in offers, suggestions, requests) 可以 kěyǐ ▸ **I could call a doctor** 我可以叫个医生 wǒ kěyǐ jiào gè yīshēng ▸ **could I borrow the car?** 我可以借一下车吗? wǒ kěyǐ jiè yīxià chē ma? ▸ **he asked if he could make a phone call** 他问是否可以打个电话 tā wèn shìfǒu kěyǐ dǎ gè diànhuà

council [ˈkaunsl] N [c] 议会 yìhuì [个 gè]

count [kaunt] I VT 1 (also: **count**

up) 数 shǔ 2 (include) 把…计算
在内 bǎ…jìsuàn zàinèi II vi 2 数
shǔ 2 (matter) 有价值 yǒu jiàzhí
▶ **to count (up) to 10** 数到10
shǔdào shí

▶ **count on** VT FUS [+ support,
help] 指望 zhǐwàng; [+ person] 依
靠 yīkào

counter ['kaʊntə'] N [c] 柜台
guìtái [个 gè]

country ['kʌntrɪ] N 1 [c] (nation)
国家 guójiā [个 gè] 2 (countryside)
▶ **the country** 乡下 xiāngxià [个
gè] 3 [c] (native land) 家乡 jiāxiāng
[个 gè]

countryside ['kʌntrɪsaɪd] N [U]
农村 nóngcūn

couple ['kʌpl] N [c] 1 (married) 夫
妻 fūqī [对 duì]; (living together) 情
侣 qínglǚ [对 duì] 2 ▶ **a couple of**
(two) 两个 liǎnggè

courage ['kʌrɪdʒ] N [U] 勇气
yǒngqì

courier ['kʊrɪə'] N 1 (messenger)
信使 xìnshǐ [个 gè] 2 (rep) 旅游团
的服务员 lǚyóutuán de fúwùyuán
[个 gè]

course [kɔːs] N 1 [c] 课程 kèchéng
[个 gè] 2 [of meal] ▶ **first/next/
last course** 第一/下一/最后一道
菜 dìyī/xiàyī/zuìhòu yīdào cài [道
dào] 3 [c] (for golf, horse-racing) 跑
场 chǎng ▶ **of course** (naturally) 自
然 zìrán; (certainly) 当然 dāngrán
▶ **of course** 没问题! méi wèntí!
▶ **of course not!** 当然不!
dāngrán bùxíng!

court [kɔːt] N 1 (Law) 法
庭 fǎtíng [个 gè] 2 (for tennis,

badminton) 球场 qiúchǎng [个 gè]

courthouse ['kɔːthaʊs] (US) N [c]
法院 fǎyuàn [个 gè]

courtyard ['kɔːtjɑːd] N [c] 庭院
tíngyuàn [个 gè]

cousin ['kʌzn] N [c] (older male on
father's side) 堂兄 tángxiōng [个
gè]; (younger male on father's side)
堂弟 tángdì [个 gè]; (older female on
father's side) 堂姐 tángjiě [个 gè];
(younger female on father's side) 堂
妹 tángmèi [个 gè]; (older male on
mother's side) 表兄 biǎoxiōng [个
gè]; (younger male on mother's side)
表弟 biǎodì [个 gè]; (older female on
mother's side) 表姐 biǎojiě [个 gè];
(younger female on mother's side) 表
妹 biǎomèi [个 gè]

cover ['kʌvə'] I vt 1 ▶ **to cover
sth (with sth)** (用某物) 盖某物
(yòng mǒuwù) gàizhe mǒuwù 2 (in
insurance) ▶ **to cover sb (against
sth)** 给某人保(某事)的险 gěi
mǒurén bǎo (mǒushì de) xiǎn II N
1 [c] 套子 tàozi [个 gè] 2 [c] (封面
fēngmiàn [个 gè] 3 [U] (insurance)
保险 bǎoxiǎn III covers NPL (on
bed) 铺盖 pūgài ▶ **to be covered
in or with sth** 被某物覆盖 bèi
mǒuwù fùgài

▶ **cover up** VT [+ facts, feelings,
mistakes] 掩饰某事 (用某事)
(yòng mǒushì) yǎnshì mǒushì

cow [kaʊ] N [c] 奶牛 nǎiniú
[头 tóu]

coward ['kaʊəd] N [c] 胆小鬼
dǎnxiǎoguǐ [个 gè]

cowboy ['kaʊbɔɪ] N [c] 牛仔
niúzǎi [个 gè]

crab [kræb] N 1 [c] (creature) 螃蟹 pángxiè [只 zhǐ] 2 [U] (meat) 蟹肉 xièròu

crack [kræk] N [c] (in cloth, paper: fold) 裂缝 lièfèng [条 tiáo]
▶ **crack down on** VT FUS 对…严惩不贷 duì...yánchéng bùdài

cracked [krækt] ADJ 破裂的 pòliè de

cracker ['krækə'] N [c] (biscuit) 薄脆饼干 báocuì bǐnggān [块 kuài]

cradle ['kreɪdl] N [c] 摇篮 yáolán [个 gè]

craft [krɑːft] N [c] (weaving, pottery etc) 工艺 gōngyì [道 dào]

cramp [kræmp] N [c/U] 抽筋 chōujīn [阵 zhèn]

crane [kreɪn] N [c] 起重机 qǐzhòngjī [部 bù]

crash [kræʃ] I N [c] 1 (of car) 撞击 zhuàngjī [下 xià]; (of plane) 坠机 zhuìjī [次 cì] 2 (noise) 哗啦声 huālā shēng [声 shēng] II VT (+ car, plane) 使撞毁 shǐ zhuànghuǐ III VI 1 (car, driver) 撞击 zhuàngjī; (plane) 坠毁 zhuìhuǐ 2 (Comput) 死机 sǐjī ▶ a car/plane crash 撞车/飞机失事 zhuàngchē/fēijī shīshì ▶ to crash into sth 猛地撞上某物 měngde zhuàngshàng mǒuwù

crawl [krɔːl] VI 爬 pá

crazy ['kreɪzɪ] (inf) ADJ 发疯的 fāfēng de ▶ to go crazy 发疯 fāfēng

cream [kriːm] I N 1 [U] (dairy cream) 奶油 nǎiyóu 2 [c/U] (for skin) 乳霜 rǔshuāng [瓶 píng] II ADJ (in colour) 乳白色的 rǔbáisè de

crease [kriːs] N [c] (in cloth, paper: fold) 折痕 zhéhén [道 dào]; (wrinkle) 皱纹 zhòuwén [条 tiáo]

create [kriː'eɪt] VT 创造 chuàngzào

creative [kriː'eɪtɪv] ADJ 有创造力的 yǒu chuàngzàolì de

creature ['kriːtʃə'] N [c] 动物 dòngwù [种 zhǒng]

crèche [krɛʃ] (Brit) N [c] 儿所 tuō'érsuǒ [个 gè]

credit ['krɛdɪt] N 1 [U] (financial) 贷款 dàikuǎn 2 [U] (recognition) 赞扬 zànyáng 3 [c] (Scol, Univ) 学分 xuéfēn [个 gè] ▶ on credit 赊账 shēzhàng

credit card N [c] 信用卡 xìnyòng kǎ [张 zhāng]

crew [kruː] N 1 [c] 全体工作人员 quántǐ gōngzuò rényuán 2 [c] (TV) 组 zǔ [个 gè]

crib [krɪb] N [c] (US) 有围栏的童床 yǒu wéilán de tóngchuáng [张 zhāng]

cricket ['krɪkɪt] N [U] (sport) 板球 bǎnqiú

CRICKET

- 在大英帝国时代，**cricket** (板球) 做为一种夏季运动引入印度，巴基斯坦和澳大利亚等国。如今，板球在这些国家依然十分盛行。两队各11名选手，通常为男性。队员通常穿传统的白色运动服。板球的规则以复杂著称。两队的每个队员力图为自己的队尽力争取最多次数的 **run**

● （跑垒），其打击者在两组称
● 为 **stump**（三门柱）的柱子
● 间跑。另一队争取在击球手
● 跑到门柱前用球击中门柱，
● 还可以在球跑地前直接接球将
● 该击球手淘汰出局。

crime [kraɪm] N 1 [c] (illegal act) 罪行 zuìxíng [种 zhǒng] **2** [U] (illegal activities) 犯罪活动 fànzuì huódòng

criminal ['krɪmɪnl] N [c] 罪犯 zuìfàn [个 gè]

crisis ['kraɪsɪs] (pl crises ['kraɪsiːz]) N [c/U] 危机 wēijī [种 zhǒng]

crisp [krɪsp] N [c] (Brit: potato crisp) 薯片 shǔpiàn [片 piàn]

critical ['krɪtɪkl] ADJ 1 (crucial) 关键的 guānjiàn de 2 (serious) 危急的 wēijí de

criticism ['krɪtɪsɪzəm] N 1 [U] (censure) 批评 pīpíng 2 [c] (complaint) 指责 zhǐzé [种 zhǒng]

criticize ['krɪtɪsaɪz] VT 批评 pīpíng

Croatia [krəʊˈeɪʃə] N 克罗地亚 Kèluódìyà

crocodile ['krɒkədaɪl] N [c] 鳄鱼 èyú [只 zhī]

crooked ['krʊkɪd] ADJ (off-centre) 歪的 wāi de

crop [krɒp] N 1 [c] (plants) 庄稼 zhuāngjia [种 zhǒng] 2 [c] (amount produced) 收成 shōucheng [个 gè]

cross [krɒs] I N [c] 1 (x shape) 交叉符号 jiāochā fúhào [个 gè]; (showing disagreement) 叉号 chāhào [个 gè] 2 (crucifix shape) 十字 shízì [个 gè] 3 (Rel) 十字架

shízìjià [个 gè] II VT [+ street, room] 横穿 héngchuān III VI [roads, lines] 相交 xiāngjiāo IV ADJ (angry) 生气的 shēngqì de

▶ **cross out** VT (delete) 取消 qǔxiāo

▶ **cross over** VI (cross the street) 过马路 guò mǎlù

crossing ['krɒsɪŋ] N [c] 1 (voyage) 横渡 héngdù [次 cì] 2 (Brit) (also: **pedestrian crossing**) 人行横道 rénxíng héngdào [个 gè]

crossroads ['krɒsrəʊdz] N [c] (pl **crossroads**) N [c] 十字路口 shízì lùkǒu [个 gè]

crosswalk ['krɒswɔːk] (US) N [c] 人行横道 rénxíng héngdào [个 gè]

crossword ['krɒswɜːd] N [c] (also: **crossword puzzle**) 填字游戏 tiánzì yóuxì [个 gè]

crowd [kraʊd] N [c] 人群 rénqún [个 gè] ▶ **crowds of people** 大批人群 dàpī rénqún

crowded ['kraʊdɪd] ADJ 拥挤的 yōngjǐ de

crown [kraʊn] N [c] 皇冠 huángguān [个 gè]

cruel [krʊəl] ADJ [+ person] 残忍的 cánrěn de; [+ treatment, behaviour] 恶毒的 èdú de ▶ **to be cruel to sb** 残酷地对待某人 cánkù de duìdài mǒurén

cruelty ['krʊəltɪ] N [U] 残忍 cánrěn

cruise [kruːz] N [c] 游船 yóuchuán [艘 sōu] ▶ **to be/go on a cruise** 乘游船旅行 chéng yóuchuán lǚxíng

crush [krʌʃ] VT 1 [+ garlic] 压碎 yāsuì 2 [+ person] 使挤在一起 shǐ jízài yiqí

cry [kraɪ] VI (weep) 哭 kū ▸**what are you crying about?** 你哭什么? nǐ kū shénme?

cub [kʌb] N [c] **1** 幼兽 yòushòu [只 zhǐ] **2** (also: **cub scout**) 幼童军 yòutóngjūn [名 míng]

cube [kjuːb] N [c] 立方体 lìfāngtǐ [个 gè]

cucumber ['kjuːkʌmbə'] N [c/u] 黄瓜 huángguā [根 gēn]

cuddle ['kʌdl] I VT, VI 搂抱 lǒubào II N [c] 拥抱 yōngbào [个 gè]

cultural ['kʌltʃərəl] ADJ 文化的 wénhuà de

culture ['kʌltʃə'] N [c/u] 文化 wénhuà [种 zhǒng]

cunning ['kʌnɪŋ] ADJ 狡猾的 jiǎohuá de

cup [kʌp] N [c] **1** (for drinking) 杯子 bēizi [个 gè] **2** (trophy) 奖杯 jiǎngbēi [个 gè] ▸**a cup of tea** 一杯茶 yìbēi chá

cupboard ['kʌbəd] N [c] 柜子 guìzi [个 gè]

curb [kəːb] N [c] (US) = **kerb**

cure [kjuə'] I VT (Med) 治好 zhìhǎo; [+ patient] 治愈 zhìyù II N [c] (Med) 疗法 liáofǎ [种 zhǒng]

curious ['kjuərɪəs] ADJ 好奇的 hàoqí de ▸**to be curious about sb/sth** 对某人/某物感到好奇 duì mǒurén/mǒuwù gǎndào hàoqí

curl [kəːl] N [c] 卷发 juǎnfà [头 tóu]

curly ['kəːlɪ] ADJ 卷曲的 juǎnqū de

currant ['kʌrnt] N [c] 无子葡萄干 wúzǐ pútáo gān [粒 lì]

currency ['kʌrnsɪ] N [c/u] 货币 huòbì [种 zhǒng]

current ['kʌrnt] I N [c] **1** (of air, water) 流 liú [股 gǔ] **2** (Elec) 电流 diànliú [股 gǔ] II ADJ [+ situation, tendency, policy] 目前的 mùqián de

current affairs NPL 时事 shíshì ▸**a current affairs programme** 时事讨论节目 shíshì tǎolùn jiémù

curriculum [kə'rɪkjuləm] (pl **curriculums** or **curricula** [kə'rɪkjulə]) N [c] **1** 全部课程 quánbù kèchéng **2** (for particular subject) 课程 kèchéng [门 mén]

curriculum vitae [-'viːtaɪ] (esp Brit) N [c] 简历 jiǎnlì [份 fèn]

curry ['kʌrɪ] N [c/u] (dish) 咖喱 gālí [种 zhǒng]

cursor ['kəːsə'] (Comput) N [c] 光标 guāngbiāo [个 gè]

curtain ['kəːtn] N [c] (esp Brit) 窗帘 chuānglián [幅 fú] ▸**to draw the curtains** (together) 拉上窗帘 lāshàng chuānglián; (apart) 拉开窗帘 lākāi chuānglián

cushion ['kuʃən] N [c] 靠垫 kàodiàn [个 gè]

custom ['kʌstəm] I N **1** [c/u] (tradition) 传统 chuántǒng [个 gè] **2** [c/u] (convention) 惯例 guànlì [个 gè] II **customs** NPL 海关 hǎiguān ▸**to go through customs** 过海关 guò hǎiguān

customer ['kʌstəmə'] N [c] 顾客 gùkè [位 wèi]

customs officer N [c] 海关官员 hǎiguān guānyuán [位 wèi]

cut [kʌt] (pt, pp **cut**) I VT **1** (injure) 切 qiē ▸**to cut one's**

hand/knee 割破手/膝盖 gēpò shǒu/xīgài 3 [+ grass, hair, nails] 修剪 xiūjiǎn 4 [+ scene, episode, paragraph] 删剪 shānjiǎn 5 [+ prices, spending] 削减 xiāojiǎn II N 1 [c] (injury) 伤口 shāngkǒu [个 gè] 2 [c] (reduction) 削减 xuējiǎn [次 cì] ▶ to cut sth in half 将某物切成两半 jiāng mǒuwù qiēchéng liǎngbàn ▶ to cut o.s. 割破自己 gēpò zìjǐ ▶ to get or have one's hair cut 剪发 jiǎnfà ▶ a cut and blow-dry 剪发吹干 jiǎnfà chuīgàn

▶ cut down VT 1 [+ tree] 砍倒 kǎndǎo 2 (reduce) 减少 jiǎnshǎo
▶ cut down on VT FUS [+ alcohol, coffee, cigarettes] 减少 jiǎnshǎo
▶ cut off VT [+ part of sth] 切掉 qiēdiào; [+ supply] 停止供应 tíngzhǐ gōngyìng
▶ cut up VT 切碎 qiēsuì

cute [kju:t] ADJ 1 (inf) [+ child, dog, house] 可爱的 kě'ài de 2 (esp US: inf: attractive) 迷人的 mírén de

cutlery ['kʌtlərɪ] (Brit) N [U] 餐具 cānjù

CV N ABBR (= curriculum vitae) 简历 jiǎnlì

cybercafé ['saɪbəkæfeɪ] N [c] 网吧 wǎngbā [家 jiā]

cycle ['saɪkl] I N [c] 自行车 zìxíngchē [辆 liàng] II VI 骑自行车 qí zìxíngchē III CPD [+ shop, helmet, ride] 自行车 zìxíngchē ▶ to go cycling 骑自行车 qí zìxíngchē

cycle lane N [c] 自行车道 zìxíngchēdào [条 tiáo]

cycling ['saɪklɪŋ] N [U] 骑自行车 qí zixíngchē

cyclist ['saɪklɪst] N [c] 骑自行车的人 qí zìxíngchē de rén [个 gè]

cylinder ['sɪlɪndəʳ] N [c] [of gas] 罐 guàn [个 gè]

cynical ['sɪnɪkl] ADJ 愤世嫉俗的 fènshìjísú de

Cyprus ['saɪprəs] N 塞浦路斯 Sàipǔlùsī

Czech Republic N ▶ the Czech Republic 捷克共和国 Jiékègònghéguó

d

dad [dæd] (inf) N [c] 爸爸 bàba [个 gè]

daffodil ['dæfədɪl] N [c] 黄水仙 huángshuǐxiān [支 zhī]

daily ['deɪlɪ] I ADJ 每日的 měirì de II ADV 每日 měirì

daisy ['deɪzɪ] N [c] 雏菊 chújú [朵 duǒ]

dam [dæm] N [c] 水坝 shuǐbà [个 gè]

damage ['dæmɪdʒ] I N [u] 损坏 sǔnhuài 2 (dents, scratches) 损伤 sǔnshāng II VT 毁坏 huǐhuài

damp [dæmp] ADJ 潮湿的 cháoshī de

dance [dɑ:ns] I N 1 [c] (waltz, tango) 舞蹈 wǔdǎo [曲 qǔ] 2 [c] (social event) 舞会 wǔhuì [个 gè] II VI 跳舞 tiàowǔ

dancer ['dɑ:nsəʳ] N [c] 舞蹈演员 wǔdǎo yǎnyuán [位 wèi]

dancing ['dɑ:nsɪŋ] N [u] 跳舞 tiàowǔ

dandruff ['dændrəf] N [u] 头皮屑 tóupíxiè

danger ['deɪndʒəʳ] N 1 [u] (unsafe situation) 危险 wēixiǎn 2 [c] (hazard, risk) 威胁 wēixié [个 gè] ▶there is a danger of/that... 有...的危险 yǒu...de wēixiǎn ▶to be in danger of doing sth 有...的危险 yǒu...de wēixiǎn

dangerous ['deɪndʒrəs] ADJ 危险的 wēixiǎn de ▶it's dangerous to... ...是危险的 ...shì wēixiǎn de

Danish ['deɪnɪʃ] I ADJ 丹麦的 Dānmài de II N [u] (language) 丹麦语 Dānmàiyǔ

dare [deəʳ] I VT ▶to dare sb to do sth 激某人做某事 jī mǒurén zuò mǒushì II VI ▶to dare (to) do sth 敢做某事 gǎn zuò mǒushì ▶I daren't tell him (Brit) 我不敢告诉他 wǒ bùgǎn gàosù tā ▶I dare say (I suppose) 我想信 wǒ xiāngxìn ▶how dare you! 你怎敢！nǐ zěngǎn!

daring ['deərɪŋ] ADJ 勇敢的 yǒnggǎn de

dark [dɑ:k] I ADJ 1 [+ room, night] 黑暗的 hēi'àn de 2 [+ eyes, hair, skin] 黑色的 hēisè de；[+ person] 头发和皮肤深色的 tóufa hé pífū shēnsè de 3 [+ suit, fabric] 深色的 shēnsè de II N ▶the dark 黑暗 hēi'àn ▶dark blue/green 深蓝色/绿色 shēnlán sè/lǜsè ▶it is/is getting dark 天黑了 tiān hēile

darling ['dɑːlɪŋ] N 亲爱的 qīn'àide

dart [dɑːt]: **darts** NPL 投掷游戏 tóubiǎo yóuxì

data ['deɪtə] NPL 数据 shùjù

database ['deɪtəbeɪs] N [c] 数据库 shùjùkù [个 gè]

date [deɪt] I N [c] 1 日期 rìqī [个 gè] 2 (meeting with friend) 约会 yuēhuì [个 gè] 3 (fruit) 海枣 hǎizǎo [颗 kē] II VT [+ letter, cheque] 给…注明日期 gěi…zhùmíng rìqī ▸ **what's the date today?, what's today's date?** 今天几号? jīntiān jǐhào? ▸ **date of birth** 出生日期 chūshēng rìqī ▸ **to be out of date** (old-fashioned) 落伍 luòwǔ; (expired) 过期 guòqī ▸ **to be up to date** (modern) 时新 shíxīn

daughter ['dɔːtə'] N [c] 女儿 nǚ'ér [个 gè]

daughter-in-law ['dɔːtərɪnlɔː] (pl **daughters-in-law**) N [c] 媳妇 xífu [个 gè]

dawn [dɔːn] N [c/u] 黎明 límíng [个 gè]

day [deɪ] N 1 [c] 天 tiān 2 [c/u] (daylight hours) 白天 báitiān [个 gè] ▸ **during the day** 在白天 zài báitiān ▸ **the day before/after** 前/后一天 qián/hòu yītiān ▸ **the day after tomorrow** 后天 hòutiān ▸ **these days** (nowadays) 现在 xiànzài ▸ **the following day** 第二天 dì'èrtiān ▸ **one day/some day/one of these days** 有一天 yǒu yītiān ▸ **by day** 在白天 zài báitiān ▸ **all day (long)** 一天到晚 yītiān dàowǎn ▸ **to work an 8** hour day 每天工作8小时 měitiān gōngzuò bā xiǎoshí

daylight ['deɪlaɪt] N [U] 白昼 báizhòu

dead [dɛd] ADJ 1 死的 sǐ de 2 [+ battery] 不能再用的 bùnéng zài yòng de ▸ **over my dead body** (inf) 绝对不行! juéduì bùxíng!

deadline ['dɛdlaɪn] N [c] 截止日期 jiézhǐ rìqī [个 gè] ▸ **to meet a deadline** 赶上期限 gǎnshàng qíxiàn

deaf [dɛf] ADJ 聋的 lóng de; (partially) 耳背的 ěrbèi de

deafening ['dɛfnɪŋ] ADJ [+ noise] 震耳欲聋的 zhèn ěr yù lóng de

deal [diːl] (pt, pp **dealt**) N [c] 协议 xiéyì [个 gè] ▸ **to do/make/strike a deal with sb** 和某人做买卖 hé mǒurén zuò mǎimài ▸ **it's a deal!** (inf) 成交! chéngjiāo! ▸ **a good or great deal (of)** 大量(的…) dàliàng(de…)
▸ **deal with** VT FUS [+ problem] 处理 chǔlǐ

dealer ['diːlə'] N [c] 1 商人 shāngrén [个 gè] 2 (in drugs) 毒品贩子 dúpǐn fànzǐ [个 gè]

dealt [dɛlt] PT, PP of **deal**

dear [dɪə'] I ADJ 1 亲爱的 qīn'ài de 2 (esp Brit: expensive) 昂贵的 ánguì de II N ▸ **(my) dear** 亲爱的 qīn'ài de III INT ▸ **oh dear/dear dear/dear me!** 呵/哎呀! hè/āiyā! ▸ **Dear Sir/Madam** (in letter) 亲爱的先生/女士 qīn'ài de xiānshēng/nǚshì ▸ **Dear Peter/Jane** 亲爱的彼得/简 qīn'ài de Bǐdé/Jiǎn

death [dɛθ] N [c/u] 死亡 sǐwáng

[个 gè] ▸**(a matter of) life and death** 生死攸关(的事情) shēngsǐ yōuguān (de shìqíng) ▸**to scare/ bore sb to death** 吓死某人/使某 人感到无聊 xiàsǐ mǒurén/shǐ mǒurén gǎndào wúliáo zhī jí

death penalty N ▸**the death penalty** 死刑 sǐxíng

debate [dɪˈbeɪt] N [c/u] 讨论 tǎolùn [次 cì]

debt [dɛt] N 1 [c] (sum of money owed) 债务 zhàiwù [笔 bǐ] 2 [u] (state of owing money) 欠债 qiànzhài ▸**to be in/get into debt** 负债 fùzhài

decade [ˈdɛkeɪd] N [c] 十年 shínián [个 gè]

decaffeinated [dɪˈkæfɪneɪtɪd] ADJ 不含咖啡因的 bù hán kāfēiyīn de

deceive [dɪˈsiːv] VT 欺骗 qīpiàn

December [dɪˈsɛmbəʳ] N [c/u] 十 二月 shíʼèryuè; see also **July**

decent [ˈdiːsənt] ADJ [+ person] 受 尊重的 shòu zūnzhòng de

decide [dɪˈsaɪd] I VT [+ question, argument] 解决 jiějué II VI 决定 juédìng ▸**to decide to do sth** 决 定做某事 juédìng zuò mǒushì ▸**I can't decide whether…** 我无 法决定是否… wǒ wúfǎ juédìng shìfǒu…

decimal [ˈdɛsɪməl] I ADJ [+ system, currency] 十进位的 shíjìnwèi de II N [c] 小数 xiǎoshù [个 gè]

decision [dɪˈsɪʒən] N [c] 决 定 juédìng [个 gè] ▸**to make a decision** 作出决定 zuòchū juédìng

deck [dɛk] N [c] 甲板 jiǎbǎn [个 gè]

deckchair [ˈdɛktʃɛəʳ] N [c] 折叠式 躺椅 zhédiéshì tǎngyǐ [把 bǎ]

declare [dɪˈklɛəʳ] VT 1 [+ intention, attitude] 宣布 xuānbù; [+ support] 表明 biǎomíng 2 (at customs) 报 关 bàoguān ▸**to declare war (on sb)** (向某人)宣战 (xiàng mǒurén) xuānzhàn

decorate [ˈdɛkəreɪt] VT 1 ▸**to decorate (with)** (用…)装饰 (yòng…) zhuāngshì 2 (paint etc) 装潢 zhuānghuáng

decoration [dɛkəˈreɪʃən] N [c/u] 装饰 zhuāngshì [种 zhǒng]

decrease [n ˈdiːkriːs, vb diːˈkriːs] I N [c] ▸**decrease (in sth)** (某 物的)减少 (mǒuwù de) jiǎnshǎo II VT, VI 减少 jiǎnshǎo

deduct [dɪˈdʌkt] VT ▸**to deduct sth (from sth)** (从某物中)减去 某物 (cóng mǒuwùzhōng) jiǎnqù mǒuwù

deep [diːp] I ADJ 1 深的 shēn de 2 [+ voice, sound] 低沉的 dīchén de 3 [+ sleep] 酣睡的 hānshuì de II ADV 深 shēn ▸**it is 1 m deep** 它有1米深 tā yǒu yīmǐ shēn ▸**to take a deep breath** 深呼吸 shēn hūxì

deeply [ˈdiːpli] ADV 1 (breathe, sigh) 深深地 shēnshēn de 2 (sleep) 沉沉 地 chénchén de

deer [dɪəʳ] (pl deer) N [c] 鹿 lù [头 tóu]

defeat [dɪˈfiːt] I N [c/u] 1 [of army] 战败 zhànbài [次 cì] 2 [of team] 击 败 jībài [次 cì] II VT 1 [+ enemy,

opposition] 战胜 zhànshèng
2 [+ team] 击败 jībài

defect [ˈdiːfekt] N [c] 缺点 quēdiǎn [个 gè]

defence, (US) **defense** [dɪˈfens] N 1 [u] (protection) 防御 fángyù 2 [u] (Mil) 国防措施 guófáng cuòshī ▸**the Ministry of Defence**, (US) **the Department of Defense** 国防部 Guófángbù

defend [dɪˈfend] vT 防御 fángyù ▸**to defend o.s.** 自卫 zìwèi

defender [dɪˈfendə'] N [c] (in team) 防守队员 fángshǒu duìyuán [个 gè]

defense [dɪˈfens] (US) N = **defence**

definite [ˈdefɪnɪt] ADJ 1 [+ plan, answer, views] 明确的 míngquè de 2 [+ improvement, possibility, advantage] 肯定的 kěndìng de ▸**is that definite?** 肯定吗？ kěndìng ma?

definitely [ˈdefɪnɪtlɪ] ADV 确定地 quèdìng de

defy [dɪˈfaɪ] vT [+ law, ban] 蔑视 miǎoshì

degree [dɪˈɡriː] N [c] 1 ▸**degree (of sth)** (level) (某事的) 程度 (mǒushì de) chéngdù [种 zhǒng] 2 (measure of temperature, angle, latitude) 度 dù 3 (at university) 学位 xuéwèi [个 gè] ▸**to some degree/a certain degree** 从某种/一定程度上来说 cóng mǒuzhǒng/yídìng chéngdù shàng lái shuō ▸**10 degrees below (zero)** 零下10度 língxià shídù ▸**a degree in maths** 数学学位

shùxué xuéwèi

delay [dɪˈleɪ] I vT 1 [+ decision, ceremony] 推迟 tuīchí 2 [+ person] 耽搁 dāngē [+ plane, train] 延误 yánwù II vI 耽搁 dāngē III N [c/u] 延误 yánwù [个 gè] ▸**to be delayed** [person, flight, departure] 被耽搁了 bèi dāngē le ▸**without delay** 立即 lìjí

delete [dɪˈliːt] vT 删除 shānchú

deliberate [dɪˈlɪbərɪt] ADJ 故意的 gùyì de ▸**it wasn't deliberate** 那不是故意的 nà bùshì gùyì de

deliberately [dɪˈlɪbərɪtlɪ] ADV 故意地 gùyì de

delicate [ˈdelɪkɪt] ADJ 1 (fragile) 易碎的 yìsuì de 2 [+ problem, situation, issue] 微妙的 wēimiào de 3 [+ colour, flavour, smell] 清淡可口的 qīngdàn kěkǒu de

delicious [dɪˈlɪʃəs] ADJ 美味的 měiwèi de

delight [dɪˈlaɪt] N [u] 快乐 kuàilè

delighted [dɪˈlaɪtɪd] ADJ ▸**delighted (at or with sth)** (对某事) 感到高兴 (duì mǒushì) gǎndào gāoxìng ▸**to be delighted to do sth** 乐意做某事 lèyì zuò mǒushì

deliver [dɪˈlɪvə'] vT 1 [+ letter, parcel] 传送 chuánsòng 2 [+ baby] 接生 jiēshēng

delivery [dɪˈlɪvərɪ] N 1 [u] 传送 chuánsòng 2 [c] (consignment) 递送的货物 dìsòng de huòwù [件 jiàn]

demand [dɪˈmɑːnd] I vT [+ apology, explanation, pay rise] 要求 yāoqiú II N 1 [c] (request) 要求 yāoqiú 2 [u] (for product)

需求量 xūqiúliàng ▸ to make demands on sb/sth 对某人/某事提出要求 duì mǒurén/mǒushì tíchū yāoqiú ▸ to be in demand 受欢迎 shòu huānyíng

democracy [dɪ'mɒkrəsɪ] N 1 [U] (system) 民主 mínzhǔ 2 [c] (country) 民主国 mínzhǔ guó [个 gè]

democratic [demə'krætɪk] ADJ 民主的 mínzhǔ de

demolish [dɪ'mɒlɪʃ] VT 拆毁 chāihuǐ

demonstrate ['demənstreɪt] I VT [+ skill, appliance] 演示 yǎnshì II VI ▸ to demonstrate (for/against sth) 示威(支持/反对某事) shìwēi (zhīchí/fǎnduì mǒushì) ▸ to demonstrate how to do sth 演示如何做某事 yǎnshì rúhé zuò mǒushì

demonstration [demən'streɪʃən] N [c] 1 示威 shìwēi [次 cì] 2 [of appliance, cooking] 演示 yǎnshì [个 gè]

demonstrator ['demənstreɪtə'] N [c] 示威者 shìwēizhě [个 gè]

denim ['denɪm] N [U] 斜纹粗棉布 xiéwén cū miánbù

Denmark ['denmɑːk] N 丹麦 Dānmài

dent [dent] N [c] 凹部 āobù [个 gè]

dental ['dentl] ADJ 牙齿的 yáchǐ de

dentist ['dentɪst] N [c] 1 (person) 牙医 yáyī [位 wèi] 2 ▸ the dentist('s) 牙医诊所 yáyī zhěnsuǒ [家 jiā]

deny [dɪ'naɪ] VT 否定 fǒudìng

deodorant [diː'əʊdərənt] N [c/U] 除臭剂 chúchòujì [种 zhǒng]

depart [dɪ'pɑːt] VI ▸ to depart (from/for somewhere) (从某地) 出发/出发 (赶往某地) (cóng mǒudì) chūfā/chūfā (gǎnwǎng mǒudì)

department [dɪ'pɑːtmənt] N 1 (in shop) 部门 bùmén [个 gè] 2 (in school or college) 系 xì [个 gè]

department store N [c] 百货商店 bǎihuò shāngdiàn [家 jiā]

departure [dɪ'pɑːtʃə'] N [c/U] 出发 chūfā

departure lounge N [c] 候机厅 hòujītīng [个 gè]

depend [dɪ'pend] VI 1 ▸ to depend on sth 依某物而定 yī mǒuwù ér dìng ▸ you can depend on me/him (rely on, trust) 你可以信赖我/他 nǐ kěyǐ xìnlài wǒ/tā 2 ▸ to depend on sth (for survival) 依靠某人/某物为生 yīkào mǒurén/mǒuwù wéishēng ▸ it (all) depends 要看具体情况而定 yào kàn qíngkuàng érdìng

deposit [dɪ'pɒzɪt] N [c] 储蓄 chǔxù [笔 bǐ]; (on house, table, when hiring) 押金 yājīn [份 fèn] ▸ to put down a deposit of 50 pounds 付50英镑的保证金 zhīfù wǔshí yīngbàng de bǎozhèngjīn

depressed [dɪ'prest] ADJ 沮丧的 jǔsàng de

depressing [dɪ'presɪŋ] ADJ 令人沮丧的 lìng rén jǔsàng de

deprive [dɪ'praɪv] VT ▸ to deprive

sb of sth 剥夺某人某物 bōduó mǒurén mǒuwù

depth [dɛpθ] N [c/u] 深 shēn ▸ **at/to/from a depth of 3 metres** 在/到/从3米深处 zài/dào/cóng sānmǐ shēnchù ▸ **to study/ analyse sth in depth** 深入研 究/分析某事 shēnrù yánjiū/fēnxī mǒushì

descend [dɪ'sɛnd] VI (frm) 下来 xiàlái ▸ **to be descended from** 是…的后裔 shì…de hòuyì

describe [dɪs'kraɪb] VT 描述 miáoshù

description [dɪs'krɪpʃən] N [c/u] 描述 miáoshù [种 zhǒng]

desert ['dɛzət] N [c/u] (Geo) 沙漠 shāmò [片 piàn] **2** [c] (fig: wasteland) 荒地 huāngdì [片 piàn]

deserve [dɪ'zə:v] VT 应受 yīngshòu ▸ **to deserve to do sth** 应该获得某事 yīnggāi huòdé mǒushì

design [dɪ'zaɪn] **I** N **1** [u] (art, process, layout, shape) 设计 shèjì **2** [c] (pattern) 图案 tú'àn [种 zhǒng] **II** VT 设计 shèjì ▸ **to be designed for sb/to do sth** 专门为某人/做某事设计 zhuānmén wèi mǒurén/zuò mǒushì shèjì

designer [dɪ'zaɪnə'] **I** N [c] 设计者 shèjìzhě [位 wèi] **II** CPD [+ clothes, label, jeans] 名师设计的 míngshī shèjì de

desk [dɛsk] N [c] **1** (in office) 办公桌 bàngōngzhuō [张 zhāng] **2** (for pupil) 书桌 shūzhuō [张 zhāng] **3** (in hotel, at airport, hospital) 服务台 fúwùtái [个 gè]

desk clerk (US) N [c] 接待员

jiēdàiyuán [位 wèi]

despair [dɪs'pɛə'] N [u] 绝望 juéwàng ▸ **in despair** 绝望地 juéwàng de

desperate ['dɛspərɪt] ADJ **1** [+ person] 绝望的 juéwàng de **2** [+ attempt, effort] 铤而走险的 tǐng ér zǒu xiǎn de **3** [+ situation] 危急的 wēijí de

desperately ['dɛspərɪtlɪ] ADV 拼命地 pīnmìng de

despise [dɪs'paɪz] VT 鄙视 bǐshì

despite [dɪs'paɪt] PREP 尽管 jǐnguǎn

dessert [dɪ'zə:t] N [c/u] 饭后甜点 fànhòu tiándiǎn [份 fèn]

destination [dɛstɪ'neɪʃən] N [c] 目的地 mùdìdì [个 gè]

destroy [dɪs'trɔɪ] VT 破坏 pòhuài

destruction [dɪs'trʌkʃən] N [u] 破坏 pòhuài

detail ['di:teɪl] **I** N [c] 细节 xìjié [个 gè] **II** **details** NPL 详情 xiángqíng ▸ **in detail** 详细地 xiángxì de

detailed ['di:teɪld] ADJ 详细的 xiángxì de

detective [dɪ'tɛktɪv] N [c] 侦探 zhēntàn [位 wèi]

detective story, detective novel N [c] 侦探小说 zhēntàn xiǎoshuō [部 bù]

detergent [dɪ'tə:dʒənt] N [c/u] 清洁剂 qīngjiéjì [种 zhǒng]

determined [dɪ'tə:mɪnd] ADJ 坚定的 jiāndìng de ▸ **to be determined to do sth** 决心做某事 juéxīn zuò mǒushì

detour ['di:tuə'] N [c] ▸ **to make**

a detour 绕道 ràodào [次 cì]
2 (US: on road) 绕行道路 ràoxíng dàolù [条 tiáo]

develop [dɪ'veləp] **I** VT
1 [+ business, idea, relationship] 发展 fāzhǎn; [+ land, resource] 开发 kāifā **2** [+ product, weapon] 开发 kāifā **2** (Phot) 冲洗 chōngxǐ
II VI [person] 成长 chéngzhǎng; [country, situation, friendship, skill] 发展 fāzhǎn

development [dɪ'veləpmənt] N
1 (U) (growth) 成长 chéngzhǎng; (political, economic) 发展 fāzhǎn
2 [c] (event) 新形势 xīn xíngshì [种 zhǒng]

devil ['dɛvl] N ▸ **the Devil** 撒旦 Sādàn [个 gè]

devoted [dɪ'vəutɪd] ADJ
1 [+ husband, daughter] 忠诚的 zhōngchéng de **2** ▸ **devoted to sth** (specialising in) 致力于某事 zhìlì yú mǒushì de

diabetes [daɪə'biːtiːz] N [U] 糖尿病 tángniàobìng

diabetic [daɪə'bɛtɪk] N [c] 糖尿病患者 tángniàobìng huànzhě [个 gè]

diagonal [daɪ'ægənl] ADJ 斜的 xié de

diagram ['daɪəgræm] N [c] 图解 tújiě [个 gè]

dial ['daɪəl] **I** N [c] (on clock or meter) 标度盘 biāodùpán [个 gè] **II** VT [+ number] 拨 bō **III** VI 拨号 bōhào

dialling code ['daɪəlɪŋ-] (Brit) N [c] 电话区号 diànhuà qūhào [个 gè]

dialogue, (US) **dialog** ['daɪəlɒg]
N [c/u] (conversation) 对话 duìhuà [次 cì]

diamond ['daɪəmənd] N [c] 钻石 zuànshí [颗 kē]

diaper ['daɪəpə*] (US) N [c] 尿布 niàobù [块 kuài]

diarrhoea, (US) **diarrhea** [daɪə'riːə] N [U] 腹泻 fùxiè ▸ **to have diarrhoea** 腹泻 fùxiè

diary ['daɪərɪ] N [c] **1** 日记簿 rìjìbù [个 gè] **2** (daily account) 日记 rìjì [篇 piān]

dice [daɪs] (pl **dice**) N [c] 骰子 shǎizi [个 gè]

dictation [dɪk'teɪʃən] N [c/u] (at school, college) 听写 tīngxiě [次 cì]

dictionary ['dɪkʃənrɪ] N [c] 词典 cídiǎn [本 běn]

did [dɪd] PT OF **do**

die [daɪ] VI 死 sǐ ▸ **to die of or from sth** 死于某事 sǐyú mǒushì ▸ **to be dying** 奄奄一息 yǎn yǎn yī xī ▸ **to be dying for sth/to do sth** 渴望某事/做某事 kěwàng mǒushì/zuò mǒushì
▸ **die out** VI **1** [custom, way of life] 灭亡 mièwáng **2** [species] 灭绝 mièjué

diesel ['diːzl] N [U] (also: **diesel oil**) 柴油 cháiyóu **2** [c] (vehicle) 柴油机驱动的车辆 cháiyóujī qūdòng de chēliàng [辆 liàng]

diet ['daɪət] **I** N **1** [c/u] (food) 饮食 yǐnshí [种 zhǒng] **2** [c/u] (slimming) 减肥饮食 jiǎnféi yǐnshí [份 fèn] **II** VI 节食 jiéshí ▸ **to be on a diet** 实行减肥节食 shíxíng jiǎnféi jiéshí

difference ['dɪfrəns] N [c] 差异

chāyì [种 zhǒng] ▶the difference in size/colour 尺寸/颜色上的差异 chǐcùn/yánsè shàng de chāyì ▶to make a/no difference (to sb/sth) (对某人/某事) 有/无影响 (duì mǒurén/mǒushì) yǒu/wú yīngxiǎng

different ['dɪfrənt] ADJ 不同的 bùtóng de

difficult ['dɪfɪkəlt] ADJ 1 困难的 kùnnán de 2 [+ person, child] 执拗的 zhíniù de ▶it is difficult for us to understand her 我们很难理解她 wǒmen hěnnán lǐjiě tā

difficulty ['dɪfɪkəltɪ] N [c] 困难 kùnnán [个 gè] ▶to have difficulty/difficulties 有困难 yǒu kùnnán

dig [dɪg] (pt, pp dug) I VT 1 [+ hole] 挖 wā 2 [+ garden] 掘土 juétǔ II VI (with spade) 挖掘 wājué ▶dig up VT [+ plant, body] 挖出来 wāchūlái

digital ['dɪdʒɪtl] ADJ 1 [+ clock, watch] 数字的 shùzì de 2 [+ recording, technology] 数码的 shùmǎ de

digital camera N [c] 数码相机 shùmǎ xiàngjī [台 tái]

digital television N [U] 数字电视 shùzì diànshì

dim [dɪm] ADJ 1 暗淡的 àndàn de 2 (inf: stupid) 迟钝的 chídùn de

dime [daɪm] (US) N [c] 一角银币 yìjiǎo yínbì [枚 méi]

dimension [daɪ'mɛnʃən] I N [c] (aspect) 方面 fāngmiàn [个 gè] II dimensions NPL (measurements) 面积 miànjī

diner ['daɪnə'] N [c] (US: restaurant) 廉价餐馆 liánjià cānguǎn [家 jiā]

dinghy ['dɪŋgɪ] N [c] (also: rubber dinghy) 橡皮筏 xiàngpífá [个 gè]

dining room N [c] 1 (in house) 饭厅 fàntīng [个 gè] 2 (in hotel) 餐厅 cāntīng [个 gè]

dinner ['dɪnə'] N 1 [c/U] 晚餐 wǎncān [顿 dùn] 2 [c] (formal meal) 正餐 zhèngcān [顿 dùn]

dinner party N [c] 宴会 yànhuì [个 gè]

dinner time N [c/U] 晚饭时间 wǎnfàn shíjiān [段 duàn]

dinosaur ['daɪnəsɔː'] N [c] 恐龙 kǒnglóng [只 zhī]

dip [dɪp] VT 蘸 zhàn

diploma [dɪ'pləumə] N [c] 毕业文凭 bìyè wénpíng [个 gè]

direct [daɪ'rɛkt] I ADJ 直达的 zhídá de II VT 1 (show) 给…指路 gěi…zhǐlù 2 (manage) 管理 guǎnlǐ 3 [+ play, film, programme] 导演 dǎoyǎn III ADV 直接地 zhíjiē de

direction [dɪ'rɛkʃən] I N 方向 fāngxiàng [个 gè] II directions NPL 1 (to get somewhere) 指路说明 zhǐlù shuōmíng 2 (for doing something) 用法说明 yòngfǎ shuōmíng ▶in the direction of 朝 cháo

director [dɪ'rɛktə'] N [c] 1 [of company] 经理 jīnglǐ [位 wèi] 2 [of organization, public authority] 主任 zhǔrèn [位 wèi] 3 [of play, film] 导演 dǎoyǎn [位 wèi]

directory [dɪ'rɛktərɪ] N [c] 电话号码簿 diànhuà hàomǎbù [个 gè]

2 (on computer) 文件名录 wénjiàn mínglù [个 gè]

dirt [dəːt] N [U] 污物 wūwù

dirty ['dəːtɪ] ADJ 脏的 zāng de

disabled [dɪs'eɪbld] ADJ **1** 伤残的 shāngcán de **2** (mentally) 残疾的 cánjí de

disadvantage [dɪsəd'vɑːntɪdʒ] N [c/u] (drawback) 不利 bùlì [种 zhǒng]

disagree [dɪsə'griː] VI ▸ **to disagree (with sb)** 不同意 (某人的观点) bù tóngyì (mǒurén de guāndiǎn) ▸ **to disagree (with sth)** (对某事表示) 不同意 (duì mǒushì biǎoshì) bù tóngyì

disagreement [dɪsə'griːmənt] N [c] (argument) 争执 zhēngzhí [个 gè]

disappear [dɪsə'pɪəʳ] VI **1** (from view) 消失 xiāoshī **2** (go missing) 失踪 shīzōng **3** (cease to exist) 消失 xiāoshī

disappearance [dɪsə'pɪərəns] N [c/u] (of person) 失踪 shīzōng [次 cì]

disappoint [dɪsə'pɔɪnt] VT [+ person] 使失望 shǐ shīwàng

disappointed [dɪsə'pɔɪntɪd] ADJ 失望的 shīwàng de

disappointment [dɪsə'pɔɪntmənt] N **1** [U] (emotion) 失望 shīwàng **2** [c] (cause) 令人失望的人/事 lìng rén shīwàng de rén/shì [个/件 gè/jiàn]

disapprove [dɪsə'pruːv] VI ▸ **to disapprove (of sb/sth)** 不同意 (某人/某事) bù tóngyì (mǒurén/mǒushì)

disaster [dɪ'zɑːstəʳ] N [c/u] **1** (earthquake, flood) 灾难 zāinàn [次 cì] **2** (accident, crash etc) 灾祸 zāihuò [场 chǎng] **3** (fiasco) 惨败 cǎnbài [次 cì] **4** (serious situation) 灾难 zāinàn [个 gè]

disastrous [dɪ'zɑːstrəs] ADJ **1** (catastrophic) 灾难性的 zāinànxìng de **2** (unsuccessful) 惨败的 cǎnbài de

disc [dɪsk] N [c] **1** 圆盘 yuánpán [个 gè] **2** (Comput) = **disk**

discipline ['dɪsɪplɪn] N [U] 纪律 jìlǜ

disc jockey N [c] 简称为DJ, 意为广播电台或迪斯科舞厅流行音乐唱片播放及介绍人

disco ['dɪskəʊ] N (event) 迪斯科 dísīkē

disconnect [dɪskə'nekt] VT **1** [+ pipe, tap, hose] 拆开 chāikāi **2** [+ computer, cooker, TV] 断开 duànkāi

discount [N 'dɪskaʊnt] N [c/u] 折扣 zhékòu [个 gè]

discourage [dɪs'kʌrɪdʒ] VT 使泄气 shǐ xièqì

discover [dɪs'kʌvəʳ] VT 发现 fāxiàn

discovery [dɪs'kʌvərɪ] N **1** [c/u] (of treasure, cure) 发现 fāxiàn **2** [c] (thing found) 被发现的事物 bèi fāxiàn de shìwù [个 gè]

discrimination [dɪskrɪmɪ'neɪʃən] N [U] 歧视 qíshì ▸ **racial/sexual discrimination** 种族/性别歧视 zhǒngzú/xìngbié qíshì

discuss [dɪs'kʌs] VT 讨论 tǎolùn

discussion [dɪs'kʌʃən] N 讨

论 tǎolùn [次 cì]

disease [dɪ'ziːz] N [C/U] (illness) 病 bìng [场 chǎng]

disgraceful [dɪs'greɪsfʊl] ADJ 可 耻的 kěchǐ de

disguise [dɪs'gaɪz] I N [c] 伪装 品 wěizhuāngpǐn [件 jiàn] II VT
▸ **(to be) disguised (as sth/sb)** (+person) 假扮成 (某物/某人) jiǎbànchéng (mǒuwù/mǒurén)
▸ **in disguise** 乔装着 qiáozhuāng zhe

disgusted [dɪs'gʌstɪd] ADJ 感到 厌恶的 gǎndào yànwù de

disgusting [dɪs'gʌstɪŋ] ADJ
1 (+food, habit) 令人作呕的 lìng rén zuò'ǒu de **2** (+behaviour, situation) 讨厌的 tǎoyàn de

dish [dɪʃ] I N [c] **1** 盘 pán [个 gè]; (for eating) 碟 dié [个 gè] **2** (recipe, food) 一道菜 yī dào cài [道 dào] **3** (also: **satellite dish**) 盘形物 pánxíngwù [个 gè] II dishes NPL 碗碟 wǎndié ▸ **to do or wash the dishes** 刷洗碗碟 shuāxǐ wǎndié

dishonest [dɪs'ɒnɪst] ADJ
1 不诚实的 bù chéngshí de
2 (+behaviour) 不正直的 bù zhèngzhí de

dishwasher ['dɪʃwɒʃə'] N [c] 洗碗 机 xǐwǎnjī [台 tái]

dishwashing liquid ['dɪʃwɒʃɪŋ-] (US) N [U] 洗洁剂 xǐjiéjì

disinfectant [dɪsɪn'fektənt] N [C/U] 消毒剂 xiāodújì [种 zhǒng]

disk [dɪsk] N [C] (Comput: hard) 硬 盘 yìngpán [个 gè]; (floppy) 软盘 ruǎnpán [张 zhāng]

dislike [dɪs'laɪk] VT 不喜欢 bù

xǐhuān ▸ **one's likes and dislikes** 某人的爱好和厌恶 mǒurén de àihào hé yànwù

dismiss [dɪs'mɪs] VT 解雇 jiěgù

disobedient [dɪsə'biːdɪənt] ADJ 不服从的 bù fúcóng de

disobey [dɪsə'beɪ] VT **1** 不顺从 bù shùncóng **2** (+order) 不服从 bù fúcóng

display [dɪs'pleɪ] I N [c] **1** (in shop, at exhibition) 陈列 chénliè [种 zhǒng] **2** (c) (information on screen) 显示 xiǎnshì [个 gè] **3** (c) (screen) 显示屏 xiǎnshìpíng [个 gè] II VT **1** (+exhibits) 陈列 chénliè **2** (+results, information) 显示 xiǎnshì

disposable [dɪs'pəuzəbl] ADJ 一 次性的 yícìxìng de

dispute [dɪs'pjuːt] (industrial) 争 执 zhēngzhí

disqualify [dɪs'kwɒlɪfaɪ] VT 取 消…的资格 qǔxiāoellipherede zìgé

disrupt [dɪs'rʌpt] VT
1 (+conversation, meeting) 扰 乱 rǎoluàn **2** (+plan, process) 妨 碍 fáng'ài

dissolve [dɪ'zɒlv] VT (in liquid) 溶 解 róngjiě

distance ['dɪstns] N [C/U] 距 离 jùlí [个 gè] ▸ **within walking distance** 步行可到 bùxíng kě dào

distinct [dɪs'tɪŋkt] ADJ
[+advantage, change] 明确的 míngquè de

distinguish [dɪs'tɪŋwɪʃ] VT
▸ **to distinguish one thing from another** 将一事物与另一事物

distract [dɪsˈtrækt] VT (+ person) 使分心 shǐ fēnxīn ▸ **to distract sb's attention** 分散某人的注意力 fēnsàn mǒurén de zhùyìlì

distribute [dɪsˈtrɪbjuːt] VT 1 (hand out) 分发 fēnfā 2 (share out) 分配 fēnpèi

district ['dɪstrɪkt] N [c] 地区 dìqū [个 gè]

disturb [dɪsˈtəːb] VT (interrupt) 打扰 dǎrǎo

disturbing [dɪsˈtəːbɪŋ] ADJ 令人不安的 lìng rén bù'ān de

ditch [dɪtʃ] N [c] 沟 gōu [条 tiáo]

dive [daɪv] VI (into water) 跳水 tiàoshuǐ 2 (under water) 潜水 qiánshuǐ

diver ['daɪvə'] N [c] 潜水员 qiánshuǐyuán [位 wèi]

diversion [daɪˈvəːʃən] N [c] (Brit) 临时改道 línshí gǎidào [次 cì]

divide [dɪˈvaɪd] VT 1 ▸ **to divide (up)** 划分 huàfēn 2 (in maths) 除 chú 3 ▸ **to divide sth between/among sb/sth** (share) 在两个/两个以上的人/物之间分配某物 zài liǎnggè/sāngè yǐshàng de rén/wù zhījiān fēnpèi mǒuwù 4 (into groups) 分开 fēnkāi ▸ **to divide sth in half** 将某物一分为二 jiāng mǒuwù yī fēn wéi èr ▸ **40 divided by 5** 40除以5 sìshí chúyǐ wǔ

diving ['daɪvɪŋ] N [u] 1 (underwater) 潜水 qiánshuǐ 2 (from board) 跳水 tiàoshuǐ

division [dɪˈvɪʒən] N 1 [u] (Math) 除法 chúfǎ 2 [u] (sharing out of

labour, resources) 分配 fēnpèi

divorce [dɪˈvɔːs] N 1 [c/u] 离婚 líhūn [次 cì] II VT (+ spouse) 与⋯离婚 yǔ⋯líhūn III VI 离婚 líhūn

divorced [dɪˈvɔːst] ADJ 离异的 líyì de ▸ **to get divorced** 离婚 líhūn

DIY (Brit) N ABBR (= **do-it-yourself**) 自己动手的活计 zìjǐ dòngshǒu de huójì ▸ **to do DIY** 自己动手做 zìjǐ dòngshǒu zuò

DIY

- 英国人对 **DIY** 很上瘾，有时幽默地称其为一种全民性消遣。**DIY** 意为 **do-it-yourself**，是指自己动手制作和修理东西，尤其是在家里。房主不雇佣专业的建筑工人，木匠或油漆匠，这样不仅省钱，还能从成功地改进家里的设备，环境中得到莫大的满足感。专门的 **DIY** 商店销售工具，油漆和木器等满足 **DIY** 爱好者嗜好的用品。

---

dizzy ['dɪzɪ] ADJ ▸ **to feel dizzy** 感到头昏 gǎndào tóuyūn

DJ N ABBR (= **disc jockey**) 简称为 DJ，意为：广播电台或迪斯科舞厅流行音乐唱片播放及介绍人

KEYWORD

do [duː] (pt **did**, pp **done**) I VT 1 做 zuò ▸ **what are you doing?** 你在做什么呢? nǐ zài zuò shénme ne? ▸ **are you doing anything tomorrow evening?**

么打算? nǐ míngwǎn yǒu shénme dǎsuàn? ▸ **what did you do with the money?** (how did you spend it) 你怎么用这笔钱的? nǐ zěnme yòng zhèbǐ qián de? ▸ **what are you going to do about this?** 你打算对此怎么办? nǐ dǎsuàn duìcǐ zěnmebàn?

2 (for a living) ▸ **what do you do?** 你做什么工作? nǐ zuò shénme gōngzuò?

3 (with noun) ▸ **to do the cooking** 做饭 zuòfàn

4 (referring to speed, distance) ▸ **the car was doing 100** 汽车以100英里的时速行进 qìchē yǐ yìbǎi yīnglǐ de shísù xíngjìn ▸ **we've done 200 km already** 我们的时速已达到了200公里 wǒmen de shísù yǐjīng dádào le èrbǎi yīnglǐ

5 (cause) ▸ **the explosion did a lot of damage** 爆炸造成了很大损失 bàozhà zàochéng le hěndà sǔnshī ▸ **a holiday will do you good** 休闲假会对你有好处 xiū cì jiā huì duì nǐ yǒu hǎochù

II VI **1** (act, behave) 做 zuò ▸ **do as I tell you** 按我告诉你的做 àn wǒ gàosù nǐ de zuò

2 (get on) 进展 jìnzhǎn ▸ **he's doing well/badly at school** 他的学习成绩很好／很差 tāde xuéxí chéngjì hěnhǎo/hěnchà ▸ **"how do you do?" — "how do you do?"** "你好" "你好" "nǐhǎo" "nǐhǎo"

3 (suit) 行 xíng ▸ **will it do?** 行吗? xíngma?

4 (be sufficient) 足够 zúgòu ▸ **will £15 do?** 15镑够吗? shíwǔ bàng

gòuma?

III AUX VB **1** (in negative constructions) ▸ **I don't understand** 我不懂 wǒ bùdǒng ▸ **she doesn't want it** 她不想要这个 tā bùxiǎng yào zhège ▸ **don't be silly!** 别傻了! bié shǎ le!

2 (to form questions) ▸ **do you like jazz?** 你喜欢爵士乐吗? nǐ xǐhuān juéshìyuè ma? ▸ **what do you think?** 你怎么想? nǐ zěnme xiǎng? ▸ **why didn't you come?** 你为什么没来? nǐ wèishénme méilái?

3 (for emphasis, in polite expressions) ▸ **do sit down/help yourself** 赶快坐啊/千万别客气 gǎnkuài zuò a/qiānwàn bié kèqì

4 (used to avoid repeating vb) 用于避免动词的重复 ▸ **they say they don't care, but they do** 他们说不在乎，但实际是在乎的 tāmen shuō bù zàihu, dàn shíjì shì zàihu de ▸ **(and) so do I** 我也是 wǒ yěshì ▸ **and neither did we** 我们也不 wǒmen yěbù ▸ **"who made this mess?" — "I did"** "是谁弄得乱七八糟的?" "是我" "shì shuí nòngde luàn qī bā zāo de" "shì wǒ"

5 (in question tags) ▸ **I don't know him, do I?** 我不认识他，是吗? wǒ bù rènshí tā, shìma? ▸ **she lives in London, doesn't she?** 她住在伦敦，不是吗? tā zhùzài Lúndūn, búshì ma?

▸ **do up** VT FUS **1** [+ laces] 系紧 jìjǐn; [+ dress, coat, buttons] 扣上 kòu shàng

2 (esp Brit) [+ room, house] 装修

zhuāngxiū

▶ **do with** VT FUS **1** (*need*) ▶ **I could do with a drink/some help** 我想喝一杯/需要帮助 wǒ xiǎng hē yìbēi/xūyào bāngzhù

2 (*be connected*) ▶ **to have it got to do with** 与……有关 yǔ……yǒuguān

▶ **what has it got to do with you?** 这跟你有什么关系? zhè gēn nǐ yǒu shénme guānxi?

▶ **do without** VT FUS 没有…也行 méiyǒu…yě xíng

dock [dɒk] N [c] (*Naut*) 船坞 chuánwù [个 gè]

doctor ['dɒktə^r] N [c] **1** 医生 yīshēng [位 wèi] **2** ▶ **the doctor's** 诊所 zhěnsuǒ [家 jiā]

document ['dɒkjumənt] N [c] **1** 文件 wénjiàn [份 fèn] **2** (*Comput*) 文档 wéndàng [个 gè]

documentary [dɒkju'mɛntəri] N [c] 记录片 jìlùpiàn [部 bù]

does [dʌz] VB *see* **do**

doesn't ['dʌznt] = **does not**

dog [dɒg] N [c] **1** 狗 gǒu [只 zhī] **2** (*male*) 雄兽 xióngshòu [头 tóu]

do-it-yourself ['du:ɪtjɔ:'self] I N [U] 自己动手的活计 zìjǐ dòngshǒu de huójì II A DJ [+*store*] 出售供购买者自行装配物品的 chūshòu gòng gòumǎizhě zìxíng zhuāngpèi wùpǐn de

dole [dəul] (*inf*) N [U] (*Brit*) ▶ **(the) dole** (*payment*) 失业救济金 shīyè jiùjìjīn ▶ **(to be) on the dole** (*Brit*) 靠失业救济金生活 kào shīyè jiùjìjīn shēnghuó

doll [dɒl] N [c] 娃娃 wáwa [个 gè]

dollar ['dɒlə^r] N [c] 元 yuán

dolphin ['dɒlfɪn] N [c] 海豚 hǎitún [只 zhī]

dominoes ['dɒmɪnəuz] N [U] 多米诺骨牌游戏 duōmǐnuò gǔpái yóuxì

donate [də'neɪt] VT **1** ▶ **to donate (to sb)** [+*money, clothes*] 捐赠 (给某人) juānzèng (gěi mǒurén) **2** [+*blood, organs*] 捐献 juānxiàn

done [dʌn] PP *of* **do**

donkey ['dɒŋkɪ] N [c] 驴 lú [头 tóu]

don't [dəunt] = **do not**

donut ['dəunʌt] (*US*) N = **doughnut**

door [dɔ:^r] N [c] 门 mén [扇 shàn] ▶ **to answer the door** 应门 yìngmén

doorbell ['dɔ:bel] N [c] 门铃 ménlíng [个 gè]

dormitory ['dɔ:mɪtrɪ] N [c] **1** (*room*) 宿舍 sùshè [间 jiān] **2** (*US: building*) 宿舍楼 sùshèlóu [座 zuò]

dose [dəus] N [c] 一剂 yíjì

dot [dɒt] N [c] 圆点 yuándiǎn [个 gè] ▶ **on the dot** (*punctually*) 准时地 zhǔnshí de

dot-com [dɒt'kɒm] N [c] 网络公司 wǎngluò gōngsī [家 jiā]

double ['dʌbl] I A DJ 双份的 shuāngfèn de [用于 *population, size*] 变成两倍 biànchéng liǎngbèi ▶ **it's spelt with a double "M"** 它的拼写有两个 "M" tā de pīnxiě zhōng yǒu liǎng gè "M" ▶ **double the size/number (of sth)** (是某物) 大小/数量的两倍 (shì mǒuwù) dàxiǎo/shùliàng de liǎngbèi

liǎngbèi

double bass N [c/u] 低音提琴 dīyīn tíqín [把 bǎ]

double-click ['dʌbl'klɪk] VI 双击 shuāngjī

double-decker ['dʌbl'dɛkəʳ] (esp Brit) N [c] (bus) 双层公共汽车 shuāngcéng gōnggòng qìchē [辆 liàng]

double glazing [-'gleɪzɪŋ] (Brit) N [u] 双层玻璃 shuāngcéng bōlí

double room N [c] 双人房 shuāngrénfáng

doubt [daʊt] I N [c/u] (uncertainty) 怀疑 huáiyí [种 zhǒng] II VT [+ person's word] 不信 bùxìn ▸ to doubt if or whether... 拿不准是否... nábùzhǔn shìfǒu... ▸I doubt it (very much) 我(很)怀疑 wǒ (hěn) huáiyí

doubtful ['daʊtful] ADJ 1 (questionable) ▸ it is doubtful that/whether... 不能确定…/是否… bùnéng quèdìng…/shìfǒu… 2 (unconvinced) ▸ to be doubtful that/whether... 怀疑…/是否… huáiyí…/shìfǒu… ▸ to be doubtful about sth 对某事有怀疑 duì mǒushì yǒu huáiyí

doughnut, (US) **donut** ['daʊnʌt] N [c] 炸面饼圈 zhá miànbǐngquān [个 gè]

down [daʊn] I ADV 1 (downwards) 向下 xiàngxià 2 (in a lower place) 在下面 zài xiàmiàn II PREP 1 (towards lower level) 沿着…往下 yánzhe…wǎng xià 2 (at lower part of) 在下面 zài xiàmiàn 3 (along) 沿着 yánzhe ▸she looked down

她向下看 tā xiàngxià kàn ▸he walked down the road 他沿街走去 tā yánjiē zǒuqù ▸ down there 在那儿 zài nàr ▸ England are two goals down (behind) 英格兰落后两球 Yīnggélán luòhòu liǎngqiú

download [daʊnləud] VT 下载 xiàzài

downstairs ['daʊn'stɛəz] ADV 1 (on or to floor below) 楼下 lóuxià 2 (on or to ground level) 在又 zài yī céng

downtown ['daʊn'taʊn] (US) I ADV 1 (be, work) 在市中心 zài shì zhōngxīn 2 (go) 去市中心 qù shì zhōngxīn II ADJ ▸ **downtown Chicago** 芝加哥的市中心 Zhījiāgē de shì zhōngxīn

dozen ['dʌzn] N [c] 一打 yìdá ▸ **two dozen eggs** 两打鸡蛋 liǎngdǎ jīdàn ▸ **dozens of** 许多 xǔduō

draft [drɑːft] N 1 [c] (first version) 草稿 cǎogǎo 2 [c] (bank draft) 汇票 huìpiào [张 zhāng]; see also **draught**

drag [dræg] VT (pull) [+ large object, body] 拖 tuō

dragon ['drægn] N [c] 龙 lóng [条 tiáo]

drain [dreɪn] I N [c] (in street) 排水沟 páishuǐgōu [条 tiáo] II VT [+ vegetables] 使…流干 shǐ…liúgān III VI [liquid] 流入 liúrù

drama ['drɑːmə] N 1 [c] (play) 一出戏剧 yīchū xìjù [幕 mù] 3 [c/u] (excitement) 戏剧性 xìjùxìng [种 zhǒng]

dramatic [drə'mætɪk] ADJ
1 (marked, sudden) 戏剧性的
xìjùxìng de (exciting, impressive)
激动人心的 jīdòng rénxīn de
3 (theatrical) 戏剧的 xìjù de

drank [dræŋk] PT of **drink**

drapes [dreɪps] (US) NPL 窗帘
chuānglián

draught, (US) **draft** [drɑːft] N [c]
气流 qìliú [股 gǔ]

draughts [drɑːfts] (Brit) N [u] 西
洋跳棋 xīyáng tiàoqí

draw [drɔː] (pt **drew**, pp **drawn**)
I VT **1** 画 huà **2** [+ curtains, blinds]
(close) 拉上 lāshàng (open) 拉
开 lākāi II VI **1** (with pen, pencil
etc) 画画 huàhuà **2** ▶ **to draw
(with/against sb)** (esp Brit: Sport)
(与某人) 打成平局 (yǔ mǒurén)
dǎ chéng píngjú III N [c] **1** (esp
Brit: Sport) 平局 píngjú [个 gè]
2 (lottery) 抽奖 chōujiǎng [次 cì]
▶ **draw up** VT [+ document, plan]
草拟 cǎonǐ

drawback ['drɔːbæk] N [c] 欠缺
qiànquē [个 gè]

drawer [drɔː^r] N [c] 抽屉 chōutì
[个 gè]

drawing ['drɔːɪŋ] N **1** [c] (picture)
素描 sùmiáo [幅 fú] **2** [u] (skill,
discipline) 绘画 huìhuà

drawing pin (Brit) N [c] 图钉
túdīng [枚 méi]

drawn [drɔːn] PP of **draw**

dread [dred] VT (fear) 惧怕 jùpà

dreadful ['dredful] ADJ 糟透的
zāotòu de

dream [driːm] (pt, pp **dreamed**
or **dreamt**) I N [c] **1** 梦 mèng

[场 chǎng] **2** (ambition) 梦想
mèngxiǎng [个 gè] II VI 做梦 zuò
mèng
▶ **dream about** (when asleep) 梦到
mèngdào

dreamt [dremt] PT, PP of **dream**

drench [drentʃ] VT (soak) 使湿透
shǐ shītòu

dress [dres] I N [c] 连衣裙
liányīqún [条 tiáo] II VT **1** [+ child]
给…穿衣 gěi…chuān yī **2** [+ salad]
拌 bàn III VI 穿衣 chuān yī ▶ **to
dress o.s., get dressed** 穿好衣服
chuānhǎo yīfu
▶ **dress up** VI **1** (wear best
clothes) 穿上盛装 chuānshàng
shèngzhuāng **2** ▶ **to dress up as**
化装成 huàzhuāng chéng

dresser ['dresə^r] N [c] **1** (Brit:
cupboard) 碗橱 wǎnchú [个 gè]
2 (US: chest of drawers) 梳妆台
shūzhuāngtái [个 gè]

dressing gown N [c] 晨衣 chényī
[套 tào]

dressing table N [c] 梳妆台
shūzhuāngtái [个 gè]

drew [druː] PT of **draw**

dried [draɪd] ADJ [+ fruit, herbs] 干
的 gān de [+ eggs, milk] 粉状的
fěnzhuàng de

drier ['draɪə^r] N = **dryer**

drill [drɪl] I N [c] 钻 zuàn [个 gè]
[of dentist] 钻头 zuàntóu [个 gè]
II VT 在…上钻孔 zài…shàng
zuānkǒng

drink [drɪŋk] (pt **drank**, pp **drunk**)
I N **1** [c] (tea, water etc) 饮料 yǐnliào
[种 zhǒng] **2** [c] (alcoholic) 酒 jiǔ
[瓶 píng] II VT 喝 hē III VI (drink
alcohol) 喝酒 hējiǔ

drink 喝一杯 hē yībēi; *(alcoholic)* 喝酒 hējiǔ

drive [draɪv] *(pt* drove, *pp* driven) I N 1 [c] *(journey)* 车程 chēchéng [段 duàn] 2 [c] *(also: driveway)* 私家车道 sījiā chēdào [条 tiáo] 3 [c] *(also: CD ROM/disk drive)* 驱动器 qūdòngqì [个 gè] II V T 1 [+ vehicle] 驾驶 jiàshǐ 2 ▸ to drive sb to the station/airport 驱车送某人去车站/飞机场 qūchē sòng mǒurén qù chēzhàn/fēijīchǎng III V I 开车 kāichē ▸ to go for a drive 开车兜风 kāichē dōufēng ▸ it's a 3-hour drive from London 到伦敦要要3个小时的车程 dào Lúndūn yào sānge xiǎoshí de chēchéng ▸ to drive sb mad/to desperation 逼得某人发疯/绝望 bīde mǒurén fāfēng/juéwàng ▸ to drive at 50 km an hour 以每小时50公里的速度驾车 yǐ měi xiǎoshí wǔshí gōnglǐ de sùdù jiàchē

driver ['draɪvə'] N [c] 1 *[of own car]* 驾驶员 jiàshǐyuán [位 wèi] 2 *[of taxi, bus, lorry, train]* 司机 sījī [位 wèi]

driver's license ['draɪvəz-] *(US)* N [c] 驾驶执照 jiàshǐ zhízhào [本 běn]

driveway ['draɪvweɪ] N [c] 车道 chēdào [条 tiáo]

driving instructor N [c] 驾驶教练 jiàshǐ jiàoliàn [位 wèi]

driving licence *(Brit)* N [c] 驾驶执照 jiàshǐ zhízhào [本 běn]

driving test N [c] 驾驶执照考试 jiàshǐ zhízhào kǎoshì [次 cì]

drizzle ['drɪzl] V I ▸ it is drizzling 下着毛毛雨 xiàzhe máomáoyǔ

drop [drɒp] I N 1 [c] *[of liquid]* 滴 dī 2 *(reduction)* ▸ a drop in sth 某物的下降 mǒuwù de xiàjiàng II V T 1 使下落下 shǐshǒu luòxià; *(deliberately)* 放 fàng 2 将…送到 jiāng…sòng dào III V I *[amount, level]* 下降 xiàjiàng; *[object]* 落下 luòxià

▸ **drop in** *(inf)* V I ▸ to drop in (on sb) 顺便拜访(某人) shùnbiàn bàifǎng (mǒurén)

▸ **drop off** V I *(fall asleep)* 睡着 shuìzháo II V T *[+ passenger]* 将…送到 jiāng…sòng dào

▸ **drop out** V I *(of college, university)* 辍学 chuòxué

drought [draʊt] N [c/u] 旱灾 hànzāi [场 chǎng]

drove [draʊv] PT *of* drive

drown [draʊn] I V T ▸ to be drowned 被淹死 bèi yānsǐ II V I *[person, animal]* 溺死 nìsǐ

drug [drʌg] N 1 *(prescribed)* 药 yào [片 piàn] 2 *(recreational)* 毒品 dúpǐn [种 zhǒng] ▸ to take drugs 吸毒 xīdú ▸ hard/soft drugs 硬/软毒品 yìng/ruǎn dúpǐn

drug addict N [c] 吸毒成瘾者 xīdú chéngyǐnzhě [个 gè]

drug dealer N [c] 毒品贩子 dúpǐn fànzi

druggist ['drʌgɪst] *(US)* N [c] 1 药剂师 yàojìshī [位 wèi] 2 ▸ druggist('s) *(shop)* 药店 yàodiàn [家 jiā]

drugstore ['drʌgstɔː'] *(US)* N [c] 杂货店 záhuòdiàn [家 jiā]

drum [drʌm] N [c] 鼓 gǔ [面

miàn] II **drums** NPL (kit) 鼓 gǔ

drummer ['drʌmə^r] N [c] 鼓手 gǔshǒu [位 wèi]

drunk [drʌŋk] I PP of **drink** II ADJ 醉的 zuì de ▸ **to get drunk** 喝醉了 hēzuì le

dry [draɪ] I ADJ 1 干的 gān de 2 [+ climate, weather, day] 干燥的 gānzào de II VT 把…弄干 bǎ…nòng gān III VI [paint, washing] 变干 biàn gān ▸ **to dry one's hands/hair** 擦干手/头发 cāgān shǒu/tóufa

dry-cleaner ['draɪ'kli:nə^r] N [c] (also: **dry cleaner's**) 干洗店 gānxǐdiàn [家 jiā]

dryer ['draɪə^r] N [c] 1 (tumble dryer, spin-dryer) 干衣机 gānyījī [台 tái] 2 (hair dryer) 吹风机 chuīfēngjī [个 gè]

duck [dʌk] N 1 [c] (bird) 鸭 yā [只 zhī] 2 [u] (as food) 鸭肉 yāròu

due [djuː] ADJ 1 ▸ **to be due** [person, train, bus] 应到 yīng dào; [baby] 预期 yùqī; [rent, payment] 应交付 yīng zhīfù II ADV ▸ **to be due north/south** 正北方/南方 zhèng běifāng/nánfāng ▸ **due to…** (because of) 由于… yóuyú…

dug [dʌg] PT, PP of **dig**

dull [dʌl] ADJ 1 [+ weather, day] 阴沉的 yīnchén de 2 (boring) 单调乏味的 dāndiào fáwèi de

dumb [dʌm] ADJ 1 哑的 yǎ de 2 (pej: stupid, foolish) 愚蠢的 yúchǔn de

dump [dʌmp] I N [c] 垃圾场 lājīchǎng [个 gè] II VT 1 (get rid of) 倾倒 qīngdào 2 (+ computer data)

转储 zhuǎn chǔ

Dumpster® ['dʌmpstə^r] (US) N [c] (用以装运工地废料的无盖） 废料箱 (yòngyǐ zhuāngyùn gōngdì fèiliào de wú gài)fèiliàotǒng [个 gè]

during ['djuərɪŋ] PREP 1 在…期间 zài…qījiān 2 (at some point in) 在…时候 zài…shíhòu

dusk [dʌsk] N [u] 黄昏 huánghūn ▸ **at dusk** 黄昏时刻 huánghūn shíkè

dust [dʌst] N [u] (dirt: outdoors) 土 chéntǔ; (: indoors) 灰尘 huīchén

dustbin ['dʌstbɪn] (Brit) N [c] 垃圾箱 lājīxiāng [个 gè]

dustman ['dʌstmən] (Brit) (pl **dustmen**) N [c] 清洁工 qīngjiégōng [位 wèi]

dusty ['dʌstɪ] ADJ 满是尘土的 mǎn shì chéntǔ de

Dutch [dʌtʃ] I ADJ 荷兰的 Hélán de II N [u] (language) 荷兰语 Hélányǔ III the **Dutch** NPL (people) 荷兰人 Hélánrén

duty ['djuːtɪ] N [c/u] 1 (responsibility) 责任 zérèn [个 gè] 2 (tax) 税 shuì [种 zhǒng] II **duties** NPL (tasks) 任务 rènwù

duty-free ['djuːtɪ'friː] ADJ [+ drink, cigarettes] 免税的 miǎnshuì de ▸ **duty-free shop** 免税商店 miǎnshuì shāngdiàn

duvet ['duːveɪ] (Brit) N [c] 羽绒被 yǔróngbèi [床 chuáng]

DVD player N [c] DVD播放器 DVD bōfàngqì [台 tái]

dye [daɪ] I N [c/u] 染料 rǎnliào [种 zhǒng] II VT 染色 rǎnsè

dynamic [daɪˈnæmɪk] ADJ 生气
  勃勃的 shēngqì bóbó de
dyslexia [dɪsˈleksɪə] N [U] 诵读困
  难 sòngdú kùnnan
dyslexic [dɪsˈleksɪk] ADJ 诵读有
  困难的 sòngdú yǒu kùnnan de

e

each [iːtʃ] I ADJ 每 měi II PRON
  (each one) 每个 měigè ▶ **each one
  of them** 他们中的每一个 tāmen
  zhōngde měiyīgè ▶ **each other** 互
  相 hùxiāng ▶ **they have 2 books
  each** 他们每人有两本书 tāmen
  měirén yǒu liǎngběnshū ▶ **they
  cost 5 pounds each** 每个售价5镑
  měigè shòujià wǔbàng

  each 表示一个群体中的每
  一个人或物，强调的是每
  一个个体。**every** 指由两
  个以上的个体组成的群体
  中的所有的人或物，强调
  的是整体。 *He listened to
  every news bulletin...an equal
  chance for every child...* 注
  意 **each** 指两个当中的任
  何一个。*Each apartment
  has two bedrooms...We each*

carried a suitcase. **each** 和 **every** 后面都只能跟名词单数形式。

ear [ɪəʳ] N [c] 耳朵 ěrduo [只 zhī]

earache [ˈɪəreɪk] N [c/u] 耳朵痛 ěrduo tòng

earlier [ˈə:lɪəʳ] I ADJ [+ date, time] 较早的 jiàozǎo de II ADV (leave, go) 提早 tízǎo ▸ **earlier this year** 今年年初 běnnián chū

early [ˈə:lɪ] I ADV 1 (in day, month) 在初期 zài chūqī 2 (before usual time: get up, go to bed, arrive, leave) 早 zǎo II ADJ 1 [+ stage, career] 早 zǎo ▸ **I usually get up early** 我通常早起床 wǒ tōngcháng zǎo qǐchuáng ▸ **early this morning** 今天一大早 jīntiān yīdàzǎo ▸ **early in the morning** 清早 qīngzǎo ▸ **you're early!** 你怎么这么早！nǐ zěnme zhème zǎo!

earn [ə:n] VT 挣得 zhèngdé ▸ **to earn one's or a living** 谋生 móushēng

earnings [ˈə:nɪŋz] NPL 收入 shōurù

earphones [ˈɪəfəunz] NPL 耳机 ěrjī

earring [ˈɪərɪŋ] N [c] 耳环 ěrhuán [只 zhī]

earth [ə:θ] N 1 [u/s] (also: the Earth) 地球 diqiú 2 [u] (land surface) 陆地 lùdì 3 [u] (soil) 泥土 nítǔ

earthquake [ˈə:θkweɪk] N [c] 地震 dìzhèn [次 cì]

easily [ˈi:zɪlɪ] ADV 不费力地 bù fèilì de

east [i:st] I N 1 [s/u] 东方

dōngfāng 2 ▸ **the East** (the Orient) 东方国家 dōngfāng guójiā II ADJ 东部的 dōngbù de III ADV 向东方 xiàng dōngfāng ▸ **the east of Spain** 西班牙东部 Xībānyá dōngbù ▸ **to the east** 以东 yǐdōng ▸ **east of ...** …以东 …yǐdōng

Easter [ˈi:stəʳ] N [u] 复活节 Fùhuó Jié ▸ **the Easter holidays** 复活节假期 Fùhuó Jié jiàqī

eastern [ˈi:stən] ADJ 1 (Geo) 东部的 dōngbù de 2 ▸ **Eastern** (oriental) 东方的 Dōngfāng de

easy [ˈi:zɪ] ADJ 1 容易的 róngyì de 2 [+ life, time] 安逸的 ānyì de ▸ **dogs are easy to train** 狗很容易训练 gǒu hěn róngyì xùnliàn ▸ **it's easy to train dogs** 训狗是容易的 xùngǒu shì róngyì de

eat [i:t] (pt ate, pp eaten [ˈi:tn]) I VT 1 吃 chī VI 1 吃 chī 2 (have a meal) 吃饭 chīfàn

eaten [ˈi:tn] PP of **eat**

echo [ˈekəu] (pl echoes) N [c] 回音 huíyīn [个 gè]

ecology [ɪˈkɔlədʒɪ] N [u] 1 (environment) 生态 shēngtài 2 (subject) 生态学 shēngtàixué

economic [i:kəˈnɔmɪk] ADJ 1 经济的 jīngjì de 2 (profitable) 有利可图的 yǒulì kětú de

economical [i:kəˈnɔmɪkl] ADJ 节约的 jiéyuē de

economics [i:kəˈnɔmɪks] N [u] 经济学 jīngjìxué

economy [ɪˈkɔnəmɪ] N 1 [c] 经济 jīngjì [种 zhǒng] 2 [u] (thrift) 节约 jiéyuē

eczema [ˈeksɪmə] N [u] 湿疹

shìzhēn

dge [ɛdʒ] N [c] **1** 边缘 biānyuán [个 gè] **2** (of table, chair) 棱 léng

ditor ['ɛdɪtər] N [c] 编辑 biānjí [个 gè]

ducate ['ɛdjʊkeɪt] VT 教育 jiàoyù

ducation [ɛdjʊ'keɪʃən] N [u/s] 教育 jiàoyù

ffect [ɪ'fɛkt] I N [c/u] 影响 yǐngxiǎng [个 gè] II **effects** NPL (Cine) 特别效果 tèbié xiàoguǒ ▶ **to take effect** [drug] 见效 jiànxiào ▶ **to have an effect on sb/sth** 对某人/某物产生影响 duì mǒurén/mǒuwù chǎnshēng yǐngxiǎng

ffective [ɪ'fɛktɪv] ADJ 有效的 yǒuxiào de

fficiency [ɪ'fɪʃənsɪ] N [u] 效率 xiàolǜ

fficient [ɪ'fɪʃənt] ADJ 效率高的 xiàolǜ gāo de

ffort ['ɛfət] N **1** [u] 努力 nǔlì **2** [c] (attempt) 尝试 chángshì [个 gè] [2 u/s] ▶ **to make an effort to do sth** 努力做某事 nǔlì zuò mǒushì

e.g. ADV ABBR (= exempli gratia) (for example) 举例来说 jǔlì lái shuō

egg [ɛg] N [c] 蛋 dàn [个 gè]

eggplant ['ɛgplɑːnt] (US) N [c/u] 茄子 qiézi [个 gè]

Egypt ['iːdʒɪpt] N 埃及 Āijí

eight [eɪt] NUM 八 bā; see also **five**

eighteen [eɪ'tiːn] NUM 十八 shíbā; see also **fifteen**

eighteenth [eɪ'tiːnθ] NUM 第十 八 dì shíbā; see also **fifth**

eighth [eɪtθ] NUM **1** 第八 dì bā

2 (fraction) 八分之一 bā fēn zhī yī; see also **fifth**

eighty ['eɪtɪ] NUM 八十 bāshí; see also **fifty**

Eire ['ɛərə] N 爱尔兰共和国 Ài'ěrlán Gònghéguó

either ['aɪðər] I ADJ **1** (one or other) 两者任一的 liǎngzhě rènyī de **2** (both, each) 两者中每一方的 liǎngzhě zhōng měiyīfāng de ▶ **on either side** 在两边 zài liǎngbiān II PRON **1** (after negative) 两者之中 任何一个 liǎngzhě zhī zhōng rènhé yīgè ▶ **I don't like either of them** 两个我都不喜欢 liǎnggè wǒ dōu bù xǐhuān **2** (after interrogative) 两者之中任何一个 liǎngzhě zhī zhōng rènhé yīgè III ADV (in negative statements) 也 yě IV CONJ ▶ **either... or...** 要么…要么… yàome...yàome... ▶ **no, I don't either** 不，我也不 bù, wǒ yě bù

elastic [ɪ'læstɪk] N [u] 橡皮 xiàngpí

elastic band (Brit) N [c] 橡皮筋 xiàngpíjīn [根 gēn]

elbow ['ɛlbəʊ] N [c] (Anat) 肘 zhǒu [个 gè]

elder ['ɛldər] ADJ [+ brother, sister] 年龄较大的 niánlíng jiào dà de

elderly ['ɛldəlɪ] I ADJ 年长的 niánzhǎng de II NPL ▶ **the elderly** 老人家 lǎorénjiā

eldest ['ɛldɪst] I ADJ 年龄最大的 niánlíng zuìdà de II [s/PL] 年龄 最大的孩子 niánlíng zuìdà de háizi

elect [ɪ'lɛkt] VT 选举 xuǎnjǔ

election [ɪ'lɛkʃən] N [c] 选 举 xuǎnjǔ [次 cì] ▶ **to hold an**

election 举行选举 jǔxíng xuǎnjǔ

electric [ɪˈlɛktrɪk] ADJ **1** 电动的 diàndòng de **2** [+ current, charge, socket] 电的 diàn de

electrical [ɪˈlɛktrɪkl] ADJ 电动的 diàndòng de

electric guitar N [c/u] 电吉他 diànjítā [把 bǎ]

electrician [ɪlɛkˈtrɪʃən] N [c] 电工 diàngōng [个 gè]

electricity [ɪlɛkˈtrɪsɪti] N [u] **1** (energy) 电 diàn **2** (supply) 供电 gòngdiàn

electric shock N [c] 触电 chùdiàn [次 cì]

electronic [ɪlɛkˈtrɒnɪk] ADJ 电子的 diànzǐ de

electronics [ɪlɛkˈtrɒnɪks] N [u] 电子学 diànzǐxué

elegant [ˈɛlɪɡənt] ADJ 优雅的 yōuyǎ de

elementary school (US) N [c/u] 小学 xiǎoxué

elephant [ˈɛlɪfənt] N [c] 大象 dàxiàng [头 tóu]

elevator [ˈɛlɪveɪtər] (US) N [c] 电梯 diàntī [部 bù]

eleven [ɪˈlɛvn] NUM 十一 shíyī; see also **five**

eleventh [ɪˈlɛvnθ] NUM 第十一 dì shíyī; see also **fifth**

eliminate [ɪˈlɪmɪneɪt] VT **1** [+ poverty] 消除 xiāochú **2** [+ team, contestant, candidate] 淘汰 táotài

else [ɛls] ADV ▸ **or else** (otherwise) 否则 fǒuzé; (threatening) 要不然 yàobùrán ▷ Don't talk to me like that again, or else 别再这样跟我说

话，要不够你受的！ bié zhème gēn wǒ shuōhuà,yàobù gòu nǐ shòu de! ▸ **something else** 其他 东西 qítā dōngxi ▸ **anything else** 任何其他东西 rènhé qítā dōngxi ▸ **what else?** 其他什么？ qítā shénme ▸ **everywhere else** 其他任何地方 qítā rènhé dìngfāng ▸ **everyone else** 其他人 qítā rén ▸ **nobody else** 没有其他人 méiyǒu qítā rén

elsewhere [ɛlsˈwɛər] ADV **1** (be) 在别处 zài biéchù **2** (go) 到别处 dào biéchù

e-mail [ˈiːmeɪl] I N [c/u] 电子邮件 diànzǐ yóujiàn [封 fēng] II VT **1** [+ person] 给…发电子邮件 gěi…fā diànzǐ yóujiàn **2** [+ file, document] 用电子邮件寄 yòng diànzǐ yóujiàn jì

e-mail account N [c] 电子邮件账号 diànzǐ yóujiàn zhànghào [个 gè]

e-mail address N [c] 电子邮件地址 diànzǐ yóujiàn dìzhǐ [个 gè]

embarrassed [ɪmˈbærəst] ADJ ▸ **to be embarrassed** 不好意思的 bùhǎo yìsi de

embarrassing [ɪmˈbærəsɪŋ] ADJ 令人尴尬的 lìng rén gāngà de

embassy [ˈɛmbəsi] N [c] 大使馆 dàshǐguǎn [个 gè]

emergency [ɪˈmɜːdʒənsɪ] N [c] (crisis) 紧急情况 jǐnjí qíngkuàng [个 gè] ▸ **in an emergency** 在紧急情况下 zài jǐnjí qíngkuàng xià

emergency room (US) N [c] 急诊室 jízhěnshì [个 gè]

emigrate [ˈɛmɪɡreɪt] VI 移居外国 yíjū wàiguó

emotion [ɪˈməʊʃən] N [c/u] 感情 gǎnqíng [种 zhǒng]

emotional [ɪˈməʊʃənl] ADJ 易动感情的 yì dòng gǎnqíng de

emperor [ˈɛmpərəʳ] N [c] 皇帝 huángdì [个 gè]

emphasize [ˈɛmfəsaɪz] VT 强调 qiángdiào

empire [ˈɛmpaɪəʳ] N [c] 帝国 dìguó [个 gè]

employ [ɪmˈplɔɪ] VT 雇用 gùyòng ▸ **he was employed as a technician** 他受雇做技师 tā shòugù zuò jìshī

employee [ɪmplɔɪˈiː] N [c] 雇员 gùyuán [个 gè]

employer [ɪmˈplɔɪəʳ] N [c] 雇主 gùzhǔ [个 gè]

employment [ɪmˈplɔɪmənt] N [u] 工作 gōngzuò

empty [ˈɛmptɪ] I ADJ 空的 kōng de II VT 倒空 dào kōng

encourage [ɪnˈkʌrɪdʒ] VT 1 [+ person] 鼓励 gǔlì 2 [+ activity, attitude] 支持 zhīchí 3 [+ growth, industry] 促进 zhùjìn ▸ **to encourage sb to do sth** 鼓励某人去做某事 gǔlì mǒurén qùzuò mǒushì

encouragement [ɪnˈkʌrɪdʒmənt] N [u] 鼓励 gǔlì

encyclop(a)edia [ɛnsaɪkləuˈpiːdɪə] N [c] 百科全书 bǎikē quánshū

end [ɛnd] I N 1 [s] [of period, event] 末期 mòqī 2 [s] [of film, book] 末尾 mòwěi 3 [c] [of street, queue, rope, table] 尽头 jìntóu [个 gè] 4 [c] [of town] 端 duān II VT [finish, stop]

终止 zhōngzhǐ III VI [meeting, film, book] 结束 jiéshù ▸ **at the end of August** 在8月末 zài bāyuè mò ▸ **to come to an end** 完结 wánjié ▸ **in the end** 最终 zuìzhōng ▸ **end up** VI ▸ **to end up in/at** [+ place] 最终到达 zuìzhōng dàodá

ending [ˈɛndɪŋ] N [c] 结局 jiéjú [个 gè] ▸ **a happy ending** 美满结局 měimǎn jiéjú

enemy [ˈɛnəmɪ] N [c] 敌人 dírén [个 gè]

energetic [ɛnəˈdʒɛtɪk] ADJ 1 精力充沛的 jīnglì chōngpèi de 2 [+ activity] 生机勃勃的 shēngjī bóbó de

energy [ˈɛnədʒɪ] N [u] 能源 néngyuán

engaged [ɪnˈgeɪdʒd] ADJ 1 (to be married) 已订婚的 yǐ dìnghūn de 2 (Brit: Tel) 被占用的 bèi zhànyòng de 3 (Brit) [+ toilet] 被占用的 bèi zhànyòng de ▸ **to get engaged (to)** (与…) 订婚 (yǔ…) dìnghūn

engagement [ɪnˈgeɪdʒmənt] N [c] (to marry) 婚约 hūnyuē [个 gè]

engagement ring N [c] 订婚戒指 dìnghūn jièzhǐ [枚 méi]

engine [ˈɛndʒɪn] N [c] 1 (Aut) 发动机 fādòngjī [台 tái] 2 (Rail) 机车 jīchē [部 bù]

engineer [ɛndʒɪˈnɪəʳ] N [c] 1 (who designs machines, bridges) 工程师 gōngchéngshī [位 wèi] 2 (who repairs machines, phones etc) 机械师 jīxièshī [位 wèi]

engineering [ɛndʒɪˈnɪərɪŋ] N [u] 1 工程 gōngchéng 2 (science) 工程

学 gōngchéngxué

England ['ɪŋɡlənd] N 英格兰 Yīnggélán

English ['ɪŋɡlɪʃ] I ADJ 英国的 Yīngguó de II N (language) 英语 Yīngyǔ III the English NPL (people) 英国人 Yīngguórén ▸an English speaker 一个讲英语的人 yīgè jiǎng yīngyǔ de rén

Englishman ['ɪŋɡlɪʃmən] (pl **Englishmen**) N [c] 英格兰男人 Yīnggélán nánrén [个 gè]

Englishwoman ['ɪŋɡlɪʃwumən] (pl **Englishwomen**) N [c] 英格兰女人 Yīnggélán nǚrén [个 gè]

enjoy [ɪn'dʒɔɪ] VT (take pleasure in) 享受…的乐趣 xiǎngshòu…de lèqù ▸to enjoy doing sth 喜欢做某事 xǐhuān zuò mǒushì ▸to enjoy o.s. 过得快活 guòde kuàihuó ▸enjoy your meal! 吃好! chīhǎo!

enjoyable [ɪn'dʒɔɪəbl] ADJ 有乐趣的 yǒu lèqù de

enormous [ɪ'nɔ:məs] ADJ 1 庞大的 pángdà de 2 [+ pleasure, success, disappointment] 巨大的 jùdà de

enough [ɪ'nʌf] I ADJ [+ time, books, people] 足够的 zúgòu de II PRON (sufficient, more than desired) 足够的东西 zúgòu de dōngxī III ADV ▸big/old/tall enough 足够大/到年龄/够高 zúgòu dà/dào niánlíng/gāo ▸enough time/money to do sth 有足够的时间/钱去做某事 yǒu zúgòu de shíjiān/jīnqián qùzuò mǒushì ▸have you got enough? 你够吗? nǐ gòu ma ▸enough to eat 够吃 gòuchī ▸will 5 be enough?

5个够吗? wǔgè gòu ma ▸I've had enough! 我受够了! wǒ shòugòu le ▸that's enough, thanks 足够了,谢谢 zúyí, xièxiè

enquiry [ɪn'kwaɪərɪ] N = **inquiry**

enrol, (US) **enroll** [ɪn'rəul] I VT 1 招…入学 zhāo…rùxué 2 (on course, in club) 注册 zhùcè II VI 1 (at school, university, on course, in club) 注册 zhùcè

en suite ['ɔnswiːt] (Brit) [+ bathroom] 接连的 jiēlián de

ensure [ɪn'ʃuə] (frm) VT 保证 bǎozhèng

enter ['ɛntə] I VT 1 [+ room, building] 进入 jìnrù 2 [+ race, competition] 参加 cānjiā 3 (Comput) [+ data] 输入 shūrù II VI 进来 jìnlái

entertain [ɛntə'teɪn] VT 1 (amuse) 给…娱乐 gěi…yúlè 2 (invite) [+ guest] 招待 zhāodài

entertainment [ɛntə'teɪnmənt] N [U] 娱乐活动 yúlè huódòng

enthusiasm [ɪn'θu:zɪæzəm] N [U] 热情 rèqíng ▸enthusiasm for sth 对某事的热情 duì mǒushì de rèqíng

enthusiastic [ɪnθu:zɪ'æstɪk] ADJ 极感兴趣的 jí gǎn xìngqù de; [+ response, reception] 热情的 rèqíng de ▸to be enthusiastic about sth 对某事满怀热情 duì mǒushì mǎnhuái rèqíng

entire [ɪn'taɪə] ADJ 整个的 zhěnggè de

entirely [ɪn'taɪəlɪ] ADV 完全地 wánquán de

entrance ['ɛntrns] N [c] 入口

rùkǒu [个 gè] ▸**the entrance to sth** 某处的入口 mǒuchù de rùkǒu

entry ['εntrɪ] N 1 [c] (way in) 入口 rùkǒu [个 gè] 2 [c] (in competition) 登记 dēngjì [个 gè] 3 [c] (item: in diary) 项目 xiàngmù [个 gè] 4 (: Comput) 输入 shūrù [项 xiàng] ▸**"no entry"** (to land, room) "禁止入内" jìnzhǐ rùnèi; (Aut) "禁止通行" jìnzhǐ tōngxíng

envelope ['εnvələup] N [c] 信封 xìnfēng [个 gè]

environment [ɪn'vaɪərnmənt] N [c/u] 环境 huánjìng [个 gè] ▸**the environment** (natural world) 自然环境 zìrán huánjìng

environmental [ɪnvaɪərn'mεntl] ADJ 环境的 huánjìng de

environmentally friendly [ɪnvaɪərn'mεntəlɪ-] ADJ 不污染环境的 bù wūrǎn huánjìng de

envy ['εnvɪ] I N [u] 羡慕 xiànmù II VT (be jealous of) 羡慕 xiànmù ▸**to envy sb sth** 羡慕某人的某物 xiànmù mǒurén de mǒuwù

epilepsy ['εpɪlεpsɪ] N [u] 癫痫 diānxián

episode ['εpɪsəud] N [c] (TV, Rad) 集 jí

equal ['i:kwl] I ADJ 1 相等的 xiāngděng de 2 [+ intensity, importance] 同样的 tóngyàng de II VT 1 [+ number, amount] 等于 děngyú 2 (match, rival) 比得上 bǐdeshàng ▸**they are roughly equal in size** 它们大小差不多 tāmen dàxiǎo chàbùduō ▸**to be equal to** (the same as) 与…相

同 yǔ...xiāngtóng ▸**79 minus 14 equals 65** 79减14等于65 qīshíjiǔ jiǎn shísì děngyú liùshíwǔ

equality [i:'kwɔlɪtɪ] N [u] 平等 píngděng

equally ['i:kwəlɪ] ADV 1 (share, divide) 平等地 píngděng de 2 (good, important) 同样地 tóngyàng de

equator [ɪ'kweɪtər] N ▸**the equator** 赤道 chìdào

equipment [ɪ'kwɪpmənt] N [u] 设备 shèbèi

equivalent [ɪ'kwɪvələnt] I ADJ 相同的 xiāngtóng de II N [c] 相当的人/物 xiāngdāng de rén/wù [个 gè]

ER N ABBR (US: Med: = emergency room) 急诊室 jízhěnshì [个 gè]

eraser [ɪ'reɪzər] N [c] (esp US) 橡皮 xiàngpí [块 kuài]

error ['εrər] N [c/u] 差错 chācuò [个 gè] ▸**to make an error** 犯错误 fàn cuòwù

escalator ['εskəleɪtər] N [c] 自动扶梯 zìdòng fútī [部 bù]

escape [ɪs'keɪp] I V 1 (get away) 逃走 táozǒu 2 (from jail) 逃跑 táopǎo 3 (from accident) ▸**to escape injury** 安然逃脱 ānrán táotuō II VT [+ injury] 避免 bìmiǎn ▸**to escape from** [+ place] 从…逃跑 cóng...táopǎo; [+ person] 避开 bìkāi

especially [ɪs'pεʃlɪ] ADV 尤其 yóuqí

essay ['εseɪ] N (Scol) 论文 lùnwén

essential [ɪ'sεnʃl] I ADJ 1 (necessary, vital) 必要的 bìyào de **2** (basic) 基本的 jīběn de

II essentials NPL (necessities) 必需品 bìxūpǐn ▸ **it is essential to...** 必须… bìxū...

estate [ɪsˈteɪt] N [c] **1** (land) 庄园 zhuāngyuán [个 gè] **2** (Brit) (also: **housing estate**) 住宅区 zhùzháiqū

estate agent (Brit) N [c] 房地产经纪人 fángdìchǎn jīngjìrén [个 gè]

estimate [n ˈɛstɪmət, vb ˈɛstɪmeɪt] **I** N [c] (reckon, calculate) 估计 gūjì [种 zhǒng] **II** VT (reckon, calculate) 估计 gūjì ▸ **the damage was estimated at 300 million pounds** 估计损失为3亿英镑 gūjì sǔnshī wéi sānyì yīngbàng

etc. (esp US) **etc.** ABBR (= et cetera) 等等 děngděng

Ethiopia [iːθɪˈəʊpɪə] N 埃塞俄比亚 Āisàiʼébǐyà

ethnic [ˈɛθnɪk] ADJ 种族的 zhǒngzú de

EU N ABBR (= European Union) ▸ **the EU** 欧洲联盟 Ōuzhōu Liánméng

euro [ˈjʊərəʊ] (pl **euros**) N [c] 欧元 Ōuyuán [个 gè]

Europe [ˈjʊərəp] N 欧洲 Ōuzhōu

European [jʊərəˈpiːən] **I** ADJ 欧洲的 Ōuzhōu de **II** N [c] (person) 欧洲人 Ōuzhōurén [个 gè]

European Union N ▸ **the European Union** 欧洲联盟 Ōuzhōu Liánméng

evacuate [ɪˈvækjueɪt] VT **1** [+ people] 疏散 shūsàn **2** [+ place] 撤离 chèlí

evaluate [ɪˈvæljueɪt] VT 评估 pínggū

even [ˈiːvn] **I** ADV 甚至 shènzhì **II** ADJ **1** (flat) 平坦的 píngtǎn de **2** [+ number] 偶数的 ǒushù de ▸ **he didn't even hear what I said** 他甚至根本没听见我的话 tā shènzhì gēnběn méi tīngjiàn wǒ de huà ▸ **even more** 甚至更多 shènzhì gèngduō ▸ **even if** 即便 jíshǐ ▸ **even though** 尽管 jǐnguǎn ▸ **not even** 连…也不 lián...yě bù ▸ **even on Sundays** 甚至星期天 shènzhì xīngqītiān

evening [ˈiːvnɪŋ] N [c/u] **1** (early) 傍晚 bàngwǎn [个 gè] **2** (late) 晚上 wǎnshang [个 gè] **3** (whole period, event) 晚上 wǎnshang [个 gè] ▸ **in the evening** 在晚上 zài wǎnshang ▸ **this evening** 今晚 jīnwǎn ▸ **tomorrow/yesterday evening** 明/昨晚 míng/zuówǎn

evening class N [c] 夜校 yèxiào [个 gè]

event [ɪˈvɛnt] N [c] 事件 shìjiàn [个 gè]

eventually [ɪˈvɛntʃuəlɪ] ADV **1** (finally) 终于 zhōngyú **2** (ultimately) 最终 zuìzhōng

请勿将 **eventually** 和 **finally** 混淆。如果某事情延迟了很久，或者经历了相当复杂的过程后终于发生了，可以说它 **eventually** 发生了，Eventually, they got to the hospital... I found Victoria Avenue eventually. **eventually** 还可以表示发生的一系列事情中的最

后一件事，通常这最后的一件事是前面一系列事情的结果。*Eventually, they were forced to return to England.* 在经历了长期的等待或期盼后，某事终于发生了，可以说定 **finally** 发生了。*Finally, I went to bed... The heat of the sun finally became too much for me.* **finally** 还可以表示发生的一系列事情当中最后的一件事。*The sky turned red, then purple, and finally black.*

ever ['ɛvə'] ADV 从来 cónglái ▶ have you ever seen it/been there *etc*? 你曾经见过它/去过那儿〔等〕吗？nǐ céngjīng jiànguò tā/qùguò nà'er〔děng〕ma? ▶ ever since (adv) 从一以来 cóng...yǐlái ▶ We have been friends ever since. 我们从那时以来一直是朋友。wǒmen cóng nàshí yǐlái yīzhí shì péngyǒu; (conj) 自从 zìcóng ▶ Jack has loved trains ever since he was a boy. 杰克自小就喜爱火车。Jiékè zìxiǎo jiù xǐ'ài huǒchē ▶ the best ever 迄今最佳 qìjīn zuìjiā ▶ hardly ever 几乎从不 jīhū cóngbù

KEYWORD

every ['ɛvrɪ] ADJ **1** (each) 每个 měigè ▶ every village should have a post office 每个村庄都应该有一个邮局 měigè cūnzhuāng dōu yīnggāi yǒu yīgè yóujú **2** (all possible) 一切可能的 yīqiè

kěnéng de ▶ recipes for every occasion 各个场合均适用的菜谱 gègè chǎnghé jūn shìyòng de càipǔ **3** (with time words) 每 měi ▶ every day/week 每天/周 měitiān/zhōu ▶ every Sunday 每个星期天 měigè xīngqītiān ▶ every now and then *or* again 不时地 bùshí de

everybody ['ɛvrɪbɒdɪ] PRON 每人 měirén ▶ everybody knows about it 谁都知道 shuí dōu zhīdào ▶ everybody else 其他所有人 qítā suǒyǒurén

everyone ['ɛvrɪwʌn] PRON = **everybody**

请勿将 **everyone** 和 **every one** 混淆。**everyone** 总是指人，并且用作单数名词。*Everyone likes him...On behalf of everyone in the school, I'd like to thank you.* 在短语 **every one** 中，**one** 是代词，在不同的上下文中，它能够指代任何人或事物。其后经常紧随单词 **of**。*We've saved seeds from every one of our plants...Every one of them phoned me.* 在这些例子当中，**every one** 是表达 **all** 的含义，而且语气更强烈。

everything ['ɛvrɪθɪŋ] PRON 所有事物 suǒyǒu shìwù ▶ is everything OK? 都还好吗？dōu hái hǎo ma ▶ everything is ready

所有都准备就绪 suǒyǒu dōu zhǔnbèi jiùxù ▶ he did everything possible 他尽了最大努力 tā jìnle zuìdà nǔlì

everywhere ['ɛvrɪwɛəʳ] I ADV 各处 gèchù II PRON 所有地方 suǒyǒu dìfang ▶ there's rubbish everywhere 到处都是垃圾 dàochù dōushì lājī ▶ everywhere you go 无论你去哪里 wúlùn nǐ qù nǎlǐ

evidence ['ɛvɪdns] N [u] 1 (proof) 根据 gēnjù 2 (signs, indications) 迹象 jìxiàng

evil ['iːvl] ADJ 邪恶的 xié'è de

ex- [ɛks] PREFIX [+ husband, president etc] 前 qián ▶ my ex-wife 我的前妻 wǒde qiánqī

exact [ɪɡˈzækt] ADJ 确切的 quèqiè de

exactly [ɪɡˈzæktlɪ] ADV 1 (precisely) 确切地 quèqiè de 2 (indicating agreement) 一点不错 yīdiǎn bùcuò ▶ at 5 o'clock exactly 在5点整时 zài wǔdiǎnzhěng shí ▶ not exactly 不完全是 bù wánquán shì

exaggerate [ɪɡˈzædʒəreɪt] I VI 夸张 kuāzhāng II VT (overemphasize) 夸大 kuādà

exam [ɪɡˈzæm] N 测验 cèyàn

pass an exam 表示考试通过, 考过通过, 用词 take 。 fail an exam 。 参加考试, 用词 take, 在英式英语中则用 sit an exam.

examination [ɪɡzæmɪˈneɪʃən] N [c] (frm: Scol, Univ) 考试 kǎoshì [次 cì] 2 [c/u] (Med) 体检 tǐjiǎn

examine [ɪɡˈzæmɪn] VT 1 (inspect) 检查 jiǎnchá 2 (Scol, Univ) 对…进行测验 duì…jìnxíng cèyàn 3 (Med) 检查 jiǎnchá

example [ɪɡˈzɑːmpl] N [c] 例子 lìzi [个 gè] ▶ for example 例如 lìrú ▶ an example of sth 某物的例子 mǒuwù de lìzi

excellence ['ɛksələns] N [u] 卓越 zhuóyuè

excellent ['ɛksələnt] I ADJ 极好的 jíhǎo de II INT ▶ excellent! 太好了! tài hǎo le!

except [ɪkˈsɛpt] PREP 除了 chúle ▶ except for 除了…外 chúle…wài ▶ except if/when …时除外 …shí liwài

exception [ɪkˈsɛpʃən] N [c] 例外 lìwài [个 gè]

exchange [ɪksˈtʃeɪndʒ] I VT 1 [+ gifts, addresses] 交换 jiāohuàn 2 ▶ to exchange sth (for sth) [+ goods] 用某物交换 (某物) yòng mǒuwù jiāohuàn (mǒuwù) II N [c/u] [of students, sportspeople] 交流 jiāoliú [次 cì] ▶ in exchange (for) 作为 (对…的) 交换 zuòwéi (duì…de) jiāohuàn

exchange rate N [c] 汇率 huìlǜ [个 gè]

excited [ɪkˈsaɪtɪd] ADJ 兴奋的 xīngfèn de ▶ to be excited about sth/about doing sth 对某事/某事感到激动 duì mǒushì/mǒushì gǎndào jīdòng ▶ to get excited 激动兴奋 jīdòng xīngfèn

excitement [ɪkˈsaɪtmənt] N [u] 兴奋 xīngfèn

exciting [ɪkˈsaɪtɪŋ] ADJ 令人兴奋的 lìng rén xīngfèn de

exclamation mark (Brit), **exclamation point** (US) N [c] 感叹号 gǎntànhào [个 gè]

excluding [ɪksˈkluːdɪŋ] PREP 不包括 bù bāokuò

excuse [n ɪksˈkjuːs, vb ɪksˈkjuːz] **I** N [c/u] 借口 jièkǒu [个 gè] **II** VT 1 (justify) 是…的正当理由 shì…de zhèngdàng lǐyóu 2 (forgive) 原谅 yuánliàng ▸**to make an excuse** 找借口 zhǎo jièkǒu ▸**excuse me!** (attracting attention) 劳驾! láojià; (as apology) 对不起! duìbuqǐ ▸**excuse me, please** 请原谅 qǐng yuánliàng ▸**excuse me?** (US) 对不起，你说什么? duìbuqǐ, nǐ shuō shénme?

exercise [ˈɛksəsaɪz] **I** N 1 [u] (physical exertion) 运动 yùndòng 2 [c] (series of movements) 练习 liànxí [个 gè] 3 [c] (Scol, Mus) 练习 liànxí [个 gè] **II** VT [+ muscles] 锻炼 duànliàn; [+ mind] 运用 yùnyòng **III** VI [person] 锻炼 duànliàn ▸**to take** or **get exercise** 做健身活动 zuò jiànshēn huódòng ▸**to do exercises** (Sport) 锻炼身体 duànliàn shēntǐ

exhaust [ɪgˈzɔːst] N (esp Brit) 1 [c] (also: **exhaust pipe**) 排气管 páiqìguǎn [根 gēn] 2 [u] (fumes) 废气 fèiqì

exhausted [ɪgˈzɔːstɪd] ADJ 精疲力竭的 jīng pí lì jié de

exhibition [ɛksɪˈbɪʃən] N [c] 展览会 zhǎnlǎnhuì [个 gè]

exist [ɪgˈzɪst] VI 1 (be present) 在 cúnzài 2 (live, subsist) 生存 shēngcún

exit [ˈɛksɪt] **I** N [c] 出口 chūkǒu [个 gè] **II** VT (Comput) 退出 tuìchū ▸**to exit from sth** [+ room, motorway] 离开某处 líkāi mǒuchù

expect [ɪksˈpɛkt] **I** VT 1 (anticipate) 预料 yùliào 2 (await) 期待 qīdài 3 [+ baby] 怀有 huáiyǒu 4 (suppose) 料想 liàoxiǎng **II** VI ▸**to be expecting** (be pregnant) 怀孕 huáiyùn ▸**to expect sth to happen** 预期某事会发生 yùqī mǒushì jiāng fāshēng ▸**I expect so** 我想会的 wǒ xiǎng huì de

expense [ɪksˈpɛns] **I** N [c/u] 费用 fèiyòng [笔 bǐ] **II expenses** NPL 经费 jīngfèi

expensive [ɪksˈpɛnsɪv] ADJ 1 昂贵的 ángguì de 2 [+ mistake] 代价高的 dàijià gāo de

experience [ɪksˈpɪərɪəns] **I** N 1 [u] (in job) 经验 jīngyàn 2 [u] (of life) 阅历 yuèlì 3 [c] (individual event) 经历 jīnglì [个 gè] **II** VT [+ feeling, problem] 体验 tǐyàn

experienced [ɪksˈpɪərɪənst] ADJ 有经验的 yǒu jīngyàn de

experiment [n ɪksˈpɛrɪmənt, vb ɪksˈpɛrɪmɛnt] **I** N [c] 1 (Sci) 实验 shíyàn [个 gè] 2 (trial) 试用 shìyòng [次 cì] **II** VI 试验 shìyàn ▸**to perform** or **conduct** or **carry out an experiment** 做实验 zuò shíyàn

expert [ˈɛkspəːt] **I** N [c] 专家 zhuānjiā [位 wèi] **II** ADJ [+ opinion, help, advice] 专家的 zhuānjiā de ▸**an expert on sth** 某事的专家

mǒushì de zhuānjiā

expertise [ˌekspə:ˈtiːz] N [U] 专门知识 zhuānmén zhīshí

expire [ɪksˈpaɪə*] VI [passport, licence] 过期 guòqī

explain [ɪksˈpleɪn] VT
1 [+ situation, contract] 解释 jiěshì 2 [+ decision, actions] 阐明 chǎnmíng ▸ **to explain why/how etc** 解释为什么/如何(等) jiěshì wèishénme/rúhé(děng) ▸ **to explain sth to sb** 向某人解释某事 xiàng mǒurén jiěshì mǒushì

explanation [ekspləˈneɪʃən] N
1 [c/u] (reason) ▸ **explanation (for)** (对…的) 解释 (duì…de) jiěshì [个 gè] 2 [c] (description) ▸ **explanation (of)** (…的) 说明 (…de) shuōmíng [个 gè]

explode [ɪksˈpləud] I VI 爆炸 bàozhà II VT [+ bomb, tank] 使爆炸 shǐ bàozhà

exploit [ɪksˈplɔɪt] VT [+ resources] 开发 kāifā; [+ person, idea] 剥削 bōxuē

explore [ɪksˈplɔː*] I VT 探索 tànsuǒ II VI 探险 tànxiǎn

explosion [ɪksˈpləuʒən] N [c] 1 爆炸 bàozhà [个 gè] 2 激增 jīzēng [个 gè]

export [vb eksˈpɔːt, n ˈekspɔːt] I VT 输出 shūchū II N 1 [u] (process) 出口 chūkǒu 2 [c] (product) 出口物 chūkǒuwù [种 zhǒng]

express [ɪksˈpres] VT 表达 biǎodá; [+ service, mail] 特快的 tèkuài de ▸ **to express o.s.** 表达自己的意思 biǎodá zìjǐ de yìsi

expression [ɪksˈpreʃən] N [c]

(word, phrase) 言辞 yáncí [种 zhǒng] 2 [c/u] (on face) 表情 biǎoqíng [种 zhǒng]

extension [ɪksˈtenʃən] N [c] 1 [of building] 扩建部分 kuòjiàn bùfen [个 gè] 2 [of contract, visa] 延期 yánqī [次 cì] 3 (Tel) 分机 fēnjī [部 bù] ▸ **extension 3718** (Tel) 3718分机

extent [ɪksˈtent] N [u/s] [of problem, damage] 程度 chéngdù ▸ **to a certain extent** 在一定程度上 zài yīdìng chéngdù shàng

extinct [ɪksˈtɪŋkt] ADJ [+ animal, plant] 灭绝的 mièjué de

extra [ˈekstrə] I ADJ 额外的 éwài de II ADV (in addition) 额外地 éwài de III N c 1 (luxury) 额外的事物 éwài de shìwù [件 jiàn] 2 (surcharge) 另外的收费 lìngwài de shōufèi [项 xiàng] ▸ **wine will cost extra** 酒另外收钱 jiǔ lìngwài shōuqián

extraordinary [ɪksˈtrɔːdnrɪ] ADJ 非凡的 fēifán de

extreme [ɪksˈtriːm] ADJ 1 极度的 jídù de 2 [+ opinions, methods] 极端的 jíduān de

extremely [ɪksˈtriːmlɪ] ADV 非常 fēicháng

extremist [ɪksˈtriːmɪst] N [c] 过激分子 guòjī fènzǐ [个 gè]

eye [aɪ] N [c] (Anat) 眼睛 yǎnjing [只 zhī] ▸ **to keep an eye on sb/sth** 密切注意某人/某事物 mìqiè zhùyì mǒurén/mǒushìwù

eyebrow [ˈaɪbrau] N [c] 眉毛 méimáo [个 gè]

eyelash [ˈaɪlæʃ] N [c] 眼睫毛

yǎnjiémáo [根 gēn]

eyelid ['aɪlɪd] N [c] 眼皮 yǎnpí [个 gè]

eyeliner ['aɪlaɪnər] N [c/u] 眼线笔 yǎnxiànbǐ

eyeshadow ['aɪʃædəu] N [c/u] 眼影 yǎnyǐng

eyesight ['aɪsaɪt] N [u] 视力 shìlì

fabric ['fæbrɪk] N [c/u] 织物 zhīwù [件 jiàn]

fabulous ['fæbjuləs] ADJ (inf) 极好的 jíhǎo de

face [feɪs] I N 1 [c] (Anat) 脸 liǎn [张 zhāng] 2 [c] (expression) 表情 biǎoqíng [个 gè] II VT 1 [+ direction] 面向 miànxiàng 2 [+ unpleasant situation] 面对 miànduì ▶I can't or couldn't face it 我应付不了 wǒ yìngfù bùliǎo ▶to come face to face with [+ person] 与…面对面 yǔ…miàn duì miàn
▶ face up to VT FUS 1 [+ truth, facts] 接受 jiēshòu 2 [+ responsibilities, duties] 承担 chéngdān

face cloth (Brit) N [c] 洗脸毛巾 xǐliǎn máojīn [条 tiáo]

facility [fə'sɪlɪtɪ] N [c] (service) 设施 shèshī [种 zhǒng]

fact [fækt] N [c] 真相 zhēnxiàng [个 gè] ▸ **in (actual) fact, as a matter of fact** (for emphasis) 实际上 shíjì shàng ▸ **facts and figures** 精确的资料 jīngquè de zīliào

factory ['fæktərɪ] N [c] 工厂 gōngchǎng [家 jiā]

fail [feɪl] I VT [+ exam, test] 没有通过 méiyǒu tōngguò II VI 1 [candidate] 没通过 méi tōngguò 2 [attempt, plan, remedy] 失败 shībài ▸ **to fail to do sth** 不能做某事 wéinéng zuò mǒushì

failure ['feɪljə] N 1 [c/u] (lack of success) 失败 shībài [次 cì] 2 [c] ▸ **failure to do sth** 没有做某事 méiyǒu zuò mǒushì

faint [feɪnt] I ADJ 1 [+ sound, light, smell, hope] 微弱的 wēiruò de 2 [+ mark, trace] 隐约的 yǐnyuē de II VI 晕倒 yūndǎo ▸ **to feel faint** 感到眩晕 gǎndào xuànyūn

fair [feə'] I ADJ 1 (just, right) 公平的 gōngpíng de 2 (quite large) 相当大的 xiāngdāng dà 3 (quite good) 大体的 dàtǐ de 4 [+ skin, complexion] 白皙的 báixī de; [+ hair] 金色的 jīnsè de II N 1 (trade fair) 交易会 jiāoyìhuì [届 jiè] 2 (Brit: also: **funfair**) 游乐场 yóulèchǎng [座 zuò] ▸ **it's not fair!** 太不公平了! tài bù gōngpíng le!

fairground ['feəgraund] N [c] 游乐场 yóulèchǎng [座 zuò]

fairly ['feəlɪ] ADV 1 (justly) 公平地 gōngpíng de 2 (quite) 相当 xiāngdāng

faith [feɪθ] N 1 [u] (trust) 信任 xìnrèn 2 [u] (religious belief) 信仰 xìnyǎng ▸ **to have faith in sb/sth** 相信某人/某事 xiāngxìn mǒurén/mǒushì

faithful ['feɪθful] ADJ 忠实的 zhōngshí de

faithfully ['feɪθfəlɪ] ADV ▸ **Yours faithfully** (Brit) 您忠实的 nín zhōngshí de

fake [feɪk] I N [c] 赝品 yànpǐn [件 jiàn] II ADJ 假的 jiǎ de

fall [fɔːl] (pt fell, pp fallen) I VI 1 掉 diào 2 [snow, rain] 下 xià 3 [price, temperature, currency] 下降 xiàjiàng II N 1 [c] [of person] 跌倒 shuāidǎo [次 cì] 2 [c] (in price, temperature) 下降 xiàjiàng [次 cì] 3 [c/u] (US: autumn) 秋天 qiūtiān [个 gè] ▸ **to fall in love (with sb/sth)** 爱上 (某人/某事) àishàng (mǒurén/mǒushì)

▸ **fall down** VI [person] 摔倒 shuāidǎo 2 [building] 倒塌 dǎotā

▸ **fall off** VI [person, object] 掉下 diàoxià

▸ **fall over** VI [person, object] 跌倒 diēdǎo

▸ **fall through** VI [plan] 落空 luòkōng

fallen ['fɔːlən] PP of **fall**

false [fɔːls] ADJ 假的 jiǎ de

fame [feɪm] N [u] 声誉 shēngyù

familiar [fə'mɪliə'] ADJ 熟悉的 shúxī de ▸ **to be familiar with** 对…熟悉 duì...shúxī

family ['fæmɪlɪ] N [c] 1 (relations) 家庭 jiātíng [个 gè] 2 (children) 孩子 háizi [个 gè]

famine ['fæmɪn] N [c/u] 饥荒 jīhuāng [阵 zhèn]

famous ['feɪməs] ADJ 著名的 zhùmíng de

fan [fæn] N [c] 1 [of pop star] 迷 mí [个 gè]; (Sport) 球迷 qiúmí [个 gè] 2 (Elec) 风扇 fēngshàn [台 tái] 3 (handheld) 扇子 shànzi [把 bǎ]

fanatic [fə'nætɪk] N [c] 狂热者 kuángrè zhě [名 míng]

fancy-dress party ['fænsɪdres-] N [c] 化装舞会 huàzhuāng wǔhuì [个 gè]

fantastic [fæn'tæstɪk] ADJ 1 极好 的 jíhǎo de 2 [+ sum, amount, profit] 巨大的 jùdà de

FAQ N ABBR (= frequently asked question) 常见问题 chángjiàn wèntí

far [fɑːʳ] I ADJ 1 远的 yuǎn de 2 ▸ the far end/side 尽头的 jìntóu de II ADV 1 远 yuǎn; (in time) 久远 jiǔyuǎn de 2 (much, greatly) …得多 …de duō ▸ as far as I know 据我所知 jùwǒ suǒzhī ▸ by far …得多 …de duō ▸ so far 迄今为止 qìjīn wéizhǐ ▸ it's not far from here 离这里不远 lí zhèlǐ bùyuǎn ▸ how far? 多远? duōyuǎn? ▸ far away 遥 远 yáoyuǎn ▸ far better 好得多 hǎodeduō

fare [fɛəʳ] N [c] 票价 piàojià [种 zhǒng]; (in taxi) 乘客 chéngkè [位 wèi] ▸ half/full fare 半/全价 bàn/quánjià

Far East N ▸ the Far East 远东 Yuǎndōng

farm [fɑːm] N [c] 农场 nóngchǎng

farmer ['fɑːməʳ] N [c] 农民 nóngmín [个 gè]

farming ['fɑːmɪŋ] N [u] 农业 nóngyè

fascinating ['fæsɪneɪtɪŋ] ADJ 迷 人的 mírén de

fashion ['fæʃən] N [u/s] 流行的式 样 liúxíng de shìyàng ▸ in fashion 流行 liúxíng

fashionable ['fæʃnəbl] ADJ 流行 的 liúxíng de

fast [fɑːst] I ADJ 1 快的 kuài de II ADV 快 kuài 2 ▸ my watch is 5 minutes fast 我的表快5分 钟 wǒde biǎo kuài wǔfēnzhōng ▸ fast asleep 酣睡 hānshuì

fasten ['fɑːsn] VT [+ coat, jacket, belt] 系上 jìshàng

fast food N [u] 快餐 kuàicān

fat [fæt] I ADJ 胖的 feìpàng de; [+ animal] 肥的 féi de II N 1 [u] (on person, animal, meat) 脂肪 zhīfáng 2 [c/u] (for cooking) 食用油 shíyòng yóu [桶 tǒng]

用 fat 形容某人胖，显 得过于直接，甚至有些 粗鲁。比较礼貌而又含 蓄的说法是 plump 或 chubby，后者更为正式。 overweight 和 obese 暗 示某人因为肥胖而有健康 问题。obese 是医学术 语，表示某人极度肥胖或 超重。一般而言，应尽量 避免当面使用任何表示肥 胖的词语。

fatal ['feɪtl] ADJ 1 致命的 zhìmíng de 2 [+ mistake] 严重

yánzhòng de

father ['fɑːðə'] N [c] 父亲 fùqīn [位 wèi]

Father Christmas (Brit) N 圣诞老人 Shèngdàn lǎorén

father-in-law ['fɑːðərɪnlɔː] (pl **fathers-in-law**) N [c] (of woman) 公公 gōnggong [位 wèi]; (of man) 岳父 yuèfù [位 wèi]

faucet ['fɔːsɪt] (US) N [c] 水龙头 shuǐlóngtóu [个 gè]

fault [fɔːlt] N 1 [c] (error) 错误 cuòwù 2 [c] (defect: in person) 缺点 quēdiǎn [个 gè]; (: in machine) 故障 gùzhàng [个 gè] ▶ **it's my fault** 是我的错 shì wǒde cuò

fava bean ['fɑːvə-] (US) N [c] 蚕豆 cándòu [颗 kē]

favour, (US) **favor** ['feɪvə'] N [c] 恩惠 ēnhuì [种 zhǒng] ▶ **to do sb a favour** 帮某人的忙 bāng mǒurén de máng ▶ **to be in favour of sth/doing sth** 赞成某事/做某事 zànchéng mǒushì/zuò mǒushì

favourite, (US) **favorite** ['feɪvrɪt] I ADJ 最喜欢的 zuì xǐhuan de II N [c] 偏爱 piān'ài [种 zhǒng]

fax [fæks] I N [c] 1 (message) 传真 chuánzhēn [份 fèn] 2 (also: **fax machine**) 传真机 chuánzhēnjī [台 tái] II VT [+ document] 用传真发送 yòng chuánzhēn fāsòng

fear [fɪə'] N 1 [c/u] (terror) 害怕 hàipà 2 [c/u] (anxiety) 焦虑 jiāolǜ [种 zhǒng]

feather ['feðə'] N [c] 羽毛 yǔmáo [根 gēn]

feature ['fiːtʃə'] N [c] 特点 tèdiǎn [个 gè]

February ['februərɪ] N [c/u] 二月 èryuè; see also **July**

fed [fed] PT, PP of **feed**

fed up (inf) ADJ ▶ **to be fed up** 厌倦 yànjuàn

fee [fiː] N [c] 费 fèi [种 zhǒng]; [+ of doctor, lawyer] 费用 fèiyòng [项 xiàng]

feeble ['fiːbl] ADJ 1 虚弱的 xūruò de 2 [+ attempt, excuse, argument] 无力的 wúlì de

feed [fiːd] (pt, pp **fed**) VT 喂 wèi

feel [fiːl] (pt, pp **felt**) VT 1 (touch) [+ object, face] 摸 mō 2 [+ pain] 感到 gǎndào 3 (think, believe) 认为 rènwéi ▶ **to feel that...** 感到⋯ gǎndào... ▶ **to feel hungry** 觉得饿 juéde è ▶ **to feel cold** 觉得冷 juéde lěng ▶ **to feel lonely/better** 感到孤独/感觉好多了 gǎndào gūdú/gǎnjué hǎo duō le ▶ **I don't feel well** 我觉得身体不适 wǒ juéde shēntǐ bùshì ▶ **to feel sorry for sb** 同情某人 tóngqíng mǒurén ▶ **to feel like** (want) 想要 xiǎng yào

feeling ['fiːlɪŋ] I N 1 [c] (emotion) 感受 gǎnshòu [种 zhǒng] 2 [c] (physical sensation) 感觉 gǎnjué [种 zhǒng] 3 [s] (impression) 感觉 gǎnjué II **feelings** NPL 1 (attitude) 看法 kànfǎ 2 (emotions) 情感 qínggǎn ▶ **I have a feeling that...** 我有种感觉⋯ wǒ yǒuzhǒng gǎnjué... ▶ **to hurt sb's feelings** 伤害某人的感情 shānghài mǒurén de gǎnqíng

feet [fiːt] NPL of **foot**

fell [fel] PT of **fall**

felt [fɛlt] PT, PP of **feel**

felt-tip pen, felt-tip ['fɛltɪp-] N [c] 毡头墨水笔 zhāntóu mòshuǐbǐ [支 zhī]

female ['fi:meɪl] I N [c] 1 (Zool) 雌兽 císhòu [头 tóu] 2 (woman) 女性 nǚxìng [位 wèi] II ADJ 1 (Zool) 雌性的 cíxìng de 2 (relating to women) 妇女的 fùnǚ de ▸ **male and female students** 男女学生 nánnǚ xuéshēng

feminine ['fɛmɪnɪn] ADJ 1 女性的 nǚxìng de 2 (Ling) 阴性的 yīnxìng de

feminist ['fɛmɪnɪst] N [c] 女权主义者 nǚquán zhǔyìzhě [位 wèi]

fence [fɛns] N [c] 篱笆 líba [道 dào]

fencing ['fɛnsɪŋ] N [U] (Sport) 击剑 jījiàn

ferry ['fɛrɪ] N [c] (small) 摆渡 bǎidù [个 gè]; (large: also: **ferryboat**) 渡船 dùchuán [艘 sōu]

festival ['fɛstɪvəl] N [c] 1 (Rel) 节日 jiérì [个 gè] 2 (Theat, Mus) 艺术节 yìshù jié [届 jiè]

fetch [fɛtʃ] VT 去拿来 qù nálái ▸ **to fetch sth for sb, fetch sb sth** 去给某人拿来某物 qù gěi mǒurén nálái mǒuwù

fever ['fi:vəʳ] N [c/U] (Med) 发烧 fāshāo

few [fju:] I ADJ 1 (not many) 少数的 shǎoshù de 2 ▸ **a few** (some) 几个 jǐ gè II PRON 1 ▸ **a few** (some) 几个 jǐ gè 2 ▸ **in the next few days** 在接下来的几天里 zài jiēxiàlái de jǐtiān lǐ ▸ **in the past few days** 在过去的几天里 zài guòqù de jǐtiān

lǐ ▸ **a few of us/them** 我们/他们 中的几个 wǒmen/tāmen zhōng de jǐgè ▸ **a few more** 再多几个 zài duō jǐgè ▸ **very few survive** 极少幸存 jíshǎo xìngcún

fewer ['fju:əʳ] ADJ 较少的 jiàoshǎo de ▸ **no fewer than** 不少于 bù shǎoyú

fiancé [fɪˈɒnseɪ] N [c] 未婚夫 wèihūnfū [个 gè]

fiancée [fɪˈɒnseɪ] N [c] 未婚妻 wèihūnqī [个 gè]

fiction ['fɪkʃən] N [U] 小说 xiǎoshuō

field [fi:ld] N [c] 1 (grassland) 草地 cǎodì [块 kuài] 2 (cultivated) 田地 tiándì [片 piàn] 3 (Sport) 场地 chǎngdì [个 gè] 4 (subject, area of interest) 领域 lǐngyù [个 gè]

fierce [fɪəs] ADJ 1 凶猛的 xiōngměng de 2 [+ loyalty, resistance, competition] 强烈的 qiángliè de

fifteen [fɪfˈtiːn] NUM 十五 shíwǔ ▸ **she's fifteen (years old)** 她15岁了 tā shíwǔ suì le

fifteenth [fɪfˈtiːnθ] NUM 第十五 dì shíwǔ; see also **fifth**

fifth [fɪfθ] NUM 1 (in series) 第五 dìwǔ 2 (fraction) 五分之一 wǔfēnzhīyī ▸ **on July fifth, on the fifth of July** 在7月5日 zài qīyuè wǔrì

fifty ['fɪftɪ] NUM 五十 wǔshí ▸ **he's in his fifties** 他50多岁 tā wǔshí duō suì

fight [faɪt] (pt, pp fought) I N [c] 1 斗殴 dòu'ōu [场 chǎng] 2 斗争 dòuzhēng [场 chǎng] II VT

figure | 336

与···对打 yǔ···duìdǎ III VI 1 战斗 zhàndòu 2 (struggle) 奋斗 fèndòu ▸to fight for/against sth 为支持/反对某事而斗争 wèi zhīchí/fǎnduì mǒushì ér dòuzhēng

figure ['fɪgə'] I N [c] 1 (number, statistic) 统计数字 tǒngjì shùzì [个 gè] 2 (digit) 数字 shùzì [个 gè] 3 (body, shape) 身材 shēncái [种 zhǒng] II VT (esp US: inf: reckon) 估计 gūjì ▸that figures (inf) 那不足为怪 nà bùzú wéiguài

file [faɪl] I N [c] 1 (dossier) 档案 dàng'àn [份 fèn] 2 (folder) 文件夹 wénjiànjiá [个 gè] 3 (Comput) 文件 wénjiàn [份 fèn] II VT 1 (also: file away) ▸that figures 把···归档 bǎ···guīdàng 2 [+ wood, metal, fingernails] 把···锉平 bǎ···cuòpíng

fill [fɪl] VT 1 [+ container] 装满 zhuāngmǎn 2 [+ space, area] 占满 zhànmǎn 3 [+ tooth] 填补 tiánbǔ ▸to fill sth with sth 用某物填满某物 yòng mǒuwù tiánmǎn mǒuwù ▸fill in VT [esp Brit] [+ form, name] 填写 tiánxiě ▸fill out VT [+ form] 填写 tiánxiě

filling ['fɪlɪŋ] N [c] (in tooth) 填补物 tiánbǔwù [种 zhǒng]

film [fɪlm] I N 1 [c] (esp Brit) 影片 yǐngpiàn [部 bù] 2 [c/u] (Phot) 胶卷 jiāojuǎn [卷 juǎn] II VT 把···拍成影片 bǎ···pāichéng yǐngpiàn

film star N [c] (esp Brit) 影星 yǐngxīng [位 wèi]

filthy ['fɪlθɪ] ADJ 污秽的 wūhuì de

final ['faɪnl] I ADJ 1 最后的 zuìhòu de 2 [+ decision, offer] 不可变更的

不可变更的 bùkě biàngēng de II N [c] (Sport) 决赛 juésài [场 chǎng]

finally ['faɪnəlɪ] ADV 1 (eventually) 终于 zhōngyú 2 (lastly) 最后 zuìhòu 3 (in conclusion) 总之 zǒngzhī

find [faɪnd] (pt, pp found) VT 1 [+ person, object, exit] 找到 zhǎodào; [+ lost object] 找回 zhǎohuí 2 (discover) [+ answer, solution] 找出 zhǎochū; [+ object, person] 发现 fāxiàn 3 [+ work, job] 得到 dédào; [+ time] 有 yǒu ▸to find sb guilty/not guilty 判决某人有罪/无罪 pànjué mǒurén yǒuzuì/wúzuì ▸to find one's way 认识路 rènde lù ▸find out I VT [+ fact, truth] 查明 chámíng II VI ▸to find out about sth (deliberately) 获知某事 huòzhī mǒushì; (by chance) 偶然发现某事 ǒurán fāxiàn mǒushì

fine [faɪn] I ADJ 1 (satisfactory) 还不错的 hái bùcuò de 2 (excellent) 好的 hǎo de 3 (in texture) 细的 xì de 4 [+ weather, day] 晴朗的 qínglǎng de II ADV (well) 不错地 bùcuò de III N [c] (Law) 罚款 fákuǎn [笔 bǐ] IV VT (Law) 处···以罚金 chǔ···yǐ fájīn ▸(I'm) fine (我)很好 (wǒ) hěnhǎo ▸(that's) fine (那) 好吧 (nà) hǎoba ▸you're doing fine 你做得很好 nǐ zuòde hěnhǎo

finger ['fɪŋgə'] N [c] 手指 shǒuzhǐ [根 gēn]

finish ['fɪnɪʃ] I N [s] (end) 结束 jiéshù 2 [c] (Sport) 终点 zhōngdiǎn [个 gè] II VT [+ work] 完成

jiéshù; [+ task, report, book] 完成 wánchéng III VI 1 [course, event] 结束 jiéshù 2 [person] 完成 wánchéng ▸ to finish doing sth 做完某事 zuòwán mǒushì

Finland ['fɪnlənd] N 芬兰 Fēnlán

fir [fɜː] N [c] (also: **fir tree**) 冷杉 lěngshān [棵 kē]

fire ['faɪə] I N 1 [u] (flames) 火 huǒ 2 [c] (in fireplace, hearth) 炉火 lúhuǒ [团 tuán] 3 [c/u] (accidental) 火灾 huǒzāi [场 cháng] II VT 1 (shoot) 射出 shèchū 2 (inf: dismiss) 解雇 jiěgù III VI (shoot) 开火 kāihuǒ ▸ to set sth on fire 放火烧某物 fànghuǒ shāo mǒuwù ▸ on fire 起火 qǐhuǒ ▸ to catch fire 着火 zháohuǒ

fire alarm N [c] 火警警报 huǒjǐng jǐngbào [个 gè]

fire brigade (Brit) N [c] 消防队 xiāofáng duì [支 zhī]

fire engine (Brit) N [c] 救火车 jiùhuǒchē [辆 liàng]

firefighter ['faɪəfaɪtə] N [c] 消防队员 xiāofáng duìyuán [位 wèi]

fireman ['faɪəmən] (pl firemen) N [c] 消防队员 xiāofáng duìyuán [位 wèi]

fire station N [c] 消防站 xiāofángzhàn [个 gè]

fire truck (US) N [c] 救火车 jiùhuǒchē [辆 liàng]

firework ['faɪəwɜːk] I N [c] 烟火 yānhuǒ [台 tái] II fireworks NPL (display) 烟火表演 yānhuǒ biǎoyǎn

firm [fɜːm] I ADJ 1 [+ mattress, ground] 硬实的 yìngshí de 2 [+ person] 坚定的 jiāndìng de II N [c] 公司 gōngsī [家 jiā]

first [fɜːst] I ADJ 1 (in series) 第一的 dìyī de 2 [+ reaction, impression] 最初的 zuìchū de 3 [+ prize, division] 头等的 tóuděng de II ADV 1 (before anyone else) 首先 shǒuxiān 2 (before other things) 首先 shǒuxiān 3 (when listing reasons) 第一 dìyī 4 (for the first time) 第一次 dìyīcì 5 (in race, competition: come, finish) 第一名 dìyīmíng ▸ at first 起先 qǐxiān ▸ the first of January 1月1号 yīyuè yīhào

first aid N [u] 急救 jíjiù

first-class [fɜːst'klɑːs] I ADJ 1 (excellent) 第一流的 dìyīliú de 2 [+ carriage, ticket, stamp] 一类的 yīlèi de II ADV (travel, send) 作为一类 zuòwéi yīlèi

firstly ['fɜːstlɪ] ADV 首先 shǒuxiān

first name N [c] 名 míng [个 gè]

fish [fɪʃ] I N 1 [c] 鱼 yú [条 tiáo] 2 [u] (food) 鱼肉 yúròu II VI (commercially) 捕鱼 bǔyú; (as sport, hobby) 钓鱼 diàoyú ▸ to go fishing 去钓鱼 qù diàoyú

fisherman ['fɪʃəmən] (pl fishermen) N [c] 渔民 yúmín [位 wèi]

fishing ['fɪʃɪŋ] N [u] 钓鱼 diàoyú

fishing boat N [c] 渔船 yúchuán [条 tiáo]

fist [fɪst] N [c] 拳 quán [个 gè]

fit [fɪt] I ADJ 1 (healthy) 健康的 jiànkāng de II VI 1 [clothes, shoes] 合身 héshēn 2 (in space, gap) 适合 shìhé ▸ to keep fit 保持健康 bǎochí jiànkāng ▸ to have a fit (Med) 癫痫病发作 diānxiánbìng

fāzuò ▸to be a good fit 很合身
hěn héshēn
▸ **fit in** I VI (lit) 容纳 róngnà II VT
[+ appointment, visitor] 定时间予
dìng shíjiān yú

fitness ['fɪtnɪs] N [U] 健康
jiànkāng

five [faɪv] NUM 五 wǔ ▸**that will
be five pounds, please** 请付
5镑 qǐng fù wǔbàng ▸**she's five
(years old)** 她5岁了 tā wǔsuì le
▸ **it's five o'clock** 5点了 wǔdiǎn le

fix [fɪks] VT 1 [+ date, price, meeting]
确定 quèdìng 2 (mend) 修理 xiūlǐ
3 [+ problem] 解决 jiějué

fizzy ['fɪzɪ] (Brit) ADJ 带气的
dàiqì de

flag [flæg] N [c] 旗 qí [面 miàn]

flame [fleɪm] N [c/u] 火焰
huǒyàn [团 tuán] ▸**in flames** 燃烧
着 ránshāo zhe

flash [flæʃ] I VI 闪光 shǎnguāng
II N [c] 1 闪光 shǎnguāng
[阵 zhèn] 2 (Phot) 闪光灯
shǎnguāngdēng [个 gè] ▸**to flash
one's headlights** 亮起车头灯
liàngqǐ chētóudēng

flashlight ['flæʃlaɪt] (esp US N)
手电筒 shǒudiàntǒng [个 gè]

flask [flɑːsk] N [c] (also: **vacuum
flask**) 保温瓶 bǎowēnpíng [个 gè]

flat [flæt] I ADJ 1 平的 píng de
2 [+ tyre, ball] 气不足的 qì bùzú de
3 (Brit) [+ battery] 没电的 méidiàn
de II N [c] (Brit) 公寓 gōngyù
[套 tào]

flatter ['flætə'] VT 奉承
fèngchéng

flavour, (US) **flavor** ['fleɪvə']

I N [c/u] 味 wèi [种 zhǒng] II VT
给...调味 gěi...tiáowèi

flea [fliː] N [c] 跳蚤 tiàozao
[只 zhī]

flew [fluː] PT OF **fly**

flexible ['flɛksəbl] ADJ 1 柔韧的
róurèn de 2 [+ person, schedule] 机
动的 jīdòng de

flight [flaɪt] N [c] 1 航班 hángbān
[个 gè] 2 (also: **flight of stairs,
flight of steps**) 一段楼梯 yīduàn
lóutī [段 duàn]

flight attendant N [c] (male) 男
空服人员 nán kōngfú rényuán
[位 wèi]; (female) 空姐 kōngjiě
[位 wèi]

float [fləut] VI 1 漂浮 piāofú
2 (stay afloat) 浮着 fúzhe

flock [flɔk] N [c] 群 qún

flood [flʌd] I N [c/u] 洪水
hóngshuǐ [次 cì] II VT 淹没
yānmò

floor [flɔːʳ] N 1 [c] 地板 dìbǎn [块
kuài] 2 [c] (storey) 楼层 lóucéng
[个 gè] ▸**on the floor** 在地板上
zài dìbǎn shàng ▸**ground floor**
(Brit) 一楼 yīlóu ▸**first floor** (Brit)
二楼 ; (US) 一楼

在英式英语中，建筑的
ground floor 是指紧贴地
面的那个楼层。它上面的
一层叫 **first floor**。在美式
英语中，**first floor** 是指
紧贴地面的楼层，它上面
的义是 **second floor**。

floppy ['flɔpɪ] N [c] (also: **floppy
disk**) 软盘 ruǎnpán [张 zhāng]

florist ['flɔrɪst] N [c] 1 花商
huāshāng [个 gè] 2 (also: **florist's**

花店 huādiàn [家 jiā]

flour ['flauə'] N [U] 面粉 miànfěn

flow [fləu] I VI 流动 liúdòng II N [c/U] 1 流动 liúdòng 2 [of traffic] 川流不息 chuānliú bùxī

flower ['flauə'] I N [c] 花 huā [朵 duǒ] II VI 开花 kāihuā ▶in flower 正开着花 zhèng kāizhe huā

flown [fləun] PP of **fly**

flu [flu:] N [U] 流感 liúgǎn

fluent ['flu:ənt] ADJ [+ speech, reading, writing] 流畅的 liúchàng de ▶to speak fluent French, be fluent in French 讲流利的法语 jiǎng liúlì de Fǎyǔ

flush [flʌʃ] VT ▶to flush the toilet 冲厕所 chōng cèsuǒ

flute [flu:t] N [c] 长笛 chángdí [支 zhī]

fly [flaɪ] (pt flew, pp flown) I VT [+ plane] 驾驶 jiàshǐ II VI 1 [bird, insect, plane] 飞 fēi 2 [passengers] 乘飞机 chéng fēijī III N [c] (insect) 苍蝇 cāngying [只 zhī]
▶fly away VI 飞走 fēizǒu

focus ['fəukəs] (pl **focuses**) I N 1 [U] (Phot) 聚焦 jùjiāo 2 [c] 重点 zhòngdiǎn [个 gè] II VI ▶to focus (on) (with camera) 聚焦（于）jùjiāo (yú) II VT (fig) 集中 (于) jízhōng (yú) ▶in focus/out of focus 焦点对准/没对准 jiāodiǎn duìzhǔn/méi duìzhǔn ▶to be the focus of attention 为关注的焦点 wéi guānzhù de jiāodiǎn

fog [fɒg] N [c/U] 雾 wù [场 chǎng]

foggy ['fɒgɪ] ADJ [+ day, climate] 有雾的 yǒuwù de ▶it's foggy 今天有雾 jīntiān yǒu wù

fold [fəuld] VT (also: **fold up**) 折叠 zhédié

folder ['fəuldə'] N [c] 文件夹 wénjiàn jiā [个 gè]

follow ['fɒləu] VT 1 跟随 gēnsuí 2 [+ example, advice, instructions] 遵循 zūnxún 3 [+ route, path] 沿着…行进 yánzhe…xíngjìn ▶I don't quite follow you 我不太理解你的意思 wǒ bùtài lǐjiě nǐde yìsi ▶as follows (when listing) 如下 rúxià; (in this way) 按如下方式 àn rúxià fāngshì ▶followed by 接着是 jiēzhe shì

following ['fɒləuɪŋ] I PREP (after) 在…之后 zàiellipherezhīhòu II ADJ 1 [+ day, week] 接着的 jiēzhe de 2 (next-mentioned) 下述的 xiàshù de

fond [fɒnd] ADJ ▶to be fond of [+ person] 喜爱 xǐ'ài; [+ food, walking] 喜欢 xǐhuan

food [fu:d] N [c/U] 食物 shíwù [种 zhǒng]

fool [fu:l] I N [c] 白痴 báichī [个 gè] II VT (deceive) 欺骗 qīpiàn

foot [fut] (pl **feet**) N 1 [c] (measure) 英尺 yīngchǐ 2 [c] [of person] 脚 jiǎo [只 zhī] ▶on foot 步行 bùxíng

football ['futbɔ:l] N [c] 1 (ball) 足球 zúqiú 2 [U] (sport) (Brit) 足球 zúqiú; (US) 美式足球 měishì zúqiú

footballer ['futbɔ:lə'] (Brit) N [c] 足球运动员 zúqiú yùndòngyuán [位 wèi]

footpath ['futpa:θ] N [c] 人行小径 rénxíng xiǎojìng [条 tiáo]

footprint ['futprɪnt] N [c]

zúji [个 gè]

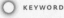

KEYWORD

for [fɔːʳ] PREP **1** 为 wèi ▸ is this for me? 这是为我准备的吗? zhè shì wèi wǒ zhǔnbèi de ma? ▸ a table for two 供两人用的桌子 gòng liǎngrén yòng de zhuōzi

2 (purpose) 为了 wèile ▸ what's it for? 它有什么用途? tā yǒu shénme yòngtú ▸ it's time for lunch 该吃午饭了 gāi chī wǔfàn le ▸ what for? 为什么呢? wèi shénme ne? ▸ a knife for chopping vegetables 用于切菜的刀 yòngyú qiēcài de dāo

3 (time) ▸ he was away for two years 他离开两年了 tā líkāi liǎngnián le ▸ it hasn't rained for three weeks 已经有3周没下雨了 yǐjīng yǒu sānzhōu méi xiàyǔ le ▸ the trip is scheduled for June 5 旅行安排在6月5日 lǚxíng ānpái zài liùyuè wǔrì

4 (in exchange for) ▸ I sold it for £50 我以50镑卖掉了它 wǒ yǐ wǔshí bàng màidiào le tā ▸ to pay 50 pence for a ticket 花50便士买票 huā wǔshí biànshì mǎi zhāng piào

5 (reason) 因为 yīnwèi

6 (on behalf of, representing) 为 wèi ▸ he works for a local firm 他为一家当地公司工作 tā wèi yījiā dāngdì gōngsī gōngzuò ▸ for George George中的G George zhōng de G

7 (destination) 前往 qiánwǎng ▸ he left for Rome 他前往罗马 tā qiánwǎng Luómǎ

8 (with infinitive clause) ▸ it is not for me to decide 这不是由我来决定的 zhè bùshì yóu wǒ lái juédìng de ▸ there is still time for you to do it 你还有时间去做 nǐ hái yǒu shíjiān qù zuò

9 (in favour of) 赞成 zànchéng

10 (referring to distance) 达 dá ▸ there are roadworks for 50 km 长跑练习长达50公里 chángpǎo liànxí chángdá wǔshí gōnglǐ

for 和 to 都可用于表示某人的目的，但后接不同的语言结构。for 用于表示目的时，后面必须跟名词。Occasionally I go to the pub for a drink. for 通常不用在动词前面。不能说 I go to the pub for to have a drink. for 在 to 的 -ing 形式前表示物的用途。...a small machine for weighing the letters... 与动词连用时，不定式前不加 for。She went off to fetch help.

forbid [fəˈbɪd] (pt **forbade** [fəˈbæd], pp **forbidden**) VT 禁止 jìnzhǐ ▸ to forbid sb to do sth 禁止某人做某事 jìnzhǐ mǒurén zuò mǒushì

forbidden [fəˈbɪdn] PP of **forbid**

force [fɔːs] I N **1** [U] (violence) 武力 wǔlì **2** [U] (strength) 力量 lìliàng II VT 强迫 qiǎngpò III **forces** NPL (Mil) 部队 bùduì ▸ to force sb to do sth 强迫某人做某事

móurén zuò móushì

forecast ['fɔːkɑːst] (pt, pp **forecast** or **forecasted**) I N [c] 预报 yùbào [个 gè] II VT (predict) 预测 yùcè

forehead ['fɒrɪd] N [c] 额 é [个 gè]

foreign ['fɒrɪn] ADJ 外国的 wàiguó de

foreigner ['fɒrɪnəʳ] N [c] 外国人 wàiguórén [个 gè]

forest ['fɒrɪst] N [c/u] 森林 sēnlín [片 piàn]

forever [fə'rɛvəʳ] ADV 永远 yǒngyuǎn

forgave [fə'geɪv] PT of **forgive**

forge [fɔːdʒ] VT [+ signature, banknote] 伪造 wěizào

forget [fə'gɛt] (pt **forgot**, pp **forgotten**) I VT 1 忘记 wàngjì 2 (leave behind) [+ object] 忘带 wàng dài II VI (fail to remember) 忘记 wàngjì ▶ **to forget to do sth** 忘记做某事 wàngjì zuò móushì ▶ **to forget that...** 忘记… wàngjì…

forgive [fə'gɪv] (pt **forgave**, pp **forgiven**) VT 原谅 yuánliàng ▶ **to forgive sb for sth** 原谅某人某事 yuánliàng móurén móushì

forgot [fə'gɒt] PT of **forget**

forgotten [fə'gɒtn] PP of **forget**

fork [fɔːk] N [c] 1 餐叉 cānchā [把 bǎ] 2 (in road, river, railway) 岔路 chàlù [条 tiáo]

form [fɔːm] I N 1 (type) 类型 lèixíng [种 zhǒng] 2 (Brit: Scol: class) 年级 niánjí [个 gè] 3 (document) 表格 biǎogé

[张 zhāng] II VT 1 (make) 组成 zǔchéng 2 (create) [+ group, organization, company] 成立 chénglì ▶ **in the form of** 通过…方式 tōngguò…fāngshì

formal ['fɔːməl] ADJ 正式的 zhèngshì de

former ['fɔːməʳ] ADJ 前任的 qiánrèn de ▶ **in former times/years** 以前 yǐqián

fortnight ['fɔːtnaɪt] (Brit) N [c] 两星期 liǎng xīngqī

fortunate ['fɔːtʃənɪt] ADJ 幸运的 xìngyùn de

fortunately ['fɔːtʃənɪtlɪ] ADV 幸运的是 xìngyùn de shì

fortune ['fɔːtʃən] N [c] 大笔钱 dàbǐqián ▶ **to make a fortune** 发大财 fā dàcái

forty ['fɔːtɪ] NUM 四十 sìshí

forward ['fɔːwəd] ADV = **forwards**

forwards ['fɔːwədz] ADV 向前 xiàngqián

fought [fɔːt] PT, PP of **fight**

found [faund] I PT, PP of **find** II VT [+ organization, company] 创办 chuàngbàn

fountain ['fauntɪn] N [c] 喷泉 pēnquán [个 gè]

four [fɔːʳ] NUM 四 sì; see also **five**

fourteen ['fɔː'tiːn] NUM 十四 shísì; see also **five**

fourteenth ['fɔː'tiːnθ] NUM 第十四 dì shísì; see also **fifth**

fourth [fɔːθ] NUM 1 第四 dìsì 2 (US: quarter) 四分之一 sìfēnzhīyī; see also **fifth**

fox [fɒks] N [c] 狐狸 húlí [只 zhī]

fragile ['frædʒaɪl] ADJ 易损的

yìsǔn de

frame [freɪm] N [c] 1 框 kuàng [个 gè] 2 (also: **frames**) [of spectacles] 眼镜架 yǎnjìngjià [副 fù]

France [frɑːns] N 法国 Fǎguó

fraud [frɔːd] N [c/u] 诈骗 zhàpiàn [种 zhǒng]

freckle ['frekl] N [c] 雀斑 quèbān [个 gè]

free [friː] ADJ 1 (costing nothing) 免费的 miǎnfèi de 2 [+ person] 自由的 zìyóu de 3 [+ time] 空闲的 kòngxián de 4 [+ seat, table] 空余的 kòngyú de ▸ free (of charge), for free 免费 miǎnfèi ▸ to be free of or from sth 没有某物 méiyǒu mǒuwù ▸ to be free to do sth 随意做某事 suíyì zuò mǒushì

freedom ['friːdəm] N [u] 自由 zìyóu

freeway ['friːweɪ] (US) N [c] 高速公路 gāosù gōnglù [条 tiáo]

freeze [friːz] (pt froze, pp frozen) I VI 1 [liquid, weather] 结冰 jiébīng 2 [pipe] 冻住 dòngzhù II VT [+ food] 冷冻 lěngdòng

freezer ['friːzər] N [c] 冰柜 bīngguì [个 gè]

freezing ['friːzɪŋ] ADJ (also: **freezing cold**) [+ day, weather] 极冷的 jílěng de; [+ person, hands] 冰凉的 bīngliáng de ▸ I'm freezing 我冻死了 wǒ dòngsǐ wǒ le

French [frentʃ] I ADJ 法国的 Fǎguó de II N [u] (language) 法语 Fǎyǔ III the French NPL (people) 法国人 Fǎguórén

French fries [-fraɪz] (esp US) NPL 炸薯条 zhá shǔtiáo

Frenchman ['frentʃmən] N [c] (pl Frenchmen) 法国男人 Fǎguó nánrén [个 gè]

Frenchwoman ['frentʃwumən] (pl Frenchwomen) N [c] 法国女人 Fǎguó nǚrén [个 gè]

frequent ['friːkwənt] ADJ 频繁的 pínfán de

fresh [freʃ] ADJ 1 新鲜的 xīnxiān de 2 [+ approach, way] 新颖的 xīnyǐng de ▸ fresh air 新鲜空气 xīnxiān kōngqì

Friday ['fraɪdɪ] N [c/u] 星期五 xīngqīwǔ [个 gè]; see also Tuesday

fridge [frɪdʒ] (Brit) N [c] 冰箱 bīngxiāng [台 tái]

fried [fraɪd] I PT, PP of fry II ADJ [+ food] 炒的 chǎo de

friend [frend] N [c] 朋友 péngyou [个 gè] ▸ to be friends with sb 与某人交朋友 yǔ mǒurén jiāo péngyou

friendly ['frendlɪ] ADJ 友善的 yǒushàn de ▸ to be friendly with 跟…友好 gēn…yǒuhǎo

friendship ['frendʃɪp] N [c] 友情 yǒuqíng [种 zhǒng]

fright [fraɪt] N [c] 惊吓 jīngxià [个 gè] ▸ to give sb a fright 吓唬某人一下 xiàhu mǒurén yīxià

frighten ['fraɪtn] VT 使惊恐 shǐ jīngkǒng

frightened ['fraɪtnd] ADJ ▸ to be frightened 被吓倒 bèi xiàdǎo ▸ to be frightened of sth or of doing sth or to do sth 害怕某事/做某事 hàipà mǒushì/zuò mǒushì

frightening ['fraɪtnɪŋ] ADJ 令人

恐惧的 kǒngjù de lìngrén kǒngjù de
frog [frɒg] (Zool) N [c] 青蛙
qīngwā [只 zhī]

KEYWORD

from [frɒm] PREP 1 (indicating
starting place) 来自 láizì ▸ **where
are you from?** 你来自哪里?
nǐ láizì nǎlǐ 2 (indicating origin) 来自 láizì ▸ **a
present/telephone call/letter
from sb** 来自某人的礼物/电话/信
láizì mǒurén de lǐwù/diànhuà/xìn
3 (with time, distance, price,
numbers) 从 cóng ▸ **from one
o'clock to** or **until two** 从1点直到
2点 cóng yīdiǎn zhídào liǎngdiǎn
▸ **it's 1 km from the beach** 从海
滩到这儿有1公里 cóng hǎitān dào
zhèr yǒu yī gōnglǐ

front [frʌnt] I N [c] (of house, dress)
前面 qiánmiàn; (of coach, train, car)
前部 qiánbù [个 gè] II ADJ 前面
的 qiánmiàn de ▸ **in front** 在前面
zài qiánmiàn ▸ **in front of** (facing)
在…前面 zài…qiánmiàn; (in the
presence of) 在…面前

front door N [c] 前门 qiánmén
[个 gè]

frontier [ˈfrʌntɪər] N [c] (Brit) 国
界 guójiè [个 gè]

front page N [c] (Publishing) 头版
tóubǎn [个 gè]

frost [frɒst] N [c] 霜 shuāng [次 cì]

frosty [ˈfrɒstɪ] ADJ 有霜冻的 yǒu
shuāngdòng de

froze [frəʊz] PT of **freeze**

frozen [ˈfrəʊzn] I PP of **freeze**
II ADJ 1 (+ food) 冷冻的 lěngdòng
de; (+ ground, lake) 结冰的 jiébīng
de 2 (+ person, fingers) 冰冷的
bīnglěng de

fruit [fruːt] (pl fruit or fruits) N
[c/u] 水果 shuǐguǒ [种 zhǒng]

frustrated [frʌsˈtreɪtɪd] ADJ 泄气的
xièqì de

fry [fraɪ] (pt, pp fried) I VT 油
煎 yóujiān II fries NPL (Culin) =
French fries

frying pan [ˈfraɪɪŋ-] N [c] 平底煎
锅 píngdǐ jiānguō [个 gè]

fuel [ˈfjʊəl] N [c/u] 燃料 ránliào
[种 zhǒng]

full [fʊl] ADJ 1 满的 mǎn de;
[+ cinema, car, restaurant] 满
的 mǎn de 2 (+ details) 全部的
quánbù de; [+ information, name]
完全的 wánquán de ▸ **I'm full (up)**
我吃饱了 wǒ chībǎo le ▸ **full of** 充
满 chōngmǎn

full stop N [c] (Brit) 句号 jù hào
[个 gè]

full-time [ˈfʊlˈtaɪm] I ADJ [+ work, study] 全职的 quánzhí
de; [+ student, staff] 全日制的
quánrìzhì de II ADV (work, study)
全日地 quánrì de

fully [ˈfʊlɪ] ADV 完全地 wánquán
de

fumes [fjuːmz] NPL 浓烈的烟气
nóngliè de yānqì

fun [fʌn] N [u] 乐趣 lèqù ▸ **to
have fun** 玩得开心 wánde kāixīn

▶**to do sth for fun** 为乐而做某事 wèi zhǎolè zuò ěr mǒushì ▶**to make fun of sb/sth** 取笑某人/某物 qǔxiào mǒurén/mǒushì

fund [fʌnd] **I** N [c] 基金 jījīn [项项 xiàng] **II funds** NPL (*money*) 资金 zījīn

funeral ['fju:nərəl] N [c] 葬礼 zànglǐ [个 gè]

funfair ['fʌnfɛəʳ] (*Brit*) N [c] 露天游乐场 lùtiān yóulèchǎng [个 gè]

funny ['fʌnɪ] ADJ **1** (*amusing*) 可笑的 kěxiào de **2** (*strange*) 奇怪的 qíguài de

fur [fəːʳ] N [c/u] 毛毛 máomáo [根 gēn]

furious ['fjuərɪəs] ADJ 大发雷霆的 dà fā léitíng de

furniture ['fəːnɪtʃəʳ] N [u] 家具 jiājù ▶**a piece of furniture** 一件家具 yījiàn jiājù

further ['fəːðəʳ] ADV 更远地 gèngyuǎn de ▶**how much further is it?** 还有多远？háiyǒu duōyuǎn?

further education N [u] 继续教育 jìxù jiàoyù

fuse, (*US*) **fuze** [fju:z] N [c] 保险丝 bǎoxiǎnsī [根 gēn] ▶**a fuse has blown** 保险丝烧断了 bǎoxiǎnsī shāoduàn le

fuss [fʌs] N [s/u] 大惊小怪 dàjīng xiǎoguài ▶**to make** or **kick up a fuss (about sth)** (对某事) 小题大做 (duì mǒushì) xiǎo tí dà zuò

future ['fju:tʃəʳ] **I** ADJ 将来的 jiānglái de **II** N **1** ▶**the future** 未来 wèilái **2** (*Ling: also:* **future tense**) ▶**the future** 将来时 jiānglái shí ▶**in (the) future** (*from now on*) 从今以后 cóngjīn yǐhòu

in the near/foreseeable future 在不久/可预见的未来 zài bùjiǔ/kě yùjiàn de wèilái

fuze [fju:z] (*US*) N [c] VT, VI = **fuse**

g

gallery ['gæləri] N [c] (also: **art gallery**) 美术馆 měishùguǎn [个 gè]

gamble ['gæmbl] I vi 1 (bet) 赌博 dǔbó 2 (take a risk) 投机 tóujī II N [c] (risk) 冒险 màoxiǎn [次 cì] ▶ **to gamble on sth** 对某事打赌 duì mǒushì dǎdǔ; [+ success, outcome] 对某事冒险 duì mǒushì màoxiǎn

gambling ['gæmblɪŋ] N [U] 赌博 dǔbó

game [geɪm] N 1 [c] (sport) 运动 yùndòng [项 xiàng] 2 [c] (activity: children's) 游戏 yóuxì [个 gè] 3 [c] (also: **board game**) 棋盘游戏 qípán yóuxì [项 xiàng]; (also: **computer game**) 电脑游戏 diànnǎo yóuxì [项 xiàng] 4 [c]

(match) 比赛 bǐsài [场 chǎng] ▶ **a game of football/tennis** 一场足球/网球赛 yīchǎng zúqiú/wǎngqiú sài

gang [gæŋ] N [c] 一帮 yī bāng

gangster ['gæŋstə^r] N [c] 歹徒 dǎitú [个 gè]

gap [gæp] N [c] 缝隙 fèngxì [个 gè]

gap year (Brit) N [c] 高中和大学之间的空隙年

> ## GAP YEAR
>
> 在高中毕业以后，进入大学继续接受高等教育之前，学生可以休息一年，这一年被称为 **gap year**。在 **gap year** 其间，很多人选择去旅游或去国外生活，也有人更愿意工作。无论如何选择，他们都能从学校学习生活之外获得宝贵的生活经验。

garage ['gæra:ʒ] N [c] 1 (of private house) 车库 chēkù [个 gè] 2 (for car repairs) 汽车修理厂 qìchē xiūlǐchǎng [个 gè] 3 (Brit: petrol station) 加油站 jiāyóuzhàn [个 gè]

garbage ['ga:bɪdʒ] N [U] 1 (esp US: rubbish) 垃圾 lājī 2 (nonsense) 废话 fèihuà

garbage can (US) N [c] 垃圾箱 lājīxiāng [个 gè]

garbage man (pl **garbage men**) (US) N [c] 清洁工 qīngjiégōng [位 wèi]

garden ['ga:dn] N [c] 花园 huāyuán [个 gè]

gardener ['gɑːdnər] N [c]
(professional) 园丁 yuándīng
[位 wèi]; (amateur) 园艺爱好者
yuányì àihàozhě [个 gè]

gardening ['gɑːdnɪŋ] N [u] 园
艺 yuányì

garlic ['gɑːlɪk] N [u] 大蒜 dàsuàn

gas [gæs] N 1 [u] (for cooking,
heating) 煤气 méiqì 2 [u] (US: also:
gasoline) 汽油 qìyóu

gasoline ['gæsəliːn] (US) N [u] 汽
油 qìyóu

gas station (US) N [c] 加油站
jiāyóuzhàn [个 gè]

gate [geɪt] N 1 [c] 门 mén [个 gè];
(of building) 大门 dàmén [个 gè]
2 (at airport) 登机口 dēngjīkǒu
[个 gè]

gather ['gæðər] I VT (understand)
▸ **to gather (that)...** 获悉…
huòxī… II VI 聚集 jùjí

gave [geɪv] PT of **give**

gay [geɪ] I ADJ 同性恋的
tóngxìngliàn de II N [c] 同性恋
tóngxìngliàn

GCSE (Brit) N ABBR (= **General
Certificate of Secondary
Education**) 普通中等教育证
书 Pǔtōng Zhōngděng Jiàoyù
Zhèngshū

gear [gɪər] N 1 [c] (of car, bicycle)
排挡 páidǎng [个 gè] 2 [u]
(equipment) 装备 zhuāngbèi 3
[u] (clothing) 服装 fúzhuāng ▸ **to
change** or (US) **shift gear** 换挡
huàndǎng

geese [giːs] NPL of **goose**

gel [dʒɛl] N [c/u] 啫 zhěli [瓶 píng]
▸ **bath/shower gel** 浴液 yùyè

Gemini ['dʒɛmɪnaɪ] N [u] (sign) 双
子座 Shuāngzǐ Zuò

general ['dʒɛnərl] ADJ 1 (overall)
[+ situation] 总的 zǒng de;
[+ decline, standard] 一般的 yìbān
de 2 [+ terms, outline, idea] 笼统的
lǒngtǒng de

general election N [c] (in Britain,
United States) 大选 dàxuǎn [届 jiè]

generally ['dʒɛnrəlɪ] ADV 1 (on
the whole) 大体上 dàtǐshang
2 (usually) 通常 tōngcháng

generation [dʒɛnə'reɪʃən] N [c]
一代人 yídàirén [代 dài]

generous ['dʒɛnərəs] ADJ 大方的
dàfāng de

genius ['dʒiːnɪəs] N [c] 天才
tiāncái [位 wèi]

gentle ['dʒɛntl] ADJ 温和的
wēnhé de

gentleman ['dʒɛntlmən] (pl
gentlemen) N [c] 先生 xiānsheng
[位 wèi]

gents [dʒɛnts] N ▸ **the gents**
(Brit: inf) 男厕 náncè

genuine ['dʒɛnjuɪn] ADJ (real) 真
正的 zhēnzhèng de; [+ emotion,
interest] 实在在的 shíshí
zàizài de

geography [dʒɪ'ɒgrəfɪ] N [u] 1 地
理 dìlǐ 2 (school/university subject)
地理学 dìlǐxué

germ [dʒəːm] (Bio) N [c] 细菌
xìjūn [种 zhǒng]

German ['dʒəːmən] I ADJ 德国的
Déguó de II N 1 (person) 德国人
Déguórén [个 gè] 2 (language)
德语 Déyǔ

Germany ['dʒəːmənɪ] N 德国

Déguó

○ KEYWORD

get [gɛt] (pt, pp **got**, (US) pp **gotten**) I VT 1 ▸ to have got see also **have, got**

2 [+ money, permission, results, information] 获得 huòdé; [+ job, flat, room] 得到 dédào ▸ he got a job in London 他在伦敦得到一份工作 tā zài Lúndūn dédào yīfèn gōngzuò

3 (fetch) 去拿 qùná ▸ to get sth for sb 为某人去拿某物 wèi mǒurén qù ná mǒuwù ▸ can I get you a coffee? 要我给你拿杯咖啡吗? yào wǒ gěi nǐ ná bēi kāfēi ma? ▸ I'll come and get you 我会来接你的 wǒ huì lái jiē nǐ de

4 [+ present, letter, prize, TV channel] 收到 shōudào ▸ what did you get for your birthday? 你生日时得到了什么礼物? nǐ shēngrìshí dédào le shénme lǐwù?

5 [+ plane, bus] 乘坐 chéngzuò ▸ I'll get the bus 我会乘坐公共汽车 wǒ huì chéngzuò gōnggòng qìchē

6 (cause to be/become) ▸ to get sth/sb ready 使某事/某人准备就绪 shǐ mǒurén/mǒushì zhǔnbèi jiùxù

7 (take, move) 把…送到 bǎ…sòngdào ▸ we must get him to hospital 我们必须把他送到医院 wǒmen bìxū bǎ tā sòngdào yīyuàn

8 (buy) 买 mǎi; (regularly) 买

到 mǎidào ▸ I'll get some milk from the supermarket 我要去超市买牛奶 wǒ yào qù chāoshì mǎi niúnǎi

9 (be infected by) [+ cold, measles] 染上 rǎnshàng ▸ you'll get a cold 你会得感冒的 nǐ huì dé gǎnmào de

10 [+ time, opportunity] 有 yǒu

11 ▸ to get sth done (do oneself) 做某事 zuò mǒushì; (have done) 完成某事 wánchéng mǒushì ▸ to get one's hair cut 理发 lǐfà ▸ to get sb to do sth 让某人做某事 ràng mǒurén zuò mǒushì

II VI 1 (become, be: +adj) 变得 biàn de ▸ to get old/tired/cold/dirty 变老/变得疲倦/变冷/变脏 biànlǎo/biànde píjuàn/biànlěng/biànzāng ▸ to get drunk 喝醉 hēzuì le

2 (go) ▸ to get to work/the airport/Beijing etc 到办公室/到达机场/到达北京 (等) dào bàngōngshì/dàodá jīchǎng/dàodá Běijīng (děng) ▸ how did you get here? 你是怎么到这儿的? nǐ shì zěnme dào zhèr de? ▸ he didn't get home till 10pm 他直到晚上10点才到家 tā zhídào wǎnshàng shídiǎn cái dàojiā ▸ how long does it take to get from London to Paris? 从伦敦到巴黎需要多久? cóng Lúndūn dào Bālí xūyào duōjiǔ?

3 (begin) ▸ to get to know sb 开始了解某人 kāishǐ liǎojiě mǒurén ▸ let's get going or started! 开始吧! kāishǐ ba!

III AUX VB 1 ▸ to have got to see

also **have, got**

2 (*passive use*) 作为构成被动语态的助动词 ▶**to get killed** 被杀 bèishā

▶ **get away** VI (*escape*) 逃跑 táopǎo

▶ **get back** I VI (*return*) 回来 huílái
II VT (*reclaim*) 重新得到 chóngxīn dédào

▶ **get back to** VT FUS (*return to*) [+ *activity, work*] 回到 huídào; [+ *subject*] 重新回到 chóngxīn huídào ▶**to get back to sleep** 重又睡着 chóng yòu shuìzháo

▶ **get in** VI I (*train, bus, plane*) 抵达 dǐdá
2 (*arrive home*) 到家 dàojiā

▶ **get into** VT FUS [+ *vehicle*] 乘坐 chéngzuò

▶ **get off** I VI (*from train, bus*) 下车 xiàchē
II VT (*as holiday*) 放假 fàngjià
III VT FUS [+ *train, bus*] 从…下来 cóng…xiàlái

▶ **get on** I VI I (*be friends*) 和睦相处 hémù xiāngchǔ ▶ **to get on well with sb** 与某人相处融洽 yǔ mǒurén xiāngchǔ róngqià
2 (*progress*) 进展 jìnzhǎn ▶ **how are you getting on?** 你进展得怎么样? nǐ guòde zěnmeyàng?
II VT FUS [+ *bus, train*] 上 shàng

▶ **get on with** VT FUS (*continue, start*) 开始继续做 kāishǐ jìxù zuò

▶ **get out** I VI (*of vehicle*) 下车 xiàchē

▶ **get out of** VT FUS [+ *vehicle*] 从…下来 cóng…xiàlái

▶ **get over** VT FUS [+ *illness, shock*] 从…中恢复过来 cóng…zhōng huīfù guòlái

▶ **get through** I VI (*Tel*) 接通 jiētōng
II VT FUS [+ *work, book*] 完成 wánchéng

▶ **get together** VI [*people*] 聚在一起 jùzài yìqǐ

▶ **get up** VI 站起来 zhànqǐlái; (*out of bed*) 起床 qǐchuáng

ghost [gəʊst] N [c] 鬼神 guǐshén [种 zhǒng]

giant [ˈdʒaɪənt] I N [c] 巨人 jùrén [个 gè] II ADJ (*huge*) 巨大的 jùdà de

gift [gɪft] N [c] I 礼物 lǐwù [件 jiàn]
2 (*talent*) 天赋 tiānfù [种 zhǒng]

gin [dʒɪn] N [U] 杜松子酒 dùsōngzǐjiǔ

ginger [ˈdʒɪndʒəʳ] I N [U] (*spice*) 姜 jiāng II ADJ (*colour*) 姜色的 jiāngsè de

girl [gəːl] N [c] I (*child*) 女孩 nǚhái [个 gè]; (*young woman, woman*) 姑娘 gūniang [个 gè] **2** (*daughter*) 女儿 nǚ'ér [个 gè]

girlfriend [ˈgəːlfrɛnd] N I [c] (*of girl*) 女性朋友 nǚxìng péngyou [个 gè] **2** (*of boy*) 女朋友 nǚ péngyou [个 gè]

◯ KEYWORD

give [gɪv] (*pt* **gave**, *pp* **given**) VT

1 ▸ **to give sb sth, give sth to sb** 给某人某物 gěi mǒurén mǒuwù; (as gift) 送给某人某物 sònggěi mǒurén mǒuwù ▸ **I gave David the book, I gave the book to David** 我把这本书送给了戴维 wǒ bǎ zhèběn shū sònggěi le Dàiwéi ▸ **give it to him** 把它送给他 bǎ tā sònggěi tā

2 [+ advice, details] 提供 tígōng ▸ **to give sb sth** [+ opportunity, surprise, shock, job] 给某人某物 gěi mǒurén mǒuwù

3 (deliver) ▸ **to give a speech/a lecture** 做演讲/讲座 zuò yǎnjiǎng/jiǎngzuò

4 (organize) ▸ **to give a party/ dinner party** etc 做东办一个聚会/宴会(等) zuòdōng bàn yī gè jùhuì/yànhuì [děng]

▸ **give back** VT 交还 jiāohuán ▸ **to give sth back to sb** 把某物交还给某人 bǎ mǒuwù jiāohuán gěi mǒurén

▸ **give in** VI (yield) 屈服 qūfú

▸ **give up** VI 放弃 fàngqì II VT [+ job] 辞掉 cídiào ▸ **to give up smoking** 戒烟 jièyān

glad [glæd] ADJ 高兴的 gāoxìng de ▸ **I'd be glad to help you** 我很愿意帮助你 wǒ hěn yuànyì bāngzhù nǐ

glamorous ['glæmərəs] ADJ 富有魅力的 fùyǒu mèilì de

glass [glɑːs] I N **1** [U] (substance) 玻璃 bōli **2** [c] (container) 玻璃杯 bōlibēi [个 gè] **3** [c] (glassful) 一杯 yī bēi II **glasses** NPL (spectacles)

眼镜 yǎnjìng ▸ **a pair of glasses** 一副眼镜 yīfù yǎnjìng

global ['ɡləʊbl] ADJ 全球的 quánqiú de

global warming [-'wɔːmɪŋ] N [U] 全球变暖 quánqiú biànnuǎn

glove [ɡlʌv] N [c] 手套 shǒutào [副 fù] ▸ **a pair of gloves** 一副手套 yīfù shǒutào

glue [ɡluː] N [c/u] 胶 jiāo [种 zhǒng]

○ **KEYWORD**

go [ɡəʊ] (pt **went**, pp **gone**, pl **goes**) I VI **1** 去 qù ▸ **he's going to New York** 他要去纽约 tā yào qù Niǔyuē ▸ **where's he gone?** 他去哪儿了？ tā qù nǎr le? ▸ **shall we go by car or train?** 我们开车去还是坐火车去？ wǒmen kāichē qù háishì zuò huǒchē qù?

2 (depart) 离开 líkāi ▸ **let's go** 我们走吧 wǒmen zǒuba ▸ **I must be going** 我必须得走了 wǒ bìxū děi zǒu le ▸ **our plane goes at 11pm** 我们的飞机晚上11点起飞 wǒmen de fēijī wǎnshàng shíyīdiǎn qǐfēi

3 (disappear) 消失 xiāoshī ▸ **all her jewellery had gone** 她的所有的珠宝首饰都不见了 tā suǒyǒu de zhūbǎo shǒushì dōu bùjiàn le

4 (attend) ▸ **to go to school/ university** 上学/上大学 shàngxué/shàng dàxué

5 (with activity) ▸ **to go for a walk** 去散步 qù sànbù ▸ **to go on a trip** 去旅行 qù lǚxíng

6 (work) 运转 yùnzhuàn

7 (become) ▸**to go pale/mouldy/bald** 变得苍白/发霉/秃顶 biàn de cāngbái/fāméi/tūdǐng

8 (be about to, intend to) ▸**are you going to come?** 你要来吗？nǐ yào lái ma? ▸**I think it's going to rain** 我想天要下雨了 wǒxiǎng tiān yào xiàyǔ le

9 (progress) 进行 jìnxíng ▸**how did it go?** 这事进展如何？ zhèshì jìnzhǎn rúhé?

10 (lead) [road, path] 通向 tōngxiàng

11 (in other expressions) ▸**there's still a week to go before the exams** 考试前还有一个星期的时间 kǎoshì qián háiyǒu yī gè xīngqī de shíjiān ▸**to keep going** 继续下去 jìxù xiàqù

II N **1** [c] (try) 尝试 chángshì [次 cì] ▸**to have a go (at sth/at doing sth)** 试一下（某事/做某事）shì yīxià (mǒushì/zuò mǒushì)

2 [c] (turn) 轮流 lúnliú [次 cì] ▸**whose go is it?** 轮到谁了？ lúndào shuí le?

▸ **go ahead** VI **1** [event] 发生 fāshēng

2 (press on) ▸**to go ahead with sth** 着手做某事 zhuóshǒu zuò mǒushì ▸**go ahead!** (encouraging) 干吧！gànba!

▸ **go around** VI **1** [news, rumour] 传播 chuánbō

2 (revolve) 转动 zhuàndòng

▸ **go away** VI **1** (leave) 离开 líkāi

2 (on holiday) 外出 wàichū

▸ **go back** VI 返回 fǎnhuí

▸ **go back to** VT FUS [+ activity, work, school] 回到 huídào

▸ **go down** I VI **1** [price, level, amount] 下降 xiàjiàng

2 [sun] 落下 luòxià

3 [computer] 死机 sǐjī

II VT FUS [+ stairs, ladder] 从…下来 cóng…xiàlái

▸ **go for** VT FUS (fetch) 去取 qùqǔ

▸ **go in** VI 进去 jìnqù

▸ **go in for** VT FUS [+ competition] 参加 cānjiā

▸ **go into** VT FUS (enter) 进入 jìnrù

▸ **go off** VI **1** (leave) 离去 líqù ▸**he's gone off to work** 他已经去上班了 tā yǐjīng qù shàngbān le

2 (explode) 爆炸 bàozhà

3 [alarm] 响起 xiǎngqǐ

4 [lights] 熄灭 xīmiè

▸ **go on** VI **1** (continue) 继续 jìxù ▸**to go on with one's work** 继续自己的工作 jìxù zìjǐ de gōngzuò ▸**to go on doing sth** 继续做某事 jìxù zuò mǒushì

2 (happen) 发生 fāshēng ▸**what's going on here?** 这里发生什么事了？ zhèlǐ fāshēng shénme shìr le?

▸ **go out** VI **1** [person] 离开 líkāi; (to party, club) 出去消遣 chūqù xiāoqiǎn ▸**are you going out tonight?** 你今晚出去吗？ nǐ jīnwǎn chūqù ma?

2 [couple] 和…交往 hé…jiāowǎng ▸**to go out with sb** 和某人交往 hé mǒurén jiāowǎng

3 [light, fire] 熄灭 xīmiè

▸ **go over** VI 过去 guòqù

▸ **go round** VI = **go around**

▸ **go through** VT FUS [+ place, town] 经过 lùguò

▶ go up VI 1 (price, level, value) 上涨 shàngzhǎng

2 (go upstairs) 上楼 shànglóu

▶ go up to VT FUS 向…走过来 xiàng…zǒuguòqù

▶ go with VT FUS (accompany) 与…相伴共存 yǔ…xiāngbàn gòngcún

▶ go without VT FUS [+ food, treats] 没有 méiyǒu…

goal [gəʊl] N [c] 1 (Sport) 进球得分 jìnqiú défēn [次 cì] 2 (aim) 目标 mùbiāo [个 gè] ▶ to score a goal 进一球 jìn yīqiú

goalkeeper ['gəʊlkiːpə'] N [c] 守门员 shǒuményuán [个 gè]

goat [gəʊt] N [c] 山羊 shānyáng [只 zhī]

God [gɒd] N 上帝 Shàngdì

goggles ['gɒglz] NPL 护目镜 hùmùjìng

gold [gəʊld] I N [U] (metal) 黄金 huángjīn II ADJ [+ ring, watch, tooth] 金的 jīn de

golf [gɒlf] N 高尔夫球 gāo'ěrfūqiú ▶ to play golf 打高尔夫球 dǎ gāo'ěrfūqiú

golf course [c] N 高尔夫球场 gāo'ěrfūqiúchǎng [个 gè]

gone [gɒn] I PP of go II ADJ 离去的 líqù de III PREP (Brit: inf: after) 过 guò ▶ the food's all gone 食物都没了 shíwù dōu méi le

good [gʊd] I ADJ 1 (pleasant) 令人愉快的 lìng rén yúkuài de 2 [+ food, school, job] 好的 hǎo de 3 (well-behaved) 乖的 guāi de 4 [+ idea, reason, advice] 好的 hǎode 5 (skilful) 好的 hǎode 6 [+ news, luck, example] 好的 hǎo de 7 (morally correct) 公正的 gōngzhèng de II N [U] (right) 善善 shàn ▶ good! 好！hǎo! ▶ to be good at (doing) sth 精于（做）某事 jīngyú (zuò) mǒushì ▶ to be no good at (doing) sth 不擅于（做）某事 bù shàncháng (zuò) mǒushì ▶ it's no good doing... 做…没有用 zuò…méiyǒu yòng ▶ it's good for you 对你有益 duì nǐ yǒuyì ▶ it's good to see you 很高兴见到你 hěn gāoxìng jiàndào nǐ ▶ good morning/afternoon! 早上/下午好！zǎoshàng/xiàwǔ hǎo! ▶ good night! (before going home) 再见！zàijiàn!; (before going to bed) 晚安！wǎn'ān! ▶ for good (forever) 永久地 yǒngjiǔ de; see also goods

goodbye [gʊd'baɪ] INT 再见 zàijiàn ▶ to say goodbye 告别 gàobié

good-looking ['gʊd'lʊkɪŋ] ADJ 好看的 hǎokàn de

goods ['gʊdz] NPL 商品 shāngpǐn

goose [guːs] (pl geese) N [c] 鹅 é [只 zhī]

gorgeous ['gɔːdʒəs] ADJ [+ weather, day] 宜人的 yírén de

gossip ['gɒsɪp] I N [U] (rumours) 流言蜚语 liúyán fēiyǔ II VI (chat) 闲谈 xiántán

got [gɒt] PT, PP of get ▶ have you got your umbrella? 你有伞吗？nǐ yǒu sǎn ma? ▶ he has got to accept the situation 他只得接受现状 tā zhǐdé jiēshòu xiànzhuàng

gotten ['gɔtn] (US) PP of **get**

government ['gʌvnmənt] N [c] (institution) 政府 zhèngfǔ [届 jiè]

GP N ABBR [c] (= general practitioner) 家庭医生 jiātíng yīshēng [位 wèi]

graceful ['greisful] ADJ 优美的 yōuměi de

grade [greid] N [c] 1 (school mark) 分数 fēnshù [个 gè] 2 (US: school class) 年级 niánjí [个 gè]

grade crossing (US) N [c] 铁路线 与公路交叉处

grade school (US) N [c/u] 小学 xiǎoxué [座 zuò]

gradual ['grædjuəl] ADJ 逐渐的 zhújiàn de

gradually ['grædjuəli] ADV 逐渐 地 zhújiàn de

gram [græm] N [c] 克 kè

grammar ['græmə'] N [u] 语 法 yǔfǎ

gramme [græm] (Brit) N = **gram**

grand [grænd] ADJ 壮丽的 zhuànglì de

grandchild ['græntʃaild] (pl **grandchildren**) N [c] (male on father's side) 孙子 sūnzi [个 gè]; (female on father's side) 孙女 sūnnǚ [个 gè]; (male on mother's side) 外 孙 wàisūn [个 gè]; (female on mother's side) 外孙女 wàisūnnǚ [个 gè]

grandfather ['grændfɑːðə'] N [c] (on mother's side) 外公 wàigōng [位 wèi]; (on father's side) 爷爷 yéye [位 wèi]

grandmother ['grænmʌðə'] N [c] (on mother's side) 外婆 wàipó [位

wèi]; (on father's side) 奶奶 nǎinai [位 wèi]

grandson ['grænsʌn] N [c] (on father's side) 孙子 sūnzi [个 gè]; (on mother's side) 外孙 wàisūn [个 gè]

grape [greip] N [c] 葡萄 pútáo [串 chuàn] ▸ a bunch of grapes 一串 葡萄 yīchuàn pútáo

grapefruit ['greipfruːt] (pl **grapefruit** or **grapefruits**) N [c/u] 葡萄柚 pútáo yòu [个 gè]

graph [grɑːf] N [c] 图表 túbiǎo [幅 fú]

graphics ['græfiks] I N [u] (design) 制图学 zhìtúxué II NPL (images) 图 形 túxíng

grass [grɑːs] N [c/u] (Bot) 草 cǎo [株 zhū] ▸ the grass (the lawn) 草 坪 cǎopíng

grate [greit] VT [+ food] 磨碎 mósuì

grateful ['greitful] ADJ 感激的 gǎnjī de ▸ to be grateful to sb for sth 为某事感激某人 wèi mǒushì gǎnjī mǒurén

grave [greiv] N [c] 坟墓 fénmù [座 zuò]

graveyard ['greivjɑːd] N [c] 墓地 mùdì [块 kuài]

gray [grei] (US) ADJ = **grey**

greasy ['griːsi] ADJ 1 [+ food] 油腻 的 yóunì de 2 [+ skin, hair] 多油脂 的 duō yóuzhīde

great [greit] I ADJ 1 (large) 巨大的 jùdà de 2 [+ success, achievement] 重大的 zhòngdà de; [+ pleasure, difficulty, value] 极大的 jídà de; [+ risk] 超乎寻常的 chāohū xúnchángde 3 [+ city, person, work *of art*] 伟大的 wěidà de **4** (*terrific*) [+ *person, place*] 好极了的 hǎojíle de; [+ *idea*] 棒极了的 bàngjíle de **II INT ▶ great!** 太好了！tàihǎole! **▶ we had a great time** 我们玩 得很快活 wǒmen wánde hěn kuàihuo

Great Britain N 大不列颠 Dàbùlièdiān

Greece [gri:s] N 希腊 Xīlà

greedy [ˈgriːdɪ] ADJ 贪心的 tānxīn de

Greek [gri:k] **I** ADJ 希腊的 Xīlà de **II** N **1** (*person*) 希腊人 Xīlàrén [个 gè] **2** [U] (*modern language*) 希 腊语 Xīlàyǔ

green [gri:n] **I** ADJ **1** 绿色的 lǜsè de **2** (*environmental*) 环保的 huánbǎo de **II** N [c/u] 绿色 lǜsè [抹 mǒ]

greengrocer [ˈgriːnˌgrəʊsər] (*esp Brit*) N [c] (*shop*) (*also:* **greengrocer's**) 果蔬店 guǒshūdiàn [家 jiā]

greenhouse [ˈgriːnhaʊs] **I** N [c] 暖房 nuǎnfáng [间 jiān] **II** CPD [+ *gas, emissions*] 温室 wēnshì

grew [gru:] PT *of* **grow**

grey, (*US*) **gray** [greɪ] **I** ADJ **1** 灰 色的 huīsè de; [+ *hair*] 灰白的 huībái de **2** [+ *weather, day*] 阴沉的 yīnchén de **II** N [c/u] 灰色 huīsè [种 zhǒng]

grey-haired [ˈgreɪˈhɛəd] ADJ 灰白 头发的 huībái tóufa de

grief [gri:f] N [u] 悲痛 bēitòng

grill [grɪl] VT (*Brit*) [+ *food*] 烤焗 kǎojú

grim [grɪm] ADJ 沙粒 shālì

groan [grəʊn] VI 呻吟 shēnyín

grocer [ˈgrəʊsər] N [c] **1** (*person*) 食品杂货商 shípǐn záhuòshāng [个 gè] **2** (*shop*: *also:* **grocer's**) 食品杂 货店 shípǐn záhuòdiàn [家 jiā]

grocery [ˈgrəʊsərɪ] N [c] (*also:* **grocery shop** (*Brit*), **grocery store** (*esp US*)) 食品杂货店 shípǐn záhuòdiàn [家 jiā] **II groceries** NPL (*provisions*) 食品杂货 shípǐn záhuò

groom [gru:m] N [c] (*also:* **bridegroom**) 新郎 xīnláng [位 wèi]

ground [graʊnd] **I** PT, PP *of* **grind II** N **1** (*floor*) **▶ the ground** 地面 dìmiàn **2** (*earth, soil, land*) **▶ the ground** 土地 tǔdì **3** [c] (*Sport*) 场 chǎng **▶ on the ground** 在地面上 zài dìmiàn shàng

ground floor N [c] 一楼 yīlóu [层 céng]

group [gru:p] N [c] **1** 组 zǔ [个 gè] **2** (*also:* **pop group, rock group**) 组合 zǔhé [个 gè] **▶ in groups** 成 组地 chéngzǔ de

grow [grəʊ] (*pt* **grew**, *pp* **grown**) **I** VI **1** [*plant, tree*] 生长 shēngzhǎng **2** [*person, animal*] 长 大 zhǎngdà **2** [*amount, feeling, problem*] 扩大 kuòdà **II** VT [+ *flowers, vegetables*] 栽种 zāizhòng **▶ to grow by 10%** 增长 10% zēngzhǎng bǎi fēn zhī shí **▶ grow up** VI (*be brought up*) 长 大 zhǎngdà; (*be mature*) 成熟 chéngshú

grown [grəʊn] PP *of* **grow**

grown-up [ˈgrəʊnˈʌp] N [c] 成年 人 chéngniánrén [个 gè]

growth [grəʊθ] N 1 [U/s] (of economy, industry) 发展 fāzhǎn 2 [U] (of child, animal, plant) 生长 shēngzhǎng ▸ **a growth in sth** 某方面的发展 mǒu fāngmiàn de fāzhǎn

grumble ['grʌmbl] VI (complain) 抱怨 bàoyuàn

guarantee [gærən'tiː] N [c] (Comm: warranty) 质保承诺 zhìbǎo chéngnuò [个 gè]

guard [gɑːd] I N [c] (sentry) 警卫 jǐngwèi [个 gè] II VT [+ building, entrance, door] 守卫 shǒuwèi; [+ person] 保护 bǎohù ▸ **to be on one's guard (against)** 提防 dīfáng

guess [gɛs] I VT, VI (conjecture) 猜测 cāicè II N [c] 猜测 cāicè [种 zhǒng] ▸ **I guess so** 我想是吧 wǒ xiǎng shì ba

guest [gɛst] N [c] (at home) 客人 kèrén [位 wèi]; (at special event) 宾客 bīnkè [位 wèi]; (in hotel) 房客 fángkè [位 wèi]

guide [gaɪd] I N [c] 1 (tour guide) 导游 dǎoyóu [位 wèi]; 2 (local guide) 向导 xiàngdǎo [位 wèi]; 3 (also: guide book) 指南 zhǐnán [本 běn] II VT 1 (round city, museum) 给…导游 gěi…dǎoyóu 2 (lead) 给…领路 gěi…lǐnglù

guidebook ['gaɪdbʊk] N [c] 旅游指南 lǚyóu zhǐnán [本 běn]

guided tour ['gaɪdɪd-] N [c] 有导游的游览 yǒu dǎoyóu de yóulǎn [次 cì]

guilty ['gɪltɪ] ADJ 1 [+ person, feelings] 内疚的 nèijiù de 2 [+ secret, conscience] 自知有过错的 zìzhī yǒu guòcuò de 3 (responsible) 有过失的 yǒu guòshī de 4 (Law) 有罪的 yǒuzuì de ▸ **guilty of murder/manslaughter** 谋杀/误杀罪 móushā/wùshā zuì

guitar [gɪ'tɑːʳ] N [c] 吉他 jítā [把 bǎ]

gum [gʌm] N 1 [c] (Anat) 牙床 yáchuáng [个 gè] 2 (also: chewing gum/bubblegum) 口香糖 kǒuxiāngtáng

gun [gʌn] N [c] (small, medium-sized) 枪 qiāng [支 zhī]; (large) 炮 pào [架 jià]

guy [gaɪ] N [c] (man) 家伙 jiāhuo [个 gè] ▸ **(you) guys** 伙计们 huǒjimen

gym [dʒɪm] N 1 [c] (also: gymnasium) 健身房 jiànshēnfáng [个 gè] 2 [U] (also: gymnastics) 体操 tǐcāo

gymnast ['dʒɪmnæst] N [c] 体操运动员 tǐcāo yùndòngyuán [位 wèi]

gymnastics [dʒɪm'næstɪks] N [U] 体操 tǐcāo

gypsy ['dʒɪpsɪ] N [c] 吉卜赛人 Jípǔsàirén [个 gè]

h

[次 cì] 2 (hairstyle) 发型 fàxíng [种 zhǒng] ▶to have or get a haircut 剪头发 jiǎn tóufa

hairdresser ['hɛədrɛsə[r]] N [c] 1 美发师 měifàshī [位 wèi] 2 (also: hairdresser's) 发廊 fàláng [个 gè]

hairdryer ['hɛədraɪə[r]] N [c] 吹风机 chuīfēngjī [个 gè]

hair gel N [u] 发胶 fàjiāo

hairspray ['hɛəspreɪ] N [u] 喷发定型剂 pēnfà dìngxíngjì

hairstyle ['hɛəstaɪl] N [c] 发型 fàxíng [种 zhǒng]

half [hɑ:f] (pl **halves**) I N, PRON [c] 1 一半 yībàn 2 (Brit: child's ticket) 半票 bànpiào [张 zhāng] II ADJ [+ bottle] 一半的 yībàn de III ADV (empty, closed, open, asleep) 半 bàn ▶to cut sth in half 把某物切成两半 bǎ mǒuwù qiēchéng liǎngbàn ▶two/three etc and a half 二/三〔等〕点五 èr/sān (děng) diǎn wǔ ▶half a pound/kilo/mile 半磅/公斤/英里 bànbàng/gōngjīn/yīnglǐ ▶a day/week/pound etc and a half 一天/星期/磅〔等〕半 yītiān/xīngqī/bàng (děng) bàn ▶half an hour 半小时 bàn xiǎoshí ▶half past four/four etc 三/四〔等〕点半 sān/sì (děng) diǎn bàn

half-hour [hɑ:fauə[r]] N [c] 半小时 bàn xiǎoshí [个 gè]

half price ['hɑ:f'praɪs] I ADJ 半价的 bànjià de II ADV 半价地 bànjià de

half-term [hɑ:f'tə:m] (Brit: Scol) N [c/u] 期中假 qīzhōng jià [段 duàn] ▶at half-term 期中假时 qīzhōng jià shí

---

habit ['hæbɪt] N [c/u] 习惯 xíguàn [个 gè] ▶to be in the habit of doing sth 有做某事的习惯 yǒu zuò mǒushì de xíguàn ▶a bad habit 坏习惯 huài xíguàn

hacker ['hækə[r]] (Comput) N [c] 黑客 hēikè

had [hæd] PT, PP of **have**

hadn't ['hædnt] = **had not**

hail [heɪl] I N [u] 冰雹 bīngbáo II VI 下雹 xiàbáo

hair [hɛə[r]] N [u] 头发 tóufa [c] (single strand) 毛发 máofà [根 gēn] ▶to do one's hair 梳头 shūtóu ▶to have or get one's hair cut 剪头发 jiǎn tóufa

hairbrush ['hɛəbrʌʃ] N [c] 发刷 fàshuā [把 bǎ]

haircut ['hɛəkʌt] N [c] 1 理发 lǐfà

half-time [hɑːˈtaɪm] (*Sport*) N [U] 半场 bànchǎng ▸**at half-time** 半场时 bànchǎng shí

halfway [ˈhɑːˈfweɪ] ADV (*between two points*) 到一半 dào yíbàn ▸**halfway through sth** 在某事过了一半时 zài mǒushì guòle yíbàn shí

hall [hɔːl] N 1 [c] (*esp Brit: entrance*) 门厅 méntīng [个 gè] 2 [c] (*room*) 礼堂 lǐtáng [个 gè]

ham [hæm] I N 火腿 huǒtuǐ II CPD [+ *sandwich, roll, salad*] 火腿 huǒtuǐ

hamburger [ˈhæmbəːgəʳ] N [c] 汉堡包 hànbǎobāo [个 gè]

hammer [ˈhæməʳ] N [c] 锤子 chuízi [把 bǎ]

hand [hænd] I N 1 [c] 手 shǒu [双 shuāng] 2 [c] [*of clock*] 指针 zhǐzhēn [个 gè] II VT 递给 dìgěi ▸**to do sth by hand** 手工制作 shǒugōng zhìzuò ▸**to give or lend sb a hand (with sth)** 帮某人（做某事）bāng mǒurén (zuò mǒushì) ▸**on the one hand…, on the other hand…** 一方面…，另一方面… yì fāngmiàn…, lìngyì fāngmiàn…
▸**hand in** VT 上交 shàngjiāo
▸**hand out** VT 分配 fēnpèi
▸**hand over** VT 交给 jiāogěi

handbag [ˈhændbæg] (*Brit*) N [c] 手包 shǒubāo [个 gè]

handcuffs [ˈhændkʌfs] NPL 手铐 shǒukào ▸**in handcuffs** 带手铐 dài shǒukào

handkerchief [ˈhæŋkətʃɪf] N [c] 手帕 shǒupà [条 tiáo]

handle [ˈhændl] I N 1 [c] [*of bag,*

手 bǎshǒu [个 gè]; [*of cup, knife, paintbrush, broom, spade*] 柄 bǐng [个 gè]; [*of door, window*] 拉手 lāshǒu [个 gè] II VT [+ *problem, job, responsibility*] 处理 chǔlǐ

handlebars [ˈhændlbɑː(z)] NPL 把手 bǎshǒu

handmade [ˈhændˈmeɪd] ADJ 手工制作的 shǒugōng zhìzuò de

handsome [ˈhænsəm] ADJ 英俊的 yīngjùn de

handwriting [ˈhændraɪtɪŋ] N [U] 笔迹 bǐjì

handy [ˈhændɪ] ADJ 1 (*useful*) 方便的 fāngbiàn de 2 (*close at hand*) 手边的 shǒubiān de

hang [hæŋ] (*pt, pp* hung) I VT 挂 guà II VI (*be suspended*) 悬挂 xuánguà
▸**hang about** VI = **hang around**
▸**hang around** (*inf*) VI 闲荡 xiándàng
▸**hang on** VI (*wait*) 稍等 shāoděng
▸**hang round** (*Brit*) VI = **hang around**
▸**hang up** I VI (*Tel*) 挂断电话 guàduàn diànhuà II VT [+ *coat, hat, clothes*] 挂起 guàqǐ

hanger [ˈhæŋəʳ] N [c] (*also:* coat hanger) 衣架 yījià [个 gè]

hangover [ˈhæŋəʊvəʳ] N [c] 宿醉 sùzuì [次 cì]

happen [ˈhæpən] VI 发生 fāshēng ▸**what will happen if…?** 如果…会怎么样？rúguǒ…huì zěnmeyàng? ▸**tell me what happened** 告诉我发生了什么事 gàosù wǒ fāshēng le shénme shì

happiness ['hæpɪnɪs] N [U] 幸福 xìngfú

happy ['hæpɪ] ADJ 1 高兴的 gāoxìng de 2 [+ life, childhood, marriage, place] 美满的 měimǎn de ▸**to be happy with sth** (satisfied) 对某事满意 duì mǒushì mǎnyì ▸**to be happy to do sth** (willing) 乐意做某事 lèyì zuò mǒushì ▸**happy birthday!** 生日快乐！ shēngrì kuàilè！▸**happy Christmas!** 圣诞快乐！ Shèngdàn kuàilè！

harassment ['hærəsmənt] N [U] 骚扰 sāorǎo

harbour, (US) **harbor** ['hɑːbər] N [C] 港口 gǎngkǒu [个 gè]

hard [hɑːd] I ADJ 1 [+ surface, object] 硬的 yìng de 2 [+ question, problem] 困难的 kùnnan de 3 [+ work] 费力的 fèilì de 3 [+ push, punch, kick] 用力的 yònglì de II ADV 1 (work, try, think) 努力地 nǔlì de 2 用力地 yònglì de ▸**it's hard to tell/say/know** 很难讲/说/知道 hěnnán jiǎng/shuō/zhīdào ▸**such events are hard to understand** 这种事很难理解 zhèzhǒng shì hěnnán lǐjiě ▸**it's hard work serving in a shop** 商店工作很难做 shāngdiàn gōngzuò hěnnán zuò

hard disk (Comput) N [C] 硬盘 yìngpán [个 gè]

hardly ['hɑːdlɪ] ADV 1 (scarcely) 几乎不 jīhū bù 2 (no sooner) ▸**he had hardly sat down when the door burst open** 他一坐下门这被被地打开了 tā yī zuòxià mén jiù bèi

měng de dǎkāi le ▸**hardly ever/any/anyone** 几乎从不/没有/没有任何人 jīhū cóngbù/méiyǒu/méiyǒu rènhé rén ▸**I can hardly believe it** 我简直不能相信 wǒ jiǎnzhí bùnéng xiāngxìn

hardware ['hɑːdwɛər] N [U] (Comput) 硬件 yìngjiàn

hardworking [hɑːd'wɜːkɪŋ] ADJ 勤奋的 qínfèn de

harm [hɑːm] VT 1 (damage) 损坏 sǔnhuài 2 (injure) 伤害 shānghài

harmful ['hɑːmful] ADJ 有害的 yǒuhài de

harp [hɑːp] N [C] (Mus) 竖琴 shùqín [架 jià]

harvest ['hɑːvɪst] N 1 [C/U] (harvest time) 收获 shōuhuò [种 zhǒng] 2 [C] (crop) 收成 shōucheng [个 gè]

has [hæz] VB see **have**

hasn't ['hæznt] = **has not**

hat [hæt] N [C] 帽子 màozi [顶 dǐng]

hate [heɪt] VT [+ person] 恨 hèn; [+ food, activity, sensation] 讨厌 tǎoyàn ▸**to hate doing/to do sth** 不喜欢做某事 bù xǐhuān zuò mǒushì

hatred ['heɪtrɪd] N [U] 仇恨 chóuhèn

KEYWORD

have [hæv] (pt, pp had) I VT 1 有 yǒu ▸**he has** or **he has got blue eyes/dark hair** 他长着蓝眼睛/黑头发 tā zhǎngzhe lán yǎnjīng/hēi tóufa ▸**do you have** or **have you**

got a car/phone? 你有车/电话吗? nǐ yǒu chē/diànhuà ma? ▶**to have** or **have got sth to do** 有必须得做的事 yǒu bìxū děi zuò de shì ▶**she had her eyes closed** 她闭上了眼睛 tā bìshàng le yǎnjīng

2 ▶**to have breakfast** 吃早饭 chī zǎofàn ▶**to have a drink/a cigarette** 喝一杯/抽支烟 hē yìbēi/chōu zhī yān

3 ▶**to have a swim/bath** 游泳/洗澡 yóuyǒng/xǐzǎo ▶**to have a meeting/party** 开会/开派对 kāihuì/kāi pàiduì

4 (receive, obtain) 得到 dédào ▶**can I have your address?** 能告诉我你的地址吗? néng gàosù wǒ nǐde dìzhǐ ma? ▶**you can have it for £5** 付5英镑它就是你的了 fù wǔ yīngbàng tā jiùshì nǐde le

5 ▶**to have a baby** 生孩子 shēng háizi

6 ▶**to have sth done** 指使/安排做某事 zhǐshǐ/ānpái zuò mǒushì ▶**to have one's hair cut** 理发 lǐfà

7 ▶**to have a headache** 头痛 tóutòng ▶**to have an operation** 动手术 dòng shǒushù

II AUX VB**1** ▶**to have arrived/gone** 到了/走了 yǐ dàole/zǒule ▶**has he told you?** 他已经告诉你了吗? tā yǐjīng gàosù nǐ le ma? ▶**when she had dressed, she went downstairs** 穿好衣服后，她下了楼 chuānhǎo yīfu hòu, tā xiàle lóu ▶**I haven't seen him for ages/since July** 我已经很久/自7月以来就没见过他了 wǒ yǐjīng hěnjiǔ/zì qīyuè yǐlái jiù méijiàn guò tā le

2 (in tag questions) ▶**you've done it, haven't you?** 你已经做了，是不是? nǐ yǐjīng zuò le, shì bùshì?

3 (in short answers and questions) ▶**yes, I have** 是的，我有/已做了 shide, wǒ yǒu/yǐzuò le ▶**no I haven't!** 不，我还没有/没做呢! bù, wǒ hái méiyǒu/méizuò ne! ▶**so have I!** 我也一样! wǒ yě yíyàng! ▶**neither have I** 我也没有过 wǒ yě méiyǒu guò ▶**I've finished, have you?** 我已经完成了，你呢? wǒ yǐjīng wánchéng le, nǐne?

4 (be obliged) ▶**to have (got) to do sth** 不得不做某事 bùdébù zuò mǒushì ▶**she has (got) to do it** 她必须得这么做 tā bìxū děi zhème zuò

▶ **have on** VT [+ clothes] 穿着 chuānzhe ▶**he didn't have anything on** 他什么都没穿 tā shénme dōu méi chuān

haven't ['hævnt] = **have not**

hay fever N [U] 花粉病 huāfěnbìng

hazel ['heɪzl] ADJ [+ eyes] 淡褐色的 dàn hèsè de

he [hi:] PRON 他 tā

head [hed] N **I** N [c] **1** 头 tóu [个 gè] **2** [of company, organization, department] 领导 lǐngdǎo [个 gè] ▶ (Brit: head teacher) 校长 xiàozhǎng [位 wèi] II VT**1** [+ list, group] 以…打头 yǐ…dǎtóu **2** (Football) [+ ball] 用头顶… tóu dǐng **3** ▶**10 pounds a** or **a**

head 每人10英镑 měirén shí yīngbàng ▶from head to foot or toe 从头到脚 cóng tóu dào jiǎo ▶heads or tails? 正面还是反面? zhèngmiàn háishì fǎnmiàn?

▶ head for VT FUS 前往 qiánwǎng ▶to be heading or headed for Glasgow 正前往格拉斯哥 zhèng qiánwǎng Gélāsīgē

headache ['hedeɪk] N [c] 头痛 tóutòng [阵 zhèn] ▶to have a headache 头痛 tóutòng

headlight ['hedlaɪt] N [c] 前灯 qiándēng [个 gè]

headline ['hedlaɪn] N [c] 标题 biāotí [个 gè] ▶the headlines (Publishing) 头条新闻 tóutiáo xīnwén; (TV, Rad) 内容提要 nèiróng tíyào

headmaster [hed'mɑ:stə] (Brit) N [c] 校长 xiàozhǎng [位 wèi]

headmistress [hed'mɪstrɪs] (Brit) N [c] 女校长 nǔ xiàozhǎng [位 wèi]

head office N [c/u] [of company] 总部 zǒngbù

headphones ['hedfəunz] NPL 耳机 ěrjī

headquarters ['hedkwɔ:təz] NPL 总部 zǒngbù

heal [hi:l] VI 痊愈 quányù

health [helθ] N [u] 健康 jiànkāng ▶to be good/bad for one's health 对某人的健康有益/不利 duì mǒurén de jiànkāng yǒuyì/bùlì ▶to drink (to) sb's health 举杯祝某人健康 jǔbēi zhù mǒurén

healthy ['helθɪ] ADJ 1 健康的

jiànkāng de 2 [+ diet, lifestyle] 对健康有益的 duì jiànkāng yǒuyì de

heap [hi:p] N [c] 堆 duī [个 gè]

hear [hɪər] (pt, pp heard [hə:d]) VT 1 听见 tīngjiàn 2 [+ news, lecture, concert] 听 tīng ▶to hear sb doing sth 听见某人做某事 tīngjiàn mǒurén zuò mǒushì 2 ▶to hear that... 听说… tīngshuō… ▶to hear about sth/sb 听说某事/某人 tīngshuō mǒushì/mǒurén ▶to hear from sb 得到某人的消息 dédào mǒurén de xiāoxi ▶I've never heard of him 我从来没听说过他 wǒ cónglái méi tīngshuō guò tā

heart [hɑ:t] N 1 [c] 心脏 xīnzàng [颗 kē] 2 [c] (emotions) 感情 gǎnqíng [种 zhǒng] 3 [c] (shape) 心形物 xīnxíng wù [个 gè] ▶to learn/know sth (off) by heart 背诵某事 bèisòng mǒushì; () ▶to break sb's heart 使某人伤心 shǐ mǒurén shāngxīn

heart attack N [c] 心脏病发作 xīnzàngbìng fāzuò [阵 zhèn] ▶to have a heart attack 心脏病发作 xīnzàngbìng fāzuò

heat [hi:t] N 1 [u] 热 rè 2 [u] (temperature) 热度 rèdù 3 [c] (Sport) (also: qualifying heat) 预赛 yùsài [场 chǎng] II VT [+ water, food] 加热 jiārè; [+ room, house] 取暖 qǔnuǎn ▶I find the heat unbearable 我实在觉得受不了热 wǒ shízài shòubùliǎo rè

▶ heat up VT [+ food] 加热 jiārè

heater ['hi:tər] N [c] (electric heater, gas heater) 供暖装置 gōngnuǎn zhuāngzhì [个 gè]; (in car) 暖气设备 nuǎnqì shèbèi [套 tào]

heating ['hi:tɪŋ] N [U] (system) 暖气 nuǎnqì

heatwave ['hi:tweɪv] N [C] 酷暑时期 kùshǔ shíqī [段 duàn]

heaven ['hɛvn] N [U] 天堂 tiāntáng

heavy ['hɛvɪ] ADJ 1 重的 zhòng de 2 [+ traffic] 拥挤的 yōngjǐ de; [+ fine, penalty, sentence] 重的 zhòng de; [+ drinking, smoking, gambling] 过度的 guòdù de; [+ rain, snow] 大的 dà de ▸ **how heavy are you/is it?** 你/它有多重? nǐ/tā yǒu duōzhòng?

he'd [hi:d] = he would, he had

hedge [hɛdʒ] N [C] 树篱 shùlí [道 dào]

heel [hi:l] N [C] 1 [of foot] 脚后跟 jiǎohòugēn [个 gè] 2 [of shoe] 鞋跟 xiégēn [个 gè]

height [haɪt] N 1 [C/U] 高度 gāodù [个 gè] 2 [C] (altitude) 高处 gāochù [个 gè] ▸ **of average/medium height** 平均/中等高度 píngjūn/zhōngděng gāodù

held [hɛld] PT, PP of hold

helicopter ['hɛlɪkɒptəʳ] N [C] 直升飞机 zhíshēng fēijī [架 jià]

hell [hɛl] I N [U] 地狱 dìyù II INT (infl) 天啊 tiān a ▸ **it was hell** (infl) 糟糕极了 zāogāo jíle

he'll [hi:l] = he will, he shall

hello [hə'ləʊ] INT 1 (as greeting) 你好 nǐhǎo; (Tel) 喂 wèi; (to attract attention) 劳驾 láojià

helmet ['hɛlmɪt] N [C] 头盔 tóukuī [个 gè]; [of soldier,

policeman, fireman] 钢盔 gāngkuī [个 gè]

help [hɛlp] I N [U] 帮助 bāngzhù II VT [+ person] 帮助 bāngzhù III VI 1 (assist) 帮助 bāngzhù 2 (be useful) 有用 yǒuyòng ▸ **thanks, you've been a great help** 谢谢，你帮了很大忙 xièxie, nǐ bāngle hěndà máng ▸ **I helped him (to) fix his car** 我帮助他修了他的车 wǒ bāngzhù tā xiūle tāde chē ▸ **help!** 救命! jiùmìng! ▸ **can I help you?** (in shop) 我能为您效劳吗? wǒ néng wèi nín xiàoláo ma? ▸ **I can't help feeling sorry for him** 我情不自禁地同情他 wǒ qíng bù zì jìn de tóngqíng tā ▸ **it can't be helped** 没办法 méi bànfǎ

helpful ['hɛlpful] ADJ 有用的 yǒuyòng de; [+ advice, suggestion] 有建设性的 yǒu jiànshèxìng de

helping ['hɛlpɪŋ] N [C] [of food] 一份 yīfèn

helpless ['hɛlplɪs] ADJ 无依无靠的 wúyīwúkào de

hen [hɛn] N [C] 母鸡 mǔjī [只 zhī]

her [hə:ʳ] I PRON 她 tā II ADJ 她的 tā de ▸ **I haven't seen her** 我还没见到她 wǒ hái méi jiàndào tā ▸ **they gave her the job** 他们给了她那份工作 tāmen gěile tā nàfèn gōngzuò ▸ **her face was very red** 她的脸很红 tāde liǎn hěnhóng

herb [ha:b, US ə:rb] N [C] 草本植物 cǎoběn zhíwù [株 zhū]

herd [hə:d] N [C] 牧群 mùqún [群 qún]

here [hɪəʳ] ADV 1 (in/to this place) 在这里 zài zhèlǐ 2 (near me) 到这

里 dào zhèlǐ ►here's my phone number 这是我的电话号码 zhèshì wǒde diànhuà hàomǎ ►here he is 他到了 tā dào le ►here you are (take this) 给你 gěi nǐ ►here and there 各处 gèchù

hero ['hɪərəʊ] (pl heroes) N [c] 1 男主人公 nán zhǔréngōng [个 gè] 2 [of battle, struggle] 英雄 yīngxióng [位 wèi]

heroin ['herəʊɪn] N [U] 海洛因 hǎiluòyīn

heroine ['herəʊɪn] N [c] 1 女主人公 nǚ zhǔréngōng [个 gè] 2 (of battle, struggle) 女英雄 nǚ yīngxióng [位 wèi]

hers [hə:z] PRON 她的 tā de ►this is hers 这是她的。zhèshì tāde ►a friend of hers 她的一个朋友 tāde yíge péngyou

herself [hə:'self] PRON 1 她自己 tā zìjǐ 2 (emphatic) 她本人 tā běnrén ►she hurt herself 她伤了自己 tā shāngle zìjǐ ►she made the dress herself 她这件衣服是 tā zìjǐ zuòde zhèjiàn liányīqún ►she lives by herself 她独自一人住 tā dúzì yīrén zhù

he's [hi:z] = he is, he has

hesitate ['hezɪteɪt] VI 犹豫 yóuyù ►he did not hesitate to take action 他毫不迟疑地采取了行动 tā háobù chíyí de cǎiqǔ le xíngdòng ►don't hesitate to contact me 请务必和我联系 qǐng wùbì héwǒ liánxì

heterosexual ['hetərəʊ'seksjuəl] N [c] 异性恋者 yìxìngliànzhě [个 gè]

hi [haɪ] INT (as greeting) 嘿 hēi; (in e-mail) 你好 nǐhǎo

hiccup ['hɪkʌp] hiccups NPL ► to have/get (the) hiccups 打嗝 dǎgé

hidden ['hɪdn] PP of hide

hide [haɪd] (pt hid, pp hidden) I VT 隐藏 yǐncáng; (+ feeling, information) 隐瞒 yǐnmán II VI 藏起来 cáng qǐlái ►to hide from sb 躲着某人 duǒzhe mǒurén

hi-fi ['haɪfaɪ] N [c] 高保真音响设备 gāobǎozhēn yīnxiǎng shèbèi [套 tào]

high [haɪ] I ADJ 高的 gāo de II ADV (reach, throw) 高高地 gāogāo de; (fly, climb) 高 gāo ►it is 20 m high 有20米高 yǒu èrshími gāo ►foods that are high in fat 脂肪含量高的食品 zhīfáng hánliàng gāo de shípǐn ►safety has always been our highest priority 安全一直是我们最重视的问题 ānquán yīzhí shì wǒmen zuì zhòngshì de wèntí ►high up 离地面高的 lí dìmiàn gāo de

high 不能用于描写人，动物和植物，而应用 tall。She was rather tall for a woman. tall 还可以用来描写建筑物，如摩天大楼等，以及其他高大得于宽度的东西。...tall pine trees...a tall glass vase...

higher education ['haɪə'-] N [U] 高等教育 gāoděng jiàoyù

high-rise ['haɪraɪz] ADJ 高层的 gāocéng de

high school N [c/U] 中学

zhōngxué [所 suǒ]

hijack ['haɪdʒæk] VT 劫持 jiéchí

hijacker ['haɪdʒækə'] N [c] 劫持者 jiéchízhě [个 gè]

hike [haɪk] N [c] 步行 bùxíng II N (walk) 徒步旅行 túbù lǚxíng [次 cì] ▶ **to go hiking** 做徒步旅行 zuò túbù lǚxíng

hiking ['haɪkɪŋ] N [u] 步行 bùxíng

hill [hɪl] N [c] 小山 xiǎoshān [座 zuò]; (slope) 坡 pō [个 gè]

him [hɪm] PRON 他 tā ▶ **I haven't seen him** 我还没看见他 wǒ hái méi kànjiàn tā ▶ **they gave him the job** 他们给了他那份工作 tāmen gěile tā nàfèn gōngzuò

himself [hɪm'sɛlf] PRON 1 他自己 tā zìjǐ 2 (emphatic) 他本人 tā běnrén ▶ **he hurt himself** 他伤了自己 tā shāngle zìjǐ ▶ **he prepared the supper himself** 他准备好了晚餐 tā zìjǐ zhǔnbèi le wǎncān ▶ **he lives by himself** 他独自一人住 tā dúzì yīrén zhù

Hindu ['hɪnduː] I N 印度教信徒 Yìndùjiào xìntú [位 wèi] II ADJ 与印度教有关的 yǔ Yìndùjiào yǒuguān de

hip [hɪp] N [c] 髋部 kuānbù [个 gè]

hippie ['hɪpɪ] N [c] 嬉皮士 xīpíshì [个 gè]

hire ['haɪə'] I VT (esp Brit) 租用 zūyòng; [+ worker] 雇用 gùyòng II N [u] (Brit: of car, hall) 租用 zūyòng

hire car (Brit) N [c] 租的车 zū de chē [辆 liàng]

his [hɪz] I ADJ 他的 tā de II PRON 他的 tā de ▶ **his face was very red** 他的脸很红 tāde liǎn hěnhóng ▶ **these are his** 这些是他的 zhèxiē shì tāde ▶ **a friend of his** 他的一个朋友 tāde yígè péngyou

history ['hɪstərɪ] N [u] 历史 lìshǐ

hit [hɪt] I VT (pp **hit**) 1 (strike) 打 dǎ 2 (collide with) 碰撞 pèngzhuàng 3 [+ target] 击中 jīzhòng II N [c] 1 (on website) 点击 diǎnjī [次 cì] 2 (hit song) 成功而风行一时的事物 chénggōng ér fēngxíng yīshí de shìwù [个 gè]

hitchhike ['hɪtʃhaɪk] VI 搭便车旅行 dā biànchē lǚxíng

hitchhiker ['hɪtʃhaɪkə'] N [c] 搭便车旅行者 dā biànchē lǚxíngzhě [个 gè]

HIV N ABBR (= **human immunodeficiency virus**) 艾滋病病毒 àizībìng bìngdú

hoarse [hɔːs] ADJ 嘶哑的 sīyǎ de

hobby ['hɔbɪ] N [c] 爱好 àihào [种 zhǒng]

hockey ['hɔkɪ] N [u] 1 (Brit) 曲棍球 qūgùnqiú 2 (US: on ice) 冰球 bīngqiú

hold [həʊld] (pt, pp **held**) I VT 1 拿 ná 2 (contain) 容纳 róngnà II VI (Tel) 等着 děngzhe III N [c] [of ship, plane] 货舱 huòcāng [个 gè] ▶ **hold the line!** (Tel) 别挂线! bié guàxiàn! ▶ **to hold sb prisoner/hostage** 扣留某人作为囚犯/人质 kòuliú mǒurén zuòwéi qiúfàn/rénzhì ▶ **to get/grab/take hold of sb/sth** 紧紧拿着/抓着/握着某人/某物 jǐnjǐn názhe/zhuāzhe/wòzhe mǒurén/mǒuwù ▶ **I need to get hold of Bob** 我需要找到鲍伯

wǒ xǔyào zhǎodào Bàobó
▶ **hold on** VI 1 (keep held) 抓牢 zhuāláo 2 等一会儿 děng yīhuìr
▶ **hold up** VT 1 (lift up) 举起 jǔqǐ 2 (delay) 耽误 dànwù

hold-up ['həʊldʌp] N [c]
1 (robbery) 持械抢劫 chíxiè qiāngjié [次 cì] 2 (in traffic) 交通阻塞 jiāotōng zǔsè [阵 zhèn]

hole [həʊl] N [c] 1 (space, gap) 洞 dòng [个 gè] 2 (tear) 破洞 pòdòng [个 gè]

holiday ['hɒlɪdeɪ] (Brit) N [c/u] 假期 jiàqī [个 gè] ▶ **public holiday** 公共假期 gōnggòng jiàqī ▶ **the school/summer/Christmas holidays** (Brit: Scol) 学校/暑/圣诞假期 xuéxiào/shǔ/Shèngdàn jiàqī ▶ **to be on holiday** 在度假 zài dùjià

Holland ['hɒlənd] N 荷兰 Hélán

hollow ['hɒləʊ] ADJ (not solid) 空 的 kōng de

holy ['həʊlɪ] ADJ 神圣的 shénshèng de

home [həʊm] I N 1 [c/u] (house) 家 jiā [个 gè] 2 [c/u] (country, area) 家乡 jiāxiāng [个 gè] 3 [c] (institution) 收容院 shōuróngyuàn [个 gè] II ADV (be, go, etc) 在家 zàijiā ▶ **at home** (in house) 在家 zàijiā

homeless ['həʊmlɪs] I ADJ 无 家可归的 wújiā kěguī de II NPL ▶ **the homeless** 无家可归的人 wújiā kěguī de rén

homepage ['həʊmpeɪdʒ] N [c] 主页 zhǔyè [个 gè]

homesick ['həʊmsɪk] ADJ 想家的 xiǎngjiā de

homework ['həʊmwəːk] N [u] 家庭作业 jiātíng zuòyè

homosexual [hɒməʊ'seksjuəl] I ADJ 同性恋的 tóngxìngliàn de II N [c] 同性恋者 tóngxìngliànzhě [个 gè]

honest ['ɒnɪst] ADJ 诚实的 chéngshí de ▶ **to be honest,...** 说实话,... shuō shíhuà, ...

honesty ['ɒnɪstɪ] N [u] 诚实 chéngshí

honey ['hʌnɪ] N [u] 蜂蜜 fēngmì

honeymoon ['hʌnɪmuːn] N [c] 蜜月 mìyuè [个 gè]

Hong Kong ['hɒŋ'kɒŋ] N 香港 Xiānggǎng

hood [hʊd] N [c] 1 兜帽 dōumào [个 gè] 2 (US) (Aut) 发动机罩 fādòngjī zhào [个 gè]

hoof [huːf] (pl hooves) N 蹄 tí

hook [hʊk] N [c] 钩 gōu [个 gè] ▶ **to take the phone off the hook** 不把电话听筒挂上 bùbǎ diànhuà tīngtǒng guàshàng

hooray [huː'reɪ] INT 好哇 hǎo wa

Hoover® ['huːvə⁺] (Brit) I N [c] 吸尘器 xīchénqì [台 tái] II VT [+carpet] 用吸尘器 yòng xīchénqì xī

hooves [huːvz] NPL of **hoof**

hop [hɒp] VI 单脚跳 dānjiǎo tiào

hope [həʊp] I VT 希望 xīwàng II VI 盼望 pànwàng III N [u] 希望 xīwàng ▶ **I hope so/not** 希望是这样/希望不会 xīwàng shì zhèyàng/xīwàng búhuì ▶ **to hope that...** 希望… xīwàng... ▶ **to hope to do**

sth 希望能做某事 xīwàng néng zuò mǒushì

hopefully ['həupfəlɪ] ADV
▸hopefully,... 如果运气好… rúguǒ yùnqi hǎo…

hopeless ['həuplɪs] ADJ
1 [+ situation, position] 糟糕的 zāogāo de 2 [inf: useless] 无能的 wúnéng de

horizon [hə'raɪzn] N ▸the horizon 地平线 dìpíngxiàn

horizontal [hɔrɪ'zɔntl] ADJ 水平的 shuǐpíng de

horn [hɔːn] N 1 [c] [of animal] 角 jiǎo [个 gè] 2 [c] (Aut) 喇叭 lǎba [个 gè]

horoscope ['hɔrəskəup] N [c] 占星术 zhānxīngshù [种 zhǒng]

horrible ['hɔrɪbl] ADJ [+ colour, food, mess] 糟透的 zāotòu de; [+ accident, crime] 可怕的 kěpà de; [+ experience, moment, situation, dream] 令人恐惧的 lìng rén kǒngjù de

horror film N [c] 恐怖片 kǒngbù piàn [部 bù]

horse [hɔːs] N [c] 马 mǎ [匹 pǐ]

horse racing N [u] 赛马 sàimǎ

hose [həuz] N [c] (also: hosepipe) 输水软管 shūshuǐ ruǎnguǎn [根 gēn]

hospital ['hɔspɪtl] N [c/u] 医院 yīyuàn [家 jiā] ▸to be in hospital or (US) in the hospital 住院 zhùyuàn

hospitality [hɔspɪ'tælɪtɪ] N [u] 好客 hàokè

host [həust] N [c] 主人 zhǔrén [位 wèi]

hostage ['hɔstɪdʒ] N [c] 人质 rénzhì [个 gè] ▸to be taken/held hostage 被绑架/扣押做人质 bèi bǎngjià/kòuyā zuò rénzhì

hostel ['hɔstl] N [c] (esp Brit) 招待所 zhāodàisuǒ [个 gè]

hostess ['həustɪs] N [c] 女主人 nǚ zhǔrén [位 wèi]

hot [hɔt] ADJ 1 [+ object] 烫的 tàng de; [+ weather, person] 热的 rè de 2 (spicy) 辣的 là de

hotel [həu'tel] N [c] 旅馆 lǚguǎn [个 gè] ▸to stay at a hotel 住旅馆 zhù lǚguǎn

hour ['auə'] I N [c] 小时 xiǎoshí [个 gè] II hours NPL (ages) 很长时间 hěncháng shíjiān ▸the buses leave on the hour 每小时正点有一班公共汽车 měi xiǎoshí zhèngdiǎn yǒu yībān gōnggòng qìchē ▸for three/four hours 三/四个小时 sān/sìgè xiǎoshí ▸(at) 60 kilometres/miles an or per hour 每小时60公里/英里 měi xiǎoshí liùshí gōnglǐ/yīnglǐ ▸to pay sb by the hour 按小时付费给某人 àn xiǎoshí fùfèi gěi mǒurén ▸lunch hour 午餐时间 wǔcān shíjiān

house [haus] N [c] 家 jiā [个 gè] ▸at/to my house 在/到我家 zài/dào wǒjiā

housewife ['hauswaɪf] (pl housewives) N [c] 家庭主妇 jiātíng zhǔfù [个 gè]

housework ['hauswəːk] N [u] 家务劳动 jiāwù láodòng

housing estate (Brit) N [c] 住宅区 zhùzhái qū [个 gè]

hovercraft ['hɒvəkrɑːft] (*pl* **hovercraft**) N [c] 气垫船 qìdiàn chuán [艘 sōu]

⊙ KEYWORD

how [hau] I ADV 1 (*in questions*) 怎样 zěnyàng ▸how did you do it? 你是怎么做的? nǐ shì zěnme zuòde? ▸how are you? 你好吗? nǐ hǎo ma? ▸how long have you lived here? 你在这儿住了多久了? nǐ zài zhèr zhùle duōjiǔ le? ▸how much milk/many people? 有多少奶/人? yǒu duōshǎo nǎi/rén? ▸how old are you? 你多大了? nǐ duōdà le? ▸how tall is he? 他有多高? tā yǒu duō gāo? 2 (*in suggestions*) ▸how about a cup of tea/a walk etc? 来杯茶/去散步(等)好吗? lái bēi chá/qù sànbù [děng] hǎo ma?

II CONJ 怎样 zěnyàng ▸I know how you did it 我知道你怎么做的 wǒ zhīdào nǐ zěnme zuòde ▸to know how to do sth 知道如何做某事 zhīdào rúhé zuò mǒushì

however [hau'evə*] ADV 1 (*but*) 但是 dànshì 2 (*with adj, adv*) 不管怎样 bùguǎn zěnyàng 3 (*in questions*) 究竟怎样 jiūjìng zěnyàng

hug [hʌɡ] I VT (*+ person*) 拥抱 yōngbào II N [c] 拥抱 yōngbào [个 gè] ▸to give sb a hug 拥抱某人 yōngbào mǒurén

huge [hjuːdʒ] ADJ 巨大的 jùdà de; [*+ amount, profit, debt*] 巨额的 jù'é de; [*+ task*] 庞大的 pángdà de

human ['hjuːmən] I ADJ 人的 rén de II N [c] (*also:* human being) 人 rén [个 gè] ▸the human race 人类 rénlèi ▸human nature 人性 rénxìng

humor ['hjuːmə*] (US) N = **humour**

humour, (US) **humor** ['hjuːmə*] N [U] 幽默 yōumò ▸sense of humour 幽默感 yōumògǎn

hundred ['hʌndrəd] I NUM 百 bǎi II hundreds NPL 几百 jǐbǎi ▸a or one hundred books/people/dollars 一百本书/个人/美元 yībǎibǎn shū/gè rén/měiyuán

hung [hʌŋ] PT, PP *of* **hang**

Hungary ['hʌŋɡərɪ] N 匈牙利 Xiōngyálì

hungry ['hʌŋɡrɪ] ADJ 饿的 jī'è de ▸to be hungry 饿了 èle

hunt [hʌnt] I VI (*for food, sport*) 打猎 dǎliè II N [c] 1 (*for food, sport*) 狩猎 shòuliè [次 cì] 2 (*for missing person*) 搜寻 sōuxún [次 cì] (*for criminal*) 追捕 zhuībǔ [次 cì]

hunting ['hʌntɪŋ] N [U] (*for food, sport*) 打猎 dǎliè ▸job/house/bargain hunting 到处找工作/住房/便宜货 dàochù zhǎo gōngzuò/zhùfáng/piányí huò

hurricane ['hʌrɪkən] N [c] 飓风 jùfēng [场 chǎng] ▸hurricane Charley/Tessa 查理/特萨号台风 Chálǐ/Tèsàhào táifēng

hurry ['hʌrɪ] I VI, VT ▸to be in a hurry (to do sth) 急于(做某事) jí yú (zuò mǒushì) ▸to do sth in a hurry 匆忙地做某事 cōngmángde zuò mǒushì

▶ **hurry up** VI 赶快 gǎnkuài

hurt [hə:t] (pt, pp **hurt**) I VT
  1 (cause pain to) 弄痛 nòngtòng
  2 (injure) 使受伤 shǐ shòushāng
  3 (emotionally) 使伤心 shǐ shāngxīn II VI (be painful) 痛 tòng III ADJ 1 (injured) 受伤的 shòushāng de 2 (emotionally) 受委屈的 shòu wěiqū de ▶ **to hurt o.s.** 伤了自己 shāngle zìjǐ ▶ **I didn't want to hurt your feelings** 我并不想伤害你的感情 wǒ bìng bùxiǎng shānghài nǐ de gǎnqíng ▶ **where does it hurt?** 哪儿疼? nǎr téng?

husband ['hʌzbənd] N [c] 丈夫 zhàngfu [个 gè]

hut [hʌt] N [c] (shed) 木棚 mùpéng [个 gè]

hyphen ['haɪfn] N [c] 连字符 liánzìfú [个 gè]

I [aɪ] PRON 我 wǒ

ice [aɪs] N [U] 冰 bīng; (for drink) 冰块 bīngkuài

iceberg ['aɪsbə:g] N [c] 冰山 bīngshān [座 zuò] ▶ **the tip of the iceberg** (fig) 冰山一角 bīngshān yījiǎo

ice cream N [c/U] 冰淇淋 bīngqílín [个 gè]

ice cube N [c] 冰块 bīngkuài [块 kuài]

ice hockey (esp Brit) N [U] 冰球 bīngqiú

Iceland ['aɪslənd] N 冰岛 Bīngdǎo

ice rink N [c] 溜冰场 liūbīngchǎng [个 gè]

ice-skating ['aɪsskeɪtɪŋ] N [U] 溜冰 liūbīng

icing (Culin) N [U] 糖霜

tángshuāng

icon ['aɪkɔn] N [c] (Comput) 图符 túfú [个 gè]

ICT (Brit) N ABBR (= information and communication technology) 通信技术 tōngxìn jìshù

ID N ABBR (= identification) 身份证明 shēnfèn zhèngmíng ▸ **do you have any ID?** 你有证件吗？nǐ yǒu zhèngjiàn ma？

I'd [aɪd] = **I would, I had**

idea [aɪ'dɪə] N 1 [c] (scheme) 主意 zhǔyi [个 gè] 2 [c] (opinion, theory) 看法 kànfǎ [种 zhǒng] 3 [c/u] (notion) 概念 gàiniàn [个 gè] ▸ **(what a) good idea!** （真是个）好主意！(zhēn shì gè) hǎo zhǔyi！▸ **I haven't the slightest or faintest idea** 我根本就不知道 wǒ gēnběn jiù bù zhīdào

ideal [aɪ'dɪəl] ADJ 理想的 lǐxiǎng de

identical [aɪ'dɛntɪkl] ADJ 完全相同的 wánquán xiāngtóng de ▸ **identical to** 和……完全相同 hé...wánquán xiāngtóng

identification [aɪdɛntɪfɪ'keɪʃən] N [u] (proof of identity) 身份证明 shēnfèn zhèngmíng

identify [aɪ'dɛntɪfaɪ] VT (recognize) 识别 shíbié

identity card N [c] 身份证 shēnfènzhèng [个 gè]

idiot ['ɪdɪət] N [c] 傻子 shǎzi [个 gè]

i.e. ABBR (= id est) 也就是 yě jiùshì

○ KEYWORD

if [ɪf] CONJ 1 (conditional use) 如果

rúguǒ ▸ **I'll go if you come with me** 如果你和我一起的话我就去 rúguǒ nǐ hé wǒ yīqǐde huà wǒ jiù qù ▸ **if I were you** 如果我是你的话 rúguǒ wǒ shì nǐ de huà ▸ **if necessary** 如有必要 rúyǒu bìyào ▸ **if so** 如果是这样的话 rúguǒ shì zhèyàng de huà ▸ **if not** 如果不行的话 rúguǒ bùxíng de huà 2 (whenever) 无论何时 wúlùn héshí ▸ **if we are in Hong Kong, we always go to see her** 我们无论何时去香港，都会去看她 wǒmen wúlùn héshí qù xiānggǎng, dōuhuì qù kàntā 3 (whether) 是否 shìfǒu ▸ **ask him if he can come** 问他是否能来 wèn tā shìfǒu néngái 4 (in expressions) ▸ **if only we had more time!** 要是我们再多点时间就好了！yàoshi wǒmen zài duōdiǎn shíjiān jiù hǎo le!

ignore [ɪg'nɔ:r] VT [+ person] 不理 bù lǐ; [+ advice, event] 不顾 bù gù

I'll [aɪl] = **I will, I shall**

ill [ɪl] I ADJ 有病的 yǒubìng de II **the ill** N PL ▸ **the mentally/terminally ill** 精神/晚期病人 jīngshén/wǎnqī bìngrén ▸ **to fall or be taken ill** 生病 shēngbìng

单词 **ill** 和 **sick** 在语意上很相近，但使用方法有很大不同。**ill** 通常不用在名词前，但可用在动词词组中，比如 **fall ill** 和 **be taken ill**。He fell ill shortly before Christmas...One of the jury members was taken *ill. sick* 经常用在名词前。*...sick children...* 在英式英语中，**ill** 比 **sick** 更为文雅和委婉。**sick** 常常指实际的身体病痛，例如晕船或呕吐。*I spent the next 24 hours in bed, groaning and being sick.* 美式英语中，**sick** 经常用在英国人说 **ill** 的地方。*Some people get hurt in accidents or get sick.*

illegal [ɪ'liːɡl] ADJ 非法的 fēifǎde

illness ['ɪlnɪs] N [c/u] 病 bìng [场 chǎng]

illusion [ɪ'luːʒən] N [c] 幻想 huànxiǎng [个 gè]

illustration [ɪlə'streɪʃən] N [c] 插图 chātú [幅 fú]

imagination [ɪmædʒɪ'neɪʃən] N 1 [c/u] 想象力 xiǎngxiànglì [种 zhǒng] 2 [c] (mind's eye) 想象 xiǎngxiàng [个 gè]

imagine [ɪ'mædʒɪn] VT 1 (envisage) 想象 xiǎngxiàng 2 (suppose) 设想 shèxiǎng

imitate ['ɪmɪteɪt] VT 1 (copy) 效仿 xiàofǎng 2 [+ person, sound, gesture] 模仿 mófǎng

imitation [ɪmɪ'teɪʃən] I N [c] 仿制品 fǎngzhìpǐn [件 jiàn] II ADJ 仿制的 fǎngzhìde

immediate [ɪ'miːdɪət] ADJ 立即的 lìjíde

immediately [ɪ'miːdɪətlɪ] I ADV 1 (at once) 立即地 lìjídi 2 II CONJ ▶ **immediately he had said it, he regretted it** 他刚一说完马上就后悔了 tā gāng yī shuōwán mǎshàng jiù hòuhuǐle

▶ **immediately before/after** 紧接着…之前/后 jǐnjiēzhe...zhīqián/hòu

immigrant ['ɪmɪɡrənt] N [c] 移民 yímín [个 gè]

immigration [ɪmɪ'ɡreɪʃən] I N [u] 1 (process) 移民 yímín 2 (also: **immigration control**) 移民局检查 yímínjú jiǎnchá II CPD [+ authorities, policy, controls, officer] 移民 yímín

impatient [ɪm'peɪʃənt] ADJ 急躁的 jízàode ▶ **to get impatient (at or with sth)** (对某事) 不耐烦 (duì mǒushì) bù nàifán

import [ɪm'pɔːt] VT 进口 jìnkǒu

importance [ɪm'pɔːtns] N [u] 1 (significance) 重要性 zhòngyàoxìng 2 (influence) 影响 yǐngxiǎng

important [ɪm'pɔːtənt] ADJ 1 重要的 zhòngyàode 2 (influential) 有影响的 yǒu yǐngxiǎng de ▶ **it is important to eat sensibly** 合理进食是很重要的 hélǐ jìnshí shì hěn zhòngyào de ▶ **it's not important** 不重要的 bù zhòngyào de

impossible [ɪm'pɒsɪbl] ADJ 不可能的 bù kěnéng de ▶ **it is impossible to understand what's going on** 不可能了解事情的进展情况 bù kěnéng liǎojiě shìqíng de jìnzhǎn qíngkuàng

impress [ɪm'prɛs] VT [+ person] 给…极深的印象 gěi...jíshēn de yìnxiàng ▶ **to be impressed by or with sb/sth** 对某人/某物印象深刻 duì mǒurén/mǒuwù yìnxiàng shēnkè

impression [ɪmˈprɛʃən] N [C] 印象 yìnxiàng N or **create a good/bad impression** 留下好/不良印象 liúxià hǎo/bùliáng yìnxiàng

impressive [ɪmˈprɛsɪv] ADJ 给人深刻印象的 gěi rén shēnkè yìnxiàng de

improve [ɪmˈpruːv] I VT 改进 gǎijìn II VI [*weather, situation*] 改善 gǎishàn; [*pupil, performance*] 进步 jìnbù

improvement [ɪmˈpruːvmənt] N [C/U] 改进 gǎijìn [个 gè] ▶**improvement in** [+ *person, thing*] 进步 jìnbù

🅚 **KEYWORD**

in [ɪn] I PREP 1 在…里 zài…lǐ ▶**it's in the house/garden/box** 它在房子/花园/盒子里 tā zài fángzi/huāyuán/hézi lǐ ▶**put it in the house/garden/box** 把它放在房子/花园/盒子里 bǎ tā fàngzài fángzi/huāyuán/hézi lǐ ▶**in here/there** 在这儿/那儿 zài zhèr/nàr 2 (*with place names*) 在 zài ▶**in London/England** 在伦敦/英格兰 zài lúndūn/yīnggélán 3 (*time: during*) 在 zài; (*within: referring to future*) 在…之后 zài…zhīhòu; (*referring to past*) 在…之内 zài…zhīnèi ▶**in 1988/ May** 在1988年/5月 zài yī jiǔ bā bā nián/wǔyuè ▶**in the morning/afternoon** 在上午/下午 zài shàngwǔ/xiàwǔ ▶**I'll see you in two weeks' time** *or* **in two weeks** 我两周后见你 wǒ liǎngzhōu hòu jiàn nǐ ▶**I did it in 3 hours/days** 我花了3小时/天完成 wǒ huàle sān xiǎoshí/tiān wánchéng 4 (*indicating manner, style etc*) 以 yǐ ▶**in pencil/ink** 用铅笔/墨水笔 yòng qiānbǐ/mòshuǐbǐ ▶**the boy in the blue shirt** 穿蓝衬衫的男孩儿 chuān lán chènshān de nánháir ▶**in the sun/rain** 在阳光下/雨中 zài yángguāng xià/yǔzhōng 5 (*with languages*) 用 yòng ▶**in English/French** 用英语/法语 yòng yīngyǔ/fǎyǔ 6 (*with ratios, numbers*) 每 měi ▶**one in ten people** 十分之一的人 shí fēn zhī yī de rén 7 (*amongst*) [+ *group, collection*] 在…中 zài…zhōng ▶**the best athlete in the team** 该队中最好的运动员 gāiduì zhōng zuìhǎo de yùndòngyuán II ADV ▶**to be in** (*at home, work*) 在 zài ▶**to ask sb in** 把某人请到家中 bǎ mǒurén qǐngdào jiāzhōng

inch [ɪntʃ] N [C] 英寸 yīngcùn

include [ɪnˈkluːd] VT 包括 bāokuò

including [ɪnˈkluːdɪŋ] PREP 包括 bāokuò ▶**nine people were injured, including two Britons** 九个人受了伤，包括两个英国人 jiǔgè rén shòule shāng, bāokuò liǎnggè Yīngguórén

income [ˈɪnkʌm] N [C/U] 收入 shōurù [笔 bǐ]

income tax N [U] 所得税 suǒdéshuì

inconvenient [ɪnkən'viːnjənt] ADJ [+ time, moment] 不合时宜的 bùhé shíyí de

incorrect [ɪnkə'rekt] ADJ 错误的 cuòwù de

increase [n 'ɪnkriːs, vb ɪn'kriːs] I N [c] 增长 zēngzhǎng [成 chéng] II VI 增长 zēngzhǎng III VT [+ price, number, level] 提高 tígāo
▶ a 5% increase, an increase of 5% 百分之五的增长 bǎi fēn zhī wǔ de zēngzhǎng

incredible [ɪn'kredɪbl] ADJ (amazing, wonderful) 不可思议的 bùkě sīyì de

indeed [ɪn'diːd] ADV (as a reply) 是 的 shì de ▶ yes indeed! 的确如此! díquè rúcǐ!

independence [ɪndɪ'pendns] N [U] 独立 dúlì

independent [ɪndɪ'pendnt] ADJ 独立的 dúlì de

index ['ɪndeks] (pl indexes) N [c] 索引 suǒyǐn [条 tiáo]

India ['ɪndɪə] N 印度 Yìndù

Indian ['ɪndɪən] I ADJ 印度的 Yìndù de II N (person from India) 印度人 Yìndùrén [个 gè]

indicate ['ɪndɪkeɪt] VT 1 表 明 biǎomíng 2 (point to) 指向 zhǐxiàng

indifferent [ɪn'dɪfrənt] ADJ 1 没 兴趣的 méi xìngqù de 2 (mediocre) 平庸的 píngyōng de

indigestion [ɪndɪ'dʒestʃən] N [U] 消化不良 xiāohuà bù liáng

individual [ɪndɪ'vɪdjuəl] I N 个 人 gèrén II ADJ (personal) 个人的 gèrén de

indoor ['ɪndɔːr] ADJ 室内的 shìnèi de

indoors [ɪn'dɔːz] ADV 在室内 zài shì nèi

industrial [ɪn'dʌstrɪəl] ADJ 工业 的 gōngyè de; [+ accident] 因工的 yīngōng de

industrial estate (Brit) N [c] 工 业区 gōngyè qū [个 gè]

industrial park (US) N [c] 工业区 gōngyè qū [个 gè]

industry ['ɪndəstrɪ] N 1 [U] (manufacturing) 工业 gōngyè 2 [c] (business) 行业 hángyè [种 zhǒng]

inevitable [ɪn'evɪtəbl] ADJ 不可 避免的 bùkě bìmiǎn de

infection [ɪn'fekʃən] N [c] 感 染 gǎnrǎn [处 chù] ▶ to have an ear/throat infection 耳朵/咽喉 感染 ěrduo/yānhóu gǎnrǎn

infectious [ɪn'fekʃəs] ADJ 传染的 chuánrǎn de

inflation [ɪn'fleɪʃən] N [U] 通货膨 胀 tōnghuò péngzhàng

influence ['ɪnfluəns] I N 1 [c/U] (power) 权势 quánshì [种 zhǒng] 2 [c] (effect) 影响 yǐngxiǎng [个 gè] II VT 影响 yǐngxiǎng

inform [ɪn'fɔːm] VT 告诉 gàosù ▶ to inform sb that... 告诉某人… gàosù mǒurén…

informal [ɪn'fɔːml] ADJ 1 (relaxed) 不拘礼节的 bùjū lǐjié de 2 [+ clothes, party] 日 常的 rìcháng de 3 [+ meeting, discussions, agreement] 非正式的 fēizhèngshì de

information [ɪnfə'meɪʃən] N [U] 信息 xìnxī ▶ a piece of

information 一条信息 yītiáo xìnxi

information technology N [U] 信息技术 xìnxī jìshù

ingredient [ɪn'griːdiənt] N [c] 配料 pèiliào [种 zhǒng]

inhabitant [ɪn'hæbɪtnt] N [c] 居民 jūmín [个 gè]

inherit [ɪn'herɪt] VT 继承 jìchéng

initial [ɪ'nɪʃl] I N [c] (letter) 首字母 shǒuzìmǔ [个 gè] II initials NPL [of name] 首字母 shǒuzìmǔ

injection [ɪn'dʒekʃən] N [c] 注射 zhùshè ▶ to give sb an injection 给某人注射 gěi mǒurén zhùshè

injure ['ɪndʒər] VT [+ person] 伤害 shānghài ▶ he was badly injured in the attack 他在进攻中受了重伤 tā zài jìngōng zhōng shòule zhòngshāng

injury ['ɪndʒəri] N [c/u] (wound) 伤害 shānghài [个 gè] ▶ to escape without injury 安然脱险 ānrán tuōxiǎn

ink [ɪŋk] N [c/u] 墨水 mòshuǐ [瓶 píng]

in-laws ['ɪnlɔːz] NPL 姻亲 yīnqīn

innocent ['ɪnəsnt] ADJ 清白的 qīngbái de

insect ['ɪnsekt] N [c] 昆虫 kūnchóng [只 zhī]

insect repellent N [c/u] 杀虫剂 shāchóngjì

inside ['ɪn'saɪd] I N 内部 nèibù II ADJ [+ wall, surface] 内部的 nèibù de III ADV 1 (go) 里面 lǐmiàn; (be) 在里面 zài lǐmiàn 2 (indoors) 在屋内 zài wū nèi IV PREP [+ place, container] 在…的 里面 zài…de lǐmiàn

insist [ɪn'sɪst] VI, VT 坚持 jiānchí ▶ to insist on sth/doing sth 坚持要求某事/做某事 jiānchí yāoqiú mǒushì/zuò mǒushì

inspector [ɪn'spektər] N [c] 1 (official) 检查员 jiǎncháyuán [位 wèi] 2 (Brit) (also: ticket inspector) 查票员 chápiàoyuán [位 wèi]

install, instal [ɪn'stɔːl] VT 安装 ānzhuāng

instalment, (US) installment [ɪn'stɔːlmənt] N [c] 分期付款 fēnqī fùkuǎn [期 qī]

instance ['ɪnstəns] N [c] (example) 例子 lìzi [个 gè] ▶ for instance 例如 lìrú

instant ['ɪnstənt] I N [c] (moment) 瞬息 shùnxí [个 gè] II ADJ 1 [+ reaction, success] 立即的 lìjí de 2 [+ coffee, soup, noodles] 速食的 sùshí de ▶ for an instant 一瞬间 yī shùnjiān

instantly ['ɪnstəntli] ADV 立即 lìjí

instead [ɪn'sted] ADV 代替 dàitì ▶ instead of 而不是 ér bùshì

instinct ['ɪnstɪŋkt] N [c/u] 本能 běnnéng [种 zhǒng]

instruct [ɪn'strʌkt] VT ▶ to instruct sb to do sth 命令某人做某事 mìnglìng mǒurén zuò mǒushì

instruction [ɪn'strʌkʃən] I CPD [+ manual, leaflet] 说明 shuōmíng II instructions NPL 说明 shuōmíng

instructor [ɪn'strʌktər] N [c] 教员 jiàoyuán [位 wèi]

instrument ['ɪnstrəmənt] N [c]

1 器械 qìxiè [件 jiàn] **2** (Mus) 乐器 yuèqì [件 jiàn]

insulin ['ɪnsjʊlɪn] N [U] 胰岛素 yídǎosù

insult [n 'ɪnsʌlt, vb ɪn'sʌlt] **I** N [c] 侮辱 wǔrǔ [个 gè] **II** VT 侮辱 wǔrǔ

insurance [ɪn'ʃʊərəns] N [U] 保险 bǎoxiǎn ▸ fire/life/health insurance 火/人寿/健康险 huǒ/rénshòu/jiànkāng xiǎn

insure [ɪn'ʃʊə'] VT [+ house, car] 给…保险 gěi…bǎoxiǎn

intelligent [ɪn'tɛlɪdʒənt] ADJ 聪明的 cōngmíng de

intend [ɪn'tɛnd] VT ▸ to intend to do sth 打算做某事 dǎsuàn zuò mǒushì

intense [ɪn'tɛns] ADJ [+ heat, pain] 剧烈的 jùliè de; [+ competition] 激烈的 jīliè de

intensive care N ▸ to be in intensive care 接受重病特别护理 jiēshòu zhòngbìng tèbié hùlǐ

intention [ɪn'tɛnʃən] N [c/U] 打算 dǎsuàn [个 gè]

interest ['ɪntrɪst] N **1** [U/s] (in subject, idea, person) 兴趣 xìngqù **2** [c] (pastime, hobby) 爱好 àihào [个 gè] **3** [U] (on loan, savings) 利息 lìxī ▸ to take an interest in sth/sb 对某事/某人感兴趣 duì mǒushì/mǒurén gǎn xìngqù

interested ['ɪntrɪstɪd] ADJ ▸ to be interested (in sth/doing sth) 对（某事/做某事）有兴趣 duì （mǒushì/zuò mǒushì） yǒu xìngqù

请勿将 **interested** 和 **interesting** 混淆。如果你 **interested in** an

说明你对它很感兴趣，很想了解或知道更多关于它的事情，或者想花更多的时间来做这件事。Not all of the children were interested in animals…She asked him how he became interested in politics. 如果你发现某事 **interesting**，表示它令人感兴趣，引人注意，使你乐于更多地了解这件事或者去做这件事。It must be an awfully interesting job…The interesting thing is that this is exactly the answer we got before.

interesting ['ɪntrɪstɪŋ] ADJ 有趣的 yǒuqù de

interfere [ɪntə'fɪə'] VI (meddle) 干涉 gānshè ▸ to interfere with sth [+ plans, career, duty] 妨碍某事 fáng'ài mǒushì

interior [ɪn'tɪərɪə'] N [c] 内部 nèibù

intermission [ɪntə'mɪʃən] N [c] (Cine) 休息时间 xiūxī shíjiān [段 duàn]

international [ɪntə'næʃənl] ADJ 国际的 guójì de

Internet ['ɪntənɛt] N ▸ the Internet 因特网 yīntèwǎng

Internet café N [c] 网吧 wǎngbā [个 gè]

interpret [ɪn'tə:prɪt] VI 口译 kǒuyì

interpreter [ɪn'tə:prɪtə'] N [c] 口译者 kǒuyìzhě [位 wèi]

interrupt [ɪntə'rʌpt] **I** VT **1** 打断 dǎduàn **2** [+ activity] 中断 zhōngduàn **II** VI (in conversation)

打岔 dǎchà

interruption [ɪntə'rʌpʃən] N [c/u] 扰 dǎrǎo [种 zhǒng]

interval ['ɪntəvl] N [c] 1 (break, pause) 间隔 jiàngé [个 gè] 2 (Brit) (Theat, Mus, Sport) 幕间休息 mùjiàn xiūxi [个 gè]

interview ['ɪntəvjuː] I N [c/u] 1 (for job) 面试 miànshì [次 cì] 2 (Publishing, Rad, TV) 采访 cǎifǎng [次 cì] II VT 1 (for job) 面试 miànshì 2 (Publishing, Rad, TV) 采访 cǎifǎng ► to go for/have an interview 参加面试 cānjiā miànshì

interviewer ['ɪntəvjuːə'] N [c] 采访者 cǎifǎngzhě [位 wèi]

intimidate [ɪn'tɪmɪdeɪt] VT 恐吓 kǒnghè

into ['ɪntu] PREP 到…里面 dào…lǐmiàn ► come into the house/garden 走进房子/花园里 zǒujìn fángzi/huāyuán lǐ ► get into the car 进入车子 jìnrù chēzi ► let's go into town 我们进城吧 wǒmen jìnchéng ba ► to translate Chinese into French 把汉语翻译成法语 bǎ Hànyǔ fānyì chéng Fǎyǔ ► research into cancer 对癌症的深入研究 duì áizhèng de shēnrù yánjiū ► I'd like to change some dollars into euros 我想把一些美元换成欧元 wǒ xiǎng bǎ yìxiē měiyuán huànchéng ōuyuán

introduce [ɪntrə'djuːs] VT 1 [+ new idea, measure, technology] 引进 yǐnjìn ► to introduce sb (to sb) 给某人介绍 (某人) jǐ

may I introduce you (to…)? 让我介绍 (认识…) 好吗? ràng wǒ jièshào nǐ (rènshi…) hǎo ma?

introduction [ɪntrə'dʌkʃən] N 1 [u] (of new idea, measure, technology) 引进 yǐnjìn 2 [c] (of person) 介绍 jièshào [个 gè] 3 [c] 引言 yǐnyán [个 gè]

invade [ɪn'veɪd] VT 侵略 qīnlüè

invalid ['ɪnvəlɪd] N [c] 病弱者 bìngruòzhě [个 gè]

invent [ɪn'vɛnt] VT 发明 fāmíng

invention [ɪn'vɛnʃən] N [c] 发明 fāmíng [项 xiàng]

investigate [ɪn'vɛstɪgeɪt] VT 调查 diàochá

investigation [ɪnvɛstɪ'geɪʃən] N [c/u] 调查 diàochá [项 xiàng]

invisible [ɪn'vɪzɪbl] ADJ 看不见的 kànbùjiàn de

invitation [ɪnvɪ'teɪʃən] N 1 [c] 邀请 yāoqǐng [个 gè] 2 [c] (card) 请柬 qǐngjiǎn [封 fēng]

invite [ɪn'vaɪt] VT 邀请 yāoqǐng ► to invite sb to do sth 邀请某人做某事 yāoqǐng mǒurén zuò mǒushì ► to invite sb to dinner 请某人赴宴 qǐng mǒurén fùyàn

involve [ɪn'vɒlv] VT 1 (entail) 包含 bāohán 2 (concern, affect) 使卷入 shǐ juǎnrù ► to involve sb (in sth) 使某人参与 (某事) shǐ mǒurén cānyù (mǒushì)

iPod® ['aɪpɒd] 数码随身听 shùmǎ suíshēntīng [个 gè]

Iran [ɪ'rɑːn] N 伊朗 Yīlǎng

Iraq [ɪ'rɑːk] N 伊拉克 Yīlākè

Iraqi [ɪ'rɑːkɪ] I ADJ 伊拉克的

Yilākè de II N [c] (person) 伊拉克
人 Yīlākèrén [名 míng]

Ireland ['aɪələnd] N 爱尔兰
Àiʼĕrlán ▶ **the Republic of Ireland**
爱尔兰共和国 Àiʼĕrlán Gònghéguó

Irish ['aɪrɪʃ] I ADJ 爱尔兰的 Àiʼĕrlán
de II N [U] (language) 爱尔兰语
Àiʼĕrlányǔ III **the Irish** NPL 爱尔兰
人 Àiʼĕrlánrén

Irishman ['aɪrɪʃmən] (pl
Irishmen) N [c] 爱尔兰男人
Àiʼĕrlán nánrén [个 gè]

Irishwoman ['aɪrɪʃwumən] (pl
Irishwomen) N [c] 爱尔兰女人
Àiʼĕrlán nǚrén [个 gè]

iron ['aɪən] I N 1 [U] (metal) 铁 tiě
2 [c] (for clothes) 熨斗 yùndǒu [个
gè] II ADJ [+ bar, railings] 铁的 tiě
de III VT [+ clothes] 熨 yùn

irresponsible [ɪrɪ'spɔnsɪbl] ADJ
[+ person, driver] 无责任感的 wú
zérèngǎn de; [+ attitude, behaviour]
不负责任的 bù fù zérèn de

irritating ['ɪrɪteɪtɪŋ] ADJ 烦人的
fánrén de

is [ɪz] VB OF **be**

Islam ['ɪzlɑːm] N 伊斯兰教
Yīsīlánjiào

Islamic [ɪz'læmɪk] ADJ [+ law,
faith] 伊斯兰教的 Yīsīlánjiào de;
[+ country] 伊斯兰的 Yīsīlán de

island ['aɪlənd] N [c] 岛 dǎo
[个 gè]

isolated ['aɪsəleɪtɪd] ADJ 1 [+ place]
孤立零落的 gūlìlíngluò de 2 [+ person]
孤立的 gūlì de 3 [+ incident, case,
example] 个例的 gèbié de

Israel ['ɪzreɪl] N 以色列 Yīsèliè

Israeli [ɪz'reɪlɪ] I ADJ 以色列的

Yīsèliè de II N [c] (person) 以色列
人 Yīsèlièrén [名 míng]

issue ['ɪʃuː] N [c] (problem, subject)
问题 wèntí [个 gè]

IT N ABBR (= Information
Technology) 信息技术 xìnxī jìshù

it [ɪt] PRON 1 (object or animal) 它
tā; (referring to baby) 他/她 tā/tā
2 (weather, date, time) ▶ **it's raining**
正在下雨。zhèngzài xiàyǔ
3 (impersonal) ▶ **it doesn't matter**
没关系。méiguānxì. ▶ **I can't
find it** 我找不到。wǒ zhǎo bù
dào ▶ **what is it?** (thing) 是什么东
西？shì shénme dōngxī?; (what's
the matter?) 怎么了？zěnme le?
▶ **"who is it?" - "it's me"** "是
谁？" "是我。" "shì shuí?"
"shìwǒ."

Italian [ɪ'tæljən] I ADJ 意大利
的 Yìdàlì de II N 1 [c] (person) 意
大利人 Yìdàlìrén [名 míng] 2 [U]
(language) 意大利语 Yìdàlìyǔ

Italy ['ɪtəlɪ] N 意大利 Yìdàlì

itch [ɪtʃ] VI 发痒 fāyǎng

itchy ['ɪtʃɪ] ADJ 发痒的 fāyǎng de

it'd ['ɪtd] = **it would, it had**

item ['aɪtəm] N [c] 项目 xiàngmù
[个 gè]; (on bill) 项目 xiàngmù [个
gè] ▶ **items of clothing** 几件衣
服 jǐjiàn yīfu

it'll ['ɪtl] = **it will**

its [ɪts] ADJ 1 (of animal) 它的 tā de
2 (of baby) 他/她的 tā/tā de

it's [ɪts] = **it is, it has**

itself [ɪt'self] PRON 1 (reflexive)
它自己 tā zìjǐ 2 (emphatic) 本身
běnshēn ▶ **it switches itself off
automatically** 它自动接通。tā
zìdòng jiētōng ▶ **I think like itself**

is a learning process 我认为生活
本身是个学习的过程。 ▸ by itself (alone)
单独地 dāndú de
I've [aɪv] = **I have**

jack [dʒæk] N [c] (Aut) 千斤顶
qiānjīndǐng [个 gè]
jacket ['dʒækɪt] N [c] 夹克 jiākè
[件 jiàn]
jail [dʒeɪl] I N [c/U] 监狱 jiānyù [个
gè] II VT 监禁 jiānjìn
jam [dʒæm] N [c/U] (Brit: preserve)
果酱 guǒjiàng [瓶 píng]
janitor ['dʒænɪtə^r] N [c] 看门人
kānménrén [个 gè]
January ['dʒænjuərɪ] N [c/U] 一
月 yīyuè; see also **July**
Japan [dʒə'pæn] N 日本 Rìběn
Japanese [dʒæpə'niːz] (pl
Japanese) I ADJ 日本的 Rìběn de
II N 1 [c] (person) 日本人 Rìběnrén
[个 gè] 2 [U] (language) 日语 Rìyǔ
jar [dʒɑː^r] N [c] 广口瓶
guǎngkǒupíng [个 gè]

jaw [dʒɔː] (Anat) I N [c] 颌 骨 [个
个] **II jaws** NPL 嘴巴 zuǐbā

jazz [dʒæz] N [U] (Mus) 爵士乐
juéshìyuè

jealous ['dʒeləs] ADJ 1 [+ husband,
wife] 爱妒忌的 ài dùjì de
2 (envious) 妒忌的 dùjì de

jeans [dʒiːnz] NPL 牛仔裤
niúzǎikù ▸ **a pair of jeans** 一条牛
仔裤 yītiáo niúzǎikù

jelly ['dʒelɪ] N [c/u] (US) 果酱
guǒjiàng [瓶 píng]

jersey ['dʒɜːzɪ] N [c] 针织毛衫
zhēnzhī máoshān [件 jiàn]

Jesus ['dʒiːzəs] N (Rel) 耶稣 Yēsū
▸ **Jesus Christ** 耶稣基督 Yēsū Jīdū

jet [dʒet] N [c] (aeroplane) 喷气式
飞机 pēnqìshì fēijī [架 jià]

jet lag N [U] 时差反应 shíchā
fǎnyìng

Jew [dʒuː] N [c] 犹太人 Yóutàirén
[个 gè]

jewel ['dʒuːəl] N [c] 宝石 bǎoshí
[块 kuài]

jewellery, (US) **jewelry** ['dʒuːəl
rɪ] N [U] 首饰 shǒushì

Jewish ['dʒuːɪʃ] ADJ 犹太的
Yóutài de

jigsaw ['dʒɪgsɔː] N [c] (also: **jigsaw
puzzle**) 拼图玩具 pīntú wánjù
[套 tào]

job [dʒɒb] N [c] **1** (position) 工作
gōngzuò [份 fèn] **2** (task) 任务
rènwù [项 xiàng] ▸ **Gladys got
a job as a secretary** 格拉迪斯
找到了一份秘书工作。Gélādísī
zhǎodào le yīfèn mìshū gōngzuò.
▸ **a part-time/full-time job** 半
职/全职工作 bànzhí/quánzhí

gōngzuò

jockey ['dʒɒkɪ] N [c] (Sport) 赛马骑
师 sàimǎ qíshī [位 wèi]

jog [dʒɒg] VI 慢跑 mànpǎo

jogging ['dʒɒgɪŋ] N [U] 慢跑
mànpǎo

join [dʒɔɪn] VT **1** [+ club, party, army,
navy, queue] 加入 jiārù **2** [+ person]
会面 huìmiàn ▸ **will you join us
for dinner?** 你想不想和我们一
起吃晚饭？nǐ xiǎng búxiǎng hé
wǒmen yīqǐ chīwǎnfàn?
▸ **join in** VI 参与 cānyù

joint [dʒɔɪnt] N [c] **1** 关节 guānjié
[个 gè], (Brit: Culin: of beef, lamb)
大块肉 dàkuàiròu [块 kuài]

joke [dʒəuk] I N [c] 笑话 xiàohuà
[个 gè] II VI 开玩笑 kāi wánxiào
▸ **you're joking** or **you must be
joking!** (inf) 你准在开玩笑〔或〕你
一定在开玩笑呢！nǐ zài kāi
wánxiào〔huò〕nǐ yīdìng zài kāi
wánxiào ba!

Jordan ['dʒɔːdən] N 约旦 Yuēdàn

journalist ['dʒɜːnəlɪst] N [c] 新
闻工作者 xīnwén gōngzuòzhě
[位 wèi]

journey ['dʒɜːnɪ] N [c] 旅程
lǚchéng [段 duàn] ▸ **a 5-hour
journey** 5个小时的路程 wǔgè
xiǎoshí de lǚchéng ▸ **to go on a
journey** 去旅行 qù lǚxíng

请勿将 **journey, voyage**
和 **trip** 混淆。**journey**
是指从一地搭乘车船或飞
机到另一地的过程。... a
journey of over 2000 miles...
如果你 **journey to** 某
地，你就是去那里。

书面的用法。*The nights became colder as they journeyed north.* **voyage** 是指从一地到一地的长途行程，通常指乘船旅行或者太空旅行。*...the voyage to the moon in 1972.* **trip** 是指从一地到一地的旅行过程，在目的地做短暂的停留后返回。*...a business trip to Milan.*

joy [dʒɔɪ] N [U] 快乐 kuàilè

judge [dʒʌdʒ] I N [C] 1 (*Law*) 法官 fǎguān [位 wèi] 2 (*in competition*) 裁判 cáipàn [个 gè] II VT [+ *exhibits, competition*] 评定 píngdìng

judo ['dʒuːdəu] N [U] 柔道 róudào

jug [dʒʌg] N [C] 壶 hú [把 bǎ]

juice [dʒuːs] N [C/U] 汁 zhī [杯 bēi]

July [dʒuˈlaɪ] N [C/U] 七月 qīyuè
▸the first of July 七月一日 qīyuè yīrì ▸at the beginning/end of July 在七月初/末 zài qīyuè chū/mò ▸each or every July 每年七月 měinián qīyuè

jump [dʒʌmp] I VI 跳 tiào II N [c] 跳 tiào ▸to jump over sth 跳过某物 tiàoguò mǒuwù ▸to jump out of a window 从窗户跳下 cóng chuānghu tiàoxià ▸to jump on/off sth 跳上/下某物 tiàoshàng/xià mǒuwù ▸to jump the queue (*Brit*) 加塞儿 jiāsāi'r

jumper ['dʒʌmpər] N [C] (*Brit*) 毛衣 máoyī [件 jiàn]

junction ['dʒʌŋkʃən] (*Brit*) N [C] 交叉点 jiāochādiǎn [个 gè]

June [dʒuːn] N [C/U] 六月 liùyuè

see also July

jungle ['dʒʌŋgl] N [C/U] 丛林 cónglín [片 piàn]

junior ['dʒuːnɪər] ADJ 级别低的 jíbié dī de ▸George Bush Junior (US) 小乔治•布什 xiǎo Qiáozhì•Bùshí

junior high, (US) **junior high school** N [C/U] 初中 chūzhōng [所 suǒ]

junior school (*Brit*) N [C/U] 小学 xiǎoxué [所 suǒ]

junk [dʒʌŋk] N [U] (*inf: rubbish*) 废旧杂物 fèijiù záwù

jury ['dʒuərɪ] N [C] 1 (*Law*) 陪审团 péishěntuán [个 gè] 2 (*in competition*) 评审团 píngshěntuán [个 gè]

just [dʒʌst] I ADJ (*frm*) [+ *decision, punishment, reward*] 公平的 gōngpíng de; [+ *society, cause*] 公正的 gōngzhèng de II ADV 1 (*exactly*) 正好 zhènghǎo 2 (*merely*) 仅仅 jǐnjǐn 3 (*for emphasis*) 简直 jiǎnzhí 4 (*in instructions, requests*) 只是 zhǐshì ▸it's just right 正合适 zhèng héshì ▸I'm just finishing this 我马上就做完了 wǒ mǎshàng jiù zuòwán le ▸we were just going 我们正要走 wǒmen zhèngyào zǒu ▸to have just done sth 刚刚做完某事 gānggāng zuòwán mǒushì ▸just now (*a moment ago*) 刚才 gāngcái; (*at the present time*) 现在 xiànzài ▸just about everything/everyone 差不多所有东西/所有人 chàbùduō suǒyǒu dōngxi/suǒyǒu rén ▸just before/after... 就在…以前/以后 jiùzài…yǐqián/yǐhòu ▶ **just enough time/money** 时间/钱正好够 shíjiān/qián zhènghǎo gòu ▶ **just a minute, just one moment** (asking someone to wait) 等一下 děng yīxià; (interrupting) 慢着 mànzhe

justice ['dʒʌstɪs] N 1 [U] (Law: system) 司法 sīfǎ 2 [U] (fairness) 正义 zhèngyì

K

K ABBR 1 (inf) (= **thousands**) 千 qiān 2 (Comput) (= **kilobytes**) 千字节 qiānzìjié

kangaroo [kæŋgə'ru:] N [C] 袋鼠 dàishǔ [只 zhī]

karaoke [kɑ:rə'əʊkɪ] N [U] 卡拉 OK kǎlā ōukèi

karate [kə'rɑ:tɪ] N [U] 空手道 kōngshǒudào

keen [ki:n] ADJ 热衷的 rèzhōng de ▶ **to be keen to do sth** 渴望做某事 kěwàng zuò mǒushì ▶ **to be keen on sth** 热衷于某事 rèzhōng yú mǒushì

keep [ki:p] (pt, pp **kept**) VT 1 [+ receipt, money, job] 保留 bǎoliú 2 (store) 保存 bǎocún 3 (detain) 留住 liúzhù ▶ **to keep doing sth** (repeatedly) 总是做某事 zǒngshì zuò mǒushì (continuously) 不停做某事 bùtíng zuò mǒushì ▸ to keep sb waiting 让某人等着 ràng mǒurén děngzhe ▸ to keep the room tidy 保持房间整洁 bǎochí fángjiān zhěngjié ▸ to keep a promise 履行诺言 lǚxíng nuòyán ▸ can you keep a secret? 你能保守秘密吗？nǐ néng bǎoshǒu mìmì ma? ▸ to keep a record (of sth) 记录(某事) jìlù (mǒushì) ▸ how are you keeping? (inf) 你还好吗？nǐ hái hǎo ma?

▸ keep away vɪ ▸ to keep away (from sth) 不接近(某处) bù jiējìn (mǒuchù)

▸ keep off vT FUS ▸ keep off the grass! 请勿进入草坪！qǐng wù jìnrù cǎopíng!

▸ keep on vɪ ▸ to keep on doing sth 继续做某事 jìxù zuò mǒushì

▸ keep up vɪ ▸ to keep up 跟上 gēnshang ▸ to keep up with sb (walking, moving) 跟上某人 gēnshàng mǒurén; (in work) 跟上某人 gēnshàng mǒurén

keep-fit [ki:p'fɪt] CPD [+ class, session, course] 健身 jiànshēn

kept [kept] PT, PP of keep

kerb, (US) curb [kə:b] N [c] 路缘 lùyuán [个 gè]

ketchup ['kɛtʃəp] N [U] 番茄酱 fānqiéjiàng

kettle ['kɛtl] N [c] 水壶 shuǐhú [把 bǎ]

key [ki:] N [c] 1 (for lock, mechanism) 钥匙 yàoshi [把 bǎ] 2 [of computer, typewriter, piano] 键 jiàn [个 gè]

keyboard ['ki:bɔ:d] N [c] 键盘 jiànpán [个 gè]

keyhole ['ki:həul] N [c] 钥匙孔 yàoshikǒng [个 gè]

kick [kɪk] ɪ vT [+ person, ball] 踢 tī ɪɪ N [c] 踢 tī ▸ kick off vɪ 开赛 kāisài

kick-off ['kɪkɔf] N [s] 开场时间 kāichǎng shíjiān

kid [kɪd] N [c] 1 (inf: child) 小孩 xiǎohái [个 gè]; (teenager) 年轻人 niánqīngrén [个 gè] ▸ you're kidding! 你一定是在开玩笑吧！nǐ yídìng shì zài kāi wánxiào ba!

kidnap ['kɪdnæp] vT 绑架 bǎngjià

kidney ['kɪdnɪ] N 1 [c] (Anat) 肾脏 shènzàng [个 gè] 2 [c/U] (Culin) 腰子 yāozi [个 gè]

kill [kɪl] vT 1 [+ person, animal, plant] 致死 zhìsǐ 2 (murder) 谋杀 móushā ▸ my back's killing me (inf) 我的背疼死了 wǒde bèi téngsǐ le

killer ['kɪlər] N [c] 凶手 xiōngshǒu [个 gè]

kilo ['ki:ləu] N [c] 公斤 gōngjīn

kilometre, (US) kilometer ['kɪləmi:tər] N [c] 公里 gōnglǐ

kind [kaɪnd] ɪ ADJ 友好的 yǒuhǎo de ɪɪ N [c] (type, sort) 种类 zhǒnglèi [个 gè] ▸ an opportunity to meet all kinds of people 与各种各样的人见面的机会 yǔ gèzhǒng gèyàng de rén jiànmiàn de jīhuì ▸ it was so kind of them to help 他们来帮忙真是太好了 tāmen lái bāngmáng zhēnshì tàihǎo le

kindness ['kaɪndnɪs] N [U] 仁慈 réncí

king [kɪŋ] N [C] 国王 guówáng
[位 wèi]

kingdom ['kɪŋdəm] N [C] 王国
wángguó [个 gè]

kiss [kɪs] I N [C] 吻 wěn [个 gè]
II VT 吻 wěn ▸ **to give sb a kiss**
吻某人一下 wěn mǒurén yīxià
▸ **to kiss sb goodbye/goodnight**
与某人吻别/吻某人一下，道晚安
yǔ mǒurén wěnbié/wěn mǒurén
yīxià, dào wǎn'ān

kit [kɪt] N [U] (esp Brit: equipment)
成套用品 chéngtào yòngpǐn;
(clothing) 服装 fúzhuāng

kitchen ['kɪtʃɪn] N [C] 厨房
chúfáng [个 gè]

kite [kaɪt] N [C] 风筝 fēngzheng
[个 gè]

kitten ['kɪtn] N [C] 小猫 xiǎomāo
[只 zhī]

knee [ni:] N [C] 膝盖 xīgài [个 gè]

kneel [ni:l] (pt, pp knelt) VI (also:
kneel down) 跪下 guìxià

knew [nju:] PT of **know**

knickers ['nɪkəz] (Brit) NPL 女
式内裤 nǚshì nèikù ▸ **a pair of
knickers** 一条女式内裤 yītiáo
nǚshì nèikù

knife [naɪf] (pl knives) N [C] 刀
dāo [把 bǎ] ▸ **knife and fork** 刀
叉 dāochā

knit [nɪt] VI 织 zhī

knives [naɪvz] NPL of **knife**

knob [nɔb] N [C] 球形把手 qiúxíng
bǎshǒu [个 gè]

knock [nɔk] I VT (strike) 碰撞
pèngzhuàng II VI (on door, window)
敲 qiāo III N [C] 1 (blow, bump) 碰
撞 pèngzhuàng 2 (on door)

敲门声 qiāoménshēng [声 shēng]
▸ **to knock sb unconscious** (blow,
blast) 把某人打晕 bǎ mǒurén
dǎyūn
▸ **knock down** VT 1 (run over) 撞
倒 zhuàngdǎo 2 (demolish) 拆除
chāichú
▸ **knock out** VT 1 (make
unconscious) 打昏 dǎhūn 2 (Boxing)
击昏 jīhūn 3 (eliminate: in game,
competition) 淘汰 táotài
▸ **knock over** VT 撞倒
zhuàngdǎo

knot [nɔt] N [C] 结 jié [个 gè] ▸ **to
tie a knot** 打个结 dǎ gè jié

know [nəu] (pt knew, pp known)
VT 1 (+ facts, dates) 知道 zhīdào
2 (+ language) 懂 dǒng 3 (+ person,
place, subject) 认识 rènshi ▸ **to
know that...** 知道…… zhīdào……
▸ **to know where/when** 知道何
处/何时…… zhīdào héchù/héshí…
▸ **to get to know sb** 逐渐开始
了解某人 zhújiàn kāishǐ liǎojiě
mǒurén ▸ **to know about sth** 听
说过某事 tīngshuō guò mǒushì
▸ **yes, I know** 对，的确如此 duì,
díquè rúcǐ ▸ **you never know** 很
难讲 hěn nánjiǎng ▸ **you know**
(used for emphasis) 你得知道 nǐ
děi zhīdào

knowledge ['nɔlɪdʒ] N [U] 知
识 zhīshi ▸ **to (the best of) my
knowledge** 据我所知 jù wǒ
suǒzhī

known [nəun] PP of **know**

Koran [kɔ'rɑ:n] N ▸ **the Koran**
《古兰经》Gǔlánjīng

Korea [kə'rɪə] N see **North Korea**,

South Korea

Korean [kəˈriən] **I** ADJ 朝鲜的 Cháoxiǎn de **II** N **1** (person) 朝鲜人 Cháoxiǎnrén **2** (language) 朝鲜语 Cháoxiǎnyǔ

label [ˈleɪbl] **I** N [c] 标签 biāoqiān [个 gè] **II** VT 用标签标明 yòng biāoqiān biāomíng

labor [ˈleɪbəʳ] (US) N = **labour**

laboratory [ləˈbɒrətərɪ] N [c] 研究室 yánjiūshì [个 gè]

labor union (US) N [c] 工会 gōnghuì [个 gè]

labour, (US) **labor** [ˈleɪbəʳ] N [U] **1** (manpower) 劳动力 láodònglì **2** ▸ **Labour** (Labour Party) 工党 Gōngdǎng ▸ **to be in labour** (Med) 处于阵痛期 chǔyú zhèntòng qī

lace [leɪs] N **1** [U] (fabric) 花边 huābiān **2** [c] (of shoe) 系带 jìdài [根 gēn]

lack [læk] **I** N [s/U] 缺乏 quēfá **II** VT [+ means, skills, experience, confidence] 缺乏 quēfá

ladder ['lædəʳ] N [c] 梯子 tīzi [个 gè]

lady ['leɪdɪ] N [c] 女士 nǚshì [位 wèi] ▶ladies and gentlemen... 女士们，先生们... ▶nǚshìmen, xiānshēngmen... ▶the ladies' (Brit), the ladies' room (US) 女厕所 nǚ cèsuǒ

lager ['lɑːɡəʳ] (Brit) N [c/u] 淡啤酒 dànpíjiǔ [瓶 píng]

laid [leɪd] PT, PP of **lay**

lain [leɪn] PP of **lie**

lake [leɪk] N [c] 湖 hú [个 gè]

lamb [læm] N 1 [c] (animal) 羔羊 gāoyáng [只 zhī] 2 [u] (meat) 羔羊肉 gāoyángròu

lamp [læmp] N [c] 灯 dēng [盏 zhǎn]

lamp-post ['læmppəʊst] (Brit) N [c] 路灯柱 lùdēngzhù [个 gè]

lampshade ['læmpʃeɪd] N [c] 灯罩 dēngzhào [个 gè]

land [lænd] N 1 [u] (area of open ground) 土地 tǔdì 2 [u] (not sea) 陆地 lùdì II V 1 (Aviat, Space) 降落 jiàngluò 2 (from ship) 登陆 dēnglù

landing ['lændɪŋ] N [c] (Aviat) 降落 jiàngluò [次 cì]

landlady ['lændleɪdɪ] N [c] 女房东 nǚfángdōng [位 wèi]

landlord ['lændlɔːd] N [c] 男房东 nánfángdōng [位 wèi]

landscape ['lændskeɪp] N [c/u] 风景 fēngjǐng [道 dào]

lane [leɪn] N 1 (in country) 小路 xiǎolù [条 tiáo] 2 (Aut: of road) 车道 chēdào [条 tiáo]

language ['læŋɡwɪdʒ] N 1 [c] (English, Russian etc) 语言 yǔyán [种 zhǒng] 2 [u] (speech) 语言表达能力 yǔyán biǎodá nénglì

language laboratory N [c] 语言实验室 yǔyán shíyànshì [个 gè]

lap [læp] N [c] 1 (of person) 大腿的上方 dàtuǐ de shàngfāng 2 (in race) 圈 quān

laptop ['læptɔp] N [c] (also: **laptop computer**) 笔记本电脑 bǐjìběn diànnǎo [个 gè]

large [lɑːdʒ] ADJ 1 [+house, person] 大的 dà de 2 [+number, amount] 大量的 dàliàng de

laser ['leɪzəʳ] N 1 [u] (beam) 激光 jīguāng [束 shù] 2 [c] (machine) 激光器 jīguāngqì [台 tái]

last [lɑːst] I ADJ 1 (most recent) 最近的 zuìjìn de [+Monday, July, weekend etc] 上 shàng 2 (final) [of series, row] 最后的 zuìhòu de II PRON (final one) 最后一个 zuìhòu yī gè III ADV 1 (most recently) 最近 zuìjìn 2 (at the end) 最后 zuìhòu 3 (in final position) 最后 zuìhòu IV V1 (continue) 持续 chíxù ▶last week 上个星期 shàng gè xīngqī ▶last night (yesterday evening) 昨晚 zuówǎn; (during the night) 昨天夜里 zuótiān yèli ▶the last time (the previous time) 上一次 shàng yīcì ▶at (long) last (finally) 终于 zhōngyú ▶our house is the last but one 我们的房子是倒数第二个 wǒmen de fángzi shì dàoshù dì'èrge ▶it lasts (for) 2 hours 持续了两个小时 chíxù le liǎngge xiǎoshí

lastly ['lɑːstlɪ] ADV 最后 zuìhòu

late [leɪt] **I** ADJ **1** (*not on time*) 迟
的 chí de **2** (*after the usual time*) 稍
晚的 shāowǎn de **II** ADV **1** (*not on
time*) 迟 chí **2** (*after the usual time*)
晚 wǎn ▶**we're late** 我们迟到了
wǒmen chídào le ▶**sorry I'm late**
对不起，我迟到了 duìbuqǐ, wǒ
chídào le ▶**to be 10 minutes late**
迟到10分钟 chídào shí fēnzhōng
▶**in late May** 5月下旬 wǔyuè
xiàxún

lately [leɪtlɪ] ADV 最近 zuìjìn

later [leɪtə] ADV 以后 yǐhòu
▶**some time/weeks/years later**
一些时候/几个星期/几年以后
yìxiē shíhou/jǐgè xīngqī/jǐnián
yǐhòu ▶**later on** 以后 yǐhòu

latest [leɪtɪst] ADJ **1** [+ *book, film,
news*] 最新的 zuìxīn de **2** (*most
up-to-date*) 最新式的 zuì xīnshì de
▶**at the latest** 最迟 zuìchí

Latin [lætɪn] N [U] 拉丁语
Lādīngyǔ

Latin America N 拉丁美洲
Lādīngměizhōu

Latin American I ADJ 拉
丁美洲的 Lādīngměizhōu de
II N [c] (*person*) 拉丁美洲人
Lādīngměizhōurén [个 gè]

latter [lætə] N ▶**the latter** 后
者 hòuzhě

laugh [lɑːf] **I** N [c] 笑 xiào [阵
zhèn] **II** VI 笑 xiào
▶**laugh at** VT FUS 对……发笑
duì……fāxiào

launch [lɔːntʃ] VT **1** [+ *rocket,
missile, satellite*] 发射 fāshè
2 [+ *product, publication*] 推出
tuīchū

laundry [lɔːndrɪ] N [U] (*dirty
washing*) 待洗的衣物 dàixǐ de
yīwù; (*clean washing*) 洗好的衣物
xǐhǎo de yīwù

laundry detergent (US) N [U/c]
洗衣粉 xǐyīfěn

lavatory [lævətərɪ] (*Brit*) N [c] 卫
生间 wèishēngjiān [个 gè]

law [lɔː] N **1** [s/U] (*legal system*) 法
律 fǎlǜ **2** [c] (*regulation*) 法规 fǎguī
[条 tiáo] ▶**against the law** 违
法 wéifǎ ▶**to break the law** 违法
wéifǎ ▶**by law** 依照法律 yīzhào
fǎlǜ ▶**to study law** 学习法律
xuéxí fǎlǜ

lawn [lɔːn] N [c] 草坪 cǎopíng
[片 piàn]

lawnmower [lɔːnməuə] N [c]
割草机 gēcǎojī [部 bù]

lawyer [lɔːjə] N [c] 律师 lǜshī
[位 wèi]

lay [leɪ] (*pt, pp* **laid**) **I** PT *of* **lie II**
(*put*) 放 fàng ▶**to lay the table**
摆放餐具 bǎifàng cānjù
▶**lay down** VT (*put down*) 放下
fàngxià
▶**lay off** VT 解雇 jiěgù

layer [leɪə] N [c] 层 céng

layout [leɪaut] N [c] 布局 bùjú
[个 gè]

lazy [leɪzɪ] ADJ 懒惰的 lǎnduò de

lead¹ [liːd] (*pt, pp* **led**) N **1** N [c]
(*esp Brit: for dog*) 皮带 pídài [条
tiáo] **2** [c] (*Elec*) 导线 dǎoxiàn [根
gēn] **II** VT [+ *group, party, organization*]
领导
lǐngdǎo; [+ *march, demonstration,
parade*] 带领 dàilǐng **III** VI (*in race,
competition*) 领先 lǐngxiān **2** (*guide*) 带领 dàilǐng

be in the lead 领先 lǐngxiān ▸**to lead the way** (lit) 引路 yǐnlù; (fig) 率先 shuàixiān

▸**lead away** VT [+ prisoner] 带走 dàizǒu

▸**lead to** VT FUS (result in) 导致 dǎozhì

lead² [lɛd] N [U] 铅 qiān

leader ['liːdəʳ] N [c] 领导人 lǐngdǎorén (位 wèi)

leaf [liːf] N (pl **leaves**) 叶 yè (片 piàn)

leaflet ['liːflɪt] N [c] (booklet) 小册子 xiǎocèzi (本 běn); (single sheet) 传单 chuándān (份 fèn)

league [liːg] N [c] (Sport) 联赛 liánsài (季 jì)

leak [liːk] I N [c] (of liquid, gas) 裂隙 lièxì (条 tiáo) II VI (shoes, pipe, liquid, gas) 漏 lòu

lean [liːn] (pt, pp **leaned** or **leant**) I VT ▸**to lean sth on/against sth** 把某物靠在某物上 bǎ mǒuwù kàozài mǒuwù shàng II ADJ [+ meat] 瘦的 shòu de ▸**to lean against** [person] 靠在某物上 kàozài mǒuwù shàng ▸**to lean forward/back** 向前/后倾 xiàngqián/hòu qīng

▸**lean on** VT FUS 倚 yǐ

leap year N [c] 闰年 rùnnián (个 gè)

learn [ləːn] (pt, pp **learned** or **learnt**) I VT (study) [+ skill] 学 xué; [+ poem, song] 背 bèi II VI 学 xué ▸**to learn about sth** (study) 学到某物 xuédào mǒuwù ▸**to learn to do sth/how to do sth** 学做事/怎样做事 xuézuò shì

learnt [ləːnt] PT, PP of **learn**

least [liːst] I ADJ (noun) 最 zuìshǎo de II ADV 1 (adjective) ▸**the least expensive/attractive/interesting** 最便宜/没有魅力/没趣的 zuì piányi/méiyǒu mèilì/méi qù de 2 (verb) 最不 zuìbù III PRON ▸**the least** 最少 zuìshǎo ▸**at least** (in expressions of quantity, comparisons) 至少 zhìshǎo

leather ['lɛðəʳ] I N [U] 皮革 pígé II CPD [+ jacket, shoes, chair] 皮 pí

leave [liːv] (pt, pp **left**) I VT 1 [+ place] 离开 líkāi 2 [+ school, job, group] 放弃 fàngqì 3 (leave behind: deliberately) 留下 liúxià; (accidentally) 落 luò 4 [+ message] 留 liú II VI 1 (depart) [person] 离开 líkāi; [bus, train] 出发 chūfā 2 (give up school) 辍学 chuòxué; (give up job) 辞职 cízhí III N [U] 休假 xiūjià; (Mil) 假期 jiàqī ▸**to leave sth to sb** 把某物留给某人 bǎ mǒuwù liúgěi mǒurén ▸**to leave sb/sth alone** 不理会某人/某物 bù lǐhuì mǒurén/mǒuwù ▸**to leave for** [+ destination] 前往 qiánwǎng

▸**leave behind** VT (forget) 忘带 wàngdài

▸**leave on** VT [+ light, heating] 开着 kāizhe

▸**leave out** VT 删掉 shāndiào

leaves [liːvz] NPL of **leaf**

Lebanon, the Lebanon ['lɛbənən] N 黎巴嫩 Líbānèn

lecture ['lɛktʃəʳ] N [c] (talk) 讲

座 jiǎngzuò [个 gè] ▸to give a lecture (on sth) 作(某方面的)讲座 zuò (mǒu fāngmiàn de) jiǎngzuò

lecturer ['lɛktʃərər'] N [c] 讲师 jiǎngshī [位 wèi]

led [lɛd] PT, PP of **lead¹**

left¹ [lɛft] I ADJ (not right) 左的 zuǒ de II N ▸ the left 左侧 zuǒcè III ADV (turn, go, look) 向左 xiàngzuǒ ▸on the left 在左边 zài zuǒbiān ▸to the left 靠左边 kào zuǒbiān

left² [lɛft] I PT, PP of **leave** II ADJ ▸to be left over 剩下 shèngxià

left-hand ['lɛfthænd] ADJ [+ side, corner] 左侧的 zuǒcè de

left-handed [lɛft'hændɪd] ADJ 左撇子的 zuǒpiězi de

left-luggage [lɛft'lʌgɪdʒ] (Brit) N [U] ▸left-luggage locker 行李寄存柜 xínglǐ jìcún guì

leg [lɛg] N 1 [c] 腿 tuǐ [条 tiáo] [c/U] 腿 tuǐ [根 gēn]

legal ['li:gl] ADJ 1 [+ system, requirement] 法律的 fǎlǜ de 2 [+ action, situation] 合法的 héfǎ de

legal holiday (US) N [c] 法定假期 fǎdìng jiàqī [个 gè]

leisure ['lɛʒər', US 'li:ʒər] N [c] 闲暇 xiánxiá

leisure centre (Brit) N [c] 娱乐中心 yúlè zhōngxīn [个 gè]

lemon ['lɛmən] N [c] 柠檬 níngméng [个 gè]

lemonade [lɛmə'neɪd] N [U] 柠檬汽水 níngméng qìshuǐ

lend [lɛnd] (pt, pp lent) VT 1 ▸to

lend sth to sb 把某物借给某人 bǎ mǒuwù jiègěi mǒurén 2 [bank] 贷 dài

length [lɛŋθ] N 1 [c/U] 长度 chángdù [个 gè]; [of sentence, article] 篇幅 piānfú [个 gè] 2 [c/U] (duration) 期间 qījiān [个 gè]

lens [lɛnz] N [c]; [of spectacles] 镜片 jìngpiàn [片 piàn]; [of telescope, camera] 镜头 jìngtóu [个 gè]

Lent [lɛnt] N [U] 大斋节 Dàzhāijié

lent [lɛnt] PT, PP of **lend**

lentil ['lɛntɪl] N [c] 小扁豆 xiǎobiǎndòu [颗 kē]

Leo ['li:əu] N [U] (sign) 狮子座 Shīzi Zuò

leopard ['lɛpəd] N [c] 豹 bào [只 zhī]

lesbian ['lɛzbɪən] I ADJ 女同性恋的 nǚ tóngxìngliàn de II N [c] 女同性恋者 nǚ tóngxìngliànzhě [个 gè]

less [lɛs] I ADJ (noun) 更少的 gèng shǎo de II ADV 1 [of adjective/adverb] 较少地 jiàoshǎo de 2 [verb] 较少 jiàoshǎo III PRON 较少的东西 jiàoshǎo de dōngxi IV PREP ▸less tax/10% discount 去掉税/10%的折扣 qùdiào shuì/bǎifēnzhīshí de zhékòu ▸less than half 不到一半 búdào yíbàn

lesson ['lɛsn] N [c] 课 kè [堂 táng]

let [lɛt] (pt, pp let) VT 1 ▸to do sth (give permission) 允许某人做某事 yǔnxǔ mǒurén zuò mǒushì 2 ▸to let sth happen 让某事发生 ràng mǒushì fāshēng ▸to let sb know that... 告诉某人…gàosù mǒurén… 3 ▸to let sb in/out 让某人进去/出去 ràng mǒurén jìnqù/

chūqù ▸**let's go/eat** 我们走/吃吧 wǒmen zǒu/chībā ▸"现房待租" "xiànfáng dàizhū"

▸**to let go** (release one's grip) 松开 sōngkāi ▸**to let sb/sth go** (release) 放走某人／某物 fàngzǒu mǒurén/mǒuwù

▸**let down** VT [+ person] 令…失望 lìng…shīwàng

▸**let in** VT 1 [+ water, air] 允许进来 yǔnxǔ jìnlái 2 [+ person] 给…开门 gěi…kāimén

letter ['lɛtə'] N [c] 1 (note) 信 xìn [封 fēng] 2 [of alphabet] 字母 zìmǔ [个 gè]

letterbox ['lɛtəbɒks] (Brit) N [c] 信箱 xìnxiāng [个 gè]

lettuce ['lɛtɪs] N [c/u] 生菜 shēngcài [棵 kē]

level ['lɛvl] I ADJ 平的 píng de I N [c] 1 (standard) 水平 shuǐpíng [种 zhǒng] 2 (height) 水位 shuǐwèi [个 gè]

level crossing (Brit) N [c] 平交道口 píngjiāodàokǒu [个 gè]

lever ['liːvə', US 'lɛvə'] N [c] 杆 gǎn [根 gēn]

liar ['laɪə'] N [c] 说谎者 shuōhuǎngzhě [个 gè]

liberal ['lɪbərl] I ADJ [+ person, attitude] ▸ 开明的 kāimíng de II N [c] (Pol) ▸ **Liberal** 自由党党员 Zìyóudǎng dǎngyuán

Libra ['liːbrə] N [u] (sign) 天秤座 Tiānchèng Zuò

librarian [laɪ'brɛərɪən] N [c] 图书管理员 túshū guǎnlǐyuán [位 wèi]

library ['laɪbrərɪ] N [c] 图书馆 túshūguǎn [个 gè]

licence, (US) **license** ['laɪsns] N [c] (permit) 许可证 xǔkězhèng [张 zhāng] 2 [c] (also: driving licence) 驾驶执照 jiàshǐ zhízhào [本 běn]

license plate (US) N [c] 车牌照 chēpáizhào [个 gè]

lick [lɪk] VT 舔 tiǎn

lid [lɪd] N [c] 1 [of box, case, pan] 盖 gài [个 gè] 2 (eyelid) 眼睑 yǎnjiǎn [个 gè]

lie¹ [laɪ] (pt lay, pp lain) VI [person] 躺 tǎng

▸**lie about** (Brit) VI = **lie around**

▸**lie around** VI 乱放 luànfàng

▸**lie down** VI [person] 躺下 tǎngxià

lie² [laɪ] I VI 说谎 shuōhuǎng II N [c] 谎言 huǎngyán [个 gè] ▸**to tell lies** 说谎 shuōhuǎng

life [laɪf] N 1 [c/u] (living, existence) 生命 shēngmìng [个 gè] 2 [c] (lifespan) 一生 yìshēng [个 gè] ▸**his personal/working life** 他的个人/工作生活 tāde gèrén/gōngzuò shēnghuó

lifeboat ['laɪfbəut] N [c] 救生艇 jiùshēngtǐng [艘 sōu]

life preserver [-prɪ'zə:və'] (US) N [c] (lifebelt) 救生用具 jiùshēng yòngjù [件 jiàn]; (life jacket) 救生衣 jiùshēngyī [件 jiàn]

lifestyle ['laɪfstaɪl] N [c/u] 生活方式 shēnghuó fāngshì [种 zhǒng]

lift [lɪft] I VT 举起 jǔqǐ II N [c] (esp Brit) 电梯 diàntī [部 bù] ▸**to give sb a lift** (esp Brit) 让某人搭便车 ràng mǒurén dā biànchē

▸**lift up** VT [+ person, thing] 举起 jǔqǐ

light [laɪt] (pt, pp lit) I N 1 [U] (from sun, moon, lamp, fire) 光 guāng 2 [c] (Elec, Aut) 灯 dēng [盏 zhǎn] 3 [s] (for cigarette) 打火机 dǎhuǒjī II VT [+ candle, fire, cigarette] 点燃 diǎnrán III ADJ 1 [+ colour] 淡的 dàn de 2 (not heavy) 轻的 qīng de IV **lights** NPL (also: **traffic lights**) 交通指示灯 jiāotōng zhǐshìdēng ▶ **to turn** or **switch the light on/off** 开/关灯 kāi/guān dēng

light bulb N [c] 灯泡 dēngpào [个 gè]

lighter ['laɪtə'] N [c] (also: **cigarette lighter**) 打火机 dǎhuǒjī [个 gè]

lighthouse ['laɪthaʊs] N [c] 灯塔 dēngtǎ [座 zuò]

lightning ['laɪtnɪŋ] N [U] 闪电 shǎndiàn

like¹ [laɪk] PREP 1 (similar to) 像 xiàng 2 (in similes) 像…一样 xiàng…yīyàng 3 (such as) 如 rú ▶ **a house like ours** 像我们这样的房子 xiàng wǒmen zhèyàng de fángzi ▶ **to be like sth/sb** 像某物/某人 xiàng mǒuwù/mǒurén ▶ **what's the weather like?** 他/天气怎么样? tā/tiānqì zěnmeyàng? ▶ **to look like** [+ person] 长得像 zhǎngde xiàng; [+ thing] 类似 lèisì ▶ **what does it look/sound/taste like?** 看/听/尝起来怎么样? kàn/tīng/chángqǐlái zěnmeyàng? ▶ **like this** 像这样 xiàng zhèyàng

like² [laɪk] I VT [+ person, thing] 喜欢 xǐhuan II N ▶ **his likes and dislikes** 他的好恶 好恶 tā de hàowù

▶ **to like doing sth** 喜欢做某事 xǐhuān zuò mǒushì ▶ **I would** or **I'd like an ice-cream/to go for a walk** 我想吃个冰激凌/去散步。wǒxiǎng chīgè bīngjílíng/qù sànbù。▶ **would you like a coffee?** 你想不想来杯咖啡? nǐ xiǎngbùxiǎng láibēi kāfēi? ▶ **if you like** (in offers, suggestions) 如果你愿意的话 rúguǒ nǐ yuànyì de huà

likely ['laɪklɪ] ADJ 很可能的 hěn kěnéng de ▶ **it is likely that…** 有可能… yǒu kěnéng… ▶ **to be likely to do sth** 很有可能做某事 hěnyǒu kěnéng zuò mǒushì

lime [laɪm] N [c] (fruit) 酸橙 suānchéng [个 gè]

limit ['lɪmɪt] N [c] 1 (maximum point) 限度 xiàndù [个 gè] 2 限定 xiàndìng [种 zhǒng]

limp [lɪmp] VI 跛行 bǒxíng

line [laɪn] N [c] 1 (long thin mark) 线 xiàn [条 tiáo] 2 排 pái 3 [+ of words] 行 háng 4 (Tel) 线路 xiànlù [条 tiáo] 5 (railway track) 铁路线路 tiělù xiànlù [条 tiáo] ▶ **hold the line please!** (Tel) 请稍等! qǐng shāoděng! ▶ **to stand** or **wait in line** 排队等候 páiduì děnghòu ▶ **on the right lines** 大体正确 dàtǐ zhèngquè

linen ['lɪnɪn] I N [U] 1 (cloth) 亚麻布 yàmábù 2 (tablecloths, sheets) 亚麻制品 yàmá zhìpǐn II CPD [+ jacket, sheets] 亚麻料 yàmáliào

lining ['laɪnɪŋ] N [c/U] 衬里 chènlǐ [个 gè]

link [lɪŋk] N [c] 1 联系 liánxì [种 zhǒng] 2 (Comput) (also: **hyperlink**)

超链接 chāoliànjiē [个 gè] II VT
1 [+ places, objects] 连接 liánjiē
2 [+ people, situations] 联系 liánxì

lion ['laɪən] N [c] 狮子 shīzi [头
tóu]

lip [lɪp] N [c] 唇 chún [个 gè]

lip-read ['lɪpriːd] VI 唇读 chúndú

lipstick ['lɪpstɪk] N [c/u] 口红
kǒuhóng [支 zhī]

liquid ['lɪkwɪd] N [c/u] 液体 yètǐ
[种 zhǒng]

liquidizer ['lɪkwɪdaɪzər] N [c] 榨
汁机 zhàzhījī [个 gè]

liquor ['lɪkər] (US) N [u] 酒 jiǔ

list [lɪst] I N [c] 单子 dānzi [个 gè]
II VT 1 (record) [person] 列出 lièchū
2 (Comput) 列出 lièchū

listen ['lɪsn] VI 1 听 tīng; (to
speaker) 听…说话 tīng…shuō
2 (follow advice) 听从 tīngcóng
▸ to listen to sb (pay attention
to) 留神听某人说话 liúshén tīng
mǒurén shuōhuà; (follow advice of)
听从某人 tīngcóng mǒurén
▸ to listen to sth 听某事 tīng mǒushì

lit [lɪt] PT, PP of light

liter ['liːtər] (US) N = litre

literature ['lɪtrɪtʃər] N [u] 文学
wénxué

litre, (US) liter ['liːtər] N [c] 升
shēng

litter ['lɪtər] N [u] 垃圾 lājī

litter bin (Brit) N [c] 垃圾箱
lājīxiāng [个 gè]

little ['lɪtl] I ADJ 1 (small) 小的 xiǎo
de 2 (young) 小的 xiǎo de
3 (younger) ▸ little brother/
sister 弟弟/妹妹 dìdi/mèimei
4 (quantifier) ▸ to have little

time/money 没有多少时间/
钱 méiyǒu duōshao shíjiān/jīnqián
II ADV 少 shǎo ▸ a little (small
amount) 一点 yìdiǎn; (noun) 一
点 yìdiǎn; (sleep, eat) 一点 yìdiǎn
▸ a little boy of 8 一个8岁的小
男孩 yígè bāsuì de xiǎo nánhái
▸ a little bit (adj) 有点 yǒudiǎn
▸ little by little 逐渐地 zhújiàn de

live¹ [lɪv] VI 1 (reside) 住 zhù
2 (lead one's life) 生活 shēnghuó
II VT [+ life] 过 guò
▸ live on VT FUS [+ money] 靠…维
持生活 kào…wéichí shēnghuó
▸ live together VI 同居 tóngjū
▸ live with VT FUS [+ partner]
与…同居 yǔ…tóngjū

live² [laɪv] I ADJ [+ animal, plant] 活
的 huó de II ADV (broadcast) 实况
地 shíkuàng de

lively ['laɪvlɪ] ADJ [+ person] 活
泼的 huópo de; [+ place, event,
discussion] 活跃的 huóyuè de

liver ['lɪvər] N 1 [c] 肝脏 gānzàng
[个 gè] 2 [c/u] (Culin) 肝 gān
[个 gè]

lives [laɪvz] NPL of life

living ['lɪvɪŋ] N [u] (life) 生活
shēnghuó ▸ for a living 作为谋生
之道 zuòwéi móushēng zhīdào ▸ to
earn or make a/one's living 谋生
móushēng

living room N [c] 起居室 qǐjūshì
[间 jiān]

load [ləud] I N [c] (thing carried)
[of vehicle] 装载量 zhuāngzàiliàng
[车 chē] II VT 1 (also: load up)
[+ vehicle, ship] 装满 zhuāngmǎn
2 [+ program, software] 下载 xiàzài

▶**loads of** or **a load of money/ people** (inf) 很多钱/人 hěnduō qián/rén

loaf [ləuf] (pl **loaves**) N [c] ▶**a loaf (of bread)** 一条(面包) yìtiáo (miànbāo)

loan [ləun] I N [c] 贷款 dàikuǎn [笔 bǐ] II VT ▶**to loan sth (out) to sb** [+ money, thing] 把某物借给某人 bǎ mǒuwù jiègěi mǒurén

loaves [ləuvz] NPL of **loaf**

local [ˈləukl] ADJ [+ council, newspaper, library] 当地的 dāngdì de; [+ residents] 本地的 běndì de

lock [lɔk] I N [c] 锁 suǒ [把 bǎ] II VT1 锁 suǒ2 [+ screen] 锁定 suǒdìng
▶**lock out** VT [+ person (deliberately)] 把…锁在外面 bǎ…suǒ zài wàimian ▶**to lock o.s. out** 把自己锁在外面 bǎ zìjǐ suǒ zài wàimian
▶**lock up** VT 锁好 suǒhǎo

locker [ˈlɔkəʳ] N [c] 小柜 xiǎoguì [个 gè]

lodger [ˈlɔdʒəʳ] N [c] 房客 fángkè [个 gè]

loft [lɔft] N [c] (attic) 阁楼 gélóu [座 zuò]

log [lɔg] N [c] (for fuel) 木柴 mùchái [根 gēn]
▶**log in, log on** (Comput) VI 登录 dēnglù
▶**log into** (Comput) VT FUS 登入 dēngrù
▶**log out, log off** (Comput) VI 退出系统 tuìchū xìtǒng

logical [ˈlɔdʒɪkl] ADJ [+ argument, analysis] 逻辑的 luójí de; [+ conclusion, result] 合逻辑的 hé

luójí de; [+ course of action] 合乎情理的 héhū qínglǐ de

London [ˈlʌndən] N 伦敦 Lúndūn

Londoner [ˈlʌndənəʳ] N [c] 伦敦人 Lúndūnrén [个 gè]

lonely [ˈləunlɪ] ADJ1 [+ person] 孤独的 gūdú de 2 [+ place] 人迹罕至的 rénjì hǎn zhì de

long [lɔŋ] I ADJ1 [+ rope, hair, table, tunnel] 长的 cháng de 2 [+ meeting, discussion, film, time] 长的 cháng de 3 [+ book, poem] 长的 cháng de II ADV (time) 长久 chángjiǔ ▶**how long is the lesson?** 这节课多长时间？zhèjiékè duōcháng shíjiān? ▶**6 metres long** 6米长 liùmǐ cháng ▶**so** or **as long as** (provided) 只要 zhǐyào ▶**long ago** 很久以前 hěnjiǔ yǐqián ▶**it won't take long** 这不需花很多时间 zhè bù xūyào huā hěnduō shíjiān ▶**a long way** 很远 hěnyuǎn

loo [lu:] (Brit: inf) N [c] 厕所 cèsuǒ [个 gè]

look [luk] I VI 1 (glance, gaze) 看 kàn 2 (search) 找 zhǎo 3 (seem, appear) 看起来 kànqǐlái II N (expression) 表情 biǎoqíng [副 fù]
▶**to look out of the window** 望向窗外 wàngxiàng chuāngwài ▶**look out!** 当心！dāngxīn! ▶**to look like sb** 长得像某人 zhǎngde xiàng mǒurén ▶**to look like sth** 看起来像某物 kànqǐlái xiàng mǒuwù ▶**it looks as if...** 看来… kànlái... ▶**to have** or **take a look at** 看一看 kànyīkàn
▶**look after** VT FUS 照顾 zhàogù

▶ **look at** VT FUS 看一看 kàn yī kàn

▶ **look for** VT FUS [+ person, thing] 寻找 xúnzhǎo

▶ **look forward to** VT FUS 盼望 pànwàng ▶ **to look forward to doing sth** 盼望做某事 pànwàng zuò mǒushì ▶ **we look forward to hearing from you** 我们盼望收到你的回音 wǒmen pànwàng shōudào nǐde huíyīn

▶ **look into** VT FUS (investigate) 调查 diàochá

▶ **look round, look around** I VI **1** (turn head) 环顾 huángù **2** (in building) 看一看 kànkàn II VT FUS [+ place, building] 游览 yóulǎn

▶ **look through** VT FUS [+ book, magazine, papers] 翻阅 fānyuè

▶ **look up** VT [+ information, meaning] 查 chá

loose [luːs] ADJ **1** [+ screw, connection, tooth] 松动的 sōngdòng de **2** [+ hair] 散开的 sǎnkāi de **3** [+ clothes, trousers] 宽松的 kuānsōng de

lord [lɔːd] (Brit) N [c] (peer) 贵族 guìzú [位 wèi]

lorry [ˈlɒrɪ] (Brit) N [c] 卡车 kǎchē [辆 liàng]

lorry driver (Brit) N [c] 卡车司机 kǎchē sījī [位 wèi]

lose [luːz] (pt, pp lost) I VT **1** (mislay) 丢失 diūshī **2** (not win) [+ contest, fight, argument] 输掉 shūdiào **3** (through death) [+ relative, wife etc] 失去 shīqù II VI 输 shū ▶ **to lose weight** 减重 jiǎnzhòng

loss [lɒs] N [c/u] 丧失 sàngshī

[种 zhǒng]

lost [lɒst] I PT, PP of lose II ADJ [+ object] 丢失的 diūshī de [+ person, animal] 走失的 zǒushī de ▶ **to get lost** 迷路 mílù

lost and found (US) N = **lost property**

lost property N [u] (Brit) **1** (things) 招领的失物 zhāolǐng de shīwù **2** (Brit: office) 失物招领处 shīwù zhāolǐngchù

lot [lɒt] N [c] ▶ **a lot** (many) 许多 xǔduō; (much) 很多 hěnduō ▶ **a lot of** 许多 xǔduō ▶ **lots of** 许多 xǔduō ▶ **he reads/smokes a lot** 他书读得/烟抽得很多 tā dúde/yān chōude hěnduō

lottery [ˈlɒtərɪ] N [c] 彩票 cǎipiào [张 zhāng]

loud [laʊd] I ADJ 响亮的 xiǎngliàng de II ADV (speak) 大声地 dàshēng de

loudly [ˈlaʊdlɪ] ADV 大声地 dàshēng de

loudspeaker [laʊdˈspiːkəʳ] N [c] 扬声器 yángshēngqì [个 gè]

lounge [laʊndʒ] N [c] **1** (in hotel) 休息室 xiūxishì [间 jiān] **2** (at airport, station) 等候室 děnghòushì [间 jiān] **3** 起居室 qǐjūshì [间 jiān]

love [lʌv] I N [u] (for partner, sweetheart) 爱情 àiqíng; (for child, pet) 爱 ài II VT [+ partner, child, pet] 爱 ài; [+ thing, food, activity] 热爱 rè'ài ▶ **to be in love (with sb)** 和（某人）恋爱 (yǔ mǒurén) liàn'ài ▶ **to fall in love (with sb)** 爱上（某人）àishàng (mǒurén)

做爱 zuò'ài ▸ love (from) Anne (on letter) 爱你的，安妮 àinǐde, Ānní ▸ to love doing/to do sth 喜欢做某事 xǐ'ài zuò mǒushì ▸ I'd love to come 我非常想来 wǒ fēicháng xiǎng lái

lovely ['lʌvlɪ] (esp Brit) ADJ
1 [+ place, person, music] 漂亮的 piàoliang de **2** [+ holiday, meal, present] 令人愉快的 lìng rén yúkuài de; [+ person] 可爱的 kě'ài de

lover ['lʌvər] N [c] 情人 qíngrén [个 gè] ▸ a lover of art or an art lover 钟爱艺术的人 zhōng'ài yìshù de rén

low [ləʊ] ADJ **1** [+ wall, hill, heel] 矮的 ǎi de **2** [+ temperature, price, level, speed] 低的 dī de **3** [+ standard, quality] 低劣的 dīliè de ▸ low in calories/salt/fat 低卡路里/盐/脂肪的 dī kǎlùlǐ/yán/zhīfáng

lower ['ləʊər] VT (reduce) 降低 jiàngdī

loyal ['lɔɪəl] ADJ 忠实的 zhōngshí de

loyalty ['lɔɪəltɪ] N [U] 忠诚 zhōngchéng

luck [lʌk] N [U] **1** (chance) 运气 yùnqì **2** (good fortune) 幸运 xìngyùn ▸ good luck 好运 hǎoyùn ▸ good luck! or best of luck! 祝你好运! zhùnǐ hǎoyùn! ▸ bad luck 不走运 bù zǒuyùn

luckily ['lʌkɪlɪ] ADV 幸运的是 xìngyùn de shì

lucky ['lʌkɪ] ADJ [+ person] 幸运的 xìngyùn de ▸ to be lucky 走

运 zǒuyùn ▸ it is lucky that... 侥幸的是… jiǎoxìng de shì... ▸ to have a lucky escape 侥幸逃脱 jiǎoxìng táotuō

luggage ['lʌgɪdʒ] N [U] 行李 xíngli ▸ piece of luggage 一件行李 yíjiàn xíngli

lunch [lʌntʃ] N **1** [c/U] (meal) 午餐 wǔcān [顿 dùn] **2** [U] (lunchtime) 午餐时间 wǔcān shíjiān ▸ to have lunch (with sb) (与某人)共进午餐 (yǔ mǒurén) gòngjìn wǔcān

lung [lʌŋ] N [c] 肺 fèi [片 piàn]

Luxembourg ['lʌksəmbɜːg] (Geo) N 卢森堡 Lúsēnbǎo

luxurious [lʌgˈzjʊərɪəs] ADJ 豪华的 háohuá de

luxury ['lʌkʃərɪ] I N [U] (comfort) 奢华 shēhuá II CPD [+ hotel, car, goods] 豪华 háohuá

lying ['laɪɪŋ] VB see **lie**¹ see **lie**²

lyrics ['lɪrɪks] NPL 词句 cíjù

m

mac [mæk] (Brit: inf) N [c] 雨衣 yǔyī [件 jiàn]

machine [məˈʃiːn] N [c] 机器 jīqì [台 tái]

machine gun N [c] 机关枪 jīguānqiāng [架 jià]

machinery [məˈʃiːnərɪ] N [U] 机器 jīqì

mad [mæd] ADJ 1 (insane) 精神失常的 jīngshén shīcháng de 2 (inf: angry) 恼怒的 nǎonù de ▸ **to go mad** 发疯 fāfēng; (get angry) 发火 fāhuǒ ▸ **to be mad about** or **on sth** (inf) 狂热地爱好某物 kuángrè de àihào mǒuwù

madam [ˈmædəm] N 女士 nǚshì ▸ **Dear Madam** 尊敬的女士 zūnjìng de nǚshì

made [meɪd] PT, PP of **make**

madness [ˈmædnɪs] N [U] 1 (insanity) 疯狂 fēngkuáng 2 (foolishness) 愚蠢 yúchǔn

magazine [mægəˈziːn] N [c] 杂志 zázhì [份 fèn]

magic [ˈmædʒɪk] I N [U] 1 魔法 mófǎ II ADJ 1 [+ formula, solution, cure] 神奇的 shénqí de 2 (supernatural) 魔法的 mófǎ de

magnet [ˈmæɡnɪt] N [c] 磁铁 cítiě [块 kuài]

maid [meɪd] N [c] (servant) 女仆 nǚpú [个 gè]

maiden name [ˈmeɪdn-] N [c] 娘家姓 niángjiā xìng [个 gè]

mail [meɪl] I N [U] 1 ▸ **the mail** 邮政 yóuzhèng 2 (letters) 邮件 yóujiàn 3 (e-mail) 电子邮件 diànzǐ yóujiàn II VT 1 (esp US: post) 寄出 jìchū 2 (e-mail) 发电邮给 fā diànyóu gěi ▸ **by mail** 以邮寄方式 yǐ yóujì fāngshì

mailbox [ˈmeɪlbɒks] N [c] 1 (US: for letters) 信箱 xìnxiāng [个 gè] 2 (US) 邮筒 yóutǒng [个 gè] 3 (Comput) 电子信箱 diànzǐ xìnxiāng [个 gè]

mailman [ˈmeɪlmæn] (pl **mailmen**) (US) N [c] 邮差 yóuchāi [个 gè]

mailwoman [ˈmeɪlwumən] (pl **mailwomen**) (US) N [c] 女邮递员 nǚ yóudìyuán [位 wèi]

main [meɪn] ADJ 主要的 zhǔyào de

main course N [c] 主菜 zhǔcài [道 dào]

mainly [ˈmeɪnlɪ] ADV 主要地 zhǔyào de

main road N [C] 主干道 zhǔ gàndào [条 tiáo]

majesty ['mædʒɪstɪ] N (title)
▸ **Your/His/Her Majesty** 陛下 bìxià

major ['meɪdʒə^r] I ADJ 重要的 zhòngyào de II N [C] 1 (Mil) 少校 shàoxiào [位 wèi] 2 (US) 专业 zhuānyè [个 gè]

majority [mə'dʒɒrɪtɪ] N [s + PL VB] 大多数 dàduōshù

make [meɪk] (pt, pp made) I VT 1 [+ object, clothes, cake] 做 zuò; [+ noise] 制造 zhìzào; [+ mistake] 犯 fàn (manufacture) 生产 shēngchǎn (cause to be) ▸ **to make sb sad** 使某人难过 shǐ mǒurén nánguò 4 (force) 促使某人做某事 cùshǐ mǒurén zuò mǒushì 5 [+ money] 挣 zhèng 6 (equal) ▸ **2 and 2 make 4** 2加2等于4 èrjiā'èr děngyú sì II N [C] (brand) 牌子 páizi [个 gè] ▸ **to make a profit/loss** 赢利/赔钱 yínglì/péiqián ▸ **what change do you make it?** 表几点了? nǐ biǎo jǐdiǎn le ▸ **it's made (out) of glass** 是玻璃做的 shì bōli zuò de
▸ **make out** VT [+ cheque] 开出 kāichū
▸ **make up** VT 1 [+ story, excuse] 捏造 niēzào 2 (with cosmetics) 化妆 huàzhuāng ▸ **to make up one's mind** 下定决心 xià dìng juéxīn ▸ **to make o.s. up** 化妆 huàzhuāng

make-up ['meɪkʌp] N [U] (cosmetics) 化妆品 huàzhuāngpǐn

Malaysia [mə'leɪzɪə] N 马来西亚 Mǎláixīyà

male [meɪl] ADJ [+ employee, child, model, friend, population] 男的 nán de; [+ animal, insect, plant, tree] 雄性的 xióngxìng de

mall [mɔːl] N [C] (also: **shopping mall**) 大型购物中心 dàxíng gòuwù zhōngxīn [个 gè]

Malta ['mɔːltə] N 马耳他 Mǎ'ěrtā

mammal ['mæml] N [C] 哺乳动物 bǔrǔ dòngwù [个 gè]

man [mæn] (pl **men**) N 1 [C] (person) 男人 nánrén [个 gè] 2 [U] (mankind) 人类 rénlèi

manage ['mænɪdʒ] I VT [+ business, shop, time, money] 管理 guǎnlǐ II VI (cope) 应付 yìngfù ▸ **to manage to do sth** 设法做到某事 shèfǎ zuòdào mǒushì

management ['mænɪdʒmənt] N 1 [U] (managing) 管理 guǎnlǐ 2 [U/S] (managers) 管理人员 guǎnlǐ rényuán

manager ['mænɪdʒə^r] N [C] 1 经理 jīnglǐ [位 wèi] 2 (Sport) 球队经理 qiúduì jīnglǐ [位 wèi]

mandarin ['mændərɪn] N 1 [U] ▸ **Mandarin (Chinese)** 普通话 Pǔtōnghuà 2 [C] (also: **mandarin orange**) 柑橘 gānjú [个 gè]

maniac ['meɪnɪæk] N [C] (lunatic) 疯子 fēngzi [个 gè]

manner ['mænə^r] I N [S] (way) 方式 fāngshì II **manners** NPL 礼貌 lǐmào ▸ **it's good/bad manners to arrive on time** 准时是有礼貌/无礼的表现 zhǔnshí shì yǒu lǐmào/wúlǐ de biǎoxiàn

manual ['mænjʊəl] N [c] (handbook) 手册 shǒu cè [本 běn]

manufacture [mænjʊ'fæktʃəʳ] VT 生产 shēngchǎn

manufacturer [mænjʊ'fæktʃərəʳ] N [c] 制造商 zhìzàoshāng [个 gè]

many ['menɪ] I ADJ (a lot of) 许多的 xǔduō de II PRON 许多的 xǔduō de ▸ how many (direct question) 多少 duōshǎo ▸ twice as many (as) (是…的) 两倍 (shì…de) liǎngbèi

map [mæp] N [c] 地图 dìtú [张 zhāng]

marathon ['mærəθən] N [c] (race) 马拉松长跑 mǎlāsōng chángpǎo [次 cì]

marble ['mɑːbl] I N [u] 大理石 dàlǐshí II marbles NPL (game) 弹子游戏 dànzǐ yóuxì

March [mɑːtʃ] N [c/u] 三月 sānyuè; see also **July**

march [mɑːtʃ] VI 行军 xíngjūn

margarine [mɑːdʒə'riːn] N [u] 人造黄油 rénzào huángyóu

marijuana [mærɪ'wɑːnə] N [u] 大麻 dàmá

mark [mɑːk] I N 1 [c] (cross, tick) 记号 jìhao [个 gè] 2 [c] (stain) 污点 wūdiǎn [个 gè] 3 [c] (Brit: grade, score) 分数 fēnshù [个 gè] II VT 1 (indicate) [+ place] 标示 biāoshì 2 (Brit: Scol) 评分 píngfēn

market ['mɑːkɪt] N [c] 集市 jíshì [个 gè]

marketing ['mɑːkɪtɪŋ] N [u] 市场营销 shìchǎng yíngxiāo

marriage ['mærɪdʒ] N 1 [c/u] (relationship, institution) 婚姻 hūnyīn 2 [c] (wedding) 婚礼 hūnlǐ [场 chǎng]

married ['mærɪd] ADJ 已婚的 yǐhūn de ▸ to be married to sb 和某人结婚 hé mǒurén jiéhūn ▸ to get married 结婚 jiéhūn

marry ['mærɪ] VT 和…结婚 hé…jiéhūn

marvellous, (US) **marvelous** ['mɑːvələs] ADJ 极好的 jíhǎo de

masculine ['mæskjʊlɪn] ADJ 1 [+ characteristic, value] 男性的 nánxìng de 2 (Ling) [+ pronoun] 阳性的 yángxìng de

mashed potato [mæʃt-] N [c/u] 土豆泥 tǔdòuní [份 fèn]

mask [mɑːsk] N [c] 1 (disguise) 面罩 miànzhào [个 gè] 2 (protection) 口罩 kǒuzhào [个 gè]

mass [mæs] N [c] (large amount, number) 大量 dàliàng ▸ **masses of** (inf) 大量 dàliàng

massage ['mæsɑːʒ] N [c/u] 按摩 ànmó [次 cì]

massive ['mæsɪv] ADJ [+ amount, increase] 巨大的 jùdà de; [+ explosion] 大规模的 dà guīmó de

master ['mɑːstəʳ] VT (learn) [+ skill, language] 掌握 zhǎngwò

masterpiece ['mɑːstəpiːs] N [c] 杰作 jiézuò [部 bù]

mat [mæt] N [c] 席 xí [张 zhāng]

match [mætʃ] I N 1 [c] (game) 比赛 bǐsài [场 chǎng] 2 [c] (for lighting fire) 火柴 huǒchái [根 gēn] II VI (go together) [colours, materials] 相配 xiāngpèi

mate [meɪt] N [c] (*animal*) 配偶
pèiǒu [个 gè]

material [məˈtɪərɪəl] I N 1 [c/u]
(*cloth*) 衣料 yīliào [块 kuài] 2 [u]
(*information, data*) 资料 zīliào
II **materials** NPL (*equipment*) 用
具 yòngjù

math [mæθ] (US) N = **maths**

mathematics [mæθəˈmætɪks]
(*frm*) N [u] 数学 shùxué

maths [mæθs] (Brit) N [u] 数学
shùxué

matter [ˈmætəʳ] I N 1 [c] 事件
shìjiàn 2 [u] (*be important*)
要紧 yàojǐn ▸**what's the
matter (with...)?** (···) 怎么了？
(···)zěnme le? ▸**it doesn't matter**
没关系 méi guānxi

mattress [ˈmætrɪs] N [c] 床垫
chuángdiàn [个 gè]

maximum [ˈmæksɪməm] I ADJ
[+ *speed, height*] 最高的 zuìgāo de;
[+ *weight*] 最重的 zuìzhòng de II N
[c] 最大量 zuìdàliàng

May [meɪ] N [c/u] 五月 wǔyuè;
see also **July**

⭕ KEYWORD

may [meɪ] AUX VB 1 (*possibility*)
▸**it may rain later** 等会儿可能
要下雨 děnghuìr kěnéng yào
xiàyǔ ▸**we may not be able to
come** 我们可能来不了 wǒmen
kěnéng lái bùliǎo ▸**he may have
hurt himself** 他可能伤了自己 tā
kěnéng shāngle zìjǐ
2 (*permission*) ▸**may I come in?**
我可以进来吗？ wǒ kěyǐ jìnlái ma?

maybe [ˈmeɪbi] ADV 1 可能
kěnéng 2 (*making suggestions*) 也
许 yěxǔ 3 (*estimating*) 大概 dàgài
▸**maybe so/not** 也许如此/不是
yěxǔ rúcǐ/bùshì

mayor [mɛəʳ] N [c] 市长 shìzhǎng
[位 wèi]

me [mi:] PRON 我 wǒ ▸**it's me** 是
我 shì wǒ

meal [mi:l] N 1 [c] (*occasion*) 一
餐 yīcān [顿 dùn]; (*food*) 膳食
shànshí [顿 dùn] ▸**to go out for a
meal** 出去吃饭 chūqù chīfàn

mean [mi:n] I VT 1 (*signify*) 表示...意思
biǎoshì...yìsi 2 (*refer to*) 意指
yìzhǐ 3 (*intend*) ▸**to mean to do
sth** 意欲做某事 yìyù zuò mǒushì
II ADJ 1 (*not generous*) 吝啬的
lìnsè de 2 (*unkind*) 刻薄的 kèbó
de ▸**what does "imperialism"
mean?** "imperialism" 是什么
意思？ "imperialism"shì shénme
yìsi? ▸**what do you mean?** 你
什么意思？ nǐ shénme yìsi?; *see
also* **means**

meaning [ˈmi:nɪŋ] N [c/u] 意思
yìsi [层 céng]; [*of symbol, dream,
gesture*] 含义 hányì [个 gè]

means [mi:nz] N [c] (*pl* **means**)
(*method*) 方法 fāngfǎ [个 gè]

meant [mɛnt] PT, PP *of* **mean**

meanwhile [ˈmi:nwaɪl] ADV 同
时 tóngshí

measles [ˈmi:zlz] N [u] 麻疹
mázhěn

measure [ˈmɛʒəʳ] VT 测量 cèliáng

measurement [ˈmɛʒəmənt] N
[c] (*length, width etc*) 尺寸 chǐcùn

meat [mi:t] N [U] 肉 ròu

Mecca ['mɛkə] N 麦加 Màijiā

mechanic [mɪ'kænɪk] N [c] 机械工 jīxiègōng [位 wèi]

medal ['mɛdl] N [c] 奖章 jiǎngzhāng [枚 méi]

media ['mi:dɪə] I PL of **medium** II NPL ▸ **the media** 媒体 méitǐ

medical ['mɛdɪkl] I ADJ 医疗的 yīliáo de II N [c] (examination) 体格检查 tǐgé jiǎnchá [次 cì]

medicine ['mɛdsɪn] N 1 [U] (science) 医学 yīxué 2 [c/U] (medication) 药 yào [种 zhǒng]

Mediterranean [mɛdɪtə'reɪnɪən] N ▸ **the Mediterranean** (sea) 地中海 Dìzhōnghǎi; (region) 地中海沿岸地区 Dìzhōnghǎi yán'àn dìqū

medium ['mi:dɪəm] ADJ 1 (average) 中等的 zhōngděng de 2 (clothing size) 中码的 zhōngmǎ de

medium-sized ['mi:dɪəm'saɪzd] ADJ 中等大小的 zhōngděng dàxiǎo de

meet [mi:t] (pt, pp met) I VT 1 (accidentally) 遇见 yùjiàn; (by arrangement) 和…见面 hé…jiànmiàn 2 (for the first time) 结识 jiéshí; (be introduced to) 认识 rènshí 3 (at station, airport) 接 jiē II VI 1 (accidentally) 相遇 xiāngyù; (by arrangement) 见面 jiànmiàn 2 (for the first time) 认识 rènshí ▸ **pleased to meet you** 见到你很高兴 jiàndào nǐ hěn gāoxìng ▸ **meet up** VI 会面 huìmiàn

meeting ['mi:tɪŋ] N 1 [c] 会议 huìyì [次 cì] 2 [c] (encounter) 会面 huìmiàn [次 cì]

megabyte ['mɛgəbaɪt] N [c] 兆字节 zhàozìjié [个 gè]

melon ['mɛlən] N [c/U] 瓜 guā [个 gè]

melt [mɛlt] I VI 融化 rónghuà II VT [+ metal, ice, snow, butter, chocolate] 使融化 shǐ rónghuà

member ['mɛmbə] N [c] 1 (of family, staff, public) 一员 yīyuán 2 (of club, party) 成员 chéngyuán [个 gè]

memorial [mɪ'mɔ:rɪəl] N [c] 纪念碑 jìniànbēi [座 zuò]

memorize ['mɛməraɪz] VT 记住 jìzhù

memory ['mɛmərɪ] N 1 [c/U] (ability to remember) 记忆力 jìyìlì [种 zhǒng] 2 [c] (thing remembered) 记忆 jìyì [个 gè] 3 [c/U] (Comput) 存储器 cúnchǔqì [个 gè] ▸ **to have a good/bad memory (for sth)** (对某事) 记忆力好/差 (duì mǒushì)jìyìlì hǎo/chà

men [mɛn] NPL of **man**

mend [mɛnd] VT 修理 xiūlǐ

mental ['mɛntl] ADJ [+ illness, health] 精神的 jīngshén de

mental hospital N [c] 精神病院 jīngshénbìngyuàn [个 gè]

mention ['mɛnʃən] VT 提到 tídào ▸ **don't mention it!** 不客气! bù kèqì!

menu ['mɛnju:] N [c] 1 菜单 càidān [个 gè] 2 (Comput) 选择菜单 xuǎnzé càidān [个 gè]

merry ['mɛrɪ] ADJ ▸ **Merry**

Christmas! 圣诞快乐!
Shèngdàn Kuàilè!

mess [mɛs] N 1 [s/U] (untidiness)
凌乱 língluàn 2 [s/U] (chaotic
situation) 混乱的局面 hùnluàn
de júmiàn
▸ **mess about, mess around**
(inf) VI 混日子 hùn rìzi

message ['mɛsɪdʒ] N [c] 消息
xiāoxi [条 tiáo] ▸ **to leave (sb) a
message** (给某人) 留个信 (gěi
mǒurén)liú gè xìn

met [mɛt] PT, PP of **meet**

metal ['mɛtl] N [c/U] 金属 jīnshǔ
[种 zhǒng]

meter ['miːtə*r*] N [c] 1 仪表 yíbiǎo
[个 gè]; (also: **parking meter**) 停
车计时器 tíngchē jìshíqì [个 gè]
2 (US: unit) = **metre**

method ['mɛθəd] N [c/U] 方法
fāngfǎ [种 zhǒng]

metre, (US) **meter** ['miːtə*r*] N [c]
(unit) 米 mǐ

metric ['mɛtrɪk] ADJ 公制的
gōngzhì de

Mexico ['mɛksɪkəʊ] N 墨西哥
Mòxīgē

mice [maɪs] NPL of **mouse**

microchip ['maɪkrəʊtʃɪp] N [c]
集成电路块 jíchéng diànlù kuài
[个 gè]

microphone ['maɪkrəfəʊn] N [c]
话筒 huàtǒng [个 gè]

microscope ['maɪkrəskəʊp] N [c]
显微镜 xiǎnwēijìng [个 gè]

microwave ['maɪkrəweɪv] N [c]
(also: **microwave oven**) 微波炉
wēibōlú [个 gè]

midday [mɪd'deɪ] N [U] 正午

zhèngwǔ ▸ **at midday** 在正午 zài
zhèngwǔ

middle ['mɪdl] I N 1 [c] (centre) 中
央 zhōngyāng [个 gè] 2 [s] 中
zhōng II ADJ (+ position, event,
period) 中间的 zhōngjiān de ▸ **in
the middle of the night** 在半夜
zài bànyè

middle-aged [mɪdl'eɪdʒd] ADJ
中年的 zhōngnián de

middle class N [c] (also: **middle-
class**) 中层社会的 zhōngcéng
shèhuì de

Middle East N ▸ **the Middle East**
中东 Zhōngdōng

middle name N [c] 中间名字
zhōngjiān míngzi [个 gè]

> MIDDLE NAME
>
> **first name** 是由父母取
> 的名字。**last name** 或
> **surname** 是家族的姓氏。
> 在说英语的国家中,名dominant
> 在姓之前。在 **first name** 和
> **last name** 之间,还可能
> 有 **middle name** (中名),
> 这是你父母给你取的第二个
> "名"。**middle name** 通常
> 只用于正式文件,例如,选
> 课或签署文件时。

midnight ['mɪdnaɪt] N [U] 半
夜 bànyè ▸ **at midnight** 在午夜
zài wǔyè

midwife ['mɪdwaɪf] (pl **midwives**)
N [c] 助产士 zhùchǎnshì [位 wèi]

might [maɪt] AUX VB (possibility)
▸ **I might get home late** 我可

能会晚点回家 wǒ kěnéng huì wǎn huíjiā ▶it might have been an accident 可能是个事故 kěnéng shì gè shìgù

migraine ['miːɡreɪn] N [C/U] 偏头痛 piāntóutòng [阵 zhèn]

mild [maɪld] ADJ 1 [+ infection, illness] 轻微的 qīngwēi de 2 [+ climate, weather] 温暖的 wēnnuǎn de

mile [maɪl] I N [C] 英里 yīnglǐ II miles NPL (inf: a long way) 很远 的距离 hěnyuǎn de jùlí ▶70 miles per or an hour 每小时70英里 měi xiǎoshí qīshí yīnglǐ

military ['mɪlɪtəri] ADJ 军事的 jūnshì de

milk [mɪlk] N [U] 奶 nǎi

milkshake ['mɪlkʃeɪk] N [C/U] 奶昔 nǎixī [份 fèn]

millimetre ['mɪlimiːtəʳ], (US) **millimeter** N [C] 毫米 háomǐ

million ['mɪljən] I NUM 百万 bǎiwàn II millions NPL (lit) 数 百万 shùbǎiwàn; (inf: fig) 无数 wúshù ▶a or one million books/people/dollars 100万本书/个人/元 yībǎiwàn běn shū/gè rén/yuán

millionaire [mɪljə'nɛəʳ] N [C] 百万富翁 bǎiwàn fùwēng [个 gè]

mind [maɪnd] I N [C] 智力 zhìlì [种 zhǒng] II VT 1 (Brit: look after) [+ child, shop] 照看 zhàokàn 2 (be careful of) 当心 dāngxīn 3 (object to) 在意 zàiyì 4 (have a preference) ▶I don't mind (what/who...) 我不在乎(什么/谁…) wǒ bù zàihu (shénme/shéi...) 5 ▶ do/would

you mind (if...)? (如果…) 你介意吗? (rúguǒ...) nǐ jièyì ma? ▶to make up one's mind or make one's mind up 下定决心 xiàdìng juéxīn ▶to change one's/sb's mind 改变主意 gǎibiàn zhǔyì ▶I wouldn't mind a coffee 我挺想喝杯咖啡 wǒ tǐngxiǎng hē bēi kāfēi ▶mind the step 小心脚下 xiǎoxīn jiǎoxià

🔘 **KEYWORD**

mine¹ [maɪn] PRON 我的 wǒ de ▶this is mine 这是我的 zhèshì wǒde ▶these are mine 这些是我的 zhèxiē shì wǒde

mine² [maɪn] N [C] 矿 kuàng [座 zuò]

mineral water [mɪnərəl-] N [U/C] 矿泉水 kuàngquánshuǐ

miniature ['mɪnətʃəʳ] ADJ 微型的 wēixíng de

minibus ['mɪnɪbʌs] N [C] 小公共汽车 xiǎo gōnggòng qìchē [辆 liàng]

MiniDisc®, minidisc ['mɪnɪdɪsk] N [C] (disc) 迷你光碟 mínǐ guāngdié [张 zhāng]

minimum ['mɪnɪməm] I ADJ 最低的 zuìdī de II N [C] 膛量 zuìshǎoliàng

miniskirt ['mɪnɪskəːt] N [C] 超短裙 chāoduǎnqún [条 tiáo]

minister ['mɪnɪstəʳ] N [C] 1 (Brit) (Pol) 部长 bùzhǎng [位 wèi] 2 (Rel) 牧师 mùshī [位 wèi]

minor ['maɪnəʳ] ADJ [+ repairs,

changes] 不重要的 bù zhòngyào de; [+ *injuries*] 不严重的 bù yánzhòng de

minority [maɪˈnɒrɪtɪ] N [s + PL VB] [*of group, society*] 少数 shǎoshù **2** [c] (*ethnic, cultural, religious*) 少数民族 shǎoshù mínzú [个 gè]

mint [mɪnt] N **1** [U] (*plant*) 薄荷 bòhe **2** [U] (*sweet*) 薄荷糖 bòhe táng

minus [ˈmaɪnəs] PREP (*inf: without*) 没有 méiyǒu ▸ **12 minus 3** (*is or equals 9*) 12减3 (等于9) shí'èr jiǎn sān (děngyú jiǔ) ▸ **minus 24** (**degrees C/F**) (*temperature*) 零下24 (摄氏/华氏) língxià èrshísì (shèshì/huáshì dù) ▸ **B minus** (*Scol*) B减 bì jiǎn

minute [ˈmɪnɪt] N [c] **1** (*unit*) 分钟 fēnzhōng **2** 一会儿, 一瞬 or *just a minute*! 等一会儿! děng yīhuǐ'r

miracle [ˈmɪrəkl] N [c] **1** (*Rel*) 圣迹 shèngjì [处 chù] **2** (*marvel*) 奇迹 qíjì [个 gè]

mirror [ˈmɪrə(r)] N [c] 镜子 jìngzi [面 miàn]; [*in car*] 后视镜 hòushìjìng [个 gè]

misbehave [mɪsbɪˈheɪv] VI 行为无礼 xíngwéi wúlǐ

miscellaneous [mɪsɪˈleɪnɪəs] ADJ 形形色色的 xíngxíng sèsè de

miserable [ˈmɪzərəbl] ADJ **1** [+ *person*] 痛苦的 tòngkǔ de **2** [+ *weather, day*] 恶劣的 èliè de

Miss [mɪs] N **1** 小姐 xiǎojiě **2** (*esp Brit: as form of address*) 小姐 xiǎojiě ▸ **Dear Miss Smith** 亲爱

的史密斯小姐 qīnài de Shǐmìsī Xiǎojiě

- **MISS, MRS, MS**

- 在说英语的国家中, **Mrs** (夫人) 用于已婚女士的姓名前。**Miss** (小姐) 用于未婚女士的姓名前。有些女士认为, 让人们知道她是否结婚并不重要, 所以往往用 **Ms** (女士) 称呼自己。与 **Mr** (先生) 类似, **Ms** 不表明任何婚姻状况。

miss [mɪs] VT **1** (*fail to hit*) 未击中 wèi jīzhòng **2** [+ *train, bus, plane*] 错过 cuòguò **3** [+ *chance, opportunity*] 错过 cuòguò ▸ **you can't miss it** 你不会找不到 nǐ bùhuì zhǎo bùdào

missing [ˈmɪsɪŋ] ADJ [+ *person*] 失踪的 shīzōng de; [+ *object*] 丢失的 diūshī de

mist [mɪst] N [c/U] 薄雾 bówù [场 chǎng]

mistake [mɪsˈteɪk] N [c] **1** (*error*) 错误 cuòwù [个 gè] **2** (*blunder*) 过失 guòshī [个 gè] ▸ **to make a mistake** 犯错 fàncuò ▸ **to do sth by mistake** 误做某事 wùzuò mǒushì

mistaken [mɪsˈteɪkən] I PP *of* **mistake** II ADJ ▸ **to be mistaken** (*about sth*) [*person*] (把某事) 搞错 (bǎ mǒushì) gǎocuò

mistook [mɪsˈtuk] PT *of* **mistake**

misty [ˈmɪstɪ] ADJ 有雾的 yǒuwù de

misunderstand
[ˌmɪsʌndə'stænd] (pt, pp
misunderstood) VT, VI 误解
wùjiě

misunderstanding
[ˌmɪsʌndə'stændɪŋ] N [c/u] 误会
wùhuì [个 gè]

misunderstood [ˌmɪsʌndə'stud]
PT, PP of **misunderstand**

mix [mɪks] I VT 混合 hùnhé II VI
(socially) ▸ to mix (with sb) (和
某人) 相处 (hé mǒurén) xiāngchǔ
III N [c] 混合 hùnhé [种 zhǒng]
▸ to mix sth with sth [+ activities]
将某物同某物混淆 jiāng mǒuwù
tóng mǒuwù hùnxiáo
▸ mix up VT [+ people] 分辨不
出 fēnbiàn bùchū; [+ things] 混
淆 hùnxiáo

mixed [mɪkst] ADJ 1 [+ salad,
herbs] 什锦的 shíjǐn de 2 [+ group,
community] 形形色色的 xíngxíng
sèsè de 3 [+ school, education] 男女
混合的 nánnǔ hùnhé de

mixture ['mɪkstʃə'] N [c/u] 混合
物 hùnhéwù [种 zhǒng]

mix-up ['mɪksʌp] (inf) N [c] 混乱
hùnluàn [种 zhǒng]

mobile phone (Brit) N [c] 手机
shǒujī [部 bù]

model ['mɒdl] I N [c] 1 (of boat,
building) 模型 móxíng 2 (fashion model)
时装模特
shízhuāng mótè [位 wèi] II ADJ
(miniature) ▸ model aircraft/
train 模型飞机/火车 móxíng
fēijī/huǒchē III VT [+ clothes] 展
示 zhǎnshì

modem ['məʊdɛm] N [c] 调制解

moderate ['mɒdərət] ADJ 中庸的
zhōngyōng de

modern ['mɒdən] ADJ 1 [+ world,
times, society] 现代的 xiàndài de
2 [+ technology, design] 新式的
xīnshì de

modern languages NPL 现代语
言 xiàndài yǔyán

modernize ['mɒdənaɪz] VT 使现
代化 shǐ xiàndàihuà

modest ['mɒdɪst] ADJ 谦虚的
qiānxū de

moisturizer ['mɔɪstʃəraɪzə']
N [c/u] 保湿霜 bǎoshīshuāng
[瓶 píng]

moment ['məʊmənt] N [c]
(period of time) 片刻 piànkè 2 [c]
(point in time) 瞬间 shùnjiān ▸ at
the/this (present) moment 此
刻/当前 cǐkè/dāngqián ▸ at the
last moment 在最后一刻 zài
zuìhòu yīkè

Monday ['mʌndɪ] N [c/u] 星期一
xīngqīyī [个 gè]; see also **Tuesday**

money ['mʌnɪ] N [u] 1 (cash) 钱
qián 2 (in the bank) 存款 cúnkuǎn
3 (currency) 货币 huòbì ▸ to make
money [person, business] 赚钱
zhuànqián

monitor ['mɒnɪtə'] N [c] 显示屏
xiǎnshìpíng [个 gè]

monkey ['mʌŋkɪ] N [c] (Zool) 猴
hóu [只 zhī]

monotonous [mə'nɒtənəs] ADJ
[+ life, job etc, voice, tune] 单调的
dāndiào de

month [mʌnθ] N [c] 月 yuè
[个 gè] ▸ every month 每个

měigè yuè

monthly ['mʌnθlɪ] **I** ADJ 每月的 měiyuè de **II** ADV (every month) 按月 ànyuè

monument ['mɒnjumənt] N [c] 纪念碑 jìniànbēi [座 zuò]

mood [muːd] N [c] 心情 xīnqíng [种 zhǒng] ▸ **to be in a good/bad/ awkward mood** 心情好/坏/不愉快 xīnqíng hǎo/huài/bù tòngkuài

moon [muːn] N ▸ **the moon** 月球 yuèqiú

moonlight ['muːnlaɪt] N [U] 月光 yuèguāng

moped ['məupɛd] N [c] 机动自行车 jīdòng zìxíngchē [辆 liàng]

moral ['mɒrl] ADJ [+ issues, values] 道德的 dàodé de; [+ behaviour, person] 品行端正的 pǐnxíng duānzhèng de

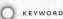

KEYWORD

more [mɔː] **I** ADJ 更多的 gèngduō de ▸ **I get more money/holidays than you do** 我比你有更多的钱/假期 wǒ bǐ nǐ yǒu gèngduō de qián/jiàqī

2 (additional) 再一些的 zài yīxiē de ▸ **would you like some more tea/peanuts?** 你要再来点茶/花生吗? nǐ yào zài lái diǎn chá/huāshēng ma? ▸ **is there any more wine?** 还有酒吗? háiyǒu jiǔ ma? ▸ **a few more weeks** 再几个星期 zài jǐge xīngqī

II PRON **1** (in comparisons) 更多的量 gèngduō de liàng ▸ **there's/ there are more than I thought** 比我想得更多 bǐ wǒ xiǎngde

gèngduō ▸ **more than 20** 大于20 dàyú èrshí ▸ **she's got more than me** 她比我得到的多 tā bǐ wǒ dédào de duō

2 (further, additional) 额外的量 éwài de liàng ▸ **is there/are there any more?** 还有多的吗? háiyǒu duōde ma? ▸ **have you got any more of it/them?** 你还有吗? nǐ háiyǒu ma? ▸ **much/many more** 多得多 duōdeduō

III ADV **1** (to form comparative) 更 gèng ▸ **more dangerous/ difficult (than)** (比...) 更危险/难 (bǐ...)gèng wēixiǎn/nán

2 (in expressions) ▸ **more and more** 越来越 yuèláiyuè ▸ **more or less** (adj, adv) 差不多 chàbùduō ▸ **more than ever** 空前的多 kōngqián de duō ▸ **once more** 再一次 zài yīcì

morning ['mɔːnɪŋ] N [c/U] (early in the morning) 早晨 zǎochén [个 gè]; (later in the morning) 上午 shàngwǔ [个 gè] ▸ **good morning!** 早上好! zǎoshang hǎo! ▸ **at 3 o'clock/7 o'clock in the morning** 凌晨3点/早上7点 língchén sāndiǎn/zǎoshang qīdiǎn ▸ **this morning** 今天上午 jīntiān shàngwǔ ▸ **on Monday morning** 星期一上午 Xīngqīyī shàngwǔ

Morocco [məˈrɒkəu] N 摩洛哥 Móluògē

mortgage ['mɔːgɪdʒ] N [c] 抵押贷款 dǐyā dàikuǎn [笔 bǐ]

Moslem ['mɒzləm] ADJ, N = **Muslim**

mosque [mɔsk] N [c] 清真寺 qīngzhēnsì [座 zuò]

mosquito [mɔsˈkiːtəʊ] (pl **mosquitoes**) N [c] 蚊 wén [只 zhī]

 KEYWORD

most [məʊst] I ADJ 1 (almost all) 大部分的 dàbùfen de ▸**most people** 大多数人 dàduōshù rén 2 (in comparisons) ▸**(the) most** 最 zuì ▸**who won the most money/prizes?** 谁赢了最多的钱/奖品? shuí yíngle zuìduō de qián/jiǎngpǐn?

II PRON 大部分 dàbùfen; (plural) 大多数 dàduōshù ▸**most of it/them** 它/他们的大部分 tā/tāmen de dà bùfen ▸**I paid the most** 我付了大部分 wǒ fùle dà bùfen ▸**to make the most of sth** 充分利用某物 chōngfèn lìyòng mǒuwù ▸**at the (very) most** 最多 zuìduō

III ADV (superlative) 1 (with verb) ▸**(the) most** 最 zuì ▸**what I miss (the) most is...** 我最想念的是… wǒ zuì xiǎngniàn de shì… 2 (with adj) ▸**the most comfortable/expensive sofa in the shop** 店里最舒服/贵的沙发 diànlǐ zuì shūfu/guì de shāfā 3 (with adv) ▸**most efficiently/effectively** 最有效率/有效地 zuì yǒuxiàolǜ/yǒuxiào de ▸**most of all** 最起码的 zuì qǐmǎ de

mother [ˈmʌðəʳ] N [c] 母亲 mǔqīn [位 wèi]

mother-in-law [ˈmʌðərɪnlɔː] (pl

mothers-in-law) N [c] (of woman) 婆婆 pópo [位 wèi]; (of man) 岳母 yuèmǔ [位 wèi]

Mother's Day (Brit) N [c/u] 母亲节 Mǔqīn Jié [个 gè]

motivated [ˈməʊtɪveɪtɪd] ADJ 士气高涨的 shìqì gāozhǎng de

motor [ˈməʊtəʳ] N [c] 发动机 fādòngjī [个 gè]

motorbike [ˈməʊtəbaɪk] N [c] 摩托车 mótuōchē [辆 liàng]

motorboat [ˈməʊtəbəʊt] N [c] 摩托艇 mótuōtǐng [艘 sōu]

motorcycle [ˈməʊtəsaɪkl] (frm) N [c] 摩托车 mótuōchē [辆 liàng]

motorcyclist [ˈməʊtəsaɪklɪst] N [c] 摩托车手 mótuōchēshǒu [位 wèi]

motorist [ˈməʊtərɪst] (esp Brit) N [c] 开汽车的人 kāi qìchē de rén [个 gè]

motor racing (Brit) N [U] 赛车 sàichē

motorway [ˈməʊtəweɪ] (Brit) N [c] 高速公路 gāosù gōnglù [条 tiáo]

mountain [ˈmaʊntɪn] N [c] 山 shān [座 zuò]

mountain bike N [c] 山地自行车 shāndì zìxíngchē [辆 liàng]

mountainous [ˈmaʊntɪnəs] ADJ 多山的 duōshān de

mouse [maʊs] (pl **mice**) N [c] 1 鼠 shǔ [只 zhī] 2 (Comput) 鼠标 shǔbiāo [个 gè]

mouse mat [ˈmaʊsmæt] N [c] 鼠标垫 shǔbiāo diàn [个 gè]

moustache, (US) **mustache** [məsˈtɑːʃ] N [c] 髭 zī [撮 cuō]

mouth [mauθ] N [c] **1** 嘴 zuǐ [张 zhāng] **2** [of river] 河口 hékǒu [个 gè]

mouthful ['mauθful] N [c] 一口 yīkǒu

move [muːv] I vɪ **1** [vehicle] 行进 xíngjìn; [person, object] 动动 dòng **2** [relocate] 搬家 bānjiā; [from activity] 改换 gǎihuàn II vᴛ **1** [+ furniture, car] 挪动 nuódòng **2** (affect emotionally) 感动 gǎndòng III N [c] 搬家 bānjiā [次 cì] **2** (in game) 一步 yíbù ▶ to **move house/jobs/offices** 搬家/换工作/更换办公地点 bānjiā/huàn gōngzuò/gēnghuàn bàngōng dìdiǎn ▶ to **get a move on** (inf) 快点 kuàidiǎn

▶ **move away** vɪ (from town, area) 离开 líkāi; (from window, door) 走开 zǒukāi

▶ **move back** vɪ **1** (return) 回来 huílái **2** (backwards) 后退 hòutuì

▶ **move forward** vɪ (person, troops, vehicle) 向前移动 xiàngqián yídòng

▶ **move in** vɪ (into house) 搬入 bānrù

▶ **move into** vᴛ ꜰᴜꜱ (house, area) 搬进 bānjìn

▶ **move out** vɪ (of house) 搬出去 bān chūqù

▶ **move over** vɪ (to make room) 让开些 ràngkāixiē

movement ['muːvmənt] N [c] **1** 团体 tuántǐ [个 gè] **2** (gesture) 动作 dòngzuò [个 gè]

movie ['muːvɪ] (US) N [c] 电影 diànyǐng [部 bù] ▶ the **movies** 电影 diànyǐng

movie theater (US) N [c] 电影院 diànyǐngyuàn [个 gè]

moving ['muːvɪŋ] ADJ **1** (emotionally) 动人的 dòngrén de **2** (not static) 活动的 huódòng de

MP N ABBR (Brit) (= Member of Parliament) 下院议员 Xiàyuàn Yìyuán

MP3 [ɛmpiːˈθriː] N **1** (format) 一种音频压缩格式 yī zhǒng yīnpín yāsuō géshì **2** (file) 以这种音频压缩格式储存的声音文件 yǐ zhè zhǒng yīnpín yāsuō géshì chǔcún de shēngyīn wénjiàn

mph ABBR (= miles per hour) 每小时...英里 měi xiǎoshí...yīnglǐ

Mr ['mɪstəʳ], (US) **Mr.** N ▶ **Mr Smith** 史密斯先生 Shǐmìsī xiānsheng

Mrs ['mɪsɪz], (US) **Mrs.** N ▶ **Mrs Smith** 史密斯太太 Shǐmìsī tàitai

Ms [mɪz], (US) **Ms.** N (Miss or Mrs) ▶ **Ms Smith** 史密斯女士 Shǐmìsī nǚshì

 KEYWORD

much [mʌtʃ] I ADJ 大量的 dàliàng de ▶ we haven't got much time/money 我们没有多少时间/钱 wǒmen méiyǒu duōshǎo shíjiān/qián

II PRON 大量 dàliàng ▶ there isn't much left 剩下的不多了 shèngxià de bùduō le ▶ he doesn't do much at the weekends 周末他不做太多事 zhōumò tā bùzuò tàiduō shì

III ADV **1** (a great deal) 许多 xǔduō ▶ he hasn't changed much 他没变很多 tā méi biàn hěnduō ▶ "did

you like her?" — "not much"
"你喜欢她吗?" — "不太喜欢"
"nǐ xǐhuan tā ma?" "bùtài xǐhuan"
2 (far) …得多 …deduō ▸ **I'm
much better now** 我感觉好多了
wǒ gǎnjué hǎoduō le
3 (often) 经常 jīngcháng ▸ **do you
go out much?** 你经常出去吗? nǐ
jīngcháng chūqù ma?

mud [mʌd] N [U] 泥泞 níní
muddle ['mʌdl] N [c/U] 1 (of papers,
figures, things) 混乱状态 hùnluàn
zhuàngtài [个 gè] 2 (situation) 糟
糕局面 zāogāo júmiàn [个 gè] ▸ **to
be in a muddle** 一片混乱 yīpiàn
hùnluàn
muddy ['mʌdɪ] ADJ 沾满烂泥的
zhānmǎn lànní de
muesli ['mjuːzlɪ] N [U] 穆兹利,
和干水果混在一起的燕麦早餐
mug [mʌg] I N [c] 大杯子 dà
bēizi [个 gè] II VT (rob) 行凶抢劫
xíngxiōng qiǎngjié
mugging ['mʌgɪŋ] N [c/U] 行凶抢
劫 xíngxiōng qiǎngjié [次 cì]
multiply ['mʌltɪplaɪ] I VT (Math)
▸ **to multiply sth (by sth)** (某
数)乘以某数 (mǒushù) chéngyǐ
mǒushù II VI (increase) 增加
zēngjiā
mum [mʌm] N (Brit: inf) 妈妈
māma
mummy ['mʌmɪ] N [c] (Brit: inf)
妈妈 māma [位 wèi]
murder ['məːdə'] I N [c/U] 谋
杀 móushā [个 gè] II VT 谋杀
móushā
murderer ['məːdərə'] N [c] 凶手

xiōngshǒu [个 gè]
muscle ['mʌsl] N [c/U] 肌肉 jīròu
[块 kuài]
museum [mjuː'zɪəm] N [c] 博物
馆 bówùguǎn [个 gè]
mushroom ['mʌʃrum] N [c] 蘑菇
mógu [个 gè]
music ['mjuːzɪk] N [U] 1 音
乐 yīnyuè 2 (Scol, Univ) 音乐课
yīnyuè kè
musical ['mjuːzɪkl] ADJ 1 (related
to music) 音乐的 yīnyuè de
2 (musically gifted) 有音乐天赋的
yǒu yīnyuè tiānfù de
musical instrument N [c] 乐器
yuèqì [件 jiàn]
musician [mjuː'zɪʃən] N [c] 音乐
家 yīnyuèjiā [位 wèi]
Muslim, Moslem ['muzlɪm] I N
[c] 穆斯林 Mùsīlín [个 gè] II ADJ
穆斯林的 Mùsīlín de
must [mʌst] AUX VB 1 (expressing
importance or necessity) 必须 bìxū
2 (expressing intention) 得 děi
3 (expressing presumption) 一定
yīdìng ▸ **you must be joking** 你
准是在开玩笑 nǐ zhǔn shì zài kāi
wánxiào ▸ **the doctor must allow
the patient to decide** 医生必
须让病人来决定。 yīshēng bìxū
ràng bìngrén lái juédìng。 ▸ **I really
must be getting back** 我真得回
去了。 wǒ zhēnděi huíqù le
mustache ['mʌstæʃ] (US) N =
moustache
mustard ['mʌstəd] N [U] 芥
末 jièmo
mustn't ['mʌsnt] = **must not**
my [maɪ] ADJ 我的 wǒ de

myself [mar'sɛlf] PRON **1** 我自己 wǒ zìjǐ **2** (me) 我 wǒ ▸ **I hurt myself** 我伤了自己。 wǒ shāngle zìjǐ ▸ **by myself** (unaided) 我独力地 wǒ dúlì de; (alone) 我独自 wǒ dúzì

mysterious [mɪs'tɪərɪəs] ADJ 神秘的 shénmì de

mystery ['mɪstərɪ] N **1** [c] (puzzle) 谜 mí [个 gè] **2** [c] (story) 推理作品 tuīlǐ zuòpǐn [部 bù]

myth [mɪθ] N [c] **1** (legend, story) 神话 shénhuà [个 gè] **2** (fallacy) 谬论 miùlùn [个 gè]

nail [neɪl] N [c] **1** (of finger, toe) 指甲 zhǐjiɑ [个 gè] **2** (for hammering) 钉子 dīngzi [个 gè]

nailfile ['neɪlfaɪl] N [c] 指甲锉 zhǐjiɑ cuò [个 gè]

nail polish N [U] 指甲油 zhǐjiɑ yóu

nail varnish (Brit) N = **nail polish**

naked ['neɪkɪd] ADJ 裸体的 luǒtǐ de

name [neɪm] N [c] 名字 míngzi [个 gè] ▸ **what's your name?** 你叫什么名字? nǐ jiào shénme míngzi? ▸ **my name is Peter** 我叫彼得 wǒ jiào bǐdé ▸ **to give one's name and address** 留下姓名和地址 liúxià xìngmíng hé dìzhǐ

nanny ['nænɪ] N [c] 保姆 bǎomǔ [个 gè]

napkin ['næpkɪn] N [c] 餐巾 cānjīn [张 zhāng]

nappy ['næpɪ] (Brit) N [c] 尿布 niàobù [块 kuài]

narrow ['nærəu] ADJ 窄的 zhǎi de

nasty ['nɑːstɪ] ADJ 1 [+ taste, smell] 恶心的 ěxīn de 2 [+ injury, accident, disease] 严重的 yánzhòng de

nation ['neɪʃən] N [c] 国家 guójiā [个 gè]

national ['næʃənl] I ADJ 国家的 guójiā de II N [c] 公民 gōngmín [个 gè]

national anthem N [c] 国歌 guógē [首 shǒu]

national holiday (US) N [c] 定假日 fǎdìng jiàqī [个 gè]

nationality [næʃə'nælɪtɪ] N [c/u] 国籍 guójí [个 gè]

national park N [c] 国家公园 guójiā gōngyuán [个 gè]

native ['neɪtɪv] ADJ 1 [+ country] 本国的 běnguó de 2 [+ language, tongue] 母语的 mǔyǔ de

natural ['nætʃrəl] ADJ 1 (normal) 正常的 zhèngcháng de 2 [+ material, product, food] 天然的 tiānrán de

naturally ['nætʃrəlɪ] ADV 1 (unsurprisingly) 自然地 zìrán de 2 (occur, happen) 自然而然地 zìrán ér rán de

nature ['neɪtʃə] N [u] (also: **Nature**) 自然界 zìránjiè

naughty ['nɔːtɪ] ADJ 淘气的 táoqì de

navy ['neɪvɪ] I N 1 ▸ **the navy** (service) 海军 hǎijūn 2 [u] (also: **navy-blue**) 藏青色 zàngqīngsè II ADJ (also: **navy-blue**) 藏青色的 zàngqīngsè de

near [nɪə] I ADJ 近的 jìn de II ADV (close) 近 jìn III PREP (also: **near to**) 1 (physically) 近 jìn 2 (just before/after) 临近 línjìn ▸ **the nearest shops are 5 km away** 最近的商店离这里有5公里远 zuìjìn de shāngdiàn lí zhèlǐ yǒu wǔ gōnglǐ yuǎn ▸ **in the near future** 在不远的将来 zài bùyuǎn de jiānglái

nearby [nɪə'baɪ] I ADJ 附近的 fùjìn de II ADV 在附近 zài fùjìn

nearly ['nɪəlɪ] ADV 差不多 chà bù duō ▸ **you're nearly as tall as I am** 你差不多高了 nǐ gēn wǒ chàbùduō gāole ▸ **nearly always** 几乎总是 jīhū zǒngshì

near-sighted [nɪə'saɪtɪd] (US) ADJ (short-sighted) 近视的 jìnshì de

neat [niːt] ADJ 1 整洁的 zhěngjié de; [+ handwriting] 工整的 gōngzhěng de 2 (US: inf: great) 绝妙的 juémiào de

neatly ['niːtlɪ] ADV 整齐地 zhěngqí de

necessarily ['nɛsɪsrɪlɪ] ADV 必然 bìrán

necessary ['nɛsɪsrɪ] ADJ 必要的 bìyào de ▸ **if/when/where necessary** 如有必要/必要时/在必要处 rú yǒu bìyào/bìyào shí/zài bìyào chù

neck [nɛk] N [c] 1 (Anat) 颈 jǐng 2 (of shirt, dress, jumper) 领子 lǐngzi [个 gè]

necklace ['nɛklɪs] N [c] 项链

xiàngliàn [条 tiáo]

necktie ['nɛktaɪ] (US) N [c] 领带 lǐngdài [条 tiáo]

need [niːd] VT 1 (require) 需要 xūyào 2 (want) [+ drink, holiday, cigarette] 想要 xiǎngyào 3 [+ a haircut, a bath, a wash] 得 děi ▸ **to need to do sth** 必须做某事 bìxū zuò mǒushì ▸ **the car needs servicing** 这辆车需要维修了 zhèliàng chē xūyào wéixiū le

needle ['niːdl] N [c] 1 (for sewing) 针 zhēn [根 gēn] 2 (for injections) 注射针 zhùshèzhēn [只 zhī]

negative ['nɛgətɪv] I ADJ 1 [+ test, result] 阴性的 yīnxìng de 2 [+ person, attitude, view] 消极的 xiāojí de 3 [+ answer, response] 否定的 fǒudìng de II N [c] (Ling) 否定词 fǒudìngcí [个 gè]

negotiate [nɪˈgəʊʃɪeɪt] VI 商讨 shāngtǎo

neighbour, (US) **neighbor** ['neɪbər] N [c] 邻居 línjū [个 gè]

neighbourhood, (US) **neighborhood** ['neɪbəhʊd] N [c] 地区 dìqū [个 gè]

neither ['naɪðər] I PRON (person) 两人都不 liǎngrén dōu bù; (thing) 两者都不 liǎngzhě dōu bù II CONJ ▸ **I didn't move and neither did John** 我和约翰都没动 wǒ hé Yuēhàn dōu méi dòng ▸ **neither do/have I** 我也不/没 wǒ yě bù/méi ▸ **neither... nor...** 既不…也 jìbù…yěbù...

> **neither** 和 **none** 作 代词的时候用法不同。 用 **neither** 指两个人或

事物，表示否定含义。 *Neither had close friends at university.* **neither of** 的 用法与之相同，后接代 词或名词词组。 *Neither of them spoke...Neither of these options is desirable.* 注意， 也可以把 **neither** 用在单 数可数名词之前。 *Neither side can win.* **none** 可以 指代三个或者三个以上的 人或事物，表示否定含 义。 *None could afford the food.* **none of** 的用法与 之相同，后接代词或名词 词组。 *None of them had learned anything.*

nephew ['nɛvjuː] N [c] (brother's son) 侄子 zhízi [个 gè]; (sister's son) 外甥 wàisheng [个 gè]

nerve [nɜːv] N 1 [c] (Anat) 神经 shénjīng [根 gēn] 2 [U] (courage) 勇气 yǒngqì ▸ **to get on sb's nerves** 使某人心烦 shǐ mǒurén xīnfán

nervous ['nɜːvəs] ADJ 紧张的 jǐnzhāng de ▸ **to be nervous about sth/about doing sth** 对 某事/做某事感到紧张不安 duì mǒushì/zuò mǒushì gǎndào jǐnzhāng bù'ān

nest [nɛst] N [c] 巢 cháo [个 gè]

net [nɛt] N 1 [c] 网 wǎng [张 zhāng] 2 (Comput) ▸ **the Net** 网络 wǎngluò [个 gè]

Netherlands ['nɛðələndz] NPL ▸ **the Netherlands** 荷兰 Hélán

network ['nɛtwɜːk] N 1 网状 系统 wǎngzhuàng xìtǒng [个

2 (system) 网络 wǎngluò [个 gè]

never ['nevə'] ADV 从未 cóngwèi ▸ we never saw him again 我们再没有见过他 wǒmen zài méiyǒu jiànguò tā

new [njuː] ADJ **1** 崭新的 zhǎnxīn de **2** [+ product, system, method] 新式的 xīnshì de **3** [+ job, address, boss, president] 新的 xīn de ▸ this concept is new to me 我对这个概念不熟悉 wǒ duì zhège gàiniàn bù shúxī

news [njuːz] N [U] 消息 xiāoxi ▸ a piece of news 一条消息 yītiáo xiāoxi ▸ good/bad news 好/坏消息 hǎo/huài xiāoxi ▸ the news (TV, Rad) 新闻 xīnwén

newsagent ['njuːzeɪdʒənt] (Brit) N [c] (also: newsagent's) 报刊店 bàokāndiàn [家 jiā]

newspaper ['njuːzpeɪpə'] N [c] 报纸 bàozhǐ [份 fèn]

New Year N [U] ▸ (the) New Year 新年 Xīnnián ▸ in the New Year 在新的一年中 zài xīnde yīnián zhōng ▸ Happy New Year! 新年快乐! Xīnnián Kuàilè!

New Year's Day, (US) **New Year's** N [U] 元旦 Yuándàn

New Year's Eve, (US) **New Year's** N [U] 元旦前夜 Yuándàn qiányè

New Zealand ['-ziːlənd] I N 新西兰 Xīnxīlán II ADJ 新西兰的 Xīnxīlán de

next [nekst] I ADJ **1** 下一个的 xiàyīgè de **2** [+ house, street, room] 旁边的 pángbiān de II ADV 接下来地 jiēxiàlái de

day/morning 第二天/天早晨 dì'èrtiān/tiān zǎochén ▸ the next five years/weeks will be very important 接下来的5年/周将是至关重要的 jiēxiàlái de wǔnián/zhōu jiāngshì zhì guān zhòngyào de ▸ the next flight/prime minister 下一次航班/下一任首相 xià yīcì hángbān/xià yīrèn shǒuxiàng ▸ next time, be a bit more careful 下一次,要更谨慎些 xià yīcì, yào gèng jǐnshèn xiē ▸ who's next? 下一位是谁? xià yīwèi shì shuí? ▸ the week after next 下下个星期 xiàxiàgè xīngqī ▸ next to (beside) 旁边 pángbiān

next door ADV 隔壁 gébì

NHS (Brit) N ABBR (= National Health Service) ▸ the NHS 英国国民医疗服务制度

nice [naɪs] ADJ **1** 好的 hǎo de **2** [+ person] (likeable) 和蔼的 hé'ǎi de; (friendly) 友好的 yǒuhǎo de ▸ to look nice 看上去不错 kànshàngqù bùcuò ▸ it's nice to see you 很高兴见到你 hěn gāoxìng jiàndào nǐ

nickname ['nɪkneɪm] N [c] 绰号 chuòhào [个 gè]

niece [niːs] N [c] (brother's daughter) 侄女 zhínǚ [个 gè]; (sister's daughter) 甥女 shēngnǚ [个 gè]

Nigeria [naɪ'dʒɪəriə] N 尼日利亚 Nírìlìyà

night [naɪt] N **1** [c/u] 黑夜 hēiyè [个 gè] **2** [c] (evening) 晚上 wǎnshang [个 gè] ▸ at night 夜间 yèjiān ▸ in/during the night

nightclub ['naɪtklʌb] N [c] 夜总
会 yèzŏnghuì [个 gè]

nightie ['naɪtɪ] N [c] 睡衣 shuìyī
[件 jiàn]

nightmare ['naɪtmɛəʳ] N [c] 恶梦
èmèng [场 chǎng]

nil [nɪl] N 1 [U] (*Brit*) (*Sport*) 零 líng
▸ **they lost two nil to Italy** 他们
以0比2输给意大利队 tāmen yǐ líng
bǐ èr shūgěi yìdàlì duì 2 ▸ **their
chances of survival are nil** 他们
没有幸存的可能 tāmen méiyŏu
xìngcún de kěnéng

nine [naɪn] NUM 九 jiǔ; *see also*
five

nineteen ['naɪn'ti:n] NUM 十九
shíjiǔ; *see also* **fifteen**

ninety ['naɪntɪ] NUM 九十 jiǔshí;
see also **fifty**

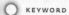

KEYWORD

no [nəʊ] (*pl* **noes**) I ADV (*opposite of
"yes"*) 不 bù ▸ **"did you see it?" —
"no (I didn't)"** "你看见了吗?" —
"不 (我没见到)" "nǐ kànjiàn le
ma?" "bù (wŏ méi jiàndào)" ▸ **no
thank you, no thanks** 不用, 谢
谢你 bùyòng, xièxiè nǐ
II ADJ (*not any*) 没有 méiyŏu ▸ **I
have no milk/books** 我没有牛
奶/书 wŏ méiyŏu niúnǎi/shū ▸ **"no
smoking"** "严禁吸烟" "yánjìn
xīyān" ▸ **no way!** 没门儿!
méiménr!

nobody ['nəʊbədɪ] PRON 没有人
méiyŏu rén

noise [nɔɪz] N 1 [c] (*sound*) 响声
xiǎngshēng [阵 zhèn] 2 [U] (*din*) 噪
音 zàoyīn

noisy ['nɔɪzɪ] ADJ 嘈杂的 cáozá
de; [+ *place*] 喧闹的 xuānnào de

none [nʌn] PRON 1 (*not one*) 没有
一个 méiyŏu yī gè 2 (*not any*) 没
有一点儿 méiyŏu yīdiǎnr ▸ **none
of us/them** 我们/他们谁也
没 wŏmen/tāmen shuí yě méi
▸ **I've/there's none left** 我一点也
没了/一点也没剩 wŏ yīdiǎn yě
méiyŏu le/yīdiǎn yě méi shèng

nonsense ['nɔnsəns] N [U] 胡说
bāshuō de

non-smoking ['nɔn'sməʊkɪŋ]
ADJ 禁烟的 jìn yān de

non-stop ['nɔn'stɔp] ADV
1 (*ceaselessly*) 不断地 bùduàn de 2
不停地 bù tíng de

noodles ['nu:dlz] NPL 面条
miàntiáo

noon [nu:n] N [U] 中午 zhōngwǔ
▸ **at noon** 中午 zhōngwǔ

no-one ['nəʊwʌn] PRON =
nobody

nor [nɔ:ʳ] CONJ 也不 yěbù; *see also*
neither

normal ['nɔ:məl] ADJ 正常的
zhèngcháng de ▸ **more/higher/
worse than normal** 比正常的
多/高/糟糕 bǐ zhèngchángde
duō/gāo/zāogāo

normally ['nɔ:məlɪ] ADV (*usually*)
通常地 tōngcháng de

north [nɔ:θ] I N [U/s] 北方
běifāng II ADJ 北部的 běibù de
III ADV 向北方 xiàng běifāng ▸ **to
the north** 以北 yǐběi

North America N 北美 Běiměi

north-east [nɔːθˈiːst] I N 东北 dōngběi II ADJ 东北的 dōngběi de III ADV 向东北 xiàng dōngběi

northern ['nɔːðən] ADJ 北方 的 běifāng de ▶the northern hemisphere 北半球banqiú

Northern Ireland N 北爱尔兰 Běi'ài'ěrlán

North Korea N 朝鲜 Cháoxiǎn

North Pole N ▶the North Pole 北极 Běijí

north-west [nɔːθˈwest] I N 西 北 xīběi II ADJ 西北的 xīběi de III ADV 向西北 xiàng xīběi

Norway ['nɔːweɪ] N 挪威 Nuówēi

nose [nəuz] N [c] 鼻子 bízi [个 gè]

not [nɒt] ADV 不 bù ▶he is not or isn't here 他不在这儿 tā bùzài zhèr ▶it's too late, isn't it? 现 在太晚了，不是吗？ xiànzài tàiwǎn le, bùshì ma? ▶he asked me not to go 他叫我不要这么 做 tā jiào wǒ bùyào zhème zuò ▶are you coming or not? 你来 不来？ nǐ láibùlái? ▶not at all (in answer to thanks) 不客气 bù kèqi ▶not yet/now 还没/现在不 háiméi/xiànzài bù ▶not really 并 不是的 bìng bùshì de

note [nəut] I N [c] 1 (message) 便 条 biàntiáo [张 zhāng] 2 (Brit: banknote) 纸币 zhǐbì [张 zhāng] II VT (observe) 留意 liúyì III notes NPL (from or for lecture) 笔记 bǐjì ▶to make a note of sth 记下某事 jìxià mǒushì ▶to take notes 记 笔记 jì bǐjì

notebook ['nəutbuk] N [c] 笔记 本 bǐjìběn [个 gè]

notepad ['nəutpæd] N [c] 1 (pad of paper) 记事本 jìshìběn [个 gè] 2 (Comput) 记事簿 jìshìbù [个 gè]

nothing ['nʌθɪŋ] PRON 什么也没 有 shénme yě méiyǒu ▶nothing new/serious/to worry about 没 有什么新的/要紧的/值得担忧 的 méiyǒu shénme xīnde/yàojǐn de/zhídé dānyōu de ▶nothing else 没有别的 méiyǒu biéde ▶for nothing 免费 miǎnfèi ▶nothing at all 什么也没有 shénme yě méiyǒu

notice ['nəutɪs] I VT 注意到 zhùyì dào II N [c] 公告 gōnggào [个 gè] ▶to notice that... 注意到… zhùyì dào... ▶to take no notice of sb/sth 不理某人/某事 bùlǐ mǒurén/mǒushì ▶without notice 不事先通知 bù shìxiān tōngzhī

noticeboard ['nəutɪsbɔːd] (Brit) N [c] 布告栏 bùgàolán [个 gè]

nought [nɔːt] (esp Brit) NUM 零 líng

noun [naun] N [c] 名词 míngcí [个 gè]

novel ['nɒvl] N [c] 小说 xiǎoshuō [个 gè]

novelist ['nɒvəlɪst] N [c] 小说家 xiǎoshuōjiā [位 wèi]

November [nəuˈvembəʳ] N [c/u] 十一月 shíyīyuè [个 gè]; see also July

now [nau] I ADV 1 现在 xiànzài 2 (these days) 如今 rújīn II CONJ ▶now (that) 既然 jìrán ▶right now 这时 zhèshí

现在 dào xiànzài ▸**just now** 眼
下 yǎnxià ▸**from now on** 从
起 cóng xiànzài qǐ ▸**that's all for
now** 就到这里 jiùdào zhèlǐ

nowhere['nəʊweə[r]] ADV 无处
wúchù ▸**nowhere else** 没有其他
地方 méiyǒu qítā dìfang

nuclear['njuːklɪə[r]] ADJ 核能的
hénéng de

nuisance['njuːsns] N ▸**to be
a nuisance** [thing] 讨厌的东西
tǎoyàn de dōngxi

numb[nʌm] ADJ 麻木的 mámù
de

number['nʌmbə[r]] I N 1 [c] (Math)
数 shù [个 gè] 2 [c] (telephone
number) 电话号码 diànhuà
hàomǎ [个 gè] 3 [c] (of house, bank
account, bus) 号 hào [个 gè] 4 [c/u]
(quantity) 数量 shùliàng II VT
[+ pages] 给…标号码 gěi…biāo
hàomǎ ▸**a number of** (several) 几
个 jǐ gè ▸**a large/small number of** 大
量/少数 dàliàng/shǎoshù

number plate (Brit) N [c] 车号牌
chēhàopái [个 gè]

nun[nʌn] N [c] 修女 xiūnǚ [名
míng]

nurse[nɜːs] N [c] 护士 hùshì [位
wèi]

nursery['nɜːsərɪ] N [c] 幼儿园
yòu'éryuán [个 gè]

nursery school N [c/u] 幼儿园
yòu'éryuán [个 gè]

nut[nʌt] N 1 [c] (Bot, Culin) 坚
果 jiānguǒ [枚 méi] 2 (Tech) 螺母
luómǔ [个 gè]

nylon['naɪlɔn] N [u] 尼龙 nílóng

O

oak[əʊk] N [c] (also: **oak tree**) 橡
树 xiàngshù [棵 kē] 2 [u] (wood) 橡
木 xiàngmù

oar[ɔː[r]] N [c] 桨 jiǎng [只 zhī]

oats[əʊts] NPL 燕麦 yànmài

obedient[ə'biːdɪənt] ADJ 顺从的
shùncóng de

obey[ə'beɪ] I VT [+ person, orders]
听从 tīngcóng; [+ law, regulations]
服从 fúcóng II VI 服从 fúcóng

object[n ˈɔbdʒɛkt, vb əbˈdʒɛkt]
I N [c] 1 [thing] 物体 wùtǐ [个 gè]
2 (Ling) 宾语 bīnyǔ [个 gè] II VI 反
对 fǎnduì

objection[əbˈdʒɛkʃən] N [c] 异议
yìyì [个 gè]

obsess[əbˈsɛs] VT 使着迷 shǐ
zháomí

obsession[əbˈsɛʃən] N [c] 着迷

zhǎomí [种 zhǒng]

obtain [əb'teɪn] VT 获得 huòdé

obvious ['ɒbvɪəs] ADJ 明显的 míngxiǎn de

obviously ['ɒbvɪəslɪ] ADV (of course) 显然地 xiǎnrán de

occasion [ə'keɪʒən] N [c] (moment) 时刻 shíkè [个 gè] **2** (event, celebration) 场合 chǎnghé [种 zhǒng]

occasionally [ə'keɪʒənəlɪ] ADV 偶尔地 ǒu'ěr de

occupation [ɒkju'peɪʃən] N [c] 职业 zhíyè [种 zhǒng]

occupy ['ɒkjupaɪ] VT1 (inhabit) [+ house, office] 占用 zhànyòng **2** ▶to be occupied [seat, place etc] 被占用 bèi zhànyòng **3** (fill) [+ time] 占用 zhànyòng

occur [ə'kɜː] VI 发生 fāshēng ▶to occur to sb 某人想到 mǒurén xiǎngdào

ocean ['əuʃən] N [c] 海洋 hǎiyáng [片 piàn]

o'clock [ə'klɒk] ADV ▶six o'clock 6点钟 liùdiǎnzhōng

October [ɒk'təubə] N [c/u] 十月 shíyuè; see also **July**

octopus ['ɒktəpəs] N [c] 章鱼 zhāngyú [只 zhī]

odd [ɒd] ADJ1 (strange) 奇怪的 qíguài de **2** [+ number] 奇数的 jīshù de

odour, (US)**odor** ['əudə] N [c/u] 气味 qìwèi [种 zhǒng]

━━━━ KEYWORD ━━━━

of [ɒv, əv] PREP1 (gen) 的 de

▶the history of China 中国历史 Zhōngguó lìshǐ ▶at the end of the street 在街的尽头 zài jiēde jìntóu ▶the city of New York 纽约城 Niǔyuēchéng

2 (expressing quantity, amount)
▶a kilo of flour 一公斤面粉 yì gōngjīn miànfěn ▶a cup of tea/vase of flowers 一杯茶/一瓶花 yìbēi chá/yìpíng huā ▶there were three of them 他们有3个 tāmen yǒu sāngè ▶an annual income of $30,000 每年3万美元的收入 měinián sānwàn měiyuán de shōurù

3 (in dates) ▶the 5th of July 7月5日 qīyuè wǔrì

4 (US: in times) ▶at five of three 3点差5分 sāndiǎn chà wǔfēn

━━━━ KEYWORD ━━━━

off [ɒf] I ADJ1 (not turned on) 关着的 guānzhe de

2 (cancelled) 取消的 qǔxiāo de
II ADV1 (away) ▶I must be off 我必须得走了 wǒ bìxū děi zǒu le ▶where are you off to? 你上哪儿去？ nǐ shàng nǎr qù?

2 (not at work) ▶to have a day off (as holiday) 休假一天 xiūjià yìtiān (because ill) 休病假一天 xiūbìngjià yìtiān

3 (Comm) ▶10% off 10%的折扣 bǎifēn zhī shí de zhékòu
III PREP (indicating motion, removal etc) ▶to take a picture off the wall 把画像从墙上取下来 bǎ

huàxiàng cóng qiáng shang qǔ xiàlái

offence, (US) **offense** [əˈfɛns] N [c] (crime) 罪行 zuìxíng [种 zhǒng]

offend [əˈfɛnd] VT (upset) 得罪 dézuì

offense [əˈfɛns] (US) N [c] = **offence**

offer [ˈɔfər] I VT 1 给 gěi 2 (bid) 出价 chūjià II N 1 [c] 1 (proposal) 提议 tíyì [项 xiàng] 2 (special deal) 特价 tèjià [个 gè]

office [ˈɔfɪs] N 1 [c] (room) 办公室 bàngōngshì [间 jiān] 2 [c] (department) 部门 bùmén [个 gè] 3 [c] (US: of doctor, dentist) 诊所 zhěnsuǒ [家 jiā]

office block N [c] 办公大楼 bàngōng dàlóu [座 zuò]

officer [ˈɔfɪsər] N [c] 1 (Mil) 军官 jūnguān [位 wèi] 2 (also: **police officer**) 警官 jǐngguān [位 wèi]

office worker N [c] 职员 zhíyuán [个 gè]

official [əˈfɪʃl] ADJ 官方的 guānfāng de

often [ˈɔfn] ADV (frequently) 经常 jīngcháng ▸**how often do you wash the car?** 你多久洗一次车? nǐ duōjiǔ xǐ yīcì chē?

oil [ɔɪl] I N [c/u] 油 yóu [桶 tǒng] II VT [+ engine, machine] 给…加油 gěi…jiāyóu

oil rig N [c] (on land) 石油钻塔 shíyóu zuàntǎ [个 gè]; (at sea) 钻井平台 zuànjǐng píngtái [个 gè]

okay [əuˈkeɪ] I ADJ 1 (acceptable) 可以的 kěyǐ de 2 (safe and well) 好

的 hǎo de II ADV (acceptably) 不错 bùcuò III INT 1 (expressing agreement) 行 xíng 2 (in questions) 好吗 hǎo ma ▸**are you okay?** 你还好吗? nǐ hái hǎoma? ▸**it's okay with** or **by me** 这对我没问题 zhè duìwǒ méi wèntí

old [əuld] ADJ 1 [+ person] 年老的 niánlǎo de 2 (not new, not recent) 古老的 gǔlǎo de 3 (worn out) 破旧的 pòjiù de 4 (former) 以前的 yǐqián de 5 [+ friend, enemy, rival] 老的 lǎo de ▸**how old are you?** 你多大了? nǐ duōdà le? ▸**he's 10 years old** 他10岁了 tā shísuì le ▸**older brother/sister** 哥哥/姐姐 gēge/jiějie

old age pensioner (Brit) N [c] 拿退休金的人 ná tuìxiūjīn de rén [位 wèi]

old-fashioned [ˈəuldˈfæʃnd] ADJ [+ object, custom, idea] 老式的 lǎoshì de; [+ person] 守旧的 shǒujiù de

olive [ˈɔlɪv] N [c] 橄榄 gǎnlǎn [棵 kē]

olive oil N [u] 橄榄油 gǎnlǎnyóu

Olympic [əuˈlɪmpɪk] I ADJ 奥林匹克的 Aolínpǐkè de II **the Olympics** NPL 奥林匹克运动会 Aolínpǐkè Yùndònghuì

omelette, (US) **omelet** [ˈɔmlɪt] N [c] 煎蛋饼 jiāndànbǐng [个 gè]

KEYWORD

on [ɔn] I PREP 1 (indicating position) 在…上 zài…shang ▸**it's on the table/wall** 它在桌上/墙上 tā zài zhuōshàng/qiángshàng ▸**the house is on the main road** 房子在主路旁 fángzi zài zhǔlù páng ▸**on the left/right** 在左边/右边 zài zuǒbiān/yòubiān ▸**on the top floor** 在顶楼 zài dǐnglóu **2** (indicating means, method, condition etc) ▸**on foot** 步行 bùxíng ▸**on the train/bus** (be, sit) 在火车/公共汽车上 zài huǒchē/gōnggòng qìchē shàng (travel, go) 乘坐 chéngzuò ▸**on the television/radio** 在电视上/广播中 zài diànshì shàng/guǎngbō zhōng ▸**on the Internet** 在因特网上 zài Yīntèwǎng shàng ▸**to be on antibiotics** 定期服用抗生素 dìngqī fúyòng kàngshēngsù **3** (referring to time) 在 zài ▸**on Friday** 在星期五 zài xīngqīwǔ ▸**on Friday, June 20th** 在6月20日，星期五 zài liùyuè èrshí rì, xīngqīwǔ

II ADV **1** (clothes) ▸**to have one's coat on** 穿着外套 chuānzhe wàitào ▸**what's she got on?** 她穿着什么？ tā chuānzhe shénme? **2** (covering, lid etc) ▸**screw the lid on tightly** 把盖子旋紧 bǎ gàizi xuánjǐn

III ADJ **1** (turned on) 打开的 dǎkāi de **2** (happening) ▸**is the meeting still on?** 会议还在进行吗？ huìyì háizài jìnxíng ma? ▸**there's a good film on at the cinema** 电影院正在上映一部好电影 diànyǐngyuàn zhèngzài shàngyìng yíbù hǎo diànyǐng

once [wʌns] **I** ADV **1** (one time only) 一次 yícì **2** (at one time) 曾经 céngjīng **3** (on one occasion) 有一次 yǒu yícì **II** CONJ (as soon as) 一旦 yídàn ▸**at once** (immediately) 立刻 lìkè ▸**once a or every month** 每月一次 měiyuè yícì ▸**once upon a time** (in stories) 很久以前 hěnjiǔ yǐqián ▸**once in a while** 偶尔 ǒu'ěr ▸**once or twice** (a few times) 一两次 yìliǎng cì

KEYWORD

one [wʌn] **I** ADJ **1** (number) 一 yī ▸**it's one o'clock** 现在1点 xiànzài yìdiǎn ▸**one hundred/thousand children** 100/1000个孩子 yìbǎi/yìqiān gè háizi **2** (same) 同一的 tóngyī de ▸**shall I put it all on the one plate?** 要我把它都放在同一个盘子里吗？ yào wǒ bǎ tā dōu fàngzài tóngyígè pánzi lǐ ma?

II PRON **1** (number) 一 yī ▸**I've already got one** 我已经有一个了 wǒ yǐjīng yǒu yígè le ▸**one of them/of the boys** 他们中的一个/男孩中的一个 tāmen zhōng de yígè/nánhái zhōng de yígè ▸**one by one** 一个一个地 yígè yígè de **2** (with adj) 一个 yígè ▸**I've already got a red one** 我已经有一个红的了 wǒ yǐjīng yǒu yígè hóngde le **3** (in generalizations) 人人 rénrén ▸**what can one do?** 一个人能做什么呢？ yīgèrén néng zuò shénme ne? ▸**this one** 这个

zhège ▸**that one** 那个 nàgè
III N (numeral) 一 yī

KEYWORD

oneself PRON 自己 zìjǐ ▸**to hurt oneself** 伤了自己 shāngle zìjǐ ▸**by oneself** (unaided) 独力地 dúlì de; (alone) 独自 dúzì

one-way ['wʌnweɪ] ADJ 1 (+ street, traffic) 单行的 dānxíng de 2 (+ ticket, trip) 单程的 dānchéng de

onion ['ʌnjən] N [c] 洋葱 yángcōng [个 gè]

online, on-line [ɒnlaɪn] (Comput) ADV (on the Internet) 网上 wǎngshang

only ['əʊnlɪ] I ADV 1 仅仅 jǐnjǐn 2 (emphasizing insignificance) 只 zhǐ II ADJ (sole) 唯一的 wéiyī de III CONJ 但是 kěshì ▸**I was only joking** 我只是在开玩笑。 wǒ zhǐshì zài kāi wánxiào ▸**not only... but (also)...** 不但…而且… bùdàn...érqiě... ▸**an only child** 独生子女 dúshēng zǐnǚ

onto, on to ['ɒntu] PREP 到…上 dào...shàng

open ['əʊpən] I ADJ 1 (+ door, window) 开着的 kāizhe de 2 (+ mouth, eyes) 张着的 zhāngzhe de 2 (+ shop) 营业的 yíngyè de II VT 1 (+ container, mouth) 打开 dǎkāi; (+ door, lid) 开开 kāikāi; (+ letter) 拆开 chāikāi; (+ book, hand, mouth, etc.) 张开 zhāngkāi III VI 1 (door, lid) 开开 kāikāi 2 (public building) 开门 kāimén

▸**in the open (air)** 在户外 zài hùwài

opening hours NPL 营业时间 yíngyè shíjiān

open-minded [əʊpn'maɪndɪd] ADJ 开明的 kāimíng de

opera ['ɒpərə] N [c] 歌剧 gējù [部 bù]

operate ['ɒpəreɪt] I VT (+ machine, vehicle, system) 操作 cāozuò II VI 1 (machine, vehicle, system) 工作 gōngzuò; (company, organization) 运作 yùnzuò 2 (Med) 动手术 dòngshǒushù ▸**to operate on sb** (Med) 给某人动手术 gěi mǒurén dòng shǒushù

operation [ɒpə'reɪʃən] N 1 [c] (procedure) 实施步骤 shíshī bùzhòu [个 gè] 2 [c] (Med) 手术 shǒushù [次 cì] ▸**to have an operation** (Med) 接受手术 jiēshòu shǒushù

operator ['ɒpəreɪtə'] N [c] (Tel) 接线员 jiēxiànyuán [位 wèi]

opinion [ə'pɪnjən] N [c] (individual view) 观点 guāndiǎn [个 gè] ▸**in my/her opinion** 按我的/她的意见 àn wǒde/tāde yìjiàn

opinion poll N 民意测验 mínyì cèyàn [次 cì]

opponent [ə'pəʊnənt] N [c] 对手 duìshǒu [个 gè]

opportunity [ɒpə'tjuːnɪtɪ] N [c/u] 机会 jīhuì [个 gè] ▸**to take the opportunity of doing sth or to do sth** 趁机会做某事 chèn jīhuì zuò mǒushì

oppose [ə'pəʊz] VT (+ person, idea) 反对 fǎnduì ▸**to be opposed to**

sth 反对某事 fǎnduì mǒushì

opposite ['ɒpəzɪt] I ADJ 1 [+ side, house] 对面的 duìmiàn de 2 [+ end, corner] 最远的 zuìyuǎn de 3 [+ meaning, direction] 相反 的 xiāngfǎn de II ADV (live, work, sit) 在对面 zài duìmiàn III PREP 在…的对面 zài…de duìmiàn IV N ▶ the opposite 对立面 duìlìmiàn ▶ the opposite sex 异性 yìxìng

opposition [ɒpə'zɪʃən] N [U] 反 对 fǎnduì

optician [ɒp'tɪʃən] N [c] 1 眼镜 商 yǎnjìngshāng [个 gè] 2 (also: **optician's**) 眼镜店 yǎnjìngdiàn [家 jiā]

optimistic [ɒptɪ'mɪstɪk] ADJ 乐观 的 lèguān de

option ['ɒpʃən] N [c] 1 (choice) 选 择 xuǎnzé [种 zhǒng] 2 (Scol, Univ) 选修课 xuǎnxiūkè [门 mén]

or [ɔː] CONJ 1 还是 háishì 2 (also: **or else**) 否则 fǒuzé

oral ['ɔːrəl] I ADJ [+ test, report] 口头的 kǒutóu de II N [c] 口试 kǒushì [次 cì]

orange ['ɒrɪndʒ] I N [c] (fruit) 柑 橘 gānjú [只 zhī] II ADJ (in colour) 橙色的 chéngsè de

orange juice ['ɒrɪndʒdʒuːs] N [U] 橙子汁 júzizhī

orchard ['ɔːtʃəd] N [c] 果园 guǒyuán [个 gè]

orchestra ['ɔːkɪstrə] N [c] 管弦乐 队 guǎnxián yuèduì [支 zhī]

order ['ɔːdə'] I N 1 [c] (command) 命令 mìnglìng [个 gè] 2 [c] (Comm) (in restaurant) 点菜 diǎncài [份 fèn] 3 [U] (sequence) 次序 cìxù

II VT 1 (command) 命令 mìnglìng 2 (Comm: from shop, company) 定 购 dìnggòu; (in restaurant) 点菜 diǎncài III VI (in restaurant) 点 菜 diǎncài ▶ in alphabetical/ numerical order 按字母/数字 顺序 àn zìmǔ/shùzì shùnxù ▶ out of order (not working) 已坏停用 yǐhuài tíngyòng ▶ in order to do sth 为了做某事 wèile zuò mǒushì ▶ to order sb to do sth 命令某 人做某事 mìnglìng mǒurén zuò mǒushì

ordinary ['ɔːdnrɪ] ADJ 普通的 pǔtōng de

organ ['ɔːgən] N [c] 1 (Anat) 器 官 qìguān [个 gè] 2 (Mus) 管风琴 guǎnfēngqín [架 jià]

organic [ɔː'gænɪk] ADJ 1 [+ food, farming] 有机的 yǒujī de 2 [+ substance] 有机物的 yǒujīwù de

organization [ɔːgənaɪ'zeɪʃən] N [c] 组织 zǔzhī [个 gè]

organize ['ɔːgənaɪz] VT 组织 zǔzhī

original [ə'rɪdʒɪnl] ADJ 1 (first, earliest) 最初的 zuìchū de 2 (imaginative) 独创的 dúchuàng de

originally [ə'rɪdʒɪnəlɪ] ADV 起 初 qǐchū

ornament ['ɔːnəmənt] N [c] 装饰 物 zhuāngshìwù [件 jiàn]

orphan ['ɔːfn] N [c] 孤儿 gū'ér [个 gè]

other ['ʌðə'] I ADJ 1 (additional) 另 外的 lìngwài de 2 (not this one) 其他的 qítā de 3 ▶ the other

(of two things or people) 另一…
lìngyī… **4** (apart from oneself) 其
他的 qítā de **II** PRON **1** (additional
one, different one) 其他 qítā de **2** (of
two things or people) 另一
个另一个 lìng yīgè ▸ **the other
day/week** (inf: recently) 几天/星
期前 jǐtiān/xīngqī qián

otherwise ['ʌðəwaɪz] ADV **1** (if
not) 否则 fǒuzé **2** (apart from that)
除此以外 chúcǐ yǐwài

ought [ɔːt] (pt ought) AUX VB
1 (indicating advisability) ▸ **you
ought to see a doctor** 你应该去
看医生 nǐ yīnggāi qù kàn yīshēng
2 (indicating likelihood) ▸ **he ought
to be there now** 他现在应该到那
儿了 tā xiànzài yīnggāi dào nàr le

our ['auəʳ] ADJ 我们的 wǒmen de

ours [auəz] PRON 我们的 wǒmen de

ourselves [auə'sɛlvz] PRON PL 我
们自己 wǒmen zìjǐ ▸ **we didn't
hurt ourselves** 我们没伤到自己
wǒmen méi shāngdào zìjǐ ▸ **by
ourselves** (unaided) 我们独力地
wǒmen dúlì de; (alone) 我们单独
地 wǒmen dāndú de

KEYWORD

out [aut] ADV **1** (outside) 在外面
zài wàimiàn ▸ **out here/there** 这
儿/那儿 zhèr/nàr
2 (absent, not in) 不在 bù zài ▸ **Mr
Green is out at the moment**
格林先生这会儿不在 Gélín
xiānshēng zhèhuìr bùzài ▸ **to
have a day/night out** 外出玩一

天/一晚 wàichū wán yītiān/yīwǎn
3 (Sport) ▸ **the ball was out** 球出
界了 qiú chūjiè le
II ADJ ▸ **to be out** (out of game) 出
局的 chūjú de; (extinguished) [fire,
light, gas] 灭了的 xīmiè de
III ▸ **out of** PREP **1** (outside: with
movement) 出 chū; (beyond)
朝…外 cháo…wài ▸ **to go/come
out of the house** 从房子里走出
去/来 cóng fángzi lǐ zǒu chūqù/lái
2 (from among) …中的 …zhōng de
▸ **one out of every three smokers**
每3个烟民中的1个 měi sāngè
yānmín zhōng de yīgè
3 (without) ▸ **to be out of
milk/petrol** 牛奶喝完了/汽油
用完了 niúnǎi hē wán le/qìyóu
yòng wán le

outdoor [aut'dɔːʳ] ADJ **1** [+ activity]
户外的 hùwài de **2** [+ swimming
pool, toilet] 露天的 lùtiān de

outdoors [aut'dɔːz] ADV 在户外
zài hùwài

outing ['autɪŋ] N [c] 出游 chūyóu
[次 cì]

outlet ['autlɛt] N [c] **1** (hole, pipe)
排放口 páifàngkǒu [个 gè] **2** (US)
(Elec) 电源插座 diànyuán chāzuò
[个 gè]

outline ['autlaɪn] N [c] **1** (shape)
轮廓 lúnkuò [个 gè] **2** (brief
explanation) 概要 gàiyào [篇 piān]

outside [aut'saɪd] N [c] 外面
wàimiàn [个 gè]; [of building] 外表
wàibiǎo [个 gè] II ADJ (exterior) 外
部的 wàibù de III ADV **1** (be, wait)
在外面 zài wàimiàn **2** (go) 向外面

xiàng wàimiàn **IV** PREP **1** [+ place] 在…外 zài…wài; [+ organization] 在…以外 zài…yǐwài **2** [+ larger place] 在…附近 zài…fùjìn

outskirts [ˈautskəːts] NPL ▸ on the outskirts 郊区 jiāoqū ▸ on the outskirts of... 在…的郊区 zài…de jiāoqū

outstanding [autˈstændɪŋ] ADJ 杰出的 jiéchū de

oval [ˈəuvl] ADJ 椭圆形的 tuǒyuánxíng de

oven [ˈʌvn] N [c] 烤箱 kǎoxiāng [个 gè]

KEYWORD

over [ˈəuvəʳ] **I** ADJ (finished) 结束的 jiéshù de
II PREP **1** (more than) 超过 chāoguò ▸ over 200 people came 超过二百人来了 zhāoguò èrbǎirén láile
2 在…上 zài…shang; (spanning) 横跨 héngkuà; (across) 穿过 chuānguò; (on the other side of) 在…对面 zài…duìmiàn ▸ a bridge over the river 横跨河流的一座桥 héngkuà héliú de yīzuò qiáo
3 (during) 在…期间 zài…qījiān ▸ we talked about it over dinner 我们边吃晚饭边讨论 wǒmen biān chī wǎnfàn biān tǎolùn
4 [+ illness, shock, trauma] 康复 kāngfù
5 ▸ all over the town/house/floor 全镇/满屋子/满地 quánzhèn/mǎn wūzi/mǎndì
III ADV **1** 过 guò ▸ over here

there 在这里/那里 zài zhèlǐ/nàlǐ
2 (more, above) 超过 chāoguò ▸ people aged 65 and over 65岁及以上年龄的人 liùshíwǔ suì jí yǐshàng niánlíng de rén
3 (US: again) 再 zài
4 ▸ all over (everywhere) 到处 dàochù

overcast [ˈəuvəkɑːst] ADJ 多云的 duōyún de

overdose [ˈəuvədəus] N [c] 过量用药 guòliàng yòngyào [剂 jì]

overseas [əuvəˈsiːz] ADV 向海外 xiàng hǎiwài

overtake [əuvəˈteɪk] (pt overtook, pp overtaken) **I** VT (esp Brit) (Aut) 超过 chāoguò **II** VI (esp Brit) (Aut) 超车 chāochē

overtime [ˈəuvətaɪm] N [U] 加班时间 jiābān shíjiān

overtook [əuvəˈtuk] PT of overtake

overweight [əuvəˈweɪt] ADJ 超重的 chāozhòng de

owe [əu] VT [+ money] 欠 qiàn ▸ to owe sb sth 欠某人某物 qiàn mǒurén mǒuwù

owing to [ˈəuɪŋ-] PREP (because of) 因为 yīnwèi

owl [aul] N [c] 猫头鹰 māotóuyīng [只 zhī]

own [əun] **I** ADJ 自己的 zìjǐ de **II** VT [+ house, land, car etc] 拥有 yōngyǒu ▸ a room of my own 我自己的房间 wǒ zìjǐ de fángjiān ▸ on one's own (alone) 独自地 dúzì de; (without help) 独立地 dúlì de

► **own up** VI (confess) 坦白 tǎnbái

owner ['əunə'] N [C] 物主 wùzhǔ
[位 wèi]

oxygen ['ɔksɪdʒən] N [U] 氧气
yǎngqì

oyster ['ɔɪstə'] N [C] 牡蛎 mǔlì
[个 gè]

ozone layer N [C] 臭氧层
chòuyǎngcéng [层 céng]

P

Pacific [pə'sɪfɪk] N ► **the Pacific
(Ocean)** 太平洋 Tàipíngyáng

pack [pæk] I VT **1** [+ clothes]
把…打包 bǎ…dǎbāo **2** [+ suitcase,
bag] 把…装箱 bǎ…zhuāngxiāng
II VI 打点行装 dǎdiǎn xíngzhuāng
III N [of cards] 副 fù
► **pack up** VI (Brit) 打点行装
dǎdiǎn xíngzhuāng

package ['pækɪdʒ] N [C] **1** 包裹
bāoguǒ [个 gè] **2** (Comput) 程序包
chéngxùbāo [个 gè]

packed [pækt] ADJ 拥挤的
yōngjǐ de

packet ['pækɪt] N [C] [of cigarettes,
biscuits] 盒 hé [个 gè]; [of crisps,
sweets, seeds] 袋 dài [个 gè]

pad [pæd] N [C] 便笺簿 biànjiānbù
[个 gè]

paddle ['pædl] N [c] 1 (for canoe) 短桨 duǎn jiǎng [个 gè] 2 (US: for table tennis) 球拍 qiúpāi [只 zhī]

padlock ['pædlɒk] N [c] 挂锁 guàsuǒ [个 gè]

paedophile, (US) **pedophile** ['piːdəfaɪl] N [c] 恋童癖者 liàntóngpǐzhě [个 gè]

page [peɪdʒ] N [c] 页 yè

pain [peɪn] N [c/u] 疼痛 téngtòng [阵 zhèn] ▶ to have a pain in one's chest/arm 胸部/胳膊疼 xiōngtòng/gēbo téng ▶ to be in pain 在苦恼中 zài kǔnǎo zhōng

painful ['peɪnful] ADJ [+ back, joint, swelling] 疼痛的 téngtòng de

painkiller ['peɪnkɪlə'] N [c] 止痛药 zhǐtòngyào [片 piàn]

paint [peɪnt] I N [c/u]
1 (decorator's) 油漆 yóuqī [桶 tǒng]
2 (artist's) 颜料 yánliào [罐 guàn]
II VT1 [+ wall, door, house] 油漆 yóuqī 2 [+ person, object] 用颜料画 yòng yánliào huà III VI (creatively) 绘画 huìhuà ▶ a tin of paint 一罐颜料 yīguàn yánliào ▶ to paint sth blue/white etc 把某物涂成蓝色/白色[等] bǎ mǒuwù túchéng lánsè/báisè [děng]

paintbrush ['peɪntbrʌʃ] N [c]
1 (decorator's) 漆刷 qīshuā [个 gè]
2 (artist's) 画笔 huàbǐ [支 zhī]

painter ['peɪntə'] N [c] 1 (artist) 画家 huàjiā [位 wèi] 2 (decorator) 油漆工 yóuqīgōng [个 gè]

painting ['peɪntɪŋ] N 1 [u] 绘画 huìhuà; (decorating walls etc)

上油漆 shàng yóuqī 2 [c] (picture) 画 huà [幅 fú]

pair [peə'] N [c] 1 [of shoes, gloves, socks] 双 shuāng 2 (two people) 对 duì ▶ a pair of scissors 一把剪刀 yībǎ jiǎndāo ▶ a pair of trousers 一条裤子 yītiáo kùzi

pajamas [pə'dʒɑːməz] (US) NPL = **pyjamas**

Pakistan [pɑːkɪ'stɑːn] N 巴基斯坦 Bājīsītǎn

Pakistani [pɑːkɪ'stɑːnɪ] I ADJ 巴基斯坦的 Bājīsītǎn de II N [c] 巴基斯坦人 Bājīsītǎn rén [个 gè]

palace ['pæləs] N [c] 宫殿 gōngdiàn [座 zuò]

pale [peɪl] ADJ 1 [+ colour] 淡的 dàn de 2 [+ skin, complexion] 白皙的 báixī de 3 (from sickness, fear) 苍白的 cāngbái de ▶ pale blue/pink/green 淡蓝色/粉红色/绿色 dàn lánsè/fěnhóngsè/lǜsè

Palestine ['pælɪstaɪn] N 巴勒斯坦 Bālèsītǎn

Palestinian [pælɪs'tɪnɪən] I ADJ 巴勒斯坦的 Bālèsītǎn de II N [c] 巴勒斯坦人 Bālèsītǎn rén [个 gè]

pan [pæn] N [c] (also: **saucepan**) 炖锅 dùnguō [口 kǒu]

pancake ['pænkeɪk] N [c] 薄煎饼 báo jiānbǐng [张 zhāng]

- **PANCAKE**

- 如果你要求英国厨师和美国
- 厨师为你做一张 **pancake**,
- 饼的样子决不会是一模
- 一样。在这两个国家里,
- **pancake** 都是扁平圆形,用

牛奶，面粉和鸡蛋打成面糊，油炸后，趁热吃。英国的饼很薄，经常卷起来，或者夹有甜味或其他口味的馅儿。很多人在 **Shrove Tuesday** (忏悔星期二) 即 **Lent** (大斋节) 开始前的一天吃饼，这一天就是人们熟知的 **Pancake Day** (煎饼节)。(**Lent** 是指复活节前的40天，从前基督教徒有在这段时间里斋戒的传统。) 在美国，**pancake** 相对较小，较厚，通常在早餐时，就着黄油和枫糖吃。

panda ['pændə] N [c] 熊猫 xióngmāo [只 zhī]

panic ['pænɪk] I N [c] 惊恐 jīngkǒng II VI 惊慌 jīnghuāng

pants [pænts] NPL 1 (Brit: underwear) 内裤 nèikù 2 (US: trousers) 长裤 chángkù

pantyhose ['pæntɪhəuz] (US) NPL 连裤袜 liánkùwà ▸ **a pair of pantyhose** 一条连裤袜 yītiáo liánkùwà

paper ['peɪpə'] N 1 [u] 纸 zhǐ 2 [c] (also: newspaper) 报纸 bàozhǐ [份 fèn] ▸ **a piece of paper** (odd bit, sheet) 一张纸 yīzhāng zhǐ

paperback ['peɪpəbæk] N [c] 平装书 píngzhuāng shū [本 běn]

paper clip N [c] 回形针 huíxíngzhēn [枚 méi]

parachute ['pærəʃuːt] N [c] 降落伞 jiàngluòsǎn [个 gè]

parade [pə'reɪd] N [c] 游行 yóuxíng [次 cì]

paradise ['pærədaɪs] N 1 [u] (Rel) 天堂 tiāntáng 2 [c/u] (fig) 乐园 lèyuán [个 gè]

paragraph ['pærəgrɑːf] N [c] 段落 duànluò [个 gè]

parallel ['pærəlɛl] ADJ 1 平行的 píngxíng de 2 (Comput) 并行的 bìngxíng de

paralysed, (US) **paralyzed** ['pærəlaɪzd] (Med) ADJ 瘫痪的 tānhuàn de

paramedic [pærə'mɛdɪk] N [c] 护理人员 hùlǐ rényuán [位 wèi]

parcel ['pɑːsl] N [c] 包裹 bāoguǒ [个 gè]

pardon ['pɑːdn] N [c] ▸ **(I beg your) pardon?**, (US) **pardon me?** 请问您刚才说什么？ qǐngwèn nín gāngcái shuō shénme?

parent ['pɛərənt] N [c] 1 (father) 父亲 fùqīn [位 wèi] 2 (mother) 母亲 mǔqīn [位 wèi] II **parents** NPL 父母 fùmǔ

park [pɑːk] I N [c] 公园 gōngyuán [个 gè] II VT 停放 tíngfàng III VI 停车 tíngchē

parking ['pɑːkɪŋ] N [u] 停车 tíngchē ▸ **"no parking"** "严禁停车" "yánjìn tíngchē"

parking lot (US) N [c] 停车场 tíngchēchǎng [个 gè]

parking meter N [c] 停车计时器 tíngchē jìshíqì [个 gè]

parking ticket N [c] 违章停车罚款单 wéizhāng tíngchē fákuǎndān [张 zhāng]

parliament ['pɑːləmənt] (Brit) N [c/u] 议会 yìhuì [个 gè]

parrot ['pærət] N [c] 鹦鹉 yīngwǔ

part 422

[只 zhī]

part [paːt] N 1 [c/u] (section, division) 部分 bùfen [个 gè] 2 [c] (of machine, vehicle) 部件 bùjiàn [个 gè] ▸ **to take part in** (participate in) 参加 cānjiā
▸ **part with** VT FUS [+ possessions] 放弃 fàngqì; [+ money, cash] 花 huā

participate [paːˈtɪsɪpeɪt] VI 参 与 cānyù ▸ **to participate in sth** [+ activity, discussion] 参加某事 cānjiā mǒushì

particular [pəˈtɪkjuləʳ] ADJ 特定 的 tèdìng de

partly [ˈpaːtlɪ] ADV 部分地 bùfen de

partner [ˈpaːtnəʳ] N [c] 1 (wife, husband, girlfriend, boyfriend) 伴 侣 bànlǚ [个 gè] 2 (in firm) 合 伙人 héhuǒrén [个 gè] 3 (Sport) 搭档 dādàng [个 gè] 4 (for cards, games) 对家 duìjiā [个 gè] 5 (at dance) 舞 伴 wǔbàn [个 gè]

part-time [ˈpaːtˈtaɪm] I ADJ 兼职 的 jiānzhí de II ADV (work, study) 部分时间地 bùfen shíjiān de

party [ˈpaːtɪ] N [c] 1 (Pol) 党 dǎng [个 gè] 2 (social event) 聚会 jùhuì [次 cì] ▸ **birthday party** 生日聚会 shēngrì jùhuì

pass [paːs] I VT 1 (hand) ▸ **to pass sb sth** [+ salt, glass, newspaper, tool] 把某物递给某人 bǎ mǒuwù dìgěi mǒurén 2 (go past) 经过 jīngguò 3 [+ exam, test] 通过 tōngguò II VI 1 (go past) 经过 jīngguò 2 (in exam) 及格 jígé ▸ **to get a pass (in sth)** (Scol, Univ) (某考试)达到及格标准

(mǒu kǎoshì)dádào jígé biāozhǔn
▸ **pass away** VI (die) 去世 qùshì

passage [ˈpæsɪdʒ] N [c] 走廊 zǒuláng [条 tiáo]

passenger [ˈpæsɪndʒəʳ] N [c] 乘 客 chéngkè [位 wèi]

passive [ˈpæsɪv] N [U] ▸ **the passive** (Ling) 被动语态 bèidòng yǔtài

passport [ˈpaːspɔːt] N [c] 护照 hùzhào [本 běn]

password [ˈpaːswəːd] N [c] 密码 mìmǎ [个 gè]

past [paːst] I PREP (in front of, beyond, later than) 过 guò II ADV (by) ▸ **to go/walk/drive past** 经/开过 jīng/kāiguò III ADJ (week, month, year) 刚过去的 gāng guòqù de IV N [c] ▸ **the past** 过去 guòqù [个 gè]; (tense) 过去 时 guòqùshí ▸ **it's past midnight** 过了午夜 guòle wǔyè ▸ **ten/(a) quarter past eight** 8点10/15分 bādiǎn shí/shíwǔ fēn ▸ **for the past few/3 days** 过去几/3天以 来 guòqù jǐ/sāntiān yǐlái ▸ **the past tense** 过去时 guòqù shí ▸ **in the past** (before now) 在过去 zài guòqù

pasta [ˈpæstə] N [U] 意大利面食 Yìdàlì miànshí

pastry [ˈpeɪstrɪ] N [U] (dough) 油 酥面团 yóusū miàntuán 2 [c] (cake) 酥皮糕点 sūpí gāodiǎn [块 kuài]

patch [pætʃ] N 1 (piece of material) 补丁 bǔdīng [个 gè] 2 (area) 斑片 bānpiàn [块 kuài]

path [paːθ] N [c] (track) 小路 xiǎolù [条 tiáo]; 小径

xiǎojìng [条 tiáo]

pathetic [pəˈθɛtɪk] ADJ (+ excuse, effort, attempt) 不足道的 bùzúdào de

patience [ˈpeɪʃns] N [U] 耐心 nàixīn

patient [ˈpeɪʃnt] I N [c] (Med) 病人 bìngrén II ADJ [+ person] 耐心的 nàixīn de

patrol [pəˈtrəʊl] VT 在…巡逻 zài…xúnluó ▸ **to be on patrol** 在巡逻中 zài xúnluó zhōng

pattern [ˈpætən] N [c] 1 花样 huāyàng [种 zhǒng] 2 (for sewing, knitting) 样式 yàngshì [个 gè]

pause [pɔːz] VI (when speaking) 停顿 tíngdùn; (when doing sth) 暂停 zàntíng

pavement [ˈpeɪvmənt] N [c] (Brit) 人行道 rénxíngdào [条 tiáo]

pay [peɪ] (pt, pp **paid**) I N [U] 工资 gōngzī II VT 1 [+ debt, bill, tax] 付 fù 2 [+ person] 发工资 fā gōngzī 3 ▸ **to pay sb sth** (as wage, salary, for goods, services) 付给某人某物 fùgěi mǒurén mǒuwù ▸ **how much did you pay for it?** 你买那个花了多少钱? nǐ mǎi nàge huāle duōshǎo qián? ▸ **pay back** VT 1 [+ money, loan] 偿还 chánghuán 2 [+ person] (with money) 还钱 huánqián ▸ **pay for** VT FUS 买 mǎi

payment [ˈpeɪmənt] N [c] 付款额 fùkuǎn é [笔 bǐ]

payphone [ˈpeɪfəʊn] N [c] 公用电话 gōngyòng diànhuà [部 bù]

PC N ABBR (= **personal computer**) 个人电脑 gèrén diànnǎo

423 | peg

PDA N ABBR (= **personal digital assistant**) 掌上电脑 zhǎngshàng diànnǎo

PE (Scol) N ABBR (= **physical education**) 体育 tǐyù

pea [piː] N [c] 豌豆 wāndòu [粒 lì]

peace [piːs] N [U] 1 (not war) 和平 hépíng 2 宁静 níngjìng

peaceful [ˈpiːsful] ADJ 安静的 ānjìng de

peach [piːtʃ] N [c] 桃 táo [个 gè]

peak [piːk] I N [c] 山顶 shāndǐng [个 gè] II ADJ [+ level, times] 高峰的 gāofēng de

peanut [ˈpiːnʌt] N [c] 花生 huāshēng [粒 lì]

pear [pɛəʳ] N [c] 梨 lí [个 gè]

pearl [pɜːl] N [c] 珍珠 zhēnzhū [颗 kē]

pebble [ˈpɛbl] N [c] 卵石 luǎnshí [块 kuài]

peculiar [pɪˈkjuːlɪəʳ] ADJ 奇怪的 qíguài de

pedal [ˈpɛdl] N [c] 1 (on bicycle) 脚蹬子 jiǎodēngzi [个 gè] 2 (in car, on piano) 踏板 tàbǎn [个 gè]

pedestrian [pɪˈdɛstrɪən] N [c] 行人 xíngrén [个 gè]

pedestrian crossing (Brit) N [c] 人行横道 rénxíng héngdào [条 tiáo]

pedophile [ˈpiːdəʊfaɪl] (US) = **paedophile**

pee [piː] (inf) VI 撒尿 sāniào

peel [piːl] I N [U] 皮 pí II VT [+ vegetables, fruit] 削 xiāo

peg [pɛg] N [c] 1 (for coat, hat, bag) 挂钩 guàdìng [枚 méi] 2 (Brit) (also: **clothes peg**) 衣夹 yījiā [个 gè]

pen [pɛn] N [c] 笔 bǐ [支 zhī]; (also: **fountain pen**) 自来水笔 zìláishuǐbǐ [支 zhī]; (also: **ballpoint pen**) 圆珠笔 yuánzhūbǐ [支 zhī]

penalty ['pɛnltɪ] N [c] 处罚 chǔfá [次 cì] **2** (Football, Rugby) 罚球 fáqiú [个 gè]

pence [pɛns] (Brit) NPL of **penny**

pencil ['pɛnsl] N [c] 铅笔 qiānbǐ [支 zhī]

pencil sharpener N [c] 铅笔刀 qiānbǐdāo [把 bǎ]

penguin ['pɛŋgwɪn] N [c] 企鹅 qǐ'é [只 zhǐ]

penicillin [pɛnɪ'sɪlɪn] N [u] 青霉素 qīngméisù

penknife ['pɛnnaɪf] (pl **penknives**) N [c] 小刀 xiǎodāo [把 bǎ]

penny ['pɛnɪ] (pl **pennies** or (Brit) **pence**) N [c] 便士 biànshì [枚 méi]

pension ['pɛnʃən] N [c] (from state) 养老金 yǎnglǎojīn [份 fèn]; (from employer) 退休金 tuìxiūjīn [份 fèn]

pensioner ['pɛnʃənə'] (Brit) N [c] 领取养老金的人 lǐngqǔ yǎnglǎojīn de rén [个 gè]

people ['piːpl] NPL **1** 人 rén **2** (generalizing) 人们 rénmen ▶ **old people** 老人 lǎorén ▶ **many people** 许多人 xǔduō rén ▶ **people say that...** 有人说… yǒurén shuō…

pepper ['pɛpə'] N **1** [u] (spice) 胡椒粉 hújiāofěn **2** [c] (vegetable) 胡椒 hújiāo [个 gè]

peppermint ['pɛpəmɪnt] N [c] 薄荷糖 bòhe táng [块 kuài]

per [pə:'] PREP 每 měi ▶ **per day**

每天 měitiān ▶ **per person** 每人 měirén ▶ **per annum** 每年 měinián

per cent, percent [pə'sɛnt] (pl **per cent**) N 百分之… bǎifēnzhī… ▶ **by 15 per cent** 以百分之15 yǐ bǎifēnzhī shíwǔ

perfect ['pə:fɪkt] I ADJ **1** (+ weather, behaviour) 完美的 wánměi de; (+ sauce, skin, teeth) 无瑕的 wúxiá de **2** (+ crime, solution, example) 理想的 lǐxiǎng de II N ▶ **the perfect (tense)** 完成(时) wánchéng(shí)

perfectly ['pə:fɪktlɪ] ADV **1** 非常好地 fēicháng hǎo de **2** (honest, reasonable, clear) 绝对地 juéduì de

perform [pə'fɔ:m] I VT 表演 biǎoyǎn II VI (function) (actor, musician, singer, dancer) 演出 yǎnchū

performance [pə'fɔ:məns] N **1** [c] (Theat: by actor, musician, singer, dancer) 表演 biǎoyǎn [次 cì]; (of play, show) 演出 yǎnchū [场 chǎng] **2** [c] (of employee, surgeon, athlete, team) 表现 biǎoxiàn

perfume ['pə:fju:m] N **1** [c/u] 香水 xiāngshuǐ [瓶 píng] **2** [c] 芳香 fāngxiāng [种 zhǒng]

perhaps [pə'hæps] ADV 可能 kěnéng ▶ **perhaps not** 未必 wèibì

period ['pɪərɪəd] N **1** (interval, stretch) 周期 zhōuqī [个 gè] **2** (time) 时期 shíqī [段 duàn] **3** (era) 时代 shídài [个 gè] **4** (esp US: punctuation mark) 句号 jùhào [个 gè] **5** (also: **menstrual period**) 月经期 yuèjīngqī [个 gè] ▶ **to have one's period** 来例假 lái lìjià

permanent ['pə:mənənt] ADJ 持久的 chíjiǔ de; [+ damage] 永久的 yǒngjiǔ de; [+ state, job, position] 长期的 chángqī de

permission [pə'mɪʃən] N [U] 1 (consent) 准许 zhǔnxǔ 2 (official authorization) 批准 pīzhǔn

permit [pə'mɪt] VT (authorization) 许可证 xǔkězhèng [个 gè]

persecute ['pə:sɪkju:t] VT 迫害 pòhài

person ['pə:sn] (pl gen **people**) N [c] 人 rén ▶ **in person** 亲自 qīnzì ▶ **first/second/third person** 第一/二/三人称 dìyī/èr/sān rénchēng

personal ['pə:snl] ADJ 1 [+ telephone number, bodyguard] 私人的 sīrén de; [+ opinion, habits] 个人的 gèrén de; [+ care, contact, appearance, appeal] 亲自的 qīnzì de 2 [+ life, matter, relationship] 私人的 sīrén de

personality [pə:sə'nælɪtɪ] N [c/u] 个性 gèxìng [种 zhǒng]

personally [pə:snəlɪ] ADV 就我个人来说 jiù wǒ gèrén láishuō

personal stereo N [c] 随身听 suíshēntīng [个 gè]

perspiration [pə:spɪ'reɪʃən] N [U] 汗ж水 hànshuǐ

persuade [pə'sweɪd] VT ▶ **to persuade sb to do sth** 劝说某人做某事 quànshuō mǒurén zuò mǒushì

pessimistic [pesɪ'mɪstɪk] ADJ 悲观的 bēiguān de

pest [pest] N [c] (insect) 害虫

hàichóng [只 zhī]

pester ['pestəʳ] VT 烦扰 fánrǎo

pet [pet] N [c] 宠物 chǒngwù [只 zhī]

petrol ['petrəl] (Brit) N [U] 汽油 qìyóu

petrol station (Brit) N [c] 加油站 jiāyóuzhàn [个 gè]

pharmacy ['fɑ:məsɪ] N 1 [c] (shop) 药店 yàodiàn [家 jiā] 2 [U] (science) 药学 yàoxué

philosophy [fɪ'lɒsəfɪ] N [U] (subject) 哲学 zhéxué

phone [fəun] I N [c] 电话 diànhuà [部 bù] II VT 打电话给 dǎ diànhuà gěi III VI 打电话 dǎ diànhuà ▶ **to be on the phone** (be calling) 在通话 ▶ **by phone** 通过电话 tōngguò diànhuà

▶ **phone back** I VT 给…回电话 gěi…huí diànhuà II VI 回电话 huídiàn

phone bill N [c] 话费单 huàfèidān [张 zhāng]

phone book N [c] 电话簿 diànhuàbù [本 běn]

phone booth (US) N [c] 电话亭 diànhuà tíng [个 gè]

phone box (Brit) N [c] 电话亭 diànhuà tíng [个 gè]

phone call N [c] 电话 diànhuà [部 bù] ▶ **to make a phone call** 打电话 dǎ diànhuà

phonecard ['fəunkɑ:d] N [c] 电话卡 diànhuà kǎ [张 zhāng]

phone number N [c] 电话号码 diànhuà hàomǎ [个 gè]

photo ['fəutəu] N [c] 照片 zhàopiàn [张 zhāng] ▶ **to take**

a photo (of sb/sth) 给(某人/某物)拍照片 gěi(mǒurén/mǒuwù)pāi zhàopiàn

photocopier ['fəʊtəʊkɒpɪəʳ] N [c] 影印机 yǐngyìnjī [台 tái]

photocopy ['fəʊtəʊkɒpɪ] I N [c] 影印本 yǐngyìnběn [个 gè] II VT [+ document, picture] 影印 yǐngyìn

photograph ['fəʊtəɡræf] N [c] 照片 zhàopiàn [张 zhāng]

photographer [fə'tɒɡrəfəʳ] N [c] 摄影师 shèyǐngshī [位 wèi]

photography [fə'tɒɡrəfɪ] N [U] 摄影 shèyǐng

phrase [freɪz] N [c] 1 (expression) 习语 xíyǔ [个 gè] 2 (in phrase book, dictionary) 短语 duǎnyǔ [个 gè]

phrase book N [c] 常用词手册 chángyòngcí shǒucè [本 běn]

physical ['fɪzɪkl] ADJ 生理的 shēnglǐ de

physician [fɪ'zɪʃən] (US) N [c] 医生 yīshēng [位 wèi]

physicist ['fɪzɪsɪst] N [c] 物理学家 wùlǐxué jiā [位 wèi]

physics ['fɪzɪks] N [U] 物理学 wùlǐxué

physiotherapist [fɪzɪəʊ'θerəpɪst] N [c] 理疗师 lǐliáoshī [位 wèi]

physiotherapy [fɪzɪəʊ'θerəpɪ] N [U] 物理疗法 wùlǐ liáofǎ

pianist ['pɪ:ənɪst] N [c] (professional) 钢琴家 gāngqínjiā [位 wèi]; (amateur) 钢琴演奏者 gāngqín yǎnzòuzhě [位 wèi]

piano [pɪ'ænəʊ] N [c] 钢琴 gāngqín [架 jià]

pick [pɪk] VT 1 (choose) 选择

xuǎnzé 2 [+ fruit, flowers] 采摘 cǎizhāi ▶ **take your pick** 随意挑选 suíyì tiāoxuǎn

▶ **pick out** VT (select) [+ person, thing] 挑中 tiāozhòng

▶ **pick up** VT 1 [+ object] (take hold of) 拿起 náqǐ; (from floor, ground) 捡起 jiǎnqǐ 2 (collect) [+ person, parcel] 接 jiē

pickpocket ['pɪkpɒkɪt] N [c] 扒手 páshǒu [个 gè]

picnic ['pɪknɪk] N [c] (meal) 野餐 yěcān [顿 dùn]

picture ['pɪktʃəʳ] I N [c] 1 (painting, drawing, print) 画 huà [幅 fú] 2 (photograph) 照片 zhàopiàn [张 zhāng] 3 (film, movie) 电影 diànyǐng [部 bù] II **the pictures** N PL (Brit: inf: the cinema) 电影院 diànyǐngyuàn

picture messaging [-'mesɪdʒɪŋ] N [U] 彩信 cǎixìn

piece [pi:s] N [c] 1 (fragment) 块 kuài 2 段 duàn 3 块 kuài ▶ **a piece of paper** 一张纸 yìzhāng zhǐ ▶ **a 10p piece** (Brit) 一枚10便士硬币 yìméi shí biànshì yìngbì

pierced [pɪəst] ADJ [+ ears, nose, lip] 穿孔的 chuānkǒng de

piercing ['pɪəsɪŋ] N [c] 人体穿孔 réntǐ chuānkǒng [个 gè]

pig [pɪg] N [c] 猪 zhū [头 tóu]

pigeon ['pɪdʒən] N [c] 鸽子 gēzi [只 zhī]

pile [paɪl] I N [c] 堆 duī [个 gè] II **pile** 堆起 duīqǐ ▶ **piles of** or **a pile of sth** (inf) 一大堆某物 yídàduī mǒuwù

pill [pɪl] N [c] 药丸 yàowán [粒 lì]

▶the pill (contraceptive pill) 避孕药 bìyùnyào ▶to be on the pill 服避孕药 fú bìyùnyào

pillow ['pɪləʊ] N [c] 枕头 zhěntou [个 gè]

pilot ['paɪlət] N [c] 飞行员 fēixíngyuán [个 gè]

*PIN [pɪn] N ABBR (= personal identification number) (also: PIN number) 密码 mìmǎ

pin [pɪn] I N [c] 1 (used in sewing) 大头针 dàtóuzhēn [枚 méi] 2 (badge) 饰针 shìzhēn [枚 méi] II VT (on wall, door, board) 钉住 dìngzhù ▶pins and needles 发麻 fāmá

pinch [pɪntʃ] VT [+ person] 捏 niē

pine [paɪn] N [c] 1 (also: pine tree) 松树 sōngshù [棵 kē] 2 [u] (wood) 松木 sōngmù

pineapple ['paɪnæpl] N [c] 菠萝 bōluó [个 gè]

pink [pɪŋk] I ADJ 粉红色的 fěnhóngsè de II N [c/u] 粉红色 fěnhóngsè [种 zhǒng]

pint [paɪnt] N [c] (measure) (Brit: 568 cc) 品脱 pǐntuō; (US: 473 cc) 品脱 pǐntuō

pipe [paɪp] N [c] 1 (for water, gas) 管子 guǎnzi [根 gēn] 2 (for smoking) 烟斗 yāndǒu [个 gè]

pirate ['paɪərət] N [c] 海盗 hǎidào [个 gè]

pirated ['paɪərətɪd] (Comm) ADJ 盗版的 dàobǎn de

Pisces ['paɪsiːz] N [u] (sign) 双鱼座 Shuāngyú Zuò

pitch [pɪtʃ] N [c] (Brit) 球场 qiúchǎng [个 gè]

pity ['pɪtɪ] I N 1 [u] (compassion)

同情 tóngqíng 2 (misfortune) ▶it is a pity that... 真遗憾... zhēn yíhàn... II VT [+ person] 同情 tóngqíng ▶what a pity! 真可惜! zhēn kěxī!

pizza ['piːtsə] N [c] 比萨饼 bǐsàbǐng [个 gè]

place [pleɪs] I N 1 [c] (location) 地方 dìfang [个 gè] 2 [c] (space) 空位 kòngwèi [个 gè]; (seat) 座位 zuòwèi [个 gè]; (at university, on course, on committee, in team) 名额 míng'é [个 gè] 3 [c] (in competition) 名次 míngcì [个 gè] 4 [u] (US: inf) ▶some/every/no/any place 某些/每个/没有/任何地方 mǒuxiē/měigè/méiyǒu/rènhé dìfang ▶in places 有几处 yǒu jǐchù ▶at sb's place (home) 在某人的家里 zài mǒurén de jiālǐ ▶to take sb's/sth's place 代替某人/某物 dàitì mǒurén/mǒuwù ▶to take place (happen) 发生 fāshēng

plain [pleɪn] I ADJ (not patterned) 无图案花纹的 wú tú'àn huāwén de II N [c] (area of land) 平原 píngyuán [个 gè]

plait [plæt] I N [c] 辫子 biànzi [条 tiáo] II VT 编 biān

plan [plæn] I N [c] 1 (scheme, project) 计划 jìhuà [个 gè] 2 (drawing) 详图 xiángtú [张 zhāng] II VT 计划 jìhuà III VI (think ahead) 打算 dǎsuàn IV PL NS (intentions) 计划 jìhuà ▶to plan to do sth 计划做某事 jìhuà zuò mǒushì

plane [pleɪn] N [c] 飞机 fēijī

[架 jià]

planet ['plænɪt] N [c] 行星 xíngxíng [个 gè]

plant [plɑːnt] N I N 1 [c] 植物 zhíwù [株 zhū] 2 [c] (factory, power station) 工厂 gōngchǎng [个 gè] II VT 栽种 zāizhòng

plaster ['plɑːstə'] N 1 [U] 灰泥 huīní [c/U] (Brit) (also: **sticking plaster**) 橡皮膏 xiàngpígāo [块 kuài] ▸**in plaster** (Brit) 打了石膏 的 dǎle shígāo de

plastic ['plæstɪk] I N [c/U] 塑料 sùliào [种 zhǒng] II ADJ [+ bucket, chair, cup] 塑料的 sùliào de

plastic wrap (US) N [U] 保鲜膜 bǎoxiānmó

plate [pleɪt] N [c] 碟 dié [个 gè]

platform ['plætfɔːm] N [c] 1 (stage) 平台 píngtái [个 gè] 2 (Rail) 站台 zhàntái [个 gè] ▸**the train leaves from platform 7** 火车从7号站台出发 huǒchē cóng qīhào zhàntái chūfā

play [pleɪ] I N [c] 戏剧 xìjù [出 chū] II VT 1 [+ game, chess] 玩 wán; [+ football] 踢 tī; [+ cricket, tennis] 打 dǎ 2 [+ team, opponent] 同…比赛 tóng…bǐsài 3 [+ part, role, character] 扮演 bànyǎn 4 [+ instrument, piece of music] 演奏 yǎnzòu 5 [+ CD, record, tape] 播放 bōfàng III VI 1 (children) 玩耍 wánshuǎ 2 (orchestra, band) 演奏 yǎnzòu ▸**to play cards** 玩纸牌 wán zhǐpái

▸**play back** VT 回放 huífàng

player ['pleɪə'] N [c] 1 (Sport) 选手 xuǎnshǒu [名 míng] 2 (Mus) ▸**a**

trumpet/flute/piano player 小号/长笛/钢琴演奏者 xiǎohào/chángdí/gāngqín yǎnzòuzhě [位 wèi]

playground ['pleɪgraund] N [c] 1 (at school) 运动场 yùndòng chǎng [个 gè]; (in park) 游戏场 yóuxì chǎng [个 gè]

playing card ['pleɪɪŋ-] N [c] 纸牌 zhǐpái [张 zhāng]

pleasant ['plɛznt] ADJ 1 (agreeable) 令人愉快的 lìngrén yúkuài de 2 (friendly) 友善的 yǒushàn de

please [pliːz] I INT 请 qǐng II VT (satisfy) 使高兴 shǐ gāoxìng ▸**yes please** 好的 hǎode

pleased [pliːzd] ADJ 开心的 kāixīn de ▸**pleased to meet you** 见到你很高兴 jiàndào nǐ hěn gāoxìng ▸**pleased with sth** 对某事满意 duì mǒushì mǎnyì

pleasure ['plɛʒə'] N 1 [U] (happiness, satisfaction) 高兴 gāoxìng 2 [U] (fun) 享乐 xiǎnglè ▸**"it's a pleasure"**, **"my pleasure"** "乐意效劳" "lèyì xiàoláo"

plenty ['plɛntɪ] PRON 1 (lots) 大量 dàliàng 2 (sufficient) 充足 chōngzú ▸**plenty of** [+ food, money, time] 很多 hěnduō; [+ jobs, people, houses] 许多 xǔduō

plot [plɔt] I N 1 [c] (secret plan) ▸**a plot (to do sth)** (做某事的)阴谋 (zuò mǒushì de) yīnmóu [个 gè] 2 [c/U] (of story, play, film) 情节 qíngjié [个 gè] II VI (conspire) 密谋 mìmóu ▸**to plot to do sth** 密谋做某事 mìmóu zuò mǒushì

plug [plʌg] N 1 (Elec: on

appliance) 插头 chātóu [个 gè]; (*socket*) 插座 chāzuò [个 gè] **2** (*in sink, bath*) 塞子 sāizi [个 gè]
▶ **plug in** (*Elec*) VT 插上…的插头 chāshang…de chātóu

plum [plʌm] N [c] (*fruit*) 梅子 méizi [颗 kē]

plumber ['plʌmə'] N [c] 管子工 guǎnzi gōng [位 wèi]

plural ['pluərl] **I** ADJ 复数的 fùshù de **II** N [c] 复数 fùshù [个 gè]

plus [plʌs] **I** CONJ **1** (*added to*) 加 jiā **2** (*as well as*) 和 hé **II** ADV (*additionally*) 此外 cǐwài **III** N [c] (*inf*) ▶ **it's a plus** 这是个附加的好处 zhè shì gè fùjiā de hǎochù [个 gè] ▶ **B plus** (*Scol*) B加 bìjiā

p.m. ADV ABBR (= *post meridiem*) 下午 xiàwǔ

pneumonia [njuː'məuniə] N [U] 肺炎 fèiyán

pocket ['pɒkɪt] N [c] 口袋 kǒudài [个 gè]; (*fig*)

pocketbook ['pɒkɪtbuk] N [c] **1** (*US: wallet*) 皮夹 píjiā [个 gè] **2** (*US: handbag*) 手提包 shǒutíbāo [个 gè]

poem ['pəuɪm] N [c] 诗 shī [首 shǒu]

poet ['pəuɪt] N [c] 诗人 shīrén [位 wèi]

poetry ['pəuɪtrɪ] N [U] **1** (*poems*) 诗 shī **2** (*form of literature*) 诗歌 shīgē

point [pɔɪnt] **I** N **1** [c] (*in report, lecture, interview*) 论点 lùndiǎn [个 gè] **2** [s] (*significant part: of argument, discussion*) 要害 yàohài **3** [s] (*purpose: of action*) 目的 mùdì

4 [c] (*place*) 位置 wèizhì [个 gè] **5** [s] (*moment*) 时刻 shíkè **6** [c] (*sharp end*) 尖端 jiānduān **7** [c] (*in score, competition, game, sport*) 分 fēn **8** [c] (*also: decimal point*) 小数点 xiǎoshùdiǎn [个 gè] **II** VI (*with finger, stick*) 指出 zhǐchū **III** VT ▶ **to point sth at sb** 把某物瞄准某人 bǎ mǒuwù miáozhǔn mǒurén ▶ **there's no point (in doing that)** (那样做) 毫无意义 (nàyàng zuò) háowú yìyì ▶ **two point five** (2.5) 二点五 èrdiǎnwǔ ▶ **to point at sth/sb** (*with finger, stick*) 指着某物/某人 zhǐzhe mǒuwù/mǒurén
▶ **point out** (*in book*) 指出 zhǐchū ▶ **to point out that...** 指出… zhǐchū…

pointless ['pɔɪntlɪs] ADJ 无意义的 wú yìyì de

poison ['pɔɪzn] **I** N [c/U] 毒药 dúyào [种 zhǒng] **II** VT 下毒 xiàdú [个 gè]

poisonous ['pɔɪznəs] ADJ (*lit*) [+ *animal, plant, fumes, chemicals*] 有毒的 yǒudú de

poker ['pəukə'] N [U] 扑克牌 pūkèpái

Poland ['pəulənd] N 波兰 Bōlán

polar bear ['pəulə'-] N [c] 北极熊 běijíxióng [头 tóu]

Pole [pəul] N [c] 波兰人 Bōlánrén [个 gè]

pole [pəul] N [c] **1** (*stick*) 杆 gān [根 gēn] **2** (*Geo*) 地极 dìjí [个 gè]

police [pə'liːs] NPL **1** (*organization*) 警方 jǐngfāng **2** (*members*) 警察 jǐngchá

policeman [pə'liːsmən] (*pl* **policemen**) N [c] 男警察 nán jǐngchá [个 gè]

police station N [c] 警察局 jǐngchá jú [个 gè]

policewoman [pəˈliːˌswʊmən] (pl **policewomen**) N [c] 女警察 nǚ jǐngchá [个 gè]

Polish [ˈpəʊlɪʃ] I ADJ 波兰的 Bōlán de II N [U] (language) 波兰 语 Bōlányǔ

polish [ˈpɒlɪʃ] I N [c/U] 1 上光 剂 shàngguāng jì [盒 hé] II VT [+ shoes] 擦亮 cāliàng; [+ furniture, floor] 上光 shàngguāng

polite [pəˈlaɪt] ADJ 有礼貌的 yǒu lǐmào de

political [pəˈlɪtɪkl] ADJ 政治的 zhèngzhì de

politician [pɒlɪˈtɪʃən] N [c] 政治 家 zhèngzhì jiā [位 wèi]

politics [ˈpɒlɪtɪks] N 1 (activity) 政治 zhèngzhì 2 (subject) 政治学 zhèngzhì xué

pollute [pəˈluːt] VT 污染 wūrǎn

polluted [pəˈluːtɪd] ADJ 被污染的 bèi wūrǎn de

pollution [pəˈluːʃən] N [U] 1 (process) 污染 wūrǎn 2 (substances) 污染物 wūrǎn wù

polythene bag [ˈpɒlɪθiːn-] N [c] 聚乙烯塑料袋 jùyǐxī sùliàodài [个 gè]

pond [pɒnd] N [c] 池塘 chítáng [个 gè]

pony [ˈpəʊnɪ] N [c] 小马 xiǎomǎ [匹 pǐ]

ponytail [ˈpəʊnɪteɪl] N [c] 马尾辫 mǎwěibiàn [条 tiáo]

pool [puːl] N 1 [c] (pond) 水 塘 shuǐtáng [个 gè] 2 (also:

swimming pool) 游泳池 yóuyǒngchí [个 gè] 3 [U] (game) 美 式台球 měishì táiqiú

poor [pʊəʳ] I ADJ 1 [+ person] 贫穷 的 pínqióng de 1 (country, area) 贫 困的 pínkùn de 2 (bad) [+ quality, performance] 低水平的 dī shuǐpíng de; [+ wages, conditions, results, attendance] 差的 chà de II NPL ▸ **the poor** 穷人 qióngrén ▸ **poor (old)** Bill 可怜的(老)比尔 kělián de (lǎo) Bǐʾěr

pop [pɒp] N 1 [U] (Mus) 流行音乐 liúxíng yīnyuè 2 [c] (US: inf: father) 爸爸 bàba [个 gè]

popcorn [ˈpɒpkɔːn] N [U] 爆米花 bàomǐhuā

pope [pəʊp] N [c] 教皇 jiàohuáng [位 wèi]

popular [ˈpɒpjʊləʳ] ADJ 1 [+ person, place, thing] 流行的 liúxíng de 2 [+ name, activity] 时髦的 shímáo de

population [pɒpjuˈleɪʃən] N [c] 人口 rénkǒu [个 gè]

pork [pɔːk] N [U] 猪肉 zhūròu

port [pɔːt] N 1 [c] (harbour) 港口 gǎngkǒu [个 gè] 2 [c] (town) 港市 gǎngshì [座 zuò]

portable [ˈpɔːtəbl] ADJ 便携式的 biànxiéshì de

porter [ˈpɔːtəʳ] N [c] 1 (Brit: doorkeeper) 门房 ménfáng [个 gè] 2 (US: on train) 列车员 lièchēyuán [个 gè]

portion [ˈpɔːʃən] N [c] 份额 fèn'é

portrait [ˈpɔːtreɪt] N [c] (picture) 画像 huàxiàng [幅 fú]

Portugal [ˈpɔːtjʊgəl] N 葡萄牙

Pútáoyá

Portuguese [pɔːtjuˈgiːz] (pl
Portuguese) I ADJ 葡萄牙的
Pútáoyá de II N 1 [c] (person) 葡
萄牙人 Pútáoyárén [个 gè] II (language) 葡萄牙语 Pútáoyáyǔ

posh [pɒʃ] (inf) ADJ [+ hotel,
restaurant, area] 豪华的 háohuá de

position [pəˈzɪʃən] N [c] 1 位置
wèizhi [个 gè] 2 (posture: of person's
body) 姿势 zīshì [个 gè]

positive [ˈpɒzɪtɪv] ADJ 1 (good) 有
益的 yǒuyì de 2 (affirmative) [+ test,
result] 阳性的 yángxìng de 3 (sure)
▶ to be positive (about sth) 确信
(某事) quèxìn (mǒushì)

possession [pəˈzɛʃən] I N [U] 拥
有 yōngyǒu II possessions NPL
财产 cáichǎn

possibility [pɒsɪˈbɪlɪtɪ] N [c]
1 (that sth is true) 可能性
kěnéngxìng [种 zhǒng]; (of sth
happening) 可能的事 kěnéng de
shì [件 jiàn] 2 (option) 可选性
kěxuǎnxìng [种 zhǒng]

possible [ˈpɒsɪbl] ADJ 1 [+ event,
reaction, effect, consequence] 可能
的 kěnéng de; [+ risk, danger] 潜
在的 qiánzài de; [+ answer, cause,
solution] 可接受的 kě jiēshòu
de ▶ it's possible (that...) 可能
(…) kěnéng… ▶ if possible 如有
可能 rúyǒu kěnéng ▶ as soon as
possible 尽快 jìnkuài

possibly [ˈpɒsɪblɪ] ADV (perhaps)
大概 dàgài

post [pəʊst] I N 1 (Brit) ▶ the post
(service, system) 邮政 yóuzhèng; (letters, delivery) 邮件 yóujiàn 2

[c] (pole) 柱子 zhùzi [根 gēn] 3
[c] (job) 职位 zhíwèi [个 gè] II VT
(Brit) [+ letter] 邮寄 yóujì ▶by
post (Brit) 以邮件的方式 yǐ yóujiàn
de fāngshì

postbox [ˈpəʊstbɒks] (Brit) N [c]
(in street) 邮筒 yóutǒng [个 gè]

postcard [ˈpəʊstkɑːd] N [c] 明信
片 míngxìnpiàn [张 zhāng]

postcode [ˈpəʊstkəʊd] (Brit) N
[c] 邮政编码 yóuzhèng biānmǎ
[个 gè]

poster [ˈpəʊstə*] N [c] 海报
hǎibào [张 zhāng]

postman [ˈpəʊstmən] (pl
postmen) (Brit) N [c] 邮递员
yóudìyuán [位 wèi]

post office N [c] 邮局 yóujú
[个 gè]

postpone [pəʊsˈpəʊn] VT 推
迟 tuīchí

postwoman [ˈpəʊstwʊmən] (pl
postwomen) (Brit) N [c] 女邮递员
nǚ yóudìyuán [位 wèi]

pot [pɒt] N 1 [c] (for cooking) 锅
guō [口 kǒu] 2 [c] (also: teapot)
茶壶 cháhú [个 gè] 3 [c] (also:
coffeepot) 咖啡壶 kāfēihú [个 gè]
4 [c] (for paint, jam, marmalade,
honey) 罐 guàn [个 gè] 5 [c] (also:
flowerpot) 花盆 huāpén [个 gè]

potato [pəˈteɪtəʊ] (pl potatoes) N
[c/u] 马铃薯 mǎlíngshǔ [个 gè]
土豆 tǔdòu [个 gè]

potato chips (US) NPL 薯片
shǔpiàn

pottery [ˈpɒtərɪ] N 1 [U] (work,
hobby) 陶艺 táoyì 2 [c] (factory,
workshop) 制陶厂 zhìtáo chǎng

[家 jiā]

pound [paund] N [c] 1 (*unit of money*) 镑 bàng 2 (*unit of weight*) 磅 bàng ▶**a pound coin** 1镑硬币 yībàng yìngbì ▶**a five-pound note** 5镑纸币 wǔbàng zhǐbì ▶**half a pound (of sth)** 半磅(某物) bànbàng (mǒuwù)

pour [pɔːˁ] VT ▶**to pour sth (into/onto sth)** 灌某物（到某物里/上）guàn mǒuwù (dào mǒuwù lǐ/shang) ▶**it is pouring (with rain), it is pouring down** 大雨如注 dàyǔ rúzhù

poverty ['pɔvətɪ] N [U] 贫穷 pínqióng

powder ['paudəˁ] N [c/u] 粉 fěn [袋 dài]

power ['pauəˁ] N [U] 1 权力 quánlì 2 (*electricity*) 电力 diànlì

powerful ['pauəful] ADJ 1 (*influential*) 有影响力的 yǒu yǐngxiǎnglì de 2 (*physically strong*) 强健的 qiángjiàn de 3 [+ *engine, machine*] 大功率的 dà gōnglǜ de

practical ['præktɪkl] ADJ 1 [+ *difficulties, experience*] 实践的 shíjiàn de 2 [+ *ideas, methods, advice, suggestions*] 切合实际的 qièhé shíjì de 3 [+ *person, mind*] 有实际经验的 yǒu shíjì jīngyàn de

practically ['præktɪklɪ] ADV 几乎 jīhū

practice ['præktɪs] I N 1 [U] (*exercise, training*) 练习 liànxí 2 [c] (*training session*) 实习 shíxí [次 cì] II VT, VI (*US*) = **practise** ▶**in practice** (*in reality*) 实际上 shíjì shàng ▶**2 hours' piano practice** 2小时的练琴时间 èr xiǎoshí de liànqín shíjiān

practise, (*US*) **practice** ['præktɪs] I VT 练习 liànxí II VI 练习 liànxí

praise [preɪz] VT 称赞 chēngzàn

pram [præm] (*Brit*) N [c] 婴儿车 yīng'érchē

prawn [prɔːn] (*Brit*) N [c] 虾 xiā [只 zhī]

pray [preɪ] VI 祷告 dǎogào

prayer [prɛəˁ] (*Rel*) N [c] (*words*) 祈祷文 qídǎowén [篇 piān]

precaution [prɪˈkɔːʃən] N [c] 预防措施 yùfáng cuòshī [项 xiàng]

precious ['prɛʃəs] ADJ [+ *time, resource, memories*] 宝贵的 bǎoguì de; (*financially*) 贵重的 guìzhòng de

precise [prɪˈsaɪs] ADJ 1 [+ *time, nature, position, circumstances*] 精确的 jīngquè de; [+ *figure, definition*] 准确的 zhǔnquè de; [+ *explanation*] 清晰的 qīngxī de 2 [+ *instructions, plans*] 详尽的 xiángjìn de

precisely [prɪˈsaɪslɪ] ADV (*exactly*) 确切地 quèqiè de; (*referring to time*) 正好 zhènghǎo

predict [prɪˈdɪkt] VT 预言 yùyán

prediction [prɪˈdɪkʃən] N [c] 预言 yùyán [种 zhǒng]

prefer [prɪˈfəːˁ] VT 偏爱 piān'ài ▶**to prefer coffee to tea** 喜欢咖啡胜于茶 xǐhuān kāfēi shèngyú chá ▶**I'd prefer to go by train** 我宁愿坐火车去 wǒ nìngyuàn zuò huǒchē qù

pregnant ['prɛgnənt] ADJ 怀孕的

huáiyùn de ▸**3 months pregnant**
怀孕3个月 huáiyùn sāngèyuè

prejudice ['predʒʊdɪs] N [C/U] 偏
见 piānjiàn [个 gè]

Premier League (Brit) (Football) N
▸**the Premier League** 超级联赛
Chāojí Liánsài

preparation [prepə'reɪʃən] I N [U]
准备 zhǔnbèi II **preparations** NPL
(arrangements) ▸**preparations
(for sth)** (为某事的)准备工作
(wèi mǒushì de) zhǔnbèi gōngzuò
▸**in preparation for sth** 为某事而
准备的 wèi mǒushì ér zhǔnbèi de

prepare [prɪ'peər] I VT 准备
zhǔnbèi; [+ food, meal] 预备 yùbèi
II VI ▸**to prepare for sth** (为
某事) 做准备 (wèi mǒushì) zuò
zhǔnbèi ▸**to prepare to do sth**
(get ready) 准备好做某事 zhǔnbèi
hǎo zuò mǒushì

prepared [prɪ'peəd] ADJ ▸**to
be prepared to do sth** (willing)
有意做某事 yǒuyì zuò mǒushì
▸**prepared (for sth)** (ready) (对某
事) 有所准备的 (duì mǒushì) yǒu
suǒ zhǔnbèi de

prescribe [prɪ'skraɪb] VT (Med)
开处 kāi

prescription [prɪ'skrɪpʃən] N [C]
(Med: slip of paper) 处方 chǔfāng
[个 gè]; (medicine) 药方 yàofāng
[个 gè]

present ['preznt] I ADJ 1 (current)
现有的 xiànyǒu de 2 (in attendance)
在场的 zàichǎng de II N 1 (not past)
▸**the present** 目前 mùqián 2 [c]
(gift) 礼物 lǐwù [件 jiàn] 3 ▸**the
present** (also: **present tense**)

在时态 xiànzài shítài [个 gè] ▸**to
be present at sth** 出席某事 chūxí
mǒushì ▸**at present** 现在 xiànzài
▸**to give sb a present** 给某人礼物
gěi mǒurén lǐwù

president ['prezɪdənt] N [C] (Pol)
总统 zǒngtǒng [位 wèi]

press [pres] I N ▸**the press** 新
闻界 xīnwén jiè II VT 1 [+ button,
switch, bell] 按 àn 2 (iron) 熨
平 yùnpíng ▸**to be pressed for
time/money** 时间紧迫/手头紧
shíjiān jǐnpò/shǒutóu jǐn

pressure ['preʃər] N 1 [U] (physical
force) 压力 yālì 2 [U] ▸**pressure
(to do sth)** (做某事的)压力 (zuò
mǒushì de) yālì 3 [c] (stress)
压力 yālì [种 zhǒng] ▸**to put
pressure on sb (to do sth)** 对某人
施加压力(去做某事) duì mǒurén
shījiā yālì (qù zuò mǒushì)

pretend [prɪ'tend] VT ▸**to
pretend to do sth/pretend
that...** 假装做某事/假装…
jiǎzhuāng zuò mǒushì/jiǎzhuāng...

pretty ['prɪtɪ] I ADJ 漂亮的
piàoliang de II ADV (good, happy,
soon etc) 相当 xiāngdāng

prevent [prɪ'vent] I ADJ [+ war,
disease, situation] 阻止 zǔzhǐ;
[+ accident, fire] 防止 fángzhǐ ▸**to
prevent sb (from) doing sth** 阻
止某人做某事 zǔzhǐ mǒurén zuò
mǒushì ▸**to prevent sth (from)
happening** 防止某事发生 fángzhǐ
mǒushì fāshēng

previous ['priːvɪəs] ADJ
1 [+ marriage, relationship,
experience, owner] 前的 qián de

2 [+ *chapter, week, day*] 以前的 yǐqián de

previously ['pri:vɪəslɪ] ADV **1** 以前 yǐqián **2** ▶ **10 days previously** 10天前 shí tiān qián

price [praɪs] N [c/u] 价格 jiàgé [种 zhǒng]

pride [praɪd] N [u] 自豪 zìháo ▶ **to take (a) pride in sb/sth** 因某人/某事而自豪 yīn mǒurén/mǒushì ér zìháo

priest [pri:st] N [c] 神职人员 shénzhí rényuán [位 wèi]

primarily ['praɪmərɪlɪ] ADV 主要 地 zhǔyào de

primary school ['praɪmərɪ-] (*Brit*) N [c/u] 小学 xiǎoxué [所 suǒ]

Prime Minister [praɪm-] N [c] 总 理 Zǒnglǐ [位 wèi]

prince [prɪns] N [c] 王子 wángzǐ [位 wèi]

princess [prɪn'ses] N [c] 公主 gōngzhǔ [位 wèi]

principal ['prɪnsɪpl] **I** ADJ 主要的 zhǔyào de **II** N [c] 校长 xiàozhǎng [位 wèi]

principle ['prɪnsɪpl] N [c/u] 准 则 zhǔnzé ▶ **in principle** (*in theory*) 原则上 yuánzé shàng

print [prɪnt] **I** N [c] (*photograph*) 照片 zhàopiàn [张 zhāng] **II** VT **1** [+ *story, article*] 出版 chūbǎn **2** (*stamp*) 印 yìn **3** (*write*) 用印刷 体写 yòng yìnshuātǐ xiě **4** (*Comput*) 打印 dǎyìn

▶ **print out** VT 打印出 dǎyìn chū

printer ['prɪntə'] N [c] 打印机 dǎyìnjī [台 tái]

printout ['prɪntaut] N [c] 打印输 出 dǎyìn shūchū [次 cì]

priority [praɪ'ɒrɪtɪ] **I** N [c] (*concern*) 重点 zhòngdiǎn [个 gè] **II** PL NPL 优先考虑的事 yōuxiān kǎolǜ de shì ▶ **to give priority to sth/sb** 给某事/某人 以先先权 gěi mǒushì/mǒurén yī yōuxiān quán

prison ['prɪzn] N **1** [c/u] (*institution*) 监狱 jiānyù [个 gè] **2** [u] (*imprisonment*) 坐牢 zuòláo ▶ **in prison** 坐牢 zuòláo

prisoner ['prɪznə'] N [c] 囚犯 qiúfàn [个 gè]

private ['praɪvɪt] ADJ **1** [+ *property, land, plane*] 私人的 sīrén de **2** [+ *education, housing, health care, industries*] 私有的 sīyǒu de **3** (*confidential*) 秘密的 mìmì de **4** [+ *life, thoughts, plans, affairs, belongings*] 私人的 sīrén de ▶ **in private** 私下 sīxià

prize [praɪz] N [c] 奖 jiǎng [个 gè]

prizewinner ['praɪzwɪnə'] N [c] 获奖者 huòjiǎngzhě [位 wèi]

pro [prəu] PREP (*in favour of*) 赞成 zànchéng

probability [prɒbə'bɪlɪtɪ] N [c/u] ▶ **probability (of sth/that...)** (某 事/…的)可能性 (mǒushì/…de) kěnéngxìng [种 zhǒng]

probable ['prɒbəbl] ADJ 可能的 kěnéng de

probably ['prɒbəblɪ] ADV 可能 kěnéng

problem ['prɒbləm] N [c] 难 题 nántí [个 gè] ▶ **what's the problem?** 有什么问题吗? yǒu shénme wèntí ma? ▶I had no problem finding her 我要找她不难 wǒ yào zhǎo tā bùnán ▶no problem! (inf) 没问题! méi wèntí!

process ['prəʊses] I N [c] 1 (procedure) 过程 guòchéng [个个 gè] II VT [Comput] [+ data] 处理 chǔlǐ ▶to be in the process of doing sth 在从事某事的过程中 zài cóngshì mǒushì de guòchéng zhōng

produce [prə'dju:s] VT 1 [+ effect, result] 促成 cùchéng 2 [+ goods, commodity] 生产 shēngchǎn 3 [+ play, film, programme] 上演 shàngyǎn

producer [prə'dju:sər] N [c] 1 制片人 zhìpiànrén [位 wèi] 2 [of food, material: country] 产地 chǎndì [个 gè]; (company) 制造商 zhìzào shāng [个 gè]

product ['prɒdʌkt] N [c] 产品 chǎnpǐn [个 gè]

production [prə'dʌkʃən] N 1 [U] 生产 shēngchǎn; (amount produced, amount grown) 产量 chǎnliàng 2 [c] (play, show) 作品 zuòpǐn [部 bù]

profession [prə'feʃən] N [c] 职业 zhíyè [种 zhǒng]

professional [prə'feʃənl] ADJ 1 [+ photographer, musician, footballer] 职业的 zhíyè de 2 [+ advice, help] 专业的 zhuānyè de 2 (skilful) 专业水平的 zhuānyè shuǐpíng de

professor [prə'fesər] N [c] 1 (Brit) 教授 jiàoshòu [位 wèi] 2 (US) 教员 jiàoyuán [位 wèi]

profit ['prɒfɪt] N [c/U] 利润 lìrùn ▶to make a profit 赚钱 zhuànqián

profitable ['prɒfɪtəbl] ADJ 有利润的 yǒu lìrùn de

program ['prəʊgræm] I N [c] 1 (also: computer program) 程序 chéngxù [个 gè] 2 (US) = programme II VT 1 (Comput) ▶to program sth (to do sth) 为某物编程(做某事) wèi mǒuwù biānchéng (zuò mǒushì) 2 (US) = programme

programme, (US) program ['prəʊgræm] I N [c] 1 (Rad, TV) 节目 jiémù [个 gè] 2 (for theatre, concert) 节目宣传册 jiémù xuānchuáncè [本 běn] 3 节目单 jiémù dān [个 gè] II VT ▶to programme sth (to do sth) [+ machine, system] 设定某事(做某事) shèdìng mǒushì (zuò mǒushì); see also program

programmer ['prəʊgræmər] (Comput) N [c] 程序员 chéngxùyuán [位 wèi]

progress ['prəʊgres] N [U] 1 (headway) 进展 jìnzhǎn 2 (advances) 进步 jìnbù ▶to make progress (with sth) (对某事)取得进步 (duì mǒushì) qǔdé jìnbù

project ['prɒdʒekt] I N [c] 工程 gōngchéng [个 gè]

promise ['prɒmɪs] I N [c] 许诺 xǔnuò [个 gè] II VI 保证 bǎozhèng III VT ▶to promise sb sth, promise sth to sb 保证给某人某物 bǎozhèng gěi mǒurén mǒuwù ▶to break/keep a promise (to do sth) 违背/遵守(做某事的)诺言 wéibèi/zūnshǒu (zuò mǒushì de) nuòyán ▸**to promise to do sth** 保证做某事 bǎozhèng zuò mǒushì

promotion [prə'məʊʃən] N [c/u] 晋级 jìnjí [次 cì]

prompt [prɒmpt] I ADJ 1 (on time) 干脆的 gāncuì de 2 (rapid) [+ action, response] 迅速的 xùnsù de II N [c] (Comput) 提示符 tíshì fú [个 gè] ▸**at 8 o'clock prompt** 8点整 bādiǎn zhěng

pronoun ['prəʊnaʊn] N [c] 代词 dàicí [个 gè]

pronounce [prə'naʊns] VT 发音 fāyīn

pronunciation [prənʌnsɪ'eɪʃən] N [c/u] 发音 fāyīn [个 gè]

proof [pruːf] N [c/u] 证据 zhèngjù

proper ['prɒpəʳ] ADJ [+ procedure, place, word] 恰当的 qiàdàng de

properly ['prɒpəlɪ] ADV 充分地 chōngfèn de 2 体面地 tǐmiàn de

property ['prɒpətɪ] N 1 [u] (possessions) 财产 cáichǎn 2 [u] (buildings and land) 地产 dìchǎn [处 chù]

prostitute ['prɒstɪtjuːt] N [c] (female) 妓女 jìnǚ [个 gè] ▸**a male prostitute** 男妓 nánjì

protect [prə'tekt] VT 保护 bǎohù ▸**to protect sb/sth from or against sth** 保护某人/某物不受某物的伤害 bǎohù mǒurén/mǒuwù bùshòu mǒuwù de shānghài

protection [prə'tekʃən] N [c/u] ▸**protection (from or against sth)** (免受某物侵害的) 保护 (miǎnshòu mǒuwù qīnhài de) bǎohù [种 zhǒng]

protest [n 'prəʊtest, vb prə'test] I N [c/u] 抗议 kàngyì [次 cì] ▸**to protest about/against/at sth** (Brit) 抗议某事 kàngyì mǒushì III VT (US: voice opposition to) 示威 shìwēi

Protestant ['prɒtɪstənt] I N [c] 新教徒 Xīnjiàotú [个 gè] II ADJ 新教的 Xīnjiào de

protester [prə'testəʳ] N [c] 抗议者 kàngyìzhě [名 míng]

proud [praʊd] ADJ 1 [+ parents, owner] 自豪的 zìháo de 2 (arrogant) 骄傲的 jiāo'ào de ▸**to be proud of sb/sth** 为某人/某事感到自豪 wèi mǒurén/mǒushì gǎndào zìháo

prove [pruːv] I VT [+ idea, theory] 证明 zhèngmíng II VI ▸**to prove that...** [person] 证明…; zhèngmíng…; [situation, experiment, calculations] 显示… xiǎnshì… ▸**to prove sb right/wrong** 证明某人是对的/错的 zhèngmíng mǒurén shì duìde/cuòde

provide [prə'vaɪd] VT [+ food, money, shelter] 供应 gōngyìng; [+ answer, opportunity, details] 提供 tígōng ▸**to provide sb with sth** 提供某人某物 tígōng mǒurén mǒuwù

provided (that) [prə'vaɪdɪd-] CONJ 假如 jiǎrú

PS ABBR (= postscript) 附言 fùyán

psychiatrist [saɪ'kaɪətrɪst] N [c] 精神病医生 jīngshénbìng yīshēng [位 wèi]

psychological [saɪkə'lɒdʒɪkl] ADJ

psychologist [saɪˈkɔlədʒɪst] N [c]
心理的 xīnlǐ de
心理学家 xīnlǐxué jiā [位 wèi]

psychology [saɪˈkɔlədʒɪ] N [U] (of person) 心理学 xīnlǐxué

PTO ABBR (= **please turn over**) 请翻过来 qǐng fān guòlái

pub [pʌb] (Brit) N [c] 酒吧 jiǔbā [个 gè]

public [ˈpʌblɪk] I ADJ 1 [+ support, opinion, interest] 公众的 gōngzhòng de 2 [+ building, service, library] 公共的 gōnggòng de 3 [+ announcement, meeting] 公开的 gōngkāi de II N [s + PL vB]
▸ **the (general) public** 民众 mínzhòng

public holiday N [c] 法定假期 fǎdìng jiàqī [个 gè]

publicity [pʌbˈlɪsɪtɪ] N [U] 1 (information, advertising) 宣传 xuānchuán 2 (attention) 关注 guānzhù

public school N [c/U] 1 (Brit: private school) 私立中学 sīlì zhōngxué [所 suǒ] 2 (US: state school) 公立学校 gōnglì xuéxiào [所 suǒ]

public transport N [U] 公共交通 gōnggòng jiāotōng

publish [ˈpʌblɪʃ] vT [+ book, magazine] 出版 chūbǎn

publisher [ˈpʌblɪʃəʳ] N [c] (company) 出版社 chūbǎnshè [家 jiā]

pudding [ˈpudɪŋ] N [c/U] (Brit: dessert in general) 甜点 tiándiǎn [份 fèn]

puddle [ˈpʌdl] N [c] 水坑 shuǐkēng [个 gè]

pull [pul] I vT 1 [+ rope, hair] 拖 tuō; [+ handle, door, cart, carriage] 拉 lā 2 [+ trigger] 扣 kòu II vI ▸ **to pull a muscle** 扭伤肌肉 niǔshāng jīròu ▸ **to pull sb's leg** (fig) 开某人的玩笑 kāi mǒurén de wánxiào
▸ **pull down** vT [+ building] 拆毁 chāihuǐ
▸ **pull in** vI (at the kerb) 停了下来 tíngle xiàlái
▸ **pull out** vI (Aut: from kerb) 开出 kāichū; (when overtaking) 超车 chāochē 2 退出 tuìchū
▸ **pull through** vI (from illness) 恢复健康 huīfù jiànkāng; (from difficulties) 渡过难关 dùguò nánguān
▸ **pull up I** vI (stop) 停下 tíngxià II vT 1 (raise) [+ socks, trousers] 拉起 lāqǐ 2 [+ plant, weed] 拔除 báchú

pull-off [ˈpulɔf] (US) N [c] 路侧停车处 lùcè tíngchēchù [个 gè]

pullover [ˈpuləuvəʳ] N [c] 套头衫 tàotóushān [件 jiàn]

pulse [pʌls] N [c] (Anat) 脉搏 màibó [下 xià] ▸ **to take** or **feel sb's pulse** 给某人诊脉 gěi mǒurén zhěnmài

pump [pʌmp] N [c] 1 (for liquid, gas) 泵 bèng [个 gè] 2 (for getting water) 抽水机 chōushuǐjī [台 tái] 3 (for inflating sth) 打气筒 dǎqìtǒng [个 gè] ▸ **water/petrol pump** 水/油泵 shuǐ/yóubèng
▸ **pump up** vT 打气 dǎqì

punch [pʌntʃ] I N [c] 拳打

quándá [顿 dùn] **I** VT **1** (hit) 用拳打击 yòng quán dǎjī **2** [+ button, keyboard] 敲击 qiāojī **3** [+ ticket, paper] 在…上打孔 zài…shang dǎkǒng

▶ **punch in** VT 敲入 qiāorù

punctual ['pʌŋktʃʊəl] ADJ 准时的 zhǔnshí de

punctuation [pʌŋktjʊ'eɪʃən] N [U] 标点 biāodiǎn

puncture ['pʌŋktʃər] **I** N [c] 刺孔 cìkǒng [个 gè] **II** VT [+ tyre, lung] 戳破 chuōpò ▶ **to have a puncture** 轮胎被扎破了 lúntāi bèi zhāpò le

punish ['pʌnɪʃ] VT 惩罚 chéngfá ▶ **to punish sb for sth/for doing sth** 因某事/做某事而惩罚某人 yīn mǒushì/zuò mǒushì ér chéngfá mǒurén

punishment ['pʌnɪʃmənt] N **1** [c/U] 惩罚 chéngfá **2** [c/U] (penalty) 处罚 chǔfá [处 chù]

pupil ['pjuːpl] N [c] 学生 xuéshēng [名 míng]

puppy ['pʌpɪ] N [c] 小狗 xiǎogǒu [只 zhī]

purchase ['pəːtʃɪs] (frm) VT 购买 gòumǎi

pure [pjʊər] ADJ **1** [+ silk, gold, wool] 纯的 chún de **2** (clean) 纯净的 chúnjìng de

purple ['pəːpl] **I** ADJ 紫色的 zǐsè de **II** N [c/U] 紫色 zǐsè [种 zhǒng]

purpose ['pəːpəs] N [c] 目的 mùdì [个 gè] [of act, meeting, visit] 意义 yìyì [个 gè] ▶ **on purpose** 故意地 gùyì de

purse [pəːs] N [c] **1** (Brit: for money)

钱包 qiánbāo [个 gè] **2** (US: handbag) 手袋 shǒudài [个 gè]

push [pʊʃ] **I** N [c] 推 tuī **II** VT **1** [+ button] 按 àn **2** [+ car, door, person] 推 tuī **II** (press) 按 àn **2** (shove) 推 tuī ▶ **at the push of a button** 只要按一下按钮 zhǐyào àn yīxià ànniǔ ▶ **to push one's way through the crowd** 挤过人群 jǐguò rénqún ▶ **to push sth/sb out of the way** 把某物/某人推开 bǎ mǒuwù/mǒurén tuīkāi ▶ **to push a door open/shut** 把门推开/上 bǎ mén tuīkāi/shàng ▶ **to be pushed for time/money** (inf) 赶时间/缺钱 gǎn shíjiān/quēqián ▶ **to push forward/push through the crowd** 挤向/过人群 jǐxiàng/guò rénqún

▶ **push in** VI (in queue) 插队 chāduì

▶ **push over** VT [+ person, wall, furniture] 推倒 tuīdǎo

▶ **push up** VT [+ total, prices] 提高 tígāo

pushchair ['pʊʃtʃeər] (Brit) N [c] 幼儿车 yòu'érchē [辆 liàng]

put [pʊt] (pt, pp put) VT **1** [+ thing] 放 fàng; [+ person] 安置 ānzhì **2** (write, type) 写 xiě ▶ **to put a lot of time/energy/effort into sth/into doing sth** 投入大量的时间/精力/努力于某事/做某事 tóurù dàliàng de shíjiān/jīnglì/nǔlì yú mǒushì/zuò mǒushì ▶ **how shall I put it?** 我该怎么说呢？wǒ gāi zěnme shuō ne?

▶ **put across, put over** VT [+ ideas, argument] 讲清 jiǎngqīng

▶ **put away** VT 把…收起 bǎ…shōuqǐ

▶ **put back** VT1 (replace) 放回 fànghuí 2 [+ watch, clock] 倒拨 dàobō

▶ **put down** VT1 (on floor, table) 放下 fàngxià 2 (in writing) 写下 xiěxià

▶ **put forward** VT [+ ideas, proposal, name] 提出 tíchū

▶ **put in** VT1 [+ request, complaint, application] 提出 tíchū 2 (install) 安装 ānzhuāng

▶ **put off** VT (delay) 推迟 tuīchí; (Brit: distract) 使分心 shǐ fēnxīn; (discourage) 使失去兴趣 shǐ shīqù xìngqù ▶ **to put off doing sth** (postpone) 推迟做某事 tuīchí zuò mǒushì

▶ **put on** VT1 [+ clothes, make-up, glasses] 穿戴 chuāndài 2 [+ light, TV, radio, oven] 开 kāi; [+ CD, video] 放 fàng ▶ **to put on weight/three kilos etc** 增重/增加了3公斤{等} zēngzhòng/zēngjiā le sān gōngjīn {děng}

▶ **put out** VT1 [+ candle, cigarette] 熄灭 xīmiè; [+ fire, blaze] 扑灭 pūmiè 2 (switch off) 关 guān 3 麻烦 máfan

▶ **put over** VT = **put across**

▶ **put through** VT (Tel) 接通 jiētōng ▶ **put me through to Miss Blair** 请帮我接布莱尔小姐 qǐng bāng wǒ jiē Bùlái'ěr xiǎojiě

▶ **put up** VT1 [+ fence, building, tent] 建造 jiànzào; [+ poster, sign] 张贴 zhāngtiē 2 [+ umbrella, hood] 撑起 chēngqǐ 3 [+ price, cost] 增加 zēngjiā 4 (accommodate) 为…提供住宿 wèi…tígōng zhùsù ▶ **to put up one's hand** 举手 jǔshǒu

▶ **put up with** VT FUS 容忍 róngrěn

puzzle ['pʌzl] N1 [C] 谜 mí [个 gè]; (toy) 测智玩具 cèzhì wánjù [套 tào] 2 [s] (mystery) 谜团 mítuán

puzzled ['pʌzld] ADJ 茫然的 mángrán de

pyjamas, (US) **pajamas** [pə'dʒɑːməz] NPL 睡衣裤 shuìyīkù ▶ **a pair of pyjamas** 一套睡衣裤 yītào shuìyīkù

pylon ['paɪlən] N [C] 电缆塔 diànlǎn tǎ [个 gè]

pyramid ['pɪrəmɪd] N [C] 金字塔 jīnzì tǎ [座 zuò]

q

qualification [kwɔlɪfɪ'keɪʃən]
N [c] 资格证明 zīgé zhèngmíng
[个 gè]

qualified ['kwɔlɪfaɪd] ADJ 合格的
hégé de ▸**fully qualified** 完全合
格的 wánquán hégé de

qualify ['kwɔlɪfaɪ] VI 1 (*pass
examinations*) 取得资格 qǔdé zīgé
2 (*in competition*) 具备资格 jùbèi
zīgé ▸**to qualify as an engineer/
a nurse** *etc* 取得工程师/护士
{等}的资格 qǔdé gōngchéngshī/
hùshì {děng} de zīgé

quality ['kwɔlɪti] N 1 [u] (*standard*)
质量 zhìliàng 2 [c] (*characteristic:
of person*) 素质 sùzhì [种 zhǒng]
▸**quality of life** 生活质量
shēnghuó zhìliàng

quantity ['kwɔntɪti] N 1 [c/u]
(*amount*) 数量 shùliàng 2 [u]
(*volume*) 容量 róngliàng ▸**in
large/small quantities** 大/少量
dà/shǎoliàng

quarantine ['kwɔrənti:n] N [u]
检疫 jiǎnyì ▸**in quarantine** 被隔
离 bèi gélí

quarrel ['kwɔrəl] I N [c] 吵架
chǎojià [场 chǎng] II VI 争吵
zhēngchǎo

quarry ['kwɔri] N [c] 采石场
cǎishí chǎng [座 zuò]

quarter ['kwɔːtəʳ] N [c] 四分之
一 sìfēnzhīyī ▸**to cut/divide sth
into quarters** 把某物切/分成
4份 bǎ mǒuwù qiē/fēnwéi sìfèn
▸**a quarter of an hour** 一刻
钟 yīkèzhōng ▸**it's a quarter to
three** *or* (*US*) **of three** 现在是三
点差一刻 xiànzài shì sāndiǎn chà
yīkè ▸**it's a quarter past three** *or*
(*US*) **after three** 现在是三点一刻
xiànzài shì sāndiǎn yīkè

quarter-final ['kwɔːtə'faɪnl] N
[c] 四分之一决赛 sìfēnzhīyī juésài
[场 chǎng]

quay [kiː] N [c] 码头 mǎtóu
[个 gè]

queen [kwiːn] N [c] 1 (*monarch*) 女
王 nǚwáng [位 wèi] 2 (*king's wife*)
王后 wánghòu [位 wèi]

query ['kwɪəri] I N [c] 疑问 yíwèn
[个 gè] II VT [+ *figures, bill, expenses*]
询问 xúnwèn

question ['kwɛstʃən] I N 1 [c]
(*query*) 问题 wèntí [个 gè] 2 [c]
(*issue*) 议题 yìtí [项 xiàng] 3 [c] (*in
written exam*) 试题 shìtí [道 dào]
II VT (*interrogate*) 盘问 pánwèn

▶**to ask sb a question, to put a question to sb** 向某人一个问题，向某人提出问题 wèn mǒurén yìgè wèntí, xiàng mǒurén tíchū wèntí

▶**to be out of the question** 不可能的 bù kěnéng de

question mark N [c] 问号 wènhào [个 gè]

questionnaire [ˌkwɛstʃə'nɛə'] N [c] 问卷 wènjuàn [份 fèn]

queue [kjuː] (esp Brit) I N [c] 队 duì [条 tiáo] II VI (also: **queue up**) 排队 páiduì ▶**to queue for sth** 为某事排队 wèi mǒushì páiduì

quick [kwɪk] I ADJ 1 (fast) 快的 kuài de 2 [+ look] 快速的 kuàisù de 3 [+ visit] 短时间的 duǎn shíjiān de 3 [+ reply, response, decision] 迅速的 xùnsùde II ADV (inf: quickly) 快地 kuài de ▶**be quick!** 快点！kuàidiǎn!

quickly ['kwɪklɪ] ADV1 快地 kuài de 2 迅速地 xùnsùde

quiet ['kwaɪət] ADJ 1 [+ voice, music] 悄声的 qiāoshēng de; [+ place] 安静的 ānjìng de 2 [+ person] 平静的 píngjìng de 3 (silent) ▶**to be quiet** 沉默的 chénmò de ▶**be quiet!** 请安静！qǐng ānjìng!

quietly ['kwaɪətlɪ] ADV1 (speak, play) 默默地 mòmò de 2 (silently) 安静地 ānjìng de

quilt [kwɪlt] N [c] 被子 bèizi [床 chuáng] 2 (Brit: duvet) 羽绒被 yǔróngbèi [床 chuáng]

quit [kwɪt] (pt, pp quit or quitted) I VT1 (esp US: give up) 放弃 fàngqì 2 (+ habit, activity) 摆脱 bǎituō 2 (inf: leave)

[+ job] 辞去 cíqù II VI1 (give up) 放弃 fàngqì 2 (resign) 辞职 cízhí

quite [kwaɪt] ADV1 (rather) 相当 xiāngdāng 2 (completely) 十分 shífēn ▶**I see them quite a lot** 我常常见到他们 wǒ chángcháng jiàndào tāmen ▶**quite a lot of money** 很多钱 hěnduō qián

▶**quite a few** 相当多 xiāngdāng duō ▶**it's not quite finished** 像是还没结束 xiàng shì hái méi jiéshù ▶**quite (so!)** 的确(是这样)！díquè (shì zhèyàng)! ▶**it was quite a sight** 景色十分了得 jǐngsè shífēn liǎodé

quite 可用在 a 或 an 之前，后接形容词加名词结构。例如，可以说 It's quite an old car 或者 The car is quite old，以及 It was quite a warm day 或者 The day was quite warm. 如前例所示，quite 应放在不定冠词之前。例如，不能说 It's a quite old car. quite 可以用来修饰形容词和副词，而且程度比 fairly 更强烈，但是比 very 弱。quite 暗示某事物的某种特性且超出预料。Nobody here's ever heard of it but it is actually quite common. 注意，不要混淆 quite 和 quiet。

quiz [kwɪz] N [c] (game) 测验 cèyàn [次 cì]

quotation [kwəʊ'teɪʃən] N [c] 1 引语 yǐnyǔ [句 jù] 2 (estimate) 报价 bàojià [个 gè]

quote [kwəʊt] **I** VT [+ *politician, author*] 引用 yǐnyòng; [+ *line*] 引述 yǐnshù **II** N [c] 引语 yǐnyǔ (句 jù] **III quotes** NPL (*inf: quotation marks*) 引号 yǐnhào ▸ **in quotes** 在引号里 zài yǐnhào lǐ

r

rabbi ['ræbaɪ] N [c] 拉比(犹太教教师或法学导师)
rabbit ['ræbɪt] N [c] 兔子 tùzi [只 zhī]
rabies ['reɪbiːz] N [U] 狂犬病 kuángquǎnbìng
race [reɪs] **I** N **1** [c] (*speed contest*) 速度竞赛 sùdù jìngsài [场 chǎng] **2** [c/u] (*ethnic group*) 种族 zhǒngzú [个 gè] **II** VI 参赛 cānsài **III** VT 与…进行速度竞赛 yǔ…jìnxíng sùdù jìngsài ▸ **a race against time** 抢时间 qiǎng shíjiān
race car (US) N = **racing car**
racecourse ['reɪskɔːs] (Brit) N [c] 赛马场 sàimǎchǎng [个 gè]
racehorse ['reɪshɔːs] N [c] 赛马 sàimǎ [匹 pǐ]
racetrack ['reɪstræk] N [c] (for

cars) 赛道 sàidào [条 tiáo]; (*US: for horses*) 赛马场 sàimǎchǎng [个 gè]

racial ['reɪʃl] ADJ 种族的 zhǒngzú de

racing driver ['reɪsɪŋ-] (Brit) N [c] 赛车手 sàichēshǒu [位 wèi]

racism ['reɪsɪzəm] N [U] 种族歧视 zhǒngzú qíshì

racist ['reɪsɪst] I ADJ [+ policy, attack, behaviour, idea] 种族主义的 zhǒngzú zhǔyì de; [+ person, organization] 有种族偏见的 yǒu zhǒngzú piānjiàn de II N [c] 种族主义者 zhǒngzú zhǔyìzhě [个 gè]

rack [ræk] N [c] 1 (*also:* **luggage rack**) 行李架 xínglǐjià [个 gè] 2 (*for hanging clothes, dishes*) 架 jià [个 gè]

racket ['rækɪt] N [c] 球拍 qiúpāi [副 fù]

racquet ['rækɪt] N [c] 球拍 qiúpāi [副 fù]

radar ['reɪdɑːʳ] N [c/u] 雷达 léidá [个 gè]

radiation [reɪdɪ'eɪʃən] N [U] 辐射 fúshè

radiator ['reɪdɪeɪtəʳ] N [c] 暖气片 nuǎnqìpiàn [个 gè]

radio ['reɪdɪəu] N 1 [c] (*receiver*) 收音机 shōuyīnjī [台 tái] 2 [U] (*broadcasting*) 广播 guǎngbō ▶**on the radio** 广播中 guǎngbō zhōng

radioactive ['reɪdɪəʊ'æktɪv] ADJ 放射性的 fàngshèxìng de

radio station N [c] 广播电台 guǎngbō diàntái [个 gè]

RAF (Brit) N ABBR (= **Royal Air Force**) ▶**the RAF** 皇家空军

Huángjiā Kōngjūn

rag [ræg] N [c/u] 破布 pòbù [块 kuài]

rage [reɪdʒ] N [c/u] 盛怒 shèngnù [阵 zhèn]

raid [reɪd] VT (*soldiers, police*) 突袭 tūxí; (*criminal*) 袭击 xíjī

rail [reɪl] N [c] 1 (*for safety on stairs*) 扶手 fúshǒu [个 gè]; (*on bridge, balcony*) 横栏 hénglán [个 gè] 2 (*for hanging clothes*) 横杆 hénggān [根 gēn] 3 (*for trains*) 铁轨 tiěguǐ [条 tiáo] ▶**by rail** 乘火车 chéng huǒchē

railroad ['reɪlrəud] (US) N [c] = **railway**

railway ['reɪlweɪ] (Brit) N [c] 1 (*system*) 铁路 tiělù 2 (*line*) 铁道 tiědào [条 tiáo]

railway line (Brit) N [c] 铁路线 tiělùxiàn [条 tiáo]

railway station (Brit) N [c] 火车站 huǒchēzhàn [个 gè]

rain [reɪn] I N [U] 雨 yǔ II VI 下雨 xiàyǔ ▶**in the rain** 在雨中 zài yǔzhōng ▶**it's raining** 正在下雨 zhèngzài xiàyǔ

rainbow ['reɪnbəu] N [c] 彩虹 cǎihóng [条 tiáo]

raincoat ['reɪnkəut] N [c] 雨衣 yǔyī [件 jiàn]

rainforest ['reɪnfɔrɪst] N [c] 雨林 yǔlín [片 piàn]

rainy ['reɪnɪ] ADJ 多雨的 duōyǔ de

raise [reɪz] I VT 1 (*lift*) [+ hand, glass] 举起 jǔqǐ 2 (*increase*) [+ salary, rate, speed limit] 增加 zēngjiā; [+ morale, standards] 提高 tígāo 3 (*rear*) [+ child, family] 抚养

fǔyǎng II N [c] (US: payrise) 加薪 jiāxīn [次 cì]

rally ['rælɪ] N [c] 1 (public meeting) 集会 jíhuì [次 cì] 2 (Aut) 拉力赛 lālìsài [场 chǎng]

rambler ['ræmblə'] N [c] (Brit) 漫步者 mànbùzhě [个 gè]

ramp [ræmp] N [c] 坡道 pōdào [条 tiáo]

ran [ræn] PT of **run**

rang [ræŋ] PT of **ring**

range [reɪndʒ] N [c] 1 [c] 范围 fànwéi [个 gè]; [of subjects, possibilities] 系列 xìliè [个 gè] 2 (also: **mountain range**) 山脉 shānmài [个 gè] ▸ **to range from... to...** 在...到...之间 zài...dào...zhījiān

rape [reɪp] I N [c/u] 强奸 qiángjiān [次 cì] II VT 强奸 qiángjiān

rapids ['ræpɪdz] NPL 湍流 tuānliú

rare [rɛə'] ADJ 1 稀有的 xīyǒu de 2 [+ steak] 半熟的 bànshóu de

rarely ['rɛəlɪ] ADV 很少 hěnshǎo

raspberry ['rɑːzbərɪ] N [c] 山莓 shānméi [只 zhī]

rat [ræt] N [c] 田鼠 tiánshǔ [只 zhī]

rather ['rɑːðə'] ADV 相当 xiāngdāng ▸ **rather a lot** 相当多 xiāngdāng duō ▸ **I would rather go than stay** 我宁愿走也不愿留下来 wǒ nìngyuàn zǒu ér bùyuàn liúxià lái ▸ **I'd rather not say** 我宁可不说 wǒ nìngkě bùshuō

raw [rɔː] ADJ 生的 shēng de

raw materials NPL 原材料 yuáncáiliào

razor ['reɪzə'] N [c] 1 (also: **safety razor**) 剃须刀 tìxūdāo [个 gè] 2 (also: **electric razor**) 电动剃须刀 diàndòng tìxūdāo [个 gè]

razor blade N [c] 剃须刀刀片 tìxūdāo dāopiàn [个 gè]

reach [riːtʃ] VT [+ place, destination] 到达 dàodá; [+ conclusion, agreement, decision] 达成 dáchéng; [+ stage, level, age] 达到 dádào ▸ **within easy reach of...** 离...很近 lí...hěnjìn

react [riːˈækt] VI 反应 fǎnyìng

reaction [riːˈækʃən] N [c/u] 反应 fǎnyìng [种 zhǒng]

reactor [riːˈæktə'] N [c] 反应器 fǎnyìngqì [个 gè]

read [riːd] (pt, pp **read** [rɛd]) I VI 阅读 yuèdú II VT 1 读 dú 2 (study at university) (Brit) 攻读 gōngdú ▸ **read through** VT 1 (quickly) 浏览 liúlǎn 2 (thoroughly) 仔细阅读 zǐxì yuèdú

reading ['riːdɪŋ] N [u] 阅读 yuèdú

ready ['rɛdɪ] ADJ 做好准备的 zuòhǎo zhǔnbèi de ▸ **to get ready** 准备好 zhǔnbèi hǎo ▸ **to get sb/ sth ready** 使某人/某物准备就绪 shǐ mǒurén/mǒuwù zhǔnbèi jiùxù ▸ **to be ready to do sth** (prepared) 准备做某事 zhǔnbèi zuò mǒushì; (willing) 愿意做某事 yuànyì zuò mǒushì

real [rɪəl] ADJ 1 [+ leather, gold] 真正的 zhēnzhèng de 2 [+ reason, interest, name] 真实的 zhēnshí de 3 [+ life, feeling] 真实的 zhēnshí de

realistic [rɪəˈlɪstɪk] ADJ 1 现实的 xiànshí de 2 (convincing) 逼真的

film, portrayal 逼真的 bīzhēn de

reality [ri:'ælɪtɪ] N [U] *(real things)* 现实 xiànshí ▸**in reality** 事实上 shìshí shàng

realize ['rɪəlaɪz] VT 意识到 yìshídào ▸**to realize that...** 意识到… yìshí dào...

really ['rɪəlɪ] ADV 1 *(very)* ▸**really good/delighted** 真好/真高兴 zhēnhǎo/zhēn gāoxìng 2 *(genuinely)* 确实 quèshí 3 *(after negative)* 真正地 zhēnzhèng de ▸**really?** *(indicating surprise, interest)* 真的吗? zhēnde ma?

realtor ['rɪəltɔːʳ] *(US)* N [c] 房地产商 fángdìchǎn shāng [个 gè]

rear [rɪəʳ] I N [s] *(back)* 后面 hòumiàn II VT [+ *cattle, chickens*] *(esp Brit)* 饲养 sìyǎng

reason ['ri:zn] N [c] 原因 yuányīn [个 gè] ▸**the reason for sth** 某事的动机 mǒushì de dòngjī ▸**the reason why** …的原因 …de yuányīn

reasonable ['ri:znəbl] ADJ 1 [+ *person, decision*] 合情合理的 héqíng hélǐ de; [+ *number, amount*] 相当的 xiāngdāng de; [+ *price*] 合理的 hélǐ de 2 *(not bad)* 凑合的 còuhe de ▸**be reasonable!** 理智些! lǐzhì xiē!

reasonably ['ri:znəblɪ] ADV *(moderately)* 相当地 xiāngdāng de

reassure [ri:ə'ʃuəʳ] VT 使安心 shǐ ānxīn

receipt [rɪ'si:t] N [c] 收据 shōujù [张 zhāng]

receive [rɪ'si:v] VT 收到 shōudào

recent ['ri:snt] ADJ 最近的 zuìjìn de

recently ['ri:sntlɪ] ADV 最近 zuìjìn ▸**until recently** 直到最近 zhídào zuìjìn

reception [rɪ'sɛpʃən] N 1 [s] *(in public building)* 接待处 jiēdàichù 2 [c] *(party)* 欢迎会 huānyínghuì [个 gè] 3 [c] *(welcome)* 反响 fǎnxiǎng [种 zhǒng]

receptionist [rɪ'sɛpʃənɪst] *(esp Brit)* N [c] 接待员 jiēdàiyuán [位 wèi]

recipe ['rɛsɪpɪ] *(Culin)* N [c] 食谱 shípǔ [个 gè]

recognize ['rɛkəgnaɪz] VT 认出 rènchū

recommend [rɛkə'mɛnd] VT 推荐 tuījiàn

record [n, adj 'rɛkɔːd, vb rɪ'kɔːd] I N [c] 1 *(sound-recording)* 唱片 chàngpiàn [张 zhāng] 2 *(unbeaten statistic)* 记录 jìlù [个 gè] II **records** NPL *(of person, area)* 记录 jìlù III VT *(make recording of)* 录制 lùzhì IV ADJ [+ *sales, profits, levels*] 创记录的 chuàng jìlù de ▸**in record time** 破记录地 pò jìlù de ▸**to keep a record of sth** 记录某事 jìlù mǒushì

recover [rɪ'kʌvəʳ] VI 恢复 huīfù

recovery [rɪ'kʌvərɪ] N [c/U] 康复 kāngfù

recycle [ri:'saɪkl] VT 再生利用 zàishēng lìyòng

recycling [ri:'saɪklɪŋ] N [U] 循环利用 xúnhuán lìyòng

red [rɛd] I ADJ 1 红色的 hóngsè de 2 [+ *face, person*] 涨红的 zhànghóng de 3 [+ *hair*] 红褐色

的 hónghèsè de **4** [+ wine] 红的
hóng de II N [C/U] 红色 hóngsè
[种 zhǒng]

Red Cross N ▸ **the Red Cross** 红
十字会 Hóngshízìhuì

red-haired [rɛd'hɛəd] ADJ 红棕色
头发的 hóngzōngsè tóufa de

reduce [rɪ'djuːs] VT 减少 jiǎnshǎo
▸ **to reduce sth by/to** 将某物
减少…/将某物减少到… jiāng
mǒuwù jiǎnshǎo…/jiāng mǒuwù
jiǎnshǎo dào…

reduction [rɪ'dʌkʃən] N **1** [C/U]
(decrease) 减少 jiǎnshǎo **2** [C]
(discount) 减价 jiǎnjià [次 cì]

redundant [rɪ'dʌndnt] ADJ (Brit)
被裁员的 bèi cáiyuán de ▸ **to be
made redundant** 被裁员 bèi
cáiyuán

refer [rɪ'fəː'] VT ▸ **to refer sb to**
[+ book] 叫某人参看 jiào mǒurén
cānkàn
 ▸ **refer to** VT FUS 提到 tídào

referee [rɛfə'riː] N [C] (Sport) 裁判
员 cáipànyuán [位 wèi]

reference ['rɛfrəns] N [C]
 1 (mention) 提到 tídào [次 cì]
 2 (for job application: letter) 证明人
zhèngmíngrén [位 wèi]

refill [riː'fɪl] VT 再装满
zàizhuāngmǎn

reflect [rɪ'flɛkt] VT [+ image] 映
出 yìngchū [+ light, heat] 反射
fǎnshè

reflection [rɪ'flɛkʃən] N **1** [C]
(image) 影像 yǐngxiàng [个 gè] **2**
[U] (thought) 沉思 chénsī

refreshing [rɪ'frɛʃɪŋ] ADJ 提神的
tíshén de

refreshments [rɪ'frɛʃmənts] NPL
饮料及小吃 yǐnliào jí xiǎochī

refrigerator [rɪ'frɪdʒəreɪtə'] N [C]
冰箱 bīngxiāng [个 gè]

refugee [rɛfju'dʒiː] N [C] 难
民 nànmín [批 pī] ▸ **a political
refugee** 政治难民 zhèngzhì
nànmín

refund [n 'riːfʌnd, vb rɪ'fʌnd] I N
[C] 退款 tuìkuǎn [笔 bǐ] II VT 偿还
chánghuán

refuse[1] [rɪ'fjuːz] VT, VI 拒绝 jùjué
 ▸ **to refuse to do sth** 拒绝做某
事 jùjué zuò mǒushì ▸ **to refuse
sb permission** 不批准某人 bù
pīzhǔn mǒurén

refuse[2] ['rɛfjuːs] N [U] 垃圾 lājī

regard [rɪ'gɑːd] I VT (consider,
view) 认为 rènwéi II N ▸ **to give
one's regards to** 表示问候
xiàng…biǎoshì wènhòu

region ['riːdʒən] N [C] 区域 qūyù
[个 gè]

regional ['riːdʒənl] ADJ 地区的
dìqū de

register ['rɛdʒɪstə'] N [C] **1** (at
hotel) 登记 dēngjì [个 gè] **2** (in
school) 注册 zhùcè [个 gè]

registered ['rɛdʒɪstəd] ADJ (Post)
挂号的 guàhào de

registration [rɛdʒɪs'treɪʃən] N
[C/U] (of birth, death, students) 登
记 dēngjì [个 gè]

regret [rɪ'grɛt] VT 后悔 hòuhuǐ
 ▸ **to have no regrets** 没有遗憾
méiyǒu yíhàn ▸ **to regret that...**
对…感到后悔 duì…gǎndào
hòuhuǐ

regular ['rɛgjulə'] ADJ

1 [+ *breathing, intervals*] 有规律的 yǒu guīlǜ de **2** [+ *event*] 有规律的 yǒu guīlǜ de; [+ *visitor*] 经常的 jīngcháng de **3** (*normal*) 正常的 zhèngcháng de

regularly [ˈrɛɡjʊləlɪ] ADV 经常 jīngcháng

regulation [rɛɡjuˈleɪʃən] N [c] 规章 guīzhāng [套 tào]

rehearsal [rɪˈhəːsəl] N [c/u] 排练 páiliàn [次 cì]

rehearse [rɪˈhəːs] VT, VI 排练 páiliàn

reject [rɪˈdʒɛkt] VT **1** 拒绝接受 jùjué jiēshòu **2** [+ *applicant, admirer*] 拒绝 jùjué

related [rɪˈleɪtɪd] ADJ [+ *people*] 有亲缘关系的 yǒu qīnyuán guānxì de ▸ **to be related to sb** 和某人有关连 hé mǒurén yǒu guānlián

relation [rɪˈleɪʃən] N [c] **1** (*relative*) 亲戚 qīnqi [个 gè] **2** (*connection*) 关系 guānxì [种 zhǒng] ▸ **in relation to** 与⋯相比 yǔ⋯xiāngbǐ

relationship [rɪˈleɪʃənʃɪp] N [c] **1** (*connection*) 关系 guānxì [个 gè] **2** (*rapport: between two people, countries*) 关系 guānxì [种 zhǒng] **3** (*affair*) 亲密的关系 qīnmì de guānxì [种 zhǒng] ▸ **to have a good relationship** 关系亲密 guānxì qīnmì

relative [ˈrɛlətɪv] N [c] 亲戚 qīnqi [个 gè]

relatively [ˈrɛlətɪvlɪ] ADV 相对 xiāngduì

relax [rɪˈlæks] VI 放松 fàngsōng

relaxation [riːlækˈseɪʃən] N [u] 消遣 xiāoqiǎn

relaxed [rɪˈlækst] ADJ 放松的 fàngsōng de; [+ *discussion, atmosphere*] 轻松的 qīngsōng de

relaxing [rɪˈlæksɪŋ] ADJ 令人放松的 lìng rén fàngsōng de

release [rɪˈliːs] N [c] 释放 shìfàng [次 cì] II VT **1** 释放 shìfàng **2** [+ *record, film*] 发行 fāxíng

relevant [ˈrɛləvənt] ADJ 切题的 qiètí de ▸ **relevant to** 和⋯有关的 hé⋯yǒuguān de

reliable [rɪˈlaɪəbl] ADJ 可靠的 kěkào de; [+ *method, machine*] 可信赖的 kěxìnlài de

relief [rɪˈliːf] N [u] 如释重负 rú shì zhòng fù

relieved [rɪˈliːvd] ADJ 宽慰的 kuānwèi de ▸ **to be relieved that...** 对⋯感到放心 duì⋯gǎndào fàngxīn

religion [rɪˈlɪdʒən] N **1** [u] (*belief*) 宗教信仰 zōngjiào xìnyǎng **2** [c] (*set of beliefs*) 宗教 zōngjiào [种 zhǒng]

religious [rɪˈlɪdʒəs] ADJ **1** [+ *activities, faith*] 宗教的 zōngjiào de **2** [+ *person*] 笃信宗教的 dǔxìn zōngjiào de

reluctant [rɪˈlʌktənt] ADJ 不情愿的 bùqíngyuàn de ▸ **to be reluctant to do sth** 不愿做某事 bùyuàn zuò mǒushì

reluctantly [rɪˈlʌktəntlɪ] ADV 不情愿地 bùqíngyuàn de

rely on [rɪˈlaɪ-] VT FUS **1** (*be dependent on*) 依赖 yīlài **2** (*trust*) 信赖 xìnlài

remain [rɪˈmeɪn] VI **1** (*continue to be*) 仍然是 réngrán shì **2** (*stay*) 逗

留 dòuliú ▶ **to remain silent/in control** 保持沉默/仍然控制局面 bǎochí chénmò/réngrán kòngzhì júmiàn

remaining [rɪ'meɪnɪŋ] ADJ 剩下的 shèngxià de

remark [rɪ'mɑːk] N [c] (*comment*) 评论 pínglùn [个 gè]

remarkable [rɪ'mɑːkəbl] ADJ 不寻常的 bù xúncháng de

remarkably [rɪ'mɑːkəblɪ] ADV 极其地 jíqí de

remember [rɪ'mɛmbəʳ] VT 1 (*+ person, name, event*) 记住 jìzhù 2 (*bring back to mind*) 回想起 huíxiǎngqǐ 3 (*bear in mind*) 牢记 láojì ▶ **she remembered to do it** 她记得要做某事 tā jìdé yào zuò mǒushì

remind [rɪ'maɪnd] VT 提醒 tíxǐng ▶ **to remind sb to do sth** 提醒某人做某事 tíxǐng mǒurén zuò mǒushì ▶ **to remind sb of sth** 使某人想起某事 shǐ mǒurén xiǎngqǐ mǒushì

remote [rɪ'məʊt] ADJ 遥远的 yáoyuǎn de

remote control N [c] 遥控器 yáokòngqì [个 gè]

remove [rɪ'muːv] VT 1 (*+ object, organ*) 移走 yízǒu 2 (*+ clothing, bandage*) 脱下 tuōxià 3 (*+ stain*) 清除 qīngchú

renew [rɪ'njuː] VT (*+ loan, contract*) 延长 yáncháng

rent [rɛnt] I N [c/u] 租金 zūjīn [笔 bǐ] II VT 1 租用 zūyòng 2 (*also:* **rent out**) (*+ house, room*) 出租 chūzū

reorganize [riːˈɔːɡənaɪz] VT 重组 chóngzǔ

rep [rɛp] N (*also:* **sales rep**) 商品经销代理 shāngpǐn jīngxiāo dàilǐ [位 wèi]

repair [rɪ'pɛəʳ] I N [c/u] 修理 xiūlǐ [次 cì] II VT 1 修补 xiūbǔ 2 (*+ damage*) 维修 wéixiū

repay [riː'peɪ] (*pt, pp* repaid) VT 偿还 chánghuán

repeat [rɪ'piːt] VT 1 重复 chóngfù 2 (*+ action, mistake*) 重做 chóngzuò

repeatedly [rɪ'piːtɪdlɪ] ADV 反复地 fǎnfù de

replace [rɪ'pleɪs] VT 1 (*put back*) 将…放回 jiāng...fànghuí 2 (*take the place of*) 代替 dàitì

replay [*n* 'riː:pleɪ, *vb* riː'pleɪ] I N [c] (*of match*) 重新比赛 chóngxīn bǐsài [场 chǎng] II VT (*+ track, song*) (*on tape*) 重新播放 chóngxīn bōfàng ▶ **to replay a match** 重新比赛 chóngxīn bǐsài

reply [rɪ'plaɪ] I N [c] 回答 huídá [个 gè] II VI 回答 dáfù ▶ **there's no reply** (*Tel*) 无人接听 wúrén jiētīng

report [rɪ'pɔːt] I N [c] 1 (*account*) 报告 bàogào [个 gè] 2 (*Brit*) (*also:* **school report**) 成绩单 chéngjìdān [个 gè] II VT (*+ theft, accident, death*) 报案 bào'àn; (*+ person*) 告发 gàofā

report card (*US*) N [c] 学生成绩报告单 xuéshēng chéngjì bàogàodān [份 fèn]

reporter [rɪ'pɔːtəʳ] N [c] 记者 jìzhě [名 míng]

represent [reprɪˈzent] VT [+ person, nation] 代表 dàibiǎo

representative [reprɪˈzentətɪv] N [c] 代表 dàibiǎo [个 gè]

republic [rɪˈpʌblɪk] N [c] 共和国 gònghéguó [个 gè]

reputation [repjuˈteɪʃən] N [c] 名声 míngshēng [种 zhǒng]

request [rɪˈkwest] I N [c] 要求 yāoqiú [个 gè] II VT 要求 yāoqiú

require [rɪˈkwaɪə²] VT (need) 需要 xūyào ▸ **to be required** [approval, permission] 必须有 bìxū yǒu

rescue [ˈreskjuː] I N [c/u] 营救 yíngjiù [次 cì] II VT 解救 jiějiù

research [rɪˈsəːtʃ] N [u] 研究 yánjiū ▸ **to do research** 从事研究 cóngshì yánjiū

resemblance [rɪˈzembləns] N [c/u] 相似 xiāngsì [种 zhǒng]

reservation [rezəˈveɪʃən] N [c] 预定 yùdìng [个 gè] ▸ **to make a reservation** (in hotel, restaurant, on train) 预订 yùdìng

reservation desk (US) N [c] 预定台 yùdìngtái [个 gè]

reserve [rɪˈzəːv] VT 预定 yùdìng

reserved [rɪˈzəːvd] ADJ 1 [+ seat] 已预定的 yǐ yùdìng de 2 (restrained) 矜持的 jīnchí de

resident [ˈrezɪdənt] N [c] 居民 jūmín [位 wèi]

resign [rɪˈzaɪn] VI 辞职 cízhí

resist [rɪˈzɪst] VT [+ temptation, urge] 克制 kèzhì

resit [riːˈsɪt] (Brit) VT [+ exam] 补考 bǔkǎo

resolution [rezəˈluːʃən] N [c/u] 决心 juéxīn ▸ **New Year's**

resolution 新年决心 Xīnnián juéxīn

resort [rɪˈzɔːt] N [c] (also: **holiday resort**) 度假胜地 dùjià shèngdì [个 gè] ▸ **a seaside/winter sports resort** 海边/冬季运动胜地 hǎibiān/dōngjì yùndòng shèngdì ▸ **as a last resort** 作为最后手段 zuòwéi zuìhòu shǒuduàn

resource [rɪˈzɔːs] N PL 1 (coal, oil) 资源 zīyuán 2 (money) 财力 cáilì ▸ **natural resources** 自然资源 zìrán zīyuán

respect [rɪsˈpekt] I N [u] 尊敬 zūnjìng II VT 尊敬 zūnjìng ▸ **to have respect for sb/sth** 对某人/某事物有敬意 duì mǒurén/mǒushì huáiyǒu jìngyì

respectable [rɪsˈpektəbl] ADJ 1 [+ area, background] 体面的 tǐmiàn de 2 [+ person] 受人尊敬的 shòurén zūnjìng de

responsibility [rɪspɒnsɪˈbɪlɪtɪ] I N 1 [s] (duty) 职责 zhízé 2 [u] (obligation) 义务 yìwù II **responsibilities** N PL 责任 zérèn

responsible [rɪsˈpɒnsɪbl] ADJ 1 (at fault) 负有责任的 fùyǒu zérèn de 2 (in charge) 负责的 fùzé de 3 (sensible, trustworthy) 可靠的 kěkào de

rest [rest] I N 1 [u] (relaxation) 休息 xiūxi 2 [c] (break) 休息 xiūxi [次 cì] 3 [s] (remainder) 剩余 shèngyú II VI (relax) 休息 xiūxi III VT [+ eyes, legs, muscles] 休息 xiūxi ▸ **to rest sth on/against sth** (lean) 把某物靠在某物上 bǎ mǒuwù kàozài mǒuwù shàng ▸**the rest (of them)** (他们当中) 其余的 (tāmen dāngzhōng)qíyú de

rest area (US) N [c] 路边服务站 lùbiān fúwùzhàn [个 gè]

restaurant [ˈrɛstərɒn] N [c] 餐馆 cānguǎn [家 jiā]

restless [ˈrɛstlɪs] ADJ (fidgety) 坐立不安的 zuòlì bù'ān de

restore [rɪˈstɔː] VT 修复 xiūfù

restrict [rɪˈstrɪkt] VT 1 [+ growth, membership, privilege] 限制 xiànzhì 2 [+ activities] 约束 yuēshù

rest room (US) N [c] 洗手间 xǐshǒujiān [个 gè]

result [rɪˈzʌlt] I N [c] (of event, action) 后果 hòuguǒ [种 zhǒng]; (of match, election, exam, competition) 结果 jiéguǒ [个 gè]; (of calculation) 答案 dá'àn [个 gè] II VI 产生 chǎnshēng ▸**to result in** 导致 dǎozhì ▸**as a result of** 由于 yóuyú ▸**to result from** 因…而产生 yīn…ér chǎnshēng

résumé [ˈreɪzjuːmeɪ] N [c] (US: CV) 简历 jiǎnlì [份 fèn]

retire [rɪˈtaɪə] VI 退休 tuìxiū

retired [rɪˈtaɪəd] ADJ 退休的 tuìxiū de

retiree [rɪtaɪəˈriː] (US) N [c] 领养老金的人 lǐng yǎnglǎojīn de rén [位 wèi]

retirement [rɪˈtaɪəmənt] N [c/u] 退休 tuìxiū

return [rɪˈtəːn] I VI 返回 fǎnhuí II VT 归还 guīhuán III N 1 [s] (of person) 返回 fǎnhuí 2 [s] (of something borrowed or stolen) 归还 guīhuán 3 [s] (Comput: key) 回车

键 huíchējiàn ▸**in return (for)** 作为 (对…)的回报 zuòwéi(duì…)de huíbào ▸**many happy returns (of the day)!** 生日快乐！shēngrì kuàilè! IV CPD (Brit) [+ journey, ticket] 往返 wǎngfǎn

reunion [riːˈjuːnɪən] N [c] 团聚 tuánjù [次 cì]

reveal [rɪˈviːl] VT (make known) 透露 tòulù

revenge [rɪˈvɛndʒ] N [u] 复仇 fùchóu ▸**to take (one's) revenge (on sb)** (对某人)进行报复 (duì mǒurén)jìnxíng bàofù

review [rɪˈvjuː] N [c] 评论 pínglùn [个 gè]

revise [rɪˈvaɪz] I VT (study) 复习 fùxí II VI (study) (Brit) 复习 fùxí

revision [rɪˈvɪʒən] N [u] (Brit: studying) 复习 fùxí

revolution [rɛvəˈluːʃən] N 1 [c/u] (Pol) 革命 gémìng [场 chǎng] 2 [c] 变革 biàngé [场 chǎng]

reward [rɪˈwɔːd] I N [c] 奖励 jiǎnglì [种 zhǒng] II VT 奖赏 jiǎngshǎng

rewarding [rɪˈwɔːdɪŋ] ADJ 值得做的 zhídé zuò de

rewind [riːˈwaɪnd] (pt, pp rewound) VT 倒带 dàodài

rhythm [ˈrɪðm] N [c/u] 节奏 jiézòu [个 gè]

rib [rɪb] N [c] 肋骨 lèigǔ [根 gēn]

ribbon [ˈrɪbən] N [c/u] 饰带 shìdài [条 tiáo]

rice [raɪs] N [c/u] 1 (grain) 大米 dàmǐ [粒 lì] 2 (when cooked) 米饭 mǐfàn [碗 wǎn]

rich [rɪtʃ] ADJ [+ person, country] 富

有的 fùyǒu de
rid [rɪd] (pt, pp **rid**) VT ▸ **to get rid of sth/sb** [+ smell, dirt, car etc] 摆脱某物/某人 bǎituō mǒuwù/mǒurén

ride [raɪd] (pt **rode**, pp **ridden** ['rɪdn]) **I** N [c] **1** (in car, on bicycle) 兜风 dōufēng [次 cì] **2** (on horse, bus, train) 出行 chūxíng [次 cì] **II** VI 骑马 qímǎ; (on bicycle) 骑自行车 qí zìxíngchē; (in car) 乘坐 chéngzuò **III** VT1 [+ horse, bicycle, motorcycle] 骑 qí **2** [+ distance] 行进 xíngjìn ▸ **to give sb a ride** (US) 让某人搭车 ràng mǒurén dāchē

ridiculous [rɪ'dɪkjələs] ADJ 荒谬的 huāngmiù de

rifle ['raɪfl] N [c] 步枪 bùqiāng [支 zhī]

right [raɪt] **I** ADJ **1** (not left) 右边的 yòubiān de **2** (correct) 正确的 zhèngquè de; [+ person, place, time] 合适的 héshì de; [+ decision, direction, time] 最适宜的 zuì shìyí de **II** N **1** [s] (not left) 右边 yòubiān **2** [c] (entitlement) 权利 quánlì [个 gè] **III** ADV1 (correctly) 正确地 zhèngquè de **2** (properly, fairly) 恰当 qiàdàng **3** (not to the left) 右边 yòubiān de **IV** INT 好吧 hǎo ba ▸ **do you have the right time?** 你的表准点了吗? nǐde biǎo jiǔdiǎn le? ▸ **to be right** [person] 正确 zhèngquè; [answer, fact] 对 duì; [clock] 准确 zhǔnquè ▸ **you did the right thing** 你做得对 nǐ zuòde duì ▸ **to** or **on the right** (position) 靠(或)在右侧 kào(huò) zài yòucè ▸ **to the right**

(movement) 向右 xiàngyòu

right-handed [raɪt'hændɪd] ADJ 惯用右手的 guànyòng yòushǒu de

ring [rɪŋ] (pt **rang**, pp **rung**) **I** N [c] (on finger) 戒指 jièzhi [枚 méi] **II** VI1 [bell] 鸣响 míngxiǎng **2** [telephone] 响 xiǎng **3** (Brit) 打电话 dǎ diànhuà **III** VT1 [+ bell, doorbell] 使…响 shǐ…xiǎng **2** (Brit: Tel) 给…打电话 gěi…dǎ diànhuà ▸ **there was a ring at the door, the doorbell rang** 有人按门铃 yǒurén àn ménlíng ▸ **to give sb a ring** (Brit: Tel) 给某人打电话 gěi mǒurén dǎ diànhuà
▸ **ring back** (Brit: Tel) **I** VT 回电话 huí diànhuà **II** VI 再打电话 zài dǎ diànhuà
▸ **ring up** (Brit: Tel) VT 给…打电话 gěi…dǎ diànhuà

rinse [rɪns] VT [+ dishes, clothes] 漂洗 piǎoxǐ

riot ['raɪət] **I** N [c] (disturbance) 暴乱 bàoluàn [次 cì] **II** VI 闹事 nàoshì

ripe [raɪp] ADJ 成熟的 chéngshú de

rise [raɪz] (pt **rose**, pp **risen** ['rɪzn]) **I** N [c] (Brit: salary increase) 加薪 jiāxīn [次 cì] **2** (in prices, temperature, crime rate) 上升 shàngshēng [次 cì] **II** VI1 (move upwards) 上升 shàngshēng **2** [prices, numbers] 上升 shàngshēng **3** [sun, moon] 升起 shēngqǐ **4** (from chair) 起身 qǐshēn

risk [rɪsk] **I** N **1** [c/u] (danger) 危险 wēixiǎn [个 gè] **2** [c] (possibility, chance) 风险 fēngxiǎn [种 zhǒng]

II VT (take the chance of) 冒险做 màoxiǎn zuò ▸ to take a risk 担风险 dān fēngxiǎn ▸ to risk it (inf) 冒险一试 màoxiǎn yīcì

rival ['raɪvl] I N [c] 竞争对手 jìngzhēng duìshǒu [个 gè] II ADJ [+ teams, groups, supporters] 对立的 duìlì de

river ['rɪvə'] N [c] 河 hé [条 tiáo]

river bank N [c] 河岸 hé'àn [个 gè]

road [rəʊd] N [c] 1 (in country) 公路 gōnglù [条 tiáo] 2 (in town) 路 lù [条 tiáo] ▸ it takes four hours by road 要花4小时的车程 yào huā sì xiǎoshí de chēchéng

road map N [c] 道路图 dàolùtú [张 zhāng]

road sign N [c] 交通标志 jiāotōng biāozhì [个 gè]

roast [rəʊst] VT 烤 kǎo

rob [rɒb] VT 抢劫 qiǎngjié ▸ to rob sb of sth 剥夺某人的某物 bōduó mǒurén de mǒuwù

robber ['rɒbə'] N [c] 强盗 qiángdào [个 gè]

robbery ['rɒbərɪ] N [c/u] 抢劫 qiǎngjié [次 cì]

robot ['rəʊbɒt] N [c] 机器人 jīqìrén [个 gè]

rock [rɒk] N 1 (c) (boulder) 巨石 jùshí [块 kuài] 2 [c] (esp US: small stone) 小石子 xiǎoshízǐ [块 kuài] 3 [u] (Mus) (also: rock music) 摇滚乐 yáogǔnyuè

rocket ['rɒkɪt] N [c] 1 (Space) 火箭 huǒjiàn [支 zhī] 2 (firework) 火箭式烟花 huǒjiànshì lǐhuā [个 gè]

rod [rɒd] N [c] 1 (pole) 杆 gān [根

gēn] 2 (also: fishing rod) 钓鱼竿 diàoyúgān [根 gēn]

rode [rəʊd] PT of **ride**

role [rəʊl] N [c] 1 (function) 作用 zuòyòng [个 gè] 2 (Theat: part) 角色 juésè [个 gè]

roll [rəʊl] I N [c] 1 一卷 yī juǎn [个 gè] 2 (also: bread roll) 小圆面包 xiǎoyuánmiànbāo [个 gè] II VT 使滚动 shǐ gǔndòng III VI (ball, stone) 滚动 gǔndòng ▸ cheese/ham roll 奶酪/火腿面包卷 nǎilào/huǒtuǐ miànbāojuǎn

rollerblades ['rəʊləbleɪdz] NPL 直排轮溜冰鞋 zhípáilún liūbīngxié

roller coaster [-'kəʊstə'] N [c] (at funfair) 过山车 guòshānchē [辆 liàng]

roller skates NPL 早冰鞋 hànbīngxié

roller skating N [u] 穿早冰鞋滑行 chuān hànbīngxié huáxíng

Roman ['rəʊmən] I ADJ 1 (of ancient Rome) 古罗马的 gǔ Luómǎ de 2 (of modern Rome) 罗马的 Luómǎ de II N [c] (in ancient Rome) 古罗马人 gǔ Luómǎrén [个 gè]

Roman Catholic I ADJ 天主教的 Tiānzhǔjiào de II N [c] 天主教教徒 Tiānzhǔjiào Jiàotú [个 gè]

romance [rə'mæns] N 1 [c] (affair) 恋情 liànqíng [种 zhǒng] 2 [u] (charm, excitement) 迷人之处 mírén zhī chù

Romania [rə'meɪnɪə] N 罗马尼亚 Luómǎníyà

Romanian [rə'meɪnɪən] I ADJ 罗马尼亚的 Luómǎníyà de II N 1 [c] (person) 罗马尼

亚人 Luómǎnǐyàrén [个 gè]
2 [U] (language) 罗马尼亚语
Luómǎnǐyàyǔ

romantic [rə'mæntɪk] ADJ
1 [+ person] 浪漫的 làngmàn de
2 (connected with love) [+ play, story
etc] 爱情的 àiqíng de **3** (charming,
exciting) [+ setting, holiday, dinner
etc] 浪漫的 làngmàn de

roof [ru:f] N [c] **1** [of building] 屋
顶 wūdǐng [个 gè] **2** [of cave, mine,
vehicle] 顶 dǐng [个 gè]

room [ru:m] N **1** [c] (in house) 室
内 shìnèi **2** [c] (also: **bedroom**)
卧室 wòshì **3** [U] (space)
空间 kōngjiān ▶**single/double
room** 单人/双人间 dānrén/
shuāngrén jiān

root [ru:t] N [c] 根 gēn [个 gè]

rope [rəup] N [c/U] 绳子 shéngzi
[根 gēn]

rose [rəuz] **I** PT of **rise** **II** N [c]
(flower) 玫瑰 méiguì [朵 duǒ]

rot [rɒt] **I** VT (cause to decay) 使腐坏
shǐ fǔhuài **II** VI (decay) [teeth, wood,
fruit] 腐烂 fǔlàn

rotten ['rɒtn] ADJ **1** (decayed) 腐
烂的 fǔlàn de **2** (inf: awful) 糟透的
zāotòu de

rough [rʌf] ADJ **1** [+ skin, surface,
cloth] 粗糙的 cūcāo de **2** [+ terrain]
崎岖的 qíqū de **3** [+ sea, crossing]
汹涛汹涌的 bōtāo xiōngyǒng de
4 (violent) [+ person] 粗鲁的 cūlǔ
de; [+ town, area] 治安混乱的
zhì'ān hùnluàn de **5** [+ outline, plan,
idea] 粗略的 cūlüè de

roughly ['rʌflɪ] ADV **1** (violently) 粗
暴地 cūbào de **2** (approximately)

大约 dàyuē ▶**roughly speaking**
粗略地说 cūlüè de shuō

round [raund] **I** ADJ **1** (circular)
圆的 yuán de **2** (spherical) 球形
的 qiúxíng de **3** [+ figure, sum] 不
计尾数的 bù jì wěishù de **II** N [c]
1 (stage: in competition) 一轮 yī
lún **2** (Golf) 一场 yī chǎng **III** PREP
1 (surrounding) 围绕 wéirào
2 (near) 在…附近 zài…fùjìn
3 (on or from the other side of) 绕
过 ràoguò ▶**to move round the
room/sail round the world** 绕
房间一周/环球航行 rào fángjiān
yī zhōu/huánqiú hángxíng ▶**all
round** 在…周围 zài…zhōuwéi
▶**to go round (sth)** 绕过(某物)
ràoguò (mǒuwù) ▶**to go round
to sb's (house)** 造访某人(的
家) zàofǎng mǒurén (de jiā) ▶**all
(the) year round** 一年到头 yīnián
dàotóu ▶**to be round at 6 o'clock**
我会在6点钟到你家 wǒ huì zài
liùdiǎnzhōng dào nǐjiā ▶**round
about** (esp Brit: approximately) 大
约 dàyuē ▶**round the clock** 连
续24小时 liánxù èrshísì xiǎoshí
▶**a round of applause** 掌声雷动
zhǎngshēng léidòng
▶**round off** VT [+ meal, evening] 圆
满结束 yuánmǎn jiéshù
▶**round up** VT **1** [+ cattle, sheep] 驱
拢 qūlǒng **2** [+ people] 围捕 wéibǔ
3 [+ price, figure] 把…调高为整数
bǎ…tiáogāo wéi zhěngshù

roundabout ['raundəbaut] N [c]
(Brit) (Aut) 环形交叉路 huánxíng
jiāochàlù [个 gè]

round trip [c] (往) 往返旅行

wǎngfǎn lùxíng [次 cì] II ADJ (US) 往返的 wǎngfǎn de

route [ruːt] N [c] 1 (*path, journey*) 路 lù [条 tiáo] 2 (*of bus, train*) 路线 lùxiàn [条 tiáo]

routine [ruːˈtiːn] N [c/u] 例行公事 lìxíng gōngshì [次 cì]

row[1] [rəʊ] N [c] 1 一排 yī pái 2 (*of seats in theatre, cinema*) 一排 yī pái II VI (*in boat*) 划船 huáchuán III VT [+ *boat*] 划 huá ▶ **in a row** 连续 liánxù

row[2] [raʊ] N 1 s (*noise*) (Brit: inf) 吵闹声 chǎonàoshēng 2 [c] (*noisy quarrel*) 吵架 chǎojià [场 chǎng]

rowboat [ˈrəʊbəʊt] (US) N [c] 划艇 huátǐng [艘 sōu]

rowing [ˈrəʊɪŋ] (Sport) N [U] 赛艇运动 sàitǐng yùndòng

rowing boat (Brit) N [c] 划艇 huátǐng [艘 sōu]

royal [ˈrɔɪəl] ADJ 皇家的 huángjiā de ▶ **the royal family** 王室 wángshì

● **ROYAL FAMILY**

royal family (英国王室) 以伊丽莎白女王二世为首。女王于1953年登基。她的丈夫是菲利普亲王，即爱丁堡公爵。他们有有四各成年子女：查尔斯王子，安妮公主，安德鲁王子和爱德华王子。查尔斯王子，即威尔士亲王是王位的继承人。他有两个孩子，威廉王子和哈里王子。他们的母亲是已故的威尔士王妃戴安娜。

rub [rʌb] VT (*with hand, fingers*) 揉 róu; (*with cloth, substance*) 擦 cā ▶ **rub out** (*erase*) 擦掉 cādiào

rubber [ˈrʌbəʳ] N 1 [U] (*substance*) 橡胶 xiàngjiāo 2 [c] (Brit) 橡皮擦 xiàngpícā [个 gè]

rubber boot (US) N [c] 橡胶长统靴 xiàngjiāo chángtǒngxuē [双 shuāng]

rubbish [ˈrʌbɪʃ] (Brit) I N [U] 1 (*refuse*) 垃圾 lājī 2 (*inferior material*) 垃圾货 lājīhuò 3 (*nonsense*) 废话 fèihuà II ADJ (Brit: inf) ▶ **I'm rubbish at golf** 我高尔夫球打得很糟糕 wǒ gāo'ěrfūqiú dǎde hěn zāogāo ▶ **rubbish!** 胡说! húshuō!

rubbish bin (Brit) N [c] 垃圾箱 lājīxiāng [个 gè]

rucksack [ˈrʌksæk] N [c] 背包 bèibāo [个 gè]

rude [ruːd] ADJ 1 无礼的 wúlǐ de 2 [+ *word, joke, noise*] 粗鄙的 cūbǐ de ▶ **to be rude to sb** 对某人无礼 duì mǒurén wúlǐ

rug [rʌg] N [c] 小地毯 xiǎodìtǎn [块 kuài]

rugby [ˈrʌgbɪ] N [U] (*also:* **rugby football**) 英式橄榄球 yīngshì gǎnlǎnqiú

ruin [ˈruːɪn] I N [U] 毁坏 huǐhuài II VT [+ *clothes, carpet*] 毁坏 huǐhuài; [+ *plans, prospects*] 葬送 zàngsòng III **ruins** NPL [*of building, castle*] 废墟 fèixū ▶ **to be in ruins** [*building, town*] 破败不堪 pòbài bùkān

rule [ruːl] N 1 [c] (*regulation*) 规则 guīzé [条 tiáo] 2 [c] (*of language,* *science*] 规则 guīzé [条 tiáo] ▸**it's against the rules** 这是不合规定 de zhèshì bùhé guīdìng de ▸**as a rule** 通常 tōngcháng

ruler [ˈruːləʳ] N [c] (*for measuring*) 直尺 zhíchǐ [把 bǎ]

rum [rʌm] N [U] 朗姆酒 lǎngmǔjiǔ

rumour, (*US*) **rumor** [ˈruːməʳ] N [c/U] 谣言 yáoyán [个 gè]

run [rʌn] (*pt* ran, *pp* run) I N [c] 1 (*as exercise, sport*) 跑步 pǎobù [次 cì] 2 (*Cricket, Baseball*) 跑动得分 pǎodòng défēn [次 cì] II VT 1 (*race, distance*) 跑 pǎo II VT 1 (*race, distance*) 跑 pǎo 2 (*operate*) [+ *business, shop, country*] 经营 jīngyíng 3 [+ *water, bath*] 流 liú 4 [+ *program, test*] 进行 jìnxíng III VI 1 跑 pǎo 2 (*flee*) 逃跑 táopǎo 3 [*bus, train*] 行驶 xíngshǐ 4 (*in combination*) 变得 biànde ▸**to go for a run** (*as exercise*) 跑步锻炼 pǎobù duànliàn ▸**in the long run** 终究 zhōngjiū ▸**I'll run you to the station** 我开车送你去车站 wǒ kāichē sòng nǐ qù chēzhàn ▸**to run on** or **off petrol/batteries** 以汽油/电池为能源 yǐ qìyóu/diànchí wéi néngyuán
▸**run after** VT FUS (*chase*) 追赶 zhuīgǎn
▸**run away** VI (*from home, situation*) 出走 chūzǒu
▸**run into** VT FUS (*meet*) [+ *person*] 偶然碰见 ǒurán pèngjiàn; [+ *trouble, problems*] 遭遇 zāoyù
▸**run off** VI 跑掉 pǎodiào
▸**run out** VI 1 [*time, money, luck*] 到 yòngwán 2 [*lease, passport*]

到期 dàoqī
▸**run out of** VT FUS 耗尽 hàojìn
▸**run over** VT (*Aut*) [+ *person*] 撞倒 zhuàngdǎo

rung [rʌŋ] PP of **ring**

runner [ˈrʌnəʳ] N [c] (*in race*) 赛跑者 sàipǎozhě [个 gè]

runner-up [ˈrʌnərˈʌp] N [c] 亚军 yàjūn [个 gè]

running [ˈrʌnɪŋ] N [U] (*sport*) 赛跑 sàipǎo ▸**6 days running** 连续6天 liánxù liùtiān

run-up [ˈrʌnʌp] N ▸**the run-up to...** …的前期 …de qiánqī

runway [ˈrʌnweɪ] N [c] 跑道 pǎodào [条 tiáo]

rush [rʌʃ] I N [s] (*hurry*) 匆忙 cōngmáng II VI [*person*] 急速前往 jísù qiánwǎng

rush hour N [c] 高峰时间 gāofēng shíjiān [段 duàn]

Russia [ˈrʌʃə] N 俄罗斯 Éluósī

Russian [ˈrʌʃən] I ADJ 俄罗斯的 Éluósī de II N 1 [c] (*person*) 俄罗斯人 Éluósīrén [个 gè] 2 [U] (*language*) 俄语 Éyǔ

rust [rʌst] N [U] 铁锈 tiěxiù

rusty [ˈrʌstɪ] ADJ 1 [+ *surface, object*] 生锈的 shēngxiù de 2 [+ *skill*] 荒疏的 huāngshū de

RV (*US*) N [c] (= *recreational vehicle*) 娱乐车 yúlèchē

rye [raɪ] N [U] (*cereal*) 黑麦 hēimài

S

sack [sæk] I N [c] 麻袋 mádài [个 gè] II VT 解雇 jiěgù

sad [sæd] ADJ 1 伤心的 shāngxīn de 2 (distressing) 令人悲伤的 lìngrén bēishāng de

saddle ['sædl] N [c] (for horse) 马鞍 mǎ'ān [副 fù]; (on bike, motorbike) 车座 chēzuò [个 gè]

safe [seɪf] I ADJ 1 (not dangerous) 安全的 ānquán de 2 (out of danger) 脱险的 tuōxiǎn de 3 [+ place] 保险的 bǎoxiǎn de II N [c] 保险箱 bǎoxiǎnxiāng [个 gè]

safety ['seɪftɪ] N [U] 安全 ānquán 2 平安 píng'ān

Sagittarius [sædʒɪ'tɛərɪəs] N (sign) 人马座 Rénmǎ Zuò

said [sɛd] PT, PP of **say**

sail [seɪl] I N [c] 帆 fān [张 zhāng]

II VI [ship] 航行 hángxíng; [passenger] 乘船航行 chéngchuán hángxíng ▸ **to go sailing** 去航行 qù hángxíng

sailing ['seɪlɪŋ] N [U] 帆船运动 fānchuán yùndòng

sailor ['seɪlə'] N [c] 水手 shuǐshǒu [位 wèi]

saint [seɪnt] N [c] 圣徒 shèngtú [个 gè]

salad ['sæləd] N [c/U] 色拉 sèlā [份 fèn]

salary ['sælərɪ] N [c/U] 薪水 xīnshuǐ [份 fèn]

sale [seɪl] I N 1 [s] (selling) 出售 chūshòu 2 [c] (with reductions) 贱卖 jiànmài [次 cì] II **sales** NPL (quantity sold) 销售量 xiāoshòuliàng ▸ **to be (up) for sale** 待售 dàishòu ▸ **to be on sale** (Brit) 上市 shàngshì; (US: reduced) 廉价出售 liánjià chūshòu

salesman ['seɪlzmən] N (pl **salesmen**) N [c] 推销员 tuīxiāo yuán [位 wèi]

salmon ['sæmən] (pl **salmon**) N [c/U] 大马哈鱼 dà mǎhā yú [条 tiáo]

salon ['sælɒn] N [c] 美发廊 měifà láng [家 jiā]

salt [sɔːlt] N [U] 盐 yán

salty ['sɔːltɪ] ADJ [+ food] 咸的 xián de

same [seɪm] I ADJ 1 [+ size, colour, age] 相同的 xiāngtóng de 2 [+ place, person, time] 同一个的 tóngyīgè de II PRON ▸ **the same** 1 (similar) 一样 yīyàng 2 (also: the **same thing**) 同样 tóngyàng ▸ **the**

same as 与…一样 yǔ…yīyàng ▸ **the same book/place as** 与…一样的书/地方 yǔ…yīyàng de shū/dìfang ▸ **at the same time** 同时 tóngshí

sample ['sɑːmpl] N [c] 样品 yàngpǐn [件 jiàn] 采样 cǎiyàng [个 gè]

sand [sænd] N [U] 沙子 shāzi

sandal ['sændl] N [c] 凉鞋 liángxié [双 shuāng]

sandwich ['sændwɪtʃ] N [c] 三明治 sānmíngzhì [份 fèn] ▸ **a cheese/ham/jam sandwich** 奶酪/火腿/果酱三明治 nǎilào/huǒtuǐ/guǒjiàng sānmíngzhì

sang [sæŋ] PT of **sing**

sanitary napkin ['sænɪtərɪ-] (US) N [c] 卫生巾 wèishēng jīn [块 kuài]

sanitary towel (Brit) N [c] 卫生巾 wèishēng jīn [块 kuài]

sank [sæŋk] PT of **sink**

Santa (Claus) ['sæntə('klɔːz)] N 圣诞老人 Shèngdàn Lǎorén

sardine [sɑː'diːn] N [c] 沙丁鱼 shādīng yú [条 tiáo]

SARS [sɑːz] N ABBR (= severe acute respiratory syndrome) 非典型性肺炎 fēi diǎnxíngxìng fèiyán

SAT N ABBR (US) (= Scholastic Aptitude Test) 学业能力倾向测试 Xuéyè Nénglì Qīngxiàng Cèshì

sat [sæt] PT, PP of **sit**

satellite ['sætəlaɪt] N 1 [c] 人造卫星 rénzào wèixīng [颗 kē] 2 [U] (also: **satellite television**) 卫星电视 wèixīng diànshì

satisfactory [sætɪs'fæktərɪ] ADJ 令人满意的 lìngrén mǎnyì de

satisfied ['sætɪsfaɪd] ADJ 满足的 mǎnzú de ▸ **to be satisfied with sth** 对某事满意 duì mǒushì mǎnyì

Saturday ['sætədɪ] N [c/U] 星期六 xīngqīliù [个 gè]; see also **Tuesday**

sauce [sɔːs] N [c/U] 酱 jiàng [种 zhǒng]

saucepan ['sɔːspən] N [c] 深平底锅 shēn píngdǐ guō [个 gè]

saucer ['sɔːsə^r] N [c] 茶杯碟 chábēi dié [个 gè]

Saudi Arabia [saudɪə'reɪbɪə] N 沙特阿拉伯 Shātè Ālābó

sausage ['sɒsɪdʒ] N [c/U] 香肠 xiāngcháng [根 gēn]

save [seɪv] I VT 1 [+ person] 救 jiù 2 (also: **save up**) 积攒 jīzǎn 3 (economize on) [+ money, time] 节省 jiéshěng 4 (Comput) 存储 cúnchǔ II VI (also: **save up**) 积攒 jīzǎn ▸ **to save sb's life** 挽救某人的生命 wǎnjiù mǒurén de shēngmìng

savings ['seɪvɪŋz] NPL (money) 存款 cúnkuǎn

savoury, (US) **savory** ['seɪvərɪ] ADJ 咸辣的 xiánlà de

saw [sɔː] (pt sawed, pp sawed or sawn) I VT see II VT 锯 jù III N [c] 锯子 jùzi [把 bǎ]

sawn [sɔːn] PP of **saw**

saxophone ['sæksəfəʊn] N [c] 萨克斯管 sàkèsī guǎn [根 gēn]

say [seɪ] (pt, pp said) VT 1 说 shuō [clock, watch] 表明 biǎomíng; [sign] 写着 xiězhe ▸ **to say sth to sb**

sb 告诉某人某事 gàosù mǒurén mǒushì ▸ **to say yes/no** 同意/不同意 tóngyì/bù tóngyì

scale [skeɪl] N [s] (*size, extent*) 规模 guīmó **scales** NPL 秤 chèng ▸ **on a large/small scale** 以大/小规模 yǐ dà/xiǎo guīmó

scandal ['skændl] N [c] 丑闻 chǒuwén [条 tiáo]

Scandinavia [skændɪ'neɪvɪə] N 斯堪的纳维亚 Sīkāndìnàwéiyà

scanner ['skænə] N [c] (*Comput*) 扫描仪 sǎomiáo yí [台 tái]

scar [skɑː] N [c] 伤疤 shāngbā [个 gè]

scarce [skeəs] ADJ 短缺的 duǎnquē de

scarcely ['skeəsli] ADV 几乎不 jīhūbù

scare [skeər] VT 使害怕 shǐ hàipà

scared ['skeəd] ADJ ▸ **to be scared (of sb/sth)** 害怕 (某人/某物) hàipà (mǒurén/mǒuwù)

scarf [skɑːf] (*pl* **scarfs** *or* **scarves**) N [c] (*long*) 围巾 wéijīn [条 tiáo]; (*square*) 头巾 tóujīn [块 kuài]

scarves [skɑːvz] NPL *of* **scarf**

scenery ['siːnəri] N [U] 风景 fēngjǐng

schedule ['ʃedjuːl, *US* 'skedjuːl] N [c] **1** (*agenda*) 日程安排 rìchéng ānpái [个 gè] **2** (*US: of trains, buses*) 时间表 shíjiān biǎo [个 gè] ▸ **on schedule** 准时 zhǔnshí ▸ **to be ahead of/behind schedule** 提前/落后于计划 tíqián/luòhòu yú jìhuà

scheme [skiːm] N [c] (*plan*) 方案 fāng'àn [个 gè]

scholarship ['skɒləʃɪp] N [c] 奖学金 jiǎngxué jīn [项 xiàng]

school [skuːl] N **1** [c/u] (*place*) 学校 xuéxiào [所 suǒ]; (*pupils and staff*) 全体师生 quántǐ shīshēng [c/u] (*US: university*) 大学 dàxué [所 suǒ] ▸ **to go to school** [child] 上学 shàngxué ▸ **to leave school** [child] 结束义务教育 jiéshù yìwù jiàoyù

schoolboy ['skuːlbɔɪ] N [c] 男生 nánshēng [个 gè]

schoolchildren ['skuːltʃɪldrən] NPL 学童 xuétóng

schoolgirl ['skuːlgɜːl] N [c] 女生 nǚshēng [个 gè]

science ['saɪəns] N **1** [U] (*scientific study*) 科学 kēxué **2** [c/u] (*branch of science, school subject*) 学科 xuékē [个 gè]

science fiction N [U] 科幻小说 kēhuàn xiǎoshuō

scientific [saɪən'tɪfɪk] ADJ 科学的 kēxué de

scientist ['saɪəntɪst] N [c] 科学家 kēxué jiā [位 wèi]

scissors ['sɪzəz] NPL 剪刀 jiǎndāo ▸ **a pair of scissors** 一把剪刀 yìbǎ jiǎndāo

scooter ['skuːtə] N [c] (*also*: **motor scooter**) 小型摩托车 xiǎoxíng mótuó chē [辆 liàng]

score [skɔː] N **1** [c] 比分 bǐfēn [个 gè] II VT [+ *goal, point*] 得 dé III VI (*in game, sport*) 得分 défēn

Scorpio ['skɔːpɪəʊ] N [c] (*sign*) 天蝎座 Tiānxiē Zuò

Scotch tape® (*US*) N [U] 透明胶带 tòumíng jiāodài

Scotland ['skɔtlənd] N 苏格兰 Sūgélán

Scottish ['skɔtɪʃ] ADJ 苏格兰的 Sūgélán de

scrambled egg ['skræmbld-] N [c/u] 炒鸡蛋 chǎo jīdàn [盘 pán]

scrap [skræp] VT 1 [+ car, ship] 报废 bàofèi 2 [+ project, idea, system, tax] 废弃 fèiqì

scratch [skrætʃ] I N [c] 1 (on car, furniture) 划痕 huáhén [条 tiáo] 2 (on body) 擦伤 cāshāng [处 chù] II VT 1 (damage) 划破 huápò 2 (because of itch) 抓 zhuā

scream [skri:m] VI 尖声喊叫 jiānshēng hǎnjiào

screen [skri:n] N [c] 1 (at cinema) 银幕 yínmù [个 gè] 2 of television, computer) 屏幕 píngmù [个 gè]

screw [skru:] N [c] 螺丝 luósī [个 gè]

screwdriver ['skru:draɪvəʳ] N [c] 螺丝起子 luósīqǐzi [把 bǎ]

sculpture ['skʌlptʃəʳ] N [u] 雕塑 diāosù

sea [si:] N ▸ **the sea** 海洋 hǎiyáng ▸ **by sea** 由海路 yóu hǎilù

seafood ['si:fu:d] N [u] 海味 hǎiwèi

seagull ['si:gʌl] N [c] 海鸥 hǎi'ōu [只 zhī]

seal [si:l] N [c] 海豹 hǎibào [只 zhī]

search [sə:tʃ] I N [c] 1 (for missing person) 搜寻 sōuxún [次 cì] 2 (Comput) 检索 jiǎnsuǒ [次 cì] II VT 搜查 sōuchá

seashore ['si:ʃɔ:ʳ] N [c] 海岸 hǎi'àn

seasick ['si:sɪk] ADJ 晕船的 yùnchuán de ▸ **to be** or **feel seasick** 感到晕船恶心 gǎndào yùnchún ěxīn

seaside ['si:saɪd] (Brit) N ▸ **the seaside** 海边 hǎibiān

season ['si:zn] N [c] 季节 jìjié [个 gè]

seat [si:t] N [c] 1 (chair) 椅子 yǐzi [把 bǎ]; (in car, theatre, cinema) 座 zuò [个 gè] 2 (place: in theatre, bus, train) 座位 zuòwèi [个 gè] ▸ **to take a/one's seat** 就座 jiùzuò ▸ **to be seated** (be sitting) 坐下 zuòxia

seat belt N [c] 安全带 ānquándài [条 tiáo]

second ['sɛkənd] I ADJ 第二的 dì'èr de II ADV 第二名地 dì'èrmíng de III N [c] (unit of time) 秒 miǎo ▸ **second floor** (Brit) 三层 sāncéng; (US) 二层 èrcéng

secondary school N [c/u] 中学 zhōngxué [所 suǒ]

second-hand ['sɛkənd'hænd] ADJ 二手的 èrshǒu de

secondly ['sɛkəndlɪ] ADV 其次 qícì

secret ['si:krɪt] I ADJ 秘密的 mìmì de II N [c] 秘密 mìmì [个 gè]

secretary ['sɛkrətərɪ] N [c] 秘书 mìshū [位 wèi]

section ['sɛkʃən] N [c] 部分 bùfen [个 gè]

security [sɪ'kjuərɪtɪ] N [u] 保安措施 bǎo'ān cuòshī

see [si:] (pt saw, pp seen) VT 1 看见 kànjiàn 2 (meet) 见 jiàn 3 [+ film, play] 看 kàn 4 (notice)

意识到 yìshí dào ▸to see sb doing/do sth 看见某人做某事 kànjiàn mǒurén zuò mǒushì ▸to go and see sb 去见某人 qùjiàn mǒurén ▸see you later! 一会儿见! yīhuǐr jiàn! ▸I see 我明白 wǒ míngbai

seed [siːd] N [c/u] 籽 zǐ [粒 lì]

seem [siːm] VI 似乎 sìhū ▸it seems that... 看来… kànlái…

seen [siːn] PP of **see**

seldom ['sɛldəm] ADV 不常 bùcháng

select [sɪ'lɛkt] VT 挑选 tiāoxuǎn

selection [sɪ'lɛkʃən] N [c] 供选择的范围 gōng xuǎnzéde fànwéi [个 gè]

self-confidence [sɛlf'kɒnfɪdns] N [u] 自信心 zìxìn xīn

selfish ['sɛlfɪʃ] ADJ 自私的 zìsī de

self-service [sɛlf'səːvɪs] ADJ 自助的 zìzhù de

sell [sɛl] (pt, pp **sold**) VT 卖卖 màimài ▸to sell sb sth, sell sth to sb 将某物卖给某人 jiāng mǒuwù màigěi mǒurén

semi-final [sɛmɪ'faɪnl] N [c] 半决赛 bàn juésài [场 chǎng]

send [sɛnd] (pt, pp **sent**) VT 1 ▸to send sth (to sb) 将某物发送（给某人）jiāng mǒuwù fāsòng (gěi mǒurén) 2 [+person] 派遣 pàiqiǎn

senior ['siːnɪəʳ] ADJ 高级的 gāojí de

senior citizen N [c] 已届退休年龄的公民 yǐjiè tuìxiū niánlíng de gōngmín [位 wèi]

senior high, (US) **senior high school** N [c] 高中 gāozhōng

[所 suǒ]

sense [sɛns] N 1 [c] (of smell, taste) 感觉官能 gǎnjué guānnéng [种 zhǒng] 2 [u] (good sense) 明智 míngzhì 3 [c] (meaning) 释义 shìyì [个 gè]

sensible ['sɛnsɪbl] ADJ 通情达理的 tōngqíng dálǐ de; [+ decision, suggestion] 明智的 míngzhì de

sensitive ['sɛnsɪtɪv] ADJ 1 善解人意的 shànjiě rényì de 2 [+ skin] 敏感的 mǐngǎn de

sent [sɛnt] PT, PP of **send**

sentence ['sɛntns] N [c] (Ling) 句子 jùzi [个 gè]

separate [adj 'sɛprɪt, vb 'sɛpəreɪt] I ADJ [+ section, piece, pile] 分开的 fēnkāi de; [+ rooms] 单独的 dāndú de II VT (split up) 分开 fēnkāi III VI [parents, couple] 分居 fēnjū ▸to be separated [couple] 分居 fēnjū

September [sɛp'tɛmbəʳ] N [c/u] 九月 jiǔyuè; see also **July**

serial ['sɪərɪəl] N [c] 连续剧 liánxùjù [部 bù]; (in magazine) 连载 liánzǎi [个 gè]

series ['sɪəriːz] (pl **series**) N [c] 1 一系列 yīxìliè [个 gè] 2 (on TV, radio) 系列节目 xìliè jiémù [个 gè]

serious ['sɪərɪəs] ADJ 1 严重的 yánzhòng de 2 (sincere) 当真的 dàngzhēn de; (solemn) 严肃的 yánsù de

serve [səːv] VT 1 (in shop, bar) 招待 zhāodài 2 [+ food, drink, meal] 端上 duānshang

service ['səːvɪs] N 1 [c] 服务 fúwù [项 xiàng] 2 [pl] (bus service) 火车/公共汽车营运 huǒchē/

gōnggòng qìchē yíngyùn [种 zhǒng] 3 [C] (Rel) 仪式 yíshì [个 gè]
▶service included/not included 含/不含小费 hán/bùhán xiǎofèi

service charge N [C] 服务费 fúwùfèi [笔 bǐ]

service station N [C] 加油站 jiāyóu zhàn [个 gè]

set [set] (pt, pp set) I N 1 [of cutlery, saucepans, books, keys] 套 tào 2 [C] (TV, Rad) 电视机 diànshìjī [台 tái] II ADJ [+ routine, time, price] 规定的 guīdìng de III VT 1 (put) 放 fàng 2 [+ table] 摆放 bǎifàng 3 [+ time, price, rules] 确定 quèdìng 4 [+ alarm] 设定 shèdìng; [+ heating, volume] 调整 tiáozhěng IV VI [sun] 落山 luòshān ▶a chess set 一副国际象棋 yīfù guójì xiàngqí
▶set off I VI ▶to set off (for) 启 程（前往）qǐchéng (qiánwǎng) II VT [+ bomb] 触发 chùfā
▶set out VI 出发 chūfā

settee [sɛ'ti:] N [C] 长沙发椅 cháng shāfāyǐ [个 gè]

settle ['sɛtl] VT [+ bill, account, debt] 支付 zhīfù

seven ['sɛvn] NUM 七 qī; see also five

seventeen [sɛvn'ti:n] NUM 十七 shíqī; see also fifteen

seventh ['sɛvnθ] NUM 第七 dìqī; see also fifth

seventy ['sɛvnti] NUM 七十 qīshí; see also fifty

several ['sɛvrəl] ADJ, PRON 几 个 jǐgè

severe [sɪ'vɪəʳ] ADJ [+ pain,

damage, shortage] 严重的 yánzhòng de 2 [+ punishment, criticism] 严厉的 yánlì de

sew [səu] (pt sewed, pp sewn) VI, VT 缝纫 féngrèn

sewing ['səuɪŋ] N [U] 缝纫 féngrèn

sewn [səun] PP of sew

sex [sɛks] N 1 [C] (gender) 性 别 xìngbié [种 zhǒng] 2 [U] (lovemaking) 性交 xìngjiāo ▶to have sex (with sb) （和某人）性 交 (hé mǒurén) xìngjiāo

sexism ['sɛksɪzəm] N [U] 性别歧 视 xìngbié qíshì

sexist ['sɛksɪst] ADJ 性别歧视的 xìngbié qíshì de

sexual ['sɛksjuəl] ADJ 性的 xìng de

sexy ['sɛksɪ] ADJ 性感的 xìnggǎn de

shade [ʃeɪd] N 1 [U] 阴凉处 yīnliáng chù 2 [C] (of colour) 色度 sèdù [种 zhǒng] 3 [C] (US) 遮阳窗帘 zhēyáng chuānglián [副 fù]

shadow ['ʃædəu] N [C] 影子 yǐngzi [个 gè]

shake [ʃeɪk] (pt shook, pp shaken ['ʃeɪkn]) I VT [+ bottle, cocktail, medicine] 摇晃 yáohuàng; [+ buildings, ground] 使震动 shǐ zhèndòng II VI [person, part of the body] 发抖 fādǒu; [building, table] 震动 zhèndòng; [ground] 震颤 zhènchàn ▶to shake one's head 摇头拒绝 yáotóu jùjué ▶to shake hands (with sb) （和某人）握手 (hé mǒurén) wòshǒu

shall [ʃæl] AUX VB 1 (indicating

future in 1st person) ▶ **I shall go** 我
要走了 wǒ yào zǒule **2** *(in 1st person
questions)* ▶ **shall I/we open the
door?** 我/我们把门打开好吗?
wǒ/wǒmen bǎ mén dǎkāi hǎoma?

shallow ['ʃæləʊ] ADJ 浅的 qiǎn de

shame [ʃeɪm] N [U] 耻辱 chǐrǔ
▶ **it is a shame that...** ...真遗憾
...zhēn yíhàn ▶ **what a shame!** 太
遗憾了! tài yíhàn le!

shampoo [ʃæm'puː] N [c/U] 洗发
液 xǐfàyè [瓶 píng]

shape [ʃeɪp] N [c] 形状
xíngzhuàng [种 zhǒng]

share [ʃeəʳ] I N [c] **1** *(part)* 一份
yífèn **2** *(Comm, Fin)* 股票 gǔpiào
[支 zhī] II VT **1** *(+ room, bed, taxi)* 合
用 héyòng **2** *(+ job, cooking, task)*
分担 fēndān
▶ **share out** VT 平均分配 píngjūn
fēnpèi

shark [ʃɑːk] N [c/U] 鲨鱼 shāyú
[条 tiáo]

sharp [ʃɑːp] I ADJ **1** *(+ knife, teeth)*
锋利的 fēnglì de; *(+ point, edge)* 尖
锐的 jiānruì de **2** *(+ curve, bend)* 急
转的 jízhuǎn de II ADV *(precisely)*
▶ **at 2 o'clock sharp** 两点整 liǎng
diǎn zhěng

shave [ʃeɪv] I VT *(+ head, legs)* 剃毛
发 tìmáofà II VI *(+)* 刮脸 guāliǎn

shaving cream N [U] 剃须膏
tìxūgāo

she [ʃiː] PRON 她 tā

she'd [ʃiːd] = **she had, she would**

sheep [ʃiːp] *(pl* **sheep)** N [c] 绵羊
miányáng [只 zhī]

sheet [ʃiːt] N [c] **1** 床单 chuángdān
[床 chuáng] **2** *(of paper)* 一张

yìzhāng

shelf [ʃelf] *(pl* **shelves)** N [c]
(bookshelf) 架子 jiàzi [个 gè]; *(in
cupboard)* 搁板 gēbǎn [块 kuài]

shell [ʃel] N [c] **1** 贝壳 bèiké [只
zhī] **2** *(of tortoise, snail, crab, egg,
nut)* 壳 ké [个 gè]

she'll [ʃiːl] = **she will**

shellfish ['ʃelfɪʃ] *(pl* **shellfish)** I N
[c/U] 贝类海产 bèilèi hǎichǎn [种
zhǒng] II NPL *(as food)* 贝类海鲜
bèilèi hǎixiān

shelter ['ʃeltəʳ] I N [c] *(building)*
遮蔽处 zhēbìchù [个 gè] II VI 躲
避 duǒbì

shelves [ʃelvz] NPL of **shelf**

she's [ʃiːz] = **she is, she has**

shift [ʃɪft] VT 移动 yídòng

shin [ʃɪn] N [c] 胫部 jìngbù

shine [ʃaɪn] *(pt, pp* **shone)** VI 照
耀 zhàoyào

ship [ʃɪp] N [c] 船 chuán [艘 sōu]

shirt [ʃəːt] N [c] 衬衫 chènshān
[件 jiàn]

shiver ['ʃɪvəʳ] VI 发抖 fādǒu

shock [ʃɔk] I N **1** [c] 震骇 zhènhài
[种 zhǒng] **2** *(Med)* 休克 xiūkè
3 [c] *(also:* **electric shock)** 触电
chùdiàn [次 cì] II VT 使厌恶 shǐ
yànwù

shocked [ʃɔkt] ADJ 感到不快的
gǎndào búkuài de

shoe [ʃuː] N [c] 鞋 xié [双 shuāng]
▶ **a pair of shoes** 一双鞋 yìshuāng
xié

shone [ʃɔn] PT, PP of **shine**

shook [ʃuk] PT of **shake**

shoot [ʃuːt] *(pt, pp* **shot)** I VT
(kill) 向...开枪 xiàng...kāiqiāng

II VI **1** (*with gun, bow*) ▶ **to shoot (at sb/sth)** （朝某人／某物）射击 (cháo mǒurén/mǒuwù) shèjī **2** (*Football etc*) 射门 shèmén

shop [ʃɒp] **I** N [c] (*esp Brit*) 商店 shāngdiàn [家 jiā] **II** VI 购物 gòuwù ▶ **to go shopping** 去买东西 qù mǎi dōngxi

shop assistant (*Brit*) N [c] 店员 diànyuán [位 wèi]

shopping [ʃɒpɪŋ] N [U] **1** (*activity*) 购物 gòuwù **2** (*goods*) 所购之物 suǒgòu zhī wù; *see also* **shop**

shopping centre, (*US*) **shopping center** N [c] 购物中心 gòuwù zhōngxīn [个 gè]

shop window N [c] 商店橱窗 shāngdiàn chúchuāng [个 gè]

shore [ʃɔː] N [c] 岸 àn [个 gè]

short [ʃɔːt] **I** ADJ **1** (*in time*) 短暂的 duǎnzàn de **2** (*in length*) 短的 duǎn de **3** (*not tall*) 矮的 ǎi de **II shorts** NPL **1** (*short trousers*) 短裤 duǎnkù **2** (*esp US: underpants*) 男用短衬裤 nányòng duǎnchènkù ▶ **a pair of shorts** 一条短裤 yìtiáo duǎnkù

shortage [ʃɔːtɪdʒ] N [c/U] 短缺 duǎnquē [种 zhǒng]

shortly [ʃɔːtlɪ] ADV 马上 mǎshàng ▶ **shortly after/before sth** 某事后/前不久 mǒushì hòu/qián bùjiǔ

short-sighted [ʃɔːtˈsaɪtɪd] ADJ (*Brit*) 近视的 jìnshì de

shot [ʃɒt] **I** PT, PP of **shoot II** N **1** [c] 射击 shèjī [阵 zhèn] **2** [c] (*Football*) 射门 shèmén [次 cì] **3** [c] (*injection*) 皮下注射 píxià zhùshè [针 zhēn]

should [ʃʊd] AUX VB **1** (*indicating*

advisability） ▶ **I should go now** 我现在应该走了 wǒ xiànzài yīnggāi zǒule **2** (*indicating obligation*) 应当 yīngdāng **3** (*indicating likelihood*) ▶ **he should be there by now/he should get there soon** 他现在该到那儿了/他该很快就到那儿了 tā xiànzài gāi dào nàr le/tā gāi hěnkuài jiù dào nàr le ▶ **you should have been more careful** 你本该更加小心 nǐ běngāi gèngjiā xiǎoxīn ▶ **he should have arrived by now** 他现在应该到了 tā xiànzài yīnggāi dàole

shoulder [ʃəʊldə] N [c] 肩膀 jiānbǎng [个 gè]

shout [ʃaʊt] VI (*also:* **shout out**) 喊叫 hǎnjiào

show [ʃəʊ] (*pt* showed, *pp* shown) **I** N [c] (*exhibition*) 展览 zhǎnlǎn [个 gè] **2** (*TV, Rad*) 节目 jiémù [个 gè] **II** VT **1** 表明 biǎomíng ▶ **to show sb sth** or **to show sth to sb** 给某人看某物（或）把某物给某人看 gěi mǒurén kàn mǒuwù（huò）bǎ mǒuwù gěi mǒurén kàn **2** (*illustrate, depict*) 描述 miáoshù ▶ **on show** 在展览中 zài zhǎnlǎn zhōng ▶ **to show that...** 表明... biǎomíng... ▶ **to show sb how to do sth** 示范某人如何做某事 shìfàn mǒurén rúhé zuò mǒushì ▶ **show around** VT 带...参观 dài...cānguān

shower [ʃaʊə] **I** N [c] (*exhibition*) 展览 zhǎnlǎn **1** 阵雨 zhènyǔ [场 chǎng] **2** (*for washing*) 淋浴器 línyùqì [个 gè] **II** VI 洗淋浴 xǐ línyù ▶ **to have** or **take a shower** 洗淋浴 xǐ línyù

shown [ʃəun] PP of **show**

shrank [ʃræŋk] PT of **shrink**

shrimp [ʃrɪmp] N [c] (small) 小虾 xiǎoxiā [只 zhǐ]; (US: bigger) 虾 xiā [只 zhǐ]

shrink [ʃrɪŋk] (pt **shrank**, pp **shrunk**) VI 缩水 suōshuǐ

shrunk [ʃrʌŋk] PP of **shrink**

shut [ʃʌt] (pt, pp **shut**) I VT 关上 guānshang; [+ shop] 关门 guānmén; [+ mouth, eyes] 闭上 bìshang II VI [shop] 打烊 dǎyàng III ADJ [+ door, drawer] 关闭的 guānbì de; [+ shop] 打烊的 dǎyàng de; [+ mouth, eyes] 闭着的 bìzhe de
▶ **shut up** VI (inf) 住口 zhùkǒu
▶ **shut up!** (inf) 闭嘴! bìzuǐ!

shuttle [ʃʌtl] N [c] (plane, bus) 穿梭航班/班车 chuānsuō bānjī/bānchē [架/辆 jià/liàng]

shy [ʃaɪ] ADJ 害羞的 hàixiū de

sick [sɪk] ADJ 1 (physically) 患病的 huànbìng de; (mentally) 令人讨厌的 lìngrén tǎoyàn de 2 ▶ **to be sick** (vomit) 呕吐 ǒutù ▶ **to feel sick** 感觉恶心 gǎnjué ěxīn

sickness [sɪknɪs] N [U] 患病 huànbìng

side [saɪd] I N [c] 1 边 biān [个 gè] 2 侧面 cèmiàn [个 gè]; [of body] 体侧 tǐcè [边 biān] 3 [of paper, face, brain] 一面 yīmiàn [个 gè]; [of tape, record] 面 miàn [个 gè] 4 边 biān [个 gè] 5 [of hill, valley] 坡 pō [个 gè] 6 (Brit: team) 队 duì [支 zhī] 7 (in conflict, contest) 一方 yīfāng II ADJ [+ door, entrance] 旁边的 pángbiān de

side of sth 在某物的另一边 zài mǒuwù de lìngyībiān

side-effect [saɪdɪfɛkt] N [c] 副作用 fù zuòyòng [个 gè]

sidewalk [saɪdwɔːk] (US) N [c] 人行道 rénxíngdào [条 tiáo]

sigh [saɪ] VI 叹气 tànqì

sight [saɪt] I N [U] 视力 shìlì [c] (spectacle) 景象 jǐngxiàng [种 zhǒng] II **sights** NPL ▶ **the sights** 景点 jǐngdiǎn

sightseeing [saɪtsiːɪŋ] N [U] 观光 guānguāng ▶ **to go sightseeing** 观光游览 guānguāng yóulǎn

sign [saɪn] I N 1 [c] 指示牌 zhǐshìpái [个 kuài] 2 [c] (also: road sign) 路标 lùbiāo [个 gè] 3 [c/u] (indication, evidence) 迹象 jìxiàng [个 gè] II VT 签署 qiānshǔ ▶ **it's a good/bad sign** 这是个好/坏兆头 zhèshì gè hǎo/huài zhàotou

signal [sɪɡnl] I N [c] 1 (to do sth) 信号 xìnhào [个 gè] 2 (Rail) 信号机 xìnhàojī [部 bù] 3 (Elec) 信号 xìnhào [个 gè] II VI (with gesture, sound) ▶ **to signal (to sb)** (向某人) 示意 (xiàng mǒurén) shìyì

signature [sɪɡnətʃəˈ] N [c] 签名 qiānmíng [个 gè]

sign language N [c/u] 手语 shǒuyǔ [种 zhǒng]

signpost [saɪnpəust] N [c] 路标 lùbiāo [个 gè]

silence [saɪləns] N [c/u] 寂静 jìjìng [片 piàn] ▶ **in silence** 鸦雀无声 yā què wú shēng

silent [saɪlənt] ADJ [+ person] 沉

默的 chénmò de

silk [sɪlk] N [c/u] 丝绸 sīchóu [块 kuài]

silly ['sɪlɪ] ADJ 愚蠢的 yúchǔn de; [+ idea, object] 可笑的 kěxiào de

silver ['sɪlvə'] I N [U] 银 yín II ADJ [+ spoon, necklace] 银的 yín de

SIM card ['sɪm-] N [c] 手机智能卡 shǒujī zhìnéngkǎ [张 zhāng]

similar ['sɪmɪlə'] ADJ 相似的 xiāngsì de ▶ **to be similar to sth** 和某事物类似 hé mǒu shìwù lèisì

simple [sɪmpl] ADJ 1 (easy) 简单的 jiǎndān de 2 [+ meal, life, cottage] 简朴的 jiǎnpǔ de

simply ['sɪmplɪ] ADV 1 (merely) 仅仅 jǐnjǐn 2 (absolutely) 完全 wánquán

since [sɪns] I ADV (from then onwards) 此后 cǐhòu II PREP 1 (from) 自…以来 zì…yǐlái 2 (after) 从…以后 cóng…yǐhòu III CONJ 1 (from when) 自从 zìcóng 2 (after) 从…以后 cóng…yǐhòu 3 (as) 因为 yīnwèi ▶ **since then** or **ever since** 从那时起 cóng nàshí qǐ ▶ **I've been here since the end of June** 我自6月底以来一直在这儿。wǒ zì liùyuè dǐ yǐlái yīzhí zài zhèr ▶ **since it was Saturday, he stayed in bed an extra hour** 因为是星期六，他在床上多躺了个小时。yīnwèi shì xīngqīliù,tā zài chuángshàng duō tǎngle yī xiǎoshí

sincere [sɪn'sɪə'] ADJ 真诚的 zhēnchéng de

sincerely [sɪn'sɪəlɪ] ADV 由衷地 yóuzhōng de ▶ **Yours sincerely** or (US) **Sincerely yours** 谨上

jǐnshàng

sing [sɪŋ] (pt **sang**, pp **sung**) I VI [person] 唱歌 chànggē; [bird] 鸣 míng II VT [+ song] 唱 chàng

Singapore [sɪŋgə'pɔː'] N 新加坡 Xīnjiāpō

singer ['sɪŋə'] N [c] 歌手 gēshǒu [位 wèi]

singing ['sɪŋɪŋ] N [U] 唱歌 chànggē

single [sɪŋgl] I ADJ 1 (solitary) 单个的 dāngè de 2 (unmarried) 单身的 dānshēn de II N [c] (Brit) (also: **single ticket**) 单程票 dānchéngpiào [张 zhāng]

singular ['sɪŋgjulə'] ADJ 单数的 dānshù de

sink [sɪŋk] (pt **sank**, pp **sunk**) I N [c] 洗涤槽 xǐdí cáo [个 gè] II VI [ship] 沉没 chénmò

sir [sə'] N 先生 xiānsheng ▶ **Dear Sir** 亲爱的先生 Qīnài de Xiānsheng ▶ **Dear Sir or Madam** 亲爱的先生或女士 Qīnài de xiānsheng huò nǚshì

siren ['saɪərn] N [c] 警报器 jǐngbàoqì [个 gè]

sister ['sɪstə'] N [c] 姐妹 jiěmèi [对 duì]; (elder) 姐姐 jiějie [个 gè]; (younger) 妹妹 mèimei [个 gè] ▶ **my brothers and sisters** 我的兄弟姐妹们 wǒde xiōngdì jiěmèi men

sister-in-law ['sɪstərɪnlɔː] (pl **sisters-in-law**) N [c] (husband's sister) 姑子 gūzi [个 gè]; (wife's sister) 姨子 yízi [个 gè]; (older brother's wife) 嫂子 shǎozi [个 gè]; (younger brother's wife) 弟媳

dìxí [个 gè]

sit [sɪt] (pt, pp **sat**) VI 1 (also: **sit down**) 坐下 zuòxià 2 (be sitting) 坐 zuò

▸ **sit down** VI 坐下 zuòxià ▸to be sitting down 就座 jiùzuò

site [saɪt] N [c] (also: **website**) 网址 wǎngzhǐ [个 gè]

sitting room (Brit) N [c] 起居室 qǐjūshì [间 jiān]

situated ['sɪtjʊeɪtɪd] ADJ ▸to be situated in/on/near sth 位于某物中/上/旁 wèiyú mǒuwù zhōng/shàng/páng

situation [sɪtjʊ'eɪʃən] N [c] 情况 qíngkuàng [种 zhǒng]

six [sɪks] NUM 六 liù; see also **five**

sixteen [sɪks'tiːn] NUM 十六 shíliù; see also **fifteen**

sixth [sɪksθ] NUM 1 (in series) 第六 dìliù 2 (fraction) 六分之一 liùfēnzhī yī; see also **fifth**

sixty ['sɪkstɪ] NUM 六十 liùshí; see also **fifty**

size [saɪz] N 1 [c/u] (of object) 大小 dàxiǎo 2 [c/u] (of clothing, shoes) 尺码 chǐmǎ [个 gè] 3 [u] (of area, building, task, loss) 大 dà ▸what size shoes do you take? 你穿几号的鞋? nǐ chuān jǐhào de xié?

skate [skeɪt] VI 1 (ice skate) 溜冰 liūbīng 2 (roller skate) 溜旱冰 liūhànbīng

skateboard ['skeɪtbɔːd] N [c] 滑板 huábǎn [个 gè]

skating ['skeɪtɪŋ] N [u] (ice-skating) 冰上运动 bīngshàng yùndòng; see also **skate**

skeleton ['skɛlɪtn] N [c] 骨骼 gǔgé [个 gè]

sketch [skɛtʃ] N [c] (drawing) 素描 sùmiáo [张 zhāng]

ski [skiː] VI 滑雪 huáxuě ▸to go skiing 去滑雪 qù huáxuě

skiing ['skiːɪŋ] N [u] 滑雪运动 huáxuě yùndòng; see also **ski**

skilful, (US) **skillful** ['skɪlful] ADJ 老练的 lǎoliàn de; [+ use, choice, management] 技巧娴熟的 jìqiǎo xiánshú de

skill [skɪl] N 1 [u] (ability) 技巧 jìqiǎo 2 [c] (acquired) 技能 jìnéng [项 xiàng]

skillful ['skɪlful] (US) ADJ = **skilful**

skin [skɪn] N [c/u] 皮肤 pífū; [of animal] 皮 pí [张 zhāng]; (complexion) 肤色 fūsè [种 zhǒng]

skip [skɪp] I VT [+ lunch, lecture] 故意不做 gùyì bùzuò II N [c] (Brit: container) 无盖用以装运工地废料的废料桶

skirt [skɜːt] N [c] 裙子 qúnzi [条 tiáo]

skull [skʌl] N [c] 颅骨 lúgǔ [个 gè]

sky [skaɪ] N [c/u] 天空 tiānkōng [片 piàn]

skyscraper ['skaɪskreɪpəʳ] N [c] 摩天大厦 mótiān dàshà [座 zuò]

slap [slæp] I N [c] 掌击 zhǎngjī [次 cì] II VT 掴 guó

sled [slɛd] (US) N [c] 雪橇 xuěqiāo [副 fù]

sledge [slɛdʒ] (Brit) N [c] 雪橇 xuěqiāo [副 fù]

sleep [sliːp] (pt, pp **slept**) I N 1 [u] 睡眠 shuìmián 2 [c] (nap) 睡觉 shuìjiào ▸to be asleep 睡着 shuì;

(*spend the night*) 过夜 guòyè ▶**to go to sleep** 去睡觉 qù shuìjiào

sleep with VT FUS 和…有性关系 hé…yǒu xìngguānxì

sleeping bag N [c] 睡袋 shuìdài [个 gè]

sleeping pill N [c] 安眠药 ānmiányào [片 piàn]

sleet [sli:t] N [U] 雨夹雪 yǔjiāxuě

sleeve [sli:v] N [c] 1 袖子 xiùzi [个 gè] 2 (*esp Brit: of record*) 唱片套 chàngpiàn tào [个 gè]

slept [slɛpt] PT, PP of **sleep**

slice [slaɪs] N [c] 片 piàn

slide [slaɪd] (*pt, pp* **slid**) I N [c] 1 (*in playground*) 滑梯 huátī [个 gè] 2 (*Brit: also: hair slide*) 发夹 fàjiā [个 gè] II VI ▶**to slide down/off/into sth** 滑下/离/进某物 huáxià/lí/jìn mǒuwù

slight [slaɪt] ADJ 微小的 wēixiǎo de

slightly ['slaɪtlɪ] ADV 略微地 lüèwēi de

slim [slɪm] I ADJ 苗条的 miáotiáo de II VI 节食减肥 jiéshí jiǎnféi

slip [slɪp] I VI (*person*) 滑跤 huájiāo; (*object*) 滑落 huáluò II N [c] (*mistake*) 差错 chācuò [个 gè]

slipper ['slɪpəʳ] N [c] 拖鞋 tuōxié [只 zhī]

slippery ['slɪpərɪ] ADJ 滑的 huá de

slot machine N [c] 投币机 tóubìjī [个 gè]; (*for gambling*) 吃角子老虎机 chījiǎozi lǎohǔjī [个 bù]

slow [sləu] I ADJ 慢的 màn de II ADV (*inf*) 缓慢地 huǎnmàn de ▶**my watch is 20 minutes slow**

我的表慢了20分钟 wǒde biǎo mànle èrshí fēnzhōng ▶**slow down** VI 放松 fàngsōng

slowly ['sləulɪ] ADV 慢慢地 mànmàn de

smack [smæk] VT (*as punishment*) 打打 dǎ dǎ

small [smɔ:l] ADJ 1 小的 xiǎo de 2 (*young*) 年幼的 niányòu de 3 [+ *mistake, problem, change*] 微不足道的 wēibùzúdào de

smart [smɑ:t] ADJ 1 (*esp Brit: neat, tidy*) 漂亮的 piàoliang de 2 (*fashionable*) 时髦的 shímáo de 3 (*clever*) 聪明的 cōngmíng de

smash [smæʃ] VT 打碎 dǎsuì

smell [smɛl] (*pt, pp* **smelled** or **smelt**) I N [c] 气味 qìwèi [种 zhǒng] II VT 闻到 wéndào III VI 1 (*have unpleasant odour*) 发臭 fāchòu 2 ▶**to smell nice/delicious/spicy** etc 闻起来香/好吃/辣(等) wén qǐlái xiāng/hǎochī/là [等] ▶**to smell of** 有…气味 yǒu…qìwèi

smelt [smɛlt] PT, PP of **smell**

smile [smaɪl] I N [c] 微笑 wēixiào [个 gè] II VI ▶**to smile (at sb)** (对某人) 微笑 (duì mǒurén) wēixiào

smoke [sməuk] I N [U] 烟 yān II VI [*person*] 吸烟 xīyān III VT [+ *cigarette, cigar, pipe*] 抽 chōu

smoker ['sməukəʳ] N [c] 吸烟者 xīyānzhě [个 gè]

smoking ['sməukɪŋ] N [U] 吸烟 xīyān ▶**"no smoking"** "禁止吸烟" "jìnzhǐ xīyān"

smooth [smu:ð] ADJ (*not rough*)

光滑的 guānghuá de

smother ['smʌðər] VT 使窒息 shǐ zhìxī

SMS N ABBR (= **short message service**) 短信息服务 duǎn xìnxī fúwù

smuggle ['smʌgl] VT 走私 zǒusī
▶ **to smuggle sth in/out** 走私进口/出口某物 zǒusī jìnkǒu/chūkǒu mǒuwù

snack [snæk] N [c] 小吃 xiǎochī [份 fèn]

snail [sneɪl] N [c] 蜗牛 wōniú [只 zhī]

snake [sneɪk] N [c] 蛇 shé [条 tiáo]

snapshot ['snæpʃɒt] N [c] 快照 kuàizhào [张 zhāng]

sneakers ['sniːkəz] (US) NPL 胶底运动鞋 jiāodǐ yùndòngxié

sneeze [sniːz] VI 打喷嚏 dǎ pēntì

snob [snɒb] (pej) N 势利小人 shìlì xiǎorén [个 gè]

snooker ['snuːkər] N [U] (Sport) 英式台球 yīngshì táiqiú

snore [snɔːr] VI 打鼾 dǎhān

snow [snəʊ] I N [U] 雪 xuě II VI 下雪 xiàxuě ▶ **it's snowing** 下雪 xiàxuě

snowball ['snəʊbɔːl] N [c] 雪球 xuěqiú [个 gè]

KEYWORD

so [səʊ] I ADV 1 (thus, likewise) 这样 zhèyàng ▶ **they do so because...** 他们这样做是因为… tāmen zhèyàng zuò shì yīnwéi... ▶ **if you don't want to go, just say so** 如果你

不想去，就说你不想去 rúguǒ nǐ bùxiǎng qù, jiù shuō nǐ bùxiǎng qù ▶ **if so** 如果这样 rúguǒ zhèyàng ▶ **I hope/think so** 我希望/认为如此必会这样 rúcǐ ▶ **so far** 迄今为止 qìjīn wéizhǐ ▶ **and so on** 等等 děngděng

2 (also) ▶ **so do I/so am I** 我也一样 wǒ yě yīyàng

3 如此 rúcǐ ▶ **so quickly/big (that)** 如此快/大(以至于) rúcǐ kuài/dà(yǐzhì yú)

4 (very) 非常 fēicháng ▶ **so much** 那么多 nàme duō ▶ **so many** 那么多 nàme duō

5 (linking events) 于是 yúshì ▶ **so I was right after all** 那终究我是对的 nà zhōngjiū wǒ shì duìde

II CONJ 1 (expressing purpose) ▶ **so (that)** 为的是 wèide shì ▶ **I brought it so (that) you could see it** 我带过来给你看 wǒ dàiguò lái gěi nǐ kàn

2 (expressing result) 因此 yīncǐ ▶ **he didn't come so I left** 他没来，因此我走了 tā méilái, yīncǐ wǒ zǒule

soaking ['səʊkɪŋ] ADJ (also: **soaking wet**) [+ person] 湿透的 shītòu de; [+ clothes] 湿淋淋的 shīlínlín de

soap [səʊp] N [c/U] 1 肥皂 féizào [块 kuài] 2 = **soap opera**

soap opera N [c] 肥皂剧 féizào jù [部 bù]

sober ['səʊbər] ADJ 未醉的 wèizuìde

soccer ['sɒkər] N [U] 足球 zúqiú

social ['səʊʃl] ADJ 社会的 shèhuì

de 2 [+ *event, function*] 社交的 shèjiāo de

socialism ['səuʃəlɪzəm] N [U] 社会主义 shèhuì zhǔyì

socialist ['səuʃəlɪst] I ADJ 社会主义的 shèhuì zhǔyì de II N [c] 社会主义者 shèhuì zhǔyìzhě [位 wèi]

social worker N [c] 社会福利工作者 shèhuì fúlì gōngzuòzhě [位 wèi]

society [sə'saɪətɪ] N [U] 社会 shèhuì

sock [sɔk] N [c] 袜子 wàzi [双 shuāng]

socket ['sɔkɪt] N [c] (Brit) 插座 chāzuò [个 gè]

sofa ['səufə] N [c] 沙发 shāfā [个 gè]

soft [sɔft] ADJ 1 [+ *towel*] 松软的 sōngruǎn de; [+ *skin*] 柔软的 róuruǎn de 2 [+ *bed, paste*] 柔软的 róuruǎn de

soft drink N [c] 软性饮料 ruǎnxìng yǐnliào [瓶 píng]

software ['sɔftwɛər] N [U] 软件 ruǎnjiàn

soil [sɔɪl] N [c/U] 土壤 tǔrǎng [种 zhǒng]

solar power N [U] 太阳能 tàiyáng néng

sold [səuld] PT, PP of **sell**

soldier ['səuldʒər] N [c] 士兵 shìbīng [位 wèi]

sole [səul] N [c] 底 dǐ [个 gè]

solicitor [sə'lɪsɪtər] (Brit) N [c] 律师 lùshī [位 wèi]

solid ['sɔlɪd] ADJ 1 (*not soft*) 坚实的 jiānshí de 2 (*not liquid*) 固体的 gùtǐ de 3 [+ *gold, oak*] 纯质的

chúnzhì de

solution [sə'luːʃən] N [c] 解决方案 jiějué fāng'àn [个 gè]

solve [sɔlv] VT 1 [+ *mystery, case*] 破解 pòjiě 2 [+ *problem*] 解决 jiějué

◯ KEYWORD

some I ADJ 1 (*a little, a few*) 一些 yìxiē ▸ **some milk/books** 一些牛奶/书 yìxiē niúnǎi/shū 2 (*certain, in contrasts*) 某些 mǒuxiē ▸ **some people say that...** 有些人说... yǒuxiē rén shuō... II PRON (*a certain amount, certain number*) 一些 yìxiē ▸ **I've got some** 我有一些 wǒ yǒu yìxiē ▸ **there was/were some left** 还剩下一些 hái shèngxià yìxiē ▸ **some of it/them** 它的一部分/他们中的一些 tāde yī bùfèn/tāmen zhōng de yīxiē

somebody ['sʌmbədɪ] PRON = **someone**

somehow ['sʌmhau] ADV 不知怎样地 bùzhī zěnyàng de

someone ['sʌmwʌn] PRON 某人 mǒurén ▸ **I saw someone in the garden** 我看见花园里有人 wǒ kànjiàn huāyuán lǐ yǒurén ▸ **someone else** 别人 biérén

someplace ['sʌmpleɪs] (US) ADV = **somewhere**

something ['sʌmθɪŋ] PRON 某事物 mǒushìwù ▸ **something else** 某些其他的事情 qítā shìqíng ▸ **would you like a sandwich or**

something? 你要来点三明治或其他什么东西吗？ nǐ yào lái diǎn sānmíngzhì huò qítā shénme dōngxi ma?

sometime ['sʌmtaɪm] ADV 某个时候 mǒugè shíhòu

请勿将 **sometime** 和 **sometime** 混淆。 **sometimes** 表示某事物只发生在某些时候，而不是总是发生。Do you visit your sister? – Sometimes... Sometimes I wish I still lived in Australia. **sometimes** 还可以表示某事物发生在特定情况下，而不是在任何情况下都会发生。Sometimes they stay for a week, sometimes just for the weekend. **sometime** 表示未来或过去某个不确定或未指明的时间。Can I come and see you sometime? ...He started his new job sometime last month.

sometimes ['sʌmtaɪmz] ADV 有时 yǒushí

somewhere ['sʌmweəʳ] ADV 在某处 zài mǒuchù ▸ I need somewhere to live 我需要找个地方住 wǒ xūyào zhǎogè dìfang zhù ▸ I must have lost it somewhere 我一定把它丢在哪儿了 wǒ yídìng bǎ bǎ diūzài nǎr le ▸ let's go somewhere quiet 我们去个安静的地方吧 wǒmen qù gè ānjìng de dìfang ba ▸ somewhere else 别的地方 biéde dìfang

son [sʌn] N [c] 儿子 érzi [个 gè]

song [sɒŋ] N [c] 歌曲 gēqǔ [首 shǒu]

son-in-law ['sʌnɪnlɔː] (pl sons-in-law) N [c] 女婿 nǚxu [个 gè]

soon [suːn] ADV 1 (in a short time) 不久 bùjiǔ 2 (a short time later) 很快 hěnkuài 3 (early) 早 zǎo ▸ soon afterwards 不久后 bùjiǔ hòu ▸ as soon as 一…就… yī…jiù… ▸ quite soon 很快 hěnkuài ▸ see you soon! 再见！ zàijiàn!

sooner ['suːnəʳ] ADV ▸ sooner or later 迟早 chízǎo ▸ the sooner the better 越快越好 yuè kuài yuè hǎo

sophomore ['sɒfəmɔːʳ] (US) N [c] 二年级学生 èr niánjí xuéshēng [个 gè]

sore [sɔːʳ] ADJ 痛的 tòng de

sorry ['sɒrɪ] ADJ 懊悔的 àohuǐ de ▸ (I'm) sorry! (apology) 对不起！ duìbuqǐ! ▸ sorry? (pardon?) 请再讲一遍 qǐng zài jiǎng yíbiàn ▸ to feel sorry for sb 对某人表示同情 duì mǒurén biǎoshì tóngqíng ▸ to be sorry about sth 对某事表示歉意 duì mǒushì biǎoshì qiànyì ▸ I'm sorry to hear that... 听到…我很伤心 tīngdào…wǒ hěn shāngxīn

sort [sɔːt] I N [c] ▸ sort (of) 种类 zhǒnglèi [个 gè] 2 (make, brand) 品牌 pǐnpái [个 gè] II VT 1 (+ papers, mail, belongings) 把…分类 bǎ…fēnlèi 2 (Comput) 整理 zhěnglǐ ▸ sort of (inf) 有点儿 yǒu diǎnr ▸ all sorts of 各种不同的 gèzhǒng bùtóng de ▸ sort out VT (separate) [+ problem] 解决 jiějué

sound [saund] I N [c]

shēngyīn [种 zhǒng] II vi 1 *(alarm, bell)* 响 xiǎng 2 *(seem)* 听起来 tīng qǐlái ▸ **to make a sound** 出声 chūshēng ▸ **that sounds like an explosion** 听起来像是爆炸声的 tīngqǐlái xiàngshì bàozhàshēng de ▸ **that sounds like a great idea** 这主意听起来妙极了 zhè zhǔyì tīngqǐlái miàojíle ▸ **it sounds as if...** 听起来似乎… tīngqǐlái sìhū…

soup [su:p] N [c/u] 汤 tāng [份 fèn]

sour ['saʊər] ADJ 1 *(bitter-tasting)* 酸的 suān de 2 [+ *milk*] 酸的 suān de

south [saʊθ] I N [s/u] 南方 nánfāng II ADJ 南部的 nánbù de III ADV 向南方 xiàng nánfāng ▸ **to the south** 以南 yǐnán ▸ **south of...** 在…以南 zài…yǐnán

South Africa N 南非 Nánfēi

South America N 南美洲 Nán měizhōu

south-east [saʊθ'i:st] I N 东南 dōngnán II ADJ 东南的 dōngnán de III ADV 向东南 xiàng dōngnán

southern ['sʌðən] ADJ 南方的 nánfāng de ▸ **the southern hemisphere** 南半球 nán bànqiú

South Korea N 韩国 Hánguó

South Pole N ▸ **the South Pole** 南极 Nánjí

south-west [saʊθ'wɛst] I N [s/u] 西南 xīnán II ADJ 西南的 xīnán de III ADV 向西南 xiàng xīnán

souvenir [su:və'nɪər] N [c] 纪念品 jìniàn pǐn [件 jiàn]

soy sauce [-ɪs-] N [u] 酱油 jiàngyóu

space [speɪs] N 1 [c/u] *(gap, place)* 空隙 kòngxì [个 gè] 2 [u] *(beyond Earth)* 太空 tàikōng ▸ **to clear a space for sth** 为某物腾地方 wèi mǒuwù téng dìfang

spade [speɪd] N [c] 锹 qiāo [把 bǎ]

spaghetti [spə'gɛti] N [u] 意大利面 yìdàlì miàn

Spain [speɪn] N 西班牙 Xībānyá

spam [spæm] *(Comput)* N [u] 垃圾邮件 lājī yóujiàn

Spanish ['spænɪʃ] I ADJ 西班牙的 Xībānyá de II N 2 *(language)* 西班牙语 Xībānyáyǔ

spanner ['spænər] *(Brit)* N [c] 扳钳 bānqián [个 gè]

spare [spɛər] I ADJ 1 *(free)* 多余的 duōyú de 2 *(extra)* 备用的 bèiyòng de II N [c] = **spare part**

spare part N [c] 备件 bèijiàn [个 gè]

spare time N [u] 业余时间 yèyú shíjiān

spat [spæt] PT, PP of **spit**

speak [spi:k] *(pt spoke, pp spoken)* I vt + *language)* 讲 jiǎng II vi 讲话 jiǎnghuà ▸ **to speak to sb about sth** 和某人谈某事 hé mǒurén tán mǒushì

special ['spɛʃl] ADJ 1 *(important)* 特别的 tèbié de 2 *(particular)* 专门的 zhuānmén de ▸ **we only use these plates on special occasions** 我们只在特别场合才用这些碟子 wǒmen zhǐzài tèbié chǎnghé cái yòng zhèxiē diézi ▸ **it's nothing special** 没什么特别的 méi shénme tèbié de

speciality [speʃɪˈælɪtɪ], (US) **specialty** ['speʃəltɪ] N [c] (food) 特制品 tèzhìpǐn [种 zhǒng]; (product) 特产 tèchǎn [种 zhǒng]

specially ['speʃlɪ] ADV 专门地 zhuānmén de

specialty ['speʃəltɪ] (US) N = **speciality**

species ['spi:ʃi:z] N [c] 种 zhǒng [个 gè]

specific [spəˈsɪfɪk] ADJ 1 (fixed) 特定的 tèdìng de 2 (exact) 具体 的 jùtǐ de

spectacles ['spɛktəklz] NPL 眼 镜 yǎnjìng

spectacular [spɛkˈtækjʊlə'] ADJ [+ view, scenery] 壮丽的 zhuànglìde; [+ rise, growth] 惊人的 jīngrénde; [+ success, result] 引人注目的 yǐnrén zhùmù de

spectator [spɛkˈteɪtə'] N [c] 观众 guānzhòng [个 gè]

speech [spi:tʃ] N [c] 演说 yǎnshuō [场 chǎng]

speed [spi:d] (pt, pp **sped** [spɛd]) N 1 [c/u] (rate, promptness) 速度 sùdù [种 zhǒng] 2 [u] (fast movement) 快速 kuàisù 3 [c] (rapidity) 迅速 xùnsù ▶at a speed of 70km/h 以时速70公里 yǐ shísù qīshí gōnglǐ

speed limit (Law) N [c] 速度极限 sùdù jíxiàn [个 gè]

spell [spɛl] (pt, pp **spelled** or **spelt**) VT 用字母拼 yòng zìmǔ pīn ▶he can't spell 他不会拼写 tā bùhuì pīnxiě

spelling ['spɛlɪŋ] N [c] (of word) 拼法 pīnfǎ [种 zhǒng] ▶spelling

mistake 拼写错误 pīnxiě cuòwù

spelt [spɛlt] PT, PP of **spell**

spend [spɛnd] (pt, pp **spent**) VT 1 [+ money] 花费 huāfèi 2 [+ time, life] 度过 dùguò ▶to spend time/energy on sth 在某事上花时间/精力 zài mǒushì shàng huā shíjiān/jīnglì ▶to spend time/energy doing sth 花时间/精力做某事 huā shíjiān/jīnglì zuò mǒushì ▶to spend the night in a hotel 在旅馆度过一晚 zài lǚguǎn dùguò yīwǎn

spent [spɛnt] PT, PP of **spend**

spicy ['spaɪsɪ] ADJ 辛辣的 xīnlà de

spider ['spaɪdə'] N [c] 蜘蛛 zhīzhū [只 zhī] ▶spider's web 蜘蛛网 zhīzhū wǎng

spill [spɪl] (pt, pp **spilt** or **spilled**) I VT 使溢出 shǐ yìchū II VI 溢出 yìchū ▶to spill sth on/over sth 将某物洒在某物上 jiāng mǒuwù sǎzài mǒuwù shàng

spinach ['spɪnɪtʃ] N [u] 菠菜 bōcài

spine [spaɪn] N [c] 脊柱 jǐzhù [根 gēn]

spit [spɪt] (pt, pp **spat**) I N [u] (saliva) 唾液 tuòyè II VI 吐唾液 tǔ tuòyè

spite [spaɪt] N [u] 恶意 èyì ▶in spite of 尽管 jǐnguǎn

splendid ['splɛndɪd] ADJ (excellent) 极好的 jíhǎo de

▶he **split** [splɪt] (pt, pp **split**) VT 1 (divide) 把…划分 bǎ...huàfēn 2 [+ work, profits] 平分 píngfēn ▶split up VI 分手 fēnshǒu

spoil [spɔɪl] (pt, pp **spoiled** or

spoilt) VT 1 (damage) 损害 sǔnhài
2 [+ child] 溺爱 nì'ài

poilt [spɔɪlt] **I** PT, PP of **spoil**
II ADJ 宠坏的 chǒnghuài de

poke [spəʊk] PT of **speak**

poken ['spəʊkn] PP of **speak**

pokesman ['spəʊksmən] (pl
spokesmen) N [c] 男发言人 nán
fāyánrén [位 wèi]

pokeswoman ['spəʊkswʊmən]
(pl **spokeswomen**) N [c] 女发言人
nǚ fāyánrén [位 wèi]

ponge [spʌndʒ] N [U] 海绵
hǎimián

poon [spuːn] N [c] 匙 chí [把 bǎ]

port [spɔːt] N 1 [c] (particular
game) 运动 yùndòng [项 xiàng] **2**
[U] (generally) 体育 tǐyù

portswear ['spɔːtswɛəʳ] N [U]
运动服 yùndòngfú

pot [spɒt] N [c] **1** (mark) 斑点
bāndiǎn [个 gè] **2** (dot) 点 diǎn [个
gè] **3** (pimple) 痘点 cìdiǎn [个 gè]
▶ **on the spot** (in that place) 在现
场 zài xiànchǎng; (immediately) 当
场 dāngchǎng

prain [spreɪn] VT ▶ **to sprain
one's ankle/wrist** 扭伤脚踝/手腕
niǔshāng jiǎohuái/shǒuwàn

pray [spreɪ] VT 1 (+ liquid) 喷
pēn **2** [+ crops] 向…喷杀虫剂
xiàng…pēn shāchóngjì

pread [spred] (pt, pp **spread**)
VT 1 ▶ **to spread sth on/over**
把某物摊在… 上 bǎ mǒuwù
tānzài…shàng **2** [+ disease] 传播
chuánbō

preadsheet ['spredʃiːt] N [c] 电
子表格 diànzǐ biǎogé [份 fèn]

spring [sprɪŋ] N 1 [c/U] (season)
春季 chūnjì [个 gè] **2** [c] (wire coil)
弹簧 tánhuáng [个 gè] ▶ **in (the)
spring** 在春季 zài chūnjì

spy [spaɪ] N [c] 间谍 jiàndié
[个 gè]

spying ['spaɪɪŋ] N [U] 当间谍
dāng jiàndié

square [skwɛəʳ] **I** N [c] **1** 正方
形 zhèngfāng xíng [个 gè] **2** (in
town) 广场 guǎngchǎng [个 gè]
3 (Math) 平方 píngfāng [个 gè]
II ADJ 正方形的 zhèngfāng xíng
de ▶ **2 square metres** 2平方米 èr
píngfāngmǐ

squash [skwɒʃ] **I** N [U] (Sport) 壁球
bìqiú **II** VT 压碎 yāsuì

squeeze [skwiːz] VT 用力捏
yònglì niē

stab [stæb] VT 刺 cì

stable ['steɪbl] **I** ADJ 稳定的
wěndìng de **II** N [c] 马厩 mǎjiù
[个 gè]

stadium ['steɪdɪəm] (pl **stadia**
['steɪdɪə] or **stadiums**) N [c] 体育
场 tǐyùchǎng [个 gè]

staff [stɑːf] N [c] 职员 zhíyuán
[名 míng]

stage [steɪdʒ] N [c] **1** (in theatre) 舞
台 wǔtái [个 gè] **2** (platform) 平台
píngtái [个 gè] ▶ **in the early/final
stages** 在早/晚期 zài zǎo/wǎnqī

stain [steɪn] **I** N [c] 污渍 wūjì [处
chù] **II** VT 沾污 zhānwū

stainless steel ['steɪnlɪs-] N [U]
不锈钢 bùxiù gāng

stair [stɛəʳ] **I** N [c] (step) 梯级 tījí
[层 céng] **II stairs** NPL (flight of
steps) 楼梯 lóutī

stall [stɔːl] N [c] 货摊 huòtān [个 gè]

stamp [stæmp] I N [c/u] 1 邮票 yóupiào [枚 méi] 2 (in passport) 章 zhāng [个 gè] II VT [+ passport, visa] 盖章于 gàizhāng yú

stand [stænd] (pt, pp stood) I VI 1 (be upright) 站立 zhànlì 2 (rise) 站起来 zhàn qǐlái 2 ▸ to stand aside/back 让开/退后 ràngkāi/tuìhòu II VT ▸ I can't stand him/it 我无法容忍他/它 wǒ wúfǎ róngrěn tā/tā
▸ stand for VT FUS [abbreviation] 代表 dàibiǎo
▸ stand out VI 醒目 xǐngmù
▸ stand up VI (rise) 起立 qǐlì

standard ['stændəd] I N [c] 1 (level) 水平 shuǐpíng [种 zhǒng] 2 (norm, criterion) 标准 biāozhǔn [个 gè] II ADJ 1 [+ size] 普通的 pǔtōng de 2 [+ procedure, practice] 标准的 biāozhǔn de 3 [+ model, feature] 规范的 guīfàn de

stank [stæŋk] PT of **stink**

star [staː^r] N [c] 1 星 xīng [颗 kē] 2 (celebrity) 明星 míngxīng [个 gè] ▸ a 4-star hotel 4星级旅馆 sì xīngjí lǚguǎn

stare [steə^r] VI ▸ to stare (at sb/sth) 盯着（某人/某物）dīngzhe (mǒurén/mǒuwù)

start [staːt] I N [c] 开始 kāishǐ [个 gè] II VT 1 (begin) 开始 kāishǐ 2 [+ business] 创建 chuàngjiàn 3 [+ engine, car] 启动 qǐdòng III VI (begin) 开始 kāishǐ ▸ to start doing or to do sth 开始做某事 kāishǐ zuò mǒushì

▸ start on VT FUS 开始 kāishǐ
▸ start over (US) VI, VT 重新开始 chóngxīn kāishǐ
▸ start up VT 创办 chuàngbàn

starter ['staːtə^r] N [c] (Brit) 开胃菜 kāiwèi cài [道 dào]

starve [staːv] VI 1 (be very hungry) 挨饿 áiè 2 (die from hunger) 饿死 èsǐ ▸ I'm starving 我饿极了 wǒ è jí le

state [steɪt] I N [c] 1 (condition) 状态 zhuàngtài [种 zhǒng] 2 [c] (country) 国家 guójiā [个 gè] 3 [c] (part of country) 州 zhōu [个 gè] II the States NPL (inf) 美国 Měiguó ▸ state of affairs 事态 shìtài

statement ['steɪtmənt] N [c] 声明 shēngmíng [个 gè]

station ['steɪʃən] N [c] 1 (railway station) 车站 chēzhàn [个 gè] 2 (radio) 电台 diàntái [个 gè]

statue ['stætjuː] N [c] 塑像 sùxiàng [尊 zūn]

stay [steɪ] I N [c] 逗留 dòuliú [次 cì] II VI 1 (in place, position) 呆着 dāizhe 2 (in town, hotel, someone's house) 逗留 dòuliú 3 (in state, situation) 保持 bǎochí III VT ▸ to stay the night 过夜 guòyè ▸ to stay with sb 在某人家暂住 zài mǒurén jiā zànzhù

▸ stay in VI 呆在家里 dāizài jiālǐ
▸ stay up VI 不去睡 bùqùshuì

steady ['stedɪ] ADJ 1 [+ progress, increase, fall] 稳定的 wěndìng de 2 [+ job, income] 固定的 gùdìng de

steak [steɪk] N [c/u] 牛排 niúpái [份 fèn]

teal [sti:l] (pt stole, pp stolen)
I VT 偷窃 tōuqiè II N 行窃
xíngqiè ▶he stole it from me 他
从我这里把它偷走了 tā cóng wǒ
zhèlǐ bǎ tā tōuzǒu le

steam [sti:m] I N [u] 蒸汽
zhēngqì II VT 蒸 zhēng

steel [sti:l] I N [u] 钢铁 gāngtiě
II CPD 钢铁 gāngtiě

steep [sti:p] ADJ 陡的 dǒu de

steering wheel N [c] 方向盘
fāngxiàng pán [个 gè]

step [step] I N I [c] (stage) 阶段
jiēduàn [个 gè] 2 [c] (of stairs) 梯
级 tíjí [层 céng] II VI ▶to step
forward/backward etc 向前/后
[等]迈步 xiàngqián/hòu [děng]
màibù
▶step aside = step down
▶step down, step aside VI 辞
职 cízhí

stepbrother ['stepbrʌðəʳ] N
[c] (with shared father) 异母兄弟
yìmǔ xiōngdì [个 gè]; (with shared
mother) 异父兄弟 yìfù xiōngdì
[个 gè]

stepdaughter ['stepdɔ:təʳ] N [c]
继女 jìnǚ [个 gè]

stepfather ['stepfɑ:ðəʳ] N [c] 继
父 jìfù [位 wèi]

stepmother ['stepmʌðəʳ] N [c]
继母 jìmǔ [位 wèi]

stepsister ['stepsɪstəʳ] N [c] (with
shared father) 异母姐妹 yìmǔ
jiěmèi [个 gè]; (with shared mother)
异父姐妹 yìfù jiěmèi [个 gè]

stepson ['stepsʌn] N [c] 继子
jìzǐ [个 gè]

stereo ['sterɪəu] N [c] 立体声装置

lìtǐ shēng zhuāngzhì [套 tào]

sterling ['stɜ:lɪŋ] I N [u] 英国货
币 Yīngguó huòbì ▶one pound
sterling 一英镑 yī yīngbàng

stew [stju:] N [c/u] 炖的食物 dùn
de shíwù [种 zhǒng]

stewardess ['stjuədes] N [c] 女
乘务员 nǚ chéngwù yuán [位 wèi]

stick [stɪk] (pt, pp stuck) I N [c]
1 (of wood) 枯枝 kūzhī [根 gēn]
2 (walking stick) 拐杖 guǎizhàng
[根 gēn] II VT ▶to stick sth on or
to sth (with glue etc) 将某物粘贴
在某物上 jiāng mǒuwù zhāntiē zài
mǒuwù shang
▶stick out VI 伸出 shēnchū

sticker ['stɪkəʳ] N [c] 不干胶标签
bù gānjiāo biāoqiān [个 gè]

sticky ['stɪkɪ] ADJ 1 (+ substance)
黏的 nián de 2 (+ tape, paper) 黏性的
de niánxìng de

stiff [stɪf] I ADJ 1 (+ person) 酸痛的
suāntòng de; (+ neck, arm etc) 僵
硬的 jiāngyìng de 2 (+ competition)
激烈的 jīliè de II ADV ▶to be
bored/scared stiff 讨厌/害怕极
了 tǎoyàn/hàipà jíle

still [stɪl] I ADJ 1 (+ person, hands)
不动的 bùdòng de 2 (Brit: not fizzy)
无气泡的 wú qìpào de II ADV
1 (up to the present) 仍然 réngrán
2 (even) 更 gèng 3 (yet) 还 hái
4 (nonetheless) 尽管如此 jǐnguǎn
rúcǐ ▶to stand/keep still 站着别
动/保持不动 zhànzhe bùdòng/bǎochí
búdòng ▶he still hasn't arrived 他还没到
tā hái méi dào

sting [stɪŋ] (pt, pp stung) I N [c]
刺 cì [根 gēn] II VT 刺 cì

stink [stɪŋk] (pt **stank**, pp **stunk**) I N [c] 恶臭 èchòu [种 zhǒng] II VI 发臭 fāchòu

stir [stɜːʳ] VT 搅动 jiǎodòng

stitch [stɪtʃ] N [c] (Med) 缝针 féngzhēn [枚 méi]

stock [stɒk] N [c] 供应物 gōngyìng wù [种 zhǒng]
  ▸ **stock up** VI ▸ **to stock up (on** or **with sth)** 储备（某物）chǔbèi (mǒuwù)

stock exchange N [c] 股票交易所 gǔpiào jiāoyì suǒ [个 gè]

stocking [stɒkɪŋ] N [c] 长统袜 chángtǒng wà [双 shuāng]

stole [stəʊl] PT of **steal**

stolen [stəʊln] PP of **steal**

stomach [stʌmək] N [c] 1 (organ) 胃 wèi [个 gè] 2 (abdomen) 腹部 fùbù [个 gè]

stomach ache N [c/u] 胃痛 wèitòng [阵 zhèn]

stone [stəʊn] N 1 [u] 石头 shítou 2 [c] (pebble) 石子 shízǐ [块 kuài]

stood [stʊd] PT, PP of **stand**

stop [stɒp] I VT 1 停止 tíngzhǐ 2 (prevent) 阻止 zǔzhǐ II VI 1 (person, vehicle) 停下来 tíng xiàlái 2 (rain, noise, activity) 停 tíng III N [c] (for bus, train) 车站 chēzhàn [个 gè] ▸ **to stop doing sth** 停止做某事 tíngzhǐ zuò mǒushì ▸ **to stop sb (from) doing sth** 阻止某人做某事 zǔzhǐ mǒurén zuò mǒushì ▸ **stop it!** 住手! zhùshǒu!

stoplight [stɒplaɪt] (US) N [c] (in road) 交通信号灯 jiāotōng xìnhào dēng [个 gè]

store [stɔːʳ] I N [c] 1 (Brit: large shop) 大商店 dà shāngdiàn [家 jiā] 2 (US: shop) 店铺 diànpù [家 jiā] II VT 1 [+ provisions, information] 存放 cúnfàng 2 [computer, brain] [+ information] 存储 cúnchǔ

storey, (US) **story** [stɔːrɪ] N [c] 层 céng

storm [stɔːm] N [c] 暴风雨 bàofēngyǔ [场 chǎng]

stormy [stɔːmɪ] ADJ 有暴风雨的 yǒu bàofēngyǔ de

story [stɔːrɪ] N [c] 1 (account) 描述 miáoshù [种 zhǒng] 2 (tale) 故事 gùshì [个 gè] 3 (in newspaper, on news broadcast) 报道 bàodào [条 tiáo] 4 (US: of building) = **storey**

stove [stəʊv] N [c] 炉子 lúzi [个 gè]

straight [streɪt] I ADJ 1 笔直的 bǐzhí de 2 [+ hair] 直的 zhí de II ADV 1 (walk, stand, look) 直 zhí 2 (immediately) 直接地 zhíjiē de

straightforward [streɪtfɔːwəd] ADJ 简单的 jiǎndān de

strain [streɪn] I N [c/u] (pressure) 负担 fùdān [个 gè] 2 [c/u] ▸ **back/ muscle strain** 背部/肌肉扭伤 bèibù/jīròu niǔshāng [处 chù] II VT [+ back, muscle] 扭伤 niǔshāng

strange [streɪndʒ] ADJ 1 (odd) 奇怪的 qíguài de 2 (unfamiliar) [+ person, place] 陌生的 mòshēng de

stranger [streɪndʒəʳ] N [c] 陌生人 mòshēng rén [个 gè]

strap [stræp] N [c] (of watch, bag) 带 dài [根 gēn]

straw [strɔː] N 1 [u] 稻草 dàocǎo

2 [c] (*drinking straw*) 吸管 xīguǎn [根 gēn]

strawberry ['strɔ:bərɪ] N [c] 草莓 cǎoméi [个 gè]

stream [stri:m] N [c] 溪流 xīliú [条 tiáo]

street [stri:t] N [c] 街道 jiēdào [条 tiáo]

streetcar ['stri:tka:'] (US) N [c] 有轨电车 yǒuguǐ diànchē [部 bù]

strength [strεŋθ] N **1** [U] 力气 lìqì **2** [U] (*of object, material*) 强度 qiángdù

stress [strεs] N [c/U] 压力 yālì [个 gè] **II** VT [+ *point, importance*] 强调 qiángdiào

stressful ['strεsful] ADJ 紧张的 jǐnzhāng de

stretch [strεtʃ] **I** VI 伸懒腰 shēn lǎnyāo **II** VT [+ *arm, leg*] 伸直 shēnzhí
▶ **stretch out** VT [+ *arm, leg*] 伸出 shēnchū

strict [strɪkt] ADJ **1** [+ *rule, instruction*] 严格的 yángé de **2** [+ *person*] 严厉的 yánlì de

strike [straɪk] (*pt, pp* struck) **I** [c] 罢工 bàgōng [场 chǎng] **II** VI **1** 罢工 bàgōng **2** (*clock*) 报时 bàoshí ▶ **to be on strike** 在罢工 zài bàgōng

striker ['straɪkə'] N [c] **1** (*person on strike*) 罢工者 bàgōng zhě [名 míng] **2** (*Football*) 前锋 qiánfēng [个 gè]

string [strɪŋ] (*pt, pp* strung) N **1** [c/U] 细绳 xìshéng [根 gēn] **2** [c] (*on guitar, violin*) 弦 xián [根 gēn]

strip [strɪp] **I** N [c] (*of paper, cloth*)

狭条 xiátiáo [条 tiáo] **II** VI (*undress*) 脱光衣服 tuōguāng yīfu; (*as entertainer*) 表演脱衣舞 biǎoyǎn tuōyī wǔ

stripe [straɪp] N [c] 条纹 tiáowén [个 gè]

striped [straɪpt] ADJ 有条纹的 yǒu tiáowén de

stroke [strəuk] **I** N [c] (*Med*) 中风 zhòngfēng [次 cì] **II** VT [+ *person, animal*] 抚摸 fǔmō

stroller ['strəulə'] (US) N [c] 婴儿小推车 yīng'ér xiǎo tuīchē [辆 liàng]

strong [strɒŋ] ADJ **1** [+ *person, arms, grip*] 有力的 yǒulì de **2** [+ *object, material*] 牢固的 láogù de **3** [+ *wind, current*] 强劲的 qiángjìng de

struck [strʌk] PT, PP *of* **strike**

struggle ['strʌgl] VI **1** (*try hard*) 尽力 jìnlì **2** (*fight*) 搏斗 bódòu

stubborn ['stʌbən] ADJ 倔强的 juéjiàng de

stuck [stʌk] **I** PT, PP *of* **stick II** ADJ
▶ **to be stuck** [*object*] 卡住 qiǎzhù; [*person*] 陷于 xiànyú

student ['stju:dənt] N [c] **1** (*at university*) 大学生 dà xuéshēng [名 míng] **2** (*at school*) 中学生 zhōng xuéshēng [名 míng] ▶ **a law/medical student** 一名法律/医学学生 yīmíng fǎlǜ/yīxué xuéshēng

studio ['stju:dɪəu] N [c] **1** (*TV, Rad, Mus*) 摄影室 shèyǐng shì [个 gè] **2** (*of artist*) 画室 huàshì [个 gè]

study ['stʌdɪ] **I** N [c] (*room*) 书房 shūfáng [间 jiān] **II** VT [+ *subject*]

攻读 gōngdú III VT 学习 xuéxí

stuff [stʌf] I N [U] 1 (things) 物品 wùpǐn 2 (substance) 东西 dōngxi II VT [+ peppers, mushrooms] 给…装馅 gěi…zhuāngxiàn; [+ chicken, turkey] 把填料塞入 bǎ tiánliào sāirù

stuffy ['stʌfɪ] ADJ 闷热的 mēnrè de

stung [stʌŋ] PT, PP of **sting**

stunk [stʌŋk] PP of **stink**

stunning ['stʌnɪŋ] ADJ 1 (impressive) 惊人的 jīngrén de 2 (beautiful) 极漂亮的 jí piàoliàng de

stupid ['stjuːpɪd] ADJ 1 笨的 bèn de 2 [+ question, idea, mistake] 愚蠢的 yúchǔn de

style [staɪl] N 1 [c] (type) 方式 fāngshì 2 [U] (elegance) 风度 fēngdù 3 [c/U] (design) 样式 yàngshì [种 zhǒng]

subject ['sʌbdʒɪkt] N [c] 1 (matter) 主题 zhǔtí [个 gè] 2 (Scol) 科目 kēmù [个 gè] 3 (Gram) 主语 zhǔyǔ [个 gè]

submarine [sʌbmə'riːn] N [c] 潜水艇 qiánshuǐtǐng [艘 sōu]

substance ['sʌbstəns] N [c] 物质 wùzhì [种 zhǒng]

substitute ['sʌbstɪtjuːt] N [c] 1 (person) 代替者 dàitì zhě 2 (thing) 代用品 dàiyòngpǐn [件 jiàn] II VT ▶ to substitute sth (for sth) 用某物代替 (某物) yòng mǒuwù dàitì (mǒuwù)

subtitles ['sʌbtaɪtlz] NPL 字幕 zìmù

subtract [səb'trækt] VT ▶ to

subtract sth (from sth) (从某数中) 减去某数 (cóng mǒushù zhōng) jiǎnqù mǒushù

suburb ['sʌbəːb] N [c] 郊区 jiāoqū [个 gè]

subway ['sʌbweɪ] N [c] (US: underground railway) 地铁 dìtiě [条 tiáo]

succeed [sək'siːd] VI 成功 chénggōng ▶ to succeed in doing sth 成功地做某事 chénggōng de zuò mǒushì

success [sək'sɛs] N [U/c] 成功 chénggōng ▶ without success 无所成 yī wú suǒ chéng

successful [sək'sɛsful] ADJ 成功的 chénggōng de

successfully [sək'sɛsfəlɪ] ADV 成功地 chénggōng de

such [sʌtʃ] ADJ 1 (of this kind) 此类的 cǐlèi de 2 (so much) 这等 zhěděng ▶ such a lot of 那么多 nàme duō ▶ such as (like) 像 xiàng

suck [sʌk] VT 含在嘴里舔吃 hánzài zuǐlǐ tiǎnchī

sudden ['sʌdn] ADJ 意外的 yìwài de

suddenly ['sʌdnlɪ] ADV 突然 tūrán

suede [sweɪd] N [U] 仿麂皮 fǎng jǐpí

suffer ['sʌfə'] VI 1 (due to pain, illness, poverty) 受损失 shòu sǔnshī 2 (be badly affected) 受苦难 shòu kǔnàn

sugar ['ʃugə'] N [U/c] 糖 táng [勺 sháo]

suggest [sə'dʒɛst] VT 建议 jiànyì

▶to suggest that... (*propose*) 建议... jiànyì...

suggestion [sə'dʒestʃən] N [C] 建议 jiànyì [条 tiáo] ▶to make a suggestion 提建议 tí jiànyì

suicide ['suːɪsaɪd] N [C/U] 自杀 zìshā ▶a suicide bomber 人肉炸弹 rénròu zhàdàn ▶to commit suicide 自杀 zìshā

suit [suːt] I N [C] 西装 xīzhuāng [套 tào] II VT 1 (*be convenient, appropriate*) 对...合适 duì...héshì 2 (*colour, clothes*) 适合 shìhé

suitable ['suːtəbl] ADJ 1 [+ *time, place*] 合适的 héshì de 2 [+ *person, clothes*] 适合的 shìhé de

suitcase ['suːtkeɪs] N [C] 手提箱 shǒutíxiāng [个 gè]

sum [sʌm] N [C] 1 (*amount*) 数额 shù'é [笔 bǐ] 2 (*calculation*) 算术题 suànshù tí [道 dào] ▶to do a sum 算算术 suàn suànshù

▶ **sum up** VI 总结 zǒngjié

summarize ['sʌməraɪz] VT 概括 gàikuò

summary ['sʌmərɪ] N [C] 摘要 zhāiyào [个 gè]

summer ['sʌmər] N [C/U] 夏季 xiàjì [个 gè] ▶in (the) summer 在夏季 zài xiàjì

summit ['sʌmɪt] N [C] 峰顶 fēngdǐng [个 gè]

sun [sʌn] N 1 [s/c] (*in the sky*) 太阳 tàiyáng [轮 lún] 2 [U] (*heat*) 太阳的光和热 tàiyáng de guāng hé rè; (*light*) 阳光 yángguāng

sunbathe ['sʌnbeɪð] VI 晒日光浴 shài rìguāngyù

sunburn ['sʌnbəːn] N [U] 晒斑

shàibān

sunburnt ['sʌnbəːnt] ADJ = **sunburned**

sunburned ['sʌnbəːnd], **sunburnt** ADJ 晒伤的 shàishāng de

Sunday ['sʌndɪ] N [C/U] 星期天 xīngqītiān [个 gè]; *see also* **Tuesday**

sung [sʌŋ] PP *of* **sing**

sunglasses ['sʌnglɑːsɪz] NPL 墨镜 mòjìng

sunk [sʌŋk] PP *of* **sink**

sunny ['sʌnɪ] ADJ 晴朗的 qínglǎng de ▶it is sunny 天气晴朗 tiānqì qínglǎng

sunrise ['sʌnraɪz] N [U] 拂晓 fúxiǎo

sunscreen ['sʌnskriːn] N [C/U] 遮光屏 zhēguāng píng [个 gè]

sunset ['sʌnset] N 1 [U] (*time*) 傍晚 bàngwǎn 2 [C] (*sky*) 日落 rìluò [次 cì]

sunshine ['sʌnʃaɪn] N [U] 阳光 yángguāng

suntan ['sʌntæn] I N [C] 晒黑 shàihēi [处 chù] II CPD [+ *lotion, cream*] 防晒 fángshài

super ['suːpər] (Brit: *inf*) ADJ 极好的 jíhǎo de

supermarket ['suːpəmɑːkɪt] N [U] 超级市场 chāojí shìchǎng

supervise ['suːpəvaɪz] VT 监督 jiāndū

supper ['sʌpər] N [C/U] 1 (*early evening*) 晚餐 wǎncān [顿 dùn] 2 (*late evening*) 夜宵 yèxiāo [顿 dùn]

supply [sə'plaɪ] I VT 提供 tígōng

II N [C/U] 供应量 gōngyìng liàng ▸**to supply sb/sth with sth** 向 某人/某物提供某物 wèi mǒurén/ mǒuwù tígōng mǒuwù

support [sə'pɔːt] VT1 (morally) 支持 zhīchí 2 (financially) 供养 gōngyǎng 3 [+ football team] 支持 zhīchí

supporter [sə'pɔːtər] N [C] 支持者 zhīchí zhě [个 gè]

suppose [sə'pəuz] VT 认为 rènwéi ▸**I suppose** 我想 wǒ xiǎng ▸**I suppose so/not** 我看 是/不是这样 wǒ kàn shì/bùshì zhèyàng ▸**he's supposed to be an expert** 人们以为他是个专家 rénmen yǐwéi tā shì gè zhuānjiā

supposing [sə'pəuzɪŋ] CONJ 假 使 jiǎshǐ

sure [ʃuər] ADJ1 有把握的 yǒu bǎwò de 2 ▸**to be sure to do sth** (certain) 肯定做某事 kěndìng zuò mǒushì ▸**to make sure that...** (take action) 保证… bǎozhèng...; (check) 查明… chámíng... ▸**sure!** (inf: of course) 当然了！ dāngrán le! ▸**I'm sure of it** 我确信对 quèxìn 2 ▸**I'm not sure how/why/ when** 我不能肯定如何/为什么/什 么时候 wǒ bùnéng kěndìng rúhé/ wèishénme/shénme shíhou

surf [sɜːf] **I** N1 拍岸的浪花 pāi'àn de lànghuā **II** VT ▸**to surf the Internet** 网上冲浪 wǎngshàng chōnglàng ▸**to go surfing** 去冲浪 qù chōnglàng

surface ['sɜːfɪs] N1 [C] [of object] 表面 biǎomiàn [个 gè] 2 [C] (top layer) 表层 biǎocéng [个 gè]

▸**on the surface** 在表面上 zài biǎomiàn shàng

surfboard ['sɜːfbɔːd] N [C] 冲浪板 chōnglàng bǎn [块 kuài]

surgeon ['sɜːdʒən] N [C] 外科医生 wàikē yīshi [位 wèi]

surgery ['sɜːdʒərɪ] N1 [U] (treatment) 外科手术 wàikē shǒushù 2 [C] (Brit: room) 诊所 zhěnsuǒ [家 jiā]

surname ['sɜːneɪm] N [C] 姓 xìng [个 gè]

surprise [sə'praɪz] **I** N1 [C] (unexpected event) 意想不到的事 物 yìxiǎng bùdào de shìwù [个 gè] 2 [U] (astonishment) 诧异 chàyì **II** VT 使感到意外 shǐ gǎndào yìwài ▸**to my (great) surprise** 使 我（很）惊奇的是 shǐ wǒ (hěn) jīngqí de shì

surprised [sə'praɪzd] ADJ 惊讶 的 jīngyà de

surprising [sə'praɪzɪŋ] ADJ 出人 意外的 chūrén yìwài de

surrender [sə'rɛndər] VI 投降 tóuxiáng

surround [sə'raund] VT 包围 bāowéi

surroundings [sə'raundɪŋz] NPL 环境 huánjìng

survey ['sɜːveɪ] N [C] 民意测验 mínyì cèyàn [项 xiàng]

survive [sə'vaɪv] VI 幸存 xìngcún

survivor [sə'vaɪvər] N [C] 幸存者 xìngcúnzhě [个 gè]

suspect [n 'sʌspɛkt, vb səs'pɛkt] **I** N [C] 嫌疑犯 xiányí fàn [个 gè] **II** VT1 [+ person] 怀疑 huáiyí 2 [+ sb's motives] 质疑 zhìyí

3 (think) 猜想 cāixiǎng ▶**to suspect that...** 怀疑… huáiyí…

suspense [səs'pɛns] N [U] 焦虑 jiāolù

suspicious [səs'pɪʃəs] ADJ [+ circumstances, death, package] 可疑的 kěyí de ▶**to be suspicious of or about sb/sth** 对某人/某事起疑心 duì mǒurén/mǒushì qǐ yíxīn

swallow ['swɔləu] VT 吞下 tūnxià

swam [swæm] PT of **swim**

swan [swɔn] N [c] 天鹅 tiān'é [只 zhī]

swap [swɔp] VT ▶**to swap sth (for)** (exchange for) (以某物) 作交换 (yǐ mǒuwù) zuò jiāohuàn; (replace with) 以…替代某物 yǐ…tìdài mǒuwù ▶**to swap places (with sb)** (与某人) 换位子 (yǔ mǒurén) huàn wèizi

swear word [swɛə'-] N [c] 骂人的话 màrén de huà [句 jù]

sweat [swɛt] VI 出汗 chūhàn

sweater ['swɛtə'] N [c] 毛衣 máoyī [件 jiàn]

sweatshirt ['swɛtʃəːt] N [c] 棉毛衫 mián máoshān [件 jiàn]

Sweden ['swiːdn] N 瑞典 Ruìdiǎn

sweep [swiːp] (pt, pp **swept**) VT 扫 sǎo

sweet [swiːt] I N (Brit) 1 [c] (chocolate, mint) 糖果 tángguǒ [颗 kē] 2 [c/U] (pudding) 甜点 tiándiǎn [份 fèn] II ADJ 1 (sugary) 甜的 tián de 2 可爱的 kě'ài de ▶**sweet and sour** 糖醋 tángcù

swept [swɛpt] PT, PP of **sweep**

swerve [swəːv] VI 突然转向 tūrán zhuǎnxiàng

swim [swɪm] (pt **swam**, pp **swum**) I VI 1 [person, animal] 游水 yóushuǐ 2 (as sport) 游泳 yóuyǒng II VT [+ distance] 游 yóu III N [c] ▶**to go for a swim** 去游泳 qù yóuyǒng [次 cì] ▶**to go swimming** 去游泳 qù yóuyǒng

swimming ['swɪmɪŋ] N [U] 游泳 yóuyǒng

swimming pool N [c] 游泳池 yóuyǒng chí [个 gè]

swimsuit ['swɪmsuːt] N [c] 游泳衣 yóuyǒng yī [套 tào]

swing [swɪŋ] (pt, pp **swung**) I N [c] 秋千 qiūqiān [副 fù] II VT [+ arms, legs] 摆动 bǎidòng III VI 1 [pendulum] 晃动 huàngdòng 2 [door] 转动 zhuǎndòng

switch [swɪtʃ] I N [c] 开关 kāiguān [个 gè] II VT (change) 改变 gǎibiàn
▶**switch off** VT 关掉 guāndiào
▶**switch on** VT [+ light, engine, radio] 开启 kāiqǐ

Switzerland ['swɪtsələnd] N 瑞士 Ruìshì

swollen ['swəulən] ADJ 肿胀的 zhǒngzhàng de

swop [swɔp] N, VT = **swap**

sword [sɔːd] N [c] 剑 jiàn [把 bǎ]

swum [swʌm] PP of **swim**

swung [swʌŋ] PT, PP of **swing**

syllabus ['sɪləbəs] (esp Brit) N [c] 教学大纲 jiàoxué dàgāng [个 gè]

symbol ['sɪmbl] N [c] 1 (sign) 象征 xiàngzhēng [种 zhǒng] 2 (Math, Chem) 符号 fúhào [个 gè]

sympathetic [sɪmpə'θɛtɪk] ADJ 有同情心的 yǒu tóngqíngxīn de

sympathy ['sɪmpəθɪ] N [U] 同情
心 tóngqíng xīn

syringe [sɪ'rɪndʒ] N [C] 注射器
zhùshè qì [支 zhī]

system ['sɪstəm] N [C]
1 (organization, set) 系统 xìtǒng
[个 gè] **2** (method) 方法 fāngfǎ
[种 zhǒng]

table ['teɪbl] N [C] 桌子 zhuōzi [张
zhāng] ▶ **to lay** or **set the table** 摆
餐桌 bǎi cānzhuō

tablecloth ['teɪblklɔθ] N [C] 桌布
zhuōbù [块 kuài]

tablespoon ['teɪblspuːn] N [C] 餐
匙 cānchí [把 bǎ]

tablet ['tæblɪt] N [C] 药片 yàopiàn
[片 piàn]

table tennis N [U] 乒乓球
pīngpāngqiú

tact [tækt] N [U] 机智 jīzhì

tactful ['tæktful] ADJ 老练的
lǎoliàn de

tactics ['tæktɪks] NPL 策略 cèluè

tadpole ['tædpəul] N [C] 蝌蚪
kēdǒu [只 zhī]

taffy ['tæfɪ] (US) N [U] 太妃糖
tàifēitáng

ag [tæg] N [C] **1** (label) 标签 biāoqiān [个 gè] **2** (electronic) 标签 biāoqiān [个 gè]

ail [teɪl] N [C] 尾巴 wěiba [条 tiáo] ▶ "heads or tails" — "tails" "正面还是背面？" "背面" "zhèngmiàn háishì bèimiàn?" "bèimiàn"

ailor ['teɪlə'] N [C] 裁缝 cáiféng [个 gè]

take [teɪk] (pt took, pp taken) VT **1** [+ holiday, vacation] 度dù; [+ shower, bath] 洗 xǐ **2** (take hold of) 拿 ná **3** (steal) 偷走 tōuzǒu **4** (accompany) 送 sòng **5** (carry, bring) 携带 xiédài **6** [+ road] 走 zǒu **7** [+ bus, train] 乘坐 chéngzuò **8** [+ size] 穿 chuān **9** [+ time] 花费 huāfèi **10** [+ exam, test] 参加 cānjiā **11** [+ drug, pill] 服用 fúyòng ▶ **don't forget to take your umbrella** 别忘了带雨伞。 bié wàngle dài yǔsǎn
▶ **take apart** VT (dismantle) [+ bicycle, radio, machine] 拆开 chāikāi
▶ **take away** VT **1** (remove) 拿走 názǒu **2** (carry off) 带走 dàizǒu
▶ **take back** VT [+ goods] 退回 tuìhuí
▶ **take down** VT (write down) 记录 jìlù
▶ **take off** VI 起飞 qǐfēi II VT [+ clothes, glasses, make-up] 脱下 tuōxià
▶ **take out** VT [+ person] 邀请 yāoqǐng
▶ **take up** VT **1** [+ hobby, sport] 开始 kāishǐ **2** [+ time, space] 占用

zhànyòng

takeaway ['teɪkəweɪ] (Brit) N [C] **1** (shop, restaurant) 外卖店 wàimàidiàn [家 jiā] **2** (food) 外卖 wàimài [个 gè]

taken ['teɪkən] PP of **take**

takeoff ['teɪkɔf] N [C] 起飞 qǐfēi [次 cì]

takeout ['teɪkaut] (US) N [C] **1** (shop, restaurant) 外卖店 wàimàidiàn [家 jiā] **2** (food) 外卖 wàimài [个 gè]

tale [teɪl] N [C] 故事 gùshì [个 gè]

talent ['tælənt] N [C/U] 才能 cáinéng [种 zhǒng]

talented ['tæləntɪd] ADJ 有才能 的 yǒu cáinéng de

talk [tɔːk] N I **1** [C] (prepared speech) 讲话 jiǎnghuà [次 cì] **2** [U] (gossip) 谣言 yáoyán **3** [C] (discussion) 交谈 jiāotán [次 cì] II VI **1** (speak) 讲话 shuōhuà **2** (chat) 聊天 liáo ▶ **to talk to** or **with sb** 跟某人谈话 gēn mǒurén tánhuà ▶ **to talk about sth** 谈论某事 tánlùn mǒushì
▶ **talk over, talk through** VT 仔细商讨 zǐxì shāngtǎo

talkative ['tɔːkətɪv] ADJ 健谈的 jiàntán de

talk show N [C] (US) 脱口秀 tuōkǒuxiù [个 gè]

tall [tɔːl] ADJ 高的 gāo de ▶ **he's 6 feet tall** 他6英尺高 tā liù yīngchǐ gāo

tame [teɪm] ADJ 驯服的 xùnfú de

tampon ['tæmpɔn] N [C] 月经棉 栓 yuèjīng miánshuān [个 gè]

tan [tæn] N [C] 晒黑的肤色 shàihēi de fùsè [种 zhǒng]

tangerine [tændʒə'ri:n] N [c] 红
橘 hóngjú [个 gè]

tank [tæŋk] N [c] 1 (Mil) 坦克
tǎnkè [部 bù] 2 (for petrol, water)
箱 xiāng [个 gè]

tanker ['tæŋkəʳ] N [c] 1 (ship) 油
轮 yóulún [艘 sōu] 2 (truck) 油罐车
yóuguànchē [辆 liàng]

tanned [tænd] ADJ 晒黑的
shàihēi de

tap [tæp] N [c] (esp Brit) 龙头
lóngtóu [个 gè]

tap-dancing ['tæpdɑ:nsɪŋ] N [U]
踢踏舞 tītàwǔ

tape [teɪp] I N [c] 1 (cassette) 磁带
cídài [盘 pán] 2 [U] (adhesive) 胶带
jiāodài II VT 1 (record) 录制 lùzhì
2 (attach) 贴 tiē

tape measure N [c] 卷尺 juǎnchǐ
[把 bǎ]

tape recorder N [c] 录音机
lùyīnjī [台 tái]

tar [tɑ:ʳ] N [U] 沥青 lìqīng

target ['tɑ:gɪt] N [c] 1 (of missile)
目标 mùbiāo [个 gè] 2 (aim) 目标
mùbiāo [个 gè]

tart [tɑ:t] N [c] 果馅饼
guǒxiànbǐng [个 gè]

tartan ['tɑ:tn] I N [U] 苏格兰方
格呢 Sūgélán fānggéní [块 kuài]
II ADJ [+ rug, scarf etc] 苏格兰方格
的 Sūgélán fānggé de

❋ TARTAN

● 是一种有图案的厚羊毛布
料,其图案是由不同宽度
和颜色的直线条垂直交叉
组成。**tartan** 用来做 **kilt**

——一种苏格兰成年男子和
男孩子在正式场合穿的特
别的短裙。这种布料起源
于 **Highlands** (苏格兰高
地)——即苏格兰群山连绵的西
北部。在那里,**tartan** 被作
为反抗英国王室的标志,并
因此在1747年至1782年期间
被禁用。不同的颜色和图案
代表着苏格兰的不同地区。

task [tɑ:sk] N [c] 任务 rènwù
[项 xiàng]

taste [teɪst] I N 1 [c] (flavour) 味道
wèidao [种 zhǒng] 2 [c]
(sample) 尝试 chángshì [次 cì]
3 [U] (choice, liking) 品位 pǐnwèi
II VI 1 to taste of/like sth 有/像
某物的味道 yǒu/xiàng mǒuwù
de wèidao

tasty ['teɪstɪ] ADJ 味美的 wèiměi
de

tattoo [tə'tu:] N [c] 纹身 wénshēn
[个 gè]

taught [tɔ:t] PT, PP of teach

Taurus ['tɔ:rəs] N [U] 金牛座
Jīnniúzuò

tax [tæks] N [c/U] 税 shuì [种
zhǒng]

taxi ['tæksɪ] N [c] 出租车
chūzūchē [辆 liàng]

taxi rank (Brit) N [c] 出租车候客
站 chūzūchē hòukèzhàn [个 gè]

taxi stand (US) N [c] 出租车候客
站 chūzūchē hòukèzhàn [个 gè]

TB N ABBR (= tuberculosis) 肺结
核 fèijiéhé

tea [ti:] N [c/U] 1 (drink) 茶 chá [杯
bēi] 2 (dried leaves) 茶 chá

piàn] 3 (Brit: evening meal) 晚饭 wǎnfàn [顿 dùn]

● TEA

● 英国人和美国人喝的茶大多
● 是红茶。通常茶里要加牛
● 奶，可能还加糖，当然也可
● 以在茶里只放两片柠檬。花
● 草茶 (herbal tea)，如薄荷
● 或甘菊茶，正风行起来。tea
● 还可以指下午小餐，通常有
● 三明治，蛋糕，还有茶。在英
● 国的一些地方，tea 还可以
● 指晚上的正餐。

teach [tiːtʃ] (pt, pp taught) I vt
1 ▸ to teach sb sth, teach sth
to sb 教某人某事，将某事教给
某人 jiāo mǒurén mǒushì, jiāng
mǒushì jiāogěi mǒurén 2 [+ pupils,
subject] 教 jiāo II vi (be a teacher)
教书 jiāoshū ▸ to teach sb to do
sth/how to do sth 教某人做某
事/怎样做某事 jiāo mǒurén zuò
mǒushì/zěnyàng zuò mǒushì
teacher ['tiːtʃəʳ] N [c] 教师 jiàoshī
[位 wèi]
team [tiːm] N [c] 1 [of people,
experts, horses] 组 zǔ [个 gè]
2 (Sport) 队 duì [个 gè]
teapot ['tiːpɔt] N [c] 茶壶 cháhú
[个 gè]
tear¹ [tɛəʳ] (pt tore, pp torn) I N [c]
(rip, hole) 裂口 lièkǒu [个 gè] II vt
撕裂 sīliè
▸ tear up 撕毁 sīhuǐ
tear² [tɪəʳ] N [c] (when crying) 眼泪
yǎnlèi [滴 dī] ▸ to burst into tears

哭起来 kū qǐlái
tease [tiːz] vt 逗弄 dòunong
teaspoon ['tiːspuːn] N [c] 茶匙
cháchí [把 bǎ]
teatime ['tiːtaɪm] (Brit) N [u] 茶
点时间 chádiǎn shíjiān
tea towel (Brit) N [c] 擦拭布
cāshìbù [块 kuài]
technical ['tɛknɪkl] ADJ
1 [+ problems, advances] 技术的
jìshù de 2 [+ terms, language] 专业
的 zhuānyè de
technician [tɛk'nɪʃən] N [c] 技师
jìshī [位 wèi]
technological [tɛknə'lɔdʒɪkl]
ADJ 工艺的 gōngyì de
technology [tɛk'nɔlədʒɪ] N [c/u]
工艺学 gōngyìxué [门 mén]
teddy (bear) ['tɛdɪ(-)] N [c] 玩具
熊 wánjùxióng [个 gè]
teenage ['tiːneɪdʒ] ADJ 十几岁的
shíjǐsuì de
teenager ['tiːneɪdʒəʳ] N [c] 青少
年 qīngshàonián [个 gè]
tee-shirt ['tiːʃəːt] N = T-shirt
teeth [tiːθ] NPL of tooth
telephone ['tɛlɪfəʊn] N [c] 电话
diànhuà [部 bù]
telephone book, telephone
directory N [c] 电话簿
diànhuàbù [个 gè]
telescope ['tɛlɪskəʊp] N [c] 望远
镜 wàngyuǎnjìng [架 jià]
television ['tɛlɪvɪʒən] N 1 [c] (also:
television set) 电视机 diànshìjī
[台 tái] 2 (system) 电视 diànshì
tell [tɛl] (pt, pp told) vt 1 (inform)
▸ to tell sb sth 告诉某人某事
gàosù mǒurén mǒushì 2 [+ story,

joke] 讲 jiǎng ▸to tell sb to do sth 指示某人做某事 zhǐshì mǒurén zuò mǒushì ▸to tell sb that... 告诉某人说… gàosù mǒurén shuō...

▸tell off VT ▸to tell sb off 斥责 某人 chìzé mǒurén

teller ['telə^r] (US) N [c] (in bank) 出 纳员 chūnàyuán [个 gè]

telly ['telɪ] (Brit: inf) N [c/u] 电视 diànshì [台 tái]

temper ['tempə^r] N [c/u] 脾气 píqì [种 zhǒng] ▸to lose one's temper 发怒 fānù

temperature ['temprətʃə^r] N 1 [c/u] (of place) 气温 qìwēn 2 [u] (of person) 体温 tǐwēn ▸to have or be running a temperature 发 烧 fāshāo

temple ['templ] N [c] 庙宇 miàoyǔ [座 zuò]

temporary ['tempərərɪ] ADJ 临 时的 línshí de

temptation [temp'teɪʃən] N [c/u] 诱惑 yòuhuò [种 zhǒng]

tempting ['temptɪŋ] ADJ 诱人的 yòurén de

ten [ten] NUM 十 shí

tend [tend] VI ▸to tend to do sth 倾向于做某事 qīngxiàng yú zuò mǒushì

tennis ['tenɪs] N [u] 网球运动 wǎngqiú yùndòng

tennis court N [c] 网球场 wǎngqiúchǎng [个 gè]

tennis player N [c] 网球手 wǎngqiúshǒu [位 wèi]

tense [tens] I ADJ 紧张的 jǐnzhāng de II N [c] (Ling) 时态 shítài [个

zhǒng]

tension ['tenʃən] N 1 [c/u] (of situation) 紧张的局势 jǐnzhāng de júshì [个 gè] 2 [u] (of person) 焦 虑 jiāolù

tent [tent] N [c] 帐篷 zhàngpeng [顶 dǐng]

tenth [tenθ] NUM 1 (in series) 第十 dì shí 2 (fraction) 十分之一 shífēn zhī yī; see also **fifth**

term [təːm] N [c] 1 学期 xuéqī [个 gè] ▸in the short/long term 短/长期 duǎn/chángqī ▸to be on good terms with sb 与某人关系 好 yǔ mǒurén guānxì hǎo

terminal ['təːmɪnl] I ADJ 晚期的 wǎnqī de II N [c] 1 (Comput) 终端 zhōngduān [个 gè] 2 (at airport) 终 点站 zhōngdiǎnzhàn [个 gè]

terminally ['təːmɪnlɪ] ADV ▸terminally ill 病入膏肓的 bìng rù gāo huāng de

terrace ['terəs] N [c] 1 (Brit: row of houses) 成排的房屋 chéngpái de fángwū [排 pái] 2 (patio) 平台 píngtái [个 gè]

terraced ['terəst] ADJ [+ house] 成 排的 chéngpái de

terrible ['terɪbl] ADJ 1 [+ accident, winter] 可怕的 kěpà de 2 (very poor) 糟糕的 zāogāo de 3 糟透的 zāotòu de

terribly ['terɪblɪ] ADV 1 (very) 非 常 fēicháng 2 (very badly) 差劲地 chàjìn de

terrific [tə'rɪfɪk] ADJ 1 [+ amount, thunderstorm, speed] 惊人的 jīngrén de 2 [+ time, party, idea] 极 好的 jíhǎo de

terrified [ˈtɛrɪfaɪd] ADJ 吓坏的 xiàhuài de

terror [ˈtɛrə*] N [U] 恐惧 kǒngjù

terrorism [ˈtɛrərɪzəm] N [U] 恐怖主义 kǒngbù zhǔyì

terrorist [ˈtɛrərɪst] I N [c] 恐怖分子 kǒngbù fènzǐ [个 gè] II ADJ 恐怖分子的 kǒngbù fènzǐ de

test [tɛst] I N [c] 1 (trial, check) 试验 shìyàn [次 cì] 2 (Med) 检验 jiǎnyàn [次 cì] 3 (Scol) 测验 cèyàn [个 gè] 4 (also: **driving test**) 驾驶考试 jiàshǐ kǎoshì [次 cì] II VT 1 (try out) 试验 shìyàn 2 (Scol) 测试 cèshì

test tube N [c] 试管 shìguǎn [根 gēn]

text [tɛkst] I N 1 [U] (written material) 正文 zhèngwén 2 [c] (book) 课本 kèběn [本 běn] 3 [c] (also: **text message**) 手机短信 shǒujī duǎnxìn [条 tiáo] II VT (on mobile phone) 发短消息 fā duǎnxiāoxī

textbook [ˈtɛkstbuk] N [c] 课本 kèběn [本 běn]

text message N [c] 短信 duǎnxìn [条 tiáo]

than [ðæn, ðən] PREP (in comparisons) 比 bǐ ▶ it's smaller than a matchbox 它比一个火柴盒还小 tā bǐ yīgè huǒcháihé hái xiǎo ▶ more/less than Paul 比保罗多/少 bǐ Bǎoluó duō/shǎo ▶ more than 20 多于20 duōyú èrshí ▶ she's older than you think 她比你想的年纪要大 tā bǐ nǐ xiǎngde niánjì yào dà

thank [θæŋk] VT [+ person] 感谢 gǎnxiè ▶ **thank you (very much)** (非常)感谢你 (fēicháng) gǎnxiè nǐ ▶ no, thank you 不，谢谢 bù, xièxie ▶ to thank sb for (doing) sth 感谢某人(做)某事 gǎnxiè mǒurén (zuò) mǒushì

thanks [θæŋks] I NPL 感谢 gǎnxiè II INT 谢谢 xièxie ▶ many thanks, thanks a lot 多谢 duōxiè ▶ no, thanks 不了，谢谢 bùle, xièxie ▶ thanks to sb/sth 多亏某人/某事 duōkuī mǒurén/mǒushì

Thanksgiving (Day) [ˈθæŋksgɪvɪŋ(-)] (US) N [c/U] 感恩节 Gǎn'ēnjié [个 gè]

⭕ **KEYWORD**

that [ðæt] (demonstrative adj, pron: pl **those**) I ADJ 那 nà ▶ **that man/woman/book** 那个男人/女人/那本书 nàgè nánrén/nǚrén/nàběnshū ▶ **that one** 那一个 nà yīgè

II PRON 1 (demonstrative) 那 nà ▶ **who's/what's that?** 那是谁/那是什么？ nàshì shuí/nàshì shénme? ▶ **is that you?** 是你吗？ shì nǐ ma? ▶ **that's my house** 那是我的房子 nàshì wǒde fángzi 2 (relative) …的 …de ▶ **the man that I saw** 我见过的那个男的 wǒ jiànguò de nàgè nánde ▶ **the woman that you spoke to** 和你说过话的那个女的 hé nǐ shuōguò huà de nàgè nǚde

III CONJ 引导宾语从句的关系代词 ▶ **he thought that I was ill** 他以为我病了 tā yǐwéi wǒ bìngle

IV ADV (so) 如此 rúcǐ ▸that
much/bad/high 如此多/糟糕/高
rúcǐ duō/zāogāo/gāo

🔵 KEYWORD

the [ðiː, ðə] DEF ART **1** 定冠词，
用于指代已知的人或物 ▸the
man/girl/house/book 男人/女
孩/房子/书 nánrén/nǚhái/fángzi/
shū ▸the men/women/houses/
books 男人/女孩/房子/书
nánrén/nǚhái/fángzi/shū ▸the
best solution 最好的解决方案
zuìhǎo de jiějué fāng'àn
2 (in dates, decades) 表示具体时
间 ▸the fifth of March 3月5日
sānyuè wǔrì ▸the nineties 90年
代 jiǔshí niándài
3 (in titles) 用于称谓中
▸Elizabeth the First 伊丽莎白一
世 Yīlìshābái Yīshì

theatre, (US) **theater** ['θɪətər]
N **1** [c] (building) 剧院 jùyuàn [座
zuò] **2** [c] (Med) (also: operating
theatre) 手术室 shǒushùshì
[间 jiān] **3** [c] (US) (also: movie
theater) 电影院 diànyǐngyuàn
[家 jiā]

theft [θɛft] N [c/u] 盗窃 dàoqiè
[次 cì]

their [ðɛər] ADJ **1** (of men, boys,
mixed group) 他们的 tāmen de; (of
women, girls) 她们的 tāmen de; (of
things, animals) 它们的 tāmen de
2 (his or her) 他/她的 tā/tā de

theirs [ðɛəz] PRON (of men, girls,

mixed group) 他们的 tāmen de;
(of women, girls) 她们的 tāmen
de; (of animals) 它们的 tāmen de
▸a friend of theirs 他们/她们的
一个朋友 tāmen/tāmen de yīgè
péngyou

them [ðɛm, ðəm] PRON (plural
referring to men, boys, mixed group)
他们 tāmen; (referring to women,
girls) 她们 tāmen; (referring to
things and animals) 它们 tāmen

theme park N [c] 主题公园 zhǔtí
gōngyuán [座 zuò]

themselves [ðəm'sɛlvz] PL PRON
1 (referring to men, boys, mixed group)
他们自己 tāmen zìjǐ; (referring to
girls, women) 她们自己 tāmen
zìjǐ; (referring to animals) 它们自
己 tāmen zìjǐ **2** (emphatic: referring
to men, boys, mixed group) 他们
本人 tāmen běnrén; (: referring
to women, girls) 她们本人 tāmen
běnrén ▸they all enjoyed
themselves 他们/她们都玩得很
开心。tāmen/tāmen dōu wánde
hěn kāixīn ▸by themselves
(unaided) 他们独立地 tā/tāmen
dúlì de; (alone) 他/她们独自地
tā/tāmen dúzì de

then [ðɛn] ADV **1** (at that time: past)
当时 dāngshí; (future) 那时 nàshí
2 (after that) 之后 zhīhòu ▸by
then 到那时 dào nàshí ▸before
then 在那之前 zài nà zhīqián
▸until then 直到那时 zhídào
nàshí ▸since then 自从那时
zìcóng nàshí ▸well/OK then 好
吧 hǎoba

there [ðɛər] ADV 那儿 nàr

▶they've lived there for 30 years 他们在那儿住了30年 tāmen zài nàr zhùle sānshí nián ▶is Shirley there please? (on telephone) 请问雪莉在吗? qǐngwèn Xuělì zàima? ▶it's over there 在那边 zài nàbian ▶there he is! 他在那儿呐! tā zài nàr ne! ▶there you are (offering something) 给你 gěinǐ ▶there is/there are 有 yǒu ▶there has been an accident 发生了一个事故 fāshēng le yīgè shìgù

therefore [ˈðɛəfɔːʳ] ADV 因此 yīncǐ

there's [ˈðɛəz] **= there is, there has**

thermometer [θəˈmɒmɪtəʳ] N [c] 温度计 wēndùjì [个 gè]

these [ðiːz] I PL ADJ (demonstrative) 这些 zhèxiē II PL PRON (demonstrative) 这些 zhèxiē ▶these days 目前 mùqián

they [ðeɪ] PL PRON 1 (referring to men, boys, mixed group) 他们 tāmen; (referring to women, girls) 她们 tāmen; (referring to animals, things) 它们 tāmen 2 (in generalizations) 人们 rénmen

they'd [ðeɪd] **= they had, they would**

they'll [ðeɪl] **= they shall, they will**

they're [ðɛəʳ] **= they are**

they've [ðeɪv] **= they have**

thick [θɪk] ADJ 1 [+ slice, line, book, clothes] 厚的 hòu de 2 [+ sauce, mud, fog] 浓的 nóng de ▶it's 20 cm thick 有20厘米粗 yǒu èrshí límǐ cū

thief [θiːf] (pl thieves [θiːvz]) N [c] 贼 zéi [个 gè]

thigh [θaɪ] N [c] 大腿 dàtuǐ [条 tiáo]

thin [θɪn] ADJ 1 [+ slice, line, book, material] 薄的 báo de 2 [+ person, animal] 瘦的 shòu de

thing [θɪŋ] I N [c] 1 事 shì [件 jiàn] 2 (physical object) 物品 wùpǐn [件 jiàn] II things NPL 1 (belongings) 东西 dōngxi 2 (in general) 情形 qíngxíng ▶a strange thing happened 发生了一件很奇怪的事。fāshēng le yījiàn hěn qíguài de shì ▶how are things going? 情形如何? qíngxíng rúhé?

think [θɪŋk] (pt, pp thought) I VI 1 (reflect) 思考 sīkǎo 2 (reason) 想 xiǎng II VT 1 (be of the opinion, believe) 认为 rènwéi 2 (believe) 以为 yǐwéi ▶what do you think of...? 你认为...怎么样? nǐ rènwéi...zěnmeyàng? ▶to think about sth/sb 想着某事物/某人 xiǎngzhe mǒu shìwù/mǒurén ▶to think of doing sth 考虑做某事物 kǎolǜ zuò mǒushì ▶I think so/not 我想是/不是的 wǒ xiǎng shì/bùshì de ▶think over VT [+ offer, suggestion] 仔细考虑 zǐxì kǎolǜ

third [θəːd] NUM 1 (in series) 第三 dì sān 2 (fraction) 三分 sānfēn ▶a third of 三分之一 sān fēn zhī yī; see also **fifth**

thirdly [ˈθəːdlɪ] ADV 第三 dì sān

Third World I N ▶the Third World 第三世界 Dì Sān Shìjiè II ADJ [+ country, debt] 第三世界的

Dì Sān Shìjiè de

thirst [θəːst] N [C/U] 口渴 kǒukě [阵 zhèn]

thirsty ['θəːstɪ] ADJ 渴的 kě de

thirteen [θəː'tiːn] NUM 十三 shísān; *see also* **fifteen**

thirteenth [θəː'tiːnθ] NUM 第十三 dì shísān; *see also* **fifth**

thirty ['θəːtɪ] NUM 三十 sānshí; *see also* **fifty**

 KEYWORD

this [ðɪs] (pl **these**) I ADJ
1 (demonstrative) 这 zhè ▶**this man** 这个男人 zhège nánrén ▶**this house** 这座房子 zhèzuò fángzi ▶**this one is better than that one** 这个比那个好 zhège bǐ nàgè hǎo
2 (with days, months, years) 这个 zhège ▶**this Sunday/month/year** 这个星期天/月/今年 zhège xīngqītiān/yuè/jīnnián
II PRON 这个 zhège ▶**who's/what's this?** 这是谁/什么? zhèshì shuí/shénme? ▶**this is Janet** (in introduction) 这是珍妮特 zhèshì Zhēnnītè; (on telephone) 我是珍妮特 wǒshì Zhēnnītè ▶**like this** 像这个一样的 xiàng zhège yīyàng de
III ADV (demonstrative) ▶**this much/high/long** 这么多/高/长 zhème duō/gāo/cháng

thorn [θɔːn] N [C] 刺 cì [根 gēn]

thorough ['θʌrə] ADJ **1** [+ search, investigation] 彻底的 chèdǐ de

2 (methodical) [+ person] 细致的 xìzhì de

those [ðəʊz] I PL ADJ 那些 nàxiē II PL PRON 那些 nàxiē ▶**those people/books** 那些人/书 nàxiē rén/shū ▶**are these yours?** 那些是你的吗? nàxiē shì nǐde ma?

though [ðəʊ] I CONJ (although) 虽然 suīrán II ADV 但是 dànshì ▶**even though** 尽管 jǐnguǎn

thought [θɔːt] I PT, PP of **think** II N [C] 想法 xiǎngfǎ [个 gè]

thoughtful ['θɔːtful] ADJ **1** (deep in thought) 深思的 shēnsī de **2** (considerate) 体贴的 tǐtiē de

thoughtless ['θɔːtlɪs] ADJ [+ behaviour, words, person] 不体贴的 bù tǐtiē de

thousand ['θaʊzənd] NUM ▶**a or one thousand** 一千 yī qiān ▶**thousands of** 许许多多 xǔ xǔ duō duō

thread [θrɛd] N [C/U] 线 xiàn [根 gēn]

threat [θrɛt] N [C/U] 威胁 wēixié [个 gè]

threaten ['θrɛtn] VT **1** (make a threat against) [+ person] 威胁 wēixié **2** (endanger) [+ life, livelihood] 使受到威胁 shǐ shòudào wēixié

three [θriː] NUM 三 sān; *see also* **five**

three-quarters [θriː'kwɔː-təz] I NPL 四分之三 sìfēn zhī sān II ADV ▶**three-quarters full/empty** 四分之三满/空 sìfēn zhīsān mǎn/kōng III PRON 四分之三 sìfēn zhī sān ▶**three-quarters**

of an hour 45分钟 sìshíwǔ fēnzhōng

threw [θruː] PT of **throw**

thriller ['θrɪlə'] N [c] 惊险 jīngxiǎn [场 chǎng]

thrilling ['θrɪlɪŋ] ADJ 令人兴奋的 lìng rén xīngfèn de

throat [θrəʊt] N [c] 1 (gullet) 咽喉 yānhóu [个 gè] 2 (neck) 脖子 bózi [个 gè] ▸ **to have a sore throat** 嗓子疼 sǎngzi téng

through [θruː] I PREP 1 [+ place] 穿过 chuānguò 2 (throughout) [+ time] 整个 zhěnggè 3 (coming from the other side of) 穿过 chuānguò II ADJ [+ ticket, train] 直达的 zhídá de ▸ **(from) Monday through Friday** (US) (从) 周一到周五 (cóng) zhōuyī dào zhōuwǔ

throughout [θruː'aʊt] PREP 1 [+ place] 遍及 biànjí 2 [+ time] 贯穿 guànchuān

throw [θrəʊ] (pt **threw**, pp **thrown**) VT 1 (toss) [+ stone, ball] 丢 diū 2 [+ person] 抛 pāo ▸ **throw away** VT 1 [+ rubbish] 扔掉 rēngdiào 2 [+ opportunity] 错过 cuòguò ▸ **throw out** VT 1 [+ rubbish] 扔掉 rēngdiào 2 (from team, organization) 赶走 gǎnzǒu ▸ **throw up** (inf) VI (vomit) 呕吐 ǒutù

thru [θruː] (US) = **through**

thumb [θʌm] N [c] 大拇指 dàmǔzhǐ [个 gè]

thumbtack ['θʌmtæk] (US) N [c] 图钉 túdīng [颗 kē]

thunder ['θʌndə'] N [u] 雷 léi

thunderstorm ['θʌndəstɔːm] N [c] 雷雨 léiyǔ [阵 zhèn]

Thursday ['θəːzdɪ] N [c/u] 星期四 xīngqīsì [个 gè]; see also **Tuesday**

tick [tɪk] N 1 (esp Brit: mark) 勾号 gōuhào [个 gè] II VI (clock, watch) 嘀嗒作响 dīdā zuòxiǎng III VT (esp Brit) [+ item on list] 打勾 dǎgōu ▸ **tick off** VT (esp Brit) [+ item on list] 打勾 dǎgōu

ticket ['tɪkɪt] N 1 [c] (for public transport, theatre, raffle) 票 piào [张 zhāng] 2 [c] (Aut) (also: **parking ticket**) 违章停车罚单 wéizhāng tíngchē fádān [张 zhāng]

ticket inspector N [c] 查票员 chápiàoyuán [位 wèi]

ticket office N [c] 售票处 shòupiàochù [个 gè]

tickle ['tɪkl] VT 挠痒 náoyǎng

tide [taɪd] N [c] 潮汐 cháoxī ▸ **high/low tide** 涨/落潮 zhǎng/luò cháo

tidy ['taɪdɪ] I ADJ 整洁的 zhěngjié de II VT (also: **tidy up**) 整理 zhěnglǐ ▸ **tidy up** VT, VI 整理 zhěnglǐ

tie [taɪ] I N 1 [c] (clothing) 领带 lǐngdài [条 tiáo] 2 (Sport) 淘汰赛 táotàisài [局 jú] 3 (draw: in competition) 平局 píngjú [个 gè] II VT (also: **tie up**) 扎 zā ▸ **tie up** VT 1 [+ parcel] 捆绑 kǔnbǎng 2 [+ dog] 拴 shuān 3 [+ person] 捆绑 kǔnbǎng

tiger ['taɪgə'] N [c] 老虎 lǎohǔ [只 zhī]

tight [taɪt] I ADJ 1 [+ shoes, clothes]

紧身的 jǐnshēn de **2** (strict)
[+ budget, schedule] 紧张的
jǐnzhāng de; [+ security, controls]
严格的 yángé de **II** ADV (hold,
squeeze, shut) 紧紧地 jǐnjǐn de

tightly ['taɪtlɪ] ADV 紧紧地
jǐnjǐn de

tights [taɪts] (Brit) NPL 连裤袜
liánkùwà

tile [taɪl] N [c] **1** (on roof) 瓦 wǎ [片
piàn] **2** (on floor, wall) 砖 zhuān
[块 kuài]

till [tɪl] **I** N [c] (Brit) 收银台
shōuyíntái [个 gè] **II** PREP, CONJ
= **until**

timber ['tɪmbə'] (Brit) N [u] 木
料 mùliào

time [taɪm] N **1** [u] 时间 shíjiān **2**
[u] (period) 时候 shíhou **3** [s] (by
clock) 时间 shíjiān **4** [c] (occasion)
次 cì ▸ **to have a good/bad time**
度过一段愉快/不愉快的时光
dùguò yíduàn yúkuài/bù yúkuài
de shíguāng ▸ **to spend one's
time doing sth** 花时间做某事 huā
shíjiān zuò mǒushì ▸ **three times
a day** 一日三次 yírì sāncì ▸ **all
the time** 总是 zǒngshì ▸ **at the
same time** (simultaneously) 同时
tóngshí ▸ **at times** (sometimes) 有
时 yǒushí ▸ **in time (for)** 正好赶
上(…) zhènghǎo gǎnshàng (…)
▸ **in a week's/month's time** 一
周/月以后 yīzhōu/yuè yǐhòu ▸ **on
time** 准时 zhǔnshí ▸ **5 times 5
is 25** 5乘5等于25 wǔ chéng wǔ
děngyú èrshíwǔ ▸ **what time is
it?, what's the time?** 几点了?
jǐdiǎn le? ▸ **time off** 休假 xiūjià

timetable ['taɪmteɪbl] N [c]
1 (Brit) (Rail etc) 时刻表 shíkèbiǎo
[个 gè] **2** (Brit) (Scol) 课程表
kèchéngbiǎo [个 gè] **3** (programme
of events) 计划表 jìhuàbiǎo [个 gè]

tin [tɪn] N **1** [u] (metal) 锡 xī **2** [c]
(Brit: can) 罐 guàn [个 gè] **3** [c]
(container: for biscuits, tobacco)
听 tīng

tin opener [-əupnə'] (Brit) N [c]
开罐器 kāiguànqì [个 gè]

tiny ['taɪnɪ] ADJ 极小的 jíxiǎo de

tip [tɪp] N [c] **1** [of branch,
paintbrush] 顶端 dǐngduān [个
gè] **2** (to waiter) 小费 xiǎofèi [笔
bǐ] **3** (Brit: for rubbish) 弃置场
qìzhìchǎng [个 gè] **4** (advice) 提
示 tíshì [个 gè] **II** VT **1** [+ waiter]
给…小费 gěi…xiǎofèi **2** (pour) 倒
出 dàochū

tiptoe ['tɪptəu] VI 踮着脚走
diǎnzhe jiǎo zǒu ▸ **on tiptoe** 踮着
脚走 diǎnzhe jiǎo zǒu

tire ['taɪə'] N (US) = **tyre**

tired ['taɪəd] ADJ 累的 lèi de ▸ **to
be tired of (doing) sth** 厌倦于
(做)某事 yànjuàn yú (zuò) mǒushì

tiring ['taɪərɪŋ] ADJ 令人疲劳的
lìng rén píláo de

tissue ['tɪʃu:] N [c] (paper
handkerchief) 纸巾 zhǐjīn [张 zhāng]

title ['taɪtl] N [c] **1** [of book, play]
题名 biāotí [个 gè] **2** (Sport) 冠军
guànjūn [个 gè]

○ KEYWORD

to [tu:, tə] **I** PREP **1** (direction)
到 dào ▸ **to France/London/**

school/the station 去法国/伦敦/学校/车站 qù Fǎguó/Lúndūn/xuéxiào/chēzhàn

2 (as far as) ▸ **from here to London** 从这儿到伦敦 cóng zhèr dào Lúndūn

3 (position) 向 xiàng ▸ **to the left/right** 向左/右 xiàng zuǒ/yòu

4 (in time expressions) ▸ **it's five/ten/a quarter to five** 差5分/10分/一刻5点 chà wǔfēn/shífēn/yīkè wǔ diǎn

5 (for, of) 的 de ▸ **a letter to his wife** 给他妻子的丁信 gěi tā qīzi de yīfēng xìn

6 (indirect object) ▸ **to give sth to sb** 给某人某物 gěi mǒurén mǒuwù ▸ **to talk to sb** 对某人说 duì mǒurén shuō ▸ **a danger to sb** 对某人的危险 duì mǒurén de wēixiǎn

7 (towards) ▸ **to be friendly/loyal to sb** 对某人友好/仁慈/忠实 duì mǒurén yǒuhǎo/réncí/zhōngshí

8 (in relation to) ▸ **30 miles to the gallon** 每加仑可行30英里 měi jiālún kě xíng sānshí yīnglǐ ▸ **three goals to two** 3比2 sān bǐ èr

9 (purpose, result) ▸ **to come to sb's aid** 来帮某人的忙 lái bāng mǒurén de máng

10 (indicating range, extent) ▸ **from... to...** 从…到… cóng…dào… ▸ **from May to September** 从5月到9月 cóng wǔyuè dào jiǔyuè

II WITH VERB **1** (simple infinitive) 与原形动词一起构成动词不定式 ▸ **to go/eat** 去/吃 qù/chī

2 (with vb omitted) 用来代替动词不定式或不定式短语,避免重复 ▸ **I don't want to** 我不想 wǒ bù xiǎng

3 (in order to) 为了 wèile ▸ **I did it to help you** 我这么做是为了帮你 wǒ zhème zuò shì wèile bāngnǐ

4 (equivalent to relative clause) 用作定语 ▸ **I have things to do** 我有事要做 wǒ yǒushì yào zuò

5 (after adjective etc) 用于某些动词,名词,形容词后构成不定式 ▸ **to be ready to go** 准备走 zhǔnbèi zǒu ▸ **too old/young to do sth** 年纪太大/太小以至于不能做某事 niánjì tàidà/tàixiǎo yǐzhì yú bùnéng zuò mǒushì ▸ **to and fro** 来来回回地 lái lái huí huí de

toast [təust] N **1** [U] (Culin) 烤面包 kǎomiànbāo **2** [c] (drink) 祝酒 zhùjiǔ [次 cì] ▸ **a piece or slice of toast** 一片烤面包 yīpiàn kǎo miànbāo ▸ **to drink a toast to sb** 为某人干杯 wèi mǒurén gānbēi

toaster ['təustə*] N [c] 烤面包机 kǎo miànbāo jī [台 tái]

tobacco [tə'bækəu] N [U] 烟草 yāncǎo

tobacconist's (shop) [tə'bækənists] N [c] 烟草店 yāncǎodiàn [家 jiā]

today [tə'deɪ] I ADV 今天 jīntiān II N [U] 今天 jīntiān ▸ **what day is it today?** 今天星期几? jīntiān xīngqījǐ? ▸ **today is the 4th of March** 今天是3月4日 jīntiān shì sānyuè sìrì

toddler ['tɒdlər] N [c] 学步的小孩 xuébù de xiǎohái [个 gè]

toe [təu] N [c] 1 [of foot] 脚趾 jiǎozhǐ [个 gè] 2 [of shoe, sock] 脚尖 处 jiǎozhǐchù [个 gè] ▸ **big/little toe** 大/小脚趾 dà/xiǎo jiǎozhǐ

toffee ['tɒfɪ] N 1 [U] (Brit: substance) 太妃糖 tàifēitáng 2 [c] (sweet) 乳脂糖 rǔzhītáng [颗 kē]

together [tə'geðər] ADV 1 (with each other) 一起 yìqǐ 2 (at the same time) 同时 tóngshí 3 (combined) 加起来 jiā qǐlái ▸ **together with** 连同 liántóng

toilet ['tɒɪlət] N [c] 1 (apparatus) 抽水马桶 chōushuǐ mǎtǒng [个 gè] 2 (Brit: room) 卫生间 wèishēngjiān [个 gè] ▸ **to go to the toilet** (esp Brit) 上厕所 shàng cèsuǒ

toilet paper N [U] 卫生纸 wèishēngzhǐ

toiletries ['tɒɪlətrɪz] NPL 卫生用品 wèishēng yòngpǐn

toilet roll N [c/U] 卫生卷纸 wèishēng juǎnzhǐ [卷 juǎn]

told [təuld] PT, PP of **tell**

toll [təul] N [c] (on road, bridge) 通行费 tōngxíngfèi [笔 bǐ]

tomato [tə'mɑːtəu] N [c] (pl **tomatoes**) 西红柿 xīhóngshì [个 gè]

tomorrow [tə'mɒrəu] I ADV 明天 míngtiān II N [U] 明天 míngtiān ▸ **the day after tomorrow** 后天 hòutiān ▸ **tomorrow morning** 明天早晨 míngtiān zǎochén

ton [tʌn] N [c] 1 (Brit) 英吨 yīngdūn 2 (US) (also: **short ton**) 美吨 měidūn 3 (metric ton) 公吨

gōngdūn

tongue [tʌŋ] N [c] (Anat) 舌头 shétou [个 gè]

tonic ['tɒnɪk] N [U] (also: **tonic water**) 奎宁水 kuíníngshuǐ

tonight [tə'naɪt] ADV N [U] 今晚 jīnwǎn

tonsil ['tɒnsl] N [c] 扁桃体 biǎntáotǐ [个 gè]

tonsillitis [tɒnsɪ'laɪtɪs] N [U] 扁桃腺炎 biǎntáoxiànyán

too [tuː] ADV 1 (excessively) 太 tài 2 (also) 也 yě ▸ **you're from Brooklyn? Me too!** 你从布鲁克林来? 我也是! nǐ cóng Bùlǔkèlín lái? Wǒ yěshì!

took [tuk] PT of **take**

tool [tuːl] N [c] 用具 yòngjù [种 zhǒng]

tooth [tuːθ] N [c] (pl **teeth**) 牙齿 yáchǐ [颗 kē]

toothache ['tuːθeɪk] N [c/U] 牙痛 yátòng [阵 zhèn] ▸ **to have toothache** 牙痛 yátòng

toothbrush ['tuːθbrʌʃ] N [c] 牙刷 yáshuā [把 bǎ]

toothpaste ['tuːθpeɪst] N [c/U] 牙膏 yágāo [管 guǎn]

top [tɒp] N 1 [c] [of mountain, building, tree, stairs] 顶部 dǐngbù [个 gè] 2 [c] [of page] 顶端 dǐngduān [个 gè] 3 [c] [of surface, table] 表面 biǎomiàn [个 gè] 4 [c] (lid: of box, jar, bottle) 盖子 gàizi [个 gè] 5 [c] (blouse) 上衣 shàngyī [件 jiàn] II ADJ 1 [+ shelf, step, storey, marks] 最高的 zuìgāo de 2 [+ executive, golfer] 顶级的 dǐngjí de ▸ **at the top of the stairs/**

page/street 在楼梯/页面的顶端/街道的尽头 zài lóutī/yèmiàn de dǐngduān/jiēdào de jìntóu ▸**to be** or **come top** 独占鳌头 dúzhàn áotóu

topic ['tɔpɪk] N [c] 话题 huàtí [个 gè]

torch [tɔːtʃ] N [c] (Brit) 手电筒 shǒudiàntǒng [个 gè]

tore [tɔːʳ] PT of **tear¹**

torn [tɔːn] PP of **tear¹**

tortoise ['tɔːtəs] N [c] 乌龟 wūguī [只 zhī]

torture ['tɔːtʃəʳ] I N [u] 酷刑 kùxíng II VT 对…施以酷刑 duì…shīyǐ kùxíng

total ['təutl] I ADJ 总的 zǒng de II N [c] 总数 zǒngshù [个 gè] ▸**in total** 总共 zǒnggòng

totally ['təutəlɪ] ADV 1 (agree, destroy) 完全地 wánquán de 2 (different, new) 绝对地 juéduì de

touch [tʌtʃ] I N [c] (contact) 触摸 chùmō [次 cì] II VT 1 (with hand, foot) 触摸 chùmō 2 (move: emotionally) 感动 gǎndòng III VI (be in contact) 接触 jiēchù ▸**to get in touch with sb** 与某人联系 yǔ mǒurén liánxì ▸**to lose touch (with sb)** (与某人) 失去联系 (yǔ mǒurén) shīqù liánxì

tough [tʌf] ADJ 1 (strong, hard-wearing) (+ material) 坚韧的 jiānrèn de 2 (+ meat) 老的 lǎo de 3 (physically) 强壮的 qiángzhuàng de 4 (rough) 无法无天的 wúfǎwútiān de

tour [tuəʳ] I N [c] 1 (journey) 旅行 lǚxíng [次 cì] 2 (of town, factory,

museum) 观光 guānguāng [次 cì] 3 (by pop group, sports team) 巡回表演 xúnhuí biǎoyǎn [个 gè] II VT (+ country, city) 观光 guānguāng ▸**to go on a tour of** (+ region) 去…旅行 qù…lǚxíng

tourism ['tuərɪzm] N [u] 旅游业 lǚyóuyè

tourist ['tuərɪst] I N [c] 游客 yóukè [位 wèi] II CPD (+ season, attraction) 旅游 lǚyóu

tow [təu] VT (+ vehicle, trailer) 拖 tuō ▸**tow away** VT (+ vehicle) 拖走 tuōzǒu

toward(s) [tə'wɔːd(z)] PREP 1 (in direction of) 朝着 cháozhe 2 (with regard to) 对于 duìyú 3 (near) 接近 jiējìn

towel ['tauəl] N [c] 毛巾 máojīn [条 tiáo]

tower ['tauəʳ] N [c] 塔 tǎ [座 zuò]

tower block (Brit) N [c] 高楼大厦 gāolóu dàshà [座 zuò]

town [taun] N [c] 城镇 chéngzhèn [个 gè]

town hall (Brit) N [c] 市政厅 shìzhèngtīng [个 gè]

tow truck (US) N [c] 拖车 tuōchē [部 bù]

toy [tɔɪ] I N [c] 玩具 wánjù [个 gè] II CPD (+ train, car) 玩具 wánjù

trace [treɪs] N [c] 痕迹 hénjì [个 gè]; (of person) 踪迹 zōngjì [个 gè]

track [træk] N [c] 1 (path) 小径 xiǎojìng [条 tiáo] 2 (Rail) 轨道 guǐdào [条 tiáo] 3 (on tape, record) 曲目 qǔmù [个 gè]

tracksuit ['træksuːt] (Brit) N [c]

运动服 yùndòngfú [套 tào]

tractor ['træktə] N [c] 拖拉机 tuōlājī [部 bù]

trade [treɪd] I N 1 [U] (buying and selling) 贸易 màoyì 2 [c] (skill, job) 谋生之道 móushēng zhī dào [种 zhǒng] II VT (exchange) ▸ **to trade sth (for sth)** (esp US) 用某物交换(某物) yòng mǒuwù jiāohuàn (mǒuwù)

trademark ['treɪdmɑːk] N [c] 商标 shāngbiāo [个 gè]

trade union (esp Brit) N [c] 工会 gōnghuì [个 gè]

tradition [trə'dɪʃən] N [c/u] 传统 chuántǒng [个 gè]

traditional [trə'dɪʃənl] ADJ 传统的 chuántǒng de

traffic ['træfɪk] N [U] 交通 jiāotōng

traffic circle (US) N [c] 转盘 zhuǎnpán [个 gè]

traffic jam N [c] 交通阻塞 jiāotōng zǔsè [阵 zhèn]

traffic lights NPL 红绿灯 hónglùdēng

traffic warden (esp Brit) N [c] 交通管理员 jiāotōng guǎnlǐyuán [位 wèi]

tragedy ['trædʒədɪ] N [c/u] 1 (disaster) 极大的不幸 jídà de búxìng [个 gè] 2 (Theat) 悲剧 bēijù [个 gè]

tragic ['trædʒɪk] ADJ 悲惨的 bēicǎn de

trailer ['treɪlə] N [c] 1 (Aut) 拖车 tuōchē [部 bù] 2 (US: caravan) 房屋式拖车 fángwū shì tuōchē [辆 liàng]

train [treɪn] I N [c] (Rail) 火车 huǒchē [辆 liàng] II VT 1 (teach skills to) 培训 péixùn 2 (+athlete) 培养 péiyǎng III VI 1 (learn a skill) 受训练 shòu xùnliàn 2 (Sport) 锻炼 duànliàn

trained [treɪnd] ADJ 经专门训练的 jīng zhuānmén xùnliàn de

trainee [treɪ'niː] N [c] 1 (apprentice) 受训者 shòuxùnzhě [位 wèi] 2 (in office, management job) 实习生 shíxíshēng [个 gè]

trainer ['treɪnə] N [c] 1 (Sport) 教练 jiàoliàn [ ] 2 (Brit: shoe) 运动鞋 yùndòngxié [双 shuāng]

training ['treɪnɪŋ] N [U] 1 (for occupation) 培训 péixùn 2 (Sport) 训练 xùnliàn

training course N [c] 培训班 péixùnbān [个 gè]

tram [træm] (Brit) N [c] (also: tramcar) 有轨电车 yǒuguǐ diànchē [辆 liàng]

tramp [træmp] N [c] 流浪者 liúlàngzhě [个 gè]

trampoline ['træmpəliːn] N [c] 蹦床 bèngchuáng [个 gè]

transfer ['trænsfə] N 1 [c/u] (of money, documents) 转移 zhuǎnyí [次 cì] 2 [c] (Sport) 转会 zhuǎnhuì [次 cì]

transit ['trænzɪt] N 1 ▸ **in transit** (people) 在途中 zài túzhōng 2 [U] (US) 运输 yùnshū

translate [trænz'leɪt] VT 翻译 fānyì

translation [trænz'leɪʃən] N 1 [c] (text) 译文 yìwén [篇 piān] 2 [U] (act of translating) 翻译 fānyì

translator [trænz'leɪtə] N [c] 译

者 yìzhě [个 gè]

transparent [træns'pærnt] ADJ 透明的 tòumíng de

transplant [vb træns'plɑ:nt, n 'trænsplɑ:nt] I VT (Med) 移植 yízhí II N [c/u] (Med: operation) 移植 yízhí [次 cì]

transport [n 'trænspɔ:t, vb træns'pɔ:t] I N [u] 交通工具 jiāotōng gōngjù II VT 运送 yùnsòng ▶ public transport (esp Brit) 公共交通 gōnggòng jiāotōng

transportation ['trænspɔ:'teɪʃən] N [u] (US: transport) 运输 yùnshū

trap [træp] I N [c] 陷阱 xiànjǐng [个 gè] II VT 1 [+ animal] 诱捕 yòubǔ 2 (in building) 困住 kùnzhù

trash [træʃ] N [u] (US) 废物 fèiwù

trash can (US) N [c] 垃圾桶 lājītǒng [个 gè]

travel ['trævl] I N [u] (travelling) 旅行 lǚxíng II VI 前往 qiánwǎng III VT [+ distance] 走过 zǒuguò

travel agency N [c] 旅行社 lǚxíngshè [个 gè]

travel agent N [c] 1 (shop, office) 旅行中介 lǚxíng zhōngjiè [个 gè] 2 (person) 旅行代理人 lǚxíng dàilǐrén [个 gè]

traveller, (US) **traveler** ['trævələr] N [c] 旅行者 lǚxíngzhě [位 wèi]

traveller's cheque, (US) **traveler's check** N [c] 旅行支票 lǚxíng zhīpiào [张 zhāng]

travelling, (US) **traveling** ['trævlɪŋ] N [u] 行程 xíngchéng

travel sickness N [u] 晕车/船/机症 yùnchē/chuán/jī zhèng

tray [treɪ] N [c] 托盘 tuōpán [个 gè]

treasure ['treʒər] N [u] 宝藏 bǎozàng

treat [tri:t] VT 1 (behave towards) [+ person, object] 对待 duìdài 2 (Med) [+ patient, illness] 医治 yīzhì

treatment ['tri:tmənt] N [c/u] (Med) 治疗 zhìliáo [次 cì]

treble ['trebl] VI 增至三倍 zēngzhì sānbèi

tree [tri:] N [c] 树 shù [棵 kē]

tremble ['trembl] VI (with fear, cold) 战栗 zhànlì

tremendous [trɪ'mendəs] ADJ 1 (enormous) 极大的 jídà de 2 (excellent) 极棒的 jíbàng de

trend [trend] N [c] 1 (tendency) 趋势 qūshì [种 zhǒng] 2 (fashion) 潮流 cháoliú [个 gè]

trendy ['trendɪ] (inf) ADJ 时髦的 shímáo de

trial ['traɪəl] N [c/u] (Law) 审理 shěnlǐ [次 cì] ▶ on trial (Law) 受审 shòushěn; (on approval) 试验 shìyàn

triangle ['traɪæŋgl] N [c] (Math) 三角 sānjiǎo [个 gè]

tribe [traɪb] N [c] 部落 bùluò [个 gè]

trick [trɪk] I N [c] 1 (by conjuror) 戏法 xìfǎ [个 gè] 2 (deception) 伎俩 jìliǎng [个 gè] II VT (deceive) 耍花招 shuǎ huāzhāo

tricky ['trɪkɪ] ADJ 棘手的 jíshǒu de

tricycle ['traɪsɪkl] N [c] 三轮车 sānlúnchē [辆 liàng]

trip [trɪp] I N [c] **1** (journey) 出行 chūxíng [次 cì] **2** (outing) 外出 wàichū [次 cì] II VI (also: **trip up**) 绊倒 bàndǎo ▸**to go on a trip** 外出旅行 wàichū lǚxíng

triple ['trɪpl] I ADJ 三部分的 sān bùfen de II VI 三倍于 sānbèi yú

triplets ['trɪplɪts] NPL 三胞胎 sānbāotāi

triumph ['traɪʌmf] N [c] 巨大的 成功 jùdà de chénggōng [个 gè]

trivial ['trɪvɪəl] ADJ 琐碎的 suǒsuì de

trolley ['trɒlɪ] N [c] **1** (Brit) 手推车 shǒutuīchē [辆 liàng] **2** (US: vehicle) 电车 diànchē [辆 liàng]

trombone [trɒm'bəʊn] N [c] 长 号 chánghào [只 zhī]

troop [tru:p] I N [c] (of people, animals) 群 qún II **troops** N [c] PL (Mil) 部队 bùduì [支 zhī]

trophy ['trəʊfɪ] N [c] 奖品 jiǎngpǐn [个 gè]

tropical ['trɒpɪkl] ADJ 热带的 rèdài de

trouble ['trʌbl] N [c/u] **1** (difficulties, bother, effort) 麻烦 máfan [个 gè] **2** (s) (problem) 问题 wèntí [个 gè] **3** (u) (unrest) 骚乱 sāoluàn ▸**to be in trouble** (with police, authorities) 惹麻烦 rě máfan ▸**the trouble is...** 问题是… wèntí shì... ▸**stomach/back trouble** 胃部/背部毛病 wèibù/bèibù máobìng

trousers ['traʊzəz] (Brit) NPL 裤子 kùzi ▸**a pair of trousers** 一条 裤子 yītiáo kùzi

trout [traʊt] N [c/u] 鳟鱼 zūnyú

[条 tiáo]

truck [trʌk] N [c] 卡车 kǎchē [辆 liàng]

truck driver N [c] 卡车司机 kǎchē sījī [位 wèi]

true [tru:] ADJ 真实的 zhēnshí de

truly ['tru:lɪ] ADV (genuinely) 确 实地 quèshí de ▸**yours truly** (in letter) 您忠诚的 nín zhōngchéng de

trumpet ['trʌmpɪt] N [c] 小号 xiǎohào [把 bǎ]

trunk [trʌŋk] I N [c] **1** (of tree) 树干 shùgàn [个 gè] **2** (of elephant) 象鼻子 xiàngbízi [个 gè] **3** (US: of car) 后备 箱 hòubèixiāng [个 gè] II **trunks** NPL (also: **swimming trunks**) 游 泳裤 yóuyǒngkù

trust [trʌst] VT 信任 xìnrèn

truth [tru:θ] N [c] 事实 shìshí

try [traɪ] I N [c] **1** (attempt) 尝试 chángshì [个 gè] II VT (make effort) 努力 nǔlì III VI (make effort) 努力 nǔlì ▸**to try to do sth, try doing sth** 尽力做某事 jìnlì zuò mǒushì ▸**try on** VT 试穿 shìchuān ▸**try out** VT 试验 shìyàn

T-shirt ['ti:ʃə:t] N [c] 短袖衫 duǎnxiùshān [件 jiàn]

tub [tʌb] N [c] **1** (container) 缸 gāng [个 gè] **2** (US) 浴缸 yùgāng [个 gè]

tube [tju:b] N [c] **1** (pipe) 管子 guǎnzi [根 gēn] **2** (container) 筒 tǒng [个 gè] **3** (Brit) ▸**the tube** (underground) 地铁 dìtiě

tuberculosis [tjubə:kju'ləʊsɪs] N [u] 肺结核 fèijiéhé

Tuesday ['tju:zdɪ] N [c] 星

期二 xīngqī'èr [个 gè] ▸**it is Tuesday 23rd March** 今天是3月 23号，星期二 jīntiān shì sānyuè èrshísān hào, xīngqī'èr ▸**on Tuesday** 在星期二 zài xīngqī'èr ▸**on Tuesdays** 每个星期二 měigè xīngqī'èr ▸**every Tuesday** 每逢星期二 měiféng xīngqī'èr ▸**last/next Tuesday** 上个/下个星期二 shànggè/xiàgè xīngqī'èr ▸**Tuesday morning/afternoon/evening** 星期二早晨/下午/晚上 xīngqī'èr zǎochén/xiàwǔ/wǎnshàng

tuition [tjuː'ɪʃən] N [U] 1 教学 jiàoxué 2 (*fees*) 学费 xuéfèi

tumble dryer [tʌmbl-] N [C] 滚筒干衣机 gǔntǒng gānyījī [台 tái]

tummy ['tʌmɪ] (*inf*) N [C] 肚子 dùzi [个 gè]

tuna ['tjuːnə] N [C/U] (*also:* **tuna fish**) 金枪鱼 jīnqiāngyú [条 tiáo]

tune [tjuːn] N [C] 曲调 qǔdiào [个 gè]

Tunisia [tjuː'nɪzɪə] N 突尼斯 Tūnísī

tunnel ['tʌnl] N [C] 隧道 suìdào [条 tiáo]

Turk [təːk] N [C] 土耳其人 Tǔ'ěrqírén [个 gè]

Turkey ['təːkɪ] N 土耳其 Tǔ'ěrqí

turkey ['təːkɪ] N 1 [C] (*bird*) 火鸡 huǒjī [只 zhī] 2 [U] (*meat*) 火鸡肉 huǒjī ròu

Turkish ['təːkɪʃ] I ADJ 土耳其的 Tǔ'ěrqí de II N [U] (*language*) 土耳其语 Tǔ'ěrqíyǔ

turn [təːn] I N [C] 1 (*in game, queue, series*) 机会 jīhuì [个 gè] II VT

1 [+ *part of body*] 转动 zhuàndòng 2 [+ *object*] 调转 diàozhuǎn 3 [+ *handle, key*] 转动 zhuàndòng 4 [+ *page*] 翻 fān III VI 1 (*rotate*) [*object, wheel*] 旋转 xuánzhuǎn 2 (*change direction*) [*person*] 转身 zhuǎnshēn 3 [*vehicle*] 转向 zhuǎnxiàng ▸**it's my turn to...** 轮到我做… lúndào wǒ zuò… ▸**to take turns** or **to take it in turns (to do sth)** 轮流做(某事) lúnliú zuò (mǒushì)

▸**turn around** VI = **turn round**

▸**turn back** VI 往回走 wǎnghuí zǒu

▸**turn down** VT [+ *heat, sound*] 调低 tiáodī

▸**turn into** VT FUS 变成 biànchéng

▸**turn off** VT 1 [+ *light, radio, tap*] 关 guān 2 [+ *engine*] 关掉 guāndiào

▸**turn on** VT [+ *light, radio, tap*] 打开 dǎkāi

▸**turn out** VT [+ *light, gas*] 关掉 guāndiào ▸**to turn out to be** (*prove to be*) 原来是 yuánlái shì

▸**turn round, turn around** VI [*person, vehicle*] 调转 diàozhuǎn

▸**turn up** VI 1 [*person*] 露面 lòumiàn 2 [*lost object*] 出现 chūxiàn II VT [+ *radio, heater*] 开大 kāidà

turning ['təːnɪŋ] N [C] (*in road*) 拐弯 guǎiwān [个 gè]

turn signal (*US*) N [U] 指示器 zhǐshìqì

turquoise ['təːkwɔɪz] ADJ [+ *colour*] 青绿色的 qīnglǜsè de

turtle ['tə:tl] (Brit) N [C] 龟 guī [只 zhī]

tutor ['tju:tə^r] N [C] 1 (Brit) (Scol) 助教 zhùjiào [位 wèi] 2 (private tutor) 家庭教师 jiātíng jiàoshī [位 wèi]

tuxedo [tʌk'si:dəʊ] (US) N [C] 男式晚礼服 nánshì wǎnlǐfú [件 jiàn]

TV N ABBR (= television) 电视 diànshì

tweezers ['twi:zəz] NPL 镊子 nièzi ▶ **a pair of tweezers** 一把镊子 yībǎ nièzi

twelfth [twelfθ] NUM (in series) 第十二 dì shí'èr; see also **fifth**

twelve [twelv] NUM 十二 shí'èr ▶ **at twelve (o'clock)** (midday) 中午12点 zhōngwǔ shí'èr diǎn; (midnight) 凌晨零点 língchén língdiǎn; see also **five**

twentieth ['twentiiθ] NUM 第二十 dì èrshí

twenty ['twenti] NUM 二十 èrshí ▶ **twenty-one** 二十一 èrshíyī; see also **fifty**

twice [twaɪs] ADV 两次 liǎngcì ▶ **twice as much/long as** 多/长至两倍 duō/chángzhì liǎngbèi

twin [twɪn] I ADJ [+ sister, brother] 孪生的 luánshēng de II N [C] 1 (person) 双胞胎 shuāngbāotāi [对 duì] 2 (also: **twin room**) 双人房 shuāngrénfáng [间 jiān]

twist [twɪst] VT 1 (turn) 扭 niǔ 2 [+ ankle] 扭伤 niǔshāng

two [tu:] NUM 二 èr; see also **five**

two-percent milk [tu:pə'sɛnt-] (US) N [U] 半脱脂奶 bàn tuōzhīnǎi

type [taɪp] I N 1 [C] (sort, kind) 类型 lèixíng [种 zhǒng] 2 [U] (Typ) 字体 zìtǐ II VT, VI 打字 dǎzì ▶ **type into** VT 录入 lùrù

typewriter ['taɪpraɪtə^r] N [C] 打字机 dǎzìjī [台 tái]

typical ['tɪpɪkl] ADJ 典型的 diǎnxíng de

tyre, (US) **tire** ['taɪə^r] N [C] 轮胎 lúntāi [个 gè]

u

UFO N ABBR (= **unidentified flying object**) 不明飞行物 bùmíng fēixíngwù

ugly ['ʌɡlɪ] ADJ 丑陋的 chǒulòu de

UK N ABBR (= **United Kingdom**)
▸ **the UK** 大不列颠及北爱尔兰联合王国 Dàbùlièdiān jí Běi'ài'ěrlán Liánhéwángguó

ulcer ['ʌlsəʳ] N [c] 溃疡 kuìyáng [处 chù]

umbrella [ʌm'brɛlə] N [c] 伞 sǎn [把 bǎ]

umpire ['ʌmpaɪəʳ] N [c] (Tennis, Cricket) 裁判员 cáipànyuán [位 wèi]

UN N ABBR (= **United Nations**)
▸ **the UN** 联合国 Liánhéguó

unable [ʌn'eɪbl] ADJ ▸ **to be unable to do sth** 不能做某事 bùnéng zuò mǒushì

unanimous [juː'nænɪməs] ADJ 一致同意的 yīzhì tóngyì de

unavoidable [ʌnə'vɔɪdəbl] ADJ 不可避免的 bùkě bìmiǎn de

unbearable [ʌn'bɛərəbl] ADJ 难以忍受的 nányǐ rěnshòu de

uncertain [ʌn'səːtn] ADJ 不确定的 bù quèdìng de ▸ **to be uncertain about sth** 对某事心无定数 duì mǒushì xīn wú dìng shù

uncle ['ʌŋkl] N [c] (father's older brother) 伯父 bófù [位 wèi]; (father's younger brother) 叔父 shūfù [位 wèi]; (father's sister's husband) 姑父 gūfù [位 wèi]; (mother's brother) 舅父 jiùfù [位 wèi]; (mother's sister's husband) 姨父 yífù [位 wèi]

uncomfortable [ʌn'kʌmfətəbl] ADJ [+ person] 不舒服的 bù shūfu de; [+ chair, room, journey] 不舒适的 bù shūshì de

unconscious [ʌn'kɔnʃəs] ADJ 失去知觉的 shīqù zhījué de

under ['ʌndəʳ] I PREP 1 (beneath) 在…下面 zài…xiàmian 2 (less than) [+ age, price] 不到 bùdào II ADV 1 (go, fly) 从下面 cóng xiàmian 2 (in age, price etc) 以下 yǐxià

underground ['ʌndəɡraʊnd] I N
▸ **the underground** (Brit: railway) 地铁 dìtiě II ADJ 地下的 dìxià de

underline [ʌndə'laɪn] (Brit) VT 在…下面划线 zài…xiàmian huàxiàn

underneath [ʌndə'niːθ] I ADV 在下面 zài xiàmian II PREP 在…下面 zài…xiàmian 2 (fig) 背后

zài…bèihòu

underpants ['ʌndəpænts] NPL 内裤 nèikù

underpass ['ʌndəpɑːs] N [c] 地下通道 dìxià tōngdào [条 tiáo]

undershirt ['ʌndəʃəːt] (US) N [c] 贴身内衣 tiēshēn nèiyī [件 jiàn]

understand [ʌndə'stænd] (pt, pp **understood**) VT 明白 míngbai; [+ foreign language] 懂 dǒng

understanding [ʌndə'stændɪŋ] ADJ 通情达理的 tōngqíng dálǐ de

understood [ʌndə'stud] PT, PP of **understand**

underwater ['ʌndə'wɔːtəʳ] ADV 在水下 zài shuǐxià

underwear ['ʌndəwɛəʳ] N [U] 内衣 nèiyī

undo [ʌn'duː] (pt undid, pp undone) VT 解开 jiěkāi

undress [ʌn'drɛs] VI 脱衣服 tuō yīfu

uneasy [ʌn'iːzɪ] ADJ 不安的 bù'ān de ▸ **to be uneasy about sth** 为某事忧虑 wèi mǒushì yōulǜ

unemployed [ʌnɪm'plɔɪd] I ADJ 失业的 shīyè de II NPL ▸ **the unemployed** 失业者 shīyèzhě

unemployment [ʌnɪm'plɔɪmənt] N [U] 失业 shīyè

unexpected [ʌnɪks'pɛktɪd] ADJ 意外的 yìwài de

unexpectedly [ʌnɪks'pɛktɪdlɪ] ADV 意外地 yìwài de

unfair [ʌn'fɛəʳ] ADJ 不公平的 bù gōngpíng de

unfamiliar [ʌnfə'mɪlɪəʳ] ADJ 陌生的 mòshēng de

unfashionable [ʌn'fæʃnəbl] ADJ

过时的 guòshí de

unfit [ʌn'fɪt] ADJ 不太健康的 bù tài jiànkāng de

unfold [ʌn'fəuld] VT 展开 zhǎnkāi

unforgettable [ʌnfə'gɛtəbl] ADJ 难忘的 nánwàng de

unfortunately [ʌn'fɔːtʃənətlɪ] ADV 不幸 búxìng

unfriendly [ʌn'frɛndlɪ] ADJ 不友善的 bù yǒushàn de

unhappy [ʌn'hæpɪ] ADJ 愁苦的 chóukǔ de

unhealthy [ʌn'hɛlθɪ] ADJ **1** [+ person] 身体不佳的 shēntǐ bùjiā de **2** [+ place, diet, lifestyle] 不利于健康的 bù lìyú jiànkāng de

uniform ['juːnɪfɔːm] N [c/u] 制服 zhìfú [套 tào]

uninhabited [ʌnɪn'hæbɪtɪd] ADJ 无人居住的 wúrén jūzhù de

union ['juːnjən] N [c] (also: **trade union**) 工会 gōnghuì [个 gè]

Union Jack N 英国国旗 Yīngguó guóqí [面 miàn]

unique [juː'niːk] ADJ 罕有的 hǎnyǒu de

unit ['juːnɪt] N [c] **1** (single whole) 单位 dānwèi [个 gè] **2** (group, centre) 小组 xiǎozǔ [个 gè] **3** (in course book) 单元 dānyuán [个 gè]

United Kingdom N ▸ **the United Kingdom** 大不列颠及北爱尔兰联合王国 Dàbùlièdiān Jí Běi'àiěrlán Liánhéwángguó

United Nations N ▸ **the United Nations** 联合国 Liánhéguó

United States (of America) N ▸ **the United States (of America)** 美利坚合众国 Měilìjiān

universe ['juːnɪvəːs] N [c] 宇宙
yǔzhòu [个 gè]

university [juːnɪ'vəːsɪtɪ] I N
[c/u] 大学 dàxué [所 suǒ] ▸ **to
go to university** 上大学 shàng
dàxué II CPD [+ student, professor,
education, year] 大学 dàxué

unkind [ʌn'kaɪnd] ADJ 刻薄的
kèbó de

unknown [ʌn'nəʊn] ADJ 1 [+ fact,
number] 未知的 wèizhī de
2 [+ writer, artist] 名不见经传的
míng bù jiàn jīngzhuàn de

unleaded [ʌn'ledɪd] I ADJ 无铅
的 wúqiān de II N [u] 无铅燃料
wúqiān ránliào

unless [ʌn'les] CONJ 除非 chúfēi

unlikely [ʌn'laɪklɪ] ADJ 未必会发
生的 wèibì huì fāshēng de ▸ **he is
unlikely to win** 他获胜的希望不
大 tā huòshèng de xīwàng bùdà

unload [ʌn'ləʊd] VT 1 [+ objects]
卸 xiè 2 [+ car, lorry] 从…上卸货
cóng…shang xièhuò

unlock [ʌn'lɒk] VT 开 kāi

unlucky [ʌn'lʌkɪ] ADJ 1 [+ person]
不幸的 búxìng de 2 [+ object,
number] 不吉利的 bù jílì de

unmarried [ʌn'mærɪd] ADJ 未婚
的 wèihūn de

unnatural [ʌn'nætʃrəl] ADJ 反常
的 fǎncháng de

unnecessary [ʌn'nesəsərɪ] ADJ
不必要的 bù bìyào de

unpack [ʌn'pæk] I VI 开包 kāibāo
II VT [+ suitcase, bag] 打开…取出
东西 dǎkāi…qǔchū dōngxi

unpleasant [ʌn'plezənt] ADJ 使

人不愉快的 shǐ rén bù yúkuài de;
[+ person, manner] 令人讨厌的 lìng
rén tǎoyàn de

unplug [ʌn'plʌg] VT 拔去…的插
头 báqù…de chātóu

unpopular [ʌn'pɒpjʊlə*] ADJ 不
受欢迎的 bù shòu huānyíng de

unrealistic ['ʌnrɪə'lɪstɪk] ADJ 不
切实际的 bù qiè shíjì de ▸ **it is
unrealistic to expect that...** 指
望…是不切实际的 zhǐwàng…shì
bùqiè shíjì de

unreasonable [ʌn'riːznəbl] ADJ
无理的 wúlǐ de

unreliable [ʌnrɪ'laɪəbl] ADJ
1 [+ person, firm] 不可信赖的 bù kě
xìnlài de 2 [+ machine, method] 不
可靠的 bù kěkào de

unroll [ʌn'rəʊl] VT 展开 zhǎnkāi

unscrew [ʌn'skruː] VT 旋开
xuánkāi

unsuccessful [ʌnsək'sesful] ADJ
1 [+ attempt, application] 失败的
shībài de 2 [+ person, applicant] 不
成功的 bù chénggōng de

unsuitable [ʌn'suːtəbl] ADJ
1 [+ place, time, clothes] 不适宜
的 bù shìyí de 2 [+ candidate,
applicant] 不合适的 bù héshì de
▸ **to be unsuitable for sth/for
doing sth** 不适于某事/做某事
shìyú mǒushì/zuò mǒushì

untidy [ʌn'taɪdɪ] ADJ 1 [+ room] 不
整洁的 bù zhěngjié de 2 [+ person,
appearance] 邋遢的 lātà de

until [ən'tɪl] I PREP 直到…时
zhídào…shí II CONJ 到…为止
dào…wéizhǐ ▸ **until now** 直到现
在 zhídào xiànzài ▸ **until** 届

时 jìeshí

unusual [ʌnˈjuːʒʊəl] ADJ 不寻常的 bù xúncháng de

unwilling [ʌnˈwɪlɪŋ] ADJ ▸ **to be unwilling to do sth** 不愿做某事 bùyuàn zuò mǒushì

unwrap [ʌnˈræp] VT 打开…的包装 dǎkāi…de bāozhuāng

KEYWORD

up [ʌp] I PREP 1 (to higher point on) 沿…向上 yán…xiàngshàng ▸ **he went up the stairs/the hill/the ladder** 他上了楼/山/梯子 tā shàngle lóu/shān/tīzi

2 (along) 沿着 yánzhe

3 (at higher point on) 在…高处 zài…gāochù; [+ road] 在…高远处 zài…gāoyuǎnchù ▸ **they live further up the street** 他们住在这条街那边儿 tāmen zhùzài zhètiáo jiē nàbiānr

II ADV 1 (towards higher point) 往上 wǎngshàng ▸ **the lift only goes up to the 12th floor** 电梯只上到12层楼 diàntī zhǐ shàngdào shí'èr céng lóu yǐshàng

2 (at higher point) 高高地 gāogāo de ▸ **up here/there** 这/那上面 zhè/nà shàngmiàn

3 ▸ **to be up** (be out of bed) 起床 qǐchuáng

4 (to/in the north) 在/向北方 zài/xiàng běifāng ▸ **they often comes up to Scotland** 他们常北上去苏格兰 tā cháng běishàng qù Sūgélán

5 (approaching) ▸ **to go/come/run up (to sb)** (朝某人)走去/过来/跑去 (cháo mǒurén) zǒuqù/guòlái/pǎoqù

6 ▸ **up to** (as far as) 直到 zhídào; (in approximations) 多达 duōdá ▸ **I can spend up to £100** 我可以花到100英镑 wǒ kěyǐ huādào yìbǎi yīngbàng

7 ▸ **up to** or **until** 直到 zhídào ▸ **I'll be here up to** or **until 5.30 pm** 我会一直呆到下午5点30分 wǒ huì yìzhí dāidào xiàwǔ wǔdiǎn sānshífēn ▸ **up to now** 直到现在 zhídào xiànzài

8 ▸ **it is up to you** (to decide) 随便你(决定) suíbiàn nǐ (juédìng)

9 ▸ **to feel up to sth/to doing sth** 感到能胜任某事/感到有力气做某事 gǎndào néng shèngrèn mǒushì/gǎndào yǒu lìqi zuò mǒushì

update [vb ʌpˈdeɪt, n ˈʌpdeɪt] I VT 更新 gēngxīn II N [c] 最新信息 zuìxīn xìnxī [条 tiáo]

uphill [ˈʌpˈhɪl] ADV (walk, push) 往坡上 wǎng pōshàng

upright [ˈʌpraɪt] ADV (sit, stand) 挺直地 tǐngzhí de

upset [ʌpˈsɛt] (pt, pp upset) I VT [+ person] 使苦恼 shǐ kǔnǎo II ADJ 1 (unhappy) 心烦意乱的 xīnfán yīluàn de 2 [+ stomach] 不舒服的 bù shūfu de ▸ **to be upset about sth** 为某事感到烦恼 wèi mǒushì fánnǎo

upside down [ʌpsaɪd-] ADV 上下颠倒地 shàngxià diāndǎo de

upstairs [ˈʌpˈstɛəz] ADV 1 (be) 在楼上 zài lóushàng 2 (go) 往楼上

wǎng lóushang

up-to-date [ˈʌptəˈdeɪt] ADJ 最新的 zuìxīn de

upwards [ˈʌpwədz] ADV 向上 xiàngshàng

urgent [ˈəːdʒənt] ADJ 紧急的 jǐnjí de

US N ABBR (= United States) ▸ **the US** 美国 Měiguó

us [ʌs] PRON 我们 wǒmen

USA N ABBR (= United States of America) ▸ **the USA** 美国 Měiguó

use [n juːs, vb juːz] I N [c/u] (purpose) 用途 yòngtú [种 zhǒng] II VT 1 [+ object, tool] 使用 shǐyòng 2 [+ word, phrase] 应用 yìngyòng ▸ **to make use of sth** 利用某物 lìyòng mǒuwù ▸ **it's no use** 没用的 méiyòng de ▸ **it's no use arguing/crying** etc 吵/哭 (等) 是没用的 chǎo/kū {děng} shì méiyòng de ▸ **to be no use (to sb)** (对某人) 毫无用处 (duì mǒurén) háowú yòngchù ▸ **she used to do it** 她过去是这么做的 tā guòqù shì zhème zuò de ▸ **I didn't use to** or **I used not to worry so much** 我过去不这么焦虑 wǒ guòqù bù zhème jiāolù ▸ **to be used to sth/to doing sth** 习惯于某事/做某事 xíguàn yú mǒushì/zuò mǒushì ▸ **to get used to sth/to doing sth** 开始习惯于某事/做某事 kāishǐ xíguàn yú mǒushì/zuò mǒushì ▸ **use up** VT 用完 yòngwán

useful [ˈjuːsful] ADJ 有用的 yǒuyòng de ▸ **to be useful for sth/doing sth** 对某事/做某事有帮助的 duì mǒushì/zuò mǒushì yǒu bāngzhù de

useless [ˈjuːslɪs] ADJ (pointless) 徒劳的 túláo de

user [ˈjuːzəʳ] N [c] 使用者 shǐyòngzhě [位 wèi]

user-friendly [ˈjuːzəˈfrendlɪ] ADJ 易于使用的 yìyú shǐyòng de

usual [ˈjuːʒuəl] ADJ 惯常的 guàncháng de ▸ **as usual** 像往常一样 xiàng wǎngcháng yíyàng ▸ **warmer/colder than usual** 比平常暖和/冷 bǐ píngcháng nuǎnhe/lěng

usually [ˈjuːʒuəlɪ] ADV 通常地 tōngcháng de

V

vacancy ['veɪkənsɪ] N [c] (*job*) 空缺 kòngquē [个 gè]; (*hotel room*) 空房 kòngfáng [间 jiān] ▸ "no vacancies" "客满" "kèmǎn"

vacant ['veɪkənt] ADJ 空着的 kòngzhe de

vacation [və'keɪʃən] N [c] (*esp US*) 休假 xiūjià [次 cì] ▸ to take a vacation 休假 xiūjià ▸ to be/go on vacation 在/去度假 zài/qù dùjià

vaccinate ['væksɪneɪt] VT ▸ to vaccinate sb (against sth) 给某人接种疫苗 (预防某疾病) gěi mǒurén jiēzhòng yìmiáo (yùfáng mǒu jíbìng)

vacuum cleaner N [c] (*also:* **vacuum**) 真空吸尘器 zhēnkōng xīchénqì [台 tái]

vague [veɪg] ADJ 不清楚的 bù qīngchǔ de

vain [veɪn] ADJ [+ *person*] 自负的 zìfù de ▸ in vain 徒然 túrán

Valentine's Day ['væləntaɪnz-] N [c/u] 情人节 Qíngrénjié [个 gè]

valid ['vælɪd] ADJ 有效的 de yǒuxiào de

valley ['vælɪ] N [c] 山谷 shāngǔ [个 gè]

valuable ['væljuəbl] ADJ 贵重的 guìzhòng de

value ['vælju:] N 1 [c/u] (*financial worth*) 价值 jiàzhí [种 zhǒng] 2 [u] (*worth in relation to price*) 价格 jiàgé

van [væn] N [c] (*Aut*) 厢式运货车 xiāngshì yùnhuòchē [辆 liàng]

vandalism ['vændəlɪzəm] N [u] 蓄意破坏公物的行为 xùyì pòhuài gōngwù de xíngwéi

vandalize ['vændəlaɪz] VT 肆意毁坏 (公共财物) sìyì huǐhuài

vanish ['vænɪʃ] VI 消失 xiāoshī

variety [və'raɪətɪ] N 1 [u] (*diversity*) 多样性 duōyàngxìng 2 [s] (*range: of objects*) 若干 ruògān

various ['vεərɪəs] ADJ 不同的 bùtóng de

vary ['vεərɪ] I VT (*make changes to*) 更改 gēnggǎi II VI (*be different*) 有差异 yǒu chāyì

vase [vɑ:z], *US* veɪs] N [c] 花瓶 huāpíng [个 gè]

VCR N ABBR (= **video cassette recorder**) 录像机 lùxiàngjī

VDT (*US*) N ABBR (= **visual display terminal**) 视频显示装置 shìpín xiǎnshì zhuāngzhì

VDU (Brit) N ABBR (= visual display unit) 视频显示装置 shìpín xiǎnshì zhuāngzhì

veal [viːl] N [U] 小牛肉 xiǎoniúròu

vegan ['viːgən] N [c] 纯素食主义者 chún sùshí zhǔyìzhě [个 gè]

vegetable ['vɛdʒtəbl] N [c] 蔬菜 shūcài [种 zhǒng]

vegetarian [vɛdʒɪ'tɛərɪən] I N [c] 素食者 sùshízhě [个 gè] II ADJ [+ diet, restaurant etc] 素的 sù de

vehicle ['viːɪkl] N [c] 机动车 jīdòngchē [辆 liàng]

vein [veɪn] N [c] 静脉 jìngmài [条 tiáo]

velvet ['vɛlvɪt] N [c/U] 天鹅绒 tiān'éróng [块 kuài]

vending machine ['vɛndɪŋ-] N [c] 自动售货机 zìdòng shòuhuòjī [部 bù]

verb [vəːb] N [c] 动词 dòngcí [个 gè]

versus ['vəːsəs] PREP 对 duì

vertical ['vəːtɪkl] ADJ 垂直的 chuízhí de

very ['vɛrɪ] ADV 1 很 hěn 2 ▶ the very end/beginning 最终/一开始 zuìzhōng/yì kāishǐ ▶ very much so 确实如此 quèshí rúcǐ ▶ very little 极少的 jíshǎo de ▶ there isn't very much (of...) (…) 不太多了 (…)bùtài duōle

vest [vɛst] N [c] 1 (Brit: underwear) 汗衫 hànshān [件 jiàn] 2 (US: waistcoat) 马甲 mǎjiǎ [件 jiàn]

vet [vɛt] N [c] (esp Brit: veterinary surgeon) 兽医 shòuyī [个 gè]

veterinarian [vɛtrɪ'nɛərɪən] (US)

N [c] 兽医 shòuyī [个 gè]

via [vaɪə] PREP 经由 jīngyóu

vicar ['vɪkəʳ] N [c] 教区牧师 jiàoqū mùshī [位 wèi]

vicious ['vɪʃəs] ADJ 1 [+ attack, blow] 剧烈的 jùliè de 2 [+ person, dog] 凶残的 xiōngcán de

victim ['vɪktɪm] N [c] 受害者 shòuhàizhě [个 gè] ▶ to be the victim of 成为…的受害者 chéngwéi…de shòuhàizhě

victory ['vɪktərɪ] N [c/U] 胜利 shènglì [次 cì]

video ['vɪdɪəʊ] I N [c] (film) 录像 lùxiàng [段 duàn] 2 [U] (system) 录像 lùxiàng 3 [c] (cassette) 录像带 lùxiàngdài [盘 pán] 4 [c] (esp Brit: machine) 录像机 lùxiàngjī [台 tái] II VT (esp Brit) 录下 lùxià

video camera N [c] 摄像机 shèxiàngjī [台 tái]

video game N [c] 电子游戏 diànzǐ yóuxì [种 zhǒng]

video recorder N [c] 录像机 lùxiàngjī [台 tái]

Vietnam ['vjɛt'næm] N 越南 Yuènán

Vietnamese [vjɛtnə'miːz] (pl Vietnamese) I ADJ 越南的 Yuènán de II N 1 [c] (person) 越南人 Yuènánrén [个 gè] 2 [U] (language) 越南语 Yuènányǔ

view [vjuː] N [c] 1 景色 jǐngsè [道 dào] 2 (opinion) 看法 kànfǎ [种 zhǒng]

village ['vɪlɪdʒ] N [c] 村庄 cūnzhuāng [个 gè]

vine [vaɪn] N [c] 葡萄藤

pútáoténg [条 tiáo]

vinegar ['vɪnɪgəʳ] N [C/U] 醋 cù [瓶 píng]

vineyard ['vɪnjɑːd] N [C] 葡萄园 pútáoyuán [座 zuò]

violence ['vaɪələns] N [U] 暴力 bàolì

violent ['vaɪələnt] ADJ 暴力的 bàolì de

violin [vaɪə'lɪn] N [C] 小提琴 xiǎotíqín [把 bǎ]

violinist [vaɪə'lɪnɪst] N [C] 小提琴手 xiǎotíqínshǒu [个 gè]

virgin ['vɜːdʒɪn] N [C] 处女 chǔnǚ [个 gè]

Virgo ['vɜːgəu] N [U] (sign) 处女座 Chǔnǚ Zuò

virus ['vaɪərəs] (Med, Comput) N [C] 病毒 bìngdú [种 zhǒng]

visa ['viːzə] N [C] 签证 qiānzhèng [个 gè]

visit ['vɪzɪt] I N [C] 1 (to person) 拜访 bàifǎng 2 (to place) 访问 fǎngwèn [次 cì] II VT 1 [+ person] 拜访 bàifǎng 2 [+ place] 游览 yóulǎn

▶ **visit with** (US) VT FUS 拜访 bàifǎng

visitor ['vɪzɪtəʳ] N [C] 1 (to city, country) 游客 yóukè [位 wèi] 2 (to person, house) 来客 láikè [位 wèi]

visual ['vɪzjuəl] ADJ 视觉的 shìjué de

vital ['vaɪtl] ADJ 至关重要的 zhìguān zhòngyào de

vitamin ['vɪtəmɪn, US 'vaɪtəmɪn] N [C] 维生素 wéishēngsù [种 zhǒng]

vivid ['vɪvɪd] ADJ 1 生动的 shēngdòng de 2 [+ colour, light] 鲜艳的 xiānyàn de

vocabulary [vəu'kæbjulərɪ] N 1 [C/U] (of person) 词汇量 cíhuìliàng 2 [C] (of language) 词汇 cíhuì [个 gè]

vodka ['vɔdkə] N [C/U] 伏特加酒 fútèjiā jiǔ [瓶 píng]

voice [vɔɪs] N [C] 嗓音 sǎngyīn [种 zhǒng]

voice mail N [U] 语音留言 yǔyīn liúyán

volcano [vɔl'keɪnəu] (pl **volcanoes**) N [C] 火山 huǒshān [座 zuò]

volleyball ['vɔlɪbɔːl] N [U] 排球 páiqiú

volume ['vɔljuːm] N [U] 音量 yīnliàng ▶ **volume one/two** (of book) 第一/二册 dìyī/èrcè

voluntary ['vɔləntərɪ] ADJ 1 (not compulsory) 自愿的 zìyuàn de 2 [+ work, worker] 志愿的 zhìyuàn de

volunteer [vɔlən'tɪəʳ] N [C] (unpaid worker) 志愿者 zhìyuànzhě [个 gè] ▶ **to volunteer to do sth** 自愿做某事 zìyuàn zuò mǒushì

vomit ['vɔmɪt] I N [U] 呕吐物 ǒutùwù II VT 吐出 tùchū III VI 呕吐 ǒutù

vote [vəut] I N [C] 选票 xuǎnpiào [张 zhāng] II VI 投票 tóupiào ▶ **to take a vote on sth** 就某事进行表决 jiù mǒushì jìnxíng biǎojué ▶ **to vote for sb** 投某人票 tóu mǒurén piào ▶ **to vote for/against sth** 投票支持/反对某事 tóupiào zhīchí/

fǎnduì mǒushì

voucher ['vautʃə'] N [C] 代金券 dàijīnquàn [张 zhāng]

vowel ['vauəl] N [C] 元音 yuányīn [个 gè]

wage [weɪdʒ] N [C] (also: **wages**) 工资 gōngzī [份 fèn]

waist [weɪst] N [C] 1 腰 yāo [个 gè] 2 [of clothing] 腰身 yāoshēn [个 gè]

waistcoat ['weɪskəut] (Brit) N [C] 马甲 mǎjiǎ [件 jiàn]

wait [weɪt] I vɪ 等待 děngdài II N [C] (interval) 等待时间 děngdài shíjiān [段 duàn] ▸ **to wait for sb/sth** 等候某人/某物 děnghòu mǒurén/mǒuwù ▸ **wait a minute!** 等一下! děngyīxià! ▸ **to keep sb waiting** 让某人等着 ràng mǒurén děngzhe

waiter ['weɪtə'] N [C] 男服务员 nán fúwùyuán [位 wèi]

waiting list ['weɪtɪŋ-] N [C] 等候者名单 děnghòuzhě míngdān

[个 gè]

waiting room ['weɪtɪŋ-] N [c] 等
候室 děnghòushì [间 jiān]

waitress ['weɪtrɪs] N [c] 女服务员
nǚ fúwùyuán [位 wèi]

wake [weɪk] (pt woke or waked,
pp woken or waked)
▸ **wake up** I VT 唤醒 huànxǐng
II VI 醒来 xǐnglái

Wales [weɪlz] N 威尔士 Wēi'ěrshì
▸ **the Prince of Wales** 威尔士王子
Wēi'ěrshì Wángzǐ

walk [wɔːk] I N [c] 1 散步 sànbù [次
cì] II VI 走 zǒu III VT [+ distance]
走 zǒu ▸ **it's 10 minutes' walk
from here** 从这儿走有10分钟的路
程 cóng zhèr zǒu yǒu shífēnzhōng
de lùchéng ▸ **to go for a walk** 去
散步 qù sànbù

walking ['wɔːkɪŋ] N [u] 步行
bùxíng

wall [wɔːl] N [c] 1 [of building, room]
墙 qiáng [堵 dǔ] 2 (around garden,
field) 围墙 wéiqiáng [圈 quān]

wallet ['wɒlɪt] N [c] 钱包 qiánbāo
[个 gè]

wallpaper ['wɔːlpeɪpər] N [c/u]
墙纸 qiángzhǐ [张 zhāng]

walnut ['wɔːlnʌt] N [c] (nut) 核桃
hétáo [个 gè]

wander ['wɒndər] VI 漫游
mànyóu

want [wɒnt] VT 1 (wish for) 想要
xiǎngyào 2 (inf: need) 需要 xūyào
▸ **to want to do sth** 想要做某事
xiǎngyào zuò mǒushì ▸ **to want
sb to do sth** 希望某人做某事
xīwàng mǒurén zuò mǒushì

war [wɔːr] N [c/u] 战争 zhànzhēng

[场 chǎng]

wardrobe ['wɔːdrəub] N [c] 衣橱
yīchú [个 gè]

warehouse ['weəhaus] N [c] 仓
库 cāngkù [间 jiān]

warm [wɔːm] ADJ 1 [+ meal,
soup, water] 温热的 wēnrè de 2
[+ day, weather] 暖和的 nuǎnhuo
de 3 [+ clothes, blankets] 保暖的
bǎonuǎn de 3 [+ applause, welcome]
热情的 rèqíng de ▸ **it's warm** 天
很暖和 tiān hěn nuǎnhuo ▸ **are you
warm enough?** 你觉得够暖和吗？
nǐ juéde gòu nuǎnhuo ma？
▸ **warm up** I VI [athlete, pianist]
热身 rèshēn II VT [+ food] 加热
jiārè

warn [wɔːn] VT ▸ **to warn sb that**
警告某人… jǐnggào mǒurén…
▸ **to warn sb not to do sth** 告诫
某人不要做某事 gàojiè mǒurén
bùyào zuò mǒushì

warning ['wɔːnɪŋ] N [c] 1 (action,
words, sign) 警告 jǐnggào [个 gè] 2
[c/u] (notice) 预兆 yùzhào [个 gè]

was [wɒz] PT of **be**

wash [wɒʃ] N 1 VT 洗 xǐ II VI [person]
洗净 xǐjìng ▸ **to wash one's
face/hands/hair** 洗脸/手/头
发 xǐliǎn/shǒu/tóufa ▸ **to have a
wash** 洗一下 xǐyīxià
▸ **wash up** VI 1 (Brit: wash dishes)
洗餐具 xǐ cānjù 2 (US: have a wash)
洗一洗 xǐyīxǐ

washbasin ['wɒʃbeɪsn] N [c] 脸盆
liǎnpén [个 gè]

washcloth ['wɒʃklɒθ] (US) N [c]
毛巾 máojīn [条 tiáo]

washing ['wɒʃɪŋ] N [u] (dirty) 待

洗衣物 dàixǐ yīwù **2** (clean) 洗好的衣物 xǐhǎo de yīwù ▸ **to do the washing** 洗衣服 xǐ yīfu

washing machine N [C] 洗衣机 xǐyījī [台 tái]

washing powder (Brit) N [C/U] 洗衣粉 xǐyīfěn [袋 dài]

wasn't ['wɒznt] = **was not**

wasp [wɒsp] N [C] 黄蜂 huángfēng [只 zhī]

waste [weɪst] I N **1** [s/U] (of resources, food, money) 浪费 làngfèi **2** [U] (rubbish) 废料 fèiliào II VT [+ money, energy, time] 浪费 làngfèi; [+ opportunity] 失去 shìqù ▸ **it's a waste of time** 这是浪费时间 zhèshì làngfèi shíjiān

wastepaper basket ['weɪstpeɪpə-] (Brit) N [C] 废纸篓 fèizhǐlǒu [个 gè]

watch [wɒtʃ] I N [C] 手表 shǒubiǎo [块 kuài] II VT **1** (look at) 注视 zhùshì; [+ match, programme, TV] 看 kàn **2** (pay attention to) 关注 guānzhù III VI 注视 zhùshì ▸ **to watch sb do/doing sth** 看着某人做某事 kànzhe mǒurén zuò mǒushì

▸ **watch out** VI 提防 dīfang

▸ **watch out!** (inf) 小心! xiǎoxīn!

water ['wɔːtə'] I N [U] 水 shuǐ II VT [+ plant] 浇水 gěi…jiāoshuǐ ▸ **a drink of water** 一杯水 yìbēishuǐ

waterfall ['wɔːtəfɔːl] N [C] 瀑布 pùbù [条 tiáo]

watermelon ['wɔːtəmɛlən] N [C] 西瓜 xīguā [个 gè]

waterproof ['wɔːtəpruːf] ADJ 防水的 fángshuǐ de

water-skiing ['wɔːtəskiːɪŋ] N [U] ▸ **to go water-skiing** 去滑水 qùhuáshuǐ

wave [weɪv] I N [C] **1** (of hand) 挥动 huīdòng [下 xià] **2** (on water) 波浪 bōlàng [个 gè] II VI 挥手示意 huīshǒu shìyì III VT [+ hand] 挥 huī ▸ **to wave goodbye to sb, wave sb goodbye** 向某人挥手告别 xiàng mǒurén huīshǒu gàobié

wax [wæks] N [U] 蜡 là

way [weɪ] I N **1** [C] (route) 路线 lùxiàn [条 tiáo] **2** [s] (distance) 距离 jùlí **3** [C] (direction) 方向 fāngxiàng [个 gè] **4** [C] (manner) 方式 fāngshì [种 zhǒng] **5** [C] (method) 方法 fāngfǎ [个 gè] II WAYS NPL (habits) 习俗 xísú ▸ **"which way?" — "this way"** "往哪边?" "这边" "wǎng nǎbiān?" "zhèbiān" ▸ **on the way** 在路上 zài lùshàng ▸ **it's a long way away** 离这儿很远 lí zhèr hěnyuǎn ▸ **to lose one's way** 迷路 mílù ▸ **the way back** 回去的路 huíqù de lù ▸ **to give way** (break, collapse) 倒塌 dǎotā ▸ **the wrong way round** (Brit) 刚好相反 gānghǎo xiāngfǎn ▸ **in a way** 在某种程度上 zài mǒuzhǒng chéngdù shàng ▸ **by the way…** 顺便道… zài tán tiáo dì… tíyìxià… ▸ **"way in"** (Brit) "入口" "rùkǒu" ▸ **"way out"** (Brit) "出口" "chūkǒu" ▸ **way of life** 生活方式 shēnghuó fāngshì ▸ **do it this way** 这么做 zhème zuò

we [wiː] PL PRON 我们 wǒmen

weak [wiːk] ADJ **1** 虚弱的 xūruò

de 2 [+ *tea, coffee, substance*] 淡
的 dàn de

wealthy ['wɛlθɪ] ADJ 富有的
fùyǒu de

weapon ['wɛpən] N [c] 武器 wǔqì
[种 zhǒng]

wear [wɛəʳ] (*pt* wore, *pp* worn)
VT 穿着 chuānzhe; [+ *spectacles,
jewellery*] 戴着 dàizhe ▶ I can't
decide what to wear 我拿不定
主意该穿什么 wǒ nábúdìng zhǔyì
gāi chuān shénme
▶ wear out VI 耗尽 hàojìn

weather ['wɛðəʳ] N [U] 天气
tiānqì ▶ what's the weather
like? 天气怎么样? tiānqì
zěnmeyàng?

weather forecast N [c] 天气预
报 tiānqì yùbào [个 gè]

web [wɛb] N 互联
网 hùliánwǎng [个 gè] ▶ on the
Web 在互联网上 zài hùliánwǎng
shàng

web page N [c] 网页 wǎngyè
[个 gè]

website ['wɛbsaɪt] N [c] 网址
wǎngzhǐ [个 gè]

we'd [wiːd] = **we had, we would**

wedding ['wɛdɪŋ] N [c] 婚礼 hūnlǐ
[场 chǎng]

Wednesday ['wɛnzdɪ] N [c/U]
星期三 xīngqīsān [个 gè]; *see also*
Tuesday

week [wiːk] N [c] 星期 xīngqī
[个 gè] ▶ this/next/last week 本
周/下/上周 běn/xià/shàngzhōu
▶ once/twice a week 一周一
次/两次 yìzhōu yícì/liǎngcì

weekday ['wiːkdeɪ] N [c] 工作日

gōngzuòrì [个 gè] ▶ on weekdays
在工作日 zài gōngzuòrì

weekend [wiːkˈɛnd] N [c] 周末
zhōumò [个 gè] ▶ at the weekend
在周末 zài zhōumò ▶ this/next/
last weekend 这个周末/下周
末/上周末 zhège zhōumò/xiàzhōu
mò/shàngzhōu mò

weigh [weɪ] I VT 称…的重量
chēng…de zhòngliàng II VI
▶ she weighs 50kg 她的体重为
50公斤 tāde tǐzhòng wéi wǔshí
gōngjīn

weight [weɪt] I N [U] 重量
zhòngliàng II **weights** NPL (*in
gym*) 举重器械 jǔzhòng qìxiè ▶ to
lose weight 体重减轻 tǐzhòng
jiǎnqīng

welcome ['wɛlkəm] I N [c] 欢
迎 huānyíng II VT 欢迎 huānyíng
▶ welcome to Beijing! 欢迎到
北京来! huānyíng dào Běijīng
lái! ▶ "thank you" — "welcome!" "谢谢你。" "别客
气!" "xièxie nǐ" "bié kèqì!" ▶ to
give sb a warm welcome 热烈欢
迎某人 rèliè huānyíng mǒurén

well [wɛl] I N [c] 井 jǐng [口 kǒu]
II VI (*to a high standard*) 好 hǎo
2 (*completely*) 充分地 chōngfēn de
III ADJ (*healthy*) 身体好的 shēntǐ
hǎo de IV VI 唔 ng ▶ to do
well [*person*] 做得好 zuòde hǎo;
[*business*] 进展顺利 jìnzhǎn shùnlì
▶ well done! 棒极了! bàngjí le!
▶ as well (*in addition*) 也 yě ▶ I
don't feel well 我觉得不舒服 wǒ
juéde bù shūfu ▶ get well soon!
早日康复! zǎorì kāngfù! ▶ well,

as I was saying... 那么，像我刚才所说的··· nàme, xiàng wǒ gāngcái suǒshuō de···

we'll [wi:l] **= we will, we shall**

well-known ['wel'nəʊn] ADJ [+ person] 有名的 yǒumíng de; [+ fact, brand] 众所周知的 zhòng suǒ zhōu zhī de

well-off ['wel'ɔf] ADJ 富裕的 fùyù de

Welsh [welʃ] I ADJ 威尔士的 Wēi'ěrshì de II N [U] (language) 威尔士语 Wēi'ěrshìyǔ III NPL ▸ **the Welsh** 威尔士人 Wēi'ěrshìrén

went [went] PT of **go**

were [wə:ʳ] PT of **be**

we're [wɪəʳ] **= we are**

weren't [wə:nt] **= were not**

west [west] I N 1 [U/s] (direction) 西方 xīfāng 2 ▸ **the West** (Pol) 西方国家 xīfāng guójiā II ADJ 西部的 xībù de III ADV 向西 xiàng xī ▸ **west of** ···以西 ···yǐxī

western ['westən] I ADJ (Geo) 西部的 xībù de II N [C] 西部影片 xībù yǐngpiàn [部 bù]

West Indian I ADJ 西印度群岛的 Xīyìndù Qúndǎo de II N [C] 西印度群岛人 Xīyìndù Qúndǎorén [个 gè]

West Indies [-'ɪndɪz] NPL ▸ **the West Indies** 西印度群岛 Xīyìndù Qúndǎo

wet [wet] ADJ 1 [+ person, clothes] 湿的shī de; [+ paint, cement, glue] 未干的 wèigān de 2 (rainy) [+ weather, day] 多雨的 duōyǔ de ▸ **to get wet** 弄湿 nòngshī

we've [wi:v] **= we have**

whale [weɪl] N [C] 鲸 jīng [头 tóu]

⬤ KEYWORD

what [wɔt] I PRON 1 什么 shénme
▸ **what is happening?** 发生了什么事？ fāshēng le shénme shì？
▸ **what is it?** 那是什么？ nàshì shénme？ ▸ **what are you doing?** 你在干什么？ nǐ zài gànshénme？
▸ **what did you say?** 你说什么？ nǐshuō shénme？
2 (in indirect questions/speech subject, object) 什么 shénme ▸ **do you know what's happening?** 你知道发生了什么事吗？ nǐ zhīdào fāshēng le shénme shì ma？
3 (relative) 所···的 suǒ···de ▸ I **saw what was on the table** 我看见了桌上的东西 wǒ kànjiàn le zhuōshàng de dōngxi
II ADJ 1 什么 shénme ▸ **what time is it?** 几点了？ jǐdiǎn le？
▸ **what size is this shirt?** 这件衬衫是几码的？ zhèjiàn chènshān shì jǐmǎ de？
2 (in exclamations) 多么 duōme ▸ **what a mess!** 真是一团糟！ zhēnshì yītuán zāo！ ▸ **what a lovely day!** 多么好的天气呀！ duōme hǎode tiānqì a！
III INT 什么 shénme ▸ **what, no coffee!** 什么，没咖啡了！ shénme, méi kāfēi le！

whatever [wɔt'evəʳ] I ADV (whatsoever) 任何 rènhé II PRON ▸ **do whatever is necessary/you**

want 做任何必要的/你想要做的事情 zuò rènhé bìyào de/nǐ xiǎngzuò de shìqíng

wheat [wiːt] N [U] 小麦 xiǎomài

wheel [wiːl] N [c] **1** 轮 lún [个 gè] **2** (also: **steering wheel**) 方向盘 fāngxiàngpán [个 gè]

wheelchair ['wiːltʃeəʳ] N [c] 轮椅 lúnyǐ [部 bù]

KEYWORD

when [wɛn] I ADV (interrogative) 什么时候 shénme shíhou ▶ **when did it happen?** 什么时候发生的? shénme shíhou fāshēng de?
II PRON (relative) **the day when** 当…的那一天 dāng…de nà yī tiān
III CONJ (in time clauses) 当…时 dāng…shí ▶ **be careful when you cross the road** 过马路时要当心 guò mǎlù shí yào dāngxīn ▶ **she was reading when I came in** 当我进来时她正在阅读 dāng wǒ jìnlái shí tā zhèngzài yuèdú ▶ **I know when it happened** 我知道什么时候发生的 wǒ zhīdào shénme shíhou fāshēng de

where [wɛəʳ] I ADV (in or to what place) 在哪里 zài nǎli II CONJ (the place in which) 哪里 nǎli ▶ **where are you from?** 你是哪里人? nǐ shì nǎli rén?

whether ['wɛðəʳ] CONJ 是否 shìfǒu ▶ **I don't know whether to accept or not** 我不知道是接受还是不接受 wǒ bù zhīdào shì jiēshòu

háishì bù jiēshòu

KEYWORD

which [wɪtʃ] I ADJ **1** (interrogative singular) 哪个 nǎge; (plural) 哪些 nǎxiē ▶ **which picture do you want?** 你要哪幅画? nǐ yào nǎfú huà? ▶ **which one/ones?** 哪个/些? nǎge/xiē?
2 (in indirect questions/speech singular) 哪个 nǎge; (plural) 哪些 nǎxiē ▶ **he asked which book I wanted** 他问我要哪本书 tā wènwǒ yào nǎběn shū
II PRON **1** (interrogative subject, object) 哪个 nǎge ▶ **which of these is yours?** 这些中的哪个是你的? zhèxiē zhōng de nǎge shì nǐde?
2 (in indirect questions/speech subject, object) 哪个 nǎge ▶ **ask him which of the models is the best** 问他哪种型号是最好的 wèn tā nǎzhǒng xínghào shì zuìhǎo de
3 (relative subject, object) …的那个… …de nǎge… ▶ **the shot which you heard/which killed him** 你听到的那一枪/杀死他的那一枪 nǐ tīngdào de nàyīqiāng/shāsǐ tā de nàyīqiāng

while [waɪl] I N [s] 一会儿 yíhuìr
II CONJ **1** (during the time that) 在…时 zài…shí **2** (although) 虽然 suīrán ▶ **While I'm very fond of him, I don't actually want to marry him.** 虽然我很喜欢他, 但我真的不想嫁给他。 suīrán wǒ hěn xǐhuān tā, dàn

wǒ zhēnde bùxiǎng jiàgěi tā. ▸**for a while** 有一会儿 yǒu yīhuǐr

whisky, (US) **whiskey** ['wɪskɪ] N [c/u] 威士忌酒 wēishìjì jiǔ [瓶 píng]

whisper ['wɪspə'] vɪ 低语 dīyǔ

whistle ['wɪsl] I vɪ 吹口哨 chuī kǒushào II N [c] 1 (device) 哨子 shàozi [个 gè] 2 (sound) 口哨声 kǒushàoshēng [声 shēng]

white [waɪt] I ADJ 1 雪白的 xuěbái de; [+ wine] 白的 bái de 2 [+ coffee] 加奶的 jiā nǎi de 3 [+ person] 白种人的 báizhǒngrén de II N [u] (colour) 白色 báisè

KEYWORD

who [hu:] PRON 1 谁 shéi ▸**who is it?** 谁呀? shéi ya? ▸**who did you discuss it with?** 你和谁讨论了? nǐ hé shuí tǎolùn le? 2 (in indirect questions/speech subject, object, after preposition) 谁 shéi ▸**I told her who I was** 我告诉了她我是谁 wǒ gàosù le tā wǒ shì shuí ▸**I don't know who he gave it to** 我不知道他把它给了谁 wǒ bù zhīdào tā bǎ tā gěile shéi 3 (relative subject, object) …的那个 … de nàgè … ▸**the girl who came in** 进来的那个女孩 jìnlái de nàgè nǚhái ▸**the man who we met in Sydney** 我们在悉尼遇到的那个男子 wǒmen zài Xīní yùdào de nàgè nánzi

whole [həul] I ADJ 整个的 zhěnggè de II N 1 [c] (entirety) 整

体 zhěngtǐ [个 gè] ▸**the whole of sth** 某物的全部 mǒuwù de quánbù [个 gè] ▸**the whole (of the) time** 所有的时间 suǒyǒu de shíjiān ▸**on the whole** 大体上 dàtǐ shàng

whom [hu:m] (frm) PRON 1 (interrogative) 谁 shéi 2 (relative) 所…的那个… suǒ…de nàgè… ▸**the man whom I saw/to whom I spoke** 我见到的/我跟他说过话的那个男的 wǒ jiàndào de/wǒ gēn tā shuō guò huà de nàgè nánde

whose [hu:z] I ADJ 1 (interrogative) 谁的 shéi de 2 (relative) …的 …de … II PRON 谁的 shéi de ▸**whose is this?** 这是谁的? zhè shì shéi de? ▸**whose book is this/coats are these?** 这本书是谁的/这些外套是谁的? zhèběnshū shì shuíde/zhèxiē wàitào shì shuíde? ▸**the woman whose car was stolen** 汽车给偷走的那个女的 qìchē gěi tōuzǒu de nàgè nǚde

KEYWORD

why [waɪ] I ADV 为什么 wèishénme ▸**why is he always late?** 为什么他总是迟到? wèishénme tā zǒngshì chídào? ▸**why not?** 为什么不呢? wèishénme bù ne? ▸**I don't know why** 我不知道为什么 wǒ bù zhīdào wèishénme II CONJ 为什么 wèishénme ▸**I wonder why he said that** 我想知道他为什么说了这么 wǒxiǎng zhīdào tā wèishénme nàme shuō

▶**the reason why he did it** 他那么做的原因 tā nàme zuò de yuányīn

wicked ['wɪkɪd] ADJ (evil) [+ person] 邪恶的 xié'è de; [+ act, crime] 罪恶的 zuì'è de

wide [waɪd] I ADJ 1 宽的 kuān de 2 [+ range, variety, publicity, choice] 广泛的 guǎngfàn de II ADV ▶**to open sth wide** 张大某物 zhāngdà mǒuwù

widow ['wɪdəu] N [c] 寡妇 guǎfù [个 gè]

widower ['wɪdəuə'] N [c] 鳏夫 guānfū [个 gè]

width [wɪdθ] N [c/u] 宽度 kuāndù [个 gè]

wife [waɪf] (pl **wives**) N [c] 妻子 qīzi [个 gè]

wild [waɪld] ADJ 1 野生的 yěshēng de 2 [+ person, behaviour] 狂野的 kuángyě de

wildlife ['waɪldlaɪf] N [u] 野生动物 yěshēng dòngwù

KEYWORD

will [wɪl] I AUX VB 1 ▶**I will call you tonight** 我今晚会给你打电话 wǒ jīnwǎn huì gěi nǐ dǎ diànhuà ▶**what will you do next?** 下面你要做什么? xiàmiàn nǐ yào zuò shénme?
2 (in conjectures, predictions) 该是 gāishì ▶**he'll be there by now** 他现在该到了 tā xiànzài gāidào le 3 (in commands, requests, offers) ▶**will you be quiet?** 你安静点?

nǐ ānjìng diǎn?
II N 1 (volition) 意志 yìzhì ▶**against his will** 违背他的意愿 wéibèi tāde yìyuàn
2 (testament) 遗嘱 yízhǔ [个 gè] ▶**to make a will** 立遗嘱 lì yízhǔ

willing ['wɪlɪŋ] ADJ ▶**to be willing to do sth** 愿意做某事 yuànyì zuò mǒushì

win [wɪn] (pt, pp **won**) I N [c] 胜利 shènglì [个 gè] II VT 1 在…中获胜 zài...zhōng huòshèng 2 [+ prize, medal] 赢得 yíngdé III VI 获胜 huòshèng

wind [wɪnd] N [c/u] 风 fēng [阵 zhèn]

window ['wɪndəu] N [c] 1 窗户 chuānghu [扇 shàn]; (in shop) 橱窗 chúchuāng [个 gè]; (in car, train) 窗 chuāng [个 gè] 2 (Comput) 视窗 shìchuāng [个 gè]

windscreen ['wɪndskri:n] (Brit) N [c] 挡风玻璃 dǎngfēng bōli [块 kuài]

windshield ['wɪndʃi:ld] (US) N [c] 挡风玻璃 dǎngfēng bōli [块 kuài]

windsurfing ['wɪndsə:fɪŋ] N [u] 帆板运动 fānbǎn yùndòng

windy ['wɪndɪ] ADJ [+ weather, day] 有风的 yǒufēng de ▶**it's windy** 今天风很大 jīntiān fēng hěndà

wine [waɪn] N [c/u] 葡萄酒 pútáojiǔ [瓶 píng]

wing [wɪŋ] N [c] 1 翅膀 chìbǎng [个 gè]; [of aeroplane] 机翼 jīyì [个 gè] 2 [of building] 侧楼 cèlóu [座 zuò]

wink [wɪŋk] VI (person) 眨眼

zhǎyǎn ▶**to give sb a wink, wink at sb** 向某人眨了眨眼 xiàng mǒurén zhǎlezhǎ yǎn

winner ['wɪnə[r]] N [c] 获胜者 huòshèngzhě [位 wèi]

winter ['wɪntə[r]] I N [c/u] 冬季 dōngjì [个 gè] II VI 过冬 guòdōng ▶**in (the) winter** 在冬季 zài dōngjì

wipe [waɪp] VT (dry, clean) 擦 cā ▶**to wipe one's nose** 擦鼻子 cā bízi
▶**wipe up** VT 把…擦干净 bǎ…cā gānjìng

wire ['waɪə[r]] N [c] (Elec: uninsulated) 电线 diànxiàn [根 gēn]; (insulated) 电缆 diànlǎn [条 tiáo]

wise [waɪz] ADJ 睿智的 ruìzhì de

wish [wɪʃ] I N [c] 愿望 yuànwàng [个 gè] II VT 但愿 dànyuàn ▶**best wishes** 良好的祝愿 liánghǎo de zhùyuàn ▶**with best wishes** 祝好 zhùhǎo ▶**give her my best wishes** 代我向她致意 dài wǒ xiàng tā zhìyì ▶**to wish to do sth** 想要做某事 xiǎngyào zuò mǒushì

◯ **KEYWORD**

with [wɪð, wɪθ] PREP 1 和…在一起 hé…zài yìqǐ ▶**with him** 我和他在一起 wǒ hé tā zài yìqǐ ▶**I'll be with you in a minute** 请稍等 qǐng shāoděng ▶**we stayed with friends** 我们和朋友们呆在一起 wǒmen hé péngyǒumen dàizài yìqǐ 2 (indicating feature, possession)

有 yǒu ▶**the man with the grey hat/blue eyes** 戴着灰帽子/有蓝眼睛的男人 dàizhe huī màozi/yǒu lán yǎnjīng de nánrén 3 (indicating means, substance) 用 yòng ▶**to walk with a stick** 拄着拐杖走 zhǔzhe guǎizhàng zǒu ▶**to fill sth with water** 在某物里装满水 zài mǒuwù lǐ zhuāngmǎn shuǐ 4 (indicating cause) ▶**red with anger** 气得涨红了脸 qìde zhànghóngle liǎn

without [wɪð'aut] PREP 没有 méiyǒu ▶**without a coat** 未穿外套 wèichuān wàitào ▶**without speaking** 不曾说话 bùcéng shuōhuà

witness ['wɪtnɪs] N [c] (gen, also in court) 目击者 mùjīzhě [位 wèi]

witty ['wɪtɪ] ADJ 诙谐的 huīxié de

wives [waɪvz] NPL of **wife**

woke [wəuk] PT of **wake**

woken ['wəukn] PP of **wake**

wolf [wulf] (pl **wolves** [wulvz]) N [c] 狼 láng [条 tiáo]

woman ['wumən] (pl **women** ['wimɪn]) N [c] 妇女 fùnǚ [位 wèi]

won [wʌn] PT, PP of **win**

wonder ['wʌndə[r]] I VT ▶**to wonder whether/why** etc 想知道是否/为什么{等} xiǎng zhīdào shìfǒu/wèishénme {děng} II VI 感到奇怪 gǎndào qíguài

wonderful ['wʌndəful] ADJ 绝妙的 juémiào de

won't [wəunt] = **will not**

wood [wud] N 1 [u] 木材 mùcái 2 [c] (forest) 树林 shùlín [棵 kē]

wool [wul] N [U] 羊毛 yángmáo

word [wəːd] N 1 [c] 词 cí [个
gè] 2 [S] (promise) 诺言 nuòyán
▸what's the word for "pen" in
French? "钢笔"这个词在法语
里怎么说? "gāngbǐ"zhège cí zài
Fǎyǔ lǐ zěnme shuō? ▸in other
words 换句话说 huàn jù huà
shuō

word processing [-'prəʊsesɪŋ] N
[U] 文字处理 wénzì chǔlǐ

word processor [-'prəʊsesəʳ] N
[c] (machine) 文字处理器 wénzì
chǔlǐqì [个 gè]

wore [wɔːʳ] PT of **wear**

work [wəːk] I N 1 [U] (tasks, duties)
事情 shìqíng 2 [U] (job) 工作
gōngzuò II VI 1 (have job, do tasks)
工作 gōngzuò 2 (function) 运
行 yùnxíng 3 (be successful) [idea,
method] 起作用 qǐ zuòyòng ▸to
go to work 去上班 qù shàngbān
▸to be out of work 失业 shīyè
▸to work hard 努力工作 nǔlì
gōngzuò

▸ **work out** I VI (Sport) 锻炼
duànliàn II VT [+ answer, solution]
努力找出 nǔlì zhǎochū; [+ plan,
details] 制订出 zhìdìng chū

worker [wəːkəʳ] N [c] 工人
gōngrén [位 wèi] ▸a hard/good
worker 工作努力/良好的人
gōngzuò nǔlì/liánghǎo de rén

work experience N [U] 工作经历
gōngzuò jīnglì

workstation [wəːksteɪʃən] N
1 (desk) 工作台 gōngzuòtái [个 gè]
2 (computer) 工作站 gōngzuòzhàn
[个 gè]

world [wəːld] I N ▸the world
世界 shìjiè II CPD [+ champion,
record, power, authority] 世界
shìjiè; [+ tour] 环球 huánqiú
▸all over the world 全世界
quán shìjiè

World-Wide Web [wəːld'waɪd-]
N ▸the World-Wide Web 万维网
Wànwéiwǎng

worn [wɔːn] PP of **wear**

worried [wʌrɪd] ADJ 闷闷不乐的
mènmèn bù lè de ▸to be worried
about sth/sb 担心某事/某人
dānxīn mǒushì/mǒurén

worry [wʌrɪ] I N 1 [U] (feeling of
anxiety) 忧虑 yōulǜ 2 [c] (cause of
anxiety) 担心 dānxīn [件 jiàn]
II VT 使担心 shǐ dānxīn III VI 担
心 dānxīn

worse [wəːs] I ADJ 更坏的
gènghuài de II ADV (comparative
of badly) 更糟地 gèngzāo de ▸to
get worse 逐渐恶化 zhújiàn
èhuà

worst [wəːst] I ADJ 最坏的 zuì
huài de II ADV (superlative of badly)
最糟地 zuì zāo de III N [s/U] 最
坏的事 zuì huài de shì ▸at worst
在最坏的情况下 zài zuìhuài de
qíngkuàng xià

worth [wəːθ] I N [U] 价值 jiàzhí
II ADJ ▸to be worth £50 值
50英镑 zhí wǔshí yīngbàng ▸it's
worth it 这是值得的 zhèshì
zhíde de ▸400 dollars' worth
of damage 价值400美元的损失
jiàzhí sìbǎi měiyuán de sǔnshī
▸it would be (well) worth
doing... (很)值得 (hěn)

zhídé zuò…

KEYWORD

would [wʊd] AUX VB1 ▶ **I would love to go to Italy** 我很愿意去意大利 wǒ hěn yuànyì qù Yìdàlì ▶ **I'm sure he wouldn't do that** 我确定他不会那么做的 wǒ quèdìng tā búhuì nàme zuòde

2 (in offers, invitations, requests) ▶ **would you like a biscuit?** 你要块饼干吗？ nǐ yào lái kuài bǐnggān ma? ▶ **would you ask him to come in?** 你要叫他进来吗？ nǐ yào jiàotā jìnlai ma?

3 (be willing to) ▶ **she wouldn't help me** 她不愿意帮助我 tā bú yuànyì bāngzhù wǒ

4 (in indirect speech) ▶ **he said he would be at home later** 他说他晚上会儿在家的 tā shuō tā wǎndiǎnr huì zàijiā de

wouldn't ['wʊdnt] = **would not**

wrap [ræp] VT 1 (cover) 包裹 bāoguǒ ▶ **wrap up** VT (pack) 包起来 bāo qǐlái

wrapping paper ['ræpɪŋ-] N [U] (gift wrap) 包装纸 bāozhuāngzhǐ

wreck [rek] I N [c] 1 (wreckage: of vehicle, ship) 残骸 cánhái 2 (US: accident) 事故 shìgù [次 cì] II VT [+ car, building] 摧毁 cuīhuǐ

wrestling ['reslɪŋ] N [U] 摔跤 shuāijiāo

wrinkled ['rɪŋkld] ADJ 布满皱纹的 bùmǎn zhòuwén de

wrist [rɪst] N [c] 手腕 shǒuwàn

[个 gè]

write [raɪt] (pt **wrote**, pp **written**) I VT 1 [+ address, number] 写下 xiěxià 2 [+ letter, note] 写 xiě 3 [+ novel, music] 创作 chuàngzuò 4 [+ cheque, receipt, prescription] 开 kāi II VI 写字 xiězì ▶ **to write to sb** 写信给某人 xiěxìn gěi mǒurén ▶ **write down** VT 记下 jìxià

writer ['raɪtəʳ] N [c] 作家 zuòjiā [位 wèi]

writing ['raɪtɪŋ] N [U] 1 (sth written) 笔迹 bǐjì 2 (handwriting) 文字 wénzì ▶ **in writing** 以书面形式 yǐ shūmiàn xíngshì

written ['rɪtn] PP of **write**

wrong [rɒŋ] I ADJ 1 [+ person, equipment, kind, job] 不合适的 bù héshì de 2 [+ answer, information, report] 错误的 cuòwù de 3 (morally bad) 不道德的 bù dàodé de II ADV (incorrectly) 错误地 cuòwù de ▶ **to be wrong** (answer) 是错的 shì cuòde; (person) 弄错了 nòngcuò le ▶ **what's wrong?** 怎么了？ zěnme le? ▶ **what's wrong with you?** 你怎么了？ nǐ zěnme le? ▶ **to go wrong** [plan] 失败 shībài; [machine] 发生故障 fāshēng gùzhàng

wrote [rəʊt] PT of **write**

WWW (Comput) N ABBR (= World-Wide Web) 万维网 Wànwéiwǎng

X y

Xmas [ˈɛksməs] N ABBR (= **Christmas**) 圣诞节 Shèngdànjié

X-ray [ˈɛksreɪ] I N [c] (*photo*) X光照片 X guāng zhàopiàn [张 zhāng] II VT 用X光检查 yòng X guāng jiǎnchá ▸ **to have an X-ray** 做一次X光检查 zuò yīcì X guāng jiǎnchá

yacht [jɒt] N [c] 1 (*sailing boat*) 帆船 fānchuán [艘 sōu] 2 (*luxury craft*) 游艇 yóutǐng [艘 sōu]

yard [jɑːd] N [c] (*US: garden*) 庭院 tíngyuàn [座 zuò]

yawn [jɔːn] I VI 打呵欠 dǎ hēqiàn II N [c] 呵欠 hēqiàn [个 gè]

year [jɪəʳ] N [c] 1 年 nián 2 (*Scol, Univ*) 学年 xuénián [个 gè]
▸ **every year** 每年 měinián ▸ **this year** 今年 jīnnián ▸ **last year** 去年 qùnián ▸ **a** *or* **per year** 每年 měinián ▸ **we lived there for years** 我们住在那儿有好多年了 wǒmen zhùzài nàr yǒu hǎoduō nián le

yellow [ˈjɛləu] I ADJ 黄色的 huángsè de II N [c/u] 黄色 huángsè [种 zhǒng]

yes [jes] I ADV 是的 shìde II N [C] (answer) 是 shì

yesterday ['jestədɪ] I ADV 昨天 zuótiān II N [U] 昨天 zuótiān
▶the day before yesterday 前天 qiántiān

yet [jet] I ADV (up to now: with negative) 还 hái; (in questions) 已经 yǐjīng II CONJ 然而 rán'ér
▶they haven't finished yet 他们还没完工。 tāmen hái méi wángōng ▶yet again 又一次 yòu yīcì

yog(h)urt ['jəugət] N [C/U] 酸奶 suānnǎi [瓶 píng]

you [ju:] PRON 1 (singular) 你 nǐ; (plural) 你们 nǐmen 2 任何人 rènhérén ▶you never know 谁知道 shuí zhīdào

young [jʌŋ] ADJ 幼小的 yòuxiǎo de ▶my younger brother/sister 我的弟弟/妹妹 wǒde dìdi/mèimei

your [jɔːʳ] ADJ (of one person) 你的 nǐ de; (of more than one person) 你们的 nǐmen de

yours [jɔːz] PRON (of one person) 你的 nǐ de; (of more than one person) 你们的 nǐmen de ▶is this yours? 这是你/你们的吗? zhèshì nǐ/nǐmen de ma? ▶yours sincerely/faithfully 你真挚的/忠实的 nǐ zhēnzhì de/zhōngshí de

yourself [jɔːˈself] PRON 1 你自己 nǐzìjǐ 2 (you) 你 nǐ ▶by yourself (unaided) 独立地 dúlì de; (alone) 独自地 dúzì de

yourselves [jɔːˈselvz] PL PRON 1 你们自己 nǐmen zìjǐ 2 (you) 你们 nǐmen ▶by yourselves (unaided)

独力地 dúlì de; (alone) 独自地 dúzì de

youth club N [C] 青年俱乐部 qīngnián jùlèbù [个 gè]

youth hostel N [C] 青年招待所 qīngnián zhāodàisuǒ [个 gè]

Z

zebra crossing ['zi:brə-] (Brit) N
[c] 斑马线 bānmǎxiàn [条 tiáo]

zero ['zɪərəu] (pl **zero** or **zeroes**)
N 1 [U/c] (number) 零 líng [个 gè]
2 [U] (nothing) 没有 méiyǒu ▶ **5
degrees below zero** 零下5度
língxià wǔdù

zip [zɪp] N [c] (Brit: fastener) 拉链
lāliàn [条 tiáo]

zip code (US) N [c] 邮政编码
yóuzhèng biānmǎ [个 gè]

zipper ['zɪpə'] (US) N [c] 拉链
lāliàn [条 tiáo]

zone [zəun] N [c] (area) 地带 dìdài
[个 gè]

zoo [zu:] (pl **zoos**) N [c] 动物园
dòngwùyuán [个 gè]

zucchini [zu:'ki:nɪ] (pl **zucchini** or
zucchinis) (US) N [c/U] 绿皮密生

Phrasefinder

常用句

Chángyòng Jù

TOPICS │ 话题 HUÀTÍ

MEETING PEOPLE | 与人会面
YǓ RÉN HUÌMIÀN

Hello!	你好！Nǐ hǎo!
Good evening!	晚上好！Wǎnshang hǎo!
Good night!	晚安！Wǎn'ān!
Goodbye!	再见！Zàijiàn!
What's your name?	你叫什么？
	Nǐ jiào shénme?
My name is ...	我叫 ...。Wǒ jiào ... .
This is my wife.	这是我妻子。
	Zhè shì wǒ qīzi.
This is my husband.	这是我丈夫。
	Zhè shì wǒ zhàngfu.
This is my partner.	这是我爱人。
	Zhè shì wǒ àiren.
Pleased to meet you.	很高兴认识你。
	Hěn gāoxìng rènshi nǐ.
Where are you from?	你是哪里人？
	Nǐ shì nǎli rén?
I come from ...	我是 ... 人。
	Wǒ shì ... rén.
How are you?	你好吗？Nǐ hǎo ma?
Fine, thanks.	我很好，谢谢。
	Wǒ hěn hǎo, xièxie.
And you?	你呢？Nǐ ne?
Do you speak English?	你说英语吗？
	Nǐ shuō Yīngyǔ ma?
Sorry, I don't understand.	对不起，我不明白。
	Duìbuqǐ, wǒ bù míngbai.
Thanks very much!	非常感谢！
	Fēicháng gǎnxiè!

Asking the Way	问路 Wènlù
Where is the nearest post office?	最近的邮局在哪儿？ Zuìjìn de yóujú zài nǎr?
How do I get there?	我怎么去那儿？ Wǒ zěnme qù nàr?
How do I get to the station?	我怎么去车站？ Wǒ zěnme qù chēzhàn?
Is it far?	远吗？Yuǎn ma?
How far is it?	有多远？Yǒu duō yuǎn?
Is this the right way to the station?	这条路是去车站的吗？ Zhè tiáo lù shì qù chēzhàn de ma?
I'm lost.	我迷路了。Wǒ mílù le.
Can you show me on the map?	你可以在地图上指给我看吗？ Nǐ kěyǐ zài dìtú shàng zhǐ gěi wǒ kàn ma?
You have to turn round.	你得调头往回走。 Nǐ děi diàotóu wǎng huí zǒu.
Go straight on.	一直往前走。 Yīzhí wǎng qián zǒu.
Turn left.	左转。Zuǒzhuǎn.
Turn right.	右转。Yòuzhuǎn.
Take the second street on the left.	左边第二个路口左转。 Zuǒbiān dì'èr gè lùkǒu zuǒzhuǎn.

Car Hire 租车 Zūchē

I want to hire a car.
我要租辆车。
Wǒ yào zū liàng chē.

An automatic, please.
请给辆自动变速车。
Qǐng gěi liàng zìdòng
biànsù chē.

How much is it for one day?
一天多少钱？
Yī tiān duōshǎo qián?

Is there a kilometre charge?
按公里数计费吗？
Àn gōnglǐ shù jìfèi ma?

What is included in the price?
价格里都包括什么？
Jiàgé lǐ dōu bāokuò shénme?

I'd like a child seat for a 2-year-old child.
我要一个两岁小孩的座椅。
Wǒ yào yīgè liǎng suì
xiǎohái de zuòyǐ.

What do I do if I have an accident?
如果出了事故我该怎么办？
Rúguǒ chū le shìgù wǒ gāi
zěnmebàn?

What do I do if I break down?
如果车出了故障我该怎么办？
Rúguǒ chē chū le gùzhàng
wǒ gāi zěnmebàn?

Breakdowns 出故障 Chū Gùzhàng

My car has broken down.
我的车坏了。
Wǒ de chē huài le.

Call the breakdown service, please.
请给紧急故障修理服务打电话。
Qǐng gěi jǐnjí gùzhàng xiūlǐ
fúwù dǎ diànhuà.

I'm on my own.	我一个人。Wǒ yīgè rén.
Where is the next garage?	下一个修车铺在哪儿？ Xià yīgè xiūchēpù zài nǎr?
The exhaust is broken.	排气坏了。Páiqì huài le.
The brakes are not working.	刹车坏了。 Shāchē huài le.
The battery is flat.	电池没电了。 Diànchí méi diàn le.
The car won't start.	车不启动。Chē bù qǐdòng.
The engine is overheating.	引擎过热。 Yǐnqíng guò rè.
The oil warning light won't go off.	机油警告灯灭不了。 Jīyóu jǐnggào dēng miè bù liǎo.
The petrol tank is leaking.	油箱漏油。 Yóuxiāng lòu yóu.
I have a flat tyre.	车胎瘪了。Chētāi biě le.
Can you repair it?	你能修吗？Nǐ néng xiū ma?
When will the car be ready?	什么时候车能修好？ Shénme shíhou chē néng xiū hǎo?

Parking 停车 Tíngchē

Can I park here?	我能在这儿停车吗？ Wǒ néng zài zhèr tíngchē ma?
How long can I park here?	我能在这儿停多久？ Wǒ néng zài zhèr tíng duō jiǔ?
Do I need to buy a car-parking ticket?	我需要买张停车票吗？ Wǒ xūyào mǎi zhāng tíngchē piào ma?

Where is the ticket machine?	停车售票机在哪儿？ Tíngchē shòupiào jī zài nǎr?
The ticket machine isn't working.	停车售票机坏了。 Tíngchē shòupiào jī huài le.
Where do I pay the fine?	我在哪儿付罚款？ Wǒ zài nǎr fù fákuǎn?

Petrol Station 加油站 Jiāyóuzhàn

Where is the nearest petrol station?	最近的加油站在哪儿？ Zuìjìn de jiāyóuzhàn zài nǎr?
Fill it up, please.	请加满。 Qǐng jiā mǎn.
30 yuan worth of diesel, please.	请加30元的柴油。 Qǐng jiā sānshí yuán de cháiyóu.
30 yuan worth of premium unleaded, please.	请加30元的优质无铅汽油。 Qǐng jiā sānshí yuán de yōuzhì wúqiān qìyóu.
Pump number 4 please.	请加4号泵。 Qǐng jiā sì hào bèng.
Please check the tyre pressure.	请检查轮胎气压。 Qǐng jiǎnchá lúntāi qìyā.
Please check the oil.	请检查油。 Qǐng jiǎnchá yóu.

Accidents 事故 Shìgù

Please call the police.	请打电话叫警察。 Qǐng dǎ diànhuà jiào jǐngchá.
Please call an ambulance.	请打电话叫救护车。 Qǐng dǎ diànhuà jiào jiùhùchē.

Here are my insurance details.	这是我的保险详细资料。 Zhè shì wǒ de bǎoxiǎn xiángxì zīliào.
Give me your insurance details, please.	请给我你的保险详细资料。 Qǐng gěi wǒ nǐ de bǎoxiǎn xiángxìzīliào.
Can you be a witness for me?	你可以做我的证人吗? Nǐ kěyǐ zuò wǒ de zhèngrén ma?
You were driving too fast.	你开得太快了。 Nǐ kāi de tài kuài le.
It wasn't your right of way.	不是你的先行权。 Búshì nǐ de xiānxíngquán.
Travelling by Car	驾车出行 Jiàchē Chūxíng
What's the best route to the airport?	去机场的最佳路线是什么? Qù jīchǎng de zuìjiā lùxiàn shì shénme?
Do you have a road map of this area?	你有这个地区的路线图吗? Nǐ yǒu zhègè dìqū de lùxiàntú ma?
Cycling	骑自行车 Qí Zìxíngchē
Is there a cycle map of this area?	有这个地区的骑车路线图吗? Yǒu zhègè dìqū de qíchē lùxiàntú ma?
My bike has been stolen.	我的自行车被偷了。 Wǒ de zìxíngchē bèi tōu le.

Where is the nearest bike repair shop?	最近的自行车修理店在哪儿？
	Zuìjìn de zìxíngchē xiūlǐdiàn zài nǎr?
The brakes aren't working.	车闸坏了。
	Chēzhá huài le.
The gears aren't working.	变速器坏了。
	Biànsùqì huài le.
The chain is broken.	链子断了。 Liànzi duàn le.
I've got a flat tyre.	我的车胎瘪了。Wǒ de chētāi biě le.
I need a puncture repair kit.	我需要个补胎工具包。
	Wǒ xūyào gè bǔtāi gōngjùbāo.

Train 火车 Huǒchē

How much is a single/return?	一张单程票/往返票多少钱？Yīzhāng dānchéng piào/wǎngfǎn piào duōshǎo qián?
Two returns to ..., please.	请要两张去 ... 的往返票。
	Qǐng yào liǎngzhāng qù ... de wǎngfǎn piào.
I would like to travel first class.	我要头等舱。
	Wǒ yào tóuděng cāng.
Is there a reduction for students?	对学生打折吗？
	Duì xuésheng dǎzhé ma?
Is there a reduction with this pass?	用这个证能打折吗？
	Yòng zhègè zhèng néng dǎzhé ma?

I'd like to reserve a seat on the train to ... please.
我要订一个去...的火车座位。
Wǒ yào dìng yīgè qù ... de huǒchē de zuòwèi.

Non smoking, please.
请订无烟车厢。
Qǐng dìng wúyān chēxiāng.

Smoking, please.
请订吸烟车厢。
Qǐng dìng xīyān chēxiāng.

Facing the front, please.
请订顺向座位。
Qǐng dìng shùnxiàng zuòwèi.

I want to book a sleeper to ...
我要订一张去...的卧铺。
Wǒ yào dìng yī zhāng qù ... de wòpù.

When is the next train to ...?
下一辆去...的火车是什么时候?
Xià yīliàng qù ... de huǒchē shì shénme shíhou?

Is there a supplement to pay?
要付附加费吗?
Yào fù fùjiāfèi ma?

Do I need to change?
我需要换车吗?
Wǒ xūyào huànchē ma?

Where do I change?
我在哪儿换车?
Wǒ zài nǎr huànchē?

Which platform does the train for ... leave from?
去...的火车从哪个站台开车?
Qù ... de huǒchē cóng nǎgè zhàntái kāichē?

Is this the train for ...?
这是去...的火车吗?
Zhè shì qù ... de huǒchē ma?

Excuse me, that's my seat.	对不起，那是我的座位。 Duìbuqǐ, nà shì wǒ de zuòwèi.
I have a reservation.	我有预订。 Wǒ yǒu yùdìng.
Is this seat free?	没有人坐这个位子吗？ Méiyǒu rén zuò zhègè wèizi ma?
Please let me know when we get to ...	当我们到 ... 的时候请叫我。 Dāng wǒmen dào ... de shíhou qǐng jiào wǒ.
Where is the buffet car?	餐车在哪儿？ Cānchē zài nǎr?
Where is coach number 43?	43号车厢在哪儿？ Sìshí sān hào chēxiāng zài nǎr?

Ferry   渡轮 Dùlún

Is there a ferry to ...?	有去 ... 的渡轮吗？ Yǒu qù ... de dùlún ma?
When is the next ferry to ...?	下一班去 ... 的渡轮是什么时候？ Xià yībān qù ... de dùlún shì shénme shíhou?
When is the last ferry to ...?	最后一班去 ... 的渡轮是什么时候？ Zuìhòu yībān qù ... de dùlún shì shénme shíhou?

How much is a single?
一张单程票多少钱？
Yīzhāng dānchéng piào duōshǎo qián?

How much is a return?
一张往返票多少钱？
Yīzhāng wǎngfǎn piào duōshǎo qián?

How much is it for a car with 2 people?
一辆车加两个人多少钱？
Yīliàng chē jiā liǎnggè rén duōshǎo qián?

Where does the boat leave from?
船从哪儿开？
Chuán cóng nǎr kāi?

How long does the crossing take?
多久能到岸？
Duōjiǔ néng dào'àn?

When do we get to ...?
我们什么时候到 ...？
Wǒmen shénme shíhou dào ...?

Where is the restaurant?
餐厅在哪儿？
Cāntīng zài nǎr?

How do I get to the car deck?
我怎么去车辆甲板？
Wǒ zěnme qù chēliàng jiǎbǎn?

Where is cabin number 28?
28号舱在哪儿？
Èrshí bā hào cāng zài nǎr?

Do you have anything for seasickness?
你有治晕船的药吗？
Nǐ yǒu zhì yùnchuán de yào ma?

Plane 飞机 Fēijī

Where is the luggage for the flight from ...?
从 ... 飞来的航班的行李在哪儿？
Cóng ... fēi lái de hángbān de xíngli zài nǎr?

Where can I change some money?	我在哪儿能换些钱？ Wǒ zài nǎr néng huàn xiē qián?
Where is the taxi rank?	出租车候车站在哪儿？ Chūzūchē hòuchēzhàn zài nǎr?
Where is the bus stop?	公共汽车站在哪儿？ Gōnggòng qìchē zhàn zài nǎr?
My luggage hasn't arrived.	我的行李还没到。 Wǒ de xíngli hái méi dào.
Where do I check in for the flight to ...?	我在哪儿办去 ... 的登机手续？ Wǒ zài nǎr bàn qù ... de dēngjī shǒuxù?
Which gate for the flight to ...?	哪个登机口是去 ... 的飞机？ Nǎge dēngjīkǒu shì qù ... de fēijī?
When does boarding begin?	什么时候开始登机？ Shénme shíhou kāishǐ dēngjī?
Window/aisle, please.	请给我靠窗/过道的位子 Qǐng gěi wǒ kào chuāng/guòdào de wèizi.
I've lost my boarding pass.	我的登机牌丢了。 Wǒ de dēngjīpái diū le.
I've lost my ticket.	我的票丢了。 Wǒ de piào diū le.
I'd like to change my flight.	我要改机票。 Wǒ yào gǎi jīpiào.

I'd like to cancel my flight.	我要取消我的机票。 Wǒ yào qǔxiāo wǒ de jīpiào.
Local Public Transport	公共交通 Gōnggòng Jiāotōng
How do I get to the centre?	我怎么去市中心？ Wǒ zěnme qù shì zhōngxīn?
Where is the bus station?	公共汽车总站在哪儿？ Gōnggòng qìchē zǒngzhàn zài nǎr?
Where is the nearest tram stop?	最近的电轨车站在哪儿？ Zuìjìn de diànguǐ chēzhàn zài nǎr?
Where is the nearest underground station?	最近的地铁站在哪儿？ Zuìjìn de dìtiě zhàn zài nǎr?
A ticket, please.	一张票。Yīzhāng piào.
To ...	去 ...。Qù ....
Is there a reduction for pensioners?	对退休人员打折吗？ Duì tuìxiū rényuán dǎzhé ma?
Is there a reduction for children?	对小孩打折吗？ Duì xiǎohái dǎzhé ma?
How does the ticket machine work?	售票机怎么使？ Shòupiào jī zěnme shǐ?
Do you have a map of the underground?	你有地铁图吗？ Nǐ yǒu dìtiě tú ma?
Please tell me when to get off.	请告诉我什么时候下车。 Qǐng gàosù wǒ shénme shíhou xiàchē.

What is the next stop?	下一站是哪儿？ Xià yīzhàn shì nǎr?
Taxi	出租车 Chūzūchē
Where can I get a taxi?	我在哪儿能打到车？ Wǒ zài nǎr néng dǎ dào chē?
Call me a taxi, please.	请给我叫辆出租车。 Qǐng gěi wǒ jiào liàng chūzūchē.
To the airport, please.	去飞机场。Qù fēijīchǎng.
To the station, please.	去火车站。 Qù huǒchēzhàn.
To the ... hotel, please.	去 ... 饭店。Qù ... fàndiàn.
To this address, please.	去这个地址。 Qù zhège dìzhǐ.
I'm in a hurry.	我有急事。Wǒ yǒu jíshì.
How much is it?	多少钱？Duōshǎo qián?
I need a receipt.	我需要一张发票。 Wǒ xūyào yīzhāng fāpiào.
I don't have anything smaller.	我没有更小的。 Wǒ méiyǒu gèng xiǎo de.
Keep the change.	不用找了。Bùyòng zhǎo le.
Stop here, please.	请在这儿停。 Qǐng zài zhèr tíng.

Camping | 露营 Lùyíng

Is there a campsite here? | 有露营地吗？
Yǒu lùyíng dì ma?

We'd like a site for a tent. | 我们要一个帐篷位。
Wǒmen yào yīgè zhàngpeng wèi.

We'd like a site for a caravan. | 我们要一个宿营车位。
Wǒmen yào yīgè sùyíngchē wèi.

We'd like to stay one night. | 我们要住一个晚上。
Wǒmen yào zhù yīgè wǎnshang.

How much is it per night? | 每晚多少钱？
Měi wǎn duōshǎo qián?

Where are the toilets? | 厕所在哪儿？
Cèsuǒ zài nǎr?

Where are the showers? | 淋浴在哪儿？
Línyù zài nǎr?

Where is the restaurant? | 餐厅在哪儿？
Cāntīng zài nǎr?

Can we park here overnight? | 我们可以在这儿停一晚吗？
Wǒmen kěyǐ zhèr tíng yī wǎn ma?

Self-Catering | 度假房 Dùjià Fáng

Where do we get the key for the apartment? | 我们从哪儿拿公寓的钥匙？
Wǒmen cóng nǎr ná gōngyù de yàoshi?

Do we have to pay extra for electricity?	我们要另附电费吗？ Wǒmen yào lìng fù diànfèi ma?
Where is the electricity meter?	电表在哪儿？ Diànbiǎo zài nǎr?
Where is the gas meter?	煤气表在哪儿？ Méiqì biǎo zài nǎr?
How does the washing machine work?	洗衣机怎么使？ Xǐyījī zěnme shǐ?
How does the heating work?	暖气怎么使？ Nuǎnqì zěnme shǐ?
Please show us how this works.	请教我们这个怎么使。 Qǐng jiāo wǒmen zhège zěnme shǐ.
Who do I contact if there are any problems?	如果出了问题我跟谁联系？ Rúguǒ chū le wèntí wǒ gēn shéi liánxì?
We need more sheets.	我们需要更多床单。 Wǒmen xūyào gèngduō chuángdān.
The gas has run out.	煤气没了。Méiqì méi le.
There is no electricity.	没电。Méi diàn.
Where do we hand in the key when we're leaving?	我们走的时候在哪儿交钥匙？ Wǒmen zǒu de shíhou zài nǎr jiāo yàoshi?
Do we have to clean the house before we leave?	我们走之前必须要打扫房间吗？ Wǒmen zǒu zhīqián bìxū yào dǎsǎo fángjiān ma?

	Hotel	饭店 Fàndiàn

Do you have a single room for tonight?
你们今晚有一个单人间吗?
Nǐmen jīnwǎn yǒu yīgè dānrénjiān ma?

Do you have a double room for tonight?
你们今晚有一个双人间吗?
Nǐmen jīnwǎn yǒu yīgè shuāngrénjiān ma?

Do you have a room with a bath?
你们有带盆浴的房间吗?
Nǐmen yǒu dài pényù de fángjiān ma?

Do you have a room with a shower?
你们有带淋浴的房间吗?
Nǐmen yǒu dài línyù de fángjiān ma?

I want to stay for one night.
我要住一个晚上。
Wǒ yào zhù yīgè wǎnshang.

I want to stay for 5 nights.
我要住5个晚上。
Wǒ yào zhù wǔgè wǎnshang.

I booked a room in the name of ...
我用 ... 这个名字订了一个房间。
Wǒ yòng ... zhège míngzì dìng le yīgè fángjiān.

I'd like another room.
我要别的房间。
Wǒ yào bié de fángjiān.

What time is breakfast?
早餐几点? Zǎocān jǐdiǎn?

Where is breakfast served?
在哪儿吃早餐?
Zài nǎr chī zǎocān?

Can I have breakfast in my room?
我可以在房间里吃早餐吗? Wǒ kěyǐ zài fángjiān lǐ chī zǎocān ma?

| Where is the restaurant? | 餐厅在哪儿？ |
| Cāntīng zài nǎr? |
| Where is the bar? | 酒吧在哪儿？ |
| Jiǔbā zài nǎr? |

Put that in the safe, please.
请把它放在保险柜里。
Qǐng bǎ tā fàng zài bǎoxiǎnguì lǐ.

I'd like an alarm call for tomorrow morning at 7 o'clock.
我要叫醒服务，明早7点。
Wǒ yào jiàoxǐng fúwù, míngzǎo qīdiǎn.

I'd like to get these things cleaned.
请把这些东西清洗了。
Qǐng bǎ zhèxiē dōngxi qīngxǐ le.

Please bring me an extra blanket.
请再给我一条毯子。
Qǐng zài gěi wǒ yītiáo tǎnzi.

The air conditioning doesn't work.
空调坏了。
Kōngtiáo huài le.

The key, please.
请给我钥匙。
Qǐng gěi wǒ yàoshi.

Room number 312
312号房间
Sān yāo èr hào fángjiān

Are there any messages for me?
有给我的留言吗？
Yǒu gěi wǒ de liúyán ma?

Please prepare the bill.
请开账单。
Qǐng kāi zhàngdān.

I'm looking for postcards.	我想买明信片。 Wǒ xiǎng mǎi míngxìnpiàn.
I'd like some toothpaste.	我要牙膏。Wǒ yào yágāo.
Do you have any batteries?	你有电池吗？ Nǐ yǒu diànchí ma?
Where is the nearest shop which sells souvenirs?	最近的卖纪念品的商店在哪儿？ Zuìjìn de mài jìniànpǐn de shāngdiàn zài nǎr?
Do you have this in another size?	这还有其它号的吗？ Zhè háiyǒu qítā hào de ma?
Do you have this in another colour?	这还有其它颜色的吗？ Zhè háiyǒu qítā yánsè de ma?
I take size ...	我要 ... 号。Wǒ yào ... hào.
My feet are a size 5½.	我的脚是39号。 Wǒ de jiǎo shì sānshí jiǔ hào.
I'll take it.	我要了。Wǒ yào le.
Do you have anything else?	你还有别的什么吗？Nǐ háiyǒu bié de shénme ma?
That's too expensive.	太贵了。Tài guì le.
I'm just looking.	我只是看看。 Wǒ zhǐshì kànkan.
Do you take credit cards?	能用信用卡吗？ Néng yòng xìnyòngkǎ ma?
Food Shopping	购买食物 Gòumǎi Shíwù
Where is the nearest supermarket?	最近的超市在哪儿？ Zuìjìn de chāoshì zài nǎr?

Where is the market?	市场在哪儿？
	Shìchǎng zài nǎr?
I'd like ...	我要 ... 。Wǒ yào ... .
a kilo of potatoes	一公斤土豆
	yī gōngjīn tǔdòu
6 slices of ham	6 片火腿 liù piàn huǒtuǐ
a litre of milk	一公升牛奶
	yī gōngshēng niúnǎi
a bottle of red wine	一瓶红葡萄酒
	yī píng hóng pútaojiǔ
a packet of crisps	一包薯片 yī bāo shǔpiàn
Post Office	邮局 Yóujú
Where is the nearest post office?	最近的邮局在哪儿？
	Zuìjìn de yóujú zài nǎr?
When does the post office open?	邮局几点开门？
	Yóujú jǐdiǎn kāimén?
Where can I buy stamps?	我在哪儿能买邮票？
	Wǒ zài nǎr néng mǎi yóupiào?
I'd like to post this letter.	我要寄这封信。
	Wǒ yào jì zhè fēng xìn.
I'd like to send this parcel.	我要寄这个包裹。
	Wǒ yào jì zhège bāoguǒ.
Is there any mail for me?	有我的信吗？
	Yǒu wǒ de xìn ma?
Where is the nearest postbox?	最近的信箱在哪儿？
	Zuìjìn de xìnxiāng zài nǎr?

Photos and Videos 相片与录像带
Xiàngpiàn yǔ Lùxiàngdài

A colour film, please. 请给我一卷彩色胶卷。
Qǐng gěi wǒ yījuǎn cǎisè jiāojuǎn.

I'd like a card for my digital camera. 我要给我的数码相机买一张记忆卡。
Wǒ yào gěi wǒ de shùmǎ xiàngjī mǎi yīzhāng jìyì kǎ.

Can I have a tape for this video camera, please? 能给我一盘这种摄像机用的摄像带吗？
Néng gěi wǒ yīpán zhèzhǒng shèxiàngjī yòng de shèxiàngdài ma?

Can you develop this film, please? 能冲这卷胶卷吗？
Néng chōng zhè juǎn jiāojuǎn ma?

I'd like the photos 10 by 15 centimetres. 我要相片15厘米长10厘米宽。
Wǒ yào xiàngpiàn shíwǔ límǐ cháng shí límǐ kuān.

When will the photos be ready? 相片什么时候好？
Xiàngpiàn shénme shíhou hǎo?

How much do the photos cost? 这些相片多少钱？
Zhèxiē xiàngpiàn duōshǎo qián?

Could you take a photo of us, please? 能给我们照张相吗？
Néng gěi wǒmen zhào zhāng xiàng ma?

Sightseeing 观光 Guānguāng

Where is the tourist office?
旅游办事处在哪儿？
Lǚyóu bànshìchù zài nǎr?

Do you have any leaflets about ...?
你们有关于 ...
的信息传单吗？
Nǐmen yǒu guānyú ... de xìnxī chuándān ma?

What sights can you visit here?
这儿有什么观光点？
Zhèr yǒu shénme guānguāngdiǎn?

Are there any sightseeing tours of the town?
有什么城市观光游吗？
Yǒu shénme chéngshì guānguāng yóu ma?

When is the museum open?
博物馆什么时候开门？
Bówùguǎn shénme shíhou kāimén?

How much does it cost to get in?
门票多少钱？
Ménpiào duōshǎo qián?

Are there any reductions for children?
对小孩打折吗？
Duì xiǎohái dǎzhé ma?

Is there a guided tour in English?
有英语导游观光团吗？
Yǒu Yīngyǔ dǎoyóu guānguāng tuán ma?

Can I take photos here?
我能在这儿照相吗？
Wǒ néng zài zhèr zhàoxiàng ma?

Can I film here?
我能在这儿摄像吗？
Wǒ néng zài zhèr shèxiàng ma?

Entertainment	娱乐 Yúlè
What is there to do here?	在这儿能干什么？ Zài zhèr néng gàn shénme?
Where can we go dancing?	我们能去哪儿跳舞？ Wǒmen néng qù nǎr tiàowǔ?
Where is there a nice bar?	哪儿有好酒吧？ Nǎr yǒu hǎo jiǔbā?
Where is there a good club?	哪儿有好的夜总会？ Nǎr yǒu hǎo de yèzǒnghuì?
What's on tonight at the cinema?	今晚电影院放什么？ Jīnwǎn diànyǐngyuàn fàng shénme?
What's on tonight at the concert hall?	今晚音乐厅演什么？ Jīnwǎn yīnyuè tīng yǎn shénme?
Where can I buy tickets for the opera?	我在哪儿能买歌剧票？ Wǒ zài nǎr néng mǎi gējù piào?
How much is it to get in?	门票多少钱？ Ménpiào duōshǎo qián?
I'd like a ticket for ...	我要买一张 ... 的票。 Wǒ yào mǎi yìzhāng ... de piào
I'd like 4 tickets for ...	我要买4张... 的票。 Wǒ yào mǎi sìzhāng ... de piào
Are there any reductions for children?	对小孩打折吗？ Duì xiǎohái dǎzhé ma?

At the Beach	在沙滩 Zài Shātān
Can you swim here?	能在这儿游泳吗？
	Néng zài zhèr yóuyǒng ma?
Where is the nearest beach?	最近的沙滩在哪儿？
	Zuìjìn de shātān zài nǎr?
Is it safe to swim here?	在这儿游泳安全吗？ Zài zhèr yóuyǒng ānquán ma?
How deep is the water?	水有多深？
	Shuǐ yǒu duō shēn?
Is there a lifeguard?	有救生员吗？
	Yǒu jiùshēng yuán ma?
Where can you go waterskiing?	在哪儿能滑水橇？
	Zài nǎr néng huá shuǐqiāo?
Where can you go diving?	在哪儿能潜水？
	Zài nǎr néng qiánshuǐ?
I'd like to hire a deckchair.	我要租一个沙滩椅。
	Wǒ yào zū yīgè shātān yǐ.
I'd like to hire a jet-ski.	我要 一个摩托艇。
	Wǒ yào zū yīgè mótuó tǐng.
I'd like to hire a rowing boat.	我要租一只手划船。
	Wǒ yào zū yīzhī shǒuhuáchuán.
Sport	运动 Yùndòng
Where can we play tennis?	我们在哪儿能打网球？
	Wǒmen zài nǎr néng dǎ wǎngqiú?
Where can we go swimming?	我们在哪儿能游泳？
	Wǒmen zài nǎr néng yóuyǒng?

Where can we go riding?	我们在哪儿能骑马？ Wǒmen zài nǎr néng qímǎ?
How much is it per hour?	每小时多少钱？ Měi xiǎoshíduōshǎo qián?
Where can I book a court?	我在哪儿能订一个球场？ Wǒ zài nǎr néng dìng yīgè qiúchǎng?
Where can I hire rackets?	我在哪儿能租球拍？ Wǒ zài nǎr néng zū qiúpāi?
I'd like to see a football match.	我想看场足球比赛。 Wǒ xiǎng kàn chǎng zúqiú bǐsài.
I'd like to see a horse race.	我想看场赛马。 Wǒ xiǎng kàn chǎng sàimǎ.

Skiing 滑雪 Huáxuě

Where can I hire skiing equipment?	我在哪儿能租滑雪用具？ Wǒ zài nǎr néng zū huáxuě yòngjù?
I'd like to hire downhill skis.	我要租下坡滑雪板。 Wǒ yào zū xiàpō huáxuě bǎn.
I'd like to hire cross-country skis.	我要租越野滑雪板。 Wǒ yào zū yuèyě huáxuě bǎn.
I'd like to hire ski boots.	我要租滑雪靴。 Wǒ yào zū huáxuě xuē.
Where can I buy a ski pass?	我在哪儿能买滑雪卡？ Wǒ zài nǎr néng mǎi huáxuě kǎ?

I'd like a ski pass for a day.	我要买一张一天的滑雪卡。Wǒ yào mǎi yīzhāng yītiān de huáxuě kǎ.
I'd like a ski pass for a week.	我要买一张一周的滑雪卡。Wǒ yào mǎi yīzhāng yīzhōu de huáxuě kǎ.
How much is a ski pass?	一张滑雪卡多少钱？Yīzhāng huáxuě kǎ duōshǎo qián?
Do you have a map of the ski runs?	你有滑雪道路线图吗？Nǐ yǒu huáxuě dào lùxiàntú ma?
Where are the beginners' slopes?	初学者坡道在哪儿？Chūxué zhě pōdào zài nǎr?
How difficult is this slope?	这个坡道有多难？Zhège pōdào yǒu duō nán?
Is there a ski school?	有滑雪学校吗？Yǒu huáxuě xuéxiào ma?
What's the weather forecast?	天气预报怎么样？Tiānqì yùbào zěnmeyàng?
What is the snow like?	雪怎么样？Xuě zěnmeyàng?
Is there a danger of avalanches?	有雪崩的危险吗？Yǒu xuěbēng de wēixiǎn ma?

A table for 4 people, please.	请来张4个人的桌子。
	Qǐng lái zhāng sìgè rén de zhuōzi.
The menu please.	请给张菜单。
	Qǐng gěi zhāng càidān.
The wine list please.	请给张酒单。
	Qǐng gěi zhāng jiǔdān.
What do you recommend?	你能推荐什么菜吗？
	Nǐ néng tuījiàn shénme cài ma?
Do you have any vegetarian dishes?	有什么素食者吃的菜吗？
	Yǒu shénme sùshízhě chī de cài ma?
Does that contain peanuts?	里面有花生吗？
	Lǐmiàn yǒu huāshēng ma?
Does that contain alcohol?	含酒精吗？
	Hán jiǔjīng ma?
Can you bring more bread, please?	请再来点面包。
	Qǐng zài lái diǎn miànbāo.
I'll have the fish.	我要鱼。Wǒ yào yú.
The bill, please.	请买单。Qǐng mǎidān.
All together, please.	一起付。Yīqǐ fù.
Separate bills, please.	分开付。Fēnkāi fù.
Keep the change.	不用找了。Bùyòng zhǎo le.
This isn't what I ordered.	我点的不是这个。
	Wǒ diǎn de bùshì zhègè.
The bill is wrong.	账单算错了。
	Zhàngdān suàn cuò le.
The food is cold.	菜是凉的。
	Cài shì liáng de.

Where can I make a phone call?	我在哪儿能打电话？ Wǒ zài nǎr néng dǎ diànhuà?
Where is the nearest card phone?	最近的磁卡电话在哪儿？ Zuìjìn de cíkǎ diànhuà zài nǎr?
Where is the nearest coin box?	最近的投币电话亭在哪儿？ Zuìjìn de tóubì diànhuà tíng zài nǎr?
I'd like a 100 yuan phone card.	我要一张100元的电话卡。 Wǒ yào yīzhāng yībǎ yuán de diànhuà kǎ.
I'd like some coins for the phone, please.	请给我些打电话的硬币。 Qǐng gěi wǒ xiē dǎ diànhuà de yìngbì.
I'd like to make a reverse charge call.	我要打个对方付费的电话。 Wǒ yào dǎ gè duìfāng fùfèi de diànhuà.
Hello.	喂！Wèi!
This is ...	我是 ... 。Wǒ shì ... .
Who's speaking, please?	请问你是谁？ Qǐngwèn nǐ shì shéi?
Can I speak to Mr ..., please?	我可以跟 ... 先生讲话吗？ Wǒ kěyǐ gēn ... xiānsheng jiǎnghuà ma?
Can I speak to Ms ..., please?	我可以跟 ... 女士讲话吗？ Wǒ kěyǐ gēn ... nǚshì jiǎnghuà ma?
Extension ..., please.	请转 ... 。Qǐng zhuǎn ... .
I'll phone back later.	我过会儿再打来。 Wǒ guòhuìr zài dǎ lái.

Can you text me your answer?	你可以把答复用短信发给我吗？
	Nǐ kěyǐ bǎ dáfù yòng duǎnxìn fā gěi wǒ ma?
Where can I charge my mobile phone?	我在哪儿能给手机充电？
	Wǒ zài nǎr néng gěi shǒujī chōngdiàn?
I need a new battery.	我需要一个新电池。
	Wǒ xūyào yīgè xīn diànchí.
Where can I buy a top-up card?	我在哪儿能买充值卡？
	Wǒ zài nǎr néng mǎi chōngzhí kǎ?
I can't get a network.	我的手机找不到网。
	Wǒ de shǒujī zhǎo búdào wǎng.

PRACTICALITIES | **实际问题**
SHÍJÌ WÈNTÍ

Passport/Customs	护照/海关
	Hùzhào/Hǎiguān
Here is my passport.	这是我的护照。
	Zhè shì wǒ de hùzhào.
Here is my identity card.	这是我的身份证。
	Zhè shì wǒ de shēnfènzhèng.
Here is my driving licence.	这是我的驾照。
	Zhè shì wǒ de jiàzhào.
Here are my vehicle documents.	这是我的车的材料。
	Zhè shì wǒ de chē de cáiliào.
The children are on this passport.	孩子在这本护照上。
	Háizi zài zhè běn hùzhào shàng.
Do I have to pay duty on this?	我要给这个上关税吗？
	Wǒ yào gěi zhège shàng guānshuì ma?
This is a present.	这是个礼物。
	Zhè shì gè lǐwù.
This is for my own personal use.	这是给我个人使用。
	Zhè shì gěi wǒ gèrén shǐyòng.
I'm on my way to …	我在去 … 的路上。
	Wǒ zài qù … de lù shàng.
At the Bank	在银行 Zài Yínháng
Where can I change money?	我在哪儿能换钱？
	Wǒ zài nǎr néng huànqián?

Is there a bank here?	这儿有银行吗？
	Zhèr yǒu yínháng ma?
Is there a bureau de change here?	这儿有外汇兑换处吗？
	Zhèr yǒu wàihuì duìhuàn chù ma?
When is the bank open?	银行什么时候开门？
	Yínháng shénme shíhou kāimén?
I'd like 2000 yuan.	我要2000元。
	Wǒ yào liǎng qiān yuán.
I'd like to change 1000 yuan into pounds.	我要把1000元换成英镑。
	Wǒ yào bǎ yīqiān yuán huànchéng Yīngbàng.
I'd like to change 1000 yuan into dollars.	我要把1000元换成美元。
	Wǒ yào bǎ yīqiān yuán huànchéng Měiyuán.
I'd like to cash these traveller's cheques.	我要把这些旅行支票兑换成现金。
	Wǒ yào bǎ zhèxiē lǚxíng zhīpiào duìhuàn chéng xiànjīn.
What's the commission?	手续费多少钱？
	Shǒuxùfèi duōshǎo qián?
Can I use my card to get cash?	我能用卡取现金吗？
	Wǒ néng yòng kǎ qǔ xiànjīn ma?
Is there a cash machine here?	这儿有取款机吗？
	Zhèr yǒu qǔkuǎnjī ma?
The cash machine swallowed my card.	取款机吞了我的卡。
	Qǔkuǎnjī tūn le wǒ de kǎ.

| 实际问题
SHÍJÌ WÈNTÍ

Can you give me some change, please?	能给我些零钱吗？ Néng gěi wǒ xiē língqián ma?
Repairs	修理 Xiūlǐ
Where can I get this repaired?	我在哪儿能修这个？ Wǒ zài nǎr néng xiūzhège?
Can you repair these shoes?	你能修这鞋吗？ Nǐ néng xiū zhè xié ma?
Can you repair this watch?	你能修这表吗？ Nǐ néng xiū zhè biǎo ma?
Is it worth repairing?	它值得修吗？ Tā zhíde xiū ma?
How much will the repairs cost?	修理费多少钱？ Xiūlǐ fèi duōshǎo qián?
When will it be ready?	什么时候好？ Shénme shíhou hǎo?
Can you do it straight away?	你能立即修吗？ Nǐ néng lìjí xiū ma?
Emergency Services	紧急服务 Jǐnjí Fúwù
Help!	救命！Jiùmìng!
Fire!	着火啦！Zháohuǒ la!
Please call the emergency doctor.	请打电话叫急救医生。 Qǐng dǎ diànhuà jiào jíjiù yīshēng.
Please call the fire brigade.	请打电话叫消防队。 Qǐng dǎ diànhuà jiào xiāofángduì.

Please call the police.	请打电话叫警察。
	Qǐng dǎ diànhuà jiào jǐngchá.
I need to make an urgent phone call.	我要打一个紧急电话。
	Wǒ yào dǎ yīgè jǐnjí diànhuà.
I need an interpreter.	我需要一个口译员。
	Wǒ xūyào yīgè kǒuyìyuán.
Where is the police station?	警察局在哪儿？
	Jǐngchájú zài nǎr?
Where is the hospital?	医院在哪儿？
	Yīyuàn zài nǎr?
I want to report a theft.	我要报个偷窃案。
	Wǒ yào bào gè tōuqiè àn.
My wallet has been stolen.	我的钱包被偷了。
	Wǒ de qiánbāo bèi tōu le.
There's been an accident.	出了个事故。
	Chū le gè shìgù.
There are 3 people injured.	3个人受伤了。
	Sāngè rén shòushāng le.
My location is …	我在 … 。 Wǒ zài … .
I've been robbed.	我被抢了。 Wǒ bèi qiǎng le.
I've been attacked.	我被打了。 Wǒ bèi dǎ le.
I've been raped.	我被强奸了。
	Wǒ bèi qiángjiān le.
I'd like to phone my embassy.	我要给我的大使馆打电话。
	Wǒ yào gěi wǒ de dàshǐguǎn dǎ diànhuà.

Pharmacy 药房 Yàofáng

Where is the nearest pharmacy?
最近的药房在哪儿?
Zuìjìn de yàofáng zài nǎr?

Which pharmacy provides emergency service?
哪个药房有紧急服务?
Nǎge yàofáng yǒu jǐnjí fúwù?

I'd like something for diarrhoea.
我要治腹泻的药。
Wǒ yào zhì fùxiè de yào.

I'd like something for a headache.
我要治头疼的药。
Wǒ yào zhì tóuténg de yào.

I'd like plasters.
我要些创可贴。
Wǒ yào xiē chuàngkětiē.

I'd like some paracetamol.
我要些扑热息痛。
Wǒ yào xiē pūrèxītòng.

I can't take aspirin.
我不能吃阿司匹林。
Wǒ bù néng chī āsīpǐlín.

Is it safe to give to children?
给孩子安全吗?
Gěi háizi ānquán ma?

How should I take it?
我怎么吃? Wǒ zěnme chī?

At the Doctor's 看病 Kànbìng

I need a doctor.
我要看医生。
Wǒ yào kàn yīshēng.

Where is casualty?
急诊室在哪儿?
Jízhěnshì zài nǎr?

I have a pain here.
我这儿疼。Wǒ zhèr téng.

I feel hot.
我觉得热。Wǒ juéde rè.

I feel cold.
我觉得冷。Wǒ juéde lěng.

I feel sick.
我觉得恶心。
Wǒ juéde ěxin.

I'm allergic to penicillin.	我对青霉素过敏。
	Wǒ duì qīngméisù guòmǐn.
I am pregnant.	我怀孕了。Wǒ huáiyùn le.
I am diabetic.	我有糖尿病。
	Wǒ yǒu tángniàobìng.
I'm on this medication.	我用这种药。
	Wǒ yòng zhèzhǒng yào.
My blood group is O positive.	我是O型血。
	Wǒ shì ōu xíng xiě.

At the Hospital 在医院 Zài Yīyuàn

I'd like to speak to a doctor.	我要和医生讲话。
	Wǒ yào hé yīshēng jiǎnghuà.
When will I be discharged?	我什么时候可以出院？
	Wǒ shénme shíhou kěyǐ chūyuàn?

At the Dentist's 在牙医诊所 Zài Yáyī Zhěnsuǒ

I need a dentist.	我要看牙医。
	Wǒ yào kàn yáyī.
This tooth hurts.	这颗牙疼。Zhè kē yá téng.
One of my fillings has fallen out.	我补的牙的填充材料掉出来了。
	Wǒ bǔ de yá de tiánchōng cáiliào diào chūlai le.
I have an abscess.	我有一个溃疡。
	Wǒ yǒu yígè kuìyáng.
I want an injection for the pain.	我要打止痛针。
	Wǒ yào dǎ zhǐtòng zhēn.

| 差旅人员
CHĀILǙ RÉNYUÁN

Business Travel 出差 Chūchāi

I'd like to arrange a meeting with ... 我要安排和 ... 开个会。
Wǒ yàoānpái hé ... kā gè huì

I have an appointment with ... 我和 ... 有一个预约。
Wǒ hé ... yǒu yīgè yùyuē.

Here is my card. 这是我的名片。
Zhè shì wǒ de míngpiàn.

I work for ... 我给 ... 工作。
Wǒ gěi ... gōngzuò.

How do I get to your office? 我怎么到你的办公室？
Wǒ zěnme dào nǐ de bàngōngshì?

I need an interpreter. 我需要一个口译员。
Wǒ xūyào yīgè kǒuyìyuán.

May I use your phone? 我可以用你的电话吗？
Wǒ kěyǐ yòng nǐ de diànhuà ma?

May I use your computer? 我可以用你的电脑吗？
Wǒ kěyǐ yòng nǐ de diànnǎo ma?

May I use your desk? 我可以用你的桌子吗？
Wǒ kěyǐ yòng nǐ de zuōzi ma?

What is your email address? 你的电子邮件地址是什么？
Nǐ de diànzǐ yóujiàn dìzhǐ shì shénme?

Is there an internet connection in the room? 这房间有因特网连接吗？
Zhè fángjiān yǒu yīntèwǎng liánjiē ma?

Is there a fax machine I can use?	有我可以用的传真机吗? Yǒu wǒ kěyǐ yòng de chuánzhēnjī ma?
Does the room have wireless internet access?	这房间可以无线上网吗? Zhè fángjiān kěyǐ wúxiàn shàngwǎng ma?
Is there anywhere I can charge up my mobile phone?	我在哪儿可以给我的手机充电? Wǒ zài nǎr kěyǐ gěi wǒ de shǒujī chōngdiàn?
Please could you book a taxi for me for 9am tomorrow morning?	请给我预定一辆明早9点的出租车。 Qǐng gěi wǒ yùdìng yīliàng míngzǎo jiǔdiǎn de chūzūchē.
Disabled Travellers	残疾差旅人员 Cánjí Chāilǚ Rényuán
Is it possible to visit ... with a wheelchair?	可以坐轮椅参观 ... 吗? Kěyǐ zuò lúnyǐ cānguān ... ma?
Where is the wheelchair-accessible entrance?	轮椅入口在哪儿? Lúnyǐ rùkǒu zài nǎr?
Is your hotel accessible to wheelchairs?	你们饭店便于轮椅出入吗? Nǐmen fàndiàn biànyú lúnyǐ chūrù ma?
I need a room on the ground floor.	我要一间在一层的房间。 Wǒ yào yījiān zài yīcéng de fángjiān.

I need a room with wheelchair access.	我要一间可供轮椅出入的房间。
	Wǒ yào yījiān kěgòng lúnyǐ chūrù de fángjiān.
Where is the disabled toilet?	残疾人专用厕所在哪儿?
	Cánjí rén zhuānyòng cèsuǒ zài nǎr?
Can you help me get on please?	你能帮我上车吗?
	Nǐ néng bāng wǒ shàngchē ma?
Where is the nearest repair shop for wheelchairs?	最近的轮椅修理店在哪儿?
	Zuìjìn de lúnyǐ xiūlǐdiàn zài nǎr?
The tyre has burst.	轮胎爆了。Lúntāi bào le.
The battery is flat.	电池没电了。
	Diànchí méi diàn le.
The wheels lock.	车轮卡住了。
	Chēlún qiǎzhù le.
Travelling with Children	带孩子旅行 Dài Háizi Lǚxíng
Is it OK to bring children here?	可以带孩子来这儿吗?
	Kěyǐ dài háizi lái zhèr ma?
Is there a reduction for children?	对小孩打折吗?
	Duì xiǎohái dǎzhé ma?
Do you have children's portions?	你们有儿童份吗?
	Nǐmen yǒu értóng fèn ma?
Do you have a high chair?	你们有儿童餐椅吗?
	Nǐmen yǒu értóng cānyǐ ma?

Do you have a cot?	你们有婴儿床吗？ Nǐmen yǒu yīng'ér chuáng ma?
Do you have a child's seat?	你们有童椅吗？ Nǐmen yǒu tóngyǐ ma?
Where can I change the baby?	我在哪儿能给孩子换尿布？ Wǒ zài nǎr néng gěi háizi huàn niàobù?
Where can I breast-feed the baby?	我在哪儿能给孩子喂奶？ Wǒ zài nǎr néng gěi háizi wèinǎi?
Can you warm this up, please?	能把这个给我加温吗？ Néng bǎ zhègè gěi wǒ jiāwēn ma?
What is there for children to do?	在那儿孩子能干什么？ Zài nàr háizi néng gàn shénme?
Where is the nearest playground?	最近的游乐场在哪儿？ Zuìjìn de yóulèchǎng zài nǎr?
Is there a child-minding service?	有照看孩子的服务吗？ Yǒu zhàokàn háizi de fúwù ma?
My child is ill.	我的孩子生病了。 Wǒ de háizi shēngbìng le.

I'd like to make a complaint.	我要投诉。Wǒ yào tóusù.
I'd like to speak to the manager, please.	我要跟经理讲话。Wǒ yào gēn jīnglǐ jiǎnghuà.
The light doesn't work.	灯坏了。Dēng huài le.
The heating doesn't work.	暖气坏了。Nuǎnqì huài le.
The shower doesn't work.	淋浴坏了。Línyù huài le.
The room is too small.	房间太小。Fángjiān tài xiǎo.
The room is too cold.	房间太冷。Fángjiān tài lěng.
Can you clean the room, please?	你可以打扫房间吗？Nǐ kěyǐ dǎsǎo fángjiān ma?
Can you turn down the TV please?	你可以把电视声音关小吗？Nǐ kěyǐ bǎ diànshì shēngyīn guānxiǎo ma?
The food is cold.	饭菜是凉的。Fàncài shì liáng de.
The food is too salty.	饭菜太咸了。Fàncài tài xián le.
This isn't what I ordered.	我点的不是这个。Wǒ diǎn de bùshì zhège.
We've been waiting for a very long time.	我们等了很长时间了。Wǒmen děng le hěn cháng shíjiān le.
The bill is wrong.	账单算错了。Zhàngdān suàn cuò le.
I want my money back.	我要退钱。Wǒ yào tuìqián.